More information about this series at http://www.springer.com/series/7407

Giovanni Squillero
Kevin Sim et al. (Eds.)

Applications of Evolutionary Computation

20th European Conference, EvoApplications 2017
Amsterdam, The Netherlands, April 19–21, 2017
Proceedings, Part I

 Springer

Editors

see next page

ISSN 0302-9743   ISSN 1611-3349 (electronic)
Lecture Notes in Computer Science
ISBN 978-3-319-55848-6   ISBN 978-3-319-55849-3 (eBook)
DOI 10.1007/978-3-319-55849-3

Library of Congress Control Number: 2017934329

LNCS Sublibrary: SL1 – Theoretical Computer Science and General Issues

Printed on acid-free paper

This Springer imprint is published by Springer Nature
The registered company is Springer International Publishing AG
The registered company address is: Gewerbestrasse 11, 6330 Cham, Switzerland

Organization

EvoApplications Coordinator

Giovanni Squillero — Politecnico di Torino, Italy

EvoApplications Publication Chair

Kevin Sim — Edinburgh Napier University, UK

Local Chairs

Evert Haasdijk — Vrije Universiteit Amsterdam, The Netherlands
Jacqueline Heinerman — Vrije Universiteit Amsterdam, The Netherlands

Publicity Chair

Pablo García Sánchez — University of Cádiz, Spain

EvoBAFIN Chairs

Anthony Brabazon — University College Dublin, Ireland
Michael Kampouridis — University of Kent, UK

EvoBIO Chairs

Jaume Bacardit — Newcastle University, UK
Federico Divina — Universidad Pablo de Olavide, Spain
Ting Hu — Memorial University, St. John's, Canada

EvoCOMNET Chairs

Ernesto Tarantino — ICAR/CNR, Italy
Fabio D'Andreagiovanni — Zuse Insitute Berlin, Germany
Giovanni Iacca — INCAS[3], The Netherlands

EvoCOMPLEX Chairs

Carlos Cotta — Universidad de Málaga, Spain
Robert Schaefer — AGH University of Science and Technology, Poland

EvoENERGY Chairs

Paul Kaufmann   University of Paderborn, Germany
Kyrre Glette   University of Oslo, Norway

EvoGAMES Chairs

Paolo Burrelli   Aalborg University Copenhagen, Denmark
Antonio M. Mora García   Universidad de Granada, Spain
Alberto Tonda   INRA, France

EvoIASP Chairs

Stefano Cagnoni   University of Parma, Italy
Mengjie Zhang   Victoria University of Wellington, New Zealand

EvoINDUSTRY Chairs

Kevin Sim   Edinburgh Napier University, UK
Neil Urquhart   Edinburgh Napier University, UK

EvoKNOW Chairs

Giovanni Iacca   INCAS^3, The Netherlands
Matt Coler   INCAS^3, The Netherlands
Gerd Ascheid   RWTH Aachen University, Germany

EvoNUM Chair

Anna I. Esparcia-Alcázar   Universitat Politècnica de València, Spain

EvoPAR Chairs

Francisco Fernández   University of Extremadura, Spain
  de Vega
J. Ignacio Hidalgo   Universidad Complutense de Madrid, Spain

EvoROBOT Chairs

Evert Haasdijk   Vrije Universiteit Amsterdam, The Netherlands
Jacqueline Heinerman Vrije Universiteit Amsterdam, The Netherlands

EvoSET Chairs

Anna I. Esparcia-Alcázar   Universitat Politècnica de València, Spain
Sara Silva   Faculdade de Ciências, Universidade de Lisboa, Portugal

EvoSTOC Chairs

Trung Thanh Nguyen   Liverpool John Moores University, UK
Michalis Mavrovouniotis   Nottingham Trent University, UK

Program Committees

Eva Alfaro   Instituto Technològico de Informàtica, Spain [EvoBAFIN]
Jhon Edgar Amaya   Universidad Nacional Experimental del Táchira, Venezuela [EvoCOMPLEX]
Michele Amoretti   University of Parma, Italy [EvoIASP]
Anca Andreica   Universitatea Babeş-Bolyai, Romania [EvoCOMPLEX]
Jarosław Arabas   Warsaw University of Technology, Poland [EvoKNOW]
Ignacio Arnaldo   PatternEx, USA [EvoPAR]
Maria Arsuaga Rios   CERN, Switzerland [EvoINDUSTRY]
Jason Atkin   University of Nottingham, UK [EvoINDUSTRY]
Joshua Auerbach   Champlain College, USA [EvoROBOT]
Jaume Bacardit   Newcastle University, UK [EvoBIO]
Lucia Ballerini   University of Edinburgh, UK [EvoIASP]
Tiago Baptista   Universidade de Coimbra, Portugal [EvoCOMPLEX]
Bahriye Basturk Akay   Erciyes University, Turkey [EvoINDUSTRY]
Vitoantonio Bevilacqua   Politecnico di Bari, Italy [EvoIASP]
Hans-Georg Beyer   Vorarlberg University of Applied Sciences, Austria [EvoNUM]
Leonardo Bocchi   University of Florence, Italy [EvoIASP]
János Botzheim   Tokyo Metropolitan University, Japan [EvoKNOW]
Nicola Bova   University of Edinburgh, UK [EvoIASP]
Anthony Brabazon   University College Dublin, Ireland [EvoBAFIN]
Juergen Branke   University of Warwick, UK [EvoSTOC]
Nicolas Bredeche   Institut des Systèmes Intelligents et de Robotique, France [EvoROBOT]
Cédric Buche   ENIB, France [EvoGAMES]
Doina Bucur   University of Twente, The Netherlands [EvoCOMNET, EvoKNOW]
Aleksander Byrski   AGH University of Science and Technology, Poland [EvoCOMPLEX]
Antonio Córdoba   Universidad de Sevilla, Spain [EvoCOMPLEX]
David Camacho   Universidad Autónoma de Madrid, Spain [EvoGAMES]
Fabio Caraffini   De Montfort University, UK [EvoKNOW]
Hui Cheng Cheng   Liverpool John Moores University, UK [EvoSTOC]
Francisco Chicano   Universidad de Málaga, Spain [EvoSET]
Anders Christensen   University Institute of Lisbon, ISCTE-IUL, Portugal [EvoROBOT]
Myra Cohen   University of Nebraska, USA [EvoSET]
José Manuel Colmenar   Universidad Rey Juan Carlos, Spain [EvoPAR]

Stefano Coniglio   University of Southampton, UK [EvoCOMNET]
Ernesto Costa   University of Coimbra, Portugal [EvoSTOC]
Sam Cramer   University of Kent, UK [EvoBAFIN]
Fabio Daolio   Shinshu University, Japan [EvoIASP]
Christian Darabos   Dartmouth College, USA [EvoBIO]
Ivanoe De Falco   ICAR-CNR, Italy [EvoIASP]
Antonio Della   Cioppa University of Salerno, Italy [EvoIASP]
Igor Deplano   Liverpool John Moores University, UK [GENERAL]
Laura Dipietro   Cambridge, USA [EvoIASP]
Federico Divina   Universidad Pablo de Olavide, Spain [EvoBIO]
Stephane Doncieux   Institut des Systèmes Intelligents et de Robotique, France
                            [EvoROBOT]
Bernabé Dorronsoro   Universidad de Cádiz, Spain [EvoCOMPLEX]
Marc Ebner   Ernst Moritz Arndt University, Greifswald, Germany
                            [EvoIASP]
Aniko Ekart   Aston University, UK [EvoINDUSTRY]
Andries P. Engelbrecht   University of Pretoria, South Africa [EvoSTOC]
Şima Etaner-Uyar   Istanbul Technical University, Turkey [EvoNUM]
Edoardo Fadda   Politecnico di Torino, Italy [GENERAL]
Carlos Fernandes   Universidade de Lisboa, Portugal [EvoCOMPLEX]
Florentino Fernandez   Universidad de Vigo, Spain [EvoBIO]
Antonio Fernández Ares   Universidad de Granada, Spain [EvoGAMES]
Antonio Fernández Leiva   Universidad de Málaga, Spain [EvoGAMES]
Gianluigui Folino   ICAR-CNR, Italy [EvoPAR]
Francesco Fontanella   University of Cassino, Italy [EvoIASP]
Gordon Fraser   University of Sheffield, UK [EvoSET]
Alex Freitas   University of Kent, UK [EvoBIO]
José Enrique Gallardo   Universidad de Málaga, Spain [EvoCOMPLEX]
Pablo García Sánchez   University of Cádiz, Spain [EvoCOMPLEX,
                            EvoGAMES]
Gregory Gay   University of South Carolina [EvoSET]
Carlos Gershenson   Universidad Nacional Autónoma de México,
                            México [EvoCOMPLEX]
Mario Giacobini   Universita di Torino, Italy [EvoBIO]
Raffaele Giancarlo   Universitá degli Studi di Palermo, Italy [EvoBIO]
Kyrre Glette   University of Oslo, Norway [EvoROBOT]
Francisco Gomez Vela   Universidad Pablo de Olavide, Spain [EvoBIO]
Antonio González Pardo   Universidad Autónoma de Madrid, Spain [EvoGAMES]
Casey Greene   University of Pennsylvania, USA [EvoBIO]
Michael Guckert   University of Applied Sciences, Germany
                            [EvoINDUSTRY]
Francisco Luis   Universidad de Granada, Spain [EvoGAMES]
  Gutiérrez Vela
Evert Haasdijk   Vrije Universiteit Amsterdam, The Netherlands
                            [EvoROBOT]
Johan Hagelback   Blekinge Tekniska Hogskola, Sweden [EvoGAMES]

John Hallam	University of Southern Denmark, Denmark [EvoGAMES]
Ahmed Hallawa	RWTH Aachen University, Germany [EvoKNOW]
Heiko Hamann	University of Paderborn, Germany [EvoROBOT]
Jin-Kao Hao	University of Angers, France [EvoBIO]
Jacqueline Heinerman	Vrije Universiteit Amsterdam, The Netherlands [EvoROBOT]
Daniel Hernández	Instituto Tecnológico Nacional, Mexico [EvoPAR]
Malcom Heywood	Dalhousie University, Canada [EvoBAFIN]
Ronald Hochreiter	WU Vienna University of Economics and Business, Austria [EvoBAFIN]
Rolf Hoffmann	Technical University Darmstadt, Germany [EvoCOMNET]
Ting Hu	Memorial University, Canada [EvoBIO]
Joost Huizinga	University of Wyoming, USA [EvoROBOT]
Óscar Ibáñez	Universidad de Granada, Spain [EvoIASP]
Juan Luis Jiménez Laredo	University of Le Havre, France [EvoCOMPLEX, EvoPAR]
Michael Kampouridis	University of Kent, UK [EvoBAFIN]
Andreas Kassler	Karlstad University, Sweden [EvoCOMNET]
Ahmed Kattan	EvoSys.biz, Saudi Arabia [EvoBAFIN]
Shayan Kavakeb	AECOM, UK [EvoSTOC]
Graham Kendall	University of Nottingham, UK [EvoCOMNET]
Marouane Kessentini	University of Michigan, USA [EvoSET]
Mario Koeppen	Kyushu Institute of Technology, Japan [EvoIASP]
Oliver Kramer	University of Oldenburg, Germany [EvoENERGY]
Wacław Kuś	Politechnika Śląska, Poland [EvoCOMPLEX]
William B. Langdon	University College London, UK [EvoNUM, EvoPAR]
Raúl Lara Cabrera	Universidad Autónoma de Madrid, Spain [EvoGAMES]
Claire Le Goues	Carnegie Mellon University, USA [EvoSET]
Kenji Leibnitz	National Institute of Information and Communications Technology, Japan [EvoCOMNET]
Changhe Li	China University of Geosciences, China [EvoSTOC]
Antonios Liapis	University of Malta, Malta [EvoGAMES]
Federico Liberatore	Universidad Carlos III, Spain [EvoGAMES]
Piotr Lipinski	University of Wroclaw, Poland [EvoBAFIN]
Francisco Luna	Universidad de Málaga, Spain [EvoPAR]
Evelyne Lutton	Inria, France [EvoIASP]
Chenjie Ma	Fraunhofer Institute for Wind Energy and Energy System Technology, Germany [EvoENERGY]
Penousal Machado	University of Coimbra, Portugal [EvoIASP]
Tobias Mahlmann	Lund University, Sweden [EvoGAMES]
Domenico Maisto	ICAR-CNR, Italy [EvoCOMNET]
Carlo Mannino	SINTEF Oslo, Norway [EvoCOMNET]
Andrea Marcelli	Politecnico di Torino, Italy [GENERAL]

Elena Marchiori	Radboud Universiteit van Nijmegen, The Netherlands [EvoBIO]
Ingo Mauser	Karlsruhe Institute of Technology, Germany [EvoENERGY]
Michalis Mavrovouniotis	Nottingham Trent University, UK [EvoSTOC]
Michael Mayo	University of Waikato, New Zealand [EvoBAFIN]
Jorn Mehnen	Cranfield University, UK [EvoSTOC]
Tim Menzies	University of Nebraska, USA [EvoSET]
Juan Julián Merelo	Universidad de Granada, Spain [EvoNUM, EvoCOMPLEX]
Pablo Mesejo	Santiago Inria, France [EvoIASP]
Krzysztof Michalak	Wroclaw University of Economics, Poland [EvoBAFIN]
Martin Middendorf	University of Leipzig, Germany [EvoENERGY]
Wiem Mkaouer	University of Michigan, USA [EvoSET]
Maizura Mokhtar	Edinburgh Napier University, UK [EvoENERGY]
Jean-Marc Montanier	Softbank Robotics Europe, France [EvoROBOT]
Roberto Montemanni	IDSIA, Switzerland [EvoCOMNET]
Jean-Baptiste Mouret	Inria Larsen Team, France [EvoROBOT, GENERAL]
Nysret Musliu	Vienna University of Technology, Austria [EvoINDUSTRY]
Boris Naujoks	TH - Köln University of Applied Sciences, Germany [EvoNUM]
Antonio Jesús Nebro	Universidad de Málaga, Spain [EvoCOMPLEX]
Ferrante Neri	De Montfort University, UK [EvoIASP, EvoKNOW, EvoNUM, EvoSTOC]
Trung Thanh Nguyen	Liverpool John Moores University, UK [EvoSTOC]
Geoff Nitschke	University of Cape Town, South Africa [EvoROBOT]
Rafael Nogueras	Universidad de Málaga, Spain [EvoCOMPLEX]
Stefano Nolfi	Institute of Cognitive Sciences and Technologies, Italy [EvoROBOT]
Gustavo Olague	CICESE, México [EvoPAR]
Kai Olav Ellefsen	University of Wyoming, USA [EvoROBOT]
Carlotta Orsenigo	Politecnico di Milano, Italy [EvoBIO]
Ender Ozcan	University of Nottingham, UK [EvoINDUSTRY]
Michael O'Neill	University College Dublin, Ireland [EvoBAFIN]
Patricia Paderewski Rodriguez	Universidad de Granada, Spain [EvoGAMES]
Peter Palensky	Technical University of Delft, The Netherlands [EvoENERGY]
Anna Paszyńska	Jagiellonian University, Poland [EvoCOMPLEX]
David Pelta	Universidad de Granada, Spain [EvoSTOC]
Justyna Petke	University College London, UK [EvoSET]
Sanja Petrovic	University of Nottingham, UK [EvoINDUSTRY]
Nelishia Pillay	University of KwaZulu-Natal, South Africa [EvoINDUSTRY]
Clara Pizzuti	ICAR-CNR, Italy [EvoBIO]

Riccardo Poli   University of Essex, UK [EvoIASP]
Arkadiusz Poteralski   Politechnika Śląska, Poland [EvoCOMPLEX]
Simon Powers   Edinburgh Napier University, UK [EvoINDUSTRY]
Petr Pošík   Czech Technical University in Prague, Czech Republic
    [EvoNUM]
Mike Preuss   University of Münster, Germany
    [EvoNUM, EvoGAMES]
Abraham Prieto   University of La Coruña, Spain [EvoROBOT]
Jianlong Qi   Ancestry, USA [EvoBIO]
Mauricio Resende   Amazon, USA [EvoCOMNET]
Jose Carlos Ribeiro   Politécnico de Leiria, Portugal [EvoPAR]
Hendrik Richter   Leipzig University of Applied Sciences, Germany
    [EvoSTOC]
Simona Rombo   Università degli Studi di Palermo, Italy [EvoBIO]
Claudio Rossi   Universidad Politecnica de Madrid, Spain [EvoROBOT]
Günter Rudolph   University of Dortmund, Germany [EvoNUM]
Jose Santos Reyes   Universidad de A Coruña, Spain [EvoBIO]
Federica Sarro   University College London, UK [EvoSET]
Ivo Fabian Sbalzarini   Max Planck Institute of Molecular Cell Biology
    and Genetics, Germany [EvoNUM]
Robert Schaefer   University of Science and Technology, Poland
    [EvoCOMNET]
Thomas Schmickl   University of Graz, Austria [EvoROBOT]
Sevil Sen   Hacettepe University, Turkey [EvoCOMNET]
Chien-Chung Shen   University of Delaware, USA [EvoCOMNET]
Sara Silva   Universidade de Lisboa, Portugal [EvoIASP]
Anabela Simões   Institute Polytechnic of Coimbra, Portugal [EvoSTOC]
Moshe Sipper   Ben-Gurion University, Israel [EvoGAMES]
Stephen Smith   University of York, UK [EvoIASP]
Maciej Smołka   AGH University of Science and Technology, Poland
    [EvoCOMPLEX]
Ana Soares   EnergyVille, VITO, Belgium [EvoENERGY]
Andy Song   RMIT, Australia [EvoIASP]
Giovanni Squillero   Politecnico di Torino, Italy [EvoIASP, GENERAL]
Marcin Szubert   Poznań University of Technology, Poland
    [EvoCOMPLEX]
Ke Tang   University of Science and Technology of China USTC,
    China [EvoNUM]
Andrea Tettamanzi   University of Nice Sophia Antipolis/I3S, France
    [EvoBAFIN]
Ruppa Thulasiram   University of Manitoba, Canada [EvoBAFIN]
Renato Tinós   Universidade de São Paulo, Brazil [EvoSTOC]
Julian Togelius   New York University, USA [EvoGAMES]
Pawel Topa   AGH University of Science and Technology, Poland
    [EvoCOMNET]

Krzysztof Trojanowski   Cardinal Stefan Wyszyński University in Warsaw,
                          Poland [EvoSTOC]
Ha Chi Trung   Liverpool John Moores University, UK [EvoSTOC]
Wojciech Turek   AGH University of Science and Technology, Poland
                          [EvoCOMPLEX]
Tommaso Urli   Csiro Data61, Australia [EvoGAMES]
Andrea Valsecchi   European Center of Soft Computing, Spain [EvoIASP]
Leonardo Vanneschi   Universidade Nova de Lisboa, Portugal [EvoBIO,
                          EvoIASP]
Sebastien Varrete   Université du Luxembourg, Luxembourg [EvoPAR]
José Manuel Velasco   Universidad Complutense de Madrid, Spain [EvoPAR]
Vinícius Veloso de Melo   UNIFESP-SJC, Brazil [EvoKNOW]
Marco Villani   University of Modena and Reggio Emilia, Italy
                          [EvoCOMNET]
Rafael Villanueva   Universitat Politècnica de València, Spain [EvoPAR]
Tanja Vos   Open University, The Netherlands [EvoSET]
Markus Wagner   University of Adelaide, Australia [EvoENERGY]
Ran Wang   Liverpool John Moores University, UK [EvoSTOC]
Jarosław Was   AGH University of Science and Technology, Poland
                          [EvoCOMNET]
David White   University College London, UK [EvoSET]
Tony White   Carleton University, Canada [EvoCOMNET]
Bing Xue   Victoria University of Wellington, New Zealand
                          [EvoBIO, EvoIASP]
Anil Yaman   Technical University of Eindhoven, The Netherlands
                          [EvoKNOW]
Shengxiang Yang   De Montfort University, UK [EvoSTOC]
Georgios N. Yannakakis   University of Malta, Malta [EvoGAMES]
Danial Yazdani   Liverpool John Moores University, UK [EvoSTOC]
Aleš Zamuda   University of Maribor, Slovenia [EvoKNOW]
Mengjie Zhang   Victoria University of Wellington, New Zealand
                          [EvoBIO]
Nur Zincir-Heywood   Dalhousie University, Canada [EvoCOMNET]

Contents – Part I

EvoCOMNET

EvoCOMPLEX

EvoENERGY

EvoGAMES

EvoIASP

EvoINDUSTRY

EvoKNOW

EvoROBOT

Contents – Part II

General

EvoBAFIN

Minimization of Systemic Risk for Directed Network Using Genetic Algorithm

Wenshuo Guo and Kwok Yip Szeto[(⊠)]

Department of Physics, The Hong Kong University of Science and Technology,
Clear Water Bay, Kowloon, Hong Kong
phszeto@ust.hk

Abstract. In directed networks, flow dynamics may lead to cascade failures due to node and link removal. The systemic risk in financial systems follows similar mechanism, where banks are connected by interbank linkages with money transfers. A mathematical model of the banking network is used to investigate the relationships between the cascade dynamics and key parameters determining the banking network structure, including the connectivity, the bank's capitalization, and the size of interbank exposure, based on analytical calculations and numerical simulations. To optimize the network topology for the minimization of systemic risk, genetic algorithm is applied to evolve the network. It is observed that the systemic risk of financial system could be decreased by increasing the degree variance of the associated network. This could be useful for financial risk management, with possible applications to other physical systems such as ecological web, where the network stability is also an important issue.

Keywords: Banking network · Systemic risk · Genetic algorithm · Network optimization

1 Introduction

Network science is now recognized to be an important area of research for interdisciplinary studies, where the network description allows us to address many important complex issues in nature, including neural science [1], social system [2], ecological web [3], internet [4], telecommunication, transportation networks [5] and many other complex systems. In this paper, we would like to address the application of network science in computational finance in the context of systemic risk.

Systemic risk in financial network is associated with financial crises triggered by sudden failure of a particular node or link [6]. Therefore, the social importance of analyzing and understanding systemic risk in banking systems cannot be ignored [7–10], while the containment of bankruptcy of a particular bank and the associated monitoring of the network to avoid disaster are also of research interests in academia. In this work, we study the relation between the topology

© Springer International Publishing AG 2017
G. Squillero and K. Sim (Eds.): EvoApplications 2017, Part I, LNCS 10199, pp. 3–16, 2017.
DOI: 10.1007/978-3-319-55849-3_1

of the financial network and its resistance of network disintegration caused by external shocks. In the original work by Albert et al. on the problem of error and attack tolerance of complex networks, they found that scale-free networks have a higher tolerance to random node removal than homogeneous networks [11,12]. These results focus on the abrupt removal of subgraphs, for example in cyber-attacks. There is also empirical study on complex network under external impacts and self-organizing effects [13]. We like to generalize these works to directed network.

In recent years, an increasing need to do risk management at the systemic level instead of focusing on individual banks in the banking systems has been emphasized. The systemic risk in banking systems has been studied with different models [9,10,14–16]. In the banking system which contains many individual banks, if a particular bank suffers a shock and the loss of assets exceeds its net capital, then this bank will default on loans and entail negative impact on its creditor banks due to the interbank capital flow. If this negative impact is sufficiently large, then a cascade failure can propagate, leading to further failures of the creditor banks. The result will be a financial tsunami, which is a disaster to the whole banking system. This process describes a natural propagation of shocks.

Apart from the analysis of bank failures, we want to optimize the network topology to alleviate the risk of cascade. One way to address this problem is the obvious solution by the addition of more links between banks, so that the increase of connectivity can provide timely assistance. However, the addition of links into the network inevitably increases cost. Therefore, we will focus on the problem of increasing the systemic stability of the network without changing the number of nodes and links. This optimization problem involves a large solution space, and genetic algorithm is the method we use to rewire the network towards one with less systemic risk. In this paper, we perform the optimization of network topology based on a mathematical model for the banking system. The resulted systematic risk is analyzed using both analytical methods and simulations.

2 Model

The mathematical model for analyzing the systemic risk in a financial system is based on the model used by Haldane and May [10]. A bank in the financial system is described by a node with features described in Fig. 1. An individual bank's assets, denoted by a, includes the external asset (investors' borrowing), denoted as e, and interbank asset (other banks' borrowing), denoted by l. For bank i, the asset therefore is the sum of its external asset and the interbank asset. A bank's liabilities are composed of customer deposits denoted by d, and interbank borrowing denoted by b, so that the total liability for bank i is $(b_i + d_i)$. The balance sheet yields the net worth $\gamma_i = (e_i + l_i) - (b_i + d_i)$. For each bank, the condition to survive is a non-negative net worth, which means: $\gamma_i \geq 0$, otherwise the bank will default.

Next we use a network to describe the relation between banks in a financial system. The proper network for banking system is a directed one, with the nodes

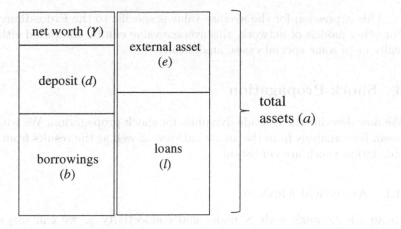

Fig. 1. The model of an individual bank.

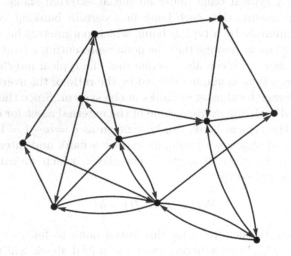

Fig. 2. A banking network example with N = 10 and p = 0.2, generated by Mathematica

or vertices of the network representing individual banks, while the links or edges of the network are the loans from one bank to another. Specifically, ingoing link means money borrowed and outgoing link means money lent. In this model, banks are interconnected in a random, Erdos–Renyi (denoted by ER) network [17], so that every bank (node) is linked to any other banks with probability p, represented by the parameter p for connectivity, as shown in Fig. 2. In such a network, a bank's average number of incoming/borrowing or outgoing/lending connections z is:

$$z = p(N - 1) \tag{1}$$

This expression for the average value is specific to the Erdos-Renyi network. For other models of network, this average value can be computed either numerically or in some special cases, analytically.

3 Shock Propagation

We now describe the cascade dynamics for shock propagation. We will provide a mean field analysis from the analytical view as well as the results from numerical simulation which are consistent.

3.1 Analytical Method

In an ER network with N nodes and connectivity p, we can use mean field approximation in statistical physics to estimate the cascade dynamics triggered by the failure of a typical bank under an initial external shock. In the mean field analysis, we assume that each bank in a certain banking system can be described approximately by a typical bank, which parameters have the average values. Specifically, as we assume that the node representing a bank has a typical coordination number z, we can also assume that the typical interbank exposure proportion θ to be a typical number defined by the ratio of the average interbank asset over the average total asset of banks in the system. Since the total asset a can be normalized to 1, the average value of the external asset for each bank, or for that matter, the typical bank, can be written as $e = a - l = 1 - \theta$ initially. To model the initial shock, we randomly choose a bank and intentionally take out a fraction f of its external assets e. The shock, which we call the Phase I shock, could be described by

$$S(I) = fe = f(1 - \theta) \tag{2}$$

Next, we define the condition for this initial bank to fail as a result of the shock it receives. The bank suffering from the initial shock will fail when the shock is bigger than its net worth γ,

$$f(1 - \theta) > \gamma \tag{3}$$

After the first failure, the creditor banks of the failed bank will experience, on the average, a total loss $(S(I) - \gamma)$ that is to be shared equally among its z creditor banks. This is because the first failed bank has absorbed γ of the initial shock $S(I)$ and the net shock propagated to its neighbors is reduced by γ. Meanwhile, the maximum loss that the creditor banks received cannot exceed b/z while $b = \theta$ is the total borrowing of the failed bank. The total loss experienced by the z creditor banks is bounded by the typical interbank exposure proportion θ. Again, based on the mean field assumption that every bank is a typical bank, each creditor bank which is connected to the failed bank will suffer $1/z$ of the total loss. Therefore, the actual loss that is received by a creditor bank is $\frac{[\theta, S(I) - \gamma]_{MIN}}{z}$. We call this second shock the Phase II shock. This loss propagating to the creditor bank can be tolerated only if it is below the creditor bank's capital. When the received loss exceeds γ, the creditor bank will fail too, triggering a cascade effect and leading to a further shock to the financial system. We call this further shock the Phase III shock and it will be analyzed later. Note that we do not specify the loss of a specific creditor bank, as in the mean field analysis they are the same as the typical bank. For a typical creditor bank, it receives a Phase II shock generated by the first failed bank which is

$$S(II) = \frac{[\theta, S(I) - \gamma]_{MIN}}{z} \tag{4}$$

The condition for this typical bank to fail is:

$$S(II) > \gamma \tag{5}$$

The second phase of failure in the cascade dynamic will occur for all the z neighbors of the first failed bank. One can then repeat this argument, based on mean field theory, to the third phase of failure, and describe the process of cascade failure. In Fig. 3, we plot the graph of interbank exposure versus net worth and show the boundary conditions for the Phase I and Phase II shock to occur. It is clear that within the triangle (with vertices $(0,0)$, $(0,1)$, $(f,0)$) the first bank will fail. If the parameters of interbank exposure and net worth fall inside the shaded triangle, Phase II failure will happen. However, if γ is large enough such that the region on the left side of point $A = \left(\frac{f}{1+(1+f)z}, \frac{zf}{1+(1+f)z} \right)$ could not be reached for all interbank exposure size θ, then Phase II failure will *not* happen for

$$\gamma > \frac{f}{1 + (1 + f)z} \tag{6}$$

The analysis for Phase III shock is more complicated because we need to consider multiple hits. In Phase I shock, there is one failed bank. After the bank has failed, it is removed from the network together with the links. In Phase II, there is $z = p(N-1)$ failed banks. Because we are using mean-field approximation here, every bank in Phase II suffers same amount of loss from the initial failed bank. Therefore, the number of surviving banks after Phase II shock is $(N - 1 - z)$. These survivors after the Phase II shock may suffer zero to z times "hits" from their neighboring failed banks. The probability $p(k)$ for the survivor to experience k hits from the z failed banks in Phase II is given by the binomial distribution,

$$p(k) = C_z^k (1 - p)^{z-k} p^k \tag{7}$$

Since the magnitude of the Phase III shock, which derivation is similar to the Phase II shock in the spirit of mean field is

$$S(III) = \frac{[\theta, S(II) - \gamma]_{MIN}}{z} \tag{8}$$

the third phase failure will occur when the cumulative loss suffered by at least one of the survivors, which is $k_{max} * S(III)$, where $k_{\max}$ is the maximum number

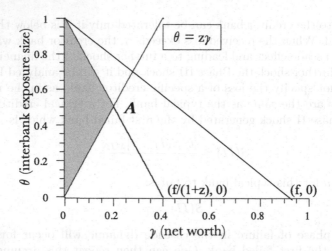

Fig. 3. Interbank exposure size θ versus bank net worth γ, for phase I shock and phase II shock

of hits suffered by the survivor, is bigger than its net worth. In another word, the condition for the Phase III failure is

$$k_{max} * S(III) > \gamma \qquad (9)$$

Note that $k_{\max}$ is the maximum value of k such that $p(k) * [N - 1 - p(N - 1)] \geq 1$. We can also define z^* as the rescaled value of the variable z in phase II to be $z^* = z/k_{\max}$ and rewrite Eq. (9) in the similar form as Phase II shock:

$$S(III) = \frac{[\theta, S(II) - \gamma]_{MIN}}{z^*} > \gamma \qquad (10)$$

Similar to Phase II, we could also plot the graph of θ versus the net worth and the region that the third phase failure will happen will be even smaller. In fact, when $N \gg z^2$, we have k_c approximately equals to 1 and $z^* = z$ approximately.

3.2   Simulation

For simulation of our model of the banking network, we need to input five parameters: the number of nodes N, the ER network probability p, the initial shock fraction f, the bank's net worth (capital) γ and the size of interbank exposure θ. For simplicity, we always fix $f = 1$ and $N = 25$. We follow the work of Nier et al. [16], and use $\theta = 0.2$, $\gamma = 0.05$, $p = 0.2$ as our benchmark values and perform numerical simulations with different value of the bank's net worth γ, the size of interbank exposure θ, and the ER probability p while keeping two of the remaining value fixed at the benchmark values. The simulation results are averaged over 100 random networks and are presented in Figs. 4, 5 and 6:

From our simulation results for shock propagation shown in Figs. 4, 5 and 6, we reach the following conclusions: a positive nonlinear correlation between

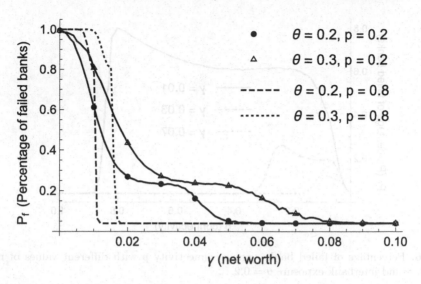

Fig. 4. Percentage of failed banks versus net worth γ with different combination of interbank exposure θ and connectivity p.

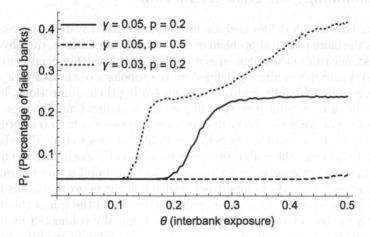

Fig. 5. Percentage of failed banks versus interbank exposure θ with different values of net worth γ and connectivity p.

the stability and net worth, a negative nonlinear relation between the systemic risk and interbank exposure size and a non-monotonic correlation between the systematic risk and connectivity. We also confirm that the transition points in the figures of numerical simulation agree well with the predicted value of mean-field approximation [18].

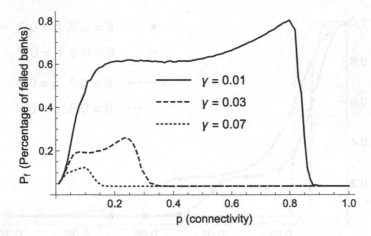

Fig. 6. Percentage of failed banks versus connectivity p with different values of net worth γ and interbank exposure $\theta = 0.2$.

4   Methodology for Risk Reduction

After describing the model for cascade failures in financial system, we would like to address the more practical problem of minimizing such failures, thereby reducing the systemic risk in the financial system. For an existing financial system, the intrinsic systemic risk is already defined by the topology of the network with N nodes representing N banks, and L links representing their connections. In order to reduce the risk, our objective is to implement a minimal modification on the topology of the network to achieve maximum reduction of risk. In real situations, the addition of links into the network inevitably increases cost. Therefore, we would like to decrease the risk of the financial system by modifying the network without changing the number of nodes and links. This implies that the only way of restructuring is to perform intelligent rewiring of the network, as this process does not change N and L. In each rewiring, the head and the tail of the link can move freely to connect two nodes that are not originally connected by another link with the same direction. A straight forward example of rewiring is shown in Fig. 7. We remove the original link from node a_4 to node a_2 and add a new link from node a_3 to node a_5. In Fig. 7, the directed bond a_4a_2 is moved to the directed bond a_3a_5. While the number of banks and money transactions remain the same in the new banking network after rewiring, we would like to investigate the change of systemic risk of this banking network under same external shocks caused by the rewiring process.

The problem in changing network topology while keeping N and L fixed involves an astronomically large configuration space where exhaustive search is prohibitive and not practical. For such problem with large solution space, genetic algorithms offer an effective way to find some good solutions, though the exact optimal solution is usually unknown due to the computation effort involved. we use genetic algorithm to find patterns of bond movements which may reduce the systemic risk

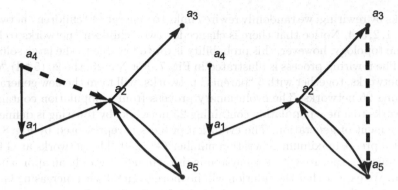

Fig. 7. Illustration of rewiring process (*left*: graph before rewiring; *right*: graph after rewiring).

as much as possible by maximally reducing the average number of failed banks caused by an initial shock for a given computation time.

Genetic algorithms (GAs) are stochastic algorithms with searching methods modelling genetic inheritance and incorporating Darwinian theory of survival of the fittest. It has been successfully applied to many optimization problems, especially when the solution space is large. The starting point is the initial population of a finite set of chromosomes. Each chromosome can be regarded as a string made of simple units, i.e. genes. Each gene controls one to several characters related to problem solving, and each chromosome in GAs represents a potential solution to a problem [19]. In our case, a chromosome is a directed network with N nodes and L links. We simply label all the possible links in this directed network from 1 to $(N * (N - 1))$, then the L actual links could be represented by an increasing sequence of L link numbers. In another word, every possible network topology corresponds to a chromosome, which is an increasing sequence of L numbers. A gene of the chromosome is the label number of an actual link among the L links. We evolve the population by mutations, which means we change the numbers in the chromosome sequence.

The evolving process of networks is illustrated in Fig. 8. First we randomly generate a population of 25 ER networks with fixed number of nodes N and number of links L. Then for each network, a node is randomly picked as the initial failed banks, triggering the cascade dynamics, and the shock propagation on this network is simulated. After the shock stops to propagate, we count the total number of failed banks for this cascade failure propagation. For a specific network structure with N nodes, the total number of failed banks for this network is averaged over at least N results by selecting node 1 to node N to be the initial failed node. According to the total number of failed banks for each network (or chromosome), we rank them and get the best 5 networks with the smallest number of failed banks. This is the fitness ranking in GA, so that a network becomes fitter the less failed banks it has. These 5 networks are selected as "parent" and these fit parents will generate new networks as their offspring. Specifically, each "parent" network generate four new networks by rewiring; we randomly rewire i links to generate 4 "children" networks for $i = 1, 2, 3, 4$. Notice that there is chance for two "children" networks to have the same topology, however, this probability is quite low due to the large solution space. The rewiring process is illustrated in Fig. 7. For N = 25, the 20 (5 * 4) "children" networks, together with 5 "parents" networks, will form the new generation containing 25 networks. The evolutionary process from a population containing 25 networks to a new population containing 25 networks by rewiring is defined as one increment of generation. The evolution process is represented by Fig. 8 and stops at a preset maximum generation number G = 250. The networks at G have the optimized structure with least systemic risk, though it is only an approximate solution. We expect that the solution will be more optimal with increasing G, but computationally we impose the stopping criterion at a finite G.

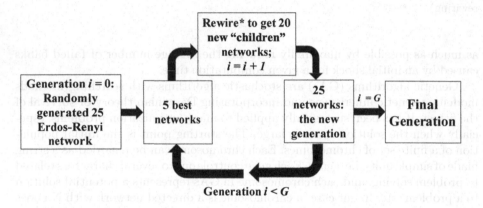

Fig. 8. Flow chart of the evolving process. (*Rewire: rewire 1–4 links in each "parent" network to get 4 "children" network; G = 250.)

5   Genetic Algorithm: Simulation Results and Analysis

Networks with 25 nodes and networks with 50 nodes are used. According to our model in Sect. 2, the banking network are determined by five parameters: the number of nodes N, the ER network probability p (or number of links L), the initial shock fraction f, the bank's level of capitalization γ and the size of interbank exposure θ. For the chosen values of other three fixed parameters except N and L, we choose parameters such that the initial network to be unstable in our simulation, which means the total number of failed banks is large. This is because we want to improve the network stability by rewiring to achieve reduction in the total number of failed banks. In Fig. 9, we use $\theta = 0.2$, $f = 1$, and the ER network probability $p = 0.2/0.5/0.8$ for both N = 25 and 50 networks. In Sect. 3, detailed analysis on these parameters have been discussed, and based on the work done in Sect. 3, we choose the value of γ such that the percentage of failed banks over all banks is above 90% initially. The choice for N = 25, p = 0.2/0.5/0.8, are $\gamma = 0.005/0.007/0.008$, and for N = 50, p = 0.2/0.5/0.8, we use $\gamma = 0.003/0.0035/0.004$. We expect that by applying our genetic algorithm, we can see clearly an increase in the network stability with generation number.

5.1   Simulation

For the simulations, the stopping criterion is defined by the maximum number of generation G = 250. In each generation, we calculate the total number of failed banks of every "parent" network and take an average over the N networks. In Fig. 9, the systemic risk indicated by the percentage of failed banks versus G is plotted. We see an obvious decrease of the failed banks' percentage with generation number, indicating our genetic algorithm can evolve the topology of the initial network towards smaller systemic risk. We also observe in Fig. 9 that the reduction in risk for networks with smaller N is faster than one with larger N. However, when p is large, e.g. $p = 0.8$, this difference between N = 25 and N = 50 becomes

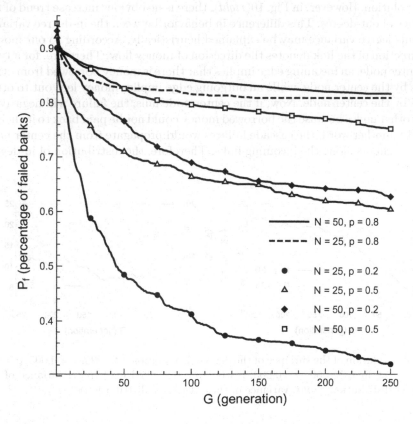

Fig. 9. Percentage of failed banks versus G (number of generation) with N = 25, p = 0.2/0.5/0.8, $\gamma = 0.005/0.007/0.008$, $\theta = 0.2$, $f = 1$; and N = 50, p = 0.2/0.5/0.8, $\gamma = 0.003/0.0035/0.004$, $\theta = 0.2$, $f = 1$.

less obvious, which is understandable since large connectivity (p) implies a smaller solution space, or the number of possible configurations is smaller, then the difference between N = 25 and N = 50 is less obvious. We see that for fixed number of nodes N and generation G, the cascade failure is more severe when the connectivity p is lower.

5.2   Analysis and Discussions

Now we discuss some general topological features of the optimized networks obtained from GA. Firstly, let us focus on the degree distribution of the network shown in Fig. 10 where we plot the variance of in-degree and out-degree for each node respectively as a function of generation.

In each generation, we have five "parents" networks. We calculate the variance of degree of each "parent" network, then take average of this variance over 5 "parents" networks. In Fig. 10(*left*), an obvious increasing trend of the variance of in-degree could be observed. Based on this, we further plot the out-degree distribution over evolution. However, in Fig. 10(*right*), there is no obvious increase trend of the variance of out-degree. This difference in behavior between the in-degree variance and out-degree variance may be explained heuristically. According to our model, the direction of the link denotes the direction of money flow. Therefore, for a typical center node, an incoming edge implies that there is money borrowed from other nodes by the center node, while an outgoing edge implies money lent out to other nodes by the center node. Now, if the center node fails, the failure will negatively affect other nodes because the borrowed money could not be paid back to its neighbors. In another word, the cascade failures would propagate from the center node to its neighbors along the incoming links. Therefore, the distribution of in-degree matters.

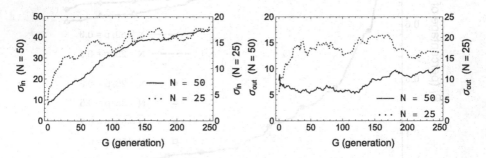

Fig. 10. Evolution of the variance of the degree distribution. (N = 25, $\gamma = 0.005$, p = 0.2, θ =0.2: dash line; N = 50, $\gamma = 0.003$, p = 0.2, $\theta = 0.2$: filled line) (*left*: variance of the in-degree distribution; *right*: variance of the out-degree distribution).

We further analyze the probability distribution function (pdf) of in-degree, we see that the in-degree distribution changes from "one peak" to "two peaks" (Fig. 11). The average value of in-degree for a node in the network with

$N = 100$ and $p = 0.2$ is $99 * 0.2 = 19.8$. Initially, for $G = 1$, we just pick 5 random generated ER network. So the variance of degree is small and the degree distribution forms a peak near the average degree as expected. However, when $G = 200$, the degree distribution has two peaks, one is formed by nodes with low degree, the other is with high degree. We now provide a heuristic interpretation for this bimodal distribution of the in-degree at long time. First of all, we emphasize that cascade failure propagates along links; thus the local topology of the failed bank is relevant. A failure of a low degree node will affect few banks, while a failed high degree node can trigger many more failures due to its high in-degree, however, the risk is shared by more nodes. We therefore expect that a network with a bimodal distribution for the in-degree has lower systemic risk than one with a unimodal distribution, since a combination of low in-degree nodes and high in-degree nodes in a network will have less failed banks as it has higher variance of in-degree, which is a feature that can be verified by combining Figs. 9, 10 and 11, concluding that network with higher degree variance is more robust to external shock.

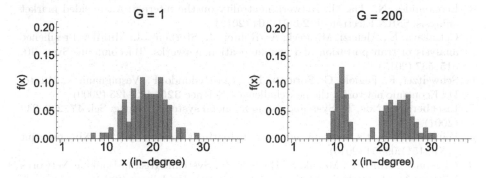

Fig. 11. Probability distribution function of in-degree. ($N = 100$, $\gamma = 0.005$, $p = 0.2$, $\theta = 0.2$, $\gamma = 0.0018$) (*left*: generation $G = 1$; *right*: generation $G = 200$).

6   Conclusions

We show numerically that genetic algorithm could offer an effective method to search for banking networks with least systemic risk under external shocks, while keeping the number of N and L unchanged. The evolution of the financial network towards one with lower systemic risk shows an increasing trend of in-degree variance at the same time. Through rewiring process, it is shown that there is a positive correlation between the variance of in-degree distribution and the stability of the network. Thus, the use of genetic algorithm provides a simple optimization procedure to obtain a stable network, with the genetic operator being the rewiring of links. Taking advantages of GA, including the elitist selection which could guarantee that the solution quality obtained by the GA will not decrease from one generation to the next, as well as the efficiency of GA which helps to narrow down the large solution space in relative few generations, we could minimize the systemic risk effectively. These numerical results also point to a guiding principle in the protocol for interbank help to reduce the risk of cascade failures, thereby lowering the probability of failure. Our method of analysis is not only useful for financial research but also is applicable to systems in other fields, where the network stability is of utmost importance. Theoretically, our results on the correlation between system stability, connectivity, capitalization, and the size of interbank exposure are of interest for further research in finance.

References

1. Rubinov, M., Sporns, O.: Complex network measures of brain connectivity: uses and interpretations. NeuroImage **52**, 1059–1069 (2010)
2. Burt, R., Kilduff, M., Tasselli, S.: Social network analysis: foundations and frontiers on advantage. Annu. Rev. Psychol. **64**, 527–547 (2013)
3. Barberán, A., Bates, S., Casamayor, E., Fierer, N.: Using network analysis to explore co-occurrence patterns in soil microbial communities. ISME J. **8**, 952 (2014)
4. Economides, N., Tåg, J.: Network neutrality on the internet: a two-sided market analysis. SSRN Electron. J. **24**, 91–104 (2012)
5. Çetinkaya, E., Alenazi, M., Peck, A., Rohrer, J., Sterbenz, J.: Multilevel resilience analysis of transportation and communication networks. Telecommun. Syst. **60**, 515–537 (2015)
6. Schweitzer, F., Fagiolo, G., Sornette, D., Vega-Redondo, F., Vespignani, A., White, D.: Economic networks: the new challenges. Science **325**, 422–425 (2009)
7. Eisenberg, L., Noe, T.: Systemic risk in financial systems. Manag. Sci. **47**, 236–249 (2001)
8. Feinstein, Z.: It's a trap: emperor palpatine's poison pill. ArXiv preprint arXiv:1511.09054 (2015)
9. Gleeson, J., Hurd, T., Melnik, S., Hackett, A.: Systemic Risk in Banking Networks Without Monte Carlo Simulation, vol. 2. Springer, Heidelberg (2012)
10. Haldane, A., May, R.: Systemic risk in banking ecosystems. Nature **469**, 351–355 (2011)
11. Albert, R., Jeong, H., Barabási, A.: Error and attack tolerance of complex networks. Nature **406**, 378–382 (2000)
12. Cohen, R., Erez, K., Ben-Avraham, D., Havlin, S.: Resilience of the internet to random breakdowns. Phys. Rev. Lett. **85**, 4626–4628 (2000)
13. Sornette, D., Deschâtres, F., Gilbert, T., Ageon, Y.: Endogenous versus exogenous shocks in complex networks: an empirical test using book sale rankings. Phys. Rev. Lett. **93**, 228701 (2004)
14. Gai, P., Kapadia, S.: Contagion in financial networks. Memeo, Bank of England (2007)
15. Iori, G., Jafarey, S., Padilla, F.: Systemic risk on the interbank market. J. Econ. Behav. Organ. **61**, 525–542 (2006)
16. Nier, E., Yang, J., Yorulmazer, T., Alentorn, A.: Network models and financial stability. J. Econ. Dyn. Control **31**, 2033–2060 (2007)
17. Erdo, P., Rényi, A.: On random graphs. Publ. Math. **6**, 290–297 (1959)
18. May, R., Arinaminpathy, N.: Systemic risk: the dynamics of model banking systems. J. R. Soc. Interface **7**, 823–838 (2009)
19. Chatterjee, S., Laudato, M.: Genetic algorithms in statistics: procedures and applications. Commun. Stat. Simul. **26**, 1617–1630 (1997)

Pricing Rainfall Based Futures Using Genetic Programming

Sam Cramer[1(✉)], Michael Kampouridis[1], Alex A. Freitas[1],
and Antonis K. Alexandridis[2]

[1] School of Computing, University of Kent, Canterbury, UK
sc649@kent.ac.uk
[2] Kent Business School, University of Kent, Canterbury, UK

Abstract. Rainfall derivatives are in their infancy since starting trading on the Chicago Mercentile Exchange (CME) since 2011. Being a relatively new class of financial instruments there is no generally recognised pricing framework used within the literature. In this paper, we propose a novel framework for pricing contracts using Genetic Programming (GP). Our novel framework requires generating a risk-neutral density of our rainfall predictions generated by GP supported by Markov chain Monte Carlo and Esscher transform. Moreover, instead of having a single rainfall model for all contracts, we propose having a separate rainfall model for each contract. We compare our novel framework with and without our proposed contract-specific models for pricing against the pricing performance of the two most commonly used methods, namely Markov chain extended with rainfall prediction (MCRP), and burn analysis (BA) across contracts available on the CME. Our goal is twofold, (i) to show that by improving the predictive accuracy of the rainfall process, the accuracy of pricing also increases. (ii) contract-specific models can further improve the pricing accuracy. Results show that both of the above goals are met, as GP is capable of pricing rainfall futures contracts closer to the CME than MCRP and BA. This shows that our novel framework for using GP is successful, which is a significant step forward in pricing rainfall derivatives.

Keywords: Rainfall derivatives · Derivative pricing · Gibbs sampler · Genetic programming

1 Introduction

Rainfall derivatives fall under the umbrella concept of weather derivatives, which are similar to regular derivatives defined as contracts between two or more parties, whose value is dependent upon the underlying asset. In the case of weather derivatives, the underlying asset is a weather type, such as temperature or rainfall. The main difference between normal derivatives and weather derivatives is that weather is not tradable. Hence, typical pricing methods that exist in the literature for other derivatives are not suitable for weather derivatives.

© Springer International Publishing AG 2017
G. Squillero and K. Sim (Eds.): EvoApplications 2017, Part I, LNCS 10199, pp. 17–33, 2017.
DOI: 10.1007/978-3-319-55849-3_2

In this problem domain the underlying asset is the accumulated rainfall over a given period, which is why it is crucial to predict rainfall as accurately as possible to reduce potential mispricing. Contracts based on the rainfall index are decisive for farmers and other users whose income is directly or indirectly affected by the rain. A lack or too much rainfall is capable of destroying a farmer's crops, hence their income. Thus, rainfall derivatives are a method for reducing the risk posed by adverse or uncertain weather circumstances. Moreover, they are a better alternative than insurance, because it can be hard to prove that the rainfall has had an impact unless it is destructive, such as severe floods or drought. Similar contracts exist for other weather variables, such as temperature.

Within the literature rainfall derivatives is split into two main parts. Firstly, predicting the level of rainfall over a specified time and secondly, pricing the derivatives based on different contract periods/length. Both aspects carry their own unique problems, with the former being a very hard time series to predict accurately, due to its volatility and redundance of its reoccurring pattern. The latter part of rainfall derivatives constitutes an incomplete market[1]. This means the standard pricing models such as the Black-Scholes model are incapable of pricing rainfall derivatives, because of the violation of the assumptions of the model; namely no arbitrage pricing. This paper focuses on pricing rainfall derivatives based on the predicted level of rainfall.

In order to predict the level of rainfall for rainfall derivatives, Markov-chain extended with rainfall prediction (MCRP) [1] and spatial-temporal rainfall (STR) models [2] have been used. More recently, Genetic Programming (GP) has been applied as an alternative predictive technique [3–5]. By predicting the underlying variable of rainfall, this increases the accuracy of pricing, which is crucial because contracts are priced ahead of time—up to a year ahead. Having the best possible predictive method reduces uncertainty in the market and boosts confidence in rainfall derivative pricing.

There is little literature on rainfall derivatives, due to being quite a new concept and rainfall being very difficult to accurately measure. The pricing techniques that have been applied so far are indifference pricing [6] and arbitrage free approach [7]. Both work in slightly different ways, with indifference pricing assuming the investor has a utility function which is a function of risk. The arbitrage free approach on the other hand is a method to change the measure of the underlying asset using the Esscher transform, taking the user from the real world to the risk neutral world through a probabilistic shift. Prior to contracts trading on the Chicago Mercantile Exchange (CME), indifference pricing was the initial technique [6,8], since contracts began trading in 2010, the arbitrage free approach has now become the standard pricing technique [7,9,10].

This paper derives contract prices for U.S.A. cities using the most recent pricing technique of the arbitrage free approach. As mentioned previously, we use the arbitrage free approach since the contracts have started to trade and are able to compare contract prices between different techniques against actual contract

---

[1] In incomplete markets, the derivative can not be replicated via cash and the underlying asset; this is because one can not store, hold or trade weather variables.

prices quoted on the CME. In order to derive contract prices, we require a technique that can maximise the accuracy of the prediction process before pricing. We use GP for three reasons, (i) GP has been shown to outperform the standard approach of MCRP in [3–5]. (ii) There is a correlation between predictive accuracy and pricing accuracy [11,12], meaning that GP should improve pricing performance. (iii) We are able to define contract specific equations, rather than a single model representing an entire year.

In this paper we use GP to predict the level of rainfall for a selection of cities from around U.S.A, which has not been done before to the best of our knowledge. Moreover, we create a novel framework for calculating the derivative prices using GP to estimate the underlying variable of rainfall. In order to do so using the arbitrage free approach, we need to generate a probability density function (PDF) out of the deterministic equations generated by GP. We develop a range of strategies in order to create a PDF, that represents the rainfall process before translating these into the risk-neutral world using the Esscher transform. The strategies consist of taking a sample of predictions across the evolution period over several runs. Thus, the computational overhead of GP is reduced.

One potential issue using a sampling approach is not having sufficient samples to generate a PDF that can adequately reflect rainfall. To cope with this issue we use Markov chain Monte Carlo (MCMC) in order to estimate the population density from a sample of our top predictive models generated from GP. The use of MCMC helps to generate a PDF that we can use with confidence.

Additionally, we show the limitation of pricing over the year using a single model. The current framework within MCRP only allows for one model to replicate rainfall over the year. On the other hand, GP is capable of producing more flexible equations that can be specifically evolved for a certain contract period. Therefore, we hypothesise that having contract-specific models will further improve the pricing accuracy, over a single GP equation for an entire year.

Hence, the contribution of this paper is a novel framework for estimating the prices under risk-neutral conditions for GP. This allows us to explore the importance of having a more suitable and robust rainfall prediction method for deriving contract prices for rainfall derivatives. Using the proposed framework with and without contract-specific models in this paper, the prices can be compared against real market data and we can evaluate how well GP is able to price rainfall derivatives.

The paper is laid out as follows. In Sect. 2 we introduce the data used in our experimentation. In Sect. 3, we give an overview of how the Esscher transform is used to derive contract prices. In Sect. 4, we introduce the methodology proposed in this paper to translate the predictions generated by GP into rainfall derivative prices. In Sect. 5, we outline the experimental setup used in this work. In Sect. 6 we show the results for both the rainfall prediction process and the pricing steps. Finally, we conclude in Sect. 7.

2   Data

We focus on the data sets that have been used for pricing derivatives on the CME. Rainfall contracts are available for 10 cities in U.S.A.: Chicago, Dallas, Des Moines, Detroit, Jacksonville, Kansas, Los Angeles, New York, Portland and Raleigh. The contracts traded for these cities are futures and options for monthly or seasonal rainfall indices.

For the monthly index, the contract is defined by the accumulated amount of rainfall within each calendar month. Whereas, the seasonal contracts are defined by the accumulated amount of rainfall between two and eight consecutive months. The contracts themselves are only available between the months March through till October. The notional value of one rainfall contract is 50 USD per 0.1 index point, where 1 index point equates to 1 in. of rainfall.

To maximise the predictive performance of GP before pricing, we use the data transformation proposed in [3] to smooth the problem landscape. As an example, Fig. 1(a) shows the original daily rainfall data for Detroit, and Fig. 1(b) shows the result of the data transformation. By making the problem landscape of rainfall prediction a simpler problem, we can enhance the rainfall prediction accuracy, which is the first of the two steps to pricing.

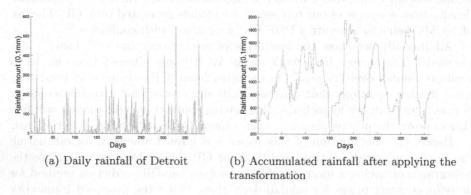

(a) Daily rainfall of Detroit   (b) Accumulated rainfall after applying the transformation

Fig. 1. A comparison between the daily rainfall time series of Detroit and after applying the data transformation from [3].

3   Pricing

One of the key characteristics of the weather derivative market is the nature of the incomplete market, whereby the underlying weather indices are non-tradable assets and can not be replicated by other risk factors. In other words, it is impossible to construct a riskless hedge portfolio containing the weather derivative. The standard approach is to price a futures contract $F(t; \tau_1, \tau_2)$ at time t with accumulation period $[\tau_1, \tau_2]$, by calculating the risk-neutral expectation Q of the rainfall index $I(\tau_1, \tau_2)$ with accumulation period $[\tau_1, \tau_2]$ based on the information set F_t available at time t. Therefore, the underlying variable is required to calculate the index over an accumulation period. We can express the price of a futures contract by the following:

$$F(t; \tau_1, \tau_2) = \exp^Q [I(\tau_1, \tau_2)|F_t] = \exp^Q \left[\sum_{\tau=\tau_2}^{\tau_2} R_\tau | F_t \right]. \tag{1}$$

Our rainfall estimates $I(\tau_1, \tau_2)$ is considered the expected price under the canonical measure P, but are within the 'risky' world. Therefore, we require $Q \sim P$ such that all tradable assets in the market are martingales after discounting. Since the market is incomplete, there will exist many different martingales (Q), where it is impossible to find a unique risk-neutral measure Q [13,14], such that Q is equivalent to the physical measure P. In order to calculate the arbitrage price under risk-neutral conditions, we require an equivalent martingale measure where $Q = Q_\theta$ using the Esscher transform [15], where θ represents the market price of risk (MPR). The MPR is the additional return or risk premium expected by investors for being exposed to undertaking the futures contract. When pricing with Black Scholes and similar pricing models, the unique equivalent martingale measure is obtained by changing the drift in the Brownian motion. The Esscher transform has been widely used across financial applications [16], more recently across rainfall derivative pricing [7,10]. To use the Esscher transform we require estimating the type of distribution for our predictions. We then apply a constant MPR to transform our distribution to find the expected price under the risk-neutral measure Q_θ, where θ is calibrated to the market data. The transformation of probability density $f(x)$ of a random variable X to a new probability density $f(x; \theta)$ with parameter θ is the Esscher transform, given by:

$$f(x; \theta) = \frac{\exp(\theta x) f(x)}{\int_{-\infty}^{\infty} \exp(\theta x) f(x) dx} \tag{2}$$

4   Adapting Genetic Programming to the Esscher Transform

The motivation behind using Genetic Programming (GP) is threefold. Firstly, GP has not been applied to the pricing of rainfall derivatives, whilst it has been shown to improve the prediction against the currently used methods. Secondly, it has been noted [11,12] that improving the prediction of the underlying variable leads to more accurate pricing. Therefore, by applying GP to the pricing domain, we aim to improve the pricing performance, which should help boost confidence in trading contracts. Finally, GP provides a flexible platform to predict rainfall contracts on a contract by contract basis. Therefore, we further tailor GP for maximising the pricing performance.

Before pricing, we need to perform an intermediate step in order for GP to calculate risk-neutral prices using the Esscher transform. One of the key aspects of the Esscher transform is the probabilistic shift under $P \sim Q$ in order to find a unique equivalent martingale close to the predicted level of rainfall. This requires constructing a probability density function (PDF) out of the predictions generated. The current approaches in rainfall derivatives are stochastic processes that simulate unique rainfall pathways on each iteration. Despite GP being a stochastic algorithm, the output is a deterministic model and can not be used to estimate the expected index of rainfall. However, GP does generate many different equations to describe the rainfall process over the evolution process.

In order to recreate the outcome of a stochastic process (e.g. MCRP), we create a subset of rainfall equations generated from GP for every run of GP we perform. By building a large enough sample using many subsets of different rainfall equations, we can form a PDF of the expected level of rainfall for each day. The PDF that is generated can be manipulated to price under the risk-neutral density using the Esscher transform. Based on the nature of rainfall, we do expect to generate a non-gaussian distribution similar to the underlying data, which is assumed to follow either a gamma or mixed-exponential distribution [1].

4.1   Strategy for Prediction Selection

To generate a PDF requires having several different observations for the same time point, but we require a sufficient number in order to determine what form the distribution takes. Using MCRP, one would typically run the chain 10,000 times in order to generate sufficient samples, which for GP is unfeasible given the computational cost to run GP 10,000 times if we were to take the final prediction from each run. To reduce the overhead, we propose taking a sample of the best solutions from the final generation. Not only will this reduce the computational cost, but is a simple method to extract the required information. One concern is that taking too many samples from the final generation may reduce the fit of a distribution, by poor predictions being selected, which will heavily skew results. Thus, we must find the best possible balance.

We present a sample of results for a contract of March using various strategies in Fig. 2. Figures 2(a–c) show the PDF of choosing between 1, 5 and 10 individuals per GP run over 50 runs and Figs. 2(d–f) show the outcome over 100 runs instead. Therefore, Fig. 2(a) contains a total of 50 samples, whereas, Fig. 2(f) contains a total of 1000 samples. We choose the sample sizes based on avoiding longer runs of GP and reducing the risk of selecting too many extreme values that may exist from poor fitting solutions. We noticed that samples of 25 or larger posed a risk of selecting extreme values. What can be seen from the figures is the nonguassianity of the predictions, which we would expect and we do not wish to exceed 100 runs of GP, due to computational overhead. In some cases we do witness that GP seems to find a modal value for the prediction with a fairly narrow distribution. From a pricing perspective this is a positive sign as GP is able to determine what it believes to be the expected outcome.

Based on the PDF's generated, we notice that in several cases no clear distribution can be easily identified, shown in Fig. 3. This is sign that not enough

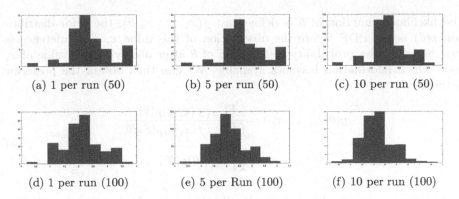

Fig. 2. The probability densities generated from GP for different strategies are shown for Detroit for the contract period of March (01/03/2011–31/03/2011). Values in brackets represents the number of GP runs, with the number per run showing how many samples are chosen to form the PDF at each run.

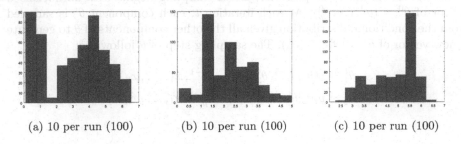

Fig. 3. Situations where a clear density can not be identified for contracts traded for Detroit in June (a), Jacksonville in June (b) and New York in April (c). Values in brackets represents the number of GP runs, with the number per run showing how many samples are chosen to form the PDF at each run.

samples have been generated and we would anticipate that generating more samples would lead to a clear distribution. However, we are attempting to reduce the computational overhead and necessity of running 10,000 separate GP runs. Hence, we employ Markov chain Monte Carlo (MCMC) to estimate the true parameters for the distribution we expect and can replicate the missing samples required to generate a PDF of our rainfall predictions.

4.2   Markov Chain Monte Carlo with Gibbs Sampling

The first key ingredient in Bayesian inference is the observation whose values are initially uncertain and described through a PDF. Another critical aspect is the previous belief about values of the parameter of interest, before observing the data. Bayesian theory is based on Bayes' Theorem, which allows new evidence to update beliefs through probabilities. Consider a random sample $x = (x_1, \ldots, x_n)$ and the parameter of interest $\theta \in \Theta$ with Θ being the parameter space.

The likelihood function of θ is defined as: $f(x_1, \ldots, x_n|\theta)$, the prior distribution $p(\theta)$ is the PDF before the observation of the value x. The inference is then based on the probability distribution of θ after observing the value of x, upon which information becomes available. We can then obtain the posterior distribution:

$$p(\theta|x_1, \ldots, x_n) = \frac{\prod_{i=1}^{n} f(x_i|\theta)p(\theta)}{\int \prod_{i=1}^{n} f(x_i|\theta)p(\theta)d\theta}$$
$$\propto \prod_{i=1}^{n} f(x_i|\theta)p(\theta). \tag{3}$$

In order to estimate the posterior distribution, using Eq. 3, we can use MCMC simulation when the posterior distribution is available. We can draw new samples of parameter $\theta = (\theta_1, \ldots, \theta_p)$ directly from the joint posterior $p(\theta|x_1, \ldots, x_n)$. We can estimate the joint posterior using Gibbs sampler, which is one type of MCMC to estimate the posterior. Gibbs sampling begins with an initialised vector of $\theta^0 = (\theta_1^0, \ldots, \theta_p^0)$. At each iteration t, each component θ_j^t is sampled from the conditional distribution given all the other components of θ to generate a new vector of $\theta^t = (\theta_1^t, \ldots, \theta_p^t)$. The sampling step of θ follows as:

$$\theta_1^t \sim p(\theta_1|\theta_2^{t-1}, \theta_3^{t-1}, \ldots, \theta_p^{t-1}, x_1, \ldots, x_n)$$
$$\theta_2^t \sim p(\theta_2|\theta_1^{t-1}, \theta_3^{t-1}, \ldots, \theta_p^{t-1}, x_1, \ldots, x_n)$$
$$\vdots$$

The sampling steps end once the last iteration has been reached, with sufficient iterations to achieve convergence. The predictive rainfall r_t of days of interest t follows an independent reparameterised Gamma distribution in the form of the mean and standard deviation of the initial rainfall predictions:

$$f(r_t|\alpha, \beta) = \frac{\beta^\alpha}{\Gamma(\alpha)} r_t^{\alpha-1} e^{-\beta r_t}, \quad \alpha = \frac{\mu^2}{\sigma^2}, \quad \beta = \frac{\mu}{\sigma^2}. \tag{4}$$

Hence the parameters of interest of the likelihood distribution in Eq. 4 are the mean and the standard deviation parameters. The prior probability distributions are the same for both parameters of interest, note that they both have vague priors, the Uniform priors $U(0, 1)$. In order to estimate the posterior of the parameters of interest, we use JAGS [17], which is an iterative MCMC simulation method, using a Gibbs sampler described previously. We run a total of 50,000 iterations including 10,000 iterations being the burn-in period.

Figure 4 shows the density plots of the Markov chains for both the shape and the rate parameters of the Gamma distribution obtained by using JAGS. Note that each posterior density, all simulated Markov chains converge to stationary, shown by the clear peak. Hence, the number of iterations and burn-in period used are sufficient to achieve convergence of the Markov chains.

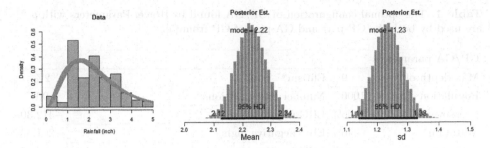

Fig. 4. The estimated kernel density of the predicted rainfall amounts and the density plots of our posterior estimates for the shape and rate parameter.

Figure 4 also shows the estimated kernel density of the predicted rainfall amounts by using the posterior means of the shape and the rate parameters in the Gamma distribution. We can see that the estimated density is representable of the target density of the rainfall prediction. This shows that using MCMC has assisted GP in creating a PDF that can be used for pricing, whilst minimising the overhead.

4.3   Pricing Using Estimated Densities

Now that the densities of our rainfall prediction under P have been estimated, we can apply the Esscher transform to shift our density to discover the expected price under the risk-neutral measure Q_θ. To do so requires one final step, which is to estimate the distribution generated and describe it under a non-guassian distribution using Normal-Inverse Gaussian (NIG) [18]. NIG is a four parameter distribution, suitable for semi-heavy tails and skewness, which can be observed from our rainfall predictions. Applying the NIG will give us the expected price under Q, whereas, our previous steps gave us the expected price under P. We require the price under Q since this is the risk-neutral level. Moreover, NIG gives us a flexible framework to price under and maintains the statistical properties after changing the MPR (θ).

NIG has been used for several applications of risk-neutral modelling across a variety of financial problems. The NIG has a PDF in the closed form of:

$$f(x|\alpha,\beta,\mu,\delta) = \frac{\alpha\delta\exp(\delta\sqrt{\alpha^2-\beta^2}+\beta(x-\mu))}{\pi\sqrt{\delta^2+(x-\mu)^2}}K_1\left(\alpha\sqrt{\delta^2+(x-\mu)^2}\right), \quad (5)$$

where K_1 denotes the modified Bessel function of the second kind. α controls the steepness, μ the location, β the skewness and δ is the scaling of the distribution. By using the Esscher transform, we manage to keep the shape of the distribution and we modify the NIG under the Esscher transform with MPR (θ) becoming NIG($\alpha, \beta + \theta, \mu, \delta$). In order to estimate the parameters for NIG, we use an optimisation algorithm of Expectation-Maximisation (EM).

Table 1. The optimal configuration of GP/GA found by iRace. Parameters with a *
are used by both the GP-part and GA-part of GP from [5].

GP/GA parameters			
Max depth of tree	9	Elitism*	2%
Population size*	1000	Number of generations*	90
Crossover*	96%	ERC negative low	−412.30
Mutation*	46%	ERC negative high	−201.63
Primitive	42%	ERC positive low	96.87
Terminal/Node bias	25%	ERC positive high	382.84
Set		Value	
Functions		ADD, SUB, MUL, DIV, POW, SQRT, LOG	
Terminals		11 r_t periods $\{r_{t-1}, r_{t-2}, \ldots, r_{t-11}\}$, 10 r_y periods $\{r_{y-1}, r_{y-2}, \ldots, r_{y-10}\}$, ERC, Constants in the range $[-4,4]$	

5   Experimental Setup

The purpose of our experiments is to compare the GP against the existing
MCRP and burn analysis (BA) against contract prices as quoted by the Chicago
Mercentile Exchange (CME). We use BA as it is the most frequently used benchmark in financial applications, where the expected prices under P are calculated
based on the cost and payout of the same contract in the previous year. It
computes the expected outcome over the accumulation period $I(\tau_1, \tau_2)$ with an
additional risk premium that may occur. Therefore, $Q = P$ and the MPR is zero.
BA can not price contracts on a daily basis, but acts as a reasonable benchmark.

For this paper we use the GP outlined in [5], which is a hybrid GP that
decomposed the problem of rainfall prediction into smaller subproblems assisted
by a Genetic Algorithm (GA). For details of this technique, hereafter referred to
as GP/GA, see [3]. GP/GA has been shown to outperform the current approach
of MCRP on European data sets. We tune the parameters for MCRP on the
historical data and tune GP/GA using a package called iRace [19] on the training
set. We present the optimal parameters along with the terminals and functions
for GP/GA in Table 1.

Evaluating the predictive performance of the algorithms at predicting rainfall
is crucial before we look at the pricing performance. We expect that the better
the rainfall prediction the better the pricing performance. Therefore, we run
the GP/GA algorithm and compare its rainfall predictive performance against
MCRP, on all 10 data sets specified in Sect. 2. This is the first time GP has been
applied to the data of U.S.A. cities that are used for rainfall derivatives.

We train GP/GA from 01/Jan/2001–31/Dec/2010 before testing on the
unseen test set (01/Jan/2011–31/Dec/2011). Recall that Sect. 4.1 discussed the
effect of different strategies. Based on previous experiments we discovered that

100 runs, saving the best 10 predictions per run, gave us the best performance in order to estimate a PDF that we can price under. Therefore, we report the average predictive performance over the 100 runs for each city. Additionally, we run MCRP 10,000 times using the mixed-exponential distribution to estimate the level of rainfall on a particular day.

6 Results

The performance of rainfall prediction of GP/GA and MCRP is shown in Table 2 based on the average RMSE performance on the testing set for each city.

Table 2. The average RMSE performance in tenths of mm for each of our approaches across each city. The best performance is shown in bold.

City	GP/GA	MCRP
Chicago	776.19	**703.05**
Dallas	**524.05**	1543.45
Des Moines	**526.55**	825.22
Detroit	653.42	**498.86**
Jacksonville	**667.10**	1098.33
Kansas	**513.59**	891.70
Los Angeles	**321.97**	941.00
New York	1087.66	**987.21**
Portland	**530.04**	636.07
Raleigh	**561.43**	829.17

GP/GA achieved the lowest RMSE over seven data sets compared to MCRP, which outperformed GP/GA three times. This is a very good result, showing that GP/GA predicts the underlying weather variable of rainfall more accurately than the most commonly used approach in the literature. This is essential to avoid problems of mispricing, which decrease the confidence within the price of derived contracts.

In order to determine whether the above results are statistically significant, we compare the two approaches by using the Wilcoxon signed-rank test. The null hypothesis that there is no significant difference between both approaches is rejected with a p value of 0.0195, which is less than the 5% level. Therefore, GP/GA provides more accurate rainfall predictions.

We now turn to pricing the contracts using GP/GA with MCRP and BA as benchmarks. Due to the limited availability of complete data from Bloomberg, we present the results of pricing for 3 of the above cities, Detroit, Jacksonville and New York over the monthly contracts for periods March to October. Based on the general performance of the algorithms from Table 2, we would expect MCRP to price more accurately in two out of these three cities. Table 3 shows

Table 3. The prices derived from GP/GA, MCRP and BA are shown with the comparison from the quoted prices on the CME for monthly contracts from March - October.

	Contract period	CME	GP/GA	MCRP	BA
Detroit	March	2.30	2.90	2.57	**2.38**
	April	2.70	2.99	3.05	**2.88**
	May	4.10	**4.18**	3.52	3.40
	June	3.50	3.23	**3.46**	3.55
	July	3.60	3.32	**3.69**	3.24
	August	3.00	**3.06**	3.60	3.31
	September	3.00	3.21	**3.09**	3.33
	October	2.40	3.44	2.91	**2.53**
Jacksonville	March	3.70	5.32	3.99	**3.87**
	April	2.40	**2.55**	2.87	2.84
	May	2.80	**2.67**	3.18	2.50
	June	7.50	**6.39**	5.72	6.16
	July	7.00	**6.91**	7.57	6.32
	August	7.00	4.10	8.29	**6.44**
	September	8.10	4.72	6.90	**8.02**
	October	2.60	**2.92**	4.19	4.03
New York	March	4.20	3.59	3.75	**4.26**
	April	4.40	3.68	3.96	**4.30**
	May	3.20	**3.71**	4.54	3.76
	June	5.00	4.37	**4.69**	4.42
	July	4.50	2.87	**4.85**	4.93
	August	4.30	**4.46**	4.53	4.52
	September	4.20	4.95	**3.99**	3.88
	October	4.60	6.06	**3.98**	3.90

the prices for each contract against the actual contract price traded on the CME. In order to generate the prices, we follow the methodology outlined in Sect. 4. Our goal is to price as close to the CME as possible.

Table 3 shows that GP/GA prices closer to the CME 9 times, while MCRP priced closer 7 times and BA priced closer 8 times. According to the Friedman test, at the 5% significance level there was no significant difference between approaches with a p value of 0.5818. This important result shows that GP/GA is able to price rainfall derivatives comparably to those on the CME. Interestingly, these findings support the hypothesis that better prediction leads to better pricing, which is shown in Table 2, where MCRP outperformed GP/GA for Detroit and New York for rainfall prediction. For each of those two cities MCRP priced closer to the CME than GP/GA. Similarly, GP/GA priced closer to the CME than MCRP for Jacksonville. For the purpose of this paper we leave the MPR constant at 0, but it would be possible to shift our predictions in line with the contract prices quoted by the CME.

Please note these prices were calculated based on all available information up to 2011 (31/12/2010) and are the result of the historical average payoff. Usually with pricing, the price changes over time depending on whether more or less rainfall is expected and trader behaviour gets nearer to maturity. Unfortunately we are unable to track the prices due to the lack of data available.

One of the drawbacks to the current procedure of having a single rainfall equation to explain a year of rainfall is the difficulty on predicting the chaotic nature of rainfall time-series data. This creates models that can not capture the dynamics of rainfall over time, but instead capture the general trend over the year. Therefore, we propose moving away from a one-size-fits-all model and have contract-specific models.

To improve the pricing under Q, we propose building individual rainfall models for each contract. From the experimentation, we noticed that having separate models should increase the predictive accuracy, as we focus on a smaller subset of data. We split the training set into 3 month partitions, where the first two months are the months prior to the contract of interest. For example, predicting a contract in March would consist of the data from 01/Jan–31/Mar. We perform this partition for every year to train our model before testing on the same partition. We provide the results of RMSE for GP (GP/GA-P) and MCRP (MCRP-P) under this partition set up in Table 4, along with the new prices of GP. The prices for MCRP remain unchanged, because the model is still the same. This is one of the weaknesses of MCRP is that it can not be used to develop dynamic models for pricing, whereas GP can take full advantage of dynamic modelling.

Using the results from Table 4, we observe better predictive accuracy when partitioning the data into 3 month segments and the behaviour of rainfall is better explained. By partitioning the data we outperform MCRP in 16 cases in terms of rainfall prediction (66.67%), which shows that having a dynamic model is better and in no case do we perform worse than GP predicting over an entire year. Based on the Wilcoxon signed rank test, GP/GA statistically outperforms MCRP at the 5% significance level with a p value of 0.0278, showing that partitioning the data does statistically lead to better predictive accuracy. Moreover, this reflects in more accurate pricing: in 19 cases we price closer to the CME than GP/GA before partitioning. Table 5 shows the results of the Friedman test and Holm post-hoc test for the results in Table 4.

Table 5 shows that partitioning the data has a really positive effect on the accuracy of our pricing, whereby GP/GA-P achieves an average rank of 1.95, compared with BA, MCRP and GP/GA (2.40, 2.73 and 2.92 respectively). Note that partitioning the time series leads to a significant increase against GP/GA for pricing with a p value of 0.0101 at the 5% significance level. GP/GA-P does not outperform MCRP at the 5% significance level for the problem of pricing at the CME, but it does so at the 10% significance level.

Table 4. The predictive accuracy of GP/GA-P and MCRP-P, along with the prices for GP/GA and GP/GA-P and CME. The bold values represents a superior performance in either rainfall prediction or pricing performance.

City	Contract	Rainfall prediction		Contract prices		CME
		GP/GA-P	MCRP-P	GP/GA-P	GP/GA	
Detroit	March	**540.62**	575.27	**2.24**	2.90	2.30
	April	606.06	**586.26**	**2.93**	2.99	2.70
	May	**562.86**	607.70	**4.18**	4.18	4.10
	June	**533.23**	538.05	**3.68**	3.23	3.50
	July	648.17	**484.01**	**3.58**	3.32	3.60
	August	738.62	**540.95**	**3.05**	3.06	3.00
	September	**791.66**	857.00	**2.86**	3.21	3.00
	October	**593.26**	827.28	3.71	**3.44**	2.40
Jacksonville	March	**459.87**	1349.03	**3.47**	5.32	3.70
	April	**361.95**	1397.80	**2.32**	2.55	2.40
	May	**570.78**	1270.63	**2.70**	2.67	2.80
	June	**535.54**	1051.15	**7.94**	6.39	7.50
	July	**571.43**	660.87	7.13	**6.91**	7.00
	August	606.88	**563.55**	**5.23**	4.10	7.00
	September	772.97	**760.28**	**6.05**	4.72	8.10
	October	**538.14**	975.60	**2.86**	2.92	2.60
New York	March	611.27	**343.46**	3.52	**3.59**	4.20
	April	512.40	**430.12**	**4.22**	3.68	4.40
	May	**462.04**	658.33	2.69	**3.71**	3.20
	June	**483.19**	955.26	**5.14**	4.37	5.00
	July	**1214.59**	1510.32	**5.21**	2.87	4.50
	August	**1885.99**	1933.50	4.50	**4.46**	4.30
	September	1921.82	**1718.51**	**4.61**	4.95	4.20
	October	**768.11**	1458.09	**4.05**	6.06	4.60

One of the issues of having contract specific equations is the increase in complexity by having multiple equations to explain the rainfall process over the year. For each city we would have eight models explaining the data rather than one model. Future work should look at condensing the concept of GP/GA-P into a single model.

To summarise, GP/GA performs very well for predicting the underlying weather variable of rainfall and for pricing against MCRP. Moreover, we have shown the benefits of having a separate GP for each contract by partitioning the time series into shorter time frames. We witness a statistical improvement over GP/GA without partitioning and MCRP and outperform (but not statistically) BA, which should be the more accurate approach for the initial pricing

Table 5. The mean ranks of the four approaches, the Friedman test statistic and the respective p values for the Holm post-hoc test (using the best method (GP/GA-P) as the control method). Significant results are shown in bold.

Friedman p-value	0.0467		
Approach	Ranks	p value	Holm score
GP/GA-P	**1.95**	-	
BA	2.40	0.2404	0.0500
MCRP	2.73	0.0386	0.0250
GP/GA	2.92	**0.0101**	0.0167

of contracts. This is a very important step within pricing, being able to predict the level of rainfall better than current approaches and to price appropriately as well, with the data sets we have available to us.

7   Conclusion

This paper introduces a novel approach for dealing with the pricing of rainfall derivatives. Our novelty is the proposed creation of probabilistic models generated from Genetic Programming (GP), with the assistance of Markov chain Monte Carlo (MCMC). By developing this approach, we are able to price rainfall derivatives using the Esscher transform, a popular technique for calculating risk premiums. The motivation for this paper comes from the work of [3–5] where GP was used to predict the rainfall time series with a range of alternative approaches across European cities. However, the work did not present information on pricing. In this paper we show the effect of pricing under GP with the assistance of MCMC in order to create a probabilistic density function, which we are able to price under risk-neutral conditions.

We evaluate the performance of rainfall prediction on U.S.A. cities using a decomposition based Genetic Programming (GP/GA) [5]. We find sufficient evidence that the algorithm has a superior predictive power than the most currently used approach within the literature of rainfall derivatives. Based on the hypothesis that better prediction leads to better pricing [12], we would expect our model to perform better for pricing in those cities where GP/GA outperformed the standard approach. We find that there is evidence to suggest that the hypothesis is true, in the contracts for cities we had available to us. In an attempt to increase the pricing performance under GP/GA we proposed generating contract-specific models, rather than a one-size-fits-all approach. We found this to significantly increase predictive accuracy and subsequently the pricing performance.

Future work will include looking at GP to produce stochastic equations to describe the rainfall time series, this would replace the sampling strategy and MCMC before applying the risk-neutral densities. More analysis on the proposed contract specific approach in an attempt to maximise the performance. Finally, upon the availability of rainfall derivative data, we can understand the pricing dynamics and how the prices change over time, which includes studying the effect that the market price of risk has on rainfall derivative contracts.

References

1. Wilks, D.S.: Multisite generalization of a daily stochastic precipitation generation model. J. Hydrol. **210**, 178–191 (1998)
2. Rodriguez-Iturbe, I., Cox, D.R., Isham, V.: Some models for rainfall based on stochastic point processes. Proc. R. Soc. Lond. A: Math. Phys. Eng. Sci. **410**(1839), 269–288 (1987)
3. Cramer, S., Kampouridis, M., Freitas, A.A., Alexandridis, A.: Predicting rainfall in the context of rainfall derivatives using genetic programming. In: 2015 IEEE Symposium Series on Computational Intelligence for Financial Engineering and Economics, pp. 711–718, December 2015
4. Cramer, S., Kampouridis, M., Freitas, A.A.: Feature engineering for improving financial derivatives-based rainfall prediction. In: Proceedings of 2016 IEEE Congress on Evolutionary Computation, Vancouver. IEEE Press, July 2016
5. Cramer, S., Kampouridis, M., Freitas, A.: A genetic decomposition algorithm for predicting rainfall within financial weather derivatives. In: Proceedings of the Genetic and Evolutionary Computation Conference 2016, GECCO 2016, pp. 885–892. ACM, New York (2016)
6. Carmona, R., Diko, P.: Pricing precipitation based derivatives. Int. J. Theor. Appl. Financ. **08**(07), 959–988 (2005)
7. Cabrera, B.L., Odening, M., Ritter, M.: Pricing rainfall futures at the CME. J. Bank. Financ. **37**(11), 4286–4298 (2013)
8. Leobacher, G., Ngare, P.: On modelling and pricing rainfall derivatives with seasonality. Appl. Math. Financ. **18**(1), 71–91 (2011)
9. Ritter, M., Mußhoff, O., Odening, M.: Minimizing geographical basis risk of weather derivatives using a multi-site rainfall model. Comput. Econ. **44**(1), 67–86 (2014)
10. Noven, R.C., Veraart, A.E.D., Gandy, A.: A lévy-driven rainfall model with applications to futures pricing. Adv. Stat. Anal. **99**(4), 403–432 (2015)
11. Jewson, S., Ziehmann, C., Brix, A.: Weather Derivative Valuation. Cambridge University Press, Cambridge (2010)
12. Alexandridis, A., Zapranis, A.: Weather Derivatives: Modeling and Pricing Weather-Related Risk. Springer, New York (2013)
13. Jenson, B., Nielsen, J.: Pricing by no arbitrage. In: Cox, D., Hinkley, D., Barndorff-Nielsen, O. (eds.) Time Series Models: In Econometrics Finance and Other Fields. Chapman & Hall/CRC/Taylor & Francis, New York (1996)
14. Benth, F.E., Benth, J.: Modelling and Pricing Derivatives on Precipitation, chap. 8, pp. 179–195. World Scientific (2012)
15. Bingham, N., Kiesel, R.: Risk-Neutral Valuation: Pricing and Hedging of Financial Derivatives. Springer Finance Textbooks. Springer, Heidelberg (2004)
16. Gerber, H., Shiu, E.S.W.: Option pricing by Esscher transforms. Insur. Math. Econ. **16**(3), 287 (1995)
17. Plummer, M.: JAGS: a program for analysis of Bayesian graphical models using Gibbs sampling. In: Proceedings of the 3rd International Workshop on Distributed Statistical Computing (2003)

18. Barndorff-Nielsen, O.E.: Normal inverse Gaussian distributions and stochastic volatility modelling. Scand. J. Stat. **24**(1), 1–13 (1997)

19. López-Ibáñez, M., Dubois-Lacoste, J., Stützle, T., Birattari, M.: The irace package: iterated racing for automatic algorithm configuration. Technical report, IRIDIA, Université Libre de Bruxelles, Belgium (2011)

Dynamic Portfolio Optimization in Ultra-High Frequency Environment

Patryk Filipiak and Piotr Lipinski[✉]

Computational Intelligence Research Group, Institute of Computer Science,
University of Wroclaw, Wroclaw, Poland
{patryk.filipiak,piotr.lipinski}@cs.uni.wroc.pl

Abstract. This paper concerns the problem of portfolio optimization in the context of ultra-high frequency environment with dynamic and frequent changes in statistics of financial assets. It aims at providing Pareto fronts of optimal portfolios and updating them when estimated return rates or risks of financial assets change. The problem is defined in terms of dynamic optimization and solved online with a proposed evolutionary algorithm. Experiments concern ultra-high frequency time series coming from the London Stock Exchange Rebuilt Order Book database and the FTSE100 index.

Keywords: Portfolio optimization · Dynamic optimization problems · Multi-objective optimization · Evolutionary algorithms · Ultra-high frequency time series

1 Introduction

One of the main goals for financial experts and stock market traders is to optimally allocate their capital among various available financial assets. Searching for optimal portfolios of stocks, which are related to random future returns, seems to pose a difficult task. It is usually formulated as a risk minimization problem under a constraint of expected portfolio return, which falls under the umbrella of multi-objective optimization, like the Modern Portfolio Theory (MPT) introduced by Markowitz [1]. Sometimes, it is further rephrased as a single-objective problem by introducing performance measures that aim at finding a good trade-off between the risk and the expected return, such as Sharpe ratio [2,3], Sortino ratio [4], Treynor ratio [5], Sterling ratio [5], or the like.

In the classic problem of portfolio optimization, introduced by Markowitz in MPT, the risk was defined by the variance of return rates. A solution to the problem stated this way can be found algebraically [1], although such a formulation was often criticized due to some artificial assumptions (that we will discuss later). In order to address these issues, a number of modifications of the classical problem were proposed. Many of them suggested alternative risk measures (such as semicovariance), or rejected certain artificial assumptions (such as unlimited short sale), or introduced a cardinality constraint. In [6],

G. Squillero and K. Sim (Eds.): EvoApplications 2017, Part I, LNCS 10199, pp. 34–50, 2017.
DOI: 10.1007/978-3-319-55849-3_3

the portfolio selection was formulated as a tri-objective optimization problem concerning risk, return and a number of securities in the portfolio. In [7], the portfolio optimization was studied with a constraint on the portfolio cardinality, whereas in [8,9], the problem was considered with minimum transaction lots. All the above approaches led to new formulations of the portfolio optimization problem, and thus required adequate solution finding techniques.

Evolutionary Algorithms (EAs) are often applied to the portfolio optimization problems [10–12]. In particular, many single- and multi-objective Genetic Algorithms (GAs) were developed for this purpose over the last decade [13,14]. In [15], a multi-objective EA was proposed for the portfolio optimization task set in the practical context that incorporated realistic constraints into the problem model and preference criterion into the evolutionary search. In [16], the envelope-based multi-objective EA, which integrated an active set algorithm with a multi-objective EA, was suggested. In [17], five multi-objective EAs, such as Niched Pareto Genetic Algorithm 2 (NPGA2), Non-dominated Sorting Genetic Algorithm 2 (NSGA-II), Pareto Envelope-based Selection Algorithm (PESA), Strength Pareto Evolutionary Algorithm 2 (SPEA2), and e-Multiobjective Evolutionary Algorithm (e-MOEA), were applied to the mean-variance cardinality constrained portfolio optimization problem (MVCCPO). Beside the EAs, there are also some approaches based on differential evolution [18], particle swarm optimization [19,20], and metaheuristics [21,22]. In [23], the problem was tackled with greedy search, simulated annealing, and ant colony optimization.

The portfolio optimization typically concerns long-term investments and is usually solved on the ground of lower frequency financial time series. Simultaneously, there is more and more attention drawn to the high frequency portfolio optimization. In [24], the portfolio optimization with high frequency data was discussed. In [25], a financial system for building long and short portfolios using intraday patterns was introduced. In [26], the minimum variance portfolio optimization with intraday data was proposed and discussed in the context of some empirical comparison with different measures on Brazilian stock market. Such a high frequency often leads to difficult computational problems and requires new efficient algorithms that are not only capable of selecting efficient portfolios, but also fast enough to provide results online.

In this paper, the problem of portfolio optimization is revisited in the context of ultra-high frequency environment with dynamic and frequent changes in statistics of financial assets. Therefore, the aim is to provide a Pareto front of optimal portfolios and to update it when estimated return rates or risks of financial assets change. The problem is formulated as a Dynamic Optimization Problem (DOP) and is solved online with a proposed EA.

2   Problem of Portfolio Optimization Revisited

Let $\mathcal{A}_1, \mathcal{A}_2, \ldots, \mathcal{A}_d$ denote $d > 0$ available financial assets. For all $i = 1, \ldots, d$ let $v_t^i \geq 0$ denote a value of the i-th asset at a given time $t \in \mathbb{N}$. The return of the i-th asset at the time t is $r_t^i = (v_t^i - v_{t-1}^i)/v_{t-1}^i$.

Given a fixed time $t_0 \in \mathbb{N}$, one may estimate the expected return rate, the variance, the covariance, and the correlation of the return rates of the assets, by considering the period of the most recent $\Delta t > 0$ time instants, i.e. the interval $\{t_0 - \Delta t + 1, ..., t_0\}$. Particularly, the expected return rate $\mathbb{E}[R]$ of an asset at the time t_0 is computed as the average return rate over the last Δt time instants. Analogously, one can obtain the variance of return rates $\mathbf{Var}[R]$, the covariance of return rates $\mathbf{Cov}[\mathbf{R}]$, etc.

2.1   Classic Portfolio Optimization

Let $\mathbf{R} = (R_1, R_2, \ldots, R_d)^T$ denote a real-valued random vector of return rates of d financial assets, as observed at a fixed time t_0. Let $\boldsymbol{\mu} = (\mu_1, \mu_2, \ldots, \mu_d)^T = \mathbb{E}[\mathbf{R}] \in \mathbb{R}^d$ denote a vector of expected return rates of these assets, and let $\boldsymbol{\Sigma} = \mathbf{Cov}[\mathbf{R}] \in \mathbb{R}^{d \times d}$ denote a corresponding covariance matrix. It is assumed that the financial assets are not risk-free, so the variance of their return rates is positive, i.e. the covariance matrix $\boldsymbol{\Sigma}$ is positively defined (hence invertible).

A portfolio is defined as a vector $\mathbf{p} = (p_1, p_2, \ldots, p_d)^T \in \mathbb{R}^d$, such that $\sum_{i=1}^d p_i = 1$. The return rate of the portfolio $\mathbf{p}$ is a random variable $R_{\mathbf{p}} = \mathbf{p}^T \mathbf{R}$. The expected return rate of the portfolio $\mathbf{p}$ equals $\mathbb{E}[R_{\mathbf{p}}] = \mathbb{E}[\mathbf{p}^T \mathbf{R}] = \mathbf{p}^T \mathbb{E}[\mathbf{R}] = \mathbf{p}^T \boldsymbol{\mu}$. The risk of the portfolio $\mathbf{p}$, defined by the variance of its return rates, equals $\mathbf{Var}[R_{\mathbf{p}}] = \mathbf{Var}[\mathbf{p}^T \mathbf{R}] = \mathbf{p}^T \mathbf{Cov}[\mathbf{R}]\mathbf{p} = \mathbf{p}^T \boldsymbol{\Sigma} \mathbf{p}$.

The optimal portfolio is the one that minimizes the risk for a given value of the expected return rate $e \geq 0$. Formally, it may be formulated as a solution to the minimization problem of the expression

$$\frac{1}{2}\mathbf{p}^T \boldsymbol{\Sigma} \mathbf{p} \quad \text{subject to} \quad \begin{cases} \mathbf{p}^T \boldsymbol{\mu} = e, \\ \mathbf{p}^T \mathbf{1} = 1. \end{cases} \tag{1}$$

Such an optimization problem may be solved using the Lagrange multipliers method, which leads to

$$\mathbf{p} = \frac{1}{D}\left[(eC - A)\boldsymbol{\Sigma}^{-1}\boldsymbol{\mu} + (B - eA)\boldsymbol{\Sigma}^{-1}\mathbf{1}\right]$$

$$= \frac{1}{D}(B\boldsymbol{\Sigma}^{-1}\mathbf{1} - A\boldsymbol{\Sigma}^{-1}\boldsymbol{\mu}) + e\frac{1}{D}(C\boldsymbol{\Sigma}^{-1}\boldsymbol{\mu} - A\boldsymbol{\Sigma}^{-1}\mathbf{1}) \tag{2}$$

with $A = \boldsymbol{\mu}^T \boldsymbol{\Sigma}^{-1} \mathbf{1}$, $B = \boldsymbol{\mu}^T \boldsymbol{\Sigma}^{-1} \boldsymbol{\mu}$, $C = \mathbf{1}^T \boldsymbol{\Sigma}^{-1} \mathbf{1}$, $D = BC - A^2$.

2.2   Modifications of the Classic Problem

The classic Markowitz model was often criticized due to certain artificial assumptions. Firstly, it allows for unlimited short sell (i.e. the components of the portfolio vector $\mathbf{p}$ may be negative), which is rarely possible in practice. Secondly, the classic risk measure, defined by the variance of return rates, although very convenient in the theoretical modeling, it does not exactly correspond with practical expectations of stock market traders. The latter tend to be more dissatisfied with returns below the expected level rather than those above it. Therefore, some extensions of the classic portfolio optimization problem were introduced, e.g. with the semicovariance risk measure, downside risk measures, or practictioner's measures based on drowdowns.

2.3 Dynamic Modeling

For the sake of simplicity, the portfolio optimization problems are typically considered at fixed time steps. On one hand such an approach may be convenient for practitioners, since financial experts and stock market traders are often interested in analyzing long-term investments in stable environments. On the other hand, the so-called high-frequency trading techniques gain increasing interest in these days. Many contemporary automatic trading systems allow for making transactions minute by minute or even more frequently. Certainly, this modern approach raises some issues that must be addressed in the portfolio optimization problem. First of all, the risk measure defined by the variance of return rates may no longer be appropriate in high-frequency time series, as it can grow excessively high in such conditions. Furthermore, the optimization algorithms must be efficient in the environments with high-frequencies of changes in order to catch up with incoming data.

In this paper we address the portfolio optimization problem defined as DOP, for which the aim is not only to find a single portfolio that is optimal at a certain time t_0, yet also a family of optimal portfolios computed for the successive time steps $t_1, t_2, \ldots, t_n$ (respectively). As a matter of fact, the above DOP can be solved in a step-wise manner, by analyzing the problem at each time step t separately. However, such a naive approach is often rather ineffective, since it tackles each sub-problem by starting from scratch, whereas the dynamic algorithms are able to reuse the knowledge gathered at the former steps.

3   Solving the Dynamic Optimization Problem

In the remainder of this paper we will concern a portfolio of $d = 101$ financial instruments being the constituents of FTSE100 [27]. The latter is a commonly used share index which comprises the 100 most highly capitalized blue chip companies listed on London Stock Exchange[1]. Despite the fact that theoretically best diversification might be achieved by considering all the instruments available on the market, it is reasonable for investors (due to practical limitations) to restrict their portfolios to certain potentially most profitable instruments like the ones above. Another practical assumption made in this study is the restriction to long-only portfolios, which reduces the number of implicit interdependencies that could bias the results, as suggested in [28].

---

[1] One of the companies, Royal Dutch Shell, was listed as two separate assets throughout the analyzed time period, thus FTSE100 essentially consisted of 101 components.

3.1   Definition of Dynamic Portfolio Optimization Problem

Mathematically, the DOP in hand is defined as follows. For all time steps $t = 1, 2, \ldots, N_{gen}$ find such weight vectors $w^{(t)} \in [0,1]^d$ that

(a) maximize the expected return function $f^{(t)}_{return}(\cdot)$, and
(b) minimize the expected risk function $f^{(t)}_{risk}(\cdot)$,

subject to $\sum_{i=1}^{d} w_i^{(t)} = 1$, where $w^{(t)} = (w_1^{(t)}, \ldots, w_d^{(t)})$. For simplicity of notation, we introduce the compound dynamic objective function $F^{(t)} : [0,1]^d \to \mathbb{R}^2$ and rephrase the above optimization criteria as follows

$$\forall_t \quad \text{minimize } F^{(t)}(\cdot) = (-f^{(t)}_{return}(\cdot), f^{(t)}_{risk}(\cdot)) \text{ in Pareto sense.} \qquad (3)$$

In compliance with the classic portfolio optimization theory [29], we define the expected return function as a weighted sum of expected returns among all the portfolio components

$$f^{(t)}_{return}(w^{(t)}) = \left[w_1^{(t)} \cdots w_d^{(t)} \right] \mathbb{E}R^{(t)} = \sum_{i=1}^{d} w_i^{(t)} \mathbb{E}R_i^{(t)} \qquad (4)$$

with the expectations calculated for the $\Delta t > 0$ most recent time steps

$$\mathbb{E}R_i^{(t)} = \frac{1}{\Delta t} \sum_{\tau=0}^{\Delta t - 1} R_i^{(t-\tau)} = \frac{1}{\Delta t} \sum_{\tau=0}^{\Delta t - 1} \frac{v_i^{(t-\tau)} - v_i^{(t-\tau-1)}}{v_i^{(t-\tau-1)}}, \qquad (5)$$

where $v_i^{(t)} \geq 0$ is the value of the i-th asset ($i = 1, \ldots, d$) at the moment t.

As it was discussed earlier, numerous expected risk measures were proposed in the literature. In this paper we consider the following three:

(a) **Covariance of Returns**

$$f^{(t)}_{cov}(w^{(t)}) = \left[w_1^{(t)} \cdots w_d^{(t)} \right] \mathbf{Cov}[R^{(t)}] \begin{bmatrix} w_1^{(t)} \\ \vdots \\ w_d^{(t)} \end{bmatrix}, \qquad (6)$$

where $\mathbf{Cov}[R^{(t)}] \in \mathbb{R}^{d \times d}$.

(b) **Semicovariance of Returns**

$$f^{(t)}_{semi}(w^{(t)}) = \left[w_1^{(t)} \cdots w_d^{(t)} \right] \mathbf{SemiCov}[R^{(t)}] \begin{bmatrix} w_1^{(t)} \\ \vdots \\ w_d^{(t)} \end{bmatrix}, \qquad (7)$$

where $\mathbf{SemiCov}[R^{(t)}] = [s_{ij}^{(t)}]_{1 \leq i,j \leq d}$ is defined as follows

$$s_{ij}^{(t)} = \frac{1}{\Delta t} \sum_{\tau=0}^{\Delta t - 1} \min\{R_i^{(t-\tau)} - \mathbb{E}R_i^{(t)}, 0\} \cdot \min\{R_j^{(t-\tau)} - \mathbb{E}R_j^{(t)}, 0\}. \qquad (8)$$

(c) **Average Maximum Drowdown**

$$f_{amd}^{(t)}(w^{(t)}) = \left[w_1^{(t)} \cdots w_d^{(t)} \right] \frac{[\max\_dd_1] + \ldots + [\max\_dd_n]}{n} \qquad (9)$$

where Δt is split into $n > 0$ equally long time intervals. In each such interval, the max_dd $\in \mathbb{R}^d$ is a vector of maximal drowdowns $(v_i^{high} - v_i^{low})/v_i^{high}$ for $i = 1, \ldots, d$ with (v_i^{high}, v_i^{low}) being a pair of arguments maximizing

$$\left\{ \left(\frac{v_i^{(t_1)} - v_i^{(t_2)}}{v_i^{(t_1)}} \right) ; \quad t_1 < t_2 \wedge v_i^{(t_1)} \geq v_i^{(t_2)} \right\} \qquad (10)$$

amid all time step pairs t_1, t_2 in a given time interval.

3.2 Dynamic Evolutionary Algorithm

Let us remind that a variant of the portfolio optimization problem analyzed in this paper is intractable analytically due to the long-only assumption and the use of semicovariance and average maximum drowdowns as risk measures. Additionally, the dynamic model defined in the previous subsection introduces an uncertainty factor imposed by time-dependent changes of the objective function $F^{(t)}$, which makes an optimum finding even more complicated.

We handle these difficulties by applying a proposed NSGA-II based EA for dynamic portfolio optimization (abbreviated as NSGA-II-DPO), which is a conglomerate of the algorithms DNSGA-II-A and DNSGA-II-B introduced in [30]. Both of them utilize simple techniques for maintaining diversity within a population in order to catch up with landscape changes. The former algorithm achieves that by performing repeatable replacements of worst individuals in a population with randomly generated candidate solutions (referred to as Random Immigrants), whereas the latter one greatly increases the mutation rate in order to prevent stagnation. The reasons why we chose these NSGA-II based EAs were due to their relative simplicity, general recognition, and the lack of criteria normalization requirement.

A pseudo-code of NSGA-II-DPO is presented in Algorithm 1. The proposed EA maintains a population P_t consisting of $M_{size} > 0$ individuals. We use a

---

Algorithm 1. NSGA-II-DPO

$P_1 = \text{RandomPopulation}(M_{size})$
for $t = 1 \rightarrow N_{gen}$ **do**
    $\text{Evaluate}(P_t)$
    $P_t = \text{Reduce}(P_t, M_{size} - M_{ri}) \cup \text{RandomImmigrants}(M_{ri})$
    for $k = 1 \rightarrow N_{sub}$ **do**
        $P_t' = \text{NSGA-II-Evolve}(P_t)$
    end for
    $P_{t+1} = \text{Reduce}(P_t \cup P_t', M_{size})$
end for

Algorithm 2. NSGA-II-Evolve(P_t)

$C_t = \text{Selection}(P_t)$
$C'_t = \text{Crossover}(C_t)$
$C''_t = \text{Mutation}(C'_t)$
$\mathcal{L} = \text{NonDominatedSorting}(P_t \cup C''_t)$
$P'_t = \emptyset, i = 1$
while $\text{size}(P'_t) + \text{size}(\mathcal{L}_i) \le M_{size}$ **do**
$\quad \text{Sort}(\mathcal{L}_i, \text{CrowdingDistance}(\mathcal{L}_i))$
$\quad P'_t = P'_t \cup \mathcal{L}_i$
$\quad i = i + 1$
end while
$\text{Sort}(\mathcal{L}_i, \text{CrowdingDistance}(\mathcal{L}_i))$
$P'_t = P'_t \cup \text{Reduce}(\mathcal{L}_i, M_{size} - \text{size}(P'_t))$
return P'_t

---

fixed number of $N_{gen} > 0$ generations as a stopping criterion, since the portfolio optimization problem has no natural termination condition by itself. Each t-th iteration of the suggested EA begins with a re-evaluation of candidate solutions and an introduction of $M_{ri} \ge 0$ random immigrants (right after making room for them by reducing the population P_t to the $M_{size} - M_{ri}$ best individuals). Next, the inner loop consisting of $N_{sub} > 0$ executions of NSGA-II-Evolve() is launched. This procedure (shown in Algorithm 2) represents exactly one iteration of the original NSGA-II (including the non-dominated sorting algorithm and the reduction technique based on Pareto dominance and/or the crowding distance) as first introduced in [31]. The role of the inner loop is purely technical. It allows to parametrize the number of generations (N_{sub}) between any two consecutive landscape changes t and $t + 1$. When the inner loop ends, the outcomes of a series of NSGA-II-Evolve() invocations, denoted as P'_t, are added to P_t. Finally, the best M_{size} solutions out of $P_t \cup P'_t$ are selected for the next generation.

The following two aspects of the evolutionary approach presented above require more detailed descriptions:

Chromosomal Representation of Solutions. The long-only assumption imposes that the problem domain is a d-dimensional simplex of the following form

$$D = \left\{ (w_1^{(t)}, \dots, w_d^{(t)}); \ \sum_{i=1}^{d} w_i^{(t)} = 1 \right\} \subset [0,1]^d \quad \text{for all } t = 1, 2, \dots, N_{gen}. \quad (11)$$

However, from the EA perspective it is more convenient to deal with the search space $[0,1]^d$. To this end, we introduce a time-invariant "genotype → phenotype" mapping $\varphi_q : [0,1]^d \to D$ defined as follows

$$\varphi_q(w_1^{(t)}, \dots, w_d^{(t)}) = \left(\frac{(w_1^{(t)})^q}{\sum_{i=1}^{d}(w_i^{(t)})^q}, \dots, \frac{(w_d^{(t)})^q}{\sum_{i=1}^{d}(w_i^{(t)})^q} \right) \quad (12)$$

where $q \in \mathbb{N}_+$ is a fixed exponent. Note that the parameter q regulates a dispersion of portfolio components. Particularly, $q = 1$ leads to a nearly uniform distribution of weights, whereas $q > 1$ amplifies the higher weights and diminishes the lower ones. We verified experimentally that the best results on the analyzed portfolio optimization tasks were achieved with $q = 5$.

Introduction of Random Immigrants. It is a common practice to generate random immigrants with a uniform distribution so that an EA could refresh its information about all the currently unobserved parts of the search space. Nonetheless, in the case of ultra-high frequency portfolio optimization one does not expect severe landscape changes. Hence, we suggest to shift from the generally good practice to the somewhat more domain-specific behavior.

The long-only assumption limits the range of each weight $w_i^{(t)}$ to the interval $[0, 1]$. As a result, at least one unit portfolio, i.e. $(0, \ldots, 0, 1, 0, \ldots, 0) \in [0, 1]^d$ must lie on a Pareto front, being the most profitable (and of course also very risky) feasible solution. Despite the fact that unit portfolios are not interesting from the perspective of investment diversification, a presence of such individuals in a population might greatly speed up an optimum finding process. We suggest then to generate random immigrants from the pool of unit portfolios only.

3.3 Performance Measure

Let $POF, POF_{true} \subset \mathbb{R}^k$ (where $k > 0$ is a number of optimization criteria) be finite subsets of an approximated- and a true Pareto front, respectively. In this study we utilize the following three performance metrics, commonly used in dynamic multi-objective optimization [32]. Each of these metrics is calculated for all time steps t and then averaged.

(a) **Hypervolume Ratio** [32] (overall performance measure)

$$\text{HVR}(POF, POF_{true}) = \frac{\text{HV}(POF)}{\text{HV}(POF_{true})}, \tag{13}$$

where $\text{HV}(X)$ for $X = \{x_1, \ldots, x_n\} \subset \mathbb{R}^k$ is a Lebesgue integral of the set

$$\bigcup_{i=1,\ldots,n} \{y \in \mathbb{R}^k \,;\, y \prec y_0 \wedge x_i \prec y\} \tag{14}$$

for a fixed reference vector $y_0 \in \mathbb{R}^k$ and a relation of Pareto dominance "$\prec$".

(b) **Maximum Spread Ratio** [32] (diversity measure)

$$\text{MSR}(POF, POF_{true}) = \frac{\text{MS}(POF)}{\text{MS}(POF_{true})}, \tag{15}$$

where

$$\text{MS}(X) = \sqrt{\sum_{j=1}^{k} \left(\max\{x_1^j, \ldots, x_n^j\} - \min\{x_1^j, \ldots, x_n^j\} \right)^2} \tag{16}$$

for $X = \{x_1, \ldots, x_n\} \subset \mathbb{R}^k$, where $x_i = (x_i^1, \ldots, x_i^k) \in \mathbb{R}^k$ for all $i = 1, \ldots, n$.

(c) **Inverted Generational Distance** [32] (accuracy measure)

$$\text{IGD}(POF, POF_{true}) = \frac{\sqrt{\sum_{y \in POF_{true}} \min_{x \in POF} \|x - y\|^2}}{\text{size}(POF_{true})} \tag{17}$$

Note that the metrics (a) and (b) compute the ratio of POF over POF_{true} (hence the outcomes lie in the interval $[0, 1]$ with the best result in 1), whereas the metric (c) captures the Euclidean distance between these fronts (hence the outcomes lie in the interval $[0, \infty)$ with the best result in 0).

4   Experiments

All the experiments were performed on the real-world data coming from the London Stock Exchange Rebuild Order Book (LSE ROB) database that contained intraday order- and transaction information for all securities listed on the London Stock Exchange.

4.1   Data Description

LSE ROB provides all orders registered and not deleted from the order book before the beginning of the trading day (the snapshot opening position), details of all orders registered and deleted from the order book within the trading day, as well as all modifications made to existing orders. It also provides the details of all transactions.

By accessing the LSE ROB database, one is able to reconstruct entire trading days of the London Stock Exchange. Such ultra-high frequency time series are expected by some economists to contain significant knowledge of the stock market [33–35]. Additionally, some computational techniques are currently in use for extracting such knowledge in financial decision support systems [36–38].

As the transactions made are far less frequent than orders submitted to the London Stock Exchange, in the ultra-high frequency approach, the value of a financial asset is better estimated by the mean price from the order book than by the price from the last made transaction. Therefore, in the experiments, the arithmetic mean of 'best ask' and 'best bid' offers was used as the value of an asset in the portfolio optimization.

4.2   Setup

Although the original data were ultra-high frequency time series with orders recorded in irregular times, for most of the 101 financial instruments under study, there were only a few orders per minute (some particular time periods) or even one order for a couple of minutes (most of the time). Therefore, the portfolio optimization problem was considered in one-minute intervals without significant loss of generality. The analyzed time series were one-minute aggregates of the values collected between 8:30AM and 4:00PM in each trading day between 1st and 15th September 2013, i.e. 10 days × 451 min = 4510 data records.

The time interval $\Delta t = 120$ min was used for estimating the expectations of return rates and risk measures, hence each test case in our scrutiny lasted for $N_{gen} = 4510 - 120 = 4390$ generations.

Since the true Pareto fronts (POF_{true}) of the examined DOPs aren't known, we obtained their best available approximations in the following manner. For all time steps $t \in \{1, ..., N_{gen}\}$ and for all exponents $q \in \{1, ..., 10\}$, we solved the (t, q)-th portfolio optimization problem instance separately by applying NSGA-II with the population of 1000 individuals, evolved for 1000 generations, such that no further improvement could be achieved afterwards. Finally, for all t, the POF_{true} was constructed out of all the non-dominated solutions from each of the runs indexed with $(t, 1)$, $(t, 2)$, ..., $(t, 10)$.

The suggested NSGA-II-DPO was run with the population of $M = 1000$ individuals and the exponent $q = 5$. We considered twenty variants of change frequencies: $N_{sub} = 1, ..., 20$; two variants of mutation rates: 0.1 and 0.9; and three variants of Random Immigrants (RI) fraction sizes: $0\%M$, $5\%M$, and All Unit Portfolios (AUP), i.e. the full spectrum of $d = 101$ unit portfolios at once.

Each combination of the input parameters specified above was tested with the three expected risk functions announced earlier (i.e. covariance of returns, semicovariance of returns, and average maximum drowdown) and repeated 30 times. The average results are summarized in Tables 1, 2 and 3 (one per each risk measure), and illustrated in Figs. 2, 3 and 4 (accordingly). In order to assure a fair comparison, the results obtained for the first trading day, treated as an initialization period, are excluded from these summaries.

4.3   Discussion of Results

A fundamental question that had to be answered first was whether the dynamic portfolio optimization in high-frequency environment was justifiable. Following [24], we wanted to verify if such an approach had a potential to retrieve some crucial information from the ultra-high frequency stock data, or would it rather

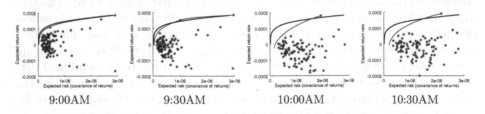

Fig. 1. Pareto optimal front obtained at 8:30AM on 3rd September (drawn with the thick line) and its interim counterparts (drawn with the thin lines) obtained at 9:00AM, 9:30AM, 10:00AM, and 10:30AM on the same day. The constituents of the FTSE100 index are marked with asterisks.

make the problem needlessly complicated without bringing any significant added value. Our experiments demonstrated that the first scenario seemed more likely.

Indeed, the Pareto optimal front that we obtained for the time instant 8:30AM on 3rd September 2013 turned out to be significantly different from the ones we computed for consecutive moments later the same day. Figure 1 illustrates that phenomenon at the time instants 9:00AM, 9:30AM, 10:00AM, and 10:30AM. Note the consecutive Pareto fronts (drawn with the thin lines) gradually drifting away from the initial front estimated at 8:30AM (drawn with the thick line). The above observation assured us that the expected risk can generally be highly volatile in the terms of minutes, hence the calculations made at the beginning of the day would no longer be accurate soon after that.

Another aim of our experiments was to assess the performance of the evolutionary approach in addressing the dynamic portfolio optimization problem. The use of NSGA-II-DPO allowed us to test a great deal of input parameters (as summarized in Tables 1, 2 and 3) and thus deduce the following:

As we expected, the landscape changes, though frequent, they were not severe. Even in the variant with the low mutation rate (0.1) and without random immigrants (0% RI) the EA was able to achieve fairly good average results according to all the three risk measures, while given enough time ($N_{sub} = 20$). Of course, such an outcome was not yet satisfactory due to the high standard deviations and too slow reactions to landscape changes.

An increase of mutation rate to 0.9 considerably improved the average performance, nevertheless the associated standard deviations remained at the relatively high level. A much greater improvement was achieved thanks to the introduction of randomly selected unit portfolios. The fraction of $M_{ri} = 5\%M = 50$ immigrants (a half of the FTSE100 constituents) sufficed to reach very good performance results in both mutation rate variants, while given $N_{sub} \geq 10$ generations per minute. Finally, a use of AUP (all of the FTSE100 constituents) outperformed all the other configuration variants, reaching very good averages with the standard deviation below 0.01 in Hypervolume Ratio and Maximum Spread Ratio, and below 0.02 in Inverted Generational Distance, for $N_{sub} \geq 5$.

Finally, we must note that all the three performance measures had to be analyzed together due to certain artifacts that might otherwise lead to false conclusions (as one may observe in Figs. 2, 3 and 4). First of all, we had to keep in mind that Maximum Spread, as such, measured the diversity of POFs regardless of their accuracy, thus in our experiments the Maximum Spread Ratio often reached very high levels (even above 1) for $N_{sub} = 1$, where POFs were highly randomized (especially with RI > 0%). Additionally, it has to be mentioned that the results obtained for various risk measures could not be compared directly, which was particularly evident in the case of Inverted Generational Distance for which the outcomes differed of even up to 10^4 amid the analyzed cases.

Table 1. Average performances and standard deviations in 30 runs of dynamic NSGA-II. The expected risk was estimated with *covariances of returns*.

Sub-iter	Mutation rate = 0.1			Mutation rate = 0.9		
	0% RI	5% RI	AUP	0% RI	5% RI	AUP
(a) Hypervolume ratio						
1	0.21 ± 0.022	0.63 ± 0.003	0.94 ± 0.001	0.52 ± 0.036	0.59 ± 0.004	0.95 ± 0.001
2	0.35 ± 0.029	0.79 ± 0.005	0.96 ± 0.001	0.71 ± 0.019	0.75 ± 0.005	0.96 ± 0.001
5	0.58 ± 0.029	0.94 ± 0.002	0.97 ± 0.001	0.88 ± 0.008	0.96 ± 0.001	0.98 ± 0.001
10	0.75 ± 0.020	0.97 ± 0.001	0.98 ± 0.001	0.94 ± 0.003	0.98 ± 0.001	0.99 ± 0.001
20	0.86 ± 0.010	0.98 ± 0.001	0.99 ± 0.001	0.97 ± 0.002	0.99 ± 0.001	0.99 ± 0.001
(b) Maximum spread ratio						
1	0.24 ± 0.018	0.82 ± 0.006	0.99 ± 0.006	0.54 ± 0.034	0.83 ± 0.006	1.02 ± 0.005
2	0.35 ± 0.025	0.84 ± 0.007	0.98 ± 0.005	0.71 ± 0.023	0.86 ± 0.005	1.01 ± 0.007
5	0.55 ± 0.027	0.93 ± 0.005	0.97 ± 0.004	0.87 ± 0.012	0.98 ± 0.005	0.99 ± 0.005
10	0.71 ± 0.021	0.95 ± 0.004	0.97 ± 0.003	0.93 ± 0.007	0.99 ± 0.004	0.99 ± 0.004
20	0.83 ± 0.012	0.96 ± 0.003	0.97 ± 0.003	0.97 ± 0.005	1.00 ± 0.005	1.00 ± 0.004
(c) Inverted generational distance $\times 10^{-4}$						
1	21.15 ± 4.256	3.11 ± 0.211	0.68 ± 0.063	7.51 ± 2.538	4.31 ± 0.271	0.85 ± 0.076
2	9.62 ± 2.566	1.21 ± 0.129	0.41 ± 0.047	3.22 ± 1.080	1.99 ± 0.133	0.61 ± 0.055
5	2.42 ± 1.180	0.32 ± 0.030	0.21 ± 0.015	0.74 ± 0.109	0.57 ± 0.049	0.31 ± 0.030
10	0.87 ± 0.405	0.21 ± 0.019	0.15 ± 0.015	0.42 ± 0.035	0.39 ± 0.028	0.21 ± 0.015
20	0.40 ± 0.067	0.19 ± 0.018	0.16 ± 0.017	0.34 ± 0.031	0.33 ± 0.021	0.22 ± 0.017

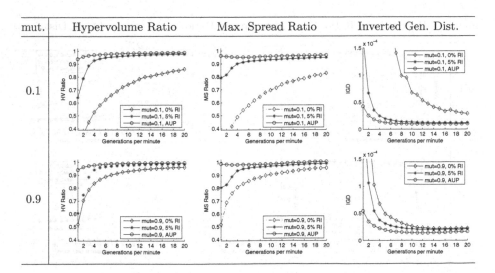

Fig. 2. Comparison of average performances in 30 runs of dynamic NSGA-II. The expected risk was estimated with *covariances of returns*.

Table 2. Average performances and standard deviations in 30 runs of dynamic NSGA-II. The expected risk was estimated with *semicovariances of returns*.

Sub-iter	Mutation rate = 0.1			Mutation rate = 0.9		
	0% RI	5% RI	AUP	0% RI	5% RI	AUP
(a) Hypervolume ratio						
1	0.24 ± 0.023	0.64 ± 0.006	0.94 ± 0.001	0.52 ± 0.036	0.61 ± 0.006	0.94 ± 0.001
2	0.36 ± 0.033	0.79 ± 0.004	0.96 ± 0.001	0.70 ± 0.021	0.75 ± 0.003	0.96 ± 0.001
5	0.58 ± 0.028	0.94 ± 0.002	0.97 ± 0.001	0.87 ± 0.007	0.96 ± 0.001	0.98 ± 0.001
10	0.74 ± 0.023	0.96 ± 0.001	0.98 ± 0.001	0.93 ± 0.003	0.98 ± 0.001	0.99 ± 0.001
20	0.86 ± 0.011	0.98 ± 0.001	0.99 ± 0.001	0.96 ± 0.002	0.99 ± 0.001	0.99 ± 0.001
(b) Maximum spread ratio						
1	0.24 ± 0.022	0.79 ± 0.005	0.96 ± 0.005	0.52 ± 0.035	0.80 ± 0.006	0.99 ± 0.005
2	0.34 ± 0.031	0.81 ± 0.007	0.96 ± 0.004	0.69 ± 0.023	0.83 ± 0.004	0.98 ± 0.003
5	0.54 ± 0.028	0.91 ± 0.003	0.95 ± 0.004	0.83 ± 0.011	0.95 ± 0.003	0.98 ± 0.004
10	0.70 ± 0.023	0.93 ± 0.004	0.96 ± 0.002	0.90 ± 0.005	0.97 ± 0.004	0.98 ± 0.004
20	0.83 ± 0.014	0.95 ± 0.002	0.97 ± 0.002	0.95 ± 0.003	0.99 ± 0.003	1.00 ± 0.003
(c) Inverted generational distance $\times 10^{-4}$						
1	22.84 ± 5.126	1.73 ± 0.186	0.42 ± 0.045	7.66 ± 3.259	2.37 ± 0.174	0.54 ± 0.060
2	12.33 ± 3.224	0.67 ± 0.071	0.25 ± 0.022	2.07 ± 0.464	1.06 ± 0.077	0.35 ± 0.029
5	2.84 ± 1.239	0.19 ± 0.017	0.12 ± 0.014	0.49 ± 0.067	0.31 ± 0.023	0.19 ± 0.016
10	0.68 ± 0.361	0.13 ± 0.013	0.10 ± 0.007	0.26 ± 0.023	0.22 ± 0.015	0.14 ± 0.011
20	0.29 ± 0.037	0.12 ± 0.009	0.10 ± 0.008	0.23 ± 0.017	0.22 ± 0.014	0.17 ± 0.011

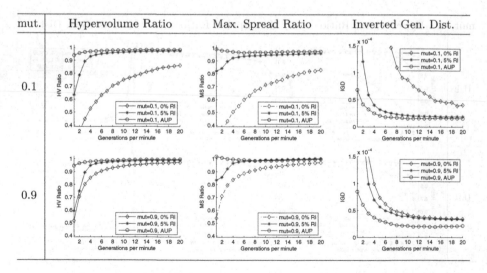

Fig. 3. Comparison of average performances in 30 runs of dynamic NSGA-II. The expected risk was estimated with *semicovariances of returns*.

Table 3. Average performances and standard deviations in 30 runs of dynamic NSGA-II. The expected risk was estimated with *average maximum drowdown*.

Sub-iter	Mutation rate = 0.1			Mutation rate = 0.9		
	0% RI	5% RI	AUP	0% RI	5% RI	AUP
(a) Hypervolume ratio						
1	0.16 ± 0.016	0.51 ± 0.007	0.91 ± 0.001	0.38 ± 0.019	0.51 ± 0.009	0.91 ± 0.001
2	0.26 ± 0.016	0.64 ± 0.010	0.95 ± 0.001	0.54 ± 0.011	0.69 ± 0.009	0.94 ± 0.001
5	0.46 ± 0.014	0.92 ± 0.003	0.97 ± 0.001	0.72 ± 0.005	0.92 ± 0.004	0.97 ± 0.001
10	0.60 ± 0.010	0.95 ± 0.003	0.98 ± 0.001	0.81 ± 0.003	0.95 ± 0.002	0.98 ± 0.001
20	0.70 ± 0.010	0.95 ± 0.002	0.98 ± 0.001	0.87 ± 0.002	0.96 ± 0.002	0.98 ± 0.001
(b) Maximum spread ratio						
1	0.35 ± 0.078	1.01 ± 0.021	0.98 ± 0.001	0.59 ± 0.067	1.01 ± 0.022	0.98 ± 0.001
2	0.46 ± 0.079	0.97 ± 0.021	0.98 ± 0.001	0.62 ± 0.028	0.96 ± 0.015	0.98 ± 0.001
5	0.60 ± 0.059	0.91 ± 0.008	0.98 ± 0.001	0.67 ± 0.013	0.91 ± 0.009	0.98 ± 0.001
10	0.65 ± 0.039	0.94 ± 0.005	0.98 ± 0.001	0.71 ± 0.007	0.94 ± 0.006	0.98 ± 0.001
20	0.69 ± 0.024	0.94 ± 0.005	0.98 ± 0.001	0.75 ± 0.007	0.94 ± 0.004	0.98 ± 0.001
(c) Inverted generational distance						
1	12.53 ± 2.204	0.44 ± 0.034	0.18 ± 0.003	4.48 ± 0.836	0.45 ± 0.038	0.19 ± 0.003
2	7.74 ± 1.232	0.28 ± 0.036	0.14 ± 0.002	1.86 ± 0.154	0.29 ± 0.026	0.15 ± 0.002
5	2.10 ± 0.427	0.13 ± 0.005	0.12 ± 0.001	0.65 ± 0.042	0.14 ± 0.005	0.12 ± 0.001
10	0.89 ± 0.121	0.13 ± 0.005	0.11 ± 0.001	0.32 ± 0.023	0.13 ± 0.004	0.11 ± 0.001
20	0.47 ± 0.040	0.13 ± 0.004	0.11 ± 0.001	0.19 ± 0.007	0.12 ± 0.003	0.10 ± 0.001

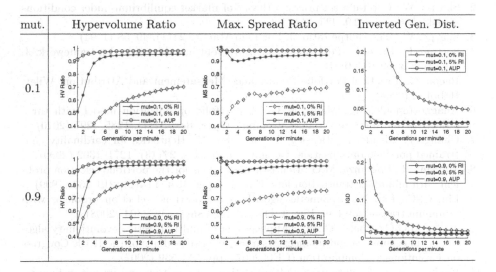

Fig. 4. Comparison of average performances in 30 runs of dynamic NSGA-II. The expected risk was estimated with *average maximum drowdown*.

5   Conclusions

In this paper, the NSGA-II based evolutionary algorithm for dynamic optimization purposes was suggested as a solver of the portfolio optimization problem defined in the ultra-high frequency environment with frequent dynamic changes.

The validation of the approach was performed on the ultra-high frequency time series taken from the London Stock Exchange Rebuilt Order Book database and the FTSE100 index. We demonstrated that there might exist a significant difference between the Pareto front obtained by solving the problem less frequently (once a trading day) and the Pareto fronts obtained on intraday basis. The proposed algorithm was fast enough to solve the optimization problem online and to provide Pareto fronts similar to the solutions of static optimization problems (obtained in much longer time).

However, further work is needed to validate the approach on larger portfolios and longer time periods. Also, we need to compare the evolutionary dynamic portfolio optimization approach with sequences of static portfolio optimization problems solved with other techniques, like linear or quadratic programming. The latter might be fast enough to find optimal portfolios in real-time as well.

Acknowledgements. Calculations have been carried out using resources provided by Wroclaw Centre for Networking and Supercomputing (http://wcss.pl), Grant No. 405.

References

1. Markowitz, H.: Portfolio selection. J. Finance **7**(1), 77–91 (1952)
2. Sharpe, W.: Capital asset prices: a theory of market equilibrium under conditions of risk. J. Finance **19**, 425–442 (1964)
3. Sharpe, W.: The sharpe ratio. J. Portfolio Manag. **21**(1), 49–58 (1994)
4. Sortino, F., Price, L.: Performance measurement in a downside risk framework. J. Investing **3**, 59–64 (1994)
5. Bacon, C.: Practical Portfolio Performance Measurement and Attribution. Wiley, Hoboken (2008)
6. Anagnostopoulos, K., Mamanis, G.: A portfolio optimization model with three objectives and discrete variables. Comput. Oper. Res. **37**(7), 1285–1297 (2010)
7. Chang, T., Meade, N., Beasley, J., Sharaiha, Y.: Heuristics for cardinality constrained portfolio optimisation. Comput. Oper. Res. **27**(13), 1271–1302 (2000)
8. Mansini, R., Speranza, M.G.: Heuristic algorithms for the portfolio selection problem with minimum transaction lots. Eur. J. Oper. Res. **114**(2), 219–233 (1999)
9. Lin, C.-C., Liu, Y.-T.: Genetic algorithms for portfolio selection problems with minimum transaction lots. Eur. J. Oper. Res. **185**(1), 393–404 (2008)
10. Tapia, M.G.C., Coello, C.A.C.: Applications of multi-objective evolutionary algorithms in economics and finance: A survey. In: Proceedings of the IEEE Congress on Evolutionary Computation (CEC 2007), pp. 532–539 (2007)
11. Coello, C.A.C.: Evolutionary multi-objective optimization and its use in finance, Handbook of Research on Nature Inspired Computing for Economy and Management (2006)

12. Ponsich, A., Jaimes, A., Coello, C.A.C.: A survey on multiobjective evolutionary algorithms for the solution of the portfolio optimization problem and other finance and economics applications. IEEE Trans. Evol. Comput. **17**(3), 321–344 (2013)
13. Skolpadungket, P., Dahal, K., Harnpornchai, N.: Portfolio optimization using multi-objective genetic algorithms. In: IEEE Congress on Evolutionary Computation, CEC 2007, pp. 516–523 (2007)
14. Streichert, F., Ulmer, H., Zell, A.: Evaluating a hybrid encoding and three crossover operators on the constrained portfolio selection problem. In: Proceedings of the IEEE Congress on Evolutionary Computation (CEC 2004), vol. 1, pp. 932–939 (2004)
15. Chiam, S., Tan, K., Al Mamum, A.: Evolutionary multi-objective portfolio optimization in practical context. Int. J. Autom. Comput. **5**(1), 67–80 (2008)
16. Branke, J., Scheckenbach, B., Stein, M., Deb, K., Schmeck, H.: Portfolio optimization with an envelope-based multi-objective evolutionary algorithm. Eur. J. Oper. Res. **199**(3), 684–693 (2009)
17. Anagnostopoulos, K., Mamanis, G.: The mean-variance cardinality constrained portfolio optimization problem: an experimental evaluation of five multiobjective evolutionary algorithms. Expert Syst. Appl. **38**(11), 14208–14217 (2011)
18. Krink, T., Paterlini, S.: Multiobjective optimization using differential evolution for real-world portfolio optimization. Comput. Manag. Sci. **8**(1–2), 157–179 (2011)
19. Cura, T.: Particle swarm optimization approach to portfolio optimization. Nonlinear Anal.: Real World Appl. **10**(4), 2396–2406 (2009)
20. Deng, G., Lin, W., Lo, C.: Markowitz-based portfolio selection with cardinality constraints using improved particle swarm optimization. Expert Syst. Appl. **39**(4), 4558–4566 (2012)
21. Di Tollo, G., Roli, A.: Metaheuristics for the portfolio selection problem. Int. J. Oper. Res. **5**(1), 13–35 (2008)
22. Gaspero, L.D., Tollo, G.D., Roli, A., Schaerf, A.: Hybrid metaheuristics for constrained portfolio selection problems. Quant. Finance **11**(10), 1473–1487 (2011)
23. Armananzas, R., Lozano, J.A.: A multiobjective approach to the portfolio optimization problem. IEEE Congress on Evolutionary Computation, vol. 2, pp. 1388–1395 (2005)
24. Liu, Q.: On portfolio optimization: how and when do we benefit from high-frequency data? J. Appl. Econ. **24**(4), 560–582 (2009)
25. Goumatianosa, N., Christoua, I., Lindgrenb, P.: Stock selection system: building long/short portfolios using intraday patterns. Proc. Econ. Finance **5**, 298–307 (2013)
26. Ziegelmann, F.A., Borges, B., Caldeira, J.F.: Selection of minimum variance portfolio using intraday data: an empirical comparison among different realized measures for BM&FBovespa data. Braz. Rev. Econ. **35**(1), 23–46 (2015)
27. http://www.ftse.com/products/indices/uk. Accessed 13 Nov 2016
28. Choueifaty, Y., Froidure, T., Reynier, J.: Properties of the most diversified portfolio. J. Investment Strat. **2**(2), 49–70 (2013)
29. Cesarone, F., Scozzari, A., Tardella, F.: Efficient algorithms for mean-variance portfolio optimization with hard real-world constraints. AFIR Colloquium (2008)
30. Deb, K., Rao N., U.B., Karthik, S.: Dynamic multi-objective optimization and decision-making using modified NSGA-II: a case study on hydro-thermal power scheduling. In: Obayashi, S., Deb, K., Poloni, C., Hiroyasu, T., Murata, T. (eds.) EMO 2007. LNCS, vol. 4403, pp. 803–817. Springer, Heidelberg (2007). doi:10.1007/978-3-540-70928-2_60

31. Deb, K., Pratap, A., Agarwal, S., Meyarivan, T.A.M.T.: A fast and elitist multi-objective genetic algorithm: NSGA-II. IEEE TEC **6**(2), 182–197 (2002)
32. Helbig, M., Engelbrecht, A.P.: Performance measures for dynamic multi-objective optimisation algorithms. Inf. Sci. **250**, 61–81 (2013)
33. Engle, R., Fleming, M., Ghysels, E., Nguyen, G.: Liquidity and Volatility in the U.S. Treasury Market: Evidence From A New Class of Dynamic Order Book Models (2001). http://www.unc.edu/maguilar/metrics/Giang.pdf. Accessed 21 Feb 2012
34. O'Hara, M.: Market Microstructure Theory. Blackwell, Oxford (1995)
35. Goodhart, C., O'Hara, M.: High frequency data in financial markets: Issues and applications. J. Empirical Finance **4**, 73–114 (1997)
36. Lipinski, P., Brabazon, A.: Pattern mining in ultra-high frequency order books with self-organizing maps. In: Esparcia-Alcázar, A.I., Mora, A.M. (eds.) EvoApplications 2014. LNCS, vol. 8602, pp. 288–298. Springer, Heidelberg (2014). doi:10. 1007/978-3-662-45523-4_24
37. Lipinski, P., Michalak, K., Lancucki, A.: Improving classification of patterns in ultra-high frequency time series with evolutionary algorithms. In: Proceedings of the Genetic and Evolutionary Computation Conference, pp. 127–128. ACM (2016)
38. Michalak, K., Lancucki, A., Lipinski, P.: Multiobjective optimization of frequent pattern models in ultra-high frequency time series: stability versus Universality. In: Proceedings of the IEEE Congress on Evolutionary Computation (CEC 2016) (2016)

EvoBIO

Integration of Reaction Kinetics Theory and Gene Expression Programming to Infer Reaction Mechanism

Jason R. White[1,2,P] and Ranjan Srivastava[1(✉)]

[1] Department of Chemical and Biomolecular Engineering,
University of Connecticut, Storrs, CT, USA
jarwhite@ucdavis.edu, rs@uconn.edu
[2] Department of Chemical Engineering, University of California,
One Shields Avenue, Davis, CA, USA

Abstract. Mechanistic mathematical models of biomolecular systems have been used to describe biological phenomena in the hope that one day these models may be used to enhance our fundamental understanding of these phenomena, as well as to optimize and engineer biological systems. An evolutionary algorithm capable of formulating mass action kinetic models of biological systems from time series data sets was developed for a system of n-species. The strategy involved using a gene expression programming (GEP) based approach and heuristics based on chemical kinetic theory. The resulting algorithm was successfully validated by recapitulating a nonlinear model of viral dynamics using only a "noisy" set of time series data. While the system analyzed for this proof-of-principle study was relatively small, the approach presented here is easily parallelizable making it amenable for use with larger systems. Additionally, greater efficiencies may potentially be realized by further taking advantage of the problem domain along with future breakthroughs in computing power and algorithmic advances.

Keywords: Evolutionary algorithm · Biochemical kinetics · Mechanistic modeling · Genetic programming · Gene expression programming

1 Introduction

Mathematical models are used in nearly all industries to describe processes, analyze data, make predictions, and propose improvements based upon those predictions. Mechanistic models describing chemical kinetic data sets are often defined by making assumptions regarding model structure. Mathematical descriptions of viral systems such as HIV-1, hepatitis B, and others have been of great interest in the hopes of developing treatment strategies based upon those models [1–8]. However, uncertainties about the systems and the manner in which species interact make developing these mechanistic models challenging.

The most comprehensive approach for determining models describing biochemical systems would be to assume no prior knowledge about the systems and the way that species interact. In theory, it should be possible to leverage an evolutionary algorithm

© Springer International Publishing AG 2017
G. Squillero and K. Sim (Eds.): EvoApplications 2017, Part I, LNCS 10199, pp. 53–66, 2017.
DOI: 10.1007/978-3-319-55849-3_4

to infer a mechanistic model describing the species and their interactions, including some interactions that may not be inherently obvious. The resulting model could then be used to make predictions about the system, as well as to test and optimize bioprocesses, development of potential therapeutics, and strategies for disease treatment. The proposed approach differs from that of model discrimination in that the best model would not be chosen from a set of pre-determined candidate models; rather the model would be inferred directly from system data.

The nature of the model inference problem is of tremendous interest. Work has been done on model generation from experimental data sets without assuming any prior knowledge about system mechanism. Sugimoto et al. has demonstrated a genetic programming approach that can infer a single equation from time-course data [9]. However, inferring mechanistic models for systems involving multiple species from noisy data has been problematic due to the discontinuous problem search space. Schmidt et al.'s Eureqa, a symbolic regression package that uses a genetic programming approach, quickly fits models to input data [10]. Although these models provide a good fit to experimental data, they often do not provide mechanistic information as to how species in a biological system interact. Chattopadhyay et al. developed an algorithm for inferring stochastic reaction mechanism from experimental data [11]. This algorithm was successful at generating correct mechanistic models on the algorithm's error-complexity Pareto front, but some knowledge of the system was required to select the correct model from a set of potential models. A study by Bazil et al. provided a method for the reverse engineering of biological networks by generating systems of ordinary differential equations from experimental data [12]. This algorithm was successful in identifying candidate pathways that were known to exist but also generated many false positive pathways, as the algorithm was designed to minimize the number of false negative pathways identified.

A common type of evolutionary algorithm used in these approaches is that of *genetic programming* [13]. Models evaluated using genetic programming are described by parse trees. An example is illustrated in the panel C of Fig. 1 (see Methods). However, there are problems associated with the parse tree structure approach. As the parse tree evolves, it may become "bloated." Bloat refers to the expansion of parse trees to very large depths [13, 14] and is the result of over-fitting data. The bloat problem can be addressed by defining the maximum depth that a tree can reach or by using a scoring function that penalizes larger solutions. Either solution to the bloat problem comes with a cost. Using the maximum depth approach, a function to check the depth of each newly generated solution is called during each iteration of the algorithm. The result is a significant increase in computational cost. When using a scoring function that penalizes larger solutions, smaller programs that may not account for the complexity of the system tend to dominate the population.

Additionally, the parse tree structure leads to a highly discontinuous model search space. Using the example equations presented in Fig. 1C, the model as defined would asymptotically approach a stable steady state after some period of time. If one of the head "−" nodes was changed to a "+" node by a point mutation, the model would move away from the steady state. As a result, some variables in the model would increase without bound, resulting in a poor fitness score and likely removal from the population of solutions. Because the tree with the "+" node is only one point mutation away from the optimal solution, it would clearly be desirable to keep it among the population of solutions. As larger systems are explored, this problem is exacerbated. Therefore, the phenotypic search space over which the algorithm must explore is highly discontinuous since changing one node or terminal can yield a major change in the quality of the solution.

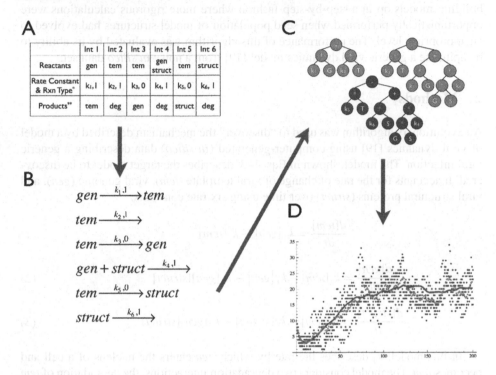

Fig. 1. Mapping of model genotype to model phenotype in evolutionary algorithm. (A) Each potential model was encoded as an interaction table describing reactants, rate constants, and products. Each interaction was also classified as a catalytic (type 0) or consumption (type 1) interaction. This table, representing a list of reactions (B), was then translated using mass action kinetic theory into a system of ordinary differential equations that could be represented as a set of parse trees (C). These equations were then simulated and scored against an experimental data set (D).

Another challenge for model inference approaches has to do with finding the best parameter set for each potential model. Studies have looked at improving parameter estimation for model selection in the context of computational biology [15, 16]. However, rigorously determining parameter sets for each potential solution in each iteration of the algorithm requires significant computational time. As a result, the viability of such an approach is limited.

For this work, it was hypothesized that by leveraging knowledge of reaction kinetic theory, mechanistic mathematical models of complex biological interactions could be inferred using an enhanced evolutionary algorithm. To test this hypothesis, the traditional genetic programming methodology was tailored to evolve mechanistic reaction kinetic models describing multi-variate data sets using a gene expression programming (GEP)-based approach [17, 18]. Models were encoded in a way that would address the discontinuous search space observed for these types of problems. They were then mapped to parse trees that could be simulated, mimicking the genotype to phenotype mapping observed in nature. The parameter estimation problem was addressed by building models up in a step-by-step fashion where more rigorous calculations were opportunistically performed when seed population of model structures had evolved to an appropriate level. The performance of this algorithm was evaluated by its ability to recapitulate a generic viral dynamics model [19] from a noisy *in silico* data set.

2   Methods

An evolutionary algorithm was used to "discover" the mechanism described by a model of viral dynamics [19] using computer-generated (*in silico*) data describing a generic viral infection. The model, shown in Eqs. 1–3, describes the target model to be discovered. It accounts for the rate of change of viral template (*tem*), viral genome (*gen*), and viral structural proteins (*struct*) over time using six rate constants.

$$\frac{d[tem]}{dt} = k_1[gen] - k_2[tem] \tag{1}$$

$$\frac{d[gen]}{dt} = k_3[tem] - k_1[gen] - k_4[gen][struct] \tag{2}$$

$$\frac{d[struct]}{dt} = k_5[tem] - k_6[struct] - k_4[gen][struct] \tag{3}$$

In this model, k_1 describes the rate by which *gen* enters the nucleus of a cell and becomes *tem*. The model considers two degradation interactions, the degradation of *tem* at a rate of k_2 and the degradation of *struct* at a rate of k_6. *tem* catalytically up-regulates *gen* at a rate of k_3 and *struct* at a rate of k_5. Finally, the interaction occurring at a rate of k_4 models the encapsulation of *gen* by *struct* to yield new viral progeny that leave the system. Parameter values for this model can be found in Table 1 (see Results) [19].

Genetic programming methods can represent programs or equations as trees made up of functions and terminals. In assembling random trees, some potential models may not include production or consumption terms for some of the mass balances. Potential models also might not include explicit rate constants for some interactions (equivalent to an assumed rate constant of 1), and some terms may include tertiary and higher-order interactions. For the evolution of reaction kinetic models, a heuristic approach limiting the search space to models that include production and consumption terms for each species was applied. Each production and consumption interaction in each candidate model was also described by a rate constant. Finally, for the biological models of interest, it was assumed that each interaction could include one or two reactants that could catalyze or be consumed to generate one or two products [20].

Table 1. Initial conditions and regression results for the viral dynamics model

Viral dynamics model conditions for data generation			
Initial condition	$[tem]_0$	$[gen]_0$	$[struct]_0$
1	1500	0	0
2	3000	0	0
3	5000	0	0
4	0	1500	0
Viral dynamics model test conditions			
Initial condition	$[tem]_0$	$[gen]_0$	$[struct]_0$
1	10000	0	0
2	0	5000	0
3	500	5000	1000
4	0	0	1000
Comparison of known equation to generated equations			
Known equations		Generated equations	
$\frac{d[tem]}{dt} = 0.025[gen] - 0.25[tem]$		$\frac{d[tem]}{dt} = 0.025[gen] - 0.25[tem]$	
$\frac{d[gen]}{dt} = [tem] - 0.025[gen]$		$\frac{d[gen]}{dt} = 0.99[tem] - 0.025[gen]$	
$-7.5 * 10^{-8}[gen][struct]$		$-7.46 * 10^{-8}[gen][struct]$	
$\frac{d[struct]}{dt} = 1000[tem]$		$\frac{d[struct]}{dt} = 2570.4[tem]$	
$-1.99[struct]$		$-5.14[struct]$	
$-7.5 * 10^{-8}[gen][struct]$		$-7.46 * 10^{-8}[gen][struct]$	

To tailor a genetic programming approach to generate desired reaction kinetic models, the structure of candidate solutions was changed from a parse tree structure to the structure shown in Fig. 1A. This representation, inspired by a GEP approach, encodes solutions as a "genotype", such as a list or collection of lists, which are then mapped to a "phenotype", such as a set of parse trees shown in Fig. 1C. Therefore, this evolutionary algorithm was used to map a list of reactants, rate constants, products, and types of reactions to parse trees describing the time series derivative of each variable under consideration. Such an approach resulted in a reduction of the size of the search space over which the evolutionary algorithm navigated to find a mechanistic mathematical model.

Another contributing factor to the large search space size was the need to search for both the optimal model structure and optimal model parameters. Even if a good model structure was found, it was unlikely that the algorithm would stochastically converge on the optimal set of rate constants. To address this problem, parameter estimation was carried out for every potential model against the experimental data during each generation of the evolutionary algorithm.

2.1 Algorithm

It was observed in early versions of the algorithm that the absence of a necessary inter-action could result in a poor scoring model that might not survive in the population of models (data not shown). This was yet another effect of the discontinuous search space associated with these types of problems. Such behavior goes against the assumption underlying evolutionary algorithms that optimal solutions could be built up gradually from suboptimal solutions containing pieces of the optimal solution. To resolve this issue, models were built up in a step-by-step fashion where only one equation was allowed to be modified at a time.

The biochemical kinetics discovery algorithm is described first for a system of n species; the general approach is shown in Fig. 2. To generate a complete kinetic model, an ordinary differential equation (ODE) describing the mass balance for a single (bio)chemical species was evolved. Simultaneously, the mass balances for the other species were described by fitted polynomials. This combination of one evolved mass balance and $n-1$ polynomial fits was called an instance. One instance was generated for each species such that every species had an instance in which it was represented by an evolved mass balance equation. The best scoring mass balance from the collection of instances was taken as the most probable result, and that mass balance equation was fixed for the next step. The species described by this result was referred to as Species A. In other words, all of the remaining instances had their Species A polynomial fit replaced by the Species A mass balance ODE. During the next step, instances of the evolutionary algorithm were carried out to evolve a mass balance for each of the remaining species one at a time. The mass balance describing Species A was fixed, and the mass balances describing the species not being evolved were described by a set of $n-2$ polynomials. Again, the best scoring result from this set of instances was fixed and this variable was defined as Species B. For a system of n species, this procedure would continue until only one species remained for which a mass balance had not yet been evolved.

The evolutionary algorithm was then used to evolve a mass balance describing this last species, while the mass balances describing the other species were fixed. This last species was defined as Species ξ, where ξ was the number of species for which a time series data set existed. After this, the mass balance for Species A was re-evolved using the evolutionary algorithm where mass balances describing Species B through ξ were fixed. The existing result for Species A and the newly evolved solution were compared by scoring with the current set of equations describing Species B through ξ and the best scoring solution was kept and fixed for subsequent steps. The mass balances for Species B through ξ were then re-evolved one at a time in the order that they were first evolved. This method was carried out cyclically until the mass balances describing Species A through ξ remained the same over one full cycle. The information gained from these steps was ultimately used to seed the first generation population of a final evolutionary step during which mass balances describing each of the species under investigation were simultaneously evolved.

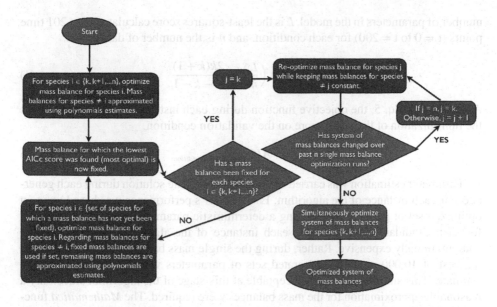

Fig. 2. Algorithm for the discovery of a biochemical kinetic model describing an n-variable system. Mass balances were evolved in a step-by-step manner to reduce the search space during a single evolutionary algorithm instance. In the initial steps, species mass balances were approximated by a set of polynomials fit to the corresponding data set until a mass balance was evolved for that variable. Once a complete model was preliminarily proposed, each species' mass balance was re-evolved one at a time until the system of mass balances had not changed over one complete cycle. The model was finalized by carrying out one final evolutionary algorithm optimization during which all mass balances were simultaneously evolved.

Inputs for this evolutionary algorithm included the maximum number of allowable interactions, the population size, the species under investigation, time series data sets describing these species, the initial conditions used to collect the data set, any fixed mass balances, and the number of generations to be run before the algorithm terminated. The number of interactions that potentially describes a system increases exponentially with the number of species under investigation. To maintain computational tractability, the number of interactions allowed to describe a model was capped by the square of the number of species (n^2) plus one. n^2 represented the maximum number of interactions allowed to occur with each of the other species, including up-regulation, consumption, and degradation. One additional interaction was allowed to provide some flexibility in accounting for second-order reactions or constitutive production interactions in the unlikely case that all n^2 interactions for a given species were used in the model.

Populations of potential solutions were generated and scored by simulating each model using *Mathematica's* ODE solver on each training condition. Each potential model was initialized with a constitutive production term and a first-order degradation term. The simulation results were compared to the training data set and scored using the corrected Akaike Information Criterion (AIC$_c$) [21] as defined by Eq. 4, where k is the number of parameters in the model, L is the least-squares score calculated over 201 time points (t = 0 to t = 200) for each condition, and n is the number of data points.

$$AIC_c = 2k + n * \ln\left(\frac{L}{n}\right) + \frac{2k(k+1)}{n-k-1} \tag{4}$$

As defined by Eq. 5, the objective function during each instance of the algorithm was the minimization of the AICc score on the validation condition.

$$minimize \ \ Score = AIC_{c,validationcondition} \tag{5}$$

Parameter estimation was carried out for each candidate solution during each generation of each instance of the algorithm. Each model's performance was based upon an optimized set of parameters. Running a deterministic parameter estimation algorithm for each candidate solution during each instance of the algorithm proved to be too computationally expensive. Rather, during the single mass balance optimization steps, the best of 10,000 randomly generated sets of parameters was selected as the initial estimate. This simplification was acceptable at this stage of the algorithm since only a reasonable approximation for the mass balances were required. The *Mathematica* function NMinimize, based on the Nelder-Mead method, was used to carry out rigorous parameter optimization of the candidate models during the final stages of the algorithm.

Evolutionary algorithms use selection, recombination, and mutation operations to generate diversity in a population of solutions and facilitate convergence towards an optimized solution. An elite selection strategy [22] was implemented where the top 20% of the best scoring solutions in the population were copied unaltered to the next generation population. The remaining 80% of the next generation population were made up of solutions randomly selected two at a time from the previous generation population that were given a chance recombine with each other, as a well as a possibility to mutate. Convergence to a local optimum brought on by decreasing diversity of solutions in the population posed a potential problem. To address this issue, the recombination rate, initiated at 90%, was decreased by 10% every x generations until it reached 0%. x was 10% of the number of generations required to terminate. Conversely, the mutation rate, initiated at 5%, was increased by 5% every x generations until it reached 50%. In this way, mutation became the favored evolutionary operation in later generations over recombination.

The algorithm is computationally intensive, and its use may be limited by the large amount of time it would take to run for systems of many species. To address this issue, the operations that could be run in parallel, such as the simulation and scoring of candidate solutions, and the execution of multiple instances of the algorithm, were parallelized. The University of Connecticut School of Engineering's high performance computing cluster consists of 768 Intel Xeon X5650 Westmere CPU cores over which parallel processes can be allocated. *Mathematica's* built-in parallelization capabilities were used to carry out this task. Due to the stochastic nature of the algorithm, instances run on a single node (16 cores) took anywhere from 0.5 to 2 days to be completed. The algorithm was not optimized to minimize runtime, but rather multiple trials were run in parallel on separate nodes.

3 Results

The biochemical kinetics discovery algorithm was implemented to evolve the known mechanism of the generic viral dynamics system as a test case. An *in silico* data set was generated as the input to the algorithm. Data was generated from the published model using four conditions, listed in Table 1, and 10% Gaussian noise. The noisy data set was used to emulate a generic viral infection as variations in species concentration. A clean data set (0% noise) had previously been used to successfully generate the published model (data not shown). Five independent samples were taken every four simulated days over a period of two hundred days. During every step of the algorithm, a population of 30 potential solutions was evolved for up to 150 generations allowing for convergence of the population. During each individual mass balance optimization step, twenty-four trials of the evolutionary algorithm were carried out. The best scoring solution across all trials, including the best result from the previous instance, was taken as the new optimized mass balance. Likewise, eight trials of the evolutionary algorithm were carried out during the final simultaneous optimization step where the best scoring result was taken as the optimized model. A maximum of four interactions were allowed to evolve during single species steps and a cap of ten interactions was used for the combined evolution step.

During the first three steps of the algorithm, a mass action kinetic equation was evolved describing the change in [*tem*] over time, then the change in [*gen*] over time, and finally the change in [*struct*] over time. The interactions described by these mass balances are shown in Fig. 3A. At this point in the evolution of the viral dynamics model, only one correct pathway had been identified (the degradation of *struct*).

The solution shown in Fig. 3B was used to seed the population for the last step during which all three mass balances were simultaneously re-evolved to determine the optimized model. The final two interactions in the seed model, shown in Fig. 3B, describing the 0th-order production of *tem* and *struct* were eliminated to allow for more new interactions to enter the population. These two interactions were chosen for elimination because both *tem* and *struct* were up-regulated in other interactions and the constitutive production of *tem* and *struct* described by this zero-order reaction was very unlikely for this intracellular viral system. If these two interactions in fact were part of the system's network structure, they could have re-entered the model during the simultaneous optimization step. After 70 generations of the simultaneous optimization step, the algorithm converged on two solutions of equal score (AICc $= -149.9$). These solutions are shown in Fig. 3C as Model 1 and Model 2. Model 1 correctly predicted the degradation of *tem* and *struct*, the consumption of *gen* to yield *tem*, and the catalytic up-regulation of *struct* by *tem*. It incorrectly predicted that *gen* was catalytically up-regulated by *struct* and that *gen* and *struct* associated to yield a net of one *struct* molecule. Model 2 correctly predicted all six interactions of the generic viral dynamics model with no additional interactions.

The performance of Models 1 and 2 on the training conditions (columns 1–3) and validation condition (column 4) are shown in Fig. 4A. As expected by the identical AICc score, both models were observed to accurately fit the *in silico* data set. To differentiate between the two models, an *in silico* data set was generated by the same procedure for four new conditions, listed in Table 1.

A
$$gen + struct \xrightarrow{k_1,1} tem$$
$$tem + struct \xrightarrow{k_2,1} struct$$
$$struct \xrightarrow{k_3,1}$$
$$struct \xrightarrow{k_4,0} gen$$
$$gen \xrightarrow{k_5,1}$$
$$tem + gen \xrightarrow{k_6,0} struct$$
$$\xrightarrow{k_7,1} tem$$
$$\xrightarrow{k_8,1} struct$$

B
$$gen + struct \xrightarrow{k_1,1} tem$$
$$tem + gen \xrightarrow{k_2,0} tem$$
$$2 * tem \xrightarrow{k_3,1}$$
$$struct \xrightarrow{k_4,1}$$
$$struct \xrightarrow{k_5,0} gen$$
$$gen \xrightarrow{k_6,1}$$
$$tem + gen \xrightarrow{k_7,0} struct$$
$$\xrightarrow{k_8,1} tem$$
$$\xrightarrow{k_9,1} struct$$

C

Model 1
$$gen + struct \xrightarrow{k_1,1} 2\,struct$$
$$tem \xrightarrow{k_2,0} struct$$
$$tem \xrightarrow{k_3,1}$$
$$struct \xrightarrow{k_4,1}$$
$$struct \xrightarrow{k_5,0} gen$$
$$gen \xrightarrow{k_6,1} tem$$

Model 2
$$gen + struct \xrightarrow{k_1,1}$$
$$tem \xrightarrow{k_2,0} struct$$
$$tem \xrightarrow{k_3,1}$$
$$struct \xrightarrow{k_4,1}$$
$$tem \xrightarrow{k_5,0} gen$$
$$gen \xrightarrow{k_6,1} tem$$

Fig. 3. Evolution of the general viral dynamics model. (A) Carrying out the first three steps of the algorithm resulted in a complete model describing the three species involved in the general viral dynamics system. (B) After additional instances of single mass balance optimization, the algorithm converged upon a model structure that was used to seed the simultaneous optimization step. (C) After the step-by-step evolution of the model was complete, the mass balances for all three species were simultaneously evolved. The result was two identical scoring models, one of which was identical to the target model.

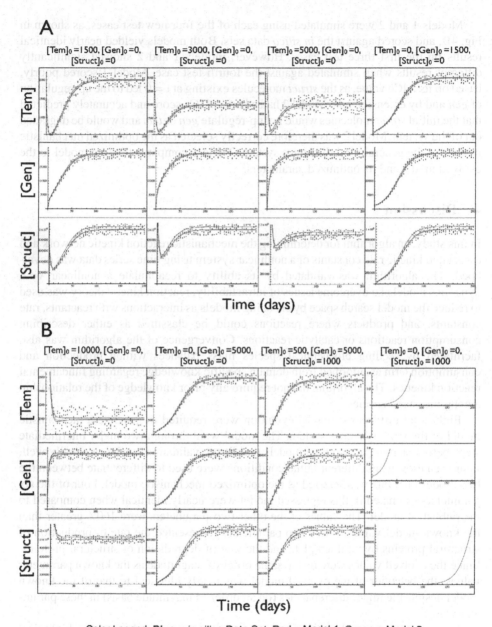

Color Legend: **Blue** = *in silico* Data Set, **Red** = Model 1, **Green** = Model 2

Fig. 4. Simulation of evolved viral dynamics models. (A) Simulation of Models 1 and 2 against *in silico* data sets generated for the three training conditions (columns 1–3) and the validation condition (column 4) are shown. Both Models 1 and 2 had an AIC_c score of -149.9 when scored against the validation condition. (B) Models 1 and 2 were tested by comparing simulation results to *in silico* data sets generated for four additional test conditions. Models 1 and 2 had nearly identical results on the first three test conditions (columns 1–3) but Model 2 significantly outperformed Model 1 on the fourth test condition (column 4). (Color figure online)

Models 1 and 2 were simulated using each of the four new test cases, as shown in Fig. 4B, and scored against the *in silico* data sets. Both models yielded nearly identical results on the first three test cases. However, models 1 and 2 showed significantly different results when simulated against the fourth test case. Model 1 scored poorly, based on its AICc value, as the *struct* molecules existing at t = 0 led to the up-regulation of *gen* and by extension *tem*. Model 2 had a better AICc score and accurately predicted that the initial *struct* molecules would not up-regulate *gen* or *tem* and would be degraded out of the system. Model 2 was therefore correctly selected as the optimized mechanistic model for the general viral dynamics system. Table 1 compares the true model to the evolved model and its optimized parameters.

4 Discussion

In this study, an algorithm for determining the mechanistic reaction kinetic network and associated kinetic rate constants of a nonlinear system using time series data was developed. The algorithm was validated by its ability to recapitulate a nonlinear viral dynamics model. To overcome issues of intractability, reaction kinetic theory was used to reduce the model search space by encoding models as interactions with reactants, rate constants, and products where reactions could be classified as either describing consumption reactions or catalytic reactions. Convergence of the algorithm was also facilitated by seeding biochemical species mass balances with a production and consumption term as informed from domain specific knowledge regarding fundamental reaction kinetics. The algorithm did not require any prior knowledge of the relationship among measured species.

Eight total instances of model evolution were required to generate a mechanistic model of the viral dynamics system. The model went through two major intermediate steps before arriving at two final models that fit the validation condition equally well. Four scenarios using different initial conditions were used to differentiate between the two models and one was selected as the optimized mechanistic model. Four of the six parameters estimated in this regressed model were nearly identical when compared to the published model. The values of the other two parameters were 160% greater than the known model values. These two parameters represented the rate of production of structural proteins by viral template and the rate of degradation of structural proteins. Since the evolved values were on the same order of magnitude as the known parameter values, the behavior of the evolved model was nearly identical to that of the known model despite the minor discrepancies (on an order of magnitude basis) in these parameter values.

Interactions between large numbers of species are commonly found in biological systems; therefore it is important that a biochemical kinetics discovery algorithm be able to analyze systems of many species. The enhancements to the traditional genetic programming algorithm used in this study have the potential to carry out such an analysis. The maximum number of interactions suggested is the square of the number of species plus one, but it is possible to specify a reasonable number of interactions specific to the system under investigation that goes beyond this value if deemed appropriate. To minimize the run time, the code is designed to monitor model evolution progress and terminate when a potential solution has not improved during a sufficient number generations. Further, this algorithm is of the class referred to as "embarrassingly parallel". As such, it could be implemented on CPUs or GPUs of large high-performance computing systems to accommodate analysis of larger and more complex biological systems. Such efforts should easily reduce computational time by an order of magnitude, with gains of up to three orders of magnitude potentially realizable. Additionally, if the code were ported to a "faster" language, such as C or Fortran, it is likely that significant speed increases would be observed. Finally, improvements to the algorithm itself are likely to have the most significant impact on decreasing computational time, allowing analysis of more complex systems.

One approach to facilitate the use of this algorithm may be to change the way by which parameters for potential solutions are trained and validated. In this study, data simulated using three different scenarios were used to infer solutions and a fourth was used to validate solutions by assigning a score using AICc. This score was then used to carry out evolutionary operations. Depending on the data set collected, it may be necessary or preferable to assign a portion of a data to the training data set. Another portion could be used as a validation data set. Such an approach is a common practice in the field of machine learning. Similarly, when multiple candidate solutions emerge, as was the case in this study, there is the potential to embed testing conditions into the algorithm. For example, a data set describing the responses of the variables of interest to a perturbation could be recorded and fed to the algorithm for this purpose.

Another avenue for potential improvement will be regarding how interactions are chosen to be involved in a potential solution. Depending on the likelihood of an interaction being present in the system, a bias may be introduced. The purpose of the bias would be to make particular interactions more or less likely to be present in a potential solution. For example, a bias against dimerization interactions could be introduced when analyzing a system such as the one in this study where such interactions were unlikely to occur. Such an improvement may prove critical in facilitating convergence of larger systems to an optimized solution.

Acknowledgements. This material is based upon work supported by the National Science Foundation under Grant No. 1137249 and 1517133.

Supporting Information. *Mathematica* source code and instructions are available from http://www.rslabs.org under a BSD open source license.

References

1. Aviran, S., Shah, P.S., Schaffer, D.V., Arkin, A.P.: Computational models of HIV-1 resistance to gene therapy elucidate therapy design principles. PLoS Comput. Biol. **6**(8), e1000883 (2010)
2. Bonhoeffer, S., Coffin, J.M., Nowak, M.A.: Human immunodeficiency virus drug therapy and virus load. J. Virol. **71**, 3275–3278 (1997)

3. Bonhoeffer, S., May, R.M., Shaw, G.M., Nowak, M.A.: Virus dynamics and drug therapy. PNAS **94**, 6971–6976 (1997)
4. Burg, D., Rong, L., Neumann, A.U., Dahari, H.: Mathematical modeling of viral kinetics under immune control during primary HIV-1 infection. J. Theor. Biol. **259**, 751–759 (2009)
5. Perelson, A.S.: Modelling viral and immune system dynamics. Nat. Rev. Immunol. **2**, 28–36 (2002)
6. Prosperi, M.C.F., D'Autilia, R., Incardona, F., De Luca, A., Zazzi, M., et al.: Stochastic modelling of genotypic drug-resistance for human immunodeficiency virus towards long-term combination therapy optimization. Bioinformatics **25**, 1040–1047 (2009)
7. Ribeiro, R.M., Bonhoeffer, S.: Production of resistant HIV mutants during antiretroviral therapy. PNAS **97**, 7681–7686 (2000)
8. von Kleist, M., Menz, S., Huisinga, W.: Drug-class specific impact of antivirals on the reproductive capacity of HIV. PLoS Comput. Biol. **6**, e1000720 (2010)
9. Sugimoto, M., Kikuchi, S., Tomita, M.: Reverse engineering of biochemical equations from time-course data by means of genetic programming. BioSystems **80**, 155–164 (2005)
10. Schmidt, M., Lipson, H.: Distilling free-form natural laws from experimental data. Science **324**, 81–85 (2009)
11. Chattopadhyay, I., Kuchina, A., Süel, G.M., Lipson, H.: Inverse gillespie for inferring stochastic reaction mechanisms from intermittent samples. PNAS **110**(32), 12990–12995 (2013)
12. Bazil, J.N., Qi, F., Beard, D.A.: A parallel algorithm for reverse engineering of biological networks. Integr. Biol. **3**(12), 1215–1223 (2011)
13. Koza, J.: Genetic Programming, p. 819. MIT Press, Cambridge (1992)
14. Iba, H.: Inference of differential equation models by genetic programming. Inf. Sci. **178**, 4453–4468 (2008)
15. Rodriguez-Fernandez, M., Rehberg, M., Banga, J.R.: Simultaneous model discrimination and parameter estimation in dynamic models of cellular systems. BMC Syst. Biol. **7**, 76–89 (2013)
16. Lillacci, G., Khammash, M.: Parameter estimation and model selection in computational biology. PLoS Comput. Biol. **6**, e1000696 (2010)
17. Ferreira, C.: Gene Expression Programming, vol. 21. Springer, Heidelberg (2006). 478 p.
18. Du, X., et al.: Convergence analysis of gener expression programming based on maintaining elitist. In: Proceedings og the first ACM/SIGEVO Summit on Genetic and Evolutionary Computation (GEC 2009), pp. 823–826. ACM, New York (2009)
19. Srivastava, R., You, L., Summers, J., Yin, J.: Stochastic vs. deterministic modeling of intracellular viral kinetics. J. Theor. Biol. **218**, 309–321 (2002)
20. Levenspiel, O.: Chemical Reaction Engineering, 2nd edn. Wiley, New York (1972)
21. Motulsky, H., Christopoulos, A.: Fitting Models to Biological Data Using Linear and Nonlinear Regression. Oxford University Press, Oxford (2004). 351 p.
22. Bautista, E.J., et al.: Semi-automated curation of metabolic models via flux balance analysis: a case study with Mycoplasma gallisepticum. PLoS Comput. Biol. **9**(9), 1003208 (2013)

De Novo DNA Assembly with a Genetic Algorithm Finds Accurate Genomes Even with Suboptimal Fitness

Doina Bucur$^{(\boxtimes)}$

University of Twente, Drienerlolaan 5, 7522 Enschede, NB, The Netherlands
d.bucur@utwente.nl

Abstract. We design an evolutionary heuristic for the combinatorial problem of de-novo DNA assembly with short, overlapping, accurately sequenced single DNA reads of uniform length, from both strands of a genome without long repeated sequences. The representation of a candidate solution is a novel *segmented permutation*: an ordering of DNA reads into contigs, and of contigs into a DNA scaffold. Mutation and crossover operators work at the contig level. The fitness function minimizes the total length of scaffold (i.e., the sum of the length of the overlapped contigs) and the number of contigs on the scaffold. We evaluate the algorithm with read libraries uniformly sampled from genomes 3835 to 48502 base pairs long, with genome coverage between 5 and 7, and verify the biological accuracy of the scaffolds obtained by comparing them against reference genomes. We find the correct genome as a contig string on the DNA scaffold in over 95% of all assembly runs. For the smaller read sets, the scaffold obtained consists of only the correct contig; for the larger read libraries, the fitness of the solution is suboptimal, with chaff contigs present; however, a simple post-processing step can realign the chaff onto the correct genome. The results support the idea that this heuristic can be used for consensus building in de-novo assembly.

Keywords: De Novo DNA assembly · Genetic algorithm · Consensus genome

1 Introduction

Sequencing technologies have increasingly low cost and feasible runtimes; they can generate deep coverage of mammal genomes within days, such that many new projects attempt to sequence previously unsequenced organisms. The raw sequence data generated in such a project is a set of overlapping, either single or paired-end DNA reads, from either of the two reverse-complementary strands of a DNA molecule. Single reads are either short (10^2 bases for most available second-generation sequencers, with high single-read accuracy: 99.9% for Illumina dye sequencing [1]) or long (10^4 bases with lower single-read accuracy: 80–90% for third-generation SMRT [2] and MinION sequencing [3], with predominantly

© Springer International Publishing AG 2017
G. Squillero and K. Sim (Eds.): EvoApplications 2017, Part I, LNCS 10199, pp. 67–82, 2017.
DOI: 10.1007/978-3-319-55849-3_5

insertion and deletion errors). Short-read second-generation sequencers are in wide use; a sufficient number of overlapping short reads need to be obtained in order to cover the underlying genome multiple times over. This coverage c is the average coverage of each base on the DNA strand, $c = n \cdot r/G$, where n is the number of reads, r the read length, and G the expected length of the genome.

We look at the problem of assembling accurate, single, short DNA reads with uniform length and a medium depth of coverage of the original genome. The overlapping DNA reads (essentially, strings over a four-letter alphabet) must be totally linearly ordered such that each pair of adjacent reads overlaps. Continuously overlapping sequences of short reads form a *DNA contig*, and the contigs obtained are ordered on a *DNA scaffold* which equates the genome. This is a combinatorial problem, yielding a computationally hard assembler; the larger the genome sequenced and the deeper its coverage, the larger the read set in input and the more difficult the computation. Some genomes and read sets are comparatively more difficult to assemble than others; current DNA assembling algorithms are themselves not optimal, and may obtain different solutions for the same input [4–6].

De-novo assembly refers to sequencing DNA reads in the absence of a *reference genome*, i.e., a closely related genome whose internal structure is essentially the best *accuracy metric* with which to verify the assembly obtained: the newly assembled genome must align back onto the reference. In absence of a reference genome, only an *estimate of the length* of the reference genome can replace it as an imperfect accuracy metric. In practice, *consensus* is used: a newly sequenced genome is considered correct if a number of different assembly algorithms (or parameter settings to the algorithms) computed it. Obtaining consensus is effectively the current accuracy metric in absence of a reference genome.

We employ all three accuracy metrics above to verify our method: the length of the genome as a fitness function, aligning back to the reference genome as a post-factum evaluator for the correctness of a single assembly, and consensus as a post-factum evaluator for the method as a whole.

The novel points in this study are:

Algorithmic. We build on prior work using Evolutionary Computation in DNA assembly. We introduce a new representation for a candidate solution which models the scaffold as a *segmented permutation*, with DNA contigs as building blocks. The corresponding genetic operators mutate and crossover DNA contigs natively, i.e., operate at macro level rather than over individual reads. This representation closely models a real genome, and allows assembly metrics to be written as computationally simple fitness functions.

Fitness functions. A new fitness function is used: the *length of the DNA scaffold*, together with the number of contigs on the scaffold (to be minimized). This fitness function is the closest option to an accuracy metric for a de-novo problem, and also makes possible to write a stopping condition for the computation when the length of the scaffold matches the estimate length of the reference genome.

Correct assemblies. We evaluate this method with read sets uniformly sampled from existing consensus genomes 3835 to 48502 base pairs long and genome coverage between 5 and 7. In over 95% of all assemblies, even with suboptimal fitness, the correct genome is obtained as a contig on a multi-contig scaffold; a simple realignment of the "chaff" contigs in the solution then yields a correct genome.

Consensus among assemblies. Since the algorithm often obtains the correct genome across repeated assemblies with different random seeds and parameter settings, the algorithm can serve effectively as a consensus builder for a new genome.

2   Related Work

On a theoretical note, assuming that the *shortest* assembled genome is desired, the assembly problem has been recast into the shortest common superstring (SCS) problem, i.e., the problem of finding, for n given finite strings $s_1, s_2, \ldots, s_n$ over an alphabet of size greater than 2, a shortest superstring S such that every string s_i can be obtained by deleting zero or more elements from S. The SCS problem is known to be NP-complete [7], as is the simpler version of SCS in which the n strings are totally ordered in a superstring [8].

In this section, we summarize results from two research areas: the performance of existing, commercial-grade assemblers, and the closely related prior work on using artificial genetic algorithms to sequence natural genetic material.

2.1   Lessons Learned from Existing Assemblers

Current short-read DNA sequencers implement heuristics which order short DNA reads onto contigs based on maximizing the overlap between adjacent reads, on maximizing the sum of overlaps across the scaffold, and on incorporating the most reads in the final assembly. As summaries of these techniques, we point to recent comparative studies such as [4–6], and give an overview of knowledge they gained from these comparative campaigns, which can act as a baseline of expectations for our own method. [4] experimented with 8 assemblers for paired-end short reads, and compared the results against reference genomes. [5] compared 43 assemblies from 21 teams over both short- and long-read, single- and paired-end read sets, without reference genomes. In [6] long-read MinION sequence data was assembled with 4 assemblers from all algorithmic classes.

No Optimal Assembly Strategy Exists. In [4], endemic problems were found across the board: the contiguity of an assembled genome varied wildly among both assemblers and genomes under sequence. When comparing the assemblies obtained to a reference genome, the following issues we found: many "chaff" contigs (of length under twice the read length), unnecessarily duplicated contigs, compressions of true repeat sequences (a widespread problem for short-read assemblers), contig "misjoins" (i.e., the assembler joined two contigs which are in fact distant in the reference genome), many indels (insertions and deletions in the assembly compared to the reference). In [5], a high degree of variability was found among assemblies, to the extent that the result of a single assembler and set of assembler parameters is not to be trusted. This supports the idea of *consensus*: an assembly obtained by different methods is likelier to be accurate.

Assembly Metrics are Error-prone; Use Accuracy Metrics. The metrics used to evaluate the assembled genome in absence of a reference genome are error-prone [4]; these *assembly metrics* (e.g., the number of contigs obtained, or various basic statistics over the sizes of the contigs) were found not to correlate very well with *accuracy metrics*, which compare the assembly against a true reference genome (when available), by computing the degree to which the reference genome is covered by the assembly, and the percentage of contigs alignable onto the reference genome. It remains unclear how to assess the quality of the assembled genomes, because no assembler performed well by all assembly metrics and all genomes [5]. In the evaluation of an assembly, one should not trust a single assembly metric. In [6], assemblies of poor accuracy were seen: for one species, all assemblers obtained very low genome coverage (between 0% and 12%); a greedy assembler had both the genome coverage and the percentage of alignment under 5% for both species.

Some Genomes and Read Sets are More Difficult to Assemble. In [4], the accuracy of the reads had larger negative effect upon the quality of the genome assembled than the assembler itself. A uniform read length r and reads uniformly distributed across the genome both improve the efficiency and accuracy of the assembly [9]. Also, a widespread problem is that genomes with repeated subsequences are more difficult to assemble: repeat sequences longer than the read length may create a gap, a misjoin, or may be compressed [4].

In consequence, we take the following decisions for this study:

- We simplify the problem to an extent by sequencing genomes or genome segments which are small and have no repeats longer than the read length.
- We control the shape of the read set by artificially sampling it using a random uniform sampler, from a reference genome.
- We use accuracy metrics (the reference genome, and consensus among assemblies) to evaluate our method both via the runtime fitness and post-factum.

2.2 Previous Genetic Representations and Operators

A major issue with prior work sequencing DNA using an evolutionary approach is that their fitness functions only model assembly metrics which state nothing about the accuracy of the result (also a widespread issue across other assemblers, per Sect. 2.1). Table 1 summarizes prior work using an evolutionary approach.

[8] builds on genetic algorithms for the TSP problem. If a candidate were to be represented as a permutation of n read identifiers, then classic two-point crossover leads to illegal offspring, so a complicated individual representation is used, not directly linked to the order in which the reads are placed in the

Table 1. Related work

	[8]	[10–12]	[13]
Candidate representation	Sorted-order representation	Permutation (array of read identifiers)	Permutation (array of read identifiers)
Mutation operators	Classic bit point mutation (micro)	Read swap (micro), contig inshift (macro), contig reverse (macro)	Read swap (micro)
Crossover operators	Classic bit two-point crossover (micro)	Edge recombination, order crossover (micro)	Order crossover (micro)
Fitness functions	Total adjacent overlap ($\uparrow$) Total distant overlap ($\downarrow$)	Total adjacent overlap ($\uparrow$) Total distant overlap ($\downarrow$)	Total adjacent overlap ($\uparrow$) Number of contigs ($\downarrow$)

assembly. In the evaluation, it was found that this candidate representation doesn't construct increasingly improved solutions, and is thus not useful.

Two fitness functions model the total overlap between adjacent fragments in a layout: $F_1 = \sum_{i=1}^{n-1} w(i, i+1)$, where $w(i,j)$ is the degree of overlap between fragments i and j (linear, and to be maximized), and F_2 (square) a variant minimizing the total degree of overlap $w(i,j)$ among all fragment pairs i and j at distant locations in the assembly. Neither of these functions, when evaluated over a candidate solution, can directly tell how closely the assembly relates to the true genome. A greedy algorithm outdid this decisively in contig counts and marginally in terms of F_1.

In [10,11] (with further parameter tuning in [12]) the fitness functions from [8] are kept, but a simpler and more effective *permutation representation* is used, i.e., an ordered list of read identifiers as appearing in the assembly. This requires specialized genetic operators listed below (in some cases renamed, to clarify that we preserve the semantics of 3 out of 5 in this work). Each operator is either *micro*, if it operates over reads, or *macro*, when at contig level:

Order crossover (micro): random read indices l and r are selected, the subsequence between l and r on the first parent is copied into the offspring preserving absolute position, and the remaining slots in the offspring are filled from left to right with the reads not yet in the offspring, in the relative order in which they appear in the second parent.

Edge recombination (micro): greedily attempts to preserve read adjacencies from the parents into the offspring. Selects the first read r from the first parent, and follows it with that read s which (i) is adjacent to r in both parents, or, failing that, (ii) has the most adjacencies left.

Swap (micro): two random reads are swapped; in [12], late swaps (to avoid local optima) become greedy by overlap rather than randomly.

Reverse-complement (macro): reverts a random contig (with the contig bounds being probabilistic in [12]).

Inshift (macro): moves a random contig between a random two previously adjacent contigs.

The number of contigs is not used as a fitness function. From the functions used, F_1 is found to be adequate (and better than F_2), but not ideal; the authors leave the design of a more appropriate function for future research. Neither function can be seen as an accuracy metric.

PALS [13] adds as fitness to F_1 the number of contigs and obtains one contig for all but the largest read set. In this candidate representation, the calculation of the number of contigs has high time complexity, and their method to estimate this is done via delta-increments from the application of operators at each iteration.

In our evaluation, we experiment with the genomes used in this prior work (under 10^5 base-pairs long, with low coverage between 5 and 7, a cutoff value for overlap of 30 base pairs, and read sets generated artificially from a reference genome without long repeats). More importantly, while all prior work makes an effort to compare against other assemblers in terms of the number of contigs obtained (and occasionally the abstract assembly metric F_1), it makes no effort to measure how well the reference genome is actually covered by the best assemblies they obtained. Here, we bridge this gap between the abstract evaluation of the algorithm, and the practical, domain-specific evaluation of the solutions.

3   Methodology

In Fig. 1 and Table 2, we summarize our design choices in terms of the genetic representation, operators, and fitness functions. Previous work borrowed from evolutionary-inspired solutions to the TSP problem, and represented a candidate solution as a simple permutation of DNA reads (a comparative overview was given in Table 1 in the related-work Sect. 2.2). This representation made it natural to then design primarily micro genetic operators, i.e., operations changing the location of individual DNA reads in the permutation. Macro operators, modifying a DNA contig, required more effort in recovering the contig structure from this representation. We build on these early designs, and lift the candidate representation and all operators to macro level, to then be able to write computationally simple fitness functions and stopping conditions, both of which reflect

Fig. 1. The representation of a candidate with reads of length 5 base pairs, 5 reads in the read set, 2 contigs currently on the scaffold, and a minimum overlap threshold of 2 base pairs. A reverse-complement bit of True is shown as a backward arrow; the reverse-complement of GGGCC is GGCCC.

Table 2. Method for this work

Candidate representation	*Segmented permutation*	
Mutation operators	(**R**) contig **reverse-complement**	(All macro)
	(**S**) contig **split**	
	(**I**) contig **inshift**	
	(**M**) contig **merge**	
Crossover operators	(**O**) one-point **order crossover** for scaffolds	
Fitness functions	Length of DNA scaffold ($\downarrow$)	
	Number of DNA contigs ($\downarrow$)	

the metrics measuring the accuracy of a DNA assembly, learnt from recent studies of commercial DNA sequencers (Sect. 2.1). These design choices are detailed in the remaining of this section.

3.1 Representation of Candidate Solution

A *segmented permutation* arranges the DNA reads in the input read set in an order, to model a DNA scaffold, as a simple permutation would also do. However, it also logically segments this scaffold into DNA contigs, where each is a subarray (of length at least one) of DNA read identifiers. This essentially memorizes the boundaries of contigs at the level of the candidate solution, and also allows to write a fitness function and a stopping condition for the evolutionary process which compare a candidate solution's scaffold length against its expected length, as given by a reference genome (i.e., an *accuracy metric* from Sect. 2.1). A candidate (with a sketch in Fig. 1) is an object with the following attributes:

DNA scaffold: a segmented permutation of the unmodified DNA reads in the input set, of which the reads in any segment (modelling a DNA contig) will have adjacent overlaps above a certain minimum overlap threshold.

Reverse-complement bits: for each DNA read, a Boolean variable which is True if the corresponding read is used it its reverse-complemented form in this candidate scaffold with respect to the input read set.

DNA contig strings: for each DNA contig on the scaffold, the overlapped contig (i.e., a relatively short string). Initially, all contigs contain a single read. The sum of the lengths of these contig strings will thus start at value $n \cdot r$, where n is the number of reads in the input set, and r is the read length, and will decrease in time, as contigs merge.

3.2 Operators Over Candidate Solutions

All genetic operators work natively over DNA contigs. This is a generalization rather than a limitation in comparison to the micro operators from the related work, since a contig here may well consist of a single read, and any DNA scaffold

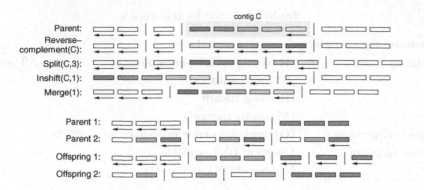

Fig. 2. Mutation (top) and crossover (bottom) operators. From the candidate representation, only the DNA scaffold and the reverse-complement bits are shown (a backward arrow models a True value). Indices are 1-indexed. This crossover example uses index 2, i.e., preserves the first two contigs from the first parent into the first offspring.

may be obtained via either set of operators. However, macro operators may be more efficient in that they apply a mutation (such as a transposition of a portion of DNA from one place in the scaffold to another) for an entire existing contig, in one step, rather than read by read.

Our set of genetic operators are listed below, and shown in Fig. 2.

Reverse-complement: as the corresponding operator in prior work [10–12]. The corresponding DNA contig string in the representation becomes the reverse-complement of the original.

Inshift: also as in prior work. It preserves the internal structure of all contigs.

Split: a randomly selected contig is split (if it consists of at least two reads) at a random point, forming two new adjacent contigs. Two new DNA contig strings are computed for the scaffold.

Random Merge: a random pair of adjacent contigs is merged into a new contig, with a new DNA contig string computed for the scaffold. The merge only occurs for pairs of contigs which overlap by a number of base pairs above a configurable threshold (the higher this threshold, the fewer the merge options are). The two contigs may overlap by a number of base pairs longer than the read length: in this case, the newly formed contig is an *interleaving* of the two original contigs. We also experimented with a variant of this operator:

Greedy Merge: among the list of all possible merges on a given candidate scaffold, the highest 50% in terms of overlap are selected, and a random choice is made out of these.

Order crossover: a random index is selected between two adjacent contigs on the first parent. All the contigs to the left of this point are preserved (in both position and internal structure) in the first offspring. The remaining reads for this offspring will come from the second parent, in the order in which that parent has them on its scaffold; two of these reads will be adjacent in the same contig only if they were arranged as such on the second parent (otherwise, they will form separate contigs).

We abbreviate these operators by their initials, **R, S, I, M, O**. They are applied in the evolutionary process to a candidate solution in a configurable order (e.g., **RSIMO**), each operator at a configurable rate of application.

With one exception, each operator performs a modification of a candidate solution which cannot be achieved by any combination of other operators—in other words, this operator set is *minimum*. The exception is the crossover operation, which may be modelled by a long sequence of mutation operators; the innate advantage of crossover is speed, i.e., it drastically raises the rate of change in the population.

The time complexity of applying each operator to a candidate with n total reads and r read length, and copying in the offspring, is up to $O(nr)$ in all cases except Greedy Merge, where an extra $O(n \log n)$ worst-case factor is needed (NB: this factor may be dominated by $O(nr)$).

3.3   Candidate Fitness

Good options for fitness functions are accuracy metrics from the literature. Since it has been observed that the assembly metrics regularly used in comparative studies do not correlate well with accuracy metrics [4], we use fitness functions which borrow from both categories.

The *length of the candidate scaffold*, i.e., *the sum of lengths of DNA contig strings*, is the main fitness, to be minimized. This is essentially an assembly metric, except if an estimate length of the reference genome is known: then it also acts as an accuracy metric.

The *number of DNA contigs* is the second, less crucial, component of the fitness, to be minimized. The two functions are summed up. This fitness reflects purely an assembly metric; unlike the first fitness component, it states nothing about the accuracy of the solution, since many assemblies may exist, of various scaffold lengths, which will have exactly one contig. For this reason, most of the early related work [8,10–12] does not use this fitness function at all, while the more recent work [13–16] uses it in conjunction with another assembly metric.

The time complexity of computing the scaffold length over a candidate with c contigs on the scaffold, in our candidate representation, is $\Theta(c)$: the length of the scaffold is the sum of the lengths of the DNA contig strings included in the representation (Sect. 3.1). Computing the number of contigs is constant-time if the length of the data structure modelling the segmented permutation is stored explicitly in the implementation.

4   Evaluation

4.1   Datasets

We obtain read libraries from existing consensus genomes. The reads are generated artificially, as in some of the prior work, rather than being selected from sequenced read libraries. This brings several advantages (argued as desirable in Sect. 2.1):

- This gives a reference genome, so we can compute accuracy metrics to evaluate any assembly obtained against the original genome itself.
- We know the raw reads to be accurate.
- We can verify that adjacent reads have an overlap above 30 base pairs.
- The genome lacks repeat sequences longer than the read length.

The genomes used in the evaluation (Table 3) were also used in the related work. X60189 and M15421 are fragments of human DNA (in the case of M15421, sequenced from messenger RNA); J02459 is the whole genome of a phage virus, the Enterobacteria phage lambda. The difference to [10,11,13,17] is that we take reads of uniform length, as uniform-length reads of length on the order of 10^2 are most common in current commercial sequencers, and we use the entirety of the J02459 (rather than the first 40% of the sequence, as done previously in [10,11,13,17]); we thus have a larger read library for J02459. We generated 10 distinct read libraries for X60189 and M15421, and one read library for J02459. Each read library was assembled 20 times, using different random seeds for the genetic algorithm.

Table 3. Reference genomes and read libraries used in the evaluation

	X60189 [18]	M15421 [19]	J02459 [20]
Genome length (base pairs)	3835	10089	48502
Read length (base pairs)	400	400	400
Coverage	5	5	7
Number of reads	48	127	849

4.2 Genetic Parameters and Implementation

Candidate solutions are selected via tournament (of tournament size 5 across all experiments), and 5 elites are kept in the population. Two stopping conditions are placed upon the evolutionary process: the fitness reaching the expected, optimal fitness for that genome (i.e., the length of the scaffold: an accuracy metric), and a stagnation condition upon the number of generations without improvement in fitness; the latter is set equal to the population size. The population size and the number of stagnating generations are always 100.

The genetic operators are applied sequentially in the basic order **RSIMOM**, i.e., with a Merge mutation after each chain of other operators which is likely to break down contigs (i.e., Split and Order crossover); the default is a Random Merge. The rates of application for the operators are 0.5 for all mutation operators, and 0.1 for the crossover.

The software implementation uses the `inspyred` [21] Python framework for bio-inspired algorithms, which is easily extensible with new candidate representations and genetic operators.

4.3   Results and Evaluation via Fitness Values

For the smallest read sets and genomes, the algorithm, when run repeatedly with different random seeds, always obtains the optimal solution. The optimal fitness value is the length of the reference genome plus one (the latter being the contig count). For the second genome, the optimal fitness is obtained in a majority of the runs; for the third, no run was optimal. We discuss this outcome later.

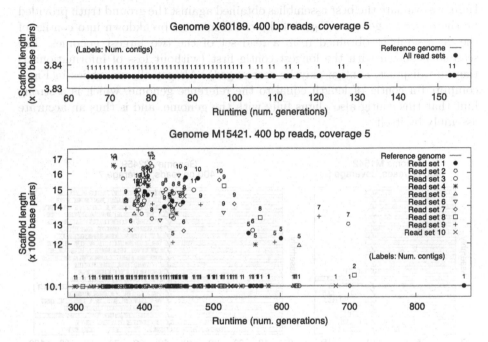

Fig. 3. Assemblies obtained for 10 different read sets sampled from the X60189 genome (top) and the M15421 genome (bottom). For each of the 10 read sets, 20 assemblies were run with different random seeds. Parameters as in Sect. 4.2. Optimal assembly length shown in red (grey in print). (Color figure online)

We first gain an insight as to the frequency and the cost of reaching the optimal fitness: in Fig. 3, we show assemblies for 10 read sets obtained from the X60189 genome, and for 10 read sets from the M15421 genome. For each of these read sets, 20 assemblies are run, with different random seeds, for a total of 200 per plot.

All assemblies used the parameter settings in Sect. 4.2. Each data point shows the best solution obtained by an assembly, in terms of fitness; the fitness is shown with its two components explicitly separate: the scaffold length (in base pairs) on the vertical axis, and the number of contigs as an annotation to each point. The optimal number of contigs is naturally one, and the optimal scaffold length is shown as a threshold line. On the horizontal axis, the number of generations required to reach the best assembly per run gives a measure of the method's runtime. For all the read sets, some or all of the assemblies found an optimal solution, i.e., the reference genome in either forward or reverse-complemented form. Not surprisingly, the smaller the read set, the likelier optimality is. For the largest genome (J02459), no assembly was optimal in fitness.

4.4   Results and Evaluation via Accuracy Metrics

Here, we evaluate the best assemblies obtained against the ground truth provided by the reference genome. Figure 4 shows the internal breakdown into contigs of the 20 assemblies obtained from a read set of the two largest genomes. The scaffold is shown with the longest contig first (without loss of information: as they are disjunct, contigs may be rearranged). Almost all assemblies in Fig. 4 computed a contig of length equal to the reference genome, which is a strong hint that this contig also aligns fully with the genome, and is thus an accurate assembly by itself.

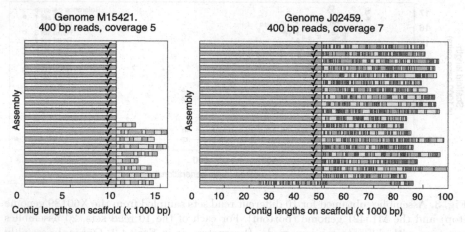

Fig. 4. Scaffolds obtained as best assemblies for the largest genomes, for one read set per genome. For each scaffold, the lengths of the internal contigs are shown, with the longest contig first. A check mark is placed on all contigs which are identical to the reference genome. Optimal assembly length shown in red (grey in print). (Color figure online)

We verify this in a separate step. All assemblies for X60189 obtained a single contig identical to the reference genome. Similarly, 131 out of 200 assemblies for M15421 obtained a single optimal contig, with the remaining assemblies consisting of a multi-contig scaffold, where the longest contig is identical to the reference; these results, together with a comparison with results from the related work and an account of the runtime of our method in the current implementation, are summarized in Table 4. The related work in [17], which also proved the optimality of the solution, is based on particle swarm optimization. We executed

Table 4. Summary of numerical results, including a comparison with related work and approximate average runtimes for our method (with sequential execution on 3-MHz computing cores). A ✓symbol is placed near a result when the single-contig assembly obtained there was verified to be the optimal solution; when not verified, no symbol is added. The full genome **J02459** was assembled before in [16], but using a smaller read library of longer, 700-bp reads, so it is not listed in the table; this related work obtained a single contig, but did not verify its accuracy.

	X60189 (5)	M15421 (5)	J02459 (7)
best num. contigs in related work	1 [10,13,16], 1 ✓ [17], 3 [22]	1 [13,16], 1 ✓ [17], 13 [22]	11 [22]
best num. contigs here	1 ✓	1 ✓	41
% runs optimal assembly	100%	66%	0%
% runs accurate contig	100%	100%	95%
average runtime per assembly	35 s	7 min	10 h

the greedy heuristic SSAKE [22] ourselves on these read sets; the parameters were -w 10 -m 20.

The results support the idea that the evolutionary algorithm can be used for consensus building.

There remains the problem of chaff contigs obtained in the assembly alongside the correct genome; the chaff can be seen in Fig. 4, and is loosely understood here as contigs of lengths shorter than 3–4 times the read length. This is a weakness of the evolutionary algorithm, also encountered in the prior work [12,13]: the best solution obtained by the GA may be suboptimal in fitness. However, suboptimal solutions are easily refinable into optimal ones: it is provable that, when a long contig is the accurate solution, a simple, deterministic, post-processing step can align each individual read left in chaff contigs back onto the long contig. This remains for future work.

4.5   Random vs. Greedy Merge

We found some variability in the results of assembly runs due to the type of the Merge operator. Figure 5 (left) shows the fitness values for the 20 assemblies of a M15421 read set, executed separately with either of the Merge operators. While a Random Merge contributed to an optimal fitness in slightly over half the runs (and did construct a correct contig in all the runs), the Greedy Merge under the same GA parameters never led to optimal fitness, but still did construct a correct contig in half the runs — Fig. 5 (right) shows the scaffolds obtained with the Greedy Merge. A greedy behaviour in this method may thus lead to local

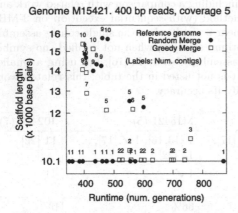
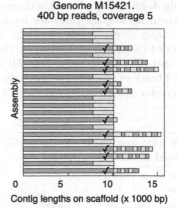

Fig. 5. The effect of the type of Merge upon assemblies over one read set for the M15421 genome. (left) 20 assembly runs with either Random Merge or Greedy Merge; (right) the scaffolds obtained with Greedy Merge. Parameters as in Sect. 4.2. Optimal assembly length shown in red (grey in print). (Color figure online)

minima, depending on the read library assembled; the type of Merge made no difference in assembling the smaller X60189 genome.

5 Conclusions

We summarize our results as follows:

- An evolutionary algorithm will often find an accurate solution to the assembly problem, for genomes and read sets of type and size used here.
- For large problems, chaff contigs is unavoidable, and an optimal fitness unattainable. However, even in these cases, the accurate genome is obtained after a simple post-processing refinement step.
- Accuracy metrics must be used to evaluate an assembly algorithm against reference genomes. De novo assemblies (without the advantage of reference genomes) can be validated by consensus.
- Evolutionary algorithms are eminently suitable as consensus builders: repeated executions will yield a number of large DNA contigs, among which the correct genome is found in majority.

Many practical difficulties remain for future work, in order that this method applies in commercial-grade assembly: (a) a uniform distribution is unlikely to be obtained in practice due to bias in some DNA fragmentation methods [9]; (b) the read sets to assemble may have far larger sizes and smaller reads, leading to a more complex problem; finally, (c) largest genomes will have long DNA repeats, which pose difficulties to all short-read assembly algorithms.

References

1. Illumina: Illumina sequencing technology, October 2016. http://www.illumina. com/documents/products/techspotlights/techspotlight_sequencing.pdf
2. Chin, C.S., Alexander, D.H., Marks, P., Klammer, A.A., Drake, J., Heiner, C., Clum, A., Copeland, A., Huddleston, J., Eichler, E.E., Turner, S.W., Korlach, J.: Nonhybrid, finished microbial genome assemblies from long-read SMRT sequencing data. Nat. Methods **10**(6), 563–569 (2013)
3. Ip, C., Loose, M., Tyson, J., de Cesare, M., Brown, B., Jain, M., Leggett, R., Eccles, D., Zalunin, V., Urban, J., Piazza, P., Bowden, R., Paten, B., Mwaigwisya, S., Batty, E., Simpson, J., Snutch, T., Birney, E., Buck, D., Goodwin, S., Jansen, H., O'Grady, J., Olsen, H.: MinION analysis and reference consortium: phase 1 data release and analysis. F1000Research **4**, 1075 (2015)
4. Salzberg, S.L., Phillippy, A.M., Zimin, A., Puiu, D., Magoc, T., Koren, S., Treangen, T.J., Schatz, M.C., Delcher, A.L., Roberts, M., Marçais, G., Pop, M., Yorke, J.A.: GAGE: a critical evaluation of genome assemblies and assembly algorithms. Genome Res. **22**(3), 557–567 (2012)
5. Bradnam, K., Fass, J., Alexandrov, A., Baranay, P., Bechner, M., Birol, I., Boisvert, S., Chapman, J., Chapuis, G., Chikhi, R., et al.: Assemblathon 2: evaluating de novo methods of genome assembly in three vertebrate species. Gigascience **2**, 10 (2013)
6. Cherukuri, Y., Janga, S.C.: Benchmarking of de novo assembly algorithms for Nanopore data reveals optimal performance of OLC approaches. BMC Genom. **17**(Suppl. 7), 507 (2016)
7. Räihä, K.J., Ukkonen, E.: The shortest common supersequence problem over binary alphabet is NP-complete. Theoret. Comput. Sci. **16**(2), 187–198 (1981)
8. Parsons, R., Burks, C., Forrest, S.: Genetic algorithms for DNA sequence assembly. In: International Conference in Intelligent Systems for Molecular Biology (1993)
9. Poptsova, M.S., Il'icheva, I.A., Nechipurenko, D.Y., Panchenko, L.A., Khodikov, M.V., Oparina, N.Y., Polozov, R.V., Nechipurenko, Y.D., Grokhovsky, S.L.: Non-random DNA fragmentation in next-generation sequencing. Sci. Rep. **4**(4532), 1697–1712 (2014)
10. Parsons, R.J., Forrest, S., Burks, C.: Genetic algorithms, operators, and DNA fragment assembly. Mach. Learn. **21**(1–2), 11–33 (1995)
11. Parsons, R., Johnson, M.E.: DNA sequence assembly and genetic algorithms - new results and puzzling insights. In: Proceedings of the Third International Conference on Intelligent Systems for Molecular Biology, Cambridge, United Kingdom, 16–19 July 1995, pp. 277–284 (1995)
12. Parsons, R., Johnson, M.E.: A case study in experimental design applied to genetic algorithms with applications to DNA sequence assembly. Am. J. Math. Manag. Sci. **17**(3–4), 369–396 (1997)
13. Alba, E., Luque, G.: A new local search algorithm for the DNA fragment assembly problem. In: Cotta, C., Hemert, J. (eds.) EvoCOP 2007. LNCS, vol. 4446, pp. 1–12. Springer, Heidelberg (2007). doi:10.1007/978-3-540-71615-0_1
14. Nebro, A., Luque, G., Luna, F., Alba, E.: DNA fragment assembly using a grid-based genetic algorithm. Comput. Oper. Res. **35**(9), 2776–2790 (2008). Part Special Issue: Bio-inspired Methods in Combinatorial Optimization
15. Dorronsoro, B., Alba, E., Luque, G., Bouvry, P.: A self-adaptive cellular memetic algorithm for the DNA fragment assembly problem. In: 2008 IEEE Congress on Evolutionary Computation (IEEE World Congress on Computational Intelligence), pp. 2651–2658, June 2008

16. Firoz, J.S., Rahman, M.S., Saha, T.K.: Bee algorithms for solving DNA fragment assembly problem with noisy and noiseless data. In: Proceedings of the 14th Annual Conference on Genetic and Evolutionary Computation, GECCO 2012, pp. 201–208. ACM, New York (2012)
17. Mallén-Fullerton, G.M., Fernández-Anaya, G.: DNA fragment assembly using optimization. In: 2013 IEEE Congress on Evolutionary Computation, pp. 1570–1577, June 2013
18. NCBI: Human MHC class III region DNA with fibronectin type-III repeats (2016). https://www.ncbi.nlm.nih.gov/nuccore/X60189
19. NCBI: Human apolipoprotein B-100 mRNA, complete cds (2016). https://www.ncbi.nlm.nih.gov/nuccore/M15421
20. NCBI: Enterobacteria phage lambda, complete genome (2016). https://www.ncbi.nlm.nih.gov/nuccore/J02459
21. Garret, A.L.: Inspyred: a framework for creating bio-inspired computational intelligence algorithms in Python (2017). https://pypi.python.org/pypi/inspyred
22. Warren, R.L., Sutton, G.G., Jones, S.J.M., Holt, R.A.: Assembling millions of short DNA sequences using SSAKE. Bioinformatics **23**(4), 500–501 (2007)

EVE: Cloud-Based Annotation of Human Genetic Variants

Brian S. Cole[⊠] and Jason H. Moore

Department of Biostatistics and Epidemiology, Perelman School of Medicine,
Institute for Biomedical Informatics, University of Pennsylvania,
Philadelphia, PA 19104-6116, USA
{colebr,jhmoore}@upenn.edu

Abstract. Annotation of human genetic variants enables genotype-phenotype association studies at the gene, pathway, and tissue level. Annotation results are difficult to reproduce across study sites due to shifting software versions and a lack of a unified hardware interface between study sites. Cloud computing offers a promising solution by integrating hardware and software into reproducible virtual appliances which may be utilized on-demand and shared across institutions. We developed ENSEMBL VEP on EC2 (EVE), a cloud-based virtual appliance for annotation of human genetic variants built around the ENSEMBL Variant Effect Predictor. We integrated virtual hardware infrastructure, open-source software, and publicly available genomic datasets to provide annotation capability for genetic variants in the context of genes/transcripts, Gene Ontology pathways, tissue-specific expression from the Gene Expression Atlas, miRNA annotations, minor allele frequencies from the 1000 Genomes Project and the Exome Aggregation Consortium, and deleteriousness scores from Combined Annotation Dependent Depletion. We demonstrate the utility of EVE by annotating the genetic variants in a case-control study of glaucoma. Cloud computing can reduce the difficulty of replicating complex software pipelines such as annotation pipelines across study sites. We provide a publicly available CloudFormation template of the EVE virtual appliance which can automatically provision and deploy a parameterized, preconfigured hardware/software stack ready for annotation of human genetic variants (github.com/epistasislab/EVE). This approach offers increased reproducibility in human genetic studies by providing a unified appliance to researchers across the world.

Keywords: Annotation · GWAS · Cloud computing · Reproducibility · Infrastructure-as-Code

1 Background

Genome-wide association studies (GWAS) have revealed the associations between genetic polymorphisms and phenotypes in thousands of studies since 2005 [1, 2]. The knowledge gained from these population-scale human association studies has contributed to advances in translational medicine, for example via drug repurposing and personalized genetic medicine, and also to our understanding of the basic biology of human cells, tissues, and organs [3, 4]. However, many GWAS studies to date have

© Springer International Publishing AG 2017
G. Squillero and K. Sim (Eds.): EvoApplications 2017, Part I, LNCS 10199, pp. 83–95, 2017.
DOI: 10.1007/978-3-319-55849-3_6

utilized additive genotype-phenotype association models, in which genetic variants contribute additively to explain variation in phenotype [5]. These additive designs have often failed to explain much of the heritability in phenotype, suggesting that other approaches may be able to more completely capture the relationship between genetic variation within a human population and a phenotype under study.

Pathway-, network-, and tissue-based analyses of genotype-phenotype association are promising approaches for many reasons [6, 7]. First, multiple genetic variants within the same biological pathway might independently contribute to the same effect at the pathway level, for example highly deleterious mutations within an intracellular signaling pathway. In such a scenario, testing the null hypothesis of no association between the aggregate mutational status of a biological pathway and a phenotype under study has the power to group the effects of many genetic variants, performing fewer total hypothesis tests in the process. Second, pathway-based approaches offer direct insights into potential drug repositioning because the results of pathway-phenotype association studies are biological pathways themselves, rather than genetic variants which must be interrogated by pathway enrichment analysis, a second layer of statistical hypothesis testing.

Annotation of genetic variants is the process of labeling a genetic variant with information derived from external sources, for instance the annotation of genetic variants with biological pathway ontology terms associated with the gene in which the genetic variant resides. Powerful open-source software such as the ENSEMBL Variant Effect Predictor (VEP) [8] and ANNOVAR [9] are capable of integrating rich, publicly-available data to annotate human genetic variants with a vast amount of information, including transcript and gene annotations, tissue-specific expression quantifications, functional genomics annotations such as miRNA loci, minor allele frequencies from population-scale sequencing datasets such as the 1000 Genomes Project and the Exome Aggregation Consortium, and deleteriousness scores including loss-of-function annotation, SIFT/PolyPHEN scores, and the Combined Annotation Dependent Depletion (CADD) score [8, 9]. These annotations, when applied to genetic variants in human studies, provide a wealth of opportunities for computational genetics researchers to integrate vast amounts of data, opening the door to new avenues of investigation.

Genotype-phenotype association studies may increase statistical power to detect significant associations through meta-analysis, an approach that combines GWAS summary statistics from individual human cohorts [10]. As a result, meta-analytical designs require separate statistical analysis of the individual cohorts, thus necessitating each cohort be analyzed using reproducible software. In the case of additive genetic models, open-source software such as PLINK and R provide high reproducibility due in part to the fact that fitting additive genetic models does not require external data sources, for instance pathway annotations [11].

Despite the fact that researchers have access to open-source annotation software and the data needed to perform annotation of genetic variants, reproducibility of annotation software is hindered by the complexity of the data sources and software, many of which are updated at different version cycles. The result is that multiple study sites annotating the same genetic variants, for instance a consortium which utilizes the same GWAS genotyping array, may generate inconsistent results both across software versions and across time, given the ongoing expansion of public datasets and databases.

The development of cloud computing has provided new opportunities for reproducible bioinformatics by tethering virtualized hardware and software together behind a unified interface, a development-operations model sometimes called Infrastructure-as-Code (IaC). This model allows researchers at independent study sites to instantiate and execute exactly the same hardware and software, providing an avenue to increase reproducibility when compared to isolated compute systems at each study site.

We developed the ENSEMBL VEP on EC2 (EVE): an on-demand virtual appliance for annotation of human genetic variants based on the ENSEMBL Variant Effect Predictor and Amazon Web Services (AWS). We provide EVE as a publicly available, open-source, version-controlled CloudFormation template that integrates AWS cloud services and machine images into a unified stack. We demonstrate the performance and utility of EVE using a human glaucoma GWAS dataset. Importantly, EVE allows researchers across the world to reproduce a unified hardware/software stack using only cloud services. EVE provides reproducible insights into human genetic variation and demonstrates the utility of cloud computing for biomedical research in a global research environment.

2 Methods

2.1 Architecting EVE on the Amazon Web Services Cloud

We designed a CloudFormation template that allows users to provision cloud resources fully configured and ready for annotation of human genetic variant data (Fig. 1). The template allows users to create an integrated hardware/software stack in the cloud. This stack includes a parameterized EC2 instance with vertically scalable resource allocations to perform computation. Attached to the EC2 instance is an Elastic Block Store (EBS) volume containing the Amazon Linux operating system, the ENSEMBL Perl application programming interface, the Variant Effect Predictor (VEP), and the system libraries and dependencies for VEP, including relational database libraries and Perl dependencies.

We next installed the current VEP cache, version 85, for the merged Homo Sapiens genome build GRCh37 using the VEP Install script [8]. This cache enables annotation of human genetic variants at a basic level, including gene and transcript annotations. In addition to this basic functionality, VEP plugins greatly expand the depth and richness of information layered onto genetic variant datasets during annotation. We selected a suite of open-source plugins to add minor allele frequency information from the Exome Aggregation Consortium [12], deleteriousness scores from the Combined Annotation Dependent Depletion [13], gene ontology terms from GO [14], tissue-specific expression information from the Gene Expression Atlas [15], and miRNA structural annotation. Together, these plugins utilize diverse strategies to annotate genetic variants (Table 1), including connection to external relational databases over the internet (GO, GXA), the ENSEMBL API itself (miRNA), and block-level access of locally attached files (CADD, ExAC). The size of the datasets required to execute this suite of plugins is too large to fit on the root filesystem volume (Fig. 1, left), so we attached a second

EBS volume to the EC2 instance provisioned in the EVE CloudFormation template to hold the plugins and their data (Fig. 1, center), the attachment of which to the EC2 instance is also parameterized.

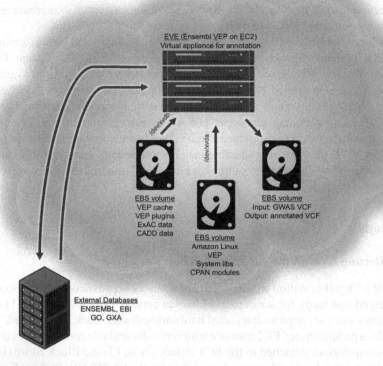

Fig. 1. Diagram of the EVE virtual appliance. A version-controlled CloudFormation template specifies the virtualized hardware to be provisioned. Preconfigured software is attached through a hardware virtual machine image based on the Amazon Linux operating system with VEP and its software dependencies preinstalled, including the tabix index utility, relational database libraries, and Perl modules from the Comprehensive Perl Archive Network (CPAN). EC2 compute instances (top) utilize these attached EBS volumes to perform annotation of human genetic variants. The plugins for the ENSEMBL VEP software used in this appliance, along with the data that they utilize, exist on a second EBS volume. A third EBS volume of parameterized size (from 1 GiB to 16 TiB) is provisioned and mounted for genetic variants and annotation output. Some plugins rely on external database connections (lower left) including relational databases (see Discussion).

We then provisioned another EBS volume to hold user genetic variant datasets in VCF format and generate output during annotation (Fig. 1, right). EBS is a virtualized device that is automatically replicated within the cloud, insulating users from adverse events such as component failures, and is therefore a durable solution for genetic variant annotation. EBS devices may also be encrypted and protected by Virtual Private Cloud

(VPC) networking configurations, providing additional security capabilities. We provide a parameterized EBS volume for user data, which enables users to load datasets of a wide range of sizes. Finally, EBS volumes provide the advantage that they are virtual devices which exist independently of the compute instances to which they are attached, providing the ability for users to make incremental snapshots of their EBS volumes for future analysis and persist the volumes while compute instances are taken offline, as opposed to ephemeral block storage.

Table 1. Annotation plugins used in EVE. Open-source plugins released under the Apache version 2.0 license use differing data retrieval strategies, requiring a system to integrate block-stored files, file access utilities (tabix), remote database connections, and the ENSEMBL API itself. Source repositories were accessed from https://github.com/Ensembl/VEP_plugins/.

Plugin	Purpose	Data retrieval strategy	Data source(s)
CADD	Deleteriousness score	Tabix-indexed EBS files	whole_genome_SNVs.tsv.gz, InDels.tsv.gz
GO	Gene Ontology term annotation	External database connection	ENSEMBL mySQL database
ExAC	Minor Allele frequencies from ExAC	Tabix-indexed EBS files	ExAC.r0.3.sites.vep.vcf.gz
GXA	Tissue-specific expression	External HTTPS query	https://www.ebi.ac.uk/gxa
miRNA	miRNA structure annotation	(ENSEMBL API)	N/A

CloudFormation templates may be launched from the web console from the us-east-1 availability zone, locally via the AWS Command Line Interface (CLI), or via one of many application programming interfaces. In addition, CloudFormation templates are JSON documents which can be managed with version control systems. We provide the EVE CloudFormation template at github.com/epistasislab/EVE/ along with a markdown walkthrough.

2.2 NEIGHBOR GWAS Study Quality Control

To benchmark cloud annotation with EVE (see Results), we utilized the NEIGHBOR case-control glaucoma GWAS study [16, 17]. We obtained Authorized Access with permission to utilize cloud computing and decrypted the data locally in a controlled and firewalled, private compute environment. We next performed individual-level and variant-level quality control [18], resulting in a total of 520,920 genetic variants in 4,969 samples. We converted the genotype data from Plink format to VCF and uploaded the VCF file to S3 cloud object storage in a private bucket. This dataset is not included with EVE.

2.3 Annotation Benchmarking and Annotation Plugins

We utilized a variety of general purpose and compute-optimized instance types to benchmark the annotation of the NEIGHBOR VCF dataset. Of all instances tried, only the c4.large instance was unable to perform the annotation of the NEIGHBOR VCF file due to insufficient memory. The resources of these instances is summarized in Table 2. We used the m4.large instance to benchmark plugins singly, and a range of compute-optimized instances to benchmark all plugins together in triplicate (see Results). The time utility was used to benchmark real compute time used by the annotation process, and the median of three results across different times of the day is visualized. These runtimes do not include the time necessary to instantiate a stack from the CloudForma-tion template or to terminate it upon completion of annotation. All benchmarking was performed in the us-east-1 region using the default availability zone.

Table 2. Instance types used for cloud annotation benchmarking. Hourly cost, vCPU count, memory capacity, and the dedicated EBS bandwidth all scale vertically within instance type families. M4 instance types are general purpose instance types, and c4 instance types are compute-optimized instance types. *Retrieved for on-demand instance pricing on 10/27/16.

Instance	vCPU	Memory (GiB)	Dedicated EBS bandwidth (Mbps)	Instance-hour cost* (USD)
m4.large	2	8	450	0.12
m4.xlarge	4	16	750	0.239
m4.2xlarge	8	32	1000	0.479
c4.large	2	3.75	500	0.105
c4.xlarge	4	7.5	750	0.209
c4.2xlarge	8	15	1000	0.419

3 Results

3.1 Cloud Instance Types for Annotation with EVE

We explored vertical scaling of EVE across compute instance types to investigate the relationship between instance type and performance, using the NEIGHBOR human glaucoma GWAS dataset as a benchmarking dataset. Using triplicate benchmarking annotation runs with no plugins applied, we tabulated the average runtime and compute cost for both general purpose and compute-optimized instances, using all vCPUs available within each instance type in parallel during annotation. We find that as instance types scale vertically, a diminishing performance benefit is achieved (Fig. 2a). We also explored cost-efficiency by tabulating the compute costs incurred at current prices using the hourly billing scheme. We find that the m4.large instance, a general purpose instance type, is the most cost-efficient (Fig. 2b) but also the slowest instance type (Fig. 2a). We also find that the compute-optimized instance types provide higher performance per vCPU count than general purpose instance types (Fig. 2b), but the c4.large instance type was not able to execute VEP due to insufficient memory (Table 2). We therefore find that the m4.large instance type is the most cost-efficient of all instance types tested, but the compute-optimized instances provide more cost-efficient vertical scaling than general purpose instance types. This vertical scaling demonstrates that users can select virtualized hardware with the goal of short runtimes or low expense. We therefore provide instance type selection as a user parameter in the EVE CloudFormation template.

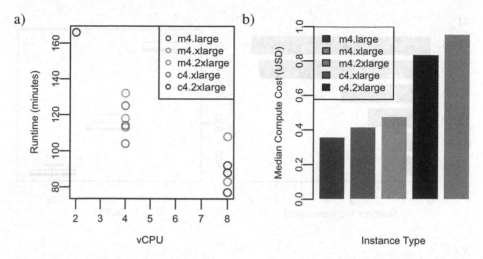

Fig. 2. Vertical scaling of EVE on general purpose and compute-optimized instance types. (a) Runtime in minutes and vCPU count across 2-, 4-, and 8-vCPU instance types from general purpose ("m4" family) and compute-optimized ("c4" family) instance types using triplicate runs and the UNIX "time" utility. Note: EBS bandwidths covary with vCPU in both instance families (see Table 2). (b) Median of triplicate compute costs computed using runtime in a). Storage and transfer costs were not included, and compute times were rounded up to the next hour as per AWS billing practice.

3.2 Plugin Benchmarking

We then evaluated the performance of adding plugins to the benchmarking runs. Plugins represent a major source of added information to the Variant Effect Predictor, including GO pathways, deleteriousness scores, tissue-specific expression, minor allele frequencies, functional genomics annotations, and more. We installed and configured plugins, dependencies, and plugin data to provide a broad suite of additional annotation functionalities (see Methods for plugin and configuration information). While these plugins expand the annotation capability of the EVE virtual appliance, some plugins require additional data sources, either local (e.g. ExAC minor allele frequencies) or remote (GO pathways via a connection to an external relational database). We then added each plugin singly and measured the increase in runtime and runcost in triplicate runs using the cost-efficient m4.large instance type (Fig. 3a). We find that some plugins, including CADD and GO, result in greater than 6× increases in runtime and run cost using the m4.large instance type. For this reason, we next explored compute-optimized instance types to decrease runtime using all plugins tested simultaneously (Fig. 3b). We identified a scaling relationship between increasing vCPU count and marginal runtime decrease, suggesting a fairly even trade-off between cost-efficiency and runtime (Fig. 3c, d).

Instance types are therefore an important parameter to balance the need for rapid execution against cost-efficiency under an hourly billing model.

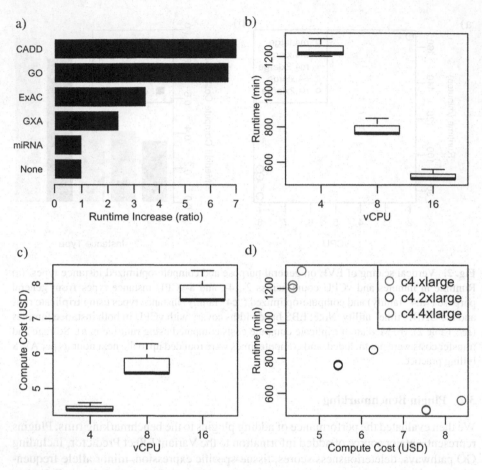

Fig. 3. Annotation plugin benchmarking. (a) Median (of triplicate) runtime increases incurred by adding plugins singly to the base annotation run with no plugins invoked, with increases expressed as a ratio over the no-plugin base annotation run. (b) Vertical scaling across compute-optimized instance types using all plugins in (a) simultaneously. Runtime vs vCPU count in compute-optimized instances (see Table 2). (c) Compute cost vs vCPU count in compute-optimized instances. Costs were calculated for EC2 computing only and do not include storage costs. Costs were tabulated from rounding the compute time up to the nearest hour, without including instance launch time and shutdown time before and after annotation. (d) Runtime versus compute cost for three compute-optimized instance types.

Using all of these plugins together generates a wealth of information layered upon the raw genotype data which serves as input to the annotation appliance. We explored the depth and richness of these annotation data in the context of the NEIGHBOR GWAS study by first annotating the NEIGHBOR genetic variants with all plugins used in

Fig. 3a (CADD, GO, ExAC, GXA, and miRNA). The annotation results relate the genetic variants genotyped in the NEIGHBOR glaucoma study to gene ontology terms including biological pathways as well as deleteriousness scores via the Combined Annotation Dependent Depletion score, providing insight into mutational burden in the context of molecular functions and biological pathways.

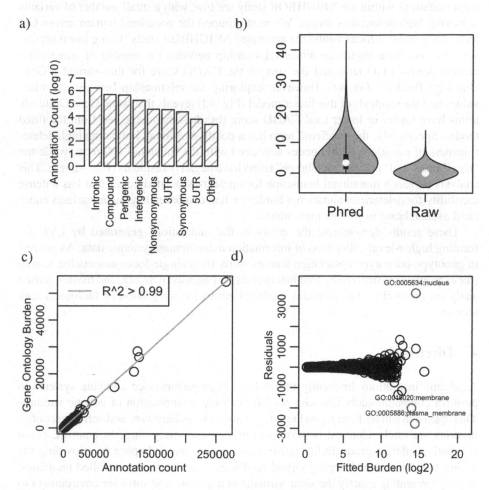

Fig. 4. EVE reveals a landscape of information within the NEIGHBOR glaucoma study. (a) Raw annotation counts per genomic feature type. One genetic variant may contribute one or more annotations by virtue of overlap with multiple genomic features, for example pre-mRNA isoforms. The sum is displayed, and compound annotations were grouped together. (b) The distribution of the CADD scores for all genetic variants within the NEIGHBOR glaucoma study. CADD reports both Phred-scaled and raw scores. (c) Burden on each GO term versus number of annotations per GO term. The y axis represents the sum of the CADD score for each GO term as a burden score. The linear regression line is displayed in gray (R-squared: 0.9915, p-value: <2.2e−16). (d) Residuals-versus-fitted plot for the linear model displayed in (c). GO terms with absolute residuals >=2000 are highlighted red. (Color figure online)

We find that the annotations generated by EVE for the genetic variants in the NEIGHBOR study are mostly intronic (Fig. 4a), but that a range of annotation types occur, including synonymous and nonsynonymous substitutions and UTR variants. We next explored the global distribution of the deleteriousness scores generated by the Combined Annotation Dependent Depletion plugin (Fig. 3a). The plugin generates two data points, a Phred-scaled and a raw score (Fig. 4b) and the deleteriousness scores of most mutations within the NEIGHBOR study are low, with a small number of variants achieving high deleterious scores. We next grouped the combined burden across GO terms for genetic variants within the annotated NEIGHBOR study. Using linear regression, we observe a significant linear relationship between the number of annotations present across a GO term and the sum of the CADD score for that variant ("Gene Ontology Burden", Fig. 4c). However, exploring the relationship between the fitted values and the residuals of this linear model (Fig. 4d) reveals that some Gene Ontology terms have higher or lower total CADD score (burden) than expected from the fitted model. Specifically, the "nucleus" term has a positive residual, indicating high deleteriousness of mutations within genes annotated with the "nucleus" GO term, while the "membrane" and "plasma_membrane" terms have negative residuals (Fig. 4d, red). This analysis reveals a mutational landscape for nuclear-associated genes that has a dense capability for deleterious mutational burdens when compared to genetic variants annotated as membrane or plasma membrane.

These results demonstrate the utility of the annotations generated by EVE for forming higher-level collections of information using human genomic data. As interest in genotype-phenotype association studies shifts from single-locus association testing (for example, as visualized by Manhattan plots) to pathway, network, and tissue-focused analyses, annotation data provides a critical nexus for integration of biological data sources.

4 Discussion

Academic institutions frequently utilize local high-performance compute systems to perform computationally intensive workflows such as annotation of genetic variants. This approach suffers from reproducibility drawbacks as hardware and software configurations are rarely identical between institutions and study sites. In contrast, cloud computing offers reproducibility advantages across time and space by providing the ability to provision and deploy virtual appliances from version-controlled templates, thereby presenting exactly the same virtualized hardware and software environment to users across diverse geographical locations, such as multiple study sites and Data Coordinating Centers in population-scale human genetic studies [19–21].

In addition to reproducibility benefits for biomedical research, the cloud provides scalable, on-demand compute requiring no capital expense. This operational-only expense model provides benefits to collaborative science by easing reliance upon enterprise hardware. Furthermore, bioinformatics in the cloud benefits from a broad array of managed cloud services including compute resource and network monitoring, billing alerts, managed encryption, controlled access to data, hardware virtual machine imaging and incremental snapshots, virtual firewalls and private networking, hybrid IT infrastructure designs, and more. In addition, cloud services continue to grow, and third-party cloud service providers continue to expand the utility of cloud computing for bioinformatics.

Annotation of human genetic variants is a nexus for integration of large, publicly available genomic and biomedical datasets. These datasets continue to evolve in size and complexity as human genomic data expands, including the Thousand Genomes Project [22], the Exome Aggregation Consortium [12], the Cancer Genome Atlas [23], and more. The scalability of cloud computing is advantageous for biomedical research to keep pace with rapidly growing and evolving datasets and databases.

Annotation is a computationally intense process which must scale not only with the size of the genetic variant space (number of variants per sample) and study size (number of samples), but also with external datasets required for data integration as part of the annotation process, for instance minor allele frequencies from the Exome Aggregation Consortium and the Thousand Genomes Project. Cloud computing offers scalable solutions for the expanding universe of human genome science.

EVE is a cloud-based virtual appliance for annotation of human genetic variants based on open-source software, publicly available datasets, and AWS cloud computing services. EVE provides on-demand annotation capability in a reproducible manner, ideal for groups of genetic researchers who require consistent annotation results across geographically distinct study sites or Data Coordinating Centers. We share an open source, version-controlled CloudFormation template to provision all the necessary resources to run EVE, including compute instances and imaged block store volume with all required software, data sources, and dependencies/libraries.

We demonstrate the performance of EVE using base annotation and a suite of plugins which greatly expand the information content of annotated genetic variants across a vertical sweep of instance types. We find a trade-off between cost-efficiency and performance using a quality-controlled human glaucoma GWAS dataset. By integrating GO pathway information with CADD deleteriousness scores, EVE enables pathway-based hypothesis testing, a promising approach for drug repurposing as well as providing mechanistic insights into disease processes. Additionally, the ENSEMBL VEP framework around which EVE is built provides a rich ecosystem of plugins that unlock data from diverse and expanding domains, including minor allele frequencies from population-scale sequencing datasets, functional genomic annotations such as miRNAs, gene and pre-mRNA annotations, codon information for nonsynonymous substitutions, and more.

EVE is an example of the benefits of cloud computing for reproducible bioinformatics. Cloud services such as CloudFormation provide abstractions for provisioning and configuring virtualized hardware and software stacks, and when coupled to images of datasets and software pipelines such as those described in this work, provide the greater research community with a unified interface to cloud resources [24]. EVE therefore provides high utility for scientific consortia, meta-analyses, and future infrastructure-as-code development and operations.

Acknowledgements. This work is supported by an Amazon Web Services Cloud Credits for Research award to BSC and NIH AI116794 to JHM.

References

1. Klein, R., Zeiss, C., Chew, E., Tsai, J.: Complement factor H polymorphism in age-related macular degeneration. Science **308**(5720), 385–389 (2005). doi:10.1126/science. 1109557.Complement
2. Welter, D., MacArthur, J., Morales, J., et al.: The NHGRI GWAS Catalog, a curated resource of SNP-trait associations. Nucleic Acids Res. **42**(D1), 1001–1006 (2014). doi:10.1093/nar/gkt1229
3. Witte, J.S.: Genome-wide association studies and beyond. Annu. Rev. Public Health **77**, 9–20 (2014). doi:10.1146/annurev.publhealth.012809.103723.Genome-Wide
4. Manolio, T.A.: Genomewide association studies and assessment of risk of disease. N. Engl. J. Med. **363**, 2076–2077 (2010). doi:10.1056/NEJMc1010310
5. Moore, J.H., Asselbergs, F.W., Williams, S.M.: Bioinformatics challenges for genome-wide association studies. Bioinformatics **26**(4), 445–455 (2010). doi:10.1093/bioinformatics/btp713
6. Greene, C.S., Voight, B.F.: Pathway and network-based strategies to translate genetic discoveries into effective therapies. Hum. Mol. Genet., 1–5 (2016). doi:10.1093/hmg/ddw160
7. Greene, C.S., Krishnan, A., Wong, A.K., et al.: Understanding multicellular function and disease with human tissue-specific networks. Nat. Genet. **47**(6) (2015). doi:10.1038/ng.3259
8. McLaren, W., Gil, L., Hunt, S.E., et al.: The ensembl variant effect predictor. Genome Biol. **17**(122) (2016). doi:10.1186/s13059-016-0974-4
9. Wang, K., Li, M., Hakonarson, H.: ANNOVAR: functional annotation of genetic variants from high-throughput sequencing data. Nucleic Acids Res. **38**(16), e164 (2010). doi:10.1093/nar/gkq603
10. Evangelou, E., Ioannidis, J.P.A.: Meta-analysis methods for genome-wide association studies and beyond. Nat. Rev. Genet. **14**(6), 379–389 (2013). doi:10.1038/nrg3472
11. Purcell, S., Neale, B., Todd-Brown, K., et al.: PLINK: a tool set for whole-genome association and population-based linkage analyses. Am. J. Hum. Genet. **81**(3), 559–575 (2007). doi:10.1086/519795
12. Lek, M., Karczewski, K.J., Minikel, E.V., et al.: Analysis of protein-coding genetic variation in 60,706 humans. Nature **536**(7616), 285–291 (2016). doi:10.1038/nature19057
13. Kircher, M.: A general framework for estimating the relative pathogenicity of human genetic variants. Nat. Genet. **46**(3), 310–315 (2014). doi:10.1038/ng.2892.A
14. Consortium TGO: Gene ontology: tool for the unification of biology. Nat. Genet. **25**(1), 25–29 (2000). doi:10.1038/75556.Gene
15. Kapushesky, M., Adamusiak, T., Burdett, T., et al.: Gene Expression Atlas update–a value-added database of microarray and sequencing-based functional genomics experiments. Nucleic Acids Res. **40**(Database issue), D1077-81 (2012). doi:10.1093/nar/gkr913
16. Wiggs, J.L., Hauser, M.A., Abdrabou, W., et al.: The NEIGHBOR consortium primary open angle glaucoma genome-wide association study: rationale, study design and clinical variables. J. Glaucoma **22**(7), 517–525 (2013). doi:10.1097/IJG.0b013e31824d4fd8
17. Wiggs, J.L., Yaspan, B.L., Hauser, M.A., et al.: Common variants at 9p21 and 8q22 are associated with increased susceptibility to optic nerve degeneration in glaucoma. PLoS Genet. **8**(4) (2012). doi:10.1371/journal.pgen.1002654

18. Anderson, C.A., Pettersson, F.H., Clarke, G.M., Cardon, L.R., Morris, A.P., Zondervan, K.T.: Data quality control in genetic case-control association studies. Nat. Protoc. **5**(9), 1564–1573 (2010). doi:10.1038/nprot.2010.116

19. Begley, C.G., Ioannidis, J.P.A.: Reproducibility in science: improving the standard for basic and preclinical research. Circ. Res. **116**(1), 116–126 (2015). doi:10.1161/CIRCRESAHA. 114.303819

20. Peng, R.D.: Reproducible research in computational science. Science **334**(6060), 1226–1227 (2011). doi:10.1126/science.1213847

21. Stein, L.D., Knopers, B.M., Campell, P., Getz, G., Korbel, J.O.: Create a cloud commons. Nature **523**, 149–151 (2015). doi:10.1038/523149a

22. Project Consortium G, Consortium Participants are arranged by project role G, by institution alphabetically then, et al.: An integrated map of genetic variation from 1,092 human genomes. Nature **490**(7422), 56–65 (2012). doi:10.1038/nature11632

23. McLendon, R., Friedman, A., Bigner, D., et al.: Comprehensive genomic characterization defines human glioblastoma genes and core pathways. Nature **455**(7216), 1061–1068 (2008). doi:10.1038/nature07385

24. Li, J., Doyle, M.A., Saeed, I., et al.: Bioinformatics pipelines for targeted resequencing and whole-exome sequencing of human and mouse genomes: a virtual appliance approach for instant deployment. PLoS One **9**(4) (2014). doi:10.1371/journal.pone.0095217

Improving the Reproducibility of Genetic Association Results Using Genotype Resampling Methods

Elizabeth R. Piette[1(✉)] and Jason H. Moore[2]

[1] Graduate Group in Genomics and Computational Biology,
Perelman School of Medicine, University of Pennsylvania,
Philadelphia, PA, USA
piette@upenn.edu
[2] Institute for Biomedical Informatics, Perelman School of Medicine,
University of Pennsylvania, Philadelphia, PA, USA
jhmoore@exchange.upenn.edu

Abstract. Replication may be an inadequate gold standard for substantiating the significance of results from genome-wide association studies (GWAS). Successful replication provides evidence supporting true results and against spurious findings, but various population attributes contribute to observed significance of a genetic effect. We hypothesize that failure to replicate an interaction observed to be significant in a GWAS of one population in a second population is sometimes attributable to differences in minor allele frequencies, and resampling the replication dataset by genotype to match the minor allele frequencies of the discovery data can improve estimates of the interaction significance. We show via simulation that resampling of the replication data produced results more concordant with the discovery findings. We recommend that failure to replicate GWAS results should not immediately be considered to refute previously-observed findings and conversely that replication does not guarantee significance, and suggest that datasets be compared more critically in biological context.

Keywords: GWAS · SNPs · Epistasis · Complex diseases · Reproducibility

1 Introduction

Replication is the gold standard for substantiating the validity of results across the spectrum of biological sciences, and is a cornerstone of rigorous hypothesis-driven research. In this era of big data and complex, computationally-intensive research, true replication may be impossible or infeasible, and reproducibility of analyses is a proximate concern [1]. Both replication and reproducibility are beset with challenges associated with a diversity of issues ranging from data access and storage, to availability of requisite computational resources, to thoughtfully implemented, high-quality code, all in the context of a constantly shifting field with high software, hardware, and ideological turnover. While advances such as portable, versioned workflows for computational environments and proposed statistical frameworks for defining replication and

© Springer International Publishing AG 2017
G. Squillero and K. Sim (Eds.): EvoApplications 2017, Part I, LNCS 10199, pp. 96–108, 2017.
DOI: 10.1007/978-3-319-55849-3_7

reproducibility themselves are addressing some of these issues, certain roadblocks to replication and reproducibility have yet to be resolved and may continue to remain impractical and inaccessible to the average researcher, such as for the analysis of datasets involving millions of parameters, multiple processors, and finite time [2–5].

In the context of genome-wide association studies, failure to replicate previously-observed findings in a second population may be attributable to a combination of statistical and biological factors. Investigating the genetic underpinnings of complex diseases presents a special challenge given the evidence for multi-locus or network-based models of disease and the increased multiple-testing burden associated with fitting interaction models over single-locus models [6]. This is in addition to considerations of the heterogeneity of disease etiology, underlying genetic architecture, and other confounding factors that vary across populations. In this study, we explore epistatic interactions as a case study of a phenomenon that may be inherently difficult to replicate, and attempt to recapitulate the power to detect epistatic interactions between single nucleotide polymorphisms (SNPs) in two populations with differing minor allele frequencies (MAFs).

Epistasis, briefly defined as interactions between genetic loci that non-additively contribute to phenotype, is suspected to be both ubiquitously implicated in susceptibility to non-Mendelian disease and difficult to detect and replicate [7]. Resampling populations so that they appear more similar for the genotypes of interest may allow us to compare them in a more meaningful way. In this study, we propose a method for improving detection of epistatic SNP-SNP interactions between genome-wide association study (GWAS) datasets with differing minor allele frequencies for the SNPs of interest via resampling by genotype such that genotypes that are underrepresented in the replication population relative to the discovery population are oversampled, and genotypes that are overrepresented are undersampled. We substantiate the efficacy of this method via simulations. Application of this method may help inform scenarios in which findings of interest with potential functional significance from a discovery population sample fail to reach statistical significance in a replication population sample.

2 Datasets and Methods

The following subsections describe our methods workflow (refer to Fig. 1 for accompanying graphical abstract). Briefly, we begin with dataset simulation for a selection of models with varying penetrance functions, minor allele frequencies for two SNPs, heritabilities, and prevalences. Then, we use the discovery penetrance tables to generate replication data with the same underlying penetrances but differing minor allele frequencies. Next, we analyze the SNP-SNP interactions for all discovery scenarios by calculating the p-value for the likelihood ratio test comparing the logistic regression models with and without the interaction between the two SNPs, and estimate power to detect the interaction over 1000 simulations. Replication datasets are resampled to match the genotype proportions of their relative discovery datasets, and interaction analysis and power estimation is performed again post-resampling. We also test negative simulations to address the possibility of erroneously significant interactions – sample datasets with significant p-values for the interaction, despite being drawn from an underlying population without a significant interaction.

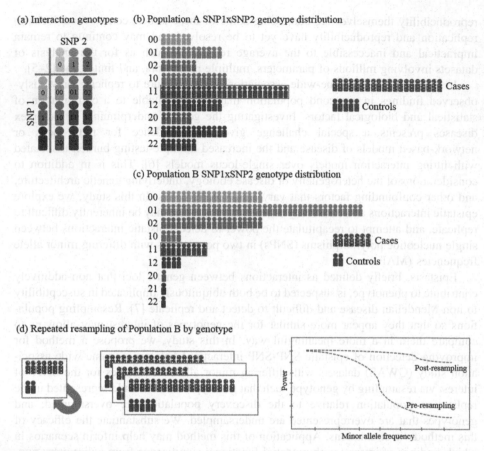

Fig. 1. Graphical abstract (a) A SNP-SNP interaction results in 9 genotypes (b) In Population A, the SNP1 minor allele frequency is 0.5, and the SNP2 minor allele frequency is also 0.5. A GWAS of Population A reveals a significant association between the '11' genotype and disease status. (c) Replication of this interaction is sought in Population B, and another GWAS is performed. However, in Population B, the SNP1 minor allele frequency is 0.1, and the SNP2 minor allele frequency is 0.5, so the relative distribution of genotypes is different. A GWAS of Population B does not reveal a significant association between the '11' genotype and disease status, despite the same penetrance for genotype '11' in Population B and in Population A, due to the low minor allele frequency of SNP1/low prevalence of genotype '11' in Population B. (d) Resampling by genotype allows us to observe what our Population B sample would look like if the minor allele frequencies for SNP1 and SNP2 were the same as in Population A. Performing resampling numerous times allows for an empirical estimation of power to detect a significant interaction.

2.1 Discovery Dataset Simulation

Penetrance functions and datasets for eight discovery scenarios were generated using GAMETES, an algorithm and software package that facilitates generation of complex epistatic models and datasets based upon these models [8]. Our test parameters (Table 1) included minor allele frequencies of 0.5 and 0.5 or 0.1 and 0.1 for two SNPs, heritabilities of 0.05 or 0.005, and prevalences of 0.5 or 0.1. Case-control datasets of size 2,000 and 4,000 were tested, and all simulation scenarios were replicated 1,000 times.

Table 1. Discovery dataset simulation parameters: minor allele frequencies, heritabililties, prevalences, and penetrance tables used to generate discovery data

	Model 1			Model 2		
SNP1 MAF:	0.5			0.5		
SNP2 MAF:	0.5			0.5		
Heritability:	0.005			0.05		
Prevalence:	0.5			0.5		
Penetrance:	0.475	0.469	0.586	0.495	0.646	0.214
	0.524	0.516	0.443	0.449	0.451	0.649
	0.476	0.498	0.528	0.608	0.451	0.498
	Model 3			Model 4		
SNP1 MAF:	0.5			0.5		
SNP2 MAF:	0.5			0.5		
Heritability:	0.005			0.05		
Prevalence:	0.1			0.1		
Penetrance:	0.145	0.092	0.071	0.130	0.105	0.061
	0.065	0.110	0.115	0.081	0.145	0.029
	0.125	0.088	0.098	0.108	0.006	0.281
	Model 5			Model 6		
SNP1 MAF:	0.1			0.1		
SNP2 MAF:	0.1			0.1		
Heritability:	0.005			0.05		
Prevalence:	0.5			0.5		
Penetrance:	0.507	0.475	0.407	0.524	0.395	0.458
	0.467	0.624	0.906	0.387	0.999	0.689
	0.548	0.274	0.692	0.604	0.033	0.462
	Model 7			Model 8		
SNP1 MAF:	0.1			0.1		
SNP2 MAF:	0.1			0.1		
Heritability:	0.005			0.05		
Prevalence:	0.1			0.1		
Penetrance:	0.097	0.113	0.102	0.115	0.036	0.029
	0.117	0.024	0.093	0.031	0.394	0.417
	0.035	0.391	0.092	0.118	0.017	0.128

2.2 Replication Dataset Simulation

Replication datasets were generated using the discovery penetrance tables to create datasets with the same underlying penetrances but differing minor allele frequencies. First, each simulated individual is assigned a value of 0, 1, or 2 for SNP 1 genotypes, with probabilities corresponding to genotype frequencies in Hardy-Weinberg equilibrium. This is repeated for SNP 2. Then, each simulated individual is assigned their case-control status based on their assigned values for SNP1 and SNP2 and the corresponding penetrance for that genotype from the discovery penetrance function. All discovery scenarios had corresponding replication scenarios with all two-SNP minor allele frequency combinations of {0.5, 0.4, 0.3, 0.2, 0.1}. We also include a finer resolution version replicating the discovery scenario with minor allele frequencies of 0.5 and 0.5, heritability of 0.005, and prevalence of 0.5 (Model 1 from Table 1) with replication SNP1 minor allele frequency fixed at 0.5, and SNP2 minor allele frequency from 0.5 to 0.01 by 0.01. 1,000 datasets of sizes 2,000 and 4,000 were generated for each replication scenario.

2.3   Interaction Analysis

For all replicates of all discovery scenarios, we calculated p-values for the likelihood ratio test comparing the logistic regression models with and without the interaction term for the two SNPs of interest, where the two models being compared are:

$$P(case) = \frac{1}{1 + e^{-(\beta_0 + \beta_1 SNP1 + \beta_2 SNP2)}} \tag{1}$$

And

$$P(case) = \frac{1}{1 + e^{-(\beta_0 + \beta_1 SNP1 + \beta_2 SNP2 + \beta_3 SNP1*SNP2)}} \tag{2}$$

Where P(case) is a binary indicator of disease status, SNP1 and SNP2 are categorical variables with values of 0, 1, or 2 corresponding to homozygous dominant, heterozygous, or homozygous recessive genotypes, and SNP1*SNP2 = {00, 01, 02, 10, 11, 12, 20, 21, 22} is the Cartesian product of SNP1 and SNP2.

2.4   Power Estimation

For the purpose of our power calculations we define power not in the traditional statistical sense, but rather as an empirical measure of the number of successes (where success is defined as a p-value of less than 0.05 for the likelihood ratio test comparing the two models above) out of the total number of simulated replication datasets for each scenario.

2.5   Replication Dataset Resampling

All replication datasets were resampled to match the genotype proportions of their corresponding discovery datasets by taking a random sample with replacement of the desired number of observations for each genotype, as follows. First, calculate desired genotype proportions from the crossproduct of discovery SNP1 proportions and discovery SNP2 proportions. Then, multiply desired genotype proportions by dataset size to obtain the desired number of observations per genotype (if the discovery and replication datasets are the same size, there are simply equal numbers of individuals per SNP-SNP genotype combination, otherwise, they are proportionate). Next, ensure that there is at least one case and one control per genotype, and if not, add single pseudo-observations to ensure non-zero case and control sampling probabilities. Finally, for each genotype, take a random sample with replacement to the desired number of observations. The resampled replication dataset is the composite of these samples by genotype. The following pseudocode outlines the resampling method.

```
INITIALIZE data frame to store resampled dataset

FOR each SNP-SNP genotype
        SUBSET all observations of the genotype from the
        replication dataset
        IF there are no case observations in this subset THEN
                APPEND a single case pseudo observation
        IF there are no control observations in this subset THEN
                APPEND a single control pseudo observation
        SAMPLE with replacement to size proportionate to
        discovery genotype
        APPEND sample to resampled dataset
```

2.6   Negative Simulation Methods

Negative simulation datasets were generated such that the SNP-SNP interaction is significant in the underlying discovery population but not the replication population. We generated 1000 discovery datasets of size 4000 with minor allele frequencies of 0.5 and 0.5 for the interacting SNPs with penetrances of 0.5 for 8 of the 9 SNP-SNP genotypes and a penetrance of 0.9 for the SNP-SNP genotype where both SNPs have two doses of the minor allele. We next generated 15,000 replication datasets, 1000 each of the 15 two-SNP minor allele frequency combinations of {0.5, 0.4, 0.3, 0.2, 0.1}. All replication datasets were generated with a penetrance of 0.5 for all SNP-SNP genotypes, that is, none of the interacting SNP-SNP genotype combinations are significant. All power calculations for the discovery and replication datasets are estimated as described above in the "Power Estimation" section, and resampling of the replication datasets that were false positives was performed as described in "Replication Dataset Resampling".

3 Results

3.1 Positive Simulation Results

We found that performing resampling of the replication datasets generally resulted in better or comparable power to detect the interaction between SNP1 and SNP2 compared to the power to detect the interaction using the unadjusted replication datasets. Figure 2 illustrates a scenario in which the minor allele frequencies of both SNP1 and SNP2 are 0.5 in the discovery dataset, and in the replication datasets the SNP1 MAF is held constant at 0.5 and only SNP2 is varied from 0.5 to 0.01 by 0.01 increments. There is increasing divergence of the unadjusted replication power to detect the interaction as the minor allele frequency of SNP2 decreases. Resampling results in better power to detect the interaction, with the worst performance observed for scenarios with the greatest difference between discovery and replication SNP2 minor allele frequency.

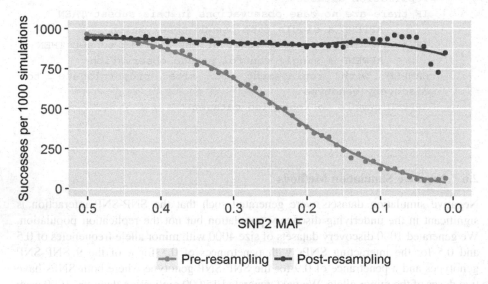

Fig. 2. Detection of a SNP-SNP interaction in unadjusted versus resampled replication datasets. Model 1: discovery SNP1 MAF = 0.5, SNP2 MAF = 0.5. Replication SNP1 MAF = 0.05, SNP2 MAF from 0.5 to 0.01 by 0.01. Heritability = 0.005 and prevalence = 0.5 for all discovery and replication datasets.

Likewise, Fig. 3 illustrates a comparable trend when both replication SNP1 and SNP2 minor allele frequencies are varied, with increasingly poor power to detect the interaction for unadjusted replication datasets with SNP1 and SNP2 minor allele frequencies that are more distant from those of the discovery dataset. Once again, we estimate replication powers to detect the interaction that are much improved after performing resampling. Table 2 tabulates the pre- and post-resampling powers for the interaction for the remainder of our test models.

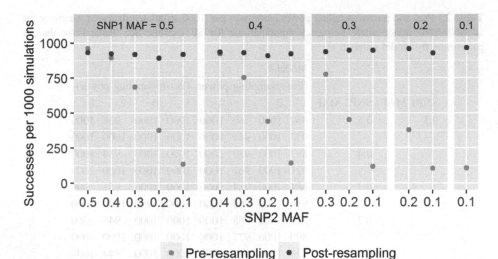

Fig. 3. Detection of a SNP-SNP interaction in unadjusted versus resampled replication datasets. Model 1: discovery SNP1 MAF = 0.5, SNP2 MAF = 0.5. Replication SNP1 MAF and SNP2 MAF combinations from 0.5 to 0.1 by 0.1. Heritability = 0.005 and prevalence = 0.5 for all discovery and replication datasets.

3.2 Negative Simulation Results

We developed a negative simulation in order to both establish that our simulated datasets have a realistic false positive rate, and to investigate the factors that contribute to why datasets may fail to recapitulate the true underlying population significance of an interaction following application of our resampling method. In the vast majority of cases, if a SNP-SNP interaction is significant in a discovery population and not significant in a replication population, we will indeed observe respectively significant and non-significant p-values for the likelihood ratio test comparing the logistic regression models with and without the interaction in samples taken from these populations. However, samples do not always provide good representations of the underlying population. For a p-value cutoff of 0.05, we expect a 5% false positive rate, and indeed, 747 of the 15,000 simulated replication datasets (4.98%) yielded false positives (e.g. the dataset yielded a significant p-value for the likelihood ratio test, even though the interaction was truly non-significant). We also expect the majority of these false positives to be unsuitable candidates for application of our resampling method because erroneous significance is driven by genotypes with so few observations that the sample penetrance is not representative of that of the underlying population, which is what we observe - 694 of the 747 false positives (92.9%) remain false positives after resampling.

Comparing the penetrances and number of observations by SNP-SNP genotype provides insight into the factors that render our resampling method inappropriate.

Table 2. Pre- and post-resampling power (successes per 1000 simulated datasets) summary for all SNP-SNP minor allele frequency combinations for all models. See Table 1 for dataset parameters by model number.

		Model #							
		(Pre-resampling power, Post-resampling power)							
SNP1 MAF	SNP2 MAF	1	2	3	4	5	6	7	8
0.5	0.5	962	1000	969	1000	1000	1000	938	1000
		932	1000	944	1000	1000	1000	1000	1000
	0.4	893	1000	989	1000	1000	1000	934	1000
		921	1000	967	1000	1000	1000	1000	1000
	0.3	684	1000	984	1000	1000	1000	951	1000
		916	1000	966	1000	1000	999	1000	1000
	0.2	375	1000	988	1000	1000	1000	946	1000
		890	1000	977	1000	1000	1000	1000	1000
	0.1	136	1000	857	999	1000	1000	944	1000
		917	1000	958	1000	1000	1000	1000	1000
0.4	0.4	923	1000	993	1000	1000	1000	941	1000
		935	1000	971	1000	1000	1000	1000	1000
	0.3	753	1000	994	1000	1000	1000	950	1000
		929	1000	965	1000	1000	999	1000	1000
	0.2	439	1000	976	1000	1000	1000	953	1000
		908	1000	984	1000	1000	1000	1000	1000
	0.1	141	998	850	999	1000	1000	952	1000
		922	1000	973	1000	1000	1000	999	1000
0.3	0.3	774	1000	991	1000	1000	1000	942	1000
		937	1000	975	1000	1000	1000	1000	1000
	0.2	451	1000	978	1000	1000	1000	967	1000
		947	1000	971	1000	1000	1000	1000	1000
	0.1	117	999	807	967	1000	1000	947	1000
		948	1000	991	1000	1000	1000	999	1000
0.2	0.2	377	1000	958	971	1000	1000	941	999
		959	1000	988	1000	1000	1000	1000	1000
	0.1	105	989	729	746	998	1000	950	1000
		928	1000	997	1000	1000	1000	999	1000
0.1	0.1	106	903	520	315	964	1000	934	999
		965	1000	998	1000	1000	1000	920	1000

In Fig. 4 one may observe that, while the mean penetrances for each genotype are comparable and centered around the expected value of 0.5 for those that do and do not successfully recapitulate the initial significance of the interaction following resampling, the variances differ significantly, particularly for the rarer genotypes. Table 3 provides a summary of the penetrance distributions and the number of observations by genotype. Recall that the minor allele frequencies of the two SNPs in the replication datasets are

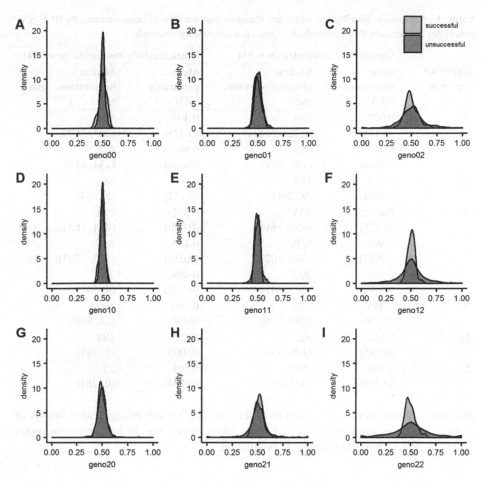

Fig. 4. Distributions of penetrances by SNP-SNP genotype. Note that 48 of the datasets that did not successfully resample had zero observations for the 22 genotype (Part I), so the density reflects only those datasets for which we can calculate penetrances.

both 0.1, so the SNP-SNP genotype where both SNPs have two doses of the minor allele is quite rare, and in some cases, replication datasets completely lacked observations for this genotype. Looking at this genotype in particular (Fig. 4, part I), the "unsuccessful" density is quite broad and flat, which stands to reason - since there are generally so few observations of this genotype, a population sample can be quite unrepresentative of the underlying population. Small perturbations in the observed number of cases per genotype can greatly skew the perceived significance of an interaction when the number of observations per genotype is quite low. In order to make reasonable inferences on the significance of an interaction, we recommend ensuring an adequate number of observations for the lowest frequency genotypes. This resampling method is only applicable if the underlying penetrances by genotype are reasonable approximations of the true population penetrances; our method simply

Table 3. Penetrance distribution summary statistics and number of observations, by SNP-SNP genotype, for datasets that successfully versus unsuccessfully resample

SNP-SNP genotype	Successfully resampled (n = 53)		Unsuccessfully resampled (n = 694)	
	Mean penetrance (SD)	Median observations (min, max)	Mean penetrance (SD)	Median observations (min, max)
00	0.502 (0.036)	489 (232, 1244)	0.499 (0.023)	904 (223, 2679)
01	0.498 (0.038)	489 (179, 817)	0.502 (0.034)	478 (154, 917)
02	0.496 (0.063)	162 (9, 269)	0.500 (0.122)	78 (5, 284)
10	0.497 (0.025)	733 (460, 1610)	0.502 (0.020)	996 (454, 1684)
11	0.495 (0.023)	920 (348, 1022)	0.498 (0.033)	618 (115, 1047)
12	0.503 (0.037)	290 (20, 534)	0.498 (0.123)	77 (4, 547)
20	0.495 (0.036)	330 (180, 815)	0.500 (0.046)	309 (21, 850)
21	0.512 (0.045)	42 (106, 537)	0.505 (0.095)	189 (2, 548)
22	0.496 (0.053)	108 (9, 263)	0.501 (0.194)	25 (0, 281)

provides a power boost for situations where we don't have enough observations of certain genotypes relative to others, but the observations we do have must be representative draws from the underlying population.

4   Discussion

This study critiques the validity of replication as the gold standard for substantiating GWAS hits, and proposes the exploration of alternative approaches that consider how differences in factors such as minor allele frequency can modulate the observed significance of SNP-SNP interactions. This may expand the usefulness of data that is already collected, which can in turn better direct our resources to future studies that will be most fruitful.

For the purposes of our positive simulations, we tested an exploratory range of heritabilities, prevalences, and sample sizes, but did not explore a wide range of differences in these parameters between populations. Small differences in minor allele frequency between discovery and replication datasets can greatly reduce the power to detect main effects, and the ability to detect this may differ by heritability, so it seems plausible that the ability to detect interactions may follow similar and possibly even more pronounced trends [9]. Future investigation into the potential joint effects of these parameters may yield further insight into the factors that affect our ability to detect and assess interactions in diverse populations, and subsequently direct study design to better control for these differences. Similarly, more negative simulations should be performed that systematically cover a range of scenarios to illuminate the conditions under which we can reliably regain power to detect interactions in replication studies; our negative simulations do not establish guidelines for across the entire space of observable population parameters.

Additional future analyses may also aim to demonstrate that shifts in interaction significance following resampling can alter which ones are selected for model inclusion, thereby modulating our ability to predict case-control status. Investigating shifts in variable inclusion following resampling is likely to yield interesting biological insight. Indeed, the future of extracting meaningful findings from GWAS is likely to be driven by investigating SNPs that are initially identified either based on expert knowledge or via bioinformatics methods incorporating prior assumptions, including hierarchical models that consider groups of SNPs and their functional relationships and interactions, in order to bypass the extreme prejudice of multiple testing burden [10–12]. Furthermore, the genome-wide significance level is unlikely to be an appropriate one-size-fits-all cutoff for multiple reasons, including evidence for the successful replication of borderline statistically significant genotype-phenotype associations [13]. It also stands to reason that diverse populations with different genetic architectures may require variable significance cutoffs that better reflect their patterns of linkage disequilibrium; hopefully, the increasing quantity of genotyped diverse populations will result in more pertinent high-quality reference genomes that will better enable identifying and replicating genetic associations between populations, enabling more accurate comparison of populations in the context of structural differences between diverse genomes [14, 15].

As new computational methods for GWAS present solutions to the various challenges associated with the accumulation of vast amounts of ever denser genetic data, and is mutually reinforced with increasing integration with clinical and epidemiological data, it is important to keep sight of the end goal of practical application of this knowledge to the betterment of both population health and personalized medicine. As such, the ultimate takeaway from this study should be that the purpose of resampling is to identify potential candidates for further biological validation, with the intention of using these findings to reduce structural inequalities in health and medicine.

Acknowledgements. This work was supported by National Institutes of Health grants LM009012, and AI116794.

References

1. Peng, R.D.: Reproducible research in computational science. Science **334**(6060), 1226–1227 (2011)
2. Boettiger, C.: An introduction to Docker for reproducible research. ACM SIGOPS Oper. Syst. Rev. **49**(1), 71–79 (2015)

3. Patil, P., Peng, R.D., Leek, J.: A statistical definition for reproducibility and replicability. bioRxiv, 066803, 1 January 2016
4. Krizhevsky, A., Sutskever, I., Hinton, G.E.: Imagenet classification with deep convolutional neural networks. In: Advances in Neural Information Processing Systems, pp. 1097–1105 (2012)
5. Russakovsky, O., Deng, J., Su, H., Krause, J., Satheesh, S., Ma, S., Huang, Z., Karpathy, A., Khosla, A., Bernstein, M., Berg, A.C.: Imagenet large scale visual recognition challenge. Int. J. Comput. Vis. **115**(3), 211–252 (2015)
6. Marchini, J., Donnelly, P., Cardon, L.R.: Genome-wide strategies for detecting multiple loci that influence complex diseases. Nat. Genet. **37**(4), 413–417 (2005)
7. Moore, J.H.: The ubiquitous nature of epistasis in determining susceptibility to common human diseases. Hum. Heredi. **56**(1–3), 73–82 (2003)
8. Urbanowicz, R.J., Kiralis, J., Sinnott-Armstrong, N.A., Heberling, T., Fisher, J.M., Moore, J.H.: GAMETES: a fast, direct algorithm for generating pure, strict, epistatic models with random architectures. BioData Min. **5**(1), 1 (2012)
9. Greene, C.S., Penrod, N.M., Williams, S.M., Moore, J.H.: Failure to replicate a genetic association may provide important clues about genetic architecture. PLoS One **4**(6), e5639 (2009)
10. Moore, J.H., Asselbergs, F.W., Williams, S.M.: Bioinformatics challenges for genome-wide association studies. Bioinformatics **26**(4), 445–455 (2010)
11. Yang, J., Ferreira, T., Morris, A.P., Medland, S.E., Madden, P.A., Heath, A.C., Martin, N.G., Montgomery, G.W., Weedon, M.N., Loos, R.J., Frayling, T.M.: Conditional and joint multiple-SNP analysis of GWAS summary statistics identifies additional variants influencing complex traits. Nat. Genet. **44**(4), 369–375 (2012)
12. Buzdugan, L., Kalisch, M., Navarro, A., Schunk, D., Fehr, E., Bühlmann, P.: Assessing statistical significance in multivariable genome wide association analysis. Bioinformatics **32**, 1990–2000 (2016)
13. Panagiotou, O.A., Ioannidis, J.P.: What should the genome-wide significance threshold be? Empirical replication of borderline genetic associations. Int. J. Epidemiol. **41**(1), 273–286 (2012)
14. Church, D.M., Schneider, V.A., Graves, T., Auger, K., Cunningham, F., Bouk, N., Chen, H.C., Agarwala, R., McLaren, W.M., Ritchie, G.R., Albracht, D.: Modernizing reference genome assemblics. PLoS Biol. **9**(7), e1001091 (2011)
15. Rosenberg, N.A., Huang, L., Jewett, E.M., Szpiech, Z.A., Jankovic, I., Boehnke, M.: Genome-wide association studies in diverse populations. Nat. Rev. Genet. **11**(5), 356–366 (2010)

Objective Assessment of Cognitive Impairment in Parkinson's Disease Using Evolutionary Algorithm

Chiara Picardi[1(✉)], Jeremy Cosgrove[2], Stephen L. Smith[1], Stuart Jamieson[2], and Jane E. Alty[2]

[1] Department of Electronics, University of York, Heslington, York, YO10 5DD, UK
{cp982,stephen.smith}@york.ac.uk
[2] Department of Neurology, Leeds Teaching Hospitals NHS Trust, Leeds, UK
{jeremycosgrove,stuart.jamieson1}@nhs.net,jane.alty@hyms.ac.uk

Abstract. Parkinson's disease (PD) is a common and disabling condition without cure. An early and accurate diagnosis is important for monitoring the disease and managing symptoms. Over time, the majority of patients with PD develop cognitive impairment, which is diagnosed using global tests of cognitive function or more detailed neuropsychological assessment. This paper presents an approach to detect PD and to discriminate different degrees of PD cognitive impairment in an objective way, considering a simple and non-invasive "reach and grasp" task performed with the patient wearing sensor-enabled data gloves recording movements in real-time. The PD patients comprised three subgroups: 22 PD patients with normal cognition (PD-NC), 23 PD patients with mild cognitive impairment (PD-MCI) and 10 PD patients with dementia (PDD). In addition, 30 age-matched healthy subjects (Controls) were also measured. From the experimental data, 25 kinematic features were extracted with the aim of generating a classifier that is able to discriminate not only between Controls and PD patients, but also between the PD cognitive subgroups. The technique used to find the best classifier was an Evolutionary Algorithm - Cartesian Genetic Programming (CGP), and this is compared with Support Vector Machine (SVM) and Artificial Neural Network (ANN). In all cases, the CGP classifiers were comparable with SVM and ANN, and in some cases performed better. The results are promising and show both the potential of the computed features and of CGP in aiding PD diagnosis.

Keywords: Classification · Genetic programming · Parkinson's disease · Machine learning · Artificial intelligence

1 Introduction

Parkinson's disease (PD) is a common disease affecting approximately one person in every 500, equating to around 127,000 people in UK [1]. The disease is caused by degeneration of dopamine producing neurons and the formation of abnormal protein aggregates called "Lewy bodies" in the brain [2]. The consequent reduction of dopamine is responsible for the abnormalities in movement. The core features of the movement

© Springer International Publishing AG 2017
G. Squillero and K. Sim (Eds.): EvoApplications 2017, Part I, LNCS 10199, pp. 109–124, 2017.
DOI: 10.1007/978-3-319-55849-3_8

disorder are a slowing of movement (bradykinesia), rigidity, tremor and postural instability.

There is currently no cure for PD and treatment is concerned with reducing the symptoms of the disease. An early and correct diagnosis is important to manage symptoms in an effective way. Conventional diagnosis is based on subjective clinical assessment, which has poor sensitivity; up to 25% of patients confidently diagnosed as having PD are ultimately found to have other conditions [3]. Many PD patients will develop mild cognitive impairment – abnormalities on tests of cognitive function without impairment of the ability to manage activities of daily living - which is a risk factor for developing Parkinson's disease dementia (PDD) [4]. Alternate methods to diagnose Parkinson's disease and also to identify early those with PD who develop cognitive impairment may be more cost efficient and reliable.

This study considers three different subgroups of Parkinson's disease patients: PD patients with normal cognition (PD-NC), PD patients with mild cognitive impairment (PD-MCI) and those with dementia (PDD). PD-MCI was formally defined in 2012 by the International Parkinson and Movement Disorder Society (MDS) [5] and it has since been shown that approximately one-third of people have PD-MCI at the time they are diagnosed with PD [6, 7].

PD-MCI is a risk factor for developing PDD [8, 9] but there is growing evidence to suggest that the progression of PD-MCI to PDD is dependent on which cognitive domains are affected. That is in turn dependent on which neurotransmitter systems in the brain are affected [10]. Cognition can be difficult to define, as it covers several different mental skills and activities [11]. It generally refers to the brain processes through which we discover and understand the world around us, and how we apply that knowledge from day to day. These include: making sense of perceptions; storing and retrieving memories; learning things; forming concepts; solving problems; planning activities; language; achieving insights; and abstract thinking [11].

Dementia is more disabling than MCI and is often a decline in multiple cognitive domains, including – but not limited to – memory. By definition, dementia of all types, including PDD, leads to an inability to independently manage activities of daily living [11].

In this paper the Evolutionary Algorithms (EAs) are used to distinguish PD patients from healthy subjects, but also to distinguish between PD cognitive subgroups. The inputs considered are kinematic features extracted from a 'reach and grasp' experiment. In a previous study [12] different reaching and grasping kinematic features were extracted to differentiate between apraxia patients and controls and also between different subgroups of apraxia patients. In our study some of these features are computed to verify if these can be useful also for the classification of the PD cognitive subgroups.

EAs are a widely used method for inducing classifiers [13–16]. Factors which make them effective for classification problems include their breadth of search, relatively low sensitivity to initial conditions, and flexibility in terms of representation and evaluation of solutions [17]. They are particularly useful for problems where there is limited prior understanding of what a solution should look like, where the method's breadth of search and ability to use relatively unconstrained solution representations permits a wide exploration of candidate solutions.

In this study a representation of Cartesian Genetic Programming (CGP) is used as the EA. CGP was first proposed by Miller and Thomson [18] and derived from Genetic programming (GP) [19]. In GP the population is composed of programs represented as trees with inputs (roots), outputs (terminal nodes) and a set of functions (internal nodes). Unlike formal methods, GP requires no knowledge about the problem that it is attempting to solve except a measure of how good a solution is. Once a GP run has been initiated it requires no human interaction. Inductive logic programming performs a local or greedy search in the solution space, usually performing a deterministic search. Instead GP performs a wider, more global search in the solution space, usually performing a stochastic search. However, GP has a bloat problem: the programs that it generates tend to become larger and larger at a rate which rises in line with a quadratic function, filling up the available space and making it almost impossible to find small and efficient solutions. Like other evolutionary computation approaches, GP has a scalability problem: increasing problem size leads to an unmanageably high increase in space and time resource requirements. CGP solves the bloat problem of GP primarily by having a fixed number of nodes defined at the design stage. Turner and Miller [20] also propose other theories of why CGP doesn't suffer of the bloat problem due to Neutral Genetic Drift and Length Bias.

CGP differs from GP simply by the representation of the programs (chromosomes) that are acyclic directed graphs instead of trees. A conventional CGP chromosome is a graph whose shape depends on the setting of the number of columns and rows. The connection between two nodes in the same columns is forbidden. In cases where there is not a specific knowledge of the problem, like in the case of this study, it is better to set the number of rows equal to one and to permit any connection between nodes.

CGP has also been used in previous studies to distinguish between PD patients and healthy subjects. In the first study [21], a figure-copying task was used, recording pen movements during the experiment. CGP was applied to find, in the acceleration of the pen, features identifying bradykinesia, the cardinal motor feature of PD. The limitations of that study are the small dataset and the choice of an experimental threshold based on the dataset. In the second study [22] 49 PD patients and 41 healthy controls performed finger tapping experiment with each hand separately while the position of the fingers was recorded in real-time. CGP was used to classify PD patients and healthy controls using as input the acceleration of the fingers to find signs of bradykinesia. The EA was able to classify both classes with an accuracy of 95%. The third study [23] also considered finger-tapping. The classifier, taking the distance between the fingers, was able to achieve an area under roc curve (AUC) [24] greater than 0.9.

In this paper EAs are used to classify between PD patients and healthy subjects, as well as between the PD subgroups. Reach and grasp is not a repetitive task, unlike finger-tapping [21–23], but rather a single ballistic movement. Some of the features computed are the same as those reported in Caselli's study [12]. Also others studies have found statistically significant differences in kinematic parameters between PD patients with normal cognition and healthy subjects when reaching and grasping. For example, in one study eight PD subjects tested whilst on medication were compared with eight age-matched healthy subjects as they reached and grasped either a small (0.7 cm) or large (8 cm) diameter dowel at three distances (15 cm, 27.5 cm and 40 cm) [25]. A similar pattern of change was observed in the PD patients as had already been demonstrated in healthy subjects [26, 27]. Despite this similarity, when the distance or the shape of the object is changed, PD patients are significantly slower than the healthy subjects.

The features computed in the Caselli's study [12] alone are not sufficiently powerful to distinguish between all the classes considered in this paper. Consequently, additional features were computed. In a previous study, Alberts et al. [28] found some differences in angular velocities and jerks (third derivative of position) between PD patients with normal cognition and healthy subjects during a "reach and grasp" experiment. Extending this study it was decided to compute some additional features relative to the angular velocity, the angular acceleration and to the jerk action.

This study has then two aims:

(1) To verify the potential of the features computed in classifying between PD patients and healthy subjects and also between PD cognitive subgroups.
(2) To establish the potential of EAs in the diagnosis of PD using a reach and grasp task.

2 Methodology

The subjects were divided into four classes: 22 PD-NC, 23 PD-MCI, 10 PDD and 30 age-matched healthy subjects (Controls). Patients were recruited from neurology clinics at Leeds Teaching Hospitals NHS Trust, UK. The average age of the PD patients measured was 69 years and the average disease duration was 6 years, while the 30 healthy subjects (controls) had an average age of 64 years. All subjects provided informed consent and the study received National Research Ethics Service and local Research and Development approval.

The experiment consisted of reaching for and grasping an 8 cm diameter cylinder (similar to a typical drinking beaker) placed 30 cm in front of the subject as shown in Fig. 1. The measurements were taken using commercially available computer data gloves manufactured by 5DT Inc. [29] in conjunction with a 6 DOF (degrees of freedom) electromagnetic tracking system manufactured by Polhemus Inc. [30]. The Polhemus sensor was placed on the wrist to provide position and orientation information at 60 Hz. The 5DT glove has one sensor on each finger measuring flexion. Each subject performed the experiment five times with the dominant hand and non-dominant hands under four different conditions as follows:

1. **Self guided reach 1 task:** a tone is the cue for the subject to start the movement in their own time at a natural speed
2. **Visually cued reach task:** movement starts when the cylinder lights up, again at a natural speed
3. **Self guided reach 2 task:** using a tone as in the first task, but with the instruction "as fast as you can"
4. **Memory guided reach task:** the subjects close their eyes, and then following an audio cue 2–5 s later, keeping their eyes closed, reach for the cylinder at a natural speed

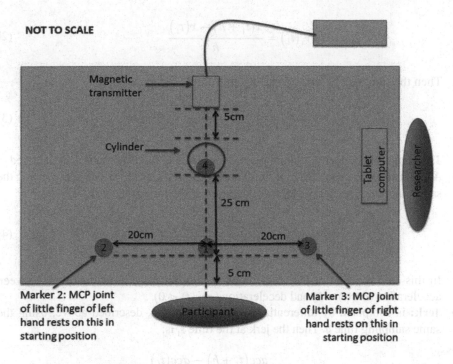

Fig. 1. A diagram of the experimental setup

In this study only the data from the memory guided condition is used as this has been found to be the best at classifying the groups.

2.1 Data Processing

Only the positional (x, y, z) and orientation (roll, pitch, yaw) data measured by the Polhemus sensor are used in this study. The data collected by the glove sensors, providing an estimation of the flexion of each finger to allow grasp features such as peak aperture or time to peak aperture to be calculated, are currently under investigation. Using the positional coordinates (x, y, z) of the wrist, the following measures are computed every 1/60 s:

- **Distance:** Euclidean distance between sensor on the wrist and Patriot source

$$dist(t) = \sqrt{x(t)^2 + y(t)^2 + z(t)^2} \tag{1}$$

- **Velocity:** each component of the velocity (v_x, v_y, v_z) is computed, differentiating each coordinate component (x, y, z) using as sampling time $h = 1/60$ s. For example the velocity along the x direction at time t_1 is:

$$v_x(t_1) = \frac{x(t_1 + h) - x(t_1)}{h} \tag{2}$$

Then the summary velocity is calculated from its components:

$$vel(t) = \sqrt{v_x(t)^2 + v_y(t)^2 + v_z(t)^2} \tag{3}$$

The sign of the velocity is not important and so only the magnitude is considered.

- **Acceleration:** is computed by differentiating the velocity, described above, using the same sampling time h. Then the acceleration at the time t_1 is:

$$acc(t_1) = \frac{vel(t_1 + h) - vel(t_1)}{h} \tag{4}$$

In this case the sign of the acceleration is significant as it distinguishes between acceleration ($acc(t) > 0$) and deceleration ($acc(t) < 0$).

- **Jerk:** is computed by differentiating the acceleration, described above, using the same sampling time h. Then the jerk at the time t_1 is:

$$jerk(t_1) = \frac{acc(t_1 + h) - acc(t_1)}{h} \tag{5}$$

Using the angular coordinates (roll, pitch, yaw) the following measures are computed every 1/60 s:

- **Angular velocity:** Given the angular coordinates $roll\ \varphi, pitch\ \theta\ and\ yaw\ \psi$ it is possible to construct the rotation matrix describing the pose of the wrist with the three rotations around ZYX. The rotation matrix was computed using the Aerospace MATLAB Toolbox [31]. From the rotation matrix $R(t)$ it is possible to find the skew-symmetric matrix $S(t)$ [32] that varies in function of the time t with the following formula:

$$S(t) = \dot{R}(t)R^T(t) \tag{6}$$

The matrix $S(t)$ is computed each 1/60 s and its symmetric elements, with respect to the main diagonal, represent the components of the angular velocity vector $\omega = [\omega_x, \omega_y, \omega_z]^T$ in the form [32]:

$$S = \begin{bmatrix} 0 & -\omega_z & \omega_y \\ \omega_z & 0 & -\omega_x \\ -\omega_y & \omega_x & 0 \end{bmatrix} \tag{7}$$

The angular velocity magnitude ω is then computed from its components:

$$\omega(t) = \sqrt{\omega_x(t)^2 + \omega_y(t)^2 + \omega_z(t)^2} \qquad (8)$$

- **Angular acceleration:** is computed by differentiating the angular velocity, described above, using the same sampling time $h = 1/60$ s. Then the angular acceleration at the time t_1 is:

$$ang\_acc(t_1) = \frac{\omega(t_1 + h) - \omega(t_1)}{h} \qquad (9)$$

All velocities and accelerations are smoothed using a Savitzky-Golay filter [33]. This filter fits successive sub-sets (windows) of adjacent data points with a low-degree polynomial using the linear least square method [33]. A window size of 35 and degree of polynomial 5 was chosen throughout experimentation.

2.2 Features Extracted

Different features are computed using the available data described in the previous subsection. The reach and grasp experiment is composed of two phases: the reach phase and the grasp phase. As explained in the previous section the grasp data is not considered in this work. Figure 2 shows the distance profile of one trial made by a control (healthy subject): on x-axis the time in seconds is reported, while on y-axis the distance in millimetres is reported. The distance decreases when the subject starts to move until a minimum is achieved when the subject reaches the object (end of the reach phase). The distance then increases when the subject lifts the cylinder and decreases at the end when the subject leaves the cylinder on the table (end of the lift phase). In the Fig. 2 the following points are highlighted:

(1) **Stimulus:** The dotted line marks the time at which the cue occurs. The cue is a sound or a light (for the visually cued task) used as a signal for the subject to start the movement.
(2) **Start of the movement:** Instant at which the subject starts to move. This point is identified as the point in which the distance between the sensor and the source starts to decrease.
(3) **End of the movement:** Instant at which the subject reaches the object. This point is identified as the first minimum of the distance between the sensor and the source.

Figure 3 considers the same movement examined in Fig. 2 with velocity (on x-axis time measured in seconds, on y-axis velocity measured in millimetres/second) and acceleration (on x-axis time measured in seconds, on y-axis acceleration measured in millimetres/second^2) derived from it. In the graph the following points are highlighted:

(1) **Peak velocity:** The maximum of the velocity identified in the interval of time between the start of the movement and the end of the movement.

(2) **Peak acceleration:** The maximum of the acceleration identified in the interval of time between the start of the movement and the end of the movement.
(3) **Peak deceleration:** The minimum of the acceleration identified in the interval of time between the start of the movement and the end of the movement.

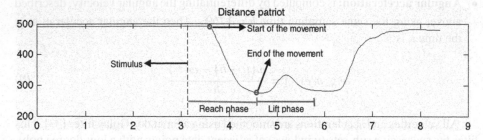

Fig. 2. Distance profile of a trial made by a control

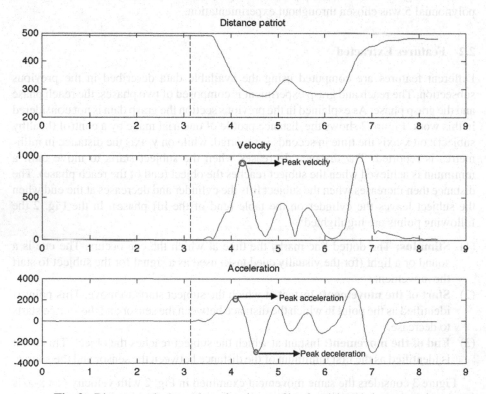

Fig. 3. Distance, velocity and acceleration profile of a trial made by a control

Using the points detailed in Figs. 2 and 3, the following features are computed:

(1) **Movement time (MT):** The time taken between the start of the movement and the end of the movement.

(2) **Reaction time as a percentage of total movement time (RT%):** The time taken between the cue and the start of the movement expressed as a percentage of the total movement time.

(3) **Peak velocity (PV):** The value of the velocity at its peak.

(4) **Time to peak velocity (TPV):** The amount of time taken from the start of the movement to the point where the velocity peak occurs.

(5) **Time to peak velocity as a percentage of total movement time (TPV%):** The amount of time taken from the start of the movement to the point where the velocity peak occurs, expressed as a percentage of the total movement time.

(6) **Peak angular velocity (PAV):** The maximum of the angular velocity found in the interval of time between start of the movement and end of the movement.

(7) **Time to peak angular velocity as a percentage of total movement time (TPAV %):** The amount of time taken from the start of the movement to the point where the angular velocity peak occurs, expressed as a percentage of the total movement time.

(8) **Time to peak angular velocity (TPAV):** The amount of time taken from the start of the movement to the point where the angular velocity peak occurs.

(9) **Peak acceleration (PA):** The value of the acceleration peak.

(10) **Time to peak acceleration as a percentage of total movement time (TPA%):** The amount of time taken from the start of the movement to the point where the acceleration peak occurs, expressed as a percentage of the total movement time.

(11) **Time to peak acceleration (TPA):** The amount of time taken from the start of the movement to the point where the acceleration peak occurs.

(12) **Peak angular acceleration (PAA):** The maximum of the angular acceleration found in the interval of time between start of the movement and end of the movement.

(13) **Time to peak angular acceleration as a percentage of total movement time (TPAA%):** The amount of time taken from the start of the movement to the point where the angular acceleration peak occurs, expressed as a percentage of the total movement time.

(14) **Time to peak angular acceleration (TPAA):** The amount of time taken from the start of the movement to the point where the angular acceleration peak occurs.

(15) **Peak deceleration (PD):** The value of the deceleration peak.

(16) **Time to peak deceleration as a percentage of total movement time (TPD%):** The amount of time taken from the start of the movement and the point where the deceleration peak occurs, expressed as percentage of the total movement time.

(17) **Time to peak deceleration (TPD):** The amount of time taken from the start of the movement and the point where the deceleration peak occurs.

(18) **Mean velocity (MV):** The mean velocity from the start of the movement and the end of the movement.

(19) **Mean angular velocity (MAV):** The mean angular velocity from the start of the movement and the end of the movement.

(20) **Mean acceleration (MA):** The mean acceleration from the start of the movement and the end of the movement.

(21) **Mean angular acceleration (MAA):** The mean angular acceleration from the start of the movement and the end of the movement.

(22) **Time lift (TL):** The amount of time from the beginning to the end of the lift phase (see Fig. 3).

(23) **Peak lift (PL):** The maximum value of the distance during the lift phase.

(24) **Total movement (TM):** The sum of the movement time and the absolute reaction time (not expressed in percentage)

(25) **Jerk score (JS):** It is a measure to quantify smoothness of the wrist path [28, 34]. Because jerk increases dramatically with movement duration [35], it is useful to normalize this quantity in time and amplitude. The following formula was used to calculate jerk score:

$$JS = \frac{1}{2} \times \int_{start\_mov}^{end\_mov} j^2(t)dt \times d^5/l^2 \qquad (10)$$

where j is the jerk computed as described before (derivative of the acceleration), d is the movement duration (time movement) and l is the movement amplitude (distance peak between start movement and end movement). We choose to use the definite integral from the start of the movement to the end of the movement to define a measure to quantify the smoothness of the wrist path during the movement.

Some of the features described above related to distance, velocity and acceleration, were also computed by Caselli et al. [12] to successfully classify apraxia patients from healthy subjects. The features related to the angular velocity and the angular acceleration are computed to appreciate also the differences of these quantities among the classes. Alberts et al. [28] in their study highlighted some differences in the angular velocity and jerk normalized profiles between PD patients and healthy subjects.

Before that the above features can be used as inputs to CGP, all are normalised by being expressed as percentage. Those features that are not yet expressed as percentage (e.g. peak velocity) are transformed considering the maximum value of the feature contained in the data. For example, the percentage of the peak velocity is computed in the following way:

$$Peak\, vel\, perc = \frac{peak\, vel}{max peak\, vel} * 100 \qquad (11)$$

Once all features are expressed as percentage they are ready to be used as inputs of the CGP in order to generate a classifier.

2.3   Classification

In the classification only the memory guided reach case is considered because, as explained before, this appears to be the condition where the differences among the classes are greatest. The data are merged together in one dataset, comprising both hands and all repetitions. For each subject there are ten repetitions (five for each hand) that are considered in the dataset as ten different samples. Unfortunately, some data had to be discarded due to measurement errors or other protocol violations.

Given the following five classes:

- All Parkinson's disease patients (PD), 453 recordings
- Parkinson's disease patients with normal cognition (PD-NC), 172 recordings
- Parkinson's disease patients with mild cognitive impairment (PD-MCI), 189 recordings
- Parkinson's disease patients with dementia (PDD), 92 recordings
- Healthy subjects (Con), 376 recordings

These six pairwise classifications cases are considered:

- PD versus Con
- PD-NC versus Con
- PD-MCI versus Con
- PDD versus Con
- PD-NC versus PD-MCI
- PD-NC versus PDD
- PD-MCI versus PDD

Each dataset, comprising the two classes considered in each classification case, was divided into five folds, and k-fold cross validation (k = 5) was performed to generalize the results.

The geometry of the programs in the population (chromosomes) has seventy-five internal nodes with a function set of four mathematical functions (+, −, *, /), 25 inputs (the features described above) and one output. Each output is considered a positive response if the value is greater than a certain threshold, negative otherwise; 18 thresholds are considered here, in multiples of 5 (5, 10, 15, ..., 90). The positive class is the first in the classification cases; for example, for the case "PD-NC versus PD-MCI", the positive class is PD-NC. Considering all thresholds using the AUC [24] of the training set and of the test set is computed for each fold of the k-fold cross validation. The mean of the training sets AUC across all levels is then computed and used as a fitness function to evaluate each of the five chromosomes in the population. The mean of the test sets AUC across all levels is instead used to evaluate the chromosome on the test set. At each generation the fittest chromosome is selected and the next generation formed with its mutated versions (mutation rate = 0.07). Evolution is stopped when 50000 iterations are reached or when the over fitting occurs. To obtain statistical significance 10 runs of the experiment were completed.

3   Results

In order to validate the results obtained, two others machine learning techniques: Artificial Neural Networks (ANN) [36] and Support Vector Machine (SVM) [37], in addition to the CGP, were used on the same datasets. The neural network used was a feed-forward back propagation network with 20 hidden layers and a tan-Sigmoid transfer function. As in CGP, also in the other methods, the datasets were divided into five folds to perform k-fold cross validation (k = 5), and 10 runs of the experiment were completed. The results for all three methods are reported in Table 1.

Table 1. Evolved classifiers AUCs of the test and the training sets (as means across the 10 runs) for the three approaches

Classes	SVM		ANN		CGP	
	Train	Test	Train	Test	Train	Test
PD versus Con	0.84	0.82	0.83	0.81	0.81	0.81
PDNC versus Con	0.84	0.76	0.84	0.79	0.78	0.78
PDMCI versus Con	0.85	0.82	0.86	0.82	0.81	0.81
PDD versus Con	0.97	0.96	0.98	0.95	0.95	0.95
PDNC versus PDMCI	0.83	0.78	0.78	0.72	0.74	0.74
PDNC versus PDD	0.89	0.83	0.86	0.79	0.85	0.83
PDMCI versus PDD	0.89	0.80	0.84	0.76	0.82	0.83

For each pair-wise classification the mean AUC of the evolved classifiers over ten runs for the training and test sets is presented. The results show that the CGP, optimising the 25 features reported in Sect. 2, is promising compared to the other methods. In all cases for CGP, the AUC of the training set is very similar to that for the test set. This demonstrates that 5-folds cross validation generalises the results well. This consideration is not true for the other approaches where in some cases (like "PD-NC versus Con") the values of the training set are much bigger than the values of the test set. This suggests that CGP has less overfitting than the other methods, evolving classifiers that able to generalise better. As the test set results are most useful in evaluating the potential of the classifier to generalise to unseen data, from this point forward discussion regarding the results will refer solely to the test set.

In all cases the results of the CGP, SVM and ANN are comparable. In "PD-NC versus PD-MCI", CGP performs slightly worse than SVM, but better than ANN. However, for "PD-MCI versus PDD", CGP evolves classifiers with better performances of SVM and ANN. Examining the results, we can see that the classification between PD (all PD patients together) and Con is around 0.81–0.82. If, instead, we consider the classification between the subgroups and Con, the situation changes. For "PD-NC versus Con" the AUC is 0.76–0.79, for "PD-MCI versus Con" it is 0.81–0.82 and for "PDD versus Con" it is 0.95–0.96. As expected, the classification between PD-NC and Controls is less certain then the other subgroups cases.

The best classification is for "PDD versus Controls" in which the generated classifiers have a very high AUC. Again, this result is expected, based on conventional clinical assessment, it is easier to distinguish between PDD and Controls than between PD-NC and Controls, or PD-MCI and Controls because those with PDD have generally had PD for longer and have more severe motor symptoms. Therefore, it can be proposed that the PD-NC class lowers the overall classification accuracy between PD and Controls, whilst the PDD class raises the classification accuracy.

Comparison of classification results for PD patient subgroups are interesting. The most challenging classification is between PD-NC and PD-MCI. This is expected because we know that patients from the two classes can perform the movement in a similar way and can be difficult to distinguish clinically. In this case CGP generated an AUC of 0.74 performing better than ANN but worse than SVM that reaches 0.78. The differentiation between PD-NC and PDD, and between PD-MCI and PDD is more pronounced. This result was also expected because we know that PDD patients have greater difficulties with respect to the other subgroups in performing the movement. As can be seen in Table 1, we note that CGP can evolve classifiers with an AUC equal to 0.83 for both cases "PD-NC versus PD-MCI" and "PD-MCI versus PDD". In particular, "PD-MCI versus PDD" CGP performs better than the other methods.

The positive aspect of CGP in respect to other the methods is that it doesn't necessary use all the inputs in the evolved classifier. Consequently, it is possible determine which are the most useful features and those features that can be ignored. In Table 2 the best classifiers evolved in the ten runs for each case are considered and the features used by them are reported. Future work will use the results of this table to determine which are the best sets of features in addressing each classification problem.

Table 2. Features used by the best classifier found across the ten runs for each case.

Classes	Features used
PD versus Con	PV, TPV%, PAV, TPAA, MV, MA, TL, PL, JS
PDNC versus Con	MT, PV, TPV%, TPAA%, PD, TPD, TL, PL, TM, JS
PDMCI versus Con	MT, PAA, TPD, MV, MAV, MA, MAA, TL, JS
PDD versus Con	RT%, TPV, TPV%, TPAV, TPD, MV, MAV, MAA, PL
PDNC versus PDMCI	MT, RT%, TPAV, TPA%, PAA, TPD%, MV, MAV, MA, MAA, TL, PL, JS
PDNC versus PDD	MT, RT%, TPV, PAV, PA, TPA, PAA, PD, MAV, MA, TL, PL, TM, JS
PDMCI versus PDD	RT%, PV, TPV, PA, TPAA%, PD, TPD%, TPD, MAV, MAA

4 Conclusions and Discussion

The first aim of this study was to verify the potential of the chosen features in addressing the classification between PD patients and Controls, and also among the PD cognitive subgroups. The results presented in Sect. 3 support the view that this has been achieved, but these results could be improved when considering additional features or using the raw data values as inputs to CGP.

The grasp data from the data gloves are another point of discussion. In this study they are not used for the reasons discussed in Sect. 2, but could be useful to find new features to improve the classification; currently, a way to use this data is under consideration. Moreover, there are other factors that could influence the results. Firstly, the patients examined were on medication to limit motor symptoms of PD, which may affect their performance. A second limitation of this study that could affect the results is the relatively small number of the patients measured and of the nature the data. Each subject performs the experiment five times with each hand. So for each subject there are ten repetitions (five for each hand) that are considered in the dataset as ten different samples. If we only considered the mean of the repetitions, the data available would be insufficient to evolve a classifier. The strategy to consider repetitions as different samples could influence the results because the same subject can perform the experiment in a similar way, reducing the variability. However, patients showed a high variability in performing the experiment, so including repetitions was justified. In future, a new memory guided reach experiment including more subjects would be useful the to overcome this limitation.

The second aim of this study was to establish the potential of EAs (CGP) in the diagnosis of PD using the "reach and grasp" task. Table 1 shows that CGP is able to evolve classifiers that is comparable with the other computer methods investigated, and in certain cases, better (e.g. PD-MCI versus PDD). Moreover, CGP has the advantage of using only the inputs useful for the classification, as showed in Table 2, giving us an indication of what features are most important in each case. The results using CGP could be improved when considering other features or using the raw data values as inputs. In particular, the use of the raw data has potential as the whole signal is considered instead of a summary represented by the features.

In conclusion, the results of this study are promising and can be used as starting point in the classification of PD patients and PD-cognitive subgroups using a reach and grasp task.

References

1. Website of the Parkinsons's UK (2016). http://www.parkinsons.org.uk
2. Gibb, W.R., Lees, A.J.: The relevance of the Lewy body to the pathogenesis of idiopathic Parkinson's disease. J. Neurol. Neurosurg. Psychiatry **51**, 745–752 (1988)
3. Playfer, J.R.: Parkinson's disease. Postgrad. Med. J. **73**, 257–264 (1997)
4. Pedersen, K.F., Larsen, J.P., Tysnes, O.B., et al.: Prognosis of mild cognitive impairment in early Parkinson disease: the Norwegian ParkWest study. JAMA Neurol. **70**, 580–586 (2013)
5. Litvan, I., Goldman, J.G., Tröster, A.I., Schmand, B.A., Weintraub, D., Petersen, R.C., Mollenhauer, B., Adler, C.H., Marder, K., Williams-Gray, C.H., Aarsland, D.: Diagnostic criteria for mild cognitive impairment in Parkinson's disease: movement disorder society task force guidelines. Mov. Disord. **27**(3), 349–356 (2012)
6. Broeders, M., De Bie, R.M.A., Velseboer, D.C., Speelman, J.D., Muslimovic, D., Schmand, B.: Evolution of mild cognitive impairment in Parkinson disease. Neurology **81**(4), 346–352 (2013)
7. Yarnall, A.J., Breen, D.P., Duncan, G.W., Khoo, T.K., Coleman, S.Y., Firbank, M.J., Nombela, C., Winder-Rhodes, S., Evans, J.R., Rowe, J.B., Mollenhauer, B.: Characterizing mild cognitive impairment in incident Parkinson disease: the ICICLE-PD study. Neurology **82**(4), 308–316 (2014)
8. Janvin, C.C., Larsen, J.P., Aarsland, D., Hugdahl, K.: Subtypes of mild cognitive impairment in Parkinson's disease: progression to dementia. Mov. Disord. **21**(9), 1343–1349 (2006)

9. Pedersen, K.F., Larsen, J.P., Tysnes, O.B., Alves, G.: Prognosis of mild cognitive impairment in early Parkinson disease: the Norwegian ParkWest study. JAMA Neurol. **70**(5), 580–586 (2013)

10. Cosgrove, J., Alty, J.E., Jamieson, S.: Cognitive impairment in Parkinson's disease. Postgrad. Med. J. **91**, 212–220 (1074)

11. Website of the Cognitive Impairment Parkinson's Disease Foundation (PDF). http://www.pdf.org/en/cognitive_impairment_pd

12. Caselli, R.J., Stelmach, G.E., Caviness, J.N., Timmann, D., Royer, T., Boeve, B.F., Parisi, J.E.: A kinematic study of progressive apraxia with and without dementia. Mov. Disord. **14**, 276–287 (1999)

13. Zhang, M., Wong, P.: Genetic programming for medical classification: a program simplification approach. Genet. Program Evolvable Mach. **9**(3), 229–255 (2008)

14. Paul, T., Iba, H.: Prediction of cancer class with majority voting genetic programming classifier using gene expression data. IEEE/ACM Trans. Comput. Biol. Bioinform. **6**(2), 353–367 (2009)

15. Winkler, S., Affenzeller, M., Wagner, S.: Using enhanced genetic programming techniques for evolving classifiers in the context of medical diagnosis. Genet. Program. Evolvable Mach. **10**(2), 111–140. http://dx.doi.org/10.1007/s10710-008-9076-8

16. Bhowan, U., Johnston, M., Zhang, M., Yao, X.: Evolving diverse ensembles using genetic programming for classification with unbalanced data. IEEE Trans. Evol. Comput. **17**(3), 368–386 (2013)

17. Freitas, A.A.: A review of evolutionary algorithms for data mining. In: Maimon, O., Rokach, L. (eds.) Soft Computing for Knowledge Discovery and Data Mining, pp. 79–111. Springer, Boston (2008)

18. Miller, J.F., Thomson, P.: Cartesian genetic programming. In: Poli, R., Banzhaf, W., Langdon, W.B., Miller, J., Nordin, P., Fogarty, T.C. (eds.) EuroGP 2000. LNCS, vol. 1802, pp. 121–132. Springer, Heidelberg (2000). doi:10.1007/978-3-540-46239-2_9

19. Banzhaf, W., et al.: Genetic Programming—An Introduction. Morgan Kaufmann, San Francisco (1998)

20. Turner, A.J., Miller, J.F.: Cartesian genetic programming: why no bloat? In: Nicolau, M., Krawiec, K., Heywood, M.I., Castelli, M., García-Sánchez, P., Merelo, J.J., Rivas Santos, V.M., Sim, K. (eds.) EuroGP 2014. LNCS, vol. 8599, pp. 222–233. Springer, Heidelberg (2014). doi:10.1007/978-3-662-44303-3_19

21. Smith, S.L., Gaughan, P., Halliday, D.M., Ju, Q., Aly, N.M., Playfer, J.R.: Diagnosis of Parkinson's disease using evolutionary algorithms. Genet. Program. Evolvable Mach. **8**, 433–447 (2007). doi:10.1007/s10710-007-9043-9

22. Lones, M.A., Smith, S.L., Alty, J.E., Lacy, S.E., Possin, K.L., Jamieson, D.R.S., Tyrrell, A.M.: Evolving classifiers to recognize the movement characteristics of Parkinson's disease patients. IEEE Trans. Evol. Comput. **18**, 559–576 (2014)

23. Lacy, S., Lones, M.A., Smith, S.L., Alty, J.E., Jamieson, S., Possin, K., Schuff, N.: Characterisation of movement disorder in Parkinson's disease using evolutionary algorithms. In: Blum, C., Alba, E. (eds.) Proceedings of the 2013 Genetic and Evolutionary Computation Conference (GECCO), pp. 1479–1486. ACM Digital Library, New York (2013)

24. Hanley, J.A., McNeil, B.J.: The meaning and use of the area under a receiver operating characteristic (ROC) curve. Radiology **143**, 29–36 (1982)

25. Castiello, U., Stelmach, G.E., Lieberman, A.N.: Temporal dissociation of the prehension pattern in Parkinson's disease. Neuropsychologia **31**(4), 395–402 (1993)

26. Jakobson, L.S., Goodale, M.A.: Factors affecting higher-order movement planning: a kinematic analysis of human prehension. Exp. Brain Res. **86**(1), 199–208 (1991)

27. Jeannerod, M.: The timing of natural prehension movements. J. Mot. Behav. **16**(3), 235–254 (1984)
28. Alberts, J.L., Saling, M., Adler, C.H., Stelmach, G.E.: Disruptions in the reach-to-grasp actions of Parkinson's patients. Exp. Brain Res. **134**(3), 353–362 (2000)
29. Website of the Fifth Dimension Technologies (5DT) (2016). http://www.5dt.com
30. Website of the Polhemus Company (2016). http://polhemus.com
31. Documentation of the Aereospace MATLAB Toolbox. http://mathworks.com/help/aerotbx/index.html
32. Siciliano, B., Sciavicco, L., Villani, L., Oriolo, G.: Robotics Modelling, pp. 106–107. Planning and Control. Springer, London (2009)
33. Luo, J., Ying, K., Bai, J.: Savitzky-Golay smoothing and differentiation filter for even number data. Sig. Process. **85**, 1429–1434 (2005)
34. Teulings, H.L., Contreras-Vidal, J.L., Stelmach, G.E., Adler, C.H.: Parkisonism reduces coordination of fingers, wrist, and arm in fine motor control. Exp. Neurol. **146**, 159–170 (1997)
35. Schneider, K., Zernicke, R.F.: Jerk-cost modulations during the practice of rapid arm movements. Biol. Cybern. **60**, 221–230 (1989)
36. Maind, S.B., Wankar, P.: Research paper on basic of artificial neural network. Int. J. Recent Innov. Trends Comput. Commun. **2**(1), 96–100 (2014)
37. Durgesh, K.S., Lekha, B.: Data classification using support vector machine. J. Theor. Appl. Inf. Technol. **12**(1), 1–7 (2010)

Characterising the Influence
of Rule-Based Knowledge Representations
in Biological Knowledge Extraction
from Transcriptomics Data

Simon Baron, Nicola Lazzarini, and Jaume Bacardit[(✉)]

School of Computing Science, Newcastle University, Claremont Tower,
Newcastle-upon-tyne, NE1 7RU, UK
jaume.bacardit@newcastle.ac.uk

Abstract. Currently, there is a wealth of biotechnologies (e.g. sequencing, proteomics, lipidomics) able to generate a broad range of data types out of biological samples. However, the knowledge gained from such data sources is constrained by the limitations of the analytics techniques. The state-of-the-art machine learning algorithms are able to capture complex patterns with high prediction capacity. However, often it is very difficult if not impossible to extract human-understandable knowledge out of these patterns. In recent years evolutionary machine learning techniques have shown that they are competent methods for biological/biomedical data analytics. They are able to generate interpretable prediction models and, beyond just prediction models, they are able to extract useful knowledge in the form of biomarkers or biological networks.

The focus of this paper is to thoroughly characterise the impact that a core component of the evolutionary machine learning process, its knowledge representations, has in the process of extracting biologically-useful knowledge out of transcriptomics datasets. Using the FuNeL evolutionary machine learning-based network inference method, we evaluate several variants of rule knowledge representations on a range of transcriptomics datasets to quantify the volume and complementarity of the knowledge that each of them can extract. Overall we show that knowledge representations, often considered a minor detail, greatly impact on the downstream biological knowledge extraction process.

Keywords: Evolutionary machine learning · Rule knowledge representations · Biological knowledge extraction

1 Introduction

Science and learning have always been built on the foundations of collecting and analysing data - in order to generate our knowledge in any field we must observe by collecting data and test by analysing that data against hypotheses. Currently, in bioinformatics, technological advances such as microarrays, high throughput

© Springer International Publishing AG 2017
G. Squillero and K. Sim (Eds.): EvoApplications 2017, Part I, LNCS 10199, pp. 125–141, 2017.
DOI: 10.1007/978-3-319-55849-3_9

sequencing and (perhaps most importantly) the sharing of information over the internet in collaborative databases, have greatly increased the amount of data we have been able to observe. Experimental technologies in transcriptomics and genomics are also designed to capture far more information than is required by the original researchers, which once again leads to a wealth of data easily available to anyone interested in studying the area further. In such an environment the focus has shifted to developing analytic tools and techniques that make the most of the data that is being collected. For this to happen we develop tools which are able to: (1) extract biological insight from raw data, (2) process large amounts of data relatively quickly and (3) produce outputs that are human readable.

Evolutionary machine learning techniques have been successfully applied for many years to analyse biological/biomedical data [4–6,9,10,13,15,16,22–24], in a variety of scenarios. In the majority of cases [4–6,9,10,13,22–24] as supervised (classification) learning, but sometimes also applied to unsupervised learning in the form of association rules [16] or bi-clustering [15]. Moreover, they have been applied to a variety of biological data, such as transcriptomics [6,10,15,16], SNPs [23,24], proteomics [22], lipidomics [9], protein structure [4,5] or clinical measurements [13]. Often, these methods are used for the core machine learning task of performing predictions, but in some cases also to extract knowledge from the data, as identifying and ranking important variables (biomarkers) [23,24], generating minimal sets of biomarkers [22], or inferring networks of interactions from data [6,16,23].

A method in this latter category, which we will use in this paper, is FuNeL [14]. FuNeL generates biological functional networks from a labelled (classification) dataset by mining the rule sets generated by the BioHEL evolutionary machine learning system [1]. In the generated networks the possible set of nodes are the attributes of the dataset (e.g. genes), and edges between two attributes are created if, in the rule sets generated by BioHEL, such pair of attributes is frequently observed. This network inference strategy is called *co-prediction*, given that attributes are connected not because they have similar values across samples (what the classic *gene co-expression principle does*) but because together these attributes make predictions on samples.

The co-prediction principle was originally used in [6], and what the authors observed in that work was that the generated network would be different depending on the core knowledge representation used in BioHEL. The standard BioHEL rules for continuous attributes are in the form of: "**If** *attributeX* $\in [2,4]$ **and** *attributeY* $\in [0,0.2]$ **and** ... **then predict** class X". That is, for each relevant attribute a rule would specify a lower and an upper bound. If the representation was subtly changed so that rules would be in the shape "**If** *attributeX* > 2 **and** *attributeY* > 0 **and** ... **then predict** class X" (where there are only lower bounds for each attribute), the networks generated by the co-prediction principle would be very different. This is a very interesting observation because it means that, by making very small changes to the core knowledge representations used in machine learning, the knowledge that can be discovered from a biological dataset can dramatically change.

The aim of this paper is to systematically assess this phenomenon, using the combination of BioHEL+FuNeL. Four different types of rule predicates are explored: (1) $AttX \in [Lower, Upper]$, (2) $AttX > Lower$, (3) $AttX < Upper$, and (4) $AttX/AttY > Threshold$. We test both the case where BioHEL can construct rules using a single (fix) type of predicate and also when the genetic algorithm (GA) is free to discover the best combination of predicate types for each rule (mix). To assess the impact of these representations we build functional networks using FuNeL and then we assess the differences between such networks in relation to the set of nodes their contain but also the differences in the biological annotation of such nodes. To evaluate our methods we use 8 microarray datasets related to several different types of cancer.

The rest of the paper is structured as follows: Sect. 2 describes the algorithms involved in this work: BioHEL, FuNeL and the set of explored knowledge representations. Section 3 details our experimental validation protocol. Section 4 reports the results of our validation. Finally, Sect. 5 summarises our findings and outlines future work.

2 Methods

2.1 BioHEL

BioHEL [1] is an evolutionary rule-based machine learning system originally designed to tackle large-scale datasets. BioHEL has been extensively used to analyse biological data of many different kinds: protein structure prediction [4,5], transcriptomics [6,10], proteomics [22] or lipidomics [9]. For brevity, we are only describing here the aspects of BioHEL that are relevant to the present work.

Learning Strategy. BioHEL generates sets of classification rules using the iterative rule learning (IRL) principle, first introduced in the context of evolutionary machine learning in the SIA [25] system. In IRL, the rules that constitute a rule set are learnt sequentially. After each rule is learnt, the examples from the training set that it covers are removed in order to force the next rule to focus on a different part of the search space. In BioHEL a generational genetic algorithm is used to learn each of these rules. Hence, BioHEL evolves a population of individual rules. The IRL process generally finishes when all the training examples have been covered. In the case of BioHEL, in which rule sets have an explicit (and predefined) default rule, the process finishes then the GA cannot learn any rule that is better than the default rule.

Existing Knowledge Representation. BioHEL uses a rule representation called *Attribute List Knowledge Representation* (ALKR) [1], which will be heavily re-factored in this work. In ALKR, each rule has an embedded feature selection: each rule specifies the subset of attributes it uses, called the attribute list. This subset may differ across rules (GA individuals). In the case of datasets with continuous attributes, each rule encodes an hyper-rectangle: for each attribute within the list, an interval, with a lower bound and an upper bound, is specified. Any attribute not present in the list will be considered as irrelevant. A class is associated with each rule to predict the label of each sample matched by such rule. Each rule in the initial GA population will randomly pick a subset of attributes (a parameter of the system specifies how many). To discover the right attributes for each rule, the GA cycle is extended with two operators that probabilistically add (specialise) or remove (generalise) attributes from the rule.

Fitness Function. The fitness function of BioHEL is designed to strike a balance between accuracy (rules should not make mistakes), coverage (rules should cover as many examples as possible) and simplicity (rules should be simple to describe, i.e. use as few attributes as possible). BioHEL uses the minimum description length principle (MDL) [19] to realise this balance. The overall fitness function F is defined in Eq. 1.

$$F = TL \times W + EL, \tag{1}$$

F (where lower is better) is comprised of two terms. The first term is the theory length (TL) which measures the simplicity of each rule. It is multiplied by a W parameter to mitigate its impact on the overall fitness formula. W is automatically adjusted following the heuristic proposed in [2]. The second term, EL, is the exception length, a measure of the quality of the rules that combines its accuracy, Acc, and its coverage, Cov. This is given by:

$$EL = (1 - Acc) + (1 - Cov). \tag{2}$$

Accuracy is measured by the proportion of training instances the rule classifies correctly to the total number of instances that it matches:

$$Acc = \frac{\text{correctly classified}}{\text{total matched}}. \tag{3}$$

Coverage is classically defined as the percentage of examples from the training set that is matched by the rule. In BioHEL this concept is refined in two directions: (1) using Recall (RC) rather than coverage and (2) with the concept of Coverage Breakpoint (CB). BioHEL employs the recall to focus only on the examples belonging to the class predicted by the rule. The recall is defined as the percentage of examples from the rule's class that are covered by the rule. Moreover, when datasets are affected by class imbalance, recall is more suitable than coverage. The recall is further filtered by specifying a system-wide parameter, called Coverage Breakpoint (CB), that indicates the rules that are *good enough*. Intuitively, this means that most of the recall reward, specified by the CR parameter, will be assigned to rules only if they reach at least CB recall. Notice that the CB parameter requires careful tuning across datasets, but it is very effective in complex and noisy datasets.

$$Cov = \begin{cases} CR \times \frac{RC}{CB}, & RC < CB \\ CR + (1 - CR) \times \frac{RC - CB}{1 - RC}, & RC \geqslant CB \end{cases} \tag{4}$$

The theory length (TL) term of the fitness function (Eq. 1) is designed to favour simple rules.

$$TL = \frac{\Sigma_{i=1}^{N_a} 1 - \text{size}(R_i)/\text{size}(D_i)}{N_a}, \tag{5}$$

where N_a is the total number of attributes in the dataset, $\text{size}(R_i)$ is the length of the interval (upper bound - lower bound) specified in a rule for attribute i, and $\text{size}(D_i)$ is the size of the domain for attribute i. TL quantifies the volume of the hyper-rectangle defined by the rule, and given that only relevant attributes contribute to the formula, it will promote rules that contains fewer attributes.

2.2 Studied Knowledge Representations

BioHEL's ALKR was re-factored to be able to explicitly specify certain types of predicates. Rather than containing a list of expressed attributes and, for each of these, an associated lower and upper bound, now the representation contains a list of predicates, which can be of four different kinds:

- *Hyper-rectangle*: $AttX \in [Lower, Upper]$
- *Greater than*: $AttX > Lower$
- *Less than*: $AttX < Upper$
- *Ratio*: $AttX/AttY > Threshold$

The types of predicates are designed to capture different biological phenomena, for example, less and greater than describe down and up regulation respectively. Similar, the ratio aims to represent the interaction between biological entities due to e.g. regulation: when the high/low presence of one e.g. gene activates the expression of another gene.

Whose abundance often regulate complex processes such as transcription or regulation.

For the first three predicate types, the range of legal values for *lower* and *upper* are determined by the min and max values observed in the training set for a given attribute. For the ratio predicates the threshold can take a value between 1 and 5. Using the presented knowledge representations, a BioHEL's rule contains a set of predicates, which can all belong to the same kind or can be mixed (belong to multiple representations). The proposed representations are illustrated in Fig. 1.

In the case of the mixed representation, the initial population of the GA would initialise rules in which all the predicate types have the same chance to appear, the evolutionary process will then identify the appropriate type for the given dataset. This change in knowledge representation impacts BioHEL in several parts of its working cycle:

- **Initialisation.** When creating initial rules a parameter specifies the expected number of predicates per rule. Once the actual number of predicates for a specific rule is decided, these are randomly created with a single constrain:

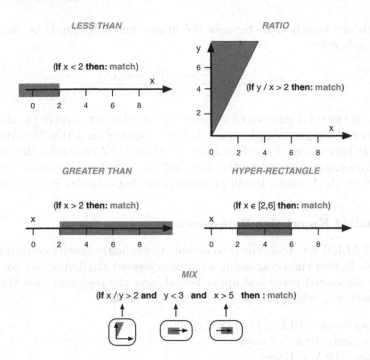

Fig. 1. Illustration of the different types of rule representations studied in this paper

we explicitly prevent the creation of incompatible predicates in the same rule.
Two predicates are declared incompatible if (1) they belong to the same type
and (2) they share the same attribute(s).

- **Crossover.** The original 1-point crossover of BioHEL is replaced with a procedure that shares some similarities with the classic uniform crossover: First
we iterate over one rule, comparing each of its predicates to the predicates of
the second rule. If the two predicates are incompatible then they are copied
to different offspring rules, randomly deciding which offspring takes each of
them. If a predicate is compatible with all predicates in the other rule, it is
randomly assigned to one of the two offspring. After all the predicates from
the first rule are assigned, any predicate from the second that was not assigned
by the incompatibility check is then randomly associated to an offspring. All
the random choices between offsprings occur with a 50–50 chance.
- **Mutation.** BioHEL uses an individual-wise mutation probability. Once an
individual is selected for mutation, one of its predicates is randomly chosen
with uniform probability to be mutated. Depending on the predicate type,
the action will be different: in *hyper-rect*, the lower and upper bounds can
be mutated. In *greater-than* only the lower bound can be mutated. In *less
than* only the upper bound, and in the *ratio* predicate with 50% chance either
(a) the threshold will be mutated or (b) the attributes in the ratio will be
inverted. Please note that the actual attributes associated to the predicate do

not change in any mutation operation. As in the original ALKR representation it will be the role of the specialise operator to create new predicates with different attributes

– **Theory length formula.** BioHEL's MDL-based fitness function needs to specify the *theory length*, an estimation of the complexity of a rule. In the original ALKR representation, the theory length was the inverse of the volume of the hyper-rectangle specified by a rule. This definition is maintained for all predicate types, and it is represented by the red area in Fig. 1.

– **Data normalisation.** The original BioHEL's representation did not require any data normalisation. However, the ratio predicate can generate strange behaviours if some of the attributes present negative values. Therefore, all datasets are normalised so variables present only values between 0 and 1.

2.3   FuNeL

FuNeL [14] is a recently proposed method to infer functional networks from rule-based machine learning models. As mentioned in the introduction, FuNeL applies the *co-prediction* principle: It infers that two biological elements (e.g. genes, in reality attributes of a dataset) need to be connected in the network if they appear together in the rules generated by BioHEL. The way in which we have used FuNeL in this paper has two stages:

1. **Rule-based network generation.** BioHEL is run 1000 times on the same data to generate 1000 different rule sets. From the analysis of the generated rule-sets: (1) all the pairs of attributes co-occurring (together) in the same rules are identified and (2) is counted the number of times that an attribute, overall, is used in the rules (called *node score*).

2. **Permutation test.** Sometimes, spurious edges might appear in the network. To prevent this situation, FuNeL employs a permutation test: a copy of the dataset (permutation) is generated by scrambling the class labels across samples. Then, BioHEL is applied to the permuted data, and the (random) *node score* is computed. The permutation test is performed using the *node score* rather than the *edge score* (number of times two attributes appear together in the same rule) because, when dealing with high dimensionality datasets such as the one employed for this work, the latter do not contain a signal strong enough to filter out the spurious elements: Even strong edges would appear very few times across rule sets and hence would be difficult to differentiate from weak edges. By repeating this permutation process 100 times, a distribution of (random) node scores is generated for each attribute. Then, using a one-tailed permutation test, FuNeL assigns to each node a p-value that represents the likelihood to draw its node score by chance (from the distribution of the permutated node scores). Th final FuNeL network contains the nodes with a p-value <0.05 with their direct neighbours.

Table 1. Eight microarray datasets which are publicly available and their sources.

Dataset	#Instances	#Attributes	Source
AML	54	12625	[26]
Breast/Colon cancer	52	22283	[8]
CNS embryonal tumour	60	7129	[18]
Diffuse large B-cell lymphoma	77	2647	[20]
Leukemia	72	7129	[11]
Lung (Harvard)	181	12534	[12]
Lung (Michigan)	96	7129	[7]
Prostate	102	12600	[21]

Table 2. BioHEL configuration

Parameter	Value
GA iterations	50
Crossover probability	0.6
Selection algorithm	Tournament
Tournament size	4
Population size	500
Individual wise mutation probability	0.6
Repetitions of rule learning process	2
Iteration of activation	10
Initial theory length ratio	0.25
Weight relax factor	0.90
Coverage ratio	0.90
Expected number of predicates in initial rules	15
Probability of generalise	0.25
Probability of specialise	0.25
Default class	majority class

3   Experimental Design

To test the new BioHEL's knowledge representations we selected eight publicly available cancer-related microarray datasets (see Table 1) as test data to demonstrate the behaviour of the new BioHEL knowledge representations. We tested five different settings for BioHEL: one setting for each predicate type, plus the mixed representation. The settings of BioHEL are represented in Table 2.

Coverage Breakpoint Calibration. As discussed in Sect. 2.1, the behaviour of BioHEL can be very sensitive to the parameters used, particularly the coverage breakpoint. For each type of predicate and dataset, we tested coverage breakpoints $\{0.05, 0.10, 0.15, 0.20\}$ in order to find the value yielding the most accurate classification. To choose the appropriate value for each scenario we employed a 10-fold cross-validation. For these experiments, in which BioHEL is used to make predictions (unlike later in the network generation process), we used an ensemble of 1000 BioHEL rule sets generated from the same training data with different random seeds, following [3]. The coverage breakpoint giving the highest cross-validation accuracy was selected for the network generation experiments.

3.1 Network Generation and Analysis

The network analysis protocol is represented in Fig. 2. Dataset by dataset, FuNeL is run using the five different BioHEL knowledge representation settings to generate five different networks. From the resulting networks, we tested the overlap of nodes across knowledge representations. The nodes in the generated networks correspond to the probes of the analysed transcriptomics data. After the network generation, we mapped each probe to the relative gene symbol (HUGO ID). Then, we analysed the Gene Ontology (GO) terms associated with each gene. We used the PANTHER database [17] to conduct an enrichment analysis which identifies the GO terms that are common to a statistically significant proportion of the genes (nodes). Finally, we performed a pairwise comparison of the GO terms to assess the knowledge representations that extracted similar biological information.

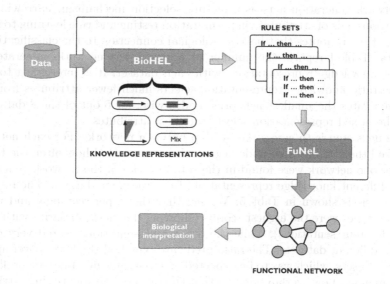

Fig. 2. Representation of the network construction and analysis protocol

4   Results

4.1   Coverage Breakpoint

In Table 3 we report, for each dataset and knowledge representation, the best coverage breakpoint and the accuracy that BioHEL obtained by using it. These coverage breakpoints were later used in the network generation process. In general, representations that operate with a higher coverage breakpoint are preferred, as this encourages rules which are more general and so counteracts any tendency of the representation to over-fit to the specifics of the training data. In average all representations prefer higher CB values (close to 0.2, the maximal tested parameter). In some cases, all CB values gave similar results. Examples are the LungM dataset where all the representations were perfect or near perfect with all the coverage breakpoints. In such cases, the largest coverage breakpoint was used to encourage the rule sets that cover more instances of the data. The mixed representation followed by the hyper-rectangle one gave the best results (obtaining the best accuracy in 5 and 4 out of the 8 datasets, respectively). Mixed is able to tap on all other representations, so it is expected to obtain better results. On the other hand, the hyper-rectangle representation is the less constrained of all predicate types and its flexibility makes it useful for making predictions. The ratio predicates are the third best representation type, and the most constrained ones, greater-than and less-than are the worst performing.

4.2   Analysis of the FuNeL Networks

The network generation acts as a feature selection mechanism, narrowing the field of thousands of attributes via permutation testing and rule learning to select the subset of attributes that have a biological connection to the classification of the data. Table 4 reports the number of nodes of the networks generated by different knowledge representations with each dataset. It is interesting to note that the ratio knowledge representation selects much fewer attributes from the data (generates the smallest networks, nodes-wise, for 5 out of the 8 datasets), while the mixed representation selects the most attributes.

The next step is to assess the overlap between networks. For each network, we ranked the attributes by node degree, then we counted how often the top 10 nodes of one network were found in the top 50 nodes of the network generated, with a different knowledge representation, from the same dataset. The result of this analysis is shown in Table 5. We see that the hyper-rectangle and mixed predicate types were the highest scorers (showing the most similarity with other knowledge representations), while the other representations scored very differently on different datasets. The ratio predicate type had the lowest overlap in 6 of the 8 datasets, which was to be expected as it operates in a fundamentally dissimilar manner. Low overlap suggests that the ratio type is identifying attributes and features that are not discovered by the other representations. Interestingly it shared most similarity with the greater than representation, even more than with the mixed type. Again, we see that the behaviour of the representations

Table 3. The coverage breakpoint parameters selected after our initial cross validation experiments and the accuracy they obtained. NP denotes that there was no preferred breakpoint parameter. Best accuracy for each dataset is marked in bold

	Hyper-rectangle	Greater than	Less than	Ratio	Mix
AML	0.05	0.15	0.10	0.20	0.15
Acc	**66.7**	64.8	61.1	65.0	64.8
B-C	0.20	0.05	0.20	0.05	0.15
Acc	**94.2**	91.1	86.5	92.0	**94.2**
CNS	0.20	0.20	0.20	0.20	0.15
Acc	70.0	50.0	**71.7**	65.0	70.0
Dlbcl	0.15	0.10	0.20	0.05	0.20
Acc	53.4	**62.0**	46.6	53.4	60.3
Leukemia	0.20	0.20	0.20	0.20	0.20
Acc	**98.6**	97.2	94.4	**98.6**	**98.6**
LungH	*NP*	*NP*	*NP*	*NP*	*NP*
Acc	98.9	98.9	98.9	**99.4**	**99.4**
LungM	*NP*	*NP*	*NP*	*NP*	*NP*
Acc	98.9	**100.0**	**100.0**	**100.0**	**100.0**
Prostate	0.20	0.20	0.20	0.15	0.20
Acc	**92.2**	91.1	87.3	90.2	**92.2**
Average	0.175	0.163	0.188	0.156	0.181
Acc	84.1	81.9	80.8	83.0	**84.9**

varies greatly from dataset to dataset, but we can also see that once again the mixed representation has very good overlap with all representations using a single predicate type, as does the hyper-rectangle representation.

The final step of the network validation is to quantify the biology captured by such network. We computed the similarity between the sets of GO terms identified by each knowledge representation on a given dataset. We queried the PANTHER database with the lists of genes identified by the probe IDs which formed nodes in each network. PANTHER identified GO terms that were statistically overrepresented among those genes. The Jaccard similarity function is used to quantify such overlap. Figure 3 shows an heatmap generated from the pairwise Jaccard indexes. We can see interesting behaviour from the ratio predicates, which overall has the lowest average overlap with the other representations, but beats all of the other single type representations for both lung cancer datasets. The two lung cancer datasets show very similar profiles despite being collected separately and having different dataset sizes (12534 attributes for the Harvard set and 7129 attributes for the Michigan set). This seems interesting and might suggest a possible particular biology related to lung cancer, however further analysis using other cases of multiple datasets associated with the same disease (e.g. prostate cancer) are necessary to fully address this observation.

Table 4. Number of nodes in the networks generated by each knowledge representation. Bold marks the knowledge representation generating the smallest network

Dataset	KR	Selected	Dataset	KR	Selected
AML (12681 attributes)	HR	2942	Leukemia (7129 attributes)	HR	1678
	GT	3540		GT	**1413**
	LT	3626		LT	1501
	R	**2131**		R	1452
	M	4011		M	2040
B-C (22282 attributes)	HR	1347	LungH (12533 attributes)	HR	**953**
	GT	1276		GT	1275
	LT	1258		LT	2238
	R	**690**		R	2804
	M	1766		M	2512
CNS (7129 attributes)	HR	3049	LungM (7129 attributes)	HR	**441**
	GT	3591		GT	693
	LT	3040		LT	1160
	R	**2339**		R	1227
	M	3770		M	919
Dlbcl (7129 attributes)	HR	2858	Prostate (12600 attributes)	HR	2991
	GT	2919		GT	3422
	LT	3061		LT	4159
	R	**1083**		R	**2786**
	M	3415		M	4120

Table 5. Overlap between the top nodes (highest degree) across networks. An average is included with emphasis for the representations that had the highest score.

AML	Hyper-rectangle	Greater than	Less than	Ratio	Mix	Mean
Hyper-rectangle	-	1	1	1	2	1.25
Greater than	2	-	0	2	7	**2.75**
Less than	0	0	-	0	4	1
Ratio	1	2	0	-	1	1
Mix	2	3	2	2	-	2.25
B-C	Hyper-rectangle	Greater than	Less than	Ratio	Mix	Mean
Hyper-rectangle	-	0	5	0	5	**2.5**
Greater than	1	-	0	2	2	1.25
Less than	9	0	-	0	3	3
Ratio	0	1	0	-	0	0.25
Mix	2	1	0	0	-	0.75

(continued)

Table 5. *(continued)*

CNS	Hyper-rectangle	Greater than	Less than	Ratio	Mix	Mean
Hyper-rectangle	-	1	6	0	8	3.75
Greater than	0	-	0	2	0	0.5
Less than	6	0	-	0	7	3.25
Ratio	0	2	0	-	0	0.5
Mix	8	0	8	0	-	**4**
Dlbcl	Hyper-rectangle	Greater than	Less than	Ratio	Mix	Mean
Hyper-rectangle	-	1	4	0	8	3.25
Greater than	3	-	0	1	3	1.75
Less than	5	0	-	0	4	2.25
Ratio	0	1	0	-	0	0.25
Mix	8	4	1	1	-	**3.5**
Leukemia	Hyper-rectangle	Greater than	Less than	Ratio	Mix	Mean
Hyper-rectangle	-	4	6	3	10	**5.75**
Greater than	5	-	0	4	6	3.75
Less than	10	0	-	0	8	4.5
Ratio	5	4	0	-	3	3
Mix	9	6	2	3	-	5
LungH	Hyper-rectangle	Greater than	Less than	Ratio	Mix	Mean
Hyper-rectangle	-	9	1	5	10	**6.25**
Greater than	8	-	0	3	10	5.25
Less than	1	0	-	0	5	1.5
Ratio	5	4	0	-	5	3.5
Mix	9	9	1	4	-	5.75
LungM	Hyper-rectangle	Greater than	Less than	Ratio	Mix	Mean
Hyper-rectangle	-	10	0	7	10	**6.75**
Greater than	9	-	0	5	8	5.5
Less than	0	0	-	0	0	0
Ratio	8	7	0	-	7	5.5
Mix	8	10	0	6	-	6
Prostate	Hyper-rectangle	Greater than	Less than	Ratio	Mix	Mean
Hyper-rectangle	-	6	4	4	10	**6**
Greater than	10	-	0	6	10	6.5
Less than	9	0	-	0	10	4.75
Ratio	4	5	0	-	4	3.25
Mix	9	6	4	4	-	5.75
Average	4.88	3.03	1.41	2.03	5.31	

AML	H	G	LT	R	M		Leukemia	H	G	LT	R	M
HR	-	65	56	56	67		HR	-	54	65	48	59
GT	65	-	56	49	69		GT	54	-	52	56	59
LT	56	56	-	46	63		LT	65	52	-	46	58
R	56	49	46	-	52		R	48	56	46	-	52
M	67	69	63	52	-		M	59	59	58	52	-

B-C	H	G	LT	R	M		LungH	H	G	LT	R	M
HR	-	49	44	44	51		HR	-	53	51	48	50
GT	49	-	33	39	46		GT	53	-	48	65	60
LT	44	33	-	30	32		LT	51	48	-	53	54
R	44	39	30	-	32		R	48	65	53	-	66
M	51	46	32	32	-		M	50	60	54	66	-

CNS	H	G	LT	R	M		LungM	H	G	LT	R	M
HR	-	71	72	64	74		HR	-	52	34	39	42
GT	71	-	66	62	75		GT	52	-	37	54	54
LT	72	66	-	65	71		LT	34	37	-	49	49
R	64	62	65	-	63		R	39	54	49	-	63
M	74	75	71	63	-		M	42	54	49	63	-

DLBCL	H	G	LT	R	M		Prostate	H	G	LT	R	M
HR	-	68	73	44	69		HR	-	67	72	66	62
GT	68	-	67	43	69		GT	67	-	63	67	65
LT	73	67	-	43	70		LT	72	63	-	63	71
R	44	43	43	-	39		R	66	67	63	-	66
M	69	69	70	39	-		M	62	65	71	66	-

Fig. 3. Heatmap representing the overlap between the biological annotation captured by different knowledge representations, quantified using the pairwise Jaccard indexes. Colouring is from white to red linearly, scaled between the minimal and maximal values for each dataset. Colour intensity is not comparable across datasets. (Color figure online)

5   Conclusions

This paper focuses on analysing the power of extracting knowledge from biological data that evolutionary rule-based machine learning has. Particularly we studied a core component of rule-based machine learning: its knowledge representation. More specifically we analysed how to define the predicates that constitute the rules created by these methods. We have implemented several types of predicates within the BioHEL evolutionary machine learning system and tested them on a set of 8 cancer-related transcriptomics datasets. To quantify the knowledge extraction power of these knowledge representations, we generated functional networks from the rule sets produced by BioHEL and then assessed the overlap between networks generated from the same dataset using different representations. Our results show that different representations generate networks of varying sizes and with relatively low overlap between important nodes. Nevertheless, the overlap between the biological annotation of different networks is much higher. This result leads to a very interesting observation: each representation is able to capture only certain patterns from the data, hence different nodes. However, these patterns are complementary parts of the same story, and this is why similar biological annotation emerged. Different knowledge representations allow us to analyse biological problems from different angles, each one interprets the data in diverse ways and gives us a unique perspective of the phenomena being analysed. Thus, it is crucial not to restrict the biological data analytics process to a reduced/specific type of knowledge representation, because it will only be able to provide partial (and probably biased) knowledge. Moreover, we observed how our results vary across datasets, meaning that different biological problems are better explained by distinct knowledge representation. Therefore, the analytics process needs to be carefully tuned so that we choose the knowledge representation that is more suitable for the range of biological questions that we are planning to address. To achieve this aim a very thorough exercise of characterising knowledge extraction across all kinds of knowledge representations and biological systems (species, tissues, processes, diseases) needs to be performed. In future work, we would also like to extend this comparison to other non-evolutionary methods of inferring biological networks as well as quantifying in much further depth the biological knowledge contained in the generated networks. Furthermore, we will try to test the proposed approach using different type of biological data. In here we employed data generated from a well-established technology (microarray), in future, we will analyse other more modern types such as RNAseq, lipidomics, proteomics etc. Finally, it would also be interesting to assess the impact of the knowledge representations in a different biological knowledge extraction task: biomarker identification [22].

Acknowledgments. This work was supported by the Engineering and Physical Sciences Research Council [EP/N031962/1]. We are grateful to the School of Computing Science of Newcastle University for the access to its High Performance Computing Cluster. We thank the anonymous reviewers for the valuable feedback received.

References

1. Bacardit, J., Burke, E.K., Krasnogor, N.: Improving the scalability of rule-based evolutionary learning. Memet. Comput. **1**, 55–67 (2009)
2. Bacardit, J., Garrell, J.M.: Bloat control and generalization pressure using the minimum description length principle for a Pittsburgh approach learning classifier system. In: Kovacs, T., Llorà, X., Takadama, K., Lanzi, P.L., Stolzmann, W., Wilson, S.W. (eds.) IWLCS 2003–2005. LNCS (LNAI), vol. 4399, pp. 59–79. Springer, Heidelberg (2007). doi:10.1007/978-3-540-71231-2_5
3. Bacardit, J., Krasnogor, N.: Empirical evaluation of ensemble techniques for a Pittsburgh learning classifier system. In: Bacardit, J., Bernadó-Mansilla, E., Butz, M.V., Kovacs, T., Llorà, X., Takadama, K. (eds.) IWLCS 2006–2007. LNCS (LNAI), vol. 4998, pp. 255–268. Springer, Heidelberg (2008). doi:10.1007/978-3-540-88138-4_15

4. Bacardit, J., Stout, M., Hirst, J.D., Valencia, A., Smith, R.E., Krasnogor, N.: Automated alphabet reduction for protein datasets. BMC Bioinform. **10**, 6 (2009)
5. Bacardit, J., Widera, P., Márquez-Chamorro, A., Divina, F., Aguilar-Ruiz, J.S., Krasnogor, N.: Contact map prediction using a large-scale ensemble of rule sets and the fusion of multiple predicted structural features. Bioinformatics **28**(19), 2441–2448 (2012)
6. Bassel, G.W., Glaab, E., Marquez, J., Holdsworth, M.J., Bacardit, J.: Functional network construction in Arabidopsis using rule-based machine learning on large-scale data sets. Plant Cell **23**(9), 3101–3116 (2011)
7. Beer, D.G., Kardia, S.L.R., Huang, C.C., Giordano, T.J., Levin, A.M., Misek, D.E., Lin, L., Chen, G., Gharib, T.G., Thomas, D.G., Lizyness, M.L., Kuick, R., Hayasaka, S., Taylor, J.M.G., Iannettoni, M.D., Orringer, M.B., Hanash, S.: Gene-expression profiles predict survival of patients with lung adenocarcinoma. Nat. Med. **8**(8), 816–824 (2002)
8. Chowdary, D., Lathrop, J., Skelton, J., Curtin, K., Briggs, T., Zhang, Y., Yu, J., Wang, Y., Mazumder, A.: Prognostic gene expression signatures can be measured in tissues collected in RNAlater preservative. J. Mol. Diagn.: JMD **8**(1), 31–39 (2006)
9. Fainberg, H.P., Bodley, K., Bacardit, J., Li, D., Wessely, F., Mongan, N.P., Symonds, M.E., Clarke, L., Mostyn, A.: Reduced neonatal mortality in Meishan piglets: a role for hepatic fatty acids? PLoS One **7**(11), 1–9 (2012)
10. Glaab, E., Bacardit, J., Garibaldi, J.M., Krasnogor, N.: Using rule-based machine learning for candidate disease gene prioritization and sample classification of cancer gene expression data. PLoS One **7**(7), e39932 (2012)
11. Golub, T.R., Slonim, D.K., Tamayo, P., Huard, C., Gaasenbeek, M., Mesirov, J.P., Coller, H., Loh, M.L., Downing, J.R., Caligiuri, M.A., Bloomfield, C.D., Lander, E.S.: Molecular classification of cancer: class discovery and class prediction by gene expression monitoring. Science **286**(5439), 531–537 (1999)
12. Gordon, G.J., Jensen, R.V., Hsiao, L.L., Gullans, S.R., Blumenstock, J.E., Ramaswamy, S., Richards, W.G., Sugarbaker, D.J., Bueno, R.: Translation of microarray data into clinically relevant cancer diagnostic tests using gene expression ratios in lung cancer and mesothelioma. Cancer Res. **62**(17), 4963–4967 (2002)
13. Hemberg, E., Veeramachaneni, K., Dernoncourt, F., Wagy, M., O'Reilly, U.M.: Efficient training set use for blood pressure prediction in a large scale learning classifier system. In: Proceedings of the 15th Annual Conference Companion on Genetic and Evolutionary Computation, GECCO 2013 Companion, pp. 1267–1274. ACM, New York (2013)
14. Lazzarini, N., Widera, P., Williamson, S., Heer, R., Krasnogor, N., Bacardit, J.: Functional networks inference from rule-based machine learning models. BioData Min. **9**(1), 28 (2016)
15. Marcozzi, M., Divina, F., Aguilar-Ruiz, J.S., Vanhoof, W.: A novel probabilistic encoding for EAs applied to biclustering of microarray data. In: Proceedings of the 13th Annual Conference on Genetic and Evolutionary Computation, GECCO 2011, pp. 339–346. ACM, New York (2011)
16. Martinez-Ballesteros, M., Nepomuceno-Chamorro, I.A., Riquelme, J.C.: Discovering gene association networks by multi-objective evolutionary quantitative association rules. J. Comput. Syst. Sci. **80**, 118–136 (2013)
17. Mi, H., Poudel, S., Muruganujan, A., Casagrande, J.T., Thomas, P.D.: Panther version 10: expanded protein families and functions, and analysis tools. Nucleic Acids Res. **44**(D1), D336–D342 (2016)

18. Pomeroy, S.L., Tamayo, P., Gaasenbeek, M., Sturla, L.M., Angelo, M., McLaughlin, M.E., Kim, J.Y.H., Goumnerova, L.C., Black, P.M., Lau, C., Allen, J.C., Zagzag, D., Olson, J.M., Curran, T., Wetmore, C., Biegel, J.A., Poggio, T., Mukherjee, S., Rifkin, R., Califano, A., Stolovitzky, G., Louis, D.N., Mesirov, J.P., Lander, E.S., Golub, T.R.: Prediction of central nervous system embryonal tumour outcome based on gene expression. Nature **415**(6870), 436–442 (2002)
19. Rissanen, J.: Modeling by shortest data description. Automatica **14**, 465–471 (1978)
20. Shipp, M.A., Ross, K.N., Tamayo, P., Weng, A.P., Kutok, J.L., Aguiar, R.C.T., Gaasenbeek, M., Angelo, M., Reich, M., Pinkus, G.S., Ray, T.S., Koval, M.A., Last, K.W., Norton, A., Lister, T.A., Mesirov, J., Neuberg, D.S., Lander, E.S., Aster, J.C., Golub, T.R.: Diffuse large B-cell lymphoma outcome prediction by gene-expression profiling and supervised machine learning. Nat. Med. **8**(1), 68–74 (2002)
21. Singh, D., Febbo, P.G., Ross, K., Jackson, D.G., Manola, J., Ladd, C., Tamayo, P., Renshaw, A.A., D'Amico, A.V., Richie, J.P., Lander, E.S., Loda, M., Kantoff, P.W., Golub, T.R., Sellers, W.R.: Gene expression correlates of clinical prostate cancer behavior. Cancer Cell **1**(2), 203–209 (2002)
22. Swan, A.L., Stekel, D.J., Hodgman, C., Allaway, D., Alqahtani, M.H., Mobasheri, A., Bacardit, J.: A machine learning heuristic to identify biologically relevant and minimal biomarker panels from omics data. BMC Genom. **16**(1), S2 (2015)
23. Urbanowicz, R.J., Granizo-Mackenzie, A., Moore, J.H.: An analysis pipeline with statistical and visualization-guided knowledge discovery for Michigan-style learning classifier systems. IEEE Comp. Int. Mag. **7**(4), 35–45 (2012)
24. Urbanowicz, R.J., Andrew, A.S., Karagas, M.R., Moore, J.H.: Role of genetic heterogeneity and epistasis in bladder cancer susceptibility and outcome: a learning classifier system approach. J. Am. Med. Inform. Assoc. **20**(4), 603612 (2013)
25. Venturini, G.: SIA: a supervised inductive algorithm with genetic search for learning attributes based concepts. In: Brazdil, P.B. (ed.) ECML 1993. LNCS, vol. 667, pp. 280–296. Springer, Heidelberg (1993). doi:10.1007/3-540-56602-3_142
26. Yagi, T., Morimoto, A., Eguchi, M., Hibi, S., Sako, M., Ishii, E., Mizutani, S., Imashuku, S., Ohki, M., Ichikawa, H.: Identification of a gene expression signature associated with pediatric AML prognosis. Blood **102**(5), 1849–1856 (2003)

Enhancing Grammatical Evolution Through Data Augmentation: Application to Blood Glucose Forecasting

Jose Manuel Velasco[1], Oscar Garnica[1], Sergio Contador[1],
Jose Manuel Colmenar[2], Esther Maqueda[3], Marta Botella[4],
Juan Lanchares[1], and J. Ignacio Hidalgo[1]([✉])

[1] Universidad Complutense de Madrid, Madrid, Spain
mvelascc@ucm.es, hidalgo@dacya.ucm.es
[2] Universidad Rey Juan Carlos, Móstoles, Spain
[3] Hospital Virgen de la Salud, Toledo, Spain
[4] Hospital U. Principe Asturias, Alcala de Henares, Spain

Abstract. Currently, Diabetes Mellitus Type 1 patients are waiting hopefully for the arrival of the Artificial Pancreas (AP) in a near future. AP systems will control the blood glucose of people that suffer the disease, improving their lives and reducing the risks they face everyday. At the core of the AP, an algorithm will forecast future glucose levels and estimate insulin bolus sizes. Grammatical Evolution (GE) has been proved as a suitable algorithm for predicting glucose levels. Nevertheless, one the main obstacles that researches have found for training the GE models is the lack of significant amounts of data. As in many other fields in medicine, the collection of data from real patients is very complex. In this paper, we propose a data augmentation algorithm that generates synthetic glucose time series from real data. The synthetic time series can be used to train a unique GE model or to produce several GE models that work together in a combining system. Our experimental results show that, in a scarce data context, Grammatical Evolution models can get more accurate and robust predictions using data augmentation.

Keywords: Grammatical Evolution · Diabetes · Time series forecasting · Data augmentation · Combining systems

1 Introduction

Diabetes Mellitus (DM) is a disease affecting more than 415 millions of people in the world. Many factors influence the appearance of Diabetes, but we can generalize saying that all patients suffer a defect in either the secretion or in the action of insulin, which is essential for the control of blood glucose levels. The result is that cells do not assimilate glucose and, as a consequence, there is a rise in blood glucose levels (or hyperglycemia). Roughly speaking we can find two main kinds of diabetes;

© Springer International Publishing AG 2017
G. Squillero and K. Sim (Eds.): EvoApplications 2017, Part I, LNCS 10199, pp. 142–157, 2017.
DOI: 10.1007/978-3-319-55849-3_10

- Type 1 Diabetes Mellitus (T1DM): cells do not produce insulin because of an autoimmune process. Currently, requires the person to inject insulin or wear an insulin pump.
- Type 2 Diabetes Mellitus (T2DM): results from insulin resistance, where cells fail to use insulin properly, sometimes combined with an absolute insulin deficiency.

Maintaining a good glycemic control is essential to avoid not only short term but also long terms complications. One of the most serious short-term complication is a diabetic coma caused by a very low level of glycemia (diabetic ketoacidosis and hypoglycemia, defined as blood glucose value less than 70 mg/dl), which can eventually conclude with the death of the patient. Among the long-term problems we can mention a set of multi-chronic complications: blindness, renal failure, sores and infections in feet, damage to nerves in the body, etc.

The good news are that most of the patient with proper control of the levels of glycemia have a normal life and avoid (or at least delay) the appearance of complications. It has been shown that a strict glycemic control in critically ill patients improves performance and reduces medical costs [1]. However, this is not an easy task. Maintaining an appropriate control of the glucose implies measures of glucose in blood using a Continous Glucose Monitoring (CGM) system or/and Glucose Meters (GM). The patient also needs to have some capacity of prediction to know what level of glucose would have if ingested a certain amount of food or injected with a quantity of an insulin of a particular kind. In fact, the objective is to avoid not only long periods of hyperglycemia (glucose levels $\geq$ 20 mg/dl) but also episodes of severe hypoglycemia (glucose levels $\leq$ 40 mg/dl) that can lead to patient death. This is the cause that a high percentage of people with diabetes (around 50%) do not achieve a real control of their glucose levels. In Fig. 1 it is shown the evolution of blood glucose during twelve days of a real diabetic patient. As we can see, almost every day, the patient oscillates over and under the thresholds of hyperglycemia and hypoglycemia which reminds us of the complexity of controlling the blood glucose levels in a safe zone.

The ideal solution would be an artificial pancreas (AP), and this is the main area of research in the field [2]. To achieve a completely autonomous glycemic control, a control algorithm (CA) receiving information from a CGM system would be necessary. By forecasting the evolution of blood glucose, using a predictive model of the response system, the CA would indicate to an insulin pump when to inject a bolus of insulin and the amount necessary. This system is usually called an AP. One of the main problems for the development of the AP is the lack of accurate models for predicting the future of the glucose. Although there are some classical approximations, there is still too much to do for predictions within a horizon of more than 90 min.

Grammatical Evolution (GE) has been proved as a suitable algorithm for predicting glucose levels. Nevertheless, one of the main obstacles that researchers have found for training the GE models is the scarcity of significant amounts of data. As in many other fields in medicine, the collection of data from real patients is very complex. One way to get around a lack of data is to augment the dataset using a Markov Chain Monte Carlo sampling algorithm [3]. This way, the models can avoid overfitting and therefore be more robust.

In this paper, we propose a data augmentation algorithm that generates synthetic glucose time series from real data. The synthetic time series can be used to train a unique GE model or to produce several GE models that work together in a combining system. As far as we know this is the first attempt to data augmentation for enhancing GE models for Time series forecasting.

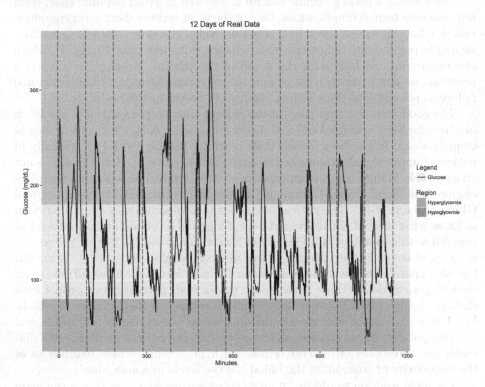

Fig. 1. Real glucose data - 12 days

The rest of the paper is organized as follows. Section 2 describes the related work whereas Sect. 3 describes the theoretical background of the techniques employed. Section 4 explains in detail our approach and the work flow that we have employed. The experimental setup and results are showed in Sects. 5 and 6. Conclusions and future work are exposed in Sect. 7.

2   Related Work

The term data Augmentation is due to Tanner and Wong [4], and it relates to methods for constructing iterative sampling algorithms that introduce unobserved data or latent variables. Although, more advanced approaches include simulation of data based on dynamic systems [5] or evolutionary systems [6].

The problem of predicting and modelling glucose levels has been an intensive area of research during the last ten years. Two are the main targets of these studies. Some of them tried to predict the glucose levels with a time horizon of up to two hours since this is usually the time step needed by the patient to be comfortable after a meal. There are also some researchers that tried to identify 24 h models. The utility of the last is different and is usually more effective when programming an insulin pump or when establishing an insulin profile for longer periods. We can find in literature some approximations providing models for the average case [7]. However, there are hardly few approaches adapted to the particularities of each patient. Most of the models in the literature apply classical modeling techniques, resulting in linear equations defined profiles, or models with a limited set of inputs [8,9]. Recently Hidalgo et al. proposed the application of GE technique to obtain customized models of patients, unlike most of the previous approaches which obtain averaged models. The proposal has been tested with in-silico patient data and results are clearly positive. Authors also present a study of four different grammars and five objective functions [10].

Other personalized control approaches were presented by the main research groups on AP. Those are proposals following the clinical practice. Treatment for subjects with T1DM uses rates of basal insulin delivery, insulin to carbohydrate ratios and individual correction factors, typically from observations of the specialist. However, those models are often inaccurate, since clinical data in T1DM are not extensive enough to identify the exact models [11]. There are also some models used in artificial pancreas systems or closed loop control models: artificial pancreas systems are closed loop control systems trying to emulate the action of a pancreas. They are based on the assumption that it is possible to reach a good control with approximate models, provided that the model is related to the control objective [12]. The main risk is hypoglycemia as a reaction to an excessive insulin administration, usually due to the lack of accurate individualized models.

3 Background

3.1 Univariate Marginal Distribution Algorithm

The Univariate Marginal Distribution Algorithm (UMDA), proposed by Pellikan and Muhlenbein [13,14] is a stochastic optimization method that belongs to a subclass of evolutive strategies that are called Estimation of Distribution Algorithms or EDAs. In the EDA's techniques, the usual genetic operators for creating new individuals (crossover and mutation) are not used. Instead, they generate a new generation of candidates, sampling a probabilistic distribution which is estimated from the best individuals of the previous generation. The UMDA algorithm is perhaps the simplest form of an EDA and the estimation of the distribution is achieved using the univariate marginal probability (that is to say, the frequency of each component in the population).

3.2   Moving Averages

A moving average (MA) is a type of finite impulse response filter which results of the convolution of the glucose values with a fixed weighting function using a rolling window. If all the weighs of the MA are equal, we have a simple MA (SMA). In this study we have used a Weighted MA (WMA) in which each weigh is different.

The simplest way of calculating the WMA in a period of N observations, is:

1. Add the values of the weighted glucose level of the last N observations.
2. Divide the result by the sum of the individual weights.

$$WMA_M = \frac{\sum_{i=M-N}^{M} w_i \times G_i}{\sum_{i=M-N}^{M} w_i} \tag{1}$$

So, Eq. 1 shows the process for finding the WMA for the last N observations, if we have a Glucose Time Series (G) consisting of at least M observations (being $N \leq M$). This process is repeated thorough the whole glucose time series.

MAs have been used historically with time series data to smooth out high-frequency variations and find the long-term trends. In Fig. 2 we can see an example of the application of a WMA to the blood glucose time series of a real patient.

3.3   Grammatical Evolution

In order to get a prediction of a patient's glucose level in the future we need a model based on data we can collect as previous glucose, carbohydrates and insulin values. Therefore, we deal with a kind of symbolic regression (SR) problem. SR tries to obtain a mathematical expression to reproduce a set of discrete data. Genetic Programming (GP) has proven effective in a number of SR problems but it also has some limitations. During last years, variants to GP like Grammatical Evolution (GE) appeared to propose different evaluation approaches. GE is an evolutionary computation technique pioneered by Conor Ryan, JJ Collins and Michael O'Neill in 1998 [15] at the BDS Group in the University of Limerick. In contrast to genetic algorithms, which work with representation of solutions, GE works (evolves) with a genetic code that determines the production process of this solution. The code translation process is determined by grammars represented in Backus-Naur Form (BNF) which is a notation for expressing context-free grammars. This way, GE allows generation of computer programs (that is to say symbolic expressions) in an arbitrary language. This is achieved by using grammars to specify the rules for obtaining the programs. In the definition of the grammars and due to its flexibility, we can insert up to a point our knowledge of the glucose-insulin interaction.

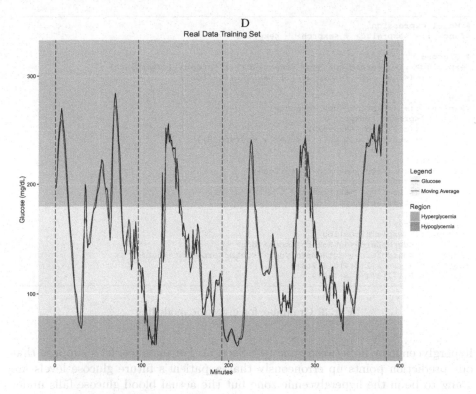

Fig. 2. Real glucose data training set with moving average

Figure 3 represents an extract of a grammar in BNF designed for finding a predicting model of future glucose levels. The code that represents an expression will consist of elements of the set of terminals T. These have been combined with the rules of the grammar. Besides, grammars can be adapted to bias the search of the evolutionary process because there is a finite number of options on each production rule, which limits the search space. So, in this case, we are limiting to two hours the previous data that can be employed in the model and the forecasting horizon is of one hour. Next, we detail the most important rules in our grammar. We search for an expression based on glucose (<exprgluc>), plus some expression regarding carbohydrates (<exprch>), minus an expression of insulin (<exprins>). The expression of glucose denoted by exprgluc is a recursive rule that may produce a complex formula using arithmetic operators (<op>), functions (<preop>) and constant values (<cte>) which, in our case, are generated through a base and an exponent built with integer values.

3.4   Error Grid Analysis

For Diabetic patients, the forecating mistakes can have a quite different impact depending on wether the actual blood glucose level is in the hypoglycemic,

```
# Model expression
<func> ::= <exprgluc> + <exprch> - <exprins>

# Glucose
<exprgluc> ::= (<exprgluc> <op> <exprgluc>) | <preop> (<exprgluc>)
          | (<cte> <op> <exprgluc>) | realData(t-<idx>)

# CH
<exprch> ::= (<exprch> <op> <exprch>)
          |<preop> (<exprch>)
          |(<cte> <op> <exprch>)
          |(getPrevData(1,t,1) * <cte> * <curvedCH>)

# Insulin:
<exprins> ::= (<exprins> <op> <exprins>)
          |<preop> (<exprins>)
          |(<cte> <op> <exprins>)
          |getVariable(2,t-<idx>)

<op> ::= +|-|*|/
<preop> ::= exp|sin|cos|log
<cte> ::= <dgtNoZero><dgtNoZero>,<dgt><dgt>
<idx> ::= <dgtNoZero>|<dgtNoZero><dgt>|<dgtNoZero><dgt><dgt>
<dgtNoZero> ::= 1|2|3|4|5|6|7|8|9
<dgt> ::= 0|1|2|3|4|5|6|7|8|9
```

Fig. 3. Grammar for glycemic modelling

hyperglycemic or in-between zone (see Sect. 1). For instance, let's suppose that our prediction points up erroneously that a patient's future glucose levels are going to be in the hyperglycemic zone but the actual blood glucose falls under the hypoglycemic threshold. In this case, the treatment for the hyperglycemic zone will get the patient deeper into the hypoglycemic zone provoking a very dangerous situation which must be avoided at all cost. In order to taking into account this kind of situations we use the method that was presented in 1987 by Clarke et al. [16] and that is known as the Clarke Error Grid (EGA). The EGA method was proposed to quantify the patient's estimates versus the values given by a blood glucose monitoring device but it has been used since then as a way to standardize the behaviour of glucose meters. In this study, we use it as a way of measuring the accuracy of the predictions of our methods.

Following the EGA method we draw a scatterplot of the experimental results. In one axis, we have the real observations and on the other, the values obtained through a forecasting method. The main diagonal represents the perfect prediction and depending on the severity of the misprediction, the rest of the points call fall into five regions:

- Region A are those values within 20% of the actual values,
- Region B contains points that are outside of 20% but would not lead to inappropriate treatment,
- Region C are those points leading to unnecessary treatment,
- Region D are those points indicating a potentially dangerous failure to detect hypoglycemia or hyperglycemia, and
- Region E are those points that would confuse treatment of hypoglycemia for hyperglycemia and vice versa.

Therefore, the lesser points that appear in the C zone, the better, being very important to avoid the E and D zones.

4 Methodology

As we have already mentioned, the aim of this paper is to enhance the ability of GE for obtaining models and predictions of glucose levels in humans. In order to achieve so, we have searched strategies to generate new time series to train the GEs. This way, we expect to get more robust models and overcome the lack of real data. In Fig. 4 we show the full work flow of our approach.

At the top of the figure, we can see twelve days of blood glucose levels from a real patient. We have divided these twelve days into three sections of four days. The first four days are used for training a GE model as it is explained deeper in Sect. 3.3. We have also employed this first four days of real data to generate synthetic time series from real data using a weighted moving average. So, in Sect. 3.2, we make a brief introduction to moving averages and our full technique is presented in Sect. 4.1. The weighs of the moving average are found using an Univariate Marginal Distribution Algorithm (UMDA); this technique is presented in Sect. 3.1. After that, we have explored two options from which the GE can benefit. On one hand, we have trained a unique GE model with both real data and synthetic data. On the other hand, we have trained several GE models, and we get a final prediction using a weighted lineal combination of each model. To find the best weighs we have employed again an UMDA algorithm (Sect. 3.1). This algorithm is trained using the second section of four days from the twelve days of real data.

Finally, we obtain the predictions of the three models during the third and last section of our real data. The experimental results are showed in Sect. 6. For comparing the results we have used the Clarke's Error Grid Analysis which is presented in Sect. 3.4. After analyzing the different options, we will be able to draw conclusions and see how to deal with future work in Sect. 7.

4.1 Synthetic Time Series Generation

In this section, we describe our methodology for generating synthetic time series that can be employed to train GE models. In essence, our idea is to find a filter that after it is applied to the real data give us two time series: a smoothed version of the blood glucose and a remainder with a Gaussian distribution. As a filter, we use a WMA whose parameters (the N weighs and the N number itself) can be found using an UMDA. When we achieve this goal, the glucose time series is segregated into a smoothed version and a remainder with a Gaussian distribution, we can generate new time series just adding up new Gaussian time series to the smoothed version of the blood glucose. The UMDA algorithm needs a fitness function to evaluate the best candidates from a population. We have experimented with different possibilities, and in this paper, we have used the p-value of the Shapiro-Wilk test [17].

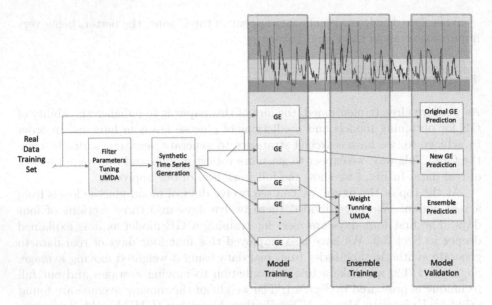

Fig. 4. Work flow

$$P = \frac{(\sum_{i=1}^{n} A_i G_i)^2}{\sum_{i=1}^{n}(G_i - MEAN(G))^2} \tag{2}$$

Equation 2 shows the Shapiro-Wilk test, where G_i are the blood glucose levels and A_i are factors obtained through a process that samples from a standard normal distribution independent and identically distributed random variables and compose them with their covariance matrix.

So, the process to get our filter are:

- First, a generation of candidates are randomly generated. Each candidate consists of the N weighs of a WMA.
- Then, we use the values stored in each individual as WMA parameters to calculate a smoothed version of the glucose time series.
- The actual glucose level minus the smoothed version are the remainders. We want that this remainder has a normal distribution so, next, we get the p-value of the Shapiro-Wilk test.
- The candidates with a higher p-value are selected, and we calculate the univariate marginal distribution for each parameter of these individuals.
- A new generation of candidates are generated using the distributions found in the previous step.
- The process is repeated for a given number of generations.

Figures 5 and 6 illustrates the histograms of the probability distribution of the remainder of the glucose after been filtered by an SMA and after been filtered by a WMA with its parameters found by the UMDA algorithm. As we can see, the first histogram shows a great Kurtosis (tailedness) and Skewness (asymmetry) and so it is far away from a normal distribution and the p-value in the Shapiro-Wilk test is very low. Nevertheless, in Fig. 6, we have what could be a sample from a Gaussian distribution and its p-value in the test is very high.

Summarizing, our technique is based on two steps:

– First, we estimate the WMA parameters using an UMDA algorithm and being the fitness function the p-value of the Shapiro-Wilk test so that the remainder of the glucose time series follows a Gaussian distribution.
– Second, we generate the synthetic time series sampling new values from a normal distribution and adding them up to the smoothed version.

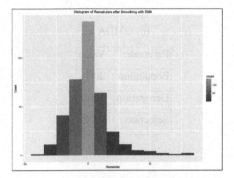

Fig. 5. Histogram of remainder after smoothing with SMA

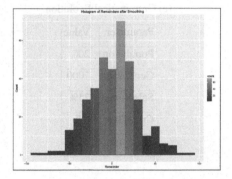

Fig. 6. Histogram of remainder after smoothing with UMDA guided WMA

5   Experimental Setup

Thanks to the staff in the Principe de Asturias Hospital at Alcala de Henares, Spain, we have been able to collect data from a real patient with a continuous glucose monitoring system (CGMS) during twelve days[1]. We have observations every fifteen minutes up to a total of 1152 measures. We also have recorded carbohydrate units ingested and insulin injected, distinguished by insulin type, for every day.

We have segregated these twelve days into three sections of four days. We have used the first section for training the GE models. Another section for training the combining system. And the last section has been targeted for validating the three systems in this study.

The models were trained rolling a window of two hours (8 observations) through the data to make a prediction with a forecasting horizon of 1 h.

---

[1] On 6 June 2012, the Clinical Research Ethics Committee of the Hospital of Alcalá de Henares (Spain) authorized the use of the data collected, provided that the privacy of the data is ensured and the informed consent of patients is made.

We run the experiment 10 times and we show here the average of the ten runs. The fitness function for the GE models were the mean squared error (MSE), that is to say, the average of the squares of the difference between actual values and model predictions.

The value of the parameters of the evolutionary algorithms used in the training phase were selected after a set of preliminary experiments. In these preliminary experiments we did a sistematic sweep of values ranging aproximately from 50% to 200% of the values shown on Table 1. These experiments also suggested to eliminate the trigonometric functions from the BNF of the grammar.

Table 1. Experimental parameters

(a) Grammatical Evolution

Parameter	Value
Population	200
Generation	2000
Selection	25%
CrossOver	0.7
Mutation	0.15

(b) UMDA

Parameter	Value
Population	200
Generation	2000
Selection	25%

6 Experimental Results

Thus, the aim of using GE is to find out a mathematical expression to model future glucose levels of a diabetic patient based on historic data (glucose, carbohydrates ingestion and insulin injection). Figure 7 shows the results of a GE model within a Clarke Error Grid. This graph is a scatterplot of real values (horizontal axis) and predicted values (vertical axis) during the third section of our real data. The forecasting horizon is one hour. The first thing that we notice is that there is a very small amount of predictions into the D and E zones which is very good news. Nevertheless, more than 80% of the values falls down into the B and C zones. We must remeber that predictions into the C zone cal lead to unnecessary treatments. This situation is the reason for searching for a method to improve the robustness of the GE mnodel.

So, as we have explained, we augmented the training data with new time series and got a new GE model trained with the original data plus ten more synthetic time series. The results of this new model are presented in Fig. 8. It is important to point out that this model decreases drastically the predictions in the C zone, being the points in the B and A zones, more than 20% and more than 70% respectively. There is a slighty increase of points in the D zone and no predictions were in the most dangerous section, the E zone.

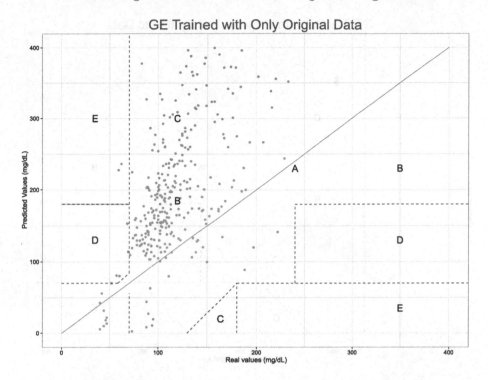

Fig. 7. Clarke Error Grid results for for GE model trained with original data

Besides, the possibility of training a unique Model with the original data plus the new time series we have experimented with another option. We have used the ten new time series to train ten new GE models. The full set of models (original model and the ten new ones) were combined into an ensemble. This way, the prediction of the ensemble is the weighted sum of every individual prediction as it is shown in Eq. 3. The final prediction $(\hat{G})$ is a lineal function of every GE model prediction $\hat{G}_i$. The prediction horizon (H) is always 1 h. To get the value of the weighs (W_i), the combining system was trained during the second section of the real data using and UMDA algorithm.

$$\hat{G}^{H=1hour} = \sum_{i=1}^{T} w_i \times \hat{G}_i^{H=1hour} \tag{3}$$

The results of the Ensemble during the validation data section are shown in Fig. 9. This combining system improves the results obtained by the unique model. As we can see, more than an 80% of the points fall into the A zone and there is a significative reduction of points into the D zone.

Finally, in Table 2 we summarize the results of the three models. The legend of this table is:

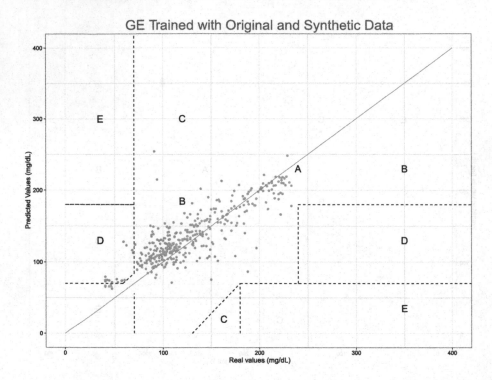

Fig. 8. Clarke Error Grid results for for GE model trained with original and synthetic data

- OrigGE, GE model trained only with original data.
- SynthGE, GE model trained with original data plus synthetic data.
- Ensemble, system that combines the predictions of eleven GE models.

The most significative differences in this table are:

- OrigGE has a 42.44% of points into the C zone, while SynthGE and Ensemble have less that 1%.
- The percentage of points into the A and B zones is about 55% for OrigGE, but it raises to 95% for SynthGE and up to 99% for Ensemble.
- Ensemble has the best results for every zone.

Table 2. Clarke zones for predicted values

Strategy	Zones percentage %				
	A	B	C	D	E
OrigGE	13.28	42.70	42.44	1.04	0.52
SynthGE	71.87	23.95	0.52	3.64	0
Ensemble	84.11	15.10	0.26	0.52	0

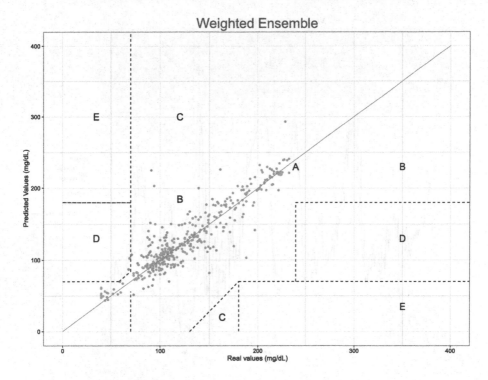

Fig. 9. Clarke Error Grid results for weighted ensemble

7 Conclusions and Future Work

The aim of this paper was to find ways for enhancing grammatical evolution models in a context of data scarcity as it is the future artificial pancreas system (AP). The AP needs of accurate predictions of future blood glucose levels in order to estimate the size of insulin bolus that it will inject into the patient's blood flow. As we have seen, a forecasting mistake could lead to a quite erronous treatment. Grammatical Evolution (GE) has been proved as a suitable algorithm for predicting glucose levels as it is not prone to obtain dangerous errors. Nevertheless, one the main obstacles that researches have found for training the GE models is the lack of significant amounts of data. As in many other fields in medicine, the collection of data from real patients is very complex.

In this paper we have presented a technique for augmenting the available glucose data. Our technique generates new time series that can be used to train the GE models. The experimental results show that the GE models trained with these synthetic time series get more robust predictions, decreasing significatively the number of hazardous predictions.

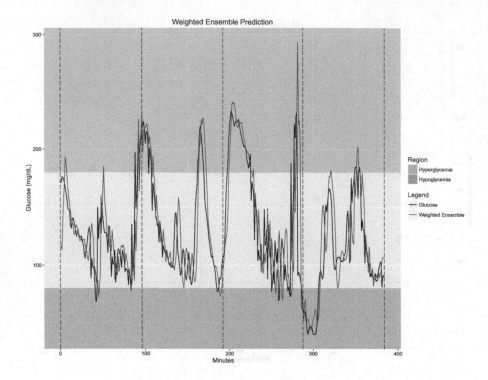

Fig. 10. Weighted ensemble prediction

Besides, we have experimented with another option: training multiple GE models using the synthetic time series. These models jointly with the original model are combined into an ensemble to produce a final prediction. Our experimental results suggests this option as the best.

In Fig. 10 is shown the Ensemble prediction time series jointly with the actual value of the glucose during the validation section of the real patient's data. Visually we can appreciate that although the results are not bad, there is still a lot of room for improvement. So, as a future work, we intend to get deeper insight into several open questions:

- What is the maximun amount of synthetic time series that can be useful?
- Where is the maximun safe prediction horizon for blood glucose?
- Are there other methods for data augmentation for glucose time series?

Acknowledgment. This research is supported by the Spanish Minister of Science and Innovation (TIN2014-54806-R).

The authors would like to thank the staff in the Principe de Asturias Hospital at Alcala de Henares for their support and assistance with this project. Special thanks also go to Maria Aranzazu Aramendi Zurimendi and Remedios Martinez Rodriguez.

References

1. Krinsley, J.S., Jones, R.L.: Cost analysis of intensive glycemic control in critically ill adult patients. Chest **129**(3), 644–650 (2006)
2. Nicolao, G.D., Magni, L., Man, C.D., Cobelli, C.: Modeling and control of diabetes: towards the artificial pancreas. In: 18th IFAC World Congress of the IFAC Proceedings Volumes, vol. 44, no. 1, pp. 7092–7101 (2011)
3. Hastings, W.: Monte Carlo sampling methods using Markov chains and their applications. J. Biometrica **57**, 97–109 (1970)
4. Tanner, M.A., Wong, W.H.: From EM to data augmentation: the emergence of MCMC Bayesian computation in the 1980s, April 2011. arXiv e-prints arXiv:1104.2210
5. Yadav, M., Malhotra, P., Vig, L., Sriram, K., Shroff, G.: ODE - augmented training improves anomaly detection in sensor data from machines. CoRR (2016). arXiv:1605.01534
6. Kumar, A., Cowen, L.: Augmented training of hidden Markov models to recognize remote homologs via simulated evolution. Bioinformatics **25**(13), 1602–1608 (2009)
7. Mays, L.: Diabetes mellitus standards of care. Nurs. Clin. North Am. **50**(4), 703–711 (2015). Pathophysiology and Care Protocols for Nursing Management
8. Messori, M., Toffanin, C., Favero, S.D., Nicolao, G.D., Cobelli, C., Magni, L.: Model individualization for artificial pancreas. Comput. Methods Programs Biomed. (2016, in press). http://dx.doi.org/10.1016/j.cmpb.2016.06.006
9. Kastorini, C.-M., Papadakis, G., Milionis, H.J., Kalantzi, K., Puddu, P.-E., Nikolaou, V., Vemmos, K.N., Goudevenos, J.A., Panagiotakos, D.B.: Comparative analysis of a-priori and a-posteriori dietary patterns using state-of-the-art classification algorithms: a case/case-control study. Artif. Intell. Med. **59**(3), 175–183 (2013)
10. Hidalgo, J.I., Maqueda, E., Risco-Martín, J.L., Cuesta-Infante, A., Colmenar, J.M., Nobel, J.: GlUCmodel: a monitoring and modeling system for chronic diseases applied to diabetes. J. Biomed. Inform. **48**, 183–192 (2014)
11. Yu, C., Zhao, C.: Rapid model identification for online glucose prediction of new subjects with type 1 diabetes using model migration method. In: IFAC World Congress of the IFAC Proceedings Volumes, vol. 47, no. 3, pp. 2094–2099 (2011)
12. Gevers, M.: Identification for control: from the early achievements to the revival of experiment design. Eur. J. Control **11**(4), 335–352 (2005)
13. Pelikan, M., Mühlenbein, H.: Marginal distributions in evolutionary algorithms. In: Proceedings of the International Conference on Genetic Algorithms Mendel, vol. 98, pp. 90–95. Citeseer (1998)
14. Mühlenbein, H.: The equation for response to selection and its use for prediction. Evol. Comput. **5**, 303–346 (1997)
15. O'Neill, M., Ryan, C.: Grammatical Evolution: Evolutionary Automatic Programming in an Arbitrary Language. Kluwer Academic Publishers, Norwell (2003)
16. Clarke, W., Cox, D., Gonder-Frederick, L., Carter, W., Pohl, S.: Evaluating clinical accuracy of systems for self-monitoring of blood glucose. Diabetes Care **10**, 622–628 (1987)
17. Shapiro, S.S., Wilk, M.B.: An analysis of variance test for normality (complete samples). Biometrika **3**(52), 591–611 (1965)

Genetic Programming Representations
for Multi-dimensional Feature Learning
in Biomedical Classification

William La Cava[1][✉], Sara Silva[2,3], Leonardo Vanneschi[4], Lee Spector[5],
and Jason Moore[1]

[1] Institute for Biomedical Informatics,
University of Pennsylvania, Philadelphia, PA, USA
lacava@upenn.edu
[2] Faculdade de Ciências, Departamento de Informática,
BioISI - Biosystems and Integrative Sciences Institute,
Universidade de Lisboa, 1749-016 Lisboa, Portugal
[3] CISUC, Department of Informatics Engineering,
University of Coimbra, Coimbra, Portugal
[4] NOVA IMS, Universidade Nova de Lisboa, 1070-312 Lisbon, Portugal
[5] School of Cognitive Science, Hampshire College, Amherst, MA, USA

Abstract. We present a new classification method that uses genetic programming (GP) to evolve feature transformations for a deterministic, distanced-based classifier. This method, called M4GP, differs from common approaches to classifier representation in GP in that it does not enforce arbitrary decision boundaries and it allows individuals to produce multiple outputs via a stack-based GP system. In comparison to typical methods of classification, M4GP can be advantageous in its ability to produce readable models. We conduct a comprehensive study of M4GP, first in comparison to other GP classifiers, and then in comparison to six common machine learning classifiers. We conduct full hyper-parameter optimization for all of the methods on a suite of 16 biomedical data sets, ranging in size and difficulty. The results indicate that M4GP outperforms other GP methods for classification. M4GP performs competitively with other machine learning methods in terms of the accuracy of the produced models for most problems. M4GP also exhibits the ability to detect epistatic interactions better than the other methods.

Keywords: Genetic programming · Feature learning · Classification

1 Introduction

Classification models are a fundamental pursuit in the biomedical field due to their widespread utility in applications such as medical diagnosis [23,29,39] and identification of genetic causes of disease [25,26]. In classification with numeric attributes, we wish to find a mapping $\hat{y}(\mathbf{x}) : \mathbb{R}^p \rightarrow C$ that associates the vector of attributes $\mathbf{x} \in \mathbb{R}^p$ with class labels from the set $C = \{c_1 \ldots c_k\}$ using n paired

© Springer International Publishing AG 2017
G. Squillero and K. Sim (Eds.): EvoApplications 2017, Part I, LNCS 10199, pp. 158–173, 2017.
DOI: 10.1007/978-3-319-55849-3_11

examples from the training set $\mathcal{T} = \{(\mathbf{x}_i, y_i), i = 1 \ldots n\}$. Central to this goal is the identification of important transformations of the original data that improve classification accuracy. Machine learning (ML) systems that conduct classification have become standardized over the last 20 years [2], and open-source packages are available for performing classification (e.g., [8,30]) according to well-known approaches such as logistic regression (LR), nearest centroid (NC), support vector classification (SVC), Bayesian Networks (e.g. naïve Bayes (NB)), k-nearest neighbors (KNN), and ensemble methods such as random forests (RF), among others. Yet three major challenges to multiclass classification persist. The first two challenges are i) the selection of and ii) transformation of features into new features (feature synthesis), derived from the original attributes, to be used for model construction. Feature selection is important for reducing large-dimension data sets and for measurement selection in some domains. Typically it is left to a pre-processing step to reduce the number of attributes to a manageable size [7]; in other words, feature selection is not an intrinsic property of most ML approaches. Regarding the second challenge, many ML methods employ projection of the original features into a new feature space, for example via kernel functions [28]. However the choice of kernel function is typically not automated, but picked by trial and error or cross-validation. The opaque nature of kernel transformations highlights a third challenge of classification: the interpretability of the resultant models. Interpretation is especially relevant in the sciences and for applications like human genomics that rely on classification as a means of inferring relationships from observations. To this end, methods with intelligible representations like decision trees use greedy simplification procedures, while acknowledging that finding a minimal decision tree is an NP-hard problem [33].

Genetic programming (GP) [14] has been proposed for classification to remedy the three challenges above [5,13]. GP is a stochastic optimization method that implicitly conducts feature selection by pressuring the model $\hat{y}(\mathbf{x})$ to use a subset of $\mathbf{x}$ most relevant to the problem solution. In addition, GP makes minimal *a priori* assumptions about the structure of the attribute space [17], admits a number of representations [21], and can be made to optimize the structure of the model such that it remains intelligible. Although it has been applied successfully to a number of binary classification problems [39], until recently [11,27] it has not been competitive with standard multiclass classification techniques. The exceptions are the recently developed methods M2GP [11] and M3GP [27] that use GP to select and synthesize features and then perform classification in the new feature space using a Mahalanobis distance-based discriminant function. In this paper, we improve upon these methods by two innovations: (i) the use of a novel program representation that simplifies the construction of multidimensional representations, and (ii) the incorporation of an advanced parent selection technique that leads to more accurate classifiers. The performance of this method, appropriately named M4GP[1], is compared to other GP representations, including M2GP, M3GP, using a set of eight benchmark classification problems. Then, M4GP is benchmarked against LR, NC, SVC, NB, KNN and

---

[1] Source code available from http://github.com/lacava/ellyn.

RF on a 16 biomedical classification problems. The experiments include a hyper-parameter optimization step for each learner, such that the comparisons consider a tuned version of each method.

2   M4GP

Recall the labeled training set $\mathcal{T} = \{(\mathbf{x}_i, y_i), i = 1 \ldots n\}$, consisting of n samples of attributes $\mathbf{x}_i \in \mathbb{R}^p$ associated with the corresponding class label y_i from the set $\mathcal{C} = \{c_1 \ldots c_k\}$. The $n \times p$ matrix of attribute samples $\mathbf{X}$ can be partitioned according to its labels into k subsets $\{\mathbf{X}_1 \ldots \mathbf{X}_k\}$, such that $\mathbf{X}_j$ is the subset of $\mathbf{X}$ tagged with class label c_j. One way to classify a new sample $\mathbf{x}' \in \mathbb{R}^p$ is by finding its nearest centroid [36], i.e. to measure the distance of $\mathbf{x}'$ to each subset $\{\mathbf{X}_1 \ldots \mathbf{X}_k\}$, and then assign the class label corresponding to the minimum distance [12], i.e.

$$\hat{y}(\mathbf{x}') = c_j, \quad \text{if} \quad j = \arg\min_\ell D(\mathbf{x}', \mathbf{X}_\ell), \quad \ell = 1, \ldots, k \qquad (1)$$

One such measure is the Mahalanobis distance, D_M,

$$D_M(\mathbf{x}', \mathbf{X}_j) = \sqrt{(\mathbf{x}' - \mu_j) \, \Sigma_j^{-1} \, (\mathbf{x}' - \mu_j)^T} \qquad (2)$$

where $\mu_j \in \mathbb{R}^p$ is the centroid of $\mathbf{X}_j$ and $\Sigma_j \in \mathbb{R}^{p \times p}$ is its covariance matrix, rendering D_M the equivalent Euclidean distance of $\mathbf{x}'$ from $\mathbf{X}_j$, scaled by the eigenvalues (variances) and rotated by the eigenvectors of Σ_j, to account for the correlation between columns of $\mathbf{X}_j$.

This approach to classification makes some assumptions about the structure of the data. First, each $\mathbf{X}_j$ must be sufficiently grouped such that samples always fall closest to their true distribution, which cannot be said of most difficult classification problems. Second, it assumes that Eq. (2) can be calculated from the original data. One can imagine that as the dimensionality of $\mathbf{X}$ increases, the calculation of D_M becomes prohibitively expensive.

In order to relax these assumptions, we wish to find a set of transformations $\Phi(\mathbf{x}) : \mathbb{R}^p \rightarrow \mathbb{R}^d$ that projects $\mathbf{x}$ into a d-dimensional space in which the samples are more easily classified according to their distribution distances. In this new space, the Mahalanobis distance takes the form $D_M(\Phi(\mathbf{x}), \Phi(\mathbf{X}_j))$, with centroid $\mu_{\Phi_j} \in \mathbb{R}^d$ and covariance matrix $\Sigma_{\Phi_j} \in \mathbb{R}^{d \times d}$.

The goal of the GP system will be to find or approximate the optimal synthesized features $\Phi^* = [\phi_1 \ldots \phi_d]$ that maximize the number of correctly classified training samples, as:

$$\Phi^*(\mathbf{x}) = \arg\max_{\Phi \in \mathbb{S}} f(\Phi, \mathcal{T}) \qquad (3)$$

$$f(\Phi, \mathcal{T}) = \frac{1}{n} \sum_{i=1}^n \delta\left(\hat{y}(\Phi(\mathbf{x}_i)), y_i\right) \qquad (4)$$

where $\mathbb{S}$ is the space of possible transformations Φ, f is the classification accuracy (used here as the GP fitness function), and $\delta = 1$ if $\hat{y}(\Phi(\mathbf{x}_i)) = y_i$, and 0 otherwise. A well-formed $\Phi(\mathbf{x})$ allows the classifier the flexibility to incorporate (linear and/or nonlinear) transformations of the original attributes in order to improve distinctions between classes compared to using the original attribute set. By using GP to estimate the features $\Phi(\mathbf{x})$, the subset of $\mathbf{x}$ used in $\Phi(\mathbf{x})$ as well as the dimensionality of Φ, $|\Phi| = d$, are optimized. Therefore, feature selection in GP can produce $d << p$ for high dimensional data sets, making Eq. (2) tractable, and also admits higher-dimensional representations $(d > p)$ in cases for which $\mathbf{x}$ is not easily mapped to y.

2.1   Genetic Programming

GP solves problems by constructing and updating a population of programs composed of building blocks that represent solution components. In this case, each program consists of a set of equations that compose the synthesized features $\Phi(\mathbf{x})$ used to estimate $\hat{y}$. For example, an individual program $\mathbf{i}$ might encode the features

$$\mathbf{i} \rightarrow \Phi(\mathbf{x}) = [x_1,\ x_2,\ x_1^2,\ x_2^2,\ x_1 x_2] \tag{5}$$

where $\phi_1 = x_1$, $\phi_2 = x_2$, $\phi_5 = x_1 x_2$, and so on. In this case, $|\Phi| = 5$, and $\mathbf{i}$ corresponds to a polynomial expansion of two attributes.

Traditionally in GP, a program is represented by a single syntax tree evaluated based on the output generated at the root node [14]. For example, ϕ_5 above could be represented by a tree $(* \ x_1 \ x_2)$, where '$*$' is the root node and x_1 and x_2 are its leaves. However, a single output cannot represent a multi-dimensional transformation. To address this, in M2GP and M3GP, program trees were modified with special nodes in order to allow for multiple outputs at the root [11,27]. This introduced unnecessary complexity to the representation. A contribution of this work is the introduction of a stack-based data flow to simplify the encoding of Φ, presented in the Representation paragraph below.

The GP population is optimized by probabilistically selecting programs based on their performance and stochastically recombining and mutating these programs to produce a new set of programs. In this work, we implement a recent selection mechanism known as lexicase selection [35] and compare its performance to a more traditional selection algorithm (tournament selection). These techniques are described in the following sections.

Representation. We implement a stack-based representation [15,31] of the equations in place of the more traditional tree-based GP representations. Programs in this representation are encoded as post-fix notation equations, e.g., $\mathbf{i} = [\ x_1 \ x_2 \ + \ ] \rightarrow \Phi = [x_1 + x_2]$. This representation is advantageous because it allows multiple outputs to be supported by default without the need for specialized instructions. This support is achieved by evaluating programs via executions on a stack, such that the program in Eq. (5) can be constructed as

$$\mathbf{i} = [\ x_1 \ x_2 \ x_1 \ x_1 \ * \ x_2 \ x_2 \ * \ x_1 \ x_2 \ * \ ]$$

The execution of program **i** is illustrated in Fig. 1. Rather than recursively evaluating the program as a tree starting at its root node, stack based evaluation proceeds left to right, pushing and pulling instructions to and from a single stack. Arguments such as x_1 are pushed to the stack, and operators such as '$*$' pull arguments from the stack and push the result. At the end of a program's execution, the entire stack represents the multi-dimensional transformation.

$$\mathbf{i} = \begin{bmatrix} x_1 & x_2 & x_1 & x_1 & * & x_2 & x_2 & * & x_1 & x_2 & * \end{bmatrix}$$
index: 1   2   3   4   5   6   7   8   9   10   11

program execution	stack
1. push (x_1):	$[\, x_1 \,]$
2. push (x_2):	$[\, x_1 \quad x_2 \,]$
3. push (x_1):	$[\, x_1 \quad x_2 \quad x_1 \,]$
4. push (x_1):	$[\, x_1 \quad x_2 \quad x_1 \quad x_1 \,]$
5. pull (x_1), (x_1); push $(x_1 \cdot x_1)$	$[\, x_1 \quad x_2 \quad x_1 x_1 \,]$
6. push (x_2):	$[\, x_1 \quad x_2 \quad x_1^2 \quad x_2 \,]$
7. push (x_2):	$[\, x_1 \quad x_2 \quad x_1^2 \quad x_2 \quad x_2 \,]$
8. pull (x_2), (x_2); push $(x_2 \cdot x_2)$	$[\, x_1 \quad x_2 \quad x_1^2 \quad x_2^2 \,]$
9. push (x_1):	$[\, x_1 \quad x_2 \quad x_1^2 \quad x_2^2 \quad x_1 \,]$
10. push (x_2):	$[\, x_1 \quad x_2 \quad x_1^2 \quad x_2^2 \quad x_1 \quad x_2 \,]$
11. pull (x_1), (x_2); push $(x_1 \cdot x_2)$	$[\, x_1 \quad x_2 \quad x_1^2 \quad x_2^2 \quad x_1 x_2 \,]$

$$\rightarrow \Phi(\mathbf{x}) = [x_1, x_2, x_1^2, x_2^2, x_1 x_2]$$

Fig. 1. Example of program representation of a multidimensional transformation. Arguments such as x_1 are pushed to the stack, and operators such as '$*$' pull arguments from the stack and push the result.

2.2 Other GP Classification Methods

In the case of M4GP, the mean and covariance of the stack outputs are used in order to make classifications for each sample according to the Mahalanobis distance (Eq. 2). However, a much simpler approach to classification could be to directly classify samples based on these outputs. This is the case with many GP-based classifiers [5]. To this end, we compare distance-based classification with two simpler alternatives: float stack classification and boolean stack classification, referred to simply as *float* and *bool* hereafter.

In the case of *float*, we take the index of the floating point stack with the highest value to be the class assignment. For example, assume the program from Fig. 1 produces the output [0.15, 2.31, 42, 6.3, 0.01] for a sample from the data. In this case the GP model would assign the 3rd class label to this sample. Thus the GP system attempts to evolve a set of equations that are maximized for the class label corresponding to their location in the program.

In the case of *bool*, we include a set of boolean operators in the function set for constructing GP programs: {AND, OR, NOT, <, >, <=, >=, ==, IF-THEN, IF-THEN-ELSE}. Boolean outputs are pushed to their own typed stack. In order to make a classification, the boolean stack is interpreted as a bit string.

For example, in the case of 2 classes, the top value of the boolean stack is interpreted as class 1 ([0]) or class 2 ([1]). For binary classification problems, this corresponds to a fairly traditional encoding for classification [32]. In the case of 4 classes, the top two values of the stack are interpreted as class 1 ([0, 0]), class 2 ([0, 1]), class 3 ([1, 0]), or class 4 ([1, 1]).

Initialization, Selection, and Variation. Programs are initialized as sets of equations varying both in individual feature size and their dimensionality. Each equation in a program is initialized recursively in an analogous fashion to the grow method (see [32]) but limited by number of nodes rather than depth. Fitness for the programs is defined in Eq. (4).

Two population selection methods are tested: tournament selection [6] and lexicase selection [9, 35]. The first, tournament selection, is a standard GP method in which individuals (in this case, two) in the current population are randomly selected (with replacement) and the one with best fitness is chosen as a parent for the next generation. Lexicase selection is described in more detail below.

Lexicase selection. Lexicase selection is a parent selection technique that pressures individuals in the population to perform well on unique combinations of training cases, i.e. samples. Each parent selection event follows this procedure:

1. The entire population is added to the selection pool.
2. The training cases are uniformly shuffled.
3. Individuals in the pool that do not have *exactly* the best fitness on the first case among the pool are removed.
4. If more than one individual remains in the pool, the first case is removed and step 2 is repeated with the next case. If only one individual remains, it is the chosen parent. If no more fitness cases are left, a parent is chosen randomly from the remaining individuals.

As can be surmised, the lexicase selection is simple to implement. It is helpful to think of the training cases as filters, and to consider each parent selection event as a randomized path through these filters. The parents returned by lexicase selection are Pareto-optimal with respect to the training cases, since they must be elite on at least one case to be selected. In turn, the selective strength of a training case is directly proportional to its difficulty because it culls the individuals from the pool that do not solve it. Therefore selective pressure shifts to cases that are not widely solved. This interaction between individuals in the pool and the training cases results in selective pressure to perform well on unique combinations of test cases. As a result, lexicase selection leads to increased population diversity observed during evolutionary runs [9, 16].

3   Related Work

Whereas GP has been proposed for evolving classification functions $\hat{y}(\mathbf{x})$ directly [5, 13, 21], M2GP proposed GP as a wrapper that evolved $\Phi(\mathbf{x})$ for a clustering method, and demonstrated in particular that Mahalanobis distance outperformed Euclidean distance in this framework [11]. M3GP extended M2GP to allow programs to change dimensionality during the run via specialized search operators that increased or decreased the dimensionality of a tree by modifying its root node [27]. M4GP removes the need for explicit root nodes by using a stack-based data flow that also preserves multi-dimensionality and allows dimensionality to change flexibly. An ensemble version of M3GP named eM3GP produced similar classification accuracies to M3GP with smaller, more legible resultant programs [34]. Together, these methods highlight the unique challenge of feature selection and its merger into learning systems [19].

A few recently developed ML methods have leveraged GP's feature-based abilities as a wrapper for regression [1,10,22]. M4GP and its ancestors differ from these regression-based approaches in that the classification does not require classes to be assigned via an arbitrarily designated range of real-valued outputs, but instead utilizes a distance metric to infer the boundaries of the transformed feature space. M4GP also incorporates a novel GP representation and advanced selection methods to improve its performance.

GP has also been proposed to fill various roles in tailored learning systems for image classification. It has been used, for example, as a way to learn image embeddings for an ensemble method [20], as an interactive learning tool for remote sensing [4], and as a binary classifier in a pulmonary nodule detection system [3]. Liu [20] noted the potential for GP to perform dimensionality reduction efficiently in large-scale settings, as we noted earlier. M4GP differs from these approaches in two ways: first, it focuses on the capacity for low- and high-dimensionality feature extraction to flexibly suit the needs of the problem, and second, it applies to general multiclass classification problems.

4   Experimental Analysis

The experimental section consists of two parts. First, we compared M4GP to other GP methods, including *bool* and *float* methods described above, M2GP, and M3GP. Second, we compared M4GP to off-the-shelf methods on a set of biomedical data sets using a full hyper-parameter optimization strategy.

The settings for the first set of experiments are shown in Table 1. The settings for the methods match those used in the M2GP and M3GP papers, with the exception of program size limits (specified in numbers of elements rather than tree depth) and initial dimensionality range. The same set of problems from the original papers are used for these experiments to facilitate the comparison. Six of the eight problems used for comparing the GP methods are from the UCI data repository [18] and are summarized in Table 1. Two others, mcd3 and mcd10, are satellite data sets from [38]. Two versions of M4GP are tested: M4GP with lexicase selection (M4GP-lx), and tournament selection (M4GP-tn). Each method is run for 30 trials, and for each trial the data is randomly partitioned into 70% training and 30% testing.

The second set of experiments are designed to compare M4GP to six common classification methods available in Scikit Learn [30]: NB, LR, KNN, SVC, RF and NC. NC uses the classification strategy of Eq. 1, and therefore provides a comparison for M4GP against using the raw feature representation with the same discriminant function. For each method, hyper-parameter optimization is conducted on the training set using 5-fold cross-validation. In order to enforce some balance in the hyper-parameter optimization step, each method is restricted to 50 parameter combinations. We report and compare classification accuracy on the test set. The experimental design is summarized in Table 2.

For this comparison, 16 biomedical data sets are used, varying from 2 to 4 classes, 88 to 3772 samples, and 7 to 1000 features. 10 of the 16 problems are open-source, real-world data sets available from the OpenML repository [40]. They consist of different biomedical tasks such as medical diagnosis, post-operative decision making, and identification of exon boundaries in DNA. Six synthetic problems generated using GAMETES [37], are included. These problems embed 2- and 3-way epistatic interactions (i.e. non-additive interaction among genes) within noisy data sets with 20 or 1000 attributes. The goal of this problem is to test the ability of ML algorithms to identify these types of interactions common in genome-wide association studies [24]. Two of the GAMETES problems also test heterogeneity by embedding two separate, semi-overlapping epistatic interactions into the data.

Table 1. Experimental setup for the comparison of GP methods.

Setting	Value
Population size	500
Max Generations	100
Crossover / Mutation	50/50%
Ephemeral random constants [14] range	[0,1]
Program size limits by # nodes	[3, 100]
Initial dimensionality range (d)	[1,33]
Termination criterion	generations or perfect training accuracy
Trials	30
Train/test split	70/30

Data Set	heart	mcd3	mcd10	movl	seg	vowel	wav	yeast
Classes	2	3	10	15	7	11	3	10
Attributes	13	6	6	90	19	13	40	8
Samples	270	322	6798	360	2310	990	5000	7797

5 Results

The results of the comparison of GP methods is first discussed in Sect. 5.1, followed by the comparison of several ML methods on the biomedical data sets in Sect. 5.2.

5.1 Comparison to Other GP Methods

As a first point of comparison, we analyze the choice of GP classification method (*bool, float* or distance) based on the test accuracy for the first set of problems in Fig. 2. The distance-based classification method, i.e. M4GP, outperforms the

Table 2. Experimental setup for the biomedical problems. The hyper-parameters that were searched are shown on the right. Below the biomedical data sets are listed. GMT stands for GAMETES data sets, which are named according to number of epistatic loci (w), number of attributes (a), noise fraction (n), and heterogeneity fraction (h).

Method	hyper-parameters
M4GP	Population size (100, 250, 500); generations (10,50,100); selection method (tournament, lexicase); max length (10, 50, 100)
Gaussian Naïve Bayes	none
Logistic Regression	Regularization coefficient (0.1,...,20); penalty (ℓ_1,ℓ_2); fit intercept (True, False); dual formulation (True, False)
Support Vector Classifier	Regularization coefficient (0.01,1,100,'auto'); γ (0.01, 10, 1000, 'auto'); kernel (linear, RBF); decision function shape ('ovo','ovr')
Random Forest Classifier	No. estimators (10, 100, 1000); minimum weight fraction for leaf (0.0, 0.25, 0.5); max features ($sqrt$, log_2, None); splitting criterion (entropy, gini)
K-Nearest Neighbor Classifier	K (1,2,...,25); weights (uniform, distance)
Nearest Centroid Classifier	distance metric (Euclidean, Mahalanobis)

Training and Test Methodology	
Hyper-parameter optimization	5-fold cross-validation
Train/Test split	50/50
Trials	30
Score	Accuracy

Data Set	Classes	Samples	Dimensions
allbp	3	3772	29
allhyper	4	3771	29
allhypo	3	3770	29
biomed	2	209	8
breast-cancer-wisconsin	2	569	30
breast-cancer	2	286	9
diabetes	2	768	8
dna	3	3186	180
GMT 2w-20a-0.1n	2	1600	20
GMT 2w-20a-0.4n	2	1600	20
GMT 3w-20a-0.2n	2	1600	20
GMT 2w-1000a-0.4n	2	1600	1000
GMT 2w-20a-0.4n-0.5h	2	1600	20
GMT 2w-20a-0.4n-0.75h	2	1600	20
liver-disorder	2	345	6
postoperative-patient-data	2	88	8

other methods on all problems, 7 out of 8 by a large margin. The distance-based method also has the advantage of less variability in its performance compared to the other methods. From these results it is clear that the distance-based classifier has a distinct advantage over *bool* and *float* methods on these problems. This validates our choice to use M4GP in comparison to other ML methods on the set of biomedical problems.

As a second point of comparison, we benchmark the results of M4GP to M2GP and M3GP in Fig. 3. The results of M4GP using lexicase selection and tournament selection are both displayed. In order to test statistical significance, pairwise Wilcoxon rank-sum tests are performed with Holm correction for multiple comparisons. We use a significance level of $p < 0.01$ in the following reporting. The results indicate that M4GP-tn significantly outperforms M2GP on 4 out of

8 problems (heart, mcd3, vowel, and wav), and significantly outperforms than M3GP on 5 out of 8 problems (heart, mcd3, vowel, wav and movl). M4GP-lx significantly outperforms M2GP on 5/8 problems and outperforms M3GP on 6/8 problems. Conversely, M3GP does not significantly outperform M4GP-lx on any problem, and only outperforms M4GP-tn on one problem (mcd10). In addition, on one problem (movl), M2GP outperforms M3GP, M4GP-tn and M4GP-lx. A closer look at these runs indicates that most finish within the first few generations due to perfect training scores, which indicates this problem is likely to be solved easily by random search. Given that M2GP begins with smaller programs, it is more likely than M4GP to not over-fit in the first few generations. In summary, M4GP-lx is able to produce significantly better results for most problems, and in other cases produce results on par with the previous methods.

The choice of selection method results in mixed performance for M4GP. M4GP-lx significantly outperforms M4GP-tn on two problems, whereas M4GP-tn outperforms M4GP-lx on one problem, meaning the selection mechanism in M4GP is problem dependent. Because the selection method is kept as a hyper-parameter for the biomedical data sets, the optimization procedure is able to test both selection methods in the subsequent set of experiments.

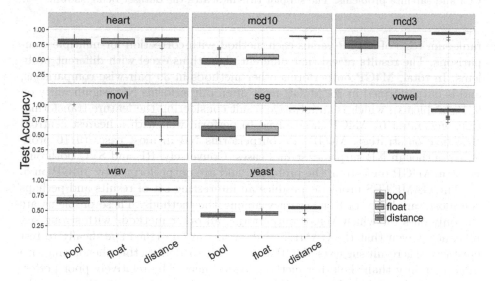

Fig. 2. Test accuracies for each GP classification method on the set of UCI and satellite problems. The distance method corresponds to the M4GP algorithm. The subplot title indicates the dataset being shown.

5.2   Comparison to Other ML Methods

The results of the ML comparisons on the biomedical problems are compared in Fig. 4. Classification accuracy on the test set for 30 trials is plotted. The statistical significance of the results is analyzed in Table 3 according to Wilcoxon

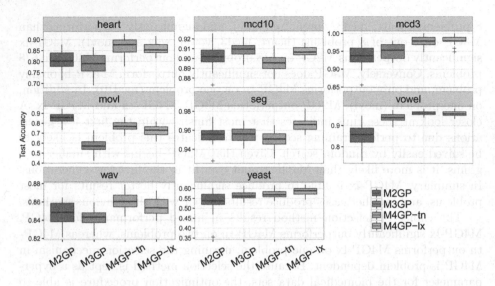

Fig. 3. Test accuracies for each Mahalanobis distance-based GP method on the set of UCI and satellite problems. The subplot title indicates the dataset being shown.

rank-sum tests of M4GP versus each method with correction for multiple comparisons. The results reveal that different algorithms excel with different problems. In total, M4GP outperforms other methods in 39 pair-wise comparisons, and is outperformed in 26. M4GP most often outperforms NC (significantly on 9/16 problems), which is an intuitive result considering the feature transformations generated by M4GP are evolved to perform well with a nearest centroid classification strategy. M4GP also outperforms NB in most cases (9/16 problems), although NB surpasses it in 2 cases. Conversely, RF and SVC both outperform M4GP on 7/16 of the problems, and are outperformed by M4GP on 5.

The GAMETES problems produce an interesting set of results and perhaps the most variability in test accuracy among the methods. These problems are the only ones for which M4GP outperforms all other methods with strong significance. Given that the GAMETES data sets are designed specifically to test epistasis, this result suggests M4GP may be able to identify this phenomena with more certainty than the other methods tested here. The relatively poor performance of most of the other tested methods is explained by their reliance on the identification of univariate correlations of the raw features with the class labels. The GAMETES data sets we tested are void of these so-called main effects, instead requiring the method to detect epistasis in the data set to produce accurate classifiers. M4GP is naturally suited for this task due to its capacity for nonlinear, multi-variate feature transformations.

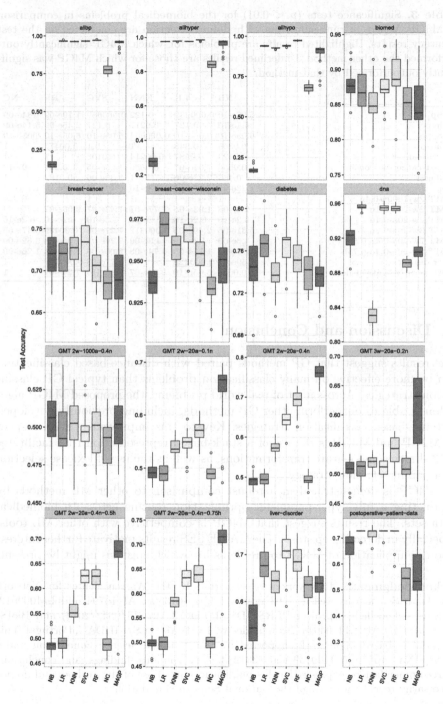

Fig. 4. Test accuracies for each method on the set of biomedical problems. The subplot title indicates the dataset being shown.

Table 3. Significance tests ($p < 0.01$) for the biomedical problems in comparison to M4GP. Wilcoxon rank-sum tests with Holm correction are conducted on the test accuracy results. Highlighted results are problems for which M4GP significantly outperformed the other method. Underlined results are those for which M4GP was significantly outperformed by that method.

	NB	LR	KNN	SVC	RF	NC
allbp	6.06e-10	0.000239	0.122	0.000659	1.19e-09	1.84e-09
allhyper	6.1e-10	0.127	0.0217	0.127	2.45e-09	5.14e-09
allhypo	6.05e-10	6.05e-10	0.000664	6.05e-10	6.05e-10	6.05e-10
biomed	0.0355	0.348	1	0.1	0.00475	1
breast-cancer	0.0123	0.0587	0.00214	0.0103	1	1
breast-cancer-wisconsin	0.0656	7.04e-07	0.0656	1.95e-05	0.231	0.012
diabetes	0.463	2.23e-06	1	3.39e-06	0.0192	1
dna	1.23e-05	6.13e-10	6.13e-10	6.13e-10	6.13e-10	1.13e-07
GMT 2w-1000a-0.4n	1	1	1	1	1	0.236
GMT 2w-20a-0.1n	2.2e-08	1.93e-08	7.77e-07	7.43e-07	9.06e-07	1.46e-08
GMT 2w-20a-0.4n	6.2e-10	6.2e-10	6.2e-10	6.2e-10	6.2e-10	6.2e-10
GMT 3w-20a-0.2n	5.31e-05	2.49e-05	0.000512	7.21e-05	0.00439	6.47e-05
GMT 2w-20a-0.4n-0.5h	4.3e-09	4.3e-09	4.3e-09	7.76e-08	4.04e-08	3.62e-09
GMT 2w-20a-0.4n-0.75h	1.76e-09	1.76e-09	4.74e-08	5.06e-08	6.51e-08	1.76e-09
liver-disorder	2.59e-06	0.000428	1	3.77e-06	0.000122	1
postoperative-patient-data	0.0016	6.65e-10	2.34e-07	6.65e-10	7.24e-09	1

6   Discussion and Conclusion

The results suggest that GP methods paired with distance-based classification can be more effective on many classification problems than typical GP classification strategies. Across a set of real-world problems, the proposed M4GP algorithm is able to outperform other GP methods, including previously developed distance-based classification strategies. Key to this improvement with respect to M2GP and M3GP is the use of a stack-based representation that facilitates multidimensional feature transformations, as well as the use of lexicase selection as a parent selection strategy.

M4GP is demonstrated in a robust comparison to other ML methods by conducting a full hyper-parameter optimization routine across 16 biomedical data sets. The results suggest that M4GP is competitive with other ML tools, especially in detecting epistasis. The GAMETES results motivate further interest into the application of M4GP to problems for which epistasis might be present.

Acknowledgments. This work was supported by the Warren Center for Network and Data Science, as well as NIH grants P30-ES013508, AI116794 and LM009012. S. Silva acknowledges project PERSEIDS (PTDC/EMS-SIS/0642/2014) and BioISI RD unit, UID/MULTI/04046/2013, funded by FCT/MCTES/PIDDAC, Portugal. This material is based upon work supported by the National Science Foundation under Grants Nos. 1617087, 1129139 and 1331283. Any opinions, findings, and conclusions or recommendations expressed in this publication are those of the authors and do not necessarily reflect the views of the National Science Foundation.

References

1. Arnaldo, I., O'Reilly, U.-M., Veeramachaneni, K.: Building predictive models via feature synthesis, pp. 983–990. ACM Press (2015)
2. Caruana, R., Niculescu-Mizil, A.: An empirical comparison of supervised learning algorithms. In: Proceedings of the 23rd International Conference on Machine Learning, pp. 161–168. ACM (2006)
3. Choi, W.-J.: Genetic programming-based feature transform and classification for the automatic detection of pulmonary nodules on computed tomography images. Inf. Sci. **212**, 57–78 (2012)
4. dos Santos, J.A., Ferreira, C.D.: A relevance feedback method based on genetic programming for classification of remote sensing images. Inf. Sci. **181**(13), 2671–2684 (2011)
5. Espejo, P.G., Ventura, S., Herrera, F.: A survey on the application of genetic programming to classification. IEEE Trans. Appl. Rev. **40**(2), 121–144 (2010)
6. Fang, Y., Li, J.: A review of tournament selection in genetic programming. In: Cai, Z., Hu, C., Kang, Z., Liu, Y. (eds.) ISICA 2010. LNCS, vol. 6382, pp. 181–192. Springer, Heidelberg (2010). doi:10.1007/978-3-642-16493-4_19
7. Guyon, I.: An introduction to variable and feature selection. J. Mach. Learn. Res. **3**, 1157–1182 (2003)
8. Hall, M., Frank, E., Holmes, G., Pfahringer, B., Reutemann, P., Witten, I.H.: The WEKA data mining software: an update. ACM SIGKDD Explor. Newsl. **11**(1), 10–18 (2009)
9. Helmuth, T., Spector, L., Matheson, J.: Solving uncompromising problems with lexicase selection. IEEE Trans. Evol. Comput. **PP**(99), 1 (2014)
10. Icke, I., Bongard, J.C.: Improving genetic programming based symbolic regression using deterministic machine learning. In: 2013 IEEE Congress on Evolutionary Computation (CEC), pp. 1763–1770. IEEE (2013)
11. Ingalalli, V., Silva, S., Castelli, M., Vanneschi, L.: A multi-dimensional genetic programming approach for multi-class classification problems. In: Nicolau, M., Krawiec, K., Heywood, M.I., Castelli, M., García-Sánchez, P., Merelo, J.J., Rivas Santos, V.M., Sim, K. (eds.) EuroGP 2014. LNCS, vol. 8599, pp. 48–60. Springer, Heidelberg (2014). doi:10.1007/978-3-662-44303-3_5
12. Jain, A.K., Murty, M.N., Flynn, P.J.: Data clustering: a review. ACM Comput. Surv. **31**(3), 264–323 (1999)
13. Kishore, J.K.: Application of genetic programming for multicategory pattern classification. IEEE Trans. Evol. Comput. **4**(3), 242–258 (2000)
14. Koza, J.R.: Genetic Programming: On the Programming of Computers by Means of Natural Selection. MIT Press, Cambridge (1992)
15. Cava, L.: Inference of compact nonlinear dynamic models by epigenetic local search. Eng. Appl. Artif. Intell. **55**, 292–306 (2016)
16. La Cava, W., Spector, L., Danai, K.: Epsilon-lexicase selection for regression. In: Proceedings of the Genetic and Evolutionary Computation Conference 2016, GECCO 2016, pp. 741–748. ACM, New York (2016)
17. Li, T.: A comparative study of feature selection and multiclass classification methods for tissue classification based on gene expression. Bioinformatics **20**(15), 2429–2437 (2004)
18. Lichman, M.: UCI Machine Learning Repository. University of California, School of Information and Computer Sciences, Irvine (2013)

19. Liu, H.: Toward integrating feature selection algorithms for classification and clustering. IEEE Trans. Knowl. Data Eng. **17**(4), 491–502 (2005)
20. Liu, L.: Evolutionary compact embedding for large-scale image classification. Inf. Sci. **316**, 567–581 (2015)
21. Loveard, T., Ciesielski, V.: Representing classification problems in genetic programming. In: Proceedings of the 2001 Congress on Evolutionary Computation, vol. 2, pp. 1070–1077. IEEE (2001)
22. McConaghy, T.: FFX fast, scalable, deterministic symbolic regression technology. In: Riolo, R., Vladislavleva, E., Moore, J.H. (eds.) Genetic Programming Theory and Practice IX, pp. 235–260. Springer, Heidelberg (2011)
23. Melin, P.: A new neural network model based on the LVQ algorithm for multi-class classification of arrhythmias. Inf. Sci. **279**, 483–497 (2014)
24. Moore, J.H.: The ubiquitous nature of epistasis in determining susceptibility to common human diseases. Hum. Hered. **56**(1–3), 73–82 (2003)
25. Moore, J.H., Asselbergs, F.W., Williams, S.M.: Bioinformatics challenges for genome-wide association studies. Bioinformatics **26**(4), 445–455 (2010)
26. Moore, J.H., Greene, C.S., Hill, D.P.: Identification of novel genetic models of glaucoma using the emergent genetic programming-based artificial intelligence system. In: Riolo, R., Worzel, W.P., Kotanchek, M. (eds.) Genetic Programming Theory and Practice XII, pp. 17–35. Springer, Heidelberg (2015)
27. Muñoz, L., Silva, S., Trujillo, L.: M3GP Multiclass Classification with GP. In: Genetic Programming, pp. 78–91. Springer, Heidelberg (2015)
28. Murphy, K.P.: Machine learning: a probabilistic perspective. a probabilistic perspective. Adaptive computation. MIT Press, Cambridge (2012)
29. Nguyen, T.: Hidden Markov models for cancer classification using gene expression profiles. Inf. Sci. **316**, 293–307 (2015)
30. Pedregosa, F., Varoquaux, G., Gramfort, A., Michel, V., Thirion, B., Grisel, O., Blondel, M., Prettenhofer, P., Weiss, R., Dubourg, V., et al.: Scikit-learn machine learning in python. J. Mach. Learn. Res. **12**(Oct), 2825–2830 (2011)
31. Perkis, T.: Stack-based genetic programming. In: Proceedings of the First IEEE Conference on Evolutionary Computation, IEEE World Congress on Computational Intelligence, pp. 148–153. IEEE (1994)
32. Poli, R.: A field guide to genetic programming. Lulu Press, Raleigh (2008). [S.I.]. http://www.lulu.com
33. Quinlan, J.R.: C4.5: Programs for Machine Learning. Elsevier, Amsterdam (2014)
34. Silva, S., Muñoz, L., Trujillo, L., Ingalalli, V., Castelli, M., Vanneschi, L.: Multiclass classificatin through multidimensional clustering. In: Riolo, R., Worzel, W.P., Kotanchek, M., Kordon, A. (eds.) Genetic Programming Theory and Practice XIII, vol. 13. Springer, Ann Arbor (2015)
35. Spector, L.: Assessment of problem modality by differential performance of lexicase selection in genetic programming: a preliminary report. In: Proceedings of the Fourteenth International Conference on Genetic and Evolutionary Computation Conference Companion, pp. 401–408 (2012)
36. Tibshirani, R.: Diagnosis of multiple cancer types by Shrunken centroids of gene expression. Proc. Natl. Acad. Sci. **99**(10), 6567–6572 (2002)
37. Urbanowicz, R.J., Kiralis, J., Sinnott-Armstrong, N.A., Heberling, T., Fisher, J.M., Moore, J.H.: GAMETES: a fast, direct algorithm for generating pure, strict, epistatic models with random architectures. BioData Min. **5**(1), 1 (2012)
38. USGS. U.S. geological survey (USGS) earth resources observation systems (EROS) data center (EDC)

39. Vanneschi, L.: Classification of oncologic data with genetic programming. J. Artif. Evol. Appl. **1–13**, 1–13 (2009)
40. Vanschoren, J., van Rijn, J.N., Bischl, B., Torgo, L.: OpenML: networked science in machine learning. SIGKDD Explor. **15**(2), 49–60 (2013)

EvoCOMNET

Meta-Heuristically Seeded Genetic Algorithm
for Independent Job Scheduling
in Grid Computing

Muhanad Tahrir Younis[✉], Shengxiang Yang, and Benjamin Passow

Centre for Computational Intelligence (CCI),
School of Computer Science and Informatics, De Montfort University,
The Gateway, Leicester LE1 9BH, UK
p14017957@my365.dmu.ac.uk, syang@dmu.ac.uk, benpassow@ieee.org

Abstract. Grid computing is an infrastructure which connects geographically distributed computers owned by various organizations allowing their resources, such as computational power and storage capabilities, to be shared, selected, and aggregated. Job scheduling problem is one of the most difficult tasks in grid computing systems. To solve this problem efficiently, new methods are required. In this paper, a seeded genetic algorithm is proposed which uses a meta-heuristic algorithm to generate its initial population. To evaluate the performance of the proposed method in terms of minimizing the makespan, the Expected Time to Compute (ETC) simulation model is used to carry out a number of experiments. The results show that the proposed algorithm performs better than other selected techniques.

Keywords: Meta-heuristic algorithms · Seeded genetic algorithm · Ant colony optimization · Job scheduling · Grid computing · Makespan

1   Introduction

Grid Computing has been defined as a type of parallel and distributed infrastructure which allows the geographically distributed autonomous and heterogeneous resources to be shared, selected and aggregated dynamically depending on their availability, capability, performance, cost, and user's quality-of-service requirements. This infrastructure offers to its users the same processing capabilities provided by supercomputers by creating a virtual supercomputer from connecting various networked and loosely coupled computers together allowing their resources to be shared among users. Computers, processing elements, software applications, printers, network interfaces, storage space and data are examples of resources. Middleware, computer software which provide basic services for resource management, security, monitoring, and so forth, are used to connect all these resources to a network. Due to the fact that resources are owned by various administrative organizations, local policies are defined to specify what is shared, who is allowed to access what and when, and under what conditions. The Grid

© Springer International Publishing AG 2017
G. Squillero and K. Sim (Eds.): EvoApplications 2017, Part I, LNCS 10199, pp. 177–189, 2017.
DOI: 10.1007/978-3-319-55849-3_12

architecture is based on the creation of Virtual Organizations (VOs), a set of rules defined by individuals and institutions to control resource sharing [8]. By sharing some or all of its resources, a physical organization can be part of one or more VOs [10]. Grid Computing has been increasingly used by commercial and non-commercial clients as a utility for solving scientific, complex mathematical, and academic problems, as well as for diverse applications [9].

In grid computing, a key concern is job scheduling. In general, job scheduling can be defined as the mapping of jobs to corresponding appropriate resources in order to process them [13]. To evaluate the job scheduling performance, an objective function should be defined such as maximizing resources utilization, minimizing the makespan, and maximizing load balancing [20]. The scheduler's efficiency strongly relays on the algorithm applied to do the scheduling. Different algorithms could be used to do the scheduling which varies from simple heuristic methods to meta-heuristic methods. However, to enhance the overall performance of the grid, the meta-heuristic approaches are more likely preferred [19].

Job scheduling in grid computing is known to be a NP-complete optimization problem, and hence, many meta-heuristic methods, which are capable of searching large search spaces very efficiently and provide optimal or near optimal solutions, have been proposed [2]. One of these methods is Ant Colony Optimization (ACO) which is a search algorithm that mimics the behavior of ants in searching for a path between their nest and a source of food [5]. While ants move back and forth from their colony to a source of food, they leave a substance called pheromone on the ground. This substance can be sensed by other ants and this allows indirect communications among them. Ants which find the shortest path to the source of food will, then, return back to their colony earlier than ants with longer paths, which means that the shortest path has been marched over more than other paths and its pheromone density will be higher. Ants will choose the path with the highest pheromone concentration, i.e. the path with high pheromone levels will attract more ants and will contain even more pheromone. However, if this path remains after the consumption of food, it would seriously obstruct the ants' ability to find food. To cope with this situation, pheromone trails evaporate over time, which is a mechanism to forget old decisions, is used [7]. The ACO algorithm has been used to solve various NP-complete optimization problems such as Travelling Salesman problem, assignment problem, graph coloring, and job-shop scheduling successfully [22]. As a result, the ACO algorithm is a good candidate for job scheduling in Grid computing.

In addition to ACO, there are many other meta-heuristic methods which have been proposed to solve the problem of job scheduling in grid computing. One of these methods is Genetic algorithm (GA), a population-based meta-heuristic search method which is inspired by the evolution of living beings. The traditional GA starts with an initial population, a group of solutions, then seeks to find the approximately best solution by applying selection, crossover and mutation operators. The simplest way to generate the initial population is the random method. However, the quality of the final solution found by GA could be effected by the quality of the initial solution as generating an initial population randomly may cause the situation where the population has more individuals with worst quality and, sometimes, infeasible solutions than best quality solutions which means more time is required to find an optimal solution, more generations are required to evolve best solution, and the convergence rate is reduced. Therefore, a new method to generate the initial generation is needed and actually, several studies have been suggested in this context [21].

A study presented by [23] developed several versions of GA and studied the different configuration issues of GA to solve the Travelling Salesman Problem (TSP) and claimed that using heuristic methods to seed the initial population can improve significantly the efficiency of GA. An improved GA for the rectilinear Steiner problem by [14] proposed a hybrid seeding population technique. The author has compared the efficiency of the proposed seeding technique with the random technique of generating the initial population of GA and concludes that the seeding technique significantly improves the performance. The authors in [11] have proposed a new method to generate the initial population of GA for the optimization of 2d and 3d truss structures. Their work has examined the effect of seeding the initial population on the performance of the GA in terms of capturing the global optimum and concluded that the proposed seeding method reduces the number of generations needed to find the optimal solution and enhances the convergence capability which consequently enhances the overall performance of the GA.

In this work, a GA for static independent job scheduling problem in grid computing is proposed. The proposed algorithm uses a meta-heuristic algorithm, which is ACO, to seed its initial population. The work focuses on minimizing the makespan and the Expected Time to Compute (ETC) model is used to test the performance. The performance of the proposed GA has been compared with Min-Min heuristic, GA with random initial generation, GA with initial population seeded by Min-Min heuristic, and ACO.

The rest of the paper is organized as follows. Section 2 presents the related work on ACO and GA in solving the problem of job scheduling in grid computing. The simulation model used to test the performance of the proposed method is described in Sect. 3. Section 4 explains the use of ACO for job scheduling in grid computing while Sect. 5 describes the proposed method. Section 6 presents the results of applying the proposed GA in grid computing. Finally, the conclusions and future works are provided in Sect. 7.

2 Related Work

An ant colony optimization based scheduler for job scheduling in grid computing was proposed by [16]. Minimization of the total job waiting time was the main goal of the proposed scheduler which consists of four steps. The proposed scheduler used local update and global update rules to update the pheromone value on each resource. In addition, the scheduler has used the Completion Time (CT), which is the time a machine needs to finish executing a job measured as clock time. The authors defined a grid environment in which jobs arrive to the system at different times, the availability of resources is regularly changing, one job could be processed by each processor per unit time and jobs are independent of each other. In the study, the performance of ACO based scheduler has been compared with First Come First Serve (FCFS), Earliest Due Date (EDD) and Earliest Release Date techniques (ERD). The results showed that ACO has the best average-case of the waiting time.

A more efficient ACO-based grid scheduling algorithm was introduced by [18]. The developed scheduler has modified the original ACO algorithm presented in [5] by changing the basic pheromone updating rule. This modification increased efficiently the algorithm performance in terms of makespan compared to the original ACO.

The authors in [22] have developed a hybrid algorithm to improve the performance of other similar techniques described in [3]. The hybrid algorithm has combined ACO with local search. The results show that the use of a local search with ACO increases the quality of the solution.

ACO is not the only algorithm used to solve the problem of job scheduling in grid computing. The literature shows that there are many other meta-heuristic methods which have been suggested in this field. One of these methods is Genetic Algorithm (GA), a population-based heuristic search method which is inspired by the evolution of living beings. GA starts with an initial population, which is a group of solutions usually generated randomly, and then seeks to find the approximately best solution by applying selection, crossover and mutation operators. GA has been quite used for solving many combinatorial optimization problems. Eleven static heuristic methods have been applied in [3] to solve the problem of job scheduling in heterogeneous environment by minimizing the makespan. The experimental results show that GA outperforms the other ten methods used in the study. The authors used a population of 200 individuals which is generated either randomly or by seeding the population with one individual generated using Min-Min heuristic method [12] and 199 individuals generated randomly.

A study proposed by [4] presented the use of GA for efficient multi-objective job scheduling in grid computing systems. To introduce diversity, two heuristics methods, which are Longest Job to Fastest Resource – Shortest Job to Fastest Resource (LJFR- SJFR) [1] and Minimum Completion Time (MCT) [17], have been used beside the random method to initialize the initial population. The authors considered two encoding schemes, namely the direct and the permutation methods, and implemented several GA operators.

A heuristic method called Min-Max has been proposed in [13] for job scheduling in heterogeneous environments. The performance of the proposed method has been compared with five popular heuristics which are: Min-Min, Max-Min, LJFR-SJFR, sufferage, and WorkQueue. The authors investigated the effect of using these heuristics for initializing simulated annealing (SA) and found that the Min-Min and Min-Max heuristics are more efficient than others.

3   Simulation Model

In order to simulate several heterogeneous scheduling scenarios in a realistic way and to allow a fair comparison of the presented methods, a well-known benchmark has been used. In this study, the Expected Time to Compute (ETC) benchmark simulation model is used which has been introduced in [3] to address the problem of static scheduling algorithms for Heterogeneous Computing (HC) such as grid computing. The expected execution time of the jobs on each machine has been assumed to be available in advance in a two dimensional array. This assumption is realistic since it is easy to gather information about the jobs requirements and the computation power of resources from the users, by predications or from historic data [25]. To capture the various characteristics of HC environments, the model defines three different types of metrics: consistency, job heterogeneity, and resource heterogeneity. A matrix is said to be consistent if it contains a resource R_n which is capable of processing a job J_k faster than another resource in the system R_m, and R_n processes all other jobs J_t faster than R_m. If a resource R_n executes some jobs faster than R_m and some slower, then the matrix is said to be inconsistent. A semi consistent matrix is an inconsistent matrix which has a sub matrix of a consistent matrix. Job heterogeneity models the statistical distribution for jobs execution times with two values high or low. Resource heterogeneity models the distribution when executing the same job in all machines, and also has two values high or low. Therefore, we need 12 distinct combinations of ETC matrix to consider all these various characteristics. Table 1 shows a 15×10 subset of the ETC matrix with semi-consistent, low job heterogeneity and low resource heterogeneity. The results provided in this study used ETC matrices of size 512×16.

The problem description under the ETC model is defined as:

1. A number of jobs, n, that has to be scheduled. These jobs are independent to each other, any job can be processed by any resource, and are non-preemptive, which means that a job must be processed entirely by a single resource.
2. A number of resources, m, to process the submitted set of independent jobs. These resources are heterogeneous.
3. The ETC matrix of size n × m, where ETC[i][j] represents the estimated time for executing the job i in the resource j.

The job scheduling problem in grid computing is known to be multi-objective, therefore, several objective functions can be considered for this problem such as makespan, load balancing, and flowtime [24]. In this study, we consider the minimization of makespan, which is defined as the finishing time of the latest job and can be calculated by Eq. (1).

$$makespan = min_{s \in Solutions} max_{j \in Jobs}(F_j) \qquad (1)$$

where Solutions is the set of all possible solutions and Jobs is the set of all jobs submitted to the system and F_j represents the time when job j is finished [15].

Table 1. A 15×10 subset of the Expected Time to Compute (ETC) matrix with semi-consistent, low job heterogeneity and low resource heterogeneity. r_i $(1 \leq i \leq 10)$ is a resource

job	r_1	r_2	r_3	r_4	r_5	r_6	r_7	r_8	r_9	r_{10}
j_1	4.3	135.9	194.5	223.8	303.0	346.6	418.4	419.0	487.5	516.7
j_2	353.5	472.9	478.4	117.5	338.8	573.7	431.4	655.5	545.8	207.0
j_3	17.2	18.9	24.5	33.2	39.7	47.2	58.4	62.1	76.2	83.5
j_4	182.2	358.3	180.1	539.6	511.8	474.3	131.0	89.7	571.8	363.1
j_5	55.3	99.7	107.0	198.0	219.1	237.3	238.0	244.3	306.8	353.1
j_6	405.8	88.7	59.9	82.9	442.6	352.3	62.9	207.1	49.5	413.2
j_7	55.8	79.0	84.7	110.2	143.9	176.0	180.7	182.5	189.3	203.8
j_8	166.6	334.4	310.1	194.7	88.5	349.0	310.6	118.6	124.6	110.5
j_9	108.2	119.3	138.7	144.7	169.7	193.5	223.4	248.1	293.3	312.9
j_{10}	109.8	127.7	30.2	125.0	136.7	56.3	92.7	25.5	89.7	187.8
j_{11}	114.1	118.3	121.8	318.0	332.2	391.5	391.7	477.3	541.0	568.9
j_{12}	186.5	635.7	727.6	308.9	747.8	563.8	146.4	485.3	728.3	205.8
j_{13}	212.8	216.0	248.4	269.2	306.1	381.9	413.4	439.2	486.6	582.6
j_{14}	250.6	70.4	106.1	136.2	163.5	100.1	211.3	108.0	113.5	174.7
j_{15}	114.9	213.2	233.7	261.5	280.4	317.3	354.6	385.0	453.0	513.1

4   Applying ACO to the Job Scheduling Problem

ACO has been applied for several problems closely related to job scheduling problem in grid computing. Therefore, it seems an appropriate candidate in this environment. An ACO-based scheduler is introduced in this section which follows the ACO algorithm design explained in [6].

The first step in any ACO algorithm is to determine what information the pheromone trail encodes. The pheromone trail allows the ants to communicate indirectly to each other and share useful information about optimal solutions. Since we have n jobs to be scheduled into m resources, a pheromone matrix, τ, of size n $\times$ m is needed in which the value of $\tau[i][j]$ represents the favorability of assigning job i to resource j. In addition to the information encoded in the pheromone trial, the ants use heuristic information to build their solutions. In this study, the following heuristic has been used:

$$\eta_{ij} = \frac{1}{free[j]} \quad (2)$$

where the function free[j] denotes the time when machine j will be free.

If free[j] is small, η_{ij} will be a very large value. Thus if a resource is free earlier, it will be more desirable.

To measure the quality of the solutions, a fitness function must be defined. As mentioned earlier, the makespan is considered in this study. The makespan

---

Algorithm 1. The ACO-based scheduler

Step 1: While (Number of generation ≤ Maximum number of generations) do steps 2–5.

Step 2: Initialization

1. Let n be the number of jobs, m be the number of resources and k be the number of ants.
2. Initialize the pheromone deposit value τ_{ij} to a small value.
3. Let free[0..m-1]=0.
4. Initialize the pheromone evaporation.

Step 3: For each ant A, do the following:

1. Randomly select the job-resource pair (i, j) and add it to the scheduled list.
2. For all unscheduled jobs, do the following:

    a. description free[j] = free[j]+ETC[i, j].
    b. Calculate the heuristic function using Eq. (2).
    c. Calculate the probability matrix using Eq. (6).
    d. Determine the highest ρ_{xy} value.
    e. Select the next job-resource pair (i=x, j=y) and add it to the scheduled list.

Step 4: Find the best solution

1. Calculate the makespan of all solutions using Eq. (1).
2. The best solution is the one with the minimum makespan.

Step 5: Pheromone update

1. Calculate F_k using Eq. (5).
2. Calculate $\Delta\tau_{ij}$ using Eq. (4).
3. Calculate the new pheromone trail using Eq. (3).

---

of a solution is a good indicator of the general throughput of the grid system. Small value of makespan means that the algorithm is finding efficient mapping of jobs to resources.

To allow the communication among ants about the current states of the resources, a rule for updating the pheromone trial is needed and it is defined by Eq. (3):

$$\tau_{ij} = \rho * \tau_{ij} + \Delta\tau_{ij} \tag{3}$$

where i, j ∈ the best solution, ρ ($0 < \rho \leq 1$) is the decay parameter which is used to allow the ants to forget poor information and $\Delta\tau_{ij}$ is the amount of pheromone deposit to the path and is defined by Eq. (4) as:

$$\Delta\tau_{ij} = \frac{1 - \rho}{F_k} \tag{4}$$

where

$$F_k = max(free[i]) \tag{5}$$

As mentioned earlier, the ants use both the information encoded in the pheromone trial and the heuristic function to build their solutions. Each ant starts with two lists: scheduled list which is empty and unscheduled list which contains n jobs. The first job-resource mapping will be selected randomly. The heuristic function η_{ij}, then, will find the best resources available to process the unscheduled jobs. A job x is selected probabilistically to be processed by resource y using the transition rule defined by Eq. (6) as follows:

$$p_{xy} = \frac{[\tau_{xy}]^\alpha * [\eta_{xy}]^\beta * \frac{1}{ETC[x,y]}}{\sum [\tau_{xy}]^\alpha * [\eta_{xy}]^\beta * \frac{1}{ETC[x,y]}} \tag{6}$$

where α and β are two parameters used to define the relative weight of the pheromone and the heuristic respectively.

This process is repeated until all unscheduled jobs have been mapped and that represents a complete solution. Each ant in the colony does the same procedure to build a solution. The colony size, which is the number of ants, is k. The pheromone trail update rule is applied as described in Eq. (3) when all k ants built their solutions. Similar to other meta-heuristics algorithms, ACO has many parameters that need to be tuned. To achieve an efficient performance, these parameters should be chosen carefully. The maximum number of generations is 5, each generation (or colony) has 50 ants. The decay parameter ρ was 0.5 while $\alpha = 2$ and $\beta = 30$. Algorithm 1 shows the complete ACO-based scheduler for job scheduling in grid computing.

5   Applying GA to the Job Scheduling Problem

Genetic Algorithm (GA), a population-based heuristic search method which is inspired by natural evolution. GA starts with an initial population, a group of solutions usually generated randomly, then seeks to find the approximately best solution by applying selection, crossover and mutation operators. GA has been quite used for solving many optimization problems closely related to the job scheduling problem.

In this study, we used the GA-based scheduler proposed in [3] to solve the problem of job scheduling in grid computing. The scheduler main steps are explained as follows:

1. The solution representation: the authors used the direct representation to encode the individuals. In direct representation, each individual is represented as a list called solution of size equals to the number of jobs. The value of solution[x] represent the resource where job x is allocated. Therefore, the values in this list are integers in the range [1, m], where m is the total number of resources.
2. The initial generation: they used a population of 200 individuals which is generated either randomly or by seeding the population with one individual generated using the Min-Min heuristic method [12] and 199 individuals generated randomly.
3. The fitness function: the makespan was used to evaluate the fitness of individuals.

4. Create a new generation by applying GA operators:

   a. The selection operator: the rank-based roulette wheel method has been used. To guarantee that the best solution remains in the population, the elitist generational was implemented.

   b. The crossover operator: the one-point scheme is used with a probability of 0.6.

   c. The mutation operator: the mutation is done with a probability of 0.4 by randomly select an individual then randomly select a job and reassign it to a different resource.

5. Repeat from step 3 until the stopping criteria are true. The proposed GA stops when one of the following conditions is occurred: (a) 1000 generations, (b) the elite individual remain the same for 150 iterations, or (c) all individuals have the same solution.

The Min-Min heuristic [12] used in generating the initial population starts by computing the minimum completing time CT[i,j] for all jobs and resources. Then finds the job x with minimum CT[i, j] and allocates it to the resource that obtains it.

In this study, a meta-heuristic method, which is ACO, will be used to seed the initial population of GA for solving the problem of static independent job scheduling in grid computing. The proposed method will run ACO first for a specific number of iterations. The solutions found by ACO, then, will be used to seed the initial population of GA together with the random method. Three versions of the GA proposed by [3] are then considered here to study the effects of seeding the initial population of GA. All the three versions follow the main steps explained above. The only difference is the way the initial population is generated, The first version, called Random-GA, uses the random method to generate the initial population while the second version, called Min-GA, generates the initial population by seeding it with one individual generated using the Min-Min heuristic and 199 individuals generated randomly. The third version, called ACO-GA, runs first the ACO meta-heuristic algorithm, then uses the 50 solutions found by the ACO and 150 individuals generated randomly to seed the initial population.

6   Experiments and Results

Experiments have been carried out using an Intel T2080 CPU @ 1.73GHz with 2 GB RAM and all programs were written in Java language. To obtain the best, worst and median values, each algorithm was executed 100 times for each instance of the 12 ETC matrices. Table 2 provides the actual makespan while Fig. 1 shows the median makespan values. In the table, the first column represents the instance name, the second column represents the type of the results, namely Best, Worst or Median, the third, fourth, fifth, sixth and seventh columns represent the makespan found by Min-Min, Rnd-GA, Min-GA, ACO, and ACO-GA. The best results are indicated in bold.

Table 2. The best, worst, and median makespan results

Instance	B/W/M	Min	Rnd-GA	Min-GA	ACO	ACO-GA
u-c-hihi	Best	16613907.00	11081565.00	9050105.00	8570055.00	**8095185.00**
	Worst	16613907.00	12423588.00	9830633.00	8845919.00	**8355396.00**
	Median	16613907.00	11709830.00	9495092.00	8680503.00	**8210842.00**
u-c-hilo	Best	254880.70	193386.30	163221.10	159259.60	**155335.40**
	Worst	254880.70	201751.70	171102.40	161058.40	**157831.00**
	Median	254880.70	196916.15	166404.4	159787.10	**155945.10**
u-c-lohi	Best	558377.30	357089.90	295008.20	279429.20	**263120.30**
	Worst	558377.30	400989.20	317053.70	289153.40	**272172.70**
	Median	558377.30	374781.20	305801.80	282148.90	**266419.40**
u-c-lolo	Best	7789.00	6463.50	5496.90	5358.20	**5221.90**
	Worst	7789.00	6758.30	5684.00	5499.60	**5289.60**
	Median	7789.00	6614.10	5574.75	5456.90	**5246.45**
u-i-hihi	Best	3943275.90	6074364.30	3239078	3253050.00	**3056285.00**
	Worst	3943275.90	7653952.60	3488099.00	3385014.00	**3232376.00**
	Median	3943275.90	7052776.30	3358354.00	3314572.00	**3132457.00**
u-i-hilo	Best	85887.20	143994.60	77287.60	78051.70	**75524.60**
	Worst	85887.20	176494.20	79323.70	80282.70	**78018.50**
	Median	85887.20	160123.45	78262.25	79462.65	**76563.10**
u-i-lohi	Best	138091.40	211945.90	110578.30	111224.20	**104657.00**
	Worst	138091.40	266207.60	118082.70	115520.40	**111124.30**
	Median	138091.40	238080.55	114355.80	113785.90	**107216.20**
u-i-lolo	Best	3112.20	4538.00	2547.10	2594.90	**2484.20**
	Worst	3112.20	5773.00	2755.60	2646.40	**2552.70**
	Median	3112.20	5182.50	2674.15	2621.20	**2513.45**
u-s-hihi	Best	10591575.00	8580789.60	6534393.00	6044180.00	**5578565.00**
	Worst	10591575.00	11212404.00	7950509.00	6405586.00	**5877259.00**
	Median	10591575.00	9492592.40	7191440.00	6133150.00	**5707337.00**
u-s-hilo	Best	150658.20	152887.30	115180.30	108923.20	**104959.00**
	Worst	150658.20	192228.80	125965.10	111047.00	**108439.20**
	Median	150658.20	175001.90	120388.80	110017.70	**106000.80**
u-s-lohi	Best	317909.00	241510.20	188685.70	169244.60	**158247.80**
	Worst	317909.00	328735.10	236169.00	180159.50	**168558.20**
	Median	317909.00	282073.55	210498.70	175702.80	**161362.30**
u-s-lolo	Best	5357.20	5320.30	3927.20	3717.50	**3589.90**
	Worst	5357.20	6600.50	4350.20	3792.40	**3681.40**
	Median	5357.20	5807.75	4167.85	3763.40	**3632.85**

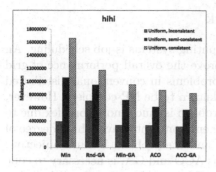

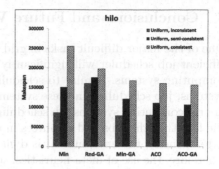

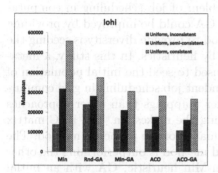

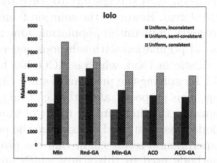

Fig. 1. Median makespan obtained by five methods in four different cases

In the table of results, the following abbreviation has been used to identify the type of ETC matric: x-y-zzww, where:

- x represents the type of probability distribution. In this study, the uniform distribution (u) has been used only.
- y represents the type of consistency, which has one of: c: consistent, i: inconsistent, s: semi-consistent.
- description zz represents the job heterogeneity, which could be either high (hi) or low (lo).
- description ww represents the resource heterogeneity, which could be either high (hi) or low (lo).

The results show clearly that ACO-GA outperforms the other approaches for all instances of ETC matrix tested in finding the minimum makespan. The performance order for all cases of the approaches used from best to worst was: ACO-GA, ACO, Min-GA, Rnd-GA, and then Min-Min. ACO provided the second best performance as it outperformed Min-GA, Rnd-GA, and Min-Min in consistent and semi-consistent cases. However, Min-GA performed better than ACO, GA, and Min-Min in some of inconsistent cases. The results also show the significant effect of seeding the initial population of GA either in the case of Min-GA which outperforms the normal Rnd-GA or in the case of ACO-GA which outperforms all other approaches used in this study.

7   Conclusions and Future Work

One of the major difficult tasks in grid computing systems is job scheduling. An efficient job scheduler will significantly improve the overall performance of grid computing systems. Similar to scheduling problems in conventional distributed systems, job scheduling in these systems is known to be NP-complete. However, in grid computing systems job scheduling problem is much more complex due to the fact that the jobs and resources in these environments have a high degree of heterogeneity, the environment is dynamic, and the problem is multi-objective. Therefore, the use of meta-heuristics, such as ACO and GA, is necessary to cope in practice with its complexity and difficulty. GA is a robust search method that has been used successfully to solve the problem of job scheduling in computational grid. However, the solution found by GA could be improved by providing diversity in its initial population. One method to provide diversity is seeding the initial population with solutions generated by heuristics. In this study, a meta-heuristic method, which is ACO, has been used to seed the initial population of GA for solving the problem of static independent job scheduling in grid computing. The proposed algorithm can find better mappings than other approaches found in the literature in terms of minimizing the makespan. The ETC matrix model has been used to examine the performance of the proposed method. The experimental results show that the proposed method is outperforming the other methods used in this study which are Min-Min heuristic, GA with an initial population generated randomly, GA with an initial population generated using Min-Min heuristic and random method, and ACO. The proposed GA seems a promising approach to scheduling in grid computing systems. However, there is much space for further improvements such as adding another objective so that the problem will be multi-objectives, adding a local search to the proposed method and testing it in a dynamic environment.

References

1. Abraham, A., Buyya, R., Nath, B.: Natures heuristics for scheduling jobs on computational grids. In: The 8th IEEE International Conference on Advanced Computing and Communications (ADCOM 2000), pp. 45–52 (2000)
2. Alobaedy, M.M., Ku-Mahamud, K.R.: Scheduling jobs in computational grid using hybrid ACS and GA approach. In: 2014 IEEE Computing, Communications and IT Applications Conference (ComComAp), pp. 223–228. IEEE (2014)
3. Braun, T.D., Siegel, H.J., Beck, N., Bölöni, L.L., Maheswaran, M., Reuther, A.I., Robertson, J.P., Theys, M.D., Yao, B., Hensgen, D., et al.: A comparison of eleven static heuristics for mapping a class of independent tasks onto heterogeneous distributed computing systems. J. Parallel Distrib. Comput. **61**(6), 810–837 (2001)
4. Carretero, J., Xhafa, F., Abraham, A.: Genetic algorithm based schedulers for grid computing systems. Int. J. Innovative Comput. Inf. Control **3**(6), 1–19 (2007)
5. Dorigo, M., Birattari, M., et al.: Swarm intelligence. Scholarpedia **2**(9), 1462 (2007)
6. Dorigo, M., Stützle, T.: The ant colony optimization metaheuristic: algorithms, applications, and advances. In: Glover, F., Kochenberger, G.A. (eds.) Handbook of Metaheuristics, vol. 57, pp. 250–285. Springer, Heidelberg (2003)

7. Eaton, J., Yang, S.: Dynamic railway junction rescheduling using population based ant colony optimisation. In: 2014 14th UK Workshop on Computational Intelligence (UKCI), pp. 1–8. IEEE (2014)
8. Foster, I., Kesselman, C.: The Grid 2: Blueprint for a New Computing Infrastructure. Elsevier, Amsterdam (2003)
9. Foster, I., Kesselman, C.: The history of the grid. Computing 20(21), 22 (2010)
10. Foster, I., Kesselman, C., Tuecke, S.: The anatomy of the grid: enabling scalable virtual organizations. Int. J. High Perform. Comput. Appl. 15(3), 200–222 (2001)
11. Guntsch, M., Middendorf, M.: Applying population based ACO to dynamic optimization problems. In: Dorigo, M., Caro, G., Sampels, M. (eds.) ANTS 2002. LNCS, vol. 2463, pp. 111–122. Springer, Heidelberg (2002). doi:10.1007/3-540-45724-0_10
12. Ibarra, O.H., Kim, C.E.: Heuristic algorithms for scheduling independent tasks on nonidentical processors. J. ACM (JACM) 24(2), 280–289 (1977)
13. Izakian, H., Abraham, A., Snasel, V.: Performance comparison of six efficient pure heuristics for scheduling meta-tasks on heterogeneous distributed environments. Neural Netw. World 19(6), 695 (2009)
14. Julstrom, B.A.: Seeding the population: improved performance in a genetic algorithm for the rectilinear Steiner problem. In: Proceedings of the 1994 ACM symposium on Applied Computing, pp. 222–226. ACM (1994)
15. Kołodziej, J., Xhafa, F.: Enhancing the genetic-based scheduling in computational grids by a structured hierarchical population. Future Gener. Comput. Syst. 27(8), 1035–1046 (2011)
16. Lorpunmanee, S., Sap, M.N., Abdullah, A.H., Chompoo-inwai, C.: An ant colony optimization for dynamic job scheduling in grid environment. Int. J. Comput. Inf. Sci. Eng. 1(4), 207–214 (2007)
17. Maheswaran, M., Ali, S., Siegel, H.J., Hensgen, D., Freund, R.F.: Dynamic mapping of a class of independent tasks onto heterogeneous computing systems. J. Parallel Distrib. Comput. 59(2), 107–131 (1999)
18. Mathiyalagan, P., Suriya, S., Sivanandam, S.: Modified ant colony algorithm for grid scheduling. Int. J. Comput. Sci. Eng. 2(02), 132–139 (2010)
19. Nesmachnow, S., Alba, E., Cancela, H.: Scheduling in heterogeneous computing and grid environments using a parallel CHC evolutionary algorithm. Comput. Intell. 28(2), 131–155 (2012)
20. Pacini, E., Mateos, C., Garino, C.G.: Distributed job scheduling based on swarm intelligence: a survey. Comput. Electr. Eng. 40(1), 252–269 (2014)
21. Paul, P.V., Ramalingam, A., Baskaran, R., Dhavachelvan, P., Vivekanandan, K., Subramanian, R.: A new population seeding technique for permutation-coded genetic algorithm: service transfer approach. J. Comput. Sci. 5(2), 277–297 (2014)
22. Ritchie, G., Levine, J.: A hybrid ant algorithm for scheduling independent jobs in heterogeneous computing environments (2004)
23. Schmitt, L.J., Amini, M.M.: Performance characteristics of alternative genetic algorithmic approaches to the traveling salesman problem using path representation: an empirical study. Eur. J. Oper. Res. 108(3), 551–570 (1998)
24. Xhafa, F., Abraham, A.: Computational models and heuristic methods for grid scheduling problems. Future Gener. Comput. Syst. 26(4), 608–621 (2010)
25. Xhafa, F., Kolodziej, J., Barolli, L., Fundo, A: A GA+ TS hybrid algorithm for independent batch scheduling in computational grids. In: 2011 14th International Conference on Network-Based Information Systems (NBiS), pp. 229–235. IEEE (2011)

Analysis of Average Communicability in Complex Networks

Qi Bu and Kwok Yip Szeto[✉]

Department of Physics, Hong Kong University of Science and Technology, Clear Water Bay, Kowloon, Hong Kong
phszeto@ust.hk

Abstract. The average communicability of a complex network is an important measure of the efficiency of information exchange in the entire network. The optimization of average communicability is a significant problem in network design for various applications in science and engineering. Since the search for the topology that achieves the highest average communicability is a very difficult problem due to the enormous size of the solution space, the genetic algorithm is a good choice for search. From numerical simulation, we discover a positive correlation between the variance of the degree distribution with the average communicability of the network. This correlation is then proven mathematically, with applications to the comparison for the average communicability of two networks with the same number of nodes and links using the largest eigenvalues of their adjacency matrices.

Keywords: Genetic algorithm · Complex networks · Communicability · Eigenvalue and eigenvector · Rewiring

1 Introduction

In the last two decades, research in network science has produced many applications that range from social systems [1, 2], food webs [3], brain networks [4], epidemic contagion [5], traffic simulations [6] to the Internet [7], where the nodes and links that form a graph become the simplest model in the description of complex systems for the investigation. In this paper, we like to address the application of network science in the design of a network that achieves maximum information flow among its N nodes, assuming the number L of links between nodes is fixed. The design of network is relevant in many real world applications such as telecommunications [8–10], computer networking [11–13], sewage systems [14], and oil and gas lines [14]. However, the network design problem is an NP-hard combinatorial optimization problem [15]. The number of possible network architectures for a given number of nodes (N) and links (L) will grow exponentially with the size of the network. Moreover, the comparison of the reliability of simple graph, is itself a difficult problem. In this paper, we focus on finding the optimal design of network structure by searching on the general large space of possible graphs. This will have application to many complex systems in real life, with high intellectual and functional importance varying from realistic transportation

© Springer International Publishing AG 2017
G. Squillero and K. Sim (Eds.): EvoApplications 2017, Part I, LNCS 10199, pp. 190–204, 2017.
DOI: 10.1007/978-3-319-55849-3_13

networks to virtual social networks, follow the so-called "web-like" structures with different properties [16–18]. In this paper we only focus on undirected and unweighted graphs with no self-loops or multiple links.

The concept of "communicability" used in this paper was introduced by Estrada and Hatano in order to measure the correlation between two nodes in a network [19]. Intuitively we can imagine that there is a solid stick and when one end of it is hit, the effect of action propagates to the other end. Then we may say that the perturbation on a molecule on the one end of the stick can be "felt" by another molecule on the other end, and the two nodes in this network are correlated [20]. The correlation effects are observed in various real complex systems such as ecological systems [21], biomolecular networks [22], etc. The measure of correlation was originally based on the shortest path length between pairs of nodes, which is built on the assumption that the interactions should occur through the shortest path mostly [23]. In a complex network, however, the information traveling from one node to another may not always follow the shortest paths but sometimes also choose longer paths, or even go back and forth before it reaches the destination [20]. It is also reasonable that two pairs of nodes with the same shortest path length may have different correlations because of global effects of the network structure. Therefore, by taking those alternative paths into account, a new measure of the correlation, i.e. the communicability between a pair of nodes in a complex network was proposed [19]:

$$C_{ij} = \sum_{k=0}^{\infty} c_k A_{ij}^k \tag{1}$$

Here C_{ij} is the communicability between node i and node j, A is the adjacency matrix of the network, and $\{c_k\}$ is a sequence with c_k a monotonically decreasing positive-valued function of k that takes into account paths of all possible lengths (k running to infinity in Eq. (1)). The monotonic decreasing nature of c_k is based on the intuitive notion that paths with length k will be more direct for communication than paths with length k' > k. Here A_{ij}^k measures the number of walks of length k between node i and node j through the network. As $\{c_k\}$ is not unique, the commonly used sequence is to choose $c_k = 1/k!$. This choice for c_k is related to the famous Estrada index [19]. The corresponding communicability, which definition we use in this article, between node i and node j is then defined as [20]:

$$C_{ij} = \sum_{k=0}^{\infty} \frac{A_{ij}^k}{k!} = e_{ij}^A \tag{2}$$

The concept of average communicability (AC) is defined by taking the mean value of the communicability over all pairs of nodes.

$$AC = \frac{1}{N(N-1)} \sum_{i,j \in V\ i \neq j} e_{ij}^A \tag{3}$$

where $G = G(V, E)$ stands for a network with a set of nodes V containing N nodes and a set of edges E having L links [24]. For simplicity, we also include the concept of "self-communicability", which represents the communicability of a node to itself, measured by the diagonal entries of the matrix e^A. The average communicability with self-communicability can then be defined mathematically as:

$$AC_s = \frac{1}{N^2} \sum_{i,j \in V} e_{ij}^A \tag{4}$$

These two definitions of average communicability Eqs. (3) and (4), have little difference in value when the size of network is large and the connectivity is not too small. We illustrate this by a numerical example of networks with $N = 10, 20, 30, 40$, and choose L between the minimum value $L_{min} = (N-1)$ to the maximum value $L_{max} = N(N-1)/2$. For each pair of numbers (N, L), we generate an ER network [25] and calculate the relative difference between the two definitions AC and AC_s as a function of the connectivity L/L_{max}. The results are shown in Fig. 1. From the figure we can conclude that the relative difference between the two definitions of average communicability is small, and becomes smaller as the number of nodes N increases. Therefore, for complex systems with large number of nodes, we simply use the average communicability with self-communicability (ACs) to stand for AC in this paper for ease of analytical calculations, as their difference should be small in general.

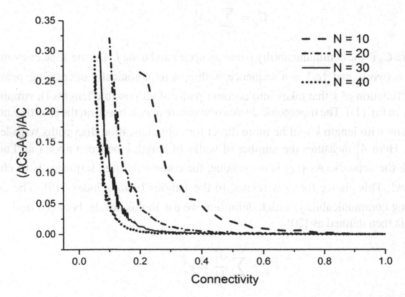

Fig. 1. Relative difference of the two definitions of average communicability versus the connectivity defined as the number of edges L over the maximum number of edges L_{max} for ER networks with $N = 10, 20, 30$ and 40

Since the average communicability of a network measures the correlation between all pairs of nodes, it is related to the efficiency of the information flow through the whole network and the ability of interaction between different parts of the network. In the rest of this article, we will focus on the problem of the optimization of the average communicability for a given complex network by restructuring, without changing the number of nodes and links. For a network with N nodes, the topology with the highest average communicability is the fully connected network with connectivity equaling to 1, for there is a link between each pair of nodes. This solution is obvious but unrealistic due to the fact that the cost involved in connecting all pair of nodes is also proportional to the number of links. Indeed, for a fully connected network, $L = L_{max} = N(N - 1)/2$, and the cost is also maximum as we need the maximum number of links. Thus, our problem should be defined as an optimization of communicability of a network with the constraint that the number of nodes and links are unchanged. This implies that the only way of restructuring is to perform intelligent rewiring of the network, as this process does not change N or L.

2 Genetic Algorithms

By rewiring one link in a network, we only change the topology of the network a little. Thus, a perturbative approach to modify the network is to perform the rewiring of a small number of edges and hope that this can achieve a rather big increase in the average communicability of the rewired network. For a network with $L < L_{max}$ links, we can choose one of the links to be removed and then link up another pair of nodes, so that the number of possible placement of this link is $L(L_{max} - L)$. Here we should note that removing a link between two nodes A and B and placing it between two originally unconnected nodes C and D can be achieved by two steps of rewiring, for example first from AB to AC and then AC to CD. This two steps operation corresponds to a bond movement in the network (AB bond is broken, and a new bond is built between CD). For a sequence of K such operations of bond movement, the complexity increases as $[L(L_{max} - L)]^K$. Therefore, for a large complex network in the real world, where L is usually large, the search for the optimal sequence of rewiring to achieve the maximal increase in the average communicability of the network is a very difficult problem. However, due to the finite nature of N and L, the existence of the optimal topology of the network that yields maximum average communicability is guaranteed. Therefore, our objective is to find an efficient way to obtain an approximate solution that is close to the optimal solution given a fixed computational resource. In this context, the use of genetic algorithm may be a good strategy to achieve relatively good results within limited steps. In the context of traditional genetic algorithms, a chromosome corresponds to a network, while the fitness of the chromosome is the average communicability of the network. The mutation operation commonly used in genetic algorithm for the search for a chromosome with maximum fitness is now represented by the choice of rewiring applied to the network. The Darwinian principle of the survival of the fittest implies that we select those networks with rewiring that has large increase in average communicability.

    In order to test whether genetic algorithm could help us find good results which are the choices of link rewiring with maximum increase in average communicability, we consider three principles in rewiring and investigate the efficiency of the combined use of these rewiring processes in the increase of average communicability. To illustrate these three principles, let's us consider the mechanism shown in Fig. 2.

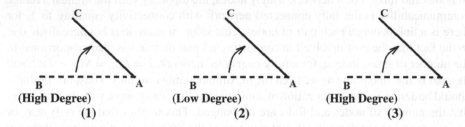

B	A	B	A	B	A
(High Degree)		(Low Degree)		(High Degree)	
(1)		(2)		(3)	

Fig. 2. A rewiring step that change the link AB between node A and node B to the link AC between nodes A and C

Let us denote the three nodes involved in one step of rewiring as nodes A, B and C. In the original network, node A and node B are connected but A and C are not. We now remove the link between A and B and use it to connect A and C. There are now three different scenarios:

(1) Node B has a low degree and node C has a high degree;
(2) Node B has a low degree and node C also has a low degree;
(3) Both node B and node C have high degrees.

Here the degree of a node is defined by the number of edges connected to it. Nodes with higher degrees have more neighbors and usually play a more important role in the communication for the network. The above three scenarios thus define three distinct principles in rewiring.

In the application of genetic algorithm, we create a population of six chromosomes, with each undergoing five steps of rewiring. Therefore, each chromosome is a string with length 5 and elements equal to "1, 2 or 3", which stand for the principles (1, 2, 3) for rewiring. In a given step, we rewire the network according to the entries of the string and each chromosome will generate a rewired network after five rewiring steps. Thus, there are in total $243 = 3^5$ possible combinations. However, depending on N and L, each rewiring can be different even if the same principle is applied, since there are in general many nodes of the same degree, so that a specific rewiring principle applied to the network in general can involve different choices of the three nodes (A, B, C).

We first randomly generate six chromosomes and then rank them according to the average communicability given by the rewired networks, which form the first generation. Then we perform mutations on the string of five integers on a given chromosome to get a new one. The chromosome with the highest average communicability is kept unchanged. For the chromosome that ranked second in the average communicability, one of the five integers in the string defining the second chromosome is mutated randomly to one of the two remaining choices of numbers. For example, if the original string is (1, 3, 2, 1, 2) and the third integer is chosen to be mutated, then the new chromosome can be either (1, 3, 1, 1, 2) or (1, 3, 3, 1, 2) because the third integer is 2 and it can only be changed to either 1 or 3. For the chromosome ranked third in average communicability, we will choose randomly two out of five integers defining the chromosome and mutate them randomly. We repeat this rule of mutation for the other chromosomes. To summarize, we choose $0 < n < 6$ integers out of the five defining the chromosome that ranked m-th for random mutation, with $n = m - 1$ and $m = 2, 3, 4, 5, 6$. Thus, the last (the sixth) chromosome will have all its five integers changed randomly. The five mutated chromosomes, together with the fittest one which is not mutated, will form the second generation of the population of chromosomes. We then rank these six chromosomes in the second generation according to the average communicability of the corresponding six networks.

For numerical testing, we start with a population consisting of six randomly generated networks with 20 nodes and 50 edges. This small network is used because we can use exhaustive search to find the optimal rewiring and compute the corresponding communicability, thereby obtaining a benchmark for comparison to the result of our best solution obtained by genetic algorithm with finite number of generations. Indeed, after 20 generations, we will be able to search with a sample of 100 chromosomes that undergo five-step rewiring. Since for each step of rewiring there are 3 choices, and each chromosome consists of 5 rewiring steps, there are totally $3^5 = 243$ possible combinations of rewiring principles, though the actual number of possible rewiring is much *larger* than that due to the possible difference in the selection of the nodes (A, B, C). The best 6 chromosomes after 20 generations are shown on Table 1 and we calculate the average communicability, the variance of degree of nodes and the largest eigenvalue of the adjacency matrix for each rewired network. We also calculate those quantities for all 3^5 combinations of rewiring principles and select the best 6 chromosomes with the largest average communicability. Comparing the results in the two tables, we find that the best quintets of rewiring resulting from the genetic algorithm in Table 1 are similar to the ones from the exhaustive search in Table 2. They all involve many rewiring principle "1" and their average communicability, variances of degree and largest eigenvalues are close to one another.

Table 1. The best 6 chromosomes after 20 generations

Chromosome					A.C.	Var.	Eigenvalue
1	3	1	1	1	11.2376	2.9474	5.5200
1	2	1	1	3	10.9853	3.0526	5.4721
1	1	3	1	1	10.6270	2.6316	5.4430
2	3	2	3	2	10.3335	2.3158	5.4254
2	1	3	1	3	10.2962	2.3158	5.4036
3	1	3	2	3	9.4281	1.7895	5.2964

Table 2. The best 6 chromosomes of all 243 possible combinations

Chromosome					A.C.	Var.	Eigenvalue
1	1	1	1	1	11.8207	3.4737	5.5696
1	2	1	1	2	11.6126	3.2632	5.5606
2	1	1	1	1	11.6055	3.1579	5.5532
1	1	2	1	2	11.5498	3.0526	5.5549
1	2	1	2	1	11.5271	3.1579	5.5441
1	1	1	3	3	11.3221	2.8421	5.5402

From these two tables, we can say that genetic algorithm is good in finding the good combination of rewiring principles that yields relatively high average communicability. We observe that chromosomes with more "1" usually have better results so that we should rewire more frequently from a low degree node B to a high degree node C for a given node A. We also observe a positive correlation between the average communicability, the variance of degree and the largest eigenvalue. We then repeat this analysis on Erdos-Renyi networks and Watts-Strogatz networks with 20 nodes and 60 edges. The results are shown in Tables 3 and 4, confirming our conclusions on randomly generated networks.

Table 3. The best 6 chromosomes after 20 generations for an ER network

Chromosome					A.C.	Var.	Eigenvalue
1	1	3	3	1	40.7726	5.3684	6.8478
2	1	3	2	1	36.9365	5.1578	6.7108
3	2	1	1	1	35.4872	4.8421	6.6603
3	1	2	1	2	35.3291	4.7368	6.6627
3	1	3	3	1	34.8849	4.4210	6.6494
1	3	1	1	2	33.8435	4.5263	6.6068

Table 4. The best 6 chromosomes after 20 generations for a WS network

Chromosome					A.C.	Var.	Eigenvalue
2	1	1	1	1	26.4966	2.1052	6.3405
2	1	2	2	2	26.1561	2.0000	6.3149
2	1	1	2	3	26.0895	2.0000	6.3163
2	2	1	2	1	25.7242	2.0000	6.2895
1	2	2	2	3	25.3684	1.4736	6.2978
2	3	3	3	1	25.2874	1.5789	6.2865

3   Testing on a "Band" Network

From the result in Sect. 2, we see that the application of rewiring principle "1" is more effective in increasing the average communicability of the network. As this rewiring principle "1" rewires edges from low degree nodes to high degree nodes, we expect the degree of a low degree node will become even lower, while the degree of a high degree node will become higher. Consequently the rewiring principle "1" increases the variance of degree of nodes. We thus formulate a hypothesis that the rewiring which increases the degree variance will increase the average communicability based on the numerical results on small network discussed in Sect. 2. In order to have a more rigorous support to our hypothesis, we turn to a network in the structure of a band shown in Fig. 3. We use this band structure because the eigenvalue spectrum of its adjacency matrix has been computed analytically by Wang and Szeto [26], which provides important insights for our understanding of the relation between rewiring and increased communicability. We now repeat the numerical experiment of Sect. 2 for the band structure in Fig. 3. After each rewiring step, we record the changes of the average communicability and the largest eigenvalue.

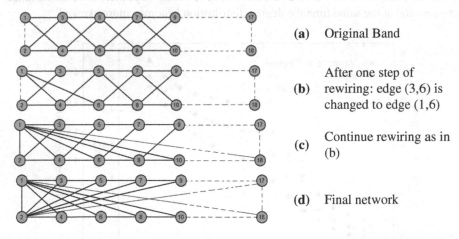

(a)   Original Band

(b)   After one step of rewiring: edge (3,6) is changed to edge (1,6)

(c)   Continue rewiring as in (b)

(d)   Final network

Fig. 3. Edge rewiring process on an originally regular network results in a structure with all even nodes linked to node 1 and all odd nodes linked to node 2

Our "band" network shown in Fig. 3 has 18 nodes and 36 edges. Each node is connected to its four neighbors and originally the variance of degree is zero as the degree distribution is a delta distribution centered at degree 4. We also label the nodes in the figures. Firstly, we remove the edge between node 3 and node 6 and then link node 6 to node 1. Hence, the degree of node 1 increases by one and the degree of node 3 decreases by one. Next we remove the edge between node 5 and node 8 and link node 8 to node 1. We keep on rewiring according to the pattern above until all nodes with even labels are linked to node 1, which is called a "hub" with a high degree. Then we choose node 2 to be another hub and rewire with similar rules until all nodes with odd labels are connected to node 2. After each step of rewiring, the numbers of nodes and edges are unchanged and the variance of the degree of nodes increases by a small amount. According to Fig. 3, we observe that the rewiring process deliberately increases the degree of node 1 and node 2 while keeping all other nodes with degree 3. The final network shown in Fig. 3(d) has a much larger variance than the original regular network in Fig. 3(a).

In Fig. 4, we show the change of the variance, the logarithm of the average communicability and the largest eigenvalue of the adjacency matrix of the network as the original network undergoes an increasing number of rewiring processes shown in Fig. 3. We observe that the variance, the largest eigenvalue and the logarithm of average communicability all increase with the number of rewiring. There is a kink during the rewiring process on all three figures, because we first rewire edges to node 1 and then rewire edges to node 2. We also observe a "drop" of the skewness versus variance. We understand this singular behavior with the following observation. Initially, all nodes have the same degree, and therefore the skewness and the variance of degree are both zero. As we rewire from other nodes to node 1, one node (node 1) has a larger degree, but more nodes move towards the low-degree side, and therefore the degree distribution function becomes skewed to the right, which leads to a positive skewness. We thus explain the first part of the curve: as the number of rewiring steps increases, the variance increases and at the same time the degree distribution becomes more skewed.

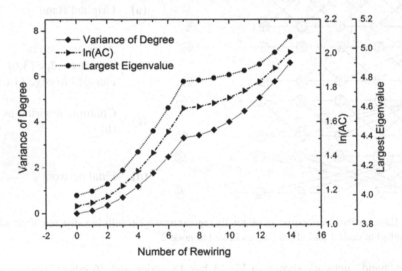

Fig. 4. The variance, the normalized third central moment of the degree distribution function of the band, and the logarithm of average communicability as a function of the number of rewiring

However, we also observe the second part of the curve in Figs. 4 and 5. Specifically, in Fig. 5b, we see a "drop" in the skewness as the number of rewiring is around 7. We notice that this corresponds to the rewiring of edges to node 2. When another node move towards the high-degree side, the degree distribution function actually becomes more "symmetric" and the skewness decreases as it is not as right-skewed as before. Therefore, the normalized third central moment decreases. Furthermore, we can extract some additional correlation between various measures of the degree distribution from the rewiring of the band in Fig. 5. We show in Fig. 5(a) how the logarithm of average communicability changes with the largest eigenvalue as well as the variance of degree distribution. A positive correlation is shown between the variance and the largest eigenvalue. From the evolution of these three quantities under rewiring, we conclude the following observations: there are positive correlations among the average communicability, the variance of degree and the largest eigenvalue. These results are consistent with the pattern we observed from the genetic algorithm on a general complex network, which shows that rewiring from low-degree nodes to high-degree nodes will increase the variance and thereby also increase the average communicability of the whole network

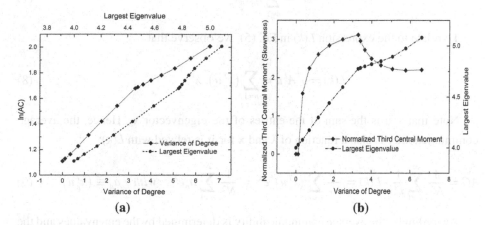

(a)   (b)

Fig. 5. (**a**) The relationship between the logarithm of the average communicability and the variance of degree as well as the largest eigenvalue of the network during the rewiring process (**b**) The normalized third central moment of degree distribution (Skewness) and the largest eigenvalue versus the variance of degree

In conclusion, with the help of the analytical calculation in [26], we confirm that the rewiring process introduced for the band in Fig. 3 can evolve the network towards one with higher average communicability.

4   Communicability, Degree Variance and Eigenvalue Spectrum

We now prove the positive correlation observed in Sect. 3 using band network. Recall that the adjacency matrix A of a network has the following property: for a certain integer k, A_{ij}^k represents the number of paths with length k between node i and node j [20]. Now we introduce the $N \times 1$ column vector $\mathbf{u} = [1111\ldots1]^T$ and write the total number of paths with length k in the network as [27]

$$L(k) = \sum_{i,j \in V} A_{ij}^k = u^T A^k u \tag{5}$$

Hence, the average communicability can be represented by $L(k)$:

$$AC = \sum_{i,j \in V} C_{ij}/N^2 = \sum_{i,j \in V} \sum_{k=0}^{\infty} (1/k!)\left(A_{ij}^k/N^2\right) = \sum_{k=0}^{\infty} (1/k!)\left[L(k)/N^2\right] \quad (6)$$

Since we only consider undirected networks [28], the adjacency matrix is symmetric and the entries are either 0 or 1, the eigenvalues and the entries of the eigenvectors of the adjacency matrix are all real. Let λ and $\mathbf{x}$ be the eigenvalues and corresponding eigenvectors of A, then

$$A^k = \sum_{n=1}^{N} \lambda_n^k x_n x_n^T \quad (7)$$

To relate to the expression $L(k)$ in Eq. (5), we observe that

$$L(k) = u^T A^k u = \sum_{n=1}^{N} \left(x_n^T u\right)^2 \lambda_n^k \quad (8)$$

Note that $x_n^T u$ is the sum of the entries of the eigenvector $\mathbf{x}_n$. Hence, the average communicability is also a function of λ and $\mathbf{x}$ for it is related with $L(k)$:

$$AC = \frac{1}{N^2} \sum_{k=0}^{\infty} \frac{1}{k!} \cdot L(k) = \frac{1}{N^2} \sum_{n=1}^{N} \left(x_n^T u\right)^2 e^{\lambda_n} = \frac{1}{N^2} \sum_{n=1}^{N} a_n e^{\lambda_n} \quad with \quad a_n \equiv \left(x_n^T u\right)^2 \quad (9)$$

Accordingly, the average communicability is determined by the eigenvalues and the sum of the entries of the eigenvectors. If we expand the last expression, we get

$$AC = \frac{1}{N^2} \sum_{n=1}^{N} a_n e^{\lambda_n} = \frac{1}{N^2}\left(a_1 e^{\lambda_1} + \sum_{n=2}^{N} a_n e^{\lambda_n} \right) \quad (10)$$

Here $\lambda_1 > \lambda_2 > \ldots > \lambda_N$ are the eigenvalues of the adjacency matrix representing the network. Taking logarithm of both sides:

$$\ln(AC) \approx \lambda_1 + \ln\left(\frac{a_1}{N^2}\right) + \frac{a_2}{a_1} e^{\lambda_2 - \lambda_1} \quad (11)$$

Equation (11) shows that the largest eigenvalue λ_1 of the adjacency matrix is a good approximation of the average communicability, while the correction term involves the second eigenvalue. Note that for large N, the term $\ln(a_1/N^2)$ is small. According to this approximation, there should be a positive correlation between the average communicability and the largest eigenvalue. Here we would like to recall the "band" network and observe the difference between the logarithm of the average communicability and the approximation based on the eigenvalue spectrum. We would like to further simplify Eq. (11) by using the fact that for a regular network, all entries of $\mathbf{x}_1$ are equal and therefore $a_1 = N$. Furthermore, the values $a_2 \sim a_n$ of a regular network are all zero [27]. Then for a band network

$$\ln(AC) \approx -\ln(N) + \lambda_1 \qquad (12)$$

and the logarithm of average communicability is approximately linear in the largest eigenvalue for the band. Actually, for all regular network, Eq. (12) is an exact equality.

We next derive the positive correlation between the average communicability and the variance of degree. By definition, the variance of degree of a network is

$$N \cdot Var = \sum_{i=1}^{N} \left(d_i - \langle d \rangle\right)^2 = \left(\sum_{i=1}^{N} d_i^2\right) - N \cdot \langle d \rangle^2 \qquad (13)$$

Here $< d >$ is the average degree of node and for undirected networks, $< d > = 2L/N$, thus

$$N \cdot Var + \frac{4L^2}{N} = \sum_{i=1}^{N} d_i^2 \qquad (14)$$

Now we may consider a node "i" with degree d_i, and for every two neighbors of node i, there is a path of length 2 between these two neighbors through node i. Therefore, the number of paths of length 2 centered at node i is d_i^2, and the total number of paths of length 2:

$$L(2) = \sum_{i=1}^{N} d_i^2 = N \cdot Var + \frac{4L^2}{N} \qquad (15)$$

Applying the spectral decomposition of the adjacency matrix in Eqs. (5, 8, 10), we have $L(2) = \sum_{n=1}^{N} a_n \lambda_n^2$ so that we can rewrite Eq. (15) as

$$N \cdot Var + \frac{4L^2}{N} = \sum_{n=1}^{N} a_n \lambda_n^2 \qquad (16)$$

We now observe that the average communicability in Eq. (10) is very similar to Eq. (16). In fact,

$$N^2 \cdot AC = \sum_{n=1}^{N} a_n e^{\lambda_n} \qquad (17)$$

Thus, the eigenvalue spectrum and their corresponding eigenvectors of the adjacency matrix of a network, shown in Eqs. (16) and (17) as the sets $\{\lambda_n\}$ and $\{a_n\}$, determine the degree variance and average communicability. We can therefore compare the average communicability (and also their degree variances) of two networks with the same number of nodes N and number of edges L by comparing the corresponding sets of $\{a_n\}$ and $\{\lambda_n\}$. In order to increase the average communicability of a network without changing N and L, one can increase the variance of the network by rewiring, since Eqs. (16) and (17) show that they are positively correlated: higher average communicability may also give out higher variance of degree.

These analytical results, inspired by the spectral analysis of the adjacency matrix of the band, is consistent with the numerical results shown in Fig. 6, where the logarithm of the average communicability and the approximation by Eq. (12) versus the number of rewiring is shown and the error of the approximation is shown in the insert. According to Fig. 6, the initial network is a regular network, thus Eq. (12) gives exactly the average communicability. As the number of rewiring increases, the network deviates from a regular network, and there is a gap between the real $\ln(AC)$ and the approximation. We see in the insert of Fig. 6 that the gap between the approximation and $\log(AC)$ is below 10% for the band network. From our band network, we can see that the numerical results shown in Fig. 6 on the evolution from a regular band to one with higher average communicability agree with our theoretical analysis.

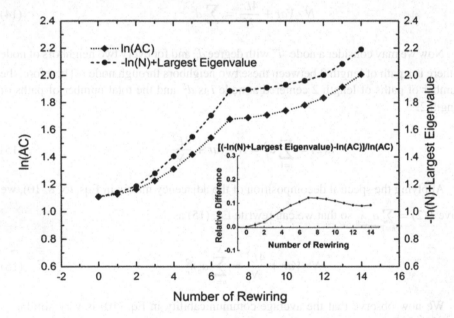

Fig. 6. The logarithm of the average communicability and the approximation by Eq. (12) versus the number of rewiring.

5   Conclusion

Based on numerical simulation on random networks, ER networks, WS networks, as well as the band network, we have found a positive correlation among the average communicability, the largest eigenvalue and the variance of degree. Besides numerical work, we also deduce these positive correlations rigorously, so that we can use them as guiding principles in the design of network with high average communicability. We should point out the importance of these mathematical results in network science, since average communicability is related to the efficiency of communication, which now can be improved by rewiring from low degree nodes to high degree nodes. Furthermore, in comparing the average communicability of the networks with the same number of nodes and edges, we may use the eigenvalue spectra and the variance of degree as references. Finally, the importance of the connectivity of the network cannot be ignored, as a fully connected network has the highest average communicability. In order to reduce cost, a network that is not fully connected can still be designed with the highest average communicability under the constraint of fixed connectivity. The result of this paper can be used to test and improve the efficiency of information flow and the communication ability of nodes in complex networks such as real-world communication networks, the Internet network, social networks [29] or even job arrangement in large companies. In realistic applications, we are often restricted to use a small number of rewiring processes. In this situation, genetic algorithm can also provide the search for a good solution with high average communicability.

References

1. Scott, J.: Social Network Analysis. Sage, New York (2012)
2. Crane, R., Sornette, D.: Robust dynamic classes revealed by measuring the response function of a social system. Proc. Natl. Acad. Sci. **105**(41), 15649–15653 (2008)
3. Dunne, J.A., Williams, R.J., Martinez, N.D.: Food-web structure and network theory: the role of connectance and size. Proc. Natl. Acad. Sci. **99**(20), 12917–12922 (2002)
4. Rubinov, M., Sporns, O.: Complex network measures of brain connectivity: uses and interpretations. Neuroimage **52**(3), 1059–1069 (2010)
5. Cai, W., Chen, L., Ghanbarnejad, F., Grassberger, P.: Avalanche outbreaks emerging in cooperative contagions. Nat. Phys. **11**(11), 936–940 (2015)
6. Rieser, M., Nagel, K.: Network breakdown 'at the edge of chaos' in multi-agent traffic simulations. Eur. Phys. J. B **63**(3), 321–327 (2008)
7. Calvert, K.L., Doar, M.B., Zegura, E.W.: Modeling internet topology. Commun. Mag. IEEE **35**(6), 160–163 (1997)
8. Aiiqullah, M.M., Rao, S.S.: Reliability optimization of communication networks using simulated annealing. Microelectron. Reliab. **33**, 1303–1319 (1993)
9. Jan, R.-H., Hwang, F.-J., Chen, S.-T.: Topological optimization of a communication network subject to a reliability constraint. IEEE Trans. Reliab. **42**, 63–70 (1993)
10. Pierre, S., Hyppolite, M.-A., Bourjolly, J.-M., Dioume, O.: Topological design of computer communication networks using simulated annealing. Eng. Appl. Artif. Intell. **8**, 61–69 (1995)
11. Aggarwal, K.K., Chopra, Y.C., Bajwa, J.S.: Topological layout of links for optimizing the overall reliability in a computer communication system. Microelectron. Reliab. **22**, 347–351 (1982)
12. Fetterolf, P.C., Anandalingam, G.: Optimal design of LAN-WAN internetworks: an approach using simulated annealing. Anna. Oper. Res. **36**, 275–298 (1992)
13. Wilkov, R.S.: Design of computer networks based on a new reliability measure. In: Fox, I. (ed.) Proceedings of the Symposium on Computer-Communications Networks and Teletraffic, pp. 371–384. Polytechnic Institute of Brooklyn, Brooklyn (1972)

14. Walters, G.A., Smith, D.K.: Evolutionary design algorithm for optimal layout of tree networks. Eng. Optim. **24**, 261–281 (1995)
15. Garey, M.R., Johnson, D.S.: Computers and Intractability: A Guide to the Theory of NP-Completeness. W.H. Freeman and Co., San Francisco, CA (1979)
16. Albert, R., Barabási, A.: Statistical mechanics of complex networks. Rev. Mod. Phys. **74**(1), 47–97 (2002)
17. da Fontoura Costa, L., Travieso Jr., G., Rodrigues, O.N., Villas Boas, P.R., Antiqueira, L., Viana, M.P., Correa Rocha, L.E.: Analyzing and modeling real-world phenomena with complex networks: a survey of applications. Adv. Phys. **60**, 329–412 (2011)
18. Boccaletti, S., Latora, V., Moreno, Y., Chavez, M., Hwang, D.-U.: Complex networks: structure and dynamics. Phys. Rep. **424**, 175–308 (2006)
19. Estrada, E., Hatano, N.: Communicability in complex networks. Phys. Rev. E **77**(3), 036111 (2008)
20. Estrada, E., Hatano, N., Benzi, M.: The physics of communicability in complex networks. Phys. Rep. **514**(3), 89–119 (2012)
21. Jordán, F., Scheuring, I.: Searching for keystones in ecological networks. Oikos **99**, 607–612 (2002)
22. Zotenko, E., Mestre, J., O'Leary, D.P., Przytycka, T.M.: Why do hubs in yeast protein interaction network tend to be essential: reexamining the connection between the network topology and essentiality. PLoS Comput. Biol. **4**, e1000140 (2008)
23. Costa, L., Rodrigues, F.: What is there between any two nodes in a complex network? Arxiv.org (2008). http://arxiv.org/abs/0801.4068. Accessed 16 Mar 2016
24. Amaral, L., Ottino, J.: Complex networks. Eur. Phys. J. B Condens. Matter **38**(2), 147–162 (2004)
25. Newman, M., Strogatz, S., Watts, D.: Random graphs with arbitrary degree distributions and their applications. Phys. Rev. E **64**(2), 026118 (2001)
26. Wang, Z., Szeto, K.Y.: Comparing the reliability of networks by spectral analysis. Eur. Phys. J. B **87**, 234 (2014). doi:10.1140/epjb/e2014-50498-0
27. Van Mieghem, P.: Graph Spectra for Complex Networks. Cambridge University Press, Cambridge (2011)
28. Biggs, N.: Algebraic Graph Theory. Cambridge University Press, London (1974)
29. Wasserman, S., Faust, K.: Social Network Analysis. Cambridge University Press, London (2016). http://www.cambridge.org/ar/academic/subjects/sociology/sociology-general-interest/social-network-analysis-methods-and-applications

Configuring Dynamic Heterogeneous Wireless Communications Networks Using a Customised Genetic Algorithm

David Lynch[1]([✉]), Michael Fenton[1], Stepan Kucera[2], Holger Claussen[2],
and Michael O'Neill[1]

[1] Natural Computing Research and Applications Group, UCD, Dublin, Ireland
david.lynch.1@ucdconnect.ie, michaelfenton1@gmail.com, m.oneill@ucd.ie
[2] Bell Laboratories Nokia-Dublin, Dublin, Ireland
{stepan.kucera,holger.claussen}@nokia-bell-labs.com

Abstract. Wireless traffic is surging due to the prevalence of smart devices, rising demand for multimedia content and the advent of the "Internet of Things". Network operators are deploying Small Cells alongside existing Macro Cells in order to satisfy demand during this era of exponential growth. Such Heterogeneous Networks (HetNets) are highly spectrally efficient because both cell tiers transmit using the same scarce and expensive bandwidth. However, load balancing and cross-tier interference issues constrain cell-edge rates in co-channel operation. Capacity can be increased by intelligently configuring Small Cell powers and biases, and the muting cycles of Macro Cells. This paper presents a customised Genetic Algorithm (GA) for reconfiguring HetNets. The GA converges within minutes so tailored settings can be pushed to cells in real time. The proposed GA lifts cell-edge (2.5th percentile) rates by 32% over a non-adaptive baseline that is used in practice. HetNets are highly dynamic environments. However, customers tend to cluster in hotspots which arise at predictable locations over the course of a typical day. An explicit memory of previously evolved solutions is maintained and used to seed fresh runs. System level simulations show that the 2.5th percentile rates are boosted to 36% over baseline when prior knowledge is utilised.

1 Introduction

Conventional wireless communications networks are served by high-powered and long-range antennas called Macro Cells (MCs). However, MC deployments are struggling to satisfy demand during an era of exponentially rising mobile traffic [1]. Small Cells (SCs) have been proposed as a scalable and cost-effective technology for boosting the capacity of MC deployments. SCs are lower-powered antennas that can be deployed in traffic hotspots to supplement the existing MC tier. When operating jointly, SCs and MCs constitute a so-called Heterogeneous Network or 'HetNet'. Network operators like Verizon Communications Inc. and AT&T Inc. are aggressively densifying with SCs. Densification is economically sensible because both cell tiers transmit across the same bandwidth, which is scarce and sells for billions of Euro at auction.

© Springer International Publishing AG 2017
G. Squillero and K. Sim (Eds.): EvoApplications 2017, Part I, LNCS 10199, pp. 205–220, 2017.
DOI: 10.1007/978-3-319-55849-3_14

The term 'User Equipment' (UE) refers to any device (e.g. a smartphone) that attaches to a cell. Now, UEs at cell edges experience low channel quality (and hence low downlink rates) due to severe cross-tier interference from MCs and other nearby SCs. Low rates may result in packet losses and poor customer satisfaction. UEs that are closer to cell centres can liberate resources without noticing a degraded quality of service. This paper proposes a customised Genetic Algorithm (GA) for configuring the cells of a HetNet so that resources are fairly distributed among all UEs.

Wireless networks are highly dynamic environments, since channel conditions fluctuate dramatically on a millisecond timescale [23], and demand from a single device varies constantly [13]. However, it is not feasible to reconfigure cells more frequently than every ten minutes or so. Insensitive manipulation of the network configuration will cause unwanted ping-pong handovers resulting in latency or dropped calls. Nonetheless, gradual changes in the traffic pattern, such as hotspots moving around or dissipating, can be tracked by an adaptive evolutionary algorithm. This paper develops a customised GA that converges on approximately the same timescale as these changes occur.

Fresh runs are seeded with individuals from an explicit memory that stores previously evolved solutions. It is hypothesised that the GA will converge to better solutions more quickly by incorporating knowledge from prior scenarios [3,8,17]. Hence, the proposed approach tailors the network configuration to the current transient conditions, but by also tapping longer term trends.

The paper is organised as follows. Section 2 introduces two paradigms for managing HetNets before formalising the optimisation problem. Previous work is reviewed in Sect. 3. Section 4 describes a customised GA that is adapted for this instance of a dynamic environment. The simulation environment and experiments are described in Sect. 5. A discussion of the results follows in Sect. 6. The paper concludes with directions for future work in Sect. 7.

2   Problem Definition

Two factors limit the capacity of channel sharing HetNets. Firstly, the SC tier is typically underutilised because low-powered SCs struggle to offload UEs from stronger MCs. Secondly, poor channel conditions manifest at the edges of SCs due to severe cross-tier interference. A standards body called the 3rd Generation Partnership Project (3GPP)[1] has proposed mechanisms for load balancing and interference mitigation in HetNets. This section specifies the optimisation problems that arise in HetNets which implement the 3GPP standard.

2.1   Load Balancing

Figure 1 depicts a single SC $s' \in S$ embedded within a MC sector $m' \in M$, where S and M denote the sets of SCs and MCs respectively. Twelve UEs attach to

---

[1] 3GPP (December 2010, http://www.3gpp.org/).

m' so that $|\mathcal{A}_{m'}| = 12$, where $\mathcal{A}_c$ is the set of UEs attached to cell $c \in \mathcal{S} \cup \mathcal{M}$. However, only $|\mathcal{A}_{s'}| = 3$ UEs attach to s', so m' is congested relative to s'. High congestion on any cell c is undesirable because the limited bandwidth must be shared among $\mathcal{A}_c$. Range expansion can be employed in this context to offload more UEs onto s'.

UE u attaches to, and hence receives data from, cell $k \in \mathcal{S} \cup \mathcal{M}$:

$$k \coloneqq \arg\max_c(Signal_{u,c} + \beta_c) = \arg\max_c(g_{u,c} + P_c + \beta_c), \ \forall c \in \mathcal{M} \cup \mathcal{S}, \qquad (1)$$

where, the signal strength $Signal_{u,c}$ experienced by u from c is given by adding the gain $g_{u,c}$ [dB] from c to u, to the transmitting power P_c [dBm] of c. The variable β_c is the Cell Selection Bias used by c, where $\beta_s \geq 0$ [dB], $\forall s \in \mathcal{S}$ and $\beta_m \coloneqq 0$ [dB], $\forall m \in \mathcal{M}$ (since MCs are rarely underutilised). Hence, the underutilised SC s' of Fig. 1.1 could absorb UEs from the adjacent hotspot by increasing $P_{s'}$, or artificially, by broadcasting a positive Cell Selection Bias $\beta_{s'}$. Figure 1.2 illustrates the expanded region that forms at the edge of s' when $\beta_{s'} > 0$. UEs in the expanded region attach to s' despite receiving a stronger signal from m'. Range expansion reduces the load imbalance from $|\mathcal{A}_{m'}| - |\mathcal{A}_{s'}| = (12 - 3) = 9$ in Fig. 1.1, to just $|\mathcal{A}_{s'}| - |\mathcal{A}_{m'}| = (9 - 6) = 3$ in Fig. 1.2.

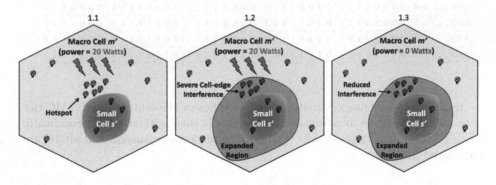

Fig. 1. Toy network containing one MC with an embedded SC.

2.2   Time Domain Interference Mitigation

Channel conditions can be very poor in the expanded regions of SCs due to severe interference from MCs (which transmit using the same bandwidth). An enhanced Inter-cell Interference Coordination (eICIC) paradigm has been proposed to mitigate cell-edge interference [15]. HetNets implementing eICIC mute MCs periodically so that SCs can transmit with dramatically reduced interference. On the other hand, $u \in \mathcal{A}_m$ receive no data when m mutes. For instance, in Fig. 1, m' should be muted regularly enough to protect $u \in \mathcal{A}_{s'}$, but m' should transmit sufficiently often to provide an acceptable quality of service for $u \in \mathcal{A}_{m'}$.

Both MCs and SCs send individual packets during 1 ms intervals called subframes. There are 40 subframes in a 'frame' $\mathcal{F}_t$, where $t \in \mathbb{N}$ is the timestep. At the end of each frame, UEs report measurements of the channel conditions that they experienced in the preceding 40 milliseconds. When a MC mutes for some $f \in \mathcal{F}_t$ we say that it executes an 'Almost Blank Subframe' (ABS) during f. Table 1 displays the seven ABS patterns that a MC can use. The feasible ABS patterns for a MC m are specified by the ABS ratio for m, or $ABS_{r,m}$. For instance, if $ABS_{r,m} = 4$ then m will mute in 20 subframes out of 40. Furthermore, $ABS_{r,m} = 4$ implies that m will adopt the muting pattern in row 4 of Table 1, where '0' in position f indicates an ABS (muted) subframe and '1' implies that the MC transmits during f. Lower ABS ratios suggest more aggressive muting.

Table 1. Possible ABS patterns for $\mathcal{F}_t$ (time increases left to right).

ABS Ratio	Subframe (f)				
	1...				...40
$ABS_{r,m} = 1$	0 0 0 0 0 0 0 1	0 0 0 0 0 0 0 1	0 0 0 0 0 0 0 1	0 0 0 0 0 0 0 1	0 0 0 0 0 0 0 1
$ABS_{r,m} = 2$	0 0 0 0 0 0 1 1	0 0 0 0 0 0 1 1	0 0 0 0 0 0 1 1	0 0 0 0 0 0 1 1	0 0 0 0 0 0 1 1
$ABS_{r,m} = 3$	0 0 0 0 0 1 1 1	0 0 0 0 0 1 1 1	0 0 0 0 0 1 1 1	0 0 0 0 0 1 1 1	0 0 0 0 0 1 1 1
$ABS_{r,m} = 4$	0 0 0 0 1 1 1 1	0 0 0 0 1 1 1 1	0 0 0 0 1 1 1 1	0 0 0 0 1 1 1 1	0 0 0 0 1 1 1 1
$ABS_{r,m} = 5$	0 0 0 1 1 1 1 1	0 0 0 1 1 1 1 1	0 0 0 1 1 1 1 1	0 0 0 1 1 1 1 1	0 0 0 1 1 1 1 1
$ABS_{r,m} = 6$	0 0 1 1 1 1 1 1	0 0 1 1 1 1 1 1	0 0 1 1 1 1 1 1	0 0 1 1 1 1 1 1	0 0 1 1 1 1 1 1
$ABS_{r,m} = 7$	0 1 1 1 1 1 1 1	0 1 1 1 1 1 1 1	0 1 1 1 1 1 1 1	0 1 1 1 1 1 1 1	0 1 1 1 1 1 1 1

In summary, cell range expansion enables efficient offloading from the MC tier onto SCs. Prohibitive interference at SC edges is then mitigated by periodically muting MCs in the time domain. The notions of range expansion and eICIC are formalised in [15].

2.3   Multi-layer Optimisation of HetNets

Let $\mathcal{C}$ denote the 'configuration' of a HetNet with $|\mathcal{M}|$ MCs and $|\mathcal{S}|$ SCs:

$$\mathcal{C} \leftarrow \left[ABS_{r,1}, \ldots, ABS_{r,|\mathcal{M}|}, P_1, \ldots, P_{|\mathcal{S}|}, \beta_1, \ldots, \beta_{|\mathcal{S}|} \right], \tag{2}$$

where, $ABS_{r,m}$ is an integer from $[1, \ldots, 7]$, P_s takes a real value in the interval $[23.0 \text{ [dBm]}, 35.0 \text{ [dBm]}]$, and β_s is a real value in $[0.0 \text{ [dB]}, 15.0 \text{ [dB]}]$. Recall that MCs do not use bias (so $\beta_m \coloneqq 0.0 \text{ [dB]}$) and $P_m \coloneqq 43.3 \text{ [dBm]}$ is invariant $\forall m \in \mathcal{M}$ during non-ABS subframes, but $P_m = 0.0 \text{ [dBm]}$ when m mutes. This paper presents a customised GA for optimising $\mathcal{C}$.

A solution $\mathcal{C}$ is evaluated with a fairness-based utility of downlink rates. Consider UE u attached to cell $k \in \mathcal{S} \cup \mathcal{M}$. Denote the channel quality experienced by u in subframe f of frame $\mathcal{F}_t$ by $Q_{u,f} = \log_2(1 + SINR_{u,f})$, where $SINR_{u,f}$ is the signal to interference and noise ratio experienced by u during f:

$$SINR_{u,f} = \frac{Signal_{u,k,f} \text{ [Watts]}}{\sum\limits_{c \in \mathcal{SUM} \backslash k} Signal_{u,c,f} \text{ [Watts]} + Noise(= 4 \times 10^{-16}) \text{ [Watts]}}. \quad (3)$$

Shannon's formula [20] then gives the (instantaneous) downlink rate for u in f,

$$R_{u,f} = \frac{20 \text{ MHz}}{|\mathcal{A}_c| - \nu_{c,f}} \times Q_{u,f}, \quad (4)$$

where, 20 MHz is the fixed bandwidth, and $|\mathcal{A}_c| - \nu_{c,f}$ is the total number of UEs that receive data from u's serving cell in f. The term $\nu_{c,f}$ is the number of UEs attached to c that cannot be scheduled in f because $Q_{u,f}$ is too low ($\nu_{c,f} = |\{u|u \in \mathcal{A}_c, SINR_{u,f} \leq -5.0 \text{ [dB]}\}|$). Intuitively, $R_{u,f}$ is high if channel conditions are favourable for u in f and if u shares the bandwidth with few UEs. The arithmetic mean of $R_{u,f}$ over $\mathcal{F}_t$ yields the 'downlink rate' ($\overline{R}_u$) for u over that frame. Notice that $\overline{R}_u$ depends on $\mathcal{C}$ through $\mathcal{A}_c$, $\nu_{c,f}$ and $Q_{u,f}$, each of which depend on the state of all cells in the network (wireless signals do not recognise cell boundaries).

Finally, the fitness of $\mathcal{C}$ over frame $\mathcal{F}_t$ is adapted from the industry standard sum-log-rates metric for evaluating HetNet control algorithms [7]:

$$fitness_{\mathcal{C}}^{\mathcal{F}_t} \leftarrow \sum_{u \in \mathcal{U}} \left(\log_e \overline{R}_u \right), \quad (5)$$

where, $\mathcal{U}$ is the set of users receiving data from the HetNet during $\mathcal{F}_t$. The logarithm is sensitive to changes in the lowest values of $\overline{R}_u$. Thus, cell configurations $\mathcal{C}$ that increase cell-edge rates will receive high fitness.

Our goal is to discover synergistic settings at the SC power and bias, and MC ABS layers of HetNets with a customised GA. This problem is non-trivial due to inter-layer and intra-layer coupling. For instance, if the SC of Fig. 1 uses a large bias then the MC should mute often to protect interfered UEs in its expanded region. Furthermore, the GA must converge quickly in order to keep pace with rapidly changing traffic patterns.

3   Previous Work

3.1   Heterogeneous Network Optimisation

Techniques for eICIC are described at the conceptual level from release 10 of 3GPP, but no algorithms are specified. As such, network operators have the freedom to interpret and implement these concepts as they see fit. The bulk of the literature on HetNet optimisation focuses on improving the effectiveness of eICIC. Self Organising Network (SON) algorithms have been proposed to modulate small cell powers and biases [9,10] and eICIC parameters such as MC ABS ratios [11]. SONs have also been designed to increase energy efficiency [22], minimise inter-cell interference [7,16,18], and maximise fairness-based utilities [21]. The authors in [2] presented a detailed survey of SONs in the context of LTE.

Our goal is to maximise fairness. Auxiliary objectives, such as improving energy efficiency, are ignored because customer satisfaction takes priority in this highly competitive industry. Deb et al. (2014) tackled the single-objective problem using non-linear programming [7]. The authors proved that optimising $\mathcal{C}$ is NP-hard, even in a network with one MC and multiple SCs. Fairness was dramatically improved by optimising β_s, $\forall s \in \mathcal{S}$, and $ABS_{r,m}$, $\forall m \in \mathcal{M}$. However, their algorithm did not modulate SC powers and it required inputs that may be difficult to obtain in real networks [14]. Our framework requires only channel gain data that are reported by UEs.

López-Pérez and Claussen (2013) proposed a method for tuning $ABS_{r,m}$ so that performance targets can be specified by the operator $\forall u \in \mathcal{A}_m$. In their approach, the bias and ABS layers were configured independently. However, HetNet layers are coupled such that, for instance, optimal MC ABS ratios depend on the size of SC expanded regions (i.e. SC biases). The framework developed in this paper jointly optimises the power, bias and ABS layers of a HetNet. Furthermore, the proposed algorithm is easily implemented on a centralised server and it requires inputs that are readily available in real networks.

3.2 Genetic Algorithms

GAs have enjoyed recent success in challenging real-world applications. For instance, Deb and Myburgh (2016) developed a customised GA to solve a billion variable problem [6]. Their findings are ground-breaking for two reasons:

1. firstly, the billion variable barrier is breached for the first time on a real-world constrained optimisation problem, and,
2. secondly, the proposed approach outperformed two commercial optimisers (`glpk` and `CPLEX`) with respect to solution quality and convergence speed. Indeed, the GA discovers near optimal solutions in a fraction of the time.

The authors concur with the critiques levelled by Deb and Myburgh (2016) regarding the use of customised heuristics. Their paper argues that the components of evolutionary heuristics should be viewed as a toolbox. Researchers should carefully select the appropriate tools for the problem at hand and avoid blindly applying canonical settings and operators that were developed for unrelated applications or toy problems. The GA in [6] was tailored for the real world problem at hand. It employed customised initialisation, re-combination, and mutation operators, which guaranteed constraint satisfiability.

An extensive literature describes the applications of GAs in dynamic environments [4,8,17]. Of the approaches that incorporate memory, Branke [4] identifies two main paradigms based on the notions of explicit and implicit memory. The former stores genetic material from previously fit individuals in a memory cache. The latter attempts to capture prior knowledge using degenerate genetic material. GAs that rely on implicit memory struggle if the environment alternates between many states [4]. On the other hand, explicit memory is beneficial when similar conditions recur frequently, as in wireless networks. The next section presents a customised GA that leverages explicit memory (see also [3,12,19]).

4   Customised Genetic Algorithm

4.1   Encoding and Mapping

Recall Eq. 2 which expressed the configuration $\mathcal{C}$ of a HetNet as a mixed type array storing the MC ABS ratios, SC powers and SC biases. Let $\mathcal{I}$ (for Individual) encode the network configuration $\mathcal{C}$. The first $|\mathcal{M}|$ elements of $\mathcal{I}$ are integers which encode $ABS_{r,m}$ for $m = 1, \ldots, |\mathcal{M}|$, the next $|\mathcal{S}|$ elements are real values encoding P_s for $s = 1, \ldots, |\mathcal{S}|$, and the remaining real-valued elements encode β_s for $s = 1, \ldots, |\mathcal{S}|$. $\mathcal{I}$ must first be mapped to $\mathcal{C}$ before it can be evaluated.

Consider again the toy network of Fig. 1 with a single MC m' containing the embedded SC s'. Let $\mathcal{I} = [11, -0.2, 4.5]$ encode the network configuration $\mathcal{C} = [ABS_{r,m'}, P_{s'}, \beta_{s'}]$. $\mathcal{I}$ is mapped to $\mathcal{C}$ as follows. The ABS ratio for m' is given by,

$$\mathcal{C}[0] = ABS_{r,m'} = ABS\_ratios\,[\mathcal{I}[0]\;\%\;12]\,,$$

where, $ABS\_ratios := [1, 2, 3, 4, 5, 6, 7, 6, 5, 4, 3, 2]$ and $\%$ is the modulo operator. Since $\mathcal{I}[0] = 11$ it follows that $\mathcal{C}[0] = ABS\_ratios\,[11\%12] = ABS\_ratios\,[11] = 2$. This implementation preserves locality in the genotype to phenotype mapping and respects the constraints on $ABS_{r,m'}$. Furthermore, $\mathcal{I}[0]$ can take any integer value and still satisfy the constraints. There is a bias against aggressive MC muting ($ABS_{r,m'} = 1$) and high activity ($ABS_{r,m'} = 7$).

$\mathcal{I}[1]$ encodes the power of SC s', which is given by,

$$\mathcal{C}[1] = P_{s'} = 23.0 + Sigmoid(\mathcal{I}[1]) \times (35.0 - 23.0),$$

where, the sigmoid function $Sigmoid(x) = 1/1 + e^{-x}$ returns a value between 0 and 1, and where the minimum and maximum powers for s' are, respectively, 23.0 dBm and 35.0 dBm. The sigmoid facilitates fine grained exploitative mutations, but occasionally it allows for large explorative steps. Similarly,

$$\mathcal{C}[2] = \beta_{s'} = 0.0 + Sigmoid(\mathcal{I}[2]) \times (15.0 - 0.0),$$

where, the minimum and maximum biases for s' are, respectively, 0.0 dB and 15.0 dB. Notice that $\mathcal{I}[1]$ and $\mathcal{I}[2]$ can adopt any real value without violating the constraints.

In summary, the individual $\mathcal{I} = [11, -0.2, 4.5]$ is mapped to the network configuration $\mathcal{C} = [ABS_{r,m'}, P_{s'}, \beta_{s'}] \approx [2, 28.40, 14.84]$.

4.2   Search Operators

Each pair of selected parents are recombined using uniform crossover to yield two children. Elements in the parent strings are swapped with a probability $p_{cross} = 0.5$ per locus, so that approximately half of the genetic material is interchanged between parents.

Each child undergoes Gaussian mutation applied with a probability $p_{mut} = 0.05$ per element. Consider the individual $\mathcal{I}$ from Sect. 4.1. Assume for the sake of exposition that each element is mutated. Then,

$$\mathfrak{I}[0] \leftarrow \mathfrak{I}[0] + \mathfrak{R} \times \left(\left| round \left(\mathcal{N} \left(0, \sigma_{ABS}^2 \right) \right) \right| + 1 \right),$$
$$\mathfrak{I}[1] \leftarrow \mathfrak{I}[1] + \mathcal{N} \left(0, \sigma_{P,\beta}^2 \right),$$
$$\mathfrak{I}[2] \leftarrow \mathfrak{I}[2] + \mathcal{N} \left(0, \sigma_{P,\beta}^2 \right),$$

where, $\mathfrak{R}$ is a random variable drawn from the set $\{-1, +1\}$, $|x| = \sqrt{x^2}$, $round(x)$ maps x to the nearest integer, and $\mathcal{N}$ is the normal distribution parametrised with zero mean and standard deviation σ_{ABS} or $\sigma_{P,\beta}$. The parameters σ_{ABS} and $\sigma_{P,\beta}$ control the severity of mutations applied to elements encoding ABS ratios, and respectively, power and bias settings. A parameter sweep on hold out data suggested that $\sigma_{ABS} = 1.0$ and $\sigma_{P,\beta} = 0.5$ gives good performance. The search parameters were not tuned exhaustively in this proof of concept study.

4.3 Fitness Assignment

Wireless signals experience some path loss gain as they propagate from a transmitting cell to a UE. Individuals are evaluated using simulated reports of these channel gains, the realistic analogues of which would be available in a physical deployment. Let $g_{u,c}^{\mathcal{F}_t}$ denote the channel gain (in [dB]) experienced by UE u from cell c during frame $\mathcal{F}_t$. These data are collected from all $|\mathcal{U}|$ UEs in the network and arranged in an $(|\mathcal{M}| + |\mathcal{S}|) \times |\mathcal{U}|$ matrix $G^{\mathcal{F}_t}$. Realistic values of $g_{u,c}^{\mathcal{F}_t}, \forall c \in \mathcal{S} \cup \mathcal{M}$, are computed by modelling the distribution buildings, waterways, streets and open spaces. The path loss model is described by the authors in [5].

The fitness of a solution $\mathcal{C}$ is calculated using $G^{\mathcal{F}_t}$ as follows. First, the signals received by UE u from each cell c are computed via,

$$Signal_{u,c} = g_{u,c}^{\mathcal{F}_t} + P_c,$$

where, P_c is the transmitting power of c (in [dBm]) as specified by $\mathcal{C}$. Then, the UE attachments are determined using Eq. 1, where again, all elements of β_c are read from $\mathcal{C}$. Next, $SINR_{u,f}$ is computed for each UE $\forall f \in \mathcal{F}_t$ using Eq. 3. Finally, Shannon's formula (Eq. 4) is invoked to calculate the downlink rates, and Eq. 5 is called to yield $fitness_{\mathcal{C}}^{\mathcal{F}_t}$ – the fitness of individual $\mathcal{C}$ based on the channel gains reported by $u \in \mathcal{U}$ during frame $\mathcal{F}_t$.

Computing $fitness_{\mathcal{C}}^{\mathcal{F}_t}$ is computationally expensive, yet new solutions are required every ten minutes or so. In order to achieve this short run time, individuals are evaluated against only five[2] channel gain matrices $G^{\mathcal{F}_t}$, from five randomly sampled recent frames. The fitness assigned to individual $\mathcal{C}$ is given by the average of $fitness_{\mathcal{C}}^{\mathcal{F}_t}$ computed over the five $G^{\mathcal{F}_t}$ that currently constitute the training set. A moving window approach is adopted whereby the training set is replenished after every five generations with the most recent reports.

---

[2] If $pop\ size = 1000$ and $gens = 100$ and runs are executed on a machine with 50 cores operating at 2.66 GHz.

4.4   Pseudocode

Algorithm 1 differs from the canonical GA in two respects. Firstly, the initial population is seeded from an explicit memory storing previously evolved solutions (line 2). Of the *pop size* individuals in the initial population, a total of $\lfloor pop\ size \times (mix/100.0) \rfloor$ are drawn from memory and the rest are randomly initialised, where $mix \in [0.0, 100.0]$. It is hypothesized that integrating knowledge from past scenarios should be beneficial since hotspots materialise at predictable locations during rush hour periods. Section 6 experimentally validates the use of explicit memory for this instance of a dynamic environment. Secondly, the training set is updated periodically during the run as described in Sect. 4.3.

Algorithm 1. Genetic Algorithm(Parameters in Table 2)

1: **procedure** OPTIMISE $\mathcal{C}$
2:     Seed *mix* [%] of the initial population $\mathcal{P}$ with individuals from memory;
3:     Sample channel gain matrices $G^{\mathcal{F}t}$ from 5 recent frames to form training set $\mathcal{T}$;
4:     **for** $gen = 1$ **to** $\#gens$ **do**
5:         **if** $gen \% 5 == 0$ **then**
6:             $\mathcal{T} \leftarrow$ update $\mathcal{T}$ with five more recent samples of $G^{\mathcal{F}t}$;
7:         Evaluate each individual in $\mathcal{P}$ against $\mathcal{T}$ as described in Sect. 4.3;
8:         Select $\frac{pop\ size - \#elites}{2}$ pairs of parents by tournament selection (size=5);
9:         Recombine each pair of selected parents using uniform crossover;
10:         Mutate both children from each crossover event;
11:         Evaluate the children against $\mathcal{T}$;
12:         Replace all but the $\#elites$ best individuals in $\mathcal{P}$ with the children;
        return the fittest individual on the final $\mathcal{T}$;

Table 2 displays the evolutionary parameters. The constants were tuned via a parameter sweep. The choice of *pop size* = 1000 and $\#gens = 100$ negotiated a satisfactory tradeoff between running time and performance for this dynamic problem.

5   Experiments

A HetNet with $|\mathcal{M}| = 21$ MCs and $|\mathcal{S}| = 63$ SCs (an average 3 per MC sector) was simulated in a $3.61\,km^2$ region of Dublin City Centre. Tri-sector MC towers were distributed on a hexagonal grid pattern. SCs were placed at random locations to mimic their ad-hoc deployment where hotspots tend to arise.

5.1   Traffic Model

The GA was trained on 100 samples of $G^{\mathcal{F}t}$ collected over the first ten minutes of 'scenarios' lasting twenty minutes. The generalisation of evolved solutions was assessed on 100 samples of $G^{\mathcal{F}t}$ from the final ten minutes of each scenario.

Table 2. Evolutionary parameters.

Parameter	Value
pop size	1000
#*gens*	100
Initialisation	Random with *mix* [%] seeded from memory
Selection	Tournament
Tournament Size	5 (= 0.5% of *pop size*)
#*elites*	10 (= 1% of *pop size*)
Mutation and Crossover	Sect. 4.2
Crossover Probability	Each pair of selected parents
Mutation Probability	Each child is mutated

Sixty hotspots were simulated in a given scenario. Half of the hotspots were placed within 10 to 20 metres of (randomly selected) SCs, and half were placed at arbitrary locations. The number of UEs in hotspot *HS* during a sampled frame $\mathcal{F}_t$ was drawn from $\mathcal{N}(\mu_{HS}(t), \sigma_{HS}(t))$. Parameters $\mu_{HS}(t)$ and $\sigma_{HS}(t)$ denote, respectively, the mean and standard deviation of the number of UEs in *HS* at timestep t. The physical size $r_{HS}(t)$ of *HS* were also varied over the 20 simulated minutes from $t = 0$ to $t = 200$. Table 3 displays the minimum and maximum values that the parameters of the traffic model can take. Parameters μ_{HS}, σ_{HS} and r_{HS} were initialised to random values in their allowed ranges at timestep $t = 0$. These values were adjusted linearly[3] until the end of the train/test period at $t = 200$. The term δ_{HS} controlled how much a parameter changed as a fraction of its allowed range; it was selected uniformly from $[-0.25, 0.25]$ for each *HS*.

Table 3. Parameters of the traffic model.

	μ_{HS}	σ_{HS}	r_{HS} [m]	δ_{HS}
min	5.0	0.5	5.0	−0.25
max	20.0	2.5	20.0	0.25

Hotspots were populated first and then the remaining UEs were distributed randomly until $|\mathcal{U}| = 1200$ existed on the map. This 'full buffer' model simulates the dynamic properties of ephemeral hotspots and the stochastic character of wireless traffic.

---

[3] This traffic model is adopted since localisation errors are tens of meters in real networks. Hence, the properties of hotspots must be estimated.

5.2 Experimental Setup

The explicit memory was initialised by executing the GA with random initial populations on 1000 different scenarios. Training and testing channel gains matrices $G^{\mathcal{F}_i}$ were then saved from 100 unique scenarios, distinct from those used to initialise the memory. The next section analyses convergence on training data and assesses the generalisation of evolved solutions on test data. Finally, a case study illustrates how complementary settings are evolved at the power, bias and ABS layers.

6 Results and Discussion

A comprehensive statistical validation of all components of the proposed framework is computationally infeasible within the scope of this proof of concept study. Instead, the memory is initialised just once as described in Sect. 5.2. The reliability of the framework is then assessed by running the GA 100 times (with and without memory) on a single scenario, using different random seeds for each run. However, performance may be sensitive to the peculiar distribution of hotspots in the scenario selected for these runs. The GA's ability to generalise across many different scenarios is assessed by executing a single run for 100 distinct scenarios (in experiments with and without memory).

6.1 Training

Reliability of the GA on a Single Scenario: Figure 2 plots the average best-of-generation fitness on a single scenario (computed over 100 runs), for the baseline method and the GA with various choices of *mix* [%]. The very thin shaded 95% confidence intervals enclosing the means implies that the GA reliably produces fit solutions.

The baseline implements constant settings of $P_s = 35$ [dBm] and $\beta_s = 10$ [dB], $\forall s \in \mathcal{S}$, and $ABS_{r,m} = 0.5, \forall m \in \mathcal{M}$. This baseline is currently used by network operators in practice. Notice that the baseline fitness jumps every time the training set is refreshed.

Interestingly, the GA's performance improves dramatically when some of the initial population is seeded from memory. Seeded runs converge faster and they yield statistically significantly better end-of-run solutions than unseeded runs ($GA_{mix=0\%}$). Furthermore, seeded runs surpass the baseline method earlier at around generation five. This result highlights the benefit of incorporating knowledge from similar frequently encountered scenarios. Convergence profiles are displayed for experiments with $mix = 0\%$, 25%, 50%, 75% and 100%. Convergence is similar and stable for all values of $mix \geq 25\%$. The best models are evolved with $mix = 50\%$.

Performance Across Multiple Scenarios: Ax. 1 in Fig. 3 indicates the mean difference in sum-log-rates between various methods versus baseline, computed over 100 scenarios, with 95% confidence intervals included. The pattern from

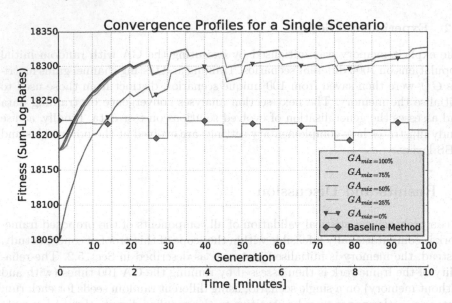

Fig. 2. The GA reliably discovers highly fit solutions.

Fig. 2 is echoed. That is, seeded runs converge to better solutions faster (blue line) than runs with random initial populations (magenta line). Seeded runs outperform the baseline after just 3 generations, compared to 13 generations for unseeded runs. The black curve on Ax. 1 indicates the difference between the blue and magenta lines. It never crosses the zero level of Ax. 1 (dotted green line). Thus, the seeded GA achieves higher mean sum-log-rates across the 100 scenarios throughout. Furthermore, the differences at each generation are significant (at $\alpha = 0.05$) based on two-sample paired t-tests (black line on Ax. 2). (Color figure online)

6.2 Benchmarking on Test Data

The proposed GA was benchmarked against an algorithm adapted from [14]. The benchmark works by first hill climbing in the SC power and bias spaces, and then using the method from [14] to establish MC ABS ratios (the lone parameter α is tuned on validation data). Initially, cells are configured using the baseline settings, such that, $P_s := 35$ [dBm] and $\beta_s := 10$ [dB], $\forall s \in \mathcal{S}$, and $ABS_{r,m} := 4$, $\forall m \in \mathcal{M}$. Then the following steps are iterated fivefold:

- P_1 (the power of SC 1) is incremented from 23 [dBm] to 35 [dBm] in steps of 1 [dBm]. Equation 5 is evaluated at each step, and hence P_1 is set to the value that maximises the sum-log-rates. The process is repeated for P_2 (after P_1 has been updated), and so on until all SC powers have been updated.
- Similarly, SC biases are updated by incrementing β_s, $\forall s \in \mathcal{S}$, from 0 [dB] to 15 [dB] in steps of 1 [dB] - selecting the setting at each SC that maximises Eq. 5.
- Finally, the rule from [14] is executed to update $ABS_{r,m}$, $\forall m \in \mathcal{M}$.

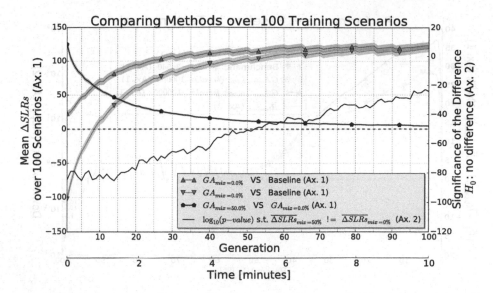

Fig. 3. The green dotted line on Ax. 1 indicates the zero level: no difference exists in the compared quantities. The black line on Ax. 2 indicates the logarithm of the p-values from paired t-tests with $H_0 : \overline{\Delta SLRs}_{mix=0\%} = \overline{\Delta SLRs}_{mix=50\%}$. (Color figure online)

Note that the training set is refreshed after every five iterations of the preceding steps, as described in Sect. 4.3.

Figure 4 compares percentiles of the downlink rates received by $\#scenarios \times \#frames \times \#UEs = 25 \times 100 \times 1200$ UEs simulated during the test intervals of 25 different scenarios. Ax. 1 represents the percentage change of downlink rates versus baseline (dotted red line). Ax. 2 plots the downlink rates in [Mbps] for the baseline (solid red line).

The unseeded GA (cyan line) increases cell-edge rates (LHS of the plot) by around 32% versus baseline. These gains are achieved by sacrificing the highest-rate cell-centre UEs (RHS of the plot) by only $\approx 20\%$. Thus, edge UEs experience greatly improved quality of service at negligible cost to their cell-centre counterparts. Seeding boosts the 2.5$^\mathrm{th}$ percentile performance by a further 4% (black line). Clearly, the GA dramatically outperforms the benchmark scheme (green line) described above.

Two-sample Kolmogorov–Smirnov tests indicate that the distributions of downlink rates for all methods are significantly ($p-values \ll 0.05$) different to that of the baseline. The following distributions are also mutually significantly different: $GA_{mix=50\%}$ v. $GA_{mix=0\%}$, and $GA_{mix=50\%}$ v. Benchmark.

6.3   Multi-layer Interactions

Figure 5 depicts a 0.05 km^2 region of the simulated network, where an umbrella MC with an embedded SC is visible. The GA was executed for; scenario 1 (LHS)

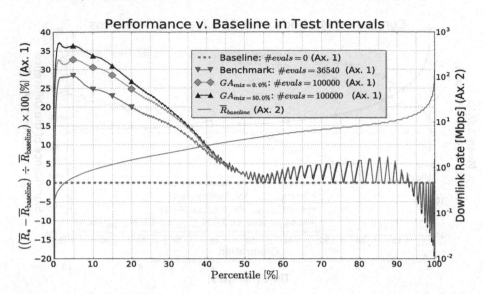

Fig. 4. Evolved settings boost cell-edge rates VS a static baseline by over 36% and outperform the benchmark scheme. The number of function evaluations required are indicated. (Color figure online)

where a hotspot containing 30 UEs is adjacent to SC 1, and scenario 2 (RHS) where the hotspot is beyond the reach of SC 1.

The GA converged on $P_1 \leftarrow 33.0$ [dBm], $\beta_1 \leftarrow 11.6$ [dB] and $ABS_{r,1} \leftarrow 1$ for scenario 1. Thus, the SC employs a large bias to absorb UEs from the adjacent hotspot. SC 1 also transmits at near maximum power so the absorbed UEs receive high channel quality. Finally, MC 1 mutes for 35 out of 40 subframes to mitigate cross-tier interference in the expanded region of SC 1.

In contrast, $P_1 \leftarrow 23.2$ [dBm], $\beta_1 \leftarrow 1.8$ [dB] and $ABS_{r,1} \leftarrow 6$ for scenario 2. Here, SC 1 cannot offload the distant hotspot from the MC tier so it uses a small bias. In addition, P_1 is reduced to mitigate small-to-macro interference.

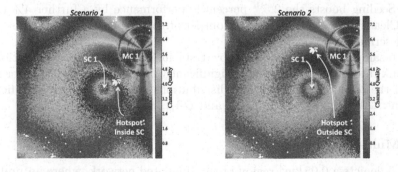

Fig. 5. Complementary settings are evolved at each layer.

MC 1 transmits often to satisfy its attached UEs. However, $ABS_{r,1} \leftarrow 6 < 7$ to protect distant SCs. Thus, the optimal settings at a particular cell depend on conditions at remote cells. In summary, the GA evolves synergistic settings at the ABS, power and bias layers in this region of the HetNet.

7   Future Work and Conclusions

HetNets must be reconfigured every few minutes to keep pace with changing traffic patterns. Such a timescale is on par with the running time of an evolutionary algorithm. This paper presented a customised GA for configuring multi-layer HetNets in real time. Cell-edge capacity was significantly increased over industry standard baselines in system level simulations. The experiments revealed that fitter solutions are evolved more rapidly when runs are seeded from an explicit memory. Smarter mechanisms for adapting the memory over time could be developed in a follow-up study.

A state of the art benchmark was significantly surpassed by the GA. The inferior performance of the greedy benchmark is unsurprising in this domain given that HetNet reconfiguration is an NP-hard problem. However, the benchmark significantly outperformed baseline settings that are currently used in practice. This result motivates future work to further explore the tradeoff between performance and running time of greedy versus non-greedy methods. Finally, this paper addressed a real-world dynamic optimisation problem that could serve as a test bed for designing novel adaptive heuristics in dynamic environments.

Acknowledgements. This research is based upon works supported by the Science Foundation Ireland under grant 13/IA/1850. The authors are grateful to the reviewers and Dr. Miguel Nicolau for their helpful comments.

References

1. Cisco Visual Networking Index: Global Mobile Data Traffic Forecast Update, 2014–2019. Cisco, White Paper (online) (2015)
2. Aliu, O.G., Imran, A., Imran, M.A., Evans, B.: A survey of self organisation in future cellular networks. IEEE Commun. Surv. Tutorials **15**(1), 336–361 (2013)
3. Branke, J.: Memory enhanced evolutionary algorithms for changing optimization problems. In: In Congress on Evolutionary Computation CEC99. Citeseer (1999)
4. Branke, J.: Evolutionary Optimization in Dynamic Environments, vol. 3. Springer Science & Business Media, Berlin (2012)
5. Claussen, H., Ho, L.: Multi-carrier cell structures with angular offset. In: 2012 IEEE 23rd International Symposium on Personal Indoor and Mobile Radio Communications (PIMRC), pp. 1179–1184. IEEE (2012)
6. Deb, K., Myburgh, C.: Breaking the billion-variable barrier in real-world optimization using a customized evolutionary algorithm. In: Proceedings of the 2016 on Genetic and Evolutionary Computation Conference, pp. 653–660. ACM (2016)
7. Deb, S., Monogioudis, P., Miernik, J., Seymour, J.P.: Algorithms for enhanced Inter-cell Interference Coordination (eICIC) in LTE HetNets. IEEE/ACM Trans. Netw. (TON) **22**(1), 137–150 (2014)

8. Dempsey, I., O'Neill, M., Brabazon, A.: Foundations in Grammatical Evolution for Dynamic Environments, vol. 194. Springer, Heidelberg (2009)

9. Fenton, M., Lynch, D., Kucera, S., Claussen, H., O'Neill, M.: Evolving coverage optimisation functions for heterogeneous networks using grammatical genetic programming. In: Squillero, G., Burelli, P. (eds.) EvoApplications 2016. LNCS, vol. 9597, pp. 219–234. Springer, Heidelberg (2016). doi:10.1007/978-3-319-31204-0_15

10. Fenton, M., Lynch, D., Kucera, S., Claussen, H., O'Neill, M.: Load balancing in heterogeneous networks using an evolutionary algorithm. In: 2015 IEEE Congress on Evolutionary Computation (CEC), pp. 70–76. IEEE (2015)

11. Hämäläinen, S., Sanneck, H., Sartori, C.: LTE Self-organising Networks (SON): Network Management Automation for Operational Efficiency. Wiley, Hoboken (2012)

12. Karaman, A., Uyar, Ş., Eryiğit, G.: The memory indexing evolutionary algorithm for dynamic environments. In: Rothlauf, F., Branke, J., Cagnoni, S., Corne, D.W., Drechsler, R., Jin, Y., Machado, P., Marchiori, E., Romero, J., Smith, G.D., Squillero, G. (eds.) EvoWorkshops 2005. LNCS, vol. 3449, pp. 563–573. Springer, Heidelberg (2005). doi:10.1007/978-3-540-32003-6_59

13. Liang, Y.: Real-time VBR video traffic prediction for dynamic bandwidth allocation. IEEE Transactions on Systems, Man, and Cybernetics, Part C (Applications and Reviews) **34**(1), 32–47 (2004)

14. López-Pérez, D., Claussen, H.: Duty cycles and load balancing in HetNets with eICIC almost blank Subframes. In: 2013 IEEE 24th International Symposium on Personal, Indoor and Mobile Radio Communications (PIMRC Workshops), pp. 173–178. IEEE (2013)

15. Lopez-Perez, D., Guvenc, I., De la Roche, G., Kountouris, M., Quek, T.Q., Zhang, J.: Enhanced intercell interference coordination challenges in heterogeneous networks. IEEE Wirel. Commun. **18**(3), 22–30 (2011)

16. Madan, R., Borran, J., Sampath, A., Bhushan, N., Khandekar, A., Ji, T.: Cell association and interference coordination in heterogeneous LTE-a cellular networks. IEEE J. Sel. Areas Commun. **28**(9), 1479–1489 (2010)

17. Morrison, R.W.: Designing Evolutionary Algorithms for Dynamic Environments. Springer Science & Business Media, Berlin (2013)

18. Peng, M., Liang, D., Wei, Y., Li, J., Chen, H.H.: Self-configuration and self-optimization in LTE-advanced heterogeneous networks. IEEE Commun. Mag. **51**(5), 36–45 (2013)

19. Ramsey, C.L., Grefenstette, J.J.: Case-based initialization of genetic algorithms. In: ICGA, pp. 84–91. Citeseer (1993)

20. Shannon, C.E.: Communication in the presence of noise. Proc. IRE **37**(1), 10–21 (1949)

21. Tall, A., Altman, Z., Altman, E.: Self organizing strategies for enhanced ICIC (eICIC). In: 2014 12th International Symposium on Modeling and Optimization in Mobile, Ad Hoc, and Wireless Networks (WiOpt), pp. 318–325. IEEE (2014)

22. Tang, J., So, D.K., Alsusa, E., Hamdi, K.A., Shojaeifard, A.: Resource allocation for energy efficiency optimization in heterogeneous networks. IEEE J. Sel. Areas Commun. **33**(10), 2104–2117 (2015)

23. Winstein, K., Sivaraman, A., Balakrishnan, H.: Stochastic forecasts achieve high throughput and low delay over cellular networks. In: Presented as part of the 10th USENIX Symposium on Networked Systems Design and Implementation (NSDI 2013), pp. 459–471 (2013)

Multi-objective Evolutionary Algorithms for Influence Maximization in Social Networks

Doina Bucur[1], Giovanni Iacca[2], Andrea Marcelli[3]([✉]), Giovanni Squillero[3], and Alberto Tonda[4]

[1] University of Twente, Drienerlolaan 5, 7522 NB Enschede, The Netherlands
d.bucur@utwente.nl
[2] INCAS, Dr. Nassaulaan 9, 9401 HJ Assen, The Netherlands
giovanni.iacca@gmail.com
[3] DAUIN, Politecnico di Torino, Corso Duca Degli Abruzzi,
24, 10129 Torino, Italy
{andrea.marcelli,giovanni.squillero}@polito.it
[4] INRA, UMR 782 GMPA, Avenue Lucien Brétignières,
78850 Thiverval-Grignon, France
alberto.tonda@grignon.inra.fr

Abstract. As the pervasiveness of social networks increases, new NP-hard related problems become interesting for the optimization community. The objective of *influence maximization* is to contact the largest possible number of nodes in a network, starting from a small set of seed nodes, and assuming a model for information propagation. This problem is of utmost practical importance for applications ranging from social studies to marketing. The influence maximization problem is typically formulated assuming that the number of the seed nodes is a parameter. Differently, in this paper, we choose to formulate it in a multi-objective fashion, considering the minimization of the number of seed nodes among the goals, and we tackle it with an evolutionary approach. As a result, we are able to identify sets of seed nodes of different size that spread influence the best, providing factual data to trade-off costs with quality of the result. The methodology is tested on two real-world case studies, using two different influence propagation models, and compared against state-of-the-art heuristic algorithms. The results show that the proposed approach is almost always able to outperform the heuristics.

Keywords: Influence maximization · Social network · Multi-objective evolutionary algorithms

1 Introduction

Social networks (SNs) are graphs modeling a society, where edges represent the channels through which information, news, ideas, trends, or advertising flow dynamically in time. Nowadays SNs can effectively model the dynamic of an important part of people's digital lives: from interactions in established giants of

© Springer International Publishing AG 2017
G. Squillero and K. Sim (Eds.): EvoApplications 2017, Part I, LNCS 10199, pp. 221–233, 2017.
DOI: 10.1007/978-3-319-55849-3_15

the field such as *Facebook* and *Google+*, or newcomers as *Twitter* and *Minds.com*; to contacts in specialized hubs dedicated to a specific target audience, such as *Academia.edu* and *ResearchGate*. As the number of users of such systems grows, so does the amount of behavioral data, and all classical network-related problems become computationally harder.

Interesting social phenomena can be studied by analyzing the underlying graph of the social network. A graph edge $a \rightarrow b$ could signify a likelihood that b will be exposed to a's opinions, or that a will support b in the election for the purpose of work-related promotions; given the initial set of network participants who broadcast information or cast a vote, the long-term opinions or the eventual outcome of the promotions may be easily foreseen. More in general, given an initial set of nodes in a SN, one can estimate the extent of their *influence* over the rest of the network. The dynamics by which the graph structure enables new information to spread varies with the nature of the SN: an edge $a \rightarrow b$ may model a fixed probability or a probability that varies according to other features of node b, such as its number of direct relationships with other nodes. Social sciences have studied a number of such probabilistic *propagation models* [13].

A common problem in SNs is the *influence maximization*: given the graph G, a discrete-time propagation model M, and a "budget" $k \geq 1$ of network nodes to be the initial "seeds", calculate the set of k nodes that will eventually produce the largest influence $\mathcal{I}$ upon the whole network. The problem was initially formulated in [19], and has been shown NP-hard for most propagation models [13].

Evolutionary algorithms (EAs) were found able to explore effectively the vast search space of all possible subsets of nodes [2], but the choice of the number of seeds was left to the user. In the present work, we instead propose to tackle the influence maximization problem using a Multi-Objective Evolutionary Algorithm (MOEA), trying to maximize the influence $\mathcal{I}$ and minimize the budget k concurrently. Including k as an explicit goal of the optimization provides users the necessary data to trade off between effort (the number of nodes that need to be influenced) and effect (the final influence over the whole network).

The proposed approach is then applied to two real-world case studies: the *ego-Facebook* network, which describes social circles from Facebook, and *ca-GrQc*, which covers scientific collaborations between authors. The networks are taken from the Stanford large network dataset [15], a popular source of benchmarks for influence maximization algorithms, and have been tested against state-of-the-art heuristics using two different influence propagation models.

The rest of the paper is organized as follows: Sect. 2 formalizes the problem, discusses existing heuristics and approximation algorithms for this problem, and briefly presents the MOEAs related work; Sect. 3 describes our MOEA method; and Sect. 4 presents the experimental results on two case studies. Finally, Sect. 5 concludes this work.

2   Background and Related Work

To introduce the scope of the current work, the basics of influence propagation and influence maximization in a SN are briefly recalled, followed by a short review on the state of the art for both heuristics and EAs applied to this problem, and a brief introduction to MOEAs.

2.1   Models for Influence Propagation and Problem Formulation

Concrete models for message forwarding in a SN are the basic building blocks to be able to evaluate the effectiveness of a set of seed nodes, i.e., how much global influence a set of nodes will have, indirectly, over the network via peer-to-peer message propagation.

Since the propagation of a message from a network user to another is a discrete event, the propagation models are also time-discrete. As the receptiveness of users to incoming messages from the network differs, we experiment with two previously studied models from the "Cascade" family of propagation models [13], which views influence as being transmitted through the network in a tree-like fashion, where the seed nodes are the roots.

The pseudo-code common to the two Cascade models: Independent Cascade (IC) and Weighted Cascade (WC) is given in Algorithm 1. IC was first studied in the marketing domain, modeling the effects that word-of-mouth communication has upon macro-level marketing [11]. Each newly "activated" node n will succeed in activating each inactive neighbor m with a fixed probability p, which is a global property of the system, equal for all edges $n \to m$ in G. WC, on the other hand, assigns non-uniform probabilities: an edge $n \to m$ has probability $p(n \to m) = \frac{1}{in\text{-}degree(m)}$ of activating m when n is active. In both models, when node n has more than one neighbor, activation is sequenced in an arbitrary order.

In the classical problem of influence maximization, the goal is to optimize the seed set S given a budget $k = |S|$ so that its eventual influence over the whole network is maximal. The influence of a seed set S is measured as the size of the set A of active nodes, $\mathbb{E}[|A|]$, obtained by the propagation model.

For both propagation models, the problem is NP-hard [13]. Furthermore, an approximation hardness result is known: approximating the optimal solution by a factor better than $1 - \frac{1}{e}$ (with e the base of the natural logarithm, which means roughly 63% approximation) is also NP-hard [13].

Further complication stems from the propagation models being stochastic: the evaluation of the expected influence of a seed set S in polynomial time will not be exact; the problem of computing this for any S over Independent Cascade was proven #P-complete in [22]. Instead, an approximate estimation can be obtained empirically, by simulating the propagation process a given number of times.

2.2   Prior Heuristics and EAs for Influence Maximization

We compare the proposed approach against two state-of-art heuristics: *High degree* (HIGHDEG), and *Single discount* (SDISC), briefly described in the

---

Algorithm 1. The **Cascade** family of propagation models. G is the network graph, S the set of "seed" nodes, and $p(n \to m)$ the probability that information will reach across a graph edge $n \to m$.

```
 1: procedure CASCADE(G, S, p)
 2:     A ← S                    ▷ A: the set of active nodes after the propagation ended
 3:     B ← S                    ▷ B: the set of nodes activated in the last time slot
 4:     while B not empty do
 5:         C ← ∅
 6:         for each n ∈ B do
 7:             for each direct neighbor m of n, where m ∉ A, do
 8:                 with probability p(n → m), add m to C
 9:             end for
10:         end for
11:         B ← C
12:         A ← A ∪ B
13:     end while
14:     return the size of A
15: end procedure
```

---

following. In general, the heuristics in literature fall into two categories: (a) heuristics which provably obey the approximation guarantee but are too time-intensive, and (b) heuristics of much better time complexity, but with either no approximation guarantees or much weaker ones. From the latter category, the *High-degree* (or degree centrality) greedy heuristic simply adds nodes n to A in order of decreasing out-degree [13]. Chen et al. [5] refine greedy "degree-discount" heuristics based on *High-degree*, using the idea that if a node n is already active and also there exists an edge $m \to n$, then, when considering whether to add node m to A, this edge should not be counted towards the out-degree of m. This heuristic (known as *Single discount*) is applicable to all cascade models.

Many other heuristics are known. Among those without optimality guarantees, Jiang et al. [12] test Simulated Annealing under Independent Cascade, and find that it has a complexity advantage over greedy heuristics, and can also find narrowly better solutions. In [2], a first attempt to tackle the influence maximization problem by a classic (single-objective) Genetic Algorithm is made, with promising results obtained in comparison with existing heuristics.

Various studies [5,12,13] evaluated the previously described heuristics comparatively on a small number of large SNs, and generally find empirically that the two degree-based, inexpensive greedy heuristics *High-degree* and *Single discount* may not reach the approximation guarantee of 63% known to be possible, but in some cases they are only a few percentage points away from the target.

2.3   Multi-objective Evolutionary Algorithms

In many optimization problems, the quality of a solution is defined by its performance in relation to several, conflicting objectives. Such conflicting goals cannot be sensibly reduced to a single value using a weighted sum or another aggregate function, but rather they must be considered independently from each other. Multi-Objective Evolutionary Algorithms (MOEAs) are a natural flavour of Evolutionary Algorithms specifically designed for tackling this kind of problems. As a result, differently from single-objective optimization where the output of an evolutionary algorithm is a unique optimal solution, the output of a MOEA is a *Pareto front*, that is, a set of *non-dominated* solutions, to choose from. In other words, a Pareto front contains a set of optimal trade-off solutions that are better than any other solution in the multi-dimensional objective space at hand.

MOEAs have been used with great success in a number of real-world applications, as surveyed for instance in [4, 6, 8]. In the SNs domain, so far MOEAs have been used mostly for community detection [16, 18, 23] and network clustering [14]. On the other hand, to the best of out knowledge no prior work exists on the application of MOEAs on the influence maximization problem, which is the main contribution of the present work.

3 Proposed Approach

In order to tackle influence maximization as a multi-objective problem, we propose to use a MOEA to optimize the conflicting goals of maximizing how much the network has been influenced by the seed nodes (i.e., the effect of the influence campaign), and of minimizing the number of such seed nodes (i.e., the cost of the campaign). As a result, the different solutions on the Pareto front provide users the necessary data to trade off between cost and effect. In what follows we present briefly the details of the MOEA used in our experimentation.

3.1 MOEA Engine

μGP (also called *MicroGP*) is a generic evolutionary algorithm, able to manage individuals encoded as multigraphs. Its original application was the creation of complex assembly-language programs for testing different microprocessors [20]. Afterward, it has been used on a wider range of problems, such as the creation of test programs for pre- and post-silicon validation; the design of Bayesian networks [21]; the analysis of the impact of network topology on routing protocols [3]; automatic software testing in mobile phones [10]; real-value parameter optimization; and even creation of *corewar* warriors [7]. μGP is freely available on SourceForge[1].

While handling complex and structured genomes is not needed for this case study, μGP is also able to self-adapt the activation probability of genetic operators, manage a genome of variable length, and perform multi-objective fitness evaluation, with a crowding distance assessment on the Pareto front similar to the state-of-the-art algorithm NSGA-II [9].

---

[1] http://ugp3.sourceforge.net/.

3.2   Representation and Fitness of a Candidate Solution

For the problem at hand, a candidate solution is a set of nodes, of variable size, which is a subset of the set of nodes in the original network. Individuals are thus unordered sequences of integer node identifiers, representing the seeds of influence in the network. A visual representation of the problem encoding is reported in Fig. 1.

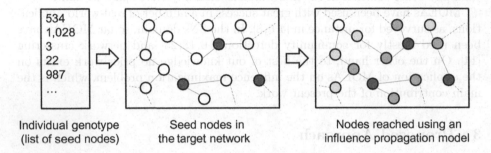

| Individual genotype | Seed nodes in | Nodes reached using an |
| (list of seed nodes) | the target network | influence propagation model |

Fig. 1. Schema of the proposed encoding. Seed nodes are internally represented as a list of integers. The fitness value is the average number of other nodes that are reached, following a given model of probabilistic influence propagation. In the example, the only node not influenced by the set of seeds is the white one, in the top left corner of the rightmost frame.

The fitness value of a candidate solution is a probabilistic metric of the number of nodes that are likely to be reached, starting from a given set of seeds of influence — according to a given model of influence propagation (Independent Cascade or Weighted Cascade, described in Sect. 2). Given the stochastic nature of both propagation models, the fitness estimation is empirical, and itself a stochastic process: repeated simulations of the network propagation model yield an extent to which the network is reached, and the final fitness value is the average among these fitness samples.

4   Experimental Evaluation

In the experimental evaluation of the algorithm, μGP uses a $(\mu + \lambda)$ MOEA, with both μ (population size) = 100 and λ (number of operators applied at each generation) = 100, and the following genetic operators:

– Recombination operators: standard one- and two-point crossover.
– Three mutation operators, that add, remove, or change one node from a candidate seed set.

The activation probabilities of the operators are self-adapted during the evolutionary run, resorting to an improved dynamic multi-armed bandit selection [1].

All nodes in a target network can be added to a solution, and μGP is used with two different configurations, generating candidate seed sets of sizes between 1 and max_nodes. As the algorithm used to estimate influence propagation (either IC or WC) is stochastic, in order to get a reliable average each individual evaluation is repeated 100 times. The resulting fitness value is the average of the 100 repetitions.

The proposed approach is tested on two real-world case studies, taken from the Stanford large network dataset [15]. The first network, labeled **ego-Facebook**, describes social circles from Facebook; the second network, labeled **ca-GrQc**, covers scientific collaborations between authors from papers submitted to General Relativity and Quantum Cosmology category, from the e-print arXiv[2]. Their notable features are reported in Table 1.

Table 1. Main features of the case studies considered for the experimental evaluation of the proposed MOEA approach.

Name	ego-Facebook	ca-GrQc
Nodes	4,039	5,242
Edges	88,234	14,496
Type of graph	undirected	undirected
Nodes in largest WCC	4,039	4,158
Nodes in largest SCC	4,039	4,158
Average clustering coefficient	0.6055	0.5296
Diameter (longest shortest path)	8	17

4.1   ego-Facebook

The MOEA algorithm is compared with the *High degree* (HIGHDEG) and *Single discount* (SDISC) heuristics on the **ego-Facebook** case study, over both the IC propagation model, using two different probabilities of influence propagation, $p = 0.01$ or $p = 0.05$, and the WC model. The evolutionary algorithm's termination condition is set to 10,000 generations, and for each influence propagation model considered (IC with $p = 0.01$, IC with $p = 0.05$, WC), two different experiments are carried out, one with max_nodes = 200 and one with max_nodes = 400.

ego-Facebook/IC. Results of the evaluation for the considered case study, using the IC model of influence propagation are reported in Fig. 2 (for $p = 0.01$) and Fig. 3 (for $p = 0.05$). In the figures, the y axis shows k, the number of seed nodes in the solution, while the x axis shows the average number of nodes reached by the seeds. The final Pareto front found by the MOEA (in red, with

---

[2] https://arxiv.org/.

early candidate evaluations in blue) outperforms the heuristics when the number of nodes in the candidate solutions exceeds 25; the MOEA is able to find solutions that are more effective, fitness-wise, than the ones created by the heuristics for the same number of nodes in the seed set. For solutions featuring a number of nodes close to the upper bound (200 or 400, depending on the experiment), it is however noticeable how the evolutionary algorithm has issues populating the Pareto front. Remarkably, some of the candidate solutions explored are still better than those provided by the heuristics (see for example Fig. 2), even if they are Pareto-dominated by others. This might be due to our choice of maintaining a relatively small population ($\mu = 100$) and give the algorithm more generations to evolve.

Intuitively, when $p = 0.05$, the number of influenced nodes is higher: however, the difference in performance between the heuristics and the MOEA also grows, as even some of the initial randomly generated individuals for high k behave better than the solutions found by HIGHDEG and SDISC, see Fig. 3. It is noticeable that the MOEA has again issues populating the higher part of the Pareto front, especially when the maximum allowed number of seed nodes is 400.

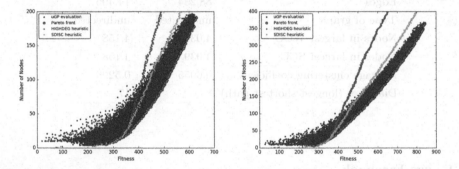

Fig. 2. Results obtained by the MOEA approach and the High Degree (HIGHDEG) and Single Discount (SDISC) heuristics on the ego-Facebook case study, using the Independent Cascade model for influence propagation, with $p = 0.01$ and an upper bound of 200 nodes (**left**) and 400 nodes (**right**) per candidate solution. (Color figure online)

ego-Facebook/WC. Results of the evaluation for the considered case study, using the WC model of influence propagation, are reported in Fig. 4 (the WC model does not use probability values p). The MOEA's results are very similar to the IC case, and while the evolutionary algorithm outperforms the heuristics on most values of k, it clearly has issues finding good solutions with a high number of nodes, especially when compared to the results of SDISC, which in this case study behaves particularly effectively.

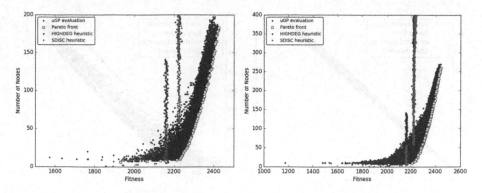

Fig. 3. Results obtained by the MOEA approach and the High Degree (HIGHDEG) and Single Discount (SDISC) heuristics on the ego-Facebook case study, using the Independent Cascade model for influence propagation, with $p = 0.05$ and an upper bound of 200 nodes (**left**) and 400 nodes (**right**) per candidate solution. (Color figure online)

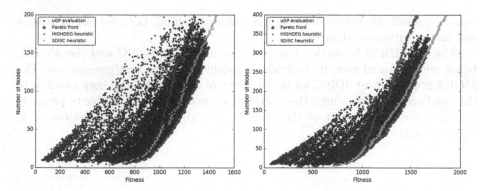

Fig. 4. Results obtained by the MOEA approach and the High Degree (HIGHDEG) and Single Discount (SDISC) heuristics on the ego-Facebook case study, using the Weighted Cascade model for influence propagation, and an upper bound of 200 nodes (**left**) and 400 nodes (**right**) per candidate solution.

4.2   ca-GrQc

As **ca-GrQc** is a simpler case study, featuring less arcs than **ego-Facebook**, we choose to evolve solutions with an upper bound of 400 candidate nodes, only (`max_nodes = 400`), and set a termination condition after 1,000 generations.

ca-GrQc/IC. Figure 5 shows results for the IC influence propagation model, using $p = 0.01$ and $p = 0.05$. Final outcomes for the two probability values are similar, even though the differences are more visible for $p = 0.05$; probably the lower value of p makes it harder for influence to spread on such a sparse network,

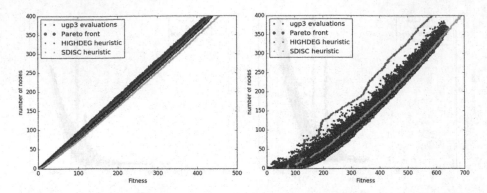

Fig. 5. Results obtained by the MOEA approach and the High Degree (HIGHDEG) and Single Discount (SDISC) heuristics on the ca-GrQc case study, using the Independent Cascade model for influence propagation, with an upper bound of 400 nodes per candidate solution, $p = 0.01$ (**left**) and $p = 0.05$ (**right**).

and as a result the fitness landscape is harder to climb, both for the heuristics and the evolutionary algorithm.

The HIGHDEG heuristic clearly lags behind both SDISC and the MOEA, being outperformed even by individuals produced in the first generations. The MOEA is able to best SDISC for the majority of values of k, with issues similar to the ego-Facebook case study: the multi-objective algorithm is unable to properly populate the highest part of the front ($k > 360$), and for small values of k, SDISC's solutions are better.

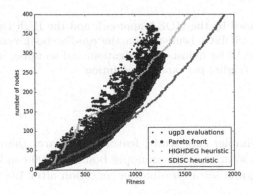

Fig. 6. Results obtained by the MOEA approach and the High Degree (HIGHDEG) and Single Discount (SDISC) heuristics on the ca-GrQc case study, using the Weighted Cascade model for influence propagation, with an upper bound of 400 nodes per candidate solution.

ca-GrQc/WC. Figure 6 shows results for the ca-GrQc case study using the WC influence model. This time, problems usually faced by the MOEA become more evident: the higher part of the Pareto front lags behind solutions found by the heuristics, already for $k > 150$; and while the MOEA clearly outperforms HIGHDEG, it cannot match the quality of seed sets found by SDISC. The general impression from this case study is that the termination condition came too early, and given more evaluations, the MOEA might have been able to populate other parts of the Pareto front: this is however counter-intuitive, as the same termination condition provided good results for the IC influence propagation model. Further analyses are required, in order to properly assess the source of these issues.

5   Conclusions

In this paper, we proposed a novel multi-objective evolutionary approach to influence maximization in social networks. A MOEA is tasked with finding the set of k seed nodes that, given a model of influence propagation, maximize the nodes reached in a target network. As minimizing the value of k is also given as an optimization objective, the MOEA is able to find a Pareto front of compromises between number of seed nodes in the set and global influence in the graph. The presented methodology is then tested on two real-world case studies, using two different influence propagation models. The MOEA is proven able to reliably outperform two state-of-the-art heuristics for intermediate values of k, facing mixed success for extremely high and low values of k.

While the results obtained are still preliminary, they nevertheless show promising outcomes. In particular, MOEAs prove to be able to overcome established heuristics for influence maximization for two real-world case studies. On the other hand, the heuristics are in general more efficient time-wise (although depending on the dataset and on the size of the seed nodes, as was shown in [2]), and still get a better performance on some corner cases. Further experimental evaluations on a wide range of social networks with different features are necessary, in order to assess the effective potential of the proposed approach; furthermore, the influence of the population size on the MOEA's performance is going to be studied. Future works will also focus on hybrid techniques, developing memetic algorithms [17] for influence maximization, which may be able to extract —and combine— the best qualities of EAs and heuristics.

Acknowledgment. Andrea Marcelli Ph.D. program at Politecnico di Torino is supported by a fellowship from TIM (Telecom Italia Group).

This article is based upon work from COST Action CA15140 'Improving Applicability of Nature-Inspired Optimisation by Joining Theory and Practice (ImAppNIO)' supported by COST (European Cooperation in Science and Technology).

References

1. Belluz, J., Gaudesi, M., Squillero, G., Tonda, A.: Operator selection using improved dynamic multi-armed bandit. In: Proceedings of the 2015 Annual Conference on Genetic and Evolutionary Computation, pp. 1311–1317. ACM (2015)
2. Bucur, D., Iacca, G.: Influence maximization in social networks with genetic algorithms. In: Squillero, G., Burelli, P. (eds.) EvoApplications 2016. LNCS, vol. 9597, pp. 379–392. Springer, Heidelberg (2016). doi:10.1007/978-3-319-31204-0_25
3. Bucur, D., Iacca, G., Squillero, G., Tonda, A.: The impact of topology on energy consumption for collection tree protocols: an experimental assessment through evolutionary computation. Appl. Soft Comput. **16**, 210–222 (2014)
4. Bucur, D., Iacca, G., Squillero, G., Tonda, A.: The tradeoffs between data delivery ratio and energy costs in wireless sensor networks: a multi-objective evolutionary framework for protocol analysis. In: Proceedings of the 2014 Annual Conference on Genetic and Evolutionary Computation, pp. 1071–1078. ACM (2014)
5. Chen, W., Wang, Y., Yang, S.: Efficient influence maximization in social networks. In: Proceedings of the 15th ACM SIGKDD International Conference on Knowledge Discovery and Data Mining, KDD 2009, NY, USA, pp. 199–208. ACM, New York (2009)
6. Coello, C.C., Lamont, G.B., van Veldhuizen, D.A.: Evolutionary Algorithms for Solving Multi-objective Problems. Springer, Heidelberg (2002)
7. Corno, F., Sanchez, E., Squillero, G.: Evolving assembly programs: how games help microprocessor validation. IEEE Trans. Evol. Computat. **9**(6), 695–706. http://dx.doi.org/10.1109/TEVC.2005.856207
8. Deb, K.: Multi-Objective Optimization Using Evolutionary Algorithms, vol. 16. Wiley, Hoboken (2001)
9. Deb, K., Pratap, A., Agarwal, S., Meyarivan, T.: A fast and elitist multiobjective genetic algorithm: NSGA-II. IEEE Trans. Evol. Comput. **6**(2), 182–197 (2002)
10. Gandini, S., Ruzzarin, W., Sanchez, E., Squillero, G., Tonda, A.: A framework for automated detection of power-related software errors in industrial verification processes. J. Electron. Test. **26**(6), 689–697 (2010)
11. Goldenberg, J., Libai, B., Muller, E.: Talk of the network: a complex systems look at the underlying process of word-of-mouth. Mark. Lett. **12**(3), 211–223 (2001)
12. Jiang, Q., Song, G., Cong, G., Wang, Y., Si, W., Xie, K.: Simulated annealing based influence maximization in social networks. In: Burgard, W., Roth, D. (eds.) AAAI. AAAI Press (2011)
13. Kempe, D., Kleinberg, J.: Éva Tardos: maximizing the spread of influence through a social network. Theor. Comput. **11**(4), 105–147 (2015)
14. Kim, K., McKay, R.B., Moon, B.R.: Multiobjective evolutionary algorithms for dynamic social network clustering. In: Proceedings of the 12th Annual Conference on Genetic and Evolutionary Computation, GECCO 2010, NY, USA, pp. 1179–1186. ACM, New York (2010)
15. Leskovec, J., Krevl, A.: SNAP Datasets: Stanford Large Network Dataset Collection (2016). http://snap.stanford.edu/data
16. Liu, C., Liu, J., Jiang, Z.: A multiobjective evolutionary algorithm based on similarity for community detection from signed social networks. IEEE Trans. Cybern. **44**(12), 2274–2287 (2014)
17. Neri, F., Cotta, C., Moscato, P.: Handbook of Memetic Algorithms. Springer, Heidelberg (2012)

18. Pizzuti, C.: A multiobjective genetic algorithm to find communities in complex networks. IEEE Trans. Evol. Comput. **16**(3), 418–430 (2012)
19. Richardson, M., Agrawal, R., Domingos, P.: Trust management for the semantic web. In: Fensel, D., Sycara, K., Mylopoulos, J. (eds.) ISWC 2003. LNCS, vol. 2870, pp. 351–368. Springer, Heidelberg (2003). doi:10.1007/978-3-540-39718-2_23
20. Squillero, G.: MicroGP - an evolutionary assembly program generator. Genet. Program. Evol. Mach. **6**(3), 247–263 (2005)
21. Tonda, A.P., Lutton, E., Reuillon, R., Squillero, G., Wuillemin, P.-H.: Bayesian network structure learning from limited datasets through graph evolution. In: Moraglio, A., Silva, S., Krawiec, K., Machado, P., Cotta, C. (eds.) EuroGP 2012. LNCS, vol. 7244, pp. 254–265. Springer, Heidelberg (2012). doi:10.1007/978-3-642-29139-5_22
22. Wang, C., Chen, W., Wang, Y.: Scalable influence maximization for independent cascade model in large-scale social networks. Data Mining Knowl. Discov. **25**(3), 545–576 (2012)
23. Zeng, Y., Liu, J.: Community detection from signed social networks using a multi-objective evolutionary algorithm. In: Handa, H., Ishibuchi, H., Ong, Y.-S., Tan, K.C. (eds.) Proceedings of the 18th Asia Pacific Symposium on Intelligent and Evolutionary Systems, Volume 1. PALO, vol. 1, pp. 259–270. Springer, Heidelberg (2015). doi:10.1007/978-3-319-13359-1_21

A Fast ILP-Based Heuristic for the Robust Design of Body Wireless Sensor Networks

Fabio D'Andreagiovanni[1(✉)], Antonella Nardin[2], and Enrico Natalizio[1]

[1] Sorbonne Universités, Université de Technologie de Compiègne,
CNRS, Heudiasyc UMR 7253, CS 60319, 60203 Compiègne, France
{d.andreagiovanni,enrico.natalizio}@hds.utc.fr
[2] Università Degli Studi Roma Tre, Via Ostiense 169, 00154 Roma, Italy
nardin.an@gmail.com

Abstract. We consider the problem of optimally designing a body wireless sensor network, while taking into account the uncertainty of data generation of biosensors. Since the related min-max robustness Integer Linear Programming (ILP) problem can be difficult to solve even for state-of-the-art commercial optimization solvers, we propose an original heuristic for its solution. The heuristic combines deterministic and probabilistic variable fixing strategies, guided by the information coming from strengthened linear relaxations of the ILP robust model, and includes a very large neighborhood search for reparation and improvement of generated solutions, formulated as an ILP problem solved exactly. Computational tests on realistic instances show that our heuristic finds solutions of much higher quality than a state-of-the-art solver and than an effective benchmark heuristic.

Keywords: Body wireless sensor networks · Network design · Integer linear programming · Robust optimization · ILP heuristic

1 Introduction

A *Wireless Sensor Network* (WSN) can be essentially described as a network of typically small and portable wireless devices, the sensors, which are spread on an area to collect data in a cooperative way and then forward the data to one or more collectors, commonly called *sinks*. Recently, the application of WSNs in healthcare has received a lot of attention and, just to cite two major examples, WSNs have been used to monitor the health conditions of patients in hospitals and to remotely monitor people under health risk when they are at home [1].

In this work, we focus attention on a topic related to healthcare applications of WSNs: the design of *body area networks*. A *Body Area Network* (BAN) is a WSN where wireless sensors (*biosensors*) are placed over or inside the body of a person to collect biomedical data. The biosensors generate data and transmit them to one or more sinks for storing or processing. For a detailed introduction to BANs, we refer the reader to the works [2,3]. Designing a BAN essentially

© Springer International Publishing AG 2017
G. Squillero and K. Sim (Eds.): EvoApplications 2017, Part I, LNCS 10199, pp. 234–250, 2017.
DOI: 10.1007/978-3-319-55849-3_16

consists in deciding the topology of the network and how data are routed from the biosensors to the sinks. This constitutes a classical WSN design problem (see e.g., [4,5]). However, since BANs are deployed on human bodies, their design need particular attention and present specific challenges that are not shared with other WSNs design problems [2,6]. A critical question is in particular constituted by the peculiar high-loss propagation behaviour of wireless signals through and over the human body: in contrast to canonical wireless networks, where high losses can be handled by increasing power emissions (see e.g., [7–9]), in BANs power emissions must be contained to both avoid damages to human tissues, due to overheating, and to preserve the charge of sensor batteries, whose substitution can result very uncomfortable for patients. Controlling energy consumption is thus a major aim in BAN design and is typically achieved through multi-hop routing, implemented through relay nodes, which are wireless devices that act as intermediate nodes between sinks and sensors and allow transmission of reduced power over shorter distances [10–12].

Nowadays there is a rich literature about BANs, in particular about technical aspects concerning the definition of energy-efficient routing protocols and the study of the peculiar propagation condition in human bodies [2,6]. In contrast, there is still a limited amount of work devoted to the design of BANs in terms of optimization models and algorithms. This fact has been highlighted also in the two relevant previous works [10,13]: in [10], the design problem of a BAN is formulated as a mixed integer linear program where multi-path routing and relay deployment is established in order to minimize the total cost of deployment of a BAN; [13] instead investigates a robust optimization model for tackling the data generation uncertainty and proposes a Mixed Integer Programming (MIP)-based heuristic for the solution of the resulting challenging optimization problem.

In this work, we consider a *scenario-based min-max* robust optimization model for the design of BANs that takes into account the uncertainty of data generation of BAN sensors. Our main original contribution is a new ILP heuristic for solving the robust design problem, based on combining deterministic and probabilistic variable fixing strategies guided by peculiar linear relaxations of the robust optimization model. In comparison to [13], our new algorithm does not just fix the variables expressing routing decisions, but also employs an initial deterministic fixing phase of the variables modelling the activation of relay nodes. Computational tests on realistic BAN instances show that our new heuristic produces solutions that are not only deeply better than those produced by a state-of-the-art optimization solver, but are also significantly better than those found by the algorithm of [13].

2   The Body Area Network Design Problem

In this section, we identify the elements of a BAN that are relevant for modelling purposes and we derive a network optimization model for the energy-efficient design of a BAN. For a more detailed description of mathematical optimization modelling for BANs, we refer the reader to [10,13].

System Elements of a BAN. Any BAN can be described as a *set of biosensors*, denoted by B, that produce biomedical data while monitoring a human body. The data are collected by a *set of sinks*, denoted by S. The biosensors and the sinks are located in positions over or inside the human body that are usually precisely pre-established (for example, one can think about the electrodes of a Holter monitor, which must be positioned on specific spots of the chest of a patient for monitoring heart activity). For each sink $s \in S$, each biosensor $b \in B$ generates a volume of data $d_{bs} \geq 0$ (typically, a *bitrate* measured in bit/s).

In order to improve energy efficiency, the biosensors do not transmit their data directly to the sink according to a single-hop direct communication, but rely on a multi-hop routing strategy. Multi-hop routing can be implemented through relay nodes, which have the task of receiving and forwarding the biomedical data. The positions of relay nodes is not fixed and can be chosen. Such positioning choice, if done wisely, can greatly improve the energy efficiency of the BAN. The optimization problem that we consider is indeed related to the optimal positioning of relays in order to minimize energy consumption. In such problem, we are given a set of candidate locations for the relays and an upper bound on the number of deployable relays and we must take two decisions: (i) establish the number of deployed relays; (ii) choose the location of the deployed relays.

We introduce a set R to represent the potentially deployable relays. Each potential relay $r \in R$ is characterized by a unique position in/over the body and we must decide whether it is deployed or not. Each r has also a capacity $c_r \geq 0$ that represents the maximum bitrate that it can manage.

The transmission of data from any BAN device (biosensor, relay node or sink) to another BAN device is based on a directional wireless link. As in [10,13], we assume that the devices employs a TDMA (Time Division Multiple Access) protocol, which allows the devices to transmit on the same frequency band without interfering. When either transmitting or receiving data, the BANs devices consume energy according to the following formulas [14]:

$$
\begin{aligned}
E_{\text{TX}}(v, \delta) &= E_{\text{TX}_{CIRC}} \cdot v + E_{\text{TX}_{AMP}}(\lambda) \cdot \delta^\lambda \cdot v \\
E_{\text{RX}}(v) &= E_{\text{RX}_{CIRC}} \cdot v
\end{aligned}
\tag{1}
$$

where E_{TX} is the total transmission energy and E_{RX} the total receiver energy (expressed in joules). We remark that $E_{\text{TX}}, E_{\text{RX}}$ are a function of the volume of transmitted/received data v (expressed in bits) and of the distance δ (expressed in meters) between the transmitter and the receiver. Additionally: $E_{\text{TX}_{CIRC}}$, $E_{\text{RX}_{CIRC}}$ are the energy consumed by the circuits to respectively transmit and receive a single bit; $E_{\text{TX}_{AMP}}(\lambda)$ is the energy consumed by the transmitting amplifier and λ is the path loss exponent in the signal attenuation formula.

A Flow-Based Integer Linear Program for BAN design. It is natural to trace back the energy-efficient design of BAN to a network flow optimization problem. Specifically, we trace it back to a variant of a Multicommodity Flow Problem (MCFP), a classical network flow problem, where the aim is to decide how to install routing capacity and how to route a set of commodities in a network, minimizing the total routing and installation cost, while not exceeding the capacity of installed network elements. For an introduction to capacitated network design and MCFPs, we refer the reader to [15,16].

The BAN can be naturally modelled through a directed graph $G(V, A)$ where:

(1) the set of *vertices* V contains one element for each wireless device of the network - biosensor, sink and relay. The set V thus corresponds to the union of three disjoint sets of vertices: (i) the set B of vertices corresponding to biosensors; (ii) the set R of vertices corresponding to potentially deployable relays; (iii) the set S of vertices corresponding to sinks. We therefore have $V = B \cup R \cup S$.

Each BAN device can communicate with other devices that are within its transmission range. The transmission range may vary on the basis of the propagation conditions and of the transmission power of the device (see e.g., [14]). We denote the subsets of devices that are within the transmission range of a device as follows: (a) for each biosensor $b \in B$, we distinguish the subsets $R_b \subseteq R$, and $S_b \subseteq S$ representing the relays and sinks within the range of b, respectively; (b) for each potential relay $r \in R$, we distinguish the subsets $R_r \subseteq R$, and $S_r \subseteq S$ representing the relays and sinks within the range of r, respectively; (c) more generally, given a vertex $i \in V$, representing any type of BAN device, we denote by $V_i \subseteq V$ the subset of vertices representing devices within the transmission range of i.[1]

(2) the set of *arcs* A contains one element for each wireless link that can be established between a pair of wireless devices. An arc $a = (i, j) \in A$ is an ordered pair of vertices that models a directional wireless link from a device $i \in V$ to another device $j \in V_i$ within the range of i. We respectively call tail and head the vertices i, j of $a = (i, j)$. The set A is the union of four disjoint sets of arcs:

   (a) the set $A_{B \to S}$ of arcs (i, j) such that the tail is a biosensor and the head is a sink within the range of the biosensor, i.e. $i \in B$, $j \in S_i$. They represent transmissions of biomedical data directly to sinks;

   (b) the set $A_{B \to R}$ of arcs (i, j) such that the tail is a biosensor and the head is a relay within the range of the biosensor, i.e. $i \in B$, $j \in R_i$. They represent transmissions from a biosensor to a relay;

   (c) the set $A_{R \leftrightarrow R}$ of arcs (i, j) such that both the tail and the head are relay nodes, i.e. $i, j \in R$ with $j \in R_i$. They represent wireless links between relays;

   (d) the set $A_{R \to S}$ of arcs (i, j) such that the tail is a relay node and the head is a sink within the range of the relay, i.e. $i \in R$, $j \in S_i$. They represent transmissions from a relay to a sink. Therefore we have $A = A_{B \to S} \cup A_{B \to R} \cup A_{R \leftrightarrow R} \cup A_{R \to S}$.

---

[1] We note that we assume that each biosensor $b \in B$ never acts as a receiver and *only generates and transmits* data. So we do not characterize the subsets $B_r, B_s \subseteq B$ of biosensors within the range of a relay r or a sink s. Furthermore, we assume that each sink s never acts as a transmitter and *only receives* data. So we do not characterize the subsets $B_s \subseteq B$, $R_s \subseteq R$ of biosensors and relays within the range of a sink s.

We can now rewrite the energy formulas (1) in terms of the graph introduced above. When data are transmitted on an arc $a = (i,j) \in A$, the energy consumed is the sum of the energy consumed by i to transmit and the energy consumed by j to receive. The energy consumed to send one unit of data from i to j is:

$$E_{ij} = E_{\text{TX}}(1, \delta_{ij}) + E_{\text{RX}}(1) = \left[E_{\text{TX}_{\text{CIRC}}} + E_{\text{TX}_{\text{AMP}}}(\lambda_{ij}) \cdot \delta_{ij}^{\lambda_{ij}} \right] + E_{\text{RX}_{\text{CIRC}}} \quad (2)$$

which is obtained from formulas (1) for $v = 1$. Here, λ_{ij} and δ_{ij} are respectively the path loss coefficient and the distance between i and j.

Using all the notation and elements introduced until now, we can formally state the BAN design problem that we consider, referring to the problem definition and modelling that has been initially provided in [13]:

Definition 1 (The Body Area Network Design Problem - BAND).
Given: (1) a BAN modeled as a directed graph $G(V, A)$, where $V = B \cup R \cup S$ is the set of vertices and $A = A_{B \to S} \cup A_{B \to R} \cup A_{R \leftrightarrow R} \cup A_{R \to S}$ is the set of arcs; (2) the bitrate $d_{bs} \geq 0$ of data generated by each biosensor $b \in B$ for each sink $s \in S$; (3) the capacity $c_r \geq 0$ of each relay $r \in R$; (4) the energy coefficients $E_{ij} \geq 0$ expressing the total energy consumed to send 1 data unit from i to j; the BAND consists in choosing which relays are activated and which single-paths are used to route the flow of data generated by each biosensor for each sink, in order to minimize the total energy consumption. □

The BAND is based on taking two decisions: (1) which relays to deploy and (2) which single-paths to use to route the data generated by each biosensor for each sink. These two decisions can be modeled through two families of binary decision variables: (1) binary *relay deployment variables* $y_r \in \{0,1\} \ \forall \ r \in R$ such that y_r equals 1 if relay r is deployed and 0 otherwise; (2) binary *unsplittable flow variables* $x_{ij}^{bs} \in \{0,1\} \ \forall \ b \in B, s \in S, (i,j) \in A$ such that x_{ij}^{bs} equals 1 if all the data generated by biosensor b for sink s are routed on arc (i,j) and 0 otherwise.

These variables are employed in the following ILP problem that we denote by BAND-ILP [13]:

$$\min \sum_{b \in B} \sum_{s \in S} \sum_{(i,j) \in A} E_{ij} \, d_{bs} \, x_{ij}^{bs} \qquad \text{(BAND-ILP)}$$

$$- \sum_{\substack{(b,j) \in \\ A_{B \to R} \cup A_{B \to S}}} d_{bs} \, x_{bj}^{bs} = -d_{bs} \qquad b \in B, s \in S \qquad (3)$$

$$\sum_{\substack{(j,r) \in \\ A_{B \to R} \cup A_{R \leftrightarrow R}}} d_{bs} \, x_{jr}^{bs} - \sum_{\substack{(r,j) \in \\ A_{R \leftrightarrow R} \cup A_{R \to S}}} d_{bs} \, x_{rj}^{bs} = 0 \qquad b \in B, s \in S, r \in R \qquad (4)$$

$$\sum_{\substack{(j,s) \in \\ A_{B \to S} \cup A_{R \to S}}} d_{bs} \, x_{js}^{bs} = d_{bs} \qquad b \in B, s \in S \qquad (5)$$

$$\sum_{\substack{(r,j)\in \\ A_{R\to R}\cup A_{R\to S}}} d_{bs}\, x^{bs}_{rj} \leq c_r\, y_r \qquad\qquad r \in R \qquad (6)$$

$$\sum_{r\in R} y_r \leq U \qquad\qquad (7)$$

$$x^{bs}_{ij} \in \{0,1\} \qquad\qquad b\in B, s\in S, (i,j)\in A$$

$$y_r \in \{0,1\} \qquad\qquad r \in R.$$

We remark that the constraints (3–5) could be simplified by dividing both sides of the inequalities by d_{bs}.

The objective function pursues the minimization of the total BAN energy consumption expressed as the sum of the energy consumed by each arc (i,j), equal to the product of the data flow and the energy E_{ij} consumed on (i,j) to transmit and receive 1 unit of data. The constraints (3–5) are flow conservation constraints essentially expressing the balance between ingoing and outgoing flows in any node of the graph. Note that we distinguish three flow balance cases, one for each type of device/vertex: (1) biosensors $b\in B$, which only transmit data, have a negative flow balance; (2) relays $r\in R$, which are transit vertices and thus retransmit all the received data, have a null flow balance; (3) sinks $s\in S$, which only receive data, have a positive flow balance. In each of these vertices, the flow balance must be considered for the data flow generated by each biosensor $b\in B$ for each sink $s\in S$. The constraints (6) express the capacity of each relay. We note that each of these constraints has a right-hand-side whose value may vary: if $y_r = 1$, then the constraint activates and the right-hand-side is equal to c_r. Otherwise, the right-hand-side is equal to 0 and forces to zero also the left-hand-side, thus preventing data flows to be received by or transmitted to r. The constraints (7) express the limit $U > 0$ on the number of deployable relays.

Protecting Against Data Uncertainty by a Robust Model. Until now, we have assumed that all the data involved in the BAND are exactly known when the problem is solved. However, this assumption does not hold in the real world: among its sensors, a BAN typically includes sensors that generate data according to an event-driven policy, thus leading to changeful and non-continuous data rates whose value is not known a priori [2]. A reduction in the expected data rate is not harmful to the designed BAN, since there is anyway sufficient transmission capacity. What can instead have very bad effects is an increase in the data rates, since the used relays may become not sufficient to handle the increased data volumes. In this case, biomedical data would be lost and this is a risk that cannot be taken at all in a BAN (as an example, one can think about the dramatic consequences that losing data produced by an early detection ischemia sensor could have on a patient).

The presence of data uncertainty in an optimization problem, namely the fact that a subset of the input data is not exactly known when the problem is solved, may result really tricky not just practically but also theoretically: as well-known from sensitivity analysis, even small deviations in the value of the input data may completely compromise the feasibility and optimality of produced solutions.

Solutions supposed to be feasible may result infeasible and thus totally useless in practice, while solutions supposed to be optimal may result instead of very bad quality. For an exhaustive introduction to the consequences of the presence of data uncertainty in optimization, we refer the reader to [17–19].

For the design of BAN under data rate uncertainty, we adopt *min-max robustness* (Min-Max) [20, 21]: this type of robust optimization paradigm is especially appropriate in problems where it is crucial to guarantee very high level of protection against data uncertainty, since infeasibility due to data variations could have dramatic effects. This is the case of BANs, where data loss due to unexpected fluctuations in data rates may lead to the death of monitored patients.

In the context of the BAND, assuming the perspective of a highly risk-averse decision maker, who wants to guarantee a fully trustable monitoring of health conditions even under data uncertainty, looks appropriate. Specifically, Min-Max can be adapted to the BAND problem by introducing a set of data generation scenarios Σ: each scenario $\sigma \in \Sigma$ specifies a vector $d^\sigma = (d_{11}^\sigma \cdots d_{bs}^\sigma \cdots d_{|B||S|}^\sigma)$ that states the bitrate between each biosensor-sink couple in σ. These scenarios can be included in the so-called *robust counterpart* of BAND-ILP, a version of BAND-ILP that we denote by Rob-BAND-ILP and that produces robust solutions, i.e. solutions protected against data fluctuations (such formulation has been introduced in [13], paper to which we refer the reader for a detailed discussion of how the model is derived following the principles of Min-Max):

$$\min \quad E \qquad \qquad \text{(Rob-BAND-ILP)} \qquad (8)$$

$$\sum_{b \in B} \sum_{s \in S} \sum_{(i,j) \in A} E_{ij} \, d_{bs}^\sigma \, x_{ij}^{bs} \leq E \qquad \qquad \sigma \in \Sigma \qquad (9)$$

$$-\sum_{\substack{(b,j) \in \\ A_{B \to R} \cup A_{B \to S}}} x_{bj}^{bs} = -1 \qquad \qquad b \in B, s \in S \qquad (10)$$

$$\sum_{\substack{(r,j) \in \\ A_{R \to R} \cup A_{R \to S}}} x_{rj}^{bs} - \sum_{\substack{(j,s) \in \\ A_{B \to R} \cup A_{R \to R}}} x_{jr}^{bs} = 0 \qquad b \in B, s \subset S, r \in R \qquad (11)$$

$$\sum_{\substack{(j,s) \in \\ A_{B \to S} \cup A_{R \to S}}} x_{js}^{bs} = 1 \qquad \qquad b \in B, s \in S \qquad (12)$$

$$\sum_{\substack{(r,j) \in \\ A_{R \to R} \cup A_{R \to S}}} d_{bs}^\sigma \, x_{rj}^{bs} \leq c_r \, y_r \qquad \qquad r \in R, \sigma \in \Sigma \qquad (13)$$

$$\sum_{r \in R} y_r \leq U \qquad \qquad (14)$$

$$x_{ij}^{bs} \in \{0, 1\} \qquad \qquad b \in B, s \in S, (i,j) \in A$$

$$y_r \in \{0, 1\} \qquad \qquad r \in R.$$

where variable $E \geq 0$ is introduced to express an upper bound on the total energy consumed by routing decisions over all the scenarios in Σ. Additionally, this robust model includes one capacity constraint (13) and one variable lower bound constraint (9) for each scenario $\sigma \in \Sigma$, as done in [13].

3   A Fast Heuristic for the Rob-BAND-ILP

The optimization problem Rob-BAND-ILP in principle can be solved by any Mixed Integer Programming (MIP) solver. However, the problem may prove (very) difficult to solve even for commercial solvers based on state-of-the-art branch-and-cut solution algorithms like IBM ILOG CPLEX [22]: these solvers can have issues in fast finding good quality solutions and tend to present a slow convergence to an optimal solution. More specifically, the optimality gap, expressing how far the best solution found is from an optimal solution during the execution of the branch-and-cut, tends to be improved slowly. Such difficulties constitute an issue for practical applications of the BAND.

To tackle such unsatisfactory performance, we propose to adopt a heuristic that is based on the sequential execution of the following three phases:

(1) a deterministic variable fixing phase that exploits the optimal solution of the (strengthened) linear relaxation of Rob-BAND-ILP and that produces a partial solution for the problem;
(2) a probabilistic variable fixing phase, guided by the combination of information coming from the optimal solutions of two distinct linear relaxations of (Rob-)BAND-ILP and that provides a complete fixing of the variables;
(3) a reparation/improvement phase based on executing an *exact large variable neighborhood search*, which aims at substituting an infeasible fixing with a feasible fixing or improving a feasible fixing, produced during phase 2. The search is called *exact* since it is expressed through the solution of an integer linear programming problem solved through an MIP solver.

We detail the features of each phase in the following subsections. Here, we just anticipate that the second phase represents the core of our algorithm and is based on an improvement of the algorithm ANTS (*Approximate Nondeterministic Tree Search*) [23], an ant colony-like algorithm. Specifically, the refinement of ANTS that we adopt is based on interpreting ant colony as a probabilistic variable fixing procedure, where the fixing is guided by optimal solutions to linear relaxations of the problem. Such interpretation has been first made in [13, 16, 24]. We stress that such interpretation actually leads to an algorithm that in spirit and substance is deeply different from ant colony algorithms and is more "well founded" on precious polyhedral considerations that come from the linear relaxation of the problem and from its strengthened version obtained after the application of cuts at the root of the branch-and-bound node.

Ant Colony Optimization (ACO) is a metaheuristic inspired by the foraging behaviour of ants that was initially proposed for combinatorial optimization by Dorigo and colleagues in [25] and later extended and improved in many works (e.g., [23, 26] - we refer the reader to [27] for an overview of theory and applications of ACO). A typical ACO algorithm has the following general structure:

while an arrest condition is *not* satisfied
   – ant-based solution construction
   – pheromone trail update
   – local search

The core of the algorithm is represented by a cycle where a number of feasible solutions are defined in a probabilistic and iterative way, taking into account the quality of solutions built in previous cycle iterations. Each solution is iteratively built by an *ant*: at each iteration, the ant is in a *state* that corresponds to a *partial solution* and can execute a so-called *move*, fixing the value of an additional variable and thus further completing the solution. The move is established probabilistically, putting together an *a-priori* and an *a-posteriori* measure of variable fixing attractiveness. In the theory of ACO, the a-priori measure is called *pheromone trail value* and is updated at the end of the construction phase on the basis of how good were the moves done. The construction cycle ends when reaching a stop condition, which commonly consists in a time limit. Then a local search is started to try improve the feasible solutions built, finding some local optimal solution.

Deterministic Fixing Phase. The first step of the first phase consists of solving the linear relaxation of problem Rob-BAND-ILP: the optimal solution of the linear relaxation, strengthened by the cuts added by CPLEX at the root node of the branch-and-bound tree, is then used to fix the value of decision variables of the problem. Specifically, the strategy is to fix to 1 the relay activation variables y_r whose value in the optimal solution of the linear relaxation is sufficiently close to 1. The rationale at the basis of this strategy is that if the value of a variable is sufficiently close to 1, then there is a quite good indication that we should fix the decision variable to 1 a good feasible solution. Formally, if we denote by y_r^{TLR} the value of variable y_r in an optimal solution of the (strengthened) linear relaxation, the fixing rule is: if $y_r^{\text{TLR}} \geq 1 - \epsilon$ then impose $y_r = 1$, where $\epsilon > 0$ is a parameter to choose. We focus on the relay activation variables as their fixing results particularly effective in reducing the difficulty of solving the complete problem Rob-BAND-ILP. Once that this fixing has been operated, we obtain a smaller version of the original problem, denoted by Rob-BAND-ILP^{FIX}, where the fixed variables y_r are no more part of the decision problem.

Probabilistic Fixing Phase. This phase is aimed at identifying the data routing paths within the BAN and consists of fixing the unsplittable flow variables x_{ij}^{bs}. As first step, let us denote by C the set of biosensor-sink pairs for which there exists at least one data scenario with positive bitrate, i.e. $C = \{(b,s) \in B \times S : \exists\ \sigma \in \Sigma \text{ with } d_{bs}^\sigma > 0\}$. We then refer to the concept of routing state.

Definition 2 (Routing state - RS [13]). *Consider a subset of biosensor-sink couples $\bar{C} \subseteq C$. We define routing state a fixing of the unsplittable flow variables $x_{ij}^{bs}\ \forall(i,j) \in E$ for each $(b,s) \in \bar{C}$ such that the fixing is feasible for the flow conservation constraints (10–12).*   □

A *routing state* assigns one routing path to each pair $(b,s) \in \bar{C}$. It is said *partial* when $\bar{C} \subset C$ (i.e., only a subset of data flows is routed), whereas it is said *complete* when $\bar{C} = C$ (i.e., all data flows are routed).

We build a complete routing state by assigning paths to biosensor-sink pairs according to the following procedure, which we call SET-PATHS. The pairs are considered according to an a-priori defined order, as done in [13]: we sort pairs $(b,s) \in C$ for decreasing value of the highest bitrate d_{bs}^σ over all the data scenarios $\sigma \in \Sigma$. Following the pair order, for each couple $c = (b,s) \in C$, we assign the entire data flow to a path p connecting b to s. The routing path for the pair c is chosen from a set of candidates P_c, defined as follows: (1) we solve the linear relaxation of Rob-BAND-ILP^{FIX}, which includes the deterministic fixing of the first phase and where we have additionally fixed the value of variables of pairs $c \in \bar{C}$ for which a path has been assigned in previous executions of the external loop; (2) using the optimal solution (x^{LR}, y^{LR}) of the linear relaxation, we define a graph $H^c(V, A^{mod})$ from $G(V, A)$: the set of vertices does not change, while in A^{mod} we keep only those arcs $(i,j) \in A$ with a positive flow, i.e. such that $x_{ij}^{LR\,c=(b,s)} > 0$. Furthermore, for each arc $(i,j) \in A^{mod}$ we define a weight $w_{ij} = x_{ij}^{LR\,c=(b,s)}$. We derive L candidate paths for the pair $c = (b,s)$ on graph $H^c(V, A^{mod})$ by iteratively modifying $H^c(V, A^{mod})$: in an internal loop, at each iteration we find the shortest path p considering the weights w_{ij} in $H^c(V, A^{mod})$, then we add p to the set P_c and we delete the arc of p with lowest weight from $H^c(V, A^{mod})$. This is a straightforward procedure that, however, can be fast implemented and that we have observed among professionals in real-world telecommunication applications. The rationale behind the exclusion of the arc with lowest weight is that, if the fractional value in the range $[0,1]$ of a binary variable is seen as the probability of fixing to 1 the variable in a good solution, then smaller values should lead to fixing to 1 of lower quality (we refer the reader to the book [28] about randomized rounding algorithms for a good discussion on looking at fractional binary solutions as measures of probability). After having established the set of candidate paths P_c for c, we compute the probability of choosing each path $p \in P_c$ to route the entire flow of couple c using the formula:

$$\mathrm{PROB}_p = \frac{\alpha\,\tau_p + (1-\alpha)\,\eta_p}{\sum_{\pi \in P_c} \alpha\,\tau_\pi + (1-\alpha)\,\eta_\pi}, \qquad (15)$$

where both τ_p and η_p are obtained as the sum of the current values of the a-priori and the a-posteriori measures τ_{ij}^c, η_{ij}^c for the edges in path p for pair c. In particular, the a-priori measures τ_{ij}^c are initialized with the values that flow variables assume in an optimal solution to the (strengthened) linear relaxation of Rob-BAND-ILP^{FIX} and are updated at the end of each construction phase (see below for more details). Instead, the a-posteriori measures η_{ij}^c are set equal to the values that flow variables assume in an optimal solution to the linear relaxation of Rob-BAND-ILP^{FIX} plus the additional fixing that have been operated while building a complete routing state. After having probabilistically chosen a path $p^* \in P_c$ through formula (15), we derive a fixing of the flow variables x^{bs}, where

$x_{ij}^{bs} = 1$ if (i, j) belongs to p^* and $x_{ij}^{bs} = 0$ otherwise. Finally, we add the couple c to the set of processed couples $\bar{C}$ for which the routing has been established.

After having executed the external loop $|C|$ times, following the ordering of the pairs, we obtain a complete routing state. However, since the procedure adopted to define a routing state does not take into account the capacity of relays, we may actually produce routing solutions that are infeasible: this can occur, for example, if many routing paths use the same relay and the sum of the data exceeds the relay capacity. Due to this possibility, we include in the algorithm a check-and-repair phase: this phase first verifies the feasibility of the routing state and, in case of infeasibility, tries to repair the solution. The reparation is attempted through the same ILP heuristic that we adopt to find better solutions (see the next subsection for a description of the ILP heuristic).

The feasibility of a complete routing state for the complete problem Rob-BAND-ILP can be fast and easily operated: we deploy all relays appearing in paths used in the routing state (i.e., we fix to 1 the corresponding relay deployment variables y_r and to 0 all the other variables y_r) and we verify the presence of relay-capacity constraints (13) violated for some data scenario in Σ. Additionally, we must check if the number of activated relays is higher than the limit expressed by constraint (14). If all constraints are satisfied, then we have built a feasible solution for Rob-BAND-ILP: the complete routing state specifies the values of the flow variables x and these allows us to also derive a feasible activation of the relay activation variables y. In contrast, any violation of a capacity or activation constraint immediately certifies that the built routing state is infeasible and we must therefore repair it.

We present the pseudocode of the heuristic in Algorithm 1. There, the energy value of a solution $(\bar{x}, \bar{y})$ is denoted by $E(\bar{x}, \bar{y})$. Additionally, we denote by (x^*, y^*) the best solution found during the entire execution of the algorithm. The heuristic includes two main loops: the external loop is executed until a time limit is reached, whereas the internal loop provides for building m feasible solutions according to the routing state construction that we have explained above. Specifically, the first task of the algorithm is to solve the (strengthened) linear relaxation of Rob-BAND-ILP that is used to execute the first deterministic fixing phase, leading to problem Rob-BAND-ILP^{FIX}. Then the (strengthened) linear relaxation of Rob-BAND-ILP^{FIX} is solved and its optimal solution is used to initialize the a-priori measure of attractiveness $\tau_{ij}^c(0)$. In each execution of the internal loop, the first task is to define a complete routing state as previously detailed. The complete routing state provides a complete valorization of the variables $\bar{x}$ and is used as basis to derive a relay installation $\bar{y}$. This leads to an integral solution $(\bar{x}, \bar{y})$ whose feasibility is not guaranteed and must thus be checked and eventually repaired through the ILP heuristic. If the solution $(\bar{x}, \bar{y})$ found is feasible and is better than the current best solution (x^B, y^B), (x^B, y^B) is updated and the internal loop continues. At the end of the internal loop, the a-priori measures τ are updated, evaluating how good the fixing resulted in the obtained solutions. The update formula uses the *optimality gap* (*OGap*) corresponding with a feasible solution of value v and a lower bound L for the optimal value v^* of the problem (since we consider a minimization problem, we have $L \leq v^* \leq v$ and $OGap(v, L) = (v - L)/v$):

$$\tau_{ij}^c(h) = \tau_{ij}^c(h - 1) + \sum_{f=1}^{F} \Delta\tau_{ij}^c \text{ with } \Delta\tau_{ij}^{c\,f} = \tau_{ij}^c(0) \cdot \left(\frac{OGap(\bar{v}, L) - OGap(v_f, L)}{OGap(\bar{v}, L)} \right)$$

(16)

where $\tau_{ij}^c(h)$ is the a-priori attractiveness of fixing variable $x_{ij}^{c=(b,s)}$ at fixing iteration h, L is the lower bound (in our case, the strengthened linear relaxation of Rob-BAND-ILP), v_f is the value of the f-th feasible solution built in the last construction cycle and $\bar{v}$ is the (moving) average of the values of the F solutions produced in the previous construction phase. $\Delta\tau_{ij}^{c\,f}$ is the penalization/reward factor for a fixing and depends upon the initialization value τ_{ij}^c of τ, combined with the relative variation in the optimality gap that v_σ implies w.r.t. $\bar{v}$. Since in (16) we use a relative gap difference, we are able to encourage or discourage fixings made in the last produced solution through a comparison with the average quality of the last F solutions produced. Once the time limit is reached, we execute the ILP heuristic for improving the best solution found and at the end of the execution we return (x^*, y^*).

Algorithm 1. Heuristic for Min-Max BAND

1: compute the strengthened linear relaxation of Rob-BAND-ILP
2: execute the deterministic fixing phase of variables y_r using a fixing threshold $\epsilon > 0$ and define Rob-BAND-ILP^{FIX}
3: compute the strengthened linear relaxation of Rob-BAND-ILP^{FIX} and initialize the values $\tau_{ij}^c(0)$ through it
4: let (x^*, y^*) denote the best solution found by the algorithm
5: **while** a global time limit is not reached **do**
6:     let (x^B, y^B) denote the best solution found in the inner loop
7:     **for** $k := 1$ to m **do**
8:         build a complete routing state $\bar{x}$ following the procedure SET-PATHS
9:         derive a relay installation $\bar{y}$ using $\bar{x}$
10:         **if** $(\bar{x}, \bar{y})$ is not feasible for Rob-BAND-ILP **then**
11:             run mod-RINS for repairing $(\bar{x}, \bar{y})$
12:         **end if**
13:         **if** $(\bar{x}, \bar{y})$ is feasible and $E(\bar{x}, \bar{y}) < E(x^B, y^B)$ **then**
14:             update the best solution found $(x^B, y^B) := (\bar{x}, \bar{y})$
15:         **end if**
16:     **end for**
17:     update $\tau_{ij}^c(t)$ according to (16)
18:     **if** $E(x^B, y^B) < E(x^*, y^*)$ **then**
19:         update the best solution found $(x^*, y^*) := (x^B, y^B)$
20:     **end if**
21: **end while**
22: run mod-RINS(x^*, y^*) for improving (x^*, y^*)
23: return (x^*, y^*)

Reparation/Improvement by an ILP Heuristic. To either repair an infeasible fixing of the decision variables or to improve a feasible solution, we rely on an ILP heuristic *exactly* executing a *very large neighborhood search*, i.e. the search is formulated as an integer linear programming problem solved through a state-of-the-art MIP solver (see also, e.g., [35]). Specifically, we rely on a modified *Relaxation Induced Neighborhood Search* (RINS) (see [29] for an exhaustive description of this search method). Let $(\bar{x}, \bar{y})$ be a solution found for Rob-BAND-ILP, (x^{TLR}, y^{TLR}) be an optimal solution of the linear relaxation of Rob-BAND-ILP^{FIX} strengthened by the cuts found by CPLEX in the root node of the branch-and-bound tree. Moreover, denote by $(\bar{x}, \bar{y})_j, (x^{TLR}, y^{TLR})_j$ the j-th component of the vectors.

The modified RINS *(mod-RINS)* that we adopt solves a subproblem of Rob-BAND-ILP where we fix the variables whose value in $(\bar{x}, \bar{y})$ and (x^{TLR}, y^{TLR}) differs of at most $\rho > 0$ according to the following rules:

$(\bar{x}, \bar{y})_j = 0 \ \wedge \ (x^{TLR}, y^{TLR}) \leq \rho \implies (x, y)_j = 0$

$(\bar{x}, \bar{y})_j = 1 \ \wedge \ (x^{TLR}, y^{TLR}) \geq 1 - \rho \implies (x, y)_j = 1$.

The resulting problem is then passed to CPLEX, which attempts at solving it within a time limit. The rationale is that CPLEX, though not being able to fast finding good quality solutions to the complete problem, is instead able to fast finding good solutions to subproblems obtained by smartly fixing variables.

4   Experimental Results

We evaluated the performance of the new heuristic on the same set of 30 instances considered in [13]. We refer the reader to that paper for a detailed description of the instances; here we just remind the major topology features of the corresponding graph: all instances consider a BAN including 16 biosensors (i.e., $|B| = 16$) and 2 sinks (i.e., $|S| = 2$). Moreover, 400 potential sites over the human body (excluding head, hands and feet) are considered for the deployment of relays (i.e., $|R| = 400$), chosen randomly over the human body.

We performed all the experiments on a 2.70 GHz machine with 8 GB, using a C/C++ code interfaced with IBM ILOG CPLEX 12.5 through Concert Technology and running with a time limit of 2400 s. The results of the computational tests are presented in Table 1, where *ID* is the identifier of the instance and where we show the performance of all the considered algorithms in terms of the optimality gap associated with the best solutions found within the time limit. Specifically, we show the optimality gaps of: (1) CPLEX (GapILP%) applied directly to solve Rob-BAND-ILP; (2) the heuristic presented in [13] (GapRB%) - we denote this heuristic by *RB*; (3) our new heuristic (GapHEU%) - we denote our heuristic by *HEU*. Finally, $\Delta Gap\%$ is the percentage increase of the optimality gap of CPLEX w.r.t. that of the heuristics. For both RB and HEU, the optimality gap is derived comparing the value of the linear relaxation of Rob-BAND-ILP computed by CPLEX with the value of the best feasible solution found by the heuristic within the time limit. For both heuristics, the number of candidate paths for each biosensor-sink routing path assignment equals 5, the

Table 1. Experimental results.

ID	GapILP%	GapRB%	GapHEU%	Δ Gap% HEU-ILP	Δ Gap HEU-RB
I1	55.22	41.63	36.85	33.2	11.5
I2	67.17	57.10	49.28	26.6	13.7
I3	40.26	35.83	32.21	19.9	10.1
I4	45.20	42.16	26.10	25.1	10.1
I5	68.60	54.54	51.65	24.7	5.3
I6	60.45	38.33	35.34	41.5	7.8
I7	45.65	34.52	33.07	27.5	4.2
I8	64.09	48.78	44.68	30.2	8.4
I9	60.66	47.77	42.13	30.5	11.8
I10	34.08	28.10	23.07	32.3	17.9
I11	61.42	48.50	32.20	46.2	14.5
I12	60.97	46.65	43.56	31.8	14.2
I13	59.96	37.66	27.27	21.2	5.8
I14	63.92	50.77	28.73	25.0	9.9
I15	34.61	28.95	32.47	10.9	21.0
I16	38.33	31.89	40.21	34.5	17.1
I17	36.45	41.10	41.23	32.3	11.6
I18	53.04	41.61	32.17	39.3	22.7
I19	36.81	31.97	28.36	22.9	11.3
I20	36.08	30.87	26.70	25.9	13.5
I21	34.89	29.03	35.96	20.4	14.7
I22	56.89	42.63	37.00	34.9	13.2
I23	52.83	43.58	39.92	24.4	8.4
I24	47.13	50.34	40.93	13.1	18.7
I25	41.50	35.06	37.34	10.0	6.5
I26	67.46	38.43	35.47	47.4	7.7
I27	34.18	29.52	24.38	28.6	17.4
I28	64.75	52.11	40.48	37.4	22.3
I29	70.31	41.25	34.61	50.7	16.1
I30	59.95	48.35	42.50	29.1	12.1

combination factor of the a-priori and a-posteriori measures α is set equal to 0.5 and the width F of the moving average is 4. To solve the linear relaxation of Rob-BAND-ILP and of BAND-ILP we used CPLEX. The threshold ϵ for the deterministic fixing threshold is set equal to 10^{-1}. The repair/improvement heuristic *mod-RINS* uses a threshold $\rho = 10^{-1}$ and runs with a time limit of 10 min for finding improvements and of 1 min when used for solution reparation.

The external cycle of HEU ran with a time limit of 30 min, which matches the time limit of CPLEX when added up to the time reserved for mod-RINS.

The optimality gaps GapILP% indicate that the instances proved challenging to solve even for a state-of-the-art solver like CPLEX, which produces solutions that are distant from the optimum at the time limit. In contrast, HEU provides solutions associated with a great reduction in the optimality gap that is on average equal to about 29% and can be sensibly over 40%, as in the case of instances I11, I26 and I29. HEU is also able to grant a significative reduction with respect to the benchmark heuristic RB, which already grants a high reduction in the optimality gap with respect to CPLEX: the average reduction in gap is about 12% and can be over 20% as for I18 and I28. We think that the better performance of HEU with respect to BR is due to the inclusion of an additional fixing phase that involve the relay activation variables, which are excluded from the linear relaxation-guided fixing of BR.

As future work, we plan to further reduce the optimality gap by considering other integration of heuristics (in particular, genetic and sequential heuristics like in [30,31]) and cutting plane methods identifying conflicts between variables, as in [32,33]. Also, we intend to evaluate biobjective versions of the problem, considering the trade-off between relay deployment cost and energy consumption and adopting an algorithm similar to [34]. Finally, we plan to investigate the adoption of another robustness paradigm, namely Multiband Robustness [19].

References

1. Ko, J., Lu, C., Srivastava, M., Stankovic, J., Terzis, A., Welsh, M.: Wireless sensor networks for healthcare. Proc. IEEE **98**, 1947–1960 (2007)
2. Chen, M., Gonzalez, S., Vasilakos, A., Cao, H., Leung, V.: Body area networks: a survey. Mob. Netw. Appl. **16**, 171–193 (2010)
3. Mitra, U., Emken, A., Lee, S., Li, M., Rozgic, V., Thatte, G., Vatsangam, H., Zois, D., Annavaram, M., Narayanan, S., Spruijt-Metz, D., Sukhatme, G.: KNOWME: a case study in wireless body area sensor network design. IEEE Commun. Mag. **50**, 116–125 (2012)
4. Guerriero, F., Violi, A., Natalizio, E., Loscri, V., Costanzo, C.: Modelling and solving optimal placement problems in wireless sensor networks. Appl. Math. Model. **35**, 230–241 (2011)
5. Natalizio, E., Loscri, V., Viterbo, E.: Optimal placement of wireless nodes for maximizing path lifetime. IEEE Commun. Lett. **12**, 362–364 (2008)
6. Negra, R., Jemilia, I., Belghith, A.: Wireless body area networks: applications and technologies. Procedia Comput. Sci. **83**, 1274–1281 (2016)
7. D'Andreagiovanni, F.: Revisiting wireless network jamming by SIR-based considerations and multiband robust optimization. Optim. Lett. **9**, 1495–1510 (2015)
8. D'Andreagiovanni, F., Mannino, C., Sassano, A.: GUB covers and power-indexed formulations for wireless network design. Manag. Sci. **59**, 142–156 (2013)
9. Gendron, B., Scutellà, M., Garroppo, R., Nencioni, G., Tavanti, L.: A branch-and-Benders-cut method for nonlinear power design in green wireless local area networks. Eur. J. Oper. Res. **255**, 151–162 (2016)
10. Elias, J.: Optimal design of energy-efficient and cost-effective wireless body area networks. Ad Hoc Netw. **13**, 560–574 (2014)

11. Tsouri, G., Prieto, A., Argade, N.: On increasing network lifetime in body area networks using global routing with energy consumption balancing. Sensors **12**, 13088–13108 (2012)
12. Yousaf, S., Javaid, N., Khan, Z., Qasim, U., Imran, M., Iftikhar, M.: Incremental relay based cooperative communication in wireless body area networks. Procedia Comp. Sci. **52**, 552–559 (2015)
13. D'Andreagiovanni, F., Nardin, A.: Towards the fast and robust optimal design of wireless body area networks. Appl. Soft Comput. **37**, 971–982 (2015)
14. Braem, B., Latre, B., Moerman, I., Blondia, C., Reusens, E., Joseph, W., Martens, L., Demeester, P.: The need for cooperation and relaying in short-range high path loss sensor networks. In: SENSORCOMM 2007, pp. 566–571 (2007)
15. Bertsekas, D.: Network Optimization: Continuous and Discrete Models. Athena Scientific, Belmont (1998)
16. D'Andreagiovanni, F., Krolikowski, J., Pulaj, J.: A fast hybrid primal heuristic for multiband robust capacitated network design with multiple time periods. Appl. Soft Comput. **26**, 497–507 (2015)
17. Bauschert, T., Büsing, C., D'Andreagiovanni, F., Koster, A.M.C.A., Kutschka, M., Steglich, U.: Network planning under demand uncertainty with robust optimization. IEEE Commun. Mag. **52**, 178–185 (2014)
18. Ben-Tal, A., El Ghaoui, L., Nemirovski, A.: Robust Optimization. Springer, Heidelberg (2009)
19. Büsing, C., D'Andreagiovanni, F.: New results about multi-band uncertainty in robust optimization. In: Klasing, R. (ed.) SEA 2012. LNCS, vol. 7276, pp. 63–74. Springer, Heidelberg (2012). doi:10.1007/978-3-642-30850-5_7
20. Aissi, H., Bazgan, C., Vanderpooten, D.: Min-max and min-max regret versions of combinatorial optimization problems. Eur. J. Oper. Res. **197**, 427–438 (2009)
21. Furini, F., Iori, M., Martello, S., Yagiura, M.: Heuristic and exact algorithms for the interval minmax regret knapsack problem. INFORMS J. Comput. **27**, 392–405 (2015)
22. IBM ILOG CPLEX. http://www-01.ibm.com/software
23. Maniezzo, V.: Exact and approximate nondeterministic tree-search procedures for the quadratic assignment problem. INFORMS J. Comp. **11**, 358–369 (1999)
24. D'Andreagiovanni, F., Krolikowski, J., Pulaj, J.: A hybrid primal heuristic for robust multiperiod network design. In: Esparcia-Alcázar, A.I., Mora, A.M. (eds.) EvoApplications 2014. LNCS, vol. 8602, pp. 15–26. Springer, Heidelberg (2014). doi:10.1007/978-3-662-45523-4_2
25. Dorigo, M., Maniezzo, V., Colorni, A.: Ant system: optimization by a colony of cooperating agents. IEEE Trans. Syst. Man Cybern. B **26**, 29–41 (1996)
26. Gambardella, L.M., Montemanni, R., Weyland, D.: Coupling ant colony systems with strong local searches. Eur. J. Oper. Res. **220**, 831–843 (2012)
27. Blum, C.: Ant colony optimization: introduction and recent trends. Phys. Life Rev. **2**, 353–373 (2005)
28. Motwani, R., Raghavan, P.: Randomized Algorithms. Cambridge University Press, New York (1995)
29. Danna, E., Rothberg, E., Le Pape, C.: Exploring relaxation induced neighborhoods to improve MIP solutions. Math. Program. **102**, 71–90 (2005)
30. D'Andreagiovanni, F.: On improving the capacity of solving large-scale wireless network design problems by genetic algorithms. In: Chio, C., et al. (eds.) EvoApplications 2011. LNCS, vol. 6625, pp. 11–20. Springer, Heidelberg (2011). doi:10.1007/978-3-642-20520-0_2

31. Dely, P., D'Andreagiovanni, F., Kassler, A.: Fair optimization of mesh-connected WLAN hotspots. Wirel. Commun. Mob. Com. **15**, 924–946 (2015)
32. Bley, A., D'Andreagiovanni, F., Karch, D.: WDM fiber replacement scheduling. Electron. Notes Discret. Math. **41**, 189–196 (2013)
33. D'Andreagiovanni, F., Mannino, C., Sassano, A.: Negative cycle separation in wireless network design. In: Pahl, J., Reiners, T., Voß, S. (eds.) INOC 2011. LNCS, vol. 6701, pp. 51–56. Springer, Heidelberg (2011). doi:10.1007/978-3-642-21527-8_7
34. Zakrzewska, A., D'Andreagiovanni, F., Ruepp, S., Berger, M.: Biobjective optimization of radio access technology selection and resource allocation in heterogeneous wireless networks. In: 2013 11th International Symposium on Modeling and Optimization in Mobile, Ad Hoc and Wireless Networks (WiOpt), pp. 652–658. IEEE (2013)
35. D'Andreagiovanni, F., Caire, G.: An unconventional clustering problem: user service profile optimization. In: 2016 IEEE International Symposium on Information Theory (ISIT). IEEE Xplore, Piscataway. IEEE (2016). doi:10.1109/ISIT.2016.7541420

EvoCOMPLEX

Lamarckian and Lifelong Memetic Search in Agent-Based Computing

Wojciech Korczynski, Marek Kisiel-Dorohinicki, and Aleksander Byrski(✉)

Department of Computer Science, AGH University of Science and Technology,
Al. Mickiewicza 30, 30-059 Krakow, Poland
{wojciech.korczynski,doroh,olekb}@agh.edu.pl

Abstract. Memetic algorithms when used with care can help in balancing exploitation and exploration of the metaheuristics, without the overhead measured by the rapidly increased number of function fitness calls. The paper tackles such balancing of use of metaheuristics in an agent-oriented setting. In particular, application of local search during a computing agent's life is researched. The results shown for selected benchmark functions are presented along with necessary statistic testing.

Keywords: Memetic algorithms · Agent-based computing · Continuous optimization · Metaheuristics

1 Introduction

When tackling difficult optimization problems, often described as *black-box* [1] ones, one has to carefully plan the search taking advantage of different aspects of well-known meta-heuristics (i.e. higher level, general heuristics—algorithms that provide "good-enough", maybe not optimal, solutions in reasonable time), in order to achieve success. Exploration and exploitation can affect to a great extent the efficiency and efficacy of such search [2], throwing the solutions all over the search space or concentrating them in one sub-optimal area, when not handled properly.

Handling memetic algorithms [3] with care (remembering of their apparent high cost measured in the overhead of the fitness function calls) can help in achieving proper balance between exploration and exploitation. Usually memetic algorithms apply the local search during reproduction (inspired by Lamarck evolution) [4] or during evaluation (inspired by Baldwin effect) [5]. However, more often use of local search might also lead to achieving interesting results, providing it is not used too-often. Doing this will of course loosen the connections to the actual biological and sociological metaphor—however there are many metaheuristics not following the actual metaphor (cf., e.g., Scatter Search [6]) that turned out to be successful.

Meta-heuristics were not fully understood, nor commonly used, until successful studies by Davis [7] and Moscato [3], who managed to prove how meta-heuristic algorithms may be efficiently used in experimental research. Another

© Springer International Publishing AG 2017
G. Squillero and K. Sim (Eds.): EvoApplications 2017, Part I, LNCS 10199, pp. 253–265, 2017.
DOI: 10.1007/978-3-319-55849-3_17

important conclusion drawn by Davis and Moscato, later confirmed in [8,9], was that meta-heuristic solver has to be adjusted to the characteristics of tackled problem—the so called *no-free-lunch theorem* requires to look for novel meta-heuristics, adjusted to given problem, since it is impossible to find "one-for-all" ultimate solution, fit for all kinds of problems. Therefore, researchers, often inspired by nature, biology, evolution or genetics, conduct incessant studies on the new meta-heuristic solvers.

In this paper we focus on an efficient, agent-based search and optimization system [10], that was proposed by Krzysztof Cetnarowicz in 1996 and extended many times since then: Evolutionary Multi-Agent System (EMAS). This system is composed of agents—pseudo-intelligent, autonomous objects [11], which are able to make decisions by themselves, based on an interaction with other agents and with environment. As main task is decomposed into sub-tasks, each of which is entrusted to an agent, EMAS is an effective implementation of distributed problem solving. To this day, EMAS proved to be much more efficient than classic evolutionary algorithm and was applied successfully to different problems—classic benchmarks [12], inverse problems [13] and other optimization tasks [14,15].

We focus on hybridization of EMAS with memetic algorithms, inspired by the meme theory [16–18]. Besides implementing the local search in a classic, Lamarckian way (as a part of reproduction process), we run the local search during the agent's life, trying to enhance the actual genotypes, keeping however caution in order not to randomize the whole population. This paper may be treated as a follow-up of [19], adding to a significant extent substantial results concerning the lifelong memetic search mechanism. In addition, profound analysis of diverse memetic parameters and their influence on results has been performed and described.

In Sect. 2 classic evolutionary algorithm, Parallel Evolutionary Algorithm (PEA), alongside with EMAS are described in detail. Hybridization of PEA and EMAS with memetic algorithms is presented in Sect. 2.2, where, furthermore, two methods of memetization in EMAS are introduced. Section 3 includes results of experiments performed on two hard high-dimensional benchmark function used first to properly parameterize the memetic mechanism used, later to tackle the benchmarks using all the available agent-based computing EMAS flavors and classic evolutionary (with memetic local search) ones. Section 4 concludes the paper and approaches a question of possible future work.

2   Agent-Based Memetic Computing

Evolutionary algorithms and similar population-based metaheuristics [2,20] are very common means of solving difficult, often black-box [1] problems. Classic evolutionary algorithms (see Fig. 1(a)) simplify several mechanisms well-known from the biological evolution, e.g. full synchronization of the reproduction while in biological systems no such phenomenon occurs. Another example would be lack of global knowledge in actual biological systems, while in evolutionary algorithms a single entity manages the whole population and synchronizes the variation operators etc. In order to try to leverage more natural phenomena in computing, EMAS was proposed (first in [21], then extended in [14,22] and many other papers).

2.1   EMAS

EMAS utilizes the totally distributed (uncontrolled globally) phenomena of death and reproduction for modelling the processes of selection and inheritance (Fig. 1(c)). Agent in EMAS carries the genotype (each agent has its own) and tries to survive competing with its neighbors (by executing the evaluation action) and proliferate (by reproduction leveraging recombination and mutation). Moreover, an agent may possess some knowledge acquired during its life, which is not inherited, yet controls the actions of the agent (e.g. sexual preferences [15]). Usually EMAS is implemented in a multi-deme model, similar to parallel evolutionary algorithm (cf. [23]).

One of the most important aspects of EMAS is distributed mechanism of selection, based on existing of non-renewable resource that is exchanged between the agents (in the process of evaluation—i.e. the better agent takes a certain part of the resource from the worse one). Later, the amount of the resource owned by a particular agent, becomes a condition for performing the action of reproduction (when the resource level is high) or death (when the resource level falls down). Moreover, the offspring overtakes certain part of the parents' energy during the reproduction.

EMAS prove to be an universal optimization tool (moreover, formal proofs of this feature have been constructed for EMAS and other computing systems, see, e.g. [24–26]), particularly with less demand on the number of the fitness function calls than its classic competitors, like PEA. However, striving to attain a truly universal computing system, being able to properly balance the exploration and exploitation phenomena, the authors started to design and develop memetic versions of EMAS.

2.2   Memetic EMAS

Population-based, in particular evolutionary algorithms may be easily hybridized with local search constituting memetic systems. Local improvements of the genotype are carried out usually during the evaluation (Baldwin effect [5]) or mutation (according to the Lamarckian model [4]). However, the local search adds an immense computational overhead, usually significantly decreasing the efficiency of such systems. In order to overcome this problem, memetic operators can be used in steady-state evolutionary algorithm [27] and similar ones, leveraging the fact that the genotype is processed once by the memetic operator—it is retained for a longer time in the population. Recent works of the authors tried to apply memetic algorithms to EMAS and presented promising results at the expense of efficiency (see, e.g. [22]), since many evaluation events were required. However, the authors presented recently a concept of efficient memetic search

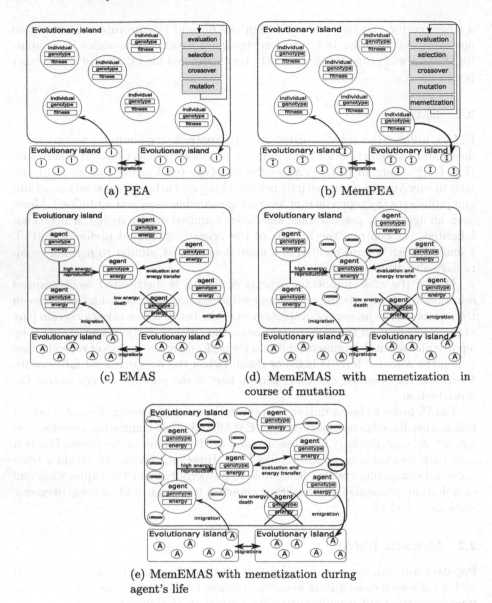

Fig. 1. Schematic presentation of the algorithms tackled in this paper

(using a buffering mechanism) [19]. In this paper the research on leveraging of the proposed efficient memetic mechanism is put forward and new results are presented.

It is common that local search methods are applied in the course of reproduction (Lamarckian memetics, local search is realized during mutation) or evaluation (Baldwinian memetics). However, agents are autonomous entities, and many of the processes are distributed under lack of global control in EMAS (e.g. onto-genesis, as many agents at the same time may die, reproduce or simply live). This fact encourages to extend the control of the agent over its genotype, e.g. making them enhance their genotypes (using Lamarckian memetic operator) in the course of their lives. Such an approach may help in balancing between explo-ration and exploitation, based on the actual parameters of the search. Generally speaking, the agent may autonomously decide, whether it should apply a local search in a certain period of time, or not. Thus the authors focus in this article on experimenting with EMAS alongside with its two memetic variants (memeti-zation in course of reproduction—MemEMAS and memetization during agent's life—MemEMAS_step) is compared with PEA algorithm and its memetic ver-sion (MemPEA). Figures 1(b), (d) and (e) illustrate schematically MemPEA, MemEMAS and MemEMAS_step algorithms respectively.

2.3 Buffered Memetics

Main drawback of local search algorithms is a computational overhead generated by radically increased number of evaluation events. Therefore, we needed to find an efficient local search mechanism not to hamper computations by exhaustive memetization.

In order to improve fitness evaluation efficiency, we decided to implement an evaluation operator based on the idea presented in [28], where a fitness function is separated into parts, each of which corresponds to the particular gene:

$$f(x) = f_1(x_1) \diamond_1 f_2(x_2) \diamond_2 \ldots \diamond_{n-1} f_n(x_n) \tag{1}$$

where $f(x) : \mathbb{R}^n \to \mathbb{R}$, $f_i(x_i) : \mathbb{R} \to \mathbb{R}, i \in [1, n], i \in \mathbb{N}, \diamond_j, j \in [1, n-1]$ is any mathematical operator. Assuming such fitness function, one can easily compute the $n - 1$ values of the partial functions $f_j(x_j), j \in [1, n] \land j \neq k, j, k \in \mathbb{N}$, leaving the value of $f_k(x_k)$ to be computed once per each mutation, when the single-point mutation is considered.

3   Experimental Results

In this part of the paper results of experiments, first focusing on determin-ing proper parameters for the memetic mechanisms used, and later comparing classic Parallel Evolutionary Algorithm, Evolutionary Multi-Agent System with properly parameterized memetic versions are presented and discussed. All exper-iments lasted 72000 s, were repeated 11 times and common statistical data were computed.

3.1   Experimental Setting

The experiments were executed on the PyAgE computing platform. PyAgE is an agent-based computing platform built upon flexible, component-based environment [29].

All of the computations have been run on AGH Cyfronet Zeus supercomputer (HP BL2x220c, Intel Xeon, 23 TB RAM, 169 TFlops).

In order to prove the ideas presented in the paper, we tried to find a global minimum of two multidimensional hard continuous benchmark functions: Rastrigin and Ackley functions defined by Eqs. 2 and 3 respectively. Figures 2(a) and (b) illustrate them in two dimensions. Global optimum for all of them equals $f(x) = 0.0$.

$$f(x) = An + \sum_{i=1}^{n} [x_i^2 - A\cos(2\pi x_i)] \tag{2}$$

$$f(x) = -a\exp\left(-b\sqrt{\frac{1}{n}\sum_{i=1}^{n} x_i^2}\right) - \exp\left(\frac{1}{n}\sum_{i=1}^{n}\cos(cx_i)\right) + a + \exp(1) \tag{3}$$

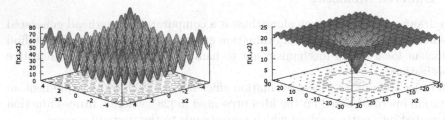

(a) Two-dimensional Rastrigin function   (b) Two-dimensional Ackley function

Fig. 2. Illustration of benchmark functions tackled in this work

Parts of the tackled functions that were cached according to the local search buffering method introduced in Sect. 2.2 were:

- $x^2 - A\cos(2\pi x)$ for Rastrigin
- x^2 and $\cos(cx)$ for Ackley

The experiments consisted in evaluating these two hard benchmark functions in 5000 dimensions on the following hypercubes:

- $x_i \in [-5.12, 5.12]$ for Rastrigin
- $x_i \in [-32.768, 32.768]$ for Ackley

Constants were assigned the following values:

- Rastrigin: $A = 10$
- Ackley: $a = 20$, $b = 0.2$, $c = 2\pi$

Table 1 includes other configuration parameters.

Table 1. Experiments configuration parameters

Parameter	EMAS	PEA
Mutation	Uniform, of one randomly chosen gene	
Crossover	Single point	
Speciation	Allopatric	
Environment	Torus-shaped, size 10 x 10	
Number of evolutionary islands	3, fully connected	
Numbers of individuals on each island	50	
Agent/individual migration probability	0.05	
Initial energy	100	-
Energy transferred from loser to winner	5	-
Agent's death energy level	0	-
Minimal energy required to reproduce	120	-
Minimal energy required to migrate	130	-
Selection	-	tournament (tournament size: 30)

3.2 Memetic Parameters Testing

First, we decided to examine how memetic parameters such as memetic mutation repetitions, mutation strength and probability of memetization during agent's life, influence on obtained results.

The memetic algorithm constituted of a certain number of phases (an algorithm's parameter). During one phase, a randomly chosen gene was changed by adding or subtracting some small, fixed value. If this change did improve fitness value, the same change was repeated as long as an improvement was noticeable. What is also worth emphasizing is that mutation strength was adapted to the increase of best fitness on current evolutionary island within last two iterations—if this change is not big enough, mutation strength is greater.

We performed extra experiments in which Rastrigin function was solved with the following algorithms: MemPEA, MemEMAS and MemEMAS_step.

Figures 3(a), (b) and (c) show how different number of memetic mutation iterations (also named "phases") impacts the solution.

Change of the number of mutation repetitions had no effect on solution found by PEA, which seemed to get stuck in some local minimum. In case of EMAS, a general rule can be observed—the more mutation repetitions, the worse final result. We can explain it by an increased computational overhead caused by more profound local search.

Figures 4(a), (b) and (c) depict an influence of mutation strength parameter value on obtained results.

As one can see, varied mutation strength in PEA had no visible influence on results as well. We may affirm that in this case memetization is not able to provide successful solution, even for various memetic solver parameters.

The parameter of mutation strength did not change final results of both memetic versions of EMAS in spite of the fact that, initially, configurations with mutation strength of values 2.0 and 3.0 could be distinguished as the most efficient ones.

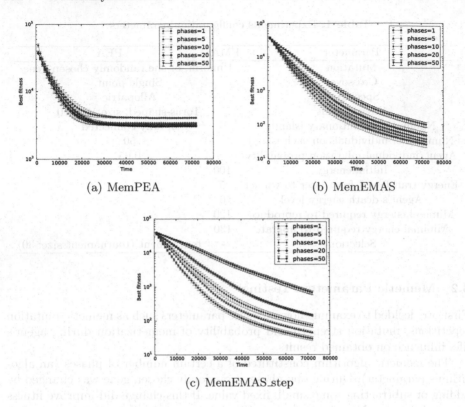

(a) MemPEA   (b) MemEMAS

(c) MemEMAS_step

Fig. 3. Influence of memetic mutation repetitions on the best fitness

An influence of the probability of memetization during EMAS agent's life has been shown in Fig. 5.

As it may be observed, more frequent memetic events during agent's life worsen MemEMAS_step algorithm efficiency because of the computational overhead generated by exhaustive local search events. One has to bear in mind the results provided in Fig. 6(a) and in Table 2, which clearly show that the best solution of Rastrigin function is found by classic EMAS. Therefore, it is not surprising that enhancement of memetization negatively impacts the results.

3.3   Comparison of Classic and Memetic System Versions

Following the results obtained during the testing of memetization mechanism, the probability of memetization at every evolutionary step (for MemEMAS_step) was performed with the probability of 0.1.

We have set the number of memetic repetitions to 10, following the observations that it gives average results—as we wanted to avoid imposing a significant computational overhead on the system, still being able to efficiently leverage the properties of the local search applied.

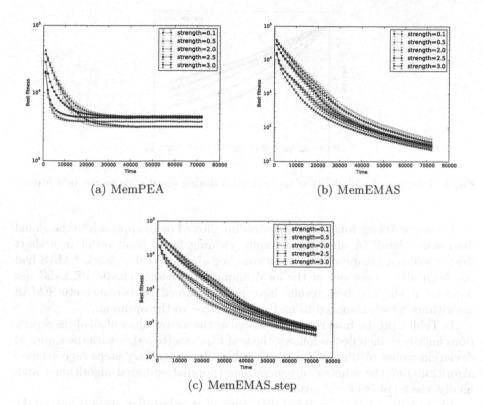

(a) MemPEA   (b) MemEMAS

(c) MemEMAS_step

Fig. 4. Influence of memetic mutation strength on the best fitness

Mutation strength was adapted depending on how the best fitness changed between the successive iterations. Its basic value equaled 0.1, but if the best fitness improvement was lower than 10.0, mutation strength was increased to 1.5 and 10.0 for Rastrigin and Ackley problems, respectively.

Results of fitness evaluation with the use of five configurations—EMAS, EMAS with memetization in the course of reproduction (MemEMAS), EMAS with memetization during agent's life (MemEMAS_step), PEA and PEA with memetization (MemPEA)—have been illustrated in Figs. 6(a) and (b). These results are presented with the use of box-and-whisker plot that provides information about lower and upper quartiles, median, minimum and maximum value of data.

In all of these experiments EMAS proved to be visibly more efficient than PEA and was able to reach much better solutions in the same time. These results confirm outcomes of research presented in e.g. [22]. Though classic EMAS reached better solution than MemEMAS and MemEMAS_step, memetic versions reached better results earlier than EMAS and later they were outrun by their counterpart (based on the observation of the dependencies of fitness functions on time). Both PEA algorithms gave promising results at the beginning but ultimately got stuck in a local optimum.

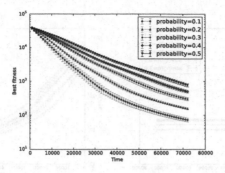

Fig. 5. Influence of probability of memetization during agent's life on the best fitness

In case of Ackley function, memetization allowed us to approach to the global minimum. MemPEA algorithm, despite yielding fairly good result in a short time, could not escape a local minimum. For about 60000 s, classic EMAS had not been able to get out of the local minimum, whereas classic PEA did not improve at all. The best results have been obtained by two memetic EMAS algorithms, which managed to find solution close to the optimum.

In Table 2 precise final results presented as the mean values of all of the repetitions have been included as follows: the best fitnesses (together with the standard deviation values of these data), the number of evolutionary steps (agent-based algorithms) or the number of generations (population-based algorithms) and, finally, the number of evaluation events.

First of all, it has to be noted that value of standard deviation is low, so the experiments are repeatable.

One of the basic conclusions that may be drawn based on the information given in Table 2 is that exploitation performed by memetic operations significantly hampers and slows down whole search process (i.e. evolution). For example, MemPEA algorithm run over 100000 less generations for Rastrigin and over

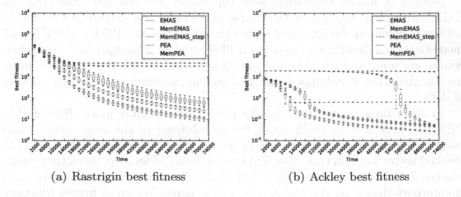

(a) Rastrigin best fitness   (b) Ackley best fitness

Fig. 6. Comparison of the best fitness values reached by PEA, EMAS and their memetic variants

Table 2. Experiments results in the 72000th second

	Result	St. Dev	Steps/gens	Evaluations
Rastrigin				
PEA	4513.99	38.98	287060.08	43059161.54
MemPEA	3236.08	34.14	177721.54	134895769.85
EMAS	11.01	1.85	6527920.00	23554647.15
MemEMAS	28.57	8.28	3990063.38	306424173.00
MemEMAS_step	63.77	16.44	2664479.54	690798501.92
Ackley				
PEA	17.19	0.77	402680.64	60402245.45
MemPEA	0.66	0.00	150125.82	113398065.45
EMAS	0.05	0.00	7110282.45	27779639.36
MemEMAS	0.03	0.00	3189123.18	246871911.27
MemEMAS_step	0.05	0.00	1773259.36	470297477.00

250000 less generations for Ackley. Therefore, it is important to properly tune the configuration of local search events.

What is more, it may be seen that efficient local search buffering method enabled to perform far more fitness evaluation events than in the memetic-less configurations. For example, in case of Rastrigin function, MemEMAS executes about 13 times more evaluations than EMAS. It should be emphasized that in most cases these are local evaluations which improve exploitation, not exploration.

Results obtained in our work confirm also the aforementioned *no free lunch theorem*, as we are not able to provide an ultimate solution for all kinds of problems.

4   Conclusion

Experiments described in this paper prove that memetic mechanism may be an efficient enhancement of search and optimization process performed by evolutionary meta-heuristics. Main drawback of memetic algorithms, i.e. extremely increased number of evaluation events that causes a substantial computational overhead, has been reduced by implementing an efficient local search operator based on buffering (or "caching") of particular parts of individuals' fitness [19]. Thereby, it was possible to handle a large number of evaluation events and not to disrupt the balance between exploration and exploitation, even in high-dimensional search space.

In the course of our experimental results we have examined the applied memetization mechanism, and later apply the resulting parameters (perceived as the best ones, or at least good ones) to the testing of two selected benchmark functions. It was proven that memetic version of EMAS turned out to be the best when tackling Ackley benchmark function, while for Rastrigin, the classic EMAS prevailed. It is to note that memetic algorithms are better suited for Ackley than for Rastrigin, due to the nature of these functions—and this turned out to be true for the algorithms used. The proposed lifelong mutation method turned out to be only a little worse than Memetic EMAS, and it will be further researched in the near future.

Furthermore, a study on application of memetic algorithms in solving hard discrete problems, such as LABS [28], is also planned. In order to further improve efficiency of memetization, it is to be run on FPGA and GPGPU architectures.

Acknowledgment. This research was supported by AGH University of Science and Technology Statutory Fund no. 11.11.230.124. This research was supported by PlGrid infrastructure.

References

1. Droste, S., Jansen, T., Wegener, I.: Upper and lower bounds for randomized search heuristics in black-box optimization. Theory Comput. Syst. **39**, 525–544 (2006)
2. Michalewicz, Z.: Genetic Algorithms Plus Data Structures Equals Evolution Programs. Springer-Verlag New York, Inc., Secaucus (1994)
3. Moscato, P.: On evolution, search, optimization, genetic algorithms and martial arts: towards memetic algorithms. Technical report Caltech Concurrent Computation Program, Report. 826, California Institute of Technology, Pasadena, California, USA (1989)
4. Eldridge, N., Gould, S.: Punctuated equilibria: an alternative to phyletic gradualism. In: Schopf, T. (ed.) Models in Paleobiology. Freeman, Cooper and Co., San Francisco (1972)
5. Hinton, G., Nolan, S.: How learning can guide evolution. Complex Syst. **1**, 495–502 (1987)
6. Glover, F.: Scatter search and path relinking. In: New Ideas in Optimization, pp. 297–316. McGraw-Hill Ltd. (1999)
7. Davis, L.: Handbook of Genetic Algorithms. Van Nostrand Reinhold Computer Library, New York (1991)
8. Hart, W., Belew, R.: Optimizing an arbitrary function is hard for the genetic algorithm. In: Belew, R., Booker, L. (eds.) Proceedings of the Fourth International Conference on Genetic Algorithms, pp. 190–195. Morgan Kaufmann, San Mateo (1991)
9. Wolpert, D., Macready, W.: No free lunch theorems for search. Technical report SFI-TR-02-010, Santa Fe Institute (1995)
10. Byrski, A.: Agent-Based Metaheuristics in Search and Optimisation. AGH University of Science and Technology Press, Kraków (2013)
11. Kisiel-Dorohinicki, M., Dobrowolski, G., Nawarecki, E.: Agent populations as computational intelligence. In: Rutkowski, L., Kacprzyk, J. (eds.) Neural Networks and Soft Computing, pp. 608–613. Physica, Heidelberg (2003)
12. Byrski, A.: Tuning of agent-based computing. Comput. Sci. **14**(3), 491 (2013)
13. Wróbel, K., Torba, P., Paszyński, M., Byrski, A.: Evolutionary multi-agent computing in inverse problems. Comput. Sci. **14**(3), 367 (2013)

14. Dreżewski, R., Siwik, L.: Multi-objective optimization technique based on co-evolutionary interactions in multi-agent system. In: Giacobini, M. (ed.) EvoWorkshops 2007. LNCS, vol. 4448, pp. 179–188. Springer, Heidelberg (2007). doi:10.1007/978-3-540-71805-5_20

15. Drezewski, R., Siwik, L.: Co-evolutionary multi-agent system for portfolio optimization. In: Brabazon, A., O'Neill, M. (eds.) Natural Computing in Computational Finance. SCI, vol. 1, pp. 271–299. Springer, Heidelberg (2008)

16. Krasnogor, N., Smith, J.: A tutorial for competent memetic algorithms: model, taxonomy, and design issues. IEEE Trans. Evol. Comput. 9(5), 474–488 (2005)

17. Moscato, P.: Memetic algorithms: a short introduction. In: Corne, D., Dorigo, M., Glover, F. (eds.) New Ideas in Optimization, pp. 219–234. McGraw-Hill, New York City (1999)

18. Moscato, P., Cotta, C.: A modern introduction to memetic algorithms. In: Gendrau, M., Potvin, J.Y. (eds.) Handbook of Metaheuristics. International Series in Operations Research and Management Science, vol. 146, 2nd edn., pp. 141–183. Springer, Heidelberg (2010)

19. Korczynski, W., Byrski, A., Kisiel-Dorohinicki, M.: Efficient memetic continuous optimization in agent-based computing. Procedia Comput. Sci. 80, 845–854 (2016). International Conference on Computational Science 2016, ICCS 2016, San Diego, California, USA, 6–8 June 2016

20. Talbi, E.G.: Metaheuristics: From Design to Implementation. Wiley, Hoboken (2009)

21. Cetnarowicz, K., Kisiel-Dorohinicki, M., Nawarecki, E.: The application of evolution process in multi-agent world (MAW) to the prediction system. In: Tokoro, M. (ed.) Proceedings of the 2nd International Conference on Multi-Agent Systems (ICMAS 1996), AAAI Press (1996)

22. Byrski, A., Korczynski, W., Kisiel-Dorohinicki, M.: Memetic multi-agent computing in difficult continuous optimisation. In: KES-AMSTA, pp. 181–190 (2013)

23. Cantú-Paz, E.: A summary of research on parallel genetic algorithms. IlliGAL Report No. 95007. University of Illinois (1995)

24. Byrski, A., Schaefer, R., Smołka, M.: Asymptotic guarantee of success for multi-agent memetic systems. Bull. Pol. Acad. Sci.-Tech. Sci. 61(1), 257–278 (2013)

25. Byrski, A., Schaefer, R.: Formal model for agent-based asynchronous evolutionary computation. In: 2009 IEEE Congress on Evolutionary Computation, pp. 78–85, May 2009

26. Schaefer, R., Byrski, A., Smolka, M.: The island model as a markov dynamic system. Int. J. Appl. Math. Comput. Sci. 22(4), 971–984 (2012)

27. Syswerda, G.: A study of reproduction in generational and steady state genetic algorithms. Found. Genet. Algorithms 2, 94–101 (1991)

28. Gallardo, J.E., Cotta, C., Fernández, A.J.: Finding low autocorrelation binary sequences with memetic algorithms. Appl. Soft Comput. 9(4), 1252–1262 (2009)

29. Kaziród, M., Korczynski, W., Byrski, A.: Agent-oriented computing platform in python. In: 2014 IEEE/WIC/ACM International Joint Conferences on Web Intelligence (WI) and Intelligent Agent Technologies (IAT), vol. 3, pp. 365–372. IEEE (2014)

Two-Phase Strategy Managing Insensitivity in Global Optimization

Jakub Sawicki[✉], Maciej Smołka, Marcin Łoś, Robert Schaefer,
and Piotr Faliszewski

AGH University of Science and Technology,
Al. Mickiewicza 30, 30-059 Kraków, Poland
{jsawicki,smolka,schaefer,faliszew}@agh.edu.pl,
marcin.los.91@gmail.com

Abstract. Solving ill-posed continuous, global optimization problems remains challenging. For example, there are no well-established methods for handling objective insensitivity in the neighborhood of solutions, which appears in many important applications, e.g., in non-invasive tumor tissue diagnosis or geophysical exploration. The paper presents a complex metaheuristic that identifies regions of objective function's insensitivity (plateaus). The strategy is composed of a multi-deme hierarchic memetic strategy coupled with random sample clustering, cluster integration, and special kind of multiwinner selection that allows to breed the demes and cover each plateau separately. We test the method on benchmarks with multiple non-convex plateaus and evaluate how well the plateaus are covered.

Keywords: Ill-posed global optimization problems · New tournament-like selection · Fitness insensitivity

1 Insensitivity in Global Optimization Problems

Formulating and solving Global Optimization Problems (GOPs) is one of the fundamental ways for modeling, planning, and optimizing important human activities. Roughly speaking, we first identify the decision variables that affect a given process, then formulate a numerical criterion that describes the process—e.g., as an objective function f of the real-valued decision variables, in such a way that the better the variables describe the desired process, the smaller is the value of f—and finally we seek variable values that minimize this function. Unfortunately, in many real-life settings the natural objective function has large regions (surrounding the global solutions) where they lose sensitivity to the parameters. Such GOPs belong to the group of *ill-conditioned* problems.

The work presented in this paper has been partially supported by National Science Centre, Poland grant no. 2015/17/B/ST6/01867 and by the AGH statutory research grant no. 11.11.230.124.

G. Squillero and K. Sim (Eds.): EvoApplications 2017, Part I, LNCS 10199, pp. 266–281, 2017.
DOI: 10.1007/978-3-319-55849-3_18

If an admissible set of decision variables $\mathcal{D}$ is equipped with a metric and a vector structure (e.g., $\mathcal{D}$ is a regular domain in $\mathbb{R}^N$), the regions of insensitivity can be studied by topological methods. Such methods may also be applicable if $\mathcal{D}$ is discrete with a topology imposed by the graph structure inside. In such cases, finding the regions of insensitivity surrounding global objective minimizers seems to be the primary task in GOP solving. If there are multiple, non-intersecting regions of low sensitivity surrounding different global minimizers, the problem becomes also *multimodal*.

Traditional approaches to handling multimodality and insensitivity in GOP solving rely on regularization methods [1]. These methods proceed by supplementing the objective function with a regularization term, making it globally convex. Unfortunately, such methods may lead to many undesirable artifacts and to the loss of information regarding the modeled process. Indeed, it can even lead to outright false solutions, forced by the regularization supplement.

A different, perhaps more reliable, approach to handling multimodality and insensitivity is based on finding approximations of the insensitivity regions that contain the global objective minimizers (plateaus). In this paper we pursue this approach by suggesting a two-phase memetic, multi-deme strategy for finding these plateaus. In the first phase, we roughly identify and separate the plateaus, while in the second phase we cover them with individuals derived from the demes bred during the first phase.

Diversity of populations and demes (see, e.g., Gupta and Ghafir [2]) plays a crucial role in both phases of our method. We ensure diversity and high efficiency of the first, global search, phase by using Hierarchic Genetic Strategy (HGS) [3]. We maintain local diversity in populations evolving in the second, local, phase by using a dedicated *multiwinner selection* operator [4].

Effective handling of insensitivity and multimodality of the objective functions is essential for solving various tasks in technology (e.g., regarding lens design [5]), in geophysics (e.g., in the calibration of conceptual Rainfall-Runoff Models [6] or for investigating oil and gas resources [7]), as well as in medical diagnosis (e.g., in tumor tissue identification [8]).

2   Formal Definition of the Problem

We consider Global Optimization Problems where the goal is to compute:

$$\arg\min_{x \in \mathcal{D}}\{f(x)\},\ \mathcal{D} \subset \mathbb{R}^\ell,\ f : \mathcal{D} \to \mathbb{R}, \tag{1}$$

where $\mathcal{D}$ is a closed, bounded domain with a nonempty interior and sufficiently regular boundary (e.g., Lipschitz boundary [9]). Let us assume that Problem (1) is ill-posed, so that its set of solutions $\mathcal{S} \subset \mathcal{D}$ is continuous and has positive Lebesgue measure (i.e., $\text{meas}(\mathcal{S}) > 0$). $\mathcal{S}$ can either be connected or composed of many connected parts.

Some minimizers $\hat{\omega} \in \mathcal{S}$ may belong to *plateaus* which are defined as the largest nonempty set of the form:

$$\mathcal{P}_{\hat{\omega}} = \{x \in \mathcal{S}|\ \exists A \subset \mathcal{S},\ A \text{ is open and connected},\ \hat{\omega}, x \in A\}. \tag{2}$$

Naturally, it holds that $\hat{\omega} \in \mathcal{P}_{\hat{\omega}}$ and $\mathrm{meas}(\mathcal{P}_{\hat{\omega}}) > 0$. By a *basin of attraction* $\mathcal{B}_{\mathcal{P}_{\hat{\omega}}} \subset \mathcal{D}$ of plateau $\mathcal{P}_{\hat{\omega}}$ we mean the single connected part of the largest level set of the objective f, so that it contains the plateau $\mathcal{P}_{\hat{\omega}} \subset \mathcal{B}_{\mathcal{P}_{\hat{\omega}}}$ and is contained in the plateau's attractor. That is, any strictly decreasing local optimization method starting from an arbitrary point in $\mathcal{B}_{\mathcal{P}_{\hat{\omega}}}$ converges to some point of $\mathcal{P}_{\hat{\omega}}$ (see [10, 11] for details).

There is no simple relation between the number of connected parts of $\mathcal{S}$ and the number of plateaus, see Fig. 1.

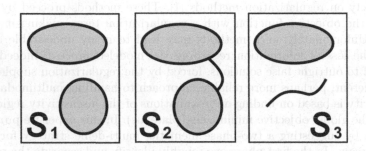

Fig. 1. The set of solutions $\mathcal{S}_1$ has two connected parts and contains two plateaus, while $\mathcal{S}_2$ is connected containing also two plateaus, $\mathcal{S}_3$ has again two connected components but contains only a single plateau.

The main goal of the strategy proposed in this paper is to cover each plateau $\mathcal{P} \subset \mathcal{S}$ and its narrow neighborhood $\mathcal{P} \subset \mathcal{C}_{\mathcal{P}} \subset \mathcal{B}_{\mathcal{P}}$ by a cluster of uniformly distributed points allowing further approximation of the shape of $\mathcal{P}$. We propose a new strategy of achieving this effect, which combines the Hierarchic Memetic Strategy (HMS) [12] and the multiwinner selection operator.

Our goal is somewhat similar to that of the Clustered Genetic Search algorithm (CGS) [13], but instead of identifying only the starting points for a local optimization method, we strive to explore the whole plateau regions.

3   Plateau Coverage Strategy

Our strategy consists of several phases, presented as Algorithm 1. First, we perform a global search using the HMS algorithm (line 1 of Algorithm 1). We continue its operation until we identify the most important regions and populate them with clusters of individuals evolving in the leaf-level demes of the HMS tree (we discuss this in detail in Sect. 4). The decision whether to continue HMS operation is based on a certain cluster quality measure. Intuitively, after the first phase we have roughly identified the basins of attraction.

In the second phase (lines 2 and 3), we cluster the first-phase individuals again and integrate the obtained clusters. The goal of this phase is to identify distinct basins of attraction which will seed populations governed by special software

---

Algorithm 1. Strategy for covering of plateau regions

---
1 execute HMS and collect individuals from the leaves
2 clusterize individuals, obtaining w clusters
3 integrate clusters, reducing their number to w'
   // the loop below can be executed in parallel
4 **for** $i \leftarrow 1$ **to** w' **do**
5 | initialize LBA_i with i'th cluster
6 | evolve LBA_i until stop condition is reached
7 **for** $i \leftarrow 1$ **to** w' **do**
8 | determine the shape of the plateau in LBA_i

---

agents called Local Basin Agents (LBAs). This process is further described in Sects. 4.2 and 4.3.

Finally, for each LBA (i.e., for each identified basin of attraction), we evolve its population to increase its local diversity. Having in mind this aim, evolution is performed using the multiwinner selection operator (see Sect. 5). This process is performed in the loop that starts in line 6.

Once local diversity is sufficiently high, we determine the plateaus' shapes using LBA's history (line 8). Currently, we perform this task with a local approximation method described in [14], but there are also other possibilities, such as the method of Wolny and Schaefer [15] that builds so-called *cluster extensions* as unions of ellipsoids, based on the cluster statistics. In this paper we only stipulate the use of local approximation, however cluster extensions play an auxiliary role in cluster merging (see below).

4   Hierarchic Memetic Strategy as a Global Search Phase

In the global phase, we want to identify all the possible basins of attraction. We do it by performing a global search with Hierarchic Memetic Strategy (HMS). This strategy is an extended version of Hierarchic Genetic Strategy (HGS), introduced by Schaefer and Kołodziej [16] and supplemented by some local search methods and data post-processing by Smołka et al. [12].

4.1   Short Description of HMS

The strategy operates on many demes, organised in a form of a tree with a set number of levels. The search at the root level is performed with the lowest accuracy, as it only serves to identify basins of attraction. The higher the level, the higher the accuracy of the search, and typically the higher the computational cost. Initially, the algorithm starts with the root deme only. When it identifies a promising region, a child deme is "sprouted" to the next level. If the sprouted deme isn't at the leaf level, it can sprout to the yet higher level.

We run the HMS search and when it identifies the optimization solutions, we integrate the leaf populations to form the input for clustering. Based on the observation that populations converge to regions of good fitness values, we can presume that the formed clusters correspond to the basins of attraction, a feature further verified by cluster integration.

The papers [3,7,12,16] and the references inside show the performance of HMS and its progenitor (HGS) by solving ill-conditioned, multimodal optimization problems in continuous domains, both benchmark and real-world ones.

4.2   Preliminary Identification of Local Minima Attraction Basins

Based on the presumption about the population's convergence to the basins of attraction, we can determine the regions of such basins by appropriate clustering of the individuals.

To perform the clustering step, we use the OPTICS-ξ algorithm described by Ankerst et al. [17]. It is a hierarchical density-based clustering method; we provide only a brief description of its workings here. (We use the implementation of the algorithm from ELKI Data Mining Framework [18].)

The OPTICS algorithm orders the points sequentially, keeping the points which may form a cluster close to each other. Moreover, each point is assigned a value of "reachability distance", i.e., a smallest distance such that a sphere of that radius centred at the point contains at least MinPts $\in \mathbb{Z}_+$ points. Because of that, points which have dense neighbourhoods have small reachability distances, while points in the less populated regions have larger ones. There are two parameters of this procedure: $\varepsilon_t \in \mathbb{R}_+$ (the maximal "reachability distance" considered) and MinPts.

We show an example of how OPTICS operates in Fig. 2. There are several clusters in the data, each containing 100 points. Two clusters are centred at point $(0,0)$ (each with different density), and another one is centered at point $(2,2)$. OPTICS identifies the clusters, with each cluster represented as a basin in the so called "reachability plot".

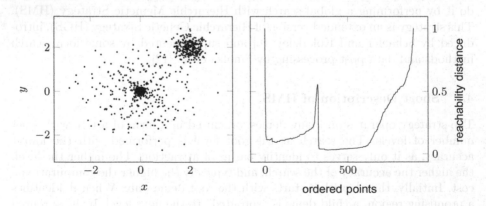

Fig. 2. An example of a clustering using the OPTICS algorithm. The line plot on the right shows the result of OPTICS run for $\varepsilon_t = 1$ and MinPts $= 20$. Three clusters are present in the data, which the algorithm is able to identify.

Now, to actually extract the cluster information from the ordering, OPTICS-ξ is used. It determines where uphill and downhill areas in the "reachability plot" are located, it uses the term of "steep-up" and "steep-down" areas. Each such steep area must have at least MinPts ξ-steep points, i.e., short areas are rejected and only steep-enough regions are accepted. The larger the ξ parameter, the larger the required steepness of "reachability distance" between consecutive points in each steep area.

The algorithm proceeds through all the ordered points, identifying the steep areas. Appropriate "steep-down" and "steep-up" areas are matched with each other to form clusters. The algorithm employs several techniques which help in removing artifact clusters and in reducing computational complexity of the search. As the result, the algorithm returns a hierarchical set of clusters. We don't want to have overlapping clusters, so we have to filter the results somehow.

Firstly, we want the clusters to be numerous enough. This limitation can be tied to the required LBA population size and MinPts value, as all the clusters are larger than MinPts, due to OPTICS-ξ nature.

Secondly, we would like the clusters to cover distinct basins of attraction. It is not possible to determine with full certainty that a cluster contains only a single basin of attraction. We try to find as many possible distinct basins of attraction as possible and then we remove the superfluous ones in the integration phase.

In order to fulfill both the requirements, we have devised a scheme presented below. In order to determine which clusters to keep we need to search the cluster tree. We do it in the DFS (Depth-First Search) order. The clusters below the set size are removed from the search, and then the remaining clusters at the leaves are collected and returned. In this way, we find clusters of appropriate sizes, while trying to collect as many of them as possible.

4.3 Cluster Integration

Some of the clusters identified in the previous stage can occupy areas belonging to common local-minima attraction basins. Hence, we apply an integration procedure to discover such cases and merge the corresponding clusters.

In the discovery phase of the procedure, we use two complementary techniques. The first one is based on the *hill-valley* function described in paper [19]. In Algorithm 2, we use it in a *hollow-ridge* version, appropriate for minimization problems.

It checks if somewhere on the interval between two points selected from different clusters the objective has value greater than for those points. If this is the case, the function returns a positive value, otherwise it returns 0. Using the hill-valley function, we check if two given clusters C_1 and C_2 can be merged as follows. We find two points, $p_1 \in C_1$ and $p_2 \in C_2$ such that the distance between them is minimal, and we merge their clusters if the value of the hill-valley function for these points is 0 (or, in a more general case, less than a prescribed "hill-valley tolerance").

The second considered merge checking method is based on the idea exploited in the Clustered Genetic Search algorithm [3,13]. Given two different clusters

---

Algorithm 2. Hill-valley function (hollow-ridge version)

Require: Points p_1, p_2 from different clusters, number of intermediate points k

1   $max \leftarrow max(fitness(p_1), fitness(p_2))$
2   **for** $j \leftarrow 1$ **to** k **do**
3   calculate intermediate point $inter_j$ on the interval $[p_1, p_2]$
4   compute $fitness(inter_j)$
5   **if** $max < fitness(inter_j)$ **then**
6   **return** $fitness(inter_j) - max$
7   **return** 0

Algorithm 3. Merge check by means of hill-valley function

Require: number of intermediate points k; clusters $C_1 \neq C_2$

1   find points $p_1 \in C_1$ and $p_2 \in C_2$ with minimal distance
2   **if** $HillValley(p_1, p_2, k) = 0$ **then**
3   C_1 and C_2 can be merged

Algorithm 4. Merge check by means of a local optimization method

Require: clusters $C_1 \neq C_2$

1   find points $p_1 \in C_1$ and $p_2 \in C_2$ with minimal distance
2   run a local optimization method $local()$ from p_1 and p_2
3   **if** $local(p_1)$ finishes in $extension(C_2)$ **or** $local(p_2)$ finishes in $extension(C_1)$
     then
4   C_1 and C_2 can be merged

C_1 and C_2, we take two points (one from each) that are closest to each other and start local optimization method runs from those points. The clusters can be merged if at least one of those runs converges to a point in the *cluster extension* of the opposite cluster, see Algorithm 4.

The idea of cluster extension is borrowed from paper [15] (see also [12]). Here it allows us to easily check if a given point belongs to a cluster "surrounding" with nonempty interior. As in [15], as cluster extensions we take ellipsoids:

$$extension(C) = \left\{ x \in \mathbb{R}^\ell : (x - \overline{x}_C)^T \Sigma_C^{-1} (x - \overline{x}_C) \leq 1 \right\}, \qquad (3)$$

where $\overline{x}_C$ is the center of C and Σ_C is the unbiased covariance matrix of C. An advantage of using ellipsoids as cluster extensions is that they are easily computable at an acceptable cost level.

5   Improved Genetic Algorithm Using Multiwinner Selection

Faliszewski et al. [4] developed a new selection operator based on the theory of multiwinner elections, and have shown a genetic algorithm that uses the operator to increase diversity within the population kept by the algorithm. While their benchmarks confirmed the method's potential for the case of not-too-small populations (over twenty individuals, say), for inverse problems it is necessary to handle yet smaller populations. Further, their algorithm required setting several non-obvious parameters. Here we provide a refined algorithm that addresses both these issues.

5.1   Key Concepts for Multiwinner Selection

Multiwinner Voting. An election $E = (C, V)$ consists of a set $C = \{c_1, \ldots, c_m\}$ of candidates and a collection $V = (v_1, \ldots, v_n)$ of voters. Each voter v_i has a linear order $\succ_i$ over the candidate set (ranking the candidates from the most to the least desired one). A multiwinner rule $\mathcal{R}$ is a function that given an election $E = (C, V)$ and an integer k outputs a size-k subset of C (referred to as the winning committee).[1] While there are various voting rules [20, 21], Faliszewski et al. [4] argued that the GreedyCC method, first suggested by Lu and Boutilier [22], should behave very well for the multiwinner selection operator. For an election $E = (C, V)$, this rule proceeds as follows. For a candidate c and voter v, by $\text{pos}(c, v)$ we mean the position of c in the preference order of v (1 if c is ranked first, m if c is ranked last). The score of some committee W, $W \subseteq C$, is $\sum_{v \in V}(|C| - \min_{c \in W} \text{pos}(c, v))$. The rule starts with an empty committee W and to elect committee of size k, it executes k rounds, in each adding to W a candidate that increases the score of W maximally (breaking the ties in an arbitrary way). This rule produces a diverse committees that covers a wide spectrum of candidates [21].

Multiwinner Selection. Multiwinner selection operator receives as input an election group, that is, a set $X = \{x^{(1)}, \ldots, x^{(n)}\}$ of individuals, each with its fitness value $f(x^{(i)})$. To apply a multiwinner voting rule, Faliszewski et al. [4] treat each individual from X both as a candidate and as a voter. To this end, for each two individuals $x^{(i)}$ and $x^{(j)}$ they define the utility of $x^{(i)}$ for selecting $x^{(j)}$ to be:

$$u_i^p(x^{(j)}) = \frac{h(f(x^{(j)}))}{d(x^{(i)}, x^{(j)})}, \tag{4}$$

where h is an *inversion function* (so that the smaller the fitness value $f(x^{(j)})$, the larger the inverted value $h(f(x^{(j)}))$), and d is the Euclidean distance (or some its power). The form of these utilities is such that a given individual assigns highest utility ($+\infty$) to being selected itself, but otherwise it balances its desires for a similar candidate (located closely to $x^{(i)}$) to be selected and for a high-fitness-value individual to be selected. For each individual $x^{(i)}$ we form its preference order by sorting all the individuals in the non-decreasing order with respect to

---

[1] In the theory of elections it is often assumed that a rule can output several tied committees, and these ties have to somehow be broken. In our application it is far simpler to assume that tie-breaking already happened within the rule and we get a unique outcome.

utilities u_i^p, and run the GreedyCC algorithm to pick k individuals (where k is a parameter of the operator).

We refer to the utility function used by Faliszewski et al. [4] as *proportional* because it is directly proportional to the (inverted) fitness value and inversely proportional to the distance. However, we noted that proportional utilities favor duplicated individuals too strongly and, instead, we propose to use utilities of the form:

$$u_i^p(x^{(j)}) = \frac{h(f(x^{(j)}))}{1 + d(x^{(i)}, x^{(j)})}. \tag{5}$$

We call them *plus-1-proportional utilities*. Their crucial feature is that an individual no longer assigns infinite value to itself or other identical individuals.

5.2 The Improved Genetic Algorithm

The algorithm proposed here uses the $(\mu + \lambda)$ scheme, i.e., the next population comprises of both parents and children, selected appropriately. In our case the offspring population has the same size $\lambda = \mu$ and is created with Vose's scheme [23]. The parents' and the offspring' populations are then merged and reduced using multiwinner selection to the size μ again. The offspring population is meant to introduce extra diversity, so, in general, we use high mutation and/or crossover rates. Diversity is then managed by the multiwinner selection operator, choosing for the next genetic epoch individuals which satisfy both the fitness and the local diversity requirements.

The described scheme is presented in Algorithm 5. A single iteration of our algorithm proceeds as follows. We use Vose's scheme to create μ new individuals by selecting two individuals from the current population X_t, using the proportional, roulette sampling procedure, crossing them arithmetically over, and mutating by moving by the vector sampled using normal probability distribution. Each such individual is placed in the *Offspring* population. Next, we merge X_t and the *Offspring* populations and select μ elements from it using multiwinner selection operator, which outputs population X_{t+1}.

This procedure gives MWS a chance to run only once an epoch, but allows it to operate on a bigger individual set than in our previous papers, where it was applied a number of times to a smaller individual pools. In a series of such small elections, the offspring was formed, but this made it more likely for individual's duplicates to make it to the output population, reducing diversity. Now, MWS can handle such cases by itself, with the help of an appropriate utility function.

6 Experimental Evaluation

In order to evaluate how the proposed strategy performs, we have run two benchmarks, that mimic the real-world problems for which the proposed strategy is dedicated. We show that the strategy achieves high local diversity, making it well-suited for providing input for the following plateau shape determination method. The first benchmark is simpler, with a single, yet non-convex, plateau

---

Algorithm 5. Outline of an improved genetic algorithm using MWS.

Notation:
$X_t = \langle x_t^{(1)}, \ldots, x_t^{(\mu)} \rangle \in \mathcal{D}^\mu \leftarrow$ the population in the t-th epoch,
$C \subseteq X_t \leftarrow$ the election group,
select(), cross(), mutate() $\leftarrow$ selection, crossover and mutation procedures
respectively,
MWS $\leftarrow$ multiwinner selection procedure.

1 Sample the initial population X_0
2 Evaluate X_0
3 $t \leftarrow 0$
   // the main loop over the epochs
4 **while** *Stopping_Condition(X_t)* **do**
5 $\quad$ *Offspring* $\leftarrow \emptyset$
   $\quad$ // the Vose's scheme
6 $\quad$ **for** $i \leftarrow 1$ **to** μ **do**
7 $\quad\quad$ $x_1 \leftarrow select(X_t)$
8 $\quad\quad$ $x_2 \leftarrow select(X_t)$
9 $\quad\quad$ $x \leftarrow cross(x_1, x_2)$
10 $\quad\quad$ $x' \leftarrow mutate(x)$
11 $\quad\quad$ *Offspring* $\leftarrow$ *Offspring* $\cup \{x'\}$
12 $\quad$ $C \leftarrow X_t \cup$ *Offspring*
13 $\quad$ $t \leftarrow t + 1$
14 $\quad$ $X_t \leftarrow \text{MWS}(C, \mu)$
15 $\quad$ Evaluate X_t
16 output X_t

---

region. This test evaluates the general features of the scheme. In the second benchmark, a more difficult, multimodal problem is considered. We asses the ability of our scheme to isolate plateau regions separately from evaluating the scheme's basic features.

The benchmark functions we consider are C-shaped valleys. Each such valley is constructed by combining three ellipsoidal plateau regions. Let r_1 and $r_2 \in \mathbb{R}_+$ be the axes of the plateau and (x_1^0, x_2^0) the point the ellipse is centred at. The respective Gaussian function alone is then defined as:

$$g_{(x_1^0, x_2^0)}^{(r_1, r_2)}(x_1, x_2) = 1 - \exp\left(-\ln 2/r_1^2(x_1 - x_1^0)^2 - \ln 2/r_2^2(x_2 - x_2^0)^2\right) . \quad (6)$$

In this way, function $g_{(x_1^0, x_2^0)}^{(r_1, r_2)}$ has value 0 in the centre, $1/2$ at distances r_1 and r_2 from the centre in the respective dimensions, and approaches 1 quickly further off. The $1/2$ property we use to create a "sliced off" modification of it later. Meanwhile, we create a combination of 3 Gaussian functions, i.e.:

$$s_{(x_1^0, x_2^0)}(x_1, x_2) = \underbrace{g_{(x_1^0, x_2^0+1.5)}^{(1, 0.5)}(x, y)}_{\text{Part 1}} \cdot \underbrace{g_{(x_1^0+1.5, x_2^0)}^{(0.5, 1)}(x, y)}_{\text{Part 2}} \cdot \underbrace{g_{(x_1^0, x_2^0-1.5)}^{(1, 0.5)}(x, y)}_{\text{Part 3}} . \quad (7)$$

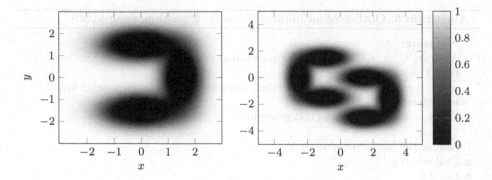

Fig. 3. The two objective functions on which the experiments were performed.

Then, in order to obtain a flat plateau region, we slice it at value $1/2$ scaling it appropriately for its values to stay in the $[0, 1]$ range, namely we set:

$$r_s(x_1, x_2) = \begin{cases} 2s(x_1, x_2) - 1 & \text{if } s(x_1, x_2) \leq 1/2 , \\ 0 & \text{otherwise,} \end{cases} \qquad (8)$$

where $s = s_{(x_1^0, x_2^0)}$. Such function forms a single C-shaped valley, it is flat in the middle and then approaches 1 quickly. The first benchmark's objective function consists of just one such region. However, in the second benchmark two such regions are placed in the domain, which is done by adding more Gaussian functions in desired locations. Both the functions are presented in Fig. 3, the parts are numbered as in Eq. (7).

6.1   Single Valley

The search domain in this case was set to $\mathcal{D} = [-10, 10] \times [-10, 10]$, with the objective function $s_{(0,0)}$, as presented in Fig. 3 (though with larger domain). Our goal was to cover the plateau region and we used the proposed two-phase search strategy.

The first, global search, phase was performed with a 2-level HMS algorithm. Once we have obtained the results from the leaves, a local LBA phase was run. The HMS's root level was configured to use 20-individuals population, with a normal mutation probability 0.5, its standard deviation 1.0, and arithmetic crossover probability 0.05 (because this level was meant to explore the domain). The fitness threshold for sprouting was set to 0.1 and a minimal distance between sprouts was set to 0.5. The second level was initialized from a single sprout seed by creating a new 20-individuals population using normal mutation with standard deviation 0.5. The mutation probability in the leaves was 0.1, its standard deviation 0.1, and crossover probability 0.5.

The global stopping condition activated after 500 fitness evaluations. Moreover, the leaves had local stopping conditions, which activated if they didn't

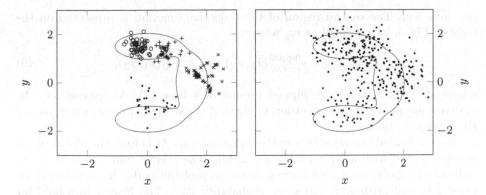

Fig. 4. Results of the first benchmark. On the left, the 4 resulting clusters are presented, each mark type represents a single cluster. On the right, integrated individuals from the LBA evolutionary phase. The isoline is placed at 0.1 objective function value.

improve their fitness in 2 evolutionary steps. In this way, the algorithm didn't spend too much resources (fitness evaluations) in the 2nd level, and was able to explore the basin of attraction.

Having merged the results from the 2nd level, we moved on to cluster the points with OPTICS-ξ. It was configured with a maximal reachability distance $\varepsilon = 2.0$, MinPts $= 20$, and the steepness factor $\xi = 0.02$. During the DFS reduction of the hierarchical clustering, the threshold cluster size was 50. Cluster integrator was configured with 3 intermediate points, maximal distance 2.0 and hill-valley tolerance 0.1.

The resulting clusters, or actually a single cluster in this case, were then processed using our improved Genetic Algorithm using multiwinner selection. The population was much larger than in the global phase, it had 100 individuals. The normal mutation probability was 1.0, its standard deviation 0.5 and no crossover was applied. The evolution was stopped after 4 evolutionary steps.

The results of such a run are presented in Fig. 4. In the first plot, the identified clusters are presented. In this case, they correspond to the leaf level demes. As they lay in a single plateau region, they have been integrated into a single cluster, which was then evolved for 4 epochs. The integrated individuals from that phase are presented on the right.

The effect of running our scheme in the single plateau case shows that the scheme is able to cover the plateau region robustly. Using a larger population size and the improved GA, we were able to cover the region approximately uniformly. There is some number of individuals outside the plateau, which would be beneficial in case we wanted to determine the shape of the plateau.

6.2 Two Valleys

Next, we proceeded to verify the scheme's characteristics on a multimodal benchmark. The domain was set to $\mathcal{D} = [-10, 10] \times [-10, 10]$, the same as in the previous test. The central region of the objective function is presented on the right of Fig. 3. It is defined as r_{s_2} where:

$$s_2(x_1, x_2) = s_{(-1,0)}^{\text{flipped}}(x_1, x_2) \cdot s_{(1.5,-1.5)}(x_1, x_2), \qquad (9)$$

where s^{flipped} is a vertically flipped version of s from (7). As we can see, the plateaus are placed near each other, to check if the strategy manages to separate the distinct regions.

We configured the algorithm in the following way. As before, the global phase was performed with a 2-level HMS algorithm. The HMS's root was using a 20-individual population, with a normal mutation probability 0.5, its standard deviation 1.0, and arithmetic crossover probability 0.05. The fitness threshold for sprouting was set to 0.1 and a minimal distance between sprouts was set to 0.5. The second level was initialized from a single sprout seed by creating a new 20-individual population using normal mutation with standard deviation 0.5. The mutation probability in the leaves was 0.1, its standard deviation 0.1, and crossover probability 0.5. The parameters used here are identical to the previous test, except that we changed the global stopping condition to allow 3000 fitness evaluations. The leaves' stopping condition remained unaltered, i.e., they were halted if no fitness improvement happened in 2 evolutionary steps.

The local phase was configured similarly too. OPTICS-ξ was configured with a maximal reachability distance $\varepsilon = 2.0$, MinPts $= 20$, and the steepness factor $\xi = 0.02$. During the DFS reduction of the hierarchical clustering, the threshold cluster size was 20. Cluster integrator was configured with 3 intermediate points, maximal distance 4.0, and hill-valley tolerance 0.1.

In the local phase, we again used the improved GA with population size 100, normal mutation probability 1.0, its standard deviation 0.5, and no crossover. The evolution was halted after 4 epochs.

Firstly, when we ran the strategy, 24 leaf-level demes were sprouted in the global phase which covered the plateau regions. In the then-following local phase, these demes' individuals were reduced to just 2 clusters, as expected. The integration strategy helped achieve that result. Further on, during the evolutionary part of the local phase, the plateau regions were covered with individuals.

For clarity, only the results from the evolutionary phase are presented in Fig. 5. On the left, the initial population is presented, i.e., the individuals resulting directly from the clustering and integration processes. It is evident, that they don't cover the region uniformly but they are a good input for the improved GA. On the right, however, the populations after 4 evolutionary epochs are presented. They cover the plateau regions uniformly, with a slight tendency to extend outwards. The latter effect is particularly important for algorithms for automatic determination of plateau region shapes.

Apart from the preceding analysis, we performed a test of "plateau coverage". That is, we attempted to measure how well the population covered the both plateaus on average. We assume the plateaus to be points with the objective fitness values of 0.1 and lower. We impose a rectangular grid of size 0.1 on the domain and then choose points with the objective function values below

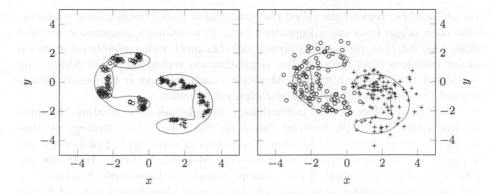

Fig. 5. The results of the LBA evolution. On the left, the initial populations, after clustering and integration, are shown. On the right, the populations after 4 evolutionary steps much better covering the plateau regions. The isoline is placed at 0.1 objective function value and different mark types designate different populations.

0.1, which will form a plateau approximation. Then, for each point from the approximation we check if there is an individual (chosen from some set defined below) within some threshold distance (we have chosen 0.2 in this case). The fraction of points for which at least one such individual exists is called the plateau coverage value. (For a more detailed description see e.g. [11].)

We choose the individual set for each strategy run as follows. The initial LBA population is discarded, as it can be too focused after the global phase, and we merge all the following populations from all the LBAs. We treat such a merged set as the input to calculate the plateau coverage. In the case of the preceding example, the mean coverage of both plateaus was equal to 94%.

We ran the strategy 10 times and collected the plateau coverage values. The average coverage was 88% ± 8% with 1-sigma normal confidence level. The plateau regions were covered well in all the cases, the minimal coverage value was 75%. In 6 cases two LBAs were started as expected, and in 2 cases three LBAs were created. In the remaining 2 runs, only a single LBA was created covering both plateaus.

The cases where 3 LBAs are started should be easy to resolve in the future with repeated integrations, i.e. repeating it after several evolutionary epochs and merging matching LBAs. More importantly, the strategy should avoid merging distinct plateaus, as their separation later is more difficult. A smart use of fitness values during the clustering and integration phases should help at achieving that.

The test shows, that the strategy is able to cover the plateau regions robustly, yet there remain issues to be tackled.

7   Conclusions

Recent development of metaheuristics allows for studying regions of admissible domains, in which the objective is insensitive with respect to the decision variables (these regions are called plateaus). Such global optimization problems take their origin from many important tasks in technology, geophysics, medical diagnosis, etc. The proposed approach delivers much more reliable information about solutions than the objective regularization technique [1], in which only single solution can be obtained. Moreover, such solution is frequently biased toward the minimum of the regularization supplement.

The paper offers a new methodology for plateau identification, by producing a random sample covering uniformly their area. This strategy is composed of several phases: (1) Locating the basins of attraction of plateaus using a global optimization algorithm (Hierarchic Memetic Strategy, HMS, in our case [12]); (2) Clustering of the random sample of individuals produced by the global optimization algorithm; (3) Integrating the clusters located in the same basins of attraction; (4) Performing the local-phase evolution to uniformly cover the plateaus. The last phase is performed individually for each plateau, using a custom-made multiwinner selection operator that we recently introduced [4,11].

We will release the source code of the algorithm and the benchmarks soon to allow reproduction, please contact any author to stay up to date in this regard.

The results of the proposed strategy will constitute input to various postprocessing steps, such as approximating the plateau area [15] and smooth local objective approximation by isoparametric splines [14].

The strategy exhibits good efficiency on the benchmarks in which the objective function contains either a single non-convex plateau or two non-convex plateaus. These benchmark results are, of course, only a preliminary assessment, the exhaustive statistical efficiency analysis is in progress. We will apply this strategy for solving various parametric inverse problems, e.g., inverting magnetotelluric measurements. The first results in this direction were reported in [10].

It is difficult to compare the proposed strategy with other methods because, to the best of our knowledge, the issue of such plateau identification has not been addressed in prior papers.

References

1. Tikhonov, A., Goncharsky, A., Stepanov, V., Yagola, A.: Numerical Methods for the Solution of Ill-Posed Problems. Kluwer, Dordrecht (1995)
2. Gupta, D., Ghafir, S.: An overview of methods maintaining diversity in genetic algorithms. Int. J. Emerg. Technol. Adv. Eng. 2(5), 56–60 (2012)
3. Telega, H.: Two-phase stochastic global optimization strategies. In: Schaefer, R. (ed.) Foundation of Genetic Global Optimization. SCI, vol. 74, pp. 153–197. Springer, Heidelberg (2007). doi:10.1007/978-3-540-73192-4_6
4. Faliszewski, P., Sawicki, J., Schaefer, R., Smołka, M.: Multiwinner voting in genetic algorithms for solving ill-posed global optimization problems. In: Squillero, G., Burelli, P. (eds.) EvoApplications 2016. LNCS, vol. 9597, pp. 409–424. Springer, Heidelberg (2016). doi:10.1007/978-3-319-31204-0_27
5. Isshiki, M., Sinclair, D., Kaneko, S.: Lens design: global optimization of both performance and tolerance sensitivity. In: International Optical Design, Optical Society of America (2006). TuA5

6. Duan, Q., Sorooshian, S., Gupta, V.: Effective and efficient global optimization for conceptual rainfall-runoff models. Water Resour. Res. **28**(4), 1015–1031 (1992)
7. Smołka, M., Gajda-Zagórska, E., Schaefer, R., Paszyński, M., Pardo, D.: A hybrid method for inversion of 3D AC logging measurements. Appl. Soft Comput. **36**, 422–456 (2015)
8. Paruch, M., Majchrzak, E.: Identification of tumor region parameters using evolutionary algorithm and multiple reciprocity boundary element method. Eng. Appl. Artif. Intell. **20**(5), 647–655 (2007)
9. Zeidler, E.: Nonlinear Functional Analysis and its Application. II/A: Linear Monotone Operators. Springer, Heidelberg (2000)
10. Sawicki, J.: Identification of low sensitivity regions for inverse problems solutions. Master's thesis, AGH University of Science and Technology, Faculty of Informatics, Electronics and Telecommunication, Kraków, Poland (2016)
11. Faliszewski, P., Sawicki, J., Schaefer, R., Smołka, M.: Multiwinner voting in genetic algorithms. Accepted to IEEE Intelligent Systems (2016)
12. Smołka, M., Schaefer, R., Paszyński, M., Pardo, D., Álvarez-Aramberri, J.: An agent-oriented hierarchic strategy for solving inverse problems. Int. J. Appl. Math. Comput. Sci. **25**(3), 483–498 (2015)
13. Schaefer, R., Adamska, K., Telega, H.: Clustered genetic search in continuous landscape exploration. Eng. Appl. Artif. Intell. **17**, 407–416 (2004)
14. Łoś, M., Schaefer, R., Sawicki, J., Smołka, M.: Local misfit approximation in memetic solving of ill-posed inverse problems. In: Squillero, G., Sim, K. (eds.) EvoApplications 2017. LNCS, vol. 10199, pp. 297–309. Springer, Heidelberg (2017)
15. Wolny, A., Schaefer, R.: Improving population-based algorithms with fitness deterioration. J. Telecommun. Inf. Technol. **4**(4), 31–44 (2011)
16. Schaefer, R., Kołodziej, J.: Genetic search reinforced by the population hierarchy. In: Foundations of Genetic Algorithms, vol. 7, pp. 383–399. Morgan Kaufman (2003)
17. Ankerst, M., Breunig, M.M., Kriegel, H.P., Sander, J.: Optics: ordering points to identify the clustering structure. SIGMOD Rec. **28**(2), 49–60 (1999)
18. Schubert, E., Koos, A., Emrich, T., Züfle, A., Schmid, K.A., Zimek, A.: A framework for clustering uncertain data. PVLDB **8**(12), 1976–1979 (2015)
19. Ursem, R.K.: Multinational evolutionary algorithms. In: Proceedings of the 1999 Congress on Evolutionary Computation, CEC 1999, vol. 3. IEEE (1999)
20. Aziz, H., Brill, M., Conitzer, V., Elkind, E., Freeman, R., Walsh, T.: Justified representation in approval-based committee voting. In: Proceedings of the 29th AAAI Conference on Artificial Intelligecne, pp. 784–790 (2015)
21. Elkind, E., Faliszewski, P., Skowron, P., Slinko, A.: Properties of multiwinner voting rules. In: Proceedings of the 13th International Conference on Autonomous Agents and Multiagent Systems, pp. 53–60, May 2014
22. Lu, T., Boutilier, C.: Budgeted social choice: from consensus to personalized decision making. In: Proceedings of the 22nd International Joint Conference on Artificial Intelligence, pp. 280–286 (2011)
23. Vose, M.: The Simple Genetic Algorithm. MIT Press, Cambridge (1999)

Avenues for the Use of Cellular Automata in Image Segmentation

Laura Dioşan[1]([✉]), Anca Andreica[1], Imre Boros[1], and Irina Voiculescu[2]

[1] Department of Computer Science, Babes-Bolyai University, Cluj-Napoca, Romania
lauras@cs.ubbcluj.ro
[2] Department of Computer Science, University of Oxford, Oxford, UK

Abstract. The majority of Cellular Automata (CA) described in the literature are binary or three-state. While several abstractions are possible to generalise to more than three states, only a negligible number of multi-state CA rules exist with concrete practical applications.

This paper proposes a generic rule for multi-state CA. The rule allows for any number of states, and allows for the states are semantically related. The rule is illustrated on the concrete example of image segmentation, where the CA agents are pixels in an image, and their states are the pixels' greyscale values.

We investigate in detail the proposed rule and some of its variations, and we also compare its effectiveness against its closest relative, the existing Greenberg–Hastings automaton. We apply the proposed methods to both synthetic and real-world images, evaluating the results with a variety of measures. The experimental results demonstrate that our proposed method can segment images accurately and effectively.

1 Introduction

For well over half a century [1], many interesting properties of Cellular Automata (CA) have been studied and described [2]. It is somewhat surprising to discover that the vast majority of work on this topic deals with binary CA, in which each cell can have one of two possible states. Papers reporting applications of multi-state CA feel like a mere handful. Various models such as the Potts model [3] is documented [4], as is the Greenberg–Hastings (GH) model [5], subsequently studied in [6,7]. The approach presented in [8] is defined as a multi-state CA but the results are all illustrated on only three states.

CA have been used mostly to model discrete processes, for example the propagation of information (such as rumour or opinion) in a colony of discrete agents [9]. They are also used to generate random numbers [10]. For such applications, it is normally enough to use binary or three-state CA.

Multi-state CA are used more naturally in image processing applications, in the sense that the greyscale level of each pixel can represent that pixel's state. Image processing in this sense includes geometric transformations, noise filtering, feature detection, edge detection. There exist also CA-based approaches to image segmentation, but attempts in the literature are scarce.

© Springer International Publishing AG 2017
G. Squillero and K. Sim (Eds.): EvoApplications 2017, Part I, LNCS 10199, pp. 282–296, 2017.
DOI: 10.1007/978-3-319-55849-3_19

One of the most frequently cited CA-based image segmentation approaches is given by the GrowCut algorithm [11]. In [12] an unsupervised Grow–Cut algorithm is developed for medical image segmentation. Grow-Cut without seeds does not require user intervention because it starts with a random number of seed points (and random seed's type) and converges to a stable configuration. Another unsupervised Grow–Cut segmentation method is proposed in [13]. The seed selection process takes place using the Grey Level Co Occurrence Matrix (GLCM), a mechanism that allows of specifying only two possible types of seeds (foreground and background). We nevertheless see the use of CA in these approaches merely as a parallelization tool, without taking advantage of the full emergence phenomenon (which yields a semantically significant global behaviour based on local rules).

It has been shown [14] that the seeded GrowCut is essentially no different from the Ford–Bellman algorithm which computes shortest paths from a cell to all the other cells in the CA. Their proof makes it clear that CA is no more than a parallelization tool.

There are other few CA-based segmentation approaches, but they have some limits. For instance, the aim of [15] was to identify and segment suspicious mass regions of mammograms. A 2D CA is used with initial state of each cell established based on the sum average feature from the initially segmented image using histogram-based thresholding. This thresholding actually involves using a binary CA. Tumour segmentation on magnetic resonance images is considered in [16]. A 3D CA is actually used with initial state set to MRI seed volume voxels (showing intensities) for foreground (tumour) and background, determined after computing a volume of interest from a line drawn by the user over the largest visible diameter of the tumour. This interactive algorithm, which offers reasonably robust segmentation, is dependent on user input and is limited by the number of classes defined in the interaction.

The focus of this paper is on CA with a large set of discrete and semantically-correlated states. We propose a novel update rule to be used with multi-state CA. The rule can be parameterized and takes into account features of neighbouring cell compared to the features of the current cell.

Our approach harnesses the CA benefits and applies these to image segmentation: easy to implement; possible to parallelize; can be applied to any number of classes (both bi-label and multi-label image segmentations are possible); easy to extend to various features extracted from images (currently, pixel intensity values have been used as state transition rules, but other image features such as texture or edges could be easily incorporated into update mechanism); dimensionality- and size-independent (the computational complexity of the segmentation process is not directly influenced by the image size or the number of image features).

The paper is organised as follows. Section 2 formalizes multi-state CA. The problem of image segmentation is described in Sect. 3. In Sect. 4 the proposed generic rule for multi-state CA is introduced. The description of used datasets and the results are discussed in Sect. 5. In Sect. 6 we conclude with a discussion around the validation results and future research directions.

2   Multi-state CA Formalism

2.1   Generic Multi-state CA

CA can be formalised as decentralized structures of simple and locally interacting elements which evolve following a set of rules, emerging into a global behaviour. A CA can be defined by a 4-tuple $(L, \mathcal{S}, n, f)$:

– the topology L (a grid of g cells, usually a lattice)
– the finite set $\mathcal{S}$ of cell states (e.g. greyscale values)
– a finite number n of neighbour indices
– a transition function $f : \mathcal{S}^n \longrightarrow \mathcal{S}$

The transition function computes the new state of each cell $c \in L$ as a function of its n neighbours, simultaneously for all cells. If we denote a configuration $C_t : L \longrightarrow \mathcal{S}^g$ of a CA as a function which associates a state to each cell at time t, then the transition function f changes C_t into C_{t+1} thus:

$$C_{t+1}(c) = f(\{C_t(v) \mid v \in N(c)\})$$

where $N(c)$ is the set of n neighbours v of each cell $c \in L$.

As an aside, there is a choice of neighbourhood shape used in two-dimensional CA. The most popular ones are *von Neumann* ($n = 4$) and *Moore* ($n = 8$). A von Neumann neighbourhood is the set of all cells that are orthogonally-adjacent to the core cell (the core cell itself may or may not be considered part of the neighbourhood, depending on the context). A Moore neighbourhood is the set of all cells which surround the core cell. Whilst our experiments work with the latter, they are easily reproducible for any neighbourhood shape.

2.2   Related Work: The Greenberg–Hastings Model

The particular case of GH automata involves a regular grid of cells in one or more dimensions. Each cell can be in one of s states $(0, 1, 2, \ldots, s - 1)$. The states $1, 2, \ldots, s - 1$ are called excited states.

The initial cell states are generated randomly. Subsequently the following rules are followed:

– a cell in a state i between 1 and $s - 2$ takes the succeeding value (namely, $i + 1$);
– a cell in state $s - 1$, takes the 0 as next state;
– a cell in state 0 takes 1 as the next state if one of its neighbours is in an excited state; it takes 0 as the next state if none of its neighbours is in an excited state.

This CA was described as a simple model generating spatio-temporal structures similar to those that can be observed in the Belousov–Zaikin–Zhabotinsky oscillating chemical reaction [5]. The first two rule items describe a reaction rule, while the last describes a diffusion rule. This model is simple in that the diffusion rule and the reaction rules do not act together for the same cell at the same time. In two dimensions, the GH automaton can exhibit complex spiralling behaviour.

While the GH automaton is also defined as multi-state, the way in which it deals with the greyscale values results in three main categories of states: pixels of values 0, 255, and anything in-between.

3   Application Domain

Although the multi-state CA contributed in this paper is a generic in nature, its behaviour is illustrated on a concrete image dataset, using image segmentation as its primary application domain.

The complete segmentation S of an image I can be defined as the *partitioning* of I in P subregions, $R^1 \ldots R^P$, such that:

$$\bigcup_{k=1}^{P} R^k = I$$

$$\forall \widetilde{x} \in R^k \quad \text{pixel label } S(\widetilde{x}) = k \qquad\qquad \forall k \in \{1, 2, \ldots, P\}$$

$$R^k \text{ is a connected set} \qquad\qquad\qquad \forall k \in \{1, 2, \ldots, P\}$$

$$R^j \cap R^k = \phi \qquad\qquad\qquad\qquad \forall j, k, \; j \neq k$$

$$\mathcal{Q}(R^k) = \text{True} \qquad\qquad\qquad\qquad \forall k \in \{1, 2, \ldots, P\}$$

$$\mathcal{Q}(R^j \cup R^k) = \text{False} \qquad\qquad\qquad \forall R^j, R^k \text{ adjacent}$$

where $\mathcal{Q}$ is a logical predicate, used for describing the objects of the image, and is defined on the points of a given region. For instance, $\mathcal{Q}$ can be related to intra-region uniformity, or inter-region signal variation.

The segmentation problem can be considered solved when every pixel has an associated label. The number of labels may or may not correspond to the number of semantic regions in the image.

4   Proposed Approach

The principal contribution of this paper is a novel update rule for a multi-state CA with a range of semantically related discrete states. We illustrate this idea on a concrete application to greyscale images, where the CA agents are pixels in an image and each greyscale value represents a separate state. Naturally, this interpretation is not unique, so the state can also represent other pixel features, such as one of the RGB channels, the gradient magnitude, etc. The difference in value between two cells can be viewed in terms of distance between the features considered. For the remainder of this paper, we work with the greyscale value, imagining the image as a contour landscape and the greyscale values as the height at a given pixel.

The proposed rule is based on the following observations:

1. Pixels with greyscale values which are close to each other normally belong to the same region; pixels with greyscale values which are further apart normally belong to different regions;
2. The state of a cell is influenced by the states of its neighbour cells;
3. A neighbour cell will give its state to the current cell if certain conditions (related to the distance between the cells of the neighbourhood) are met.

Thus, the transition rule that we propose is conditioned not only by the geometry of the CA and the size and shape of each neighbourhood, but also by the state space.

The formalism of the proposed CA rule relies on the following notations:

M current cell to be updated according to the values of its neighbouring cells;
C_1 neighbour of M of closest greyscale value, with value less than that of M;
C_2 neighbour of M of closest greyscale value, with value greater than that of M;
D_1 neighbour of M of furthest greyscale value, with value less than that of M;
D_2 neighbour of M of furthest greyscale value, with value greater than that of M.

A family of rules for our CA can be derived from the existence or absence of these special neighbours. We present and analyse three related versions of the rule.

4.1   Close Attraction Rule (CAR)

The main intuition for our proposed rule is that a given cell changes its own state according to relative greyscale values in its neighbourhood. Agent M moves to take the value of its neighbour of closest value on either side, according to "attraction" forces from other cells in its neighbourhood (see Algorithm 1).

Algorithm 1. CAR

if C_1 exists and C_2 does not exist **then**
    $M \leftarrow C_1$
if C_2 exists **and** C_1 does not exist **then**
    $M \leftarrow C_2$
if both C_1 **and** C_2 exist **then**
    if M is closer to D_1 than to D_2 **then**
        $M \leftarrow C_1$
    if M is closer to D_2 than to D_1 **then**
        $M \leftarrow C_2$

Algorithm 2. FAR

---

if C_1 exists **and** C_2 does not exist **then**
    $M \leftarrow C_1$
if C_2 exists **and** C_1 does not exist **then**
    $M \leftarrow C_2$
if both C_1 and C_2 exist **then**
    if M is equidistant from C_1 than to C_2 **then**
        if M is closer to D_1 than to D_2 **then**
            $M \leftarrow D_1$
        else
            $M \leftarrow D_2$
    else
        if M is closer to C_1 than to C_2 **then**
            $M \leftarrow C_1$
        else
            $M \leftarrow C_2$

4.2 Far Attraction Rule (FAR)

Similar to CAR, the FAR rule allows the cell to take values from neighbours. Rather than taking values from its closest neighbours, each cell aims to progress at a faster rate by taking the values from the "attraction poles" themselves, which are further away in greyscale value (see Algorithm 2).

4.3 Fine-Tuned Attraction Rule (FTAR)

While CAR and FAR give acceptable results, common sense dictates that the results will always depend on the distance between the neighbours closer in value and the neighbours further in value. This observation yields the fine-tuned rule which takes into account distance parameters (see Algorithm 3).

In particular, a neighbour cell will give its state to the current cell only if:

- the difference between their state values is less than a threshold ε, and
- the difference in state value between the neighbour cell with the closest value and the neighbour cell with the furthest value is higher than a given threshold δ.

The FTAR rule causes the state of each pixel to evolve away from the greyscale values of its neighbours which look very different (because this could mean that they belong to a different region). Its application relies inherently on the size of each neighbourhood. The resulting automaton is able strongly to outline regions in an image, regardless of their dimension or shape.

In our experiments, the values $\varepsilon = 3$ and $\delta = 5$ have been established empirically for a particular class of images. In separate study [17] we illustrate the relative difference and choices to be made for these parameters.

Algorithm 3. FTAR

> **if** C_1 exists **and** C_2 does not exist **then**
>> **if** $dist(M, C_1) < \varepsilon$ **and** $dist(C_1, D_1) > \delta$ **then**
>>> $M \leftarrow C_1$
>
> **if** C_2 exists **and** C_1 does not exist **then**
>> **if** $dist(M, C_2) < \varepsilon$ **and** $dist(C_2, D_2) > \delta$ **then**
>>> $M \leftarrow C_2$
>
> **if** both C_1 and C_2 exist **then**
>> **if** M is equidistant from C_1 than to C_2 **then**
>>> **if** M is closer to D_1 than to D_2 **and** M is closer to C_1 than to C_2 **and**
>>> $dist(M, C_1) < \varepsilon$ **and** $dist(C_1, D_1) > \delta$ **then**
>>>> $M \leftarrow C_1$
>>>
>>> **if** M is closer to D_2 than to D_1 **and** M is closer to C_2 than to C_1 **and**
>>> $dist(M, C_2) < \varepsilon$ **and** $dist(C_2, D_2) > \delta$ **then**
>>>> $M \leftarrow C_2$

---

5   Numerical Experiments

A series of systematic experiments on synthetic and real data reveal that the new rule shows more stability when comparing it to established rules such as GH.

We first analyse the performance of the proposed rule on a set of 2D two-region synthetic images. Synthetic images are an appropriate tool for evaluating such techniques and putting bounds on their performance. Our synthetic images are arrays of 500×500 greyscale values. A selection of foreground shapes (square, rectangle, disk) were generated automatically, with uniform intensity and with the option of added noise. These feature in the leftmost column of Fig. 1.

We then move on to segment *real-world images*, namely the Berkeley Segmentation Dataset [18], which contains natural images with corresponding human segmentations (ground-truth). We have used 100 of these images in order to validate our approach.

Two medical images have also been sampled in order to illustrate the holy grail of our method. Since no ground-truth contours were available for these images, the assessment can only be carried out visually.

5.1   CA Specification

Our experiments have been carried out using a *two-dimensional* CA. The process relies on a static CA based on a grid of cells. The width and height of the grid correspond to the size of the image to be segmented. The set of cells and their interconnection pattern do not change with time.

Each cell of the CA can have one of 256 possible states which correspond to greyscale values. Even if the initial configuration (construction or random generation) often conditions the evolution of a CA, in our case the cells are initialized by the greyscale value of each pixel.

Conventional limit conditions for CA can be periodic, reflective or with fixed value. We have chosen to work with fixed value borders. No boundary conditions are imposed for the evolution of the CA. Border cells simply have fewer neighbours than other cells.

Each of the three versions of the proposed update rule have been compared against the conventional GH update.

5.2 Evaluation Measures

Segmented regions and their boundaries can be compact, discontinuous, smooth, etc. For increased reliability we have also looked at how (a label associate to) the greyscale value of each pixel in the segmented image compares against some gold standard or ground truth.[1] Given two segmentations:

- reference segmentation (gold standard) S_r
- machine segmentation S_m

Each image point (pixel) can be classified as:

- true positive (TP): $S_r(x,y)$ is 1 $\wedge$ $S_m(x,y)$ is 1
- false positive (FP): $S_r(x,y)$ is 0 $\wedge$ $S_m(x,y)$ is 1
- true negative (TN): $S_r(x,y)$ is 0 $\wedge$ $S_m(x,y)$ is 0
- false negative (FN): $S_r(x,y)$ is 1 $\wedge$ $S_m(x,y)$ is 0

The four basic cardinalities of the so-called *confusion matrix*, namely the true positives (TP), the false positives (FP), the true negatives (TN), and the false negatives (FN) are defined as follows. Let $I(x,y) : R^2 \to R$ be a 2D image and $S(I(x,y)) : R^2 \to \Omega$, $\Omega = \{0, 1, 2, \ldots, k-1\}$, be a k-ry decision segmentation of the image $I(x,y)$.

Each of these segmentations are composed by k segments, or regions, or classes (e.g. if $k = 2$, then the two segments are represented by the class of interest and the background; if $k = 3$, then two classes of interest and the background will represent possible segments). In the case of $k = 2$ segments, the confusion matrix can be represented as shown in Table 1.

Table 1. Confusion matrix

		Real segments	
		Positive seg	Negative seg
Computed segments	Positive seg	TP	FN
	Negative seg	FN	TN

---

[1] In order to call the reference segmentation *ground truth* we have to be certain that it is so. Manual reference segmentations drawn by experts normally approximate ground truth, in which case it can be used as gold standard, but not as the ground truth itself.

Dice Coefficient was used as one of the evaluation metrics [19] not so much due to its reliability as its popularity. Dice computes the overlap between regions, quantifying the similarity of two segmentations.

$$\text{Coeff}_{\text{Dice}}(S_m, S_r) = \frac{2\,|S_r \cap S_m|}{|S_r| + |S_m|} = \frac{2TP}{2TP + FP + FN}$$

F-measure is an alternative evaluation measure which can be expressed as a percentage; its values range between 0 (no overlap) and 1 (perfect agreement) using the values below. It is also called the *overlap index* and makes it possible to quantify reproducibility. An equivalent of the Dice coefficient is, therefore, the F_β measure with $\beta = 1$.

$$F_\beta = \frac{(\beta^2 + 1) * \text{Precision} * \text{Recall}}{\beta^2 * \text{Precision} + \text{Recall}}$$

Precision (defined as $\frac{TP}{TP+FP}$) is another measure that can be used to evaluate the quality of segmentation.

Recall (defined as $\frac{TP}{TP+FN}$) is computed as the ratio between the number of positive hits in the reference image and the number of pixels in the segmented image which should be positive hits.

Specificity (defined as $\frac{TN}{TN+FP}$) is computed as the ratio between the number of negative hits in the reference image and the number of pixels in the segmented image which should be negative hits.

There are two other related measures, namely Fallout $= \frac{FP}{FP+TN} = 1 -$ Specificity and the false negative rate FNR $= \frac{FN}{FN+TP} = 1 -$ Recall.

Since the latter two are equivalent to Specificity and Recall, only one pair ((Recall, Specificity) or (Fallout, FNR)) are ever used to evaluate segmentation performance.

Recall is also known as Sensitivity or True Positive Rate (TPR). Specificity is True Negative Rate (TNR). Fallout is false positive rate (FPR).

Global Consistency Error (GCE) is an error-based measure [18] which is the complement to similarity measures, in that two segmentations are identical if an error-based measure is 0.

This measure is computed as an average over the error of pixels belonging to two segmentations. It compares partitions of the same image and it is tolerant to one partition refining the other (e.g. by splitting or merging regions). For an image I of n pixels ($n = |I|$) and a segmented region S, we denote the set of all neighbour pixels to pixel p which belong to the same segmentation region S by $R(S, p)$. For two segmentations, one computed S_c and one reference segmentation S_r, the asymmetric Local Refinement Error at pixel p [18] is LRE$(S_c, S_r, p) = \frac{|R(S_c,p) - R(S_r,p)|}{|R(S_c,p)|}$.

The GCE between segmentations can be defined as a mean over the error of all points (pixels):

$$\text{GCE}(S_1, S_2) = \frac{1}{|I|} \times \min\left\{ \sum_{i=1}^{|I|} LRE(S_1, S_2, p), \sum_{i=1}^{|I|} LRE(S_2, S_1, p) \right\}$$

Using the cardinalities previously introduced, GCE can be expressed as follows:

$$\text{GCE}(S_c, S_r) = \frac{1}{|I|} \times$$

$$\min\left\{ \frac{FN(FN + 2TP)}{TP + FN} + \frac{FP(FP + 2TN)}{TN + FP}, \right.$$
$$\left. \frac{FP(FP + 2TP)}{TP + FP} + \frac{FN(FN + 2TN)}{TN + FN} \right\}$$

This measure is able to quantify the consistency between image segmentations of differing granularities. It has the advantage of being tolerant to (label) refinement. It makes most sense to use this measure when the two segmentations being compared have comparable numbers of segments [20].

5.3   Numerical Results and Discussion

Synthetic Data. We have analysed the results obtained by running our three proposed variations (CAR, FAR, FTAR) on a simple synthetic dataset. For completeness, we have also compared our results against the performance of the existing GH CA.

Results obtained with noise-free images are all similar, and close to the optimal value of all considered evaluation measures. It therefore seems spurious to detail these results here. These preliminary results merely constitute a basic validation of our CA-based approach to image segmentation.

When the synthetic images were peppered with random noise as illustrated in the leftmost column of Fig. 1, the resulting segmentations are more meaningful. We illustrate those obtained after 70 iterations of the proposed CA on noisy synthetic data.

Visual inspection is enough to point out the way in which segmentations performed by our proposed family of rules (CAR, FAR, FTAR) are very close to the ground truth, while the GH automaton is unable to process the noisy images successfully. Once again, when assessed systematically, the evaluation measures obtained by CAR, FAR, FTAR are very close to their optimal values, while those obtained by GH are considerably weaker.

General Real Data. The bulk of our analysis, however, consisted of a thorough and systematic analysis of 100 real-world examples from the Berkeley Segmentation Dataset, together with their corresponding ground truths. The evaluation

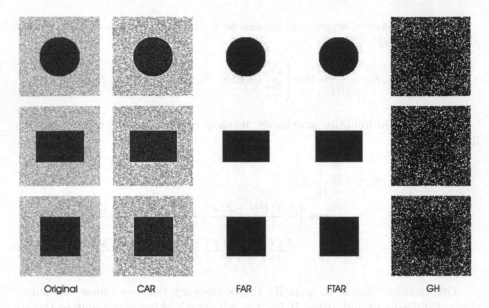

Fig. 1. Synthetic 2D images with added noise, and their respective segmentation results

measures obtained by all considered algorithms on this dataset are depicted in Fig. 2. For each of the evaluation measures we give a graph illustrating the mean (over all images) and the corresponding confidence interval considered at the same discrete timesteps over (up to) 70 CA iterations.

On close inspection of the graphs, it is worth noting the following:

- The Dice value for CAR and FAR decreases with the iteration index, while the Dice value for FTAR and GH not only outperform CAR and FAR from the early iterations, but they also increase as the iterations progress.
- The same underperforming behaviour of CAR and FAR (described for the Dice metric) can also be observed from the perspective of consistency error, as the metric values undesirably increase with the number of iterations. The errors obtained by FTAR are almost constant as the iterations progress, while those of GH rise and fall. Moreover, FTAR performs slightly better than GH.
- In the early stages of the execution, there is no significant difference between FAR and CAR measured with FPR; however the later stages indicate that FAR outperforms CAR. Moreover, the difference between FTAR and GH is statistically significant under the fallout measure, FTAR considerably outperforming GH.
- The Sensitivity results are very similar to FPR, with the main difference that, under this measure, GH offers the best performance.
- In the case of Specificity, FTAR outperforms all the other CA; under this measure the performance of GH appears significantly weaker. CAR and FAR perform better than GH, their Specificity measure decreasing at a slower rate with the number of iterations.

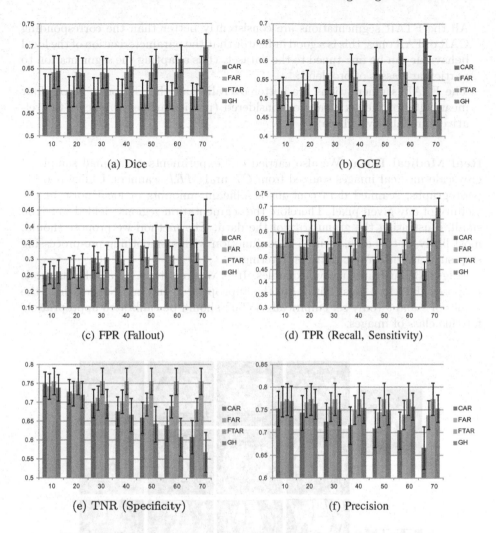

Fig. 2. Performance measures for the Berkeley Segmentation Dataset

- Precision ranks FTAR slightly better than GH, but the difference between them is not statistically significant. Whilst FAR outperforms CAR, the results obtained by CAR and FAR are even weaker than those of GH.

From the above observations we can conclude that:

- GH exhibits a fluctuating behaviour across the selection of measures: sometimes it yields the best results, whilst other times it is measured as weakest);
- Unsurprisingly, FAR outperforms CAR in five out of the six evaluation measures considered; this can be regarded as an example of convergence acceleration;

– All the FTAR segmentations are consistently better than the corresponding CAR or FAR ones; this is a good indicator that the parameterization of the local behaviour can be fine-tuned to the dataset, thus adapting the segmentation to particular classes of problems;
– The FTAR segmentations are better overall than the GH ones, across four meaningful of the six measures considered (particularly experiencing the relative unreliability of Dice).

Real Medical Data. We also carried out experiments on a small sample of greyscale medical images sourced from CT and MRI scanners. Unlike real-life photographs, scanned data contains significant amounts of local noise in the vicinity of any given pixel. Therefore the segmentation regions yielded were too small, illustrating the granularity of the data. The method we propose should, most likely, in this case, be used in conjunction with a smoothing pre-processing step such as anisotropic diffusion filtering.

Figure 3 illustrates a few examples. It is obvious that, of all the methods proposed, FTAR is most faithful to the appropriate contours. Nevertheless, the values of ε and δ (only set empirically so far) should be calibrated appropriately for this class of images.

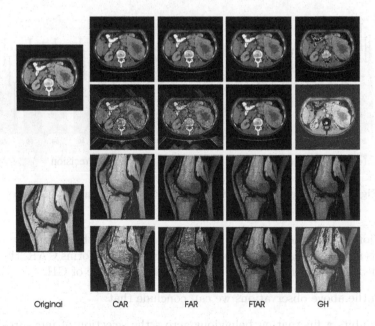

Original   CAR   FAR   FTAR   GH

Fig. 3. Medical images: originals on the left, and various CA-based segmentations (after one and 70 iterations respectively) on each row

6 Conclusions and Further Work

We have illustrated the family of CA update rules for the intuitive case of image segmentation. The rules are relatively easy to generalise and adapt to other applications, as well as to other classes of images. Future work will revolve around the calibration parameters ε and δ and their tuning to the case of medical image segmentation.

Acknowledgment. This work was supported by a grant of the Romanian National Authority for Scientific Research and Innovation, CNCS – UEFISCDI, project number PN-II-RU-TE-2014-4-1130.

References

1. von Neumann, J.: Theory of Self-reproducing Automata. University of Illinois Press, Urbana (1966). Edited and Completed by Arthur W. Burks
2. Wolfram, S.: A New Kind of Science. Wolfram Media Inc., Champaign (2002)
3. Potts, R.B.: Some generalized order-disorder transformations. Math. Proc. Camb. Philos. Soc. **48**(1), 106–109 (1952)
4. Wu, F.Y.: The potts model. Rev. Mod. Phys. **54**, 235–268 (1982)
5. Greenberg, J.M., Hastings, S.P.: Spatial patterns for discrete models of diffusion in excitable media. SIAM J. Appl. Math. **34**, 515–523 (1978)
6. Fisch, R., Gravner, J., Griffeath, D.: Metastability in the Greenberg-Hastings model. Ann. Appl. Probab. **3**(4), 935–967 (1993)
7. Fisch, R., Gravner, J.: One-dimensional deterministic Greenberg-Hastings models. Complex Syst. **9**, 329–348 (1995)
8. Baetens, J.M., Baets, B.: Towards a comprehensive understanding of multi-state cellular automata. In: Wąs, J., Sirakoulis, G.C., Bandini, S. (eds.) ACRI 2014. LNCS, vol. 8751, pp. 16–24. Springer, Heidelberg (2014). doi:10.1007/978-3-319-11520-7_3
9. dos Santos, R.M.Z., Coutinho, S.: Dynamics of HIV infection: a cellular automata approach. Phys. Rev. Lett. **87**, 168102 (2001)
10. Chaudhuri, P.P., Chowdhury, D.R., Nandi, S., Chattopadhyay, S.: Additive Cellular Automata: Theory and Applications. Wiley-IEEE Computer Society Press, Hoboken (1997)
11. Vezhnevets, V., Konouchine, V.: Growcut - interactive multi-label N-D image segmentation by cellular automata (2005)
12. Ghosh, P., Antani, S.K., Long, L.R., Thoma, G.R.: Unsupervised grow-cut: cellular automata-based medical image segmentation. In: 2011 First IEEE International Conference on Healthcare Informatics, Imaging and Systems Biology (HISB), pp. 40–47. IEEE (2011)
13. RajKumar, R., Niranjana, G.: Image segmentation and classification of MRI brain tumor based on cellular automata and neural networks. IJREAT Int. J. Res. Eng. Adv. Technol. **1**(1), 323–327 (2013)
14. Kauffmann, C., Piche, N.: Seeded ND medical image segmentation by cellular automaton on GPU. Int. J. Comput. Assist. Radiol. Surg. **5**(3), 251–262 (2010)
15. Anitha, J., Peter, J.D.: Mammogram segmentation using maximal cell strength updation in cellular automata. Med. Biol. Eng. Comput. **53**(8), 737–749 (2015)

16. Hamamci, A., Kucuk, N., Karaman, K., Engin, K., Ünal, G.B.: Tumor-Cut: segmentation of brain tumors on contrast enhanced MR images for radiosurgery applications. IEEE Trans. Med. Imaging **31**(3), 790–804 (2012)
17. Diosan, L., Andreica, A., Voiculescu, I.: Parameterized cellular automata in image segmentation. In: 18th International Symposium on Symbolic and Numeric Algorithms for Scientific Computing (SYNASC) (2016)
18. Martin, D.R., Fowlkes, C.C., Tal, D., Malik, J.: A database of human segmented natural images and its application to evaluating segmentation algorithms and measuring ecological statistics. In: ICCV, vol. II, pp. 416–423 (2001)
19. Dice, L.R.: Measures of the amount of ecologic association between species. Ecology **26**(3), 297–302 (1945)
20. Unnikrishnan, R., Pantofaru, C., Hebert, M.: Toward objective evaluation of image segmentation algorithms. IEEE Trans. Pattern Anal. Mach. Intell. **29**(6), 929–944 (2007)

Local Misfit Approximation in Memetic Solving of Ill-Posed Inverse Problems

Marcin Łoś[✉], Robert Schaefer, Jakub Sawicki, and Maciej Smołka

AGH University of Science and Technology,
Al. Mickiewicza 30, 30-059 Kraków, Poland
marcin.los.91@gmail.com, {schaefer,jsawicki,smolka}@agh.edu.pl

Abstract. The approximation of the objective function is a well known method of speeding up optimization process, especially if the objective evaluation is costly. This is the case of inverse parametric problems formulated as global optimization ones, in which we recover partial differential equation parameters by minimizing the misfit between its measured and simulated solutions. Typically, the approximation used to build the surrogate objective is rough but globally applicable in the whole admissible domain. The authors try to carry out a different task of detailed misfit approximation in the regions of low sensitivity (plateaus). The proposed complex method consists of independent C^0 Lagrange approximation of the misfit and its gradient, based on the nodes obtained during the dedicated memetic process, and the subsequent projection of the obtained components (single or both) on the space of B-splines. The resulting approximation is globally C^1, which allows us to use fast gradient-based local optimization methods. Another goal attained in this way is the estimation of the shape of plateau as an appropriate level set of the approximated objective. The proposed strategy can be applied for solving ill-conditioned real world inverse problems, e.g., appearing in the oil deposit investigation. We show the results of preliminary tests of the method on two benchmarks featuring convex and non-convex U-shaped plateaus.

Keywords: Ill-posed global optimization problems · Objective approximation · Fitness insensitivity

1 Motivation and State-of-the-Art

The *parametric inverse problems* under consideration consist in recovering coefficient functions (inverse solutions) describing physical features of phenomena modeled by partial differential equations (PDE), from the measurements of the state, which correspond to the solutions of the related PDE (forward solutions).

This work is supported by National Science Centre, Poland grant no. 2015/17/B/ST6/01867.

G. Squillero and K. Sim (Eds.): EvoApplications 2017, Part I, LNCS 10199, pp. 297–309, 2017.
DOI: 10.1007/978-3-319-55849-3_20

Such tasks are frequently formulated as global optimization problems, in which one minimizes the misfit between the measurements and simulated forward solution over the set of admissible coefficient representations (see, e.g., [1]).

The main difficulty in solving inverse problems is the usual ill-conditioning, which typically is the misfit multimodality and insensitivity with respect to some parameters, even over the subsets of positive Lebesgue measure (plateaus). Such a type of ill-conditioning can be observed in the electric field intensity measurement inversion used in the search for hydrocarbon deposits [2,3].

There are generally two ways to manage the multimodality and insensitivity:

- the elimination of excess solutions by misfit regularization [4], which may lead to replacing real minimizers by artificial ones imposed by the regularization term, or
- finding all solutions, letting experts in the area select reasonable ones and reject artifacts.

If we select the second, more general way, the following task have to be carried out: separate attraction basins of different plateaus in the misfit landscape and individually approximate the area of each plateau. The first task might be performed by means of multimodal genetic optimization methods [5] or by using simple Clustered Genetic Search CGS [6,7]. There are not, however, any well established methodologies constructing a reasonable (i.e., time and memory efficient) plateau approximation. Some attempts in this direction are the methods of approximating central parts of misfit minimizer attraction basins (see [6,7]).

This paper puts forward a new method of recognizing plateau as a level set of the local misfit approximation covering the narrow subdomain in which the plateau is located. Input data for this approximation are delivered by a deme distinguished from a memetic strategy solving inverse problem and specially tuned towards filling uniformly plateau regions [8,9].

The approximation of fitness function in evolutionary searches has been applied since '80s of the 20th century (see Grefenstette and Fitzpatrick 1985 [10]), whereas the general idea of the objective approximation was known much earlier in the optimization. The development of the misfit approximation methods was summarized and characterized in several survey papers (see e.g. [11–13]). Typically, the approximation is used as a *fitness surrogate* (called also *meta-model, proxy*) if the original one is costly to execute or/and contains stochastic noise component and its evaluation requires multiple executions. Another goal is to obtain a sufficiently smooth surrogate function allowing use of gradient-based methods or/and to avoid local minima and reduce the insensitivity. The most popular approximation methods applied are 2nd degree polynomials fitted by least squares, Kriging (typically with a constant trend) as well as the neural perceptrons.

However, the plateau recognition task needs a much more accurate method, which can be applied locally, in a roughly restricted region of the admissible search domain. These circumstances suggested the authors to apply two approximation methods widely accepted in the Finite Element Method of solving PDEs:

H^1-regular one utilizing the linear splines on Delaunay's simplexes and C^∞ isoparametric one, defined on cuboid subdomains.

2   Definition of the Problem and Solving Strategy

The class of parametric inverse problems will be defined as follows:

$$\arg\min_{\omega\in\mathcal{D}}\{f(u_0, u(\omega)); \ A(u(\omega)) = 0\} \tag{1}$$

where $u(\omega) \in U$ is the forward solution for ω that belongs to the admissible set of parameter representations $\mathcal{D} \subset \mathbb{R}^N$, $u_0 \in \mathcal{O}$ is the forward solution observation and $f : \mathcal{O} \times U \to \mathbb{R}_+$ is the misfit function. Moreover, $A : U \to U'$ stands for the forward problem operator, whereas U, U' are the space of forward solutions and its conjugate space, respectively. Typically, the set of observations $\mathcal{O}$ contains specific, discrete representations of the forward solutions $u \in U$.

Let us denote by $\mathcal{S} \subset \mathcal{D}$ the set of solutions to (1). We will call the set $\mathcal{P}_{\hat{\omega}} \subset \mathcal{S}$ the *plateau* associated with the minimizer $\hat{\omega} \in \mathcal{S}$ if it is the largest nonempty set such that for each $x \in \mathcal{P}_{\hat{\omega}}$ there exists an open, connected set $A \subset S$ such that $x, \hat{\omega} \in A \subset \mathcal{P}_{\hat{\omega}}$ (see [9,14]). The above definition imposes that $\hat{\omega} \in \mathcal{P}_{\hat{\omega}}$, moreover $\mathrm{meas}(\mathcal{P}_{\hat{\omega}}) > 0$.

By a *basin of attraction* of plateau $\mathcal{B}_{\mathcal{P}_{\hat{\omega}}} \subset \mathcal{D}$, we mean a single connected part of the largest level set of the objective f, such that it contains the plateau $\mathcal{P}_{\hat{\omega}} \subset \mathcal{B}_{\mathcal{P}_{\hat{\omega}}}$ and it is contained in the plateau's attractor, i.e., any strictly decreasing local optimization method starting from an arbitrary point in $\mathcal{B}_{\mathcal{P}_{\hat{\omega}}}$ converges to some point of $\mathcal{P}_{\hat{\omega}}$ (see [14] for details).

The problem of our interest is the following: given a subpopulation $P_{\hat{\omega}} \subset \mathcal{B}_{\hat{\omega}}$ covering the plateau $P_{\hat{\omega}}$ together with computed values of misfit $(f)^x$ (and possibly also values of its gradient $(Df)^x$) for $x \in P_{\hat{\omega}}$, find an approximation of $\mathcal{P}_{\hat{\omega}}$.

The strategy we propose consists of constructing an approximation of the misfit in the vicinity of $\mathcal{P}_{\hat{\omega}}$ and obtaining a representation of the plateau as its level set.

It is important to note that there is a class of inverse parametric problems of a great engineering significance, in which the misfit function is continuously differentiable in the strong (i.e., Fréchet) sense and the misfit gradient can be numerically evaluated together with the misfit value, using, e.g., the goal-oriented version of the Finite Element Method. The additional computational cost is linear with respect to the number of degrees of freedom (see, e.g., [15,16] and references therein).

3   Memetic Multi-deme Global Search

The approximation technique which is the main subject of this paper is thought to be a component of a complex hybrid inverse solver called Hierarchic Memetic

Strategy (HMS) [17]. Currently, the latter is built upon a multi-deme evolutionary global search engine. Each deme executes its own evolutionary engine: in the current implementation it is the Simple Evolutionary Algorithm, i.e., a common type of evolutionary algorithm with floating-point encoding, Gaussian mutation, arithmetic crossover and fitness-proportional selection. The demes form a parent-child tree-like hierarchy where the accuracy of performed search is determined by the tree level. The single population at the root level is the most explorative, so its search is the least accurate. The search accuracy increases while going towards the leaves, where the search is the most focused. The tree itself has a self-organization ability thanks to an operation performed by its demes, called sprouting. It works as follows: after a fixed number of evolutionary epochs a deme tries to start a child deme around the individual with the currently-best misfit value. However, the sprouting is performed only unless there is another deme at the child level exploring the area around the mentioned individual.

The HMS stopping condition consists of a local component controlling the evolution in non-root demes and a global component estimating the maturity of the global search. The local stopping condition stops demes non revealing noticeable progress. The global stopping condition stops the whole strategy if for a given number of epochs no new demes are sprouted and if all leaves have been stopped.

But HMS goes beyond the evolutionary paradigm. Namely, it contains a number of memetic extensions. One of them is the optional accuracy-boosting machinery of running local optimization methods in leaf demes (for details we refer the reader to [17]). Another utilized technique is the clustering of the population gathered from leaves. The aim of this mechanism is a preliminary identification of local minima attraction basins as well as plateaus in the misfit landscape. The clustering is supported by a post-processor which merges clusters apparently occupying the same plateaus. The populations of integrated clusters are then subject to an additional evolution phase using a multi-winner selection operator [9]. Its aim is to provide better coverage of the clusters. The final populations form then the input for the plateau recovery stage utilizing the approximation method described in the sequel.

4   Misfit Approximation Strategies

Since the purpose of the misfit approximation is the reduction of the misfit computation cost, it needs to be efficient to evaluate and, to a lesser degree, to construct. While our main intent is to utilize it to determine the plateau regions, it might also be beneficial to use the approximation as a surrogate objective for local gradient-based convex optimization methods. A desirable property of the approximation is then the global C^1 class. Moreover, a continuously differentiable approximation can better preserve the geometrical properties of the graph of an actual continuously differentiable objective [15, 16].

To satisfy all these requirements we use a tensor product B-spline approximation. It is relatively cheap to evaluate and smoothness of B-spline functions guarantees global C^1 approximation. Let us denote by $Q_{\hat{\omega}}$ the minimal hyperrectangle with edges parallel to the coordinate axes that contains $P_{\hat{\omega}}$. Furthermore, let $\{B_i^{(1)}\}_{i=1}^{K_1}, \ldots, \{B_i^{(N)}\}_{i=1}^{K_N}$ denote one-dimensional B-spline bases corresponding to each dimension of $Q_{\hat{\omega}}$, where K_i is the number of basis B-splines used for each dimension. Formally, the sought approximation is an element of the space $\mathcal{V}_{\hat{\omega}}$ spanned by basis functions of the form

$$B_I(x_1, \ldots, x_N) = B_{i_1}^{(1)}(x_1) \cdots B_{i_N}^{(N)}(x_N) \tag{2}$$

where $I = (i_1, \ldots, i_N)$ are multi-indices ranging over the one-dimensional bases.

We propose and compare two variants of the method – one using only values of misfit function and the other utilizing the gradient. In both cases the process of constructing the approximation consists of two stages – first we construct a non-smooth auxiliary approximation and then approximate it with B-spline basis.

4.1 Approximation Using Misfit Values

The simpler approach using only misfit values at the population points is to create a continuous misfit approximation $\tilde{f}_{\hat{\omega}} \in C^0(V_{\hat{\omega}})$, which can be regularly extended to $C^0(Q_{\hat{\omega}})$, and project it onto B-spline space $\mathcal{V}_{\hat{\omega}} \subset C^1(Q_{\hat{\omega}})$ using scalar product inherited from $L^2(Q_{\hat{\omega}})$, which results in the local, smooth misfit approximation $\overline{f}_{\hat{\omega}} \in C^1(Q_{\hat{\omega}})$.

To create non-smooth approximation $\tilde{f}_{\hat{\omega}}$, Delaunay triangulation of the point set $P_{\hat{\omega}}$ is computed and piecewise linear Lagrange interpolation is used on each of thus obtained simplices. The resulting approximation is C^∞ inside each simplex and C^0 globally (see e.g. [18]).

Computing L^2-projection requires numerical integration of expressions involving projected function, which renders projecting misfit directly infeasible due to prohibitive evaluation cost and thus necessitates using the auxiliary Lagrange interpolation.

In the context of general Hilbert spaces the projection of element $x \in H$ onto a subspace $V \subset H$, i.e. $x_0 \in V$ with minimal distance to x is well known to be the unique x_0 such that $x - x_0$ is orthogonal to V [19, Theorem 5.24]. For a finite dimensional V finding such x_0 requires solving a system of linear equations with Gram matrix of the basis of V. Projecting $\tilde{f}_{\hat{\omega}}$ onto $\mathcal{V}_{\hat{\omega}}$ thus involves solving system of linear equations with Gram matrix of the basis of $\mathcal{V}_{\hat{\omega}}$, which can be done efficiently using ADS algorithm thanks to the tensor product structure of the chosen basis [20].

This work uses a sequential version of ADS solver. There are currently parallel versions of alternating direction solver under development, targeting the shared-memory Linux cluster nodes in GALOIS environment [21], distributed memory Linux clusters [22]. The alternating direct solver has been also applied for solution of a sequence of isogeometric L^2-projections resulting from explicit dynamics simulations [23,24].

4.2   Approximation Using Misfit Values and Gradients

The second strategy is similar to the first, but it does not discard information about gradient values. In addition to $\tilde{f}_{\hat{\omega}}$, we construct piecewise linear approximations of components of the gradient $\widetilde{Df}_{\hat{\omega}} \in (C^0(V_{\hat{\omega}}))^N$ in the same manner. These approximations are not necessarily coherent in the sense that the distributional derivative $D\tilde{f}_{\hat{\omega}}$ coincides $\widetilde{Df}_{\hat{\omega}}$ almost everywhere in $V_{\hat{\omega}}$, but we can nevertheless use $\tilde{f}_{\hat{\omega}}$ and $\widetilde{Df}_{\hat{\omega}}$ as approximations of misfit and its gradient to compute its H^1-projection onto $V_{\hat{\omega}}$.

Coefficients $u = (u_I)$ of the H^1-projection of misfit f would ideally be computed by solving system of equations of the form

$$Mu = F \tag{3}$$

where M is the Gram matrix of the basis, i.e. $M_{IJ} = (B_I, B_J)_{H^1}$ and F is the vector containing H^1-products of f and basis functions – $F_I = (B_I, f)_{H^1}$. Expanding the definition of H^1 product,

$$F_I = \int_{Q_{\hat{\omega}}} B_I f \, dx + \int_{Q_{\hat{\omega}}} \nabla B_I \cdot \nabla f \, dx \tag{4}$$

Since we cannot afford to evaluate the misfit function enough times to compute the integrals, we replace f with $\tilde{f}_{\hat{\omega}}$ and ∇f with $\widetilde{Df}_{\hat{\omega}}$ and solve the system $Mu = \tilde{F}$, where

$$\tilde{F}_I = \int_{Q_{\hat{\omega}}} B_I \tilde{f}_{\hat{\omega}} \, dx + \int_{Q_{\hat{\omega}}} \nabla B_I \cdot \widetilde{Df}_{\hat{\omega}} \, dx \tag{5}$$

The resulting local smooth misfit approximation satisfies again $\overline{\overline{f}}_{\hat{\omega}} \in C^1(Q_{\hat{\omega}})$, but can be much more accurate than $\overline{f}_{\hat{\omega}}$ because of the additional, independent information about the misfit behavior utilized.

5   Numerical Results

We have applied both aforementioned misfit approximation strategies to two benchmark problems – one relatively simple with a convex plateau, and one with non-convex, U-shaped plateau. In both cases the approximations were built using the populations generated by HMS. We studied the quality of obtained approximations with particular attention to plateau regions they yield. Both benchmark functions assume values between 0 and 1. Approximations of the plateau region are constructed as level sets of the misfit approximations – points with misfit below 0.1 are considered to be elements of the plateau. As a quality metric when comparing plateau approximations we used its Hausdorff distance to the level-set based plateau constructed using the exact misfit.

5.1   Convex Plateau

In the first test the function that mimics misfit is given by

$$f(\mathbf{x}) = \phi(\tilde{r}(\mathbf{x})) \tag{6}$$

where

$$\phi(a) = \exp\left(1 - \frac{1}{1 - a^2}\right)$$

$$\tilde{r}(\mathbf{x}) = \begin{cases} \|\mathbf{x}\| - 0.3 & \text{if } \|\mathbf{x}\| > 0.3 \\ 0 & \text{otherwise} \end{cases} \tag{7}$$

It is a C^∞ function with values between 0 and 1 and has value 0 in the disk with radius 0.3 centered at $(0,0)$. Plot of the function is presented in Fig. 1a.

The Lagrange interpolation of misfit value used to construct L^2 and H^1 projections is presented in Fig. 1b. The shape of the plateau and its borders is visibly distorted and sharp edges can be noticed. L^2 projection (Fig. 1c) is built purely using this value interpolation and as such shares its flaws – while the sharp edges are absent due to B-splines being C^1, the same distortions can be observed. Figure 1d presents H^1 projection built using both value and gradient interpolations. No sharp edges can be observed and the approximations seems "smoother" than L^2-projection. This can be easily seen on the error plots (Fig. 1e and f) – error of H^1-projection is significantly more evenly distributed, while error of L^2-projection exhibits large variation and spikes.

Furthermore, L^2-projection error depends heavily on the distribution of evaluation points – it is nearly zero at evaluation points (since it is purely a projection of interpolation of values) and grows significantly in regions between these points. Error of H^1-projection on the other hand does not seem to display such clear dependence on evaluation points.

Overall, H^1 projection is slightly more accurate considering mean L^2 error (Table 1). The difference is more significant when we measure error using H^1 norm – error of L^2-projection is about 50% higher than for H^1-projection.

Plateau region approximations produced by both methods are displayed and compared to the one obtained using exact misfit in Fig. 2. L^2-projection produces superior plateau border approximation in certain regions, but in others it is heavily distorted. Plateau approximation obtained using H^1-projection has the correct shape (no distortions), but does not cover the whole exact plateau region. Comparison of Hausdorff distances of both approximations to the exact plateau slightly favors H^1-projection (Table 1).

Table 1. Errors for convex plateau.

Method	L^2 error	H^1 error	Plateau error
L^2-projection	0.0512	0.3943	0.1723
H^1-projection	0.0491	0.2884	0.1501

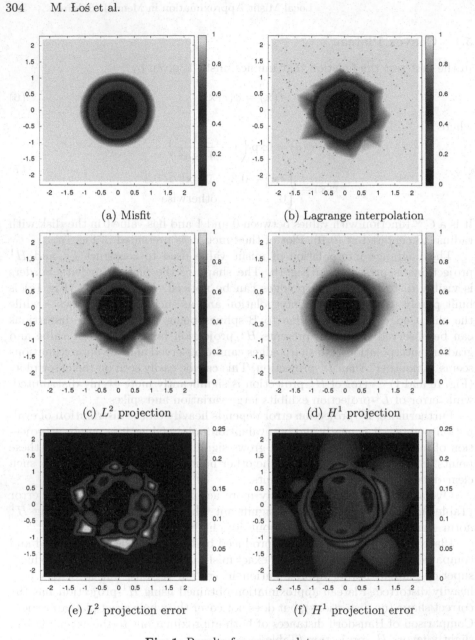

(a) Misfit

(b) Lagrange interpolation

(c) L^2 projection

(d) H^1 projection

(e) L^2 projection error

(f) H^1 projection error

Fig. 1. Results for convex plateau

The approximations were constructed using 300 evaluations (first three epochs of HMS evolution). Points of evaluation are displayed in the plots in Fig. 1.

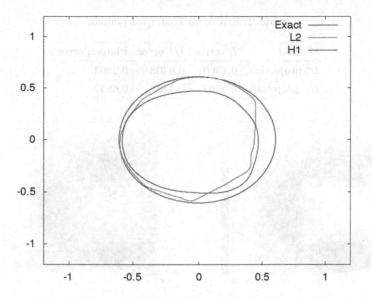

Fig. 2. Convex plateau approximation comparison

5.2   U-Shaped Plateau

In the second test the function that mimics misfit is given by

$$f(\mathbf{x}) = \begin{cases} 2s(\mathbf{x}) - 1 & \text{if } s(\mathbf{x}) < \frac{1}{2} \\ 0 & \text{otherwise} \end{cases} \tag{8}$$

where

$$s(\mathbf{x}) = g_{(0,1.5)}^{(1,0.5)}(\mathbf{x})\, g_{(1.5,0)}^{(0.5,1)}(\mathbf{x})\, g_{(0,-1.5)}^{(1,0.5)}(\mathbf{x})$$

$$g_{(x_1^0,x_2^0)}^{(r_1,r_2)}(x_1,x_2) = 2^{-\left(\frac{x_1-x_1^0}{r_1}\right)^2 - \left(\frac{x_2-x_2^0}{r_2}\right)^2} \tag{9}$$

Plot of this function is presented in Fig. 3a.

The Lagrange interpolation of misfit value used to construct L^2 and H^1 projections is presented in Fig. 3b. As in the previous example, L^2-projection (Fig. 3c) retains much of the irregularities exhibited by the Lagrange interpolation (Fig. 3b), while H^1-projection (Fig. 3d) matches the smoothness of exact misfit significantly better. L^2-projection error has large variation and depends heavily on the distribution of evaluation points, unlike for the H^1-projection.

Once again, H^1 projection is more accurate considering mean L^2 and H^1 errors (Table 2), but this time the difference is more significant – the errors of H^1 projection are roughly twice smaller.

Plateau region approximations produced by both methods are displayed and compared to the one obtained using exact misfit in Fig. 2. Both L^2 and H^1-projections produce plateau that closely matches the exact plateau except for the lower left part. In this example L^2-projection gives better overall plateau

Table 2. Errors for U-shaped plateau.

Method	L^2 error	H^1 error	Plateau error
L^2-projection	0.1360	0.9408	0.2803
H^1-projection	0.0692	0.4408	0.6892

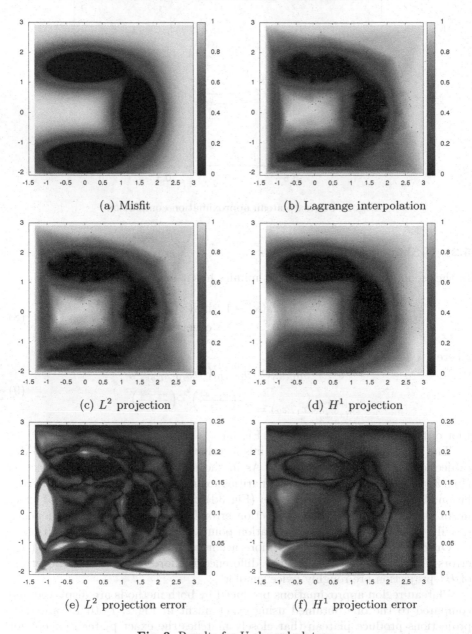

(a) Misfit (b) Lagrange interpolation

(c) L^2 projection (d) H^1 projection

(e) L^2 projection error (f) H^1 projection error

Fig. 3. Results for U-shaped plateau

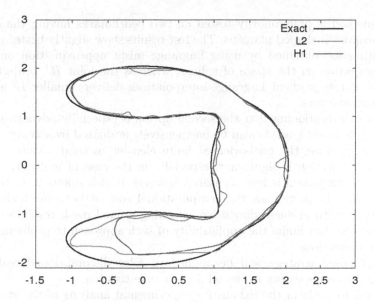

Fig. 4. U-shaped plateau approximation comparison

approximation (Table 2) although its border exhibits more irregularities than the one obtained from H^1-projection.

As in the first example, the approximations were constructed using 300 evaluations at points produced by HMS algorithm. Points of evaluation are displayed in the plots in Fig. 3.

6   Conclusions

There are typically two ways of managing the multimodality and insensitivity in solving parametric inverse problems: the first one related to the misfit regularization which reduces the number of solutions using an appropriate misfit supplement and the second, more general, in which we find all solutions, letting the domain experts select reasonable ones and reject artifacts. The proposed method follows the second approach, by using an accurate smooth approximation of the misfit function in the regions of potential solutions, which are plateaus in the misfit landscape. It consist of two steps: independent C^0 Lagrange approximation of the misfit and its gradient, based on the nodes obtained during the dedicated memetic process, and the projection of single or both components on the space of B-splines. The resulting approximation is globally C^1, which allows us to use fast gradient methods of local optimization. Another goal attained in this way is the estimation of the shape of plateau by an appropriate level set of the final approximation.

We currently work on releasing the source code of the algorithm and the benchmarks. If interested, please contact any of the authors, so you will be informed once the code is released.

The method is preliminarily tested on two benchmarks having the convex and non-convex U-shaped plateaus. The test results show slightly better plateau shape estimation obtained by using Lagrange misfit approximation only and the L^2 projection on the space of splines, whereas the joint H^1 projection of the misfit and its gradient Lagrange interpolations delivers smaller L^2 and H^1 approximation errors.

It is worth mentioning that the second option is especially advantageous in case when the misfit gradient can be inexpensively evaluated by solving forward problem (e.g., using the goal-oriented finite element method). Moreover, the cost of H^1 projection is significant, especially in the case of multidimensional problems. L^2 projection is less expensive, however, it also suffers from the high dimensionality. In particular, the computational cost of both methods grows exponentially with problem dimension assuming a fixed mesh resolution in all directions. This fact limits the applicability of such approach to problems up to about ten dimensions.

The proposed strategy will be applied to solve ill-conditioned real-world inverse problems appearing in the oil deposit investigation.

We plan to perform the exhaustive experimental analysis of the strategy's scalability (misfit approximation error, plateau approximation accuracy, computational cost) with respect to the dimension of the admissible set of parameters. As far as the applied evolutionary sampling method HMS works well, we will check the performance of the proposed local misfit approximation method coupled with other, state-of-the-art stochastic population based optimizers.

In the authors' opinion, it is difficult to compare the proposed strategy with other objective approximation methods, because of radically different goals which they intend to achieve. To the best of the authors' knowledge, the problems of the misfit approximation in the plateau area and the estimation of plateau shape have not been considered before.

References

1. Tarantola, A.: Inverse Problem Theory. Mathematics and Its Applications. Society for Industrial and Applied Mathematics, Philadelphia (2005)
2. Gajda-Zagórska, E., Schaefer, R., Smołka, M., Paszyński, M., Pardo, D.: A hybrid method for inversion of 3D DC logging measurements. Nat. Comput. **3**, 355–374 (2014)
3. Smołka, M., Gajda-Zagórska, E., Schaefer, R., Paszyński, M., Pardo, D.: A hybrid method for inversion of 3D AC logging measurements. Appl. Soft Comput. **36**, 422–456 (2015)
4. Tikhonov, A., Goncharsky, A., Stepanov, V., Yagola, A.: Numerical Methods for the Solution of Ill-Posed Problems. Kluwer, Dordrecht (1995)
5. Preuss, M.: Multimodal Optimization by Means of Evolutionary Algorithms. Natural Computing. Springer, Heidelberg (2015)
6. Schaefer, R., Adamska, K., Telega, H.: Genetic clustering in continuous landscape exploration. Eng. Appl. Artif. Intell. (EAAI) **17**, 407–416 (2004)
7. Wolny, A., Schaefer, R.: Improving population-based algorithms with fitness deterioration. J. Telecommun. Inf. Technol. 4, 31–44 (2011)

8. Faliszewski, P., Sawicki, J., Schaefer, R., Smołka, M.: Multiwinner voting in genetic algorithms for solving Ill-posed global optimization problems. In: Squillero, G., Burelli, P. (eds.) EvoApplications 2016. LNCS, vol. 9597, pp. 409–424. Springer, Heidelberg (2016). doi:10.1007/978-3-319-31204-0_27

9. Faliszewski, P., Sawicki, J., Schaefer, R., Smołka, M.: Multiwinner voting in genetic algorithms. IEEE Intell. Syst. (2016, accepted)

10. Grefenstette, J., Fitzpatrick, J.: Genetic search with approximate fitness evaluations. In: Proceedings of the International Conference on Genetic Algorithms and Their Applications, pp. 112–120 (1985)

11. Jin, Y.: A comprehensive survey of fitness approximation in evolutionary computation. Soft. Comput. **9**(1), 53–59 (2005)

12. Bhattachaya, M.: Evolutionary approaches to expensive optimization. Int. J. Adv. Res. Artif. Intell. **2**(3), 3–12 (2013)

13. Brownlee, A., Woodward, J., Swan, J.: Metaheuristic design pattern: surrogate fitness functions. In: GECCO 2015 Proceedings, pp. 1261–1264. ACM Press, July 2015

14. Sawicki, J.: Identification of low sensitivity regions for inverse problems solutions. Master's thesis, AGH University of Science and Technology, Faculty of Informatics, Electronics and Telecommunication, Kraków, Poland (2016)

15. Dierkes, T., Dorn, O., Natterer, F., Palamodov, V., Sielschott, H.: Fréchet derivatives for some bilinear inverse problems. SIAM J. Appl. Math. **62**(6), 2092–2113 (2002)

16. Smołka, M.: Differentiability of the objective in a class of coefficient inverse problems. Comput. Math. Appl. (submitted)

17. Smołka, M., Schaefer, R., Paszyński, M., Pardo, D., Álvarez-Aramberri, J.: An agent-oriented hierarchic strategy for solving inverse problems. Int. J. Appl. Math. Comput. Sci. **25**(3), 483–498 (2015)

18. Ciarlet, P.G.: The Finite Element Method for Elliptic Problems. North-Holland, New York (1978)

19. Folland, G.B.: Real Analysis. Pure and Applied Mathematics, 2nd edn. Wiley, New York (1999). Modern Techniques and Their Applications, A Wiley-Interscience Publication

20. Gao, L., Calo, V.M.: Fast isogeometric solvers for explicit dynamics. Comput. Methods Appl. Mech. Eng. **274**, 19–41 (2014)

21. Łoś, M., Woźniak, M., Paszyński, M., Hassaan, M.A., Lenharth, A., Pingali, K.: IGA-ADS: parallel explicit dynamics GALOIS solver using isogeometric L^2 projections. Comput. Phys. Commun. (submitted)

22. Woźniak, M., Łoś, M., Paszyński, M., Dalcin, L., Calo, V.M.: Parallel three dimensional isogeometric l^2-projection solver. Comput. Inform. (accepted)

23. Łoś, M., Woźniak, M., Paszyński, M., Dalcin, L., Calo, V.M.: Dynamics with matrices possesing Kronecker product structure. Procedia Comput. Sci. **51**, 286–295 (2015)

24. Łoś, M., Paszyński, M., Kłusek, A., Dzwinel, W.: Application of fast isogeometric L^2 projection solver for tumor growth simulations. Comput. Methods Appl. Mech. Eng. (submitted)

The Two Regimes of Neutral Evolution: Localization on Hubs and Delocalized Diffusion

David Shorten[1,2]([✉]) and Geoff Nitschke[1,2]

[1] CAIR, CSIR Meraka, Building 43a, CSIR,
Meiring Naude Road, Brummeria, Pretoria, South Africa
[2] Department of Computer Science,
University of Cape Town, Rondebosch 7700, South Africa
{dshorten,gnitschke}@cs.uct.ac.za

Abstract. It has been argued that much of evolution takes place in the absence of fitness gradients. Such periods of evolution can be analysed by examining the mutational network formed by sequences of equal fitness, that is the neutral network. It has been demonstrated that, in large populations under a high mutation rate, the population distribution over the neutral network and average mutational robustness are given by the principle eigenvector and eigenvalue, respectively, of the network's adjacency matrix. However, little progress has been made towards understanding the manner in which the topology of the neutral network influences the resulting population distribution and robustness. In this work, we build on recent results from spectral graph theory and utilize numerical methods to demonstrate that there exist two regimes of behaviour: convergence on hubs and diffusion over the network. We also derive approximations for the population's behaviour under these regimes. This challenges the widespread assumption that neutral evolution always leads to exploration of the neutral network and elucidates the conditions which result in the evolution of robust organisms.

1 Introduction

When evolution reaches fitness plateaus, the evolutionary dynamics are governed by the topology of the neutral network [37]. In monomorphic populations, where the population size and mutation rate are low, the population performs a random walk on this network [39]. Conversely, in polymorphic populations, at equilibrium, the distribution of the population on the neutral network is given by the principle eigenvector of the network's adjacency matrix [37]. However, there is very little work examining the manner in which the topology of the neutral network influences this population distribution. This paper investigates polymorphic evolution on neutral networks by analyzing the influence of network topology on the principle eigenvector of the neutral network.

When organisms undergo natural evolution, mutation does not act directly on their form, but rather on the genetic code. Similarly, in *Evolutionary Computing* (EC), a *representation* of the problem, upon which mutation can occur, must

© Springer International Publishing AG 2017
G. Squillero and K. Sim (Eds.): EvoApplications 2017, Part I, LNCS 10199, pp. 310–325, 2017.
DOI: 10.1007/978-3-319-55849-3_21

be identified. The problem of choosing such a representation, the *representation problem*, has been identified as a critical issue within EC [11], as well as artificial intelligence in general [25].

This necessitates a mapping between the genetic code or representation (genotype) and the organism or resulting problem solution (pheontype): the $G \rightarrow P$ map. The developmental process which translates genetic information into various biological organisms is not well understood [30]. Yet, it has become clear that this mapping is neither one-to-one nor linear [14]. In many organisms and *Ribonucleic Acid* (RNA) folding [10], it has been found that genetic change resulting from mutation is not proportional to phenotypic change [28,30,38]. Moreover, the $G \rightarrow P$ map is highly degenerate, that is many genotypes might encode for an identical phenotype [30].

There exists great variation in the mappings between representations and candidate solutions used in EC. On the one hand, in genetic algorithms, the relationship between representation and solution is often somewhat straightforward [11]. However, within the field of *generative and developmental systems* [8], many highly complicated mappings between representations and evolved forms have been proposed. Such mappings have been applied to a variety of tasks, including robot morphologies and organisms in artificial life studies [34]. Although the properties of individual mappings depend on their definition, some have been shown to be highly degenerate.

Degeneracy introduces the possibility that, when mutated, a genotype will still map to the same phenotype. This implies that the mutation has no effect on fitness and so can be labeled as *neutral*. Kimura [18], along with King and Jukes [19], brought the importance of neutral mutations to the attention of the scientific community through what has come to be known as the *neutral theory of molecular evolution*. This posits that the majority of evolutionary change is the result of the fixation of neutral mutations, as opposed to mutations which confer a selective advantage. Although the level of importance that such genetic drift has on evolution has been controversial [23], it is beyond doubt that certain mutations of certain organisms and structures are selectively neutral [4,27,40].

If the genetic code is a string of characters, as opposed to, say, a vector of real numbers, then one can construct networks out of genotypes coding for a given phenotype [37]. Here the vertices represent genotypes, and an edge connects two vertices if there exists a point mutation between their associated genotypes, that is their genetic codes are a hamming distance of one apart. Such *neutral networks* have been studied extensively [1,4,27,37] and it has been shown that, under certain assumptions, these networks permeate sequence space and that any common phenotype can be reached by traveling along them [32].

An important associated concept is that of *mutational robustness* [35]. This refers to the proportion of mutations which leave the phenotype unchanged. The greater the mutational robustness of the genotypes, the larger their neutral networks will be [39]. This has an impact on the *evolvability* of these genotypes, as they can access a greater variety of phenotypes through neutral drift. Moreover, populations can evolve so as to occupy the most connected parts of the network [37], thus increasing their average robustness.

If one assumes that evolution has reached a fitness plateau, that is that the fitness of all genotypes off the network is lower than that of those on it, then two behavioural regimes emerge. Given a population size M and a mutation rate μ, then if $M\mu \ll 1$ the population is *monomorphic* [3]. Mutations either fix or disappear, that is they either become present in the entire population or none of it. Thus, the entire population is concentrated on a single node of the neutral network. Throughout the neutral epoch the population performs a random walk over the network. On the other hand, if $M\mu \gg 1$, the population is polymorphic and spreads out over the neutral network [39]. Populations of self-replicating RNA, viruses and bacteria are polymorphic, whereas larger organisms are monomorphic [39]. Given the simple dynamics of the monomorphic case, this work focuses exclusively on polymorphic populations.

In their seminal work, van Nimwegen et al. [37] showed that the equilibrium distribution of a polymorphic population is given by the principle eigenvector of the adjacency matrix of the neutral network and that the average robustness of the population is given by the principle eigenvalue. Despite the insight of this result, little work has been conducted towards determining the manner in which the topology of the neutral network influences the resulting population distribution over the network.

Reeves et al. [31] were able to derive an upper limit to the principle eigenvalue in terms of the size of the network, by utilising the fact that neutral networks are subgraphs of a hypercube graph. This work, however, said nothing about the effect of other topological features and, moreover, has no implications for the principle eigenvector. Noirel and Simonson [27] were able to show, in simulation, that degree assortativity and the existence of hubs increased the average robustness of populations.

The principle eigenvectors and eigenvalues of graphs are of great importance to a variety of problems [33], principally synchronization phenomena and the spread of epidemics. Since the publication of van Nimwegen et al.'s seminal paper, there has been significant progress towards describing the behaviour of these two quantities in terms of network topology [6,15,20,29]. To the best of the authors' knowledge, there has been no work published which examines the implications of these results on the neutral evolution of polymorphic populations.

In this paper, we build on the above-mentioned results, both analytically and numerically, in order to elucidate the effect of neutral network topology on the equilibrium distribution and average robustness of polymorphic populations evolving on neutral networks. The principle finding is that there are two distinct behavioural regimes. If the network contains a hub of sufficiently high degree, then the population localizes on this hub. That is the vast majority of the population is found on the hub node and its neighbours. The neutral networks of proteins have been found to have high degree hubs and simulations of neutral evolution have shown that populations converge on these hubs [4,27,40]. However, these models also incorporated the stability of the proteins, which acts as a type of fitness. In most instances, the stability of the sequences correlates with their neutral degree in what is known as a *superfunnel*. Here we show, generally, that this behaviour occurs in the absence of a fitness advantage conferred by hubs so long as the hubs' degree is sufficiently large. Moreover, we demonstrate that, in large networks, the extent of the localization can be much greater than in the smaller networks analyzed in these studies.

This mode of behaviour casts the discussion on the relationship between robustness and evolvability in a new light. Many arguments are based on the assumption that populations spread out over the neutral network. While this is true for monomorphic populations and polymorphic populations evolving on networks that lack high degree hubs, we demonstrate that polymorphic populations evolving on networks with hubs cluster within a very small region of the network. Specifically, there have been two main arguments for how robustness facilitates evolvability. In the first, it is proposed that, when polymporphic populations spread out over the network, the population gains cryptic variation [21]. This variation allows the population to better adapt to changes in the environment. In the second, it is argued that robust genotypes create larger neutral networks. This creates more "stepping off points", and so the population can access more phenotypic variation [38]. Neither of these arguments hold if the population is tightly clustered around a hub. Furthermore, as demonstrated below, when the population clusters around a hub, its average robustness can be substantially higher than the average degree of the network. Thus, this is a case in which robustness and evolvability have a firmly antagonistic relationship.

The second behavioural regime encountered by polymorphic populations is diffusion over the network. We show that such populations are distributed roughly evenly over the network and we derive an expression for the average mutational robustness of the population. This expression shows that the population's robustness is largely determined by two biases: the edge sampling bias caused by mutations and the degree assortativity of the network. Although robustness itself represents a type of mutational bias, one can question the existence and role of higher order mutational biases, that is biases towards biases. Indeed, mutations on the neutral network, that is mutations that lead to viable genotypes, are biased towards higher degree nodes due to the friendship paradox [13]. This effect is named after the phenomenon where, in social networks, the average number of friends of friends is higher than the average number of friends. Moreover, this effect is present in all networks, where the average number of neighbors of neighbors is higher than the average number of neighbors of nodes in the network. The cause of this paradox is that sampling the degrees of neighbors is equivalent to sampling the degrees of nodes at the end of edges, which is biased towards higher degree nodes. The relationship between these two averages can be expressed as [13]:

$$\hat{\lambda} = \langle k \rangle + \frac{\sigma_n^2}{\langle k \rangle} = \frac{\langle k^2 \rangle}{\langle k \rangle} \tag{1}$$

where $\langle k \rangle$ is the average degree (robustness) of genotypes on the neutral network, σ_n^2 is the variance of these degrees and $\hat{\lambda}$ is the average degree of single mutation neighbors. An implication of this result, as demonstrated by van Nimwegen et al. [37], is that random walks on neutral networks result in an average neutrality equal to $\hat{\lambda}$.

Intuitively, we would not expect populations to converge on an average level of robustness substantially lower than what a random walk provides. Although robust genotypes have a selective advantage in that they produce more viable offspring, if these offspring themselves are not robust it is difficult to see how the population could converge on this lineage. Therefore, the selection of robustness is facilitated by the existence of highly robust nodes whose offspring are also highly robust. This sort of higher order mutational bias is provided by network assortativity, that is, correlation in the degrees of the nodes at the end of edges [24]. By deriving an expression for the average population robustness, we show that it is equal to the mutational sampling bias and rises above or below this figure depending on whether the network has positive or negative degree assortativity.

2   Localization on Hubs

In the context of graph spectra, localization refers to the phenomenon whereby the normalisation weight of an eigenvector ($\sum f_i^2(\lambda)$, where λ is the eigenvalue and $\boldsymbol{f}(\lambda)$ is the eigenvector) is concentrated on a small number of nodes that does not scale with the size of the network [29]. Some authors have suggested using the inverse participation ratio $Y(\lambda)$.

$$Y(\lambda) = \sum_{i=1}^{N} f_i^4(\lambda) \tag{2}$$

as a quantitative measure of localization where, in this case, $\boldsymbol{f}(\lambda)$ is the normalised eigenvector. If, in the limit $N \to \infty$, $Y(\lambda) \sim 1$ then the state is localized. On the other hand, if $Y(\lambda) \to 0$ then the state is delocalized. There are a number of results relating aspects of network topology to localization. Chung et al. [6] showed that the principle eigenvalue, for a random graph model characterised by a given degree distribution, is given by.

$$\lambda_1 = \begin{cases} \hat{\lambda}, & \hat{\lambda} > \sqrt{k_{max}} \log N \\ \sqrt{k_{max}}, & \sqrt{k_{max}} > \hat{\lambda} \log^2 N \end{cases} \tag{3}$$

where $\hat{\lambda} = \langle k^2 \rangle / \langle k \rangle$ ($\langle k \rangle$ being the average degree and $\langle k^2 \rangle$ being the mean of the squares of the degrees). $\lambda_1 = \hat{\lambda}$ corresponds to the delocalized state and $\lambda_1 = \sqrt{k_{max}}$ corresponds to the localized state.

Goltsev et al. [15] showed that, for unassortative scale-free networks with degree distribution $P(k) \sim k^{-\gamma}$, the principle eigenstate is localized for $\gamma > \frac{5}{2}$ and delocalized otherwise. The principle eigenvalue is given by $\sqrt{k_{max}}$ and $\hat{\lambda}$ for the localized and delocalized states, respectively.

Martin et al. [20] demonstrated that for a hub connected to an Erdős-Renyi network, localization occurs when $\sqrt{k_{max}} > \langle q \rangle$ where $\langle q \rangle$ is the average degree of the original Erdős-Renyi network, without the hub. Furthermore, they showed that the eigenvector component on the hub, f_h is given by

$$f_h = \sqrt{\frac{k_{max} - 2\langle q \rangle}{2k_{max} - 2\langle q \rangle}} \tag{4}$$

Where the average of the components neighbouring the hub, $\langle f_n \rangle$ is given by

$$\langle f_o \rangle = \frac{f_h}{\sqrt{k_{max} - \langle q \rangle}} \tag{5}$$

and the average of all non-hub components $\langle f_j \rangle$ is

$$\langle f_j \rangle = \frac{1}{N-1} \frac{f_h}{\sqrt{k_{max} - \langle q \rangle}} \tag{6}$$

Finally, Pastor-Satorras and Castellano [29] have shown that a form of less severe localization can occur on scale-free networks where $\gamma < \frac{5}{2}$.

This then begs the question of whether the neutral networks encountered in natural and artificial evolution meet the topological criteria for localization. Given the wide variety of possible fitness landscapes, it is fair to assume that at least some of them will contain neutral networks with localized principle eigenvectors. However, there is a dearth of mapped-out neutral networks. The authors know of none within EC. Fortunately, some neutral networks of protein [4,27,40] and RNA folding [2] have been mapped. RNA neutral networks would seem to be fairly homogeneous, with narrow degree distributions. However, the neutral networks induced by protein folding contain high-degree hubs. This makes them candidates for localization behaviour.

Moreover, it was reported that localization-like behaviour was observed when evolution was simulated on these neutral networks. However, those simulations incorporated the stability of the proteins, which acts as a type of fitness. The stability of the proteins was strongly correlated with the robustness, that is the highest degree node also had the greatest stability. This has been labeled as the *superfunnel* paradigm [27] and it contains the further assumption that robustness and, by implication, the stability of the sequences decreases with increasing distance from the hub, or 'prototype' sequence. This can be visualized as a funnel, with the bottom placed over the prototype sequence.

The above results concerning the localization of eigenvectors demonstrate that the localization of populations can occur in the absence of the fitness advantage conferred by stability and the anticorrelation of robustness and distance from the prototype sequence. The crucial feature is high degree hubs. Although none of the networks reported on in these studies satisfy the stringent conditions of Chung et al. [6], some of those analyzed by Bornberg-Bauer [4] easily satisfy the criteria of Martin et al. [20] that $\sqrt{k_{max}} > \langle q \rangle$. However, it is unclear how close the topology of the observed networks is to the model of Martin et al. [20]. Although we do not have access to the full topology of all of the networks studied by these authors, inspection of those for which they presented diagrams leads us to believe that they do conform to this model. Moreover, it is worth bearing in mind that the model of Martin et al. [20] is considering hubs connected to a *maximally random* network.

2.1 Connected Hubs

The topology of the neutral network of the haemagglutinin protein of the influenza A virus (H3N2) as explored by Wagner [40] appears to conform to a somewhat different topology. Although it easily satisfies the criteria that $\sqrt{k_{max}} > \langle q \rangle$, it would seem to be composed of hubs attached to one another.

In order to shed light on this type of topology, we studied the localization behaviour of a model of random networks, whereby hubs (star networks) were connected by non-preferential attachment. Specifically, a high degree hub of degree m was instantiated by connecting m nodes to a hub node. Further to this, 30 lower degree hubs, of degree $n = 5$ were created. All the hubs were then connected through non-preferential attachment, beginning with the maximum degree hub. Specifically, one low degree hub was connected to the high degree hub and then each subsequent low degree hub was connected to a randomly chosen hub in this connected graph. Figure 1 shows that the localization transition occurs at around $m = 35$.

3 Delocalized Regime

In the delocalized regime, progress on approximating the population's distribution and robustness can be made by assuming that, at equilibrium, for every node in the network, the average population concentration on nodes at a given distance l is equal. That is we utilise a mean-field approximation at a given distance l. This average concentration is the uniform concentration, that is the population size divided by the number of nodes. This is equivalent to assuming that the correlation length for the degrees is low. It has been found that, for most real-world networks, the correlation length is low [22]. Using this assumption we can approximate the proportion of the population which mutates onto a given node, and hence the population distribution and average robustness.

For the cases $l = 2$ and $l = 3$ we make use of the *annealed network approximation* [9], whereby all nodes with a given degree k are approximated as having the same nearest neighbour degree distribution, which is the aggregate distribution over the neighbours of all nodes with degree k. This has the implication that all nodes of degree k have the same average nearest neighbours degree, that is $\bar{k}_{nn}(i) = \bar{k}_{nn}(k_i)$, where i is a node's index and k_i the associated degree. We also use the approximation:

$$\bar{k}_{nn}(k) \approx \hat{\lambda} + \left(k - \hat{\lambda} \right) r \tag{7}$$

Where $\bar{k}_{nn}(k)$ is the average nearest-neighbour degree of nodes of degree k, $\hat{\lambda} = \langle k^2 \rangle / \langle k \rangle$ ($\langle k \rangle$ being the average degree $\langle k^2 \rangle$ being the average of the squares of the degrees) and r is the assortativity coefficient (the Pearson correlation between the degrees at either end of an edge) [24]. This approximation is derived by considering that r is the root of the coefficient of determination of the linear regression between the degrees of the nodes at either end of an edge.

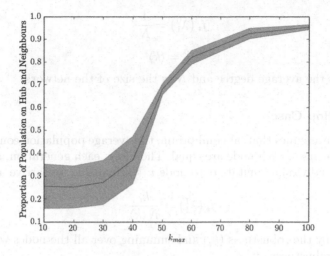

Fig. 1. The proportion of the population found on the largest hub node and its neighbours for our model of connected-hub networks. 30 star networks of degree 5 and a larger star whose degree is plotted on the x axis were connected via non-preferential attachment. The shaded region shows the standard deviation.

We introduce the notation λ_1^l to denote the approximation of the principle eigenvalue (population average robustness) based on the assumption of equal average distribution at distance l. Similarly, we use $f_i\left(\lambda_1^l\right)$ to denote the ith component of the principle eigenvector (the proportion of the population having the genotype represented by the ith node), based on the assumption of equal average distribution at distance l.

Some of the below reasoning is based on the particulars of the model of van Nimwegen et al. [37]. In this model, the population of constant size M resides on a neutral network of size N. The total number of neighbours, neutral and non-neutral, that a given genotype can have is given by U, this limit is determined by the length of the genetic code and the size of the alphabet. Each generation, M genotypes are selected with replacement from the population. These individuals then undergo mutation. With probability k_i/U the individual remains on the network, where k_i is the degree of the node representing the individual's genotype. If the individual stays on the network, it moves to one of its neighbouring nodes, chosen at random. If it mutates off the network then it is ineligible for selection in the subsequent generation.

3.1 Zero-Hop Case

The simplest case is that we assume that the average population concentration at a distance zero from each node is equal, that is we assume that the population is uniformly distributed. The average robustness of the population is therefore, trivially, the average degree. Thus, we have:

$$f_i\left(\lambda_1^0\right) = \frac{1}{N} \tag{8}$$

$$\lambda_1^0 = \langle k \rangle \tag{9}$$

Where $\langle k \rangle$ is the average degree and N is the size of the network.

3.2 One-Hop Case

The next case assumes that, at equilibrium, the average population concentration of the neighbours of each node are equal. Therefore, each generation, an average of $k_i M/NU$ individuals mutate onto node i. Normalizing, we arrive at

$$f_i\left(\lambda_1^1\right) = \frac{k_i}{N\langle k \rangle} \tag{10}$$

Multiplying by the robustness (k_i) and summing over all the nodes we arrive at the average robustness of:

$$\lambda_1^1 = \frac{\langle k^2 \rangle}{\langle k \rangle} = \hat{\lambda} \tag{11}$$

3.3 Two-Hop Case

If we assume an average uniform population concentration two hops from each node, then, each generation, by the annealed network approximation, the nodes neighbouring node i will receive, on average, $\bar{k}_{nn}\left(k_i\right) M/NU$ mutants. This implies that node i will receive $k_i \bar{k}_{nn}\left(k_i\right) M/NU^2$ individuals. Substituting in Eq. (7) and normalizing we arrive at

$$f_i\left(\lambda_1^2\right) = \frac{1}{N\langle k^2 \rangle}\left(k_i\hat{\lambda} + k_i\left(k_i - \hat{\lambda}\right)r\right) \tag{12}$$

Multiplying through by the node's robustness (k_i) and summing over the nodes, we arrive at

$$\lambda_1^2 = \hat{\lambda} + \frac{r\sigma_e^2}{\hat{\lambda}} \tag{13}$$

Where $\sigma_e^2 = \langle k^3 \rangle/\langle k \rangle - \langle k^2 \rangle^2/\langle k \rangle^2$ is the variance of the node's degrees when sampled by following edges. (13) is equivalent to the approximation derived by Goltsev et al. [15] through the use of a power iteration.

3.4 Three-Hop Case

Our final approximation is based on the assumption that, from any given node, the average population density at nodes three hops away is equal. We consider the node i', a neighbour of i. Each generation, this node will receive an average of $k_{i'}\bar{k}_{nn}\left(k_{i'}\right) M/NU^2$ mutants from its neighbours. We then average this over all neighbours i' of node i, that is we want to find

$$I = \frac{M}{NU^2}\left\langle k_{i'}\hat{\lambda} + k_{i'}^2 r - k_{i'}\hat{\lambda}r \right\rangle_{i'} \tag{14}$$

Using the fact that $\langle k_{i'}^2 \rangle_{i'} \approx \sigma_e^2 + \langle k_{i'} \rangle_{i'}^2$, where the equality is approximate as σ_e^2 is the global variance and not specific to the neighbours of nodes of degree $k_{i'}$, we can arrive at

$$I \approx \frac{M}{NU^2} \left(\hat{\lambda}^2 + \hat{\lambda} \left(k_i - \hat{\lambda} \right) r + \hat{\lambda} \left(k_i - \hat{\lambda} \right) r^2 + \left(k_i - \hat{\lambda} \right)^2 r^3 + \sigma_e^2 r \right) \qquad (15)$$

The number of mutants that a node i receives is $k_i I / U$. When we come to normalise this, we find that the total population is

$$P \approx \frac{M}{U^3} \left(\langle k \rangle \hat{\lambda}^2 + \left\langle k \left(k - \hat{\lambda} \right)^2 \right\rangle r^3 + \langle k \rangle \hat{\sigma}_e^2 r \right) \qquad (16)$$

The second two terms in the parentheses are much smaller than the first and so, for mathematical expediency, we ignore them. This results in

$$f_i \left(\lambda_1^3 \right) \approx \frac{1}{N \langle k^2 \rangle} \left(k_i \hat{\lambda} + k_i \left(k_i - \hat{\lambda} \right) r + k_i \left(k_i - \hat{\lambda} \right) r^2 + \frac{k_i \left(k_i - \hat{\lambda} \right)^2 r^3}{\hat{\lambda}} + \frac{k_i \sigma_e^2 r}{\hat{\lambda}} \right) \qquad (17)$$

As previously, we multiply by each node's robustness (k_i) and sum over all nodes to arrive at the approximation for the eigenvalue (population average robustness).

$$\lambda_1^3 \approx \hat{\lambda} + \frac{2r\sigma_e^2}{\hat{\lambda}} + \frac{r^2 \sigma_e^2}{\hat{\lambda}} + \frac{r^3 \left(\langle k^4 \rangle - 2\hat{\lambda} \langle k^3 \rangle + \hat{\lambda}^2 \langle k^2 \rangle \right)}{\langle k^2 \rangle \hat{\lambda}} \qquad (18)$$

3.5   Numerical Verification

Random networks conforming to the Erdős-Renyi model [12] were created in order to measure the accuracy of the approximations. We needed to test these approximations for various values of the assortativity coefficient (r), however, the expected value of r for Erdős-Renyi networks is 0 [24]. In order to both increase and decrease the assortativity, the rewiring algorithm of van Miegham et al. [36], was used. This algorithm operates by iteratively picking two edges at random and observing the degrees of the four nodes at their endpoints. If the goal is to increase assortativity, the two nodes with the highest degrees are connected by an edge and, likewise, the lowest degree nodes are also connected. Moreover, the original two edges are removed from the network. Similarly, if the goal is to decrease assortativity, the maximum degree node is connected to the minimum degree node and the remaining two nodes are also connected. Rewiring does not take place if the desired connectivity arrangement between the four nodes was already present. This iterative process is repeated until the desired value of r is achieved.

We chose 15 values of r on which to test: those between –0.7 and 0.7, inclusive, at intervals of 0.1. 100 networks, each with $N = 1000$ nodes and average degree of $\langle k \rangle = 10$ were instantiated for each of these values. Figure 2 shows the relative error of the derived approximations. It shows that, for positive values of r, the approximation λ_1^3 is more accurate than that of Goltsev et al. [15] (which is equivalent to λ_1^2).

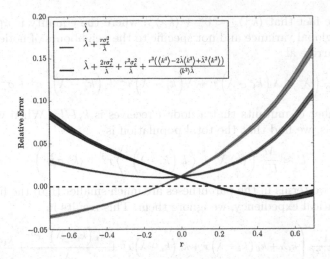

Fig. 2. The relative error of the approximations of the principle eigenvalue measured on Erdős-Renyi networks which have been subjected to a rewiring algorithm [36] in order to display various values of degree assortativity. The shaded region shows the standard deviation.

4   Discussion

In this work, we set out to incorporate and build upon recent results concerning the behaviour of the principle eigenvectors, and associated eigenvalues, of the adjacency matrices of networks in the context of the study of the dynamics of polymorphic populations evolving on neutral networks.

Much of the discussion surrounding neutral evolution has functioned on the assumption that there is only one regime of polymorphic neutral evolution. In this regime, the population explores much of the network and, in the words of van Nimwegen et al. [37] "seeks out the most connected areas of the neutral network". This intuition is echoed by many authors, for instance "the population will tend to congregate in regions of a neutral network that have more robust genotypes" [39] and the population will "evolve toward regions denser in neutral genotypes" [1]. Moreover, this is plausible, given that the principle eigenvector (which specifies the population's distribution) is used as a measure of centrality: the *eigenvector centrality* [20].

Our most salient finding is that there are actually two distinct behavioural regimes. Moreover, each of these regimes differ from the above intuition in important ways.

The first regime involves the localization of the population onto a hub and its neighbouring nodes. Here the average mutational robustness of the population is approximated by the square root of the degree of the hub and the number of nodes upon which the bulk of the population resides does not scale with the size of the network.

This has important ramifications for the understanding of neutral evolution. Firstly, under localization, the eigenvector centrality ceases to be a useful measure [20]. This can be illuminated by considering a star network connected to an Erdős-Renyi [12] network by a single edge. Following the arguments outlined in Sect. 2, so long as the degree d of the star's hub is greater than the average degree of the original network $\langle q \rangle$, the population will localize on the star. As a star network has one more edge than vertices (in this case two more, due to the connection to the Erdős-Renyi network), the average degree of this network is approximately two. Therefore, so long as the original Erdős-Renyi network has an average degree greater than two, the majority of the population will be concentrated on a region of the network with below average degree. It is thus concentrated on a region which is neither "most connected" nor "denser in neutral genotypes".

It is useful to query why our intuition failed in this case. After all, the population's average robustness ($\sqrt{k_{max}}$) can be much higher than the network's average degree, even though the population is occupying a region of below average degree. This is due to the fact that such a large proportion of the population is found on the hub itself. Referring again to Sect. 2, we see that, in the case of a star connected to an Erdős-Renyi network, in the limit of large d, around half of the entire population is found on the hub genotype. This concentration is self-reinforcing, as a substantial proportion of the hub's mutants will mutate back onto it, leading to the localization phenomenon [20].

This regime of behaviour has particular relevance to arguments concerning the relationship between robustness and evolvability. These arguments are predicated on the fact that robust genotypes form larger neutral networks [39]. This then allows for the population to accumulate more cryptic variation as it spreads over the network [21], allowing it to better adapt to changes in its environment. Moreover, it creates more "stepping off points" for the population, allowing it to access more phenotypic variation [38]. However, these arguments fail to take into account the proportion of the network occupied by the population. By definition, localization occurs when the normalization weight of the principle eigenvector is concentrated at a number of nodes that does not scale with the size of the network [29]. Therefore, the cryptic variation in the population and the amount of phenotypic variation accessible to it does not scale with the robustness of the genotypes of which the network is composed. Furthermore, as the population's average robustness is determined solely by the degree of the hub, it is entirely possible to have populations with extremely high average robustness, and very low cryptic variation and access to phenotypic variation. The access to phenotypic variation is particularly poor in this regime, given that such a large proportion of the population is concentrated on the hub and that the hub has such a high proportion of neutral neighbours. It is worth noting that these arguments relating robustness and evolvability are still valid, so long as the robustness of genotypes is homogeneously distributed, in order to avoid localization.

The delocalized case has more in common with the traditional intuition. A principle difference, however, is the level to which concentration on regions of better connected genotypes occurs. Firstly, such a region needs to exist. This requirement will be met in networks with degree assortativity, however, disassortative mixing will result in genotypes with high robustness mutating to those with low robustness, thwarting evolution's attempts at settling on robust nodes. Specifically, by examining Eqs. (10), (12) and (17) we see that, in unassortative networks, the proportion of the population on a given node scales with its degree. This implies that, on relatively homogeneous networks, there will be little difference in the population concentration on various nodes. Furthermore, as shown in (17), disassortative mixing decreases the number of individuals occupying a node in proportion to both the square and cube of its degree. Although we do expect to see a certain degree of concentration of the population in more robust regions of the neutral network in the case that the network exhibits assortative mixing, the severity of this concentration will be relatively mild. Given that, for networks of reasonably high average degree, $\hat{\lambda}$ is substantially larger than r, the latter terms in Eq. (17) will only play a significant role when k_i is much larger than $\hat{\lambda}$.

We further propose that it is fruitful to think of the delocalized regime of neutral evolution more in terms of a biased sampling process of the genotypes on the network, resulting from mutational biases, as opposed to a population moving between regions of the network. From Eqs. (11), (13) and (18) we can see that, in the absence of assortativity, the population's average robustness is approximated by $\hat{\lambda}$. This is exactly the average robustness which we would expect from performing a random sampling of all possible mutations on the network, as implied by the friendship paradox [13]. Assortative and disassorative mixing by degree will increase or decrease the population's average robustness above or below this level. Assortativity represents a further mutational bias towards higher or lower degree nodes, dependent on the degree of the node from which the mutation originates.

Given that it is suspected that much of evolution occurs on neutral networks [23] along with the importance of mutational robustness to the survival of organisms and its relationship with evolvability, understanding the impact of the topology of neutral networks on the dynamics of neutral evolution and the resulting robustness of organisms is of great importance. This work has provided insight into these issues in the case of polymorphic populations: large populations evolving at high mutation rate. The directed, neutral, evolution of bio-molecules [7,16] along with viruses overcoming immunity through neutral evolution [26] fall within this category. These results have potential applicability to these problems. For instance, the neutral evolution of large libraries of molecules [17] will be greatly aided by delocalization, whereas a virus's attempt to escape immunity might be thwarted if its population localizes on a hub.

5   Conclusion

This paper investigated the manner in which neutral network topology influences the resulting population distribution and robustness during neutral evolution at high mutation rates in large populations. In such cases, the population distribution is given by the principle eigenvector of the adjacency matrix of the neutral network and, similarly, the average mutational robustness of the individuals in the population is given by the principle eigenvalue [37]. Hence, we utilized, and built upon, recent results concerning the behaviour of these values from studies concerning the spread of epidemics on networks [15] as well as more general work [20].

It was found that, on homogeneous neutral networks, the population's behaviour could be described in terms of mutational biases. For unassortative neutral networks, it was found that the average mutational robustness was equal to the sampling bias provided by the friendship paradox [13]. Assortative and disassortative mixing by degree raised the robustness above or below this value, respectively. Furthermore, in the process of demonstrating this, we derived a new approximation for the principle eigenvalue of a network in terms of its assortativity and the moments of its degree distribution.

Conversely, for heterogeneous neutral networks with high degree hubs, it was found that the population become concentrated on the nodes around the hub and thus the number of nodes occupied does not scale with the size of the network. Furthermore, the average robustness of the population is given by the square root of the network's maximum degree. These results are particularly relevant to various arguments concerning the relationship between robustness and evolvability [21,38], which assume that the number of nodes occupied by the population scales with the size of the network.

These results are relevant to the directed evolution of bio-molecules [7,16], where they can be used to evolve more robust molecules as well as facilitate the evolution of greater variety. Moreover, they can also further our understanding of the factors that allow viruses to escape immunity along neutral networks [26].

Computations were performed using facilities provided by the University of Cape Town's ICTS High Performance Computing team: http://hpc.uct.ac.za.

References

1. Aguirre, J., Buldú, J.M., Manrubia, S.C.: Evolutionary dynamics on networks of selectively neutral genotypes: effects of topology and sequence stability. Phys. Rev. E **80**(6), 066112 (2009)
2. Aguirre, J., Buldú, J.M., Stich, M., Manrubia, S.C.: Topological structure of the space of phenotypes: the case of RNA neutral networks. PLoS One **6**(10), e26324 (2011)
3. Bloom, J.D., Lu, Z., Chen, D., Raval, A., Venturelli, O.S., Arnold, F.H.: Evolution favors protein mutational robustness in sufficiently large populations. BMC Biol. **5**(1), 1 (2007)
4. Bornberg-Bauer, E.: How are model protein structures distributed in sequence space? Biophys. J. **73**(5), 2393 (1997)
5. Bornberg-Bauer, E., Chan, H.S.: Modeling evolutionary landscapes: mutational stability, topology, and superfunnels in sequence space. Proc. Natl. Acad. Sci. **96**(19), 10689–10694 (1999)

6. Chung, F., Lu, L., Vu, V.: Spectra of random graphs with given expected degrees. Proc. Natl. Acad. Sci. **100**(11), 6313–6318 (2003)
7. Currin, A., Swainston, N., Day, P.J., Kell, D.B.: Synthetic biology for the directed evolution of protein biocatalysts: navigating sequence space intelligently. Chem. Soc. Rev. **44**(5), 1172–1239 (2015)
8. Devert, A.: When and why development is needed: generative and developmental systems. In: Proceedings of the 11th Annual Conference on Genetic and Evolutionary Computation, pp. 1843–1844. ACM (2009)
9. Dorogovtsev, S.N., Goltsev, A.V., Mendes, J.F.: Critical phenomena in complex networks. Rev. Mod. Phys. **80**(4), 1275 (2008)
10. Draper, D.: The RNA-folding problem. Acc. Chem. Res. **25**(4), 201–207 (1992)
11. Eiben, A., Smith, J.: Introduction to Evolutionary Computing. Springer, Berlin (2003)
12. Erdős, P., Renyi, A.: On random graphs i. Publ. Math. Debr. **6**, 290–297 (1959)
13. Feld, S.: Why your friends have more friends than you do. Am. J. Sociol. **96**(6), 1464–1477 (1991)
14. Gjuvsland, A., Vik, J., Beard, D., Hunter, P., Omholt, S.: Bridging the genotype-phenotype gap: what does it take? J. Physiol. **591**(8), 2055–2066 (2013)
15. Goltsev, A.V., Dorogovtsev, S.N., Oliveira, J., Mendes, J.F.: Localization and spreading of diseases in complex networks. Phys. Rev. Lett. **109**(12), 128702 (2012)
16. Jäckel, C., Hilvert, D.: Biocatalysts by evolution. Curr. Opin. Biotechnol. **21**(6), 753–759 (2010)
17. Kaltenbach, M., Tokuriki, N.: Generation of effective libraries by neutral drift. Dir. Evol. Libr. Creat.: Methods Protoc. **1179**, 69–81 (2014)
18. Kimura, M., et al.: Evolutionary rate at the molecular level. Nature **217**(5129), 624–626 (1968)
19. King, J.L., Jukes, T.H.: Non-Darwinian evolution. Science **164**(3881), 788–798 (1969)
20. Martin, T., Zhang, X., Newman, M.: Localization and centrality in networks. Phys. Rev. E **90**(5), 052808 (2014)
21. Masel, J., Trotter, M.V.: Robustness and evolvability. Trends Genet. **26**(9), 406–414 (2010)
22. Mayo, M., Abdelzaher, A., Ghosh, P.: Long-range degree correlations in complex networks. Comput. Soc. Netw. **2**(1), 1 (2015)
23. Nei, M.: Selectionism and neutralism in molecular evolution. Mol. Biol. Evol. **22**(12), 2318–2342 (2005)
24. Newman, M.: Assortative mixing in networks. Phys. Rev. Lett. **89**(20), 208701 (2002)
25. Nilsson, N.J.: The Quest for Artificial Intelligence. Cambridge University Press, Cambridge (2009)
26. van Nimwegen, E.: Influenza escapes immunity along neutral networks. Science **314**(5807), 1884–1886 (2006)
27. Noirel, J., Simonson, T.: Neutral evolution of proteins: the superfunnel in sequence space and its relation to mutational robustness. J. Chem. Phys. **129**(18), 185104 (2008)
28. Parter, M., Kashtan, N., Alon, U.: Facilitated variation: how evolution learns from past environments to generalize to new environments. PLoS Comput. Biol. **4**(11), e1000206 (2008)
29. Pastor-Satorras, R., Castellano, C.: Distinct types of eigenvector localization in networks. Sci. Rep. **6**, 18847 (2016)

30. Pigliucci, M.: Genotype-phenotype mapping and the end of the 'genes as blueprint' metaphor. Philos. Trans. R. Soc. Lond. B: Biol. Sci. **365**(1540), 557–566 (2010)
31. Reeves, T., Farr, R., Blundell, J., Gallagher, A., Fink, T.: Eigenvalues of neutral networks: interpolating between hypercubes. Discret. Math. **339**(4), 1283–1290 (2016)
32. Reidys, C., Stadler, P.F., Schuster, P.: Generic properties of combinatory maps: neutral networks of RNA secondary structures. Bull. Math. Biol. **59**(2), 339–397 (1997)
33. Restrepo, J.G., Ott, E., Hunt, B.R.: Approximating the largest eigenvalue of network adjacency matrices. Phys. Rev. E **76**(5), 056119 (2007)
34. Stanley, K.O., Miikkulainen, R.: A taxonomy for artificial embryogeny. Artif. Life **9**(2), 93–130 (2003)
35. Taverna, D.M., Goldstein, R.A.: Why are proteins so robust to site mutations? J. Mol. Biol. **315**(3), 479–484 (2002)
36. Van Mieghem, P., Wang, H., Ge, X., Tang, S., Kuipers, F.: Influence of assortativity and degree-preserving rewiring on the spectra of networks. Eur. Phys. J. B **76**(4), 643–652 (2010)
37. Van Nimwegen, E., Crutchfield, J., Huynen, M.: Neutral evolution of mutational robustness. Proc. Natl. Acad. Sci. **96**(17), 9716–9720 (1999)
38. Wagner, A.: Robustness and evolvability: a paradox resolved. Proc. R. Soc. Lond. B: Biol. Sci. **275**(1630), 91–100 (2008)
39. Wagner, A.: The Origins of Evolutionary Innovations: A Theory of Transformative Change in Living Systems. OUP, Oxford (2011)
40. Wagner, A.: A genotype network reveals homoplastic cycles of convergent evolution in influenza a (H3N2) haemagglutinin. Proc. R. Soc. Lond. B: Biol. Sci. **281**(1786), 20132763 (2014)

EvoENERGY

Adaptive Batteries Exploiting On-Line Steady-State Evolution Strategy

Edoardo Fadda[1]($\boxtimes$), Guido Perboli[1,2], and Giovanni Squillero[1]

[1] Politecnico di Torino, Corso Duca Degli Abruzzi 24, Torino, Italy
edoardo.fadd@polito.it
[2] CIRRELT, Montreal, Canada

Abstract. In energy distribution systems, uncertainty is the major single cause of power outages. In this paper, we consider the usage of electric batteries in order to mitigate it. We describe an intelligent battery able to maximize its own lifetime while guaranteeing to satisfy all the electric demand peaks. The battery exploits a customized steady-state evolution strategy to dynamically adapt its recharge strategy to changing environments. Experimental results on both synthetic and real data demonstrate the efficacy of the proposed solution.

Keywords: Evolutionary strategy · Battery · Intelligent systems · Optimisation

1 Introduction

Uncertainty is the major single cause of power outages in energy distribution systems, and, in North America alone, such power outages cause annual losses of up to \$180 billion [1]. The main causes of power outages are demand peaks that the power generation systems are unable to satisfy. Furthermore, during demand peaks the producers of energy use power generator systems able to rapidly ramped. This kind of generators use more expensive fuels, are less efficient and have higher marginal carbon emissions [2]. In order to solve this problem energy storages can be used. Energy storages are commonly used at various levels: batteries are used to integrate renewable sources for domestic use and to mitigate the variations of consumption between day and night.

The usual behaviour of an energy storage is to provide energy when needed, and to accumulate energy whenever possible. Some examples of energy storages are electric batteries and hydroelectric power plants. However, switching from discharge to charge does not come for free: the hydroelectric power plants have to use electricity to pump the water, and batteries lose a part of their lives because of electrodes degradation. As the cost of such a battery is not negligible, the market is actively seeking more clever battery management systems as well as other method to control energy demand such as demand side management.

In this paper, we focus on the case of electric batteries located in the medium- to low-voltage (MV/LV) cabin, that is, batteries connected to a small set of

G. Squillero and K. Sim (Eds.): EvoApplications 2017, Part I, LNCS 10199, pp. 329–341, 2017.
DOI: 10.1007/978-3-319-55849-3_22

buildings. We propose a battery that uses a threshold T to optimize the discharge/charge operations: when a surplus of energy is available, the battery will start charging only if its energy is below T, otherwise it simply does not discharge. The threshold T is automatically adapted using an evolution strategy (ES) to maximize battery's life, while guaranteeing that the units connected to MV/LV cabin never exceed the assigned energy budget[1]. Batteries in MV/LV cabins are connected to different agents, and no central controller can reliably share data among them. Thus, the proposed strategy is entirely local: it uses the history of the energy requested to the battery by the elements directly connected to it, and its actual internal energy.

Experimental results show the efficacy of the proposed approach both on synthetic benchmarks, and on a real data taken from the EU-founded project *FlexMeter*[2]. The rest of the paper is organized as follows: in Sect. 2 we present a small literature review about the problem, in Sect. 3 we define the problem, in Sect. 4 we present our approach, in Sect. 5 we show the experimental results and the performances of our method, in Sect. 6 we discuss the results and in Sect. 7 we conclude our work by describing future development of our work.

2   Background

Batteries are basically containers of energy, and their use to mitigate the fluctuations of energy demand has been thoroughly analysed in the literature. The capacity of a battery is defined as the quantity of charge that it can release in the network at a given voltage, and it is usually measured in *ampere hour* (Ah) or *kilocoulombs* (kC). Usually the batteries have a maximum amount of capacity that they can absorb or release in a given time. The choice of using Ah is not practical and, without loss of generality we can consider this quantity to be expressed in Wh, kWh or in Ws because the voltage of the network is fixed.

Generally speaking, the performance of a battery depends on many factors such as the technology of the battery, the environmental temperature and if it keeps for a lot of time a high level of charge. In the following, we take into account the technology of the battery for determining how a recharge cycle affects its residual life, but we suppose that all batteries work in a controlled environment with stable temperature. Different kinds of batteries can be used in an energy network, namely, batteries for domestic use, and batteries for mitigating the fluctuations for a small group of buildings. Similarly, the optimisation of their lives has been tackled in different ways. Some authors focus on the optimisation of the physical components [5,6]. Others, optimize the activity of batteries able to integrate the energy from small renewable power plant [7]. More recently, in studies of increasing relevance, electric cars are used as energy storages for small group of buildings [8].

---

[1] An area that never exceeds the part of energy assigned to it by the network is called *independent*; the more independent parts a network has, the more it is robust and do not risk a power outage see [3,4].

[2] See http://flexmeter.polito.it/.

The strategies and operations of the batteries can be optimized with regard to different factors. For example, the use of fuzzy rules has been investigated to control the battery behaviour relating to the wind condition [9]. Optimisation and prediction can be combined with the feedback control of closed-loop controllers [7]. Other works exploit approximate dynamic programming [8], or a stochastic multi-stage programming [10]. Most papers have in common that the optimisation of charge discharge operations is done every fifteen to sixty minutes, and further examples of this choice are [11,12]. In very few cases the optimisation is done every five minute [13].

3 Problem Definition

We tackle a network composed by a non renewable energy source with a constant production, a set of buildings with a noisy, almost periodic load profile, and a battery inside a MV/LV cabin connected to these buildings. We choose the MV/LV cabin because we consider as main stakeholder of the peak cutting service the distribution system operator. In the following we will call agent every part of the energy network different from the connection links.

Batteries are the only agents able to both drain and release energy, their purpose is to provide energy when the network needs it. The proposed batteries do charge only if their internal energy is below a threshold T. Other, much simpler, yet still widely used, batteries always charge whenever a surplus of energy is available (this is equal to a battery with a threshold equal to the capacity). The threshold T influences the life of the battery: the higher it is, the more times the battery will charge and the more life it will lose.

All agents that ask for energy are labelled as *buildings*. We assume that the load profile is the algebraic sum between their internal production and their consumption, in order to have a realistic load profile and inspired by the data in [14] we assume that the load profile is described by

$$l_t = \min\left[A_1(1+X_t^1)e^{-\frac{([t]_{24}-8+d_t^1)^2}{\delta_1}} + A_2(1+X_t^2)e^{-\frac{([t]_{24}-20+d_t^2)^2}{\delta_2}} + \epsilon_t, \hat{\gamma}\right] \quad (1)$$

where A_1 and A_2 are the amplitudes of the requests in the peaks near to 8 am and near to 20 pm. X_t^1, X_t^2 are independent and identically distributed random variables uniformly distributed between -0.1 and 0.1 (X_t^1, X_t^2 iid $\mathcal{U}(-0.1, 0.1)$) that modify the amplitude of the two peaks. Further, d_t^1, d_t^2 are independent random variables uniformly distributed between 1 and -1 (d_t^1, d_t^2 iid $\mathcal{U}(-1,1)$) that describe a possible delay in the peaks. Finally, ϵ_t is a random noise such that the sequence $\{\epsilon_t\}_{t=1:T}$ is composed by independent and identically distributed random variables distributed following a distribution with 0 mean and σ_l^2 variance ϵ_t iid $N(0, \sigma_l^2)$ and $\hat{\gamma}$ is the minimum request of the house.

4 Proposed Approach

In this paper, we consider the optimisation of the charge/discharge operations of a battery located in a MV/LV cabin. The battery can safely store energy in the interval $E \in [E^{\min}, E^{\max}]$, where both $E^{\min}$ and $E^{\max}$ are constants dependent on the technology of the battery; in each *time step*, it can be charged by an amount δ_C or discharged by an amount δ_D. We define as *life time* the number of charge/discharge cycles possible before the battery's cells fail to operate satisfactorily. We denote this number with L, and the loss of life time with $\mathcal{L}$.

The battery can be in different states: charging ($\mathcal{C}$), when it is draining power from the network to increase its internal energy; or discharging ($\mathcal{D}$), when it is providing energy. When the battery neither drains nor provides energy, we define an additional state: idle ($\mathcal{I}$) (discharging, paused). Every battery has an internal threshold T that is used to decide when to charge: if a surplus of energy becomes available, the battery switches from discharge to charge ($\mathcal{D} \to \mathcal{C}$) only if its internal energy is below the threshold ($E < T$), otherwise it simply stops discharging ($\mathcal{D} \to \mathcal{I}$). Further, the battery must provide energy whenever requested, regardless if currently charging ($\mathcal{C} \to \mathcal{D}$) or idle ($\mathcal{I} \to \mathcal{D}$). Hence, the threshold influences only the charge operation since the discharge operations are impose by the environment.

4.1   Basic Evolution Strategy

The adaptive battery records the past energy availability and requests, and tweaks its internal threshold T using a self-adaptive, steady-state evolution strategy $(1 + \lambda)$-ES. In every time step, it generates a set of possible thresholds $\mathbf{O} = \{T^0, \ldots, T^n\}$, it simulates the performance of each of these thresholds by using the recorded history, and it sets T equal to the threshold T_i with the best performance.

In more details, an individual encode the candidate threshold and the standard deviation used to calculate it $\mathbf{I} = (T, \sigma)$. Let T_t be the threshold used in time frame t and σ_t its associated standard deviation; after one time step, the ES first generates λ small variations $(i = 0, \ldots, \lambda - 1)$ of the standard deviation $\sigma_{t+1}^i = \sigma_t \cdot (1 + Z)$ with Z random variable uniformly distributed between -0.1 and 0.1 i.e. $Z \sim \mathcal{U}(-0.1, 0.1)$ (the values σ_{t+1}^λ is fixed in order to assure a reasonable exploration of the solution space even when the algorithm has converged). Then, it generates new thresholds $T_{t+1}^i \ i = 0, \ldots, \lambda$ from a realization of a normal distribution with mean T_t and variance $(\sigma_{t+1}^i)^2$ i.e. $T_{t+1}^i \sim \mathcal{N}(T_t, (\sigma_{t+1}^i)^2)$. The new thresholds are eventually adjusted to fit into the interval $[T^{\min}, T^{\max}]$. In the beginning, $T^{\min} = E^{\min}$ and $T^{\max} = E^{\max}$, but $T^{\min}$ is subsequently modified during the optimisation process. In particular, as soon as a threshold T_{t+1}^i causes a power outage, the lower bound of acceptable thresholds is updated: $T^{\min} = (1 + \epsilon) \cdot T_{t+1}^i$, where ϵ is a small constant like 10^{-2} or 10^{-3} (its exact value is not so relevant). As a result, the optimizer is prevented from exploring non-feasible region of the solution space. As past records older than I^{LIMIT} are discarded, the threshold's lower bound may need to be re-evaluated. Thus, every I^{LIMIT} time steps, a realization threshold $\tilde{T}$ is generated from $\mathcal{U}[0, T^{\min}]$, and if it did not cause a power outage then it is used as new lower bound: $T^{\min} = \tilde{T}$.

At the end, the optimizer checks all these new thresholds against the past observations, and determines the one that would have yield the best results.

Eventually, if the fitness of the best threshold among the newly generated (T^*_{t+1}) outperforms the current one (T_t), it updates the threshold inside the battery $(T_{t+1} = T^*_{t+1})$ and stores the deviation used to calculate it σ^*_{t+1}. This optimisation procedure is repeated for N_{gen} generations in each time step. Note that the best threshold generated in each generation T^*_{t+1} is not necessarily the threshold that the battery will eventually use during the next period T_{t+1}. In fact, the threshold that the battery will choose is the best among the current threshold T_t and the values found during all the generations. This difference is shown in Fig. 1 and in Fig. 2: on the left there is the instant best thresholds found in each generation and their associated variance, while on the right there is the real threshold/variance picked by the battery.

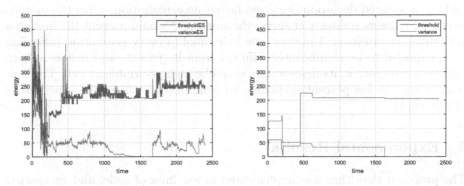

Fig. 1. On the left: best threshold and variance found in each generation. On the right: threshold and standard deviation actually used by the battery. The time is expressed in hours and the energy in kWh

The fitness function used to evaluate a threshold is based on the expected life of the battery. In more details, the fitness measures the residual life in the initial time of the simulation (i.e., the time when the battery was attached to the system), thus, the fitness of the solution found decreases as time progresses. The goal of the algorithm is to find the highest fitness, that is, reducing the loss of life. For each past time step u:

- If the battery is asked to give some energy, the fitness is decreased by one unit $\Delta F_u = 1$, modelling the usual wearing.
- If the battery starts to charge $(\mathcal{D} \to \mathcal{C})$, the fitness is decreased by the current energy of the battery $\Delta F_u = E_u$. This roughly models the *battery memory* (or *lazy battery*) effect observed in nickel-cadmium and nickel-metal hydride rechargeable batteries: units gradually lose their maximum energy capacity if they are repeatedly recharged after being only partially discharged.
- If there is a power outage, the fitness is decreased by the maximum capacity of the battery multiplied by a given constant $\Delta F_u = K_{out} \cdot (E^{\min} + C)$. The exact value of the constant K_{out} is not relevant, as its only purpose is to mark the event as highly undesirable. In the experiments we used $K_{out} = 100$.

To handle both the inherent variability of the demand, and the existence of short patterns, like a particularly hot week or a long holiday, the battery weights recent records more than old ones. Furthermore, all time steps prior to $t^* = \max(0, t - I^{\mathrm{LIMIT}})$ are completely ignored, while the fitness losses are discounted relatively to the time instant i_u in which they occur by an exponential factor: $\Delta F_t^{TOT} = \sum_{u=t^*}^{t-1} \Delta F_u \cdot e^{\beta(t-i_u)}$. The constant β weights the past results. We analyse the behaviour of the algorithm with respect to different value of β in the Sect. 6.

Moreover, differently from standard $(1 + \lambda)$-ES, in every generation one individual among the offspring is generated with a high, fixed deviation $\sigma_t^\lambda = \gamma \cdot T^{\max}$. This tweak allows adapting to abrupt changes in the pattern of energy requests. In a stable situation, the ES is quickly able to find the optimal threshold T^{opt}, and the associated deviation decreases favouring exploitation; when the pattern of energy requests suddenly changes, the small σ^{opt} would prevent the finding a very different threshold. However, one individual in every generation (offspring λ) is expected to be significantly different from its parent, and if it is able to outperform its parent, its descendants would be highly-variable as well. The constant γ is set to few percentage points, for example $\gamma = 0.05$ in the experiments of this paper.

5   Experimental Results

The proposed algorithm was implemented in few lines of code, and we created a simulator to test experimentally the approach. It was implemented in C++, and consists of about 7,000 lines of code for 17 classes. The source code is freely available under the *GNU Public License*[3].

Agents are all active elements that can be connected with the battery (e.g. houses, factories, renewable energy plants, batteries, shops, ...). The simulator represents the situation as a playground where different agents strive, hence the name of the project "Electric Games". In each turn, the simulation manager asks all the agents the amount of energy that they need to absorb, it computes the global energy request, and the energy that agents will produce to compute the global energy offer.

If the total amount of energy offered is more than the total amount of energy requested, the manager first satisfies all requests from buildings. Then, the remaining energy is offered to batteries, and eventually equally divided between the players that accepted the offer. Conversely, if the total amount of energy offered is less than the amount of energy requested, the manager takes the missing energy forcing all batteries to discharge. If batteries are unable to provide the necessary amount of energy, a power outage is recorded. In the tests that we performed, we consider a network composed by three elements:

---

[3] https://bitbucket.org/EdoFadda/electricgame/.

- A non-renewable power plant generator, able to generate 100 kW each time instant.
- A battery with a life L of 500 change discharge operations, a capacity of 1,000 kWh, $E^{\min} = 0$ kWh and $E^{\max}$ equals to the capacity of the battery. In our experiments we consider batteries with fixed threshold and batteries that update this value by using the approach presented in Sect. 4.
- A single building with a load profile changing from simulation to simulation.

For the battery implementing the evolution strategy we set $\lambda = 10$, $N_{\text{gen}} = 60$, $\beta = 0.01$ and $I^{\text{LIMIT}} = 48$. Further, we set δ_D equal to the capacity of the battery while δ_C changes in the various experiments. In the following we present the results of three experiments. The first one generates synthetic (even unrealistic) scenarios in order to test the capacity of our strategy to adapt to different conditions. The second experiment asses the influence of the variance σ_l^2 on the threshold that the battery adopts. The final experiment tests our approach on real data. In each of them we interpret the single time step as an hour of real time.

5.1 Synthetic Scenarios

To assess the characteristic of the proposed approach, we consider five different synthetic scenarios. In every scenario we assume that δ_C is set to the 10% of the capacity.

- **Scenario 1** is deterministic: the battery has an initial energy of 0.5% of the capacity (it is almost empty), and the non-renewable energy production satisfies the building request. The optimal strategy in such a situation is never to recharge. The time horizon is 30 days.
- **Scenario 2** is deterministic: the battery starts with zero initial energy. During the 13th hour, the building requests abruptly 900 kW, and during the 17th hour, it request 450 kW, in the other hours there is no request of energy. The optimal strategy for the battery is to have threshold above the 200 kWh. The time horizon is 30 days.
- **Scenario 3** is deterministic: the battery starts with zero initial energy. During the 13th hour, the building requests abruptly 200 kW and during the 17th hour it requests 1050 kW. The optimal strategy for the battery is to have threshold of 900 kWh. The time horizon is 30 days.
- **Scenario 4** models the request of the building, as in formula (1) with $A_1 = \frac{2}{3}A_2$ and $A_2 = 150$ kW, $\sigma_l = 50$ kW, $\delta_1 = 2$, $\delta_2 = 3$ and, X_1, X_2 iid $\mathcal{U}(-0.1, 0.1)$. In this setting there is no a best fixed threshold strategy. The time horizon is 100 days.
- **Scenario 5** models a situation where the load profile formula (1) is time dependent. In particular, we consider that the coefficients A_1 and A_2 change during the simulation. In the first quarter, $A_1 = \frac{2}{3}A_2$ and $A_2 = 120$ kW, $\sigma_l = 20$ kW, X_1, X_2 iid $\mathcal{U}(-0.1, 0.1)$, while in the second half $A_1 = \frac{2}{3}A_2$ and $A_2 = 150$ kW $\sigma_l = 50$ kW while X_1, X_2. The change occurs during the 1800th hour. The time horizon is 100 days.

In each scenario, we compared the adaptive battery against batteries with fixed threshold set to 0%, 25%, 50%, 75% and 100% of the capacity. Note that the battery with $T = 0\%$ never asks for energy. We included this case because in the first experiment this limit case is the best strategy. In the real setting, this is the best strategy during periods when people are not at home for a long period (e.g. during summer holidays in a north Italy city). On the opposite, the battery with $T = 100\%$ threshold always charges, a quite common behaviour. Table 1 summarizes the results.

Table 1. Table shows the average loss of battery life ($\mathcal{L}_{avg}$) and the corresponding standard deviation ($\mathcal{L}_\sigma$) for each kind of battery in the various scenarios, the $n.a.$ (not applicable) value is set when, during the simulation, a power outage occurs. Experiments have been repeated 100 times.

	Scenario 1		Scenario 2		Scenario 3		Scenario 4		Scenario 5	
	$\mathcal{L}_{avg}$	$\mathcal{L}_\sigma$	$\mathcal{L}_{avg}$	$\mathcal{L}_\sigma$	$\mathcal{L}_{avg}$	$\mathcal{L}_\sigma$	$\mathcal{L}_{avg}$	$\mathcal{L}_\sigma$	$\mathcal{L}_{avg}$	$\mathcal{L}_\sigma$
Adaptive	0.000	0.000	0.300	0.000	0.300	0.000	0.068	0.004	0.035	0.004
Fixed $T = 0\%$	0.000	0.000	$n.a.$		$n.a.$		$n.a.$		$n.a.$	
Fixed $T = 25\%$	0.010	0.000	0.300	0.000	$n.a.$		$n.a.$		$n.a.$	
Fixed $T = 50\%$	0.010	0.000	0.300	0.000	$n.a.$		0.073	0.002	0.0414	0.0028
Fixed $T = 75\%$	0.010	0.000	0.300	0.000	$n.a.$		0.121	0.006	0.0754	0.0054
Fixed $T = 100\%$	0.010	0.000	0.300	0.000	0.300	0.000	0.489	0.001	0.3694	0.0011

In Scenario 1, the best thresholds are all the values below the 0.5% of the capacity, i.e., the strategy that does nothing. As we can see from the results in Table 1, the best devices are the adaptive battery and the battery with $T = 0\%$. This result is true for an initial threshold of the adaptive battery below the initial energy because if the initial threshold is above, the battery starts to charge and it loses life. Nevertheless, in less than one day it is able to find the optimal threshold. Due to this dependency on the initial condition, in the results, we do not consider the first day of simulation. In Scenario 2, as expected, all the batteries with a threshold greater than 200 kWh work perfectly. As in Scenario 3, batteries with a threshold greater than 900 kWh. The same discussion about the initial condition of the scenario 1 must be done in this case. In this scenario we decide to have different thresholds and then to discard the first 10% of observations in order to delete the effect of the initial conditions. In Scenario 4 the adaptive battery has the best performance and it is able to adapt to the different request conditions in the different parts of the day. As in Scenario 2 and Scenario 3 we discard the first 10% of observations in order to delete the effect of the initial conditions. Scenario 5 confirms that the adaptive battery is able to change its internal threshold. The evolution is shown in Fig. 2. This experiment was failed by the adaptive battery before the insertion of the fixed value of the variance. The reason of this change is described in Sect. 4.

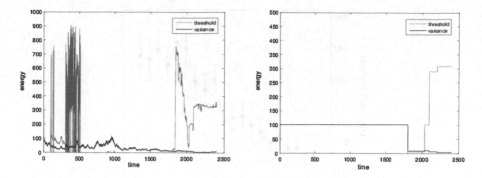

Fig. 2. On the left: best threshold and variance generated in each generation in scenario 5, on the right: evolution of the threshold and standard deviation that the battery uses in each time in scenario 5. On the x-axis there is the time, expressed in hours. On the y-axis there is the energy, expressed in kWh

Table 1 shows batteries' residual life (mean and standard deviations) in the different scenarios. If a power outage occurs then we set in the cell the value *n.a.* (not applicable).

5.2   Variance Analysis

In order to study the behaviour of the threshold that the battery choose with respect to the variance of the load profile of the building we ran 100 simulations for each value of $\sigma_l^2 \in [0, 5, 10, 15,\dots, 100]$ kW (the variance of the noise related to the ask for the building in Eq. (1)). As in Sect. 5.1, we consider that each time step is one hour. Further, we assume that δ_C is set equal to the 10% of the capacity. Figure 3 shows the results of these simulations. It is reasonable that optimal threshold increases as the value of σ_l^2 increases: as the more unstable the environment conditions are, the more energy is wise to store to cope with unexpected request.

5.3   Real Data

In this section we compare the batteries with a fixed threshold with the one implementing our customize evolution strategy on realistic data (the daily load profile is shown in Fig. 4), gather from the FlexMeter project.

In this experiment we do not consider any bound in the charge-discharge quantities that the battery can exchange in one hour i.e. $\delta_D = \delta_C$ and they both are equal to the capacity of the battery. The reasons of this choice is that modern batteries such that the one with the lithium iron phosphate ($LiFePO_4$) technology can be fully discharged and charged in less than one minute [15]. Further, we consider that the network provides the 60th percentile amount of energy request by the building. The time horizon of this experiment is 30 days. The battery implementing the evolutionary strategy updates the threshold every

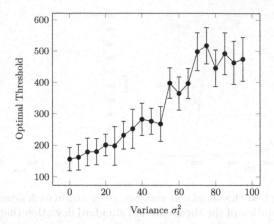

Fig. 3. Value of convergence of the adaptive battery's threshold for different value of building variance. The variance is expressed in kW, while the optimal threshold is expressed in kWh

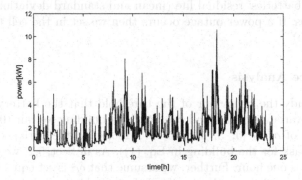

Fig. 4. Daily load profile

hour and it creates a generation every minute. Table 2 shows the results obtained by running fifty times the experiments with different monthly load profiles. The first column reports the life lost by the battery in its activity. The second column reports the standard deviations of the values in the first column and the third column reports the probability of power outage calculated as number of time that we register a power outage over the number of simulations (50).

Form Table 2 emerges that the adaptive battery does not produce any power outage during the 50 runs and all the deterministic batteries performances are worse. In particular, the deterministic battery with more similar performance is the one with threshold at the 50% of the capacity. Nevertheless, it losses the 11.2% of life in 30 days while the adaptive battery loses 8.6%.

Table 2. The table shows the average loss of battery life ($\mathcal{L}_{\text{avg}}$), the corresponding standard deviation ($\mathcal{L}_{\sigma}$), and the frequency of power outages (f_{PO}) for each kind of battery in a real scenario for 30 days. Experiments have been repeated 100 times.

	$\mathcal{L}_{\text{avg}}$	$\mathcal{L}_{\sigma}$	f_{PO}
Adaptive	0.086	0.006	0.00
Fixed $T = 0\%$	0.000	0.000	1.00
Fixed $T = 25\%$	0.099	0.002	0.30
Fixed $T = 50\%$	0.112	0.000	0.05
Fixed $T = 75\%$	0.140	0.000	0.00
Fixed $T = 100\%$	0.200	0.000	0.00

6   Discussion

In this section we provide some qualitative analysis of the behaviour of our approach with respect to the values of different parameters. In particular, the evolution strategy proposed needs the parameter β and the initial conditions to be set (initial threshold, initial energy and the initial standard deviations). As previously said, β rules how fast the battery forgets the previous history. A high value of β produces convergence problems because the battery over fits the present consumption values and forgets its history. A low value can be too preventive and can lead the battery to consider only the major energy requests. For this reason, we suggest to choose the coefficient β lower than 0.01. As an example of the effect of this parameter, in Fig. 5, we show the best threshold and variance found in each generation for a simulation with $\beta = 0.05$ and for a simulation with $\beta = 0.1$. In the plot obtained with $\beta = 0.05$ the convergence is faster than with $\beta = 0.1$. Nevertheless, in both cases there are more oscillations and the variance converges slowly than in Fig. 2 (where we have used $\beta = 0.01$).

We do not suggest any lower bound on β because it depends by two factors: the frequency of extreme values and how much the user wants to prevent power outages. For examples, if there are a lot of extreme values and power outages must be avoid we suggest to use $\beta = 0$. In this way, the battery sets the threshold in order to deal with these spikes. If some power outages is reasonable (even with really low probability), then we can use positive values of β. In this way the battery is more likely to decrease its internal threshold in calm conditions. In order to avoid power outages and to produce the best performances the initial energy, the initial threshold and the initial standard deviation are really important. Good initial values for these parameters enable the battery to converge to the optimal value in a fast way. While, bad initial conditions can produce failure of the convergence. Concerning the initial energy, we suggest to choose this value as big as possible (the best situation is when the initial energy is equal to the capacity of the battery). The reason of this choice is that during the first time steps the battery has no information regarding the network energy requests and, for this reason, it has not yet a reasonable threshold. Then, it is possible that the

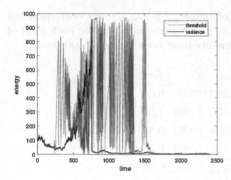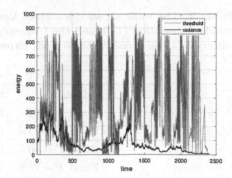

Fig. 5. On the left: value of the best threshold and standard in each generation for $\beta = 0.05$, on the right: value of the best threshold and standard in each generation for $\beta = 0.1$. On the x-axis there is the time, expressed in hours. On the y-axis there is the energy, expressed in kWh

battery faces unexpected energy requests that can be fulfilled only if the battery has a sufficient quantity of energy. Concerning the initial threshold, with the same arguments as above, we suggest to use a high value for this parameter. The best is to set it to be equal to the capacity of the battery.

Finally, we analyse the choice of the initial standard deviation. This value influences the exploration of the solution space. Hence, it is the most important parameter to be set. A low value of the standard deviation deprives the battery of the opportunity to change the threshold in a significant way. Therefore, the simulation is likely to end with a threshold almost equal to the initial one. A value of the standard deviation higher than half of the capacity of the battery is useless because the convergence to a small value could take a lot of iterations. Then, we suggest to use initial standard deviation around the 20% of the capacity.

7 Conclusions and Future Works

In this paper, we present a customized steady-state evolution strategy in order to optimize the life of the battery while maintaining an acceptable level of performance. In particular, we found that our approach loses less life than the batteries with fixed threshold in all the generated synthetic scenarios and in the real scenarios. Further, even if the battery implementing our strategy is not deterministic we have not registered any power outages. Due to this result we can claim that all the buildings connected to the battery do not need more energy from the network when they generate demand peaks. Hence, the batteries implementing our strategy increase the robustness to power outages of the network.

From the methodological point of view, we have found very effective to create, in every generation, one individual among the offspring from a high, fixed deviation $\sigma_t^\lambda = \gamma \cdot T^{\max}$. This change allows the battery to be more reactive with respect to the change in energy demand. Further, this strategy combined with the right choice of the parameter β provides a very effective strategy.

Future studies will be to consider batteries trying to cut peaks in energy offer, to consider a real multi-agent system approach, as defined in [16] and to study the behaviour of more batteries in the same network with and without the possibility to communicate. Further, an interesting characteristic that we have not considered in this paper is that batteries lose a part of their charge during time.

References

1. Matthewman, S., Byrd, H.: Blackouts: a sociology of electrical power failure. Soc. Space Sci. J. **1** (2014)
2. Alt, L.: Energy Utility Rate Setting. Lulu.com, Raleigh (2006)
3. Pasqualetti, F., Bicchi, A., Bullo, F.: A graph-theoretical characterization of power network vulnerabilities. In: American Control Conference (ACC), pp. 3918–3923 (2011)
4. Abad Torres, J., Sandip, R.: Stabilization and destabilization of network processes by sparse remote feedback: graph-theoretic approach. In: American Control Conference (ACC), pp. 3984–3989 (2014)
5. Ahmadi, P., Rosen, M.A., Dincer, I.: Multi-objective exergy-based optimization of a polygeneration energy system using an evolutionary algorithm. Energy **46**(1), 21–31 (2012)
6. Kavvadias, K., Maroulis, Z.: Multi-objective optimization of a trigeneration plant. Energy Policy **38**(2), 945–954 (2010)
7. Müller, J., März, M., Mauser, I., Schmeck, H.: Optimization of operation and control strategies for battery energy storage systems by evolutionary algorithms. In: Applications of Evolutionary Computation (2016)
8. Branimir, K., Joko, D.: Dynamic programming-based optimisation of charging an electric vehicle fleet system represented by an aggregate battery model. Energy **92**(Part 3), 456–465 (2015). (Sustainable Development of Energy, Water and Environment Systems)
9. Cheol-Hee, Y., Il-Yop, C., Hak-Ju, L., Sung-Soo, H.: Intelligent control of battery energy storage for multi-agent based microgrid energy management. Energies **6**, 4956–4979 (2013)
10. Li, H., Fu, B., Yang, C., Zhao, B., Tang, X.: Power optimization distribution and control strategies of multistage vanadium redox flow battery energy storage systems. Proc. Chin. Soc. Electr. Eng. **33**(16), 70–77 (2013)
11. Toersche, H., Hurink, J., Konsman, M.: Energy management with TRIANA on FPAI. In: IEEE Eindhoven PowerTech, pp. 1–6 (2015)
12. Ha, D.L., Joumaa, H., Ploix, S., Jacomino, M.: An optimal approach for electrical management problem in dwellings. Energy Build. **45**(1), 1–14 (2012)
13. Chen, Z., Wu, L., Fu, Y.: Real-time price-based demand response management for residential appliances via stochastic optimization and robust optimization. IEEE Trans. Smart Grid **3**(4), 1822–1831 (2012)
14. Arif, M.T., Amanullah, M.T.O.: Estimation of energy storage and its feasibility analysis. In: Zobaa, A., Shawkat Ali, A.B.M. (eds.) Energy Storage - Technologies and Applications. InTech, Rijeka (2013)
15. Kang, B., Ceder, G.: Battery materials for ultrafast charging and discharging. Nature **458**(7235), 190–193 (2009)
16. Lagorse, J., Simoes, M., Miraoui, A.: A multiagent fuzzy-logic-based energy management of hybrid systems. IEEE Trans. Ind. Appl. **45**, 2123–2129 (2009)

Hybrid Multi-ensemble Scheduling

Jörg Bremer$^{(\boxtimes)}$ and Sebastian Lehnhoff

University of Oldenburg, 26129 Oldenburg, Germany
{joerg.bremer,sebastian.lehnhoff}@uni-oldenburg.de

Abstract. A steadily increasing pervasion of the electrical distribution grid with rather small renewable energy resources imposes fluctuating and hardly predictable feed-in, a partly reverse load flow and demands new predictive load planning strategies. For predictive scheduling with high penetration of renewable energy resources, agent-based approaches using classifier-based decoders for modeling individual flexibilities have shown good performance. On the other hand, such decoder-based methods are currently designed for single entities and not able to cope with ensembles of energy resources. Combining training sets sampled from individually modeled energy units, results in folded distributions with unfavorable properties for training a decoder. Nevertheless, this happens to be a quite frequent use case, e. g. when a hotel, a small business, a school or similar with an ensemble of co-generation, heat pump, solar power, and controllable consumers wants to take part in decentralized predictive scheduling. In this paper, we propose an extension to an established agent approach for scheduling individual single energy units by extending the agents' decision routine with a covariance matrix adaption evolution strategy that is hybridized with decoders. In this way, locally managed ensembles of energy units can be included. We show the applicability of our approach by conducting several simulation studies.

Keywords: Predictive scheduling · CMA-ES · Multi-agent system · Smart grid

1 Introduction

In European countries, especially in Germany where currently a financial security of guaranteed feed-in prices is granted, the share of distributed energy resources (DER) is rapidly rising. Following the goal defined by the European Commission [1], concepts for integration into electricity markets will quickly become indispensable for both: active power provision as well as ancillary services to reduce subsidy dependence [2,3]. Consequently, combining smart measurement technologies for decentralized information gathering on current operational grid state, new telecontrol techniques, communication standards and decentralized self-organized control schemes will lead to a so called smart grid with decentralized power conditioning and control of the production and distribution of electricity managed without central control; as in the vision of [4] or similar for Europe [5].

© Springer International Publishing AG 2017
G. Squillero and K. Sim (Eds.): EvoApplications 2017, Part I, LNCS 10199, pp. 342–358, 2017.
DOI: 10.1007/978-3-319-55849-3_23

As the smart grid will have to delegate many control tasks to small and distributed energy units, new control algorithms are required that are able to cope with large problem sizes and distributed and only locally available information. Virtual power plants (VPP) are a well-known instrument for aggregating and controlling DER [6]. Concepts for several purposes (commercial as well as technical) have been developed. A usual use case commonly emerging within VPP control is the need for scheduling the operation of participating DER. Predictive scheduling [7] describes the optimization problem for day-ahead planning of energy generation in VPPs, where the goal is to select a schedule for each energy unit – from an individual search space of feasible schedules with respect to a future planning horizon – such that a global objective function (e. g. resembling a target power profile for the VPP) is optimized.

Recently, distributed approaches gained more and more importance for VPP control. Different works proposed hierarchical and decentralized architectures based on multi-agent systems and market-based computing [8,9]. Newer approaches try to establish self-organization between actors within the grid [10–12]. In contrast, today's commercial VPP are often operated by a single authority that at the same time is the owner of (and responsible for) all distributed energy resources in this rather static unit ensemble. Independently from a concrete implementation for predictive scheduling, the dispatch algorithm has to choose a schedule for each DER in the VPP such that all objectives are met.

In order to choose an appropriate schedule for each participating DER, the algorithm must know from each DER, which schedules are actually operable and which are not. Depending on the type of DER, different constraints restrict possible operations. The information about individual local feasibility of schedules has to be modeled appropriately in (distributed) optimization scenarios, in order to allow unit independent algorithm development. For this purpose, meta-models of constrained spaces of operable schedules have been shown indispensable as a means for independently modeling constraints and feasible regions of flexibility. Each energy unit has its own individual flexibility – i. e. the set of schedules that might be operated without violating any technical operational constraint – based on the capabilities of the unit, operation conditions (weather, etc.), cost restrictions and so forth. Integrating these constraints to possible operations of an arbitrary energy unit demands a means for meta-modeling that allows model independent access to feasibility information. [13] introduced a support vector based model that captures individual feasible regions from training sets of operable example schedules. Figures 1 and 2 show example training sets for a co-generation plant and a heat pump respectively. An extending use case for these models has been introduced in [14]. Agent-based approaches can derive a so called support vector decoder automatically from the surrogate model and use them as a means for generating feasible solutions without domain knowledge on the (possible, situational) operations of the controlled energy resource.

Examples for using decoders in optimization within the smart grid can be found in [15–18]. In general, the idea works in two successive stages – a decoder training phase and the actual planning phase – as follows [7]: During the training phase a decoder is calculated for each unit. These calculations can be done fully parallel. During the succeeding load planning phase, these decoders may be used by an optimization algorithm that determines the optimal partition of a given active power target schedule into schedules for each single unit. The decoder automatically generates feasible solutions and thus the solver does not need any domain knowledge about the energy units, their individual constraints, or possible operation.

An example for a recently developed agent approach for fully decentralized predictive scheduling is given by the combinatorial heuristics for distributed agents (COHDA). In COHDA [19] each agent is responsible for exactly one energy unit and uses a decoder to locally decide on feasible schedules for the represented unit. The algorithm has shown excellent performance [16,19,20]. But, as soon as an agent has to represent a local ensemble of energy units instead of a single device, a problem arises because usually only flexibility models of single units are available. Generating a single decoder for handling all constraints and feasible operations of the whole ensemble is hardly possible due to statistical problems when combining training sets from individually sampled flexibility models. Due to the folded densities only a very small portion from the interior of the feasible region (the dense region) is captured by the machine learning process. But, a combined training set is needed if one wants to train a single decoder for each agent.

For this reason, we propose to exchange the single decoder part that generates suitable and feasible schedules for the negotiating agent by an evolution strategy that does this job by solving the problem using individual decoders (one for each unit in the ensemble). In this way, an optimization problem has to be solved instead of a single mapping with a decoder for each agent decision during the negotiation, but with harnessing the full flexibility of the ensemble. Hence, we contribute a new decision method to the agent approach based on a covariance matrix adaption evolution strategy that widens the applicability to including multiple local ensembles of DER into the VPP without changing the underlying negotiation between the agents.

The rest of the paper is organized as follows. We start with an outline on predictive scheduling and related work regarding the decoder approach and the decentralized, agent-based method for solving. We derive the necessity of integrating a heuristic approach into the agent method for ensembles and present this integration in detail. We conclude with several simulation studies showing the effectiveness of the hybrid approach.

2   Related Work

2.1   Predictive Scheduling

As related work, the solution to predictive scheduling with decoders has to be discussed in the context of agent-based approaches prior to deriving the root cause that raises the problem when extending scheduling to participants that

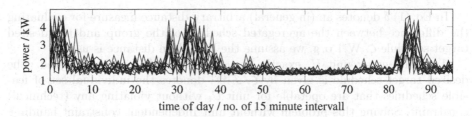

Fig. 1. Example for a training set of schedules for a co-generation plant. A state-of-charge of 50% at night and an increased thermal demand for showering in the morning and dish washing in the evening result in higher flexibilities during these periods.

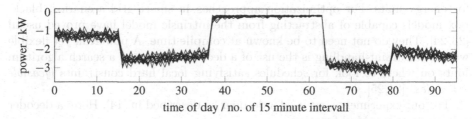

Fig. 2. Example for a training set of schedules for a heat pump with a maximum deviation of 500 Wh from the integral of set thermal demand.

locally have to control more than one single energy unit. We start with a definition of the general predictive scheduling problem.

As opposed to the usual time series model, we regard a schedule as real valued vector $\boldsymbol{p} = (p_1, \ldots, p_d) \in \mathbb{R}^d$ with each element p_j denoting mean active power generated (positive values) or consumed (negative values) during the j-th of d time intervals. Starting time and width of each time interval are assumed to be known from context information. The feasibility of a schedule $\boldsymbol{p}$ is defined by sets of unit specific technical and economic constraints.

One of the crucial challenges in operating a VPP arises from the complexity of the scheduling task due to the large amount of (small) energy units in the distribution grid [21]. In the following, we consider predictive scheduling, where the goal is to select exactly one schedule $\boldsymbol{p}_i$ for each energy unit U_i from a search space $\mathcal{F}^{(U)}$ of feasible schedules specific to the possible operations and technical constraints of unit U and with respect to a future planning horizon, such that a global objective function (e. g. resembling a target power profile) is optimized by the sum of individual contributions [22]. A basic formulation of the scheduling problem is given by

$$\delta \left(\sum_{i=1}^{m} \boldsymbol{p}_i, \boldsymbol{\zeta} \right) \to \min; \text{ s.t. } \boldsymbol{p}_i \in \mathcal{F}^{(U_i)} \ \forall U_i \in \mathcal{U}. \tag{1}$$

In Eq. (1) δ denotes an (in general) arbitrary distance measure for evaluating the difference between the aggregated schedule of the group and the desired target schedule ζ. W. l. o. g. we assume the Euclidean distance is used.

To each energy unit U_i exactly one schedule p_i has to be assigned. The desired target schedule is given by ζ. $\mathcal{F}^{(U_i)}$ denotes the individual set of feasible schedules that are operable for unit U_i without violating any (technical) constraint. Solving this problem without unit independent constraint handling leads to specific implementations that are not suitable for handling changes in VPP composition or unit setup without having changes in the implementation of the scheduling algorithm [16].

Flexibility modelling can be understood as the task of modelling constraints for energy units. For optimization approaches in smart grid scenarios, black-box models capable of abstracting from the intrinsic model have proved useful [23,24]. They do not need to be known at compile time. A powerful, yet flexible way of constraint-handling is the use of a decoder that gives a search algorithm hints on where to look for schedules satisfying local hard constraints (*feasible schedules*) [24,25].

For our experiments, we used a decoder as described in [14]. Here, a decoder γ is given as mapping function

$$\gamma : \mathbb{R}^d \to \mathbb{R}^d; \; \gamma(\boldsymbol{p}) \mapsto \boldsymbol{p}^*. \tag{2}$$

With $\boldsymbol{p}^*$ having the following properties:

- $\boldsymbol{p}^*$ is operable by the respective energy unit without violating any constraint,
- the distance $\|\boldsymbol{p} - \boldsymbol{p}^*\|$ is small; where the term small depends on the problem at hand and often denotes the smallest distance of $\boldsymbol{p}$ to the feasible region.

With such decoder concept for constraint handling one can now reformulate the optimization problem as

$$\delta \left(\sum_{i=1}^{m} \gamma_i(\boldsymbol{p}_i), \zeta \right) \to \min, \tag{3}$$

where γ_i is the decoder function of unit i that produces feasible, schedules from $\boldsymbol{p} \in [0, p_{max}]^d$ resulting in schedules that are operable by that unit. Please note, that this is a constraint free formulation. With this problem formulation, many standard algorithms for optimization can be easily adapted as there are no constraints (apart from a simple box constraint $\boldsymbol{p} \in [0, p_{max}]^d$) to be handled and no domain specific implementation (regarding the energy units and their operation schedules) has to be integrated. Equation (3) is used as a surrogate objective to find the solution to the constrained optimization problem Eq. (1).

2.2   COHDA

The Combinatorial Optimization Heuristics for Distributed Agents (COHDA) was originally introduced in [26,27]. Since then it has been applied to a variety of smart grid applications [16,22,28,29]. With our explanations we follow [27].

Originally, COHDA has been designed as a fully distributed solution to the predictive scheduling problem (as distributed constraint optimization formulation) in smart grid management [26]. In this scenario, each agent in the multi-agent system is in charge of controlling exactly one distributed energy resource (generator or controllable consumer) with procuration for negotiating the energy. All energy resources are drawn together to a virtual power plant and the controlling agents form a coalition that has to control the VPP in a distributed way. It is the goal for the predictive scheduling problem to find exactly one schedule for each energy unit such that

1. each assigned schedule can be operated by the respective energy unit without violating any hard technical constraint, and
2. the difference between the sum of all targets and a desired given target schedule is minimized.

The target schedule usually comprises 96 time intervals of 15 min each with a given amount of energy (or equivalently mean active power) for each time interval, but might also be constituted for a shorter time frame by a given energy product that the coalition has to deliver.

An agent in COHDA does not represent a complete solution as it is the case for instance in population-based approaches [30,31]. Each agent represents a class within a multiple choice knapsack combinatorial problem [32]. Applied to predictive scheduling each class refers to the feasible region in the solution space of the respective energy unit. Each agent chooses schedules as solution candidate only from the set of feasible schedules that belongs to the DER controlled by this agent. Each agent is connected with a rather small subset of other agents from the multi-agent system and may only communicate with agents from this limited neighborhood. The neighborhood (communication network) is defined by a small world graph [33]. As long as this graph is at least simply connected, each agent collects information from the direct neighborhood and as each received message also contains (not necessarily up-to-date) information from the transitive neighborhood, each agent may accumulate information about the choices of other agents and thus gains his own local belief of the aggregated schedule that the other agents are going to operate. With this belief, each agent may choose a schedule for the own controlled energy unit in a way that the coalition is put forward best while at the same time own constraints are obeyed and own interests are pursued.

All choices for own schedules are rooted in incomplete knowledge and beliefs in what other agents are probably going to do; gathered from received messages. The taken own choice (together with the basis for decision-making) is communicated to all neighbors and in this way knowledge is successively spread throughout the coalition without any central memory. This process is repeated. Because all spread information about schedule choices is labeled with an age, each agent may decide easily whether the own knowledge repository has to be updated. Any update results in recalculating of the own best schedule contribution and spreading it to the direct neighbors. By and by all agents accumulate

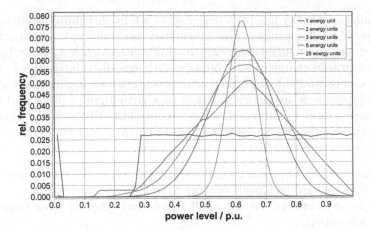

Fig. 3. Probability density of different numbers of folded distributions of operable power levels for co-generation plants.

complete information and as soon as no agent is capable of offering a schedule that results in a better solution, the algorithm converges and terminates. Convergence has been proved in [19].

More formally, each time an agent receives a message, three successive steps are conducted. First, during the perceive phase an agent a_j updates its own working memory κ_j with the received working memory κ_i from agent a_i. From the foreign working memory the objective of the optimization (i.e. the target schedule) is imported (if not already known) as well as the configuration that constitutes the calculation base of a neighboring agent a_i. An update is conducted if the received configuration is larger or has achieved a better objective value. In this way, schedules that reflect the so far best choices of other agents and that are not already known in the own working memory are imported from the received memory.

During the following decision phase agent a_j has to decide on the best choice for his own schedule based on the updated belief about the system state Γ_k. Index k indicates the age of the system state information. The agent knows which schedules of a subset of other agents (or all) are going to operate. Thus, the schedule that fills the gap to the desired target schedule exactly can be easily identified. Due to operational constraints of the controlled DER, this optimal schedule can usually not be operated. Thus, each agent is equipped with a decoder that automatically maps the identified optimal schedule to a nearby feasible schedule that is operable by the DER and thus feasible. In this way, the decision routine of the agent reduces simply to a mapping call of the decoder. Based on a set of feasible schedules sampled from an appropriate simulation model for flexibility prediction [34], the decoder can be built by learning a support vector model after the approach of [14].

If the objective value for the configuration with this new candidate is better, this new solution candidate is kept as selected one. Finally, if a new solution candidate has been found, the working memory with this new configuration is sent to all agents in the local neighborhood. The procedure terminates, as soon as all agents reach the same system state and no new messages are generated. In this case no agent is able to find a better solution. Finally, all agents know the same final result.

As the whole procedure is based exclusively on local decisions, each agent decides privately which schedules are taken. Private interest and preferences can be included and all information on the flexibility of the local DER is kept private. The same must hold true for agents controlling an ensemble of energy units.

3 Ensemble Scheduling

3.1 Problem

Sometimes the technical equipment of a single participant in a virtual power plant consists of more than just a single generator (or prosumer or controllable consumption). Nevertheless, the owner as operator is still represented by a single controlling agent when embedded into a decentralized agent-based control scheme inside a virtual power plant. In this case that agent has to handle the ensemble of energy units as a single unit (in a sense as a single sub VPP) and negotiate to the other agents with the aggregated flexibility. Nevertheless, there is usually no joint model of the whole ensemble, and thus the agent has to use an individual model of each unit and thus a set of individual decoders for deciding on an aggregated schedule for the ensemble.

If an agent covers a set of energy units instead of a single unit, a decoder for the joint feasible region of the group of units has to be used. A model of the operation of the ensemble of units is usually not available. Using the training sets of individual energy units and randomly combining them (adding up exactly one from each training set) to joint schedules in order to gain a training set for the joint behavior is not targeted. The problem is that all source trainings sets are independent random samples and thus the resulting training set exhibits a density (of operable power levels) that results from folding the source distributions. Figure 3 shows an example. Uniformly (except for the gap between zero and minimum engine velocity) distributed values for levels of power as in the case of an co-generation plant with sufficient buffer capacity fold up – in case of ensembles with more than one CHP – to an multi-modal Irvin-Hall-distribution [35]. This distribution has some similarities to a sharp normal distribution and the more samples (number of energy units in the ensemble) are folded the more leptokurtic the pdf gets. This leads to a sample with a very high density in the middle of the feasible region. At the outskirts the sample is extremely sparse. Thus, almost all instances from the outer parts are neglected as outliers from the support vector approach that generates the surrogate model and the decoder.

For this reason, a decoder trained from such a training sample reproduces only a very small, inner portion of the feasible region. In this way, most of the flexibility that an ensemble could bring in into virtual power plant control is neglected.

3.2   CMAES with Decoder

The covariance matrix adaption evolution strategy [36,37] (CMA-ES) is a well known evolution strategy for solving multi modal black box problems.

CMA-ES aims at learning lessons from previous successful evolution steps for future search directions. A new population of solution candidates is sampled from a multi variate normal distribution $\mathcal{N}(0, C)$ with covariance matrix C which is adapted in a way that maximizes the occurrence of improving steps according to previously seen distributions for good steps. Sampling is weighted by a selection of solutions of the parent generation. In a way, the method learns a second order model of the objective function and exploits it for structure information and for reducing calls of objective evaluations. An a priori parametrization with structure knowledge of the problem by the user is not necessary as the method is capable of adapting unsupervised. A good introduction can for example be found in [38]. Especially for non-linear, non-convex black-box problems, the approach has shown excellent performance [38]. CMA-ES is initially not designed for integrated constraint handling in constrained optimization. Nevertheless, some approaches for integrating constraint handling have been developed. In [39] a CMA-ES is introduced that learns constraint function models and rotates mutation distributions accordingly. In [40] an approximation of the directions of the local normal vectors of the constraint boundaries is built by accumulating steps that violate the respective constraints. Then, the variances of these directions are reduced for mutation.

We want to use CMA-ES for solving the internal optimization problem that arises when an agent has to decide on the best possible joint schedule to offer during the decision phase of the COHDA negotiation for virtual power plants. In case the agent has to control an ensemble with more the one local unit, a decoder cannot be used directly as in the case of a single unit. For this reason, a local optimization problem has to be solved: find the closest aggregated schedule that the local ensemble can operate. This is essentially the same problem as for predictive scheduling Eq. 1. Because the operation of several decoders that model the different feasible regions of the local ensemble has to be involved, a heuristic that uses only a small number of objective evaluations is advantageous. CMA-ES is well known for this characteristic [38]. For handling the constraints, the readily available decoders can be used. Thus, we adapted and employed the decoder technique also to the CMA-ES part.

In each iteration g of CMA-ES a multivariate distribution is sampled to generate a new offspring solution population:

$$x_k^{(g+1)} \sim m^{(g)} + \sigma^{(g)} \mathcal{N}(0, C^{(g)}), \ k = 1, \ldots, \lambda. \tag{4}$$

$C^{(g)} \in \mathbb{R}^{n \times n}$ defines the covariance matrix of the search distribution at generation (iteration) g with overall standard deviation $\sigma^{(g)}$ which can also be interpreted in terms of an adaptive step size. The mean of the multivariate distribution is denoted by $m^{(g)}$, $\lambda \geq 2$ denotes the population size.

The new mean $m^{(g+1)}$ for generating the sample of the next generation in CMA-ES is calculated as weighted average

$$m^{(g+1)} = \sum_{i=1}^{\mu} w_i x_{i:\lambda}^{(g+1)}, \quad \sum w_i = 0, \ w_i > 0, \tag{5}$$

of the best (in terms of objective function evaluation) individuals form the current sample $x_i^{(g)}, \ldots, x_{\lambda}^{(g)}$. In order to introduce the decoder into CMA-ES, ranking is done with the help of the decoder mapping γ:

$$f(\gamma(x_{1:\lambda}^{(g)})), \ldots, f(\gamma(x_{\lambda:\lambda}^{(g)})), \ \lambda \geq \mu, \tag{6}$$

to define $x_{i:\lambda}^{(g)}$ as the ith ranked best individual. In our ensemble scheduling example x as solution candidate is the concatenation of schedules

$$x = p_1 p_2 \ldots p_m = (p_{11}, p_{12}, \ldots, p_{1d}, p_{21}, \ldots, p_{2d}, \ldots, p_{md}) \tag{7}$$

with $p_1, \ldots, p_m$ denoting schedules for the units in the ensemble.

Finally, the covariance matrix is updated as usual, but also based on the decoder based ranking Eq. 6:

$$C_{\mu}^{(g+1)} = \sum_{i=1}^{\mu} w_i \left(x_{i:\lambda}^{(g+1)} - m^{(g)} \right) \left(x_{i:\lambda}^{(g+1)} - m^{(g)} \right)^{\top}. \tag{8}$$

CMA-ES has a set of parameters that can be tweaked to some degree for a problem specific adaption. Nevertheless, default values that are applicable for a wide range of problems are usually available. For our experiments, we used the following default settings for the CMA-ES part. The (external) strategy parameters are $\lambda, \mu, w_{i=1\ldots\mu}$, controlling selection and recombination; c_σ and d_σ for step size control and c_c and μ_{cov} controlling the covariance matrix adaption. We have chosen to set these values after [38]:

$$\lambda = 4 + \lfloor 3 \ln n \rfloor, \quad \mu = \left[\frac{\lambda}{2} \right], \tag{9}$$

$$w_i = \frac{\ln(\frac{\lambda}{2} + 0.5) - \ln i}{\sum_{\mu}^{j=1} \frac{\lambda}{2} + 0.5) - \ln i}, \ i = 1, \ldots, \mu \tag{10}$$

$$C_c = \frac{4}{n+4}, \quad \mu_{\text{cov}} = \mu_{eff}, \tag{11}$$

$$C_{\text{cov}} = \frac{1}{\mu_{\text{cov}}} \frac{2}{(n + \sqrt{2})^2}$$
$$+ \left(1 - \frac{1}{\mu_{\text{cov}}} \right) \min \left(1, \frac{2\mu_{\text{cov}} - 1}{(n+2)^2 + \mu_{\text{cov}}} \right). \tag{12}$$

An in-depth discussion of these parameters is also given in [41]. These settings are specific to the dimension N of the objective function. In our case is $N = d \cdot m$ related to the number of agents and the dimension of the assigned schedules in the test cases that are discussed in the following section.

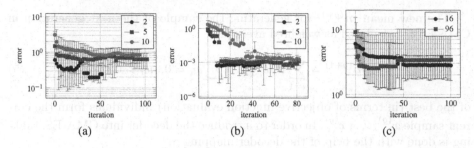

Fig. 4. Convergence behavior of different (mixed and homogeneous) energy unit ensembles. (a) shows differently sized groups of only co-generation for problems with 32-dimensional time horizons and 96-dimensional schedules in (b); (c) compares the behavior for mixed scenarios with 3 co-generation plants, 3 boilers and 3 cool storages each of 16- and 96-dimensional schedules.

4 Results

Evaluation was done by simulation with a setup comprising a set of simulated energy resources and a multi-agent system for control. The agent system was implemented after [19]. Each agent is responsible for conducting local decisions and communication with other agents in charge of controlling a small local ensemble of jointly controlled energy resources. Each agent is equipped with the described CMA-ES approach for local decisions on operation.

As a first model for distributed energy resources we used a model for co-generation plants that has already served in several studies and projects for evaluation [14,28,29,42,43]. This model comprises a micro CHP with 4.7 kW of rated electrical power (12.6 kW thermal power) bundled with a thermal buffer store. Constraints restrict power band, buffer charging, gradients, min. on and off times, and satisfaction of thermal demand. Thermal demand is determined by simulating losses of a detached house (including hot water drawing) according to given weather profiles. For each agent the model is individually (randomly) configured with state of charge, weather condition, temperature range, allowed operation gradients, and similar. From these model instances, the respective training sets for building the decoders have been generated with the sampling approach from [34].

In addition, we used models for heat pumps and boilers for hot water provision [44]. For each agent the model is individually (randomly) configured with state of charge, weather condition, temperature range, allowed operation gradients, and similar. A fourth model simulates the flexibilities of a cool storage.

Prior to integrating the hybrid CMA-ES decoder solver into the agent-based COHDA algorithm, we tested speed and behavior of convergence on single ensembles of energy resources. As the process of finding the best combination of schedules for an ensemble has to be conducted in every execution of the agent-based negotiation algorithm for finding the joint orchestration of the group of all ensembles, speed of convergence and thus execution time is an important criterion.

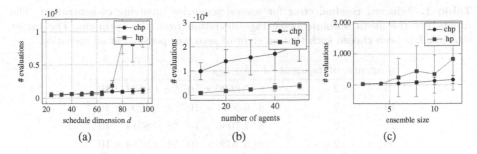

Fig. 5. Sensitivity to different parameters: tested have been schedule dimension 5(a) ranging from 24 to 96 15-minute intervals (10 agents, 2 units each), number of agents 5(b) ranging from 10 to 50 (each with 2 units, time horizon 8 intervals) and number of units per agent (ensemble size) 5(c) (96 dimensions).

Figure 4 shows the result for two different scenarios: for ensembles with only co-generation and for mixed scenarios with ensembles consisting of co-generation, boilers and cool storages. The experiment has been conducted for different group sizes and schedule dimension. By hybridizing with a decoder, obviously quick convergence can be achieved because the decoder guides the CMA-ES right from the beginning to the region with feasible solutions and as – specifically in the case of predictive scheduling with distributed energy resources – the feasible region is usually extremely small [42], the start solutions is already quite good. In this way, the decoder takes over parts of the optimization and CMA-ES may converge quicker. Adaption to a good enough solution can be achieved in a rather low number of iterations. Thus, a threshold (achieved solution quality) can be set to stop CMA-ES earlier for accelerating the agent procedure. Empirically, we found that stopping CMA-ES as soon as the residual error falls below 10^{-4} (L^2 of residual distance to target) yields sufficiently good solutions in practice. Next, we scrutinized the performance when integrated into the agents' decision routine.

Table 1 shows the results for several test scenarios with co-generation plants. In these scenarios each agent is responsible for controlling an ensemble of 2 to 4 co-generation plants; each of which is optimized using CMA-ES with a decoder that has been trained with a training set generated after the sampling approach in [34]. In order to be able to compare results from different problem sizes we used the mean absolute percentage error (MAPE)

$$\delta_{MAPE} = \delta(\boldsymbol{x}, \boldsymbol{\zeta}) = \frac{100}{d} \sum_{i=1}^{d} \left| \frac{\zeta_i - x_i}{\zeta_i} \right|. \tag{13}$$

Thus, in a scenario with 100 co-generation plants (last row in Table 1) an error of $\delta_{MAPE} \approx 6.8 \times 10^{-3}$ means a mean deviation of ~32 W. The scrutinized scenarios comprise different numbers of sites (and thus agents) and different time horizons (and thus schedule dimensions). The problem size N that the CMA-ES had to solve results from the product of schedule dimension and number of units

Table 1. Achieved residual error for several scenarios involving co-generation. The results list the mean absolute percentage deviation from the optimum. The target schedule has been chosen such that an error of zero was possible in all scenarios.

# agents	units/agent	d	δ_{MAPE}
5	2	8	$5.8620 \times 10^{-1} \pm 1.0533 \times 10^{0}$
10	2	8	$6.5071 \times 10^{-2} \pm 5.1203 \times 10^{-2}$
25	2	8	$7.7086 \times 10^{-3} \pm 4.8514 \times 10^{-3}$
50	2	8	$5.4036 \times 10^{-3} \pm 2.8514 \times 10^{-2}$
25	2	16	$1.3340 \times 10^{-1} \pm 1.3718 \times 10^{-1}$
25	2	96	$4.6533 \times 10^{-1} \pm 2.2456 \times 10^{-1}$
10	3	8	$3.9156 \times 10^{-2} \pm 2.7225 \times 10^{-2}$
25	3	8	$6.8898 \times 10^{-2} \pm 4.4228 \times 10^{-1}$
10	4	8	$5.1316 \times 10^{-2} \pm 6.4731 \times 10^{-2}$
25	4	8	$6.8771 \times 10^{-3} \pm 4.1621 \times 10^{-3}$

Table 2. Residual mean absolute percentage error for different mixed scenarios involving co-generation (chp), water heater (boiler), heat pumps and cool storages (cooler). Each agent is responsible for up to 4 units (at least one), P denotes the likelihood of having the respective unit in the ensemble.

P(chp)	P(boiler)	P(heatpump)	P(cooler)	δ_{MAPE}
25%	25%	25%	25%	$1.6701 \times 10^{-1} \pm 2.0922 \times 10^{-1}$
50%	50%	0%	0%	$6.4937 \times 10^{-2} \pm 1.2252 \times 10^{-1}$
50%	0%	0%	50%	$1.2247 \times 10^{-1} \pm 1.4329 \times 10^{-1}$
0%	0%	50%	50%	$2.1977 \times 10^{-2} \pm 2.4932 \times 10^{-2}$
25%	0%	50%	25%	$1.1427 \times 10^{-1} \pm 1.8387 \times 10^{-1}$
0%	50%	50%	0%	$3.1922 \times 10^{-2} \pm 3.1491 \times 10^{-2}$

(CHPs per agent) and ranges in these scenarios from 16 to 198. Table 2 shows the results for several mixed scenarios comprising a mix of co-generation, heat pumps, boilers, and cool storages at each site.

Figure 5 shows the sensitivity of the hybrid CMA-ES to schedule dimension, number of agents and size of the ensembles. The impact on the used number of objective evaluations is acceptably small. As an exceptional case the sensitivity of the schedule length in the case of the heat pump in Fig. 5(a) should be noticed. Obviously this effect is due to the general sharp changes in behavior of the heat pump at specific points in time. Schedules with and without such change points obviously show some different behavior.

In general, the performance is independent of the schedule dimension because the decoder repairs all dimensions at the same time in one mapping, but finding good combinations seems to exhibit steps in difficulty as schedules have steps in behavior.

5   Conclusion

We presented a hybrid approach to overcome the problem of folded densities when training decoders for ensembles of energy resources in predictive scheduling. To achieve this, we embedded a CMA-ES solver in the decision routine of an established agent-based solution.

With our approach also households, hotels, small businesses, schools or similar with an ensemble of co-generation, heat pump, solar power, and controllable consumers can take part in agent-based decentralized predictive scheduling for providing energy services in future smart grid architectures without a need for an (expensive) individual link of each single device in the ensemble. By using a hybrid approach of evolution strategy and support vector based decoder, such ensemble based participants in virtual power plants can easily be represented by a single agent. Moreover, agents with our decision method still implement the same interface as single unit agents and can thus be easily integrated with the standard COHDA protocol.

Our simulations showed that CMA-ES is well suitable for being hybridized with a decoder in order to build a system that may operate with arbitrary energy units regardless of individual constraints that restrict feasible operation. CMA-ES performs satisfactorily on reasonable large ensembles. Based on these results the inclusion of secondary, local optimization objectives like cost or preferences are a consequentially next step in future work.

References

1. European Parliament & Council: Directive 2009/28/ec of 23 april 2009 on the promotion of the use of energy from renewable sources and amending and subsequently repealing directives 2001/77/ec and 2003/30/ec
2. Abarrategui, O., Marti, J., Gonzalez, A.: Constructing the active European power grid. In: Proceedings of WCPEE 2009, Cairo (2009)
3. Niee, A., Lehnhoff, S., Trschel, M., Uslar, M., Wissing, C., Appelrath, H.J., Sonnenschein, M.: Market-based self-organized provision of active power and ancillary services: an agent-based approach for smart distribution grids. In: Complexity in Engineering (COMPENG 2012), pp. 1–5, June 2012
4. Vinay Kumar, K., Balakrishna, R.: Smart grid: advanced metering infrastructure (AMI) & distribution management systems (DMS). Int. J. Comput. Sci. Eng. 3(11), 19–22 (2015)
5. Colak, I., Fulli, G., Sagiroglu, S., Yesilbudak, M., Covrig, C.F.: Smart grid projects in Europe: current status, maturity and future scenarios. Appl. Energy 152, 58–70 (2015)
6. Awerbuch, S., Preston, A.M. (eds.): The Virtual Utility: Accounting, Technology & Competitive Aspects of the Emerging Industry. Topics in Regulatory Economics and Policy, vol. 26. Kluwer Academic Publishers, Heidelberg (1997)
7. Sonnenschein, M., Lünsdorf, O., Bremer, J., Tröschel, M.: Decentralized control of units in smart grids for the support of renewable energy supply. Environ. Impact Assess. Rev. (2014, in press)

8. Kamphuis, R., Warmer, C., Hommelberg, M., Kok, K.: Massive coordination of dispersed generation using powermatcher based software agents. In: 19th International Conference on Electricity Distribution, May 2007

9. Kok, K., Derzsi, Z., Gordijn, J., Hommelberg, M., Warmer, C., Kamphuis, R., Akkermans, H.: Agent-based electricity balancing with distributed energy resources, a multiperspective case study. In: Hawaii International Conference on System Sciences, p. 173 (2008)

10. Kamper, A., Esser, A.: Strategies for decentralised balancing power. In: Lewis, A., Mostaghim, S., Randall, M. (eds.) Biologically-Inspired Optimisation Methods: Parallel Algorithms, Systems and Applications. Studies in Computational Intelligence, vol. 210, pp. 261–289. Springer, Heidelberg (2009)

11. Mihailescu, R.-C., Vasirani, M., Ossowski, S.: Dynamic coalition adaptation for efficient agent-based virtual power plants. In: Klügl, F., Ossowski, S. (eds.) MATES 2011. LNCS (LNAI), vol. 6973, pp. 101–112. Springer, Heidelberg (2011). doi:10.1007/978-3-642-24603-6_11

12. Ramchurn, S.D., Vytelingum, P., Rogers, A., Jennings, N.R.: Agent-based control for decentralised demand side management in the smart grid. In: Sonenberg, L., Stone, P., Tumer, K., Yolum, P. (eds.) AAMAS, IFAAMAS, pp. 5–12 (2011)

13. Bremer, J., Rapp, B., Sonnenschein, M.: Support vector based encoding of distributed energy resources' feasible load spaces. In: IEEE PES Conference on Innovative Smart Grid Technologies Europe, Chalmers Lindholmen, Gothenburg, Sweden (2010)

14. Bremer, J., Sonnenschein, M.: Constraint-handling for optimization with support vector surrogate models - a novel decoder approach. In: Filipe, J., Fred, A. (eds.) Proceedings of the 5th International Conference on Agents and Artificial Intelligence, ICAART 2013, Barcelona, Spain, vol. 2, pp. 91–105. SciTePress (2013)

15. Nieße, A., Sonnenschein, M.: A fully distributed continuous planning approach for decentralized energy units. In: Cunningham, D.W., Hofstedt, P., Meer, K., Schmitt, I. (eds.) Informatik 2015. GI-Edition - Lecture Notes in Informatics, 246 edn., pp. 151–165. Bonner Köllen Verlag, Bonn (2015).

16. Nieße, A., Beer, S., Bremer, J., Hinrichs, C., Lünsdorf, O., Sonnenschein, M.: Conjoint dynamic aggrgation and scheduling for dynamic virtual power plants. In: Ganzha, M., Maciaszek, L.A., Paprzycki, M. (eds.) Federated Conference on Computer Science and Information Systems - FedCSIS 2014, Warsaw, Poland, September 2014

17. Bremer, J., Sonnenschein, M.: Parallel tempering for constrained many criteria optimization in dynamic virtual power plants. In: 2014 IEEE Symposium on Computational Intelligence Applications in Smart Grid (CIASG), pp. 1–8, December 2014

18. Schiendorfer, A., Steghöfer, J.P., Reif, W.: Synthesised constraint models for distributed energy management. In: Ganzha, M., Maciaszek, L.A., Paprzycki, M. (eds.) Proceedings of the 2014 Federated Conference on Computer Science and Information Systems, Warsaw, Poland, 7–10 September 2014, pp. 1529–1538 (2014)

19. Hinrichs, C.: Selbstorganisierte Einsatzplanung dezentraler Akteure im Smart Grid. Ph.D. thesis, Carl von Ossietzky Universitt Oldenburg (2014)

20. Bremer, J., Lehnhoff, S.: Decentralized coalition formation in agent-based smart grid applications. In: Bajo, J., et al. (eds.) PAAMS 2016. CCIS, vol. 616, pp. 343–355. Springer, Heidelberg (2016). doi:10.1007/978-3-319-39387-2_29

21. McArthur, S., Davidson, E., Catterson, V., Dimeas, A., Hatziargyriou, N., Ponci, F., Funabashi, T.: Multi-agent systems for power engineering applications - Part I: concepts, approaches, and technical challenges. IEEE Trans. Power Syst. **22**(4), 1743–1752 (2007)
22. Sonnenschein, M., Hinrichs, C., Nieße, A., Vogel, U.: Supporting renewable power supply through distributed coordination of energy resources. In: Hilty, L.M., Aebischer, B. (eds.) ICT Innovations for Sustainability. AISC, vol. 310, pp. 387–404. Springer, Heidelberg (2015). doi:10.1007/978-3-319-09228-7_23
23. Gieseke, F., Kramer, O.: Towards non-linear constraint estimation for expensive optimization. In: Esparcia-Alcázar, A.I. (ed.) EvoApplications 2013. LNCS, vol. 7835, pp. 459–468. Springer, Heidelberg (2013). doi:10.1007/978-3-642-37192-9_46
24. Bremer, J., Sonnenschein, M.: Model-based integration of constrained search spaces into distributed planning of active power provision. Comput. Sci. Inf. Syst. **10**(4), 1823–1854 (2013)
25. Coello, C.A.C.: Theoretical and numerical constraint-handling techniques used with evolutionary algorithms: a survey of the state of the art. Comput. Methods Appl. Mech. Eng. **191**(11–12), 1245–1287 (2002)
26. Hinrichs, C., Sonnenschein, M., Lehnhoff, S.: Evaluation of a self-organizing heuristic for interdependent distributed search spaces. In: Filipe, J., Fred, A.L.N. (eds.) International Conference on Agents and Artificial Intelligence (ICAART 2013), vol. 1, pp. 25–34. SciTePress (2013)
27. Hinrichs, C., Lehnhoff, S., Sonnenschein, M.: A decentralized heuristic for multiple-choice combinatorial optimization problems. In: Helber, S., et al. (eds.) Operations Research Proceedings 2012, pp. 297–302. Springer, Heidelberg (2014)
28. Hinrichs, C., Bremer, J., Sonnenschein, M.: Distributed hybrid constraint handling in large scale virtual power plants. In: IEEE PES Conference on Innovative Smart Grid Technologies Europe (ISGT Europe 2013). IEEE Power & Energy Society (2013)
29. Nieße, A., Sonnenschein, M.: A fully distributed continuous planning approach for decentralized energy units. In: Cunningham, D.W., Hofstedt, P., Meer, K., Schmitt, I., eds.: Informatik 2015. GI-Edition - Lecture Notes in Informatics (LNI), vol. 246, pp. 151–165. Bonner Köllen Verlag, Bonn (2015)
30. Poli, R., Kennedy, J., Blackwell, T.: Particle swarm optimization. Swarm Intell. **1**(1), 33–57 (2007)
31. Karaboga, D., Basturk, B.: A powerful and efficient algorithm for numerical function optimization: artificial bee colony (ABC) algorithm. J. Glob. Optim. **39**(3), 459–471 (2007)
32. Lust, T., Teghem, J.: The multiobjective multidimensional knapsack problem: a survey and a new approach. CoRR abs/1007.4063 (2010)
33. Watts, D., Strogatz, S.: Collective dynamics of 'small-world' networks. Nature **393**(6684), 440–442 (1998)
34. Bremer, J., Sonnenschein, M.: Sampling the search space of energy resources for self-organized, agent-based planning of active power provision. In: Page, B., Fleischer, A.G., Göbel, J., Wohlgemuth, V. (eds.) 27th International Conference on Environmental Informatics for Environmental Protection, EnviroInfo 2013, Shaker, pp. 214–222 (2013)
35. Hall, P.: The distribution of means for samples of size n drawn from a population in which the variate takes values between 0 and 1, all such values being equally probable. Biometrika **19**(3/4), 240–245 (1927)
36. Ostermeier, A., Gawelczyk, A., Hansen, N.: A derandomized approach to self-adaptation of evolution strategies. Evol. Comput. **2**(4), 369–380 (1994)

37. Hansen, N.: The CMA evolution strategy: a comparing review. In: Lozano, J., Larranaga, P., Inza, I., Bengoetxea, E. (eds.) Towards a New Evolutionary Computation: Advances in the Estimation of Distribution Algorithms. Studies in Fuzziness and Soft Computing, vol. 192, pp. 75–102. Springer, Heidelberg (2006)
38. Hansen, N.: The CMA evolution strategy: a tutorial. Technical report (2011)
39. Kramer, O., Barthelmes, A., Rudolph, G.: Surrogate constraint functions for CMA evolution strategies. In: Mertsching, B., Hund, M., Aziz, Z. (eds.) KI 2009. LNCS (LNAI), vol. 5803, pp. 169–176. Springer, Heidelberg (2009). doi:10.1007/978-3-642-04617-9_22
40. Arnold, D.V., Hansen, N.: A (1+1)-CMA-ES for constrained optimisation. In: Proceedings of the 14th Annual Conference on Genetic and Evolutionary Computation, GECCO 2012, pp. 297–304. ACM, New York (2012)
41. Hansen, N., Ostermeier, A.: Completely derandomized self-adaptation in evolution strategies. Evol. Comput. 9(2), 159–195 (2001)
42. Bremer, J., Rapp, B., Sonnenschein, M.: Encoding distributed search spaces for virtual power plants. In: IEEE Symposium Series on Computational Intelligence 2011 (SSCI 2011), Paris, France, April 2011
43. Neugebauer, J., Kramer, O., Sonnenschein, M.: Classification cascades of overlapping feature ensembles for energy time series data. In: Woon, W.L., Aung, Z., Madnick, S. (eds.) DARE 2015. LNCS (LNAI), vol. 9518, pp. 76–93. Springer, Heidelberg (2015). doi:10.1007/978-3-319-27430-0_6
44. Sonnenschein, M., Appelrath, H.J., Canders, W.R., Henke, M., Uslar, M., Beer, S., Bremer, J., Lünsdorf, O., Nieße, A., Psola, J.H., et al.: Decentralized provision of active power. In: Smart Nord - Final Report. Hartmann GmbH, Hannover (2015)

EvoGAMES

Driving in TORCS Using Modular Fuzzy Controllers

Mohammed Salem[1]([⊠]), Antonio Miguel Mora[2], Juan Julian Merelo[2],
and Pablo García-Sánchez[3]

[1] University of Mascara, Mascara, Algeria
salemohammed@gmail.com
[2] Department of Architecture and Computer Technology,
University of Granada, Granada, Spain
amorag@geneura.ugr.es, jjmerelo@gmail.com
[3] Universiy of Cádiz, Cádiz, Spain
fergunet@gmail.com

Abstract. When driving a car it is essential to take into account all possible factors; even more so when, like in the TORCS simulated race game, the objective is not only to avoid collisions, but also to win the race within a limited budget. In this paper, we present the design of an autonomous driver for racing car in a simulated race. Unlike previous controllers, that only used fuzzy logic approaches for either acceleration or steering, the proposed driver uses simultaneously two fuzzy controllers for steering and computing the target speed of the car at every moment of the race. They use the track border sensors as inputs and besides, for enhanced safety, it has also taken into account the relative position of the other competitors. The proposed fuzzy driver is evaluated in practise and timed races giving good results across a wide variety of racing tracks, mainly those that have many turning points.

Keywords: Videogames · Fuzzy controller · TORCS · Steering control · Speed computation

1 Introduction

The Open Racing Car Simulator (TORCS) [19] is a three-dimensional racing video game created by Eric Espié and Christophe Guionneau, whose objective is to be used as a framework to develop and test Artificial Intelligence (AI) models for autonomous drivers, named *controllers* or bots. It is one of the most popular car racing simulators among the scientific community, and due to its open-source philosophy, there are several designers and programmers constantly improving it [11].

Even if it does not have the graphic quality of commercial games, it presents several advantages for academic purposes, such as [11]:

- Its complexity lies between an advanced simulator, like recent commercial car racing games, and a fully customisable environment, like the ones typically used by computational intelligence researchers for benchmark purposes.

G. Squillero and K. Sim (Eds.): EvoApplications 2017, Part I, LNCS 10199, pp. 361–376, 2017.
DOI: 10.1007/978-3-319-55849-3_24

- It features a sophisticated physics engine that includes aerodynamics, fuel consumption, traction, as well as a 3D graphics engine for the visualization of the races.
- It was not conceived as a free alternative to commercial racing games, but it was specifically devised to make it as easy as possible to develop and test your own controller. In fact, controllers are implemented as separated software pieces with a modular architecture, so it is easy to develop a new one and to plug it into the game.

Even in simulation mode, driving a car with a bot as a human would do is a hard task, because the agent has to control several actions such as the steer, gear and brake/acceleration using the data related to the car and its environment (detected by means of sensors).

Hence, Computational Intelligence (CI) methods are interesting to be applied to the problem of implementing a car controller in TORCS [4,5,14,17]. Among these techniques, Fuzzy logic [1] with its adaptation and ability of imitating the human behaviour, is an interesting tool to design these drivers. It could be integrated in any controller module (steering, gear change, acceleration and brake, stuck) to give a human-like 'appeal' to the bot driver [15,16].

In each simulation tick, the autonomous driver must make a decision, for instance, to direct the car (steer) on the track and select a target speed. This problem is much harder when the car is near to a curve where it has to choose a compromise between going faster and avoiding the car slips and goes out of the track. The overall idea is to move the car towards the farthest track border to avoid prematurely breaking.

This complex problem could be solved by means of Fuzzy Logic, due to its adaptive control and ability to deal with noise (in sensors [11]) and uncertainty (non-deterministic opponents' decisions in the race). Indeed, several researchers have taken advantage of this technique to design TORCS controllers, for example [9,15,16]. All the existing works used a specific fuzzy module with a concrete objective inside the controller's operation, such as computing the optimal acceleration, turning angle, or speed at every moment.

However, this work presents a novel fuzzy-based controller, which implements two modular sub-controllers, each of them devoted to infer a specific target, namely: maximum speed and optimal steering for the car at every simulation tick. They consider the track sensors, to find the farthest border; and the opponents' position in the race, for collision avoidance and overtaking.

2   Background and State of the Art

In the last years, several researchers have focused on driving a racing car using computational intelligence techniques. Among them, Artificial Neural Networks (ANN) have been one of the most prolific techniques successfully applied to this problem. For instance, using supervised methods it is possible to create controllers by the imitation of an existing bot [4]. However, their performance decreases if they drive on circuits not previously used for training. In those cases, some authors have proposed automatic on-line (during the game) learning approaches, such as Quadflieg et al. [17], who implemented a recognition system based on a simple classifier to identify the part of the track where the car is; or Cardamone et al. [5], that proposed a neuroevolutionary method to adapt a controller to a new (unknown) track.

Human data can also be used for training ANNs, or for example, to model a human-like controller [14]. Although several scripts can be used to avoid noise, the problem to create a human-like driver is difficult, and again, their performance in circuits not known will be reduced, so a learning approach should be applied.

These models can be improved using meta-optimization techniques, such as Evolutionary Algorithms (EAs). These have been applied to 'refine' the parameters [3] considered in the different methods (being them hand-coded or not), or to improve the structure/architecture of the models [18]. Thus, this can optimize the controllers' behavioural modules, and yield bots that might even win competitions [3,15]. EAs can also been used online during the game, to adapt a controller to the player skills [5,20]. Other approaches try to generate the source code of the controller from scratch using Genetic Programming [2], although in the same evaluation time these approaches normally behave worse than standard ANN-based controllers. In these cases, higher population sizes might aid to outperform the latter.

Another prolific technique has been Fuzzy Logic (FL), which has been widely used since the year 2008. For instance, Fujii et al. in [6] examined the performance of fuzzy rule-based systems for high-level decision making in a controller, along with the effect and influence of sensory information. In [16], a fuzzy controller was designed to obtain the target position for the car, whereas the steering was computed using a crisp formula. This work and its improvement [15] have some common points with our proposal, as the controller is pretty similar, however, in this work two different specialized fuzzy modules have been implemented instead of just one.

Some approaches are based on context-dependant hybrid fuzzy-sets, avoiding training and dealing with input variables [21]. These authors claim that using Machine Learning techniques and fuzzy approaches may reduce the training time. Although their approaches were applied to a different simulation environment, not to TORCS.

EAs have been also used to optimize the fuzzy set parameters, although the maximum values of the sets may not be achieved following this approach [9]. In that work, the authors obtain improved fuzzy models to infer the acceleration and turning angle, but they are not specialized as the proposed here.

In [7], a fuzzy rule-based car controller for Car Racing Competition was built and tuned with co-evolutionary genetic algorithms. Indeed, two fuzzy controllers were designed: the first one to compute the acceleration using the velocity and distance and the second one to get the turning angle. But their approach was applied to a simpler simulator than TORCS.

In this paper, we go a step further in the state of the art of TORCS fuzzy controllers, proposing a bot with modular or specialized fuzzy sub-modules for inferring on-line the target speed and the optimal steering at every point of the race.

3 Problem Description: TORCS

The Open Racing Car Simulator (TORCS)[19] is a standalone application mainly designed as a framework or testbed for bots/controllers, which are built as separate modules loaded into the main memory when a race takes place [13], so they are quite independent for the game engine itself. The main features of the architecture of TORCS are [11]:

- TORCS is a client-server application, where the bots are run as external processes connected to the server through UDP connections.
- The simulation is achieved in real time with 20 ms per game tick. So, the server sends the values of the sensors to every controller and waits 10 ms (real time) to receive an action to conduct from the bot. If there is not a new action, the simulation continues and the last action is repeated.
- The TORCS software makes a physical separation between the driver code and the simulator itself. Hence, it defines an abstract layer that gives complete freedom of choice of the programming language used to implement the bots, and just gives access to some information.

There are several competitions which use TORCS as a base. During a competition, the bot perceives the race environment by means of a number of sensors, that provide information such as the status of the car, the status of the race, opponents' positions and track borders [10,11]. Table 1 presents a complete list of available sensors with a description of each one.

Every TORCS driver bot is controlled by means of a set of actuators: the steering wheel 'Steer', the accelerator 'accel', the brake pedal and the gearbox. In addition, a meta-action is available to request a restart of the race to the server. Table 2 details the available actions/actuators and their representation.

Hence, a controller is a program, which run inside TORCS, that automatically drives a car. It gets as input information about the current state of the car and its situation on the track. These collected data are used to compute actions to do in the next simulation tick; like steer, gear changes, acceleration or brake and clutch. A client may request a restart of the race by sending a special action on the server: Restart or shutdown [11].

The basic architecture of a controller consists of five simple modules (see Fig. 1), which are continuously working during a race.

TORCS comes with a simple example driver often used to validate new designed controllers [10,16]. It presents very basic functions for controlling the race car to give developers an idea of what the controller should look like. It includes simple functions to control the speed, steering angle and speed without dealing with opponents. We have used it as a baseline for comparison, as we will see later on.

Table 1. Description of available sensors in TORCS [13].

Sensor	Name	Range (unit)	Data type
1	angle	$[-\pi,+\pi]$	Double
2	curLapTime	$[0,+\infty]$ (s)	Double
3	damage	$[0,+\infty)$(point)	Double
4	distFromStart	$[0,+\infty)$ (m)	Double
5	distRaced	$[0,+\infty)$ (m)	Double
6	focus	$[0,200]$ (m)	Double
7	fuel	$[0,+\infty)$ (l)	Double
8	gear	$\{-1,0,1,.. 6\}$g	Integer
9	lastLapTime	$[0,+1]$ (s)	Double
10	opponents	$[0,200]$ (m)	Double
10	racePos	$\{1,2,...,N\}$	Double
11	rpm	$[0,+\infty)$ (rpm)	Double
13	speedX	$(-\infty,+\infty)$ (km/h)	Double
14	speedY	$(-\infty,+\infty)$ (km/h)	Double
15	speedZ	$(-\infty,+\infty)$ (km/h)	Double
16	track	$[0,200]$	Double
17	trackPos	$(-\infty,+\infty)$	Double
18	wheelSpinVel	$[0,+\infty)$ (rad/s)	Double
19	z	$(-\infty,+\infty)$ (m)	Double

Table 2. TORCS actuators [15].

Action	Range (unit)	Data type
Acceleration	$[0,+1]$	Double
Brake	$[0,+1]$	Double
Gear	$-1..0..+6$	Double
Steer	$[-1,+1]$	Double
Clutch	$[-1,+1]$	Double

4   Proposed Fuzzy Controller

The proposed controller has the same modular architecture as the simple driver, and has some common functions of this approach. However, the target speed and steering angle are computed by means of two modular and specialised fuzzy controllers, which consider five position sensors.

In the following sections, each sub-controller is described.

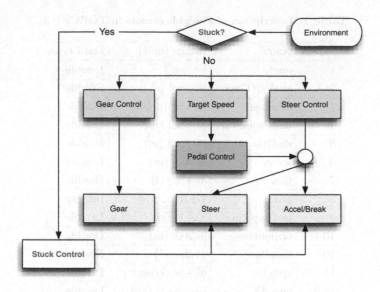

Fig. 1. Basic architecture of a controller.

4.1   Fuzzy Target Speed Sub-controller

The first proposed fuzzy sub-controller aims to estimate the optimal target speed of the car, both in straight parts and curves of the track, taking into account two criteria: moving as faster as possible and secure the car. This estimation is based on fuzzy rules, so two general cases are considered, following the simple driver approach:

- If the car is in a straight line, the target speed will take a maximum value (*maxSpeed* km/h).
- If it is close to a curve, the controller will decrease the current speed to a value included in the interval *[minSpeed; maxSpeed]* km/h.

Thus, in case the car is out of the track or near a curve, the brake system is activated, and ABS (Anti-Block System) and TCL (Traction Control Limit) will be loaded to avoid the car skidding. The obtained target speed will be used for computing the value of acceleration, following - as the simple driver do - the expression:

$$Gas(speed - Target_{speed}) = -1 + \frac{2}{1 + e^{speed - Target_{speed}}} \qquad (1)$$

Gas function refers to acceleration, *speed* is the current speed of the car.

This fuzzy controller has three input values and one output: the target speed (see Fig. 2).

The controller presented in that figure is a Mamdani-based fuzzy system [8] with trapezoidal Membership Functions (MF) for input variables, because it

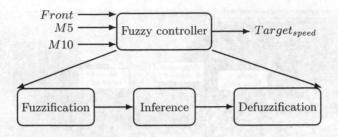

Fig. 2. Fuzzy controller of target speed.

avoids sudden changes in input values. It considers three values among the 19 track sensors (see Fig. 3):

- Front = Track[9]: the front distance between the car and the border of the track (angle 0°).
- M5 = max (Track[8], Track[10]): the max distance to the track limits in an angle of +5° and −5° with respect to Front.
- M10 = max (Track[7], Track[11]): the max distance to the border in an angle of +10° and −10°.

The set of sensors was chosen considering those used in previous works [15], but refining it after an exhaustive systematic experimentation phase. Thus, the final set of sensors are those which yielded the best results in a wider amount of tracks.

Each input variable is represented by three membership functions: Low, Medium and High. The description of fuzzy inputs and output are represented in Table 3.

Table 3. Fuzzy variables description.

Variable	Range	Name	MF	Low	Medium	High
Input	[0–100] m	Front	Trapezoidal	[0–50]	[20–80]	[60–100]
Input	[0–100] m	M5	Trapezoidal	[0–40]	[10–70]	[50–100]
Input	[0–100] m	M10	Trapezoidal	[0–30]	[20–60]	[50–100]
Output	[0–200] m/s	TargetSpeed	Singleton	/	/	/

The base of rules has been composed modelling the behaviour of a human expert driver, refining them also. Thus, this set is designed so that if the frontal distance is maximal, then the target speed should be the maximum. Its value should be lower when the frontal distance is shorter. The fuzzy rules are listed below:

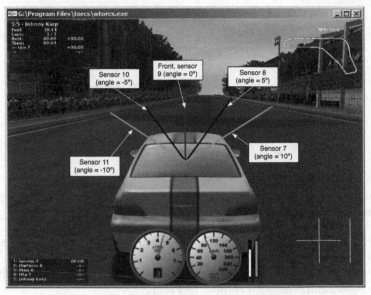

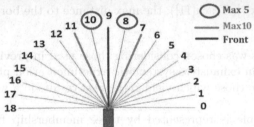

Fig. 3. Inputs considered in the fuzzy sub-controllers.

- IF Front is High THEN TargetSpeed is TS1
- IF Front is Medium THEN TargetSpeed is TS2
- IF Front is Low and M5 is High THEN TargetSpeed is TS3
- IF Front is Low and M5 is Medium THEN TargetSpeed is TS4
- IF Front is Low and M5 is Low and M10 is High THEN TargetSpeed is TS5
- IF Front is Low and M5 is Low and M10 is Medium THEN TargetSpeed is TS6
- IF Front is Low and M5 is Low and M10 is Low THEN TargetSpeed is TS7
  In addition, a crisp rule is added to rule base to obtain a maximum value of the target speed when the three input variables are as big as possible:
- IF Front = MAXDISTSPEED or M5 = MAXDISTSPEED or M10 = MAXDISTSPEED THEN TargetSpeed = MAXSPEED

MAXDISTSPEED is the a longest possible value for the track sensors, and MAXSPEED, which is related to the car's properties, is the maximal car speed. For example in the case of car-trb1 model, MAXSPEED = 300.

The output value is encoded by seven singletons TS1 to TS7, being respectively: 280, 240, 220, 180, 120, 60 and 30.

4.2 Fuzzy Steering Control Sub-controller

In addition to the speed sub-controller, another fuzzy approach has been applied to control the steering, estimating and determining the target position of the car.

The architecture of this sub-controller is similar to the one shown in Fig. 2, but with the steering as output. The set of sensors considered are the same as in the speed case, described in Table 3.

Then, if the car is in a straight line, it will set as target position half width of the race track (central position of the lane). Whereas, if the car is near a right curve, it will approach the path leading to the right, with a space between the car and the border of the track to avoid the loss of control. The same approach is considered if the car is near a left curve.

In order to detect the curves, the controller focuses on the sensor values (M10, M5, and Front). So, if the value on Front sensor is the longest, there is a straight road; whereas if the values of M5 and M10 with positive angles (+5 and +10) are the longest, there is right curve; and the other way round.

The base of rules has been defined again modelling the behaviour of a human driver, so, for this controller is:

- IF Front is High THEN steer is S1
- IF Front is Medium AND M10 is High THEN steer is S2
- IF Front is Medium AND M10 is Medium AND M5 is Medium THEN steer is S2
- IF Front is Medium AND M10 is Medium AND M5 is Low THEN steer is S3
- IF Front is Low AND M10 is High THEN steer is S3
- IF Front is Low AND M10 is Medium AND M5 is Medium THEN steer is S4
- IF Front is Low AND M10 is Medium AND M5 is Low THEN steer is S4

The values for S1 to S4 are respectively: 0, 0.25, 0.5, and 1. When M10 = Track[7] we will take negative values of the steer (sterr = −steer).

Once the controllers have been described, they will be tested and compared with the standard one y several races. The obtained results are presented in the following section.

5   Simulation Results

In this section we present all the experiments that we performed in order to measure the performance of our controller, called *AD (Automatic Driver)*. We first, describe the methodology we have used and next, we present the experimental results of the implementation of the fuzzy driver, including opponents and using special criteria in each case.

We have compared the proposed controller with the simple driver included in TORCS, so we have run every controller in several races in different tracks. We will start by an individual race by setting the laps number first and then a time trial race. The last test is a real test against TORCS drivers.

5.1   Simulation Settings

TORCS provides several tracks to choose which have been designed in order to test the performance of the controllers on different difficulty circuits and on different types of roads. In our case, we chose four circuits:

- Two road tracks: *E-Road* and *CG-Speedway Number1*, with a different associated difficulty, regarding the amount of curves and width of the road. Concretely *E-Road* has been selected to check the performance of our controller on sinuous circuits, which are normally the hardest for other approaches.
- A dirt road track: which increases the difficulty due to the lower grip of the dirty asphalt. *Dirt1* has a good variety of curves, which also add an extra difficulty.
- An oval track: *E-Track5* seems to be the most interesting, as it has curves in both directions.

Table 4 presents the properties and description of each selected track.

Table 4. Description of selected tracks

Track name	E-Track5	Dirt1	E-Road	CG-Speedway Number1
Shape				
Track Type	Oval	Dirty	Road	Road
Length	1621.73 m	3260.43 m	3260.43 m	2057.56 m
Width	20.0 m	16.0 m	16.0 m	15.0 m

The aim of this selection is to test the value of AD in a wide set of situations, in order to check its potential as a global controller.

Cars Settings. The car considered is *car1-tbr1* of SCR 1 Server, which is a NASCAR car part of the SCR Server team. It has a weight of 1150 KG, max fuel: 94 KG, length: 4.25 m and width: 1.94 m, with 300 km/h as maximal speed. This is a fair car, i.e. not the fastest, but a quite fast. Anyway, the obtained results represents the quality of the controllers and could be extrapolated to any other car.

Controllers Settings. We have tested the different sub-controller features in a separated way, in order to see which one has the highest influence on the success or failure of AD. Thus, we have considered the following bots in the experiments:

- AD-SP: Fuzzy speed controller.
- AD-SC: Fuzzy steering controller.
- AD-SSOP: Fuzzy speed and steering controller. This controller also takes the opponent into account. Thus, it considers the sensors that give the distance to the opponents from the car. If this distance is smaller than the distance to the border or the track (track sensor), it is used in the fuzzy rules.
- SD: Simple driver.

Since the speed controller is similar to previous approaches, it was expected to work properly. Hence, we have checked the basic version of our controller AD-SP and compared it with modified/improved versions, such as AD-SC and AD-SSOP. As stated before, SD has been taken as a baseline for comparisons.

5.2   Results of 20 Laps Practise Race

We firstly test our controllers in the simplest case, a practise race without rivals. We conducted a 20 laps race in the four tracks, aiming to check if the controllers are able to perform well in these 'warm up' races. 20 have been considered as it is the maximum number of laps a car can perform without doing a pit stop, because our controller is not prepared to plan and manage this event.

The Table 5 shows that among the four drivers, the minimum time has been achieved by the AD-SSOP controller in each of the four tracks. This was due to the steering unit of the controller, which allows late braking, and thus, getting and maintaining a maximal speed (as it can be seen on the third row of every table), along with following optimal paths to earn race time.

The target position allows the car to safely adjust the required steering angle with the maximum speed so the controller AD-SSOP gave the best time. However, taking a smaller target angle required a greater distance to cover by the car which follows a less efficient trajectory. In addition, the number of times the car was off the road on Dirt1 was higher for AD-SSOP and thus, this controller gets a higher damage due to the collision with the outer walls of the track.

The simple SD driver finished the race without damage, while AD-SSOP was able to complete E-Track5 track safely and with damage for the others. The damage was also a little high for the AD-SP driver.

Regarding the Fuel consumption, it depends on shocks rate and category of tracks, because it is required to accelerate more after a collision or depending on the grip, for instance.

AD-SC gets quite bad results, even in the comparison with the simple driver, so it means that the use of only the steering controller is not recommended, and it must be combined with any other.

The novel controllers seem to be robust in the sense that they obtain their best marks from their first laps, as a difference to the SD, which usually requires a higher amount of laps to improve its times.

Table 5. Results for 20 laps in practise races.

E-Track5	SD	AD-SP	AD-SC	AD-SSOP
Best time	01:05:15	01:21:24	04:33:24	29:87
Topspeed	149	148	203	199
Minspeed	46	44	60	172
Best lap	14	2	18	8
Damage	0	0	0	0
Fuel	71.22	71.25	77.45	77.02
Dirt1	SD	AD-SP	AD-SC	AD-SSOP
Best time	01:12:96	50:43	02:23:12	35:51
Topspeed	132	126	136	139
Minspeed	21	-52	-43	-54
Best lap	14	7	1	5
Damage	0	7438	905	9274
Fuel	65.04	79.26	79.98	66.06
E-Road	SD	AD-SP	AD-SC	AD-SSOP
Best time	02:44:93	02:11:39	04:33:59	01:25:66
Topspeed	149	202	203	207
Minspeed	24	-58	32	-55
Best lap	3	3	17	3
Damage	0	6056	7309	2239
Fuel	62.11	78.25	79.25	55.22
CG-Speedway Number1	SD	AD-SP	AD-SC	AD-SSOP
Best time	01:25:00	01:12:99	01:12:23	53:61
Topspeed	149	191	194	178
Minspeed	49	57	32	-51
Best lap	12	20	2	2
Damage	0	0	0	114
Fuel	66.66	62.58	73.38	60.65

5.3 Time Trial Race

In the second experiment, the race stopping criterion is set to 300 s, so, after that time, the simulation stops. There are no opponents again. Once the race has ended, the distances covered by each controller are checked.

The results are shown in Table 6 where it could be seen that the AD-SSOP controller has yielded the best results in the oval and road tracks. However, in the dirty one, it was a disaster, since it was extremely damaged and TORCS simulator had to stop it. For this reason, the distance covered by this controller is the smallest.

Table 6. Results of the controllers in 300 s time trial race.

E-Track5	Best Time Lap	Distance	Top speed
AD-SP	01:11:98	4540.844	155
AD-SC	02:15:26	8803.161	155
AD-SSOP	29:30	32600	199
Dirt1	Best Time Lap	Distance	Top speed
AD-SP	04:49:12	7825.032	126
AD-SC	03:45:02	5202.99	134
AD-SSOP	01:36:14	4620.25	153
E-Road	Best Time Lap	Distance	Top speed
AD-SP	03:62:33	11586.2	160
AD-SC	02:41:41	11588	208
AD-SSOP	01:15:16	23139	217
CG-Speedway Number1	Best Time Lap	Distance	Top speed
AD-SP	01:15:19	23136	195
AD-SC	01:15:80	17352.2	193
AD-SSOP	44:67	28921.6	206

This happened to the lack of grip in this kind of tracks and the damages which were caused by the crashes/collisions with the track border. AD-SC also showed problems in the same circuit so this lead us to reinforce the fact the fuzzy steering control module is too much sensitive to the bad conditions of the road. This is a point of improvement that we will address in a close future.

5.4   Real Race

Finally, a real race test has been conducted. Our main goal is to test the performance of our best controller, AD-SSOP, in a race, and answer the following questions: Could we have a perfect driving in a race with AD-SSOP only with the track borders and opponents' sensors? Can we win the race with AD-SSOP?

In this context we tested this controller in 5 tracks against *berniw, bt, damned, inferno* and *tita* teams which are integrated TORCS controllers with different strategies and slightly modifications. Moreover, *bt* controller comes with advanced machine learning methods [12].

After the launch of every race, AD-SSOP against the 10 cars of each team for 20 laps in each track, we obtained the results presented in Table 7.

From Table 7, we noticed that our controller has won the race in E-Track5 (oval track), and also got good positions against all the teams but inferno. This lead us to think that it is quite good for this type of circuit, due to the optimal trajectory in curves computed by means of the steering sub-controller, which also allows braking as late as possible. Furthermore, the target speed sub-controller

Table 7. Results of AD-SSOP in a real race.

E-Track5	Against berniw team	Against bt team	Against damned team	Against inferno team	Against tita team
Ranking	1/11	2/11	1/11	7/11	4/11
Best time	29:90	30:28	30:28	30:59	30:53
Maxspeed	198	198	198	199	198
Damage	2267	7939	5888	5232	8043
Dirt1	Against berniw team	Against bt team	Against damned team	Against inferno team	Against tita team
Ranking	10/11	11/11	11/11	11/11	10/11
Best time	05:11:45	05:07:79	05:39:33	05:27:96	05:37:16
Maxspeed	146	141	145	145	145
Damage	10017	6462	39	226	5593
E-Road	Against berniw team	Against bt team	Against damned team	Against inferno team	Against tita team
Ranking	2/11	2/11	8/11	7/11	10/11
Best time	01:21:29	01:29:92	01:39:54	01:27:27	01:48:18
Maxspeed	205	201	212	211	208
Damage	9979	10362	4421	7685	5593
CG-SpeedWay Number1	Against berniw team	Against bt team	Against damned team	Against inferno team	Against tita team
Ranking	2/11	4/11	1/11	5/11	6/11
Best time	46:16	48:56	47:23	46:06	03:41:41
Maxspeed	205	202	199	200	198
Damage	5533	3096	5093	5501	4345

allowed to go as fast as possible. In E-Road and CG-SpeedWay Number1 the results are also very competitive, except against the teams *inferno* and *tita*.

The obtained damage happens because when our controller is in parallel with its opponent, close to it in a narrow track they shock between them. According to damage results, despite our controller can win the race on the E-track5 and CG-SpeedWay Number1, it had a higher crash rates in several cases. We observed also that in the majority of cases our car is very slow compared to the other cars in each team.

In the Dirt1 which has the difficulty of a lower grip, the drawbacks of the proposed controller had clearly affected the results.

6   Conclusions and Future Work

In this work, a novel fuzzy driver for TORCS has been presented. It is based on two fuzzy sub-controllers, able to compute the target speed and the steering respectively. The aim of the proposed controller is to direct the car to the farthest side of the track in curves so to keep the target speed as high as possible.

This approach differs from others in the state of the art due to the combination of both sub-controllers, which is a novel variation.

The designed controller has been evaluated in four circuits with different shapes and conditions and considering three different scenarios: a practise race, a time trial race, and a real race against tough opponents belonging to TORCS teams. Three different combinations of the fuzzy modules have been tested, namely one with the target speed computation (AD-SP), one with just steering control (AD-SC), and one with both of them plus the consideration of the opponents (AD-SSOP), when there exist.

The obtained results have been very good in practise and time limit races, mainly for AD-SSOP. It has also behaved very well in the real races in one of the circuits (an oval one), ranked in the first positions. It has happened because the optimal trajectory computation conducted by the steering sub-controller, which allows late braking. However, this approach tends to receive too much damage, due to the crash with rivals or with the borders of the tracks, mainly when the road is not in optimal conditions, e.g. it is dirty. This is the main point of improvement that we will address in the close future.

In addition, in future work we also aim to improve the controller to design a smarter racing car driver. This could be enhanced by tuning its parameters using an evolutionary algorithm or/and combine it with a learning tool (neural networks) to recognize the track parts and plan in advance.

Acknowledgements. This work has been supported in part by projects EPHEMECH (TIN2014-56494-C4-3-P, Spanish Ministerio de Economy Competitividad), PROY-PP2015-06 (Plan Propio 2015 UGR), PETRA (SPIP2014-01437, funded by Dirección General de Tráfico), CEI2015-MP-V17 (awarded by CEI BioTIC Granada), and PRY142/14 (funded by Fundación Pública Andaluza Centro de Estudios Andaluces en la IX Convocatoria de Proyectos de Investigación).

References

1. Abraham, A.: Neuro fuzzy systems: state-of-the-art modeling techniques. In: Mira, J., Prieto, A. (eds.) IWANN 2001. LNCS, vol. 2084, pp. 269–276. Springer, Heidelberg (2001). doi:10.1007/3-540-45720-8_30
2. Agapitos, A., Togelius, J., Lucas, S.M.: Evolving controllers for simulated car racing using object oriented genetic programming. In: Lipson, H. (ed.) Genetic and Evolutionary Computation Conference, GECCO 2007, Proceedings, London, England, UK, 7–11 July 2007, pp. 1543–1550. ACM (2007)
3. Butz, M.V., Lönneker, T.D.: Optimized sensory-motor couplings plus strategy extensions for the TORCS car racing challenge. In: Lanzi, P.L. (ed.) Proceedings of the 2009 IEEE Symposium on Computational Intelligence and Games, CIG 2009, Milano, Italy, 7–10 September 2009, pp. 317–324. IEEE (2009)
4. Cardamone, L., Loiacono, D., Lanzi, P.L.: Learning drivers for TORCS through imitation using supervised methods. In: Lanzi, P.L. (ed.) Proceedings of the 2009 IEEE Symposium on Computational Intelligence and Games, CIG 2009, Milano, Italy, 7–10 September 2009, pp. 148–155. IEEE (2009)
5. Cardamone, L., Loiacono, D., Lanzi, P.L.: On-line neuroevolution applied to the open racing car simulator. In: Proceedings of the Eleventh Conference on Congress on Evolutionary Computation, CEC 2009, pp. 2622–2629. IEEE Press, Piscataway (2009)
6. Fujii, S., Nakashima, T., Ishibuchi, H.: A study on constructing fuzzy systems for high-level decision making in a car racing game. In: IEEE World Congress on Computational Intelligence. IEEE, June 2008

7. Guadarrama.S, Vazquez, R.: Tuning a fuzzy racing car by coevolution. In: Genetic and Evolving Systems, GEFS 2008. IEEE, March 2008
8. Iancu, I.: A Mamdani Type Fuzzy Logic Controller. InTech, Rijeka (2012). pp. 325–352
9. Liébana, D.P., Recio, G., Sáez, Y., Isasi, P.: Evolving a fuzzy controller for a car racing competition. In: Lanzi, P.L. (ed.) Proceedings of the 2009 IEEE Symposium on Computational Intelligence and Games, CIG 2009, Milano, Italy, 7–10 September 2009, pp. 263–270. IEEE (2009)
10. Loiacono, D., Cardamone, L., Lanzi, P.: Software manual of the car racing competition. TORCS news (2009). http://cig.dei.polimi.it/wpcontent/uploads/2008/04/manualv03.pdf
11. Loiacono, D., Cardamone, L., Lanzi, P.: Simulated car racing championship competition software manual. TORCS news (2013)
12. Loiacono, D., Lanzi, P.L., Togelius, J., Onieva, E., Pelta, D.A., Butz, M., Lonneker, T.D., Cardamone, L., Perez, D., Saez, Y., Preuss, M., Quadflieg, J.: The 2009 simulated car racing championship. IEEE Trans. Comput. Intell. AI Games 2(2), 131–147 (2010)
13. Loiacono, D., Cardamone, L., Butz, M., Lanzi, P.L.: The 2011 simulated car racing championship @ cig-2011. TORCS news (2011). http://cig.dei.polimi.it/wpcontent/
14. Muñoz, J., Gutiérrez, G., Sanchis, A.: A human-like TORCS controller for the simulated car racing championship. In: Yannakakis, G.N., Togelius, J. (eds.) Proceedings of the 2010 IEEE Conference on Computational Intelligence and Games, CIG 2010, Copenhagen, Denmark, 18–21 August 2010, pp. 473–480. IEEE (2010)
15. Onieva, E., Pelta, D., Godoy, J., Milanés, V., Rastelli, J.: An evolutionary tuned driving system for virtual car racing games: the autopia driver. Int. J. Intell. Syst. 27, 217–241 (2012)
16. Onieva, E., Pelta, D.A., Alonso, J., Milanés, V., Pérez, J.: A modular parametric architecture for the TORCS racing engine. In: Proceedings of the 5th IEEE Symposium on Computational Intelligence and Games (CIG 2009), pp. 256–262. IEEE Press, Piscataway (2009)
17. Quadflieg, J., Preuss, M., Kramer, O., Rudolph, G.: Learning the track and planning ahead in a car racing controller. In: Proceedings of the 6th IEEE Symposium on Computational Intelligence and Games (CIG 2010), pp. 395–402. IEEE Press (2010)
18. SeongKim, T., Na, J.C., Kim, K.J.: Optimization of an autonomous car controller using a self-adaptive evolutionary strategy. Int. J. Adv. Robot. Syst. 9, 73 (2012)
19. Sourceforge: Web torcs. Web, November 2016. http://torcs.sourceforge.net/
20. Tan, C.H., Ang, J.H., Tan, K.C., Tay, A.: Online adaptive controller for simulated car racing. In: Proceedings of the IEEE Congress on Evolutionary Computation, CEC 2008, 1–6 June 2008, Hong Kong, China, pp. 2239–2245. IEEE (2008)
21. Thang, H.D., Garibaldi, J.M.: A novel fuzzy inferencing methodology for simulated car racing. In: FUZZ-IEEE 2008, IEEE International Conference on Fuzzy Systems, Hong Kong, China, 1–6 June 2008, Proceedings, pp. 1907–1914. IEEE (2008)

Automated Game Balancing in Ms PacMan and StarCraft Using Evolutionary Algorithms

Mihail Morosan$^{(\boxtimes)}$ and Riccardo Poli

University of Essex, Colchester, UK
{mmoros,rpoli}@essex.ac.uk

Abstract. Games, particularly online games, have an ongoing requirement to exhibit the ability to react to player behaviour and change their
mechanics and available tools to keep their audience both entertained
and feeling that their strategic choices and in-game decisions have value.
Game designers invest time both gathering data and analysing it to introduce minor changes that bring their game closer to a state of balance,
a task with a lot of potential that has recently come to the attention
of researchers. This paper first provides a method for automating the
process of finding the best game parameters to reduce the difficulty of
Ms PacMan through the use of evolutionary algorithms and then applies
the same method to a much more complex and commercially successful
PC game, *StarCraft*, to curb the prowess of a dominant strategy. Results
show both significant promise and several avenues for future improvement that may lead to a useful balancing tool for the games industry.

Keywords: Evolutionary algorithms · Game balance · Automation ·
PacMan · StarCraft

1 Game Balance

1.1 Introduction

The literature presents different notions of "balance", perhaps because different
games, or even genres, naturally lead to (or need) slightly different versions of
the concept. The most generic definition, supplied by Schreiber [24], is that game
balance "is mostly about figuring out what numbers to use in a game". Some
have argued that a measure of balance can be derived from how interesting,
while also uncertain, a game is during its play [9,18]. This will be discussed in
more detail in Sect. 1.2.

Players will reliably find their own state of balance after investing enough
time in the game. This can involve learning what the best strategies are and what
game elements are strongest. This gives experienced players a clear advantage
over novices, while the best players will have a fair battleground to fight on.

M.Morosan—This work is supported by the EPSRC Centre for Doctoral Training
in Intelligent Games & Game Intelligence (IGGI) [EP/L015846/1].

© Springer International Publishing AG 2017
G. Squillero and K. Sim (Eds.): EvoApplications 2017, Part I, LNCS 10199, pp. 377–392, 2017.
DOI: 10.1007/978-3-319-55849-3_25

Although this is definitely a state of balance, it is not the same concept as a balanced game, as there might exist game elements that are not used at all, resulting in wasted design space and game assets, as well as a potential lack of any strategic breadth.

Game designers can directly impact the strengths and weaknesses of their game's entities, but they cannot control player behaviour. By optimising the parameters of a game, they force players to adapt to the new environment and rediscover the state of balance described previously.

1.2 Balance Definitions

Defining what is and is not balanced is not an easy task, especially when a mathematical representation of the game's mechanics is unavailable and one has to rely on statistics and word of mouth [5]. In popular multiplayer games, both designers and players analyse how often a game entity (e.g., a champion in *League of Legends* or a gun in *Counter-Strike*) has impacted a player's chance of winning the game.

Sirlin [27] considers game balancing as the iterative task of bringing a game to a state where the options presented to a player are not only reasonably many, but also viable.

One way of looking at balance is to see it as a function of many variables, each representing a different facet of the game, that needs to be optimised [24]. However, the greater the complexity of the game, the more difficult it is to derive an explicit formulation for such a function or that the solution currently used in a game is optimal. Indeed, optimising game balance is difficult and game designers tend to use a sort of hill-climbing approach based on small steps where some of their games' parameters are changed in tiny increments or decrements, hoping the new values will bring the game closer to their definition of balance.

Complex games allow for much variation in play style, decisions to be taken and different start configurations. Balance is almost impossible and often highly dependent on player opinion [5]. While some might consider an element of a game to be imbalanced, there will often be many bringing good arguments towards the contrary. What is almost consistently true is that, in a competitive game, players will constantly look for the strongest options and abuse them.

However, people's understanding of games is highly subjective and designers have different understandings of what makes their game balanced or not. For the purpose of this research, the definition used by Beyer *et al.* is the one that is followed, as it is the most general available and is reported below [4].

Definition 1. *Game balancing is the process of systematically modifying parameters of game components and operational rules in order to determine satisfactory configurations regarding predefined goals.*

1.3 Balance Through the Use of Computational Intelligence

Computational intelligence can be used to aid in many areas, from medical diagnosis [7], to improving search results or more efficient antenna designs [16].

This sparked the question of whether there is potential for use in helping game designers as well. It has also been applied by Mahlmann et al. [18] and Volz et al. [29] to generate game environments from a pool of existing mechanics and game assets using a selection of different AI agents, based on various representations of fitness to describe what makes a game balanced and fun. These studies used different approaches and both were successful.

Very similar to the work done in this study are the results from Beyer et al. on describing an integrated process for game balancing [4]. The work offers great insight on the challenges presented by automated balancing and offers advice on how such algorithms can be used to facilitate the work of games designers. One very important conclusion from this work is that, at this time, most artificial agents do not play like humans and so the suggestions offered by an automated system based on such agents may or may not work for human players. Thus designers must always double check what they are doing to their games.

This paper seeks to further explore how computational intelligence, in particular genetic algorithms (GA), can aid in the process of game design by altering a couple of existing commercial games to fit optimised requirements. There has been work in the area of designing game variations through use of GAs.

Mahlmann et al. [18] worked on matching game elements from Dominion, a popular board game, to create interesting variations of it for players. They successfully used GAs and AI agents to essentially create new games in the Dominion design space.

Chen et al. [8] applied GAs to find balanced character skills for role-playing games. It is done on a very small scale, with a minimal custom game model used and a simple rules-based agent controlling behaviour. The approach does not consider how their methodology would apply to real games or the presence of noise generated by humans or AI agents.

GAs are capable of finding interesting, often innovative [11,22,23], ways of solving given problems. They do not always generate perfect solutions, but not all tasks require perfect optimality in the first place. Given that games can have many parameters, each with its own limits as to the values it can have, as well as a wide variety of relationships between them, the search space is immense. GAs thrive in these scenarios.

When deciding how balance is affected by the game parameters, this paper aims for two "interesting" games, where it uses a similar understanding of interesting as Cincotti et al. [9], where uncertainty creates a more enjoyable experience. It is interpreted as the requirement to not have any dominant strategy and, as a result, no way to crown a winner early in the game, assuming equally skilled players.

2   Methodology

The adjustment of two games' parameters was sought: *Ms PacMan* for a proof of concept and *StarCraft* as the main target.

2.1   Ms PacMan

Ms PacMan is a single player game played on a 2-dimensional board, where the player controls the "PacMan" and has the goal of collecting as many points as possible while navigating a maze-like map. There are 4 "ghosts" opposing the player.

The ghosts follow predictable strategies, but their movements can be random at times, making for an unpredictable game every time it is played. This means deterministic AI agents will not always achieve the same score in consecutive games. Figure 1 highlights the distribution of scores a simple rules-based agent can achieve.

This rules-based agent is a greedy-random agent based on work done by Thompson *et al.* [28], with modifications by Shelton [26].

There are many AI agents available for *Ms PacMan*, from simple rules-based agents, to strong Q-learning [13], neural network [17] or MCTS agents [21]. For this experiment, to see if this method is applicable to the game, the quick rules-based agent mentioned above is used, as it can represent a lower-level human player and many more games can be simulated in a short amount of time.

For *Ms PacMan*, the elements of the game that are immediately quantifiable are the speeds at which each of the characters moves, with two different values available for the ghosts: when chasing the PacMan and when being chased by the PacMan. Another variable available is the duration of the power-up when a power pill is eaten, but in this study, it was left at its default value.

For this experiment, the game's rules were altered slightly. Instead of aiming for a high score, the game is "won" once the player achieves a certain amount of points, 1500 for this study. As a result, players can have a win-rate associated to their performance instead of an average score and performance can be evaluated based on that.

Given this change to the game's mechanics, the rules-based agent would win the game only 19.63% of the time (see Fig. 1). This data is a result of 10000 game simulations. The distribution of these scores presented in Fig. 1 was generated using the Parzen window method, using a Gaussian kernel estimator.

2.2   StarCraft

StarCraft is a real-time strategy game from Blizzard Entertainment, known for its e-sports environment, but more importantly, its AI development community [1]. The game involves three distinct races, the Terran, the Protoss and the Zerg, each with its own available units, strategies and strengths. It is played from a top-down perspective, with the player managing both an economy and an army.

The game is played in real-time, meaning that both players must act with some degree of urgency in issuing their commands, while paying attention to multiple areas of the game. These areas can include the workers that gather resources, the military unit production facilities, the environment and the natural defences offered by it, such as cliffs or bridges, and access areas where the enemy might make an attack through. Each player can only see parts of the map where

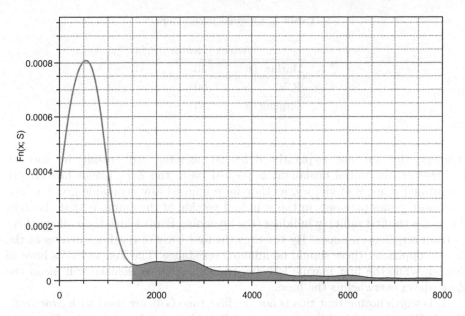

Fig. 1. Distribution of scores achieved by a rules-based agent in *Ms PacMan* (see text). The area highlighted in red represents winning scores according to our altered rules

it has units or buildings, thus, for most of the game, do not see what their opponents are doing. This is a very important element of the game, as a player will not know what strategy their opponent is employing for quite some time and will have minimal time to adapt to it should it be strong against them.

The important units in *StarCraft* for this study are:

- the Terran SCV, the basic worker of the Terran faction. They are weak in combat, but are the only resource-gathering unit.
- the Terran Marine, the cheapest military unit available to the Terran faction. They are efficient in multiple numbers, attack from range and move at a medium speed.
- the Zerg Zergling, the cheapest military unit available to the Zerg faction. They are very efficient in multiple numbers, attack from melee range and are very fast.

There is one Zerg AI agent, called ZZZKBot, written by Chris Coxe [10], that has a very high win-rate against most other AI agents and intermediate or novice human players [2]. Prior knowledge of ZZZKBot's strategy, or an experienced player, are required to successfully defend against it. This study seeks to change the game to make this AI bot's strategy not as dominant without completely nullifying it.

ZZZKBot employs the 4-pool zergling rush strategy. It makes the cheapest offensive units in bulk as quickly as possible, sending them to attack the opponent as soon as they are complete. This is a very aggressive

Table 1. Original parameters

	Attack	Health
Marine	6	40
SCV	5	60
Zergling	5	35

strategy that, if not explicitly defended against, will result in success. If, however, the initial onslaught is pushed back, the Zerg player has greatly diminished chances of victory, as they have ignored any economic growth. The way most games play out, in the standard version of the game, is that the Zerg AI rushes the first military building (the Spawning Pool) which then allows them to train zerglings en-masse. By the time the first wave of zerglings arrives at the Terran opponent, there should be minimal resistance. The Terran SCVs have to defend, while the first marine is being trained. A failed defence will mean the Zerg player overwhelms the base.

It is worth noting that this is not the first time GAs are used with *StarCraft*. García-Sánchez *et al.* [14] were successfully able to evolve strategies for an AI to play the game at a higher level than many other artificial agents. Their goals were, however, very different from what we are attempting.

The game's relevant parameters, for this study, are how strong the marine, SCV and zergling units are, in regards to their available hit points (how hard they are to kill) and their attack damage (how strong their attacks are) (Table 1). Of course, there are many more units whose defence and attack could be evolved, as well as several other parameters, such as how long it takes to train or build them, what their costs are, and so on. We will explore their optimisation in future research.

2.3 Tools Used

Multiple tools, some made by third parties and others specifically developed for this research, were used to simulate *Ms PacMan* and to gain control of *StarCraft* and facilitate this study. These are described below.

For *Ms PacMan*, an adaptation of existing code by Shelton was used [25] and is available on GitHub [20]. This is a faithful recreation of the original game, with the added ability to be run without any graphical rendering or pause between frames. As a result, hundreds of games can be simulated every second when quick agents control it.

By having access to the source code, we were able to directly alter the game's parameters, bypassing any requirement for editing running memory or binary files. When referencing the *Ms PacMan* experiment, the original values and evolved values will be represented in this paper as the array $(PS, GS_1, GS_2, GS_3, GS_4, GF_1, GF_2, GF_3, GF_4)$, where PS represents the player's speed, GS represents the respective ghost's chase speed, and GF represents the respective ghost's flee speed.

For *StarCraft*, BWAPI [6] is an open-source piece of software that allows third-party applications to access and interact with *StarCraft* in real time, resulting in the possibility of creating AI agents for the game. For this study, BWAPI required a couple of patches that would allow multiple independent instances of the game to run in parallel.

ChaosLauncher [19] is a tool written in Pascal that injects third-party libraries, such as BWAPI, into *StarCraft*'s executable, to facilitate their functionality. Similarly to BWAPI, changes to the original code were required to allow multiple instances of *StarCraft* to run at the same time.

With the changes mentioned above, multiple games of *StarCraft* can be played in parallel, each with its own AI agents and different maps.

The GA we used to perform the balancing (more on this in the next section) evolves arrays of parameters. When calculating the fitness of an individual, these are sent to a custom C++ application that alters the corresponding unit attack and defence parameters in the game. This is done by replacing several binary values in the targeted *StarCraft* map file and repacking it properly, to allow it to be read by the game. To achieve this, the open source StormLib library [30] was used to unpack and repack maps, modified with own code for replacing the game's parameters. The game itself remains unchanged, but the map file tells it to use the new set of parameters rather than the default ones. When discussing the *StarCraft* experiments, the original values and evolved values will be represented in this paper as the array $(A_1, A_2, A_3, H_1, H_2, H_3)$, where A represents Attack and H represents Health.

2.4 Genetic Algorithm

The evolutionary algorithm employed is a variant of a generational GA with two-point crossover [15] (applied with a rate of 40%), a specialised mutation operator (applied with a per-individual rate of 40%) and elitism (applied to the top 20% of the population).

The mutation operator for *Ms PacMan* was applied with a (per allele) mutation rate of 0.5 (meaning that on average 50% of the elements of an individual would be mutated). At each application of the operator, a displacement is randomly generated by a random number generator within the range of -0.1 and $+0.1$ and added to the corresponding parameter value. Should the new value be outside the range of accepted values, it is clamped to be within those values.

The mutation operator for *StarCraft* was also applied with a (per allele) mutation rate of 0.5. At each application of the operator, a displacement (to be added to an allele's value) is randomly drawn from a discrete distribution where ± 1 has a probability of approximately 36.4%, ± 2 has a probability of approximately 27.3%, ± 3 has a probability of approximately 18.2%, ± 4 has a probability of approximately 9.1% and ± 5 has a probability of approximately 9.1%.

Experiments for both games used tournament selection, with a tournament size of 6. The population size was 50, with no more than 100 generations for each run.

Each evolved vector was constrained to only contain values between 0 and 8 for *Ms PacMan* and between 1 and 80 for *StarCraft*. Values outside of these ranges are not realistic for the tested scenarios.

2.5 Fitness Evaluation

In both games, the parameters in an individual were decoded and games were played on a corresponding version of the game.

In *Ms PacMan*, 100 games were played for each individual, storing all the scores the agent achieved. Any scores above or equal to 1500 were counted as a win, while any scores below that were considered losses. That represented the individual's win-rate.

For *StarCraft*, the map was created, then 7 or 11 games were run in sequence (7 for the first experiment and 11 for the second experiment), storing the end-result (win or loss) of the Zerg AI and the duration of the game. The Zerg AI played against the game's highest difficulty Terran player.

From a game designer's standpoint, the end goal is to control two features: how often the main agent wins (the Zerg AI for *StarCraft* and the rules-based AI in *Ms PacMan*) and how big the changes are to the original game parameters. The smaller the changes are to the original game parameters, the less likely it is that the game's players would become dissatisfied with the changes.

So, fitness is a multi-objective function of the win-rate and the absolute difference between the default game parameters and the newly evolved ones. The closer the win-rate is to the desired one, the better the fitness. Also, the smaller the difference between the original parameters and the evolved parameters, the better the fitness, as it is preferred to have incremental changes rather than big ones. This is the immediate result of wanting to optimise an existing game rather than creating a new one from existing mechanics.

The objective of optimising the win-rate could be further split into multiple game scenarios, each one dealing with different AI agents or maps, but we decided to keep it straightforward and focus on methodology by using only two AI agents (ZZZKBot and the default *StarCraft* Terran AI).

Our GA considers smaller fitness values to be better, with 0 representing a perfect solution.

Formally, the fitness function can be written as:

$$Fitness = W + \Delta_P \tag{1}$$

$$W = |WR - DWR| \times C_W \tag{2}$$

$$\Delta_P = \sum_{i=0}^{n} |\Delta_i| \times C_\Delta \tag{3}$$

In the win-rate optimisation function W, WR = Win-Rate (from 0 to 1), DWR = desired win-rate, C_W = win-rate bias factor. In the parameter optimisation function Δ_P, Δ_i = difference between the original ith parameter and the evolved ith parameter, C_Δ = value difference bias factor.

2.6   Experiments

We performed four experiments.

The first experiment we ran was on *Ms PacMan*, to test the algorithm in an environment where changes and fixes can be done quickly and where multiple runs can be done in little time. The designer requirement for this experiment was to make the game easier for the novice player, but not too much easier than the original version. Considering the original win-rate of 19.67%, we wanted the game to be won around 50% of the time.

The second experiment we ran had the purpose of assessing whether this GA can, for the much more complex *StarCraft* scenario, completely nullify the ZZZKBot AI's strategy, thus achieve 0% win-rate. Intuition says that pushing the Zergling's attack damage as low as possible, or, alternatively, increasing the SCVs attack high enough, would be sufficient to neutralize the Zerg AI strategy. If the GA arrived at a similar conclusion, it would be a sanity check for its ability to alter the game appropriately.

The third experiment was the main one, where the game had to evolve in such a way as to make the AI's strategy only successful 50% of the time. This is a much more complex task, and there is no immediately obvious solution to it. It is also very likely that there might be multiple ways of achieving this goal, and these could be found by different GA runs. The reason behind choosing 50% as the target win-rate is due to the definition supplied earlier in the paper on what is an interesting game. By removing the dominant strategy, the game should once again allow for multiple strategies to be viable.

Finally, once a good set of parameters was computed in the third experiment, in a fourth experiment, the corresponding version of *StarCraft* was played by people of varying skills, to assess its viability with respect to the original version. Players had to play as the Terran race and face ZZZKBot in two best of 3 series, one with the original parameters, and one with a parameter set identified by the GA, then describe which parameter set they considered the fairest and most entertaining to play with, as well as any strategic considerations that they made as a result of the changes.

3   Results

3.1   Experiment 1: Altering the Difficulty in Ms PacMan

For *Ms PacMan* 10 runs were done, with the parameters described in the previous section, $DWR = 0.5$, $C2 = 100$ and $C = 1000$. The best parameters generated by each run, as well as the fitness components, can be seen in Table 2. Each run had other good solutions, but for this task we will focus on only the ones with the highest fitness.

The Δ_P values (see Eq. 3) of the best individuals in each run averaged 188.2 (±117.77), with a median of 158.5 (see also box-plot in Fig. 2). The win-rate component W (see Eq. 2) of the fitness function was optimal in 6 of the 10 best-of-run individuals.

Table 2. Main *Ms PacMan* experiment results, with the best solution in bold

Run	Parameters	Δ_P	Win-rate
1	(3.58, 3.32, 2.64, 2.46, 2.37, 1.51, 1.54, 1.51, 1.41)	218	50%
2	(3.83, 3.56, 2.37, 2.80, 2.83, 1.41, 1.49, 1.47, 1.87)	255	50%
3	(2.57, 2.53, 2.69, 2.53, 2.78, 1.48, 1.50, 1.47, 1.46)	119	51%
4	**(3.07, 2.81, 2.82, 2.64, 2.86, 1.45, 1.5, 1.56, 1.41)**	**51**	**50%**
5	(4.64, 4.03, 3.03, 2.64, 2.86, 1.48, 1.50, 1.44, 1.50)	339	50%
6	(4.60, 4.01, 2.50, 2.60, 2.33, 1.47, 1.25, 1.54, 1.50)	409	50%
7	(3.05, 2.79, 3.21, 2.58, 2.82, 1.49, 1.56, 1.51, 1.54)	84	47%
8	(3.74, 3.45, 2.57, 2.82, 2.79, 1.50, 1.54, 1.34, 1.44)	191	50%
9	(3.31, 3.07, 3.07, 2.82, 2.77, 1.53, 1.70, 1.44, 1.44)	126	40%
10	(2.96, 2.77, 2.86, 3.02, 2.70, 1.53, 1.85, 1.51, 1.43)	90	48%
Orig	(3.00, 2.80, 2.80, 2.80, 2.80, 1.50, 1.50, 1.50, 1.50)	0	19.67%

Some of the best individuals made minor changes to the game's mechanics, but these changes resulted in a much easier game for the rules-based agent. It is worth noting that in the runs, the GA found 4 different methods of balancing the game towards the required designer metric.

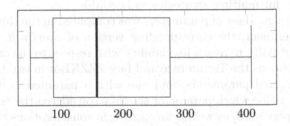

Fig. 2. Boxplot of fitnesses for best individual in each of the 10 *Ms PacMan* runs

The first strategy (runs 1, 2, 5, 6 and 8) is to make the main player and one ghost faster (up to 30% faster), while barely altering the other ghosts. This is a worthy avenue to take by a designer, but might not be the best one available due to physical reaction time differences between AI agents and humans.

The second strategy (runs 3 and 10) is to slow everyone down by a bit. The ghosts are slowed down less than the player, which seems to allow for more points to be gathered, thus winning the game more often. It is very likely the average score would decrease, should we return to the original version of the game, but that is a side effect of the new goal.

The strategy that run 4 found is very mild tweaks to all values. Surprisingly, this fits the requirements very well, while changing the game the least out of all the presented options. This would be the solution a designer would be most interested in at first glance.

Runs 7 and 9 have various variations of speeding up both the player and some of the ghosts. No obvious pattern can be noticed that would warrant further exploration. Their fitness is not great either and can thus be considered unlucky runs.

Given this array of suggestions, a designer can run diagnostics with different AI agents or human testers and assess the value of the ones they found most interesting. They can be further adjusted manually or the fitness function can be altered to reflect a better understanding of the task.

These results were both interesting and promising and prompted the application of our balancing technique to the much more complex game of *StarCraft*.

3.2   Experiment 2: Completely Nullifying the ZZZKBot in StarCraft

For *StarCraft* a single run was done, with the objective of completely disabling the ZZZKBot's strategy. This was done just as a test of the much more complex version of our system required by the game, with the parameters described in the previous section, $DWR = 0.0$ and $C2 = 1$.

The best set of parameters computed was $(7, 5, 1, 39, 60, 35)$. This individual had a W of 0, which means ZZZKBot lost all 7 of the games it played, and a Δ_P of 6. With these parameters, the game's default Terran AI agents consistently defeat ZZZKBot, while also diverging from the game's default parameters by very little, as was required.

This result is in line with the intuitive solution a game designer would come up with to solve the task. While, for this example, the Marine and SCV parameters did not require any changes, it highlights the GA's ability to come to the same conclusion and focus on changing the relevant unit parameters only, in this case the zergling's attack.

3.3   Experiment 3: Balancing the ZZZKBot Strategy in StarCraft

In the third experiment 10 runs were done, each with a different seed and C win-rate bias factor, but the same fitness function and GA parameters as in experiment 2 and $DWR = 0.5$. The different win-rate bias factors control how much more the algorithm values win-rate against absolute difference between original and evolved values.

Given the complex setup, each generation required approximately 20 min to complete when run on an octa-core computing cluster. Consequently, each run took approximately 33 h to finalise. Some runs were ended early due to low likelihood of them improving any further given the lack of improvement over many generations, or, alternatively, due to a very good result being achieved early. Results can be seen in Table 3.

The Δ_P values of the best individuals in each run averaged 43 (± 18.4), with a median of 44.5 (see also box-plot in Fig. 3). The win-rate component of the

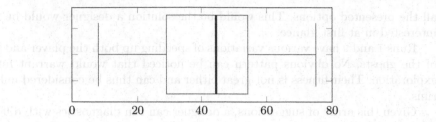

Fig. 3. Boxplot of Δ_P fitness component for all 10 *StarCraft* runs

fitness function consistently achieved the optimal value, as a result of having
won 5 or 6 out of 11 games.

Table 3. Main *StarCraft* experiment results, with best individual in bold

Run	Parameters	Δ_P	Win-rate	Generations	C
1	(33, 4, 14, 39, 60, 31)	42	5/11	100	500
2	(5, 37, 10, 26, 62, 36)	55	5/11	80	500
3	(7, 18, 9, 47, 54, 12)	54	6/11	100	500
4	(12, 2, 4, 44, 60, 19)	30	5/11	80	500
5	(28, 5, 18, 41, 58, 28)	45	6/11	100	1000
6	(30, 7, 15, 40, 63, 30)	44	5/11	100	1000
7	**(6, 6, 7, 43, 59, 36)**	**8**	**6/11**	**60**	**2000**
8	(9, 12, 2, 37, 67, 38)	26	6/11	100	2000
9	(38, 13, 15, 41, 37, 36)	75	5/11	100	2000
10	(38, 7, 15, 42, 58, 32)	51	6/11	100	2000
Orig	(6, 5, 5, 40, 60, 35)	0	11/11		

With all of the evolved parameter sets, the game's default Terran AI agent
has a chance to defend against ZZZKBot in approximately 50% of their encounters. The difference between the default parameters and the computed ones is
generally substantial in most runs, with a single run finding a solution very close
to the initial values. Each run consistently managed to optimise the win-rate
objective W of the fitness function.

Looking at the results, we can notice several different strategies to modifying
the game. The most common one (runs 1, 5, 6, 9 and 10) is to greatly increase
the power of the Terran marine and to also increase the attack power of the Zerg
zergling, while changing the Terran SCV only slightly, if at all in some cases.

The best performing run, by the given requirements, is run 7. It showed
constant improvement over time, eventually finding a result that is very close to
the original values and might realistically be possible to implement as an official
patch, assuming no other balance requirements.

One common observation about all runs is how the average fitness over time behaved. Just as described in the previous experiment, given a fit solution, minor changes to that parameter set, such as those done through mutation, could completely push the new set out of the appropriate range and greatly affect its fitness. As a result, the average fitness did not improve over time after several generations, but varied between two limits quite far apart.

Overall these results show that our approach was successful, as the different GA runs didn't just give us several different solutions that fit the requirements but also made clear what strategies designers can choose when balancing their games.

3.4   Experiment 4: Human Play-Testing

Five people, one with thousands of hours of experience in the game, 2 with intermediate experience and 2 novices, were asked to play between 2 and 6 games of *StarCraft* against ZZZKBot, half of those games using the vanilla parameters and the other half using the evolved parameters from run 7. Using ChaosLauncher and BWAPI, the whole setup was automated. Players were asked to play to the best of their abilities, that the games would be short and that one map had some parameters modified compared to the other, as well as that they would play against a fairly aggressive Zerg player. Results can be seen in Fig. 4.

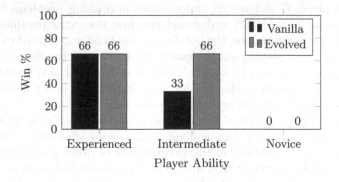

Fig. 4. Win-rate % after human play-testing

The novice players consistently lost in both versions of the game, but, after realising they could defend with the workers, often found it easier to survive slightly longer on the evolved map that gave their SCV workers a slight increase in attack power. This does highlight the fact that balancing the game against the insane difficulty AI means weaker players do not benefit as much from minor changes in their favour. This is worth considering for the future, as a multi-objective fitness evaluation can be used to balance against multiple difficulties at once, each potentially having its own requirements and target optimal values. Of course, it is also representative of how humans do attempt to adapt to changes and make use of them to their advantage through trial and error.

The intermediate players took better advantage of the changes, successfully defending using both workers and an alternate strategy on the modified map, but finding it more challenging on the vanilla version of the game. They reported that the stronger workers were something beneficial, but also stated that they could have won more reliably on the unchanged map were they able to micro-manage their units more effectively, an ability that requires a lot of practice.

The experienced player did not make any use of the stronger workers, opting to always use an optimal strategy that involved marines and a bunker (a building that allows marines to shoot from safety until it is destroyed) in all scenarios. They still lost a game on both versions of the map due to positioning mistakes, but reliably showcased how one could beat the Zerg rush strategy and keep a healthy economy to eventually win the game. This is as expected, as the employed Zerg strategy, while very strong, is not a dominant one when playing against high-level opponents.

4   Conclusion and Future Work

For the purpose of this study, in the *StarCraft* experiments, only a subset of its parameters were taken in consideration. Other available variables, pertaining to the 3 units considered, are "Time to train", "Mineral cost" and "Armour". Of course, the build times and costs of the Terran Barracks or the Zerg Spawning Pool (the buildings required to actively train the units considered), could have also been evolved. GAs have no major issues optimising problems with many more than 6 variables [3,12] and would not find the extra parameters overly problematic. For performance, the bottleneck was in no way related to the length of the arrays, but in playing out the games themselves for the fitness evaluation. Better hardware or access to a game's source code would also greatly increase the speed of an evaluation, allowing for more individuals in a population, more games to be played, or more generations to be run.

The results do show a lot of promise, as the methodology proposed could not only be useful in balancing a game itself, but, as seen after testing with human players, could aid in calibrating the performance of other intelligent agents to displaying a desired level of skill and expertise. Instead of evolving the game parameters, one could evolve the AI parameters and run a virtually unchanged set of fitness tests, hoping to optimise it to behave at a required level, for instance to the purpose of creating opponents of different difficulty levels for games.

The area of automated game balancing is being explored in depth at this point in time by many researchers and this can only benefit the games development world. Manual testing will, most likely, never be obsolete, but designers will be able to focus on much more interesting tasks while letting computational intelligence do the less exciting elements of balance.

This study has further shown that GA are viable tools for use in game design, complementing human intuition and offering a tool for future problem-solving of complex scenarios.

At the time of writing, this work is being applied to a commercial game as part of its development. *ComPet*, a game from MindArk Sweden, is making use of this research to find possible issues in their game's campaign pacing. Early work has resulted in a lot of valuable feedback to improving the system for mainstream use. These findings will be studied and reported in future publications. We believe our current methodology and understanding of design requirements to be a good starting point for future work that will be valuable to the industry.

References

1. StarCraft AI, the StarCraft BroodWar Resource for Custom AIs. http://www. starcraftai.com/
2. AIIDE: 2015 AIIDE StarCraft AI Competition Report (2015). https://www.cs. mun.ca/~dchurchill/starcraftaicomp/report2015.shtml
3. Back, T., Fogel, D.B., Michalewicz, Z.: Handbook of Evolutionary Computation. IOP Publishing Ltd., Bristol (1997)
4. Beyer, M., Agureikin, A., Anokhin, A., Laenger, C., Nolte, F., Winterberg, J., Renka, M., Rieger, M., Pflanzl, N., Preuss, M., Volz, V.: An Integrated process for game balancing. In: IEEE Conference on Computational Intelligence and Games (2016)
5. Burgun, K.: Understanding Balance in Video Games (2011). http://www. gamasutra.com/view/feature/134768/
6. BWAPI: BWAPI https://bwapi.github.io/
7. Cagnoni, S., Dobrzeniecki, A.B., Poli, R., Yanch, J.C.: Genetic algorithm-based interactive segmentation of 3D medical images. Image Vis. Comput. 17(12), 881–895 (1999)
8. Chen, H., Mori, Y., Matsuba, I.: Solving the balance problem of on-line role-playing games using evolutionary algorithms. J. Softw. Eng. Appl. 05(08), 574–582 (2012). http://www.scirp.org/journal/PaperDownload.aspx?DOI=10.4236/jsea.2012.58066
9. Cincotti, A., Iida, H., Cincotti, A., Iida, H.: Outcome uncertainty and interestedness in game-playing: a case study using synchronized hex. New Math. Nat. Comput. (NMNC) 02(02), 173–181 (2006)
10. Coxe, C.: ZZZKBot (2015). https://github.com/chriscoxe/ZZZKBot
11. David, O.E., van den Herik, H.J., Koppel, M., Netanyahu, N.S.: Genetic algorithms for evolving computer chess programs. IEEE Trans. Evol. Comput. 18(5), 779–789 (2014)
12. Davis, L.: Handbook of Genetic Algorithms (1991)
13. DeLooze, L.L., Viner, W.R.: Fuzzy Q-learning in a nondeterministic environment: developing an intelligent Ms. Pac-Man agent. In: 2009 IEEE Symposium on Computational Intelligence and Games, pp. 162–169. IEEE, September 2009. http:// ieeexplore.ieee.org/document/5286478/
14. Garcia-Sanchez, P., Tonda, A., Mora, A.M., Squillero, G., Merelo, J.: Towards automatic StarCraft strategy generation using genetic programming. In: 2015 IEEE Conference on Computational Intelligence and Games (CIG), pp. 284–291. IEEE, August 2015. http://ieeexplore.ieee.org/document/7317940/
15. Goldberg, D.E., et al.: Genetic Algorithms in Search Optimization and Machine Learning, vol. 412. Addison-Wesley, Reading (1989)
16. Linden, D.S., Altshuler, E.E.: Automating wire antenna design using genetic algorithms. Microw. J. 39(3), 74–81 (1996)
17. Lucas, S.: Evolving a neural network location evaluator to play Ms. Pac-Man. In: IEEE Symposium on Computational Intelligence and Games, pp. 203–210 (2005)

18. Mahlmann, T., Togelius, J., Yannakakis, G.N.: Evolving card sets towards balancing dominion. In: 2012 IEEE Congress on Evolutionary Computation, pp. 1–8 (2012)
19. MasterOfChaos: Chaoslauncher (2011). https://github.com/mihail-morosan/Chaoslauncher
20. Morosan, M.: PacMan-CSharp. https://github.com/mihail-morosan/PacMan-CSharp
21. Pepels, T., Winands, M.H.M., Lanctot, M.: Real-time Monte Carlo tree search in Ms Pac-Man. IEEE Trans. Comput. Intell. AI Games 6(3), 245–257 (2014). http://ieeexplore.ieee.org/document/6731713/
22. Preble, S., Lipson, M., Lipson, H.: Two-dimensional photonic crystals designed by evolutionary algorithms. Appl. Phys. Lett. 86(6), 61111 (2005)
23. Ramos, J.I.E., Vázquez, R.A.: Locating seismic-sense stations through genetic algorithms. Proc. GECCO 11, 941–948 (2011)
24. Schreiber, I.: Game Balance Concepts (2010). https://gamebalanceconcepts.wordpress.com/2010/07/07/level-1-intro-to-game-balance/
25. Shelton, L.: PacmanAI-MCTS. https://github.com/LoveDuckie/PacmanAI-MCTS
26. Shelton, L.: Implementation of high-level strategy formulating AI in Ms Pac-Man. Technical report (2013). http://lucshelton.com/assets/Uploads/Dissertation-Main-Copy.pdf
27. Sirlin, D.: Balancing Multiplayer Games (2009). http://www.sirlin.net/articles/balancing-multiplayer-games-part-1-definitions
28. Thompson, T., McMillan, L., Levine, J., Andrew, A.: An evaluation of the benefits of look-ahead in Pac-Man. In: 2008 IEEE Symposium Computational Intelligence and Games, pp. 310–315. IEEE (2008)
29. Volz, V., Rudolph, G., Naujoks, B.: Demonstrating the Feasibility of Automatic Game Balancing, March 2016. http://arxiv.org/abs/1603.03795
30. Zezula, L.: StormLib. https://github.com/ladislav-zezula/StormLib

Evolving Game-Specific UCB Alternatives for General Video Game Playing

Ivan Bravi[1]([✉]), Ahmed Khalifa[2], Christoffer Holmgård[2], and Julian Togelius[2]

[1] Dipartimento di Elettronica, Informatica e Bioingegneria,
Politecnico di Milano, Milano, Italy
ivan.bravi@gmail.com
[2] Tandon School of Engineering, New York University, New York City, USA
{ahmed.khalifa,holmgard}@nyu.edu, julian@togelius.com

Abstract. At the core of the most popular version of the Monte Carlo Tree Search (MCTS) algorithm is the UCB1 (Upper Confidence Bound) equation. This equation decides which node to explore next, and therefore shapes the behavior of the search process. If the UCB1 equation is replaced with another equation, the behavior of the MCTS algorithm changes, which might increase its performance on certain problems (and decrease it on others). In this paper, we use genetic programming to evolve replacements to the UCB1 equation targeted at playing individual games in the General Video Game AI (GVGAI) Framework. Each equation is evolved to maximize playing strength in a single game, but is then also tested on all other games in our test set. For every game included in the experiments, we found a UCB replacement that performs significantly better than standard UCB1. Additionally, evolved UCB replacements also tend to improve performance in some GVGAI games for which they are not evolved, showing that improvements generalize across games to clusters of games with similar game mechanics or algorithmic performance. Such an evolved portfolio of UCB variations could be useful for a hyper-heuristic game-playing agent, allowing it to select the most appropriate heuristics for particular games or problems in general.

Keywords: General AI · Genetic programming · Monte-Carlo Tree Search

1 Introduction

Monte Carlo Tree Search (MCTS) is a relatively new and very popular stochastic tree search algorithm, which has been used with great success to solve a large number of single-agent and adversarial planning problems [5]. Unlike most tree search algorithms, MCTS builds unbalanced trees; it spends more time exploring those branches which seem most promising. To do this, the algorithm must balance exploitation and exploration when deciding which node to expand next.

In the canonical formulation of MCTS, the UCB1 equation is used to select which node to expand [1]. It does this by trying to maximize expected reward

© Springer International Publishing AG 2017
G. Squillero and K. Sim (Eds.): EvoApplications 2017, Part I, LNCS 10199, pp. 393–406, 2017.
DOI: 10.1007/978-3-319-55849-3_26

while also making sure that nodes are not underexplored, so that promising paths are not missed.

While MCTS is a general-purpose algorithm, in practice there are modifications to the algorithm that make it perform better on various problems. In the decade since MCTS was invented (in the context of Computer Go [22]), numerous modifications have been proposed to allow it to play better in games as different as Chess [3] and Super Mario Bros [10], and for tasks as different as real-value optimization and real-world planning. While some of these modifications concern relatively peripheral aspects of the algorithm, others change or replace the UCB1 equation at the heart of it.

The large number of different MCTS modifications that have been shown to improve performance on different problems poses the question whether we can automate the search for modifications suitable for particular problems. If we could do that, we could drastically simplify the effort of adapting MCTS to work in a new domain. It also poses the question whether we can find modifications that improve performance compared to the existing UCB1 not just on a single problem, but on a larger class of problems. If we can identify the class of problems on which a particular MCTS version works better, we can then use algorithm selection [12, 21] or hyper-heuristics [6] to select the best MCTS version for a particular problem. And regardless of practical improvements, searching the space of node selection equations helps us understand the MCTS algorithm by characterizing the space of viable modifications.

In this paper, we describe a number of experiments in generating replacements for the UCB1 equation using genetic programming. We use the General Video Game AI (GVGAI) framework as a testbed. We first evolve UCB replacements with the target being performance on individual games, and then we investigate the performance of the evolved equations on all games within the framework. We evolve equations under three different conditions: (1) only given access to the same information as UCB1 (UCB_+); (2) given access to additional game-independent information (UCB_{++}); and (3) given access to game-specific information ($UCB_\#$).

2 Background

2.1 Monte Carlo Tree Search

Monte Carlo Tree Search (MCTS) is a relatively recently proposed algorithm for planning and game playing. It is a tree search algorithm which selects which nodes to explore in a best-first manner, which means that unlike Minimax (for two-player games) and breadth-first search (for single-player games) Monte Carlo Tree Search focuses on promising parts of the search tree first, while still conducting targeted exploration of under-explored parts. This balance between exploitation and exploration is usually handled through the application of the Upper Confidence Bound for Trees (UCT) algorithm which applies UCB1 to the search tree.

The basic formulation of UCB1 is given in Eq. 1, but many variations exist [1,5,15].

$$UCB1 = \overline{X_j} + \sqrt{\frac{\ln n}{n_j}} \tag{1}$$

These variations change UCB1 by e.g. optimizing it for single-player games or incorporating feature selection to name a few variations. However, when we use MCTS for general game playing it becomes impossible to know if we are better off using "plain UCB" or some specialized version, since we do not know which game we will encounter.

Ideally, we need some way of searching through the different possible variations of tree selection policies to find one that is well suited for the particular game in question. We propose addressing this problem by evolving tree selection policies to find specific formulations that are well suited for specific games. If successful, this would allow us to automatically generate adapted versions of UCB for games we have never met, potentially leading to better general game playing performance.

2.2 Combinations of Evolution and MCTS

Evolutionary computation is the use of algorithms inspired by Darwinian evolution for search, optimization, and/or design. Such algorithms have a very wide range of applications due to their domain-generality; with an appropriate fitness function and representation, evolutionary algorithms can be successfully applied to optimization tasks in a variety of fields.

There are several different ways in which evolutionary computation could be combined with MCTS for game playing. Perhaps the most obvious combination is to evolve game state evaluators. In many cases, it is not possible for the rollouts of MCTS to reach a terminal game state; in those cases, the search needs to "bottom out" in some kind of state evaluation heuristic. This state evaluator needs to correctly estimate the quality of a game state, which is a non-trivial task. Therefore the state evaluator can be evolved; the fitness function is how well the MCTS agent plays the game using the state evaluator [19].

Of particular interest for the current investigation is Cazenave's work on evolving UCB1 alternatives for Go [7]. It was found that it was possible to evolve heuristics that significantly outperformed the standard UCB1 formulation; given the appropriate primitives, it could also outperform more sophisticated UCB variants specifically aimed at Go. While successful, Cazenave's work only concerned a single game, and one which is very different from a video game.

MCTS can be used for many of the same tasks as evolutionary algorithms, such as content generation [4,5] and continuous optimization [14]. Evolutionary algorithms have also been used for real-time planning in single-player [16] and two-player games [11].

2.3 General Video Game Playing

The problem of General Video Game Playing (GVGP) [13] is to play unseen games. Agents are evaluated on their performance on a number of games which the designer of the agent did not know about before submitting the agent. GVGP focuses on real time games compared to board games (turn based) in General Game Playing. In this paper, we use the General Video Game AI framework (GVGAI), which is the software framework associated with the GVGP competition [17,18]. In the competition, competitors submit agents which are scored on playing ten unseen games which resemble (and in some cases are modeled on) classic arcade games from the seventies and eighties.

It has been shown that for most of these games, simple modifications to the basic MCTS formulation can provide significant performance improvements. However, these modifications are non-transitive; a modification that increases the performance of MCTS on one game is just as likely to decrease its performance on another [9]. This points to the need for finding the right modification for each individual game, manually or automatically.

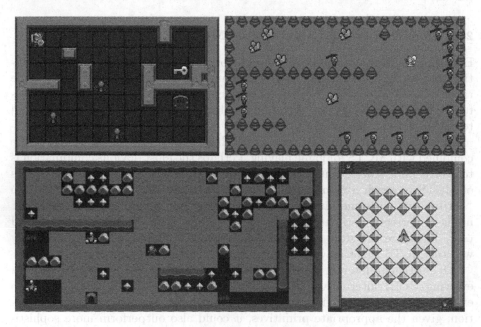

Fig. 1. Each screen represent a different GVGAI game. Games in order from top left to bottom right: Zelda, Butterflies, Boulderdash, and Solarfox

We selected five different games from the framework as testbeds for our experiments:

– **Boulderdash:** is a VGDL (Video Game Description Language) port of Boulderdash. The player's goal is to collect at least ten diamonds then reach the goal while not getting killed by enemies or boulders.

- **Butterflies:** is an arcade game developed specifically for the framework. The player's goal is to collect all the butterflies before they destroy all the flowers.
- **Missile Command:** is a VGDL port of Missile Command. The player's goal is to protect at least one city building from being destroyed by the incoming missiles.
- **Solar Fox:** is a VGDL port of Solar Fox. The player's goal is to collect all the diamonds and avoid hitting the side walls or the enemy bullets. The player has to move continuously which makes the game harder.
- **Zelda:** is a VGDL port of The legend of Zelda dungeon system. The goal is to reach the exit without getting killed by enemies. The player can kill enemies using his sword.

Figure 1 shows some levels of these games. These games require very different strategies from agents for successful play providing varied testbeds for the approach. They also have in common that standard MCTS with the UCB1 equation does not play these games perfectly (or even very well) and in the past it has been shown that other agents play them better than MCTS.

2.4 Genetic Programming

Genetic Programming (GP) [20] is a branch of evolutionary algorithms [2,8] which evolves computer programs as a solution to the current problem. GP is essentially the application of genetic algorithms (GA) [23] to computer programs. Like GAs, GP evolves solutions based on Darwinian theory of evolution. A GP run starts with a population of possible solutions called chromosomes. Each chromosome is evaluated for its fitness (how well it solves the problem). In GP, chromosomes are most commonly represented as syntax trees where inner nodes are functions (e.g. addition, subtraction, conditions) while leaf nodes are terminals (e.g. constants, variables). Fitness is calculated by running the current program and seeing how well it solves the problem. GP uses Crossover and Mutation to evolve the new chromosomes. Crossover in GP combines two different programs at a selected node by swapping the subtrees at these nodes, and mutation in GP alters a node value.

3 Methods

In the GP algorithm, chromosomes are represented as syntax trees where nodes are either *unary* or *binary functions* while leaves are either *constant values* or *variables*. The binary functions available are addition, subtraction, multiplication, division and power; instead the unary functions are square root, absolute value, multiplicative inverse and natural logarithm. The constant values can be 0.1, 0.25, 0.5, 1, 2, 5, 10, 30 and their opposites. The formula can be composed of variables belonging to three different sets:

- *Tree Variables*: represent the state of the tree built by MCTS, i.e. the variables that are used by the UCB1 formula;

– *Agent Variables*: related to the agent behavior;
– *Game Variables*: describe the state of the game.

The fitness function is a linear combination of two parameters, *win ratio* and *average score*, coming from the simulation of multiple playthroughs of one level of a single game. Equation 2 shows how these two parameters are combined. We used the same formula used in the GVGAI competition to rank agents, with *win ratio* having higher priority than *average score*.

$$Fitness = 1000 * win\_ratio + avg\_score \qquad (2)$$

In the process of evolving a game-specific equation each chromosome is tested over 100 playthroughs. Rank-based selection creates the pool of chromosomes used to generate the next generation. Two chromosomes are selected and subtree crossover is applied to the couple, later a mutation operator is applied to each new chromosome. The mutation can be either a constant mutation, point mutation, or a subtree mutation. Constant mutation selects a constant,

Table 1. Descriptive statistics for all the tested games. Mean, Median, Min, Max, and SD all relate to the score attained using $UCB1$, UCB_+, UCB_{++}, and $UCB_\#$, respectively. A **bold** value is significantly better than $UCB1$ ($p < 0.05$).

Game	Tree policy	Mean	Median	Min	Max	SD	Win ratio
Boulderdash	$UCB1$	5.30	4.00	0	186	5.22	0
Boulderdash	UCB_+	5.05	4.00	0	18	2.85	0
Boulderdash	UCB_{++}	**28.48**	3.0	−1.0	36.0	23.92	**0.018**
Boulderdash	$UCB_\#$	**27.03**	3.0	−1.0	36.0	21.85	**0.014**
Butterflies	$UCB1$	37.39	32.00	8	86	18.92	0.902
Butterflies	UCB_+	36.34	30.00	8	88	18.68	0.89
Butterflies	UCB_{++}	35.84	30.00	8	80	18.43	**0.914**
Butterflies	$UCB_\#$	22.302	18.0	12.0	48.0	8.13	**0.993**
Missile Command	$UCB1$	2.88	2.00	2	8	1.37	0.641
Missile Command	UCB_+	**3.03**	2.00	2	8	1.44	**0.653**
Missile Command	UCB_{++}	**4.95**	5.00	2	8	2.13	**0.785**
Missile Command	$UCB_\#$	**8.0**	8.0	8.0	8.0	0.0	**1.0**
Solarfox	$UCB1$	6.31	5.00	0	32	6.06	0.00565
Solarfox	UCB_+	**6.49**	5.00	0	32	5.81	**0.0075**
Solarfox	UCB_{++}	**7.765**	6.0	−7.0	32.0	9.152	**0.067**
Solarfox	$UCB_\#$	**18.57**	18.0	−5.0	32.0	12.318	**0.412**
Zelda	$UCB1$	3.58	4.00	0	8	1.85	0.088
Zelda	UCB_+	**6.32**	6.00	0	8	1.26	**0.155**
Zelda	UCB_{++}	**6.906**	8.0	−1.0	8.0	1.623	**0.633**
Zelda	$UCB_\#$	**6.661**	7.0	−1.0	8.0	1.731	**0.613**

if present, from the tree and changes it with new value between the ones available in the *constants values* set. Point mutation consists in selecting a node with a 0.05 probability and swapping it with a node of the same type (either unary node, binary node, variable or constant). Subtree mutation picks a subtree and substitutes it with another tree of depth randomly distributed between 1 and 3.

In the population of the first generation contains 1 $UCB1$ chromosome and 99 random ones. $UCB1$ is injected in the initial population in order to push the GP to possibly converge faster to a better equation. We run the GP for 30 generations. Between one generation and the next a 10% elitism is applied to guarantee that the best chromosomes are carried out to the next generation.

The performance of the best equations, between all the chromosomes evolved by the genetic algorithm, is validated through the simulation of 2000 playthroughs.

For Boulderdash, Butterflies, Missile Command, Solar Fox, and Zelda we evolved new formulae under three different conditions:

- UCB_+, using only Tree Variables;
- UCB_{++}, using both Tree and Agent Variables;
- $UCB_\#$, using Tree, Agent and Game Variables.

4   Results

Table 1 shows the results of all the evolved equations compared to $UCB1$. We can see that $UCB_\#$ is almost always better than all the others equations, followed by UCB_{++}, then UCB_+, finally $UCB1$. This was expected as the later equations have more information about the current game than the previous. Interestingly, almost all evolved equations can be said to implement the core idea behind UCB1 Eq. 1, in that they consist of two parts: exploitation and exploration.

4.1   Evolved Equations

In this section we will discuss and try to interpret every equation evolved for each game. We describe the best formula found in each experimental condition (UCB_+, UCB_{++}, and $UCB_\#$) for each game. All variables and their meanings can be found in Table 2.

Boulderdash

$$UCB_+ = max(X_j)(max(X_j)^9 d_j + 1) - 0.25 \tag{3}$$

Equation 3 pushes MCTS to exploit more without having any exploration. The reason is that the Boulderdash map is huge compared to other games, with a small number of diamonds scattered throughout the map. GP finds that exploiting the best path is far better than wasting time steps in exploring the rest of the tree.

$$UCB_{++} = max(X_j) + d_j + \frac{1}{E_{xy}} + 1.25 \qquad (4)$$

Equation 4 consists of two exploitation terms and one exploration term. The exploitation term tries to focus on the deepest explored node with the highest value, while the exploration pushes MCTS to explored nodes that are least visited in the game space.

$$UCB_\# = max(X_j) + \frac{N_{port}}{min(D_{port}) \cdot \sqrt{E_{xy}}} \qquad (5)$$

Equation 5 consists of two main parts. The first part makes the agent more courageous and it seeks actions that increase his maximum reward regardless of anything else. The second part pushes the agent toward exploring the map while staying close to the exit door. This equation reflects the goal of the game, we can say the first part makes the player collect gems, while the second part pushes the agent towards the exit.

Butterflies

$$UCB_+ = \overline{X_j} + \frac{1}{n_j^2 \cdot \sqrt{d_j}(d_j \cdot \sqrt{0.2 \cdot d_j \cdot max(X_j)} + 1)} \qquad (6)$$

Equation 6 is similar to MCTS with exploitation and exploration terms. The exploitation term is similar to UCB1 while the exploration term is more complex. The exploration term tries to explore the shallowest least visited nodes in the tree with the least maximum value. The huge map of the game with butterflies spread all over it leads MCTS to explore the worst shallowest least visited node. The value of the exploration term is very small compared to the exploitation one so it will make a difference only between similar valued nodes.

$$UCB_{++} = \sqrt{max(X_j)} + 2\overline{X_j} - \frac{X_j}{R_j} - \left(\frac{\ln X_j}{\sqrt{max(E_{xy}) + X_j^{-0.25}}} + \sqrt{U_j}\right)^{max(E_{xy})} \qquad (7)$$

Equation 7 is similar to MCTS with the mixmax modification [9]. The first two terms resemble mixmax with different balancing between average child value and maximum child value. The other two terms force the MCTS to search for nodes with the least useless moves and with the highest number of reverse moves. The useless moves force the agent to go deeper in branches that have more moves, while the number of reverse moves in *butterflies* forces the agent to move similarly to the butterflies in the game which leads to capture more of them.

$$UCB_\# = \overline{X_j} + \frac{1}{\Sigma D_{npc}} \qquad (8)$$

Equation 8 consists of two main parts. The first part is similar to the exploitation term in MCTS. The second part makes the agent get closer to the butterflies.

This equation reflects the goal of the game, we can say the first term makes the agent collect the butterflies, while the second term makes the agent get closer to them.

MissileCommand

$$UCB_+ = \overline{X_j} + (10 + \frac{X_j^{X_j}}{n})^{-1/\ln n} \tag{9}$$

Equation 9 has the same exploitation term as $UCB1$. Although the second term is very complex, it forces MCTS to pick nodes with less value. This second term is very small compared to the first term so it's relevant only when two nodes have nearly identical values.

$$UCB_{++} = \overline{X_j} + \frac{max(X_j)}{n \cdot E_{xy} \cdot (2X_j)^{0.2n_j}} \cdot \tag{10}$$
$$(d_j - \frac{1}{2/max(X_j) + 2U_j/X_j + 2\ln X_j + 1/n})^{-1}$$

Equation 10 has the same exploitation term from $UCB1$. Even though the second term is very complex, it forces MCTS to explore the least spatially visited node with the least depth. This solution is most likely evolved due to the simplicity of *Missile Command* which allows GP to generate an overfitted equation that suits this particular game.

$$UCB_\# = \overline{X_j} + \frac{1}{min(D_{npc})} \tag{11}$$

Equation 11 is similar to Butterflies Eq. 8 with a very small difference. The difference is that the second term instead of summing all the distances, it just goes toward the nearest missile. One of the reasons is that the goals of both games are similar: the agent wants to get closer to the moving entity (either its a butterfly or a missile). In Butterflies, the agent wins only if it collects (destroys) all butterflies while in MissileCommand, the agent wins if it destroys at least one missile. This is the reason for having a more loose equation for MissileCommand than Butterflies.

Solarfox

$$UCB_+ = \overline{X_j} + \frac{\sqrt{d_j}}{n_j} \tag{12}$$

Equation 12 is a variant of the original UCB1 equation. The exploitation term is the same while the exploration term is simplified to select the deepest least selected node regardless of anything else.

$$UCB_{++} = \overline{X_j} + 2 \cdot \frac{E_{xy}}{X_j} \tag{13}$$

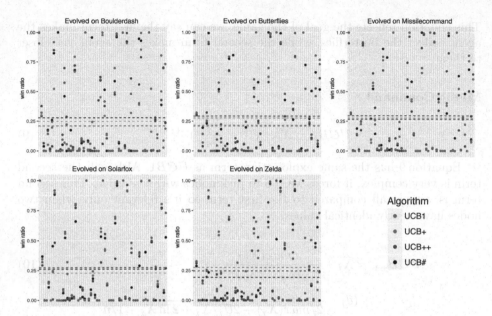

Fig. 2. Each graph shows the win ratio in all the games of the equations evolved and UCB1. Each column in a graph is a game and each dot in the column represents a win ratio. The dotted lines show the average win ratio across all the games.

Equation 13 consists of two parts. The first part is similar to the exploitation term in the $UCB1$ Eq. 1. The second part pushes the agent towards the most visited position with the least total reward.

$$UCB_\# = 2 \cdot \overline{X_j} + \frac{1}{min(D_{mov})} \tag{14}$$

Equation 14 is similar to the MissileCommand Eq. 11 but with a different target. It focuses more on the exploitation term (increase the average score) than on getting closer to movable objects. The reason for this is that in Solarfox, the movable objects can be gems, enemies, and missiles. The agent is not able to differentiate between these three movable objects.

Zelda

$$UCB_+ = (n + max(X_j))^{(n+max(X_j))} \tag{15}$$

Equation 15 is pure exploitation. This equation selects the node with maximum value. This new equation leads the player to be more courageous which then leads to a higher win rate and a higher score than $UCB1$.

$$UCB_{++} = 0.1 \cdot max(X_j) \cdot (\frac{1}{\sqrt{n_j}} - R_j - \sqrt{0.5 \cdot U_j} + \frac{n_j^{0.25} \cdot (2 \cdot d_j + 1)}{30 + E_{xy} - max(E_{xy})}) \tag{16}$$

Equation 16 is a very complex equation but it consists of two parts. The first one is exploitation using max value which forces the agent to be more courageous. The second part consists of multiple parts which are all related to exploration. These parts push the agent to explore the least visited node with the least repetition of the same action, the least useless actions, and the least visited position on the map. The main reason of having a very complex equation is Zelda being a hard game with multiple objectives: navigating the level, avoiding or killing enemies, getting the key then reach goal.

$$UCB_{\#} = \sqrt{max(X_j - 0.25)} + (\Sigma D_{res})^{0.5 \cdot max(D_{mov})}$$
$$+ (max(X_j) \cdot \Sigma D_{immov})^{-0.5 \cdot E_{xy}} + 0.1 \cdot n \qquad (17)$$

Equation 17 consists of three main parts as $0.1 \cdot n$ is equal for all children of the same node. The first part is the exploitation term, while the others are very complex terms for exploration and evading the enemies. The reason of having a very complex equation is the same for Eq. 16.

4.2   Testing Evolved Equations on All Other Games

We ran all evolved equations on all 62 public games in GVGAI framework to see if any of these equations can be generalized. All the results are shown in Fig. 2. The average win ratio of the evolved equations is generally rather similar to $UCB1$ on average. In particular the two $UCB_{\#}$ equations evolved for Butterflies and Missile Command are better than $UCB1$ over all games, in the latter case with a gain of 0.02 (2%) for the win ratio. The only $UCB_{\#}$ that performs poorly compared to the others is the one evolved for Zelda. The probable reason is that the evolved formula for Zelda, a complex game, overfit to this game (as evidenced by the complexity and length of the formula).

For over 20 games, excluded the ones used in the evolutionary process, one of the evolved equation could score an improvement in the win ratio of 0.05 (5%). In particular in some cases the gain is more than 0.6 (60%), resulting in the algorithm mastering the game. For example, $UCB_{\#}$ evolved for Boulderdash in the games Frogs, Camel Race and Zelda is remarkable, as it takes MCTS to win rates of 96%, 100% and 70% respectively. This happens because the evolved formula embeds important information about the game: the benefit of decreasing the distance from portals.

Another great example is $UCB_{\#}$ evolved for Butterflies, which encapsulates the importance of staying close to NPCs (either to collect resources or to kill enemies) in the games of DigDug (80%), Missile Command (100%), Survive Zombies (72%) and Wait For Breakfast (50%).

Table 2. Variables used in the formula and their meanings, as well as what type of variable it is (tree variable, agent variable or game variable).

Variables		
d_j	Tree	Child depth
n	Tree	Parent visits
n_j	Tree	Child visits
X_j	Tree	Child value
U_j	Agent	Useless moves for this child
E_{xy}	Agent	Number of visits of the current tile
R_j	Agent	Repeated actions as the current
RV_j	Agent	Opposite action count to the current
D_{mov}	Game	Distance from movable object
D_{immov}	Game	Distance from immovable object
D_{npc}	Game	Distance from NPC
D_{port}	Game	Distance from portal
N_{port}	Game	Number of portals

5   Discussion and Conclusion

In this paper we have presented a system to evolve heuristics, used in the node selection phase of MCTS, for specific games. The evolutionary process implements a Genetic Programming technique that promotes chromosomes with the highest win rate. The goal is to examine the possibility of systematically finding UCB alternatives.

Our data supports the hypothesis that it is possible to find significantly enhance heuristics. Moreover, we can argue that embedding knowledge about the game ($UCB_{\#}$) and about the agent's behavior (both UCB_{++} and $UCB_{\#}$) allows to get exceptional improvements. With either UCB_{++} or $UCB_{\#}$ we were able to beat $UCB1$ in all the five games used in our experiments; UCB_+ was able to beat $UCB1$ for three games, while using the same information. This supports the idea of developing a portfolio of equations that can conveniently be selected by an hyper-heuristic agent or through algorithm selection to achieve higher performance.

Many of the UCB alternatives evolved still resemble the exploitation/exploration structure of the original UCB. While the exploitation term is still the same, although sporadically swapped or enhanced by the mixmax modification, the equations instead push the concept of exploration toward different meanings, such as spatial exploration and game-element hunt, embodying in the equation some general knowledge of the domain of games. One might even use the evolved formula to better understand the games.

Subsequently we tested the evolved equations across all games currently available in the GVG-AI framework. We could notice an overall slight improvement for $UCB_\#$ evolved for Missile Command and Butterflies. We also noted how a single clean equation can behave very well on games that share some design aspect. This encourages us to evolve heuristics not just for a single game but for clusters of games.

References

1. Auer, P., Cesa-Bianchi, N., Fischer, P.: Finite-time analysis of the multiarmed bandit problem. Mach. Learn. **47**(2–3), 235–256 (2002)
2. Bäck, T., Schwefel, H.P.: An overview of evolutionary algorithms for parameter optimization. Evol. Comput. **1**(1), 1–23 (1993)
3. Baier, H., Winands, M.H.: Monte-Carlo Tree Search and minimax hybrids. In: 2013 IEEE Conference on Computational Intelligence in Games (CIG), pp. 1–8. IEEE (2013)
4. Browne, C.: Towards MCTS for creative domains. In: Proceedings of the International Conference on Computational Creativity, Mexico City, Mexico, pp. 96–101 (2011)
5. Browne, C.B., Powley, E., Whitehouse, D., Lucas, S.M., Cowling, P.I., Rohlfshagen, P., Tavener, S., Perez, D., Samothrakis, S., Colton, S.: A survey of Monte Carlo Tree Search methods. IEEE Trans. Comput. Intell. AI Games **4**(1), 1–43 (2012)
6. Burke, E.K., Gendreau, M., Hyde, M., Kendall, G., Ochoa, G., Özcan, E., Qu, R.: Hyper-heuristics: a survey of the state of the art. J. Oper. Res. Soc. **64**(12), 1695–1724 (2013)
7. Cazenave, T.: Evolving Monte Carlo Tree Search Algorithms. Dept. Inf., Univ. Paris 8 (2007)
8. Eiben, A.E., Smith, J.E.: Introduction to Evolutionary Computing, vol. 53. Springer, Heidelberg (2003)
9. Frydenberg, F., Andersen, K.R., Risi, S., Togelius, J.: Investigating MCTS modifications in general video game playing. In: 2015 IEEE Conference on Computational Intelligence and Games (CIG), pp. 107–113. IEEE (2015)
10. Jacobsen, E.J., Greve, R., Togelius, J.: Monte Mario: platforming with MCTS. In: Proceedings of the 2014 Conference on Genetic and Evolutionary Computation, pp. 293–300. ACM (2014)
11. Justesen, N., Mahlmann, T., Togelius, J.: Online evolution for multi-action adversarial games. In: Squillero, G., Burelli, P. (eds.) EvoApplications 2016. LNCS, vol. 9597, pp. 590–603. Springer, Cham (2016). doi:10.1007/978-3-319-31204-0_38
12. Kotthoff, L.: Algorithm selection for combinatorial search problems: a survey. AI Mag. **35**(3), 48–60 (2014)
13. Levine, J., Congdon, C.B., Ebner, M., Kendall, G., Lucas, S.M., Miikkulainen, R., Schaul, T., Thompson, T.: General video game playing. Dagstuhl Follow-Ups **6** (2013)
14. McGuinness, C.: Monte Carlo Tree Search: Analysis and Applications. Ph.D. thesis (2016)
15. Park, H., Kim, K.J.: MCTS with influence map for general video game playing. In: 2015 IEEE Conference on Computational Intelligence and Games (CIG), pp. 534–535. IEEE (2015)
16. Perez, D., Samothrakis, S., Lucas, S., Rohlfshagen, P.: Rolling horizon evolution versus tree search for navigation in single-player real-time games. In: Proceedings of the 15th Annual Conference on Genetic and Evolutionary Computation, pp. 351–358. ACM (2013)

17. Perez, D., Samothrakis, S., Togelius, J., Schaul, T., Lucas, S., Couëtoux, A., Lee, J., Lim, C.U., Thompson, T.: The 2014 General Video Game Playing Competition (2015)
18. Perez-Liebana, D., Samothrakis, S., Togelius, J., Schaul, T., Lucas, S.M.: General Video Game AI: Competition, Challenges and Opportunities (2016)
19. Pettit, J., Helmbold, D.: Evolutionary learning of policies for MCTS simulations. In: Proceedings of the International Conference on the Foundations of Digital Games, pp. 212–219. ACM (2012)
20. Poli, R., Langdon, W.B., McPhee, N.F., Koza, J.R.: A Field Guide to Genetic Programming. Lulu.com, Raleigh (2008)
21. Rice, J.R.: The algorithm selection problem. Adv. Comput. **15**, 65–118 (1976)
22. Rimmel, A., Teytaud, O., Lee, C.S., Yen, S.J., Wang, M.H., Tsai, S.R.: Current frontiers in computer go. IEEE Trans. Comput. Intell. AI Games **2**(4), 229–238 (2010)
23. Whitley, D.: A genetic algorithm tutorial. Stat. Comput. **4**(2), 65–85 (1994)

Relief Camp Manager: A Serious Game Using the World Health Organization's Relief Camp Guidelines

Hamna Aslam^(⊠), Anton Sidorov, Nikita Bogomazov, Fedor Berezyuk,
and Joseph Alexander Brown

Artificial Intelligence in Games Development Lab,
Innopolis University, Innopolis 420500, Russian Federation
{h.aslam,j.brown}@innopolis.ru

Abstract. Emergency management plans rely on training in order to provide support to first responders, government planners, and affected persons in potential disaster zone. Serious Games have proved to be useful in capturing and invoking people's attention and emergency management education is also being delivered through games. The paper presents a relief camp game developed using the figures from World Health Organization's (WHO) report on water, sanitation and hygiene guidelines in emergencies. The game play provides player an understanding of the management of relief camps by giving them a supervisory role to design and organize camp areas. It also encourages players to introduce their own ideas in setting up relief camps. The player is competing against evolutionary computation algorithm. The aims are to create awareness about relief camp management strategies and improving the present approaches for better plans via human competitive testing.

Keywords: Serious games · Relief camp management · Emergency management · Evolutionary computation · Disaster management

1 Introduction

Serious games are an effective tool for education, training and research [1]. Research on the application of serious games is extending areas where these can be useful in achieving the desired research objectives. [2] describes the benefits and challenges of conducting emergency management research using serious gaming technology and simulations. Serious games for training and research purposes are cost effective and provide benefits of changing control variables to generate the maximum possibilities and also allows repetition of the process to analyze outcomes over different settings. There are some challenges, the most prominent one is the difficulty of accurate analysis of different aspects of outcome in relation to the natural environment. The outcome generated from a virtual environment may not align with the outcome in a real emergency situation. A solution to this problem is to list the differences between the virtual

© Springer International Publishing AG 2017
G. Squillero and K. Sim (Eds.): EvoApplications 2017, Part I, LNCS 10199, pp. 407–417, 2017.
DOI: 10.1007/978-3-319-55849-3_27

and real settings. [3] presents SONNA, a research project analyzes the impact of serious games and social media as tools for education and effective learning. It investigates the implications of gaming technology and social network on educating individuals of different age groups. For this purpose, two games are being developed related to citizenship education and bioethics. [4] also considers business games an effective tool to teach and train engineering students for future professional and industrial activities.

In the same manner [5] focuses on game based language learning and teaching. It describes the importance of humor and fun as a strategy for enhancing the learning process. Incorporation of fun element into serious games is a difficult task because of the multi-cultural diversity of the players. It also states that humor should be easily perceivable by all the players so they can enjoy the fun elements in the game.

Serious games are now a significant element in health systems too. [6] presents a modular system that supports serious games targeted for physical therapy by using a back office system for the remote physical therapy programs. As it states, the functions and features of a back office system are accessible by authenticated users. The doctors handle patient profiles and decide their therapy program with the therapist. The health professionals along with the patients work in a systematic configuration. With the back office system, health professionals have an easy access to any patient's statistics and ongoing therapy results. This project is one of the finest display of remote patient monitoring. Also [7,8] are using whack-a-mole, for an on-going clinical study to check age related cognitive decline. Results from the game have suggested that serious games are a useful way to measure cognitive ability of individuals and provide accurate results. For emergency decision making, sequential games can help take dynamic decisions and modify relief plans according to the situations. Games allow for testing decision plans for all the possible crises states and under different sets of information [9]. [10] presents a serious game; Disaster In My Backyard, to introduce people to disaster management and how information dissemination takes place during disasters. The game presents a flood due to heavy rains. It allows player to process information and communicate with other teams to make decisions about evacuation plans and manage resources. The game has several features such as deciding location, adding volunteers and managing budget and resources to help victims.

Examining tools from games, Procedural Content Generation (PCG) is any algorithmic method for the development of game assets without or with minimal human development, see [11]. Numerous researchers have examined problems in games and architectural settings involving the placement and design of buildings to meet with user constraints [12–14]. To examine evolutionary techniques, [15] used Genetic Programming (GP) to place rooms inside of a dungeon level.

This paper presents a serious game, Relief camp manager (RCM), for the building of relief camps. RCM is a construction and management simulator for refugee relief camps. The player is the manager of the relief camp area and their tasks include setting up camps as well as managing and optimizing available resources. There is a competition between the player and the computer driven opponent which is the Evolutionary Algorithm (EA), see [16] for an overview of methods. The game has been developed for two purposes; first promoting awareness and training about the management of relief camps and second to improve current organization plans and introduce new strategies for relief camps establishment and operations by using human competitive testing.

The remainder of this paper is organized as follows. Section 2 explains our motivation behind developing RCM game by describing the need of organized relief camps via the statistics of the displaced people in disasters. The information which has been adopted from the report by WHO, as game playing strategy for the evolutionary computation algorithm has also been described. Section 3 discusses evolutionary computation algorithm. Section 4 illustrates the game design and play process. Section 5 details the purpose and research benefit of human competitive testing for the establishment of relief camps. And finally Sect. 6 draws some conclusions and give some ideas for further research and development.

2   WHO's Guidelines on Water, Sanitation and Hygiene

Presently 2.6 million refugees live in camps worldwide [17]. Since 2008 an average of 26.4 million people are displaced by disasters every year, which is equivalent to one person displaced every second [18].

Table 1 shows figure of refugees and conflict-related internally displaced people (IDPs) from the year 2011–2015 by Global Internal Displacement Database [18].

Table 1. Global internal displacement database; refugees and conflict-related IDPs [18]

Year	Refugees	Conflict-related IDPs
2011	15.2 M	26.4 M
2012	15.4 M	28.8 M
2013	16.7 M	33.3 M
2014	19.5 M	38.0 M
2015	21.3 M	40.8 M

In these circumstances, relief camps have become indispensable shelters to displaced people. Currently, a relief camp is not just a roof for temporary shelter but an organized management system. The unpredictable severity and dynamics of the situation has made relief camp management quite challenging. It is difficult to estimate the exact number and needs of the displaced as natural disasters and emergencies create unpredictable circumstances. The high unpredictability and chaos can be mitigated with careful preparations beforehand. We need a systematic approach to deal with the challenges of relief establishment problems.

The similar problem is addressed by [19] in terms of mathematical modelling of the military contingency base camp design. The model does the resource estimation for the base camps by using linear equations and a visualization of the design in a 3D tool.

In the same manner, Our goal is to make relief camps;

An organized place of shelter capable of running till the duration of displacement; providing the atmosphere and basic necessities of survival by optimizing available resources.

The World Health Organization's report on water, sanitation and hygiene specifications [20] details individual requirements of water for fulfilling basic necessities as well as instructions for relief camps setup to maintain hygienic conditions. It also shows sample calculations of water demand for survival and long term solutions for maintaining relief camps. This report provides a structure to maintain healthy conditions for relief camps. RCM is developed using these guidelines. The player has to provide these basic facilities to all the residents of relief camp in a consistent way in order to earn points. Table 2 shows some of the figures implemented in the game from WHO and United Nations High Commissioner for Refugees (UNHCR) emergency handbook [21]

The challenge of resource optimization must be dealt with using wise strategies when available resources would be less than the needs of the people. The provision of resources according to the figures shown in Table 2 will earn high points for the player.

Table 2. Guidlines and figures by WHO and UNHCR implemented in the game [20,21]

Basic necessities	Provision guideline
Drinking water (per person)	3 litres per day approx
Tent to water point distance	500 m (max)
Distance between toilets and tents	50 m
Distance between toilets and water container	30 m (min)

3 Evolutionary Algorithms

Evolutionary algorithms [16,22] utilize the phenomenon of natural selection to evolve pathways towards the goal. It incorporates techniques such as crossover and mutations to find various possible solutions to the problem and ultimately the fittest solution survives.

The computer opponent is played by the evolutionary algorithm to generate relief camp designs. The algorithm has the following specifications.

Representation

The population of data structures consists of water distribution among people and relief tent placements with respect to each other as well as to water container and toilets.

Evaluation

A data structure is evaluated as the sum of all happiness.

Happiness is the feedback from the residents of the relief camps on 0 to 100% scale, about the satisfaction related to the amount of water they are getting from the camp manager as well as the placement of structures (i.e. toilets, water containers) in the camps.

The happiness level of refugees at the end of simulation is calculated. The parameters for happiness calculation along with their maximum values are shown in Table 2. Death of refugees give zero happiness and may impact on others happiness as well. Ability to maintain all functions of life according to the standard values over the entire simulation scores 100.

Selection

We have applied single tournament selection technique [16] such as population is shuffled randomly and divided into two small groups and two most fit data structures among each group are chosen to be parents for crossover.

Variance

The Variance operators are one point crossover and two point mutation [16].

Crossover takes two parents as shown in Fig. 1 and selects some properties from each parent by toggling the bits to produce two children, see Fig. 2.

Where $\alpha(x, y)$ corresponds to placements of tents in the field area
$\beta(x, y)$, placements of toilets in the field area
$\gamma(x, y)$, placements of water containers
And 'W' refers to water distribution per person.

The Bits, 1s and 0s are randomly toggled and a '0' corresponds to parent 1 and a '1' corresponds to parent 2. Parameters corresponding to bit 0 are taken from parent 1 and corresponding to bit 1 are taken from parent 2 to produce child 1 and child 2, see Fig. 3.

Mutation can be of two types, changing the placement of the tents, water tanks and toilets or replace these structures with each other.

Replacement

Replacement happens according to absolute fitness replacement technique that replaces lowest fitness members of the population with the children [16].

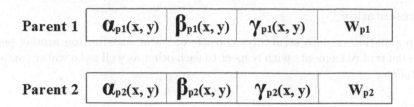

Fig. 1. Parents for crossover

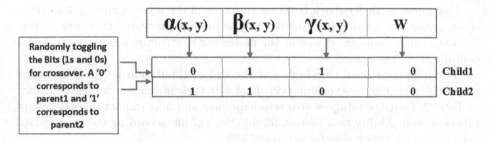

Fig. 2. Toggling bits for crossover, Bit 0 represents Parent 1 and Bit 1 represents Parent 2

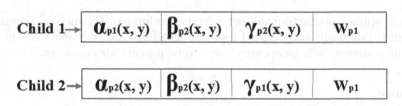

Fig. 3. Child 1 and child 2 after crossover

4 Game Play

Relief camp manager game initially displays a start screen where a player can see a menu on the left side of the screen where amount of resources can be set as shown in Fig. 4. After specifying value for the resources the player presses the start button and game shifts to the next screen as shown in Fig. 5.

In Fig. 5 upper left corner shows number of tents, toilets and water containers that must be placed on the field. The bottom left corner shows total number of people for the camp and the amount of water available in liters.

The player can see the happiness of the camp at the upper right corner of the screen, after placing all the resources. Player can also change the placement of tents and water containers etc. after placing them on the field. The right click on any of the items such as tents, toilets and water containers show the distance of them with respect to all other placements. So, the player can easily adjust the distance between different type of items.

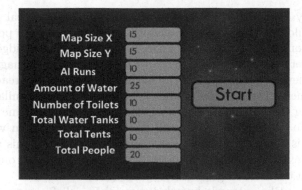

Fig. 4. Start screen of the RCM game

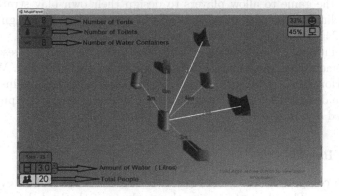

Fig. 5. Game play interface

5 Human Competitive Testing

The player versus opponent approach is implying sandboxing (i.e. minimal restrictions on the player) versus evolutionary computation algorithm. The play will be a competition between the player who is playing entirely according to his own ideas and the computer driven opponent which is the evolutionary computation algorithm trying to achieve WHO's strategies for setting up relief camps.

The significance of sandboxing is not just limited to getting an entertainment element, it allows to benefit from the knowledge of the players. Games featuring a possibility of different moves other than the standard play directions helps in exploring better plans. In this way, implications of serious gaming will not be limited to training and education but also helps in exploring more ways to carry out a task and at the same time allows to benefit from the knowledge of the players for an improved plan.

[23] emphasizes upon realizing the importance of integrating local people's knowledge in disaster preparedness plans. Some examples are presented where members of the community had more awareness about the geology of the area

and probability of the occurrence of disasters than the technical people. Lives and money could have been saved if attention was paid to local people's advice while making construction decisions. There is a strong need to bridge the communication gap between community members and emergency management policy makers. Interviews and surveys are the most common ways to reach out to the people and benefit from the useful knowledge they possess. Similarly, with the trend of adding realism to the serious games, it has also become necessary to allow players to speak their minds and try things in their own way to get to the goal. This is especially true for the management games. This approach has advantages of exploring maximum possible means of carrying out a plan and benefiting from the knowledge and ideas of players.

We want to utilize player's knowledge to make relief camps establishment and management a highly organized system and have incorporated sandboxing features in the game to allow players to design their own play strategies. It is also compelling for the players as game poses no limitations on design and setup strategies [24].

The evolutionary computation algorithm is trying to optimize resources and camp placements using standard directions provided by the WHO. We want to see the performance of evolutionary computation algorithms against humans. The scheme designed by the player and through evolutionary computation can be compared or combined to get the near optimal solution.

5.1   Test Results

The human competitive test was done with 30 playtesters and 30 evolutionary algorithm runs. The playtesters were the students of the bachelors program in information technology and have the average age of 21. All of them were not familiar with the relief camp design methods. Players were given 20 min before starting the playtest so that they familiarize themselves with the game.

The test was conducted on five problem cases, starting from the easier settings to the complex. The evolutionary algorithm was also run on the five problem case settings. The results of the human competitive testing are shown in Table 3.

The average and 95% confidence interval (CI) for the 30 human tests and evolutionary algorithm runs shows that evolutionary algorithm had maximum score on each run. In all cases the algorithm performed statistically significantly better than the human player.

Comparing players test results with each other over different settings and with the algorithm is significant as the first test showed a considerable difference between human and algorithm results. The game settings were the easiest in the first set to get high percentage in result. The considerably low average of result percentage in the first test by players is due to the fact that they were not familiar with the relief camp design in the beginning and the game play results also showed an improvement in players performances as they played successive levels of the game settings.

Players were given a questionnaire at the end of the playtesting. They were asked about the idea they got from the game and were they able to understand the game more as they played successive levels. Ninety percent of the participants were able to understand that the purpose of the game is to find the optimal relief camp design. They also mentioned that they were familiarized about the relief camp designs through the game. A few participants thought that the game is about residential area management. The participants also provided feedback regarding the entertainment element in the game saying that they enjoyed the game but it can be more fun if graphics are improved and some background music had been added. The playtest and questionnaire results show that serious game can be used as an effective tool for relief camp design and management training.

Table 3. Human competitive test results

Problem case	Humans (Average ± CI)	Evolutionary algorithm (Average ± CI)
1	49.7 ± 9.56	100 ± 0.00
2	78.56 ± 7.20	100 ± 0.00
3	86.46 ± 7.47	100 ± 0.00
4	80.66 ± 3.20	100 ± 0.00
5	73.8 ± 5.92	98.9 ± 3.46

6   Conclusions and Future Recommendations

Our work uses a serious game and evolutionary computation algorithm for relief camps design and training. The serious game based training for relief camps opens many possibilities for the camp design and resource placements through which bad as well as effective camp designs can be observed. The evolutionary algorithm is developed to generate the optimal design according to the quantity of resources available. Both approaches, serious game based training as well as evolutionary generation of camp designs have significance to get advantageous solutions. The human solution can be optimized by comparing it to evolutionary computation outcomes and people can be trained against all the possibilities through serious gaming.

The motivation for this research is to make relief camp establishment a systematic process starting from its design to operations and management. We have achieved the first goal of systematic design of a camp which is meant to assure that residents of the camp are as comfortable as possible with the placements of the resources and they do not have to bear unnecessary difficulties in accessing the facilities provided. Also keeping in check that camp design must assure maintenance of hygienic conditions.

The work has already been done in terms of figures and guidelines from the UN agencies and the WHO. We have the standards and benchmarks to get the optimal camp design; however the practical implementation of these guidelines is challenging due to time constraints and each relief camp has different field area, different number of displaced people and available resources. This requires optimization according to the available resources. As a result of which the best solution may not be able to accommodate the exact figures from the WHO guidelines; however it tries to implement the standards as near as possible. The evolutionary algorithm generates the solutions according to the standards and while facing resource constraints, it generates the optimal solutions through fitness function.

Presently, we incorporate resource placements for the camp and water distribution among people. In future the work can be extended to take into account other logistics for the camps such as provision of medicines, electricity, fire breaks management and refusal management. The dynamics can also be added both to the game and the algorithm to manage the changing number of resources and residents of relief camps.

References

1. Wong, W.L., Shen, C., Nocera, L., Carriazo, E., Tang, F., Bugga, S., Narayanan, H., Wang, H., Ritterfeld, U.: Serious video game effectiveness. In: Proceedings of the International Conference on Advances in Computer Entertainment Technology, pp. 49–55. ACM (2007)
2. Van Ruijven, T.: Serious games as experiments for emergency management research: a review. In: ISCRAM 2011: Proceedings of the 8th International Conference on Information Systems for Crisis Response and Management, Lisbon, Portugal, pp. 8–11. ISCRAM (2011)
3. Carrozzino, M., Evangelista, C., Brondi, R., Lorenzini, C., Bergamasco, M.: Social networks and web-based serious games as novel educational tools. Procedia Comput. Sci. **15**, 303–306 (2012)
4. Khrushchev, Y., Batseva, N., Fix, N., Chesnokova, I., Khar kovskaya, V.: Business games in training engineering students. Procedia-Soc. Behav. Sci. **206**, 267–271 (2015)
5. Lombardi, I.: Not-so-serious games for language learning. now with 99, 9% more humour on top. Procedia Comput. Sci. **15**, 148–158 (2012)
6. Martins, T., Carvalho, V., Soares, F.: Web platform for serious games management. Procedia Comput. Sci. **64**, 1115–1123 (2015)
7. Tong, T., Chignell, M., Sieminowski, T.: Case study: a serious game for neurorehabilitation assessment. Procedia Comput. Sci. **69**, 125–131 (2015)
8. Tong, T., Guana, V., Jovanovic, A., Tran, F., Mozafari, G., Chignell, M., Stroulia, E.: Rapid deployment and evaluation of mobile serious games: a cognitive assessment case study. Procedia Comput. Sci. **69**, 96–103 (2015)
9. Yang, J., Xu, C.: Emergency decision engineering model based on sequential games. Syst. Eng. Procedia **5**, 276–282 (2012)
10. Meesters, K., van de Walle, B.: Disaster in my backyard: a serious game introduction to disaster information management. In: Comes, T., Fiedrich, F., Fortier, S., Geldermann, J., Müller, T. (eds.) Proceedings of the 10th International ISCRAM Conference-Baden-Baden, Germany (2013)

11. Togelius, J., Yannakakis, G., Stanley, K., Browne, C.: Search-based procedural content generation: a taxonomy and survey. IEEE Trans. Computat. Intell. AI Games **3**(3), 172–186 (2011)
12. Hahn, E., Bose, P., Whitehead, A.: Lazy generation of building interiors in realtime. In: Canadian Conference on Electrical and Computer Engineering, CCECE 2006, pp. 2441–2444 (2006)
13. Merrell, P., Schkufza, E., Koltun, V.: Computer-generated residential building layouts. In: ACM SIGGRAPH Asia 2010 Papers, SIGGRAPH ASIA 2010, pp. 181:1–181:12. ACM, New York (2010)
14. Flack, R.W.J., Ross, B.J.: Evolution of architectural floor plans. In: Chio, C., et al. (eds.) EvoApplications 2011. LNCS, vol. 6625, pp. 313–322. Springer, Heidelberg (2011). doi:10.1007/978-3-642-20520-0_32
15. Valtchanov, V., Brown, J.A.: Evolving dungeon crawler levels with relative placement. In: Proceedings of the Fifth International C* Conference on Computer Science and Software Engineering. C3S2E 2012, pp. 27–35. ACM, New York (2012)
16. Ashlock, D.A.: Evolutionary Computation for Modeling and Optimization. Springer, New York (2006)
17. UNHCR: 'Shelter'. UNHCR (2016). Accessed 6 Oct 2016
18. Yonetani, M., Lavell, C., Bower, E., Meneghetti, L., OConnor, K.: Global estimates 2015, people displaced by disasters. In: IDMC, Internal Displacement Monitoring Centre (2016). Accessed 6 Oct 2016
19. Poreddy, B.R., Daniels, B.: Mathematical model of sub-system interactions for forward operating bases. In: IIE Annual Conference. Proceedings, Institute of Industrial Engineers-Publisher, p. 1 (2012)
20. Reed, R., Godfrey, S., Kayaga, S., Reed, B., Rouse, J., Fisher, J., Vilholth, K., Odhiambo, F.: Technical notes on drinking-water, sanitation and hygiene in emergencies (2013)
21. UNHCR: Comparison of humanitarian standards, the sphere project and UNHCR emergency handbook (2001). Accessed 26 Oct 2016
22. De Jong, K.A.: Evolutionary Computation: A Unified Approach. MIT Press, Cambridge (2006)
23. Dekens, J.: Herders of chitral the lost messengers, community risk assessment (CRA) toolkit (2007)
24. Ocio, S., Brugos, J.A.L.: Multi-agent systems and sandbox games. AISB 2009 (2009)

Analysis of Vanilla Rolling Horizon Evolution Parameters in General Video Game Playing

Raluca D. Gaina(✉), Jialin Liu, Simon M. Lucas, and Diego Pérez-Liébana

School of Computer Science and Electronic Engineering,
University of Essex, Colchester CO4 3SQ, UK
{rdgain,jialin.liu,sml,dperez}@essex.ac.uk

Abstract. Monte Carlo Tree Search techniques have generally dominated General Video Game Playing, but recent research has started looking at Evolutionary Algorithms and their potential at matching Tree Search level of play or even outperforming these methods. Online or Rolling Horizon Evolution is one of the options available to evolve sequences of actions for planning in General Video Game Playing, but no research has been done up to date that explores the capabilities of the vanilla version of this algorithm in multiple games. This study aims to critically analyse the different configurations regarding population size and individual length in a set of 20 games from the General Video Game AI corpus. Distinctions are made between deterministic and stochastic games, and the implications of using superior time budgets are studied. Results show that there is scope for the use of these techniques, which in some configurations outperform Monte Carlo Tree Search, and also suggest that further research in these methods could boost their performance.

Keywords: General Video Game Playing · Rolling Horizon Evolution · Games · Monte Carlo Tree Search · Random search

1 Introduction

General Video Game Playing (GVGP) is a sub-domain of Artificial General Intelligence (AGI), which aims to create an agent capable of achieving a high level of play in any given environment, that was potentially previously unknown. It uses video games as testbeds for this purpose because of their complex nature, offering practical problems in a constrained environment where it is easy to quantify results and observe performance. In contrast with other domains such as robotics, where errors are expensive to correct, video games are cheap alternatives for testing AI algorithms, as well as having the possibility of multiple tests run very quickly (due to modern computational power).

The General Video Game AI Competition (GVGAI) [22,23] offers a large corpus of games described in a plain text language, making it easy to run general AI agents in several different environments and analyse their performance.

© Springer International Publishing AG 2017
G. Squillero and K. Sim (Eds.): EvoApplications 2017, Part I, LNCS 10199, pp. 418–434, 2017.
DOI: 10.1007/978-3-319-55849-3_28

The competition has already completed three editions of its single player track (starting in 2014), with two additional tracks running in 2016 for two player games [7] and level generation [11]. Therefore, it is attracting a large interest on an international scale, with close to a hundred participants every year across its different tracks.

This competition is becoming a popular way of benchmarking AI algorithms such as enforced hill climbing [2], algorithms employing advanced path finding or using the knowledge gained during the game in interesting ways [6,19], or dominant Monte Carlo Tree Search techniques [18]. All of the authors appear to agree on the complexity of the problem proposed, as well as its importance, going beyond the realm of video games towards that of AGI.

Among the techniques employed over the last years of the GVGAI, one of the most promising is that of Rolling Horizon Evolutionary Algorithms (RHEA). These methods, rather than basing the search on game tree structures, use influences from biological sciences to evolve a population of individuals until a suitable one, corresponding to a solution to the problem, is obtained. The way they are applied to the domain of GVGP is by encoding sequences of in-game actions as individuals, using heuristics to analyse the value of each sequence [20].

Up to date, there is no in depth evaluation of the vanilla version of RHEA on the GVGAI framework, attending to certain crucial parameters such as population size and individual length. It is hardly possible that the same parameter setting would work equally well for all of the assorted games of the GVGAI corpus: on one hand, these games can vary in many forms, such as their level of stochasticity, average duration of a game, presence or absence of other NPCs, etc., but on the other hand, variations of the population size and the lengths of the action sequences explored may be sensitive to variations in the game design space.

The first objective of this paper is to perform an analysis of the vanilla version of RHEA (see Sect. 3.2) on a subset of 20 GVGAI games, with special focus on the population size and the individual length of this technique. This analysis is performed attending to the different games presented, and their stochastic nature. Additionally, this study aims to make a comparison with the sample Open Loop Monte Carlo Tree Search (OLMCTS), the best sample agent included in the GVGAI framework, which is actually the starting point of several winners of the competition in past editions.

The rest of this paper is structured as follows: Sect. 2 reviews work already present in the literature on this topic, with Sect. 3 detailing background information on the framework and algorithms used. Section 4 describes the approach taken and the experimental setup, while Sect. 5 presents the results obtained from this experiment. The paper concludes in Sect. 6 with a discussion of the results and notes on future work that will be undertaken as a consequence of this study.

2   Relevant Research

The popularity of General Game Playing (GGP) has increased in the last decade, since M. Genesereth et al. [8] organised the first GGP competition allowing participants to submit game agents to play in a diverse collection of board games. Sharma et al. [25] motivates research in this area by bringing to attention how agents trained without prior knowledge of the game and excelling in specific games, such as TD-Gammon in Backgammon [26] and Blondie24 in Checkers [1], cannot be successfully applied in other scenarios or environments.

The problem is further expanded to video games in General Video Game Playing (GVGP [12]), which provide the agents with new and possibly more complex challenges due to a higher and continuous, in practice, rate of actions. One of the first frameworks to allow testing of such general agents was the Arcade Learning Environment (ALE) [3], later used as benchmark for applying Deep Q-Learning to achieve human level of play on the Atari 2600 collection [16]. The way the world was presented to the agents in this framework was via screen capture; they would return an action to be performed and the next game state would be processed by the system.

Monte Carlo Tree Search methods have dominated GVGP so far, and their variations have been explored in various works [5]. However, Evolutionary Algorithms (EA) show great promise at obtaining just as good, if not better, performance. Perez et al. [21] compare EA techniques with tree search on the Physical Salesman Travelling Problem, and their results are satisfactory, encouraging research in the area. In their work, the authors employ several techniques to improve the state evaluation function, such as avoiding opposite actions, movement blocks and pheromone exploration.

Samothrakis et al. [24] compare two variations of the Rolling Horizon setting of EAs in a number of continuous environments, including a Lunar Lander game. The first algorithm uses a co-variance matrix, while the second employs a value optimisation algorithm. The Rolling Horizon refers to evolving plans of actions and, at each game step, executing the first action that appears to be the best at present, while starting fresh and creating a new plan for the next move, sequentially increasing the "horizon". Their research suggests EAs to be viable algorithms in general environments, and that a deeper exploration should be performed with an emphasis on heuristic improvement.

N. Justesen et al. [10] used online evolution for action decision in Hero Academy, a game in which each player counts on multiple units to move in a single turn, presenting a branching factor of a million actions. In this study, groups of actions are evolved for a single turn, to be performed by up to 6 different units. With a fixed population of 100 individuals, the authors show that online evolution is able to beat MCTS and other greedy methods. Later, Wang et al. [27] employed a modified version of online evolution using a portfolio of script to play Starcraft micro. In this work, rather than evolving groups or sequences of actions, the algorithm evolved plans to determine which script (among a set of available ones) each unit should use at each time step. Each gene in the individual represents a script that will be executed by a given unit in the next turn.

Other different approaches to EAs have been explored in the past, such as combining them with other techniques in order to produce hybrids, and take advantage of the benefits of each algorithm [9]. For example, evolution was used during the simulation phase in a Monte Carlo Tree Search algorithm by Perez et al. [19], or, for a different effect, the MCTS parameters were adjusted with evolutionary methods [14]. There has been recent work that has attempted to give more focus to the evolutionary process and instead integrates tree structures into EAs, or uses N-armed bandit techniques and Upper Confidence Bounds (UCB) for informing and guiding the evolution process [13].

3   Background

3.1   The GVGAI Framework

The experiments presented in this paper were run within the General Video Game AI framework[1], frequently used in recent literature for benchmarking Artificial Intelligence agents due to its large and constantly increasing collection of games. This framework currently includes 100 single player and 40 two-player games, of both deterministic and stochastic nature. All of them are real time games, where the agents receive a 1 s time budget for initialisation purposes and a $40ms$ budget for selecting an action to be performed during each game step.

The action space available to the agents is limited to a maximum of 5, although it can vary across games. The agents may choose to perform no action (ACTION_NIL; it is important to note that this is not equivalent to the avatar stopping movement), to move in a certain direction (ACTION_LEFT or RIGHT, UP or DOWN, correspondingly), or to perform a special action (ACTION_USE) that depends on the game, and may range from shooting to creating or activating various game objects.

Concrete information about the game rules is not available to the agents, although they do have access to details about the current game state through a State Observation object. This includes the current score, game tick, a description of the state of the avatar (such as position, orientation, resources etc.), and data about other game objects (such as NPCs, portals or static objects).

Another tool available to the agents through this framework is a Forward Model (FM), which allows for simulation of possible future states of the game (this simulated state may not be accurate in stochastic games). In order to advance the Forward Model, the agent must supply one of the legal actions of the game to an *advance* function, which would roll the state of the game forward following this move.

Games vary in nature not only in their probabilistic states, but also in the presence of certain game objects (e.g. NPCs and portals), scoring methods (binary, in which 1 point is awarded for winning, 0 otherwise; incremental, which sees continuous small rewards spread out in the game; or discontinuous, in which certain actions or sequences of actions may produce a sudden large gain), or the conditions which lead to an end state (e.g. counters, timers or exit doors). This results in a great variety of games, which truly tests the abilities of general agents. Figure 1 shows a few examples of games included in this framework, which were also employed in this study.

---

[1] www.gvgai.net.

The ranking of controllers in the GVGAI competition used for the results analysis of this paper employs a Formula 1 point system per game: agents are sorted based on their performance (win percentage, score and time steps, in this order, with the secondary ones used as tiebreakers if needed) for each game, then awarded a number of points depending on their position: 25 for the first, then 18, 15, 12, 10, 8, 6, 4, 2, 1 and 0 for all subsequent entries. The points are then summed to a total used to determine the position in the overall rankings. This system is meant to emphasise the generic aspect of the competition, as achieving a high average win rate is not equivalent to performing well across all games.

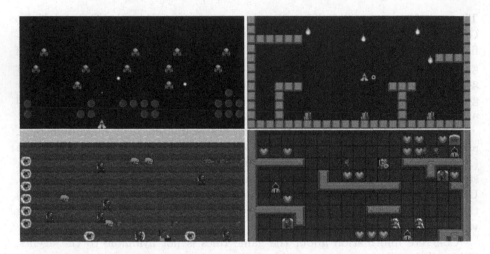

Fig. 1. Games in GVGAI Framework: Aliens, Missile Command, Sea Quest and Survive Zombies (from left corner, clockwise).

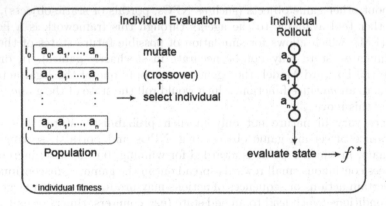

Fig. 2. Rolling Horizon Evolutionary Algorithm cycle.

3.2 Rolling Horizon Evolutionary Algorithms

Rolling Horizon Evolutionary Algorithms (RHEA) [21] are a subset of EAs which use populations of individuals representing action plans or sequences of actions. The individuals are evaluated by simulating moves ahead using a Forward Model. From the current state of the games, all actions (genes of the individual) are executed in order, until a terminal state or the length of the individual is reached. The state reached at that point is then evaluated with a heuristic function and the value assigned as the fitness of the individual (Fig. 2).

In general, the algorithm starts with a random population of individuals. At each game step it applies traditional genetic operators (such as mutation, randomly changing some actions in the sequence, and cross-over, combining individuals in different ways) to obtain new individuals for the next generation of the population. Each one of them is then evaluated and assigned a fitness, according to which the population is sorted and only the best are carried forward to subsequent generations. This process ends when an end condition is satisfied, such as a time or memory limit reached or a certain number of iterations have been performed. The action selected by the algorithm is represented by the first gene in the best individual found at the end of the evolutionary process. The action is played in the game, a new state is received in the next step by the agent, and new iterations are performed to evolve new action plans.

As the agents have a limited amount of time to make decisions in real-time games, one of the popular methods in the literature consists of generating only one new individual at each generation, therefore making it possible to interrupt the process at any point. The most basic form this algorithm can take is that of a Random Mutation Hill Climber [15], where the population size is only 1, using the mutation operator as the only way to navigate through the search space.

3.3 Open Loop Monte Carlo Tree Search (OLMCTS)

Open Loop Monte Carlo Tree Search (OLMCTS) is an MCTS implementation for the GVGAI framework. This particular agent does not store the states of the

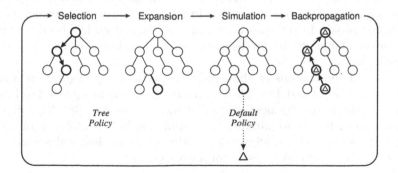

Fig. 3. Monte Carlo Tree Search steps [5]

game in the nodes of the tree, but instead uses the forward model to reevaluate each action. OLMCTS uses four simple steps to produce a high level of play: selection (using a tree policy to select one of the current leaves of the tree, which is not yet fully expanded), expansion (adding a new child of the selected node to the tree), simulation (a Monte Carlo process using the forward model to advance through the game with random actions) and back-propagation (the state reached after the MC simulation is evaluated using a heuristic and its value backed up the tree to the root node, updating all other parent nodes). The steps of the MCTS algorithm are depicted in Fig. 3.

When reaching the limit of its execution budget (memory, time, iterations, or, as is the case of this paper, number of calls to the forward model *advance* function), the algorithm returns action to apply via a recommendation policy. In the GVGAI implementation of this agent, the action returned is that of the child of the root node that has been selected more often. For an in depth description of Monte Carlo Tree Search, variants, improvements, and applications, the reader is referred to [5].

4   Approach and Experimental Setup

4.1   Methods

This paper analyses how modifying the population size (P) and individual length (L) configuration of the vanilla Rolling Horizon Evolutionary Algorithm (RHEA) impacts performance in a generic setting. Exhaustive experiments were run on all combinations between population sizes $P = \{1, 2, 5, 7, 10, 13, 20\}$ and individual lengths $L = \{6, 8, 10, 12, 14, 16, 20\}$. The budget defined for planning at each game step was set as 480 Forward Model calls to the *advance* function, the average number of calls OLMCTS is able to perform in $40ms$ of thinking time in the games of this framework[2]. Larger values for either individual length or population size were not considered due to the limited budget and the complete nature of the experiment (analysis of all combinations); values above 24 would not allow in certain cases for a full evaluation of even one population.

The fitness function used by RHEA evaluates the state reached after executing the sequence of actions in an individual, and returns the current in-game score of the player. In the case where an end-game state has been reached, it instead gives a large penalty for losing the game (or, alternatively, a high reward for winning).

To expand the analysis of the results, a particular configuration was also tested, using $P = 24$ and $L = 20$. Effectively, given the budget of 480 Forward Model calls, this is an equivalent method of Random Search (RS). The algorithm only has enough budget to initialise the population before applying any genetic operator. In essence, this configuration evaluates 24 random walks and returns the first action of the best sequence of moves found.

---

[2] Using these forward model calls instead of real execution time is more robust to fluctuations on the machine used to run the experiments, making it time independent and results comparable across different architectures.

The algorithm itself begins with the initialisation of the population, which sets each individual to a sequence of actions selected uniformly at random. The genes of the individual take integer values in the interval [0, N-1], where N is the number of available actions in that particular game state, therefore each value corresponding to an in-game legal action. The evolutionary process then proceeds in a slightly different way depending on the population size. For the case in which there is only one individual in a population, one new individual is mutated at each iteration and it replaces the first if its fitness is higher (RHEA is set to maximize the fitness provided by the value function).

For a population of size 2, the best individual is passed on to the next generation unchanged (elitism of 1), then uniform crossover and mutation are applied to the 2 individuals to generate the second solution for the new population. If the population contains 3 or more individuals, similar rules apply, but the 2 parents are selected for crossover through a tournament of size 2. The mutation operator always modifies one gene of the individual, chosen uniformly at random. It is important to note that the initialisation is counted in the budget received for evolution, in order to ensure that there is a trade-off in higher population sizes.

In order to validate the results, Open Loop Monte Carlo Tree Search was also tested on the same set of 20 games, under the same budget conditions. OLMCTS has proven to be the dominating technique out of the sample ones provided in the GVGAI competition, with numerous participants using it as a basis for their entries before adding various enhancements on top of its vanilla form. The winner of the first edition of the competition in 2014, Adrien Couëtoux [23], employed an Open Loop technique quite similar to this algorithm.

4.2 Games

All of the combinations explored in this study were run on 20 games of the GVGAI corpus, on all 5 levels, 20 times each, resulting in 100 games played per configuration. The games were selected using two different classifications present in literature in order to balance the game set and analyse performance on an assorted selection of different games. The first classification was that generated by Mark Nelson [17] in his analysis of the vanilla Monte Carlo Tree Search algorithm in 62 of the games in the framework, sorted using the win rate of MCTS as a simple criterion. The second classification considered for this study was the clustering of 49 games by Bontrager et al. [4], which separated the games into groups based on their similarity in terms of game features. Combining these two lists and uniformly sampling from both provided a diverse subset appropriate for this experiment, which contains 10 stochastic and 10 deterministic games. See Table 1 for the name of these games and the indices used in later figures in this document.

5 Results and Discussion

This section presents and analyses the results obtained from different angles. Observations are made attending to the nature of the game and variations of

Table 1. Names, indexes and types of the 20 games from the subset selected. Legend:
S - Stochastic, D - Deterministic.

Idx	Name	Type	Idx	Name	Type	Idx	Name	Type	Idx	Name	Type
0	Aliens	S	4	Bait	D	13	Butterflies	S	15	Camel Race	D
18	Chase	D	22	Chopper	S	25	Crossfire	S	29	Dig Dug	S
36	Escape	D	46	Hungry Birds	D	49	Infection	S	50	Intersection	S
58	Lemmings	D	60	Missile Command	D	61	Modality	D	67	Plaque Attack	D
75	Roguelike	S	77	Sea Quest	S	84	Survive Zombies	S	91	Wait for Breakfast	D

the population size and individual length. Section 5.1 compares the performance
using smaller or larger population, while Sect. 5.2 discusses the impact of individual length. Later, the performance of RHEA is also compared to RS employing
different budgets (Sect. 5.3) and OLMCTS (Sect. 5.4) as supplied by the GVGAI
framework. As the game set used is divided equally between deterministic and
stochastic games, an in-depth analysis is carried out on each game type, although
it is not implied the trend would carry through in other games of the same type
(Tables 3 and 4).

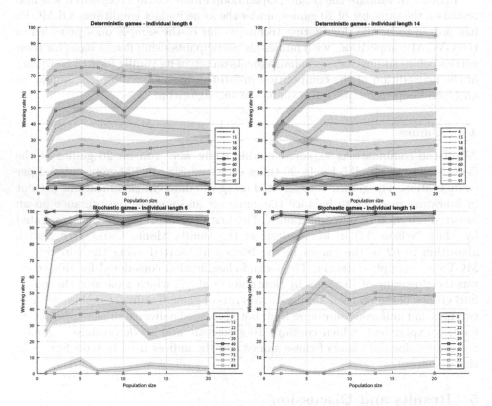

Fig. 4. Change in winning rate as population size increases, for individual lengths
$L = 6$ and $L = 14$, in all games tested for this paper. The Standard Error is shown
by the shaded boundary. Please refer to Table 1 for the names of the game indexes
presented here.

Table 2. Winning rate for different values of population size (P) and individual length (L), in all 20 tested games. Average of standard errors indicated between brackets. Highlighted in bold style is the best result.

P	L = 6	L = 8	L = 10	L = 12	L = 14	L = 16	L = 20
1	35.45(2.54)	38.25(2.54)	37.95(2.47)	36.70(2.58)	34.20(2.42)	33.55(2.57)	33.15(2.60)
2	39.95(2.62)	40.95(2.55)	41.05(2.62)	40.25(2.48)	39.50(2.56)	38.75(2.56)	36.80(2.60)
5	42.55(2.57)	43.50(2.39)	44.65(2.40)	44.25(2.38)	43.80(2.34)	44.95(2.53)	46.05(2.54)
7	43.00(2.49)	42.60(2.43)	44.65(2.36)	44.35(2.45)	45.30(2.23)	44.80(2.47)	47.05(2.56)
10	42.25(2.53)	43.60(2.49)	44.05(2.26)	45.80(2.47)	45.05(2.35)	46.60(2.45)	46.80(2.49)
13	42.65(2.43)	45.15(2.48)	45.15(2.47)	45.00(2.42)	46.25(2.41)	47.40(2.30)	47.05(2.42)
20	42.75(2.51)	43.20(2.60)	44.75(2.31)	45.50(2.34)	46.45(2.32)	46.30(2.32)	**47.50(2.33)**

Table 3. Winning rate for different values of population size (P) and individual length (L), in the 10 deterministic tested games. Average of standard errors indicated between brackets. Highlighted in bold style is the best result.

P	L = 6	L = 8	L = 10	L = 12	L = 14	L = 16	L = 20
1	22.30(2.88)	26.80(2.95)	26.90(2.93)	25.30(2.91)	24.20(2.84)	23.00(3.01)	22.50(2.99)
2	26.40(3.13)	26.80(3.08)	27.90(3.05)	27.90(2.92)	27.10(2.91)	26.80(2.93)	24.50(2.99)
5	28.70(3.08)	29.70(3.10)	31.90(3.18)	31.80(2.88)	30.00(2.86)	32.00(3.04)	32.20(3.19)
7	28.80(3.26)	29.00(3.00)	30.80(3.09)	30.40(3.01)	31.70(2.82)	32.00(2.99)	34.30(3.12)
10	27.70(3.18)	31.00(3.27)	29.50(2.90)	33.00(3.03)	32.60(2.94)	32.40(3.11)	33.20(3.05)
13	28.90(3.19)	32.20(3.32)	32.10(3.06)	31.80(3.07)	33.30(3.18)	**34.70(2.88)**	34.00(2.97)
20	28.60(3.19)	29.90(3.34)	31.50(2.87)	32.30(3.05)	33.10(3.11)	32.10(2.84)	34.30(3.02)

Table 4. Winning rate for different values of population size (P) and individual length (L), in the 10 stochastic tested games. Average of standard errors indicated between brackets. Highlighted in bold style is the best result.

P	L = 6	L = 8	L = 10	L = 12	L = 14	L = 16	L = 20
1	48.60(2.20)	49.70(2.13)	49.00(2.01)	48.10(2.25)	44.20(2.00)	44.10(2.12)	43.80(2.22)
2	53.50(2.12)	55.10(2.02)	54.20(2.20)	52.60(2.05)	51.90(2.20)	50.70(2.20)	49.10(2.22)
5	56.40(2.07)	57.30(1.68)	57.40(1.61)	56.70(1.88)	57.60(1.81)	57.90(2.01)	59.90(1.89)
7	57.20(1.72)	56.20(1.85)	58.50(1.64)	58.30(1.90)	58.90(1.63)	57.60(1.95)	59.80(2.00)
10	56.80(1.88)	56.20(1.71)	58.60(1.63)	58.60(1.91)	57.50(1.77)	**60.80(1.79)**	60.40(1.93)
13	56.40(1.68)	58.10(1.65)	58.20(1.88)	58.20(1.76)	59.20(1.63)	60.10(1.71)	60.10(1.86)
20	56.90(1.83)	56.50(1.86)	58.00(1.74)	58.70(1.64)	59.80(1.53)	60.50(1.80)	60.70(1.64)

Additionally, a Mann-Whitney non-parametric test was used to measure the statistical significance of results for each game (p-value $= 0.05$). Table 2 summarises the winning rates of all configurations tested in this study.

5.1 Population Variation

Figure 4 shows the change in winning rate as population size increases, for $L = 6$ and $L = 14$ (figures for other individual lengths have been omitted for the sake of space). Each of the 20 games that these algorithm configurations were tested on showed different performance and variations. There is a trend noticed in most of the games, with win rate increasing, regardless of the game type (c.f. Table 4). Exceptions are for games where the win rate starts at 100%, therefore leaving no room for improvement (games with indexes 0 and 50, *Aliens* and *Intersection*, respectively) or, on the contrary, when the win rate stays very close to 0% due to outstanding difficulty (game index 75, *Roguelike*). The winning rate on game with index 25, *Crossfire*, increases significantly from 0 to 10% (p-value = 0.02) along with the increase in population size. This suggests that games which a priori seem unsolvable, can be approached by exploring more with a larger population.

Deterministic games. Winning rate increases progressively in most of the tested deterministic games (Fig. 4, top). A high diversity of the performance over the tested games is observed, with the concrete winning rate having a high dependency on the given game. The games with indexes 60 and 91 (*Missile Command* and *Wait for Breakfast*, respectively), stand out in these cases as they achieve a larger increase in performance, particularly with longer individuals.

Stochastic games. Regarding stochastic games (Fig. 4, bottom) in particular, it is important to separate them based on their probabilistic elements and their impact on the outcome of the game. For example, the game with index 84, *Survive Zombies*, has numerous random NPCs and probabilistic spawn points for all object types, in contrast with game numbered 0, *Aliens*, where its stochastic nature comes only from the NPCs dropping bombs in irregular intervals.

In games numbered 13 and 22 (*Butterflies* and *Chopper* respectively), a big improvement in terms of winning rate is observed by increasing the population size from 2 (the case in which there is no tournament) to 1, and this remains stable with larger populations.

When the length of the individual is fixed to a small value, increasing the population size is not beneficial in all cases, sometimes having the opposite effect and causing a drop in win rate (games with indexes 77 and 84, *Sea Quest* and *Survive Zombies*, respectively). On the contrary, the game with index 22, *Chopper*, sees a great improvement (from an average of 29% in population size $P = 1$ to 98% in population size $P = 20$, p-value $\ll 0.001$, for both win rate and scores achieved).

In general, a conclusion that could be drawn from these experiments is that increasing the population size rarely hinders the agent to find good solutions. In fact, in some cases it makes the difference between a very poor and a very successful performance (from 29% to 98% in *Chopper*). An explanation for this phenomena could be that the higher diversity in the population allows the algorithm to perform a better exploration of the search space.

5.2   Individual Variation

Figure 5 illustrates the change of the winning rate in each of the 20 games as individual length increases, for population sizes $P = 1$ and $P = 5$. The full

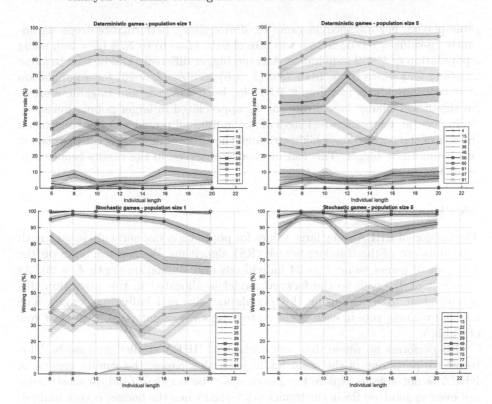

Fig. 5. Change of the winning rate as individual length increases, for population sizes $P = 1$ and $P = 5$, in all games tested for this paper. The standard error is shown by the shaded boundary. Please refer to Table 1 for the names of the game indexes presented here.

results using a variety of population size and individual length are given in Table 2. Using identical numbers of individuals when the population size is large ($P \geq 5$) and increasing the individual length, i.e., simulation depth, leads to a growth of winning rate (c.f. Table 2).

Deterministic games. When there is only one individual in the population, thus no crossover is involved, the winning rate experiences a significant increase followed by a drop along with the increase of individual length. This is due to the fact that the size of search space of solutions increases exponentially with the individual length. With few individuals evaluated, the algorithm struggles to find optimal solutions. This issue can be solved by increasing the population size, as shown in Fig. 5 (top). For instance, the game with index 67, *Plaque Attack*, sees a variation from 68% to 83% to 55% with population size $P = 1$; while with population size $P = 5$, there is a constant increase from 79% to 97%.

Stochastic games. In stochastic games, however, matters are different. In this case, the performance of the different variants of RHEA depends greatly on the game played. For instance, in game 13 (*Butterflies*), performance drops significantly (*p*-value = 0.001) from a win rate of 91% ($L = 6$) to 75% ($L = 20$), using a population of $P = 2$ individuals. An even bigger difference can be seen in game 22 (*Chopper*) which drops from 78% ($L = 6$) to 30% ($L = 20$) for a population of $P = 2$ individuals (*p*-value $\ll 0.001$ for both win rate and in-game scores). No significant change in win rate can be appreciated in larger population sizes.

In general, increasing the length of the individual provides better solutions if the size of the population is high, although the effect of increasing the population size seems to be bigger. This can be clearly observed in the results reported in Table 4.

5.3   Random Search

The version of RHEA using large values for population size and individual length is reminiscent of the Random Search (RS) algorithm. We perform a RS on the same set of games using $P = 24$ individuals and simulation depth $L = 20$. As a budget of 480 calls to the forward model is allocated to this algorithm, RS is equivalent to RHEA using this population size and individual length. The average winning rate in each of the tested games is summarized in the last row of Table 5.

RS performs no worse than any variant of RHEA studied previously. This result supports one of the main findings on this paper: the vanilla version of RHEA is not able to explore the search space better than (and, in most cases, not even as good as) RS in the framework tested when the budget is very limited. In order to test the limits and potential benefits of evolution, an additional set of experiments was run, using the same $P = 24$, $L = 20$ configuration, but increasing the forward model budget from 480 *advance* calls to 960, 1440 and 1920. It's notable that, for these new budgets, the population is evolved during 2, 3 and 4 generations, respectively.

The results, presented in Table 5, suggest that the solution recommended by RHEA at the end of optimisation converges towards the optimal solution while increasing the budget. As the budget becomes higher, the win rate increases first, to then stabilise when it reaches the highest budget tested. The difference observed is smaller than that given by the search in terms of population sizes and individual lengths.

Table 5. Comparison of winning rates and points achieved by RHEA with different budgets and OLMCTS. It shows rates and points for all games (T), deterministic (D) and stochastic (S). With budget 480, the RS is equivalent to a RHEA using 24 individuals and individual length 20.

Algorithm	Average wins (T)	Points (T)	Average wins (D)	Points (D)	Average wins (S)	Points (S)
RHEA-1920	48.25(2.36)	351	36.30(2.88)	181	60.20(1.84)	170
RHEA-1440	48.05(2.23)	339	35.40(2.82)	177	60.70(1.65)	162
RHEA-960	47.85(2.39)	323	34.60(2.99)	162	61.10(1.79)	161
OLMCTS-480	41.45(1.89)	316	22.20(2.45)	149	60.70(1.34)	167
RHEA/RS-480	46.60(2.40)	271	32.90(3.04)	131	60.30(1.76)	140

In stochastic games, there is no difference observed in the average winning rate, but there is a small increase in ranking points, which vary according to the budget. However, there is a clearer improvement in performance distinguished in deterministic games. This may be due to the fact that resampling an individual is useless in deterministic games, whilst a single evaluation of a solution in a stochastic environment may be inaccurate.

5.4 RHEA vs OLMCTS

Table 5 also includes the performance of the GVGAI sample OLMCTS agent. The sample OLMCTS agent uses a playout depth of 10, hence the comparisons presented here relate to RHEA configurations with individual length $L = 10$. Results show that, although RHEA is significantly worse when its population size is small, it outperforms OLMCTS when the number of individuals per population is increased ($P > 5$). A second interesting contribution of this paper is that it is possible to create an RHEA capable of achieving a higher level of play than OLMCTS, which is the base of most dominating algorithms in the GVGAI literature.

In addition, OLMCTS also falls short when comparing it to RS with regards to the average percentage of victories. However, it does manage to gain a higher number of ranking points in these games against the other 4 agents. Considering the fact that points are awarded for each game in order to value their generic capabilities, this result suggests that OLMCTS is more general than the vanilla version of RHEA.

Finally, if an analysis is carried out per game type, OLMCTS appears to be similar to RS in stochastic games but, not surprisingly, its performance is much worse than RS in deterministic games, becoming comparable to the worst configuration of RHEA found during these experiments (population size $P = 1$ and individual length $L = 20$).

6 Conclusions and Future Work

This paper presents an analysis of population size and individual length of the vanilla version of Rolling Horizon Evolutionary Algorithm (RHEA). The performance of this algorithm is measured in terms of winning rate in a subset of 20 games of the General Video Game AI corpus. These games were selected based on their difficulty and game features, in order to present a reduced set of challenges as assorted as possible. Games were also chosen so there would be a split between deterministic and stochastic ones.

One of the main findings of this research is the fact that RHEA is unable to find better solutions than Random Search (RS) in the settings explored, being worse than RS in many cases. Rather than an indication of RHEA being not suitable for GVGAI, these results suggest that the vanilla version of the algorithm is not able to explore the search space quickly enough given the limited budget. Therefore, this finding motivates research in RHEA, in order to find operators and techniques able to evolve sequences of actions in a more efficient way. The results presented in this paper with higher execution budgets are an indication that this is possible.

At the same time, this paper highlights another interesting conclusion: given the same length for the sequence of actions and the same budget (480 calls to the forward model), RHEA is able to outperform Open Loop Monte Carlo Tree Search (OLMCTS) hen configured with a high population size. Most of the entries of the GVGAI competition, including some of the winners, base their entries in OLMCTS or similar tree search methods. Thus, RHEA presents itself as a valuable alternative with a potentially promising future.

Finally, this study analyses the performance of the different versions of the algorithm in a game per game basis, and it is clear that in some games the agent performance shows a trend after increasing the population size or the individual length. For instance, in most games the agent benefits from using larger populations, but, in some of them, it works better with fewer individuals. Similarly, a long sequence of actions typically helps finding better solutions, but some games form the exception and RHEA performs better with shorter individual lengths. In general, however, it has been observed that an increase in the population size has a higher impact on the performance than considering a further look ahead (longer individuals).

Therefore, although the general finding is that bigger populations and longer individuals improve the performance of RHEA on average, it should be possible to devise methods that could identify the type of game being played, and employ different (or, maybe, modify dynamically) parameter settings. In a form of a meta-heuristic, an agent could be able to select which configuration better fits the game being played at the moment and increases the average performance in this domain.

The most straightforward line of future work, however, is the improvement of the vanilla RHEA in this general setting. The objectives are twofold: first, seeking bigger improvements of action sequences during the evolution phase, without the need of having too broad an exploration as in the case of RS; and second, being able to better handle long individual lengths in order for them to not hinder the evolutionary process. Additionally, further analysis could be conducted on stochastic games, considering the effects of more elite members in the population or resampling individuals, in order to alleviate the effect of noise in the evaluations.

References

1. Al-Khateeb, B., Kendall, G.: The importance of a piece difference feature to blondie 24. In: UK Workshop on Computational Intelligence (UKCI), pp. 1–6 (2010)
2. Babadi, A., Omoomi, B., Kendall, G.: EnHiC: An enforced hill climbing based system for general game playing. In: IEEE Conference on Computational Intelligence and Games (CIG), vol. 1, pp. 193–199 (2015)
3. Bellemare, M.G., Naddaf, Y., Veness, J., Bowling, M.: The arcade learning environment: an evaluation platform for general agents. J. Artif. Intell. Res. 47, 253–279 (2013)

4. Bontrager, P., Khalifa, A., Mendes, A., Togelius, J.: Matching games and algorithms for General Video Game Playing. In: Twelfth Artificial Intelligence and Interactive Digital Entertainment Conference, pp. 122–128 (2016)
5. Browne, C.B., Powley, E., Whitehouse, D., Lucas, S.M., Cowling, P.I., Rohlfshagen, P., Tavener, S., Perez, D., Samothrakis, S., Colton, S.: A survey of Monte Carlo Tree Search methods. IEEE Trans. Comput. Intell. AI Games **4**, 1–43 (2014)
6. Chu, C.Y., Hashizume, H., Guo, Z., Harada, T., Thawonmas, R.: Combining pathfinding algorithm with knowledge-based monte-carlo tree search in General Video Game Playing. In: IEEE Conference on Computational Intelligence and Games (CIG), vol. 1, pp. 523–529 (2015)
7. Gaina, R.D., Perez-Liebana, D., Lucas, S.M.: General video game for 2 players: framework and competition. In: Proceedings of the IEEE Computer Science and Electronic Engineering Conference (CEEC) (2016)
8. Genesereth, M., Love, N., Pell, B.: General game playing: overview of the AAAI competition. AI Mag. **26**, 62 (2005)
9. Horn, H., Volz, V., Perez-Liebana, D., Preuss, M.: MCTS/EA hybrid GVGAI players and game difficulty estimation. In: Proceedings of the IEEE Conference on Computational Intelligence and Games (CIG) (2016)
10. Justesen, N., Mahlmann, T., Togelius, J.: Online evolution for multi-action adversarial games. In: Squillero, G., Burelli, P. (eds.) EvoApplications 2016. LNCS, vol. 9597, pp. 590–603. Springer, Cham (2016). doi:10.1007/978-3-319-31204-0_38
11. Khalifa, A., Perez-Liebana, D., Lucas, S., and J.T.: General video game level generation. In: Proceedings of the Genetic and Evolutionary Computation Conference (GECCO) (2016)
12. Levine, J., Lucas, S.M., Mateas, M., Preuss, M., Spronck, P., Togelius, J.: General Video Game Playing. In: Artificial and Computational Intelligence in Games, Dagstuhl Follow-Ups, vol. 6, pp. 1–7 (2013)
13. Liu, J., Liebana, D.P., Lucas, S.M.: Bandit-Based Random Mutation Hill-Climbing. CoRR abs/1606.06041 (2016). http://arxiv.org/abs/1606.06041
14. Lucas, S.M., Samothrakis, S., Perez, D.: Fast evolutionary adaptation for Monte Carlo Tree Search. In: EvoGames (2014)
15. Mitchell, M.: An Introduction to Genetic Algorithms. MIT Press, Cambridge (1998)
16. Mnih, V., Kavukcuoglu, K., Silver, D., Rusu, A.A., Veness, J., Bellemare, M.G., Graves, A., Riedmiller, M., Fidjeland, A.K., Ostrovski, G., Petersen, S., Beattie, C., Sadik, A., Antonoglou, I., King, H., Kumaran, D., Wierstra, D., Legg, S., Hassabis, D.: Human-level control through deep reinforcement learning. Nature **518**(7540), 529–533 (2015)
17. Nelson, M.J.: Investigating vanilla MCTS scaling on the GVG-AI game corpus. In: Proceedings of the 2016 IEEE Conference on Computational Intelligence and Games (2016)
18. Park, H., Kim, K.J.: MCTS with influence map for General Video Game Playing. In: IEEE Conference on Computational Intelligence and Games (CIG), vol. 1, pp. 534–535 (2015)
19. Perez, D., Samothrakis, S., Lucas, S.M.: Knowledge-based fast evolutionary MCTS for General Video Game Playing. In: IEEE Conference on Computational Intelligence and Games, pp. 1–8 (2014)
20. Perez-Liebana, D., Dieskau, J., Hnermund, M., Mostaghim, S., Lucas, S.M.: Open loop search for General Video Game Playing. In: Proceedings of the Genetic and Evolutionary Computation Conference (GECCO), pp. 337–344 (2015)

21. Perez-Liebana, D., Samothrakis, S., Lucas, S.M., Rolfshagen, P.: Rolling Horizon Evolution versus tree search for navigation in single-player real-time games. In: Proceedings of the Genetic and Evolutionary Computation Conference (GECCO), pp. 351–358 (2013)
22. Perez-Liebana, D., Samothrakis, S., Togelius, J., Lucas, S.M., Schaul, T.: General video game AI: competition, challenges and opportunities. In: Thirtieth AAAI Conference on Artificial Intelligence (2016)
23. Perez-Liebana, D., Samothrakis, S., Togelius, J., Schaul, T., Lucas, S., Couetoux, A., Lee, J., Lim, C.U., Thompson, T.: The 2014 General Video Game Playing competition. IEEE Trans. Comput. Intell. AI Games **PP**, 1 (2015)
24. Samothrakis, S., Roberts, S.A., Perez, D., Lucas, S.: Rolling Horizon methods for games with continuous states and actions. In: Proceedings of the Conference on Computational Intelligence and Games (CIG), August 2014
25. Sharma, S., Kobti, Z., Goodwin, S.D.: General game playing: an overview and open problems. In: IEEE International Conference on Computing, Engineering and Information, pp. 257–260 (2009)
26. Tesauro, G.J.: Temporal difference learning and TD-gammon. In: IEEE Conference on Computational Intelligence and Games, pp. 58–68 (1995)
27. Wang, C., Chen, P., Li, Y., Holmgård, C., Togelius, J.: Portfolio online evolution in starcraft. In: Twelfth Artificial Intelligence and Interactive Digital Entertainment Conference (2016)

Darwin's Demons: Does Evolution Improve the Game?

Terence Soule[✉], Samantha Heck, Thomas E. Haynes, Nicholas Wood,
and Barrie D. Robison

University of Idaho, Moscow, ID 83844, USA
tsoule@cs.uidaho.edu

Abstract. It is widely assumed that evolution has the potential to make
better video games. However, relatively few commercial games have been
released that use evolution as a core game mechanic, and of these games
only a very small sub-set have shown that evolution occurs as expected
and improves game play as intended. Thus, there remains a critical gap
between studies showing the clear potential of evolution to improve video
games and studies showing that evolution did improve game play in a
commercially released game.

We have developed Darwin's Demons, a space shooter inspired by
old style arcade games, with the added feature of evolving enemies. In
August, 2016 Darwin's Demons was Green-lit for sale on Steam, a standard benchmark for commercialization of games. In this paper we present
and test four hypotheses that form the basis for the claim that evolution occurs and improves game play in Darwin's Demons. More generally, these hypotheses can be used to confirm that evolution meets the
intended design goals for other evolutionary games.

Our results support the hypotheses that evolution makes Darwin's
Demons get progressively more difficult over the course of a game, and
that the fitness function, player choices, and player strategy all affect
the evolutionary trajectory during a single game. This suggests that in
Darwin's Demons, the enemies adapt to the player's decisions and strategy, making the game interesting and increasing its replayability.

Keywords: Evolution · Games · Procedural generation

1 Introduction

Polymorphic Games, a game design studio at the University of Idaho, recently
completed Darwin's Demons, an arcade style video game that uses evolution
of the opponents as the core game mechanic (Fig. 1). Our central hypothesis is

This material is based in part upon work supported by the National Science Foundation under Cooperative Agreement No. DBI-0939454, the Vandal Ideas Project, and
by NSF Grant DMS-1029485. Any opinions, findings, and conclusions or recommendations expressed in this material are those of the author(s) and do not necessarily
reflect the views of the National Science Foundation.

© Springer International Publishing AG 2017
G. Squillero and K. Sim (Eds.): EvoApplications 2017, Part I, LNCS 10199, pp. 435–451, 2017.
DOI: 10.1007/978-3-319-55849-3_29

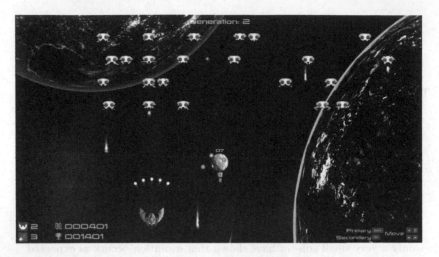

Fig. 1. Screenshot from Darwin's Demons, in which the player must defeat generations of evolving opponents.

that this game mechanic should make the game more challenging and compelling because the enemy population will adapt to the players' decisions and strategies. This hypothesis makes a series of important predictions:

1. Evolution causes the game to get progressively more difficult.
2. Changing the fitness function leads to different evolutionary trajectories.
3. Different player decisions (e.g. ship choice) lead to different evolutionary trajectories.
4. Different player strategies lead to different evolutionary trajectories.

These predictions do not directly measure "fun", largely because fun is subjective and varies from player to player. Instead they help determine whether evolution has succeeded in meeting our goals regarding player challenge and re-playability. The first prediction determines whether the came increases in difficulty, which is a requirement of most, if not all, arcade style games. A game that doesn't increase in difficulty isn't fun because either the game is too hard and the player either immediately fails or it is too easy and the player can play indefinitely without challenge. Thus, it is important to confirm that the evolution of opponents does cause the game to become increasingly challenging.

The second prediction determines whether we, as the game's designers, can adjust the game, its difficulty, and how it progresses by modifying the fitness function. If this prediction is confirmed, it means that evolution is a method by which to change the players' experience. For example, changing the fitness function to change game difficulty or the diversity of game experiences.

The third and fourth predictions relate to the players' experience and the re-playability of the game. If the evolutionary outcomes are a function of players' decisions and strategies then the game is responding to the player - as opposed to simply following a pre-programmed script or fixed evolutionary trajectory. Generally, a more responsive game is considered a more interesting one. These predictions also impact re-playability. If the player experiences a different evolutionary trajectory by adopting a different strategy or by making different decisions then each re-play is a more novel, and hopefully fun and compelling, experience than if the game followed a (randomized) script. Of course, some players might prefer a carefully scripted game that they can memorize and exploit. This is part of the reason we do not attempt to measure "fun" directly - fun is a subjective measure that varies from player to player.

These predictions are intentionally general. We reason that for any game in which the core evolutionary mechanic is the evolution of the opponents, testing these predictions can be used to support the claim that the evolutionary mechanic is improving the game experience.

2   Background

Evolution has great potential for improving video games in a wide range of areas. Some of the most promising include generating levels and environments, making games more affective, evolving opponents strategies, and evolving content. Despite the potential advantages there are relatively few commercial games that incorporate evolution as a core mechanic [1]. Furthermore, the most successful commercial games that emphasize evolution in their advertising (e.g. Spore^{TM}, Evolve^{TM}, and Pokemon^{TM} evolution) do not actually use evolution. Even in cases where evolution is used it is often applied pre-release to create intelligent, but static, opponents, which undermines perhaps the largest advantage of evolution, that if can be used to create a game that adapts, either competitively or cooperatively, to the player [2].

A few video games in which accurate evolutionary processes fulfill a significant role in the game do exist. Creatures by Creatures Lab is an artificial life game in which the player trains and breeds creature called Norns. In this game the evolutionary mechanic is accurate, but lifetime learning is at least as important and much of the evolution is via player controlled breeding.

Petalz is a Facebook game in which players breed flowers that they can share or sell through an on-line market place [3,4]. Flowers are generated via a neural network whose structure is evolved via Neuroevolution of Augmenting Topologies (NEAT). Players crossbreed existing flowers to drive the evolutionary process. A number of studies have confirmed the evolutionary aspect of Petalz in the context of human directed breeding.

Although it has not been released commercially the NeuroEvolving Robotic Operatives (NERO) video game is a well developed example of a game that incorporates evolution [5,6]. In NERO players evolve the behavior of agents by putting them in different training scenarios. The goal is to evolve/train agents to solve a particular problem or set of problems. Nero has also been used in a number of research projects that confirm the evolutionary mechanic is meeting the design goals of the game - allowing the player to evolve the behavior of their troops. EvoCommander builds on the idea of NERO by allowing the player to evolve multiple "brains" (literally different artificial neural networks) during the training phase and then manually switch between them during battles [7]. This gives the player a more active role in the games' battles as well as encouraging them to try to evolve multiple, specialized, and complementary behaviors.

In these games evolution is driven more or less intentionally by the player. In contrast, in Galactic Arms Race by Evolutionary Games evolution is used to procedurally generate new weapons for the player [1]. The player can influence this process by preferentially using some weapons over others, but even if they chose to focus only on the other aspects of the game new weapons are still evolved. This is a prime example of procedural content generation that is tuned to the player's preference by the evolutionary process. A slightly different approach is taken in [8], there players select the spaceship designs they prefer and the fitness function is modified so that higher fitnesses are assigned to the preferred ships. This allows evolution to run in the background using a fitness function that is tailored to the player. In related work it was shown that including a novelty component in the evolutionary search process significantly improved diversity in evolved spaceship designs [9]. Other research has successfully tied the evolution of game visuals, such as the evolved fire patterns in Galactic Arms Race, to the background music being played [10,11].

Species, is an evolutionary, a life game that is in early alpha release [12]. Currently Species is primarily an evolutionary, simulation in which the "player" takes on the role of observer, but can, to a limited extent, influence the evolutionary process, mostly on a creature by creature basis.

Perhaps surprisingly the opponents do not directly evolve during game play in any of these games (in NERO teams of evolved agents can be pitted against each other), which is a particularly promising application of evolution to video games [13]. [14] discusses the use of evolution in Tower Defense games and includes preliminary experiments suggesting that the opponents (creeps) could be evolved, but it was done in test runs without a human player being involved. Thus, in developing Darwin's Demons it was important to develop and test a set of hypotheses that would confirm that the game mechanic of evolving opponents was meeting our design goals.

3   Darwin's Demons

Darwin's Demons is based on classic arcade games in which the player has to defeat waves of opponents. The evolutionary component was included by assigning each opponent a fitness based on how well it performed against the player and by making each "wave" in the game a generation in a generational evolutionary algorithm. Each opponent has its own genome that determines its characteristics: appearance, behavior, fire type and rate, projectile speed, and entry time during the generation (dominance). The player controls a space ship, and must kill all of the opponents in each generation. The player has a limited number of lives and loses one each time either the ship is hit by an opponent's projectile, an opponent reaches the bottom of the screen, or the ship is hit by an opponent (some ships are immune to hits from the side, allowing them to move into and destroy, opponents that move too far down the screen).

3.1   The Development Team

Darwin's Demons was developed by Polymorphic Games, a game design studio at the University of Idaho, with funding from the BEACON Center for Evolution in Action. The majority of the development process took place in the summer of 2016 with major development starting in mid-May and approval on Steam Greenlight received in mid-August. Prior to the major development push Drs. Robison and Soule, and the project lead, Nicholas Wood (a Virtual Technology Design (VTD) graduate student) developed a fairly detailed design document to guide the development process. In addition to Robison, Soule, and Wood the development team included two full time programmers (CS majors), two full time and one half time artists (VTD majors), a communications coordinator (English major), one full time and one half time musicians (Music majors), and two research assistants (Biology majors who collected data on the evolutionary behavior of the game). All of these students were undergraduates.

4   The Player

In Darwin's Demons the player has a range of ships, secondary weapons, defenses, and perks/augmentations to choose from (Fig. 2). Each ship has a unique appearance, movement characteristics, and primary weapon. Types of primary weapons include direct fire, homing missiles, piercing weapons, burst area weapons, boomeranging weapons, and weapons that have a larger impact when charged. Secondary weapons generally have a limited number of uses and greater impact, including large burst areas or multiple projectiles. The secondary weapons also includes some purely defensive options, such as personal shields that can briefly block opponents' projectiles. Defense options include stationary shields in different configurations and active, firing "turrets". Perks are general improvements such as extra initial lives, increased fire rates, etc.

Between each generation the player has the opportunity to upgrade their ship, secondary weapon, defenses, or to buy additional lives (Fig. 3). These upgrades are paid for with "biomatter", which is collected when opponents are killed. Biomatter is one of the two monetary systems in the game. The other is "credits", which are used to unlock additional ships, secondary weapons, etc.

Although the design studio's primary goal in incorporating evolution was to improve game play, a secondary goal was to encourage players to learn about evolution. To help meet this goal data on evolution is included in the upgrades screen. The upper left panel (Fig. 3) shows the five most fit opponents from the previous generation. Because these opponents are the ones likely to contribute the most offspring to the next generation, players who understand the basics of evolution will understand that these opponents are a preview of the type of opponent they are likely to see in the next generation.

Fig. 2. The selection screen. Players choose their ship, secondary weapon, defensive shields, and augmentation by rotating the arc. Many choices must be unlocked with credits earned during game play or through in game achievements.

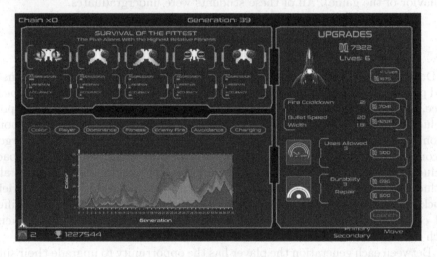

Fig. 3. Screenshot from Darwin's Demons showing the upgrade screen. Here players can spend "biomatter", which is collected as they play, to improve their ship or to purchase extra lives (right side panel). In addition, to emphasize the evolutionary nature of the game, the screen shows the five fittest opponents from the previous generation (upper left panel) and graphs showing the evolution of different traits (bottom left panel).

Additionally, in the lower left panel of the upgrades screen (Fig. 3) the player can toggle through graphs that display data illustrating the evolutionary trajectory of the current game, including the evolution of particular types of fire, dominance, charging behaviors, and other traits that effect game play. A player that understands evolution can use these graphs to predict the types and behaviors of the opponents that they are likely to see in the next generation.

Finally, the complete genome of every opponent in a game can be written to a CSV file for post-game analysis. Although we do not expect the typical player to take advantage of this feature, it is very useful for analyzing evolution within the game. It also greatly enhances the possibility of using the game for educational and research purposes.

4.1 Experiment Mode

To facilitate research using Darwin's Demons the game includes an experiment mode in which the player can set a number of parameters. Adjustable parameters include those relevant to evolution, such as population size, mutation rate, etc. and parameters that are relevant to game play, which can be used to create experiments based on different game conditions. These parameters include the number of lives the player has, whether migrants appear (see Sect. 5.7), etc.

5   The Opponents

In Darwin's Demons the opponents are members of an alien species called the *Protean Swarm*. Each opponent's appearance, behavior, fire type and rate, projectile speed, and entry time during the generation (dominance) are determined by it's genome. They follow basic, evolved movement patterns and fire evolvable types of projectiles at the player.

5.1   Movement and Firing

On each time step each opponent can choose to move either left or right one step and on every twentieth time step each opponent can choose to move either up or down one step. The restriction on up and down movement is to keep the opponents from dive bombing the player too quickly. Opponents cannot move through each other and an opponent that attempts to move into another opponent's space fails to move.

Opponents decide their direction of movement (left or right and up or down) based on several factors: the position of the player's ship, the position of the nearest player projectile, the height of the opponent, and the opponents last movement. These factors are weighted based on evolved weights (using a linear equation) to determine the direction of movement.

Similar factors are used by the opponent to determine whether or not to fire. However, opponents cannot fire through each other, preventing opponents with a conspecific below them from firing. In addition, each opponent has an evolved maximum rate of fire that it cannot exceed. Thus, an opponent may "decide" to fire, but not actually fire either because it would exceed its rate of fire or because their is another opponent below it.

5.2 Projectile Type

There are six types of opponents with six general appearances and six corresponding types of projectiles. The six types of projectiles that can evolve are:

1. A basic projectile that fires straight down. All of the opponents in the initial generation use this type of projectile.
2. A projectile that follows a sine wave trajectory. The amplitude of the sine wave is evolved.
3. A projectile that is aimed at the current location of the player. The maximum angle at which the projectile can be aimed is evolved.
4. Twin projectiles, each of which moves away from the opponent at a particular angle. The angle between the projectiles is evolved.
5. A projectile that splits into three projectiles partway down the screen. The delay before splitting is evolved.
6. A projectile that homes in on the player's ship, homing strength is evolved.

There is one gene for each of the five projectile types (not including the basic projectile type). The gene with the largest (absolute) value determines the projectile type for that opponent.

5.3 Appearance

In Darwin's Demons there are eleven base body types, represented by animated sprites. These sprites are used to determine the appearance of each opponent. Each sprite is a two frame animation. Figure 4 shows a sample sprite sheet.

Fig. 4. The sprite sheet used to define the base body types in Darwin's Demons. There are eleven basic sprites, one for the basic opponent (left most column) and two for each of the possible projectile types. In addition, there are separate sprites for the top half and bottom half of opponents. (All opponents are symmetrical so only the left half of the sprite is defined.)

Each opponent consists of a top half sprite and a bottom half sprite, both of which are determined by the opponent's genome. The bottom half of the sprite is determined by the same genes that control the type of projectile, with one sprite for positive values of the gene and one sprite for negative values of the gene. For example, an opponent with a large, positive genetic value for homing projectiles incorporates a specific sprite into its appearance and an opponent with a large negative value incorporates a different sprite into its appearance.

To create an opponent's appearance, a weighted mixture of the sprites corresponding to the two projectile types with the largest absolute value are merged. For example, if the genes for a sine wave projectile and a homing projectile have the largest values then the opponent's appearance is a mixture of these two body types. In addition, the value of the gene is a factor in how strongly the sprite is represented. So, an opponent with a very large genetic value for the sine wave projectile and a relatively small value for the homing projectile will look like an almost "pure" sine wave opponent. Whereas an opponent with nearly equal values for both genes will look like a hybrid. Finally, the color and shape of the eyes is determined by the projectile type gene with the highest value.

Overall, this approach means that there is a strong connection between an opponent's appearance and the type of projectile it fires. This allows players to identify the type of opponent they are playing against.

5.4 Dominance

At the beginning of a generation, 26 opponents drop into the screen. After the first 13 opponents are killed, 13 more opponents drop in. This is repeated until the maximum population size is reached. Maximum population size varies across game types, but ranges from a minimum of 65 to a maximum of 130. The order in which the opponents drop in is determined by their *dominance* gene. Opponents with the highest value of the dominance gene enter the screen first, and entry priority proceeds in a ranked fashion, with the opponent with the lowest dominance entering last.

5.5 Fitness

At the end of each generation, each opponent can be assigned a fitness based on three factors:

1. Lifetime - how long the opponent survived.
2. Aggression - the average vertical screen position of the opponent
3. Accuracy - a combination of the number of projectiles fired and how close they came to the player's ship.

The fitness components are added together to determine the overall fitness of each enemy. Some of these fitness components are in conflict. For example, an opponent that charges down the screen is likely to get a high aggression score, but is also likely to be shot by the player leading to a low lifetime score. This makes the underlying fitness landscape quite complex and creates a wide variety of successful strategies that can be evolved.

5.6 Evolution

The Protean Swarm have a diploid genome encoded by 34 floating point values at each locus. They are hermaphroditic, and offspring receive one "chromosome" from each parent that is generated using a free recombination model. Evolution follows a generational model with between 65 and 130 individuals per generation, depending on game type. Tournament selection is used at the end of each generation to determine the parents of the next generation. The default tournament size for the game is 20, but parameters relating to evolution can be changed in the game's experiment mode.

During reproduction each gene has a chance equal to the mutation rate to acquire a mutation drawn from a Gaussian distribution with mean zero. The mutation rate and standard deviation of the Gaussian are adjustable parameters that depend on the game type. Mutation rates generally range from 0.1 to 0.2, and standard deviations from 0.7 to 1.5. In easy mode (as opposed to normal mode) the player also receives extra lives and the maximum speed of the opponents projectiles is slightly reduced.

5.7 Migrants

In addition to the standard opponents, migrants, or genetic anomalies, occasionally appear. Migrants are opponents whose genetics are pre-determined to represent difficult opponents, e.g. their genome defines a high rate of fire or particularly aggressive behavior, etc. In addition, they have a "shield" that requires them to be shot five times to be destroyed. They contribute to the next generation in the same way as any other opponent. This means that if the player fails to kill them quickly the next generation is likely to contain many offspring from the (more powerful) migrant.

The migrants give the player an additional choice to make, focus on the migrant to avoid having it reproduce or pursue their normal attack strategy. This type of choice is considered to be important in making a game interesting and engaging [15]. Migrants also help emphasize the evolutionary nature of the game. Players can observe the migrant in one generation and, if they fail to kill it quickly, its offspring stand out in the next generation. A clear indication of the role of inheritance in evolution.

6 Methods

To test our four predictions we played Darwin's Demons in a replicated experiment. We chose game settings that represent an intermediate value for most game parameters that a player would experience in the game. The player used the personal shield as the secondary "weapon". This shield can be used three times per generation to protect the player from all incoming projectiles for one second. The player used the basic planetary defense shield, which is a set of three destructible shields that protect the player from incoming projectiles. No perks or augmentations were used. The ships were not up-graded during play. We chose these game play settings because they are available in the free demo of the game, and thus could be reproduced.

The mutation rate was 0.1 per gene. Mutations were drawn from a Gaussian distribution with a mean of zero and a standard deviation of one. The tournament size was 15. Each generation started with 26 opponents, once 13 opponents were destroyed 13 more opponents are added. This addition was repeated 6 times for a total population size of $104(26 + 6 * 13)$. This is slightly larger than the standard population size to reduce the amount of drift caused by very small populations sizes reducing the number of replications required to obtain statistically significant results. Any player can use experiment mode to set the same, or other, parameters. No genetic anomalies/migrants were included. The player started with 100 lives, and play ended after 20 generations.

Two ships were used: the *needle* and the *stingray*. These ships were chosen because their primary weapons are quite different and have the potential to generate very different evolutionary trajectories. The *needle* has a low rate of fire, but fires missiles that have weak homing capabilities. In contrast the *stingray* has a high rate of fire, and fires very fast "lasers" that travel in a straight line, but can occasionally pierce more than one opponent. It is possible to up-grade the ships' primary weapons, but this was not done during the experiments to minimize the number of variables involved.

Experiment 1. We ran 24 replicates with selection based on the three fitness factors described previously (accuracy, aggression, and lifetime), and with no fitness function (i.e. genetic drift). These data were used to test the first two predictions:

1. Evolution causes the game to get progressively more difficult.
2. Changing the fitness function leads to different evolutionary trajectories.

Experiment 2. We compared the data from the two ships to address our third prediction:

3. Different player decisions (e.g. ship choice) lead to different evolutionary trajectories.

We conducted statistical tests for different evolutionary outcomes based on ship type and fitness function using the terminal generation for which we had data in all replicates (generation 17). Using the lmer() function in R, we fit a mixed model with Ship and Fitness function as fixed effects, and replicate as a random effect. P values are from a Wald Chi square test of the model results using the anova() function in R.

Experiment 3. To test the fourth prediction:

4. Different player strategies lead to different evolutionary trajectories.

an additional set of replicates were collected in which a different player used a specific strategy designed to "domesticate" the opponents. The strategy that the player followed consisted of the following rules for prioritizing the targeting of opponents:

- Target opponents with a non-base fire type.
- Target opponents that follow the player.
- Target opponents that move to the lower half of the screen.
- Target opponents that stay near the middle of the screen.
- Target opponents that shoot more often than average.

In addition, for opponents that shoot basic projectiles (not homing, splitting, etc.) and that don't follow the player, their projectiles were allowed to get near the player (increasing their accuracy fitness).

This strategy was designed to increase the fitness of opponents that stay in the upper corners of the screen, shoot rarely, and shoot base projectiles, by allowing them to collect the most lifetime and accuracy fitness. Only the stingray was used for these replicates because its fast, direct fire makes it easier for the player to implement the domestication strategy. The results of these replicates were compared to the replicates that used the stingray to determine whether the player's choice of strategy effected the evolutionary trajectory.

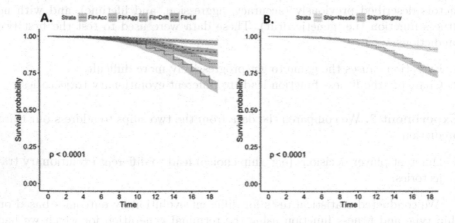

Fig. 5. A. Probability of survival (per player life) over 20 generations of game play under four fitness functions. With no fitness function (genetic drift), the probability of survival is almost 1.00 indicating that the game is quite easy - very few lives are lost. In general, selection of any kind makes the game increase in difficulty over time and different fitness functions lead to different difficulty curves. The differences between the outcomes are significant according to a log-rank test ($p < 0.0001$). B. Probability of survival (per player life) over 20 generations of game play as a function of the ship selected. With the Needle the survival probability is significantly higher ($p < 0.0001$).

Using the lmer() function in R, we fit a mixed model with Player and Fitness function as fixed effects, and replicate as a random effect. P values are from a Wald Chi square test of the model results using the anova() function in R.

7 Results

We began by looking at how the fitness function affects game difficulty. To test the prediction that evolution makes Darwin's Demons get progressively more difficult, we measured difficulty using survivorship curves of fleet size as a function of the generation number. The control case was random selection (i.e. drift) in which evolution by natural selection was not occurring.

Figure 5 shows the results of this experiment. A log rank test indicated that the fitness function has a significant impact on the probability of survival (p < 0.0001). The highest survival rates are for drift and survival rates are lower for each of the three fitness functions. This confirms that the inclusion of evolution does cause the game to become increasingly difficult. It also shows that the progressive difficulty of the game can be adjusted via the fitness function.

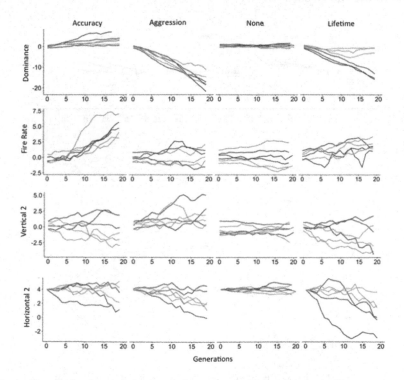

Fig. 6. A. Trends for four of the genes (dominance, fire rate, vertical movement 2, and horizontal movement 2) as a function of ship (red = Needle, blue = Stingray) and fitness function (columns). For some genes the evolutionary trajectory depends on the fitness function. For example, the direction of selection on the dominance gene varies between fitness based on accuracy and fitness based on aggression. The evolutionary trajectory also varies by ship, most obviously for the dominance gene with the lifetime fitness function (top right graph). (Color figure online)

Figure 5 also shows the survival probability as a function of ship type. A log rank test indicates that ship choice has a significant effect on survival probability (p < 0.0001). This strongly suggests that the player's choices, at least in selecting a ship, have a significant effect on the evolutionary trajectory. However, without examining individual genes (see below) it remains possible that evolution is following the same general trajectory, but at different "rates".

Figure 5 also suggests that the Needle is a "better" ship than the Stingray. This is clearly useful information to the game designers as it either means that the ships need to rebalanced or possibly that the Needle should be "locked" and only be made available to the player later in the game. However, it is important to note that there are two possible interpretations of the data. One is that the Needle is an inherently better ship. The other possibility is that the Stingray drives evolution faster, leading to harder opponents sooner than if the player chooses to use the Needle.

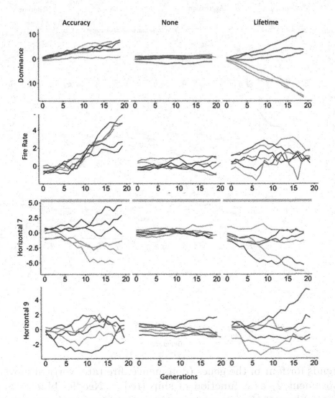

Fig. 7. Evolution for four of the genes (dominance, fire rate, horizontal movement 7, and horizontal movement 9) as a function of player strategy (line color) and fitness function (columns). The blue lines are for the player using the domestication strategy. All of the trials were run using the same ship (the Stingray). Notice that for some fitness functions the player's strategy had a significant effect on some genes. (Color figure online)

We tested whether the fitness function and ship choice affected the evolutionary trajectory of all genes. The results show that the fitness function has a significant effect on the evolutionary trajectory of some genes. Particularly notable is the evolution of the dominance gene, which depends markedly ($p \ll 0.0001$) on the fitness function (Fig. 6). Similarly, the evolution of the fire rate gene changes significantly ($p \ll 0.0001$) when the accuracy fitness function is used. The evolution of the horizontal2 ($p = 0.0002$) and vertical2 ($p = 0.0055$) genes was also significantly effected by the fitness function. These two genes determine the reaction of an enemy to the position of the player, positive values cause movement towards the player, and negative values cause movement away from the player. In aggregate, these data confirm that different fitness functions lead to different evolutionary trajectories and outcomes in Darwin's Demons. Ultimately, the data suggests that the evolutionary mechanism gives the game designers an additional tool (the fitness function) with which to change the player's experience.

For many genes and phenotypes, we observed a significant interaction between ship and player. This indicates that different ships drive different evolutionary trajectories depending on the fitness function used. For example, Fig. 6 also shows that the evolutionary trajectory does depend on the player's choices. This is shown most clearly by the dominance gene (Interaction $p \ll 0.0001$) when lifetime fitness is used (Fig. 6 upper-right graph).

Figure 7 shows the genetic values of four of the genes as a function of player strategy and fitness function. The same ship, the Stingray, was used for all of these trials. The results strongly support the prediction that the evolutionary trajectory depends on the player's strategy. This is most clearly seen in the dominance gene when fitness is based on lifetime, here direction of selection (for positive or negative values) depends on the player's strategy (a significant interaction between player and fitness function, $p \ll 0.0001$). A similar, if slightly less pronounced, result can be seen for the Horizontal 7 gene when selection is based on accuracy ($p = 0.005$). This gene affects the movement of the enemy relative to the player position in the previous timestep.

8 Conclusions

We have developed Darwin's Demons, a commercial (Green-lit on Steam and scheduled for release in Q1 2017) video game that uses evolution as a core mechanic. To confirm our hypothesis that evolution contributes to improvements in gameplay, we tested four predictions. Our results suggest that:

- The evolutionary mechanic causes the game to become more difficult over time.
- The evolutionary trajectory of the game depends on the choice of fitness function, providing a way to customize and diversify the player's experience.
- The player's choices, e.g. the choice of ship, affects the evolutionary trajectory increasing the replayability of the game; if a player choses to replay the game with a different ship they are likely to have a different play experience.

– The player's strategy affects the evolutionary trajectory of the game, showing that the game responds to the player's strategy. This generally makes a game more interesting and challenging. It can also increase replayability; if the player tries a different strategy they are likely to have a different experience.

Importantly, the results also show that there is variation in the evolutionary trajectory even for the same player decisions and strategy. Evolution is finding different solutions for the same player challenge. This keeps Darwin's Demons from being overly predictable. Based on these results we conclude that the evolutionary mechanic in Darwin's Demons is meeting the design goals of making a game that is challenging and responsive to the player without being predictable.

References

1. Hastings, E.J., Guha, R.K., Stanley, K.O.: Evolving content in the galactic arms race video game. In: 2009 IEEE Symposium on Computational Intelligence and Games, pp. 241–248. IEEE (2009)
2. Muñoz-Avila, H., Bauckhage, C., Bida, M., Congdon, C.B., Kendall, G.: Learning and game AI. Dagstuhl Follow-Ups 6 (2013)
3. Risi, S., Lehman, J., D'Ambrosio, D.B., Hall, R., Stanley, K.O.: Combining search-based procedural content generation and social gaming in the petalz video game. In: Aiide. Citeseer (2012)
4. Risi, S., Lehman, J., D'Ambrosio, D., Hall, R., Stanley, K.: Petalz: search-based procedural content generation for the casual gamer (2015)
5. Stanley, K.O., Bryant, B.D., Miikkulainen, R.: Real-time neuroevolution in the nero video game. IEEE Trans. Evol. Comput. 9(6), 653–668 (2005)
6. Stanley, K.O., Bryant, B.D., Karpov, I., Miikkulainen, R.: Real-time evolution of neural networks in the nero video game. In: AAAI, vol. 6, pp. 1671–1674 (2006)
7. Jallov, D., Risi, S., Togelius, J.: Evocommander: a novel game based on evolving and switching between artificial brains. IEEE Trans. Comput. Intell. AI Games (2016)
8. Liapis, A., Yannakakis, G.N., Togelius, J.: Adapting models of visual aesthetics for personalized content creation. IEEE Trans. Comput. Intell. AI Games 4(3), 213–228 (2012)
9. Liapis, A., Martınez, H.P., Togelius, J., Yannakakis, G.N.: Transforming exploratory creativity with delenox. In: Proceedings of the Fourth International Conference on Computational Creativity, pp. 56–63. AAAI Press (2013)
10. Cachia, W., Aquilina, L., Martínez, H.P., Yannakakis, G.N.: Procedural generation of music-guided weapons. In: 2014 IEEE Conference on Computational Intelligence and Games (CIG), pp. 1–2. IEEE (2014)
11. Hoover, A.K., Cachia, W., Liapis, A., Yannakakis, G.N.: AudioInSpace: exploring the creative fusion of generative audio, visuals and gameplay. In: Johnson, C., Carballal, A., Correia, J. (eds.) EvoMUSART 2015. LNCS, vol. 9027, pp. 101–112. Springer, Cham (2015). doi:10.1007/978-3-319-16498-4_10
12. Schumacher, J.: Species (2016)
13. Schrum, J., Miikkulainen, R.: Constructing game agents through simulated evolution (2015)

14. Avery, P., Togelius, J., Alistar, E., Van Leeuwen, R.P.: Computational intelligence and tower defense games. In: 2011 IEEE Congress on Evolutionary Computation (CEC), pp. 1084–1091. IEEE (2011)
15. Schell, J.: The Art of Game Design: A Book of Lenses. CRC Press, Boca Raton (2014)

EvoIASP

Evolutionary Art Using the Fly Algorithm

Zainab Ali Abbood, Othman Amlal, and Franck P. Vidal$^{(\boxtimes)}$

School of Computer Science, Bangor University, Bangor, UK
{z.a.abbood,f.vidal}@bangor.ac.uk, attumy.22022@gmail.com

Abstract. This study is about Evolutionary art such as digital mosaics. The most common techniques to generate a digital mosaic effect heavily rely on Centroidal Voronoi diagrams. Our method generates artistic images as an optimisation problem without the introduction of any *a priori* knowledge or constraint other than the input image. We adapt a cooperative co-evolution strategy based on the Parisian evolution approach, the Fly algorithm, to produce artistic visual effects from an input image (e.g. a photograph). The primary usage of the Fly algorithm is in computer vision, especially stereo-vision in robotics. It has also been used in image reconstruction for tomography. Until now the individuals correspond to simplistic primitives: Infinitely small 3-D points. In this paper, the individuals have a much more complex representation and represent tiles in a mosaic. They have their own position, size, colour, and rotation angle. We take advantage of graphics processing units (GPUs) to generate the images using the modern OpenGL Shading Language. Different types of tiles are implemented, some with transparency, to generate different visual effects, such as digital mosaic and spray paint. A user study has been conducted to evaluate some of our results. We also compare results with those obtained with GIMP, an open-source software for image manipulation.

Keywords: Digital mosaic · Evolutionary art · Fly algorithm · Parisian evolution · Cooperative co-evolution

1 Introduction

The boundaries between artists and computer scientists may become thinner as the technology becomes more and more ubiquitous. A relatively new field of computer graphics (CG) is called non-photorealistic rendering (NPR). One of the main goals of NPR is to produce "digital art" that can benefit the artistic community as well as the scientific community, e.g. in scientific and medical visualisation [1]. Rendering algorithms have been proposed to simulate multiple forms of traditional art, e.g. digital watercolours [2], line art drawing [3], expressive painting [4], and Celtic art [5]. This paper focuses on the most ancient of classical art forms, mosaics, but also includes other types such as spray paint.

A digital mosaic tries to provide artistic touches to a source image by covering it by tens, hundreds, or thousands of small coloured square tiles in a way that

© Springer International Publishing AG 2017
G. Squillero and K. Sim (Eds.): EvoApplications 2017, Part I, LNCS 10199, pp. 455–470, 2017.
DOI: 10.1007/978-3-319-55849-3_30

resembles ancient mosaics or stained-glass windows. The main goal is to generate a discrete coloured image that still gives the same impression as the real image. To design a piece of mosaic, an artist needs to precisely decompose the original image into tiles with different size, colour, and orientation. The artist requires a large area where to fit the tiles together like a jigsaw forming a special image (it is not unusual to have mosaics over several square metres) [6,7].

In image processing and computer vision, the approach consists of building an algorithm that produces an image with mosaic effects automatically or with as little user intervention as possible. The produced mosaic image should replicate the features of the real image [8]. One of the difficulties in digital mosaic generation is that the same original image may be visualised into various mosaics. Therefore, choosing an appropriate tile data set (including tile number, position, size, colour and rotation of every tile) will impact onto the final mosaic image.

Mosaic images can be categorised into four types: (i) crystallization mosaic, (ii) ancient mosaic, (iii) photo mosaic, and (iv) puzzle image mosaic. The first two types of mosaics are traditional. The mosaic is the reconstruction of a real image using small square tiles. The last two types are obtained by aggregating multiple small images to approximate the real image.

In this article, we revisit digital mosaic-like image generation. Our method is also suitable for other effects, such as spray paint. The image generation is considered as an optimisation problem (image reconstruction) and we propose to solve it using artificial evolution (AE), in a particular cooperative co-evolution (CoCo) strategy. Our method relies on the Fly algorithm [9]. To validate our results, a user study has been conducted. It is used to ascertain which version of our algorithm produces the most visually appealing results. We also demonstrate the ability of the algorithm to preserve edges and compared some of our results with similar ones produced with GNU Image Manipulation Program (GIMP) (http://www.gimp.org/), an open-source software for image editing.

Section 2 discusses previous work. It primarily focuses on digital mosaic, which is the problem the closest to the one considered in this paper. The following section is a general overview of the "Parisian evolution" strategy and of the Fly algorithm. Section 4 describes our approach. It explains how the Fly algorithm can be adapted from robotic applications and medical tomography reconstruction into an evolutionary art generator. The penultimate section presents our results. Several images have been generated with different versions of the algorithm. We conducted an experiment with 25 participants to judge some these results. Concluding remarks are given in the last section.

2   Previous Work

To our knowledge Haeberli is the first researcher who worked on digital mosaic [10]. He created attractive images using an ordered collection of brush strokes to create mosaic and paint effects. He generated images by regulating the colour, shape, size, and orientation of individual brush strokes. To control the mosaic effect his method heavily relies on Voronoi diagrams. One of the main limitations of his algorithm at the time is that it took several hours to produce a satisfactory image. However, much less time should be required with today's "massively parallel processors". This is actually the approach followed by Hoff and his colleagues to overcome the limitation mentioned above. They presented an implementation to compute discrete Voronoi diagrams on graphics processing units (GPUs) [11]. The method starts with a set of random points representing various sites in the image. They are used as the basis to create polygonal meshes that can be rendered in OpenGL to create the Voronoi diagrams. Their approach relies on a metrics based on the Euclidean distance for each site, which computes the distance from any point to that site. Each site has a unique colour.

Hausner improved Hoff's method to use regular and square tiles only. The aim is to create images that have an effect similar to actual mosaics [12]. Each tile may have a different size, colour, and orientation based on the image considered. This approach relies on Centroidal Voronoi (CV) diagrams, which usually order points in regular hexagonal grids. Instead of using the Euclidean distance as a metrics, the Manhattan distance is preferred to place the tiles in different orientation following the edges of the original image.

Lai et al. [13] extended Hausner's work by trying to place mosaic tiles on a surface. The tiles are located over a mesh model that is created using a CV diagram and the Manhattan distance. The size of tiles is regular, i.e all the tiles have the same shape (rectangle) and size. The orientation of tiles depends on a vector field, which is interpolated over the surface based on control vectors. The algorithm is sensitive to sharp creases, open boundaries, and boundaries between regions of different colours, which may affect the orientation of tiles.

Lu et al. presented a hybrid method that combines Centroidal Voronoi Tessellation (CVT) and Monte Carlo with minimisation (MCM). CVT places the tiles on a mesh surface. Because of local minima, MCM is applied to optimise the result of CVT on a global basis, which improves the final results [14].

In 2015, Hu and his colleagues presented an algorithm for the reconstruction of digital surface mosaics based on irregularly shaped tiles [15]. They use a hybrid optimisation paradigm, which includes continuous configuration optimisation and discrete combinatorial optimisation. In the continuous configuration optimisation scheme, the tiles are adjusted using iterative relaxation. The aim is to adapt their position, orientation, and scale to fit onto approximated Voronoi regions. The aims of the discrete combinatorial optimisation are to reduce the amount of overlapping tiles and to increase the surface coverage.

Nguyen et al. [16] produced digital images using an evolutionary algorithm (EA) based on (MAP-Elites). Their aim was to demonstrate that deep neural networks (DNNs) can be easily fooled. Their implementation evolves a population to produce a tremendous diversity of images with a strong chance that DNN can classify the objects correctly.

Another approach is the use of Evolutionary art [17]. In this context, an EA somehow generates images. Artificial evolution is used to modify the images (e.g. by mutation and recombination). Evolutionary art is often an interactive task where the user/artist plays the role of a selection operator. Our work follows the Evolutionary art paradigm. We provide a method without the need of any user interaction, without constraints such as the requirement to generate a Voronoi diagram, and limit the amount of *a priori* knowledge to the input image.

3   Fly Algorithm Paradigm

We saw in the previous section various approaches to translate an input image into a digital mosaic. The problem can be defined as follows:

Given a rectangular region I^2 in the plane $\mathbb{R}^2$, a dataset of N tiles, a set of constraints, and a vector field $\phi(x, y)$ defined on that region, find N sites $P_i(x_i, y_i)$ in I^2 to place the N tiles, one at each site P_i, such that all tiles are disjoint, the area they cover is maximized and the constraints are verified as much as possible.

In this context, image generation can be studied as a special case of the *set cover problem*, which is NP-complete [18]. It can be solved as an optimisation problem [7,12]: Find the best set of tiles to generate a rectangular region to approximate a coloured image. Each tile has a colour that represents the specific part of the image it covers. For more realistic reconstruction, the tiles can rotate at a given angle $\phi(x, y)$ following the direction field for that region and may have sightly different sizes. If there are N tiles to place, as each tile has 9 parameters (3-D position, 3 colour components, width, height, and rotation angle), the search space has $9 \times N$ dimensions.

In addition to being a difficult optimisation problem to solve, the digital mosaic generation is also related to topics in computer graphics and visualisation. In particular we saw in Sect. 2 that most of the mosaic synthesis methods are based on Centroidal Voronoi. In this paper, we propose to solve such a problem without the use of any Voronoi diagram. Instead we rely on an unsupervised EA based on cooperative co-evolution principles.

The approach we follow is called "Parisian evolution". In classical EAs the best individual of the population corresponds to the solution of the optimisation problem, i.e a global optimum. In the Parisian approach all the individuals of the population (or at least a subset of the population) is the solution: Each individual only encodes a part of the solution, and they have to collaborate to build the final solution. Fig. 1 illustrates the mechanics of the Parisian evolution. A Parisian EA usually contains all the usual components of an EA (i.e. genetic operators such as selection, mutation, and recombination), plus the additional components as follows:

- 2 levels of fitness
  - *Global fitness* computed on the whole population,
  - *Local fitness* computed on each individual to assess their own contribution to the global solution.

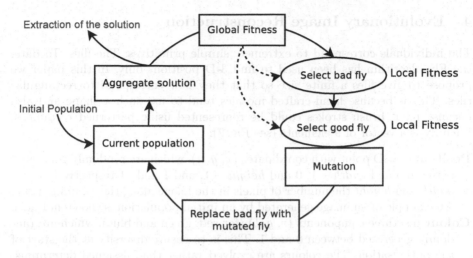

Fig. 1. Steady-state Parisian evolution algorithm.

The global fitness may be the sum (or a complex combination) of the local fitnesses but not necessarily. The local fitness of an individual may be defined as its marginal contribution to the global fitness.

- **A diversity mechanism** to avoid individuals gathering in only a few areas of the search space.

The Parisian approach shares many similarities with the Cooperative Co-Evolution Algorithm (CCEA). Similar internal evolutionary engines are considered in classical EA, CCEA and Parisian evolution. The difference between CCEA and Parisian evolution resides in the population's semantics. CCEA divides a big problem into sub-problems (groups of individuals) and solves them separately toward the big problem [19]. There is no interaction/breeding between individuals of the different sub-populations, only with individuals of the same sub-population. However, Parisian EAs solve a whole problem as a big component. All population's individuals cooperate together to drive the whole population toward attractive areas of the search space.

One good example of Parisian EA is the Fly algorithm. Here an individual is a 3-D point. The position of each fly is optimised using the repetitive application of genetic operators. The global and local fitness functions are the key elements of the algorithm. The final set of points is the solution of the optimisation problem.

It has first been applied in computer vision, particularly stereovision, and robotics [9], where flies are projected to gather on the surface of objects. It has been successfully applied to autonomous robots for obstacle avoidance [20,21] and to self localisation and mapping (SLAM) [22]. Another computer vision application is related to hand gesture recognition [23]. Computer vision is not the only field where the Fly algorithm has been applied. It has been tried in tomography reconstruction in nuclear medicine, where the concentration of flies approximate a radioactive concentration within the human body [24]. Our approach is closely related to this work.

4   Evolutionary Image Reconstruction

The individuals correspond to extremely simple primitives: The flies. To date, the Fly algorithm has been used to find 3-D positions only. In this paper we propose to give flies a finite size so that they now correspond to rectangular tiles. This is because hand-crafted mosaics tend to use such a shape and also because paint brush strokes could be represented using patterned rectangles. Each fly is a vector of 9 elements (see Fig. 2):

Position is a 3D point with coordinates (x, y, z), which are randomly generated between 0 and $width - 1$, 0 and $height - 1$, and 1 and -1 respectively (with $width$ and $height$ the number of pixels in the image along the x- and y-axes). An example of an image generated by an initial population is shown in Fig. 3.

Colour has three components (r, g, b) (for red, green and blue), which are randomly generated between 0 and 1. This is to ensure diversity at the start of the optimisation. Tile colours are evolved rather than assigned deterministically. It leads to better results in term of sharpness when tiles are located at edges between different regions of the image (see the difference between Figs. 6(a) and (b), when tile colours are evolved, and Figs. 6(c) and (d), when the tile colours are not evolved).

Rotation Angle is randomly generated between 0 and 360.

Scaling factor has two components (w, h), which control the size of the tile along its horizontal and vertical axes.

Local fitness measures its marginal contribution toward the global solution.

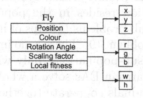

Fig. 2. Structure of the fly data.

The initial scaling factors are set to make sure the tiles could cover the totality of the image [12]. If there are N individuals, the scaling factors are:

$$d = \sqrt{(width \times height)/N} \tag{1}$$

Due to the randomness in the initial tile positions, tiles overlap. It creates holes in Fig. 3. They progressively disappear during the evolution process, which aims to optimise the 9 parameters (position, colour, scale, and rotation) of all the N individuals. To achieve this, the algorithm minimises the global fitness function. To assess how good the population is, we compare the input image (ref) with the image generated using the tiles corresponding to the population (pop).

Fig. 3. Random initial population.

We use the sum of absolute error (SAE) (also known as Manhattan distance) to quantify the error between ref and the computed image pop:

$$\text{SAE}(pop, ref) = \sum_i \sum_j |ref(i,j) - pop(i,j)| \qquad (2)$$

To improve the population's performance, we need a large proportion of good individuals. The performance of a single fly is evaluated using the local fitness function, which is used during the selection process. In our context, the local fitness is called "marginal fitness", F_m) (see Eq. 3). It measures the impact of the selected fly on the global performance of the population. To measure how good or bad the contribution of Fly i is, we use the SAE metrics with the leave-one-out cross-validation method:

$$F_m(i) = \text{SAE}(pop - \{i\}, ref) - \text{SAE}(pop, ref)) \qquad (3)$$

with $pop - \{i\}$ the image computed with all individuals but Fly i. The numerical value of $F_m(i)$ can be easily interpreted by looking at its sign:

- If the error is greater with Fly i than without, $\text{sgn}(F_m(i)) < 0$, then Fly i damages the performance of the population.
- If the error is smaller with Fly i than without, $\text{sgn}(F_m(i)) > 0$, then Fly i has a positive impact on the performance of the population.
- If the error is the same, $\text{sgn}(F_m(i)) = 0$, then Fly i is not beneficial nor detrimental. It may happen when Fly i is covering similar flies.

We use this principle in our *Threshold selection* operator [24]. To find a fly to kill, pick a random number i between 0 and $N - 1$. If $F_m(i) \leq 0$, then Fly i can be killed, if not pick another random number i until $F_m(i) \leq 0$. To find a fly to reproduce, find one whose fitness $F_m(i)$ is strictly positive. During the evolution process, the number of flies whose fitness is negative or null will decrease. There will be more and more good flies; and fewer and fewer bad flies: It gives a good stopping criteria to the algorithm as the selection operator will struggle to find bad flies to kill.

Computing the marginal fitness for the problem considered here is time consuming on a central processing unit (CPU). Therefore, all the computations to generate images are performed on a GPU using the OpenGL Shading

Language (GLSL). The image is stored in a 2-D texture using a framebuffer object (FBO). The texture is then passed to a shader program to compute the pixel-wise absolute error between ref and pop. The sum is also performed on the GPU using the OpenCL implementation of the reduction operator in Boost.Compute [25, 26]. It provides the SAE in an effective manner.

Our implementation is based on a steady state evolutionary strategy (see Fig. 1). At each iteration of the optimisation process, a bad fly is selected for death and replaced with another one. We use a mutation operator to produce a new fly that is slightly different from the selected good fly. The aim is to create a new fly in the vicinity of a good fly. In this way the new fly is likely to be a good one too. Crossover is not used: If we consider two good flies located at the opposite corners of the image, a new fly in between is very likely to be bad.

The algorithm stops when a stopping criterion is met, e.g. maximum number of iterations, when the evolution process does not improve the performance of the whole population, or when the Threshold selection becomes too slow to find bad flies. A restart mechanism is eventually used to further improve the results. It allows the algorithm to leave a local minima (see Fig. 5).

5   Results

In this section we evaluate our method using the results obtained with five test images of increasing complexity (see Row 0 in Fig. 4). We consider the image reconstruction with 12 different schemes (see Table 1) using:

- Different image sizes: 256×256 or 512×512;
- Different colour quantisations: 60 colours or full RGB colours (i.e. 2^{24});
- Different types of tiles: square with a border, square without a border, set of lines, or flower;
- With or without restart mechanism.

For each test image, evolutionary reconstructions are obtained with these schemes:

- As a feasibility study, the first two images (Star and Yin & Yang) are relatively simple and have a relatively low resolution. 6 schemes of Table 1 are used.
- Three other test images are more complex. They are used to evaluate the 12 schemes.

Schemes 1 to 4 uses the algorithm presented in Fig. 1. The flies correspond to uniform rectangles (see "one shader" in Table 1). Schemes 5 to 8 uses the algorithm presented in Fig. 1 twice, with one restart between the two runs. The initial population of the first run is random (as in Fig. 3). The initial population of the second run is the best population of the first run. The flies correspond to complex shapes (see "two shaders" in Table 1). Examples of template shapes are given in Fig. 7. Different shader programs can be used to generate different effects depending on the pixel colour/intensity of the templates. Schemes 9 to 12 are almost similar to Schemes 5 to 8. The only difference is that the flies are

Table 1. Summary of all the possible configurations used in Fig. 4.

#	256 × 256	512 × 512	60 colours	Full colour	One shader	Two shaders	Restart
1	✓			✓	✓		
2	✓		✓		✓		
3		✓		✓	✓		
4		✓	✓		✓		
5	✓			✓		✓	
6	✓		✓			✓	
7		✓		✓		✓	
8		✓	✓			✓	
9	✓			✓	✓	✓	✓
10	✓		✓		✓	✓	✓
11		✓		✓	✓	✓	✓
12		✓	✓		✓	✓	✓

uniform rectangles during the first run and complex shapes during the second run. The aim is to speed-up computations.

The algorithm is tested with two sets of parameters (see Table 2), one with a 22500-D search space, and the other one with a 45000-D search space. We fix the mutation probability to 100% because, as we saw previously, crossover is not suitable in our case. In practice, the only parameters chosen by the user are the image (and its size) and the number of individuals. The initial size of tiles is computed depending on the images size and the number of individuals (see Eq. 1). Note that the sizes will then encompass evolution. We empirically estimated suitable population sizes for different image resolutions. We balanced the number of flies and image size to avoid a premature convergence that would slow down the entire process.

Table 2. Parameters used to generate the images in Fig. 4.

Image size	256 × 256	512 × 512
Number of flies	2500	5000
Number of generations	40000	40000
Probability of mutation	100%	100%
Probability of crossover	0.0%	0.0%
Corresponding scheme	1, 2, 5, 6, 9 and 10	3, 4, 7, 8, 11 and 12
Number of unknowns	$9 \times 2,500 = 22,500$	$9 \times 5,000 = 45,000$

To assess which scheme from Table 1 is the most suitable one, Fig. 4 was printed on A3 paper and we individually asked 25 participants to indicate which

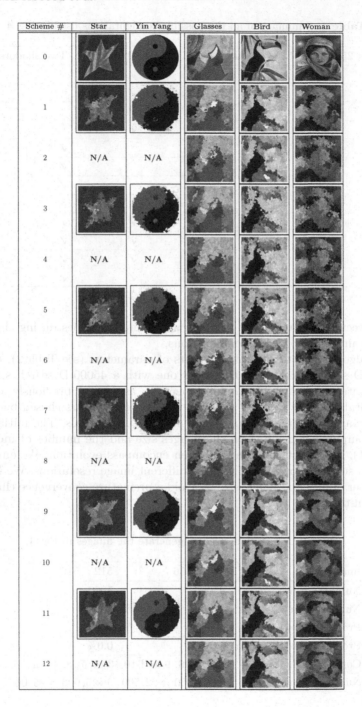

Fig. 4. Evolutionary art using schemes of Table 1. The woman image (Fatima) is from the artist Lubna Ashrafis. Other test images are from the Open Images Dataset (https://github.com/openimages/dataset) under CC BY 4.0 license.

Table 3. Vote results (25 participants voted for their preferred image for each column in Fig. 4).

Scheme #	Star	Yin Yang	Glasses	Bird	Woman
3	0%	12%	20%	0%	0%
4	0%	0%	0%	0%	4%
9	12%	4%	8%	24%	4%
10	0%	0%	20%	**32%**	0%
11	**88%**	**84%**	**36%**	20%	**48%**
12	0%	0%	16%	24%	44%

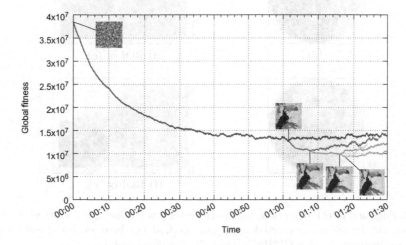

Fig. 5. Evolution of the global fitness with 4 restarts. Images were computed using a Macbook Laptop with a 2.6 GHz Intel Core i5 CPU with an Intel Iris 5100 GPU. (Color figure online)

image in each column they prefer. Table 3 shows the results in percentages. Strategies 11 and 12 are particularly popular among participants. To a lesser exten, the 10th scheme is also popular, the 3rd and 9th also received some votes. Other schemes did not. Schemes 10, 11, and 12 use two shader programs and a restart mechanism. Scheme 11 uses full-colour in the original image, Scheme 12 did not.

Figure 5 shows the evolution of global fitness with and without restart. It is well known that restart is useful in classical evolutionary algorithms where the solution of the optimisation problem is the best individual of the population. However, very little has been done for the cooperative co-evolution scheme of the Fly algorithm. In [24] a mitosis operator is used to double the size of the population. Here we keep the size of the population constant. When restart is not used, the evolution reaches a plateau then stagnates (see purple curve). After the first restart, the global fitness decreases (see green curve). After the

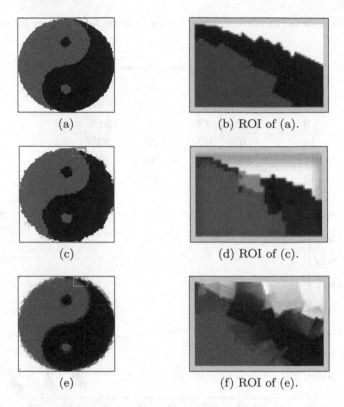

(a)

(b) ROI of (a).

(c)

(d) ROI of (c).

(e)

(f) ROI of (e).

Fig. 6. Edge and depth detection: (a) Image reconstructed using our method (evolving colours); (b) Image reconstructed using our method (without evolving colours); (c) Image reconstructed using GIMPressionist. (Color figure online)

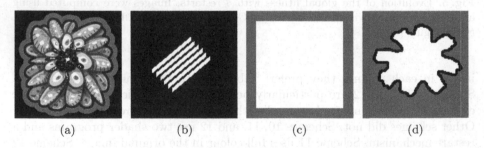

(a)   (b)   (c)   (d)

Fig. 7. Examples of tile templates.

global minimum is found, it is possible that the global fitness increases. A similar phenomenon is observed for the subsequent restarts (see blue, yellow, and orange curves). This experiment demonstrates the benefit of a few restarts in the Fly algorithm.

During the generation of the images, tiles can be located at different depth to determine the colour of the closest (visible) tile. It is efficiently implemented

(a) Mask: Flower (Fig. 7a).

(b) Mask: Flower (Fig. 7a).

(c) Mask: Set of lines (Fig. 7b).

(d) Mask: Set of lines (Fig. 7b).

(e) Mask: square (Fig. 7c).

(f) Mask: Flower (Fig. 7d).

Fig. 8. More appealing visual effects using different masks and shader programs.

using OpenGL's Z-buffer. Depending on the properties of the regions of the image, black tiles may be located behind red tiles, or *vice versa*. The algorithm picks up the discriminated edge between the black and red regions, no matter how small the regions are in the original image compared to the minimum size of a tile. For example, in Fig. 6(b) red tiles are over black tiles that are larger than the actual region in the original image. It also shows that our evolutionary algorithm chooses the right rotation angle to follow the curvature of the edges in the original image when colours are evolved. This is not as accurate when colours are picked up directly from the original image as in Fig. 6(d). Edges are even blurrier in images generated using GIMP's filter (GIMPressionist) (see Fig. 6(f)).

In the following examples, four shapes (or masks) (see Fig. 7) to generate tiles: Square, flowers and stripes. Figure 8 shows the results using the toucan as a test image. The shader program to generate the images can be altered to create different visual effects. The aim is to generate more appealing images. Figure 8(a) and (b) have been produced using the same mask (Fig. 7(a)) but with slightly different shader programs. Figure 8(c) and (d) have been generated using Fig. 7(b) as mask, but with a much bigger size and without considering the rotation angle of the tiles in the second image. The masks used in Fig. 8(e) and (f) include an edge. More results are available as videos on YouTube at http://tinyurl.com/ho5kfvb.

To demonstrate the usefulness of our approach, further comparison examples have been done between the proposed algorithm and GIMP using two types of mask: Flower and stripe (see Figs. 8(d), (f) and 9). Our method leads to better reconstructions in term of edges and colours (brightness).

(a) Mask: Set of lines (Fig. 7b).

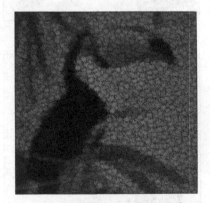

(b) Mask: Flower (Fig. 7d).

Fig. 9. Example of images produced with GIMP's filter (GIMPressionist).

6   Conclusion

The problem tackled here lies within the field of Evolutionary art. Our method relies on techniques inherited from CG, AE and scientific computing. We used an AE strategy based on the Fly algorithm for creating visual effects on an image in a fully-automatic fashion. The algorithm optimises the location of tiles in the 3-D space to approximate an input image. We used real-time CG rendering to generate the image data, and GPU computing to calculate the fitness functions. The algorithm can be modified to introduce multiple artistic visual effects. Different templates are used (square, flower, stripes) to define the shape of tiles.

Our initial proof-of-concept shows that the Fly algorithm can be used in Evolutionary Arts. Our implementation could be refined to take advantage of more advanced genetic operators, for example to speed-up computations, and to recover fine details. Further work will also include a more robust evaluation to ascertain that the resulting images are visually appealing. It will include a more extensive comparison study and an user evaluation survey. A friendly graphical user interface (GUI) will be added to introduce an optional level of user interaction. It will allow the user to control some parameters of the output image, e.g. shape of tiles, number of tiles, etc. A plugin for an image manipulation program, such as GIMP, will be released to make it available to potential users.

Acknowledgements. This work was partially supported by the European Commission, Grant no. 321968 (http://fly4pet.fpvidal.net), and the Iraqi Ministry of Higher Education and Scientific Research (MOHESR).

References

1. Isenberg, T.: A survey of illustrative visualization techniques for diffusion-weighted MRI tractography. In: Hotz, I., Schultz, T. (eds.) Visualization and Processing of Higher Order Descriptors for Multi-valued Data, pp. 235–256. Springer, Cham (2015)
2. Devinck, F., Spillmann, L.: The watercolor effect: spacing constraints. Vis. Res. **49**(24), 2911–2917 (2009)
3. Li, Z., Qin, S., Jin, X., Yu, Z., Lin, J.: Skeleton-enhanced line drawings for 3D models. Graph Models **76**(6), 620–632 (2014)
4. Chu, N.S.H., Tai, C.L.: Real-time painting with an expressive virtual Chinese brush. IEEE Comput. Graph **24**(5), 76–85 (2004)
5. Kaplan, M., Cohen, E.: Computer generated celtic design. In: Proceedings of the 14th Eurographics Workshop on Rendering, vol. 44, pp. 9–19 (2003)
6. Elber, G., Wolberg, G.: Rendering traditional mosaics. Visual Comput. **19**(1), 67–78 (2003)
7. Battiato, S., Blasi, G.D., Farinella, G.M., Gallo, G.: Digital mosaic frameworks - an overview. Comput. Graph Forum **26**(4), 794–812 (2007)
8. Faustino, G.M., De Figueiredo, L.H.: Simple adaptive mosaic effects. In: Brazilian Symposium of Computer Graphic and Image Processing, pp. 315–322 (2005)

9. Louchet, J.: Stereo analysis using individual evolution strategy. In: Proceedings of the International Conference on Pattern Recognition, ICPR 2000, vol. 1, pp. 908–911 (2000)
10. Haeberli, P.: Paint by numbers: abstract image representations. SIGGRAPH Comput. Graph. **24**(4), 207–214 (1990)
11. Hoff III., K.E., Keyser, J., Lin, M., Manocha, D., Culver, T.: Fast computation of generalized Voronoi diagrams using graphics hardware. In: Proceedings of SIGGRAPH 1999, pp. 277–286 (1999)
12. Hausner, A.: Simulating decorative mosaics. In: Proceedings of SIGGRAPH 2001, pp. 573–580 (2001)
13. Lai, Y.K., Hu, S.M., Martin, R.R.: Surface mosaics. Visual Comput. **22**(9), 604–611 (2006)
14. Lu, L., Sun, F., Pan, H., Wang, W.: Global optimization of centroidal voronoi tessellation with monte carlo approach. IEEE T Vis. Comput. Gr. **18**(11), 1880–1890 (2012)
15. Hu, W., Chen, Z., Pan, H., Yu, Y., Grinspun, E., Wang, W.: Surface mosaic synthesis with irregular tiles. IEEE Trans. Vis. Comput. Gr. **22**(3), 1302–1313 (2016)
16. Nguyen, A., Yosinski, J., Clune, J.: Deep neural networks are easily fooled: high confidence predictions for unrecognizable images. In: IEEE Conference on Computer Vision and Pattern Recognition (CVPR), pp. 427–436 (2015)
17. Collomosse, J.: Evolutionary search for the artistic rendering of photographs. In: Romero, J., Machado, P. (eds.) The Art of Artificial Evolution: A Handbook on Evolutionary Art and Music, pp. 39–62. Springer, Heidelberg (2007)
18. Karp, R.M.: Reducibility among combinatorial problems. In: Miller, R.E., Thatcher, J.W., Bohlinger, J.D. (eds.) Complexity of Computer Computations, pp. 85–103. Springer, New York (1972)
19. Mesejo, P., Ibáñez, O., Fernández-Blanco, E., Pazos, A., Porto-Pazos, A.B., Cedrón, F.: Artificial neuron-glia networks learning approach based on cooperative coevolution. Int. J. Neural Syst. **25**(4), 1550012 (2015)
20. Boumaza, A.M., Louchet, J.: Dynamic flies: using real-time parisian evolution in robotics. In: Boers, E.J.W. (ed.) EvoWorkshops 2001. LNCS, vol. 2037, pp. 288–297. Springer, Heidelberg (2001). doi:10.1007/3-540-45365-2_30
21. Louchet, J., Guyon, M., Lesot, M.J., Boumaza, A.: Dynamic flies: a new pattern recognition tool applied to stereo sequence processing. Pattern Recogn. Lett. **23**(1–3), 335–345 (2002)
22. Louchet, J., Sapin, E.: Flies open a door to SLAM. In: Applications of Evolutionary Computation: EvoApplicatons 2009, pp. 385–394 (2010)
23. Kaufmann, B., Louchet, J., Lutton, E.: Hand posture recognition using real-time artificial evolution. In: Applications of Evolutionary Computation: EvoApplicatons 2010, pp. 251–260 (2010)
24. Vidal, F.P., Louchet, J., Rocchisani, J.M., Lutton, É.: New genetic operators in the fly algorithm: application to medical PET image reconstruction. In: Applicationsof Evolutionary Computation: EvoApplicatons 2010, pp. 292–301 (2010)
25. Lutz, K.: Boost.Compute (2016). http://boostorg.github.io/compute/. Accessed 26 Oct 2016
26. Gaster, B., Howes, L., Kaeli, D.R., Mistry, P., Schaa, D.: Heterogeneous Computing with OpenCL. 1edn. Morgan Kaufmann, USA (2011)

Bagging and Feature Selection for Classification with Incomplete Data

Cao Truong Tran[⊠], Mengjie Zhang, Peter Andreae, and Bing Xue

School of Engineering and Computer Science, Victoria University of Wellington,
PO Box 600, Wellington 6140, New Zealand
{cao.truong.tran,mengjie.zhang,peter.andreae,bing.xue}@ecs.vuw.ac.nz

Abstract. Missing values are an unavoidable issue of many real-world datasets. Dealing with missing values is an essential requirement in classification problem, because inadequate treatment with missing values often leads to large classification errors. Some classifiers can directly work with incomplete data, but they often result in big classification errors and generate complex models. Feature selection and bagging have been successfully used to improve classification, but they are mainly applied to complete data. This paper proposes a combination of bagging and feature selection to improve classification with incomplete data. To achieve this purpose, a wrapper-based feature selection which can directly work with incomplete data is used to select suitable feature subsets for bagging. The experiments on eight incomplete datasets were designed to compare the proposed method with three other popular methods that are able to deal with incomplete data using C4.5/REPTree as classifiers and using Particle Swam Optimisation as a search technique in feature selection. Results show that the combination of bagging and feature selection can not only achieve better classification accuracy than the other methods but also generate less complex models compared to the bagging method.

Keywords: Incomplete data · Ensemble · Feature selection · Classification · Particle swarm optimisation · C4.5 · REPTree

1 Introduction

Classification is one of the main tasks in machine learning and data mining, and has been successfully applied to many areas such as computer science, engineering and biology. Moreover, classification has been continuously received a great attention. However, there are still open issues in classification, and one of the issues is classification with incomplete data [6,9].

Incomplete data is data which contains some fields without values. Missing values are a common problem in many datasets. For example, 45% of the datasets in UCI machine learning repository, which is one of the most popular collection of benchmark datasets for machine learning, contain missing values [6]. Reasons for datastes containing missing values are various. For example, social survey sheets often contain missing values because respondents refuse to answer some

© Springer International Publishing AG 2017
G. Squillero and K. Sim (Eds.): EvoApplications 2017, Part I, LNCS 10199, pp. 471–486, 2017.
DOI: 10.1007/978-3-319-55849-3_31

questions; medical patient records also usually have missing values because all tests often cannot be done on patients [13].

Missing values cause serious problems for classification. One of the most serious problems is the non-applicability of majority classifiers with incomplete data. Majority classifiers require complete data; therefore, they cannot directly work with incomplete data. Moreover, missing values often lead to big classification errors [6,20].

One of the most popular approaches to solving classification with incomplete data is to use a classifier which can directly classify incomplete data. For example, C4.5 can directly deal with incomplete data in both training and testing process. Although this approach can tackle incomplete data to some extent, it often results in more complex learnt models and bigger classification errors [19]. Therefore, further approaches to improving classifiers able to directly classify incomplete data should be investigated.

Feature selection is the process to select a suitable feature subset from the original features. Feature selection has been proven capable of improving classification accuracy and reducing the complexity of learnt models [14]. Although feature selection is mainly applied to complete data, it is also used to improve classification with incomplete data [18,22].

Ensemble is a machine learning method that builds a set of classifiers instead of a single classifier for classification tasks. Ensemble methods have been demonstrated to enhance classification accuracy [4]. One of the most popular ensemble methods is bagging. Although bagging helps improve classification accuracy, it often generates more complex learnt models [17]. Moreover, bagging is mainly applied to complete data. Therefore, researches on improving bagging for classification with incomplete data should be investigated.

1.1   Research Goals

The goal of this paper is to propose a new method which improves bagging for classification with incomplete data. In order to achieve the goal, a combination of bagging and feature selection is proposed to classify incomplete data. The proposed method is compared with three benchmark methods for classification with incomplete data. The first benchmark method is to use a classifier which can directly classify incomplete data. The second benchmark method is to combine feature selection and a classifier which can directly classify incomplete data. The third benchmark method is to combine bagging and a classifier which can directly classify incomplete data. The experimental results are used to address the following objectives:

1. Whether the combination of bagging and feature selection can achieve better classification accuracy compared to the other methods for classification with incomplete data.
2. Whether the combination of bagging and feature selection can generate less complex learnt models compared to bagging with all features for classification with incomplete data.

1.2 Organisation

The rest of this paper is organised as follows. Section 2 outlines related work. Section 3 presents the proposed method. After that, Sect. 4 presents comparison method and experiment design. Section 5 shows results and analysis. Finally, Sect. 6 presents conclusions and future work.

2 Related Work

This section outlines related work including classification with incomplete data, feature selection and ensemble learning.

2.1 Classification with Incomplete Data

There are two main approaches to classification with incomplete data. One approach is to use imputation methods to transform incomplete data to complete data before using classification algorithms. The other approach is to use classification algorithms which can directly work with incomplete data without using imputation methods [6].

The purpose of imputation methods is to replace missing values with plausible values. For example, mean imputation fills all missing values in each feature with the average of all complete values in the same feature. The main benefit of using imputation methods is that they can provide complete data which can be used by any classification algorithm. However, simple imputation methods such as mean imputation often lead to the big classification error. Moreover, more sophisticated imputation methods are often computationally intensive to estimate missing values before using classification algorithms [20].

The majority of classification algorithms cannot directly work with incomplete data. However, there are some classification algorithms which are able to directly classify incomplete data. For example, C4.5 [19] use a probabilistic approach to tackle missing values in both the training set and test set. The main benefit of using classification algorithms able to directly classify incomplete data is that the classification algorithms do not require any time for estimating missing values. However, when the classification algorithms work with incomplete data, they often generate more complexed models and lead to large classification errors [20]. Therefore, further approaches to improving the classification algorithms should be investigated.

2.2 Feature Selection

Feature selection is the process of selecting a relevant subset of features from the original features. The underlying reason for using feature selection is that the data often contains redundant/irrelevant features, which should be removed without much loss of information. By removing redundant/irrelevant features, feature selection can help improve classification accuracy. Moreover, thanks to providing a smaller number of features, feature selection can help to speed up the training process and make simpler learnt classifiers which are easier to interpret [1,14,24].

Feature selection includes two main procedures: a search procedure and an evaluation procedure. The search procedure is used to search feature subsets while the evaluation procedure is used to measure the quality of feature subsets. The performance of feature selection strongly depends on the quality of both of the procedures [1,14,24].

Search methods for feature selection can be categorised into traditional search methods and evolutionary search methods. For example, sequential forward selection and sequential backward selection are two common traditional search methods for feature selection. In recent times, evolutionary algorithms have been successfully used as search methods in feature selection. Genetic algorithms and particle swarm optimisation (PSO) are two popular evolutionary search methods for feature selection [24].

Evaluation methods for feature selection can be categorised into wrapper methods and filter methods. A wrapper method uses a classifier to evaluate feature subsets while a filter method uses a measure such as information gain to evaluate. In order to evaluate each feature subset, wrapper methods need to train a classifier and then test its performance; therefore, they are often computationally expensive. In contrast, evaluation measures in filter methods are often computationally cheap; therefore, filter methods are often more efficient and general than wrapper methods. However, wrapper methods are often more accurate than filter methods [1,14,24].

Particle swarm optimisation (PSO) is a swarm intelligent algorithm proposed by Kennedy and Eberhart in 1995 [10]. Recently, PSO has been widely used as a search method for feature selection. Continuous PSO is usually used for feature selection, where the dimensionality of each particle is equal to the total number of features and a threshold θ is often used to determine whether or not a feature is selected. If the value is smaller than θ, the corresponding feature is not selected, otherwise, it is selected. PSO has been used for both wrapper and filter. In a PSO-based wrapper, a classifier is required to evaluate particles, and the fitness of each particle is the accuracy of the classifier by using selected features. In a PSO-based filter, an evaluation measure is required to evaluate particles, and the fitness of each particle is estimated by the measure with selected features [24].

Feature selection methods have been mainly applied to complete data. However, in recent times, there are some feature selection approaches to incomplete data. In [5], the mutual information criterion which is based on k-nearest neighbours is expanded to tackle with missing values. The experimental results show that the method can select important feature subsets without using any imputation method and help enhance the performance of the prediction models. In [18], a combination of the mutual information measure and rough sets is proposed to evaluate feature subsets with incomplete data. The empirical results show that the proposed method is effective for selecting feature subsets with incomplete data. A wrapper-based feature selection for incomplete data is proposed in [22], where PSO is used as a search technique and C4.5 which is able to directly classify incomplete data is used to evaluate feature subsets. The experimental results show that the proposed methods not only can improve the accuracy of the classifier, but it also can reduce the complexity of the classifier.

2.3 Ensemble Learning

Ensemble learning is a machine learning method which constructs a set of classifiers for a classification task. It classifies a new instance by voting the decision of individual classifiers. The set of classifiers has been proved capable of achieving higher accuracy than any of the individual classifiers [4].

An ensemble of classifiers is accurate if the individual classifiers in the ensemble is accurate and diverse. Two popular methods to construct accurate ensembles are Bagging and Boosting. Both of the methods use "resampling" techniques to construct different training sets for each of the classifier. Bagging manipulates the original training data by randomly drawing with replacement instances. Consequently, some of the original instances might appear multiple times in the resulting training data while others might disappear. Bagging is usually helpful with "unstable"classification algorithms like neural networks and decision trees where small changes in the training data often result in major changes in predictions. Experimental results reveal that Bagging ensemble almost always achieves better accuracy than a single classifier. Boosting also manipulates the original training data by drawing with replacement, but it uses the performance of the previous classifier(s) to calculate the probability of selecting each instance. Boosting tries to construct new classifiers that are better to classify instances for which the current ensemble's performance is poor. Therefore, in Boosting, instances which are incorrectly classified by previous classifiers are more often selected than instances which are correctly classified. Experimental results reveal that with little or no classification noise, Boosting ensemble also almost always achieve better accuracy than a single classifier, and it is sometimes more accurate than Bagging ensemble. However, with substantial classification noise, Boosting ensemble is often less accurate than a single classifier since Boosting ensemble often overfits noisy datasets [16].

Feature selection also has been used to improve ensemble learning. In [17], a genetic algorithm (GA) is used to search a suitable set of feature subsets for ensemble. Initially, a set of classifiers is generated where each classifier is built by randomly picking a set of features. After that, new classifiers are created by using the genetic operators. Finally, the best fit individuals are chosen to build an appropriate set of feature subsets which is then used to create an ensemble. Neural network is used as a classifier and the fitness of each individual is the combination of accuracy and diversity. Experiment results show that the feature selection ensemble can achieve better accuracy than the popular and powerful ensembles of Bagging and Boosting. In [7], GA is also applied to search a set of feature subsets for ensemble, where the GA runs multiple times with different training data to provide different feature subsets. C4.5 and Euclidean Decision Tables are used as classifiers and the fitness of each individual is the classification accuracy. Experiments show that the feature selection ensemble is more accurate than other existing ensemble methods. In [15], a multi-objective GA is used to select a set of feature subsets which is used to construct a set of classifiers. After that the multi-objective GA is used again to select an optimal set of classifiers. The experimental results show that the proposed method is more effective than Boosting and Bagging for the handwriting recognition problem.

Ensemble learning also has been used to solve classification with incomplete data. In [11], a set of classifiers is constructed to classify incomplete data, where each base classifier is trained with a random subset of features. In [2], incomplete data is firstly grouped into complete subsets, and then each subset is used to train one classifier. Although the two methods can tackle incomplete data in some extent, they cannot ensure to classify all incomplete instances.

Popular ensemble methods such as bagging/boosting have been mainly applied to complete data. Therefore, the application of popular ensemble methods for incomplete data should be investigated. Moreover, combining popular ensemble methods with feature selection has not been investigated. Feature selection can improve the performance of classification with incomplete data. Therefore, a combination of popular ensemble methods with feature selection for incomplete data also need be investigated.

3   The Proposed Method

The key idea of the proposed method is that bagging is combined with feature selection to improve the accuracy and diversity of a set of learnt classifiers. The underlying reason is that to construct a set of classifiers, bagging repeatedly resamples the training dataset to build a set of training resampled datasets. The resampled datasets often contain redundant/irrelavant features. Moreover, feature selection has been proven capable of remove redundant/irrelavant features. Therefore, feature selection could be applied to each resampled dataset to eliminate redundant/irrelavant features. By eliminating redundant/irrelavant features, feature selection can help improve resampled datasets which in turn can help build more accurate and less complex learnt classifiers.

Figure 1 shows main steps of the training process of the proposed method. In the training process, firstly, the training dataset is put into a resampling procedure several times to generate a set of training resampled datasets.

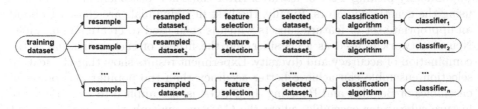

Fig. 1. The training process of classification with incomplete data by combining bagging and feature selection.

After that, each training resampled dataset is put into a feature selection procedure to select a suitable feature subset which is then used to transform the training resampled dataset into the training selected dataset. Subsequently, each the training selected dataset is used by a classification algorithm to learn a classifier. As a result, the training process generates a set of classifiers. In the application process, the set of classifiers is combined to classify a new instance.

The main steps of the proposed method are presented in the following subsections.

3.1 Resampling Data

The purpose of each time resampling training dataset is to create a random redistribution of the training dataset. Each training resampled dataset is generated by randomly choosing with replacement the same number of instances in the original training dataset. As a result, many of the original instances might be repeated in the training resampled dataset while others might be left out.

3.2 Feature Selection

The key difference between the proposed method and bagging is this step. Bagging immediately uses a set of training resampled datasets to build a set of classifiers. In contrast, the proposed method applies feature selection to eliminate redundant/irrelevant features in each training resampled dataset before building a set of classifiers.

In order to remove redundant/irrelevant features in incomplete data, any search technique can be used to find feature subsets. However, to evaluate a feature subset which may contain incomplete features, the feature selection procedure requires a feature subset evaluation method which can deal with incomplete data. In [22,23], a combination of PSO and a classifier able to classify incomplete data has been successfully used to remove redundant/irrelevant features in incomplete data. Therefore, in the proposed method, PSO will be used to search feature subsets and a classifier which is able to classify incomplete data such as C4.5 will be used to evaluate feature subsets.

3.3 Combining Classifiers

A set of classifiers which is built in the training process is combined to classify new instances in the application process. The majority vote chooses a class label with the most votes from the ensemble members as the ensemble output. The majority is a simple and powerful voting method [16]. Therefore, in the proposed method, the majority vote will be used to combine classifiers.

4   Method and Experiment Design

This section shows the comparison method and experiment design including datasets used in the experiment, parameter settings for feature selection and classification algorithm.

4.1   The Comparison Method

Experiments are conducted to evaluate the effectiveness of the combination of bagging and feature selection for classification with incomplete data. In order to achieve the goal, a combination of bagging and feature selection for classification with incomplete data as shown in Fig. 1 is compared with three other common methods for classification with incomplete data as shown in Figs. 2, 3 and 4. Figure 2 shows the training process of classification with incomplete data by using a classifier able to directly classify with incomplete data. Figure 3 shows the training process of classification with incomplete data by combining feature selection and a classifier able to directly classify with incomplete data. Figure 4 shows the training process of classification with incomplete data by combining bagging and a classifier able to directly classify with incomplete data.

Fig. 2. The training process of classification with incomplete data by directly using a classifier able to classify incomplete data.

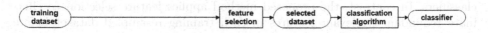

Fig. 3. The training process of classification with incomplete data by using feature selection.

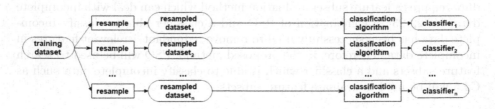

Fig. 4. The training process of classification with incomplete data by using bagging.

In the four setups, firstly, incomplete dataset is divided into training dataset and testing dataset. In the proposed setup shown in Fig. 1, the training dataset is used by bagging and feature selection to build a set of classifiers which is used to classify the testing dataset. In the setup shown in Fig. 2, the training dataset is directly put into a classification algorithm to learn a classifier which is then used to classify the testing dataset. In the setup shown in Fig. 3, the training dataset is put into a feature selection procedure to select a suitable feature subset which is used to transform the training dataset into the training selected dataset. After that, the training selected dataset is used by a classification algorithm to learn a classifier which is used to classify the testing dataset. In the setup shown

Fig. 4, the training dataset is put into a resampling procedure to generate a set of training resampled dataset. After that the set of training resampled dataset is used by a classification algorithm to build a set of classifiers which is then used to classify the testing dataset.

4.2   Datasets

The experiments used eight benchmark incomplete datasets chosen from UCI Repository of Machine Learning Databases [12]. Table 1 presents main characteristics of these datasets which include the name, the number of features (R:real/I: integer/N:nominal values), the number of classes, the number of instances and the percentage of incomplete instances which contain at least one missing field.

Table 1. Datasets used in the experiments.

Name	#Features(R/I/N)	#Classes	#Instances	Incomplete instances (%)
Breast	9 (0/0/9)	2	286	3.15
Cleveland	13 (13/0/0)	5	303	1.98
Crx	15 (3/3/9)	2	690	5.36
Dermatology	34 (0/34/0)	6	366	2.19
Hepatitis	19 (2/17/0)	2	155	48.39
Mammographic	5 (0/5/0)	2	961	13.63
Marketing	13 (0/13/0)	9	8993	23.54
Wisconsin	9 (0/9/0)	2	699	2.29

These datsets were carefully chosen to represent classification tasks with incomplete data of varying difficulty, dimensionality, feature types and number of classes. These datasets have varying levels of incomplete instances (Cleveland has 1.98% incomplete instances while Hepatitis has 48.39% incomplete instances). These problems also range low and high dimensionality (Mammographic has five features while Dermatology has 34 features), different feature types and binary classification and multi-class classification.

None of the datasets has a specific test set. Furthermore, the number of instances in some datasets is relatively small. Consequently, the ten-fold cross-validation method was applied to measure the performance of the learnt classifiers. In the experiments, with each dataset, the ten-fold cross-validation method was done 30 times. Therefore, with each dataset, 300 pairs of training set and test set were generated to evaluate the performance of the algorithms.

4.3   Classification Algorithms

In the experiments, we used C4.5 [19] and REPTree [21] to classify data and evaluate the quality of feature subsets in the feature selection procedure.

Both of the algorithms are able to directly classify incomplete data. The WEKA [8] was used to implement the algorithms by setting its parameters as the default values. Following [16], in the proposed method and the original bagging method, the number of classifiers was set 10.

4.4 PSO Parameter Settings

The experiments used continuous PSO to search feature subsets in the feature selection procedure. The PSO parameters were set as common parameter settings proposed by Clerc and Kennedy [3]. The detailed parameter settings are shown as follows: inertia weight (ω) was set 0.729844, the cognitive parameter (c_1) and the social parameter (c_2) were set 1.49618, population size was set to 30, the maximum iteration was set to 50 and the fully connected topology. The classification accuracy was used to evaluate the quality of particles. The threshold θ was set 0.8 to determine whether or not a feature is selected.

5   Results and Analysis

This section shows the comparison of the proposed method with the other methods on classification accuracy and the complexity of learnt classifiers. This section also mentions some reasons for the experimental results.

5.1   Classification Accuracy

Table 2 shows the average of classification accuracy and standard deviation of the four methods with the two classifiers on the eight incomplete datasets. The average of classification accuracy is the average of accuracies of 30 times performing ten-fold cross-validation on each dataset. In the table, *BaFS* column presents the average of accuracy from the proposed setup shown in Fig. 1; *All* column presents the average of accuracy from the setup shown in Fig. 2; *FS* column presents the average of accuracy from the setup shown in Fig. 3, and *BaAll* column presents the average of accuracy from the setup shown in Fig. 4.

To compare the performance of the proposed method with the other methods, the Wilcoxon signed-ranks tests at 95% confidence interval is used to compare the classification accuracy achieved by BaFS with the other methods. "T"columns in Table 2 show significant test of the columns before them against BaFS, where "+", "="and "−" mean BaFS is significantly more accurate, not significantly different, and significantly less accurate, respectively. The bold ones mean the best results for each dataset.

It is clear from Table 2 that in most cases, the proposed method can achieve the best classification accuracy. In all cases, the proposed method achieves significantly better classification accuracy than using all features as shown in Fig. 2. In all cases, the proposed method also achieves significantly better classification accuracy than using selected features as shown in Fig. 3. Compared to bagging as shown in Fig. 4, in 16 cases, the proposed method achieves significantly better

Table 2. The classification accuracy of different methods.

Dataset	Algorithm	BaFS	All	T	FS	T	BaAll	T
Breast	C4.5	**96.19 ± 0.53**	94.64 ± 0.43	+	94.40 ± 0.61	+	95.89 ± 0.42	+
	REPTree	**95.98 ± 0.45**	94.42 ± 0.42	+	94.16 ± 0.58	+	95.75 ± 0.39	=
Clevelant	C4.5	**58.67 ± 1.34**	54.45 ± 2.00	+	57.68 ± 1.58	+	57.06 ± 1.56	+
	REPTree	58.68 ± 1.10	56.63 ± 1.49	+	57.60 ± 1.54	+	**59.03 ± 1.17**	=
Crx	C4.5	**85.89 ± 0.41**	84.98 ± 0.80	+	84.62 ± 0.68	+	85.89 ± 0.61	=
	REPTree	**86.03 ± 0.41**	84.55 ± 0.83	+	84.91 ± 0.46	+	84.90 ± 0.63	+
Dermatology	C4.5	96.67 ± 0.72	95.66 ± 0.48	+	92.35 ± 1.20	+	**96.84 ± 0.56**	=
	REPTree	**96.23 ± 0.67**	94.75 ± 0.71	+	92.09 ± 1.50	+	95.67 ± 0.56	+
Hepatitis	C4.5	**83.04 ± 1.78**	78.87 ± 1.89	+	80.58 ± 1.73	+	80.97 ± 1.30	+
	REPTree	**82.71 ± 1.69**	80.21 ± 2.23	+	80.14 ± 1.77	+	81.69 ± 1.96	+
Mammographic	C4.5	**82.84 ± 0.48**	82.08 ± 0.36	+	82.17 ± 0.48	+	82.67 ± 0.45	=
	REPTree	82.60 ± 0.50	82.00 ± 0.68	+	81.76 ± 0.59	+	**82.65 ± 0.50**	=
Marketing	C4.5	**33.14 ± 0.35**	30.86 ± 0.41	+	32.04 ± 0.49	+	31.54 ± 0.28	+
	REPTree	**33.66 ± 0.31**	32.75 ± 0.42	+	32.16 ± 0.59	+	33.04 ± 0.35	+
Wisconsin	C4.5	**96.19 ± 0.32**	94.61 ± 0.49	+	94.42 ± 0.51	+	95.76 ± 0.44	+
	REPTree	**96.03 ± 0.42**	94.45 ± 0.48	+	94.00 ± 0.67	+	95.68 ± 0.45	+

Bold values indicate the best results for each dataset

classification accuracy than bagging in 10 cases, similar classification accuracy to bagging in 6 cases and never significantly worse classification accuracy than bagging.

In summary, the combination of bagging and feature selection is able to help significantly improve accuracy of classification with incomplete data.

5.2 Classifier Size

Table 3 shows the average size of decision trees(the number of nodes in the trees) of the four methods with two classifiers on the eight incomplete datasets. The average size of decision trees is the average size of 30 times performing ten-fold cross-validation on each dataset. In the table, *BaFS* column presents the average size from the proposed setup shown in Fig. 1; *All* column presents the average size from the setup shown in Fig. 2; *FS* column presents the average size from the setup shown in Fig. 3, and *BaAll* column presents the average size from the setup shown in Fig. 4.

Figure 5 summaries Table 3 by showing the average of tree size ratio between the other methods and the proposed method with C4.5 and REPTree (bigger than one means bigger tree, otherwise equal or smaller tree). It can be seen from Fig. 5 that the feature selection with original data shown in Fig. 3 provides the smallest trees. Moreover, it is clear from Fig. 5 that with both C4.5 and REPTree, the average of tree size generated by bagging with all features is bigger than the combination of bagging and feature selection. In other words, the combination

Table 3. The tree size of different methods.

Dataset	Algorithm	BaFS	All	FS	BaAll
Breast	C4.5	18.67	22.96	14.89	22.81
	REPTree	14.54	13.35	13.12	14.86
Clevelant	C4.5	71.33	79.19	18.13	73.36
	REPTree	30.33	17.42	11.61	32.24
Crx	C4.5	38.08	29.00	9.45	48.85
	REPTree	30.76	22.76	13.10	46.76
Dermatology	C4.5	20.88	15.20	17.28	17.43
	REPTree	15.66	15.66	13.85	15.24
Hepatitis	C4.5	11.40	17.46	7.04	15.17
	REPTree	8.55	6.42	7.18	8.91
Mammographic	C4.5	15.88	10.49	8.78	31.75
	REPTree	22.75	13.99	11.08	35.54
Marketing	C4.5	1031.61	1372.32	186.12	1713.21
	REPTree	442.72	361.64	163.12	724.25
Wisconsin	C4.5	18.93	22.95	15.26	23.09
	REPTree	14.50	13.12	12.51	14.87

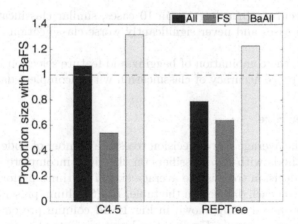

Fig. 5. Tree size ratio between the other methods and BaFS

of bagging and feature selection helps reduce the complexity of learnt classifiers from bagging.

In summary, the combination of bagging and feature selection not only help improve classification accuracy of bagging, but also helps reduce the complexity of the learn classifiers compared with the standard bagging method.

5.3   Further Analysis

To understand how the combination of bagging and feature selection can achieve better classification and smaller trees than bagging with all features, we looked carefully at the trees generated by C4.5 bagging with all features and bagging with selected features on Hepatitis dataset which has 19 features (*Age, Sex, Steroid, Antivirals, Fatigue, Malaise, Anorexia, LiverBig, LiverFirm, SpleenPalpable, Spiders, Ascites, Varices, Bilirubin, AlkPhosphate, Sgot, AlbuMin, ProTime, Histology*). The Hepatitis dataset was chosen since the trees generated on Hepatitis are not too big to analyse. Figures 6 and 7 present two typical pattern trees we observed.

It is clear from Figs. 6 and 7 that the combination of bagging and feature selection can generate more accurate and less complex trees than bagging with all features. The reason might be that classifiers like C4.5 are greedy algorithms which make the locally optimal choice at each stage. Therefore, they may provide locally optimal solutions. The purpose of feature selection is to search for more suitable feature subsets. Therefore, feature selection can help reduce the limitation of greedy algorithms. For example, in Fig. 6, with a training resampled data, when C4.5 bagging uses all features, the information gain of feature Spiders and feature Sex are higher than the information gain of feature Age, so feature Spiders and feature Sex are chosen to build the right tree before choosing feature Age. When feature selection is applied to the training resampled data, only three features Age, Ascite and LiverBig are selected. Consequently, feature Age is chosen to develop the right tree instead of feature Spiders or feature Sex. As a result, bagging with selected features generates more accurate and less complex trees than bagging with all features.

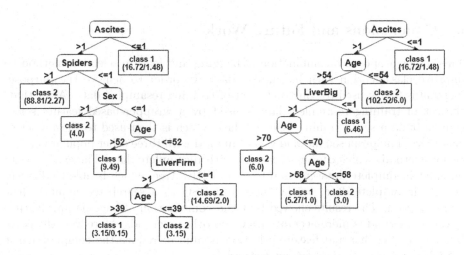

Fig. 6. Left tree with 90.0% of accuracy generated by C4.5 bagging with all features and right tree with 92.14% of accuracy generated by C4.5 bagging with selected features

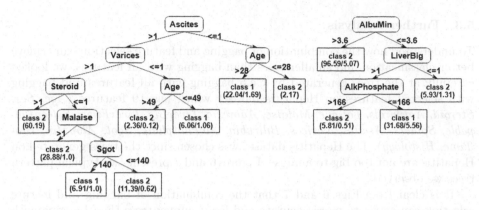

Fig. 7. Left tree with 86.42.0% of accuracy generated by C4.5 bagging with all features and right tree with 91.42% of accuracy generated by C4.5 bagging with selected features

It also can be seen from Figs. 6 and 7 that the combination of bagging and feature selection can generate more diverse trees than bagging with all features. For example, the right tree on Fig. 6 uses the same feature Ascites in the *first level* as the right tree on Fig. 7. However, the left tree on Fig. 6 uses different feature in the *first level* from the right tree on Fig. 7. By generating more diverse trees, feature selection helps improve the bagging method.

In summary, bagging with selected features can generate more accurate, less complex and more diverse learnt models than bagging with all features. Therefore, the combination of bagging and feature selection helps improve the traditional bagging method.

6   Conclusions and Future Work

This paper proposed a combination of bagging and feature selection method to improve classification with incomplete data. In order to achieve the purpose, bagging is firstly used to construct a set of training resampled data. After that, the set of training resampled data is used by a wrapper-based feature selection to build a set of training selected data which is then used to learn a set of classifiers. The proposed method was compared with three other popular classification methods which can directly work with incomplete data. The experiments on eight incomplete datasets used C4.5 and REPTree, which is able to directly classify incomplete data, as classifiers and PSO as a search technique in feature selection. The results showed that the combination of bagging and feature selection method is more accurate than the other methods. Moreover, the combination of bagging and feature selection is able to reduce the complex learnt models generated by the bagging method.

One of the other most popular ensemble methods is boosting. We already tried to use the same process as the proposed method to combine boosting and feature section for classification with incomplete data. However, experimental results were not promising. Therefore, future work could be to investigate more suitable approaches to combining boosting and feature selection, and check which ensemble methods are more suitable to what kinds of problems.

References

1. Chandrashekar, G., Sahin, F.: A survey on feature selection methods. Comput. Electr. Eng. **40**(1), 16–28 (2014)
2. Chen, H., Du, Y., Jiang, K.: Classification of incomplete data using classifier ensembles. In: 2012 International Conference on Systems and Informatics (ICSAI), pp. 2229–2232 (2012)
3. Clerc, M., Kennedy, J.: The particle swarm-explosion, stability, and convergence in a multidimensional complex space. IEEE Trans. Evol. Comput. **6**, 58–73 (2002)
4. Dietterich, T.G.: Ensemble methods in machine learning. In: International Workshop on Multiple Classifier Systems, pp. 1–15 (2000)
5. Doquire, G., Verleysen, M.: Feature selection with missing data using mutual information estimators. Neurocomputing **90**, 3–11 (2012)
6. García-Laencina, P.J., Sancho-Gómez, J.L., Figueiras-Vidal, A.R.: Pattern classification with missing data: a review. Neural Comput. Appl. **19**, 263–282 (2010)
7. Guerra-Salcedo, C., Whitley, D.: Feature selection mechanisms for ensemble creation: a genetic search perspective. In: Data Mining with Evolutionary Algorithms: Research Directions. Papers from the AAAI Workshop (1999)
8. Hall, M., Frank, E., Holmes, G., Pfahringer, B., Reutemann, P., Witten, I.H.: The weka data mining software: An update. SIGKDD Explor. Newsl. **11**, 10–18 (2009)
9. Han, J., Pei, J., Kamber, M.: Data Mining: Concepts and Techniques. Elsevier, Waltham (2011)
10. Kennedy, J.: Particle swarm optimization. In: Encyclopedia of Machine Learning, pp. 760–766 (2011)
11. Krause, S., Polikar, R.: An ensemble of classifiers approach for the missing feature problem. In: 2003 Proceedings of the International Joint Conference on Neural Networks, vol. 1, pp. 553–558 (2003)
12. Lichman, M.: UCI machine learning repository (2013). http://archive.ics.uci.edu/ml
13. Little, R.J., Rubin, D.B.: Statistical Analysis with Missing Data. Wiley, New York (2014)
14. Liu, H., Motoda, H.: Feature Selection for Knowledge Discovery and Data Mining, vol. 454. Springer, Heidelberg (2012)
15. Oliveira, L.S., Morita, M., Sabourin, R.: Feature selection for ensembles applied to handwriting recognition. Int. J. Doc. Anal. Recogn. (IJDAR) **8**, 262–279 (2006)
16. Opitz, D., Maclin, R.: Popular ensemble methods: An empirical study. J. Artif. Intell. Res. **11**, 169–198 (1999)
17. Opitz, D.W.: Feature selection for ensembles. In: AAAI/IAAI 379–384 (1999)
18. Qian, W., Shu, W.: Mutual information criterion for feature selection from incomplete data. Neurocomputing **168**, 210–220 (2015)
19. Quinlan, J.R.: C4.5: Programs for Machine Learning. Elsevier, New York (2014)
20. Saar-Tsechansky, M., Provost, F.: Handling missing values when applying classification models. J. Mach. Learn. Res. **8**, 1623–1657 (2007)
21. Su, J., Zhang, H.: A fast decision tree learning algorithm. In: Proceedings of the 21st National Conference on Artificial Intelligence, vol. 1, pp. 500–505 (2006)

22. Tran, C.T., Zhang, M., Andreae, P., Xue, B.: Improving performance for classification with incomplete data using wrapper-based feature selection. Evol. Intell. **9**, 81–94 (2016)
23. Tran, C.T., Zhang, M., Andreae, P., Xue, B.: A wrapper feature selection approach to classification with missing data. In: Squillero, G., Burelli, P. (eds.) EvoApplications 2016. LNCS, vol. 9597, pp. 685–700. Springer, Cham (2016). doi:10.1007/978-3-319-31204-0_44
24. Xue, B., Zhang, M., Browne, W., Yao, X.: A survey on evolutionary computation approaches to feature selection. IEEE Trans. Evol. Comput. **20**, 606–626 (2016)

Surrogate-Model Based Particle Swarm Optimisation with Local Search for Feature Selection in Classification

Hoai Bach Nguyen[(✉)], Bing Xue, and Peter Andreae

School of Engineering and Computer Science, Victoria University of Wellington,
Wellington, New Zealand
{Hoai.Bach.Nguyen,Bing.Xue,Peter.Andreae}@ecs.vuw.ac.nz

Abstract. Evolutionary computation (EC) techniques have been applied widely to many problems because of their powerful search ability. However, EC based algorithms are usually computationally intensive, especially with an expensive fitness function. In order to solve this issue, many surrogate models have been proposed to reduce the computation time by approximating the fitness function, but they are hardly applied to EC based feature selection. This paper develops a surrogate model for particle swarm optimisation based wrapper feature selection by selecting a small number of instances to create a surrogate training set. Furthermore, based on the surrogate model, we propose a sampling local search, which improves the current best solution by utilising information from the previous evolutionary iterations. Experiments on 10 datasets show that the surrogate training set can reduce the computation time without affecting the classification performance. Meanwhile the sampling local search results in a significantly smaller number of features, especially on large datasets. The combination of the two proposed ideas successfully reduces the number of features and achieves better performance than using all features, a recent sequential feature selection algorithm, original PSO, and PSO with one of them only on most datasets.

Keywords: Feature selection · Particle swarm optimization · Surrogate model · Instance selection

1 Introduction

In classification, a set of training instances is used to build a classifier, which assigns a pre-defined class label to unseen instances. However in many classification problems, each instance is described by a large number of features, which causes difficulties to the training process due to the "curse of dimensionality". Therefore, feature selection is proposed to select a small number of features while maintain or even improve the classification performance. However, feature selection is not an easy task because of its huge search space, which increases exponentially with respect to the number of features. It is also challenging to

© Springer International Publishing AG 2017
G. Squillero and K. Sim (Eds.): EvoApplications 2017, Part I, LNCS 10199, pp. 487–505, 2017.
DOI: 10.1007/978-3-319-55849-3_32

capture complex interactions between features [1]. The two issues are usually handled by two main components, a search mechanism and an evaluation criterion, respectively. The search mechanism is used to generate candidate feature subsets, which are then evaluated by the evaluation criterion.

Based on the evaluation measure, feature selection methods can be divided into wrapper approaches and filter approaches [1]. In wrappers, a classification algorithm is used to measure the candidate feature subsets' performance, which often results in promising classification performance. However wrappers are usually computationally intensive and the selected feature subsets are only for a specific classification algorithm. Meanwhile, in filter approaches, feature subsets are evaluated based on the characteristics of data, which are captured by some filter measures such as information measure or correlation measure. Filters are usually faster and selects more general features than wrappers. However, in terms of classification accuracy, filter approaches often can not achieve as good results as wrappers.

In terms of the search mechanism, evolutionary computation (EC) techniques have been widely applied to feature selection because of their potential global search ability. Compared with other EC techniques like genetic algorithms (GAs), memetic algorithms, PSO evolves better solutions in more efficient computation time on many problems [2]. Therefore, this work uses PSO as the search mechanism to find optimal feature subsets.

A common problem of EC based algorithms is the expensive computation cost since the fitness evaluation is performed on many individuals. Surrogate models have been used to reduce the computation cost in many expensive problems [3]. The main idea is to partly replace the highly cost fitness function using its cheap estimation. Despite of being applied widely, surrogate models have seldom been applied to feature selection, which also has an expensive fitness evaluation. To the best of our knowledge, this work will be the first attempt to develop a surrogate model for PSO based wrapper feature selection.

Although PSO is a global search technique, it easily converges prematurely and stuck at local optima when applying to feature selection, whose search space is complex with many local optima. Furthermore, PSO only considers the current best solutions, while useful information from the previous generations might be discarded. Therefore, this work investigates on improving the evolved feature subsets by applying an efficient local search, which uses information of the best solutions from all iterations so far to prevent the premature convergence.

1.1   Goals

This paper aims to develop a new PSO based feature selection approach with the goal of maintaining or improving the classification accuracy of wrappers while significantly reducing the computational cost and the number of features. To achieve this goal, firstly a surrogate training set is built by applying an instance selection algorithm. The expectation is to reduce the computation cost and maintain the information of the whole training set by selecting a small number of informative instances. Based on the surrogate training set, to improve the quality of the current best solution, a local search is developed to utilise features selected by the best feature subsets in the previous iterations to sample new candidate feature subsets, which will compete with and might replace the current best solution. The proposed approach will be evaluated and compared with a PSO based pure wrapper method and a sequential feature selection method. Specifically, we will investigate:

- whether the surrogate training set can reduce the computation cost while maintain or improve the performance over using the whole training set,
- whether the local search can assist PSO to evolve smaller feature subsets with similar or better classification accuracy, and
- whether combining the local search and the surrogate model can achieve better classification performance and scalability than using all instances and a state-of-the-art sequential feature selection algorithm.

2   Background

2.1   Particle Swarm Optimisation

Particle Swarm Optimisation (PSO) was originally proposed by Kennedy [4] to solve continuous problems. In PSO, an optimisation problem is solved by using a set of particles, called swarm, in which each particle represents a candidate solution. Particles move around the search space by updating their positions using velocities, which are based on their best position, called *pbest* and their neighbours's best position, named *gbest*. In order to solve binary problems, Sticky PSO [5] was proposed, which replaced the velocity vector by a probability vector. Each element of the probability vector represents the chance of flipping the corresponding position's bit. The probability element consists of three components: cognitive factor determined by *pbest*, social factor determined by *gbest*, and a stickiness property, which is a new binary momentum. The stickiness property is defined as a tendency to stay with the current position. It has the maximum value of 1 if its corresponding bit is just flipped to a new value, and decays in the following iterations if the bit's value is not changed. This idea is implemented by a variable called *currentLife*, which records the number of iterations after the bit was flipped. *maxLife* is the upper limit of *currentLife*, which ensures that the stickiness is not negative. After a number of iterations without flipping, the bit's stickiness becomes 0. The position and flipping probability vector of a particle, denoted by x and p, are updated according to the following equations:

$$
x_d^{t+1} = \begin{cases} 1, \text{ if } rand() < \frac{1}{1+e^{-v_d^{t+1}}} \\ 0, \text{ otherwise} \end{cases}
\tag{1}
$$

$$
p_d = i_m * (1 - stickiness_d) + i_p * |pbest_d - x_d| + i_g * |gbest_d - x_d|
\tag{2}
$$

$$
stickiness_d = 1 - \frac{currentLife_d}{maxLife}
\tag{3}
$$

where t is the tth iteration, and d is the dth dimension in the search space. i_m, i_p and i_g are used to control the proportions of the stickiness, cognitive and social components in the flipping probability, respectively. By redefining the velocity and momentum concepts, Sticky PSO can cope with binary search spaces to search more efficiently and effectively. Specifically, Sticky PSO can evolve better solutions than PBPSO [6], a state-of-the-art binary PSO, on two well-known types of binary problems: knapsack and feature selection. Therefore, Sticky PSO is selected as the search mechanism in this work.

2.2   Related Work on Feature Selection

Feature Selection Using Non-EC Techniques: Sequential forward selection (SFS) [7]/backward selection (SBS) [8] are two well-known traditional feature selection algorithms, which starts with an empty/full feature subset and incrementally adds/removes a feature which gives the best performance improvement. The process of adding/removing continues until the performance can not be improved. Although these techniques are more efficient than considering all possible feature subsets, they suffer the "nesting" problem. Specifically, once a feature is added or removed from the feature subset, it can not be removed or added later. To overcome this issue, "plus-l-take away -r" is proposed in [9], which iteratively does l forward steps followed by r backward steps. The pair (l,r) is determined dynamically in [10]. Later, Nakariyakul et al. [11] propose a method named IFFS which further improves the sequential searches using an additional step replacing weak features in the current feature subset by an unselected feature. The experimental results show that IFFS achieves better performance than other sequential search algorithms. Therefore, IFFS is chosen to compare against our proposed method.

PSO Based Feature Selection: Many works attempt to improve PSO based feature selection algorithms by modifying initialisation, representation or fitness function. In [12], an opposition chaotic method is applied to improve the initialisation of PSO. Specifically, two candidate feature subsets are generated on two opposite sides of the search space and the better side is used to initialise a particle in the swarm. In addition, opposition chaotic also assists to define PSO parameters dynamically and update $gbest$ to avoid being stagnation in local optima. A representation of PSO is proposed by Vieira et al. [13] to simultaneously optimise support vector machine's parameters and select a feature subset. However, the length of this representation is longer than the traditional one since it needs extra bits for the parameters. The results indicate that the proposed representation achieves better performance than other binary PSO and GAs based feature selection algorithms. Based on statistical feature clustering, Nguyen et al. [14] propose a representation which is shorter than the traditional one. Firstly, similar features are grouped into the same feature cluster. For each feature cluster, a maximum number of selected features from the cluster are predefined. Each position's bit belongs to a cluster and indicates which feature is selected from that cluster. The experimental results show that the proposed algorithm selects a smaller number of features while improves the classification performance over two other PSO based algorithms.

Premature convergence is a typical problem of PSO based feature selection algorithms. To address this problem, a *gbest* resetting mechanism is proposed in [15]. Specifically, if the *gbest* is not changed for a certain number of iterations, its position entries are reset to 0. This mechanism is utilised in [16] along with a local search to simultaneously reduce both classification error and the size of feature subsets. In addition, to speed up the fitness calculation, the proposed algorithm only considers the changed features. In [17], PSO is even used with GAs to solve feature selection problems, where in each iteration, the swarm is divided into two parts which are enhanced by PSO and GAs, respectively. The combination of two EC algorithms enhances the population variety, which results in informative feature subsets. Nguyen et al. [18] aim to improve *gbest* by applying a local search called filter based backward elimination. Features selected by the current *gbest* are ranked by mutual information. The elimination process mimics the backward selection to remove the less informative and redundant features. The proposed algorithm reduces the number of features and achieves significantly better performance than other recent PSO based algorithms. A comprehensive survey on EC based feature selection is provided by Xue et al. [1].

There have been many works attempting to improve the efficiency of PSO based feature selection algorithms by modifying the representation and fitness function. Recently, the surrogate model is applied to many EC techniques to reduce the computation time. However, it has never been applied to PSO based feature selection algorithms. This will be the first time that the surrogate model is investigated in PSO based feature selection. In addition, the current PSO based feature selection algorithms do not use the feature subsets selected by *gbest* in previous generations, which might contain information about good features.

3   Proposed Feature Selection Approach

Wrappers usually achieve high classification performance feature subsets with an intensive computation cost. To alleviate the problem, we propose a surrogate model and a local search to improve the PSO based wrapper feature selection algorithm.

3.1   Surrogate Model for Feature Selection

Surrogate Training Set: A large training set is one of the reasons for a long classification process i.e. long time for wrapper feature selection. There might be some noisy instances which may deteriorate the classification performance. In order to alleviate the expensive computation cost and at least maintain the accuracy, an instance selection algorithm can be used to select a small number of representative instances to form a new instance set, called a surrogate training set, which is expected to contain all essential information from the original training set. The fitness function calculated on the *surrogate training set* is called a *surrogate fitness function*, which can be considered an estimation of the original fitness function.

K nearest neighbours (KNN) is a simple and powerful instance based classification algorithm [19], so it is chosen to evaluate feature subsets. Wilson et al. [20] propose several instance selection algorithms for KNN. Among the proposed algorithms, it has been shown in [21] that DROP3 achieves good performance with respect to KNN. In general, DROP3 reduces the number of instances by removing central instances and retaining border instances. The main reason is that the internal instances do not affect on the decision boundaries as much as the border points. Therefore, removing the central instances affects the classification performance less than removing the border instances.

DROP3 starts with filtering out all noisy instances, which are assigned to wrong class labels by their K nearest neighbours. This step also removes instances in the middle of two or more class boundaries, which creates a smoother decision boundary. For each remaining instance, there is an "enemy" instance, which is the closest instance with a different class label. The distance from an instance to its "enemy" instance is called an "enemy" distance. Therefore, the larger "enemy" distance an instance has, the farther the instance is to its class label boundary. All remaining instances will be sorted according to their "enemy" distances so that the internal instances, which are far from their class label boundary, are removed first. For each instance, its removing process relates to its associated instances, which have the instance as one of their K nearest neighbours. If removing the instance does not reduce the number of correctly classified associated instances, then the instance will be removed. The set of selected instances is used as the *surrogate training set* for KNN in this work.

Surrogate Training Process: Surrogate models for fitness evaluations can be roughly divided into three categories: individual based, generation based and population based [22]. In individual based approaches, some individuals from the population are calculated by using the original fitness function and other individuals are evaluated by the surrogate fitness function. Population based approaches have more than one sub-populations, which might use different surrogate fitness functions. The communication and exchanging individuals from different sub-populations are allowed. For generation based, the surrogate fitness function is used in some of the generations before the original fitness function is used in the rest of the generations. In PSO, the swarm starts by exploring the search space to locate promising areas, which are then exploited in the later iterations. So it can be said that in early iterations the swarm tries to estimate the possible regions of global optima. In the sense of estimation, it would be safe to use the surrogate model at the beginning of a PSO algorithm to locate promising areas before using the original fitness function to find out the exact optima. Therefore, the idea of generation based approach is suitable here. Specifically, the particles are evaluated using the surrogate training set in the first I_s iterations, while in rest of the iterations, the whole training set is used. Given I is the maximum number of iterations, the task is to figure out the value of I_s iterations so that the classification performance is still maintained or even improved over using the original fitness function. The rate between I_s and I is called the surrogate rate α_s, i.e. $\alpha_s = \frac{I_s}{I}$.

3.2   Local Search: Sampling on *gbest*

In a PSO algorithm, the main idea is to use the current *gbest* and *pbest* to guide the particles to follow promising trajectories. However, the *gbest* from the previous generations might contain some useful information, which can assist the swarm to achieve better solutions. For instance, in feature selection, features which appear in *gbest* for many iterations tend to be good features. Moreover, since feature selection has a large and complex search space, some good features might not be selected together in the *gbest* solutions. These features might be complementary features, which provide even more information about the class label when appearing in one feature subset. Therefore the main idea of the local search is to keep features selected on all *gbest* and use them to improve the current *gbest*.

Suppose that S_{best} is the set of features which are selected in all *gbest* from previous iterations. Each feature from S_{best} has a score (explained later and shown in Eq. 4). The local search constructs $\frac{P}{2}$ candidate solutions by using S_{best}, where P is the population size. $|gbest|$, the number of features in the current *gbest*, is the maximum number of features in each candidate feature subsets. Specifically, based on the calculated scores, a tournament selection is used to select $|gbest|$ features from S_{best}, which form a sampled feature subset. The higher a feature's score is, the more chance that feature is selected. In addition, in $|gbest|$ selected features, there might be some duplicated features, which means that the size of the sampled feature subset can be less than $|gbest|$. All sampled feature subsets are then compared with each other based on their surrogate fitness values to find the best candidate feature subset. In this way, the local search utilises the surrogate training set to approximate a good solution in a short time. After that, the best candidate subset and the current *gbest* compete on the current fitness function, $fitness_{cur}$, which is the surrogate fitness function in the first I_s iterations or the original fitness function in the last $(I-I_s)$ iterations. The winner becomes *gbest*.

The task now is to define the scores of features in S_{best}. The main idea is to give more scores to features, which are selected more frequently and recently by *gbest*. The first component of the score is $freq$, which measures the number of iterations, in which a feature is selected in *gbest*. The higher $freq$ a feature has, the better the feature's quality. Before contributing to the score, $freq$ is normalised to $freq_n$ so that the total $freq_n$ of all features from S_{best} is 1. The second component of the score is related to the current *gbest*, called gc. If a feature in S_{best} is also selected in the current *gbest*, its gc is set to $\frac{1}{|gbest|}$. Otherwise its gc is 0. The score of the fth feature in S_{best} is the sum of its $freq_n$ and gc, which can be seen in Eq. (4).

$$score_f = freq_{nf} + gc_f \tag{4}$$

where

$$freq_{nf} = \frac{freq_f}{\sum_{f=1}^{|S_{best}|} freq_f}$$

$$gc_f = \begin{cases} \frac{1}{|gbest|} & \text{if } f \in gbest \\ 0 & \text{otherwise} \end{cases}$$

As illustrated in Eq. (4), given the same $freq_n$, the gc component gives more scores to features which are recently selected. In addition, since the best sampled subset might replace the current $gbest$, it is preferred to keep the sampled subset close to the current $gbest$ so that the swarm is not distracted. The gc component lets the features from the current $gbest$ to have more chance to be chosen, which allows to build new feature subsets not far from the current $gbest$. The local search is applied after the $gbest$ of the current iteration is determined and before that $gbest$ is informed to all particles.

3.3   Overall Algorithm

In this work, Sticky PSO, a binary PSO algorithm, is applied to achieve feature selection, in which each position entry corresponds to one original feature. The value 1 of a position entry indicates that the corresponding feature is selected. Otherwise the corresponding feature is not selected. In this work, a feature subset is evaluated by the fitness function given in Eq. (5)

$$fitness = \gamma * ClassificationError + (1 - \gamma)\frac{\#\text{selected features}}{\#\text{all features}} \tag{5}$$

where PSO needs to minimise the classification error determined by a classification algorithm and the number of selected features. The proportions of the two objectives are controlled by γ. If the classification algorithm is trained on the surrogate training set, the corresponding fitness function is a surrogate fitness function, denoted by $fitness_{sur}$. If the whole training set is used to build the classifier then the fitness function is the original one, called $fitness_{ori}$. In terms of PSO's representation, each feature corresponds to a position entry, whose value is either 1 or 0, indicating the feature is selected or not selected, respectively. The overall proposed algorithm, named SurSammPSO, is described in Fig. 1, in which the contribution of this work is marked in blue. So_{can} is a sampled feature subset, So_{best} is the best So_{can} generated by the sampling process, and P is the swarm size.

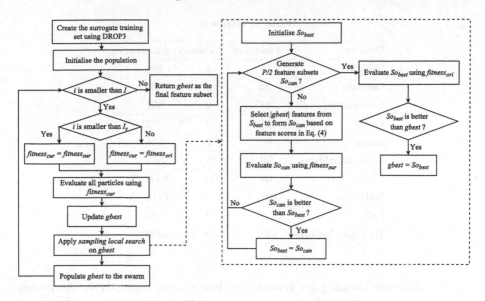

Fig. 1. Overall algorithm

4 Experiment Design

4.1 Datasets

Ten datasets (Table 1) with various numbers of features, classes and instances chosen from the UCI machine learning repository [23] are used in the experiments. Each dataset is randomly divided into two parts for training and test purpose, which preserve the original class distribution and contain 70% and 30% instances, respectively. DROP3 [20] is applied on the training set to create the surrogate training set. During the training process, a 10-fold cross validation is used on the training set or surrogate training set to calculate the classification accuracy. On each dataset, feature selection algorithms are executed 40 independent times.

4.2 Parameter Settings

A KNN classification algorithm is used to classify instances, where K = 3, which is recommended in [20]. The weight γ in Eq. (5) is set to 0.9 so that the search process focuses more on the classification performance than the number of features. For sticky PSO, i_m, i_p and i_g are set to 0.1154, 0.4423 and 0.4423, respectively, which ensures that *pbest* and *gbest* contribute more to a particle's movement than *momentum*. *maxLife* is set to 40. The population size is equal to the number of features and limited by 100. The maximum number of iterations is 100.

In order to find out the best α_s, different values of α_s ranging from 0.0 to 1.0 with a step of 0.25 are tested on different datasets. The value of 0.0 or 1.0 mean

Table 1. Datasets.

Dataset	#features	#classes	#instances
Vehicle	18	4	496
German	24	2	1000
Ionosphere	34	2	351
Lung	56	2	32
Sonar	60	2	208
Movementlibras	90	15	360
Plant	64	100	1600
Hillvalley	101	2	1213
LSVT	310	2	126
Multiple features	649	10	2000

that the surrogate training set is never or always used, respectively. According to the results, $\alpha_s = 0.75$ gives the similar or better classification performance with the shortest running time. So the value of 0.75 is set to α_s in this work, which is given 100 iterations, the surrogate training set is used in the first 75 iterations.

The PSO based feature selection algorithm, which uses purely the original fitness function, is called OriPSO. SurPSO applies the surrogate training set in the first 75 iterations while OriSamPSO uses the sampling local search in OriPSO. The combination of the local search and the surrogate training model results in SurSamPSO. The classification accuracies of different algorithms are compared by a statistical significance test called Wilcoxon test with significance level set to 0.05.

5 Experiment Results

This section presents the results of SurPSO, OriSamPSO and SurSamPSO. In all tables, NF, Ave and Std stand for the average number of features, the average and standard deviation of the classification accuracy over 40 independent runs. T shows the significant test results. All means using all features.

5.1 Effect of the Surrogate Training Set

To analyse the effect of the surrogate training set, SurPSO will be compared with OriPSO, which only uses the original fitness function to evaluate feature subsets. The comparison can be seen from Table 2, in which "+"/"−"/"=" indicate that OriPSO or using all features are significantly better/worse/similar to SurPSO.

In comparison with using all features, SurPSO selects from 5% to 20% of the original features while still achieves significantly better test performance on 8 out of the 10 datasets. For example, on the LSVT dataset, SurPSO reduces more than 90% of the features and achieves around 1% better accuracy than using all features.

As can be seen from the table, in terms of training accuracy, SurPSO achieves similar or better performance than OriPSO on 7 out of the 10 datasets. SurPSO's test accuracies are better than that of OriPSO on 2 datasets. For example, on the Hillvalley dataset, SurPSO selects 2.5 features fewer than OriPSO, but its classification performance is about 1.1% better. On the rest of the datasets, SurPSO achieves similar test performance in comparison with OriPSO. In terms of the number of selected features, except for the last dataset with a large number of features, the size of feature subsets selected by the two algorithms are roughly equal. Despite of maintaining or improving the classification performance, SurPSO's evolutionary processes are much shorter than that of OriPSO. Specifically, on most of datasets SurPSO spends 70% less time than OriPSO to evolve a feature subset. Although OriPSO is already quite fast on the Lung dataset (only 707 ms), SurPSO is still able to reduce about 40% of the OriPSO's computation time. So the surrogate training set significantly reduces the computation cost without deteriorating the test performance. On some datasets, SurPSO even improves the performance due to the DROP3's intention to remove noisy instances.

5.2   Effect of the Sampling Local Search

To analyse the effect of the proposed local search, OriSamPSO, which applies the local search to the original fitness function is compared with using all features and OriPSO. The comparisons are illustrated in Table 3.

As can be seen from the table, applying the sampling local search not only reduces the number of features on all datasets but also maintains or even improves the test accuracy on 8 out of the 10 datasets. Especially, on the largest dataset, Multiple Features, OriSamPSO selects less than 10% of the original features and still achieves better performance than using all features.

According to the significant test results, the local search maintains or improves training performance on all datasets. Especially, on the large datasets, the training accuracy is significantly improved, for example on the LSVT dataset, OriSamPSO achieves almost 3% better accuracy than OriPSO. Although test accuracies are not significantly better, the local search assists PSO to evolve smaller number of features on 8 out of the 10 datasets. This pattern is obvious in the largest dataset, Multiple Features, where OriSamPSO selects only 59.8 features, which is two times smaller than the feature subset evolved by OriPSO. Despite of spending time on the local search, OriSamPSO still has comparative computation time in comparison with OriPSO on all datasets. OriSamPSO is even more efficient on 4 out of 10 datasets, for instance on Multiple Features, OriSamPSO is 15% more efficient than OriPSO. The main reason is that the local search is cheap since it mainly works on the surrogate training set. Meanwhile, it can reduce the number of features significantly, which leads to shorter calculation time for the original fitness function.

Table 2. Results of OriPSO and SurPSO

Dataset	NF	Training results AveTrain ± Std	T	Test results AveTest ± Std	T	Time (ms)
Vehicle						
All	18.0	89.44 ± 0.00	−	83.07 ± 0.00	−	
OriPSO	4.8	91.41 ± 0.69	=	84.66 ± 1.29	−	113187.62
SurPSO	5.1	91.43 ± 0.69		85.23 ± 0.82		34294.93
German						
All	24.0	83.14 ± 0.00	−	65.33 ± 0.00	−	
OriPSO	5.6	78.70 ± 0.52	−	67.63 ± 1.90	=	229110.30
SurPSO	6.4	84.33 ± 0.52		68.35 ± 0.75		60600.90
Ionosphere						
All	34.0	90.24 ± 0.00	−	86.67 ± 0.00	−	
OriPSO	4.8	95.27 ± 0.81	+	88.48 ± 2.12	=	33564.40
SurPSO	4.0	94.64 ± 0.81		88.38 ± 2.61		9903.90
Lung						
All	56.0	86.36 ± 0.00	−	80.00 ± 0.00	=	
OriPSO	5.1	99.89 ± 1.73	+	79.50 ± 4.44	=	707.38
SurPSO	4.4	99.20 ± 1.73		79.50 ± 5.45		451.75
Sonar						
All	60.0	88.97 ± 0.00	−	84.13 ± 0.00	+	
OriPSO	14.8	95.55 ± 1.78	+	81.94 ± 3.32	=	23605.65
SurPSO	12.4	93.55 ± 1.78		82.58 ± 3.14		7291.62
Movementlibras						
All	90.0	98.52 ± 0.00	−	95.06 ± 0.00	−	
OriPSO	9.2	98.54 ± 0.16	=	95.33 ± 0.41	=	105780.20
SurPSO	9.4	98.63 ± 0.16		95.29 ± 0.32		41165.30
Plant						
All	64.0	99.55 ± 0.00	+	99.10 ± 0.00	+	
OriPSO	3.0	99.24 ± 0.04	=	98.67 ± 0.03	=	1756442.18
SurPSO	3.1	99.26 ± 0.04		98.68 ± 0.05		566479.72
Hillvalley						
All	100.0	79.83 ± 0.00	−	59.07 ± 0.00	−	
OriPSO	24.8	81.54 ± 0.83	=	58.85 ± 1.88	−	1557361.75
SurPSO	22.3	81.16 ± 0.83		59.92 ± 1.46		443232.00
LSVT						
All	310.0	79.55 ± 0.00	−	55.26 ± 0.00	−	
OriPSO	27.9	85.45 ± 4.72	=	65.53 ± 1.53	=	18240.05
SurPSO	27.4	85.11 ± 4.72		65.07 ± 4.89		4708.20
Multiple features						
All	649.0	99.49 ± 0.00	−	98.57 ± 0.00	−	
OriPSO	118.2	99.66 ± 0.05	=	99.04 ± 0.10	=	7203332.90
SurPSO	143.6	99.65 ± 0.05		99.05 ± 0.12		2068439.52

Table 3. Results of OriPSO and OriSamPSO

Dataset	NF	Training results		Test results		Time (ms)
		AveTrain ± Std	T	AveTest ± Std	T	
Vehicle						
All	18.0	89.44 ± 0.00	−	83.07 ± 0.00	−	
OriPSO	4.8	91.41 ± 0.73	=	84.66 ± 1.29	=	113187.62
OriSamPSO	4.7	91.40 ± 0.73		84.83 ± 1.10		117337.07
German						
All	24.0	83.14 ± 0.00	+	65.33 ± 0.00	−	
OriPSO	5.6	78.70 ± 4.90	=	67.63 ± 1.90	=	229110.30
OriSamPSO	5.4	79.26 ± 4.90		67.33 ± 1.98		226021.25
Ionosphere						
All	34.0	90.24 ± 0.00	−	86.67 ± 0.00	−	
OriPSO	4.8	95.27 ± 0.42	=	88.48 ± 2.12	+	33564.40
OriSamPSO	4.3	95.19 ± 0.42		87.31 ± 1.68		39497.60
Lung						
All	56.0	86.36 ± 0.00	−	80.00 ± 0.00	=	
OriPSO	5.1	99.89 ± 0.00	=	79.50 ± 4.44	=	707.38
OriSamPSO	4.5	100.00 ± 0.00		80.75 ± 2.63		833.70
Sonar						
All	60.0	88.97 ± 0.00	−	84.13 ± 0.00	+	
OriPSO	14.8	95.55 ± 1.54	=	81.94 ± 3.32	=	23605.65
OriSamPSO	14.6	95.60 ± 1.54		81.83 ± 3.27		23992.17
Movementlibras						
All	90.0	98.52 ± 0.00	=	95.06 ± 0.00	−	
OriPSO	9.2	98.54 ± 0.20	=	95.33 ± 0.41	=	105780.20
OriSamPSO	9.0	98.55 ± 0.20		95.21 ± 0.36		107488.62
Plant						
All	64.0	99.55 ± 0.00	+	99.10 ± 0.00	+	
OriPSO	3.0	99.24 ± 0.02	−	98.67 ± 0.03	=	1756442.18
OriSamPSO	3.0	99.25 ± 0.02		98.67 ± 0.04		1703456.68
Hillvalley						
All	100.0	79.83 ± 0.00	−	59.07 ± 0.00	=	
OriPSO	24.8	81.54 ± 1.01	=	58.85 ± 1.88	=	1557361.75
OriSamPSO	23.3	81.81 ± 1.01		59.48 ± 1.46		1553409.23
LSVT						
All	310.0	79.55 ± 0.00	−	55.26 ± 0.00	−	
OriPSO	27.9	85.45 ± 2.75	−	65.53 ± 1.53	=	18240.05
OriSamPSO	38.1	88.38 ± 2.75		66.51 ± 4.40		19069.62
Multiple features						
All	649.0	99.49 ± 0.00	−	98.57 ± 0.00	−	
OriPSO	118.2	99.66 ± 0.04	−	99.04 ± 0.10	=	7203332.90
OriSamPSO	59.8	99.67 ± 0.04		99.03 ± 0.12		6260769.17

The experimental results show that the local search using the surrogate training set reduces the number of selected features significantly while maintains the classification performance. The main reason is that the sampling process generates feature subsets containing at most the same number of features as the current *gbest*. Therefore, if a sampling feature subset replaces the current *gbest*, it achieves similar or better fitness with a smaller number of features than the current *gbest*.

5.3   Combining Sampling Local Search and Surrogate Training Set

In the above sections, it can be seen that both surrogate model and local search reduces either the computation time or the number of features significantly while maintains or improves the classification performance. This section analyses the effect of combining them together in one algorithm called SurSamPSO. It is expected that SurSamPSO can take the advantages of these two components. SurSamPSO is compared against OriPSO and using all features, which is shown in Table 4.

According to the experimental results, SurSamPSO successfully reduces the number of features on all datasets while improves the classification accuracy over using all features on 7 out of the 10 datasets. Although using all features achieves better performance on two datasets, Sonar and Plant, SurSamPSO selects less than 20% and 5% of the original features, respectively.

As can be seen from the table, although being trained on the surrogate training set for 75 iterations, SurSamPSO still evolves comparative feature subsets in terms of the training accuracy, which is calculated on the whole training set. Particularly, SurSamPSO is significantly better on 3 datasets while maintaining the training performance on 5 datasets. The largest difference between training accuracies of the two algorithms is on LSVT where SurSamPSO is 3.5% more accurate. In terms of the test performance, SurSamPSO is always similar or better than OriPSO, especially on LSVT, SurSamPSO improves about 5% over OriPSO. The local search still maintains its effect on SurSamPSO, in which the number of features is reduced significantly on 8 out of the 10 datasets. This pattern is more obvious on the large dataset. For example on Multiple Features, SurSamPSO selects 50% less features than OriPSO. In comparison with OriPSO, SurSamPSO is able to reduce up to 70% computation time.

5.4   Overall Comparisons

The comparisons between OriPSO, OriSamPSO, SurPSO and SurSamPSO are summarised in Fig. 2. The comparisons are based on 4 criteria: training error, test error, number of selected features and computation time, which need to be minimised. For making an easy comparison, all values are normalised in the range [0,1], where 0 is the best value and 1 is the worst value. It can be seen that SurSamPSO achieves the best test accuracy on 7 out of the 10 datasets, which is followed by SurPSO with two times of being the best. Meanwhile OriSamPSO is not the best one on any dataset despite of using both original fitness function

Table 4. Results of OriPSO and SurSamPSO

Dataset	NF	Training results		Test results		Time (ms)
		AveTrain ± Std	T	AveTest ± Std	T	
Vehicle						
All	18.0	89.44 ± 0.00	−	83.07 ± 0.00	−	
OriPSO	4.8	91.41 ± 0.46	−	84.66 ± 1.29	−	113187.62
SurSamPSO	5.0	91.79 ± 0.46		85.44 ± 0.72		36255.28
German						
All	24.0	83.14 ± 0.00	−	65.33 ± 0.00	−	
OriPSO	5.6	78.70 ± 0.38	−	67.63 ± 1.90	=	229110.30
SurSamPSO	6.5	84.44 ± 0.38		68.22 ± 0.68		69631.98
Ionosphere						
All	34.0	90.24 ± 0.00	−	86.67 ± 0.00	−	
OriPSO	4.8	95.27 ± 0.80	+	88.48 ± 2.12	=	33564.40
SurSamPSO	3.7	94.51 ± 0.80		88.93 ± 2.45		9867.20
Lung						
All	56.0	86.36 ± 0.00	−	80.00 ± 0.00	−	
OriPSO	5.1	99.89 ± 1.62	=	79.50 ± 4.44	−	707.38
SurSamPSO	4.2	99.32 ± 1.62		81.50 ± 4.21		559.83
Sonar						
All	60.0	88.97 ± 0.00	−	84.13 ± 0.00	+	
OriPSO	14.8	95.55 ± 1.45	+	81.94 ± 3.32	=	23605.65
SurSamPSO	11.6	94.46 ± 1.45		81.67 ± 2.58		8337.40
Movementlibras						
All	90.0	98.52 ± 0.00	−	95.06 ± 0.00	−	
OriPSO	9.2	98.54 ± 0.20	=	95.33 ± 0.41	=	105780.20
SurSamPSO	9.0	98.58 ± 0.20		95.29 ± 0.31		45424.00
Plant						
All	64.0	99.55 ± 0.00 .	+	99.10 ± 0.00	+	
OriPSO	3.0	99.24 ± 0.03	=	98.67 ± 0.03	=	1756442.18
SurSamPSO	3.0	99.25 ± 0.03		98.68 ± 0.04		647379.50
Hillvalley						
All	100.0	79.83 ± 0.00	−	59.07 ± 0.00	=	
OriPSO	24.8	81.54 ± 0.96	=	58.85 ± 1.88	=	1557361.75
SurSamPSO	19.7	81.24 ± 0.96		59.27 ± 1.99		458048.42
LSVT						
All	310.0	79.55 ± 0.00	−	55.26 ± 0.00	−	
OriPSO	27.9	85.45 ± 3.72	−	65.53 ± 1.53	−	18240.05
SurSamPSO	22.2	89.09 ± 3.72		70.39 ± 5.76		4883.50
Multiple features						
All	649.0	99.49 ± 0.00	−	98.57 ± 0.00	−	
OriPSO	118.2	99.66 ± 0.04	=	99.04 ± 0.10	=	7203332.90
SurSamPSO	61.8	99.66 ± 0.04		99.07 ± 0.14		1674807.10

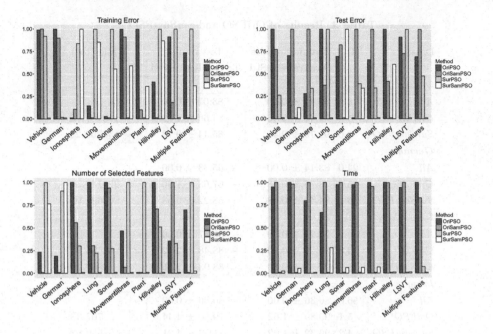

Fig. 2. Comparisons between all algorithms

and the sampling local search. The reason might be the inconsistency between the fitness function of the local search and the main fitness function of PSO. In addition, it can be seen that both algorithms using the surrogate training set evolve more promising performance than the others with the whole training set. In other words, selecting instances helps to select more general features by removing noisy instances in the training set. Besides the test accuracy, Sur-SamPSO also shows its strength on the number of selected features criterion. Specifically, SurSamPSO selects the least number of features on 7 out of the 10 datasets. OriSamPSO achieves the smallest number of features on 4 datasets. These results illustrate that the sampling local search is good at reducing the number of features. Filtering out instances also helps to reduce the number of features since the small instance set might require fewer features to classify the instances correctly. The last but not least criterion is the computation time, where SurPSO is the fastest algorithm on 9 out of the 10 datasets. SurPSO loses its first position to SurSamPSO on Multiple Features. As can be seen from Fig. 2, SurSamPSO follows SurPSO quite closely. It is even faster than SurPSO on Multiple Features because it selects much fewer features.

Overall the combination of the surrogate model and the sampling local search results in a more efficient, effective and scalable feature selection algorithm.

5.5 Comparison with IFFS

The comparison between SurSamPSO and IFFS is shown in Table 5. In the table, "+"/"−"/"=" mean that SurSamPSO is significantly better/worse/similar to IFFS. As can be seen from the table, SurSamPSO achieves better performance on 8 out of the 10 datasets. The reason is that IFFS usually selects a small number of features since it stops when adding more features does not improve the fitness value. Although IFFS attempts to capture more feature interactions than other traditional sequential methods, it still considers only one feature at a step, which cause difficulty to find out blocks of complimentary features. Furthermore, IFFS is not scalable with respect to the number of features. This can be seen on the Multiple Features dataset, where SurSamPSO is about 30 times faster while still achieves better classification performance.

Table 5. Comparison between SurSamPSO and IFFS

Dataset	Method	NF	AveTest	Std	T	Time (ms)
Vehicle	IFFS	4.0	81.69			15923.00
	SurSamPSO	5.0	85.44	0.72	+	36255.28
German	IFFS	2.0	66.00			11312.00
	SurSamPSO	6.5	68.22	0.68	+	69631.98
Ionosphere	IFFS	4.0	86.67			8442.00
	SurSamPSO	3.7	88.93	2.45	+	9867.20
Lung	IFFS	2.0	90.00			30.00
	SurSamPSO	4.2	81.50	4.21	−	559.83
Sonar	IFFS	3.0	77.78			2143.00
	SurSamPSO	11.6	81.67	2.58	+	8337.40
Movementlibras	IFFS	6.0	94.32			114080.00
	SurSamPSO	9.0	95.29	0.31	+	45424.00
Plant	IFFS	3.0	98.67			258225.00
	SurSamPSO	3.0	98.68	0.04	+	647379.50
Hillvalley	IFFS	5.0	59.07			525402.00
	SurSamPSO	19.7	59.27	1.99	=	458048.42
LSVT	IFFS	3.0	63.16			3507.00
	SurSamPSO	22.2	70.39	5.76	+	4883.50
Multiple features	IFFS	12.0	98.73			48614670.00
	SurSamPSO	61.8	99.07	0.14	+	1674807.10

6 Conclusions and Future Work

The goal of this paper was to develop a PSO based feature selection algorithm, which could select a small number of features in an efficient way while maintaining or improving the classification performance. This goal has been achieved firstly by applying an instance selection algorithm to create a surrogate training set, which is smaller than the original training set. In the first 75% of the selection process, feature subsets are evaluated on the surrogate set to reduce the computation time. In addition to the surrogate training set, a sampling local search is designed to utilise all features selected by *gbest* so far to improve the current *gbest*. The results show that the surrogate training set can significantly reduce the computation time while maintain or even improve the classification performance. The sampling local search assists PSO to evolve a much smaller number of features with similar or better classification performance. The combination of the two components leads to a more effective and efficient PSO based algorithm, especially on datasets with a large number of features. In comparison with a recent sequential feature selection method, the proposed algorithm is better at balancing between the classification performance and the number of selected features. Especially on the largest dataset, the proposed algorithm is even more efficient than the improved sequential algorithm.

From the results, it is evident that the local search focuses more on reducing the number of features while mainly maintaining the classification accuracy. In the future, we will further improve the balance between the two objectives so that the local search can significantly enhance the classification performance. We will also investigate more on the relationship between fitness landscapes of the surrogate and original fitness functions to not only shorten the computation time but also strengthen the classification ability.

References

1. Xue, B., Zhang, M., Browne, W.N., Yao, X.: A survey on evolutionary computation approaches to feature selection. IEEE Trans. Evol. Comput. **20**(4), 606–626 (2016)
2. Hu, M., Wu, T., Weir, J.D.: An adaptive particle swarm optimization with multiple adaptive methods. IEEE Trans. Evol. Comput. **17**(5), 705–720 (2013)
3. Tabatabaei, M., Hakanen, J., Hartikainen, M., Miettinen, K., Sindhya, K.: A survey on handling computationally expensive multiobjective optimization problems using surrogates: non-nature inspired methods. Struct. Multi. Optim. **52**(1), 1–25 (2015)
4. Kennedy, J.: Particle swarm optimization. In: Sammut, C., Webb, G.I. (eds.) Encyclopedia of Machine Learning, pp. 760–766. Springer, Heidelberg (2011)
5. Nguyen, B.H., Xue, B., Andreae, P.: A novel binary particle swarm optimization algorithm and its applications on knapsack and feature selection problems. In: Leu, G., Singh, H., Elsayed, S. (eds.) Intelligent and Evolutionary Systems: The 20th Asia Pacific Symposium, IES 2016, Canberra, Australia, pp. 319–332. Springer, Heidelberg (2017)
6. Xue, B., Nguyen, S., Zhang, M.: A new binary particle swarm optimisation algorithm for feature selection. In: Esparcia-Alcázar, A.I., Mora, A.M. (eds.) EvoApplications 2014. LNCS, vol. 8602, pp. 501–513. Springer, Heidelberg (2014). doi:10.1007/978-3-662-45523-4_41
7. Whitney, A.W.: A direct method of nonparametric measurement selection. IEEE Trans. Comput. **100**(9), 1100–1103 (1971)
8. Marill, T., Green, D.M.: On the effectiveness of receptors in recognition systems. IEEE Trans. Inf. Theory **9**(1), 11–17 (1963)

9. Stearns, S.D.: On selecting features for pattern classifiers. In: Proceedings of the 3rd International Conference on Pattern Recognition (ICPR), Coronado, CA, pp. 71–75 (1976)
10. Pudil, P., Novovičová, J., Kittler, J.: Floating search methods in feature selection. Pattern Recogn. Lett. 15(11), 1119–1125 (1994)
11. Nakariyakul, S., Casasent, D.P.: An improvement on floating search algorithms for feature subset selection. Pattern Recogn. 42(9), 1932–1940 (2009)
12. Bharti, K.K., Singh, P.K.: Opposition chaotic fitness mutation based adaptive inertia weight BPSO for feature selection in text clustering. Appl. Soft Comput. 43, 20–34 (2016)
13. Vieira, S.M., Mendonça, L.F., Farinha, G.J., Sousa, J.M.: Modified binary PSO for feature selection using SVM applied to mortality prediction of septic patients. Appl. Soft Comput. 13(8), 3494–3504 (2013)
14. Nguyen, H.B., Xue, B., Liu, I., Zhang, M.: PSO and statistical clustering for feature selection: A new representation. In: Dick, G., Browne, W.N., Whigham, P., Zhang, M., Bui, L.T., Ishibuchi, H., Jin, Y., Li, X., Shi, Y., Singh, P., Tan, K.C., Tang, K. (eds.) SEAL 2014. LNCS, vol. 8886, pp. 569–581. Springer, Cham (2014). doi:10.1007/978-3-319-13563-2_48
15. Chuang, L.Y., Chang, H.W., Tu, C.J., Yang, C.H.: Improved binary PSO for feature selection using gene expression data. Comput. Biol. Chem. 32(1), 29–38 (2008)
16. Tran, B., Xue, B., Zhang, M.: Improved PSO for feature selection on high-dimensional datasets. In: Dick, G., Browne, W.N., Whigham, P., Zhang, M., Bui, L.T., Ishibuchi, H., Jin, Y., Li, X., Shi, Y., Singh, P., Tan, K.C., Tang, K. (eds.) SEAL 2014. LNCS, vol. 8886, pp. 503–515. Springer, Cham (2014). doi:10.1007/978-3-319-13563-2_43
17. Ghamisi, P., Benediktsson, J.A.: Feature selection based on hybridization of genetic algorithm and particle swarm optimization. IEEE Geosci. Remote Sens. Lett. 12(2), 309–313 (2015)
18. Nguyen, H., Xue, B., Liu, I., Zhang, M.: Filter based backward elimination in wrapper based PSO for feature selection in classification. In: IEEE Congress on Evolutionary Computation (CEC 2014), pp. 3111–3118 (2014)
19. Liu, H., Zhang, S., Zhao, J., Zhao, X., Mo, Y.: A new classification algorithm using mutual nearest neighbors. In: Ninth International Conference on Grid and Cloud Computing, pp. 52–57 (2010)
20. Wilson, D.R., Martinez, T.R.: Reduction techniques for instance-based learning algorithms. Mach. Learn. 38(3), 257–286 (2000)
21. Olvera-López, J.A., Carrasco-Ochoa, J.A., Martínez-Trinidad, J.F., Kittler, J.: A review of instance selection methods. Artif. Intell. Rev. 34(2), 133–143 (2010)
22. Jin, Y.: Surrogate-assisted evolutionary computation: Recent advances and future challenges. Swarm Evol. Comput. 1(2), 61–70 (2011)
23. Lichman, M.: UCI machine learning repository. University of California, School of Information and Computer Sciences, Irvine, CA (2013). http://archive.ics.uci.edu/ml

Feature Selection in High Dimensional Data by a Filter-Based Genetic Algorithm

Claudio De Stefano, Francesco Fontanella$^{(\boxtimes)}$, and Alessandra Scotto di Freca

Dipartimento di Ingegneria Elettrica e dell'Informazione (DIEI),
Università di Cassino e del Lazio meridionale, Via G. Di Biasio,
43 02043 Cassino, FR, Italy
{destefano,fontanella,a.scotto}@unicas.it

Abstract. In classification and clustering problems, feature selection techniques can be used to reduce the dimensionality of the data and increase the performances. However, feature selection is a challenging task, especially when hundred or thousands of features are involved. In this framework, we present a new approach for improving the performance of a filter-based genetic algorithm. The proposed approach consists of two steps: first, the available features are ranked according to a univariate evaluation function; then the search space represented by the first M features in the ranking is searched using a filter-based genetic algorithm for finding feature subsets with a high discriminative power.

Experimental results demonstrated the effectiveness of our approach in dealing with high dimensional data, both in terms of recognition rate and feature number reduction.

1 Introduction

Recent years have seen a strong growth of applications dealing with huge amounts of data, such as data mining and medical data processing [23]. This kind of application often imply classification or clustering problems where the objects to be classified or clustered are represented as feature vectors. The feature selection problem consists in selecting, from the whole set of available features, the subset of them providing the most discriminative power. The choice of a good feature subset is crucial since if the selected features do not contain enough information to discriminate patterns belonging to different classes, the performances may be unsatisfactory, regardless of the effectiveness of the classification system employed. Moreover, irrelevant and noisy features unnecessarily enlarge the search space, increasing both the time and the complexity of the learning process.

Feature selection algorithms usually imply the definition of an evaluation function and of a search procedure. Evaluation functions can be divided into two broad classes: *univariate* and *multivariate* measures. Univariate measures evaluate the effectiveness of each single feature in discriminating samples belonging to different classes and are used to rank the available features. Once the features

© Springer International Publishing AG 2017
G. Squillero and K. Sim (Eds.): EvoApplications 2017, Part I, LNCS 10199, pp. 506–521, 2017.
DOI: 10.1007/978-3-319-55849-3_33

have been evaluated, the subset search procedure is straightforward: the features are ranked according to their merit and the best M features are selected. The parameter M is specified by the user. These kind of approaches are very fast and can be used to cope with problems involving even hundreds of thousands of features. The main drawback of these measures is that they cannot consider interactions that may occur between two or more features. For this reason, features which perform well when used in conjunction with other features, are discarded if they perform poorly when used alone. Additionally, the features with the highest scores (merits) are usually similar. Therefore, these measures tend to select redundant features [6].

Multivariate measures, instead, evaluate feature subsets by measuring how well patterns belonging to different classes are discriminated when projected in the subspace represented by the subset to be evaluated. These measures are generally classified into two categories: *filter* and *wrapper* [8]. Wrapper approaches use classification algorithms, to evaluate the goodness of the subsets. This leads to high computational costs when a large number of evaluations is required, especially when large datasets are involved. Filter approaches, instead, are independent of any classification algorithm and, in most of the cases, are computationally less expensive and more general than wrapper algorithms.

As concerns the search strategies, given a measure, the optimal subset can be found by exhaustively evaluating all the possible solutions. Unfortunately, the exhaustive search is impracticable when the cardinality N of the whole set of features Y is high ($N > 50$). This is due to the fact that the search space, made of all the 2^N possible subsets of Y, exponentially grows with N. For this reason, many heuristic algorithms have been proposed for finding near-optimal solutions [4,8,21]. Among these algorithms, greedy strategies that incrementally generate feature subsets have been proposed. Since these algorithms do not take into account complex interactions among the features, in most of the cases they lead to sub-optimal solutions.

Evolutionary computation (EC) based techniques have been widely used to cope with the feature selection problem [21]. Among the EC based approaches, Genetic Algorithms (GAs) have been widely used. GA binary vectors provide a natural and straightforward representation for feature subsets: the value 1 or 0 of the chromosome i-th element indicates whether the i-th feature is included or not. Most of the GA approaches use wrapper evaluation functions [21]. For these approaches different classification algorithms have been adopted, among them: Support Vector Machines (SVMs) [16], K-Nearest Neighbor (KNN) [13] and Artificial Neural Networks (ANNs) [22]. As mentioned above, wrapper evaluation functions lead to high computational costs since their computational complexity depends on the number of samples actually used for training the classifier. As consequence, such approaches are not well suited to deal with problems involving a huge number of instances and features.

Also filter fitness functions have been used; the approach presented in [19] uses an information theory based evaluation function, while in [11] the authors adopt a consistency measure. Moreover, in [3,5] the authors present a filter fitness function that extends the Fisher's linear discriminant.

Recently, in order to reduce the search space size for high-dimensional datasets, different strategies have been adopted [18,20,21] for GA-based algorithms. In [18], the search space reduction for the GA is performed by using different filter approaches. The information provided by these approaches is used to build a part of the individuals making up the initial population. Then, individuals are evaluated by means of a neural network based wrapper function. The approach has been tested on a credit assessment risk problem involving just 33 features. In [20] the authors present a new GA-based approach for feature selection which uses three different ranking algorithms for reducing the search space for the GA, which uses a SVM based wrapper as fitness function. However, in this case, the GA algorithm is used in a very limited way because the search space is reduced to only 12 features. Moreover, in [10,12] two different GA-based hybrid approaches that use wrapper fitness functions are proposed and tested on data with no more than 100 features. Finally, in [2] a two steps procedure is used to deal with data involving up to thousands of features. In the first step, the whole set of features is ranked according to an univariate measure; in the second step, the final subset is built by incrementally adding the i-th ranked feature. The process continues until the added feature improves the performance of the classifier used for the subset evaluation.

In this paper we present a new GA-based algorithm for feature selection that exploits the advantages of both feature ranking and GAs. The goal is to build a high performance feature selection system that selects a small number of features, with respect to the total number of available features. For this purpose, we built a two-module system that combines a feature ranking algorithm with a GA. The proposed system allows us to greatly reduce the number of features to be used in the classification phase. More specifically, the first module uses a feature ranking algorithm to greatly reduce the number of features to be taken into account by the second module; it considers only a given number M (a priori fixed) of features that are promising, according to the univariate measure used for ranking the whole feature set given in input to the system. The second GA-based module seeks, in the search space consisting of the feature subsets made of the features provided by the first module, the best feature subset by using a filter fitness function that evaluates feature subsets. The layout of the proposed system is shown in Fig. 1.

Because of the reduction performed by the feature ranking, the search space provided to the GA module is much smaller than that made of all the possible subsets of the whole feature set. The proposed system is based on the hypothesis that this reduced search space still contains most of the "promising areas", i.e. those containing good and near-optimal solutions (subsets). In practice, the "filtering" performed by the ranking module does not discard those features that performs well only when used in combination with other ones; this allows the second GA-based module to focus its search on these more promising areas.

As concerns the univariate measures for the feature ranking, we used the Chi-square measure introduced in [15]. As evaluation function for the GA module we used that introduced in [9], namely the Correlation based Feature Selection function (CFS). This function evaluates the merit of a subset by considering

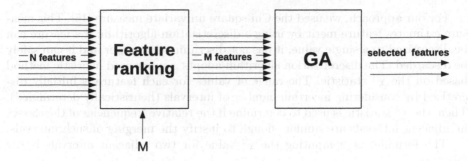

Fig. 1. The layout of the proposed system.

both the correlation between the class labels and the single features, and the inter-correlation among the selected features. The CFS function computation is made of two steps: (i) the class-features correlation vector and the features correlation matrix are a priori computed for all the features and properly stored; (ii) the subsequent computations of the CFS function can be computed by accessing to the vector and matrix a priori computed. It is worth noting that these computations are independent of the training set size.

The effectiveness of the proposed approach has been tested on four different datasets publicly available, whose total number of features ranges from 500 to 10000. Two kinds of comparison were performed: in the former the results of our approach were compared with those achieved by using different feature selection strategies; in the latter, our results were compared with those obtained by a wrapper based approach.

The remainder of the paper is organized as follows: in Sect. 2 the feature evaluation functions are described, Sect. 3 illustrates the GA used to implement the second module. In Sect. 4 the experimental results are detailed. Finally, Sect. 5 is devoted to the conclusions.

2   Feature Evaluation Function

As mentioned in the Introduction, feature evaluation functions can be broadly divided into two classes, namely *univariate* measures and *multivariate* measures. In the following, the univariate measure adopted for the ranking module and the subset evaluation criterion used as fitness function of the GA module are detailed.

2.1   Univariate Measures

Univariate measures evaluate the effectiveness of a single feature in discriminating samples belonging to different classes and can be used to sort the whole set of available features. The feature selection approaches which use this kind of measure do not need a search procedure In fact, once the features have been sorted, the best subset of M features consists of the first M features of the ranking. Note that the value of M must be chosen by the user.

For our approach, we used the Chi-square univariate measure [15]. This measure estimates feature merit by using a discretization algorithm: if a feature can be discretized to a single value, it has not discriminative power and it can safely be discarded. The discretization algorithm adopts a supervised heuristic method based on the χ^2 statistic. The range of values for each feature is initially discretized by considering a certain number of intervals (heuristically determined). Then, the χ^2 statistic is used to determine if the relative frequencies of the classes in adjacent intervals are similar enough to justify the merging of such intervals.

The formula for computing the χ^2 value for two adjacent intervals is the following:

$$\chi^2 = \sum_{i=1}^{2} \sum_{j=1}^{C} \frac{(A_{ij} - E_{ij})^2}{E_{ij}} \tag{1}$$

where C is the number of classes, A_{ij} is the instance number of the j-th class in the i-th interval and E_{ij} is the expected frequency of A_{ij} given by the formula: $E_{ij} = R_i C_j / N_T$ where R_i is the number of instances in the i-th interval and C_j and N_T are the instance number of the j-th class and the total number of instances, respectively, in both intervals.

The extent of the merging process is controlled by a threshold, whose value represent the maximum admissible difference among the occurrence frequencies of the samples in adjacent intervals. The value of this threshold has been heuristically set during preliminary experiments.

2.2   Subset Evaluation Functions

Multivariate methods for feature subset evaluation, can in turn be divided into two classes: *filter* and *wrapper*. The former are based on statistical measures and their outcomes are independent from the classifier actually used. The latter, instead, are based on the classification results achieved by a certain classifier, trained on the subset to be evaluated. Wrapper methods are usually computationally more expensive than the filter ones, as they require the training of the classifier used for each evaluation, making them unsuitable to solve "big data" tasks, where huge datasets must be processed. Moreover, while filter-based evaluations are more general, as they give statistical information on the data, wrapper-based evaluations may give raise to loss of generality because they depend on the specific classifier used.

In order to introduce the subset evaluation function adopted, let us briefly recall the well known information-theory concept of entropy. Given a discrete variable X, which can assume the values $\{x_1, x_2, \ldots, x_n\}$, its entropy $H(X)$ is defined as:

$$H(X) = -\sum_{i=1}^{n} p(x_i) \log_2 p(x_i) \tag{2}$$

where $p(x_i)$ is the probability mass function of the value x_i. The quantity $H(X)$ represents an estimate of the uncertainty of the random variable X. The concept of entropy can be used to define the conditional entropy of two random variables X and Y taking the values x_i and y_j respectively, as:

$$H(X|Y) = -\sum_{i,j} p(x_i, y_j) \log \frac{p(y_j)}{p(x_i, y_j)} \tag{3}$$

where $p(x_i, y_j)$ is the joint probability that at same time $X = x_i$ and $Y = y_j$. The quantity in (3) represents the amount of randomness in the random variable X when the value of Y is known.

Given two features X and Y, their correlation r_{XY} is computed as follows[1]:

$$r_{XY} = 2.0 \cdot \frac{H(X) + H(Y) - H(X, Y)}{H(X) + H(Y)} \tag{4}$$

As fitness function for the GA module we chose a filter called CFS (Correlation-based Feature Selection) [9], which uses a correlation based heuristic to evaluate feature subset quality. This function takes into account the usefulness of the single features for predicting class labels along with the level of inter-correlation among them. The idea behind this approach is that good subsets contain features highly correlated with the class and uncorrelated with each other.

Given a feature selection problem in which the patterns are represented by means of a set Y of N features, the CFS function computes the merit of the generic subset $X \subseteq Y$, made of k features, as follows:

$$f_{CFS}(X) = \frac{k \cdot \overline{r_{cf}}}{\sqrt{k + k \cdot (k-1) \cdot \overline{r_{ff}}}} \tag{5}$$

where $\overline{r_{cf}}$ is the average feature-class correlation, and $\overline{r_{ff}}$ is the feature-feature correlation. Note that the numerator estimates the discriminative power of the features in X, whereas the denominator assesses the redundancy among them. The CFS function allows the GA to discard irrelevant and redundant features. The former because they are poor in discriminating the different classes at the hand; the latter because they are highly correlated with one or more of the other features. In contrast to previously presented approaches [10,18], this fitness function is able to automatically find the number of features and does not need the setting of any parameter.

Finally, given a dataset $\mathcal{D}$ to estimate the quantities in (4) and a feature subset X to be evaluated, the computation of $f_{CFS}(X)$ $(X \subseteq Y)$ can be made very fast. In fact, before starting the search procedure (the GA in our case), the correlation vector V_{cf}, containing N elements, and the $N \times N$ symmetric correlation matrix M_{ff} can be computed. The i-th element of V_{cf} contains the value of the correlation between the i-th feature and the class, whereas the element $M_{ff}[i, j]$ represents the correlation between the i-th and the j-th feature. Once the values of V_{cf} and M_{ff} have been computed, given a subset X containing k features, the computation of $f_{CFS}(X)$ only requires $2k$ memory accesses.

---

[1] Note that the same holds also for the feature-class correlation.

3   Genetic Algorithms for Feature Selection

In the last decades, Evolutionary Computation techniques have shown to be very effective as methodology for solving optimization problems whose search space are discontinuous and very complex. In this field, GAs represent a subset of these optimization techniques and have been applied to a wide variety of both numerical and combinatorial optimization problems [12]. In a GA the solutions are represented as binary vectors and operators such as crossover and mutation are applied to explore the search space made of all possible solutions.

GAs can be easily applied to the problem of feature selection: given a set Y having cardinality equal to N, a subset X of Y ($X \subseteq Y$) can be represented by a binary vector of N elements whose i-th element is set to 1 if the i-th features is included in X, 0 otherwise. Besides the simplicity in the solution encoding, GAs are well suited for this class of problems as the search in this exponential space is very hard since interactions among features can be highly complex and strongly nonlinear. Some studies on the GAs effectiveness in solving features selection problems can be found in [12,21].

The second module of the system presented here has been implemented by using a generational GA. In order to reduce the computational complexity of the fitness function (see Subsect. 2.2) the class-feature correlation vector V_{CF} and the feature-feature correlation matrix M_{FF} are pre-computed. Then the GA starts by randomly generating a population of P individuals. Afterwards, the fitness of the generated individuals is evaluated according to the formula in (5). After this preliminary evaluation phase, a new population is generated by selecting $P/2$ couples of individuals using the roulette wheel method. The one point crossover operator is then applied to each of the selected couples, according to a given probability factor p_c. Afterwards, the mutation operator is applied with a probability p_m. The value of p_m has been set to $1/N$, where N is the chromosome length, i.e. the total number of the available features for the problem at hand. This probability value allows, on average, the modification of only one chromosome element. This value has been suggested in [17] as optimal mutation rate below the error threshold of replication. Finally these individuals are added to the new population. The process just described is repeated for N_g generations.

4   Experimental Results

We tested the proposed approach on high dimensional data (from 500 up to 10000 features). For each dataset, a set of values for the parameter M (see Fig. 1) has been tested. For each value of M, 30 runs have been performed for the GA module. At the end of every run, the feature subset encoded by the individual with the best fitness, has been used to built a Multilayer Perceptron classifier (MLP in the following), trained by using the back propagation algorithm. The classification performances of the classifiers built have been obtained by using the 10-fold cross-validation approach. The results reported in the following have been obtained averaging the performance of the 30 MLP's built.

Table 1. The values of the GA module parameters used in the experiments. Note that p_m depends on the chromosome length, i.e. the total number of available features N_F.

Parameter	Symbol	Value
Population size	$\mathcal{P}$	100
Crossover probability	p_c	0.4
Mutation probability	p_m	$1/N_F$
Number of generations	N_g	500

Some preliminary trials have been performed to set the parameters of the GA and of the MLP, reported in Tables 1 and 2 respectively. These two sets of parameters have been used for all the experiments reported below.

Table 2. The values of the parameters used for the training of the MLP's. Note that the number of hidden neurons depends on both the number of input attributes N_a and the output classes N_c.

Parameter	Value
Learning rate	0.3
Momentum	0.2
Hidden neurons	$(N_a + N_c)/2$
Epochs	500

4.1 The Datasets

The proposed approach has been tested on the following, publicly available, datasets: *Arcene, Gisette, Madelon* [1] and *Ucihar* [14]. The characteristics of the datasets are summarized in Table 3. They present different characteristics as regards the number of attributes, the number of classes (two or multiple classes problems) and the number of samples. In particular, Arcene contains mass-spectrometric data from medical tests for cancer diagnosis (ovarian or prostate cancer); it is a two-class classification problem with continuous input variables. Gisette contains images of confusable handwritten digits: the four and

Table 3. The datasets used in the experiments.

Datasets	Attributes	Samples	Classes
Arcene	10000	100	2
Gisette	5000	6000	2
Madelon	500	2000	2
Ucihar	561	10299	6

the nine. The dataset was constructed from the MNIST data made available by Yann LeCun of the NEC Research Institute; it is a two-class classification problem with sparse continuous input variables. Madelon contains two-class synthetic data with sparse binary attributes; each class contains a certain number of Gaussian clusters, independently generated. It also contains some redundant and useless features. Finally, the Ucihar dataset contains data representing signals from smartphone sensors (accelerometer and gyroscope), recorded from 30 persons wearing a smartphone on the waist. Each person performed six activities, each representing a class of the problem: walking, walking upstairs, walking downstairs, sitting, standing and laying.

4.2 Comparison Findings

In order to test the effectiveness of our system, we performed two sets of comparisons. In the first set, we compared the results of the proposed system with those obtained by three different feature selection approaches:

- The feature ranking represented by the first module of our system (Fig. 1): given the whole set of N features, it gives as output the best M feature, according to the univariate measure adopted; it will be denoted as RNK in the following.
- the GA used in the second module of the proposed system (Fig. 1): given the whole set of N features, it searches for the best solution (subset) by using the GA algorithm detailed in Sect. 3. It will be denoted as GA in the following.
- The third approach taken into account for the comparison, instead, is quite similar to our approach but uses the sequential forward floating selection as search strategy of the second module. This strategy searches the solution space by using a greedy hill-climbing technique. It starts with the empty set of features and, at each step, selects the best feature that satisfies the evaluation function; The algorithm also verifies the possibility of improvement of the criterion if a feature is excluded. In this case, the worst feature, according to the evaluation function, is excluded from the set. We used an improved version of this algorithm, presented in [7]. It will be denoted as RNK-SFS in the following.

The purpose of the first comparison was to test the effectiveness of the proposed approach in improving the performance obtained by using only the feature ranking approach. As regards the second comparison, its aim was to validate our hypothesis: a feature ranking algorithm can be used to improve the performance of a standard GA, by locating the promising areas of the whole search space consisting of all the available features. Finally, the goal of the third comparison was to assess the ability of the GA in finding good solutions in the search space provided by the feature ranking module. For all the comparisons, the performance have been evaluated in terms of recognition rate and feature reduction.

As concerns the second set of comparisons, we compared the results of our system with those presented in [2]. The approach taken account for this comparison is called $IWSS$ and, as mentioned in the introduction, it is wrapper-based and is able to deal with problems involving thousands of features.

With the purpose of investigating how the value of the parameter M affects the performance of the presented system, we tested several M values. Moreover, since the number of attributes of the datasets taken into account differs widely, we considered two sets of values. The set $\{100, 200, 500, 1000, 2000\}$ has been considered for the datasets Arcene and Gisette, whose samples are described by 10000 and 5000 attributes, respectively. The set $\{20, 50, 100, 200, 300\}$ has been used for the datasets Madelon and Ucihar, having 500 and 561 attributes, respectively.

First Set of Comparisons. Since the approaches RNK and RNK-SFS are deterministic, for each value of M, they generated a single feature subset. However, in order to perform a fair comparison with the proposed approach, for each subset generated, 30 MLP's have been trained with different, randomly generated, initial weights. The trained MLP's have been evaluated by using the 10-fold cross-validation approach. The results reported in the following have been obtained averaging the performance of the 30 MLP's learned. Also in this case we used the parameters reported in Table 2.

As concerns the results of the GA approach, they have been obtained by using the methodology adopted for our approach, so as described at the beginning of the present section.

Note that to statistically validate the comparison results, we performed the non-parametric Wilcoxon rank-sum test ($\alpha = 0.05$) over 30 runs.

The comparison results have been grouped according to the different values of M used, and are reported in Tables 4 (Arcene and Gisette) and 5 (Madelon and Ucihar). In both tables, the second column shows the values of the parameter M, while the recognition rate (RR) and the number of selected features (NF), are reported for each method. It is worth noting that for the RNK method the number of selected features have not been reported because it coincides with the value of M actually used.

In each table, the recognition rates in bold highlight the results which are significantly better with respect to the second best results (values starred in the table), according to the Wilcoxon test. As concerns the results that do not present a statistically significant difference, the best two results are both starred. Moreover, for each method, in the case that two or more results do not present statistically significant difference, the result achieved with the minimum number of features has been considered. Finally, note that for our approach, we used the abbreviation *RNK-GA*.

The comparison results for the Arcene and Gisette datasets are shown in Table 4. From the table it can be seen that the proposed approach achieves better performance for both datasets. In more detail, for the Arcene dataset a recognition rate of 92.3% has been obtained by using only 465 out of the 10000 features provided in input to the system. This result has been achieved with a value of M equal to 2000 and it is significantly better than those obtained with smaller values. This seems to suggest that for these smaller values the ranking module discards features that, although they score poorly according to the χ^2

Table 4. Comparison results for the Arcene and Gisette datasets. Bold values represent the best statistically significant results.

Dataset	M	RNK-GA		GA		RNK	RNK-SFS	
		RR	NF	RR	NF	RR	RR	NF
Arcene	100	78.5	8.3	80.1	990	81.4	80.1	8
	200	83	12.5			86.4	82.9	11
	500	85.2	35			87.4*	82.7	18
	1000	88.1	110.7			87.2	83.7	34
	2000	**92.3**	465			79	85.7	53
Gisette	100	92.55	22.6	95.7*	370	94.68	92.8	31
	200	94.55	29.9			95.57*	94.7	42
	500	**96.7**	41.9			94.93	95.6*	73
	1000	96.76	103.8			94.52	95.4	74
	2000	95.4	190.8			90.1	95.5	77

measure, are relevant for the classification task when used in conjunction with other features.

Nonetheless, the search space reduction performed by the ranking module with $M = 2000$ (from $\approx 10^{3000}$ to $\approx 10^{670}$) allowed a strong improvement of the performance with respect to the GA, which searched the whole search space. As concerns the second best result, the RNK approach reached a recognition rate of 87.4%, by using 500 features which coincides with the value of M. Note that for $M = 2000$ the RNK approach performs poorly, indicating that only some of the first 2000 ranked features are actually relevant, while most of them are irrelevant or redundant, and training the MLP with all of them leads to poor classification performance. As for the RNK-SFS method, which got its best result with $M = 2000$, it performs significantly worse than our approach, showing that the GA has a better searching ability than RNK-SFS. For the Gisette dataset, the best two results of our system ($M = 500$ and $M = 1000$) were not significantly different and, according to the criterion mentioned above, we considered that which used 41.9 features, which achieved a recognition rate of 96.7% ($M = 500$). The results of the other methods were not significantly different each other.

In this case, the GA approach got good results, but selected much more features than RNK-GA. This result shows that, even if the GA selected most of the relevant features, it was not able to discard the redundant and irrelevant ones. This is due to the fact that the GA searched the whole space of solutions and could not benefit of the "filtering action" performed by the ranking module.

As regards the RNK-SFS, it got the best performance with three different results ($M = 500$, $M = 100$ and $M = 2000$), which did not exhibit any statistically significant difference. The result chosen ($M = 500$) reached a recognition rate of 95.6%, by selecting 73 features. These results exhibit slight differences also

Table 5. Comparison results for the Madelon and Ucihar datasets. Bold values represent the best statistically significant results.

Dataset	M	RNK-GA		GA		RNK	RNK-SFS	
		RR	NF	RR	NF	RR	RR	NF
Madelon	20	76.11	9	76.4*	10.7	76.25*	76.14	9
	50	76.17	9			68.82	75.88	9
	100	76.01	8.9			63.97	76.15	9
	200	76.3*	8.7			62.01	76.09	9
	300	76.41	9.1			59.8	76.21*	9
Ucihar	20	81.65	7	95.67*	74.5	86.63	81.83	7
	50	93.85	19.0			94.07	93.8	18
	100	94.21	22.7			93.78	93.7	20
	200	95.51*	27.7			91.9	95.26*	21
	300	94.99	29.6			88.56	93.97	21

in terms of number of features. This seems to suggest that the SFS algorithm, starting from the 500 features case, got stuck in suboptimal areas of the search space, and it was not able to locate new areas containing solutions consisting of a greater number of features.

The results just described seem to confirm that as the search space (exponentially) grows with M, the GA module of the proposed approach is able to locate new areas of the search space containing better solutions, which includes the new features progressively added. In particular, in the case of the Arcene dataset, our system was able to find solutions whose cardinality strongly grows as M increases, obtaining a strong increase of the performance in terms of recognition rate. For the Gisette dataset, instead, the fitness increment of the new solutions found did not lead to a significant improvement in terms of recognition rate.

The comparison results for the Madelon and Ucihar datasets are shown in Table 5. From the table it can be observed that for both datasets the proposed system did not significantly outperform the compared systems.

As concerns the Madelon dataset, the RNK approach reached its best performance by using the first 20 ranked features. This suggests that the Madelon whole set of features contains a small set of features that, even when they are taken separately, have a high discriminative power. This set can be easily identified, either by using RNK which selected the best 20 features, according to χ^2 measure (Eq. (1)), or by the GA, despite it searched the whole search space.

As for the Ucihar results, RNK-GA, RNK-SFS and GA outperformed RNK, but achieved performances that did not exhibit any statistically significant difference. RNK-GA and RNK-SFS obtained their best results with $M = 200$, using a comparable number of features. The GA selected much more features than RNK-GA and RNK-SFS (about three times), confirming that it wasn't able to

Table 6. Comparison results with the IWSS approach.

(a) C4.5 algorithm

Dataset	RNK-GA			IWSS	
	M	RR	NF	RR	NF
Arcene	500	**86.75**	35.0	80.00	5.4
Gisette	2000	**94.58**	190.8	93.75	35.8
Madelon	50	74.09	9.0	**78.10**	12
(b) K Nearest Neighbor					
Arcene	200	**85.20**	12.5	77.00	5.2
Gisette	1000	**96.74**	103.8	96.05	71.6
Madelon	200	77.78	8.7	**88.70**	11.7
(c) Naive Bayes					
Arcene	100	**86.95**	8.3	72.00	6.2
Gisette	500	90.38	41.9	**94.68**	112.6
Madelon	50	**61.05**	9.0	60.50	8

discard redundant and irrelevant features. Nonetheless, in this case, these features did not affect the MLP training process. These results seems to suggest that when the number of features to be dealt with is not too large: (i) even less effective search algorithms like the SFS can find good solutions in the reduced search space provided by the first module; (ii) the GA alone is still able to locate search space areas containing good solutions, but they may contain redundant or irrelevant features.

Second Set of Comparisons. In [2], the proposed approach (IWSS) has been tested on three classifiers: Naive Bayes (NB), KNN ($K = 1$) and C4.5. Moreover, in [2], among the others, three of the four datasets reported in Table 3 have been tested: Arcene, Gisette and Madelon. The comparison results are shown in Table 6. Note that the second column shows the values of the parameter M that obtained the best result among those tested (the same used for the first set of comparison). The recognition rate (RR) and the number of selected features (NF), are also reported. Since the IWSS approach is deterministic, the results reported in [2], refer to a single feature subset and have been obtained using the 10-fold cross-validation technique. For this reason, in order to statistically validate the comparison results we performed the one sample Wilcoxon rank-sum test ($\alpha = 0.05$), comparing the single result of IWSS with the results of RNK-GA, on the 30 runs. The values in bold highlight the best result, according to the Wilcoxon test.

From the table it can be seen that for the Arcene dataset (10000 features), the proposed system greatly outperforms the IWSS approach on the three classifiers considered. As concerns the Gisette dataset (5000 features), for the C4.5

and KNN classifiers, the performance of our approach are better than those of IWSS. Finally, as for the Madelon dataset (500 features), IWSS achieves better performance for the C4.5 and KNN classifiers, whereas for the NB classifier our system performs slightly better.

The above results confirms the effectiveness of proposed approach to deal with high dimensional data. In fact, on the Arcene dataset our system largely outperforms the IWSS approach, in spite of the fact that IWSS uses a wrapper evaluation function. This is confirmed by the results on the Gisette dataset, where our system obtained better performances on two of the three classifiers. In this case, the differences in terms of recognition rates are much smaller than those of the Arcene dataset. However, these results are similar to those reported in Table 4, where the recognition rate differences for the MLP classifier are not greater than 1%. Only for the NB classifier IWSS significantly outperforms our approach, but nonetheless this performance is worse than that obtained by our approach with the MLP.

Finally, as for the Madelon dataset, as mentioned above, it is characterized by a small set of discriminative features that can be easily identified by univariate measures. Then, in this case, the IWSS approach is favored because it first ranks the features and then incrementally build the feature subset by using a greedy strategy.

4.3   Discussion

From the results shown above it can be seen that the univariate measure used in the first module is able to identify most of the relevant features even though the adopted measure evaluates the relevance of each feature, without taking into account any feature interaction. In practice, what happens is that these "interacting features" that are singularly little relevant, but that become useful when taken with other features, do not appear at the bottom of the ranking. Thus, these features can always be included by suitably incrementing the value of M. It is worth noting that, because of the exponentially growth of the search space, even high values of M allows a strong reduction of the search space. An interesting property of our system is that, once the number of M has been correctly set, the GA of the second module is able to discard redundant features. In fact, our approach selected much less features than those given in input or those selected by the GA taken into account for the comparison.

We want to remark that, the above results confirm the assumptions underlying our method: (i) a feature ranking algorithm can be used to "preselect" a number, a priori fixed, of features among the whole set of available features; (ii) the search space consisting of the subsets made of these selected features contains most of the good and near-optimal solutions (subsets). In practice, the filtering performed by the feature ranking module makes easier the task of searching for good solutions and this filtering is crucial in improving the performance of the GA when thousands of features are involved.

5   Conclusions

We present a novel GA-based approach for feature selection which is able to deal with thousands of features. The approach consists of two modules. The first uses a feature ranking based approach that reduces the search space made of the whole set of available features. This reduction is performed by discarding the features that, according the univariate measure employed, are less useful for discriminating among the different classes at hand. The second module uses a genetic algorithm to search in the solution space provided by the first module. This module employs a correlation based heuristic function to evaluate the worth of the feature subsets encoded by the individuals.

Since we used only filter evaluation functions, the proposed approach shows the following interesting properties: (i) it is independent of the classification system used; (ii) once that the correlation data have been computed in the initialization step of the GA, the computational cost of the fitness function does not depend on the training set size. The second property makes our system particularly suitable for problems involving a huge number of instances.

The effectiveness of the proposed system has been tested on data represented in high dimensional spaces. The achieved results have been compared with those obtained by different feature selection strategies, both wrapper and filter. For the datasets containing thousands of features, our method obtain better results than the other methods both in terms of accuracy and number of selected features.

Future works will investigate different feature evaluation function, both for the ranking (univariate) and for the GA (multivariate). Moreover, system performance will be evaluated also for different classification schemes.

References

1. Nips 2003 workshop on feature extraction and feature selection challenge (2003). http://clopinet.com/isabelle/Projects/NIPS2003
2. Bermejo, P., Gámez, J.A., Puerta, J.M.: Improving incremental wrapper-based subset selection via replacement and early stopping. IJPRAI **25**(5), 605–625 (2011)
3. Cordella, L.P., De Stefano, C., Fontanella, F., Marrocco, C., Scotto di Freca, A.: Combining single class features for improving performance of a two stage classifier. In: 20th International Conference on Pattern Recognition (ICPR 2010), pp. 4352–4355. IEEE Computer Society (2010)
4. Dash, M., Liu, H.: Feature selection for classification. Intell. Data Anal. **1**(1–4), 131–156 (1997)
5. De Stefano, C., Fontanella, F., Marrocco, C.: A GA-based feature selection algorithm for remote sensing images. In: Giacobini, M., et al. (eds.) EvoWorkshops 2008. LNCS, vol. 4974, pp. 285–294. Springer, Heidelberg (2008). doi:10.1007/978-3-540-78761-7_29
6. De Stefano, C., Fontanella, F., Maniaci, M., Scotto di Freca, A.: A method for scribe distinction in medieval manuscripts using page layout features. In: Maino, G., Foresti, G.L. (eds.) ICIAP 2011. LNCS, vol. 6978, pp. 393–402. Springer, Heidelberg (2011). doi:10.1007/978-3-642-24085-0_41

7. Gütlein, M., Frank, E., Hall, M., Karwath, A.: Large scale attribute selection using wrappers. In: Proceedings of the IEEE Symposium on Computational Intelligence and Data Mining (CIDM 2009) (2009)
8. Guyon, I., Elisseeff, A.: An introduction to variable and feature selection. J. Mach. Learn. Res. **3**, 1157–1182 (2003)
9. Hall, M.A.: Correlation-based feature selection for discrete and numeric class machine learning. In: Proceedings of the Seventeenth International Conference on Machine Learning, pp. 359–366. Morgan Kaufmann Publishers Inc., San Francisco (2000)
10. Huang, J., Cai, Y., Xu, X.: A hybrid genetic algorithm for feature selection wrapper based on mutual information. Pattern Recogn. Lett. **28**(13), 1825–1844 (2007)
11. Lanzi, P.: Fast feature selection with genetic algorithms: a filter approach. In: IEEE International Conference on Evolutionary Computation, pp. 537–540, April 1997
12. Lee, J.S., Oh, I.S., Moon, B.R.: Hybrid genetic algorithms for feature selection. IEEE Trans. Pattern Anal. Mach. Intell. **26**(11), 1424–1437 (2004)
13. Li, R., Lu, J., Zhang, Y., Zhao, T.: Dynamic adaboost learning with feature selection based on parallel genetic algorithm for image annotation. Knowl. Based Syst. **23**(3), 195–201 (2010)
14. Lichman, M.: UCI machine learning repository (2013). http://archive.ics.uci.edu/ml
15. Liu, H., Setiono, R.: Chi2: Feature selection and discretization of numeric attributes. In: ICTAI, pp. 88–91. IEEE Computer Society, Washington, DC (1995)
16. Manimala, K., Selvi, K., Ahila, R.: Hybrid soft computing techniques for feature selection and parameter optimization in power quality data mining. Appl. Soft Comput. **11**(8), 5485–5497 (2011). http://www.sciencedirect.com/science/article/pii/S1568494611001694
17. Ochoa, G.: Error thresholds in genetic algorithms. Evol. Comput. **14**(2), 157–182 (2006)
18. Oreski, S., Oreski, G.: Genetic algorithm-based heuristic for feature selection in credit risk assessment. Expert Syst. Appl. **41**(4, Part 2), 2052–2064 (2014)
19. Spolaôr, N., Lorena, A.C., Lee, H.D.: Multi-objective genetic algorithm evaluation in feature selection. In: Takahashi, R.H.C., Deb, K., Wanner, E.F., Greco, S. (eds.) EMO 2011. LNCS, vol. 6576, pp. 462–476. Springer, Heidelberg (2011). doi:10.1007/978-3-642-19893-9_32
20. Tan, F., Fu, X., Zhang, Y., Bourgeois, A.G.: A genetic algorithm-based method for feature subset selection. Soft Comput. **12**(2), 111–120 (2007)
21. Xue, B., Zhang, M., Browne, W.N., Yao, X.: A survey on evolutionary computation approaches to feature selection. IEEE Trans. Evol. Comput. **20**(4), 606–626 (2016)
22. Yusta, S.C.: Different metaheuristic strategies to solve the feature selection problem. Pattern Recogn. Lett. **30**(5), 525–534 (2009)
23. Zhai, Y., Ong, Y.S., Tsang, I.: The emerging "big dimensionality". IEEE Comput. Intell. Mag. **9**(3), 14–26 (2014)

Brain Programming and the Random Search in Object Categorization

Gustavo Olague[1](✉), Eddie Clemente[2], Daniel E. Hernández[3],
and Aaron Barrera[1]

[1] Centro de Investigación Científica y de Educación Superior de Ensenada,
Ensenada, BC, Mexico
gustavo.olague@gmail.com, abarrera@cicese.edu.mx
[2] Instituto Tecnológico de Ensenada, Ensenada, BC, Mexico
eclemente@ite.edu.mx
[3] Instituto Tecnológico de Tijuana, Tijuana, BC, Mexico
daniel.hernandezm@tectijuana.edu.mx

Abstract. Computational neuroscience lays the foundations of intelligent behavior through the application of machine learning approaches. Brain programming, which derives from such approaches, is emerging as a new evolutionary computing paradigm for solving computer vision and pattern recognition problems. Primate brains have several distinctive features that are obtained by a complex arrangement of highly interconnected and numerous cortical visual areas. This paper describes a virtual system that mimics the complex structure of primate brains composed of an artificial dorsal pathway – or "where" stream – and an artificial ventral pathway – or "what" stream – that are fused to recreate an artificial visual cortex. The goal is to show that brain programming is able to discover numerous heterogeneous functions that are applied within a hierarchical structure of our virtual brain. Thus, the proposal applies two key ideas: first, object recognition can be achieved by a hierarchical structure in combination with the concept of function composition; second, the functions can be discovered through multiple random runs of the search process. This last point is important since is the first step in any evolutionary algorithm; in this way, enhancing the possibilities for solving hard optimization problems.

Keywords: Object recognition · Random search · Brain programming

1 Introduction

Object recognition is a fundamental task for humans and all living beings endowed with the sense of sight, since it allows the interaction of the organism with the surrounding environment and the understanding of a given object. In the last two decades computer vision and evolutionary algorithms have seen a growing interest from the scientific community [1]. In general, the human visual system is able to recognize and classify an object according to its category with ease.

© Springer International Publishing AG 2017
G. Squillero and K. Sim (Eds.): EvoApplications 2017, Part I, LNCS 10199, pp. 522–537, 2017.
DOI: 10.1007/978-3-319-55849-3_34

Both tasks consider that the set of attributes or features extracted from the images are general enough to classify the object as part of the category, while maintaining in memory the features that serve to identify that particular object within a given scene [2–4]. The aim of this paper is to present a new model inspired by the transformations that take place within the visual cortex for the solution of the object classification task.

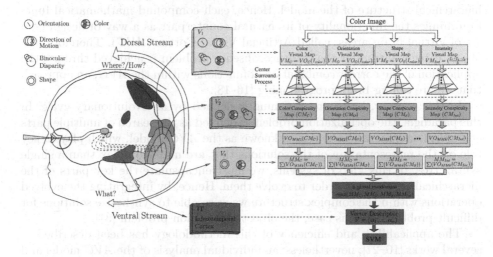

Fig. 1. Conceptual Model of the Artificial Visual Cortex. The color image is decomposed into four dimensions (color, orientation, shape and intensity). Then, a hierarchical structure is charged of solving the object classification problem through a function driven paradigm.

Ungerleider and Mishkin in 1982 proposed the existence of two routes in the visual cortex. These pathways have been called dorsal and ventral streams, the functionality of the dorsal stream provides the location of an object within the scene, while the ventral stream is dedicated to the task of object recognition. Thus, efficient visual functionality is achieved by a high interchange of information between the two streams [5–10]. In this way, object recognition involves processes performed along the dorsal stream such as selectivity that is defined as the ability to filter unwanted information, and those performed in the ventral stream in charge of describing the objects. Thus, the approach proposed in this work is suggested by a computational model based in these two information streams of the visual cortex. This approach differs from those of the state-of-the-art where a data-driven principle is applied using a set of patches – image regions – while creating a dictionary of visual words like in a bag-of-words approach [11–15]. In our work, the first hypothesis is that the dictionary of visual words can be replaced by a set of visual operators which are built with a group of mathematical functions. The second idea is based on the integration of properties responsible for the visual attention process – or selectivity – that is related to the creation of conspicuity maps (*CMs*) and the center surround process together with description and combination of maximum responses executed by a *max* operation of the functions that select features, which categorize the object; see Fig. 1. In this way, this model sees the brain as a collection of functions joined into a structural unit that serves to the purpose of object recognition, where the functionality of each area or layer in the visual cortex is represented by a kind of mathematical function, and the interconnection among them is given by the hierarchical structure of the model. Hence, each compound mathematical function mimics the functionality of its natural counterpart as a way of designing a set of virtual brain areas, called Artificial Visual Cortex (*AVC*). Therefore, the object categorization for the presence/absence problem is achieved through the application of the correct combination of functions within the *AVC*; an approach that we are calling brain programming [16–18].

In this manner, brain programming is defined by an evolutionary cycle. In this paradigm, the optimization problem is defined as the search of multiple parts embedded on a hierarchical system known as the *AVC* model, which plays a key role on the representation of the solutions that are more complex than a single syntax tree. In this kind of systems, we must encapsulate the key parts of the hierarchical structure in order to evolve them. Hence, by integrating the evolved operations within the complex structure we were able to synthesize solutions for difficult problems; in this case, the object recognition problem [31].

The applicability and efficiency of this methodology has been described in several works [16–21], nevertheless, an individual analysis of the *AVC* model and the brain programming methodology has not been done. As in many optimization paradigms, we propose to compare brain programming with a random search approach, in order to characterize the benefits of the *AVC* model by itself and the improvement brought by the evolutionary approach. This paper focus on the random search and we will explore the whole algorithm in a future article.

1.1 Research Contributions

This paper outlines the following research contributions:

- First, in the proposed approach the total number of visual operators made of mathematical functions and embedded within the hierarchical structure can be discovered through a small number of random trials, while actually achieving outstanding results on an standard testbed. This article provides evidence that the hierarchical structure plays a significant role on the solution of visual problems.
- Second, a comparison of the random search with state-of-the-art algorithms and the whole evolutionary cycle gives us a clear picture of the benefit of applying brain programming.

1.2 Related Work

Most of the works are divided in two basic approaches, the first is regarding visual attention conducted along the dorsal stream, while a second approach is related on object recognition held in the ventral stream. Nevertheless, there are a few works that attempted to integrate the two approaches. For example, Fukushima in 1987 implemented a hierarchical neural network that serves as a model for selective attention and object recognition [22]. In this case, when several patterns are presented simultaneously, the model performs a selective attention to each one, segmenting it from the rest and recognizing it separately. Afterwards, Olshausen *et al.* in 1993 defined a biologically plausible model that combines an attentional mechanism with an object recognition process to form position and scale invariant representations in the visual world [23]. Then, Walther *et al.* suggested a combined model for spatial attention and object recognition [24]. In their work, visual attention follows the computational model proposed by Itti and Koch [15] and object recognition is achieved through the *HMAX* model of Riesenhuber and Poggio [25]. Their information stream follows the whole visual attention process and the final saliency map is fed into the S2 layer of the *HMAX* model to accomplish the task of object detection. This model was applied to the problem of recognizing artificial paperclips. Next, Walther and Koch in 2007 suggested, with a computational model, that features learned by the *HMAX* model used for the recognition of a particular object category may also serve for top-down attention tasks [26]. Finally, Heinke and Humphteys applied a model called SAIM for visual search involving simple lines and letters [27]. This model, in a first stage selects the object within the image and subsequently performs an object identification step using a template matching technique.

In our work, we propose a hierarchical model following the preattentive stage of visual attention described in [28] in order to locate the conspicuity regions within the image. Then, a description process is performed using the max operator in combination with a series of functions that emulate the functionality of the V4 area in the visual cortex. This approach differs from traditional models for object recognition [4, 12, 13, 25–27] where a set of patches – or visual words – are used to identify the object. In contrast, in our proposed approach the discovered functions provide the functionality of multiple patches; hence, helping in the creation of a straightforward process as will be shown in the experimental results.

2   The *AVC* Algorithm

In the natural system the interrelation between the layers of the visual cortex is not fully understood; nevertheless, the functionality at each stage has been described on previous works. Figure 1 depicts the proposed model based on these processes. The *AVC* is divided in two main parts. In the first stage the proposed system executes the acquisition and transformation of features. Then, in a second stage the *AVC* performs description and classification associated to the studied object.

2.1   Acquisition and Transformation of Features

The first step of our algorithm is represented by the image acquired with the camera, whose natural counterpart is the retina. Here, the system considers

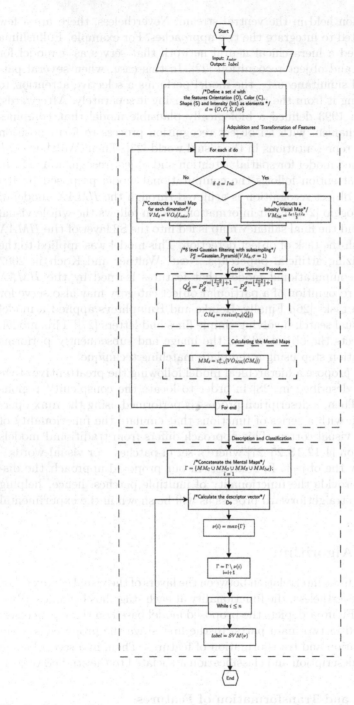

Fig. 2. Schematic representation of the computational algorithm whose output is a label that represents the membership to a specific class.

digital color images in the RGB color model, which are later transformed into the CMYK and HSV color models; see Fig. 2. In this way, the color image is decomposed into multiple color channels. The idea is to build the set $I_{color} = \{I_r, I_g, I_b, I_c, I_m, I_y, I_k, I_h, I_s, I_v\}$, which corresponds to the *red, green, blue, cyan, magenta, yellow, black, hue, saturation, and value* components of their respective color models and which are used to provide the initial representation of the scene. In our work, the input images in I_{color} are transformed by four visual operators (VOs) applied independently to emphasize specific image features. The transformations are performed to recreate the feature extraction process of the brain; resulting into a visual map (VM) per dimension [28].

2.2 Feature Dimensions

The VOs are defined with the aim of classifying specific image features along several dimensions: color, shape, orientation and intensity; hence, $d \in \{C, S, O, Int\}$. Figure 2 shows that features are extracted sequentially one at a time by applying the corresponding operator VO_d.

2.3 Center Surround Process

The center surround method is based on the functionality of the ganglion cells that measure the difference between the firing rates at the center and surrounding areas of their receptive fields. The goal of this process is to generate a conspicuity map (CM) per dimension according to the model proposed in [29]. The algorithm consists of a two step process where the information is built to emulate its natural counterpart as follows; see Fig. 2. First, the computation of the CMs is modeled as the difference between fine and coarse scales, which are computed through a pyramid of nine levels $P_d^g = \{P_d^{\sigma=0}, P_d^{\sigma=1}, P_d^{\sigma=2}, P_d^{\sigma=3}, \ldots, P_d^{\sigma=8}\}$. Each pyramid is calculated from its corresponding VM_d using a Gaussian smoothing filter resulting in an image that is half of the input map size and the process is repeated recursively eight times to complete the nine level pyramid. Second, the pyramid P_d^g is used as input to a center surround procedure to derive six new maps that result from the difference between some of the pyramid levels that are calculated as follows.

$$Q_d^j = P_d^{\sigma=\lfloor \frac{j+9}{2} \rfloor+1} - P_d^{\sigma=\lfloor \frac{j+2}{2} \rfloor+1},$$

where $j = \{1, 2, \ldots, 6\}$. Note that the levels of P_d^g have different size and are scaled down to the size of the top level to calculate their difference. Next, each of these six maps are normalized and combined into a unique map through the summation operation, which is then normalized and scaled up to the VM_d maps' original size using a polynomial interpolation to define the final CM_d.

2.4 Description and Classification Stage

After the construction of the CMs, the next stage along the AVC is to define a descriptor vector that will be used as input to a support vector machine (SVM) model for classification purposes.

2.5   Computation of the Mental Maps

In this stage of the process a single set of visual operators is used to produce a mental map (MM_d) per dimension; see Fig. 2. After the computation of the conspicuity maps a set of visual operators VO_{MM} is applied with the aim of describing the image content. Note that the proposed visual operators are homogeneous and independently applied to each feature dimension. This operation is defined as follows:

$$MM_d = \sum_{i=1}^{k}(VO_{MM_i}(CM_d)), \tag{1}$$

where d is the dimension index and k represents the cardinality of the set VO_{MM}. Each summation is applied to integrate the output of all operations VO_{MM_k} to produce a MM_d per dimension. Thereafter, the four Mental Maps are concatenated into a single array and the n highest values are selected to define the vector $\vec{\nu}$ that describes the image.

In contrast to our proposal, the state-of-the-art methodologies [11–15] are based on a template matching paradigm with the goal of learning a set of prototype image patches. Traditionally, the idea is to learn such a set by using what is known as the bag-of-words model, which is applied to identify a given object category. In this way, our approach substitutes the set of templates with the set of visual operators to characterize one object class with excellent results as we will show in the experiments.

3   Experiments and Results

We use the CalTech 5 and CalTech 101 image databases, despite many serious concerns raised about them [30,31]. Nevertheless, that test is still widely used in the object recognition community and thus most state-of-the-art algorithms report their classification results [12,13,32–36].

3.1   Methodology to Obtain an *AVC* Solution

The methodology that was used to generate the AVC programs followed the algorithm of Sect. 2, where an important step is the construction of VOs. These operators consist of syntax trees made of internal and leaf nodes, which are defined by a set of primitive elements also called function set (see Table 1) and the terminal set defined by the domain of each function. In our work, each tree has its own sets of functions and terminals that were carefully chosen according to the desired functionality that we attempt to emulate within the AVC. All VOs were generated through a random procedure with a maximum depth of 5 levels, where half of the trees were balance trees and the other half were constructed as arbitrary trees adding nodes until the maximum depth is reached.

The proposed methodology for designing $AVCs$ to study the absent/present classification problem is divided in three steps. The first two steps define the training stage while the last one is devoted to the testing stage. In this way, all image databases were randomly divided into three subsets for each class; one per step. This process is detailed next.

Table 1. Functions for the visual operators (VOs).

Function	Description
$A + B,\ A - B,\ A \times B,\ A/B$	Arithmetic functions between two images A and B
$log(A),\ exp(A)$	Transcendental functions over the image A
$(A)^2$	Square function over the image A
$\sqrt{A}$	Square root function over the image A
$(A)^c$	Image complement over the image A
$Op_{r-g}(I),\ Op_{b-y}(I)$	Color opponency Red - Green and Blue - Yellow
$thr(A)$	Dynamic threshold function over the image A
$k + A,\ k - A,\ k \times A,\ A/k$	Arithmetic functions between an image A and a constant k
$round(A),\ half,\ \lfloor A \rfloor,\ \lceil A \rceil$	Round, half, floor and ceil functions over the image A
$A \oplus SE_d,\ A \oplus SE_s,\ A \oplus SE_{dm}$	Dilation operator with disk, square, and diamond structure element (SE)
$A \ominus SE_d,\ A \ominus SE_s,\ A \ominus SE_{dm}$	Erosion operator with disk, square, and diamond structure element (SE)
$Sk(A)$	Skeleton operator over the image A
$Perim(A)$	Find perimeter of objects in the image A
$A \circledast SE_d,\ A \circledast SE_s,\ A \circledast SE_{dm}$	Hit or miss transformation with disk, square, and diamond structures
$T_{hat}(A),\ B_{hat}(A)$	Performs morphological top-hat and bottom-hat filtering over the image A
$A \odot SE_s,\ A \odot SE_s$	Opening and closing morphological operators on A
$\|A\|,\ \|A + B\|,\ \|A - B\|$	Absolute value applied to A, and the addition and subtraction operators
$inf(A, B),\ sup(A, B)$	Infimum and supremum functions between the images A and B
$G_{\sigma=1}(A),\ G_{\sigma=2}(A)$	Convolution of the image A and a Gaussian filter with $\sigma = 1$ or 2
$D_x(A),\ D_y(A)$	Derivative of the image A along direction x and y

1. The first step starts by randomly generating a set of VOs to be used inside the AVC structure. Then, it proceeds to the training stage of the SVM using the images from the first subset, called training-A. As a constraint, if the SVM achieves a given threshold in classification accuracy during its training, the process continues to step 2; on the other hand, the VOs together with the SVM are discarded and the process is restarted.

2. At step 2 the system uses the set of VOs found in step 1 but it trains a new SVM with the second image subset, called training-B. Once again, if the SVM scores the given threshold in classification accuracy the process continues to step 3 and the AVC structure is considered as the solution; on the other hand, both VOs and SVM are discarded and the search continues at step 1.

3. In the last step, the best AVC structures are tested by classifying the third image subset. The testing is performed with the estimated SVM from step 2 and the VOs from step 1. The whole process is repeated until the best set of solutions are discovered.

Finally, all experimental results are provided in the following sections.

Table 2. Total number of random runs needed to discover 100 solutions per class for all subset sizes.

Class	Size of the training set						
	10	20	30	40	50	60	70
Airplanes	2501	3219	1916	2088	1993	1971	3253
Cars	7294	11032	6652	10674	4447	4845	22037
Faces	1811	3041	1489	2148	1556	1462	1940
Leaves	1781	1960	1392	1843	1893	1355	1763
Motorcycles	10419	23131	12871	20214	9386	6662	39470

Airplanes   Cars   Faces   Leaves   Motorcycles   Background

Fig. 3. Sample images from CalTech-5 database, and the category background from CalTech-101 database.

3.2 Experimental Evaluation of the AVC for Classification of Color Images

In a first experiment, the performance of the proposed model was evaluated through a binary test using five classes from the Caltech-5 database in combination with the Google background of Caltech-101, see Fig. 3. The goal is to analyze the effect on the recognition performance by using training sets of different sizes. Thus, the AVC model was trained with randomly selected positive images used to define the training-A subset of size: 1, 10, 20, 30, 40, 50, 60, and 70; while using a constant subset of 50 negative images for all experiments. In the case of one positive training image and after 7500 randomly possible evaluations an *AVC* was never found; hence, it was discarded from further tests. Thus, the numbers of images selected for training-B were set to 50 positive images and 50 negative images. In this way, Table 2 provides the number of random runs that were necessary to discover the solutions. This experiment was repeated until 100 *AVC*s were found for each training-B subset producing a total of 700 solutions with 100% accuracy during the training stage per class. All these solutions were tested and the mean and standard deviation are reported in the following section.

3.3 Testing the Performance of the Random Search

Table 3 presents the summary of the experiment showing the average, standard deviation, maximum and minimum performance for the testing stage. All results were normalized between 0 and 1 in such a way that 1 represents 100% of classification accuracy. The best solutions were obtained for the airplanes, faces and leaves classes scoring 95%, 99% and 97% respectively; while in the case of cars and motorcycles classes the best solutions scored a classification accuracy of 77% and 75% respectively. Note that these final scores are similar regardless of the subset size that is applied during the training stage. Moreover, the solutions whose scores are highlighted in bold at Table 3 are provided with their corresponding formulae in Table 4.

Table 3. This table shows a summary of the results of the *AVC* testing which were obtained with a random search and using the color category background from CalTech-101 database.

Images on training	Airplane class				Cars class				Faces class			
	Mean	Std	Max	Min	Mean	Std	Max	Min	Mean	Std	Max	Min
10	0.64	0.08	0.87	0.50	0.57	0.06	0.76	0.46	0.66	0.15	0.98	0.48
20	0.61	0.08	0.83	0.50	0.55	0.05	**0.77**	0.45	0.67	0.14	0.99	0.45
30	0.62	0.09	0.88	0.45	0.56	0.05	0.71	0.47	0.65	0.13	0.98	0.50
40	0.61	0.09	**0.95**	0.50	0.57	0.06	0.75	0.45	0.64	0.12	0.98	0.45
50	0.61	0.08	0.88	0.49	0.55	0.05	0.74	0.46	0.64	0.14	0.98	0.50
60	0.57	0.07	0.83	0.49	0.54	0.05	0.74	0.46	0.58	0.10	**0.99**	0.46
70	0.61	0.08	0.92	0.50	0.55	0.04	0.73	0.47	0.62	0.12	0.98	0.50
	Leaves class				Motorcycle class							
	Mean	Std	Max	Min	Mean	Std	Max	Min				
10	0.68	0.14	0.97	0.48	0.58	0.05	0.75	0.46				
20	0.67	0.12	0.95	0.48	0.58	0.06	**0.75**	0.46				
30	0.64	0.12	0.95	0.50	0.56	0.05	0.70	0.44				
40	0.65	0.13	**0.97**	0.49	0.55	0.05	0.71	0.47				
50	0.59	0.09	0.93	0.48	0.54	0.04	0.74	0.47				
60	0.62	0.11	0.97	0.48	0.54	0.04	0.70	0.46				
70	0.61	0.09	0.94	0.50	0.57	0.06	0.74	0.47				

Table 4. This table shows the best solutions that were discovered after a random process.

Name	VO	VO_{MMk}	Evaluation
AVC_{A1}	$VO_O = round(D_{xy}(I_k))$ $VO_C = I_r$ $VO_S = \lfloor I_r \rfloor$	$VO_{MM1} = D_{yy}(CM_d)$ $VO_{MM2} = G_{\sigma=2}(D_{xx}(CM_d))$ $VO_{MM3} = \sqrt{D_{xy}(CM_d)}$ $VO_{MM4} = D_{xx}(CM_d)$ $VO_{MM5} = D_y(CM_d)$ $VO_{MM6} = |D_{xy}(CM) - D_x(CM_d)|$ $VO_{MM7} = G_{\sigma=2}(D_{yy}(CM_d))$ $VO_{MM8} = D_{xx}(CM_d)$ $VO_{MM9} = log(D_{xx}(CM_d))$	$Tr = 100\%$ $Tst = 95\%$
AVC_{C1}	$VO_O = D_y(I_v)$ $VO_C = \dfrac{I_b}{I_r}$ $VO_S = \lfloor I_c \rfloor$	$VO_{MM1} = D_x(CM_d)$ $VO_{MM2} = log(CM_d)$ $VO_{MM3} = D_{xx}(CM_d)$ $VO_{MM4} = D_{xy}(CM_d)$ $VO_{MM5} = D_{xy}(CM_d)$ $VO_{MM6} = D_{yy}(CM_d)$ $VO_{MM7} = G_{\sigma=1}(D_y(CM_d))$ $VO_{MM8} = D_y(CM_d)$ $VO_{MM9} = CM_d$ $VO_{MM10} = D_{xy}(CM_d)$ $VO_{MM11} = log(D_y(CM_d))$ $VO_{MM12} = G_{\sigma=2}(D_{yy}(CM_d))$	$Tr = 100\%$ $Tst = 77\%$
AVC_{F1}	$VO_O = round(D_{xx}(I_m))$ $VO_C = \sqrt{I_k}$ $VO_S = 0.45 * (I_b)$	$VO_{MM1} = (D_{xx}(CM_d))^2$	$Tr = 100\%$ $Tst = 99\%$
AVC_{L1}	$VO_O = \sqrt{D_x(I_b)}$ $VO_C = I_b * I_g$ $VO_S = \lfloor I_h \rfloor$	$VO_{MM1} = 0.5 * (D_y(CM_d))$ $VO_{MM2} = Dyy(CM_d) - D_y(CM_d)$	$Tr = 100\%$ $Tst = 97\%$
AVC_{M1}	$VO_O = G_{\sigma=1}(D_x(I_y)^2)$ $VO_C = \dfrac{I_b^c}{I_g - I_r}$ $VO_S = (I_v - 0.21) \oplus SE_{dm}$	$VO_{MM1} = \dfrac{D_{xx}(CM_d)}{D_{xx}(CM_d)} - log(D_x(CM_d))$	$Tr = 100\%$ $Tst = 75\%$

3.4   Comparison Between the *AVC* and *HMAX* Models

The *HMAX* model was used in a second series of tests based on the experimental design proposed in [12], in order to compare our results with the state-of-the-art. Thus, once again, the solutions from the first experiment were tested, in the object present/absent experiment, with a new random set of images considering 50 positive images for the object classes selected earlier, as well as 50 negative images selected from the Caltech-5 background database. The aim is to investigate the effect on the 700 final solutions per class using the recognition performance based on the accuracy. Note that for this test the background images are in gray scale; hence, the color components of the image were initialized

Table 5. This table summarizes the classification results achieved on testing using the background Caltech-5 database as the negative class. Note that the performance is better than the previous experiment, since the background is built by gray tone images.

Images on training	Airplane class				Cars class				Faces class			
	Mean	Std	Max	Min	Mean	Std	Max	Min	Mean	Std	Max	Min
10	0.64	0.10	0.95	0.50	0.59	0.07	0.78	0.47	0.66	0.15	0.97	0.43
20	0.63	0.09	0.90	0.49	0.61	0.12	0.97	0.45	0.67	0.14	0.98	0.47
30	0.63	0.10	0.86	0.48	0.60	0.09	0.97	0.50	0.66	0.13	0.99	0.47
40	0.62	0.09	**0.97**	0.50	0.59	0.09	0.92	0.45	0.64	0.13	0.97	0.46
50	0.62	0.10	0.96	0.49	0.61	0.11	0.96	0.47	0.65	0.14	**1.00**	0.48
60	0.59	0.10	0.95	0.50	0.57	0.09	0.92	0.46	0.60	0.13	0.97	0.42
70	0.64	0.11	0.96	0.50	0.60	0.10	**0.98**	0.46	0.63	0.12	0.99	0.47

	Leaves class				Motorcycle class							
	Mean	Std	Max	Min	Mean	Std	Max	Min				
10	0.70	0.14	**0.98**	0.50	0.62	0.12	0.95	0.43				
20	0.67	0.13	0.97	0.49	0.61	0.12	0.98	0.48				
30	0.65	0.12	0.91	0.47	0.58	0.08	0.97	0.46				
40	0.66	0.13	0.95	0.46	0.59	0.10	0.96	0.47				
50	0.59	0.11	0.97	0.45	0.59	0.11	0.96	0.45				
60	0.63	0.13	0.96	0.46	0.55	0.07	0.90	0.45				
70	0.61	0.11	0.92	0.47	0.61	0.12	**1.00**	0.41				

with the same value. The results summary is shown in Table 5. The comparison between our model and the *HMAX* model is provided in Table 6. We report the error rate at equilibrium point as the measure performance in these experiments. For the sake of showing that the differences between the performances of the proposed *AVC* and the *HMAX-SVM* models are statistically significant, we used two non-parametric statistical tests: the Wilcoxon rank sum [37] and a two-sample Kolmogorov-Smirnov test [38]. These last experiments were tested on the 30 best random solutions out of the 700 found for each class.

Table 6. This table shows a comparison of the performance achieved among the *HMAX* model, considering the boost and *SVM* classifiers, and the *AVC* model. Note that in the case of the *HMAX* model a learning process was applied in order to identify the best patches. However, for the *AVC* model only a random sampling was used to discover the best solution.

Datasets	Performance of *HMAX*		Artificial V. C	Statistical Significance	
	boost	*SVM*		K-S test	Wilcoxon test
Airplanes	96.7	94.9	98.6	4.9×10^{-15}	1.1×10^{-7}
Cars	99.7	99.8	98.1	2.1×10^{-13}	3.9×10^{-8}
Faces	98.2	98.1	100	1.8×10^{-15}	1.3×10^{-10}
Leaves	97.0	95.9	96.2	7.9×10^{-17}	6.3×10^{-12}
Motorcycles	98.0	97.4	100	5.4×10^{-13}	9.6×10^{-6}

Using the whole evolutionary process, we present in Table 7 the solutions that were discovered by the brain programming. The selection process was implemented following the *roulette-wheel* strategy, which consists in assigning to each individual a probability of selection proportional to its fitness value. Termination criteria was defined using a a maximum number of generations; 30 in this case and 30 solutions per generation. Thus, the aim is that each evolutionary process reaches an optimal AVC program at each single run. Note that the performance of each solution in testing is 100% in classification accuracy.

Table 7. This table shows some solutions that were discovered after of evolutionary process of the brain programming.

Solution	EVO	EVO_{MMk}	Accuracy
Airplanes	$EVO_O = D_{xy}(I_r)$ $EVO_C = Op_{b-y}(I)$ $EVO_S = \frac{I_r \ominus SE_{dm}}{K}$	$EVO_{MM_1} = 0.5 * (D_x(MC))$	$Tr. = 100\%$ $Val. = 100\%$ $Tst. = 100\%$
Cars	$EVO_O = \sqrt{0.33 * D_{yy}(I_y)}$ $EVO_C = ((Op_{r-g}(I))^c)^2$ $EVO_S = Sk(I_v) - 0.33 * I_m$	$EVO_{MM_1} = |0.5 * (D_x(MC))|$	$Tr. = 100\%$ $Val. = 100\%$ $Tst. = 100\%$
Faces	$EVO_O = G_{\sigma=2}(0.5 * D_{yy}(I_r))$ $EVO_C = \frac{Op_{r-g}(I)}{I_k * \sqrt{I_m}}$ $EVO_S = T_{hat}(I_h \ominus SE_s)$	$EVO_{MM_1} = log(D_{xx}(MC))$	$Tr. = 100\%$ $Val. = 100\%$ $Tst. = 100\%$
Leaves	$EVO_O = D_x(log(I_h - I_s))$ $EVO_C = (I_k)^2$ $EVO_S = 0.13 * ((I_h \oplus SE_s) \oplus SE_s)$	$EVO_{MM_1} = 0.5 * |\sqrt{MC} - (D_{yy}(MC) - D_x(MC))|$ $EVO_{MM_2} = \frac{|D_y(MC) - D_y(MC)|}{D_y(MC) - MC}$	$Tr. = 100\%$ $Val. = 100\%$ $Tst. = 100\%$
Motorcycles	$EVO_O = sup(\sqrt{D_x(I_r)}, thr(D_x(I_r)))$ $EVO_C = \sqrt{\sqrt{(I_r)^2}}$ $EVO_S = I_g - I_m$	$EVO_{MM_1} = log(|D_{xy}(MC) + D_x(MC)|)$ $EVO_{MM_2} = 0.5 * (G_{\sigma=1}(D_{xy}(MC)))$	$Tr. = 99.5\%$ $Val. = 99.66\%$ $Tst. = 100\%$

4   Conclusions and Future Work

This paper presented a computational model of the visual cortex following the hierarchical structure of previous visual attention and object recognition proposals. As a result, the proposed methodology replicates the initial stages of the artificial dorsal stream using four dimensions: color, shape, orientation and intensity, in combination with the final stages of an artificial ventral stream, which are used to approach the task of object categorization. The overall approach considers that the process of visual information extraction and description can be enforced by function composition through a set of mathematical operations that are used in the aforementioned stages. According to the results all functions embedded within the hierarchical structure of the AVC can be easily discovered through random search while achieving excellent results on the Caltech database. In this sense, we presented examples that illustrate the behavior of the discovered *AVC*s for the problems of faces and motorcycles of the Caltech categorization problem. Finally, we provide a comparison with the *HMAX* model that is considered as the reference for these kind of approaches and found that the *AVC* model was superior according to the results obtained for the Caltech testbed.

As a conclusion, we can say that the *AVC* methodology offers a new perspective to study the development of artificial brains since the structural complexity can be improved because the approach is susceptible of being framed as an optimization problem. This article provides some results of the whole evolutionary cycle for the studied database. Indeed, the results score perfect accuracy except for one case. In this way, we can synthesize new structures according to the task at hand. In particular, as future research we would like to test the approach with more complex datasets, such as the GRAZ and the VOC challenge datasets. Additionally, since the methodology is computationally costly, we propose to undergo a change towards a parallel computing implementation of the *AVC* model through the application of GPGPU technology [39]. Finally, we would like to explore the application of this new paradigm to problems of humanoid robotics.

Acknowledgments. This research was founded by CONACyT through the Project 155045 - "Programación cerebral aplicada al estudio del pensamiento y la visión". This work is also supported by ITE-TecNM through the project 5748.16-P, "Optimización de controladores aplicados a la navegación de un robot móvil, utilizando cómputo evolutivo".

References

1. Olague, G.: Evolutionary Computer Vision: The First Footprints. Springer, Heidelberg (2016)
2. Logothetis, N.K., Sheinberg, D.L.: Visual object recognition. Ann. Rev. Neurosci. **19**, 577–621 (1996)
3. DiCarlo, J.J., Zoccolan, D., Rust, N.C.: How does the brain solve visual object recognition? Neuron **73**(3), 415–434 (2012)
4. Riesenhuber, M., Poggio, T.: Models of object recognition. Nat. Neurosci. **3**, 1199–1204 (2000)
5. Rees, G., Frackowiak, R., Frith, C.: Two modulatory effects of attention that mediate object categorization in human cortex. Science. **275**(5301), 835–8 (1997)
6. Desimone, R., Duncan, J.: Neural mechanisms of selective visual attention. Ann. Rev. Neurosci. **18**, 193–222 (1995)
7. Kastner, S., Ungerleider, L.G.: Mechanisms of visual attention in the human cortex. Ann. Rev. Neurosci. **23**, 315–341 (2000)
8. Milner, A.D., Goodale, M.A.: The Visual Brain in Action, 2nd edn. Oxford University Press, Oxford (2006)
9. Creem, S.H., Proffitt, D.R.: Defining the cortical visual systems: "what", "where", and "how". Acta Psychol. **107**(1–3), 43–68 (2001)
10. Farivar, R.: Dorsal-ventral integration in object recognition. Brain Res. Rev. **61**(2), 144–153 (2009)

11. Fukushima, K.: Neocognitron: a self-organizing neural network model for a mechanism of pattern recognition unaffected by shift in position. Biol. Cybern. **36**(4), 193–202 (1980)
12. Serre, T., Kouh, C., Cadieu, M., Knoblich, G., Kreiman, U., Poggio, T.: Theory of object recognition: computations and circuits in the feedforward path of the ventral stream in primate visual cortex. Technical report, Massachusetts Institute of Technology Computer Science and Artificial Intelligence Laboratory (2005)
13. Mutch, J., Lowe, D.G.: Object class recognition and localization using sparse features with limited receptive fields. Int. J. Comput. Vis. **80**(1), 45–57 (2008)
14. Mel, B.W.: Seemore: combining color, shape, and texture histogramming in a neurally inspired approach to visual object recognition. Neural Comput. **9**(4), 777–804 (1997)
15. Itti, L., Koch, C.: Computational modeling of visual attention. Nat. Rev. Neurosci. **2**(3), 194–203 (2001)
16. Clemente, E., Olague, G., Dozal, L., Mancilla, M.: Object recognition with an optimized ventral stream model using genetic programming. In: Chio, C., et al. (eds.) EvoApplications 2012. LNCS, vol. 7248, pp. 315–325. Springer, Heidelberg (2012). doi:10.1007/978-3-642-29178-4_32
17. Clemente, E., Olague, G., Dozal, L.: Purposive evolution for object recognition using an artificial visual cortex. In: Schuetze, O., Coello, C.A.C., Tantar, A.-A., Tantar, E., Bouvry, P., Del Moral, P., Legrand, P. (eds.) EVOLVE - A Bridge between Probability, Set Oriented Numerics, and Evolutionary Computation II, pp. 355–370. Springer, Heidelberg (2013)
18. Olague, G., Clemente, E., Dozal, L., Hernádez, D.E.: Evolving an artificial visual cortex for object recognition with brain programming. In: Schuetze, O., Coello, C.A.C., Tantar, A.-A., Tantar, E., Bouvry, P., Del Moral, P., Legrand, P., et al. (eds.) EVOLVE - A Bridge between Probability, Set Oriented Numerics, and Evolutionary Computation III. Springer, Heidelberg (2014)
19. Dozal, L., Olague, G., Clemente, E., Hernandez, D.E.: Brain programming for the evolution of an articial dorsal stream. Cognit. Comput. **6**(3), 528–557 (2014)
20. Hernandez, D.E., Clemente, E., Olague, G., Briseño, J.L.: Evolutionary multiobjective visual cortex for object classification in natural images. J. Comput. Sci. **17**(1), 216–233 (2016)
21. Clemente, E., Chavez, F., Fernandez de Vega, F., Olague, G.: Self-adjusting focus of attention in combination with a genetic fuzzy system for improving a laser environment control device system. Appl. Soft Comput. **32**, 250–265 (2015)
22. Fukushima, K.: Neural network model for selective attention in visual pattern recognition and associative recall. Appl. Opt. **26**(23), 4985–4992 (1987)
23. Olshausen, B.A., Anderson, C.H., Van Essen, D.C.: A neurobiological model of visual attention and invariant pattern recognition based on dynamic routing of information. J. Neurosci. **13**(11), 4700–4719 (1993)
24. Walther, D., Itti, L., Riesenhuber, M., Poggio, T., Koch, C.: Attentional selection for object recognition — a gentle way. In: Bülthoff, H.H., Wallraven, C., Lee, S.-W., Poggio, T.A. (eds.) BMCV 2002. LNCS, vol. 2525, pp. 472–479. Springer, Heidelberg (2002). doi:10.1007/3-540-36181-2_47
25. Riesenhuber, M., Poggio, T.: Hierarchical models of object recognition in cortex. Nat. Neurosci. **2**(11), 1019–1025 (1999)
26. Walther, D., Koch, C.: Attention in hierarchical models of object recognition. Progr. Brain Res. **165**, 57–78 (2007)

27. Heinke, D., Humphteys, G.W.: Attention, spatial representation, and visual neglect: simulating emergent attention and spatial memory in the selective attention for identification model (SAIM). Psychol. Rev. **110**(1), 29–87 (2003)
28. Treisman, A.M., Gelade, G.: A feature-integration theory of attention. Cogn. Psychol. **12**(1), 97–136 (1980)
29. Walther, D., Koch, C.: Modeling attention to salient proto-objects. Neural Netw. **19**(9), 1395–407 (2006)
30. Pinto, N., Cox, D.D., DiCarlo, J.J.: Why is real-world visual object recognition hard? PLoS Comput. Biol. **4**(1), 151–156 (2008)
31. Ponce, J., et al.: Dataset issues in object recognition. In: Ponce, J., Hebert, M., Schmid, C., Zisserman, A. (eds.) Toward Category-Level Object Recognition. LNCS, vol. 4170, pp. 29–48. Springer, Heidelberg (2006). doi:10.1007/11957959_2
32. Wang, Z., Feng, J.: Multi-class learning from class proportions. Neurocomputing **119**, 273–280 (2013)
33. Ji, Z., Wang, J., Su, Y., Song, Z., Xing, S.: Balance between object and background: object-enhanced features for scene image classification. Neurocomputing **120**, 15–23 (2013)
34. Chen, B., Polatkan, G., Sapiro, G., Blei, D., Dunson, D., Carin, L.: Deep learning with hierarchical convolutional factor analysis. IEEE Trans. Pattern Anal. Mach. Intell. **8**(35), 1887–1901 (2013)
35. Xu, B., Hu, R., Guo, P.: Combining affinity propagation with supervised dictionary learning for image classification. Neural Comput. Appl. **22**(7–8), 1301–1308 (2013)
36. Chandra, S., Kumar, S., Jawahar, C.V.: Learning hierarchical bag of words using naive bayes clustering. In: Lee, K.M., Matsushita, Y., Rehg, J.M., Hu, Z. (eds.) ACCV 2012. LNCS, vol. 7724, pp. 382–395. Springer, Heidelberg (2013). doi:10.1007/978-3-642-37331-2_29
37. Wilcoxon, F.: Individual comparison by ranking methods. Biometr. Bull. **1**(6), 80–83 (1945)
38. Massey, F.J.: The Kolmogorov-Smirnov test for goodness of fit. J. Am. Stat. Assoc. **46**(253), 68–78 (1951)
39. Hernandez, D.E., Olague, G., Hernandez, B., Clemente, E.: CUDA-based parallelization of a bio-inspired model for fast object classification. Neural Comput. Appl. (2017). doi:10.1007/s00521-017-2873-3

Using Particle Swarm Optimisation and the Silhouette Metric to Estimate the Number of Clusters, Select Features, and Perform Clustering

Andrew Lensen[✉], Bing Xue, and Mengjie Zhang

School of Engineering and Computer Science, Victoria University of Wellington,
PO Box 600, Wellington 6140, New Zealand
{Andrew.Lensen,Bing.Xue,Mengjie.Zhang}@ecs.vuw.ac.nz

Abstract. One of the most difficult problems in clustering, the task of grouping similar instances in a dataset, is automatically determining the number of clusters that should be created. When a dataset has a large number of attributes (features), this task becomes even more difficult due to the relationship between the number of features and the number of clusters produced. One method of addressing this is feature selection, the process of selecting a subset of features to be used. Evolutionary computation techniques have been used very effectively for solving clustering problems, but have seen little use for simultaneously performing the three tasks of clustering, feature selection, and determining the number of clusters. Furthermore, only a small number of existing methods exist, but they have a number of limitations that affect their performance and scalability. In this work, we introduce a number of novel techniques for improving the performance of these three tasks using particle swarm optimisation and statistical techniques. We conduct a series of experiments across a range of datasets with clustering problems of varying difficulty. The results show our proposed methods achieve significantly better clustering performance than existing methods, while only using a small number of features and automatically determining the number of clusters more accurately.

Keywords: Particle swarm optimisation · Clustering · Feature selection · Automatic clustering · Silhouette

1 Introduction

One of the fundamental challenges in clustering (the task of grouping similar items/instances of a dataset together) is determining the number of clusters (K) to be produced. Many traditional methods such as k-means require K to be pre-defined by the user. Requiring a pre-defined K makes an algorithm less useful, as domain knowledge of a dataset is required to choose an appropriate K. Often, when clustering is used as an exploratory method in the knowledge

© Springer International Publishing AG 2017
G. Squillero and K. Sim (Eds.): EvoApplications 2017, Part I, LNCS 10199, pp. 538–554, 2017.
DOI: 10.1007/978-3-319-55849-3_35

discovery process, there may be no domain experts available, or there may be no specific goal in mind (so no sensible K can be determined). Hence, there is a need for clustering algorithms that are able to automatically find a suitable K.

Datasets have become increasingly larger in terms of the number of features (m) they contain. Many existing methods such as k-means perform poorly on large feature sets due to the curse of dimensionality. One common technique to reduce dimensionality is feature selection, the process of selecting a subset of features to be used in the data mining process. Performing feature selection removes irrelevant, redundant, and misleading features [1] while reducing the search space size.

Evolutionary Computation (EC) methods are stochastic population-based techniques inspired by natural evolution which produce solutions to difficult problems. EC has been extensively applied to clustering [2] and feature selection [1], but has been rarely used for performing clustering and feature selection simultaneously [3–5]. All of the work in this area uses a single-stage approach where K is either pre-defined [4], or is found during the EC search process [3,5]. When K is found automatically by the EC method, the search algorithm must optimise three criteria: the number of clusters, the clustering performance, and the number of features used. Such an approach has two significant issues.

The first issue is that a very large search space must be searched on large datasets with many features and instances. If we consider that K is allowed to vary between 2 (a single cluster is not allowed) and K_{max} (often defined as $\sqrt{n}$ for n instances [6]), each value of K is likely to have different optimal feature subsets and different clustering solutions. Even with the powerful population-based search techniques in EC, exploring such a search space thoroughly is difficult.

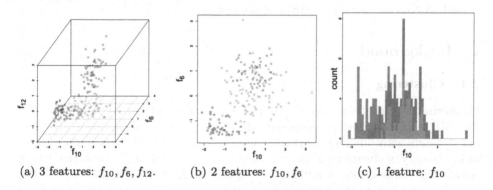

(a) 3 features: f_{10}, f_6, f_{12}.　　(b) 2 features: f_{10}, f_6　　(c) 1 feature: f_{10}

Fig. 1. Wine dataset projected across varying numbers of features.

There is also an inherent dependency between the number of features selected (m') and K. A larger m' will encourage a larger K and vice versa; the more information (i.e. features) available, the more easily the data can be divided into a larger number of smaller clusters instead of a few big clusters [7]. For example, consider the three plots shown in Fig. 1, which show the Wine dataset (containing three classes, 13 features, and 178 instances) projected using different numbers of features. The three colours represent the three classes of the Wine dataset. When three features are used in Fig. 1a, it is easy to distinguish all three classes as distinct clusters. When one feature is removed in Fig. 1b, the blue class still appears as a homogeneous cluster, however, the red and green classes are much closer and have enough overlap so that they may be considered as a single cluster. When only a single feature is considered in Fig. 1c, all three classes overlap considerably and it is difficult to choose two thresholds that would split the three classes into three clusters well. As m' is minimised to encourage selecting few features, the evolutionary search will be biased towards picking smaller K, reducing performance on datasets which have large K.

1.1 Goals

In this work, we propose a multi-stage algorithm which extends an existing single-stage approach [5] in order to automatically find K more accurately, improve clustering performance, and decrease the number of selected features. We will:

- Propose a new two-stage approach where an estimate of K (called K_{est}) is computed in the first stage, and then PSO is used to perform clustering, feature selection, and refine K_{est} in the second stage.
- Propose a third stage for fine-tuning the clusters produced in the second stage using a pseudo-local PSO search technique.
- Enhance the existing fitness function [5] to improve feature selection performance and to penalise solutions with K values far away from K_{est}.
- Evaluate our new approach compared to the existing single-stage approach, and to k-means, across a variety of datasets.

2 Background

2.1 Clustering

Clustering is perhaps the most researched of all unsupervised learning tasks [8] with many approaches proposed which are effective on a range of different datasets with different properties and clustering objectives. The most common category of clustering algorithms is partitional clustering algorithms, which divide the dataset into a number of clusters such that each instance lies in exactly **one** cluster. Clusters which are tightly packed and are far away from other clusters are generally regarded to be of high-quality; although other metrics such as connectedness and density have also been used to indicate cluster quality. k-means is the most well-known of the partitional clustering algorithms; it produces compact clusters by repetitively assigning instances to the closest cluster prototype and then re-computing cluster centres to minimise the intra-cluster variance. Other categories of clustering algorithms include density (e.g. DBSCAN), graph-based, and hierarchical (e.g. complete-linkage) algorithms [8].

2.2 Estimating K

A wide range of statistical techniques for estimating the number of clusters (K_{est}) in a given dataset have been proposed [9]. While studies have compared the efficacy of many techniques [9], there is no consensus on the best technique for the general case. One of the most popular methods is the silhouette criterion, which measures how well a given instance is matched to its cluster. It is defined as follows:

$$Silhouette(i) = \frac{b(i) - a(i)}{max\{a(i), b(i)\}} \tag{1}$$

where $a(i)$ is the average distance between instance i and all other instances in its cluster; $b(i)$ is the *minimum* average distance between instance i and the instances in each other cluster. A silhouette value of 1 indicates an instance is perfectly clustered; a value of -1 indicates it should be in a neighbouring cluster; a value of 0 indicates it is on the border of two clusters. The average silhouette computed across all instances in a partition gives a measure of how good the partition is, and implicitly balances both the intra- and inter-cluster metrics.

The silhouette criterion can be used to give K_{est} by performing clustering for each potential K and then choosing the K for which the average silhouette is highest. This can be computationally expensive due to the need to compute the pair-wise distance between all instances in a dataset. However, this computation only needs to be performed once at the start of the algorithm.

2.3 Feature Selection

EC techniques have been used widely for feature selection [1], with PSO and Genetic Algorithms (GAs) being used for filter, wrapper, and hybrid approaches. Genetic Programming (GP) has also been used for performing embedded feature selection [10]. Wrapper methods are ones which uses a learning algorithm to evaluate the quality of a feature subset and choose the one that gives the highest performance on the learning algorithm. Filter methods take a different approach where the quality of a feature subset is measured more explicitly using a metric such as information gain or entropy [11]. Filter methods tend to give inferior results to wrapper methods, but are usually quicker in terms of computational time required [12]. Hybrid approaches combine both filter and wrapper methods to give better performance than filter methods while being quicker to run than wrapper methods. Embedded approaches perform feature selection as part of the learning algorithm being used, and so can be designed efficiently while being tailored to the algorithm being used; however, they tend to be more problem-specific. While EC has been used extensively for feature selection in classification tasks, little work has used it for clustering, despite clustering generally being regarded as a more difficult task with a larger search space.

2.4 Related Work

NMA_CFS [3] was the first EC method which could simultaneously perform clustering and feature selection while automatically determining K. The authors proposed a single-stage approach using a GA which had a variable length representation based on the number of clusters in a given solution. While this method was shown to give good results, it was only tested on datasets with relatively low K (up to $K = 7$) and small number of features (up to $m = 30$). The variable-length centroid representation is unlikely to scale well as K becomes larger due to the reasons discussed in [5] which are not repeated here due to space constraints.

Lensen et al. [5] compared a number of medoid- and centroid-based representations for simultaneous clustering and feature selection. It was shown that a medoid representation generally had the best performance over a range of datasets when K was pre-fixed, and also allowed for K to be automatically found by the EC algorithm while maintaining a fixed-length representation (the Dynamic Medoid method, i.e. D-PSO). While the D-PSO method showed promise, it was concluded that it struggled to accurately find K on difficult synthetic datasets which contained a large number of clusters.

Another PSO-based method [4] has also been proposed for simultaneously performing clustering and feature selection when K is pre-fixed. Although the authors used a more advanced fitness function than that of NMA_CFS to improve clustering performance, their reliance on K being known means their approach is not generally comparable to methods which automatically determine K as the latter is a much more difficult problem.

3   The Proposed Method

Our proposed method consists of multiple stages. In the first stage, an estimate of K, called K_{est}, is determined using a statistical measure. The second stage then performs simultaneous clustering and feature selection, while using K_{est} as a guide for finding K. K is still dynamic and so can be optimised by the evolutionary search, but individuals which have a K that varies too far from K_{est} will have their fitness punished correspondingly. As methods used to generate K_{est} in the first stage may not give perfect estimates, allowing minor variations to K_{est} allows the EC method to fine-tune the K value. The (optional) third stage then performs a pseudo-local search using a centroid representation to fine-tune the solution produced by the second stage.

The following subsections discuss the design of each of the stages in detail.

3.1   First Stage

The Silhouette method described in Sect. 2.2 was used in this study to produce K_{est} in the first stage as it was empirically found to be the most accurate method tested. k-means was used to cluster the data in the first stage for each potential k in the range $[2, \sqrt{n}]$, as suggested in [6], and then the average silhouette for each K was computed. The K with the highest average silhouette is chosen as K_{est}. The silhouette method is non-deterministic and produces a large variation in K_{est} values across different runs. To address this we run the algorithm 30 times and take the median K_{est} to reduce variation, producing more consistent K_{est} values.

3.2   Second Stage

PSO Representation: The output of the first stage is a single K_{est} value. The second stage uses this value as a heuristic to guide the search by PSO for the number of clusters. We use the medoid (an instance that acts as a cluster proto-type) representation introduced in [5], which allows for simultaneous clustering, feature selection and selection of K automatically within a single particle, as shown in Fig. 2. Using such a medoid representation has been shown to give good clustering and feature selection performance, while allowing a fixed-length representation even when K is allowed to vary [5].

Fig. 2. Medoid representation for simultaneous clustering and feature selection.

The first m dimensions represent whether each of the m features in the dataset is selected. The last n dimensions represent whether each of the n instances is chosen as a medoid. A feature is considered to be selected if its corresponding position value is non-negative. An instance is considered to be a medoid if its position value is greater than Θ, a threshold that is directly encoded (and automatically evolved) in the particle representation. All positions take floating-point values.

Fitness Function: Another novel component of this work is the fitness function to use to evaluate the goodness of solutions produced during the PSO search process. As previously discussed, there are three key criteria required to measure the quality of a given PSO solution: the clustering performance, the number of features used, and how far K deviates from the heuristic K_{est}. As such, we propose that a suitable fitness function should take the following form:

$$\text{Overall Fitness} = \text{Cluster Performance} \times \text{Feature Weighting} \times K \text{ Weighting} \quad (2)$$

We discuss the design of each of the three components below:

(1) Measuring cluster performance: The clustering performance can be measured using many metrics, most of which attempt to minimise the intra-cluster variation while maximising the inter-cluster separation. We use the same metric as in [5], which was shown to give good clustering results. This metric is defined below:

$$\text{Cluster Performance} = \frac{Between_{sum}}{Within_{sum}} \quad (3)$$

$$Within_{sum} = \frac{1}{n} \sum_{i=1}^{K} \sum_{I_a \in C_i} d(I_a, Z_i)^2 \quad (4)$$

$$Between_{sum} = \sum_{i=1}^{K} \frac{|C_i|}{n} d(Z_i, Z^*)^2 \tag{5}$$

where C_i and Z_i represent the ith cluster and the mean of the ith cluster respectively. The dataset mean (Z^*) is the mean across all instances in the dataset. $d(I_a, I_b)$ is the Euclidean distance between two instances I_a and I_b:

$$d(I_a, I_b) = \sqrt{(I_{a1} - I_{b1})^2 + (I_{a2} - I_{b2})^2 + ... + (I_{am} - I_{bm})^2} \tag{6}$$

where a_i and b_i give the ith feature value of instances a and b. The distance function considers **all features**, even those that have not been selected by the algorithm. This is done to prevent feature selection introducing a bias towards a low number of clusters (as discussed previously).

(2) Measuring feature selection performance: The most common metric for measuring the goodness of a feature subset is to apply a weighting based on the number of features selected. This is usually expressed as a simple fraction in the form $\frac{m-m'}{m}$ for m total features and m' selected features. Such a weighting applies a linear penalty to the fitness of a given particle with respect to the percentage of features selected. An issue found with this approach is that the search process will tend to over-emphasise minimising m' at the cost of cluster performance—it is usually "easier" to improve fitness by reducing m' than by improving cluster performance. Furthermore, the goal of feature selection is generally to reduce the number of features used to an acceptable level; the user may not differentiate between 5% or 10% features being selected as both values of m' are acceptably small. Hence, a linear weighting mechanism may not be ideal; ideally we would like to apply little penalty when m' is below a threshold and then apply an increasing amount of penalty as m' increases. To achieve this we propose using an elliptical function as shown in Fig. 3a.

The equation used to determine the feature weighting is as follows:

$$\text{Feature weighting} = \frac{1}{m} \sqrt{m^2 - (m')^2} \tag{7}$$

We trial using both this method and the normal linear method for the feature weighting component of the fitness function in our experiments.

(3) Restricting the search space of K: The final decision required is how to penalise particles which have a K value varying significantly from the K_{est} heuristic. As K_{est} is not a perfect estimate, we allow small variations from it without any significant penalty. As the variations increase, we should penalise at a higher rate. The use of a Gaussian function was found to give a good balance of these two objectives. Figure 3b shows an example of a Gaussian function with $\mu = K_{est}$ and $\sigma = \frac{K_{est}}{1.5}$ where the output is scaled to give 1 (no penalty) when $K = K_{est}$. As shown, the fitness weighting is small for K values between 8 and 12 or so, but becomes large when K is 5 or 15. The standard deviation must be a function of K_{est} to ensure the function scales effectively; the denominator of 1.5 was chosen empirically. The use of different denominators (e.g. 1 or 2) will increase/decrease the rate of penalty as K varies from K_{est}. We use this

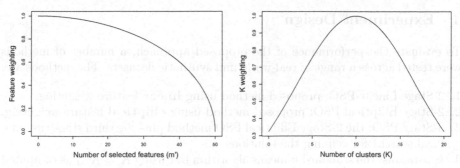

(a) Elliptical fitness weighting for a dataset (b) K fitness weighting for a dataset with
containing 50 features. K_{est} of 10 using a std. dev. of $\frac{K_{est}}{1.5}$.

Fig. 3. Fitness weightings for balancing the number of features and clusters.

Gaussian function as the third component of the fitness function in the second stage.

3.3 Third Stage (pseudo-local search)

One key limitation of a medoid-based representation is that cluster prototypes are restricted to the instances in the dataset. It is possible that better clusters may be formed using cluster prototypes that lie elsewhere in the feature space (e.g. halfway between two instances). To address this limitation, while still maintaining the benefits of a medoid approach, we propose the use of a third-stage where the medoid representation is converted to a centroid representation and then the centroids are fine-tuned using another PSO search process. We call this procedure a "pseudo-local search", as particles are initialised to the best solution found in the second stage, but are allowed to explore the search space freely.

Fig. 4. Centroid representation used in the third stage.

Figure 4 shows the representation used in the third stage. Each of the K medoids in the best solution from the second stage are used to initialise the position of the particles in the third stage—each medoid is converted to a centroid with length equal to the number of selected features (m') where the centroid contains the feature values for each of the selected features. Each particle's velocity is randomly initialised. Hence, particles will initially spread out in different directions from the second stage's *gbest* before beginning to converge again. It is hoped this will allow fine-tuning of the cluster centres, while focusing the majority of the search in an area which is known to give good performance.

4 Experiment Design

To evaluate the performance of the proposed approach, a number of methods were tested across a range of real-world and synthetic datasets. The methods are:

1. 2-Stage Linear PSO: proposed method using **linear** feature weighting.
2. 2-Stage Elliptical PSO: proposed method using **elliptical** feature weighting.
3. 3-Stage PSO: the 2-Stage Elliptical PSO method plus the third stage (pseudo-local search) for refining the solutions.
4. k_{est}-means: the standard k-means algorithm but using $K = K_{est}$ as computed by the first stage of the proposed approach. This algorithm is used to evaluate how well the proposed approach is able to refine K based on the heuristic and how well it can perform feature selection.
5. k-means: the standard k-means algorithm, initialised with centroids drawing from instances in the dataset. Note that K is **known**, and so this algorithm is being run on a much easier task.
6. D-PSO Scaled: The single-stage medoid approach proposed previously [5].

All methods are non-deterministic and so were run 30 times on each dataset for 500 iterations to ensure search convergence. The PSO methods had a swarm size of 100 and used standard PSO parameters [13]: $w = 0.729844$, $C_1 = C_2 = 1.49618$, and velocity clamped between -6 and 6. A fully connected PSO topology was used; *gbest* after 500 iterations gives the best solution. Feature values were scaled linearly to fall between 0 and 1 based on their minimum and maximum values.

4.1 Evaluation Metrics

We evaluate our proposed methods using two internal metrics (which measure clustering quality based on properties of the clusters produced), and two external metrics (which compare the clusters produced to the known class labels). The internal metrics are the scatter metric, which considers both the within-cluster scatter (S_w, i.e. compactness) and between-cluster variation (S_b, i.e. separability), and the $\sum$ *Intra metric*, which measures the total distance from all instances to their cluster means (i.e. net compactness). The external metrics are class purity, which measures the homogeneity of each cluster using its instance's class labels, and the F-measure, which measures how well pairs of instances agree on their class labels and cluster memberships. Each of these metrics is defined below.

1. Scatter trace criterion:

$$Scatter = trace(S_W^{-1} S_B) \tag{8}$$

$$S_w = \frac{1}{n} \sum_{i=1}^{K} \sum_{I_a \in C_i} (I_a - Z_i)(I_a - Z_i)^T \tag{9} \quad S_b = \sum_{i=1}^{K} \frac{|C_i|}{n}(Z_i - Z^*)(Z_i - Z^*)^T \tag{10}$$

where C_i represents the ith cluster and Z_i and $|C_i|$ are the mean of the ith cluster and the number of instances in the ith cluster respectively. I_a is an instance within cluster C_i. The dataset mean is given by Z^*.

2. Sum intra-cluster distance:

$$\sum Intra = \sum_{i=1}^{K} \sum_{I_a \in C_i} d(I_a, Z_i) \tag{11}$$

3. Class purity: computed according to the following steps:
   (a) For each cluster, find the majority class label of the instances in the cluster.
   (b) Count the number of correctly classified instances, where an instance is correctly classified if it belongs to the majority class.
   (c) Class purity is the fraction of correctly classified instances in the partition.
4. F-measure: We adapt the F-measure used in classification tasks. We consider each pair of instances in turn (it is not possible to directly decide if an instance is in the "right" cluster) and choose which of the following cases apply:
   (a) Same class label, belong to the same cluster: true positive (TP).
   (b) Same class label, belong to the **different** clusters: alse negative (FN).
   (c) **Different** class labels, belong to **different** clusters: true negative (TN).
   (d) **Different** class labels, belong to the same cluster: false positive (FP).
   The F-measure is then calculated in the normal way using the total number of TPs, FPs, and FNs, as follows:

$$\text{F-measure} = 2 \times \frac{precision \times recall}{precision + recall} \tag{12}$$

$$precision = \frac{TPs}{TPs + FPs} \tag{13} \qquad recall = \frac{TPs}{TPs + FNs} \tag{14}$$

4.2   Datasets

To comprehensively evaluate our proposed methods, we selected a variety of real-world and synthetic datasets which are shown in Table 1. The real-world datasets are sourced from the UCI machine learning repository [14], which contains several datasets often used for clustering [3,5]. These datasets are classification datasets (i.e. class labels are provided), but as is common in the clustering literature, we exclude the class labels from the training process and only use them to evaluate the final cluster against the known classes. The synthetic datasets have been specifically designed for evaluating clustering algorithms, with 10, 20, or 40 clusters and between 1014 and 2893 instances in each dataset. The synthetic datasets with large K (e.g. $K = 40$) and many features (e.g. $m = 100$) are very challenging for traditional methods such as k-means due to the large search space; it is hoped that our proposed methods will show clear improvements on these datasets.

Table 1. Datasets used in the experiments.

Real-World UCI datasets from [14].				Synthetic datasets from [15].			
Name	No. of Features	No. of Instances	No. of Classes	Name	No. of Features	No. of Instances	No. of Classes
Iris	4	150	3	10d10c	10	2730	10
Wine	13	178	3	10d20c	10	1014	20
Movement	90	360	15	10d40c	10	1938	40
Libras				50d10c	50	2699	10
Breast	9	683	2	50d20c	50	1255	20
Cancer				50d40c	50	2335	40
Image	18	683	7	100d10c	100	2893	10
Segmentation				100d20c	100	1339	20
Dermatology	34	359	6	100d40c	100	2212	40

5 Results and Discussion

The results of the experiments are shown in Tables 2 and 3 for the real-world and synthetic datasets respectively. Each table shows the **mean** number of features selected and clusters produced by each method (note that these are constant for k-means) as well as the method's average performance according to a number of evaluation metrics. The $\sum$ *Intra* metric is the only one which should be minimised—it is labelled with a $*$ to indicate this. For each of the proposed methods, each result is labelled with a "+" or a "−" if it is significantly better or worse than the k-means baseline according to a Student's t-test performed with a 95% confidence interval. A lack of a "+" or "−" indicates no significant difference was found. A label of ↑ or ↓ indicates a result is significantly better or worse than the existing D-PSO Scaled method [5] according to the same test. The results are analysed on the real-world and synthetic datasets separately in the following subsections, and then some general trends are discussed.

5.1 Real-World Data

Our proposed methods are competitive with k-means on the external metrics and often have superior performance on the internal metrics for the first four real-world datasets, while using a much smaller number of features. The methods also generally outperform D-PSO on the external metrics on four of the six datasets. The proposed methods perform significantly worse than k-means and D-PSO across all metrics on the Image Segmentation dataset due to incorrectly choosing $K = 3$. As the value of K_{est} is 2 on average, PSO is only able to vary K to be 3 without fitness being overly affected. On the Dermatology dataset, the proposed methods achieve a significantly better F-measure value compared to k-means and D-PSO, despite incorrectly estimating K. This is likely due to the estimated K allowing better-formed clusters; on real-world data, class

Table 2. Real-world datasets

Dataset	Method	m'	K	Scatter	$\sum$ Intra *	Purity	FM
Iris	2-Stage Linear PSO	1	3	$26.78^{+\downarrow}$	$29.99^{\downarrow}$	$0.9436^{+\uparrow}$	$0.8962^{+\uparrow}$
	2-Stage Elliptical PSO	1	3	$27.4^{+\downarrow}$	$29.96^{\downarrow}$	$0.9493^{+\uparrow}$	$0.9055^{+\uparrow}$
	3-Stage PSO	1	3	$26.9^{+\downarrow}$	$29.99^{\downarrow}$	$0.9449^{+\uparrow}$	$0.898^{+\uparrow}$
	k_{est}-means	4	2	9.8	37.23	0.6667	0.7462
	k-means	4	3	16.37	30.58	0.8404	0.7751
	D-PSO Scaled	1	3.6	35.03	28.29	0.9191	0.8229
Wine	2-Stage Linear PSO	2.27	3.37	$12.53^{\uparrow}$	$89.28^{-\uparrow}$	0.9161^{-}	$0.8152^{-\downarrow}$
	2-Stage Elliptical PSO	3.57	3.4	$13.96^{+\uparrow}$	$88.14^{+\uparrow}$	$0.9418^{\uparrow}$	0.8523^{-}
	3-Stage PSO	3.67	3.4	$14.55^{+\uparrow}$	$87.67^{+\uparrow}$	$0.9541^{+\uparrow}$	$0.8749^{-\uparrow}$
	k_{est}-means	13	2	4.92	104.2	0.6073	0.6357
	k-means	13	3	12.68	88.75	0.9464	0.8947
	D-PSO Scaled	2.27	3	11.14	90.26	0.9167	0.8414
Move. Libras	2-Stage Linear PSO	14.5	17.77	$45.62^{+\uparrow}$	$388.1^{+\uparrow}$	$0.5017^{+\uparrow}$	$0.3423^{\uparrow}$
	2-Stage Elliptical PSO	26.7	17.9	$47.14^{+\uparrow}$	$383.9^{+\uparrow}$	$0.5005^{+\uparrow}$	$0.3501^{\uparrow}$
	3-Stage PSO	26.5	17.73	$49.01^{+\uparrow}$	$380.0^{+\uparrow}$	$0.5012^{+\uparrow}$	$0.3596^{+\uparrow}$
	k_{est}-means	90	12.27	31.28	434.6	0.4226	0.3278
	k-means	90	15	39.01	409.4	0.4705	0.347
	D-PSO Scaled	12.5	6.13	15.21	515.6	0.2859	0.2518
Breast Cancer	2-Stage Linear PSO	1.53	2	$6.062^{-\downarrow}$	$344.2^{-\downarrow}$	0.9407^{-}	$0.8994^{-\uparrow}$
	2-Stage Elliptical PSO	2.5	2	$7.547^{-\downarrow}$	335.6^{-}	$0.9571^{-\uparrow}$	$0.9251^{-\uparrow}$
	3-Stage PSO	2.43	2	$7.807^{-\downarrow}$	334.7^{-}	$0.9573^{-\uparrow}$	$0.9254^{-\uparrow}$
	k_{est}-means	9	2	8.2	332.0	0.9609	0.9313
	k-means	9	2	8.211	332.0	0.9611	0.9316
	D-PSO Scaled	1.6	2.7	10.17	331.0	0.9441	0.8744
Image Seg.	2-Stage Linear PSO	1.33	3	$19.33^{-\downarrow}$	$1245.0^{-\downarrow}$	$0.4251^{-\downarrow}$	$0.4536^{-\downarrow}$
	2-Stage Elliptical PSO	2.13	3	$19.18^{-\downarrow}$	$1242.0^{-\downarrow}$	$0.4275^{-\downarrow}$	$0.4583^{-\downarrow}$
	3-Stage PSO	1.8	3	$19.36^{-\downarrow}$	$1241.0^{-\downarrow}$	$0.4276^{-\downarrow}$	$0.4595^{-\downarrow}$
	k_{est}-means	18	2	4.063	1482.0	0.2857	0.3362
	k-means	18	7	60.86	898.3	0.6426	0.5583
	D-PSO Scaled	2.23	5.23	63.53	984.4	0.6089	0.5725
Derm.	2-Stage Linear PSO	4.53	3.97	68.03^{-}	405.5^{-}	$0.7837^{-\uparrow}$	$0.7886^{+\uparrow}$
	2-Stage Elliptical PSO	7.13	4	$79.26^{-\uparrow}$	$401.6^{-\uparrow}$	$0.8025^{\uparrow}$	$0.8206^{+\uparrow}$
	3-Stage PSO	7.07	4	$81.22^{-\uparrow}$	$400.9^{-\uparrow}$	$0.8083^{\uparrow}$	$0.8311^{+\uparrow}$
	k_{est}-means	34	2.73	55.69	457.3	0.612	0.6113
	k-means	34	6	93.58	387.6	0.8278	0.7351
	D-PSO Scaled	4.37	3.8	68.77	409.4	0.7602	0.7587

labels are produced by a human expert and may not correspond well to hyperspherical clusters.

Another important consideration is that a clustering partition that differs from the known classification is not necessarily a "wrong" clustering—there are many ways to group a dataset based on different characteristics (i.e. feature subsets). Hence, it may be better to consider the performance in terms of the internal metrics as a better measurement of how well the proposed approach performs. If we consider the internal metrics, then it is clear that the proposed approach is able to achieve similar to or better results than k-means on the Iris, Wine, Movement Libras, and Breast Cancer datasets, while using a much smaller number of features. On the other two datasets, the performance is far superior to the k_{est}-means method, while again using a small number of features.

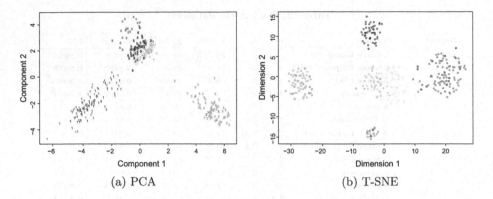

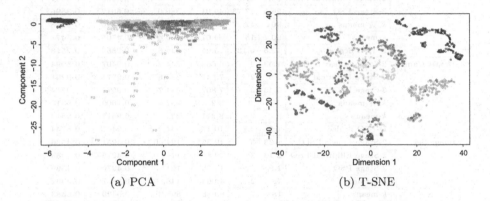

Fig. 5. Visualisations of Dermatology dataset. (Color figure online)

Fig. 6. Visualisations of Image Segmentation dataset. (Color figure online)

To analyse why K was being inaccurately estimated on the Image Segmentation and Dermatology datasets, we visualised these datasets using the principal component analysis (PCA) and t-distributed stochastic neighbour embedding (T-SNE) visualisation methods, as shown in Figs. 5 and 6. Each sub-figure shows the results of applying one of these methods to one of the datasets, where the colours represent the class labels of the dataset.

On the Dermatology dataset (which has 6 classes), PCA clearly separates the red and green classes into two distinct clusters. The remaining classes appear as one tightly packed cluster, with the pink class potentially a fourth cluster. This gives 3–4 clusters on this dataset, consistent with the 4 average clusters found by the proposed methods. T-SNE more clearly separates the classes into clusters, but there is still overlap between the teal and yellow classes, giving 5 distinct clusters.

The visualisations on the Image Segmentation dataset are much more unclear; PCA produce a poor visualisation, with only the purple class being clearly separated. T-SNE is clearer— the aquamarine and purple classes are separated well, but the remaining classes all have a fair amount of overlap. This suggests why the proposed methods find 3 clusters—two of the classes fit into two clusters well, and the remaining instances have sufficient overlap to produce a single cluster.

In summary, both the linear and elliptical two-stage methods successfully select a small m' on all real-world datasets. The elliptical method has slightly better performance than the linear method while selecting additional features. If the minimum number of features is desired while achieving good performance, then the linear method is best; however, if better performance is preferred at the cost of slightly higher complexity, the elliptical method should be used. The 3-stage method has slightly higher performance than the 2-stage elliptical method across all metrics, which shows the pseudo-local search is able to further refine solutions.

5.2 Synthetic Data

Unlike the real-world datasets, the synthetic datasets have classes which map well to hyper-spherical clusters. Thus the external metrics are useful for measuring the performance of the proposed approach, which clearly outperforms k-means and k_{est}-means on all of the synthetic datasets (except 10d10c) while achieving a low m', especially on the datasets with high m. The proposed approach scales to large datasets more effectively than the k-means algorithm, despite not performing only clustering, but also feature selection and determining K in the same search process. It also performs better than k-means on the internal metrics across the 50d and 100d datasets, where it selects the most useful features to improve clustering.

Despite performing well, the proposed methods are inaccurate in predicting K on several of the synthetic datasets, such as 50d20c and 100d20c where they select $35 - 36$ clusters instead of 20. However, compared to the D-PSO method, the proposed methods predict K more accurately on 7 of the 9 datasets. The D-PSO method predicts values of K close to 20 on all the 50d and 100d datasets despite K actually varying from 20 to 40. This suggests that D-PSO cannot search for the true K value as effectively as the proposed methods. It is interesting to note that the K values produced by the proposed methods are always higher than the K_{est} generated by the first stage. This suggests that the fitness function encourages a higher number of clusters, perhaps due to the clustering performance metric used. This behaviour is useful in some cases, where K_{est} is below the actual K (e.g. 10d10c, 10d20c and 10d40c), but on the other synthetic datasets where $K_{est} > K_{actual}$, it means that the proposed methods are not able to correctly lower the K found. It would be useful to investigate changing the clustering performance metric in the fitness function to encourage searching values on both sides of K_{est}.

Table 3. Synthetic datasets

Dataset	Method	m'	K	Scatter	$\sum$ Intra *	Purity	FM
10d10c	2-Stage Linear PSO	3.63	8.97	$15.04^{-\uparrow}$	$782.6^{-\uparrow}$	$0.8051^{-\uparrow}$	0.763^{-}
	2-Stage Elliptical PSO	4.93	9.57	$15.63^{-\uparrow}$	$750.0^{-\uparrow}$	$0.8604^{-\uparrow}$	$0.8196^{\uparrow}$
	3-Stage PSO	4.9	9.07	$16.11^{-\uparrow}$	$739.9^{-\uparrow}$	$0.8872^{-\uparrow}$	$0.8678^{+\uparrow}$
	k_{est}-means	10	5.43	11.49	815.9	0.7743	0.7786
	k-means	10	10	17.7	715.7	0.9175	0.833
	D-PSO Scaled	3.3	6.97	12.63	817.7	0.7718	0.7481
10d20c	2-Stage Linear PSO	5.07	20.1	$75.32^{+\uparrow}$	$226.9^{+\uparrow}$	$0.9587^{+\uparrow}$	$0.9408^{+\uparrow}$
	2-Stage Elliptical PSO	6.1	20.17	$85.2^{+\uparrow}$	$216.8^{+\uparrow}$	$0.9828^{+\uparrow}$	$0.9721^{+\uparrow}$
	3-Stage PSO	6.07	20	$90.17^{+\uparrow}$	$213.3^{+\uparrow}$	$0.9953^{+\uparrow}$	$0.9928^{+\uparrow}$
	k_{est}-means	10	15.13	53.31	292.7	0.7907	0.7651
	k-means	10	20	70.02	248.5	0.8887	0.8218
	D-PSO Scaled	4.4	14.7	51.65	282.7	0.8249	0.8305
10d40c	2-Stage Linear PSO	5.47	39.73	$67.26^{-\uparrow}$	$452.0^{-\uparrow}$	$0.9182^{\uparrow}$	$0.8699^{\uparrow}$
	2-Stage Elliptical PSO	6.87	39.7	$78.29^{+\uparrow}$	$417.3^{+\uparrow}$	$0.9615^{+\uparrow}$	$0.9437^{+\uparrow}$
	3-Stage PSO	6.87	40.1	$85.66^{+\uparrow}$	$402.9^{+\uparrow}$	$0.9824^{+\uparrow}$	$0.97^{+\uparrow}$
	k_{est}-means	10	29.83	55.58	499.9	0.8385	0.8234
	k-means	10	40	74.5	433.7	0.9219	0.8657
	D-PSO Scaled	3.83	15.6	27.08	756.4	0.5692	0.5477
50d10c	2-Stage Linear PSO	9.3	13.5	$93.48^{+\downarrow}$	$1072.0^{+\downarrow}$	$0.8191^{+\downarrow}$	0.5197^{+}
	2-Stage Elliptical PSO	14.87	13.23	$96.76^{+\downarrow}$	$1071.0^{+\downarrow}$	$0.8174^{+\downarrow}$	0.5172^{+}
	3-Stage PSO	14.23	13.5	$104.5^{+\downarrow}$	$1045.0^{+\downarrow}$	$0.8152^{+\downarrow}$	0.5125^{+}
	k_{est}-means	50	11.53	88.84	1242.0	0.7679	0.4978
	k-means	50	10	72.87	1306.0	0.7426	0.4865
	D-PSO Scaled	9.07	18.5	144.2	930.6	0.8824	0.5196
50d20c	2-Stage Linear PSO	10.87	34.63	$250.2^{+\uparrow}$	$372.4^{+\uparrow}$	$0.8622^{+\uparrow}$	$0.525^{+\uparrow}$
	2-Stage Elliptical PSO	17.43	34.67	$261.8^{+\uparrow}$	$366.1^{+\uparrow}$	$0.8692^{+\uparrow}$	$0.5171^{+\uparrow}$
	3-Stage PSO	17.33	34.6	$283.1^{+\uparrow}$	$356.8^{+\uparrow}$	$0.858^{+\uparrow}$	$0.4835^{+\uparrow}$
	k_{est}-means	50	28.8	211.3	432.5	0.8057	0.4713
	k-means	50	20	137.5	548.6	0.6858	0.3581
	D-PSO Scaled	10.63	17.43	99.65	539.6	0.7165	0.4167
50d40c	2-Stage Linear PSO	13.57	48	$200.4^{+\uparrow}$	$756.9^{+\uparrow}$	$0.7724^{+\uparrow}$	$0.4888^{+\uparrow}$
	2-Stage Elliptical PSO	19.87	48	$211.7^{+\uparrow}$	$738.8^{+\uparrow}$	$0.788^{+\uparrow}$	$0.4949^{+\uparrow}$
	3-Stage PSO	20.43	48	$230.3^{+\uparrow}$	$708.5^{+\uparrow}$	$0.761^{+\uparrow}$	$0.3669^{+\uparrow}$
	k_{est}-means	50	44.7	214.5	822.6	0.7099	0.2841
	k-means	50	40	192.4	871.9	0.6749	0.2586
	D-PSO Scaled	11.33	26.03	104.5	1062.0	0.5546	0.2455
100d10c	2-Stage Linear PSO	20	15.87	$148.3^{+\downarrow}$	$1401.0^{+\downarrow}$	$0.8655^{+\downarrow}$	0.5648^{+}
	2-Stage Elliptical PSO	29.4	15.77	$150.9^{+\downarrow}$	$1395.0^{+\downarrow}$	$0.8676^{+\downarrow}$	$0.5707^{+\uparrow}$
	3-Stage PSO	28.9	15.73	$153.4^{+\downarrow}$	$1376.0^{+\downarrow}$	$0.8567^{+\downarrow}$	0.5557^{+}
	k_{est}-means	100	11.27	115.2	1807.0	0.794	0.5623
	k-means	100	10	103.5	2036.0	0.7436	0.5194
	D-PSO Scaled	17.3	18.97	206.1	1287.0	0.9137	0.5549
100d20c	2-Stage Linear PSO	21.9	36	$358.9^{+\uparrow}$	$559.9^{+\uparrow}$	$0.8945^{+\uparrow}$	$0.5627^{+\uparrow}$
	2-Stage Elliptical PSO	33.4	36	$381.9^{+\uparrow}$	$548.2^{+\uparrow}$	$0.8943^{+\uparrow}$	$0.5466^{+\uparrow}$
	3-Stage PSO	34.17	35.93	$399.9^{+\uparrow}$	$536.1^{+\uparrow}$	$0.8858^{+\uparrow}$	$0.5256^{+\uparrow}$
	k_{est}-means	100	26.2	260.4	707.5	0.7865	0.4505
	k-means	100	20	188.1	841.0	0.7011	0.3799
	D-PSO Scaled	19.53	20.23	162.7	748.6	0.7568	0.4435
100d40c	2-Stage Linear PSO	27.37	47	$304.4^{\uparrow}$	$991.7^{+\uparrow}$	$0.7968^{+\uparrow}$	$0.5116^{+\uparrow}$
	2-Stage Elliptical PSO	39.07	47	$315.8^{+\uparrow}$	$980.4^{+\uparrow}$	$0.8057^{+\uparrow}$	$0.5012^{+\uparrow}$
	3-Stage PSO	37.9	47	$338.6^{+\uparrow}$	$940.5^{+\uparrow}$	$0.7624^{+\uparrow}$	$0.3305^{+\uparrow}$
	k_{est}-means	100	42.87	332.0	1146.0	0.7073	0.2837
	k-means	100	40	301.4	1176.0	0.6923	0.2689
	D-PSO Scaled	22.47	23	142.7	1442.0	0.5426	0.1997

5.3   Further Analysis

The two variations of the two-stage approach perform better on different datasets: the elliptical approach is best on datasets with small feature sets (Wine, Breast Cancer, Dermatology, 10d) where the linear fitness function selects fewer features at the expense of cluster quality. On the larger feature sets, the elliptical approach selects extra features without increasing performance. This is due to the ellipse used: on large feature sets, e.g. the 50 features seen in Fig. 3a, the feature weighting is close to 1 for m between 0 and 10, and above 0.9 even when 20 features are selected—indeed, on the synthetic datasets with 50 features, this method selects 15 to 20 features. On smaller feature sets, this effect is less noticeable, as only a few features are able to be selected before the feature weighting decreases significantly. Investigating a way of dynamically altering the shape of the ellipse used based on the size of the feature set would ensure that the weighting "drop-off" begins earlier on bigger datasets. The two-stage methods have similar values of K across all datasets, indicating that neither is being overly affected by the correlation between m' and K. If this had occurred, the elliptical approach would have higher K on the datasets where it selected more features than the linear approach.

The three-stage approach is an improvement compared to the two-stage elliptical approach on the internal metrics across all of the datasets (and especially on the hardest synthetic ones). This suggests that fine-tuning the solutions produced with a pseudo-local search is effective, increasing cluster quality. However, the results on the external metrics are much worse for the three-stage approach on the 50d40c and 100d40c synthetic datasets, contrary to that of the internal metrics. It is not obvious why this occurs—one explanation is that the noise present in the synthetic datasets has a significant effect when K is large (i.e. $K = 40$); as a centroid can take any possible co-ordinates (unlike a medoid), it may be much more sensitive to the noise in the dataset, producing overly specific clusters.

6   Conclusion

This work introduced a comprehensive and coherent two-/three-stage approach for performing simultaneous clustering and feature selection while automatically finding the K required. A number of novel techniques were proposed, including: using an estimate of K, K_{est}, to guide the PSO search process; a multi-faceted fitness function which encourages good cluster quality, minimises m', and reduces the search space of K; and a pseudo-local search which refines the clusters produced by the second stage. We showed that our approach gave good performance across several difficult datasets compared to existing methods, while selecting as few features as needed. In particular, our approach was shown to be effective on datasets with large K, which existing approaches largely fail to address. Our approach was successful at reducing dimensionality on large feature sets, consistently selecting under 40% of features on datasets with 100 features and 10 to 40 clusters.

In future work, we will further refine our fitness function by taking a multi-objective approach in order to allow more intelligent balancing of all three of cluster performance, feature selection, and deduction of K. We would also like to investigate other methods of measuring cluster performance (perhaps using multi-objective techniques), such as connectedness or density. There is also scope for improving performance further with other methods for estimating K, penalising the number of features produced, or using other EC techniques or representations.

References

1. Xue, B., Zhang, M., Browne, W.N., Yao, X.: A survey on evolutionary computation approaches to feature selection. IEEE Trans. Evol. Comput. **20**(4), 606–626 (2016)
2. García, A.J., Gómez-Flores, W.: Automatic clustering using nature-inspired meta-heuristics: a survey. Appl. Soft Comput. **41**, 192–213 (2016)
3. Sheng, W., Liu, X., Fairhurst, M.C.: A niching memetic algorithm for simultaneous clustering and feature selection. IEEE Trans. Knowl. Data Eng. **20**(7), 868–879 (2008)
4. Javani, M., Faez, K., Aghlmandi, D.: Clustering and feature selection via PSO algorithm. In: International Symposium on Artificial Intelligence and Signal Processing (AISP), pp. 71–76. IEEE (2011)
5. Lensen, A., Xue, B., Zhang, M.: Particle swarm optimisation representations for simultaneous clustering and feature selection. In: Proceedings of the Symposium Series on Computational Intelligence. IEEE (2016, to appear)
6. Pal, N.R., Bezdek, J.C.: On cluster validity for the fuzzy c-means model. IEEE Trans. Fuzzy Syst. **3**(3), 370–379 (1995)
7. Alelyani, S., Tang, J., Liu, H.: Feature selection for clustering: a review. In: Data Clustering: Algorithms and Applications, pp. 29–60 (2013)
8. Aggarwal, C.C., Reddy, C.K. (eds.): Data Clustering: Algorithms and Applications. CRC Press (2014)
9. Chiang, M.M., Mirkin, B.G.: Intelligent choice of the number of clusters in K-means clustering: an experimental study with different cluster spreads. J. Classif. **27**(1), 3–40 (2010)
10. Muni, D.P., Pal, N.R., Das, J.: Genetic programming for simultaneous feature selection and classifier design. IEEE Trans. Syst. Man Cybern. Part B **36**(1), 106–117 (2006)
11. Guyon, I., Elisseeff, A.: An introduction to variable and feature selection. J. Mach. Learn. Res. **3**, 1157–1182 (2003)
12. Liu, H., Motoda, H., Setiono, R., Zhao, Z.: Feature selection: an ever evolving frontier in data mining. In: Proceedings of the Fourth International Workshop on Feature Selection in Data Mining, pp. 4–13 (2010)
13. Van Den Bergh, F.: An analysis of particle swarm optimizers. PhD thesis, University of Pretoria (2006)
14. Lichman, M.: UCI machine learning repository (2013)
15. Handl, J., Knowles, J.D.: An evolutionary approach to multiobjective clustering. IEEE Trans. Evol. Comput. **11**(1), 56–76 (2007)

EvoINDUSTRY

Container Vessel Stowage Planning System Using Genetic Algorithm

Miri Weiss Cohen[1(✉)], Vitor Nazário Coelho[2,3], Adi Dahan[1], and Izzik Kaspi[1]

[1] Department of Software Engineering,
Braude College of Engineering, Karmiel, Israel
miri@braude.ac.il, Mail.adidahan@gmail.com, izziKal@gmail.com
[2] Institute of Computer Science, Universidade Federal Fluminense,
Niterói, RJ, Brazil
vncoelho@gmail.com
[3] Brazil Grupo da Causa Humana, Ouro Preto, MG, Brazil

Abstract. This paper deals with the container stowage planning problem, an important and a complex problem in maritime logistic optimization. The variant tackled in this work involves several constraints, inspired by real-life problems and application found in the literature. Given the complexity of the problem, which belongs to the class of $\mathcal{NP}$-hard problems, a novel evolutionary metaheuristic algorithm is developed and designed. Considering the ability and flexibility of Genetic Algorithm (GA). The approach is based on a two-phase procedure, one for master planning and the other for allocation of the containers into slots. GA parameters are analyzed to achieve practical and best results. The system offers stowage allocation solutions for both phases, thus offering flexibility for a wide variety of vessels and route combinations.

Keywords: Container vessel stowage planning · Genetic Algorithm · Metaheuristic · Constraint optimization

1 Introduction

Since the world's economy changed to a global economy, linear shipping companies have faced the increasing shipping demand by building larger ships that can carry up to 22000 containers. The vessel stowage loading plans of containers must be optimized so that costs can be reduced. Moreover, load and discharge operations at container terminals are costly. Hence, reducing the number of moves and the total time in port is essential to achieve cost reductions In the, the vessel stowage loading plans of containers must be optimized so that costs can be reduced. A relevant question formalized by Pacino is: "Can container ship stowage plans with high enough quality for practical usage be computed on standard equipment within the time required by the work processes of stowage coordinators?" [18].

Our research and software development focus on answering this relevant question and developing this topic. We believe that genetic algorithms implemented

G. Squillero and K. Sim (Eds.): EvoApplications 2017, Part I, LNCS 10199, pp. 557–572, 2017.
DOI: 10.1007/978-3-319-55849-3_36

in a software system that enables developers and users to define and facilitate a specific case will provide sufficient deployment and a good solution within a relevant run time. A flexible software system has the advantage of offering a range of solutions for users, and the ability to make decisions interactively where needed.

Container stowage planning usually known as Master Bay Plan Problem (MBPP), which belongs to the class of $\mathcal{NP}$-hard problems [2]. This problem can be defined as follows [3]: given a set C of n containers of different types to load on a ship and a set S of m available locations within the ship, we need to determine the assignment of the containers to the ship locations in order to satisfy the given structural and operational constraints related both to the ship and to the containers as well as to minimize the total loading time

A number of approaches have been introduced in the past two decades. Most of them focus on a single best solution solved offline with limited interaction from a stowage coordinator. The approaches are characterized by area of the vessel stowage loading plans, the number of phases of the solution and the optimization method. Single phase solutions include IP methods [4,6,15,18], Heuristic approaches [20,22,25] and GA [10,14]. Two-phase solutions distribute the bulk of containers into the bays, with planning for allocating each container in the specific slot solved in the second stage [1,2]. Jensen et al. [13] introduce a software and approach for interactively modifying a stowage plan. Their work considers only the lower deck of the vessel. Many limitations are covered in each one of the approaches, but only a few studies cover all the restrictions and limitations defined in [8,19]. A pioneer binary linear programming formulation was proposed by Avriel and Penn [5], but showed to be limited due to the huge number of binary variables and constraints on its formulation. Other binary linear formulation, considering stability, mixture and weight constraints can be found in other works in the literature [3,8]. GA were investigated by Dubrovsky et al. [10], Yang and Kim [24] and Imai et al. [11].

Other meta heuristic based optimization algorithms have been also applied in order to solve different variations of the stowage planning problem [1,23]. Sciomachen and Tanfani [21] presented a heuristic method for solving MBPP based on its relation with the three-dimensional bin packing problem (3D-BPP).

Recently, Ding and Chou [9] considered stowage planning problem of a container ship visiting, sequentially, a series of ports. Containers should be moved temporarily in some port in order to allow discharge of other lower containers, shifting moves, since they can only be accessed from the top of the stacks.

In this current paper, different real-life constraints are taken into account. By implementing the evolutionary framework, the proposed approach can serve as a final plan solution or an interactive system for users. In our study we made an attempt to cover as many of the known constraints for the MBPP as possible by implementing small cases of study, inspired by real-life.

2   Container Stowage Planning Problem

A container ship transports cargo in containers, and the ship layout varies from vessel to vessel. The space on a vessel is divided into bays [8]. Each bay consists of container stacks placed along the length of the ship. All bays are divided into an over deck and an under deck area, separated by structures called hatches [8]. In order to gain access to the containers stored under deck, we must remove all the containers on the deck, including the hatch cover.

On the under deck, the parts of a bay are divided into stacks/slots that are one container wide, and are composed of two Twenty-foot Equivalent Unit (TEU) stacks and a single Forty-foot Equivalent Unit (FEU) stack [17]. Some slots that have power plugs are known as reefer slots. A standard ISO container is usually 20 or 40 ft long, 8 ft wide and 8.6 ft high. 40 foot containers can be 8.6 ft high, or 9.6 ft high for high-cube containers. Each container has a weight, height, length and port where it has to be unloaded (discharge port). Aside from the standard ISO container described, several other container types exist. The major ones are:

- High-cube containers – usually refers to containers that are 9.6 ft tall, but containers of other non-standard heights exist.
- Reefer containers – having refrigeration module installed. They need a connection to the ship's power-supply [1].
- IMO containers – containing hazardous material. These containers have to be physically separated from other containers of the same type [1].

All containers are equipped with reinforced castings in each corner called corner casting, designed to withstand great force. They carry the weight of containers stacked on top of each other. It should be noted that 20' containers cannot be stacked on top of 40' containers due to their lack of castings in the middle.

2.1 Container Stowage Constraints

In real life situations, stowage planning is mainly carried out by human planners. Those planners have years of experience on board and they are familiar with the stowage instruction for containers in port terminals. However, due to the high number existing combinations for stowing all the containers on the vessel, as well as different constraints, meta heuristic algorithms have been required for solving this problem. The following constraints are detailed:

Over-Stowage. In sea transportation, container vessels visit several ports according to their planned routes. The vessel loads and unloads additional containers in each port on the route of the ship. The arrangement of the cargo on the vessel and the loading and unloading order is determined before the vessel arrives at each port. A stowage plan specifies the position of each container on the vessel [1,16]. Poorly planned stowage might cause unnecessary handling. This unnecessary handling operation is called shifting. Shifting is temporary unloading and reloading of containers from or onto the vessel. Over stowage is defined as follows: If a container is required to be unloaded at the current port, and is stacked under a container that its port of destination is in the future (Fig. 1), the container that has to be temporarily removed, is over stowing. Multiple shifts may be necessary to reach an over stowed container. Over stowage is considered very expensive, since it requires many crane shifts, which are time and energy consuming.

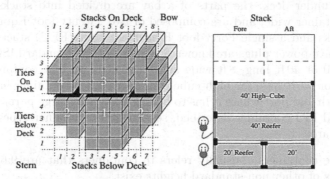

Fig. 1. Left: loaded on deck and under deck containers. Right: stack partially loaded with regular and reefer slots, figure taken from [8].

Ship Stability. Vessel stability and safety are very important in the containers stowage problem. A container ship becomes unstable if the vessels weight distribution is unbalanced.

When a vessel sails it needs to be "seaworthy", which means that its stability must be correct and all stress force should be within limits. During sailing, the draft of the vessel (the distance between the keel, the bottom of the vessel, and the waterline [1]) needs to be parallel to the waterline. For each vessel there are two draft lines (fore and aft). For the vessel to be seaworthy, vertical, transverse and longitudinal weights of cargo are measured and balanced according to the length of the arm.

Container Constraints. Containers and the cargo they carry, are constrained by many restrictions that must be considered when making a stowage plan. The first restriction is the container's weight, when containers are stacked on top of each other, the order of their weight must be considered. For that reason it is preferable to have a light container at the top of the stack and heavier containers at the bottom [8].

The second restriction refers to the different container sizes and structures. Each container has a corner casting at the top and the bottom. These castings are made for the stability of the stack. When two 20' containers are placed on top of a 40' container, both in-between castings cannot be used, and therefore the stack is unstable [19], as can be seen in Fig. 1.

The third restriction refers to reefer containers. These containers must be located in special slots that are equipped with power plugs. The location of these slots is indicated in the vessel's profile, and it is usually at the bottom tier. It is important that reefer slots be used only for this purpose (Fig. 1).

For containers that contain hazardous material (IMO containers), it is very important to allocate enough space between these containers to ensure the crew's safety in case of emergencies. Containers with special requirements such as IMO containers and reefer containers have a major effect on the planning process. IMO containers are usually stowed in a special bay towards the bow of the vessel

Line of sight: When containers are stacked on deck, the line of sight must be visible. The line of sight is an imaginary line from the bridge to the sea whose distance is equal to twice the length of the vessel or to 500 meters, whichever is smallest.

Wind force: When a container vessel sails at sea, the wind affects its performance and the safety of the cargo it carries. High winds can easily cause containers to fall off a ship. Different shipping companies have different on-deck stacking rules. Most of the companies do not allow stacks to be more than one tier higher/ lower than the ones supporting them on the sides. Our work is an extension of the basic model described in [8,14] in that we attempt to solve the planning not only for the bays below but for the entire vessel.

In this work we take into consideration the following: [14]: Both 20' and 40' containers, reefer containers are stowed in cells with power plugs, container stacking rules, trim and draft within the limit, wind and line of sight.

3   Two Phase Optimization Strategy

In order to tackle the stowage problem, the proposed approach divides the resolution of the problem into two phases. The first phase is the master bay planning phase, which allocates containers to be stowed at each bay. The second phase is the slot planning phase, which allocates a specific slot for each container within each bay.

For each one of the phases, a different evaluation function is defined. The evaluation function is composed of relevant parameters and an array of penalties which are defined. On the basis of the parameters in the IP mode solved in [8], we have imposed a heuristic penalty approach and values. The process of evaluating various values of penalties and converging to the results was accomplished through the software system, after numerous simulations were conducted and tested.

The motivation for using Genetic Algorithm (GA) is its advantage as a stochastic search algorithm and a problem-solving methodology. It has advantages such as flexibility, adaptation, global search capability, and its suitability for parallel computation. GA's have been used to solve difficult problems with objective functions that are multi model and multi constrained. A widely range of genetic operators can be used to perform the crossover, mutations, reinsertion of potential solutions, among others, in order to generate the offspring's population. Some encoding may cause the algorithm to create unfeasible solutions, or may change and enlarge the search space making it difficult to converge. In this paper

we will research and analyze these parameters for solving the stowage problem.
Results are described in Sect. 4.1.

3.1   Master Bay Planning

Since the stowage problem is a highly complex problem, first, we will focus on
allocating containers into bays. The constraints considers here are: the destination ports, reefer slots and ships stability.

For master bay planning encoding, tree encoding is used [7,12,14,16]. The
root of the tree represents the entire ship, and each leaf represents a bay. The
root also contains the total ship weight. Each leaf (bay) contains the total weight
of the bay, the total number of ports it needs to deploy, the number of reefer
slots it contains and an array of containers.

For creating the initial population, we will randomly assign all our containers
into random bays.

The following parameters are considered in the proposed model, described
by Eqs. (1) and (2), inspired from the IP model of Delgado et al. [8].

- B – all the bays in the vessel;
- B_i – containers in bay i;
- C_j^D – destination of container j;
- B_i^C – bay i is being used;
- B_i^R – number of reefer slots in bay i;
- C_j^R – container j is reefer;
- B_i^X – bay i exceeded its weight limit;
- C_j^W – container j's weight.

$$f(x) = \sum_{i \in B} \sum_{j \in B \wedge C_j^D \neq B_i^p} T_p + B_p \sum_{i \in B} B_i^C + R_p \sum_{i \in B} B_i^R - \sum_{j \in B_i} C_j^R$$

$$+ B_p^W \sum_{i \in B} B_i^X \left(\sum_{j \in B_i} C_j^W - B_i^{WL} \right) \tag{1}$$

$$Evaluation(x) = \frac{1}{f(x)} \tag{2}$$

This is a minimization problem, where all of the values are greater than one.
Therefore, Eq. (3) gives the fitness function:

$$Fitness(x) = \frac{Evaluation(x)}{\sum_{i \in B} Evaluation(i)} \tag{3}$$

For each bay (x), the target port with the maximum number of containers is
defined as the main target for that bay – B_i^p. Each container that is targeted to a
different port is assigned a penalty of $T_f = 20$ points. Since we want to be able to
stow more containers in further ports, we want to maintain as many empty bays

as possible. Thus, for each bay we use, we assign a penalty of $B_f = 10$ points. The weight limit is B_i^{WL}. Every ton exceeding that limit is assigned a penalty of $B_F^W = 50$ points. Although the containers are not allocated in this phase, if the number of reefer containers is greater than the number of reefer slots in a bay, a penalty of $R_f = 50$ points is assigned. For every bay the following is calculated:

1. if a bay is overweight: add weight_penalty * exceeded weight;
2. if a bay is open: add opening_bay_penalty;
3. add to penalty: ABS(reefer cells – reefer container) * reefer_penalty.
4. for every container destination which is not the main destination: add main destination penalty.

The evaluation function is one of the important functions in genetic algorithms. Its purpose is to evaluate each chromosome independently.

3.2   Slot Planning

In this phase, the allocation of a specific slot for each container is done. The restrictions we need to take into consideration for this stage include partial constraints from the master bay phase, such as: stability, reefer slots and over-stowage. Moreover, new restrictions must be considered, such as container size, line of sight and wind forces [19].

For each bay, a tree configuration for each bay stack is defined. Two arrays are defined, – on-deck and below-deck containers, moreover, the maximum allowed height, number and location of reefer slots and number of slots, are defined and monitored.

The evaluation function measures the quality of a specific bay stowage. A summation of all bays is done in order to analyze the complete solution. The first restriction is over-stowage. For each container that over-stows another container, we assign a penalty of $O_p = 40$. When a container above the deck over-stows a container below the deck, we add a penalty of $O_p^{AB} = 20$.

For every reefer container that is not stowed at the reefer slot or the opposite slot, we assign a penalty of $R_p = 50$, the same as in the master bay stage.

For each pair with a height difference of more than one container, we assign a penalty of $W_p = 40$. To ensure trim stability, each stack is assigned its own weight limit. For every ton exceeding that limit, we assign a penalty of $S_p^W = 50$. Due to casting restriction, a 20' container cannot be stowed above a 40' container. Thus, for every container violating this restriction, we assign a penalty of $S_p = 80$. The last restriction is based on heuristics to allow flexibility in future ports [16]. For every new stack we use in a bay - $S_{jB_i}^C$, a penalty of $NS_p = 15$ is assigned, for a stack above the deck, and a penalty of $NS_p = 10$ for below the deck. All penalties, for both stages are a result of numerous attempts to calculate and simulate, range of scores to achieve feasible solutions. Formalizing the above, is detailed in Eq. (4):

$$f(i) = O_p \sum_{j \in B_i^S} \sum_{c_1 \in S_j} \sum_{c_2 \in S_j - \{c_1\}} O_{C_1, C_2} + R_p \left(\sum_{j \in B_i} R_j C_j^{NR} + \sum_{j \in B_i^{slot}} SL_j^R SL_j^{NRC} \right)$$

$$+ W_p \sum_{j \in B_i^S}^{B_i^S - 1} H_{j,j+1} + S_p^W \sum_{j \in B_i^S} S_{jB_i}^X \left(\sum_{l \in S_j} C_l^W - S_{jB_i}^{WL} \right) + O_p^{AB} \sum_{c_1 \in Below, c_2 \in Above} O_{C_1, C_2}$$

$$+ S_p \sum_{j \in B_i^S} \left(\sum_{l \in j_A} \sum_{k \in j_A - \{l\}} A_{l,m} C_{m,l}^S + \sum_{l \in j_B} \sum_{k \in j_B - \{l\}} A_{l,m} C_{m,l}^S \right) + NS_p \sum_{j \in B_i^S} S_{jB_i}^C$$

$$\tag{4}$$

where:

- $S_{jB_i}^{WL}$ – weight limit of stack j in bay i;
- $SWL_j^{B_i}$ – weight limit of bay i;
- $S_{jB_i}^x \in [0,1]$ – stack j in bay i exceeds weight limit;
- $B_i^{slot} \in [slot_1, ..., slot_n]$ – group of all slots in bay i;
- $SL_j^{RC} \in [0,1]$ – container j is reefer;
- $O_{x,y} \in [0,1]$ – container x is over stowage y;
- $H_{S_1, S_2} \in [0,1]$ – stack S_1 over one container higher than S_2;
- $SL_j^R \in [0,1]$ – slot j is a reefer;
- $SL_j^{NRC} \in [0,1]$ – slot j is a non-reefer;
- $S_j \in [container_1, c_2, ..., c_m]$ – set of containers in stack j;
- $C_j^{NR} \in [0,1]$ – container j is not stowed in a reefer slot;
- $A_{l,m} \in [0,1]$ – container l is higher than m;
- $C_{m,l}^S \in [0,1]$ – container m is larger than container l;
- j_A – set of on deck containers in stack j;
- j_B – set of below deck containers in stack j.

The fitness function is described in Eqs. (5) and (6):

$$Evaluation(x) = \frac{1}{\sum_{i \in B} f(i)} \tag{5}$$

$$Fitness(x) = \frac{Evaluation(x)}{\sum_{i \in G} Evaluation(i)} \tag{6}$$

where, G – is a group of all the solutions in the current generation. In summary, the following procedure is done:

1. For every stack in a chromosome:
   (a) if stack is overweight: add weight_penalty * exceeded weight;
   (b) if stack above is open: add opening_stack_above_penalty;
   (c) if stack below is open: add opening_stack_below_penalty;

    (d) For every cell in stack:
        i. if a container in a stack is a reefer the and cell isn't reefer cell add reefer_penalty;
        ii. Else if cell is reefer and container isn't add reefer_penalty.
    (e) for every container in the stack:
        i. if container size is TEU and is on container FEU:
           A. add size_miss_size_penaly * the number of container lying on the TEU container.
    (f) For each container in the stack:
        i. add over stowage_penalty * number of container under over stowing.
2. For each destination below deck:
    (a) If there is container above deck that over stowage that destination add below_hach_overstowage * number of container above deck.
3. For 1 to stack number:
    (a) if abs(stack[i]-stack[i-1]) bigger than one:
        (i) Add abs($stack[i] - stack[i-1]$) * hight_diffrance_penalty.
    (b) Return penalty.

For the slot planning fitness function, each solution was compatible with various solutions of the same bay.

4 Computational Experiments

The software system developed requires the algorithm to run in reasonable time, acording o the complexity of the cargo and routing. We identified the bottleneck computational procedures which could be processed in a paralleled manner and designed them to work simultaneously, resulting a configuration which can handle a large number of threads to run parallel. We used an Intel® Xeon® server with 4–3.4 GHz CPUs, 15-cores each, with HyperThreading support, allowing up to 120 threads to run in parallel. This stage was used to configure the best GA parameters, serving the future usage of the software. The only stage of user interaction is done in loading the ship booklet and all necessary data such as: fixed route and a container list.

4.1 Genetic Algorithm Parameters

Population Size for Master Bay Planning. During our research we examined how population size and generations affect the results, taking into consideration that the software processing time is a crucial criterion. We used population sizes between 100–15000 for the master bay planning and 100–5000 for the slot planning to determine the outcome results. The analysis goal was to decide the population size versus the quality solution. Figure 2 depict only two examples, but a wide range was tested. The number of generations versus the penalty scores of the solution is depicted in both figures. As shown in Fig. 2 (left), for a population size of 100, the graph stops declining around 11,000 generations. As depicted in Fig. 2 (right), for a population size of 500, the number of generations required to reach the best solution decreases significantly to 3500. With a population value of 5000 chromosomes, the graph reaches its peak point around generation 1400 (not shown), while with a population value of 10,000 the best value in generation 1300 (not shown). The software system is flexible for developers demands and restrictions, resulting, as expected, in run time and solution efficiency. In conclusion, in the analysis we used a population of 500 chromosomes, resulting in a run time of less than 2 seconds for final container deployment results for both stages of the algorithm.

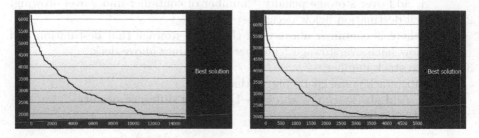

Fig. 2. GA evolution and penalty scores

Population Size for the Slot Planning. After the master bay distribution of the containers is determined, each bay is solved for individual deployment by searching for the best solution. In Fig. 3 (left and right) each bay was tested for a fixed population size, and the influence of generations vs. the penalty scores was tested and analyzed. The motivation is to determine, once again, the best solution according to run time constraints. Each figure depicts seven bays (each in a different color), each showing the progression of the solution until a minimal penalty score is achieved. With a population size of 100 (left), the graph began to freeze around generation 1200, and the best result was improved from the first evaluation in about 20%–30% of the cases. However, with a population size of 500 (right), the graph began to freeze around generation 400, and improved most of the bays in about 50%–60% of cases. Therefore, we used a population size of 500 in the results example, but offer the user the flexibility to define size of the population and generation if the restrictions are valid.

Mutation Ratio Analysis for the Master Bay and Slot Planning. Different mutation ratios were tested on fixed population sizes of 500 chromosomes and a fixed number of generations. For master bay planning we used 5000 generations and compared mutation ratios of 0.05, 0.1, 0.25, 0.35 and 0.5, resulting in minor changes among the penalty scores values. The value of 0.35 was chosen because of better results. For the slot planning problem, 350 generations were analyzed, resulting in a considerable effect. This result is straightforward and is explained by the fact that switching between two container locations in a bay can cause over-stowage or violation of stacking rules, thus influencing minimization of the penalty scores.

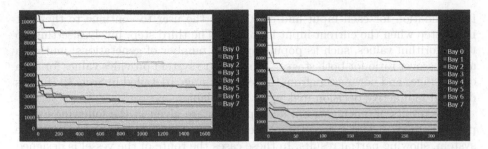

Fig. 3. Population size for slot planning

Crossover Ratio Analysis. For the master bay planning problem, crossover ratios between 0.3, 0.4 and 0.5 were tested, resulting in penalty scores of 1500, 1260 and 2240, respectively. The results show that the best ratio for the first phase was 0.4. Testing the crossover operator for the slot planning revealed a great deal of versatility. One of the reasons for this effect is that after placing the containers from the crossover segment in one of the parents, there are plenty of containers in which the original cell is no longer valid, so that we must allocate a new cell for them. Thus, when such an operation is performed, the original stack hierarchy is greatly changed. Figure 4 (left and right) depict the results for seven bays for crossover ratios of 0.3 (left)and 0.5 (right), respectively.

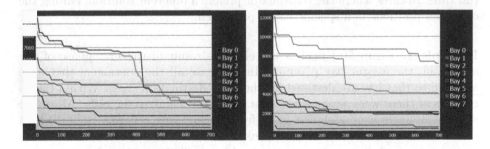

Fig. 4. Crossover ratio of 0.3 (left) and 0.5 (right)

5   Examples

The GUI was developed and computed from scratch, making it possible for each variable to be defined by the developers/users. The software is intended for use in the offices of shipping companies by trained workers that are familiar with it. Nonetheless, our software user interface is user friendly and provides validation for every input from the user. After the ship booklet has been loaded, the next step is to load all necessary data, which includes a fixed route, a contact list and a container list. The first port on the route is automatically selected as the next destination; however, the user can select a different port as the next destination. This stage involves a great deal of interaction with the user. Therefore it provides full validation for each input and only allows the user to continue to the next input step when the current input is correct. The third step, involves setting up the algorithm values, such as population size, number of generations, mutation and crossover ratio for both stages. The software system provides values for each of the stages and parameters from the learning stage (detailed in Sect. 3). If users demand interactive decision making, it is available.

The results of our algorithm and approach are given in the following examples. Figures 5, 6 and 7 are examples of cases we simulated using the software system, showing partial results. In these cases the route of the vessel is designed for four ports, each depicted in a different color. Containers are colored according to the destination port. In the figures, the layout and deployment of the upper and the lower deck are divided by a black line, which represents the hatch. The small squares in the figures represent reefer slots and containers, differentiated by color. Grey represents a reefer slot with a deployed container for which a reefer is not obligatory, green represents a match between reefer containers and slots, and red represents a reefer container in a slot that does not meet the requirement. The bar on the right side of the screen shot indicated the values of the parameters considered for the vessel and containers and the results of the deployment. These values include weight limits, actual weights, over-stowage and reefer misplacement.

Our GA approach and algorithm provides the stowage coordinator full vessel deployment for the input provided, resulting a sufficient solution in admissible run time. In cases where the coordinator prefers a different solution, editing the container positions in a specific bay is permitted.

Example 1. Figure 5(a) depicts the effective result of the first phase of our algorithm, the master bay planning. In this case all the containers that were assigned to that bay are destined for the same destination (red). Within the 56 containers there were seven reefer containers and eight reefer cells. All of the reefer containers were assigned to reefer cells and one cell was assigned to a standard container. This solution is considered sufficient due to the fact that no over-stowing containers and no weight and height limits were violated

Example 2. The second example of Fig. 5(b) depicts a result for 49 containers, of these, 35 were destined to C (yellow), 12 to the U (green) and two to the N (red). The route of the ship is I $\rightarrow$ N $\rightarrow$ U $\rightarrow$ C (the bottom line of the Figure). The result of the algorithm avoided unnecessary movements of containers and unnecessary opening of hatch covers by placing all containers that are destined to a single destination in the inner part of the ship, which is not over-stowed. Note that there is a reefer container below the hatch that is not stowed in a reefer cell.

Within that bay, there is no way to solve this without replacing it with the reefer cell from above the hatch, which is destined for the U. This will create over-stowage for that container and will force us to remove all the containers above it when arriving in the U (green). Since this is a much more expensive operation,

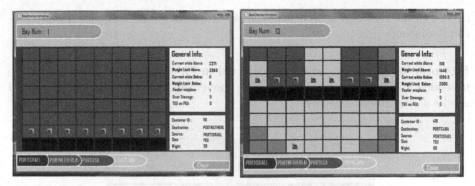

a) First stage of master bay planning   b) Bay/Slot deployment

Fig. 5. Examples 1 and 2 (Color figure online)

the algorithm yielded a less expensive solution. In this case, the stowage controller can choose to interactively switch between the two containers and solve this with a more efficient solution.

Example 3. Figure 6 depicts an example in which the system generated a non-optimal solution. A single container in the below deck area has a different port (red vs. yellow). This solution, though considered sufficient, violates the most important consideration of stowing containers for the same destination within a single bay. This solution can engender large expenses in crane motion for unloading and loading in the first port of the route.

As depicted, most containers are destined to yellow. Yet there are still four containers that are destined to red. In this case, the stowage controller might

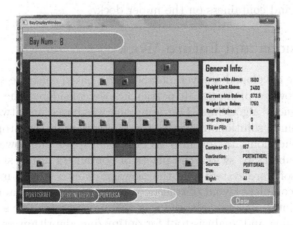

Fig. 6. Example 3 – bay deployment (Color figure online)

choose to interactively switch between two containers and solve for a more efficient solution.

Example 4. In the this example, depicted in Fig. 7, the red containers will be unloaded efficiently with minimal crane movement, with the ability to unload stacks of containers together.

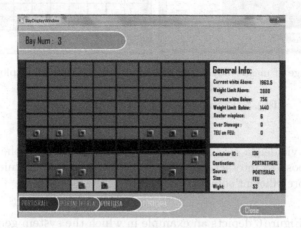

Fig. 7. Example 4 – an incomplete solution (Color figure online)

This example is presented to show an incomplete example. The solution is not optimal for reefer containers, where we suggest two optional solutions. The first raises the penalty cost for reefer container deployment if positioned in a non-reefer slot. In our experiments this solution conveyed a better result. The second solution is for the stowage coordinator to switch between containers on the lower deck and containers on the upper deck.

6   Conclusions and Future Work

In this work, we developed a novel metaheuristic based software system for container vessel stowage planning. In particular, we considered the flexibility and power of the genetic algorithms. Our approach was based on a two-phase procedure. The obtained solutions motivate the application of the proposed strategy in real-life applications, taking into account the upper and lower levels of the vessel and the ability to switch the places of containers in the slots. This novel approach and software system help the stowage planner in two manners: firstly, by providing a complete layout of containers as a planning tool; and also allowing the planner to interactively make changes, when necessary. The software system provides a learning and analysis tool for optimizing algorithm parameters.

Further work includes expanding the software for more complex routes (the route is currently restricted to four ports), including cycles. Furthermore, an interesting topic would be to include the ability of considering dynamic environments changes, such as crises, lack of electricity and other unexpected phenomena, which would require to proposed tool to offer partial solutions based on these dynamic changes.

The authors would like to thank the FP7 CORDIS, "New Horizons for Multi Criteria Decision Making", for supporting the development of this work.

References

1. Ambrosino, D., Anghinolfi, D., Paolucci, M., Sciomachen, A.: A new three-step heuristic for the master bay plan problem. Marit. Econ. Logistics **11**(1), 98–120 (2009)
2. Ambrosino, D., Anghinolfi, D., Paolucci, M., Sciomachen, A.: An experimental comparison of different heuristics for the master bay plan problem. In: Festa, P. (ed.) SEA 2010. LNCS, vol. 6049, pp. 314–325. Springer, Heidelberg (2010). doi:10. 1007/978-3-642-13193-6_27
3. Ambrosino, D., Sciomachen, A., Tanfani, E.: A decomposition heuristics for the container ship stowage problem. J. Heuristics **12**(3), 211–233 (2006)
4. Avriel, M., Penn, M., Shpirer, N.: Container ship stowage problem: complexity and connection to the coloring of circle graphs. Discrete Appl. Math. **103**(1–3), 271–279 (2000)
5. Avriel, M., Penn, M., Shpirer, N., Witteboon, S.: Stowage planning for container ships to reduce the number of shifts. Ann. Oper. Res. **76**, 55–71 (1998)
6. Botter, R.C., Brinati, M.A.: Stowage container planning: a model for getting an optimal solution. In: Proceedings of the IFIP TC5/WG5.6 Seventh International Conference on Computer Applications in the Automation of Shipyard Operation and Ship Design, vol. 7, pp. 217–229. North-Holland Publishing Co. (1992). http://dl.acm.org/citation.cfm?id=647138.717368
7. Carrano, E., Fonseca, C., Takahashi, R., Pimenta, L., Neto, O.: A preliminary comparison of tree encoding schemes for evolutionary algorithms. In: IEEE International Conference on Systems, Man and Cybernetics, pp. 1969–1974. ISIC, October 2007
8. Delgado, A., Jensen, R.M., Janstrup, K., Rose, T.H., Andersen, K.H.: A constraint programming model for fast optimal stowage of container vessel bays. Eur. J. Oper. Res. **220**(1), 251–261 (2012)
9. Ding, D., Chou, M.C.: Stowage planning for container ships: a heuristic algorithm to reduce the number of shifts. Eur. J. Oper. Res. **246**(1), 242–249 (2015)
10. Dubrovsky, O., Levitin, G., Penn, M.: A genetic algorithm with a compact solution encoding for the container ship stowage problem. J. Heuristics **8**(6), 585–599 (2002)
11. Imai, A., Sasaki, K., Nishimura, E., Papadimitriou, S.: Multi-objective simultaneous stowage and load planning for a container ship with container rehandle in yard stacks. Eur. J. Oper. Res. **171**(2), 373–389 (2006)
12. Kang, J.-G., Kim, Y.-D.: Stowage planning in maritime container transportation. J. Oper. Res. Soc. **53**(4), 415–426 (2002). http://www.jstor.org/stable/822825
13. Jensen, R.M., Leknes, E., Bebbington, T.: Fast interactive decision support for modifying stowage plans using binary decision diagrams. In: International Multiconference of Engineers and Computer Scientists (2012)
14. Kumar, R., Gopal, G., Kumar, R.: Novel crossover operator for genetic algorithm for permutation problems. Int. J. Soft Comput. Eng. (IJSCE) **3**(2), 252–258 (2013)

15. Li, F., Tian, C., Cao, R., Ding, W.: An integer linear programming for container stowage problem. In: Bubak, M., Albada, G.D., Dongarra, J., Sloot, P.M.A. (eds.) ICCS 2008. LNCS, vol. 5101, pp. 853–862. Springer, Heidelberg (2008). doi:10.1007/978-3-540-69384-0_90

16. Malhotra, R., Singh, N., Singh, Y.: Genetic algorithms: concepts, design for optimization of process controllers. Comput. Inf. Sci. 4(2), 39–59 (2011)

17. Pacino, D.: Fast generation of container vessel stowage plans. Ph.D. thesis, IT University of Copenhagen (2012)

18. Pacino, D., Delgado, A., Jensen, R.M., Bebbington, T.: Fast generation of near-optimal plans for eco-efficient stowage of large container vessels. In: Böse, J.W., Hu, H., Jahn, C., Shi, X., Stahlbock, R., Voß, S. (eds.) ICCL 2011. LNCS, vol. 6971, pp. 286–301. Springer, Heidelberg (2011). doi:10.1007/978-3-642-24264-9_22

19. Rodrigo, J.: Container ship safety, maritime Law (UPC). http://upcommons.upc.edu/e-prints/handle/2117/3051

20. Sciomachen, A., Tanfani, E.: The master bay plan problem: a solution method based on its connection to the three-dimensional bin packing problem. IMA J. Manage. Math. 14(3), 251–269 (2003)

21. Sciomachen, A., Tanfani, E.: A 3D-BPP approach for optimising stowage plans and terminal productivity. Eur. J. Oper. Res. 183(3), 1433–1446 (2007)

22. Wei-ying, Z., Yan, L., Zhuo-shang, J.: Model and algorithm for container ship stowage planning based on bin-packing problem. J. Mar. Sci. Appl. 4(3), 30–36 (2005)

23. Wilson, I., Roach, P., Ware, J.: Container stowage pre-planning: using search to generate solutions, a case study. Knowl. Based Syst. 14(3–4), 137–145 (2001)

24. Yang, J.H., Kim, K.H.: A grouped storage method for minimizing relocations in block stacking systems. J. Intell. Manuf. 17(4), 453–463 (2006)

25. Yoke, M., Low, H., Xiao, X., Liu, F., Huang, S.Y., Hsu, W.J., Li, Z.: An automated stowage planning system for large container ships. In: Proceedings of the 4th Virtual International Conference on Intelligent Production Machines and Systems (2009)

The Artificial Immune Ecosystem:
A Bio-Inspired Meta-Algorithm for Boosting
Time Series Anomaly Detection
with Expert Input

Fabio Guigou[1,2,4]($\boxtimes$), Pierre Collet[2,4], and Pierre Parrend[2,3,4]

[1] IPLine, Caluire-et-cuire, France
fguigou@ipline.fr
[2] ICube Laboratory, Université de Strasbourg, Strasbourg, France
pierre.collet@unistra.fr
[3] ECAM Strasbourg-Europe, Schiltigheim, France
pierre.parrend@ecam-strasbourg.eu
[4] Complex System Digital Campus (UNESCO Unitwin), Paris, France
http://cs-dc.org/

Abstract. One of the challenges in machine learning, especially in the Big Data era, is to obtain labeled data sets. Indeed, the difficulty of labeling large amounts of data had lead to an increasing reliance on unsupervised classifiers, such as deep autoencoders. In this paper, we study the problem of involving a human expert in the training of a classifier instead of using labeled data. We use anomaly detection in network monitoring as a field of application. We demonstrate how using crude, already existing monitoring software as a heuristic to choose which points to label can boost the classification rate with respect to both the monitoring software and the classifier trained on a fully labeled data set, with a very low computational cost. We introduce the Artificial Immune Ecosystem meta-algorithm as a generic framework integrating the expert, the heuristic and the classifier.

Keywords: Artificial immune system · Boosting · Anomaly detection · Time series · Machine learning

1 Introduction

Immune-inspired algorithms, generally referred to as Artificial Immune Systems (AIS), have been used in various contexts and applications, often with a focus on anomaly or intrusion detection. Being parallel and dynamic by design, i.e. able

The work presented here has been funded by IPLine SAS, by the French ANRT in the frame of CIFRE contract 2015/0079, and by the French Banque Publique d'Investissement (BPI) under program FUI-AAP-19 in the frame of the HuMa project.

© Springer International Publishing AG 2017
G. Squillero and K. Sim (Eds.): EvoApplications 2017, Part I, LNCS 10199, pp. 573–588, 2017.
DOI: 10.1007/978-3-319-55849-3_37

to learn online, they attracted some attention but suffered from their overly high computational cost.

In this paper, we present the Artificial Immune Ecosystem (AIE) model, a framework based on the same biological ground as the AIS. However, instead of trying to match an *algorithm* to the immune metaphor, we use it as a guide to build a *meta-algorithm* that integrates the notions of innate and acquired immunity, online learning and boosting.

More precisely, we develop a framework that augments the standard monitoring process, i.e. measures fed to a detector yielding alarms processed by an expert, to implement feedback and learning and improve the overall performance of the process. Figure 1 in Sect. 3 illustrates both processes. We show that this framework is generic enough to adapt to any machine learning algorithm and monitoring system, as long as it is biased towards false positives rather than false negatives.

In the context of cloud computing and IT monitoring, anomaly detection systems, to which we refer to as *detectors*, are mostly crude, being optimized for speed rather than accuracy. The AIE meta-algorithm, starting with such a "dumb" anomaly detector, and using some corrective input, evolves a higher-order, "smart" detector. We expect the AIE to be a viable building block of real-time monitoring systems, either by generating smart detectors or by keeping the feedback loop constantly active and having the ecosystem constantly improving.

The final goal of the AIE is to efficiently – in terms of computational cost and detection time – identify anomalous patterns in real-time streaming data. We expect our system to scale up to tens of thousands of simultaneous series, which is standard for datacenter monitoring. Industrial software designed to work at that scale either uses custom hardware and immense amounts of computational power (e.g. intrusion detection systems) or crude detectors (generally no more than an alarm threshold). These two extremes are symptomatic of two equally extreme approaches to complexity: brute force and discarding. We propose a third way that, through collaboration and learning, achieves much better results than what the IT world has come to accept, at almost the same computational cost.

Instead of trying to manually tune a detector and searching for the best parameters, we rely on the interaction of our system with *experts*, which can be users or other software components, to learn from its own errors. This way, we can use a simple, low-cost anomaly detector and, through online learning, steer down its false positive rate.

The rest of the paper is organized as follows: in Sect. 2, we review previous work on the topics of immune-inspired algorithms, anomaly detection, online learning and boosting. In Sect. 3, we state the problem the AIE is designed to solve, with the associated hypotheses. In Sect. 4, we present the core of our contribution: the AIE meta-algorithm. We evaluate it under various experimental settings in Sect. 5. Section 6 concludes this work.

2   Related Work

2.1   Immune-Inspired Algorithms

Artificial immune systems, also known as computer immunology, have been around since the early 1990s, based on the idiotypic network theory proposed by Ehrlich [1] in the late 19th century. In the earliest models, the biological process of matching antigens with antibodies, modelled by binary strings, was applied to the self vs. non-self discrimination in computer data sets [2]. Models later refined the immune metaphor to include multiple signals [3] and draw on the danger theory [4] to improve the detection rate.

While these models achieved some good results in particular problems, they failed to gain the acceptance of neural networks, evolutionary algorithms or swarm computing. Some of their downsides, such as their computational cost and conceptual similarity to genetic algorithms, provided the field from ever growing at the same pace as its most successful cousins in bio-inspired computing. Many authors have tried to update the AIS models to accommodate new machine learning problems, with some success [5,6].

We argue that, while the immune metaphor actually makes sense in the context of machine learning and classification, it was taken at the wrong conceptual level: it inspired algorithms when it should have inspired frameworks and architectures. Focusing on the matching process of antigen and antibodies, or on the detection and lymphocyte cloning process, provided no conceptual advance nor performance benefit over other methods. However, the bigger picture — how the innate and acquired immune systems complete each other, how feedback from an aggression is incorporated into the system to improve detection — can be the ground of meta-algorithms particularly well-suited for anomaly detection in time series.

2.2   Time Series Classification and Anomaly Detection

As a very specific data type, time series are notoriously hard to use with traditional classifiers. As a result, specific techniques had to be developed to reduce the dimensionality of the data and adapt new classifiers. A survey of many time series-specific classifiers using numerosity reduction, i.e. time and value space quantization, can be found in [7]. In recent years, local techniques such as shapelets [8,9], created specifically for time series classification, have also been successfully applied. However, in this paper, we are only concerned by a small subset of classification, namely anomaly detection.

Many approaches have been developed to detect anomalies in time series, either by looking for local discords or creating a model for the data and finding the samples that don't match it. Since the early 2000s, most algorithms have been using symbolic representations of the series instead of the raw samples, to filter high-frequency noise and make the analysis less CPU-intensive. The most popular representation is SAX (Symbolic Aggregate approXimation) [10].

Symbolic representations allow for fast distance computation, which in turn speeds up local similarity search [11]. Other algorithms use grammar inference and dictionary coding to measure the novelty of local patterns [12]. While these methods are known to yield good results, we found them insufficient for real-time processing, for a number of reasons. Firstly, as SAX collapses multiple (usually around 10) data points into a single symbol, symbolic approximation creates lag: assuming a new data point is polled every minute, it takes 10 min to generate a single symbol, and even more for an anomaly to spread across enough symbols to be detected. Secondly, many algorithms rate the degree of anomaly of a sample using some time window extending not only to the left of the point, but also to the right, which requires buffering and delays analysis considerably.

We wish to highlight the effectiveness of these algorithms, even on monitoring data. They can be seen as transformations from a raw samples stream to a stream of anomaly score, making the classification into normal or abnormal patterns easy. Unfortunately, the excessive delay before an actual event is detected, in the order of hours or days, makes them impractical in our real-time context.

2.3 Boosting Meta-Algorithms

Boosting meta-algorithms, sometimes referred to as metaheuristics, have been developed in the 1990's. They use a population of weak learners and efficiently weigh and combine their decisions to produce a single strong learner. The most well-known is probably AdaBoost [13]; others have been designed specifically for online learning [14]. However, the base assumption remains the same: an arbitrary low error rate can be achieved by increasing the number of weak learners [15]. In our context, where a single detector is typically available, boosting, in its traditional understanding, cannot be applied. Still, our efforts tend towards the same goal of providing a framework to improve the performance of algorithms running unaltered.

While such methods have reached a tremendous success, especially in the Big Data era, their main use remains in analysis of data at rest, replacing batch learning only to cope with large data sets that cannot fit in main memory. In particular, the application of online learning to stream mining is still rather limited [16]. Stream learning for fast query has been studied in [17], where ensemble learning is performed by a modified AdaBoost algorithm. The data, however, has to be split into chunks, therefore delaying analysis and making real-time applications unrealistic.

Boosting has also seen applications in multi-classifier time series classification [18]. Multiple classifier approaches, sometimes combined with multiple data representations, are a strong research topic in the boosting community [19]. However, these techniques are highly complex to implement, and therefore unrealistic in production environments where the deployment and tuning of a classifier must remain simple and generic.

2.4   Online Semi-supervised Learning

The task of labeling a stream of data, most of which is unlabeled, with an occasional feedback providing some labels, is called online semi-supervised learning. Both online *and* semi-supervised learning have a long history, but their combination has only become an active research field in the late 2000s. Many models use an adjacency graph to propagate labels from labeled points to their neighbors [20]. The main drawback of this approach is its high computational power and memory requirements. Others methods use dictionary coding [21] to infer the proximity of unlabeled points.

However, none of these solutions is a perfect fit to our specific context. In particular, the way labeled samples are provided may not be realistic, some methods requiring the whole training set to be provided offline [22]. Furthermore, all these algorithms use some form of clustering, which we consider too costly given the sheer size of our target data sets (tens of thousands of series samples at one point per minute, with at least a month of history) and may not always be necessary.

2.5   Machine Learning in Monitoring and Security

Though the field of IT network monitoring has spawned little research in the recent years, its close neighbor, network security, is at the core of current research. In particular, integrating semi-supervised classifiers with expert feedback to train self-defending network components is a topic of high interest.

In [23], the authors present AI^2, a framework designed to detect intrusions using web and firewall logs and expert feedback. They derive metrics from events in log files and use statistical methods to detect outliers in these metrics, then estimate the probability of a security event taking place; the expert feedback is then requested and injected into a systemic model.

In contrast to AI^2, the AIE reuses existing software, usually built upon simple business rules and thresholds, to detect potential anomalies, and can train any user-defined supervised classifier. In this regard, its focus is on integration, simplicity and low computational overhead, rather than system modelling and behavioral anomaly detection.

3   Problem Statement and Hypotheses

3.1   Role of the Expert

While machine learning has been used in the past to learn patterns and discover anomalies, most implementations worked under the assumption that either labeled – or at least partially labeled – data was available (supervised learning, a.k.a. classification), or no label ever existed (unsupervised learning, a.k.a. clustering). The former requires a field expert to manually go through the painstaking process of actually labeling the comprehensive time series, while the latter uses no expert knowledge at all, instead relying solely on structural variations to detect change.

In many applications such as network infrastructure monitoring, experts may not be available for the batch job of building a labeled data set; crude anomaly detection software may also be available, though having a rather low accuracy. Under these assumptions, three incidents can happen:

- Monitoring raises an alarm. The expert acknowledges it as a true problem and goes ahead with solving it.
- Monitoring raises an alarm. The expert discards it as a false positive.
- Some failure is detected, either by experts or customers, though no alarm was raised. Once analyzed, the expert can often track the fault to a minor event in the time series that remained undetected.

One problem we identified in the field of IT monitoring is the lack of reuse of expert knowledge. While experts are consulted at design time to set the parameters of the monitoring system (e.g. metrics to keep track of, alerting thresholds...) and have the ability to tune them later at runtime, their ability to discriminate between benign anomalies that trigger alerts and real problems, often just by looking at the time series over some time, is not captured: alerts are either discarded or the real problem corrected, but this classification is not fed back into the system. The data flow is illustrated in Fig. 1 (left).

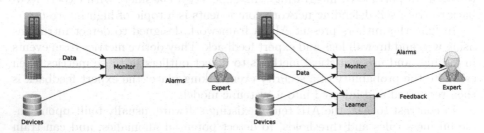

Fig. 1. *(left)* Standard data flow for monitoring. Expert classification is discarded. *(right)* AIE data flow. Expert classification is fed to a learning subsystem.

In this work, we only focus on the former two events. Discarding the third possibility – the event of a false negative – can be justified in three ways. Firstly, the action of labeling the exact location of a time series where an undetected anomaly occured is way more demanding from the expert, creates a rupture in his workflow, and is unrealistic in a real production environment. Secondly, the label would be positioned at an imprecise location, which would make the learning process more complex. Thirdly, the ability to silently discard false alarms allows the monitoring system to be tuned to more sensitive settings, reducing the false negative rate.

We capture knowledge by using the expert's classification of alerts as true or false positive as labels. The corresponding data is the raw time series captured over a period of time before the alert (e.g. 15 min). This way, it becomes possible to learn some features of a particular time series and help the monitoring system by filtering out false alerts.

Since alerts are a rare event, such a data set will typically be small, with at most a few points collected monthly on any given time series. This implies the need to perform learning on a small set and to somehow aggregate multiple time series to create a more complete set and use less classifiers. Learning each series independently is indeed inefficient and cumbersome; learning *classes* of series is a more appealing approach, as it creates diversity and thus generality: if a new series is added to a class, e.g. when a new device is added in a datacenter, its metrics can be analyzed by the existing classifier immediately.

The other factor to be considered is expert availability. As in any machine learning scenario, we need to build a labeled training set. In this case, only the expert is able to actually label the alerts. However, experts are seldom available to label a full data set ahead-of-time. Therefore, we need to adapt, using online learning, to a just-in-time labeling of data points.

3.2 Low-Resource Environment

The main constraint in Cloud monitoring is that service providers are not keen on allocating resources to it, generally running the software on old commodity servers[1]. This has historically not been an issue, as no heavy computations are performed on the collected data. However, if machine learning is to be implemented, this can become a limitation. It creates yet another incentive to work on small data sets with only a few classifiers.

3.3 Dumb Detector

The concept of detector is used to designate the monitoring software that is already in place (e.g. Nagios, ntop, PRTG...) and generates the alerts. It can easily be simulated by a process checking on devices by means of the *ping* command to measure response times, and SNMP (Simple Network Management Protocol, used to retrieve a number of useful metrics), inserting the data in some database and, when a measure crosses a user-defined threshold, send an email or a message over some messaging bus. The idea behind such detectors is that they are configured to generate false positives rather than miss potentially harmful events. We use this property to allow us to classify alerts as true or false positive, rather than labeling each data point.

3.4 Learning the Border

The usual way of dealing with imbalanced data sets is to artificially balance them, either by undersampling the majority class [24], oversampling the minority class [25], or both. However, undersampling at random results in a loss of potentialy

---

[1] Personal experience of the author as a software engineer for a Cloud service provider.

important points, while oversampling increases the size of an already large data set. Our approach is to selectively undersample the majority class, i.e. the *normal* class, by only considering those samples that generate a false alarm. In this regard, we use the "dumb" detector as a heuristic to determine how to train the classifier.

We argue that a small set of well-chosen points can carry the same information, and hence train a predictor of equal performance, as a large set of randomly selected points. Points contribute to the training when they are close to the border between two classes. Conversely, a point far from the border is of little help when it comes to discriminating a sample. This problem is highlighted in [26] as a cause for boundary skew in SVMs.

Though we did not study this notion quantitatively, it seems obvious that not all points carry useful information to determine the inter-class border, and that selecting points with a high discriminatory power in a learning set is paramount. This strategy is part of the active learning approach; though it has not spawned a large research field, similar efforts have been made in surrounding fields, such as expert evaluation of road safety [27]. Semi-supervised active learning has also been applied more recently in the field of computer security and log file analysis [23].

4   The Artificial Immune Ecosystem

4.1   The Meta-Algorithm

The Artificial Immune Ecosystem simulates the development of regulation in the immune system, as carried out by regulatory T-cells. The role of these cells is to eliminate self-matches, i.e. prevent auto-immune reactions. Our AIE classifies "immune" reactions of a "naïve immune system" as self-matches or non-self-matches. In monitoring terms, we classify alerts as true or false positive. When non-self-matches occur, they are remembered and the same match at a later time does not trigger an immune response. This long-term memory is provided by a classifier that learns the expert feedback on alerts. The system is described in Algorithm 1 and the corresponding data flow in Fig. 1 (right).

The AIE is capable of building a training data set online, i.e. while operating and sending alarms when required, to use expert feedback to label this set and to train a classifier in order to filter out the false alarms. When the data set is large enough and the classifier is trained, it is used as a predictor to decide whether an alarm should be raised or ignored, i.e. to classify it as a true or false alarm.

Because the classifier is only trained on positive samples, it cannot possibly lower the false positive rate; in fact, the increased precision will necessarily come at the cost of some false negatives. However, two facts moderate this consequence: on the one hand, a high false positive rate allows for a sufficiently large training set and enough failure examples to learn generic failure models. On the other hand, as stated in Sect. 3.1, the presence of the AIE allows the detector to be tuned to less conservative settings, hence the false negative rate should be considered with respect to a different baseline.

Algorithm 1. The Artificial Immune Ecosystem meta-algorithm

---

procedure AIE(T raw time series, N lookback, k training set size, C classifier)
    Initialize empty training DB
    for all alarm **do**
        Send alarm to expert
        Collect previous N samples from T
        Get expert feedback (true or false alarm)
        Add tuple (samples, label) to DB
        if $|DB_{true}| \geq k$ and $|DB_{false}| \geq k$ **then** Goto NEXT
NEXT:
    Train C on training DB
    for all alarm **do**
        Collect previous N samples from T
        if Predicted class for samples is TRUE **then**
            Send alarm to expert
        else
            Discard alarm

4.2 Boosting

Boosting is accomplished by pre-selecting the learning set. When enough alarms have been classified, a number of points of the time series have been consumed. We show experimentally that learning on the small pre-selected data set yields better performance than learning on all consumed points. Empirically, about 10,000 points are required to provide a roughly balanced data set of 20 to 50 points per class.

As the AIE improves the performance of a user-defined classifier, i.e. of any system capable of learning labeled data, it is indeed a boosting meta-algorithm.

4.3 Life Cycle of a Smart Detector and Parallelism

After the training phase, the subsystem containing the detector and the trained classifier can be exported as a smart detector. At this point, this subsystem is no longer able to learn or to adapt: it can, however, operate with the same level of genericity as the original detector, little computational overhead and better accuracy.

At this point, copies of the smart detector can be distributed and operate in parallel the same way as the dumb detector did. In the regard, though the training phase is only as parallel as the classifier, later operation is fully parallel.

5 Experimental Evaluation

5.1 Meta-Algorithm Implementation

We implemented the AIE as 3 interacting components: a monitoring system, designed in a way very similar to production monitoring software, a simulated expert applying rules to classify the alarms, and a classifier. Data is fed into the monitoring system, which calls the expert when an alarm occurs and sends him the last 15 min of data. The expert decision is recorded and associated with this data.

5.2   Settings

We first tested our system on CPU load time series. The load is sampled every minute for two months, yielding a total length of about 90,000 real-valued data points scaled between 0 and 100. To simulate real-time acquisition, we process the points one by one, without any batch processing. To evaluate our approach, we use the following rules:

– If the mean load over 15 min, i.e. the mean of a 15-points circular buffer, is above 90, some anomaly is going on. This rule is used by the simulated expert and is the ground truth. These settings are realistic in the context of server monitoring.
– As a weak detector, we use a similar rule with a threshold at 80, therefore generating a lot of false positives. While this is an unrealistic use case, it is useful as a first proof-of-concept.

The learner used here is a naive Bayesian classifier, suggested in [28] to be a good choice with small learning sets. Some sample data is shown in Fig. 2.

Since any anomaly detection data set is naturally heavily biased towards "normal" behavior, a metric such as accuracy is unable to efficiently discriminate between a good and a poor classifier (simply predicting the "normal" class is sufficient, in our case, to reach a 90 to 95% accuracy). Instead, we use the F-score [29], defined as the harmonic mean of precision and recall, to evaluate the performance of our various settings.

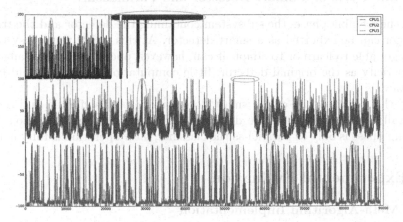

Fig. 2. Example time series used, later refered to as CPU1 to CPU3. Typical anomalies are highlighted in orange. (Color figure online)

5.3 Validating the Role of the Expert

During our first tests, we evaluated the impact of several design parameters. The first is the effect of having the expert send feedback to the system:

- in case of false alarm only, or
- also when an alarm that should have been raised is not (false negative).

Interestingly, we found out that using both false positives and negatives provides no significant improvement in terms of detection and has a negative impact on running time. This discovery is very promising for the AIE: it solves the problem of the expert not accurately positioning an undetected anomaly in the series, locating it at the wrong index, potentially hindering the learning process by introducing classification noise.

Then, using as settings the purely positive learning and running the classifier for each point, we evaluated the importance of having a highly available expert, i.e. a large training set. In a real scenario, it is unrealistic to expect a human expert to deal with thousands of errors. We simulated the limited availability of the expert by stopping his feedback after he has classified a fixed number of alarms as real or false. To cope with the limited number of data points, we still force a minimum of 10 real and 10 false alarms to train the AIE. The results are summarized in Table 1. We observe no phenomenon of overfitting, as expected given the size of the training set.

Table 1. Impact of limited expert availability

Max. expert calls	20	30	50	100	500	Unlimited
F-score	.36	.70	.72	.72	.78	.78

5.4 Reuse of a Smart Detector

In more complex settings, we wish to train a single detector to be reused on different time series with similar range and "shape", such as CPU graphs from multiple servers and devices. We examine the performance of a detector trained with one series on another.

We switch to a different classifier, trading off speed for generalization and accuracy. The following experiment uses a k-NN classifier (with $k = 5$). We conducted a series of benchmarks using 3 different CPU graphs recorded over 2 months from different devices, each time training the AIE on one and evaluating the classification on another. The results are shown in Table 2.

From these results, we can see that an AIE performs very well on series statistically similar to the one it was trained on, but also that some notion of "difficulty" exists: the CPU3 series is only poorly predicted (though better than without machine learning) by an AIE trained on other series, but an AIE trained on CPU3 successfully predicts the other two. These results indicate a good generalization ability.

Table 2. Results of smart detector reuse: F-score vs testing/training series

Test	Train			
	None	CPU1	CPU2	CPU3
CPU1	0.029	—	0.991	0.997
CPU2	0.056	0.996	—	0.999
CPU3	0.115	0.323	0.158	—

5.5 Supporting Various Classifiers

To further study the AIE and validate whether it is generic enough to accommodate any learning algorithm, we compare the results of different classifiers and learning set sizes. The F-scores are summarized in Table 3 and Fig. 3. They have been averaged over 6 different series of 90,000 points. Running times vary between 1 and 13 s.

In order to get a realistic overview of the actual gain provided by the AIE, we adjusted the detector settings to real production values. It now checks the last 3 collected points and raises an alarm if all 3 are above 85%. As a result, the performance figures are lower than the previous experiment, with some classifiers actually performing *worse* than the detector alone, and others still providing a much better classification rate.

Table 3. F-score and percent improvement over the detector for each predictor and learning set size

Size	K-NN	Naive Bayesian	Decision trees	Extra trees	Neural net	SVM
10	0.719 / +15.41%	0.104 / −83.38%	0.727 / +16.69%	0.724 / +16.18%	0.548 / −12.12%	0.361 / −42.11%
20	0.724 / +16.16%	0.18 / −71.18%	0.713 / +14.44%	0.753 / =20.82%	0.43 / −31%	0.252 / −59.56%
30	0.796 / +27.79%	0.084 / −86.49%	0.767 / +23.04%	0.739 / +18.56%	0.448 / −28.17%	0.236 / −62.2%
40	0.8 / +28.35%	0.168 / −73.05%	0.785 / +25.95%	0.739 / +18.66%	0.375 / −39.86%	0.238 / −61.77%
50	0.791 / +26.97%	0.174 / −72.07%	0.797 / +27.94%	0.801 / +28.48%	0.359 / −42.46%	0.249 / −60.02%
60	0.78 / +25.1%	0.271 / −56.45%	0.748 / +20.05%	0.761 / +22.06%	0.378 / −39.36%	0.272 / −56.39%
70	0.773 / +24.06%	0.275 / −55.85%	0.763 / +22.51%	0.766 / +22.94%	0.463 / −25.71%	0.288 / −53.74%
150	0.81 / +30.03%	0.586 / −5.9%	0.731 / +22.51%	0.726 / +16.55%	0.319 / −48.85%	0.467 / −25.13%
250	0.791 / +26.86%	0.627 / +0.67%	0.753 / +17.33%	0.688 / +10.42%	0.391 / −37.24%	0.514 / −17.52%

We then study the boosting ability of the AIE. To this end, we set the training set size to 40 samples, which we found to be optimal, and compared the performance of the classifier when trained with the points selected by the AIE and on the raw series, i.e. on average 500 times more points. The results are summarized in Fig. 4.

This experiment shows that, with the exception of the naive Bayesian classifier, all classifiers perform equally well or better when trained on a small, relatively balanced data set selected by the detector than on the original time

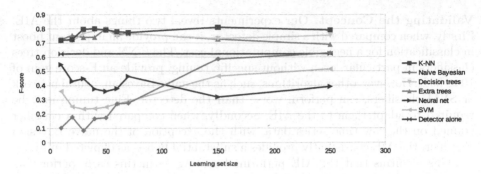

Fig. 3. Comparison of F-score with various classifiers and learning set size

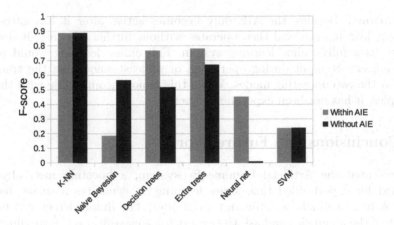

Fig. 4. F-score with AIE preselection (40 points labeled by expert) and regular learning (first 10,000 points labeled)

series. The consequence of using 40 points per class is also a much shorter running time, in the order of 10 s for the AIE and minutes to tens of minutes for the classifier operating on the full time series.

5.6 Discussion

Support for Various Classifiers. The support of various classifier was studied in Sect. 5.5. To give a meaning to those results, we compare them to the performance of the detector alone, which yields an F-score of .62. The results in Table 3 show that k-NN and the extremely randomized trees (extra trees) meta-heuristic [30] are most suited, with an optimal learning set size of 40 points per class. It is useful to note that some classifiers, under realistic settings, perform far worse than the detector alone.

Validating the Concept. Our experiments reveal two things about the AIE. Firstly, when compared with a simple detector, it can provide an important boost in classification for a negligible computational cost. The k-NN and decision trees classifiers in particular, even without specific tuning, provide an F-score gain of 10 to 30%. However, other algorithms, such as the naive Bayesian, neural network or SVM classifiers, can perform worse than the detector. Fine tuning may be required to adapt them to the AIE. Secondly, when compared with a classifier trained on the raw time series data, with the exception of the naive Bayesian classifier, the AIE consistently provides a substantial boost, as depicted in Fig. 4.

This confirms that the AIE performs boosting — in this case, performing better than the classifier alone with a training set 500 times smaller. This makes the AIE a potentially powerful tool to deal with large unbalanced data sets.

Limitations. Because the AIE only becomes active after it has gathered a sufficient learning set, and then operates without further learning, it does not operate as a fully online learning system. Full online learning would require accepting expert input during operation, or at least smoothing the transition between the two operating modes. While this is not incompatible with the AIE principles, it has not been experimented yet.

6   Conclusions and Future Work

We presented the Artificial Immune Ecosystem, a boosting meta-algorithm designed for expert-aided time series learning. It generates a smart anomaly detector from a dumb detector and a classifier. The dumb detector is used to pre-select the anomalies and ask the expert for a classification. Experiments, as depicted in Fig. 4, show that for some classifiers, the small learning set constituted during this process yields a better accuracy than a learning set 500 times larger created by labeling each data point, which is infeasible in realistic applications. In this regard, the AIE is a potential tool in any application in which labeling data is expensive and there is a way to pre-select relevant data points.

As previously stated, the AIE operation could be made fully online, i.e. integrate expert evaluation even while filtering alarms from the dumb detector. We did not evaluate this approach, as the primary scope of this paper was to devise a way to improve IT monitoring in a redistributable fashion, i.e. to turn dumb detectors into smart ones.

Evaluating the online approach is complex, as it requires careful overfitting monitoring and the detector lifecycle might include an aging process during which the changing data set becomes too large to create a clean border between normal behavior and anomaly. However, the full life of an online detector could be the scope of another study.

References

1. Silverstein, A.M.: Paul ehrlich, archives and the history of immunology. Nat. Immunol. **6**(7), 639–639 (2005)
2. Forrest, S., Perelson, A.S., Allen, L., Cherukuri, R.: Self-nonself discrimination in a computer. In: Proceedings of the 1994 IEEE Symposium on Security and Privacy, p. 202. IEEE (1994)
3. Hofmeyr, S.A., Forrest, S.: An immunological model of distributed detection and its application to computer security. The University of New Mexico (1999)
4. Aickelin, U., Cayzer, S.: The danger theory and its application to artificial immune systems (2008). arXiv preprint arXiv:0801.3549
5. Freitas, A.A., Timmis, J.: Revisiting the foundations of artificial immune systems for data mining. IEEE Trans. Evol. Comput. **11**(4), 521–540 (2007)
6. Montechiesi, L., Cocconcelli, M., Rubini, R.: Artificial immune system via euclidean distance minimization for anomaly detection in bearings. Mech. Syst. Signal Process. **76–77**, 380–393 (2015)
7. Xi, X., Keogh, E., Shelton, C., Wei, L., Ratanamahatana, C.A.: Fast time series classification using numerosity reduction. In: Proceedings of the 23rd International Conference on Machine Learning, pp. 1033–1040. ACM (2006)
8. Hills, J., Lines, J., Baranauskas, E., Mapp, J., Bagnall, A.: Classification of time series by shapelet transformation. Data Min. Knowl. Disc. **28**(4), 851–881 (2014)
9. Bagnall, A., Janacek, G.: A run length transformation for discriminating between auto regressive time series. J. Classif. **31**(2), 154–178 (2014)
10. Lin, J., Keogh, E., Lonardi, S., Chiu, B.: A symbolic representation of time series, with implications for streaming algorithms. In: Proceedings of the 8th ACM SIGMOD Workshop on Research Issues in Data Mining and Knowledge Discovery, pp. 2–11. ACM (2003)
11. Wei, L., Kumar, N., Lolla, V.N., Keogh, E.J., Lonardi, S., Ratanamahatana, C.A.: Assumption-free anomaly detection in time series. In: SSDBM 2005, vol. 5, pp. 237–242 (2005)
12. Senin, P., Lin, J., Wang, X., Oates, T., Gandhi, S., Boedihardjo, A.P., Chen, C., Frankenstein, S.: Time series anomaly discovery with grammar-based compression. In: EDBT, pp. 481–492 (2015)
13. Freund, Y., Schapire, R.E.: A desicion-theoretic generalization of on-line learning and an application to boosting. In: Vitányi, P. (ed.) EuroCOLT 1995. LNCS, vol. 904, pp. 23–37. Springer, Heidelberg (1995). doi:10.1007/3-540-59119-2_166
14. Babenko, B., Yang, M.H., Belongie, S.: A family of online boosting algorithms. In: 2009 IEEE 12th International Conference on Computer Vision Workshops (ICCV Workshops), pp. 1346–1353. IEEE (2009)
15. Beygelzimer, A., Kale, S., Luo, H.: Optimal and adaptive algorithms for online boosting (2015). arXiv preprint arXiv:1502.02651
16. Volkova, S.: Data stream mining: A review of learning methods and frameworks (2012)
17. Chu, F., Zaniolo, C.: Fast and light boosting for adaptive mining of data streams. In: Dai, H., Srikant, R., Zhang, C. (eds.) PAKDD 2004. LNCS (LNAI), vol. 3056, pp. 282–292. Springer, Heidelberg (2004). doi:10.1007/978-3-540-24775-3_36
18. Chen, L., Kamel, M.S.: Design of multiple classifier systems for time series data. In: Oza, N.C., Polikar, R., Kittler, J., Roli, F. (eds.) MCS 2005. LNCS, vol. 3541, pp. 216–225. Springer, Heidelberg (2005). doi:10.1007/11494683_22

19. Woźniak, M., Graña, M., Corchado, E.: A survey of multiple classifier systems as hybrid systems. Inf. Fusion **16**, 3–17 (2014)
20. Valko, M., Kveton, B., Huang, L., Ting, D.: Online semi-supervised learning on quantized graphs (2012). arXiv preprint arXiv:1203.3522
21. Zhang, G., Jiang, Z., Davis, L.S.: Online semi-supervised discriminative dictionary learning for sparse representation. In: Lee, K.M., Matsushita, Y., Rehg, J.M., Hu, Z. (eds.) ACCV 2012. LNCS, vol. 7724, pp. 259–273. Springer, Heidelberg (2013). doi:10.1007/978-3-642-37331-2_20
22. Kveton, B., Philipose, M., Valko, M., Huang, L.: Online semi-supervised perception: Real-time learning without explicit feedback. In: 2010 IEEE Computer Society Conference on Computer Vision and Pattern Recognition-Workshops, pp. 15–21. IEEE (2010)
23. Veeramachaneni, K., Arnaldo, I.: AI2: Training a big data machine to defend. In: 2016 IEEE 2nd International Conference on Big Data Security on Cloud (Big-DataSecurity), April 2016
24. Liu, X.Y., Wu, J., Zhou, Z.H.: Exploratory undersampling for class-imbalance learning. IEEE Trans. Syst. Man Cybern. Part B (Cybern.) **39**(2), 539–550 (2009)
25. Mi, Y.: Imbalanced classification based on active learning smote. Res. J. Appl. Sci. Eng. Technol. **5**, 944–949 (2013)
26. Akbani, R., Kwek, S., Japkowicz, N.: Applying support vector machines to imbalanced datasets. In: Boulicaut, J.-F., Esposito, F., Giannotti, F., Pedreschi, D. (eds.) ECML 2004. LNCS (LNAI), vol. 3201, pp. 39–50. Springer, Heidelberg (2004). doi:10.1007/978-3-540-30115-8_7
27. Saunier, N., Midenet, S., Grumbach, A.: Stream-based learning through data selection in a road safety application. In: STAIRS 2004, Proceedings of the Second Starting AI Researchers Symposium, vol. 109, pp. 107–117(2004)
28. Forman, G., Cohen, I.: Learning from little: Comparison of classifiers given little training. In: Boulicaut, J.-F., Esposito, F., Giannotti, F., Pedreschi, D. (eds.) PKDD 2004. LNCS (LNAI), vol. 3202, pp. 161–172. Springer, Heidelberg (2004). doi:10.1007/978-3-540-30116-5_17
29. Chinchor, N., Sundheim, B.: MUC-5 evaluation metrics. In: Proceedings of the 5th Conference on Message Understanding, pp. 69–78. Association for Computational Linguistics (1993)
30. Geurts, P., Ernst, D., Wehenkel, L.: Extremely randomized trees. Mach. Learn. **63**(1), 3–42 (2006)

Empirical Analysis of Optimization Methods for the Real-World Dial-a-Ride Problem

Dilek Arıkan[1]([⊠]), Çetin Öztoprak[2], and Sanem Sarıel[1]

[1] Department of Computer Engineering,
Istanbul Technical University, Istanbul, Turkey
{arikand,sariel}@itu.edu.tr
[2] Kapgel, Istanbul, Turkey
cetin@kapgel.com

Abstract. This paper deals with solving the Dial-a-Ride Problem (DARP) for an on-demand delivery start-up company which delivers products to its customers from their corresponding pick-up points within guaranteed time intervals. The primary goal of the company is to minimize its operational costs while fulfilling the orders under the constraints on time window, duration, carrier capacity and ride time. This problem is formulated as the real-world DARP, and two methods are empirically evaluated by using Mixed Integer Programming (MIP) and Genetic Algorithm (GA) frameworks. The experiments are done on the simulated data provided by the company. The results show that a heuristic approach is more suitable for the real-world problem to meet the time window limitations.

Keywords: Dial-a-Ride Problem · Combinatorial optimization · Genetic Algorithm · Mixed integer programming · Transportation

1 Introduction

In the *Dial-a-Ride Problem (DARP)*, user requests taken from specific origin points are dispatched to specific destination points within a given time interval [5]. Transportation is performed by vehicles. The aim of the DARP is to find the best routing schedules for the vehicles so that the total routing cost is minimized, and user inconvenience is minimized under the given constraints. Total cost is usually calculated as the total distance travelled by the vehicles in order to pick-up and deliver all the orders from and to the requested origin and destination points, respectively. User inconvenience to be minimized is determined as a function of the excess ride time and the waiting time for the customers [2]. Excess ride time is calculated as the time for travelling between two points and the waiting time for the customers is determined by the total time that a request is handled by a carrier. In this paper, we formulate the real-world on-demand product delivery problem as the DARP. In this problem, the products obtained from corresponding pick-up points are to be delivered by

© Springer International Publishing AG 2017
G. Squillero and K. Sim (Eds.): EvoApplications 2017, Part I, LNCS 10199, pp. 589–600, 2017.
DOI: 10.1007/978-3-319-55849-3_38

carriers to their customers within guaranteed time intervals. Since the DARP is a generalized version of the Travelling Salesman Problem with Time Windows (TSPTW) and also Vehicle Routing Problem with Pick-up and Delivery (VRPPD) which are both NP-Hard problems, DARP is also an NP-Hard problem. We have implemented the problem formulation under two frameworks to empirically analyse the performances on the data provided by the company. The first is the Mixed Integer Programming formulation as a single-objective multi-vehicle DARP formulation [1]. MIP formulation is implemented using universal Linear Programming (LP) solver CPLEX[1]. The second is a heuristic method based on a classical cluster-first, route-second approach. In the classical heuristic approach, standard construction and improvement methods are applied to the solution. These approaches perform limited exploration of the search space and typically produce good results within modest computing times. [7] In the cluster-first, route-second approach formulation, since the constraints are represented as soft constraints, multi-criteria multi-vehicle DARP formulation [2] is used to minimize the user inconvenience using excess ride time and waiting time for the customers. Both MIP and heuristic methods are evaluated on simulated data generated by the company based on its real customer requests.

The DARP can be modelled as static or dynamic. In the static case, all the requests with the origin and destination points and the earliest pick-up and the latest drop-off times are known in advance. Rather, in the dynamic case, the data appear online during daytime depending on the requests by the user. The focus of the paper is on static DARP yet still providing an analysis on the suitability of the methods for the dynamic case which is left as future work.

Th rest of the paper is organized as follows. The formal definition of the DARP, notation and formulation are presented in Sect. 3. Then, MIP and heuristic methods to solve DARP are introduced, and the results obtained from both methods are given with a comparison. Finally, the paper is concluded with the possible future works.

2   Problem Definition

DARP is an NP-Hard problem that generalizes the TSPTW and VRPPD. The items ordered by customers are transported within specific time windows from their pick-up points to the specified drop-off points determined by the customers. Transportation is carried out by carriers (vehicles). Time window for an order is started at the point when the user creates the request, and it ends after a fixed amount of time determined by the company (1 h in our case study). A task which corresponds to a customer order with its pick-up, drop-off coordinates, and its time stamp is called a request in the problem formulation. A vehicle can serve for more than one request simultaneously to reduce the operational costs. However, each request must be completed under the given time frame which directly affects user convenience as a function of excess ride time. Carriers start from a depot and return to this depot once their tasks are done.

---

[1] http://www-01.ibm.com/software/commerce/optimization/cplex-optimizer/.

This problem is investigated from both a linear programming perspective and a heuristic perspective to analyse their suitability to the real-world application.

2.1 Notation

The constraints and the variables for the real-world DARP meeting the company's needs is adopted from [5]. The problem is formulated as single-objective and multi-objective multi-vehicle DARP as follows:

n	: The number of customer requests
$P = \{1, ..., n\}$	: Pick-up coordinates of requests
$D = \{n + 1, ..., 2n\}$	: Drop-off coordinates of requests
$N = P \cup D \cup \{0, 2n+1\}$	: Pick-up, drop-off, origin and destination coordinates
A	: Arcs connecting coordinates
$G = (N, A)$	: Directed graph on which the problem is constructed
K	: Set of carriers
Q_k	: Load amount allowed for carrier k
T_k	: Ride time limit for the carrier k
q_i	: Amount loaded by a carrier at node i
d_i	: Service duration at node i
$[e_i, l_i]$	: Time window for node i
L	: Ride time limit for a request
c_{ij}	: Cost of traveling between the nodes i and j
t_{ij}	: Required time to travel between the nodes i and j
V	: Set of carriers used in the solution satisfying $V \subset K$
m	: Number of carriers used in solution, i.e. $|V| = m$

As given above, n denotes the number of customer requests. The DARP is defined on the graph $G = (N, A)$. The sets P and D include pick-up and drop-off points, respectively. N is the set including the origin point, destination point and pick-up and drop-off points. 0 is the origin node and $2n + 1$ is the destination node. Carriers start their routes at the origin node and go to the destination nodes after they deliver all the requests they are responsible for. K is the set of carriers. Q_k is the load amount that is allowed for carrier k. T_k is the ride time limit for carrier k and none of the carriers are allowed to exceed this time limit. In this paper, T_k is defined as 9 h and identical for each k. q_i is the loaded amount at node i, and each $i \in N$ is associated with a load q_i satisfying the equations $q_0 = q_{2n+1} = 0$ and $q_i = -q_{n+i}(i = 1, ..., n)$. These equations mean that an order picked-up at node i should be dropped-off at node $n + i$, the load amount of each carrier at the origin and the destination points is zero. d_i is the service duration at node i. Since there is no service at the origin and destination nodes, service duration at the origin and destination nodes are zero. The equation $d_0 = d_{2n+1} = 0$ is satisfied. Time window is given as $[e_i, l_i]$ for each $i \in N$, where e_i represents the order time, l_i represents the latest time that the request is allowed to be delivered. Time window can not exceed the duration defined as L. This duration is defined as 1 h by the company. For each arc $(i, j) \in A$, c_{ij} is the cost and t_{ij} is the time duration to traverse the arc. The average speed for the carriers is defined as 30 km/h, and t_{ij} is calculated depending on this speed. Note that in the dynamic version of the problem, these values are subject to change.

In the heuristic algorithm, V is the set of carriers determined by the optimization procedure. The less the carriers are used, the more the objective function is minimized, and the better solution we have. m, is introduced as a necessity for the heuristic algorithm depending on the new variable V representing the number of carriers used in the solution (i.e., $|V| = m$ and is to be minimized inside the objective function).

Decision variables used in the MIP for the single-criterion multi-vehicle DARP model are given as follows.

x_{ij}^k : Variable taking the value 1, if carrier k is going from node i to node j; 0 if not
B_i^k : Time point that carrier k visits node i
Q_i^k : Amount of load left in the carrier's vehicle after it visits node i
L_i^k : Total ride time of request i by carrier k

x_{ij}^k is a binary variable, while B_i^k, Q_i^k and L_i^k are fractional variables [4].

In the heuristic version of the DARP, some relaxations to the constraints are required. While the constraints are relaxed, the objective function is expanded with a new mathematical expression. For the multi-criteria multi-vehicle DARP model, the following weight values are introduced to be used as coefficients for each expression to be minimized [2].

w_1 : Weight on the customer transportation time
w_2 : Weight on the number of vehicles used
w_3 : Weight on the route duration
w_4 : Weight on the customer excess ride time
w_5 : Weight on the waiting time for a customer

3   Mixed Integer Programming Formulation

Based on the given notation, the mathematical formulation of the DARP as a Mixed Integer Programming (MIP) problem as follows [5]:

Objective Function:

$$min \sum_{k \in K} \sum_{i \in N} \sum_{j \in N} c_{ij}^k x_{ij}^k \tag{1}$$

constraints:

$$\sum_{k \in K} \sum_{j \in N} x_{ij}^k = 1 \qquad\qquad \forall i \in P \tag{2}$$

$$\sum_{j \in N} x_{ij}^k - \sum_{j \in N} x_{n+i,j}^k = 0 \qquad\qquad \forall i \in P, \forall k \in K \tag{3}$$

$$\sum_{j \epsilon N} x_{0j}^k = 1 \qquad\qquad \forall k \in K \qquad (4)$$

$$\sum_{j \epsilon N} x_{ji}^k - \sum_{j \epsilon N} x_{ij}^k = 0 \qquad\qquad \forall i \in P \cup D, \forall k \in K \quad (5)$$

$$\sum_{i \epsilon N} x_{i,2n+1}^k = 1 \qquad\qquad \forall k \in K \qquad (6)$$

$$B_j^k \geq (B_i^k + d_i + t_{ij}) x_{ij}^k \qquad \forall i,j \in N, \forall k \in K \qquad (7)$$

$$Q_j^k \geq (Q_i^k + q_j) x_{ij}^k \qquad\qquad \forall i,j \in N, \forall k \in K \qquad (8)$$

$$L_i^k = B_{n+i}^k - (B_i^k + d_i) \qquad\qquad \forall i \in P, \forall k \in K \qquad (9)$$

$$B_{2n+1}^k - B_0^k \leq T_k \qquad\qquad \forall k \in K \qquad (10)$$

$$e_i \leq B_i^k \leq l_i \qquad \forall i \in N, \qquad\qquad \forall k \in K \qquad (11)$$

$$t_{i,n+i} \leq L_i^k \leq L \qquad \forall i \in P, \qquad\qquad \forall k \in K \qquad (12)$$

$$max\{0, q_i\} \leq Q_i^k \leq min\{Q_k, Q_k + q_i\} \qquad \forall i \in N, \forall k \in K \qquad (13)$$

$$x_{ij}^k \in \{0,1\} \qquad\qquad \forall i,j \in N, \forall k \in K \qquad (14)$$

The objective function minimizes the total routing cost using the variables c_{ij}^k and x_{ij}^k [5]. Routes are found by assigning the number of carriers for each request. Constraint 2 ensures that each request is served exactly once. Constraint 3 guarantees that an order is picked-up and dropped-off by the same carrier. Each carrier starts to its route at the origin node (constraint 4) and ends at the destination node (constraint 6). The carrier who enters a node should leave the same node (constraint 5). Visiting time is identified by constraints 7 and 11. Similarly, time restrictions are identified with constraints 9 and 12. Ride time for a route is bounded by the equation given in constraint 10. Load limitations are represented by constraints 8 and 13. x_{ij}^k is defined as a binary variable with constraint 14.

3.1   Implementation

The values of the variables in the problem formulation are set based on the company's needs. The sets N, P and D include longitude and latitude coordinates for the points i and j. Origin and destination points are fixed and unique. Haversine formula [8] is used to calculate the distance between two nodes, and the values are assigned to the cost matrix c_{ij}. The Haversine formula is an equation important in navigation, giving great-circle distances between two points on a sphere from their longitudes and latitudes [8]. Since the formulation needs an average speed for the vehicles in order to calculate the ride time between the nodes, average speed for a vehicle is assumed to be 30 km/h. Maximum amount of load Q_k is defined as 10 packages for a vehicle. Service duration d_i defined as 5 min represents the time that a carrier is used at the pick-up point for each node except origin and destination nodes. The formulation is linearized as introduced in the original paper [2].

4 Heuristic Algorithm Formulation

The solution method used to solve the DARP with a heuristic algorithm is based on cluster-first, route-second principle [2–4]. This method is divided into two parts. In the first part, a clustering process is performed in order to distribute the requests to the carriers. A genetic algorithm (GA) based clustering method is used in the first part where each request is assigned to one and only one carrier. In the second part, routes are created for carriers depending on the requests assigned to them. The modified space-time Nearest Neighbor Heuristic (NNH) [2] is used for the routing part. The nearest neighbor heuristic uses the pick-up and drop-off locations and time windows. After the routing schedule is completed for each carrier, the costs are calculated.

The mathematical formulation of the multi-objective optimization formulation for the heuristic method is adopted from [2] as follows:

Objective Function:

$$
\begin{aligned}
min \quad & w_1 \sum_{k \in V} \sum_{i \in N} \sum_{j \in N} c_{ij}^k x_{ij}^k + w_2 m + \\
& w_3 \sum_{k \in V} (B_{2n+1}^k - B_0^k) + \\
& w_4 \sum_{k \in V} \sum_{i \in P} (B_{n+i}^k - d_i - B_i^k - t_{i,n+i}) + \\
& w_5 \sum_{k \in V} \sum_{i \in P \cup D} L_i^k (Q_i^k - q_i)
\end{aligned}
\tag{15}
$$

In addition to the constraints 2, 3, 5, 10, 11, 13 and 14 used in the MIP formulation, the following constraints are used for the heuristic algorithm formulation. additional constraints:

$$
\sum_{j \in P \cup 2n+1} x_{0j}^k = m \qquad\qquad \forall k \in V \tag{16}
$$

$$
\sum_{i \in D \cup 0} x_{i,2n+1}^k = m \qquad\qquad \forall k \in V \tag{17}
$$

$$
(B_i^k + d_i + t_{ij}) x_{ij}^k \leq x_{ij}^k (B_j^k - W_j^k) \qquad \forall i, j \in N, \forall k \in V \tag{18}
$$

$$
(Q_i^k + q_j - Q_j^k) x_{ij}^k = 0 \qquad\qquad \forall i, j \in N, \forall k \in V \tag{19}
$$

$$
t_{i,n+i} + W_j^k - (B_i^k + d_i) \leq B_{n+i}^k - (B_i^k + d_i) \qquad \forall i \in P, \forall k \in V \tag{20}
$$

$$
B_{n+i}^k + B_i^k \leq L \qquad\qquad \forall i \in P, \forall k \in V \tag{21}
$$

Since it is difficult to solve the DARP with an exact function, an LP relaxation has been performed on the following constraints: Maximum route duration constraint, maximum ride times constraint, time windows constraints [2]. An acceptable modification for these constraints is made on the model in order to solve the problem using heuristic algorithms. Within these relaxations, the softened constraints are added to the objective function to be minimized and the DARP formulation introduced in the MIP formulation is turned out to be a multi-objective DARP with the new multi-criteria objective function.

Objective function (Eq. 15) used in the heuristic formulation of the DARP minimizes both the total cost and the user inconvenience [2]. The total cost is measured with the total distance travelled by all carriers in order to serve all requests, the number of carriers used in the final solution, and the total time taken by the carriers in order to serve all requests. The details about user inconvenience expressions are as introduced in the original paper [2]. Since the constraints are very similar to the ones used in the MIP approach, the rest of the formulation will not be repeated here.

4.1   Implementation

As mentioned before, the heuristic algorithm is split into two parts and solved using two different heuristics.

Clustering via Genetic Algorithm. In the clustering part, the given requests are assigned to the carriers using the Genetic Algorithm (GA). Each request is associated to only one carrier since it has to be picked-up and dropped-off by the same carrier.

Requests are grouped together using a binary chromosome representation as a matrix form where each row describes the requests associated to a carrier. In the chromosome representation, there should be as many rows as there are available vehicles and as many columns as there are requests and depot. [2] Since each request can be assigned to only one carrier, the sum of each column is 1 except the depot column. This information helps the algorithm to perform a verification. While generating the chromosome, constraints that the number of rows equals to the number of available vehicles, the number of columns equals to the number of requests, the sum of each row except depot row is 1, the sum of the row of the depot equals to the number of vehicles are checked. Once these constraints are satisfied, it means that the assignment of each request to exactly one vehicle is performed, and the clustering is completed.

A sample representation for 8 requests and 4 carriers is given in Table 1. As seen in the table, each row (i.e., the route) includes the depot since all the carriers should start from the depot and need to go back to the depot after delivering all the requests. This means that the sum of the depot column should be equal to the number of the carriers used in the candidate solution.

With the consideration that each request must be assigned to only one carrier, the initial population is generated randomly with 50 chromosomes. The population replacement proportion for the next generation is 0.10.

With an empirical analysis which is performed on an instance pointing that the problem instance with the number of requests is 20 and the number of vehicles is 5, the number of generations is determined as 15000.

The stopping criteria is chosen as the maximum iteration number (i.e., 15000). The fitness of an individual is solely its objective function value. A simple

Table 1. Chromosome representation used in GA. Each row corresponds to the requests assigned to a carrier.

depot	Req1	Req2	Req3	Req4	Req5	Req6	Req7	Req8
1	0	0	1	0	1	0	0	1
1	1	0	0	1	0	0	0	0
1	0	1	0	0	0	0	1	0
1	0	0	0	0	0	1	0	0

crossover operator with probability 0.60 is used. This procedure is repeated until each of the requests is allocated to exactly one vehicle [2]. A standard mutation operator with probability 0.05 is used which moves one random customer from its current cluster to another random cluster (i.e., carrier).

Routing via Space-Time Nearest Neighbor Heuristic Algorithm. The modified space-time nearest neighbour heuristic [1] is used in the routing part to create routes for the carriers. The algorithm starts at the node at which the pick-up time is the earliest, then calculates the costs of the other nodes in order to make a choice for the next move. The cost of a node is calculated by a weighted sum of the travel time between the nodes and the time window violation at the destination node. The next move is determined to be the unvisited node adding the lowest cost. The route is constructed for each carrier accordingly. A sample route created for the first carrier from Table 1 is given in Table 2. The request number is concatenated with either 1 or 2 indicating a pick up or delivery, respectively. This carrier handles all requests at the same time by sequentially picking up orders 3, 5 and 8; and dropping them off with the order 3, 8 and 5, respectively. In this way, a possible route for this carrier is constructed by Table 2.

Table 2. The constructed route for carrier 1 from Table 1

depot	3.1	5.1	8.1	3.2	8.2	5.2	depot

5   Empirical Analysis

5.1   Experiment Setup

The algorithms for the MIP and GA were applied on two sets of generated instances. The first set includes 2 carriers while the second set includes 3 carriers. At each trial, the number of requests is increased by 2 for different instances until MIP is stuck. The results are obtained and compared.

Both algorithms were applied to the DARP on NetBeans IDE 8.1[2] using the programming language Java[3]. MIP formulation is implemented using universal Linear Programming (LP) solver IBM ILOG Cplex Optimization Studio 12.6 (See footnote 1). Both algorithms ran on a 2.49 GHz Intel Xeon E312xx processor and 4.00 GB memory (RAM). No runtime is defined as a limit in order to be able to see the characteristic of the runtime while the request number is increasing.

5.2   Data

A simulated data is generated by the company Kapgel so that it is quite similar to the real-world data. The data file includes time stamps, pick-up and drop-off coordinates for the requests as latitude and longitude. Time stamps are given without date since all the orders given in the same day. The used sample data set for 14 requests ($n = 14$) is given in Table 1. Actual used data includes more accurate numbers of coordinates. Abbreviations *D.Lat.*, *D.Lon.*, *P.Lat.* and *P.Lon.* given in the table implies *Drop-off Latitude, Drop-off Longitude, Pick-up Latitude* and *Pick-up Longitude*, respectively (Table 3).

The average and best fitness values are analyzed for a sample run with 20 requests and 5 carriers. In order to determine the number of generations, multiple runs are carried out on the mentioned data. While the number of generations are set to be increased, the program is ran 100 times at each step, and the average and best results are obtained. The plot representing these values are given in Fig. 1. As seen in the figure, starting with the number of generations 10000, the average and best values are nearly stable. Since larger generation numbers are unacceptable for the problem, the results of this analysis also show that the selected maximum number of generations as 15000 is suitable for finding a feasible solution.

5.3   Results

Table 4 indicates the results obtained using MIP and the heuristic algorithm where n, k, Q and L identify the number of requests, the number of carriers, the maximum allowed amount of load and the time limit, respectively. *MIP Cost, MIP RT[s], HA Cost, HA RT[s]* mean *Mixed Integer Programming Cost, Mixed Integer Programming CPU Runtime in seconds, Heuristic Algorithm Cost* and *Heuristic Algorithm CPU Runtime in seconds*, respectively. Here *cost* implies the objective function value obtained from the associated instance.

---

[2] https://netbeans.org/.
[3] https://www.java.com.

Table 3. Sample data set

Order time	D. Lat.	D. Long.	P. Lat.	P. Long.
2015.10.23 07:01:00	41.07229665	29.00858021	41.0679290	28.998334
2015.10.23 07:02:00	41.07973364	29.00261594	41.0683038	28.995370
2015.10.23 07:02:00	41.11138302	29.02498088	41.1103170	29.025015
2015.10.23 07:04:00	41.04422181	28.99857499	41.0492424	28.994820
2015.10.23 07:07:00	41.03666225	28.98240609	41.0509730	28.992405
2015.10.23 07:10:00	41.04648808	29.00000021	41.0509730	28.992405
2015.10.23 07:21:00	41.09853598	29.00666582	41.1089660	29.019145
2015.10.23 07:21:00	41.04648081	29.00456804	41.0506640	28.994785
2015.10.23 07:25:00	41.05389792	29.00851407	41.0478833	28.994217
2015.10.23 07:30:00	41.04309879	28.97850662	41.0464000	28.986510
2015.10.23 07:31:00	41.03159294	28.99582617	41.0463760	28.986622
2015.10.23 07:35:00	41.07401257	28.99822703	41.0611558	28.988009
2015.10.23 07:36:00	41.05204563	28.98962944	41.0508389	28.992600
2015.10.23 07:41:00	41.12461287	29.05163578	41.1103020	29.032298

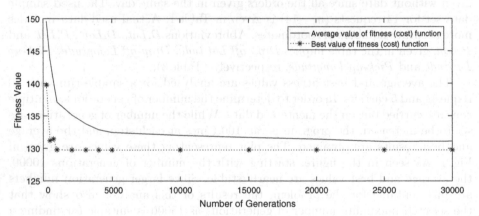

Fig. 1. The average and best cost values change with the number of generations

5.4   Analysis of the Results

The results are analyzed in terms of cost and runtime. As expected, for both mixed integer programming and heuristic algorithm, the objective function value (cost) increase for the increasing number of requests. Heuristic algorithm performs better than MIP in the overall. There are some cases in the small number of instances that the heuristic algorithm costs are smaller than that of MIP. This is because of the relaxations made in the heuristic algorithm while all the constraints are hard constraints in MIP. The heuristic algorithm includes some soft constraints. For example, time window violation is allowed in the heuristic

Table 4. The results for the generated instances

Instance	n	k	Q	L	MIP Cost	MIP RT[s]	HA Cost	HA RT[s]
a4-2	4	2	10	60	33.18	0.27	23.52	14.04
a6-2	6	2	10	60	33.18	1.13	33.12	15.24
a8-2	8	2	10	60	35.74	14.28	46.90	15.74
a10-2	10	2	10	60	44.17	223.92	51.26	20.19
a4-3	4	3	10	60	33.18	0.16	23.52	19.35
a6-3	6	3	10	60	33.18	0.97	33.12	18.97
a8-3	8	3	10	60	35.70	3.47	46.90	22.61
a10-3	10	3	10	60	44.17	206	51.26	24.21
a12-3	12	3	10	60	53.71	13940.55	70.24	25.07
a14-3	14	3	10	60	60.95	25456.7	88.82	28.35
a16-3	16	3	10	60	-	-	105.77	63.09
a18-3	18	3	10	60	-	-	117.99	54.23
a20-3	20	3	10	60	-	-	130.83	54.55
a16-4	16	3	10	60	-	-	105.77	73.61
a18-4	18	3	10	60	-	-	118.36	63.54
a20-4	20	3	10	60	-	-	129.74	62.68
a16-5	16	5	10	60	-	-	107.26	77.20
a18-5	18	5	10	60	-	-	119.73	75.16
a20-5	20	5	10	60	-	-	131.48	85.84

algorithm while it is not possible in MIP. It is also seen that while the number of requests is bigger than 14, MIP is not able to find a feasible solution. Runtime characteristics are also investigated, and it has been seen that the CPU runtime for MIP rise exponentially. These results show that MIP cannot be implemented for the company Kapgel because of the runtimes since there is a time limit to deliver the requests. On the other hand, GA is shown to be applicable since it gives quite similar results to that of the MIP results while it keeps the runtime under 30 s for 14 requests.

6   Conclusion

In this paper, the focus has been to model a real-world vehicle routing problem as a static Dial-a-Ride Problem and solving the problem using linear programming and heuristic methods. The problem is modelled as a Dial-a-Ride Problem since the objective function and the constraints of the DARP totally comply with the needs of the company. Existing MIP and heuristic method formulations are adopted and implemented in order to find feasible solutions to the problem and the results are compared. The results show that although MIP finds optimal solutions and minimizes the costs, it is not applicable because of the excessive runtimes for the increasing number of requests. Nevertheless, the heuristic algorithm results are quite similar to that of the MIP results in terms of the costs while it keeps the runtime at about 30 s. This is the first empirical step in solving the real-world DARP problem. The future work includes a more detailed analysis of the methods compared to the other heuristic methods. Then, the system will be ported to work for the dynamic DARP efficiently.

References

1. Baugh Jr., J.W., Kakivaya, G.K.R., Stone, J.R.: Intractability of the dial-a-ride problem and a multiobjective solution using simulated annealing. Eng. Optim. **30**(2), 91–123 (1998)
2. Bergvinsdottir, K., Larsen, J., Jørgensen, R.: Solving the dial-a-ride problem using genetic algorithms. Informatics and Mathematical Modelling, Technical University of Denmark, DTU (2004)
3. Bodin, L.D., Sexton, T.: The multi-vehicle subscriber dial-a-ride problem. TIMS Stud. Manage. Sci. **2**, 73–86 (1986)
4. Cordeau, J.F., Laporte, G.: A tabu search heuristic for the static multi-vehicle dial-a-ride problem. Transp. Res. Part B Methodol. **37**(6), 579–594 (2003)
5. Cordeau, J.F.: A branch-and-cut algorithm for the dial-a-ride problem. Oper. Res. **54**(3), 573–586 (2006)
6. Røpke, S.: The dial a ride problem (DARP). Ph.D. thesis, Datalogisk Institut Københavns Universitet (2005). https://www.itu.dk/people/pagh/CAOS/DARP.pdf
7. Sariel, S.: An integrated planning, scheduling and execution framework for multi-robot cooperation and coordination. Dissertation, Istanbul Technical University (2007). http://web.itu.edu.tr/sariel/thesis/sariel_PhD_Thesis_2007.pdf
8. Van Brummelen, G.: Heavenly Mathematics: The Forgotten Art of Spherical Trigonometry. Princeton University Press (2013). https://books.google.co.uk/books?id=0BCCz8Sx5wkC
9. Williams, H.P.: Integer programming, pp. 25–70. Springer US, Boston, MA (2009). doi:10.1007/978-0-387-92280-5_2

EvoKNOW

Presenting the ECO:
Evolutionary Computation Ontology

Anil Yaman[1,2], Ahmed Hallawa[3], Matt Coler[2,4], and Giovanni Iacca[2(✉)]

[1] Department of Mathematics and Computer Science, Eindhoven University
of Technology, P.O. Box 513, 5600 MB Eindhoven, The Netherlands
a.yaman@tue.nl
[2] INCAS3, P.O. Box 797, 9400 AT Assen, The Netherlands
m.coler@rug.nl, giovanni.iacca@gmail.com
[3] Chair for Integrated Signal Processing Systems, RWTH Aachen University,
52056 Aachen, Germany
hallawa@ice.rwth-aachen.de
[4] Campus Fryslân, University of Groningen, Sophialaaan 1, 8911 AE Leeuwarden,
The Netherlands

Abstract. A well-established notion in Evolutionary Computation
(EC) is the importance of the balance between exploration and exploitation. Data structures (e.g. for solution encoding), evolutionary operators,
selection and fitness evaluation facilitate this balance. Furthermore, the
ability of an Evolutionary Algorithm (EA) to provide efficient solutions
typically depends on the specific type of problem. In order to obtain
the most efficient search, it is often needed to incorporate any available
knowledge (both at algorithmic and domain level) into the EA. In this
work, we develop an ontology to formally represent knowledge in EAs.
Our approach makes use of knowledge in the EC literature, and can be
used for suggesting efficient strategies for solving problems by means of
EC. We call our ontology "Evolutionary Computation Ontology" (ECO).
In this contribution, we show one possible use of it, i.e. to establish a link
between algorithm settings and problem types. We also show that the
ECO can be used as an alternative to the available parameter selection
methods and as a supporting tool for algorithmic design.

Keywords: Ontology · Knowledge representation · Evolutionary computation

1 Introduction

Ontologies are a type of formal knowledge representation that make it possible to
represent kinds of knowledge for different applications [1]. Ontologies structure
data as a network of objects and their relations. These objects refer to entities
and events (also known as concepts) in the real world, and their relations represent the semantic relations between entities. Thus, ontologies can be represented
as a graph structure similar to semantic networks [2].

© Springer International Publishing AG 2017
G. Squillero and K. Sim (Eds.): EvoApplications 2017, Part I, LNCS 10199, pp. 603–619, 2017.
DOI: 10.1007/978-3-319-55849-3_39

Ontologies have been used successfully in a number of applications, such as knowledge modeling [3] and decision support for medical diagnosis [4]. A comprehensive survey of such application was performed by [5]. The goal of building an ontology depends normally on its use: for instance, in Evolutionary Computation (EC), ontologies can be used to represent knowledge about the evolutionary operators and their parameters, as well as the problem features and their fitness landscapes. Knowledge plays a key role in various aspects of EC including encoding, population initialization, evolutionary operators [6]. For instance, individual representations facilitate implicit knowledge, while population initialization, fitness evaluation, and evolutionary operators facilitate explicit knowledge incorporation [7]. Knowledge incorporation is in turn beneficial for an efficient search, by balancing the trade-off between exploration and exploitation. In the literature there are a number of works where knowledge incorporation has been used, for instance in the design of evolutionary operators [7], in the selection of the algorithm parameters [8] and in the selection process in Interactive Evolutionary Computation (IEC) [9].

In this work, we present the "Evolutionary Computation Ontology" (ECO), an ontology that is primarily designed to include available knowledge in EC and problem domains, and to establish a link between algorithmic and domain knowledge; in this sense, it can provide the background for reasoning methods such as case-based and analogical reasoning. As we will see in Sect. 3, some motivating use cases for the ECO are operator and parameter selection, human-made selection in IEC, user guidance in EC software tools [10], and teaching and self-learning of EC-related topics [11].

As a proof-of-concept, we show how the ECO can be used for instance to define efficient strategies (i.e., algorithm settings, see Table 2 in Sect. 4 for a complete definition) based on the type of the problem. In particular, we focus on the strategies for *parameter selection*. First, we make use of the existing literature in EC to collect these strategies. However, since most of the proposed strategies are defined as vague rules that rarely are applicable off-the-shelf, we perform an empirical analysis to specify such rules in concrete terms. We then populate our ontology with concrete rules to be used for parameter selection. We describe the development process of our ontology in Sect. 4, and perform experiments to demonstrate the performance of the ECO. We then present our experimental results in Sect. 5. In these experiments, we used the ontology to extract rules established on benchmark functions, and compared the results of an evolutionary algorithm based on such rules, with the performance of a control algorithm whose parameters are chosen arbitrarily. Finally, we discuss our concluding remarks and the future work in Sect. 6.

2   Background

The term "ontology" is used in computer science to describe a type of knowledge representation that explicitly defines what exists in a domain. Ontologies represent knowledge by defining concepts, their properties and relations, and the individuals [12]. The properties of concepts describe their features; and, the relations define how concepts semantically relate to one another. These components are essential for representing knowledge. For example, taxonomic relations are one of the fundamental relations, as they establish the concept class hierarchy using "is-a" relation. The individuals are instances of the concept classes.

A general guideline of the practical steps for developing an ontology is provided by Noy et al. [13]. An initial step for developing ontologies is to identify the domain and scope of the ontology. It is impossible to represent everything; therefore, it is required to define its scope [14]. Thereafter, the concepts in the domain are identified and hierarchically structured. Next, the properties of the concepts and the relations between them are defined. In the final step, individuals are added to the ontology.

To guarantee the interoperability across different ontologies from different domains, a number of standardized formal representation languages have been proposed for developing ontologies. These include the Resource Description Framework (RDF) [15], a framework for structuring the data as an easy-to-process graph and the Web Ontology Language (OWL) [16], an ontology development language endorsed by World Wide Web Consortium (W3C) [17]. Once ontologies are developed, the knowledge can then be retrieved by query languages such as the SPARQL Protocol or the RDF Query Language (SPARQL), a standard query language for querying RDF structured data [18].

3   Motivating Use Cases

In this section, we motivate knowledge incorporation into Evolutionary Computation by discussing some possible use cases and applications.

3.1   Operator and Parameter Selection

The knowledge involved into the evolutionary operator and parameter selection plays a key role for balancing the trade-off between the exploration and exploitation processes, a fundamental aspect for an efficient search [19]. In addition, the availability of any additional knowledge about the problem domain offers a great source of information for suggesting efficient strategies for evolutionary search. There are several approaches listed in Table 1 that can be used for selecting the evolutionary operators and adjusting their parameters.

The approaches listed in (1)–(8) are outlined by Črepinšek et al. [19]. We included an additional approach (9). Ontologies can be designed to include the knowledge involved in the approaches (2), (4), (5), (6) and (9). The ECO is designed to include the knowledge involved in (2) and (5), but it is also applicable to the approaches (4) and (9). It is applicable to (4) (also known as case-based reasoning [20]) because it establishes the links between (2) and (5), and makes it possible to reuse these links on similar problems; it is also applicable to (9) because it allows the structural mappings between different knowledge representations from different domains. Although there has been extensive research in

Table 1. Approaches to evolutionary operator/parameter selection (adapted from [19])

#	Approach
(1)	Trial and error
(2)	Following guidelines from the literature [21,22]
(3)	Parameter-less EA [23]
(4)	Using experience from previous similar problems [24]
(5)	Identifying fitness landscape's features to propose suitable parameters [25,26]
(6)	Analyzing the parameters and their effects statistically [27]
(7)	Mathematical modeling
(8)	Optimizing the parameters algorithmically [28,29]
(9)	Adapting solutions to the problems from different domains

the literature focused on evolutionary operators and parameters, to the best of our knowledge (as also demonstrated by [19]) there is no application that makes direct use of such knowledge in the approaches given in (4) and (9). Our work here aims at collecting (part of) this knowledge accumulated over many decades of EC literature, and make it available —in a structured and consistent way— for future developments in Evolutionary Computing.

We hypothesize that it is beneficial to use the existing knowledge in the ECO, i.e. that similar strategies can solve similar problems. Under this assumption, transferring the algorithm settings obtained from past problems to new problems should produce an advantage in terms of optimization. In this scenario, the ontology can be populated with example problems (representing different problem types: unimodal vs multimodal, separable vs non-separable, etc.) and their landscape properties can be described by using the concepts in the ECO. Using the links between the concepts related to problem types and strategies present in the ontology, specific strategies that apply to specific problem types can then be identified.

By leveraging the ECO, all this existent knowledge can be collected and used automatically for selecting the most efficient strategies for a problem. Using the knowledge included in the ECO, the following example questions can be answered (the definitions of the concepts mentioned in the example questions can be found in Table 2, see Sect. 4):

- What is the best strategy for unimodal functions?
- What are the operators and their parameters that cause low exploration?
- Which crossover operator is the best for mutimodal functions when the evolutionary process is in is "maturation" phase?

3.2 Human-Made Selection in Interactive Evolutionary Computation

Another example task that involves knowledge is in Interactive Evolutionary Computation, where experts and users can involve directly into the evolutionary process to select the individuals they find interesting, in order to pass their genes to the next generation [9]. However, this process is often extremely time-consuming and requires a significant effort to perform the individual selection manually. Also, it is often impossible to monitor all individuals for thousands of generations, especially if the population is large. The ECO can provide support for improving the speed of IEC processes, thus reducing the effort spent by users. For instance, the knowledge of how selection is performed by humans can be represented in the ECO, and used automatically in the selection process to find similar individuals that satisfy the user's interests or preferences.

3.3 Guidance in Software Tools Based on Evolutionary Computation

Evolutionary algorithms are now widely available in several optimization software packages [10,30,31]. In general, it is straightforward to apply evolutionary algorithms to custom problems using these tools. However, it is not always so easy to adjust their settings if the user does not have any expertise in the EC field. As we discussed in Sect. 3.1, parameter selection requires extensive expertise regarding what concerns the algorithm configuration, the problem type, and the strategies that should be applied. Therefore in many cases it can be useful that these software tools are able to provide some guidance to users from different expertise domains.

In this sense, the ECO defines the knowledge required for supporting smart human computer interaction. Explicit relations between the concepts in the evolutionary algorithms, the problem types and the strategies can make the expert knowledge available in the software packages making use of evolutionary algorithms. For instance, the ECO can be used to recommend a suitable algorithm, as well as its operator and parameter configuration, based on the problem that is introduced by a user. The ECO is a good candidate for providing this support in software.

3.4 Teaching and Self-learning

Ontologies are well suited also for introducing new topics to students. In the literature, an example use of the ontologies for education in EAs was demonstrated by Kaur and Chaudhary [11], who included useful knowledge about the background and history in evolutionary algorithms into their ontology. It should be noted, however, that the main difference between the ontology proposed in [11] and that one proposed in this work is: while the ECO proposed by Kaur and Chaudhary is only limited to historic knowledge and education purposes, whereas, our ECO extends that knowledge, and includes efficient strategies and problem types which is used for parameter selection problem. As such, our ECO is dynamically updatable, and extensible that support a lifetime learning and knowledge-based optimization.

4   Evolutionary Computation Ontology

The development process of the ECO involves the steps elaborated in Sect. 2. In this work, we focus on representing the knowledge for problem solving making use of the literature in EC. To structure the knowledge formalized in the ECO, we manually parsed 50 of the most cited research papers in the field. We then identified the relevant concepts, as shown in Table 2, and we extracted concrete strategy instances to populate the ontology.

There are different "knowledge categories" in ECO that describe the concepts in Evolutionary Computation. These are broadly categorized under: *evolutionary algorithms*, *evolutionary processes*, *problem types*, *search properties*, and *strategies*.

Evolutionary Algorithms. One of the earliest taxonomies of evolutionary algorithms is provided by Bäck and Schwefel [34]. We limit our ontology to the algorithms provided in their overview, with the addition of genetic programming. Thus, the domain knowledge covered in this area describes four main classes of evolutionary algorithms, namely, Genetic Algorithms (GA), Genetic Programming (GP), Evolutionary Programming (EP) and Evolutionary Strategies (ES). Each class of algorithms originates from a different research line, and has different characteristics. The properties of these classes define the algorithmic characteristics (i.e. data structure, population parameters, evolutionary operators), which

Table 2. Some example concepts represented in the ECO, and their definitions

Concept	Definition
Modality	A feature of a fitness landscape representing the no. of optima [32]
Maturation phase	One of the four phases of an evolutionary run: initial, sub-maturation, maturation and convergence [33]
Strategy	Algorithm settings that can be applied to an evolutionary algorithm for solving a problem. The settings of an algorithm define the data structure, the evolutionary operators and their parameters, the selection operator, the population size and the initialization methods
Percentage of performed evaluations	The number of evaluations performed at any point of an evolutionary run, divided by the total number of evaluations allotted to the EA
Exploration	A property of a search process that aims to visit as many search space regions as possible

are in turn included in concept classes. The concepts of the evolutionary operators and parameters are represented as algorithm-independent and therefore can be manipulated and plugged into any suitable evolutionary algorithm.

Evolutionary Processes. This knowledge area includes the properties related to the runtime of the evolutionary processes. Percentage of performed evaluations, convergence rate, average, minimum and maximum fitness values are some of the properties that describe an evolutionary run. These properties are univocally determined, except the convergence rate [35] which can be used e.g. for defining the phases of an evolutionary run. For example, Zhang et al. [33] measures the convergence rate by finding the relative sizes of the clusters (subpopulations) that include the worst and the best individual. In their work, they used this rate to identify the phases of an evolutionary process which they divided into *initial, sub-maturation, maturation* and *convergence*. We find it appropriate to include these concepts into our ontology, although the methods that define the convergence rate and the evolutionary phases are not restricted to these examples. For instance, the evolutionary phases can also be split based on the percentage of performed evaluations.

Problem Types. We define here the concepts linked to the fitness landscapes properties. We include the following types of functions: unimodal, multimodal, separable, non-separable, symmetric and non-symmetric [32]. An instance of a problem can be linked to one or more of these types.

Search Properties. This category includes two main concepts, namely "Exploration" and "Exploitation". Such concepts define special properties of the search where exploration refers to the process of visiting areas of the search space that have not been visited before; exploitation defines the process of visiting neighboring solutions to those that have been visited during an evolutionary run. There is a well-established knowledge in the correlation between the problem types and the suggested amount of computational budget dedicated to each of the two search regimes. These suggestions often are coupled with an evolutionary phase that they apply to, or to the specific problem type (see the example strategies defined below).

Strategies. Finally, we define the *strategies* to establish a link between the operator/parameter settings of evolutionary algorithms and the problem types they apply to. The strategies suggested in the literature are usually conditional on some of the runtime properties. Therefore, we include the conditions that can be defined to trigger a strategy. These conditions can be based e.g. on percentage of performed evaluations, convergence rate, and/or population diversity.

To populate our ontology, we extracted strategies that are suggested in the literature. Some of these strategies are presented in Table 3. There are various levels of specificity in these statements. For example, the strategies given in (1)

Table 3. Example strategies (with references)

#	Strategy
(1)	For unimodal functions, the mutation rate is constant and there is an optimal value which is $1/l$ where l is the string length. This value is quite low because there is no need to invest more into exploration [22,36]
(2)	"For deceptive trap functions of order k, the best mutation rate is k/l" [22,36]
(3)	"If only local variation operators are used, e.g., mutation flipping only a single bit, it is easy to see that then sub-functions in a separable function are optimized independently and in parallel" [37]
(4)	"High mutation rate can help within the first phase of the evolution, but it becomes useless when we get close to the best solution" [22,36]
(5)	"[...] in the early stages a larger population is needed than in the later stages, when fine tuning of sub-optimal solutions is done."[19]
(6)	Selection can mainly be used for exploitation. Adjusting the selection pressure in the selection operator changes the level of exploitation. The selection operators can be ranked by increasing selection pressure: proportional selection, linear ranking, tournament selection, and (μ, λ)- and $(\mu + \lambda)$-selection [19,38]

and (2) are quite specific as they suggest certain mutation rates that should be used for unimodal and deceptive functions; however, the strategies given in (4) and (5) are open to different interpretations, since they use categorical terms like "high" and "large" while their definitions are not explicit. For instance the statement given in (4) suggests starting with a "high" mutation rate in the beginning and decreasing it in later stages of the evolutionary process. It is also important to note that the concept of "high" mutation rate can be dependent on the problem (e.g. number of dimensions), as well as the other parameter settings (e.g. population size, crossover, etc.).

To translate these statements to readily applicable strategies in our ontology, we then performed a systematic set of preliminary experiments, and assessed the ranges of the categorical concepts to use. For illustration purposes, we picked a unimodal and a multimodal function, namely the Sphere and the Rastrigin's functions (F_1 and F_9 in [39]), in $D = 10$ dimensions, to observe examples of performance obtained with different parameter settings on different kinds of functions. Following an experimental setting similar to that performed in [40], we consider population sizes $n \in \{10, 30, 50, 100, 200\}$, Gaussian mutation with mutation rates $p_m \in \{0.0005, 0.001, 0.002, 0.005, 0.01, 0.02, 0.05, 0.1, 0.2, 0.5\}$, elite counts $e \in \{0, 1\}$, selection operator fixed as "roulette selection", and crossover rate fixed at 0.8. With these experimental settings, we aim to establish concrete, optimal ranges for the concepts { "high", "medium", "low"}.

The Supporting Information **SI.1**[1] presents the results we obtained on the Sphere and Rastrigin's functions using different mutation rates, population sizes and elite counts. All the experiments were implemented in Matlab, using the

---

[1] Available online at: http://www.goo.gl/xSgVvv.

Genetic Algorithm Toolbox [31]. Tables (a), (b), (c), and (d) present results for the Sphere function with elite count 0, the Rastrigin's function with elite count 0, the Sphere function with elite count 1 and the Rastrigin's function with elite count 1, respectively. The columns and the rows of the tables are organized w.r.t. mutation rates population sizes in ascending order. We follow the evaluation criteria presented in [39]. We set the maximum number of evaluations to $D \times 10^4$, and record the fitness of the best individual for the checkpoints at 1st, 10^3th, 10^4th and 10^5th generations. We run an evolutionary algorithm 25 times for each specified parameter settings for the two selected functions, and found the average best fitness values for each checkpoint.

We defined the concept "EvolutionaryProcessPhases" based on these checkpoints. We then refer to the evolutionary process between the checkpoints 1st and 10^3th, 10^3th and 10^4th, 10^4th and 10^5th as "Initial", "Maturation", and "Convergence" respectively. Our aim is to identify how a parameter set performs within each evolutionary phase. Therefore, we find the difference between the average fitness values at the start and the end point of each phase, and divide this delta by the number of evaluations performed in each phase. In other words, this value indicates the average change of fitness per evaluation observed within a phase.

With reference to **SI.1**, the color (gray in print) intensity level in each cell indicates the magnitude of the average fitness difference observed in each phase (scaled across the values within each row). With elite count 0, some parameter settings produced negative fitness differences, which we represented as zeros for the sake of illustration.

For the Sphere function with elite count 0 and pop. sizes $\{10, 30, 50, 100, 200\}$, mutation rates $\{0.2, 0.1, 0.2, 0.2, 0.1\}$ perform better in phase 1, respectively. However, when a larger population size is used, the difference in the performance obtained with a high mutation rate gradually decreases. The comparisons between phases 1 and 2, and between phases 2 and 3, reveal that in further phases lower mutation rates generally perform better. Moreover, we observe a clear pattern within phases 2 and 3, which indicates that for larger population sizes lower mutation rates perform better. The behavioral pattern of the algorithm persists on the Sphere function using an elite count 1. On the other hand, the range of better performing mutation rates shift to the left to cover the lower values, and the performance differences among different mutation rates for each row becomes more distinct and sharp relative to table (a). If we fix the mutation rate and we compare the preferred population sizes across different phases, we observe that in the later stages smaller population sizes perform better in general.

For the Rastrigin's function, we observe similar patterns observed for the Sphere function in phase 1, for both elite counts 0 and 1. Also in this case, in the initial phase of the evolutionary process higher mutation rates are preferable. The pattern observed on the population sizes (i.e., lower population sizes are better for later stages of the evolutionary process) also persists. Moreover, we observe the trade-off between the population sizes and mutation rates specifically in table (d) where higher mutation rates work best with lower population sizes, and lower mutation rates work best with higher population sizes. These observations support

Table 4. Optimal parameters (population size and mutation rate) defined using categorical concepts for different phases and elite count 0

		Sphere function	Rastirigin's function
	Pop.Size	Mutation rate	Mutation rate
Phase 1	Small	High	–
	Medium	Medium-High	Medium
	Large	Low-Medium-High	Low-Medium
Phase 2	Small	Medium	Low-Medium
	Medium	Low-Medium	Medium
	Large	Low	Medium-High
Phase 3	Small	Medium	Low-Medium
	Medium	Low	Low-Medium
	Large	Low	Medium-High

the literature on shrinking the mutation rate [7] and population size [41, 42] during an evolutionary run and comply with the suggestions presented in Table 3.

Based on these initial experiments, we then define population sizes {"Small", "Medium", "Large"} as {10, 50, 200}, and mutation rates {"Low", "Low-Medium", "Medium","Medium-High","High"} as {[0.001, 0.002), [0.002, 0.01), [0.01, 0.05), [0.05, 0.2), [0.2, 0.5]}, respectively. We map the optimal population sizes and mutation rates to their categories for each function and elite count using the experimental results given in **SI.1**. As an example, we illustrate the mapping results in Table 4 for elite count 0. On the Rastrigin's function, none of the mutation rates produced a fitness improvement for small population size; this is shown as a "–" in the table.

Finally, we populate our ontology with the rules summarized in Table 4 associated to the function types (e.g. unimodal, multimodal, etc.) represented by the two chosen benchmark functions. For example, for unimodal functions with "Small" population size our ontology would suggests starting with "High" mutation rate in phase 1, and modifying it to "Medium" in phase 2 and 3. The suggested strategies are retrieved from the ontology using the SPARQL query language. Questions such as *"What is the mutation rate for unimodal functions when the evolutionary process is in maturation phase?"* are converted into a SPARQL query (see Query 1.1). The query returns the list of mutation rates that are stored in the ontology.

```
SELECT ?MutationRate
WHERE {
  ?strategy initializes ?MutationRate.
  ?strategy suggestedFor UnimodalFunction.
  ?strategy conditionedOn MaturationPhase
}
```

Query 1.1. An example SPARQL query

For the sake of completeness, we provide a detailed scheme of our ontology and a partial illustration of the ECO as Supporting Information **SI.2** and **SI.3**[2].

5   Experimental Validation

In this section, we use the strategies in the ECO in a parameter selection example to demonstrate the advantage of incorporating knowledge into the EA. We select three test functions that were not used in the experiments performed for populating the strategy instances represented in the ECO. These functions are the Schwefel's, Rosenbrock's, and Ackley's functions (F_2, F_6 and F_8 in [39]). The Schwefel's function is unimodal while the Rosenbrock's and Ackley's functions are multimodal. Thus, we test the strategies we derived and represented for unimodal and multimodal functions correspondingly. A list of tested strategies is given in Table 5. The strategies labeled as (1), (2) and (3) were retrieved from the ECO, with strategy (1) suggested for unimodal functions and strategies (2) and (3) suggested for multimodal functions. The rest of the strategies {(4), (5), (6)} are used as control strategies, selected arbitrarily as if no prior knowledge existed on the function types.

The numerical results are summarized in Table 6. Each column in the table shows the performance of a selected strategy on a selected test function. Strategies are labeled as in Table 5. For testing, we used elite count 1 for all the selected functions. We only compared the strategies that are retrieved from the ECO with the ones that are defined arbitrarily, i.e. we did not compare the performance of all strategies across different functions. As for the mutation rates, we considered the lowest value of the categories defined above. The rows labeled as 1, 1e+03, 1e+04 and 1e+05 indicate the generations (checkpoints) when we record the best fitness value. We present the results of 1st, 7th, 13th and 25th best fitness values, and the mean and standard deviations for 25 separate evolutionary runs using the same strategy. In the table, for each function and phase the boldface indicates the strategy showing the best performance (on average, across 25 runs).

Table 5. Selected strategies for testing

Phase	Strategy (1)		Strategy (2)		Strategy (3)	
	Pop.Size	Mut.Rate	Pop.Size	Mut.Rate	Pop.Size	Mut.Rate
1	Medium	Medium-High	Medium	Medium-High	Large	Medium
2	Medium	Low	Medium	Medium	Medium	Medium
3	Medium	Low	Medium	Medium	Small	Medium
Phase	Strategy (4)		Strategy (5)		Strategy (6)	
	Pop.Size	Mut.Rate	Pop.Size	Mut.Rate	Pop.Size	Mut.Rate
1	Medium	Medium-High	Medium	Medium	Medium	Medium
2	Medium	Medium-High	Medium	Medium	Medium	Low
3	Medium	Medium-High	Medium	Medium	Medium	Low

---

[2] Available online at: http://www.goo.gl/xSgVvv.

Table 6. The performance of different strategies

Function	Strategy	F2	F2	F2	F2	F6	F6	F6	F6	F6	F8	F8	F8	F8	F8
		1	4	5	6	2	3	4	5	6	2	3	4	5	6
1	1st	7.88E+03	8.68E+03	6.66E+03	6.81E+03	9.35E+02	7.50E+02	5.71E+02	4.83E+02	5.89E+02	7.89E+02	6.80E+03	6.02E+03	9.38E+03	9.08E+03
	7th	1.00E+04	1.18E+04	1.03E+04	1.28E+04	1.35E+04	9.79E+02	1.15E+03	1.21E+03	1.18E+03	1.24E+04	1.03E+04	1.21E+04	1.26E+04	1.32E+04
	13th	1.30E+04	1.34E+04	1.43E+04	1.42E+04	1.62E+04	1.15E+03	1.34E+03	1.39E+03	1.47E+03	1.49E+04	1.12E+04	1.39E+04	1.44E+04	1.47E+04
	25th	1.98E+04	1.77E+04	2.09E+04	1.86E+04	1.96E+04	1.52E+03	2.18E+03	2.02E+03	2.05E+03	2.07E+04	1.44E+04	1.97E+04	2.01E+04	2.04E+04
	Mean	1.32E+04	1.34E+04	1.38E+04	1.40E+04	1.55E+04	1.14E+03	1.42E+03	1.40E+03	1.43E+03	1.43E+04	1.10E+04	1.34E+04	1.50E+04	1.46E+04
	Std.	3.41E+03	2.39E+04	4.16E+03	2.82E+03	2.64E+02	2.20E+02	4.23E+02	3.41E+02	3.53E+02	3.42E+02	1.91E+03	3.26E+03	3.02E+03	3.11E+03
1E3	1st	2.08E-02	7.08E-02	7.38E-03	4.27E-03	3.18E+00	6.62E-03	8.17E-02	1.49E-02	2.13E-02	1.02E+01	2.50E+00	3.53E+01	8.91E+00	8.45E+00
	7th	7.12E-02	1.87E-01	2.06E-02	2.14E-02	4.36E-01	1.21E-02	1.30E-01	3.22E-02	3.31E-02	1.85E+01	8.15E+01	7.16E+01	8.74E+02	9.41E+00
	13th	1.08E-01	3.41E-01	2.56E-01	1.48E-01	9.14E+00	1.59E-02	1.59E-01	5.39E-01	4.21E-02	3.49E+01	1.33E+02	1.31E+02	3.16E+02	1.13E+02
	25th	2.81E-01	7.71E-01	2.18E+03	1.89E+03	2.11E+01	3.07E-02	3.93E-01	1.62E+01	1.21E+01	6.17E+03	8.17E+03	8.07E+03	9.06E+05	9.22E+03
	Mean	**1.17E-01**	3.68E-01	2.94E+02	2.26E+02	1.18E+01	**1.76E-02**	1.80E-01	4.69E+00	5.30E-01	**9.06E+02**	1.11E+03	9.39E+02	9.96E+04	2.05E+04
	Std.	6.02E-02	2.06E-01	5.91E+02	4.81E+02	7.61E+00	7.19E-03	7.17E-02	6.00E+00	2.41E+00	1.56E+03	2.17E+03	1.91E+03	2.41E+05	3.29E+03
1E4	1st	1.17E-07	1.14E-03	1.57E-05	3.04E-07	1.50E-01	4.60E-04	5.59E-03	5.04E-04	6.18E-05	1.57E-02	3.02E-02	5.26E+00	4.85E+00	7.05E-02
	7th	3.62E-07	3.34E-03	4.36E-05	5.11E-07	2.81E-01	8.74E-04	9.20E-03	1.06E-03	1.17E-04	4.61E+00	5.88E+00	7.13E+00	5.65E+00	1.76E-01
	13th	5.56E-07	5.24E-03	5.90E-05	7.63E-07	4.83E-01	1.21E-03	1.34E-02	1.39E-03	1.76E-04	5.37E+00	3.50E+01	1.06E+01	6.22E+01	8.41E-01
	25th	4.24E-06	2.01E-02	2.54E-04	6.34E-05	2.11E+00	2.24E-03	2.57E-02	2.48E-03	1.02E+01	2.60E+01	9.23E+02	1.20E+02	1.01E+02	7.03E+03
	Mean	**8.05E-07**	5.64E-03	8.25E-05	4.38E-06	6.86E+00	**1.23E-03**	1.37E-02	1.45E-03	4.08E-01	**5.70E+00**	1.55E+02	2.63E+01	1.74E+02	1.15E+03
	Std.	8.23E-07	3.74E-03	5.87E-05	1.29E-05	9.67E+00	4.58E-04	5.14E-04	5.14E-04	2.04E+00	4.78E+00	2.54E+02	3.44E+01	3.20E+02	2.43E+03
1E5	1st	3.68E-09	1.37E-05	1.53E-07	3.03E-09	1.68E-01	3.04E-04	5.80E-04	7.18E-05	6.61E-06	1.41E-02	1.26E-02	7.99E-01	1.30E+00	3.69E-03
	7th	8.47E-09	3.06E-05	4.19E-05	7.34E-09	2.91E-01	4.38E-04	1.04E-03	8.82E-05	1.16E-05	2.97E+00	3.94E+00	3.62E+00	3.74E+00	5.65E-03
	13th	9.52E-09	7.01E-05	6.53E-07	9.14E-09	3.65E-01	5.95E-04	1.31E-03	1.18E-04	1.55E-05	3.34E+00	4.48E+00	6.67E+00	4.01E+00	8.74E-03
	25th	2.56E-08	2.05E-04	2.05E-06	2.82E-08	2.13E+01	1.26E-03	2.96E-03	2.09E-04	1.02E+01	6.62E+00	2.46E+02	8.52E+02	5.25E+01	2.80E+02
	Mean	1.01E-08	7.64E-05	8.07E-07	**9.49E-09**	6.14E+00	6.53E-04	1.36E-03	1.25E-04	4.08E-01	**3.14E+00**	2.65E+01	1.39E+01	8.67E+00	1.73E+01
	Std.	4.30E-09	5.09E-05	5.01E-07	4.98E-09	9.49E+00	2.74E-04	4.87E-04	4.07E-05	2.04E+00	1.38E+00	5.03E+01	2.09E+01	1.33E+02	5.76E+01

We omit the boldface for the 1st evaluation, due to the random initialization of the evolutionary algorithm.

The first four columns show the result on the unimodal function (Schwefel's function [39]). On average, the strategy suggested by the ECO performs better than the arbitrarily selected strategies labeled as (4), (5) and (6) in the first two phases. In the last phase, the strategy (6) performs better than the strategy (1), on average. However, this fact may be ignored since two of these strategies implement the same mutation rate for the final phase. We should note that the strategy (4) is often recommended by the literature (see (1) in Table 3); however, in our experiments we observe that the strategy (1) performs better than the strategy (4) (see (4) in Table 3).

As for for multimodal functions, the ECO suggests the strategies labeled as (2) and (3). Therefore, we tested the strategies (2) and (3) on F_6 and F_8. On F_6, the strategy (3) shows the best performance. The empirical results point out that for multimodal functions, population reduction in further phases of the evolutionary process is a good strategy. However, it is interesting to see the contradiction where the strategy (5) performs better than the strategy (3). When we take a closer look, the strategy (3) performs better than (5) in phase 1 and 2. On the other hand, the results show that during the last phase a small population size caused the strategy (3) to slow down in terms of fitness improvement; whereas, a medium population size caused (5) to catch up. This suggests that in the last phase of strategy (3), a slightly higher population size might be preferable (e.g. as a last attempt to introduce diversity). Finally, from the comparison among the strategies evaluated on F_8 we can observe that the strategy (2) performs significantly better in all three phases.

6   Conclusions

In this work, we presented the ECO, an ontology designed to represent domain and algorithmic knowledge in evolutionary algorithms. As such, the ECO includes concepts relevant to evolutionary algorithms, problem domains and strategies. The strategies are defined as general guidelines in EC that were extracted from the literature. To populate the ontology, we collected the knowledge available in fifty research papers from the specialized EC-related literature. We then described some possible uses of the ontology in parameter selection, Interactive Evolutionary Computation, software design and education. We finally demonstrated numerically the performance of an evolutionary algorithm with parameters driven by the ECO on three different functions. Our results show that the incorporation of knowledge (coming from different sources, i.e. literature and/or empirical experiments) into evolutionary algorithms can improve their performance consistently. Furthermore, the use of a common ontology guarantees a systematic way of collecting, representing and sharing this knowledge among researchers, among algorithms, and across different application domains.

The main limitation of the ECO is the uncertainty that characterizes knowledge in EC. While parsing the literature, we noted that most of the strategy statements that we found use non-specific wordings such as "high mutation rate facilitates more exploration". Clearly, the exact parameter values that should be used are not defined. Here, to define the range of these values in the ECO, we performed preliminary experiments on a unimodal (Sphere) and a multimodal (Rastrigin) function and we observed, for instance, that some mutation rates are expected to perform better depending on the population size, and vice versa. In this work, we assigned a crisp value for each category based on the experimental data. However, in future works we aim to include representation methods that can deal with gradual ranges for categories, such as fuzzy logic [33]. Another source of uncertainty is due to the fact that multiple strategies (characterized by different combinations of operators and parameters) may be equally efficient in an optimization scenario. Currently, querying over the ECO yields a list of suitable strategies. These strategies are conditional on the type of problem and other properties of the evolutionary process, e.g. its phase. However, the list of suggested strategies should be aggregated to recommend one single strategy. This aggregation is *probabilistic* in nature, because in general it summarizes conflicting and vague strategies available in the knowledge base. Moreover, different strategies may have different levels of confidence, depending on how well they perform in specific settings. Future research will focus on specific methods for providing aggregated probabilistic results into our query processing.

Another limitation of the present work obviously consists in the limited set of unimodal and multimodal functions we used for testing. However, these limited experiments were shown here as a simple proof-of-concept. In order to derive statistically rigorous conclusions and generalize the experimental results, so to transfer these generalizations to a broader set of optimization functions, we will need to perform more experiments on a much larger set of benchmark functions.

In future works, we also aim to extend our strategies to cover different kinds of evolutionary operators and different evolutionary algorithms. We believe that a similar experimental analysis would improve our current understanding of the effects of different evolutionary operators and parameter settings.

 Acknowledgments. This project has received funding from the European Union's Horizon 2020 research and innovation programme under grant agreement No 665347.

References

1. Gruber, T.R.: A translation approach to portable ontology specifications. Knowl. Acquis. **5**(2), 199–220 (1993)
2. Sowa, J.F.: Principles of Semantic Networks: Explorations in the Representation of Knowledge. Morgan Kaufmann, San Mateo (2014)
3. Studer, R., Benjamins, V.R., Fensel, D.: Knowledge engineering: principles and methods. Data Knowl. Eng. **25**(1), 161–197 (1998)
4. Riaño, D., Real, F., López-Vallverdú, J.A., Campana, F., Ercolani, S., Mecocci, P., Annicchiarico, R., Caltagirone, C.: An ontology-based personalization of health-care knowledge to support clinical decisions for chronically ill patients. J. Biomed. Inf. **45**(3), 429–446 (2012)

5. Liao, S.H.: Expert system methodologies and applications-a decade review from 1995 to 2004. Expert Syst. Appl. **28**(1), 93–103 (2005)
6. Jin, Y.: Knowledge Incorporation in Evolutionary Computation, vol. 167. Springer, Heidelberg (2013)
7. Bonissone, P.P., Subbu, R., Eklund, N., Kiehl, T.R.: Evolutionary algorithms + domain knowledge = real-world evolutionary computation. IEEE Trans. Evol. Comput. **10**(3), 256–280 (2006)
8. Eiben, A.E., Hinterding, R., Michalewicz, Z.: Parameter control in evolutionary algorithms. IEEE Trans. Evol. Comput. **3**(2), 124–141 (1999)
9. Takagi, H.: Interactive evolutionary computation: fusion of the capabilities of EC optimization and human evaluation. Proc. IEEE **89**(9), 1275–1296 (2001)
10. Wagner, S., Kronberger, G., Beham, A., Kommenda, M., Scheibenpflug, A., Pitzer, E., Vonolfen, S., Kofler, M., Winkler, S., Dorfer, V., Affenzeller, M.: Architecture and design of the heuristiclab optimization environment. In: Klempous, R., Nikodem, J., Jacak, W., Chaczko, Z. (eds.) Advanced Methods and Applications in Computational Intelligence, vol. 6, pp. 197–261. Springer International Publishing, Heidelberg (2014)
11. Kaur, G., Chaudhary, D.: Evolutionary computation ontology: e-learning system. In: 2015 4th International Conference on Reliability, Infocom Technologies and Optimization (ICRITO) (Trends and Future Directions), pp. 1–6, September 2015
12. Roussey, C., Pinet, F., Kang, M.A., Corcho, O.: An introduction to ontologies and ontology engineering. In: Falquet, G., Métral, C., Teller, J., Tweed, C. (eds.) Ontologies in Urban Development Projects, vol. 1, pp. 9–38. Springer, London (2011)
13. Noy, N.F., McGuinness, D.L., et al.: Ontology development 101: a guide to creating your first ontology (2001)
14. Davis, R., Shrobe, H., Szolovits, P.: What is a knowledge representation? AI Mag. **14**(1), 17 (1993)
15. Pan, J.Z.: Resource description framework. In: Staab, S., Studer, R. (eds.) Handbook on Ontologies, pp. 71–90. Springer, Heidelberg (2009)
16. McGuinness, D.L., Van Harmelen, F., et al.: OWL web ontology language overview. W3C recommendation **10**(10) (2004)
17. The World Wide Web Consortium (W3C) (2016). Accessed 14 Aug 2016. https://www.w3.org/
18. Quilitz, B., Leser, U.: Querying distributed RDF data sources with SPARQL. In: Bechhofer, S., Hauswirth, M., Hoffmann, J., Koubarakis, M. (eds.) ESWC 2008. LNCS, vol. 5021, pp. 524–538. Springer, Heidelberg (2008). doi:10.1007/978-3-540-68234-9_39
19. Črepinšek, M., Liu, S.H., Mernik, M.: Exploration and exploitation in evolutionary algorithms: a survey. ACM Comput. Surv. **45**(3), 35:1–35:33 (2013)
20. Johnson, J., Louis, S.J.: Case-initialized genetic algorithms for knowledge extraction and incorporation. In: Jin, Y. (ed.) Knowledge Incorporation in Evolutionary Computation, pp. 57–79. Springer, Heidelberg (2005)
21. De Jong, K.A., Spears, W.M.: A formal analysis of the role of multi-point crossover in genetic algorithms. Ann. Math. Artif. Intell. **5**(1), 1–26 (1992)
22. Falco, I.D., Cioppa, A.D., Tarantino, E.: Mutation-based genetic algorithm: performance evaluation. Appl. Soft Comput. **1**(4), 285–299 (2002)

23. Bäck, T., Eiben, A.E., van der Vaart, N.A.L.: An empirical study on GAs "without parameters". In: Schoenauer, M., Deb, K., Rudolph, G., Yao, X., Lutton, E., Merelo, J.J., Schwefel, H.-P. (eds.) Proceedings of the 6th International Conference on Parallel Problem Solving from Nature (PPSN VI), London, UK, pp. 315–324. Springer-Verlag (2000). ISBN: 3-540-41056-2
24. Yeguas, E., Luzón, M., Pavón, R., Laza, R., Arroyo, G., Díaz, F.: Automatic parameter tuning for evolutionary algorithms using a bayesian case-based reasoning system. Appl. Soft Comput. **18**, 185–195 (2014)
25. Picek, S., Jakobovic, D.: From fitness landscape to crossover operator choice. In: Proceedings of the 2014 Annual Conference on Genetic and Evolutionary Computation, pp. 815–822. ACM (2014)
26. Asmus, J., Borchmann, D., Sbalzarini, I.F., Walther, D.: Towards an FCA-based recommender system for black-box optimization. In: Workshop Notes, p. 35 (2014)
27. Czarn, A., MacNish, C., Vijayan, K., Turlach, B., Gupta, R.: Statistical exploratory analysis of genetic algorithms. IEEE Trans. Evol. Comput. **8**(4), 405–421 (2004)
28. Eiben, A., Smit, S.: Parameter tuning for configuring and analyzing evolutionary algorithms. Swarm Evol. Comput. **1**(1), 19–31 (2011)
29. Neumüller, C., Wagner, S., Kronberger, G., Affenzeller, M.: Parameter meta-optimization of metaheuristic optimization algorithms. In: Moreno-Díaz, R., Pichler, F., Quesada-Arencibia, A. (eds.) EUROCAST 2011. LNCS, vol. 6927, pp. 367–374. Springer, Heidelberg (2012). doi:10.1007/978-3-642-27549-4_47
30. Inspyred: Bio-inspired Algorithms in Python (2016). Accessed 11 Nov 2016. http://pythonhosted.org/inspyred/
31. Matlab Genetic Algorithm Toolbox (2016). Accessed 11 Nov 2016. https://www.mathworks.com/help/gads/genetic-algorithm.html
32. Finck, S., Hansen, N., Ros, R., Auger, A.: Real-parameter black-box optimization benchmarking 2009: presentation of the noiseless functions. Technical report, Citeseer (2010)
33. Zhang, J., Chung, H.S., Lo, A.W., Hu, B.: Fuzzy knowledge incorporation in crossover and mutation. In: Jin, Y. (ed.) Knowledge Incorporation in Evolutionary Computation, vol. 167, pp. 123–143. Springer, Heidelberg (2005)
34. Bäck, T., Schwefel, H.P.: An overview of evolutionary algorithms for parameter optimization. Evol. Comput. **1**(1), 1–23 (1993)
35. He, J., Kang, L.: On the convergence rates of genetic algorithms. Theor. Comput. Sci. **229**(1), 23–39 (1999)
36. Mühlenbein, H.: How genetic algorithms really work: mutation and hillclimbing. PPSN **92**, 15–25 (1992)
37. Doerr, B., Sudholt, D., Witt, C.: When do evolutionary algorithms optimize separable functions in parallel?. In: Proceedings of the Twelfth Workshop on Foundations of Genetic Algorithms XII, FOGA XII 2013, pp. 51–64. ACM, New York (2013)
38. Back, T.: Selective pressure in evolutionary algorithms: a characterization of selection mechanisms. In: Proceedings of the First IEEE Conference on Evolutionary Computation, 1994, IEEE World Congress on Computational Intelligence, vol. 1, pp. 57–62, June 1994
39. Suganthan, P.N., Hansen, N., Liang, J.J., Deb, K., Chen, Y.P., Auger, A., Tiwari, S.: Problem definitions and evaluation criteria for the CEC 2006 special session on constrained real-parameter optimization. Technical Report, Nanyang Technological University, Singapore, AND KanGAL Report 2005005, IIT Kanpur, India, May 2005

40. Gates, G.H., Merkle, L.D., Lamont, G.B., Pachter, R.: Simple genetic algorithm parameter selection for protein structure prediction. In: IEEE International Conference on Evolutionary Computation, vol. 2, pp. 620–624. IEEE (1995)
41. Iacca, G., Mallipeddi, R., Mininno, E., Neri, F., Suganthan, P.N.: Super-fit and population size reduction in compact differential evolution. In: 2011 IEEE Workshop on Memetic Computing (MC), pp. 1–8. IEEE (2011)
42. Tanabe, R., Fukunaga, A.S.: Improving the search performance of shade using linear population size reduction. In: IEEE Congress on Evolutionary Computation (CEC), pp. 1658–1665. IEEE (2014)

A New Evolutionary Algorithm
for Synchronization

Jakub Kowalski[1([⊠])] and Adam Roman[2]

[1] Institute of Computer Science, University of Wrocław, Wrocław, Poland
jko@cs.uni.wroc.pl
[2] Institute of Computer Science, Jagiellonian University, Cracow, Poland
roman@ii.uj.edu.pl

Abstract. A synchronizing word brings all states of a finite automaton to the one particular state. From practical reasons the synchronizing words should be as short as possible. Unfortunately, the decision version of the problem is NP-complete. In this paper we present a new evolutionary approach for finding possibly short synchronizing words for a given automaton. As the optimization problem has two contradicting goals (the word's length and the word's rank) we use a 2 population feasible-infeasible approach. It is based on the knowledge on words' ranks of all prefixes of a given word. This knowledge makes the genetic operators more efficient than in case of the standard letter-based operators.

Keywords: Genetic algorithm · Automata synchronization · Knowledge-based evolution

1 Introduction

The synchronization problem is to find a word that brings all states of a finite automaton to the one, fixed state. Such word is called a synchronizing word and an automaton for which it exists is called synchronizing. In 1964 Černý [1] conjectured that for every synchronizing automaton with n states there exists a synchronizing word of length at most $(n-1)^2$. This conjecture remains open and it stimulated a huge research in the field of automata theory.

Synchronization is not only a theoretical problem, but has many practical applications. Some most important examples are:

- model-based testing of reactive systems, where we test conformance of a system under test with its model [2,3]
- biocomputing, where a computing process is modeled by a "soup of automata" built with DNA molecules and after the computations all automata need to be restarted to the initial state [4]

J. Kowalski—Supported in part by the National Science Centre, Poland under project number 2014/13/N/ST6/01817.
A. Roman—Supported in part by the National Science Centre, Poland under project number 2015/17/B/ST6/01893.

© Springer International Publishing AG 2017
G. Squillero and K. Sim (Eds.): EvoApplications 2017, Part I, LNCS 10199, pp. 620–635, 2017.
DOI: 10.1007/978-3-319-55849-3_40

– part orienting problem, where some parts of a defined shape arrive at manufacturing sites and they need to be sorted and oriented before assembly [5,6].

It is clear that for the practical reasons we need to find – for a given automaton – the shortest possible synchronizing word. Unfortunately, the decision version of this problem is NP-complete [5,7]. There exist some heuristic algorithms
to compute the synchronizing word ([5,8–10]), but they do not guarantee the
optimal solution. Of course, the algorithms that are able to return the shortest synchronizing word are exponential, thus not very practical (for example
[11–13]). Finally, there are some attempts that utilize artificial intelligence, like
simple genetic algorithm [14] in which chromosomes directly represent synchronizing words.

In this paper we continue the research on the artificial intelligence methods
for finding shortest possible synchronizing words. The evolutionary algorithm
we present in this paper realizes a good trade-off between the runtime and the
quality of results measured in terms of the length of a synchronizing word found.

Instead of the plain GA approach we used a more sophisticated algorithm, FI-
2POP [15], and found it better suited for the task of synchronization. Moreover,
we introduce domain-knowledge-based operators which significantly improve the
quality of synchronizing words produced.

The paper is organized as follows. In Sect. 2 we introduce the basic definitions
on automata and synchronization. We also present some ideas from [14] that
show how it is possible to represent the problem of finding a short reset word in
terms of a genetic algorithm machinery. In Sect. 3 we present our approach to the
synchronization problem. We give the details about the evolutionary algorithm
and its features constructed in a way to make the process of searching the space of
possible solutions efficient and effective. Section 4 is devoted to the experiments
and comparison of our approach with other known algorithms. Finally, Sect. 5
gives some conclusions and final remarks.

2 Automata Synchronization

2.1 Basic Notions and Definitions

A *finite automaton* is a triple (Q, Σ, δ), where Q is a finite, nonempty set of
states, Σ is a finite, nonempty set of input symbols (called an *alphabet*) and
$\delta : Q \times \Sigma \to Q$ is a *transition function*. By Σ^* we denote the free monoid over
Σ, that is the set of all words over Σ. The *length* of a word $w \in \Sigma^*$ is the
number of its letters. An empty word $\varepsilon \in \Sigma^*$ has length 0. Without introducing
any ambiguities, the transition function can be naturally extended to the set 2^Q
of states from Q and to words over A: $\delta(P, \varepsilon) = P$, $\delta(P, aw) = \delta(\delta(P, a), w)$ for
all $P \subseteq Q$, $a \in \Sigma$, $w \in \Sigma^*$.

For a given $\mathcal{A} = (Q, \Sigma, \delta)$ and $w \in \Sigma^*$ we define the *deficiency* of w as
$df(w) = |Q| - |\delta(Q, w)|$. The deficiency may be viewed as a "completeness" of
the synchronization process. For an empty word we have $df(\varepsilon) = 0$. If w is a
synchronizing word, then we achieve the maximal deficiency, $df(w) = |Q| - 1$.

A *rank* of the word w is defined as $rk(w) = |Q| - df(w) = |\delta(Q, w)|$. For a word $w = a_1 a_2 ... a_k$ let us put $r_i = rk(a_1...a_i)$ for $1 \le i \le k$, $r_0 := |Q|$, $r_t := 0$ for $t > k$. We say that a subword $v = a_i a_{i+1}...a_j$ of w $(i < j)$ is a *compressing word* if $r_{i-1} > r_i = r_{i+1} = ... = r_{j-1} > r_j$. A single letter a_i is a compressing word if $r_{i-1} > r_i > r_{i+1}$.

Let $\mathcal{A} = (Q, A, \delta)$ be a finite automaton. We say that a word $w \in \Sigma^*$ *synchronizes* $\mathcal{A}$ iff $|\delta(Q, w)| = 1$ or, equivalently, that $\forall p, q \in Q$ $\delta(p, w) = \delta(q, w)$. Such w is called a *synchronizing word*. Notice that if w is a synchronizing word, then so is any word of the form uwv, $u, v \in \Sigma^*$. Therefore, it is natural to ask about the shortest possible synchronizing word. Such a word is called a *minimal synchronizing word*. The famous Černý conjecture states, that the length of a minimal synchronizing word for the n-state synchronizing automaton does not exceed $(n-1)^2$.

For the sake of simplicity, when it is clear what is the transition function, we will use the notation Qw instead of $\delta(Q, w)$.

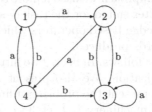

Fig. 1. An exemplary 4-state synchronizing automaton over 2-letter alphabet.

Let us consider the automaton $\mathcal{A} = (\{1, 2, 3, 4\}, \{a, b\}, \delta)$ from Fig. 1. It is easy to check that the word $w = bbaabb$ is a synchronizing word, because for each state $q \in Q$ we have $\delta(q, bbaabb) = 3$. It can be shown that this is also the minimal synchronizing word for this automaton.

2.2 Genetic Algorithm for Synchronization

Simple Genetic Algorithm (SGA) operates on the populations of possible solutions S to a given problem in a way that imitates nature. A population P consists of a number of chromosomes. Each chromosome $c \in P \subset S$ encodes a possible solution to a problem. To evaluate the quality of this solution, a fitness function $f : S \to [0, \infty)$ is introduced. It is used to perform the selection of the best individuals that are further subjected to genetic operators: crossover and mutation.

The idea of a crossover is to construct from two good individuals c_1, c_2 a third one, c_3, that is possibly better than its parents, that is $f(c_3) > f(c_i)$ for $i = 1, 2$. The mutation allows us to introduce the diversity to the population. This way the genetic algorithm is able to effectively explore a potentially very big solution search space.

In case of a synchronization problem we search for a word w that is a possibly short synchronizing word for a given automaton $\mathcal{A} = (Q, \Sigma, \delta)$. As each word is a linear representation of its letters, $w = a_1 a_2 \ldots a_n$, $a_i \in \Sigma$, $i = 1, \ldots, n$, we may represent w directly as a chromosome with genes $a_i \in \Sigma$. Notice that we do not need to encode the solution: the chromosome *is* already a solution.

In [14] a modified version of SGA, named SynchroGA, was used for the problem of finding the short synchronizing words. Two most important modifications were:

- the variable length of the chromosome – as we evaluate the solutions by their length,
- the number of possible genes – SGA operates on a binary alphabet of two genes: 0 and 1; in case of synchronization each gene corresponds to one letter from Σ, so the number of different genes is equal to the size $|\Sigma|$ of the input alphabet.

The modified SGA also used an experimentally constructed fitness function:

$$f(w) = \frac{df^4(w)}{\sqrt[4]{|w|}}.$$

The fitness function evaluated two things at the same time: the deficiency of the found word (the larger, the better) and the length of this word (the shorter, the better). This approach is not very effective, because it imposes fixed coefficients that represent the importance of these two factors.

3   Algorithm

In this section we describe in details our evolutionary SynchroGA-2POP algorithm. We provide arguments for using 2-population GA, point out the improvements from the previous approaches and present the set of implemented operators.

3.1   Feasible-Infeasible 2-Population Approach

The feasible-infeasible two population (FI-2POP) genetic algorithm [15] seems naturally well-suited for the task of DFA synchronization, as it has been developed especially to handle constrained optimization problems. The FI-2POP algorithm has been successfully used especially for search-based procedural content generation [16], including game level generation [17,18] and music generation [19].

In the synchronization problem, there exist two types of words, synchronizing and non-synchronizing, corresponding to feasible and infeasible population respectively. Non-synchronizing words can be very close to the optimal solution (e.g. by one letter deletion). Let us consider again the automaton from Fig. 1. A word *babaabb* brings the whole set of states to its subset $\{2, 3\}$. However, when we remove the first occurrence of a, the word *bbaabb* becomes a synchronizing one.

The goals for both populations are different, which encourages us to use different operators. To improve the non-synchronizing word and advance to the feasible population, we have to reduce its rank (which can be easiest achieved by making it longer). To improve a synchronizing word, from the other hand, we have to reduce its length. As stated in [15], maintaining two distinct populations is more natural in such case than using e.g. penalty functions, as it was done in SynchroGA [14].

3.2   Rank-Based Model

Let $\mathcal{A}$ be a deterministic finite automaton with $|Q| = n$ states and the alphabet of size k. For a given word w, checking if w synchronizes $\mathcal{A}$ is equal to computing Qw, which requires $\Theta(n|w|)$ time. We have that $rk(w) = |Qw|$ is a word's rank, and w is synchronizing iff $rk(w) = 1$.

The natural model used in the previous approach utilizing a genetic algorithm [14] was to base fitness function on the word's rank. However, this information turns out to be very limited. In particular, knowing that $w = va$ is synchronizing, we have no information if v is synchronizing. Thus in many cases computed words can be trivially improved. This problem was raised as one of the conclusions in [14].

Our solution is to extend the output given by the checking procedure, without increasing its complexity. Instead of returning just the rank for a word w, the procedure returns the ranks of all prefixes of w (which are computed anyway, as they are required to compute the rank of the whole word). So, for a word $w = a_1 a_2 \ldots a_{|w|}$, we compute $r_1, r_2, \ldots, r_{|w|}$ (recall that for every $i \leq |w|$, r_i is the rank of the word $a_1 a_2 \ldots a_i$).

This information allows us not only to remove the unnecessary suffixes of synchronizing words but also to introduce more sophisticated genetic operators, based on the compressing words.

3.3   Operators

In our algorithm we have implemented multiple genetic operators, to choose the combinations which provide the best results. Apart from the standard operators based on the plain strings, in most cases we also defined their rank-based counterparts.

Initialization. Let P be the size of the entire population. The initialization operator generates $2P$ random words. It is twice much as the population size in order to increase the chance of generating the feasible words and to have the feasible and infeasible populations more balanced. The *uniform(l)* operator creates the words of length $l \cdot n$, where every letter is chosen with the uniform probability.

The rank of a letter a is the size of the $|Qa|$ set. The *rank-based(l)* initialization creates the words of length $l \cdot n$, where every letter is chosen using the roulette wheel method, using letter rank as the weight. Alternatively, *reverse-rank-based(l)* operator uses as the roulette wheel weights the values $n - r_a + 1$, where r_a is the rank of letter a. Adding one in this formula ensures that the probability will be nonzero in case of letters being the permutations of states.

Selection. For every subpopulation (feasible and infeasible) of size P', the $\lfloor \frac{P'}{2} \rfloor$ pairs of parents are chosen. The *tournament(s)* selection operator chooses every parent as the best among s randomly selected individuals. The tournaments are repeated until a pair containing different parents is chosen. The mostly used *uniform* selection operator, is the special case of the tournament selection with s equal to one. The sampling is performed with repetitions.

Crossover. We have tested standard crossover operators: *one-point, two-point* and *uniform*. Each one has also its rank-based equivalent. For the rank-based crossovers, the cutting points have to be defined at the end of the compressing words.

Mutation. It is the main operator whose task is to push a given population to its goal. Thus, we mostly use different mutations for the feasible and infeasible population.

The *letter-exchange(p)* mutation changes every letter in a word with a given probability p. The new letter is chosen with the uniform probability among the letters different than the actual one.

The first operator designed for the infeasible population is the *letter-insertion(p)* mutation. After every existing letter it inserts, with a probability p, a new, uniformly chosen letter. The *adaptive* version of the operator makes the probability dependent on the best fitness value among the individual's parents. Let r be the lowest rank of the parent's words. The probability of the individual letter insertion is equal to $\min\{p \cdot r, 1\}$.

Let $LC(P_f)$ be the set of the last compressing words for all elements of the feasible population P_f. The *lastwords* operator extends the chromosome by adding at the end one randomly chosen element from $LC(P_f)$. If the feasible population is empty, it uses a random word of length $0.1n$.

The *compressing-word-insertion* inserts one random compressing word of length ≥ 5 (not necessarily the last one) from the current feasible population, or a random word of length $0.1n$ if it is empty. The word is inserted always between the existing compressing words. We use the heuristic stating that the rank based crossovers preserve compressing words (which is certainly true only before the first cutting point).

Finally, the *letter-deletion(p)* mutation, designed for the feasible population, removes a letter with a given probability. The *adaptive* version uses the probability $\min\{p \cdot l/l_{min}, 1\}$, where l is the length of the shortest parent word and l_{min} the length of the shortest word in the feasible population.

Replication. All our experiments use one replication operator. From the joint population of the parents and offsprings with removed duplicates it chooses best $\frac{P}{2}$ synchronizing words for the new feasible population, and best $\frac{P}{2}$ non-synchronizing words for the new infeasible population. If there are no valid individuals to fill one of the populations, the other one is properly extended to always maintain P individuals in total.

Fitness Function and Termination Criteria. We used two fitness functions: the word's rank for the infeasible population, and the word's length for the feasible population. The goal for every population is to minimize its fitness function value. The evolution stops after a given generation.

3.4   Preliminary Experiments

The preliminary experiments were intended to choose the best combination of operators. They have been performed using randomly generated automata: over binary alphabet with 25, 50, 75, 100 states, and over 3 and 4 letters alphabet with 25, 50, and 75 states. Each sample contained 100 automata and each automaton has been tested 100 times. We have used the population of size 60 (30 feasible + 30 infeasible), and the maximum generation has been set to 500.

The parameter settings were tested using the hill climbing strategy. After the initial run containing different combinations of operators, in each turn we modified the individual operators in a few most promising settings, evaluated the new settings, and repeated the process a few times, until no score increase has been observed.

In total, we have tested more than 110 settings. The partial results are presented in Table 1. For every tested combination of operators we have calculated the fraction of cases where a minimal synchronizing word has been found (column 2). The average generation in which it happened is presented in column 3. Let us point out that in all cases we were able to find some synchronizing word. The next columns show the ratio of the length of the found synchronizing word and the lengths returned by the other algorithms. MLSW stands for the length of a minimal synchronizing word calculated using the exponential algorithm [11]. COFFLSW stands for the result of Cut-Off IBFS$_n$ [10], which is so far the most accurate heuristic algorithm described. EPPLSW denotes the length provided by the classical Eppstein algorithm [5]. Ratio below 1 means that our algorithm provides shorter synchronizing words than the algorithm we are comparing to.

The next four columns show the average percent of advancements between the succeeding populations. IF→FI is counted when a child of infeasible parents is feasible. IF++ is counted when a child of infeasible parents is improved, i.e. it is feasible or its rank is lower than the lowest rank of its parents. Similarly, FI→FI is counted when a child remains in feasible population, and FI++ when it is improved (it is shorter then the shortest of its parents). Remaining columns describe the operators used. For all presented combinations we used the uniform selection operator.

Table 1. Results for preliminary selection of operators. The table presents the best 20 combinations of operators according to % of MLSW found by the evolutionary algorithm with this set of operators. The last row presents the best setting that does not use any rank-based operator. Abbreviations used in the table: Init = initialization operator (uni = uniform, rb = rank-based, rrb = reverse-rank-based); C_{FI} = feasible population crossover, C_{IF} = infeasible population crossover (1pL = one-point standard, i.e. letter-based, 1pRB = one-point rank-based, 2pRB = two-point rank-based); M_{FI} = feasible population mutation (ald(p) = adaptive letter-deletion with probability p); M_{IF} = infeasible population mutation (lw = lastwords, cwi = compressing-word-insertion, ali(p) = adaptive letter-insertion with probability p).

Rank	% MLSW	avg. gen.	Ratio between LSW and: MLSW	COFFLSW	EPPLSW	IF→FI	IF++	FI→FI	FI++	Operators Init	C_{FI}	C_{IF}	M_{FI}	M_{IF}
1	75.68	87.54	1.0233	1.0124	0.6880	12.53	12.55	6.15	0.57	rb(1.0)	1pL	2pRB	ald(0.065)	lw
2	75.67	86.19	1.0229	1.0121	0.6878	12.86	12.86	6.24	0.62	spl(2.0)	1pL	2pRB	ald(0.065)	lw
3	75.52	86.14	1.0231	1.0123	0.6879	12.90	12.91	6.25	0.63	spl(2.5)	1pL	2pRB	ald(0.065)	lw
4	75.50	87.14	1.0232	1.0124	0.6880	12.89	12.90	6.23	0.62	rb(2.0)	1pL	2pRB	ald(0.065)	lw
5	75.50	85.76	1.0231	1.0123	0.6879	12.45	12.47	6.16	0.56	spl(1.0)	1pL	2pRB	ald(0.065)	lw
6	75.46	84.41	1.0234	1.0126	0.6881	12.25	12.28	8.40	0.63	spl(1.0)	1pL	2pRB	ald(0.050)	lw
7	75.45	86.71	1.0231	1.0123	0.6879	11.87	12.21	6.12	0.50	rb(0.5)	1pL	2pRB	ald(0.065)	lw
8	75.36	87.60	1.0231	1.0123	0.6880	12.81	12.83	4.57	0.50	spl(1.0)	1pL	2pRB	ald(0.080)	lw
9	75.36	85.81	1.0232	1.0124	0.6880	12.76	12.77	6.22	0.60	spl(1.5)	1pL	2pRB	ald(0.065)	lw
10	75.27	84.76	1.0233	1.0124	0.6880	11.87	12.21	6.15	0.50	spl(0.5)	1pL	2pRB	ald(0.065)	lw
11	75.16	83.55	1.0239	1.0130	0.6884	12.29	12.31	10.37	0.68	spl(1.0)	1pL	2pRB	ald(0.040)	lw
12	75.06	85.41	1.0234	1.0126	0.6881	12.95	12.96	6.34	0.62	rrb(2.0)	1pL	2pRB	ald(0.065)	lw
13	75.03	85.17	1.0234	1.0126	0.6882	12.58	12.61	6.29	0.57	rrb(1.0)	1pL	2pRB	ald(0.065)	lw
14	74.93	88.96	1.0236	1.0128	0.6883	13.07	13.07	4.14	0.60	spl(2.0)	2pRB	2pRB	ald(0.065)	lw
15	74.87	89.11	1.0236	1.0128	0.6883	12.67	12.69	4.07	0.54	spl(1.0)	2pRB	2pRB	ald(0.065)	lw
16	74.87	90.50	1.0239	1.0130	0.6884	12.71	12.73	4.05	0.54	rb(1.0)	2pRB	2pRB	ald(0.065)	lw
17	74.82	90.25	1.0239	1.0131	0.6884	13.04	13.05	4.11	0.59	rb(2.0)	2pRB	2pRB	ald(0.065)	lw
18	74.82	91.39	1.0237	1.0129	0.6883	13.08	13.10	3.07	0.48	spl(1.0)	2pRB	2pRB	ald(0.080)	lw
19	74.79	88.85	1.0249	1.0140	0.6891	18.38	18.38	6.06	0.61	spl(1.5)	1pL	1pRB	ald(0.065)	cwi
20	74.78	88.85	1.0249	1.0140	0.6891	18.27	18.29	6.02	0.57	spl(1.0)	1pL	1pRB	ald(0.065)	cwi
52	73.75	97.08	1.0260	1.0152	0.6898	4.10	4.12	6.12	0.62	spl(1.0)	1pL	1pL	ald(0.065)	ali(0.04)

All leading operator settings have very similar performance. The difference in the percent of founded MLSW between the leader and the first ten settings is less than 0.5%, and for the first twenty it is less than 1%. The first combination of operators which does not contain any rank-based operator has been classified as 52 with the score nearly 2% worse than the leader. On the other hand, some of the tested combinations, using e.g. 3 elements tournament selection and letter-exchange mutation obtained MLSW scores below 60%.

Let us discuss the performance of the individual operators. It seems that the initial population size (ranging from $0.5n$ to $2.5n$, where n is the number of states) does not have any significant impact on the number of generations. Performance of the rank-based and uniform initialization operators is alike, which is expected due to the fact that the probability values they use are similar for the random automata. However, the reverse-rank-based initialization which differentiate probabilities more, scores visibly worse (positions 12 and 13 at best).

Surprisingly, the dominant crossover operator for the feasible individuals is not based on the knowledge on compressing words, but it is a standard *one-point crossover*. It seems that the only top-score alternative is the *two-point rank-based crossover* within an entry ranked as 14. The best rank-based equivalent of the one-point crossover achieved the score of 74.6% and is ranked as 29th. No other operator appears in the table unless close to the bottom.

On the other hand, the rank-based crossovers seems to be the only reasonable choice for the infeasible parents, especially the *two-point crossover*. The best letter-based crossover is the one ranked 52. Also, we have to point out that the uniform crossovers, both letter- and rank-based, do not work well for the task of synchronization. They tend to destroy word's structure too much, and failed for both population types.

The only operator directly suited to improving feasible individuals is *letter-deletion*. The *letter-exchange* mutation preserves the word length, so the score increase mostly relies on the crossover operation. We have tested different probability values combined with both adaptive and non-adaptive version. We observed that the adaptive version behaves better, as it is more cautious for short synchronizing words while simultaneously more aggressive for the long words. The best combination of operators using *non-adaptive letter-deletion* is ranked 68th. We also found that the slightly higher or slightly lower probability values usually result in a worse score. Note that increasing the probability actually decreases a chance to preserve or improve a feasible individual.

The *lastwords* operator totally dominates the other options for the infeasible individuals mutation. The heuristic that the last compression words tend to synchronize the remaining, thus the hardest to synchronize, states is surprisingly effective. Note that the compressing word insertion has significantly higher percent factor of improving the infeasible population, so we can assume that the *lastwords* seems to prefer quality over the quantity. The first entry with a *letter-insertion* operator is ranked as 49, with less than 74% of found MLSW and population improvement factor below 3%. Similarly, as in case of the *letter-deletion* operator, the adaptive version results in undeniably better scores.

For the further experiments we usually use just the combination of operators ranked as first. However, in some cases we also test the behavior of other operator sets which are same how representative (ranked 2nd, 14th, 19th, and 52nd).

4 Experiments and Results

In this section we provide the results of three experiments with our algorithm. First one checks the algorithm performance for the so-called *extremal automata*. These are the automata with very long ($\Omega(|Q|^2)$) minimal synchronizing words, thus they are the 'hardest to synchronize'. We use some well-known series of such automata, for which it is known what is the exact length of their MLSW, hence, we are able to compare the algorithm results with the optimal solutions.

The second experiment compares our approach with the genetic algorithm from [14]. We perform this experiment on the same set of the extremal automata, so the results of the first two experiments are put together in the next subsection.

The third experiment checks how our algorithm deals with the random automata having large number of states. We also compare it with the Eppstein and Cut-Off IBFS algorithms.

We do not provide running time comparisons because of the used architecture. Implementations of all other algorithms are written in the highly optimized C++ code, while our SynchroGA2-POP is mainly written in Lua, and refers to C++ implementation only when testing ranks of the words.

4.1 Extremal Automata and Comparison with SynchroGA

In this section we present the comparison of our approach with the genetic algorithm from [14]. We tested both algorithms for the series of extremal automata B, C, D', D'', E, F, G, H, W and two simpler series a and b (see Table 2 for the details) for 11, 21, 31, 41, 51 and 61 states.

There are two main reasons for testing these automata. First, they are hard to synchronize. Second, for each type we can construct an automaton with an arbitrary number of states and we know exactly what are the minimal synchronizing words for all these automata (for proofs, see the 'Reference' column in Table 2).

For each automaton of a given type and number of states both algorithms were run 20 times. Each run included 1000 steps. Population size was 40 in case of the genetic algorithm and 20 feasible + 20 infeasible in case of our approach. After each run we collected the following information:

- rk – the minimal rank among the ranks of all the words from all populations for this run,
- length – the length of the word with minimal rank,
- firstPop – the number of the first population in which the best word was found.

Table 2. Description of the extreme automata series and two special series a and b analyzed in the experiment.

Symbol	MSW	MSW length	References
$B_n,\ n = 2k+1 > 3$	$(ab^{2k-1})^{k-1}ab^{2k-2}(ab^{2k-1})^{k-1}a$	$n^2 - 3n + 2$	[20]
C_n	$(ba^{n-1})^{n-2}b$	$(n-1)^2$	[1]
D'_n	$(ab^{n-2})^{n-2}ba$	$n^2 - 3n + 4$	[21,22]
D''_n	$(ba^{n-1})^{n-3}ba$	$n^2 - 3n + 2$	[21,22]
E_n	$(a^2b^{n-2})^{n-3}a^2$	$n^2 - 3n + 2$	[22]
F_n	$(ab^{n-2})^{n-2}a$	$n^2 - 3n + 3$	[22]
$G_n,\ n = 2k+1 > 3$	$a^2(baba^{n-3})^{n-4}baba^2$	$n^2 - 4n + 7$	[22]
H_n	$b(ab^{n-2})^{n-3}ab$	$n^2 - 4n + 6$	[22]
W_n	$(ab^{n-2})^{n-2}a$	$n^2 - 3n + 3$	[23]
a_n	a^{n-1}	$n-1$	[14]
$b_n,\ n = 2k+1$	$a(ba)^{\frac{n-1}{2}}$	n	[14]

Based on this information we were able to compare the algorithms in three different ways: (1) comparison for the optimal runs, where only the runs with the minimal synchronizing words found were analyzed; (2) comparison for the runs in which any synchronizing word was found; (3) general comparison, taking into account all the runs. The results are presented respectively in Tables 3, 4 and Fig. 2.

As for the optimal runs we can see that our algorithm was able to find the minimal synchronizing words in case of D'_{21}, D''_{11}, D''_{21}, G_{11}, G_{21}, W_{11} and for all a and b automata. The genetic algorithm was not able to find the synchronizing word for a_{51}, a_{61}, b_{51} and b_{61}, despite the fact that their MLSW are relatively short (linear in the number of states). We may also observe that for a and b automata our algorithm was able to find the minimal synchronizing words much faster than SynchroGA.

When comparing the runs in which any (not necessarily minimal) synchronizing word was found we may observe that in case of SynchroGA the algorithm was usually not able to find a synchronizing word for automata with large number of states. Our algorithm found the synchronizing word for all types of automata, but the differences between their lengths and the MLSW values increase with the number of states.

The analysis of all runs shows that our algorithm deals generally much better than SynchroGA. First, it was able to find the synchronizing words for all types and sizes of the analyzed automata. Only in few cases the mean rank of the best word found is greater than 1, which means that in some (out of 20) runs for some automata types our algorithm was not able to find the synchronizing word. The results for SynchroGA are much worse. For some automata (B_{41}, C_{31}, C_{41}, D''_{41}, E_{31}, E_{41}, F_{41}, H_{31}) it was not able to find a synchronizing word within all 20 runs.

Table 3. Comparison of algorithms for runs in which minimal synchronizing words were found. SGA2 = our SynchroGA-2POP approach, SGA = SynchroGA.

Automaton	MLSW	% of optimal runs		avg. firstPop	
		SGA2	SGA	SGA2	SGA
D'_{11}	92	0	5	–	1
D'_{21}	382	65	10	217	3.5
D''_{11}	90	65	0	237	–
D''_{21}	380	5	0	934	–
F_{11}	91	0	5	–	9
G_{11}	84	70	0	277	–
G_{21}	364	5	0	932	–
W_{11}	91	45	15	276	217
W_{31}	871	0	5	–	570
W_{41}	1561	0	5	–	116
a_{11}	10	100	95	7.5	148
a_{21}	20	100	40	17	178
a_{31}	30	100	10	25.4	448
a_{41}	40	100	10	33.7	251
a_{51}	50	100	0	43.3	–
a_{61}	60	100	0	46	–
b_{11}	10	100	100	7	43.5
b_{21}	20	100	100	18.3	239.9
b_{31}	30	100	80	38.9	516.2
b_{41}	40	100	55	61.2	697.8
b_{51}	50	100	0	103.4	–
b_{61}	60	100	0	137.4	–

4.2 Computing Reset Words of Large Automata

The next test was performed for the large random automata over 2-letter alphabet. In this case, computing the length of a minimal synchronizing word is computationally too expensive, and instead of the exact algorithm the heuristic procedures are used to obtain as good approximation as possible. We have tested how SynchroGA-2POP behaves for such large data, and compared it against the Eppstein algorithm and Cut-Off IBFS$_n$.

We tested automata with the number of states n between 100 and 600 (with step 100). For each n we tested 1000 automata, and for each automaton we run our algorithm 10 times. The results of the experiment are presented in Fig. 3. We used the same settings as in the preliminary experiments, i.e. population of size 60 and generation limit set to 500. We run the experiment using various operator combinations, which are appointed by the rank presented in Fig. 1.

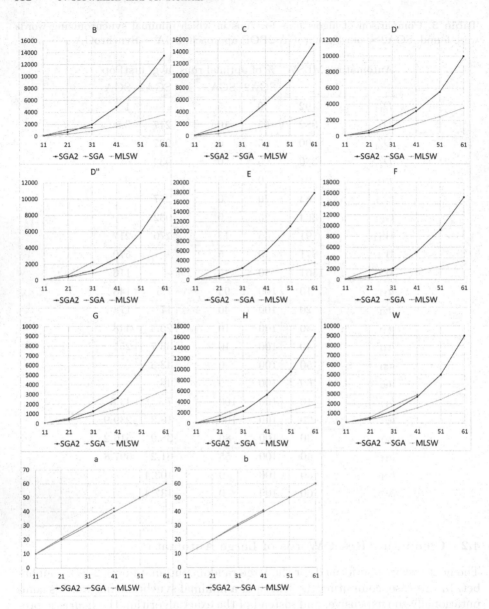

Fig. 2. Comparison of algorithms for runs in which any synchronizing words was found.

It can be seen that the difference between the best three selected variants is very small, and all of them performed better than the Eppstein algorithm for DFA with less than 400 states. On the other hand, the difference between them, and the variant ranked as 19, which differs mainly in the mutation operator for the infeasible population, is clearly visible. The results of Cut-Off IBFS$_n$ are very close to the estimated length of a minimal reset word proposed in [11],

Table 4. Comparison of algorithms for all runs. SGA2 = our SynchroGA-2POP approach, SGA = SynchroGA.

$\mathcal{A}$	best rk		mean rk		$\mathcal{A}$	best rk		mean rk		$\mathcal{A}$	best rk		mean rk	
	SGA2	SGA	SGA2	SGA		SGA2	SGA	SGA2	SGA		SGA2	SGA	SGA2	SGA
B_{11}	1	1	1.45	1	D_{11}''	1	1	1.45	1	G_{11}	1	1	1.05	1
B_{21}	1	1	1.05	1	D_{21}''	1	1	1.05	1	G_{21}	1	1	1	1
B_{31}	1	1	1	1.90	D_{31}''	1	1	1	1.35	G_{31}	1	1	1	1.1
B_{41}	1	2	1	2.75	D_{41}''	1	2	1	2	G_{41}	1	1	1	2
B_{51}	1	–	1	–	D_{51}''	1	–	1	–	G_{51}	1	–	1	–
B_{61}	1	–	1	–	D_{61}''	1	–	1	–	G_{61}	1	–	1	–
C_{11}	1	1	1	1	E_{11}	1	1	1	1	H_{11}	1	1	1.15	1
C_{21}	1	1	1	1	E_{21}	1	1	1	1.14	H_{21}	1	1	1	1
C_{31}	1	2	1	2.35	E_{31}	1	3	1	3.95	H_{31}	1	1	1	2.3
C_{41}	1	4	1	5.30	E_{41}	1	4	1	7.40	H_{41}	1	3	1	4.75
C_{51}	1	–	1	–	E_{51}	1	–	1	–	H_{51}	1	–	1	–
C_{61}	1	–	1	–	E_{61}	1	–	1	–	H_{61}	1	–	1	–
D_{11}'	1	1	1.05	1	F_{11}	1	1	1.05	1	W_{11}	1	1	1	1
D_{21}'	1	1	1	1	F_{21}	1	1	1	1	W_{21}	1	1	1	1
D_{31}'	1	1	1	1.1	F_{31}	1	1	1	2.2	W_{31}	1	1	1	1.1
D_{41}'	1	1	1	1.9	F_{41}	1	4	1	4.8	W_{41}	1	1	1	1.75
D_{51}'	1	–	1	–	F_{51}	1	–	1	–	W_{51}	1	–	1	–
D_{61}'	1	–	1	–	F_{61}	1	–	1	–	W_{61}	1	–	1	–

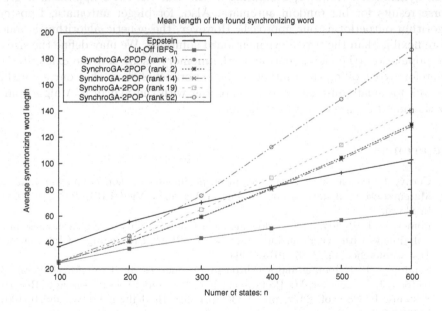

Fig. 3. The mean found length by the algorithms for random binary automata.

and SynchroGA-2POP reaches comparable lengths only for $n \leq 100$. Lastly, the quality of the results provided by the best letter-based-only variant (ranked as 52 in the preliminary experiment) emphasizes the benefits from using more sophisticated rank-based operators.

5   Conclusions

In this paper we presented a new heuristic algorithm for finding short synchronizing words. We used a 2 population feasible-infeasible approach. This allowed us to manage two usually contradicting goals when considering them as the components of the fitness function: rank of the word and its length. Usually, for random words, short ones have large ranks. From the other hand, providing the words with low rank requires them to be very long.

In [14] both these contradicting goals were put into one fitness function. In our approach we used the 2 population scheme, which allowed us to 'split' the fitness function into two independent components. The mutation operator for the feasible population took into account the result from the infeasible one, therefore it was able to 'adapt' to a given automaton and allowed to mutated words to be still synchronizing, but shorter.

The performed experiments show that our algorithm generally works better than SynchroGA. However, comparing to the Cut Off-IBFS approach, it gives worse results for big random automata. Also, for bigger automata, Eppstein algorithm outperforms our approach. However, the genetic algorithm is much more flexible than the two above mentioned solutions. We may define the size of the population (therefore, controlling the memory used) and the exit criterion (therefore, controlling the runtime). The experiments show that our algorithm fits well for small automata and – comparing with the SynchroGA algorithm – for the ones that are hard to synchronize.

References

1. Černý, J.: Poznámka k homogénnym eksperimentom s konečnými automatami. Matematicko-fyzikálny Časopis Slovenskej Akadémie Vied **14**(3), 208–216 (1964). In Slovak
2. Pomeranz, I., Reddy, S.: On achieving complete testability of synchronous sequential circuits with synchronizing sequences. In: IEEE Proceedings of International Test Conference, pp. 1007–1016 (1994)
3. Sandberg, S.: 1 Homing and synchronizing sequences. In: Broy, M., Jonsson, B., Katoen, J.-P., Leucker, M., Pretschner, A. (eds.) Model-Based Testing of Reactive Systems. LNCS, vol. 3472, pp. 5–33. Springer, Heidelberg (2005). doi:10.1007/11498490_2
4. Benenson, Y., Adar, R., Paz-Elizur, T., Livneh, Z., Shapiro, E.: DNA molecule provides a computing machine with both data and fuel. Proc. Natl. Acad. Sci. **100**(5), 2191–2196 (2003)
5. Eppstein, D.: Reset sequences for monotonic automata. SIAM J. Comput. **19**, 500–510 (1990)

6. Goldberg, K.Y.: Orienting polygonal parts without sensors. Algorithmica **10**(2–4), 201–225 (1993)
7. Berlinkov, M.V.: Approximating the minimum length of synchronizing words is hard. Theory Comput. Syst. **54**(2), 211–223 (2014)
8. Kowalski, J., Szykuła, M.: A new heuristic synchronizing algorithm (2013). http://arxiv.org/abs/1308.1978
9. Roman, A.: Synchronizing finite automata with short reset words. In: Applied Mathematics and Computation. ICCMSE-2005, vol. 209, pp. 125–136 (2009)
10. Roman, A., Szykuła, M.: Forward and backward synchronizing algorithms. Expert Syst. Appl. **42**(24), 9512–9527 (2015)
11. Kisielewicz, A., Kowalski, J., Szykuła, M.: A fast algorithm finding the shortest reset words. In: Du, D.-Z., Zhang, G. (eds.) COCOON 2013. LNCS, vol. 7936, pp. 182–196. Springer, Heidelberg (2013). doi:10.1007/978-3-642-38768-5_18
12. Kisielewicz, A., Kowalski, J., Szykuła, M.: Computing the shortest reset words of synchronizing automata. J. Comb. Optim. **29**(1), 88–124 (2015)
13. Trahtman, A.N.: An efficient algorithm finds noticeable trends and examples concerning the Černy conjecture. In: Královič, R., Urzyczyn, P. (eds.) MFCS 2006. LNCS, vol. 4162, pp. 789–800. Springer, Heidelberg (2006). doi:10.1007/11821069_68
14. Roman, A.: Genetic algorithm for synchronization. In: Dediu, A.H., Ionescu, A.M., Martín-Vide, C. (eds.) LATA 2009. LNCS, vol. 5457, pp. 684–695. Springer, Heidelberg (2009). doi:10.1007/978-3-642-00982-2_58
15. Kimbrough, S.O., Koehler, G.J., Lu, M., Wood, D.H.: On a feasible-infeasible two-population (FI-2Pop) genetic algorithm for constrained optimization: distance tracing and no free lunch. Eur. J. Oper. Res. **190**(2), 310–327 (2008)
16. Togelius, J., Yannakakis, G.N., Stanley, K.O., Browne, C.: Search-based procedural content generation: a taxonomy and survey. IEEE Trans. Comput. Intell. AI Games **3**(3), 172–186 (2011)
17. Liapis, A., Yannakakis, G.N., Togelius, J.: Sentient sketchbook: computer-aided game level authoring. In: Conference on the Foundations of Digital Games, pp. 213–220 (2013)
18. Liapis, A., Holmgård, C., Yannakakis, G.N., Togelius, J.: Procedural personas as critics for dungeon generation. In: Mora, A.M., Squillero, G. (eds.) EvoApplications 2015. LNCS, vol. 9028, pp. 331–343. Springer, Cham (2015). doi:10.1007/978-3-319-16549-3_27
19. Scirea, M., Togelius, J., Eklund, P., Risi, S.: MetaCompose: a compositional evolutionary music composer. In: Johnson, C., Ciesielski, V., Correia, J., Machado, P. (eds.) EvoMUSART 2016. LNCS, vol. 9596, pp. 202–217. Springer, Cham (2016). doi:10.1007/978-3-319-31008-4_14
20. Ananichev, D.S., Volkov, M.V., Zaks, Y.I.: Synchronizing automata with a letter of deficiency 2. In: Ibarra, O.H., Dang, Z. (eds.) DLT 2006. LNCS, vol. 4036, pp. 433–442. Springer, Heidelberg (2006). doi:10.1007/11779148_39
21. Ananichev, D., Gusev, V., Volkov, M.: Slowly synchronizing automata and digraphs. In: Hliněný, P., Kučera, A. (eds.) MFCS 2010. LNCS, vol. 6281, pp. 55–65. Springer, Heidelberg (2010). doi:10.1007/978-3-642-15155-2_7
22. Ananichev, D.S., Volkov, M.V., Gusev, V.V.: Primitive digraphs with large exponents and slowly synchronizing automata. J, Math. Sci. **192**(3), 263–278 (2013)
23. Wielandt, H.: Unzerlegbare, nicht negative Matrizen. Math. Z. **52**, 642–648 (1950)

Large Scale Problems in Practice:
The Effect of Dimensionality on the
Interaction Among Variables

Fabio Caraffini[1,2], Ferrante Neri[1,2], and Giovanni Iacca[1,2(✉)]

[1] Centre for Computational Intelligence,
De Montfort University, The Gateway, Leicester LE1 9BH, UK
{fabio.caraffini,fneri}@dmu.ac.uk
[2] INCAS3, Dr. Nassaulaan 9, 9401 HJ Assen, The Netherlands
giovanni.iacca@gmail.com

Abstract. This article performs a study on correlation between pairs of variables in dependence on the problem dimensionality. Two tests, based on Pearson and Spearman coefficients, have been designed and used in this work. In total, 86 test problems ranging between 10 and 1000 variables have been studied. If the most commonly used experimental conditions are used, the correlation between pairs of variables appears, from the perspective of the search algorithm, to consistently decrease. This effect is not due to the fact that the dimensionality modifies the nature of the problem but is a consequence of the experimental conditions: the computational feasibility of the experiments imposes an extremely shallow search in case of high dimensions. An exponential increase of budget and population with the dimensionality is still practically impossible. Nonetheless, since real-world application may require that large scale problems are tackled despite of the limited budget, an algorithm can quickly improve upon initial guesses if it integrates the knowledge that an apparent weak correlation between pairs of variables occurs, regardless the nature of the problem.

Keywords: Large scale optimization · Covariance matrix · Correlation

1 Introduction

Dimensionality is a problem feature that is, in most cases, explicitly available when an optimization problem is formulated. It follows that a good algorithmic design should take into account the knowledge about the problem dimensionality to efficiently solve the problems at hand.

Optimization problems in many dimensions radically differ from low dimensional problems since the size of a domain grows exponentially with the number

The original version of this chapter was revised: An acknowledgment has been added. The erratum to this publication is available online at https://doi.org/10.1007/978-3-319-55849-3_58

G. Squillero and K. Sim (Eds.): EvoApplications 2017, Part I, LNCS 10199, pp. 636–652, 2017.
DOI: 10.1007/978-3-319-55849-3_41

of dimensions. To remark this fact, let us consider a uni-dimensional decision space $\mathbf{D}$. Let $\mathbf{D}$ be a set composed of 100 points (candidate solutions). Let us consider now a function f defined over the set $\mathbf{D}$. Without loss of generality, let us assume that there exists a solution $\mathbf{x}^* \in \mathbf{D}$ such that $f(\mathbf{x}^*)$ is minimal. Hence, in order to find the global minimum $\mathbf{x}^*$, an optimization algorithm needs at most 100 samples (or like it is often indicated in nature-inspired algorithms, fitness evaluations, see [1]). This problem would be very easy for a modern computer. On the other hand, if the problem is scaled up to two dimensions, there will be one optimum $\mathbf{x}^*$ in a space composed of $100^2 = 10000$ candidate solutions. If the problem is scaled up to 1000 dimensions, the optimum will be only one point in a space of 100^{1000} solutions. With an exhaustive search, the latter problem would be extremely hard to solve in a feasible time. Thus a specifically designed algorithm will be required to tackle it. In other words, since the decision space grows exponentially with the problem dimensionality, the detection of the optimal solution in high dimensions is like the search of a needle in a haystack, and requires some specific strategies.

In addition to that, the problem dimensionality affects not only the number of candidate solutions in the search space, but also other intrinsic features of the search space itself. For example, a unitary radius sphere in a 3-dimensional Euclidean space has area of the surface $S_2 = 4\pi$ and volume $V_3 = \frac{4}{3}\pi$. In the generic n-dimensional space, it can be easily proved that the ratio between volume and surface is $\frac{1}{n}$. This means that if we consider a unitary radius sphere in high dimensions and randomly sample some points within it, most of them will be located on its surface as its volume is a small fraction of it.

An optimization problem characterized by a high number of dimensions is known as Large Scale Optimization Problem (LSOP). Large scale problems can be hard to solve as some optimization algorithms that easily solve a problem in e.g. 30 dimensions can display a poor performance to solve the same problem scaled up to e.g. 300 dimensions. The deterioration in the performance of optimization algorithms as the dimensionality of the search space increases is commonly called "curse of dimensionality", see [2], and generally affects every kind of search logic. For example, several studies show that Differential Evolution (DE) and Particle Swarm Optimization (PSO) can easily display a poor performance when applied to solve LSOPs, see e.g. [2,3].

Furthermore, the dimensionality has a direct impact on the computational cost of the optimization, see [4]. In general, this is true because, due to the large decision space, a large budget is usually necessary to detect a solution with a high performance. Moreover, due to high dimensionality, algorithms which perform a search within the neighborhood of a candidate solution (e.g. Hooke-Jeeves Algorithm, [5]) might require a very large number of fitness evaluations at each step of the search, while population based algorithms are likely to either prematurely converge to suboptimal solutions, or stagnate due to an inability to generate new promising search directions. Other approaches that inspect the interaction between pairs or variables in order to perform an exploratory move, see e.g. [6], can be computationally onerous and in some cases, see e.g. [7], unacceptably expensive for modern computers.

A trivial but overlooked consideration regarding the scalability of optimization problems is that the parameter setting of the algorithm and the experimental setup should take the dimensionality into account. At first, if a population-based algorithm is used, an exponential increase in the population size should be performed to keep the domain coverage constant. For example, if a DE algorithm is run with a population size of 30 individuals in 10 dimensions, to reproduce the same coverage in 50 dimensions, $30^{50-10} \approx 1.22 \times 10^{59}$ solutions would be needed. A population of this size is in practice impossible to use in the vast majority of problems. Hence, metaheuristics in high dimensions cover only a minimal part of the decision space.

A similar consideration can be done on the computational budget. Let us consider a DE algorithm run to solve a 10−dimensional problem with a budget of 50000 fitness evaluations. In order to explore/visit the same portion of decision space in 50 dimensions a budget of $50000^{40} \approx 9.1 \times 10^{187}$ fitness evaluations. Also this setting would be infeasible.

While in some cases scalability can simply be addressed by heuristic rules that scale up the algorithm parameters (e.g. by imposing that the computational budget is proportional to the problem dimensionality), as we have seen this strategy is not always possible, let alone efficient. Nevertheless, in real-world applications LSOPs must often be tackled efficiently in order to achieve a solution with a reasonable performance, e.g. in scheduling [8], chemical engineering [9,10], and in engineering design [11,12]. To address the aforementioned feasibility issues in terms of computational cost, several algorithms have been therefore proposed in the literature for handling this kind of problems.

In this paper, we present a study on the effect of dimensionality in optimization problems when the usual experimental conditions are set. Our purpose is to shed light on some specific characteristics that we consider especially interesting in large scale optimization and that, according to our empirical results, are common -to some extent- to most LSOPs. Among the features that can be used to analyze the fitness landscape in LSOPs, we focus on the correlation between pairs of problem variables. In particular, we study how the pairwise correlation changes in dependence on the dimensionality of the problem, in an attempt to address the research question: *On the basis of the usual algorithm and experimental setting, what happens to the correlation among the variables when the dimensionality grows?*

To address this question we illustrate a procedure to estimate the correlation between pairs of variables, an averaging technique to extract a unique measure that the describes the overall correlation among variables, and a sensitivity analysis of this measure with respect to the problem dimensionality. We applied the proposed analysis over a number of scalable problems commonly used in continuous optimization benchmarks, with dimensionality ranging between 10 and 1000 dimensions.

The remainder of this paper is organized in the following way. Section 2 shows successful strategies proposed in the literature to tackle LSOPs. Section 3 gives the implementation details of the procedure for estimating the correlation between pairs of variables. Section 4 shows the numerical results on a broad set of benchmark functions. Finally, Sect. 5 concludes this work.

2   Background: A Literature Review on Large Scale Optimization

In recent years, several modern metaheuristics have been proposed in order to tackle LSOPs, such as some modified versions of Ant Colony Optimization (ACO) [13] and Artificial Bee Colony Algorithm (ABC) [14]. In our view, the methods for tackling LSOPs can be roughly divided into two main categories:

– **Methods that intensively exploit promising search directions.** These algorithms with an apparent counterintuitive action, instead of exploring the large decision space, give up the search for the global optimum and use an intensive exploitation to improve upon a set of initial solutions to detect a solution with a high quality (regardless its optimality). Two popular ways to implement this approach have been proposed in the literature. The first way to achieve this aim is by using population-based algorithms with very small populations, see [15–18], or with a population that shrinks during the run, see [19–22]. The second way to achieve this aim is by using highly exploitative local search algorithms by combining them with other algorithms and integrating them within population based structures. In particular, a coordination of multiple local search components is used to tackle LSOPs in [23]. This logic, a part or a modification of it has been coupled and integrated within other algorithmic frameworks in [24–28]. It must be remarked that these algorithms tend to use a simple local search component that exploits the decision space by perturbing the candidate solution along the axes. Another interesting study belonging to this category has been presented in [29], where a modified version of Covariance Matrix Adaptation Evolution Strategy (CMA-ES) is proposed for tackling separable problems. In this case, the proposed algorithm makes use of a diagonal matrix to determine the newly sampled points and then the search directions. Hence, this modified version of CMA-ES performs moves along the axes to solve separable problems. It was shown that this algorithmic scheme appeared especially promising in high dimensional cases.
– **Methods that decompose the search space.** Some other papers propose a technique, namely cooperative coevolution, originally defined in [30] and subsequently developed in other works, see e.g. [31,32]. The concept of the cooperative coevolution is to decompose a LSOP into a set of low-dimensional problems which can be separately solved and then recombined in order to compose the solution of the original problem. It is obvious that if the fitness function is separable, then the problem decomposition can be trivial, while for non-separable functions the problem decomposition can turn out to be a very difficult task. However, some techniques for performing the decomposition of non-separable functions have been developed, see [33]. Recently, cooperative coevolution procedures have been successfully integrated within DE frameworks for solving LSOPs, see e.g. [34–38]. Another very successful implementation of cooperative coevolution has been integrated within a PSO framework in [39].

A common denominator in these approaches is that the algorithm attempts to quickly achieve improvements by exploiting the search directions. In other words, since the budget is very limited and there is a large margin of improvement with respect to an initial sampling, every effective modern metaheuristic for LSOPs gives up the search for the global optimum and simply tries to enhance as much as possible upon an initial sampling.

3 Procedure for Estimating the Correlation Between Pairs of Variables

The proposed correlation estimation procedure is performed in two steps: (1) a preliminary sampling process, needed to sample a set of solutions in the search space and *evolve* them for a given number of generations; and (2) an estimation of the correlation among the variables in the final set of solutions obtained at the end of the evolutionary process performed in the first step. In this paper we use two different correlation measures, while the sampling mechanism is the same for both measures.

3.1 First Step: Covariance Matrix Adaptation Evolution Strategy

During the preliminary step, the Covariance Matrix Adaptation Evolution Strategy (CMA-ES) with rank-μ-update and weighted recombination, see [40], is applied for $n \times 1000$ fitness evaluations. Briefly, the CMA-ES consists of sampling from a multivariate distribution λ points, computing their fitness values and updating the shape of the distribution in order to progressively adapt to the basins of attraction. The sampling rule of the individual k at the generation $g + 1$ is given by:

$$x_k^{(g+1)} \sim \mathcal{N}\left(\langle \mathbf{x} \rangle_w^g, (\sigma^g)^2 \, \mathbf{C}^g\right) \tag{1}$$

where $\mathcal{N}\left(\mathbf{m}, \sigma^2 \mathbf{C}\right)$ is a multivariate normal distribution of mean $\mathbf{m}$, step size σ, and estimated covariance matrix $\mathbf{C}$. The mean value $\langle \mathbf{x} \rangle_w^g$ is a weighted sum of the μ candidate solutions ($\mu \leq \lambda$) displaying the best performance at the generation g (those individuals that are associated to the lowest fitness values $f(\mathbf{x})$). This vector corresponds to a recombination result, see [40] for details. At each gth generation, the values of step size σ and covariance matrix $\mathbf{C}$ are updated. The two update rules are determined by a vector $\mathbf{p_c}$, named evolution path. The evolution path $\mathbf{p_c}$ is updated first, according to the following rule:

$$\mathbf{p_c}^{g+1} = (1 - c_c)\mathbf{p_c}^g + H_\sigma \sqrt{c_c (2 - c_c)} \frac{\sqrt{\mu_{eff}}}{\sigma^g} \left(\langle \mathbf{x} \rangle_w^{g+1} - \langle \mathbf{x} \rangle_w^g\right)$$

where $\mu_{eff} = \frac{1}{\sum_1^\mu w_i^2}$, c_c is a parameter, and H_σ is a discrete function that can take either the value 0 or 1. The step size is then updated according to the following rule:

$$\sigma^{g+1} = \sigma^g \exp\left(\frac{c_c}{d_c}\left(\frac{\|\mathbf{p_c}\|}{E\|(\mathcal{N}(\emptyset, \mathbf{I}))\|} - 1\right)\right)$$

where d_d is a damping factor, usually close to one, and $\|\dots\|$ indicates the 2-norm (see [41] for further explanations). Finally, $\mathbf{C}$ is updated according to the following rule:

$$\mathbf{C}^{g+1} = (1 - c_1 - c_\mu + c_s)\mathbf{C}^g + c_1 \mathbf{p_c}^{g+1} \left(\mathbf{p_c}^{g+1}\right)^T$$

$$+ c_\mu \sum_{i=1}^{\mu} w_i \left(\frac{\mathbf{x}_{i:\lambda}^{g+1} - \langle\mathbf{x}\rangle_w^g}{\sigma^g}\right) \left(\frac{\mathbf{x}_{i:\lambda}^{g+1} - \langle\mathbf{x}\rangle_w^g}{\sigma^g}\right)^T$$

where c_1, c_μ and c_s are learning parameters. At the end of each generation, the μ individuals displaying the best performance are selected and used to compute $\langle\mathbf{x}\rangle_w^{g+1}$. Implementation details about the CMA-ES structure and functioning can be found in [40, 42, 43].

According to the philosophy of CMA-ES, the matrix $\mathbf{C}$ evolves and reliably approximates the theoretical covariance matrix. A covariance matrix is a correlation matrix, i.e. a matrix that describes the correlation between pairs of variables and, at the same time, approximates the shape of the basins of attraction, i.e. those regions of the fitness landscape surrounding the fitness minima. In this way, CMA-ES samples new points from a distribution that adapts to the fitness landscape itself. In our tests, we empirically chose the CMA-ES budget ($n \times 1000$ fitness evaluations) so to have a reliable estimation of the covariance matrix, even though the convergence condition is likely still to be met. In other words, after this budget, the CMA-ES is likely to still sample points in a large portion of the decision space and not only a local basin of attraction. Due to the curse of dimensionality, this statement becomes progressively more true as the problem dimensionality grows (since the complexity grows exponentially while the CMA-ES budget is assigned by means of a linear formula).

3.2 Second Step: Correlation Estimation

Once the estimated covariance matrix $\mathbf{C}$ has been computed (i.e. after the given number of fitness evaluations), we calculate the pairwise correlation among the decision variables. Here we use, independently, two alternative correlation measures, namely the Pearson [44] and the Spearman correlation coefficients [45]. To calculate the Pearson coefficients, we take each element of the matrix $C_{i,j}$ and apply the following transformation:

$$\rho_{i,j} = \frac{C_{i,j}}{\sqrt{C_{i,i}C_{j,j}}}. \tag{2}$$

where $\rho_{i,j}$ define the Pearson correlation coefficients. These coefficients vary between -1 and 1 and measure the linear correlation between pairs of variables. When $\rho_{i,j} = 0$, there is no correlation at all between the ith and j^{th} variables. When $|\rho_{i,j}| = 1$, there is a perfect correlation between the variables. More specifically, when $\rho_{i,j} = 1$, it means that to an increase of the ith variable corresponds the same (linear) increase of the jth variable; when $\rho_{i,j} = -1$, it means that to an increase of the ith variable corresponds the same (linear) decrease of the

j^{th} variable. The matrix ρ composed of elements $\rho_{i,j}$ is the Pearson correlation matrix. The Pearson correlation matrix is more intuitive than the covariance matrix because its elements are limited and normalized within the $[-1, 1]$ interval, thus allowing an immediate interpretation. Since there is no interest, within this study, to distinguish between positive and negative correlation, the absolute value of the Pearson correlation matrix $|\rho|$ is computed. Moreover, since the correlation between variables is a symmetric relation and the self-correlation is the maximum possible correlation, the Pearson matrix has the following structure:

$$|\rho| = \begin{pmatrix} 1 & |\rho_{1,2}| & |\rho_{1,3}| & \cdots & |\rho_{1,n}| \\ X & 1 & |\rho_{2,3}| & \cdots & |\rho_{2,n}| \\ X & X & 1 & \cdots & |\rho_{3,n}| \\ \cdots & \cdots & \cdots & \cdots & \cdots \\ X & X & X & X & 1 \end{pmatrix}.$$

Thus, only $\frac{(n^2-n)}{2}$ elements of the matrix $|\rho|$ are of interest. In order to extract an index that performs an estimation of the average correlation among the variables, we simply average the elements of the matrix $|\rho|$:

$$\varsigma = \frac{2}{n^2-n} \sum_{i=1}^{n-1} \sum_{j=i+1}^{n} |\rho_{i,j}|. \tag{3}$$

The Spearman correlation estimate consists of the following. By means of the covariance matrix $\mathbf{C}$, m points are sampled within the decision space. Considering that each point $\mathbf{x} = (x_1, x_2, \ldots, x_n)$ is a vector having n elements, these m points compose the following $m \times n$ matrix:

$$\mathbf{X} = \begin{pmatrix} x_{1,1} & x_{1,2} & x_{1,3} & \cdots & x_{1,n} \\ x_{2,1} & x_{2,2} & x_{2,3} & \cdots & x_{2,n} \\ \cdots & \cdots & \cdots & \cdots & \cdots \\ x_{m,1} & x_{m,2} & x_{m,3} & \cdots & x_{m,n} \end{pmatrix} = (\mathbf{X^1}, \mathbf{X^2}, \ldots, \mathbf{X^n})$$

where $\mathbf{X^j}$ is the generic j^{th} column vector of the matrix $\mathbf{X}$.

For each column vector, the elements are substituted with their ranking. More specifically, for the generic column vector $\mathbf{X^j}$ the lowest value is replaced with its ranking 1, the second lowest with 2, and so on until the highest value is replaced with n. If l elements have the same value, an average ranking is assigned. For example if three elements corresponding to the rank 3, 4, and 5 have the same value, the ranking 4 is assigned to all of them. This procedure can be seen as a matrix transformation that associates to the matrix $\mathbf{X}$ a new rank matrix $\mathbf{R}$ where the element $x_{i,j}$ is replaced with its rank $r_{i,j}$:

$$\mathbf{R} = \begin{pmatrix} r_{1,1} & r_{1,2} & r_{1,3} & \cdots & r_{1,n} \\ r_{2,1} & r_{2,2} & r_{2,3} & \cdots & r_{2,n} \\ \cdots & \cdots & \cdots & \cdots & \cdots \\ r_{m,1} & r_{m,2} & r_{m,3} & \cdots & r_{m,n} \end{pmatrix} = (\mathbf{R^1}, \mathbf{R^2}, \ldots, \mathbf{R^n}).$$

From the rank matrix $\mathbf{R}$, a new matrix $\mathbf{T}$ is calculated by computing the Pearson correlation coefficients of the ranks. More specifically, the correlation between the ith and j^{th} variables is given by:

$$\tau_{i,j} = \frac{\sum_{k=1}^{m} \left(r_{k,i} - \bar{\mathbf{R}}^{\mathbf{i}}\right) \sum_{k=1}^{m} \left(r_{k,j} - \bar{\mathbf{R}}^{\mathbf{j}}\right)}{\sqrt{\sum_{k=1}^{m} \left(r_{k,i} - \bar{\mathbf{R}}^{\mathbf{i}}\right)^2 \sum_{k=1}^{m} \left(r_{k,j} - \bar{\mathbf{R}}^{\mathbf{j}}\right)^2}} \tag{4}$$

where $\bar{\mathbf{R}}^{\mathbf{i}}$ and $\bar{\mathbf{R}}^{\mathbf{j}}$ are the mean values of the ith and j^{th} column vectors, respectively. $\tau_{i,i} = 1$ define the Spearman coefficients.

Considering that $\forall i, j$, it results that $\tau_{i,i} = 1$ and $\tau_{i,j} = \tau_{j,i}$, the matrix $\mathbf{T}$ is symmetric and displays unitary diagonal elements. Since, analogous to the Pearson coefficient, we are not interested in the sign of the correlation, the absolute value of the matrix $\mathbf{T}$ is calculated:

$$|\mathbf{T}| = \begin{pmatrix} 1 & |\tau_{1,2}| & |\tau_{1,3}| & \dots & |\tau_{1,n}| \\ X & 1 & |\tau_{2,3}| & \dots & |\tau_{2,n}| \\ X & X & 1 & \dots & |\tau_{3,n}| \\ \dots & \dots & \dots & \dots & \dots \\ X & X & X & X & 1 \end{pmatrix}.$$

We then compute the average Spearman correlation index φ as the average value of the $\frac{(n^2-n)}{2}$ elements of the matrix $\mathbf{T}$ under consideration:

$$\varphi = \frac{2}{n^2 - n} \sum_{i=1}^{n-1} \sum_{j=i+1}^{n} |\tau_{i,j}|. \tag{5}$$

Before discussing the results, it is worth mentioning why we use two different correlation coefficients here. As explained in [46], the Pearson coefficient is more accurate if the pairwise correlation can be approximated to be linear. This circumstance realistically occurs in several -but not all- cases, in which the Pearson coefficient is reliable [47]. On the other hand, the Spearman coefficient is not a measure of the linear correlation between two variables, but rather it simply assesses how well the relationship between two variables can be described using a monotonic (not necessarily linear) function. Moreover the Spearman coefficient is non-parametric (distribution free), i.e. it does not require any assumption on the statistical process, it is less sensitive to outliers than the Pearson coefficient, but its calculation is computationally more expensive.

4 Numerical Results

We initially tested the procedure illustrated above over the 19 scalable test problems introduced in the Test Suite for the *Special Issue of Soft Computing on Scalability of Evolutionary Algorithms and other Metaheuristics for Large Scale Continuous Optimization Problems* [48], hereafter SISC2010. We calculated both Pearson and Spearman correlation coefficients over these 19 test problems in 10, 30, 50, 100, 500 and 1000 dimensions. To obtain robust correlation indications (which are affected by the stochastic nature of the sampling process), we calculated each aggregate index (ς and φ) 50 times per problem/dimension. In the following, we will explicitly refer to the dimensionality of the corresponding problem every time we will mention an index. For example, to indicate the ς value for a problem in 30 dimensions we will write ς_{30n}.

In order to find the optimal number of samples to be drawn from the distribution to have a reliable calculation of correlation, we performed a preliminary experiment on SISC2010 in the aforementioned dimensionality values, with sample sizes proportional to the dimensionality of the problem. We tested four configurations, namely n, $5n$, $10n$ and $100n$, and for each of them we calculated the corresponding index values ς and φ. We observed that, regardless of the problem dimension, a set of 100 points, for the Pearson index, and 1000, for the Spearman index, provide an index as stable and reliable as that obtained by a higher number of points.

Following the indications of this preliminary experiment, we set the population size for CMA-ES equal to 100, which also allowed us to keep the experimental setup quite simple and computationally affordable. In case of Spearman index, the final population is sampled 10 times.

Table 1 displays the average correlation indices (calculated over the 50 runs available) and the corresponding standard deviation obtained on the entire SISC2010 benchmark. As it can immediately be observed, both the proposed indices appear to be closely related to the problem dimensionality. More specifically, regardless of the nature of the problem, the correlation amongst variables appear to decay with the dimensionality. All the problems display the maximum values of Pearson and Spearman indices in low dimensions, while these indices tend to take small values in large scale cases being nearly null in 1000 dimensions.

Moreover, we can observe that the correlation between pairs of variables appears somehow related to the separability of the problem, i.e. it tends to be lower when the problem is separable, as also noted in [49]. Although we admit that the concepts of correlation and separability are not strictly linked, we have conjectured the following explanation for the relation between these two concepts: since separable functions in n variables can be expressed as the sum of n functions in one variable, the problem is somehow characterized by a low correlation among variables. However, the opposite is not necessarily true: a low correlation among variables does not implicate problem separability. Some non-separable problems can still be characterized by a low variable correlation.

In order to confirm that the obtained results are not biased by the chosen testbed, we performed the same tests also over the *2013 IEEE Congress on Evolutionary Computation* (CEC2013) testbed, see [50] and the *2010 Black Box Optimization Benchmarking* (BBOB2010) testbed, see [51]. The first is scalable only for a limited amount of dimensionality values, that is 10, 30, and 50 dimensions. The second testbed is scalable in 10, 30, 50 and 100 dimensions. We performed the tests on the two testbeds over all problems in all the available dimensionality values, again with each test repeated 50 times. Numerical results on the CEC2013 testbed, showing the correlation indices averaged over the 50 runs available, are reported in Table 2 for both Pearson and Spearman indices. Numerical results on the BBOB2010 testbed are given in Table 3. On both testbeds and indices, it can be observed the same trend seen for SISC2010.

Table 1. Average Pearson (ς) and Spearman (φ) correlation indices $\pm$ standard deviation values for SISC2010 over increasing dimensionality values

	$\varsigma10n$	$\varsigma30n$	$\varsigma50n$	$\varsigma100n$	$\varsigma500n$	$\varsigma1000n$	Separable
f_1	0.054 ± 0.006	0.032 ± 0.001	0.025 ± 0.001	0.015 ± 0.001	0.002 ± 0.000	0.001 ± 0.000	YES
f_2	0.068 ± 0.008	0.043 ± 0.002	0.034 ± 0.001	0.021 ± 0.001	0.014 ± 0.0015	0.021 ± 0.001	$-$
f_3	0.178 ± 0.077	$0.072 \pm .0190$	0.035 ± 0.002	0.020 ± 0.002	0.002 ± 0.000	0.001 ± 0.000	$-$
f_4	0.058 ± 0.014	0.036 ± 0.005	0.026 ± 0.001	0.019 ± 0.002	0.004 ± 0.000	0.002 ± 0.000	YES
f_5	0.053 ± 0.007	0.033 ± 0.001	0.026 ± 0.001	0.017 ± 0.000	0.003 ± 0.000	0.001 ± 0.000	$-$
f_6	0.058 ± 0.010	0.038 ± 0.002	0.030 ± 0.008	0.017 ± 0.004	0.003 ± 0.001	0.002 ± 0.000	YES
f_7	0.059 ± 0.018	0.033 ± 0.001	0.035 ± 0.001	0.019 ± 0.001	0.003 ± 0.000	0.001 ± 0.000	YES
f_8	0.146 ± 0.008	0.069 ± 0.002	0.067 ± 0.002	0.053 ± 0.004	0.007 ± 0.002	0.003 ± 0.000	$-$
f_9	0.508 ± 0.428	0.073 ± 0.084	0.069 ± 0.064	0.094 ± 0.039	0.040 ± 0.015	0.025 ± 0.003	$-$
f_{10}	0.051 ± 0.004	0.033 ± 0.001	0.024 ± 0.001	0.016 ± 0.003	0.004 ± 0.000	0.002 ± 0.000	$-$
f_{11}	0.276 ± 0.272	0.092 ± 0.056	0.097 ± 0.066	0.068 ± 0.040	0.037 ± 0.0031	0.021 ± 0.006	$-$
f_{12}	0.109 ± 0.029	0.055 ± 0.008	0.041 ± 0.006	0.032 ± 0.009	0.008 ± 0.0006	0.005 ± 0.001	$-$
f_{13}	0.241 ± 0.077	0.075 ± 0.021	0.058 ± 0.003	0.046 ± 0.004	0.014 ± 0.0006	0.010 ± 0.001	$-$
f_{14}	0.091 ± 0.010	0.055 ± 0.005	0.040 ± 0.004	0.031 ± 0.007	0.010 ± 0.0015	0.007 ± 0.001	$-$
f_{15}	0.056 ± 0.008	0.040 ± 0.002	0.029 ± 0.000	0.025 ± 0.010	0.008 ± 0.0017	0.006 ± 0.001	$-$
f_{16}	0.094 ± 0.011	0.092 ± 0.024	0.084 ± 0.028	0.048 ± 0.013	0.017 ± 0.0021	0.013 ± 0.004	$-$
f_{17}	0.206 ± 0.121	0.144 ± 0.050	0.078 ± 0.011	0.061 ± 0.013	0.024 ± 0.0021	0.015 ± 0.002	$-$
f_{18}	0.226 ± 0.224	0.074 ± 0.024	0.049 ± 0.021	0.053 ± 0.034	0.036 ± 0.0099	0.022 ± 0.001	$-$
f_{19}	0.066 ± 0.006	0.063 ± 0.007	0.045 ± 0.007	0.027 ± 0.012	0.006 ± 0.0006	0.004 ± 0.001	$-$
	$\varphi10n$	$\varphi30n$	$\varphi50n$	$\varphi100n$	$\varphi500n$	$\varphi1000n$	Separable
f_1	0.093 ± 0.011	0.085 ± 0.003	0.084 ± 0.002	0.082 ± 0.001	0.080 ± 0.001	0.014 ± 0.000	YES
f_2	0.099 ± 0.010	0.091 ± 0.003	0.089 ± 0.002	0.083 ± 0.001	0.082 ± 0.001	0.016 ± 0.001	$-$
f_3	0.219 ± 0.062	0.113 ± 0.018	0.092 ± 0.005	0.084 ± 0.002	0.081 ± 0.002	0.014 ± 0.000	$-$
f_4	0.127 ± 0.017	0.091 ± 0.004	0.085 ± 0.003	0.083 ± 0.001	0.080 ± 0.001	0.014 ± 0.000	YES
f_5	0.103 ± 0.012	0.086 ± 0.002	0.083 ± 0.001	0.081 ± 0.001	0.080 ± 0.001	0.014 ± 0.000	$-$
f_6	0.096 ± 0.009	0.089 ± 0.004	0.085 ± 0.004	0.082 ± 0.001	0.080 ± 0.001	0.014 ± 0.000	YES
f_7	0.103 ± 0.018	0.086 ± 0.004	0.086 ± 0.002	0.083 ± 0.001	0.080 ± 0.001	0.014 ± 0.000	YES
f_8	0.186 ± 0.019	0.116 ± 0.002	0.116 ± 0.003	0.097 ± 0.003	0.081 ± 0.003	0.014 ± 0.000	$-$
f_9	0.675 ± 0.417	0.128 ± 0.061	0.112 ± 0.046	0.127 ± 0.029	0.096 ± 0.029	0.022 ± 0.002	$-$
f_{10}	0.097 ± 0.010	0.088 ± 0.004	0.084 ± 0.002	0.082 ± 0.001	0.081 ± 0.001	0.014 ± 0.000	$-$
f_{11}	0.577 ± 0.404	0.187 ± 0.101	0.112 ± 0.057	0.115 ± 0.010	0.098 ± 0.030	0.022 ± 0.001	$-$
f_{12}	0.160 ± 0.020	0.102 ± 0.007	0.096 ± 0.005	0.093 ± 0.007	0.084 ± 0.007	0.017 ± 0.001	$-$
f_{13}	0.237 ± 0.069	0.130 ± 0.014	0.130 ± 0.006	0.085 ± 0.004	0.089 ± 0.004	0.019 ± 0.001	$-$
f_{14}	0.123 ± 0.011	0.101 ± 0.008	0.098 ± 0.005	0.093 ± 0.004	0.087 ± 0.004	0.018 ± 0.002	$-$
f_{15}	0.105 ± 0.015	0.089 ± 0.036	0.089 ± 0.003	0.084 ± 0.003	0.081 ± 0.003	0.022 ± 0.000	$-$
f_{16}	0.132 ± 0.014	0.142 ± 0.030	0.128 ± 0.021	0.105 ± 0.008	0.089 ± 0.008	0.020 ± 0.003	$-$
f_{17}	0.210 ± 0.138	0.189 ± 0.067	0.123 ± 0.014	0.109 ± 0.011	0.088 ± 0.011	0.018 ± 0.001	$-$
f_{18}	0.386 ± 0.229	0.134 ± 0.067	0.098 ± 0.015	0.106 ± 0.025	0.096 ± 0.025	0.020 ± 0.002	$-$
f_{19}	0.108 ± 0.011	0.102 ± 0.009	0.102 ± 0.004	0.085 ± 0.009	0.081 ± 0.009	0.014 ± 0.001	$-$

Finally, we have taken into account the testbed for *Large Scale Global Optimization* introduced at CEC2013 (CEC2013-LSGO), for a further check. This testbed is available only at 1000 dimensions and its results are reported in Table 4. Again, the displayed indices have been averaged over 50 independent runs. As shown in Table 4, the results reported for the other testbeds are further confirmed. In this large scale case, all the indices tend to take a low value regardless of the fact the corresponding problem is separable or non-separable.

Table 2. Average Pearson (ς) and Spearman (φ) correlation indices $\pm$ standard deviation values for CEC2013 over increasing dimensionality values

	$\varsigma 10n$	$\varsigma 30n$	$\varsigma 50n$	$\varphi 10n$	$\varphi 30n$	$\varphi 50n$	Separable
f_1	0.054 ± 0.007	0.032 ± 0.001	0.027 ± 0.001	0.099 ± 0.010	0.085 ± 0.005	0.084 ± 0.001	YES
f_2	0.563 ± 0.036	0.256 ± 0.025	0.238 ± 0.024	0.543 ± 0.053	0.293 ± 0.038	0.242 ± 0.030	$-$
f_3	0.271 ± 0.147	0.116 ± 0.019	0.059 ± 0.025	0.267 ± 0.108	0.127 ± 0.023	0.112 ± 0.027	$-$
f_4	0.110 ± 0.028	0.085 ± 0.011	0.091 ± 0.009	0.154 ± 0.061	0.121 ± 0.006	0.121 ± 0.013	$-$
f_5	0.072 ± 0.010	0.058 ± 0.008	0.045 ± 0.004	0.113 ± 0.015	0.100 ± 0.006	0.091 ± 0.007	YES
f_6	0.601 ± 0.222	0.315 ± 0.045	0.164 ± 0.010	0.543 ± 0.224	0.305 ± 0.075	0.187 ± 0.015	$-$
f_7	0.303 ± 0.208	0.100 ± 0.019	0.060 ± 0.006	0.176 ± 0.268	0.117 ± 0.013	0.098 ± 0.005	$-$
f_8	0.413 ± 0.061	0.142 ± 0.011	0.076 ± 0.004	0.409 ± 0.086	0.158 ± 0.010	0.108 ± 0.005	$-$
f_9	0.325 ± 0.106	0.119 ± 0.020	0.076 ± 0.013	0.372 ± 0.178	0.150 ± 0.020	0.107 ± 0.003	$-$
f_{10}	0.187 ± 0.010	0.093 ± 0.001	0.065 ± 0.001	0.201 ± 0.021	0.120 ± 0.003	0.103 ± 0.004	$-$
f_{11}	0.081 ± 0.047	0.038 ± 0.007	0.028 ± 0.002	0.132 ± 0.044	0.087 ± 0.003	0.084 ± 0.002	YES
f_{12}	0.277 ± 0.075	0.085 ± 0.004	0.055 ± 0.001	0.257 ± 0.051	0.115 ± 0.007	0.097 ± 0.004	$-$
f_{13}	0.235 ± 0.068	0.113 ± 0.029	0.066 ± 0.009	0.261 ± 0.066	0.121 ± 0.025	0.106 ± 0.005	$-$
f_{14}	0.057 ± 0.011	0.037 ± 0.010	0.036 ± 0.010	0.093 ± 0.011	0.090 ± 0.013	0.092 ± 0.006	$-$
f_{15}	0.194 ± 0.025	0.091 ± 0.005	0.065 ± 0.006	0.205 ± 0.031	0.119 ± 0.011	0.100 ± 0.010	$-$
f_{16}	0.435 ± 0.110	0.345 ± 0.137	0.273 ± 0.162	0.354 ± 0.145	0.285 ± 0.022	0.245 ± 0.093	$-$
f_{17}	0.210 ± 0.062	0.099 ± 0.015	0.051 ± 0.009	0.197 ± 0.069	0.117 ± 0.014	0.094 ± 0.005	$-$
f_{18}	0.283 ± 0.032	0.120 ± 0.016	0.082 ± 0.021	0.264 ± 0.038	0.150 ± 0.019	0.115 ± 0.015	$-$
f_{19}	0.255 ± 0.043	0.094 ± 0.011	0.073 ± 0.019	0.288 ± 0.059	0.124 ± 0.006	0.105 ± 0.010	$-$
f_{20}	0.360 ± 0.127	0.140 ± 0.006	0.076 ± 0.003	0.319 ± 0.046	0.156 ± 0.008	0.109 ± 0.006	$-$
f_{21}	0.075 ± 0.011	0.032 ± 0.002	0.031 ± 0.008	0.107 ± 0.012	0.088 ± 0.004	0.085 ± 0.002	$-$
f_{22}	0.058 ± 0.011	0.046 ± 0.017	0.045 ± 0.010	0.100 ± 0.014	0.089 ± 0.009	0.091 ± 0.005	YES
f_{23}	0.252 ± 0.147	0.097 ± 0.011	0.087 ± 0.052	0.219 ± 0.062	0.130 ± 0.029	0.122 ± 0.011	$-$
f_{24}	0.224 ± 0.074	0.067 ± 0.016	0.057 ± 0.013	0.262 ± 0.131	0.110 ± 0.018	0.094 ± 0.010	$-$
f_{25}	0.218 ± 0.122	0.115 ± 0.010	0.065 ± 0.008	0.197 ± 0.048	0.138 ± 0.010	0.102 ± 0.004	$-$
f_{26}	0.253 ± 0.087	0.068 ± 0.009	0.082 ± 0.069	0.301 ± 0.010	0.152 ± 0.011	0.150 ± 0.075	$-$
f_{27}	0.142 ± 0.093	0.082 ± 0.032	0.065 ± 0.021	0.138 ± 0.077	0.118 ± 0.032	0.105 ± 0.011	$-$
f_{28}	0.084 ± 0.063	0.033 ± 0.001	0.028 ± 0.013	0.118 ± 0.012	0.086 ± 0.003	0.085 ± 0.002	$-$

For all the 86 problems considered in this study, it appears clear that the correlation amongst variables (both Pearson and Spearman indices) tends to decay when the dimensionality increases. As a general trend, optimization problems with at least 100 dimensions seem characterized by a weak correlation. Optimization problems in 500 and 1000 dimensions show a nearly null correlation amongst the variables.

The phenomenon of the decrease of the correlation indices when the dimensionality increases is depicted in Figs. 1 and 2. It can be observed that all the trends decrease towards zero. In addition, we noticed that while for separable functions the indices have comparatively low values already in 10 dimensions and further become smaller with the increase of dimensionality, non-separable functions are characterized by a major drop in the correlation indices when the dimensionality increases (see Figs. 1 and 2).

Thus, our experimental study suggests that large scale optimization problems, regardless of the specific problem, have a lot in common with each other in terms of correlation among the variables and that all the LSOPs appear always

Table 3. Average Pearson (ς) and Spearman (φ) correlation indices ± standard deviation values for BBOB2010 over increasing dimensionality values

	$\varsigma 10n$	$\varsigma 30n$	$\varsigma 50n$	$\varsigma 100n$	$\varphi 10n$	$\varphi 30n$	$\varphi 50n$	$\varphi 100n$	Separable
f_1	0.054 ± 0.004	0.045 ± 0.035	0.028 ± 0.001	0.015 ± 0.000	0.095 ± 0.009	0.087 ± 0.003	0.084 ± 0.002	0.082 ± 0.001	YES
f_2	0.051 ± 0.006	0.034 ± 0.002	0.028 ± 0.001	0.015 ± 0.000	0.096 ± 0.008	0.087 ± 0.004	0.084 ± 0.002	0.081 ± 0.001	YES
f_3	0.054 ± 0.007	0.045 ± 0.040	0.030 ± 0.012	0.015 ± 0.000	0.096 ± 0.009	0.087 ± 0.003	0.084 ± 0.001	0.082 ± 0.001	YES
f_4	0.055 ± 0.007	0.045 ± 0.002	0.027 ± 0.001	0.015 ± 0.000	0.090 ± 0.008	0.087 ± 0.004	0.085 ± 0.002	0.081 ± 0.001	YES
f_5	0.058 ± 0.004	0.035 ± 0.002	0.027 ± 0.001	0.015 ± 0.000	0.092 ± 0.011	0.086 ± 0.003	0.084 ± 0.002	0.082 ± 0.001	YES
f_6	0.051 ± 0.006	0.042 ± 0.030	0.031 ± 0.015	0.015 ± 0.000	0.099 ± 0.016	0.084 ± 0.004	0.083 ± 0.002	0.082 ± 0.001	–
f_7	0.053 ± 0.005	0.033 ± 0.002	0.027 ± 0.001	0.015 ± 0.000	0.099 ± 0.013	0.087 ± 0.004	0.086 ± 0.001	0.081 ± 0.001	–
f_8	0.055 ± 0.006	0.034 ± 0.002	0.028 ± 0.001	0.015 ± 0.000	0.094 ± 0.010	0.086 ± 0.003	0.085 ± 0.002	0.081 ± 0.001	–
f_9	0.054 ± 0.005	0.039 ± 0.015	0.027 ± 0.001	0.015 ± 0.000	0.099 ± 0.010	0.089 ± 0.004	0.085 ± 0.001	0.082 ± 0.000	–
f_{10}	0.055 ± 0.007	0.034 ± 0.001	0.028 ± 0.001	0.015 ± 0.000	0.102 ± 0.018	0.087 ± 0.003	0.087 ± 0.008	0.082 ± 0.001	–
f_{11}	0.051 ± 0.005	0.043 ± 0.034	0.029 ± 0.008	0.015 ± 0.000	0.094 ± 0.011	0.087 ± 0.003	0.085 ± 0.001	0.082 ± 0.001	–
f_{12}	0.053 ± 0.005	0.034 ± 0.002	0.028 ± 0.001	0.015 ± 0.000	0.093 ± 0.014	0.088 ± 0.003	0.085 ± 0.002	0.082 ± 0.001	–
f_{13}	0.055 ± 0.007	0.035 ± 0.002	0.027 ± 0.001	0.015 ± 0.000	0.095 ± 0.011	0.086 ± 0.004	0.083 ± 0.002	0.081 ± 0.001	–
f_{14}	0.054 ± 0.007	0.034 ± 0.002	0.027 ± 0.001	0.015 ± 0.000	0.097 ± 0.009	0.088 ± 0.004	0.084 ± 0.001	0.082 ± 0.001	–
f_{15}	0.053 ± 0.007	0.035 ± 0.001	0.028 ± 0.001	0.015 ± 0.000	0.097 ± 0.008	0.086 ± 0.003	0.085 ± 0.001	0.082 ± 0.001	–
f_{16}	0.051 ± 0.004	0.054 ± 0.046	0.027 ± 0.001	0.015 ± 0.000	0.093 ± 0.013	0.085 ± 0.003	0.084 ± 0.002	0.082 ± 0.001	–
f_{17}	0.051 ± 0.004	0.035 ± 0.002	0.027 ± 0.001	0.015 ± 0.000	0.092 ± 0.013	0.087 ± 0.004	0.084 ± 0.003	0.082 ± 0.001	–
f_{18}	0.052 ± 0.006	0.039 ± 0.012	0.028 ± 0.001	0.015 ± 0.000	0.100 ± 0.012	0.089 ± 0.004	0.085 ± 0.003	0.082 ± 0.001	–
f_{19}	0.052 ± 0.006	0.034 ± 0.001	0.028 ± 0.001	0.015 ± 0.000	0.097 ± 0.008	0.087 ± 0.002	0.085 ± 0.002	0.082 ± 0.001	–
f_{20}	0.051 ± 0.006	0.034 ± 0.001	0.028 ± 0.001	0.015 ± 0.000	0.093 ± 0.009	0.086 ± 0.003	0.084 ± 0.001	0.082 ± 0.001	–
f_{21}	0.052 ± 0.006	0.034 ± 0.001	0.027 ± 0.001	0.015 ± 0.000	0.088 ± 0.008	0.087 ± 0.004	0.084 ± 0.002	0.082 ± 0.001	–
f_{22}	0.051 ± 0.004	0.038 ± 0.013	0.027 ± 0.001	0.015 ± 0.000	0.098 ± 0.010	0.086 ± 0.003	0.083 ± 0.002	0.082 ± 0.001	–
f_{23}	0.054 ± 0.007	0.035 ± 0.001	0.027 ± 0.001	0.015 ± 0.000	0.092 ± 0.011	0.091 ± 0.009	0.084 ± 0.003	0.082 ± 0.001	–
f_{24}	0.053 ± 0.005	0.033 ± 0.002	0.027 ± 0.001	0.015 ± 0.000	0.096 ± 0.008	0.086 ± 0.003	0.084 ± 0.002	0.082 ± 0.001	–

Table 4. Average Pearson (ς) and Spearman (φ) correlation indices $\pm$ standard deviation values for CEC2013-LSGO in 1000 dimensions

	ς_{1000n}	φ_{1000n}	Separable
f_1	0.015 ± 0.001	0.085 ± 0.001	YES
f_2	0.003 ± 0.000	0.080 ± 0.000	YES
f_3	0.002 ± 0.000	0.080 ± 0.000	YES
f_4	0.015 ± 0.001	0.085 ± 0.001	$-$
f_5	0.003 ± 0.000	0.080 ± 0.000	$-$
f_6	0.002 ± 0.000	0.080 ± 0.000	$-$
f_7	0.015 ± 0.001	0.085 ± 0.001	$-$
f_8	0.016 ± 0.001	0.085 ± 0.001	$-$
f_9	0.003 ± 0.000	0.080 ± 0.000	$-$
f_{10}	0.002 ± 0.000	0.080 ± 0.000	$-$
f_{11}	0.015 ± 0.001	0.086 ± 0.001	$-$
f_{12}	0.015 ± 0.002	0.085 ± 0.001	YES
f_{13}	0.015 ± 0.001	0.085 ± 0.001	$-$
f_{14}	0.015 ± 0.001	0.085 ± 0.002	$-$
f_{15}	0.015 ± 0.001	0.085 ± 0.001	$-$

characterized by uncorrelated variables. This fact has an effect on the design strategy since uncorrelated variables could be perturbed/optimised separately.

We are not concluding, however, that the nature of the problem changes with its dimensionality. In other words, we are not concluding that LSOPs are

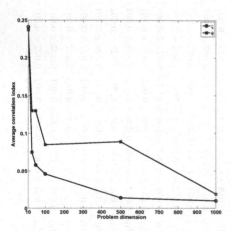

Fig. 1. Correlation indices for f_{13} of SISC2010

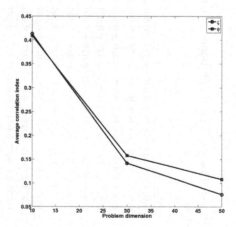

Fig. 2. Correlation indices for f_8 of CEC2013.

characterized by a weak correlation between pairs of variables. On the other hand, the experimental conditions imposed by the computational restrictions make LSOPs appear characterized by a low correlation since the search on this problems has to be much more shallow (i.e., it can cover a much smaller portion of the decision space) than the same problem in low dimensions. From a practical viewpoint, our conclusion is that since we know that in high dimensions we do not (and cannot) truly explore the decision space but we only attempt to improve upon some solutions with a very modest budget, the most effective way to quickly achieve an improvement would be to take into account this apparent weak correlation between pairs of variables. Although a further investigation is needed, the result of this study can be exploited during the algorithm design by employing exploitative techniques which perturb the variables one by one.

5   Conclusion

This paper proposed a technique based on two statical tests, based Pearson and Spearman correlation coefficients respectively, to measure the correlation between pairs of variables. These tests have been applied to measure the correlation between pairs of variables in different dimensionality scenarios. The standard experimental conditions used in the literature and popular competitions have been reproduced.

We noted that, in practice, such experimental conditions impose a growing shallowness of the search with the increase of dimensionality, i.e. only a very restricted portion of the decision space is explored in high dimensions. We observed that under these conditions, problems tend to appear, regardless of their nature, characterized by a weak correlation of variables.

Thus, if the budget is limited, a practically efficient approach could be, according to our conjecture, to avoid the use of exploratory components and simultaneous variations of multiple variables (diagonal moves). On the contrary, the exploitation of the search along each variable can enhance in the short term and for the limited budget the efficiency of the search. This conjecture is in accordance with the most popular and successful methods for large scale optimisation.

Further studies will propose specific algorithmic components which will make use of the knowledge gained in this study to leverage the (apparent) weak correlation between pairs of variables within their search logic.

 Acknowledgments. This project has received funding from the European Union's Horizon 2020 research and innovation programme under grant agreement No 665347.

References

1. Eiben, A.E., Smith, J.E.: Introduction to Evolutionary Computation. Natural Computing Series. Springer, Berlin (2003)
2. van den Bergh, F., Engelbrecht, A.P.: A cooperative approach to particle swarm optimization. IEEE Trans. Evol. Comput. **8**(3), 225–239 (2004)

3. Neri, F., Tirronen, V.: Recent advances in differential evolution: a review and experimental analysis. Artif. Intell. Rev. **33**(1–2), 61–106 (2010)
4. Li, S., Wei, D.: Extremely high-dimensional feature selection via feature generating samplings. IEEE Trans. Cybern. **44**(6), 737–747 (2014)
5. Hooke, R., Jeeves, T.A.: Direct search solution of numerical and statistical problems. J. ACM **8**, 212–229 (1961)
6. Auger, A., Hansen, N.: A restart CMA evolution strategy with increasing population size. In: Proceedings of the IEEE Congress on Evolutionary Computation, pp. 1769–1776 (2005)
7. Molina, D., Lozano, M., Garcia-Martinez, C., Herrera, F.: Memetic algorithms for continuous optimization based on local search chains. Evol. Comput. **18**(1), 27–63 (2010)
8. Marchiori, E., Steenbeek, A.: An evolutionary algorithm for large scale set covering problems with application to airline crew scheduling. In: Cagnoni, S. (ed.) EvoWorkshops 2000. LNCS, vol. 1803, pp. 370–384. Springer, Heidelberg (2000). doi:10.1007/3-540-45561-2_36
9. Kononova, A.V., Hughes, K.J., Pourkashanian, M., Ingham, D.B.: Fitness diversity based adaptive memetic algorithm for solving inverse problems of chemical kinetics. In: Proceedings of the IEEE Congress on Evolutionary Computation, pp. 2366–2373 (2007)
10. Kononova, A.V., Ingham, D.B., Pourkashanian, M.: Simple scheduled memetic algorithm for inverse problems in higher dimensions: application to chemical kinetics. In: Proceedings of the IEEE World Congress on Computational Intelligence, pp. 3906–3913 (2008)
11. Akay, B., Karaboga, D.: Artificial bee colony algorithm for large-scale problems and engineering design optimization. J. Intell. Manufact. **23**(4), 1001–1014 (2012)
12. Iacca, G., Caraffini, F., Neri, F.: Multi-strategy coevolving aging particle optimization. Int. J. Neural Syst. **24**(1), 1450008 (2014)
13. Korošec, P., Šilc, J.: The differential ant-stigmergy algorithm for large scale real-parameter optimization. In: Dorigo, M., Birattari, M., Blum, C., Clerc, M., Stützle, T., Winfield, A.F.T. (eds.) ANTS 2008. LNCS, vol. 5217, pp. 413–414. Springer, Heidelberg (2008). doi:10.1007/978-3-540-87527-7_51
14. Fister, I., Jr., I.F., Brest, J., Zumer, V.: Memetic artificial bee colony algorithm for large-scale global optimization. In: Proceedings of the IEEE Congress on Evolutionary Computation, pp. 1–8 (2012)
15. Parsopoulos, K.E.: Cooperative micro-differential evolution for high-dimensional problems. In: Proceedings of the Conference on Genetic and Evolutionary Computation, pp. 531–538 (2009)
16. Parsopoulos, K.E.: Cooperative micro-particle swarm optimization. In: Proceedings of the First ACM/SIGEVO Summit on Genetic and Evolutionary Computation, pp. 467–474. ACM (2009)
17. Rajasekhar, A., Das, S., Das, S.: Abc: a micro artificial bee colony algorithm for large scale global optimization. In: GECCO (Companion), pp. 1399–1400 (2012)
18. Dasgupta, S., Biswas, A., Das, S., Panigrahi, B.K., Abraham, A.: A micro-bacterial foraging algorithm for high-dimensional optimization. In: IEEE Congress on Evolutionary Computation, pp. 785–792 (2009)
19. Brest, J., Maučec, M.S.: Population size reduction for the differential evolution algorithm. Appl. Intell. **29**(3), 228–247 (2008)

20. Zamuda, A., Brest, J., Bošković, B., Žumer, V.: High-dimensional real-parameter optimization using self-adaptive differential evolution algorithm with population size reduction. In: Proceedings of the IEEE World Congress on Computational Intelligence, pp. 2032–2039 (2008)
21. Iacca, G., Mallipeddi, R., Mininno, E., Neri, F., Suganthan, P.N.: Super-fit and population size reduction mechanisms in compact differential evolution. In: Proceedings of IEEE Symposium on Memetic Computing, pp. 21–28 (2011)
22. Brest, J., Maucec, M.S.: Self-adaptive differential evolution algorithm using population size reduction and three strategies. Soft Comput. 15(11), 2157–2174 (2011)
23. Tseng, L.Y., Chen, C.: Multiple trajectory search for large scale global optimization. In: Proceedings of the IEEE Congress on Evolutionary Computation, pp. 3052–3059 (2008)
24. Zhao, S.Z., Suganthan, P.N., Das, S.: Self-adaptive differential evolution with multi-trajectory search for large-scale optimization. Soft Comput. 15(11), 2175–2185 (2011)
25. Caraffini, F., Neri, F., Poikolainen, I.: Micro-differential evolution with extra moves along the axes. In: Proceedings of the IEEE Symposium Series on Computational Intelligence, pp. 46–53 (2013)
26. Iacca, G., Neri, F., Mininno, E., Ong, Y.S., Lim, M.H.: Ockham's razor in memetic computing: three stage optimal memetic exploration. Inf. Sci. 188, 17–43 (2012)
27. Caraffini, F., Neri, F., Iacca, G., Mol, A.: Parallel memetic structures. Inf. Sci. 227, 60–82 (2013)
28. Caraffini, F., Neri, F., Passow, B., Iacca, G.: Re-sampled inheritance search: high performance despite the simplicity. Soft Comput. 17(12), 2235–2256 (2014)
29. Ros, R., Hansen, N.: A simple modification in CMA-ES achieving linear time and space complexity. In: Proceedings of the Parallel Problem Solving in Nature, pp. 296–305 (2008)
30. Potter, M.A., Jong, K.A.: A cooperative coevolutionary approach to function optimization. In: Davidor, Y., Schwefel, H.-P., Männer, R. (eds.) PPSN 1994. LNCS, vol. 866, pp. 249–257. Springer, Heidelberg (1994). doi:10.1007/3-540-58484-6_269
31. Liu, Y., Zhao, Q.: Scaling up fast evolutionary programming with cooperative coevolution. In: Proceedings of the IEEE Congress on Evolutionary Computation, pp. 1101–1108 (2001)
32. Sofge, D., De Jong, K., Schultz, A.: A blended population approach to cooperative coevolution for decomposition of complex problems. In: Proceedings of the IEEE Congress on Evolutionary Computation, pp. 413–418 (2002)
33. Potter, M.A., De Jong, K.: Cooperative coevolution: an architecture for evolving coadapted subcomponents. Evol. Comput. 8(1), 1–29 (2000)
34. Shi, Y., Teng, H., Li, Z.: Cooperative co-evolutionary differential evolution for function optimization. In: Wang, L., Chen, K., Ong, Y.S. (eds.) ICNC 2005. LNCS, vol. 3611, pp. 1080–1088. Springer, Heidelberg (2005). doi:10.1007/11539117_147
35. Yang, Z., Tang, K., Yao, X.: Differential evolution for high-dimensional function optimization. In: Proceedings of the IEEE Congress on Evolutionary Computation, pp. 3523–3530 (2007)
36. Zamuda, A., Brest, J., Bošković, B., Žumer, V.: Large scale global optimization using differential evolution with self-adaptation and cooperative co-evolution. In: Proceedings of the IEEE World Congress on Computational Intelligence, pp. 3719–3726 (2008)
37. Olorunda, O., Engelbrecht, A.P.: Differential evolution in high-dimensional search spaces. In: Proceedings of the IEEE Congress on Evolutionary Computation, pp. 1934–1941 (2007)

38. Yang, Z., Tang, K., Yao, X.: Large scale evolutionary optimization using cooperative coevolution. Inf. Sci. **178**(15), 2985–2999 (2008)
39. Li, X., Yao, X.: Cooperatively coevolving particle swarms for large scale optimization. IEEE Trans. Evol. Comput. **16**(2), 210–224 (2012)
40. Hansen, N., Müller, S.D., Koumoutsakos, P.: Reducing the time complexity of the derandomized evolution strategy with covariance matrix adaptation (CMA-ES). Evol. Comput. **11**(1), 1–18 (2003)
41. Hansen, N., Kern, S.: Evaluating the CMA evolution strategy on multimodal test functions. In: Yao, X., et al. (eds.) PPSN 2004. LNCS, vol. 3242, pp. 282–291. Springer, Heidelberg (2004). doi:10.1007/978-3-540-30217-9_29
42. Hansen, N., Ostermeier, A.: Adapting arbitrary normal mutation distributions in evolution strategies: the covariance matrix adaptation. In: Proceedings of the IEEE International Conference on Evolutionary Computation, pp. 312–317 (1996)
43. Hansen, N., Ostermeier, A.: Completely derandomized self-adaptation in evolution strategies. Evol. Comput. **9**(2), 159–195 (2001)
44. Pearson, K.: Mathematical contributions to the theory of evolution. XI. on the influence of natural selection on the variability and correlation of organs. Philos. Trans. Roy. Soc. Lon. Ser. A, Contain. Papers Math. Phys. Char. **200**, 1–66 (1903)
45. Spearman, C.: The proof and measurement of association between two things. Am. J. Psychol. **15**(1), 72–101 (1904)
46. Hauke, J., Kossowski, T.: Comparison of values of pearson's and spearman's correlation coefficients on the same sets of data. Quaestiones Geographicae **2**, 87–93 (2011)
47. Cox, D.R., Hinkley, D.: Theoretical Statistics. Chapman & Hall, London (1974)
48. Lozano, M., Molina, D., Herrera, F.: Editorial scalability of evolutionary algorithms and other metaheuristics for large-scale continuous optimization problems. Soft Comput. **15**(11), 2085–2087 (2011)
49. Caraffini, F., Neri, F., Picinali, L.: An analysis on separability for memetic computing automatic design. Inf. Sci. **265**, 1–22 (2014)
50. Liang, J.J., Qu, B.Y., Suganthan, P.N., Hernández-Díaz, A.G. : Problem definitions and evaluation criteria for the CEC 2013 special session on real-parameter optimization. Technical report 201212, Zhengzhou University and Nanyang Technological University, Zhengzhou China and Singapore (2013)
51. Hansen, N., Auger, A., Finck, S., Ros, R., et al.: Real-parameter black-box optimization benchmarking 2010: noiseless functions definitions. Technical report RR-6829, INRIA (2010)

A Framework for Knowledge Integrated Evolutionary Algorithms

Ahmed Hallawa[1]([✉]), Anil Yaman[2,3], Giovanni Iacca[2], and Gerd Ascheid[1]

[1] Chair for Integrated Signal Processing Systems,
RWTH Aachen University, 52056 Aachen, Germany
{hallawa,ascheid}@ice.rwth-aachen.de
[2] INCAS3, P.O. Box 797, 9400 AT Assen, The Netherlands
giovanni.iacca@gmail.com
[3] Department of Mathematics and Computer Science, Eindhoven University
of Technology, P.O. Box 513, 5600 MB Eindhoven, The Netherlands
a.yaman@tue.nl

Abstract. One of the main reasons for the success of Evolutionary Algorithms (EAs) is their general-purposeness, i.e. the fact that they can be applied in a straight forward manner to a broad range of optimization problems, without any specific prior knowledge. On the other hand, it has been shown that incorporating a priori knowledge, such as expert knowledge or empirical findings, can significantly improve the performance of an EA. However, integrating knowledge in EAs poses numerous challenges. It is often the case that the features of the search space are unknown, hence any knowledge associated with the search space properties can be hardly used. In addition, a priori knowledge is typically problem-specific and hard to generalize. In this paper, we propose a framework, called Knowledge Integrated Evolutionary Algorithm (KIEA), which facilitates the integration of existing knowledge into EAs. Notably, the KIEA framework is EA-agnostic, i.e. it works with any evolutionary algorithm, problem-independent, i.e. it is not dedicated to a specific type of problems and expandable, i.e. its knowledge base can grow over time. Furthermore, the framework integrates knowledge while the EA is running, thus optimizing the consumption of computational power. In the preliminary experiments shown here, we observe that the KIEA framework produces in the worst case an 80% improvement on the converge time, w.r.t. the corresponding "knowledge-free" EA counterpart.

Keywords: Evolutionary algorithms · Knowledge incorporation · Landscape analysis · Evolutionary algorithm fingerprint

1 Introduction

Evolutionary Algorithms (EAs) are considered nowadays a valuable search and optimization tool suitable for many real-world problems characterized by complex multidimensional search spaces. Among the many applications of EAs, some

© Springer International Publishing AG 2017
G. Squillero and K. Sim (Eds.): EvoApplications 2017, Part I, LNCS 10199, pp. 653–669, 2017.
DOI: 10.1007/978-3-319-55849-3_42

notable examples include the optimal design of electronic circuits [1], software [2,3], and even antennas for satellites orbiting outer space [4,5].

Despite the EAs' versatility, the theoretical limitations stated by the "No free lunch" (NFL) [6] pose a limit to their efficiency and applicability. As a possible mitigation for this problem, an EA can be made efficient and effective across a wide range of problems by endowing it with adaptive behavior with respect to the problem structure, thus with problem-specific mechanisms.

Such adaptation typically involves the EA's operators and tunable parameters, which play a pivotal role in the performance of the algorithm. In fact, there are several methods that can be used to optimize the behavior of EA. In a recent survey published by Črepinšek et al. [7], a number of approaches that can be used for this purpose are presented. Traditionally, researchers have used trial-and-error approaches in the attempt to find the best settings of the EA operators that can solve optimization problems most efficiently [8,9]. However, these approaches are typically computationally expensive, because they require numerous iterations (and in many cases it is not feasible to try all possible parametric combinations), and some are problem-specific, thus they can not be generalized to use on problems other than the one for which the tuning was performed. Furthermore, proposed frameworks which offer an adaptive behavior such as in some modulated versions of Differential Evolution (DE) algorithms, as in jDE [10] and JADE [11], does not offer a comprehensive strategy for all tunable parameters. Other approaches uses hyper-heuristics, i.e. they find the optimal EA settings by using an optimization algorithm [7,12].

One of the approaches that have not yet been explored, however, is to use experiences from previous problems with similar population behavior in the EA run [7]. In this work, we propose a framework that is a first attempt in this direction, where we also combine the approaches of "following general guidelines" accumulated in the literature, and "identifying the features of the landscape by a classifier, in order to propose good control parameters" [7].

The framework we propose is dubbed as *Knowledge Integrated Evolutionary Algorithm* (KIEA). Its main component is a *knowledge base* that maintains the knowledge of how various functions, i.e. optimization problems can be efficiently solved. These functions are named as *pilot functions*, and the associated knowledge to optimally tune the EA for solving those functions is named a *strategy*. The framework collects characteristics of the EA population behavior across generations. These characteristics are named *EA fingerprints*, and they are used to classify any unknown function under investigation w.r.t. each of the pilot functions (under the implicit hypothesis that such fingerprints can be used to assess the similarity between different functions). The strategy associated to the classified pilot function is then reused on the unknown function at hand, in the attempt of solving it in the most efficient way possible.

The approach we propose is novel in the following ways: Firstly, it allows the incorporation of various types of knowledge into the EA, allowing the algorithm to adjust its behavior based on the knowledge in the knowledge base. Initially, experts can bootstrap the system with their knowledge on the pilot functions. Secondly, the experience gained by the EA by solving problems generates valuable empirical knowledge that can also be added to the knowledge base for further use. This can be done by extending the pilot functions or changing the strategies associated with them. As a result, the knowledge base grows by accumulating the experience gained by solving multiple problems. The accumulated knowledge is then "plugged" into the problems that are similar to the ones encountered before. Moreover, the KIEA approach is generalizable as it conducts the problem classification only based on the behavior of the population in the EA run, independently from what this population is representing, i.e. the solution encoding and the genotype/phenotype mapping.

To assess the performance of KIEA, you see preliminary experiments on a small set of benchmark optimization problems. More specifically, we measure the fingerprint-based classification accuracy on different pilot functions by using different fingerprint properties. In addition to that, we compare the difference in terms of convergence time obtained in the experiments with and without KIEA.

The rest of the paper is organized as follows: Sect. 2 summarizes the previous works on knowledge integration in EAs, Sect. 3 presents the mathematical foundation of the EA fingerprint and the classification process. Section 4 demonstrates and discusses performance evaluations of our approach. Finally, Sect. 5 concludes with the paper.

2   Background

Different knowledge incorporation methodologies available in the literature aim to optimize EAs in order to enhance their performance. One of the key elements where knowledge plays a role is the balance between exploration and exploitation, a crucial aspect for an efficient search [7,13]. If there is, for example, more influence of exploration then the search becomes more like a random search; on the other hand, if exploitation is stronger than exploration then the search space could not be explored, and the behavior of the search becomes similar to the behavior of hill climbing [7].

In EAs, the balance between exploration and exploitation is typically adjusted by the evolutionary operators and their parameters. However, different evolutionary operators and different parameter values influence the process differently; and their combinations may have different, hard-to-analyze effects. One general interpretation considers the mutation and crossover as exploration operators[1], since they make (pseudo-)random changes in the genotype of individuals and cause random jumps in the search space; on the other hand, the selection operator is usually seen as an exploitation operator, because it focuses on specific places by selecting the individuals to reproduce. Moreover, the population size plays an important role in the EA behavior. Generally, re-sizing population

---

[1] It should be noted, however, that some literature considers the crossover operator as an exploitation mechanism. Generally, mutation and crossover have an effect on both exploration and exploitation, although this effect varies depending on the implementation and the fitness landscape at hand.

can be used to direct evolution process towards exploration or exploitation [14–16], this method is widely used in CMA-ES, DE, and PSO. In that regard, it is also important to highlight that the increase of the population size does not necessarily improve exploration. Conversely, it has shown that there is strong link between population size and structural bias of the algorithm [17]. Consequently, this component has to be taken into consideration when designing self-adapting EA.

The performance of a search process is also closely dependent on the features of the search space and the fitness landscape. There have been many works in the literature that aim to classify the landscapes based on their geometrical and topological features. Most of these works are linked to specific features such as modality, symmetry, etc., such as in [18–21]. There have also been several studies that aim to suggest optimal algorithms, or optimal algorithm parameters, based on the features of the landscape of the search space. For example, Asmus et al. [22] proposed a system for recommending suitable algorithms for a given black-box optimization problem. Muoz et al. [23] introduced a model that links the landscape analysis measures and the algorithm parameters (used CMA-ES) to predict the performance of the algorithm parameters. Picek and Jakobovic [24] performed a thorough study focused on the correlation between fitness landscapes and crossover operators.

Clearly, it would be extremely beneficial to leverage this wide range of knowledge from the literature for tuning the evolutionary operators parameters based on the landscape features. However, applying this knowledge often requires that such features are captured first, in order to choose the proper strategies. Unfortunately though, this is not always possible since either the search space is completely unknown, or hard to characterize.

Moreover, many of the existing works offer knowledge that is problem-specific and therefore hard to generalize and use with other problems. Another difficulty arises from the fact that this knowledge is often scattered over different levels of granularity, from too general to extremely detailed, which makes it hard to have comprehensive strategies.

The objective of the presented work is to propose a way of integrating existing *algorithmic knowledge* into a single, comprehensive evolutionary framework, and test the effect of such knowledge on the optimization performance. Here, with "algorithmic knowledge" we generally refer to the knowledge encompassing the categorizations of problems based on their landscape features, the types of strategies related to the adaptation of evolutionary operators and parameters, and the link between problem types and strategies, i.e. which strategies work best on a specific type. In the next section a detailed description of the framework is presented.

3   Methods

The KIEA methodology is straightforward and its implementation is relatively simple (see Algorithm 1). For completeness, we also report a conceptual scheme of the proposed KIEA in Fig. 1.

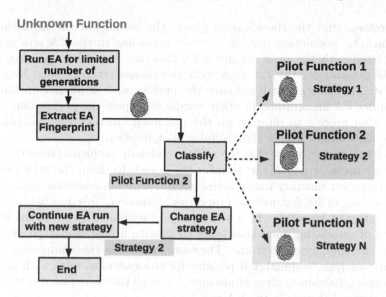

Fig. 1. Conceptual scheme of KIEA

The whole process can be considered as a single run of an EA divided into two stages: in the **first stage**, for a predefined number of generations, G_C, the unknown function under investigation undergoes an EA run with an arbitrary parameter setting (basically, population size, mutation and crossover probability). These settings are set as the initial EA strategy S_0. In each generation evolved in this first stage, a set of properties describing the population behavior is calculated to be used later for classification. These population behavior properties are termed *EA fingerprint* (see Sect. 3.1 for details). The first stage stops when the allotted number of generations G_C is reached.

In the **second stage**, a classification based on the EA fingerprint is performed as follows. The unknown function's fingerprint produced from the first stage is compared with the fingerprint obtained by the same initial strategy S_0 on a set of *pilot functions*, i.e. benchmark functions that are chosen a priori as representative of different categories of problems. Based on fingerprint similarities, the unknown function is then classified as the most similar pilot function. Detailed insights on the classification process are provided in Sect. 3.2.

Associated to each pilot function, the system maintains an EA *strategy*. Here, we refer to "strategy" as a set of changes (adaptation rules) in the EA parameters (e.g. a population size reduction/shrinking, mutation probability update rules, etc.) and when these changes should be implemented within the evolutionary run in order to enhance the optimization performance. These strategies are organized in a *knowledge base*, such that for each pilot function, its associated strategy is the one that according to our empirical experiments (see Sect. 4.1) showed the best performance.

Therefore, after the classification phase, the settings of the algorithm, i.e. mutation rate, population size, etc. are set according to the EA strategy that is associated with the most similar pilot function. For the remaining of the available generations, the EA runs with the chosen strategy. The hypothesis is that similar strategies can enhance the performance of an EA on functions with similar EA fingerprints; in other words, we expect the performance of the optimization process to improve on the unknown function after adopting the strategy associated with the most similar pilot function.

It is important to notice that the ability to classify problems based on the EA fingerprint makes it possible to transfer the knowledge from the pilot functions to any unknown function under investigation, without assuming any previous understanding of its features or properties. Moreover, this mechanism allows generalization of knowledge to a wide range of optimization problems without the need of associating such knowledge to specific fitness landscape properties such as modality, symmetry, etc. Therefore, it avoids the complexity due to landscape analysis, and makes it possible for the system to work with functions with complex, hard-to-analyze landscapes, since all that is required is to capture the population behavior in the EA run.

Algorithm 1. High-level description of the KIEA framework

```
1: procedure KIEA
2:     initialize total no. of generations G
3:     initialize no. of generations for classification G_C
4:     initialize generation counter g = 0
5:     set initial EA strategy S_0
6:     initialize population P
7:     while g < G_C do
8:         F ← evaluate (P)
9:         P ← select (P, F)
10:        P ← reproduce (P, F, S_0)
11:        f ← getFingerprint(P, F)              ▷ Store fingerprint
12:        g = g + 1
13:    end while
14:    Pilot_i ← classify(f)                      ▷ Classification
15:    S_i ← getStrategy(Pilot_i)                 ▷ Retrieve strategy
16:    while g < R_T do
17:        F ← evaluate (P)
18:        P ← select (P, F)
19:        P ← reproduce (P, F, S_i)
20:        g = g + 1
21:    end while
22: end procedure
```

In the following sections, we cover the mathematical details of the EA fingerprints and the classification procedure. In Table 1, we summarize the main symbols used in the text, with the related explanation.

Table 1. Symbols used in the paper

Symbol	Explanation
N	Total number of individuals in population
G	Total number of generations
G_C	Number of generations allocated for classification
$\mathbf{i}_l^g \in \mathbb{R}^n$	Individual belongs to cluster l at generation g
$\mathbf{c}_l^g \in \mathbb{R}^n$	Cluster l center individual at generation g
c_{min}	Minimum number of individuals to form a cluster
r_{max}	Maximum radius of the sphere S^n that a cluster can occupy
C_l^g	Set of individuals in cluster l at generation g
$|C_l^g|$	Number of individuals in cluster l at generation g
C_c^g	Set of cluster centers at generation g
$\mathcal{P}_l$	A tuple with the number of individuals in cluster l
d_{ij}^g	Euclidean distance between $\mathbf{c}_i^g$ and $\mathbf{c}_j^g$ at generation g
T_l	Population trend tuple of cluster l
$G_{d_{ij,\epsilon}}^g$	Set of points that have equal Euclidean distance $d_{ij} \pm \epsilon$ at generation g
S_i	EA Strategy i

3.1 EA Fingerprint

In the previous section we defined the EA fingerprint as a set of properties that characterize the population behavior. While in principle this could be done at individual level, in practice following all individuals in the population would be extremely computationally expensive, especially in high dimensions. For example, a simple task as finding the pair of points in a set with smallest distance between them (known as *closest pair of points problem*) has time complexity of $O(n^2 D/log^2 D)$ for D dimensions and n points using a divide and conquer approach [25]. Therefore, we define here EA fingerprints that are based on *clustering* the population and following the resulting clusters properties.

A cluster emerges when a predefined minimum number of individuals c_{min} from the population are grouped in a predefined maximum space r_{max} in the search space. This minimum number of individuals constituting a cluster and the corresponding maximum space used to designate it are set as a percentage of the population size N, e.g. $c_{min} = 5\%$ of N.

An EA fingerprint is grouped into two main groups: Clusters Emergence Characteristics (CEC) and Clusters Constellation Characteristics (CCC). CEC is designed to capture 5 features: number of clusters, number of individuals in each cluster, population trend in each cluster, fitness value of the fittest individual of each cluster, and its position. On the other hand, CEC captures the geometric properties of clusters, which include equidistant cluster topology and the corresponding distances between equidistant clusters in the search space.

In CCC, the first step is recognizing emerging clusters. The procedures for that are described as follows:

1. All individuals $\mathbf{i}_l^g \in \mathbb{R}^n \ \forall \, l = 1 \ldots N$ at generation g are sorted in descending order with respect to fitness.
2. The highest value is designated as a potential cluster center $\mathbf{c}_l^g$ forming the first point in the potential cluster set C_l^g.
3. Going through all population, each individual $\mathbf{i}_l^g$ is assigned to C_l^g with center point $\mathbf{c}_i^g$ if and only if:

$$\|\mathbf{i}_i^g - \mathbf{c}_j^g\| < r_{max}, \quad \forall j \neq i \wedge j = 1 \ldots N \tag{1}$$

where r_{max} is the maximum radius of the sphere S^n that a cluster can occupy, $S^n = \{x \in \mathbb{R}^{n+1} : \|x\| = r_{max}\}$. r_{max} is chosen adequately, e.g. 5% of the smallest search domain across all search variables.

4. A cluster C_l^g is designated with the center $\mathbf{c}_i^g$ if and only if the number of individuals assigned to it, $|C_l^g|$, is bigger than or equal to the minimum cluster size $c_{\min}$:

$$|C_l^g| \geq c_{\min} \tag{2}$$

where $c_{\min}$ is chosen as a percentage of the total population size N, e.g. 5%.
5. All individuals that were previous assigned to a cluster or picked as a potential cluster center are then discarded, steps (3) to (5) are repeated again until all N individuals in the population are considered.

These procedures are executed for each generation, until G_C is exhausted. For each generation g, all cluster centers $\mathbf{c}_l^g$, $l = 1, 2, \ldots$, are kept in a set C_c^g. Furthermore, due to sorting population in the first step in the procedures, $\mathbf{c}_l^g$ are also the fittest points in cluster l. This will be used later for comparing clusters with similar highest fitness points. In addition, for each generation the corresponding fitness value of each cluster center $\mathbf{c}_l^g$ are stored in a fitness set F_c^g. A tuple $\mathcal{P}_l$ with the number of individuals in cluster l through out all generations until a given generation m is defined as follows:

$$\mathcal{P}_l^m = <\,|C_l^1|, |C_l^2| \ldots, |C_l^{m-1}|, |C_l^m|\,> \tag{3}$$

where m can take any value from 1 to total number of generations G. In order to capture the changes in each cluster throughout different generations until a given generation m, for each $\mathcal{P}_l^m$, there exists a population trend tuple T_l^m defined as:

$$T_l^m = \begin{cases} 1, & \text{for } |C_l^k| - |C_l^{k+1}| < 0 \\ 0, & \text{for } |C_l^k| - |C_l^{k+1}| > 0 \end{cases} \quad \forall k = 1 \ldots m - 1 \tag{4}$$

Now, all the aforementioned CEC properties can be defined: the number of clusters for each generation g in $|C_l^g|$, the number of individuals in each cluster l in $\mathcal{P}_l$, the population trend across all generations in each cluster in T_l, the fitness value of the fittest individual (which is also the center) of each cluster in F_c^g, and its position in C_c^g for each generation g.

The second fingerprint component's, CCC, is meant to capture the geometric properties of clusters. Firstly, we define the Euclidean distance between all cluster centers in each generation g as:

$$d_{ij}^g = \|\mathbf{c}_i^g - \mathbf{c}_j^g\| \tag{5}$$

Then, we group equidistant cluster center points as follows:

$$G_{d_{kl,\epsilon}}^g = \{(\mathbf{c}_i^g, \mathbf{c}_j^g) \in C_c^{g^2} \ \forall i \neq j, \ d_{kl} - \epsilon < \|\mathbf{c}_i^g - \mathbf{c}_j^g\| < d_{kl} + \epsilon\} \tag{6}$$

where ϵ is a margin of tolerance adequately chosen as a percentage of the domains of each search variable.

Both d_{ij}^g and $G_{d_{kl,\epsilon}}$ constitute the CCC properties. Now that we have defined all the elements of the EA fingerprint, we can show how we use them for classification.

3.2   Classification

The objective of the classification process is to find the closest pilot function to the unknown function under investigation. This is conducted by comparing the EA fingerprints with the fingerprint of each pilot function. In the following description, ψ_k^g indicates the comparison of feature k at generation g.

The first comparison ψ_1^g is the difference in cluster numbers at each generation. This difference is multiplied by the ratio between the smallest cluster number over the biggest, as follows:

$$\psi_1 = \||C_l^g|_u - |C_l^g|_p\| \times \frac{\min(|C_l^g|_u, |C_l^g|_p)}{\max(|C_l^g|_u, |C_l^g|_p)} \tag{7}$$

where $|C_l^g|_u$ and $|C_l^g|_p$ are the numbers of clusters on the unknown function and the pilot function, respectively.

The second comparison ψ_2^g is the difference in the position between each center point $\mathbf{c}_l^g$ in the unknown function and the closest cluster center point position in the pilot functions. Only points whose distance from $\mathbf{c}_l^g$ is at most r_{max} are considered, to ensure that the closest point found in the pilot function cannot be chosen more than once, since there cannot exist two center cluster points within the same cluster sphere S^n which has maximum radius r_{max}. Consequently, ψ_2^g is defined as the sum of all the minimum distances between $\mathbf{c}_l^g$ of unknown function and pilot function, as follows:

$$\psi_2^g = \sum_{\mathbf{c}_i^g \in {}^u C_l^g} \min_{\mathbf{c}_j^g \in {}^P C_l^g} \|\mathbf{c}_i^g - \mathbf{c}_j^g\| \text{ with } d_{ij} < r_{max} \tag{8}$$

where ${}^u C_l^g$ and ${}^P C_l^g$ are sets with center points $\mathbf{c}_l^g$ at generation g for the unknown function and pilot function, respectively. The inequality $d_{ij} < r_{max}$ is the minimum distance condition explained earlier.

The third comparison is defined to capture the difference in population trends between the unknown function and the pilot function for clusters with similar fittest point values, i.e. clusters which have close center fitness values across all generations. Center cluster points with similar fitness values are identified as follows:

$$^{u}T^{g}_{f_0+k\epsilon} = \{f_l \in F^{g}_{u} | f_l - \epsilon \le f_0 + k\epsilon \le f_l + \epsilon\} \; \forall k \in \mathbb{N} \tag{9}$$

where f_0 is the least fit cluster center $\mathbf{c}^{g}_{l}$ in the unknown function at generation g, and F^{g}_{u} is the fitness set of the unknown function at generation g. $^{u}T^{g}_{f_0+k\epsilon}$ is a set of all points within range $f_0 + k\epsilon$, $\forall k \in \mathbb{N}$. The analogous value for the pilot functions, $^{p}T^{g}_{f_0+k\epsilon}$ is calculated similarly:

$$^{p}T^{g}_{f_0+k\epsilon} = \{f_l \in F^{g}_{p} | f_l - \epsilon \le f_0 + k\epsilon \le f_l + \epsilon\} \; \forall k \in \mathbb{N} \tag{10}$$

where f_0 is least fit cluster center $\mathbf{c}^{g}_{l}$ in the unknown function at generation g (same as in Eq. 9), and F^{g}_{p} is the fitness set of the pilot function at generation g. Then ψ^{g}_{3} is defined as:

$$\psi^{g}_{3} = \sum_{k \in \mathbb{N}} \frac{\min(|^{u}T^{g}_{f_0+k\epsilon}|, |^{p}T^{g}_{f_0+k\epsilon}|)}{\max(|^{u}T^{g}_{f_0+k\epsilon}|, |^{p}T^{g}_{f_0+k\epsilon}|)} \times \frac{\min(|C^{g}_{l}|_{u}, |C^{g}_{l}|_{p})}{\max(|C^{g}_{l}|_{u}, |C^{g}_{l}|_{p})} \tag{11}$$

where ψ^{g}_{3} is the summation of the ratio of number of points in range $f_o + k\epsilon$ in the unknown function and pilot function $\forall k$, normalized w.r.t. the ratio of cluster sizes, exactly like in ψ^{g}_{1}. The reason why the min and max operators are used instead of simply having $|^{u}T^{g}_{f_0+k\epsilon}|$ in the numerator and $|^{p}T^{g}_{f_0+k\epsilon}|$ in the denominator, is to ensure that the value of the fraction is always less than one and therefore ψ^{g}_{3} is comparable with other cases, regardless the fact that $|^{u}T^{g}_{f_0+k\epsilon}|$ is greater than $|^{p}T^{g}_{f_0+k\epsilon}|$ or vice versa.

The fourth comparison is used to capture the difference between the equidistant cluster center points, as follows:

$$\psi^{g}_{4} = \frac{\min(|\,G^{g}_{d_{ij,\epsilon}}\,|_{u}, |\,G^{g}_{d_{kl,\epsilon}}\,|_{p})}{\max(|\,G^{g}_{d_{ij,\epsilon}}\,|_{u}, |\,G^{g}_{d_{kl,\epsilon}}\,|_{p})} \text{ with } d_{kl} - \epsilon \le d_{ij} \le d_{kl} + \epsilon \tag{12}$$

where $G^{g}_{d_{ij,\epsilon}}$ is the set of equidistant cluster centers within the margin of tolerance ϵ at generation g.

The fifth comparison captures the trend of the population within clusters. Its definition reflects similarities in the change of population within clusters with similar fitness values. f^{g}_{l} is the highest fitness point in each cluster l at generation g, and there might exist a f^{g}_{l} in the pilot function at the same generation g with fitness value that is within ϵ range from it, a set that includes all these pairs of points is defined as:

$$M^{g} = \{(i,j) \in \mathbb{N}^{2} | \; \forall f_i \in F^{g}_{u}, f_j \in F^{g}_{p}, \; \|f^{g}_{i} - f^{g}_{j}\| \le \epsilon\} \tag{13}$$

where F^{g}_{u} and F^{g}_{p} are the fitness sets of the unknown function and pilot function respectively. M^{g} includes all cluster id pairs unknown function and pilot function that have highest fitness values difference less than ϵ. From Eq. 17, each item at position k in the tuple reflects the change in population between generation k and $k + 1$, its value be either zero for no change in population or one for increase in population or negative one for a decrease in population. For each pair identified in M^g, a comparison in the population number history up to generation g is defined as follows:

$$\psi_5^g = \sum_{(i,j) \in M} T_i^g \odot T_j^g \tag{14}$$

where T_i^g and T_j^g are the trend tuples of the unknown function and pilot function respectively and $\odot$ is defined here as an XNOR logic operator which produces 1 if operands are equal and 0 otherwise.

The sixth comparison captures the difference in the number of clusters per generation, as follows:

$$\psi_6^g = \sum_{g=1}^{G} \frac{\min(|C_l^g|_u, |C_l^g|_p)}{\max(|C_l^g|_u, |C_l^g|_p)} \tag{15}$$

Finally, the classification process is concluded based on ψ_1 to ψ_6, using a weighted sum as follows:

$$\psi_{Total} = \sum_{i=1}^{6} w_i \psi_i \tag{16}$$

where w_i is the weight of property i, which is set as follows:

$$w_i = \begin{cases} 1, & \text{for } i = 3, \\ -1, & otherwise \end{cases} \quad \forall i = 1 \ldots 6 \tag{17}$$

as with exception to ψ_3, the lesser the value the better the match with the pilot function. Finally, the total value is then compared with each pilot function, and the highest value leads to the winning pilot function, which then leads to the unknown function adapting its strategy.

4   Results

As a proof-of-concept, we now present the numerical results obtained by KIEA on a small set of benchmark functions. First, we explain the algorithmic setup and the strategy initialization in Sect. 4.1. Then, in Sect. 4.2 we illustrate the effect of different fingerprint properties on classification. Finally, Sect. 4.3 evaluates the performance of KIEA in terms of convergence time.

4.1   System Setup and Strategy Initialization

Although the KIEA framework is algorithmically agnostic and can be used with any EA, for testing purposes we use a classic Genetic Algorithm (GA). In the prototype we implemented, we focused on strategies expressed in terms of population size and mutation rates. Figures 2 and 3 show a preliminary performance analysis for two simple benchmark functions, namely the Ackley and the Gaussian function. It can be seen that for the Ackley function, population size 60 and mutation rate 0.01 is the most suitable strategy, while for the Gaussian function population size 40 and mutation rate 0.1 offer a more suitable strategy.

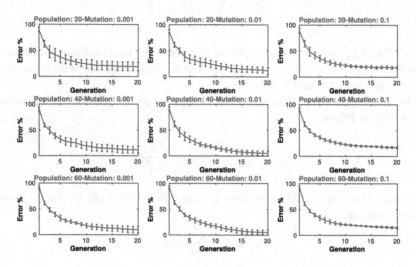

Fig. 2. Strategy analysis on the Ackley function

4.2   Effect of Fingerprints

To test the ability to classify a function based on its fingerprint, we conducted a four tests in total. In the first two, the objective was to classify the two pilot functions (Ackley and Gaussian) as if they were unknown. Moreover, we considered two additional unknown functions (Rastrigin and Rosenbrock), different from the pilot functions. Figures 4, 5, 6 and 7 show the classification of the Ackley, Gaussian, Rastrigin, and Rosenbrock functions, respectively. Each classification test was done by first extracting 50 different fingerprints for each pilot function, and then comparing each of the 50 fingerprints from the unknown function, thus with a total of 2500 comparisons (50 pilot functions fingerprints × 50 unknown function fingerprints). It is important to highlight that each property in the fingerprint contributes to the classification process, i.e. they are all needed and their contribution varies depending on the function at hand, while keeping the overall successful classification rate 90% to 98%. Moreover, their variance is relatively small (3% on average), which shows the good reliability of the proposed classification process.

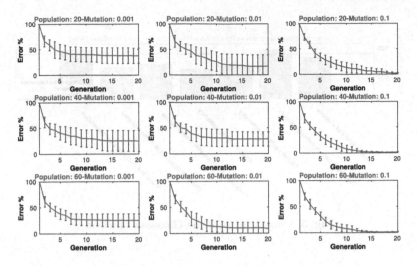

Fig. 3. Strategy analysis on the Gaussian function

4.3   KIEA Performance

We conclude the experimental validation of KIEA by measuring the performance gain in terms of convergence time. Table 2 summarizes the convergence time on the Ackley and Gaussian function in 10 dimensions, with and without KIEA. Tests are done 25 times per function and the 1st, 7th, 13th, 19th and 25th best convergence times out of the 25 runs are captured. All runs are done with FES $= 10^3$ and termination error $= 10^{-6}$. It is clear that there a decrease across all the best times when using KIEA, which reaches a 80% decrease in the worst case. Moreover, there is a significant decrease in standard deviation across all the runs, which suggests a more reliable performance when using KIEA.

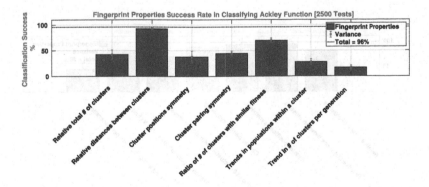

Fig. 4. Classification of the Ackley function

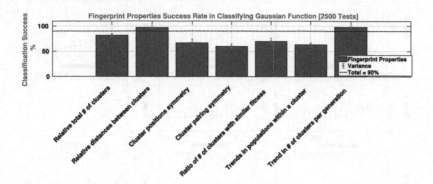

Fig. 5. Classification of the Gaussian function

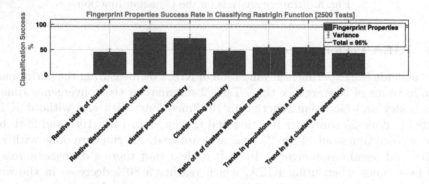

Fig. 6. Classification of the Rastrigin function

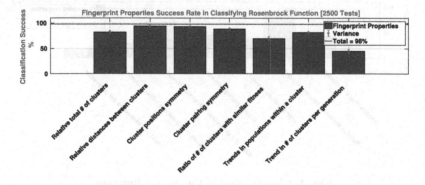

Fig. 7. Classification of the Rosenbrock Function

Table 2. Convergence time T [s] with and without KIEA

	Ackley (w/o KIEA)	Ackley (w/ KIEA)	Gaussian (w/o KIEA)	Gaussian (w/ KIEA)
1st	1.439	1.261	0.232	0.1179
7th	2.994	2.890	0.131	0.1194
13th	3.014	2.905	0.137	0.1200
19th	3.053	2.929	0.14	0.1283
25th	10.056	2.990	0.191	0.1658
Mean	3.677	2.791	0.1662	0.1303
Std	2.324	0.388	0.0439	0.0203

5   Conclusions

In this work, we have introduced a framework for knowledge integration in evolutionary algorithms. The framework, named KIEA, is based on the concept of *EA fingerprint*, i.e. a set of a properties that capture the population behavior in the solution space while the EA is running. In addition to the algorithmic description of the framework, we presented a mathematical formalization of the properties constituting the fingerprint.

In the preliminary experiments conducted in this study, the framework prototype showed a successful classification probability between 90% and 98%, depending on the function to optimize. Furthermore, the comparison of the convergence time on functions optimized with and without KIEA proved that the presented framework consistently enhances the convergence time, reaching a worst-case improvement of nearly 80%.

In addition to the improved numerical performance, the presented framework has the advantage of being fully expandable, since it is possible to add new pilot functions and strategies in a straightforward manner. Furthermore, KIEA is suitable for any evolutionary algorithm as it is not strictly bound to any specific EA implementation. In future works, we will test this framework on a wider range of optimization problems, and we will expand our knowledge base of pilot functions and corresponding strategies. Finally, we plan to perform tests with different kinds of state-of-the-art EAs, to show the general applicability of KIEA.

Acknowledgments. This project has received funding from the European Union's Horizon 2020 research and innovation program under grant agreement No. 665347. We also gratefully acknowledge the computational resources provided by RWTH Compute Cluster from RWTH Aachen University under project RWTH0118.

References

1. Koza, J.R., Keane, M.A., Streeter, M.J.: What's ai done for me lately? genetic programming's human-competitive results. IEEE Intell. Syst. **3**, 25–31 (2003)
2. Arcuri, A., Yao, X.: Co-evolutionary automatic programming for software development. Inf. Sci. **259**, 412–432 (2014)
3. Squillero, G.: MicroGP - an evolutionary assembly program generator. Program. Evol. Mach. **6**(3), 247–263 (2005)
4. Hornby, G.S., Globus, A., Linden, D.S., Lohn, J.D.: Automated antenna design with evolutionary algorithms. In: AIAA Space, pp. 19–21 (2006)
5. Lohn, J.D., Linden, D.S., Hornby, G.S., Kraus, W.F., Rodriguez-Arroyo, A.: Evolutionary design of an X-band antenna for NASA's space technology 5 mission. In: null, vol. 155. IEEE (2003)
6. Wolpert, D.H., Macready, W.G.: No free lunch theorems for optimization. IEEE Trans. Evol. Comput. **1**(1), 67–82 (1997)
7. Črepinšek, M., Liu, S.H., Mernik, M.: Exploration and exploitation in evolutionary algorithms: a survey. ACM Comput. Surv. (CSUR) **45**(3), 35 (2013)
8. Bäck, T.: Selective pressure in evolutionary algorithms: A characterization of selection mechanisms. In: Proceedings of the First IEEE Conference on Evolutionary Computation, IEEE World Congress on Computational Intelligence, 57–62. IEEE (1994)
9. Gates, G.H., Merkle, L.D., Lamont, G.B., Pachter, R.: Simple genetic algorithm parameter selection for protein structure prediction. In: IEEE International Conference on Evolutionary Computation, vol. 2, pp. 620–624. IEEE (1995)
10. Yang, M., Cai, Z., Li, C., Guan, J.: An improved adaptive differential evolution algorithm with population adaptation. In: Proceedings of the 15th Annual Conference on Genetic and Evolutionary Computation, pp. 145–152. ACM (2013)
11. Caorsi, S., Massa, A., Pastorino, M., Randazzo, A.: Optimization of the difference patterns for monopulse antennas by a hybrid real/integer-coded differential evolution method. IEEE Trans. Antenna Propag. **53**(1), 372–376 (2005)
12. Eiben, A.E., Hinterding, R., Michalewicz, Z.: Parameter control in evolutionary algorithms. IEEE Trans. Evol. Comput. **3**(2), 124–141 (1999)
13. Eiben, A.E., Schippers, C.A.: On evolutionary exploration and exploitation. Fundamenta Informaticae **35**(1–4), 35–50 (1998)
14. Harik, G.R., Lobo, F.G.: A parameter-less genetic algorithm. In: Proceedings of the 1st Annual Conference on Genetic and Evolutionary Computation-Volume 1, pp. 258–265. Morgan Kaufmann Publishers Inc. (1999)
15. Harik, G.R., Lobo, F.G., Goldberg, D.E.: The compact genetic algorithm. IEEE Trans. Evol. Comput. **3**(4), 287–297 (1999)
16. Iacca, G., Mallipeddi, R., Mininno, E., Neri, F., Suganthan, P.N.: Super-fit and population size reduction in compact differential evolution. In: IEEE Workshop on Memetic Computing (MC), pp. 1–8. IEEE (2011)
17. Kononova, A.V., Corne, D.W., Wilde, P., Shneer, V., Caraffini, F.: Structural bias in population-based algorithms. Inf. Sci. **298**, 468–490 (2015)
18. Beyer, H.G., Schwefel, H.P.: Evolution strategies-a comprehensive introduction. Nat. Comput. **1**(1), 3–52 (2002)
19. Casas, N.: Genetic algorithms for multimodal optimization: a review. arXiv preprint arXiv:1508.05342 (2015)
20. Miller, B.L., Shaw, M.J.: Genetic algorithms with dynamic niche sharing for multimodal function optimization. In: Proceedings of IEEE International Conference on Evolutionary Computation, pp. 786–791. IEEE (1996)

21. Sareni, B., Krahenbuhl, L.: Fitness sharing and niching methods revisited. IEEE Trans. Evol. Comput. **2**(3), 97–106 (1998)
22. Asmus, J., Borchmann, D., Sbalzarini, I.F., Walther, D.: Towards an FCA-based recommender system for black-box optimization. In: Workshop Notes, p. 35 (2014)
23. Muñoz, M.A., Kirley, M., Halgamuge, S.K.: A meta-learning prediction model of algorithm performance for continuous optimization problems. In: Coello, C.A.C., Cutello, V., Deb, K., Forrest, S., Nicosia, G., Pavone, M. (eds.) PPSN 2012. LNCS, vol. 7491, pp. 226–235. Springer, Heidelberg (2012). doi:10.1007/978-3-642-32937-1_23
24. Picek, S., Jakobovic, D.: From fitness landscape to crossover operator choice. In: Proceedings of the 2014 Annual Conference on Genetic and Evolutionary Computation, pp. 815–822. ACM (2014)
25. Min, K., Kao, M.-Y., Zhu, H.: The closest pair problem under the hamming metric. In: Ngo, H.Q. (ed.) COCOON 2009. LNCS, vol. 5609, pp. 205–214. Springer, Heidelberg (2009). doi:10.1007/978-3-642-02882-3_21

DICE: A New Family of Bivariate Estimation of Distribution Algorithms Based on Dichotomised Multivariate Gaussian Distributions

Fergal Lane[1(✉)], R. Muhammad Atif Azad[2], and Conor Ryan[1]

[1] CSIS Department, University of Limerick, Limerick, Ireland
{Fergal.Lane,Conor.Ryan}@ul.ie
[2] School of Computing and Digital Technology,
Birmingham City University, Birmingham, UK
atif.azad@bcu.ac.uk

Abstract. A new family of *Estimation of Distribution Algorithms* (EDAs) for discrete search spaces is presented. The proposed algorithms, which we label DICE (*Discrete Correlated Estimation* of distribution algorithms) are based, like previous bivariate EDAs such as MIMIC and BMDA, on bivariate marginal distribution models. However, bivariate models previously used in similar discrete EDAs were only able to exploit an $O(d)$ subset of all the $O(d^2)$ bivariate variable dependencies between d variables. We introduce, and utilize in DICE, a model based on *dichotomised multivariate Gaussian distributions*. These models are able to capture and make use of all $O(d^2)$ bivariate variable interactions in binary and multary search spaces. This paper tests the performances of these new EDA models and algorithms on a suite of challenging combinatorial optimization problems, and compares their performances to previously used discrete-space bivariate EDA models. EDAs utilizing these new *dichotomised Gaussian* (DG) models exhibit significantly superior optimization performances, with the performance gap becoming more marked with increasing dimensionality.

Keywords: Dichotomised Gaussian models · EDAs · Combinatorial optimization

1 Introduction

Estimation of Distribution Algorithms (EDAs), often also called *Probabilistic Model Building Genetic Algorithms* (PMBGAs), are an important optimization paradigm within Evolutionary Computation. They are stochastic optimization methods that guide the search for a global optimum by building and sampling explicit probabilistic models. Traditional search operators like mutation and crossover are instead replaced by a probabilistic model. The intent is that such models identify and capture pertinent data dependencies and other structures within fitter more promising candidate solutions. At each iteration, the model

© Springer International Publishing AG 2017
G. Squillero and K. Sim (Eds.): EvoApplications 2017, Part I, LNCS 10199, pp. 670–685, 2017.
DOI: 10.1007/978-3-319-55849-3_43

is used to generate a population of new candidate solutions. These are evaluated and the fitter solutions selected. These, then, are used to update the probabilistic model for the next iteration. Pseudocode for a canonical EDA is shown in Algorithm 1.

Algorithm 1. Pseudocode for a canonical EDA

1: set $t \longleftarrow 0$ (uniformly randomly generate an initial population P_0 composed of n individuals)
2: **while** termination condition not met **do**
3:     Select a collection P_t^* of m candidate solutions from the current population P_t
4:     create an updated probabilistic model M_t using P_t^*
5:     generate a new population by sampling from the probabilistic model M_t
6:     set $t \longleftarrow t + 1$
7: **end while**

Many different types of EDAs have been proposed for optimization in both continuous and discrete problem domains. Some of the earliest EDAs used relatively simple univariate models. Examples would include *Population-Based Incremental Learning* (PBIL) [3], the *Compact Genetic Algorithm* (cGA) [19] and the *Univariate Marginal Distribution Algorithm* (UMDA) [33]. Obviously, such simple models were going to be inadequate when used in the optimization of more complex problem domains. There was a natural progression in the use of models able to capture more complex problem dependencies and structures.

EDA utilizing models that could capture and exploit bivariate marginal distributions appeared fairly early on in the development of this field. For discrete spaces, the principal examples would be *Mutual Information Maximizing Input Clustering* (MIMIC) [10], *Combining Optimizers with Mutual Information Trees* (COMIT) [4], and the *Bivariate Marginal Distribution Algorithm* (BMDA) [35]. COMIT was essentially an extension of MIMIC. Whereas, for d-dimensional problems with d dependent variables, MIMIC greedily constructed a sequential chain of $O(d)$ individual bivariate marginal distributions, COMIT used a more general $O(d)$ dependency tree structure. An example of a bivariate EDA for continuous spaces would be the *Estimation of Multivariate Normal Algorithm* (EMNA) [29], which operates using an underlying multivariate Gaussian distribution model.

However, successively more expressive models, capable of capturing ever more complicated problem features, have been investigated. The *Extended Compact Genetic Algorithm* (ECGA) [20] used a marginal product model where the search space variables were partitioned into several variable groupings (using the *minimum description length* criterion) with the overall model being a product of multivariate marginal distributions. The use of graphical models and Bayesian networks has been the most popular approach. Some discrete search space examples would be the *Bayesian Optimization Algorithm* (BOA) [34] and the *Estimation of Bayesian Networks Algorithm* (EBNA) [12], and, in continuous search spaces, the *Estimation of Gaussian Network Algorithm* (EGNA) [28].

In this paper, we propose an EDA approach for discrete search spaces based on dichotomised multivariate Gaussian distributions. These models can construct and generate candidate solutions relatively efficiently (with a cost complexity of $O(d^3)$). They also have the attractive property of capturing and using all of the possible $O(d^2)$ bivariate interactions between the d variables of a problem. As far as these authors are aware, all bivariate marginal distribution models previously used in discrete space EDAs have been restricted to using just $O(d)$ of these bivariate interactions.

The structure of the paper is as follows. Section 2 looks at related past work with bivariate EDAs. Section 3 begins with a short survey of the literature related to the simulation of correlated multivariate Bernoulli variables. This field is the source of the *dichotomised Gaussian* (DG) technique we apply here. The remainder of Sect. 3 describes this method in detail.

Section 4 details our suite of combinatorial optimization problem domains and the configuration of the EDA algorithms we test and compare on them. Section 5 presents results and analysis for these experiments. Finally, in Sect. 6, we give some conclusions and lay out some ideas for future work.

2 Bivariate EDAs

2.1 Minimum Spanning Tree Techniques

In continuous spaces, models capable of efficiently capturing all bivariate marginal distributions are readily available and easy to use, e.g. the family of multivariate Gaussian distributions. EDAs like EMNA and the *Covariance Matrix Adaptation Evolution Strategy* (CMA-ES)[1] [18], which utilize such models have, therefore, long been widely available and used.

For discrete spaces, the only bivariate EDAs available up-to-now use restricted bivariate interaction models. MIMIC, COMIT and BMDA are all based on chains or trees of $d - 1$ individual bivariate marginal distributions. COMIT, in effect, builds a Chow-Liu tree [8]. This procedure scores all pairwise interaction densities based on an estimate of their *mutual information* (MI). An efficient *Minimum Spanning Tree* (MST) algorithm is then applied to a matrix of these scores to greedily construct an MST. The cost of this MST algorithm for arbitrary matrices is $O(d^2)$, which also gives the overall cost for the procedure. This tree along with the $d - 1$ pairwise bivariate distributions involved is then used to generate new individuals. Chow-Liu trees can be viewed as a particularly simple and constrained form of Bayesian network (where a child can have at most one parent). They also have certain optimality properties. Out of the all such restricted trees or chains of $O(d)$ connections, they are the unique model that minimizes Kullback– Leibler divergence from the original probability distribution. However, even if this approach identifies and makes use of the $O(d)$ most

---

[1] Strictly speaking, CMA-ES does not quite fall into the canonical EDA framework as given in Algorithm 1. However, it shares almost all of the core features of a typical EDA.

significant pairwise interactions, it still is the case that the vast majority are discarded. This increasingly impacts on model accuracy as problem dimensionality increases. The BMDA algorithm also uses essentially the same procedure. The principal difference is that it uses Pearson's chi-squared estimator instead of mutual information to score bivariate variable interactions.

In [41], an interesting variation on such tree-based algorithms is given. Their algorithm, *EDA based on Mixtures* (EDAM), simply uses random trees (avoiding this costly $O(d^2)$ step). A mixture of ten such random trees was used as their EDA model in experiments. Despite randomly constructing the dependency trees, they claim their algorithm, nonetheless, performed similarly to MIMIC on tests.

2.2 Copula EDAs

An interesting relatively-recent development in EDAs is the use of copula techniques (see [17] for a survey). Copulas are a statistical tool that allow a multivariate dependency to be decomposed into a univariate marginal distribution function and a *copula*, which describes the dependence structure between the variables. Both aspects can then be modelled separately. This can allow particular EDA models to be applied to a wider set of problem domains. For example, copulas might allow a Gaussian distribution model to be used even when the problem univariate marginal distribution itself is not Gaussian. One application of copulas techniques to bivariate EDAs was the development of a more general copula-based version of the MIMIC algorithm in [40].

A small number of authors have previously used multivariate Gaussian copulas models in EDAs. An example of this, which has some relevance to our work is [24]. There are some similarities between the general approach of the algorithm given in Sect. 3 of that paper and our method here. Their algorithm is potentially capable of learning and exploiting all the bivariate marginal dependencies in the continuous problem domains examined in their paper. However, it would be difficult and very expensive to apply the rejection sampling procedure they describe to discrete spaces. That would involve the computation of rectangular integrals of arbitrary multivariate Gaussians. As pointed out in Alan Genz's book [14], beyond a very small number of dimensions, exact computation of these is difficult and expensive. Therefore, this method, while useful in continuous spaces, is not practical as a technique in discrete search spaces.

2.3 Computational Cost

A seeming advantage of the MST or chain techniques that have been used in all discrete bivariate EDAs up to now, is their relatively low $O(d^2)$ cost (the main cost bottleneck is in the construction of the MST) in building such a model. However, this does not factor in the $O(d^2n)$ cost in estimating all $O(d^2)$ bivariate interactions in a population of n candidate solutions. It is hard to see how this $O(d^2n)$ cost can be computationally escaped, particularly for algorithms that seek to use all such interactions. MIMIC, BMDA and previous algorithms (except for EDAM) necessarily need to perform such operations (they still need to measure and score all such interactions in order to find and use the $O(d)$ most significant ones). Therefore, there is certainly scope to increase the cost complexity of the EDA model used to a similar order of $O(d^2n)$ and yet still maintain the same overall time cost complexity of the EDA.

The cost complexity of our new *dichotomised Gaussian* (DG) bivariate EDA model, which will be described in detail later, is $O(d^3)$. However, generally, to have a reasonable chance of accurately estimating all $O(d^2)$ bivariate interaction parameters, it is expected that the population size n should at minimum be at least d. Therefore, the computational cost of the DG model normally is still of the same order as this unavoidable $O(d^2n)$ bivariate EDA generational cost. This extra computational scope was one of the primary motivations that spurred us to seek more accurate discrete bivariate models.

2.4   Kernel Methods

A second motivation has been our interest in the use of kernel methods [39] in the principled design of *Evolutionary Algorithms* (EA) and EA search operators [26,27]. At the core of every kernel model is a *kernel function* that is chosen to match the inherent statistical characteristics of the problem domain at hand. The core strategy of kernel methods is the so-called *kernel trick* [1]. This allows primarily linear algorithms, which principally operate using inner products, to be extended to implicitly and cheaply operate in richer and higher-dimensional kernel feature spaces $\mathcal{V}$ where the original problem is easier to linearly separate and/or model. For example, a standard linear classifier that could not effectively separate data in the original space might successfully separate these in some higher dimensional feature space via a kernel; this is the basis of *Support Vector Machine* (SVM) techniques [9] in classification and *Gaussian Random Functions* (GRFs) [39] in machine learning (also known as *Gaussian Processes*).

Our longer range goal is the use of kernel methods and the kernel trick in EDA design. The very earliest EDAs primarily used simple linear univariate models. The kernel trick is a way of non-linearly extending linear algorithms that work primarily via inner products. We feel a similar strategy might successfully be used to construct a new family of non-linear EDAs, which are capable of being easily tailored to the problem at hand via learnable kernel functions.

The family of polynomial kernel functions [16] and, in particular, the quadratic kernel function [7], which is quite popular in natural language processing, represent probably the very simplest kernel function special case (only just beyond basic linearity). It is possible to recast and reformulate existing continuous bivariate EDAs like CMA-ES and EMNA as kernelized versions of simpler linear algorithms (using as a framework such quadratic kernels and their associated feature spaces). We wished to do the same for the discrete bivariate EDA case, which sparked our interest in these DG models. Having tools like the DG model to deal with the basic quadratic kernel case seems essential if we are to hope to later construct even more general and powerful kernel EDAs.

3   Dichotomised Multivariate Gaussian Distribution Models

3.1   Simulation of Correlated Multivariate Bernoulli Variables

The literature concerning the generation of correlated binary vectors has a long history. A multivariate Bernoulli variable is, in principle, fully specified by $2^d - 1$ parameters (in effect, the individual probabilities for every possible bitstring of length d it can generate). There is usually little practical hope of accurately learning so many parameters from data. A more realistic goal is to learn the univariate marginal distributions of the variables and the $O(d^2)$ correlations between those variables. Then, one constructs a multivariate Bernoulli variable with those same univariate distribution and correlation characteristics.

Usually, the ideal choice would be use the maximum entropy distribution for the situation where means and correlations for the set of d binary variables are constrained to the desired target values. In this case, the maximum entropy distribution is actually the Ising model. Unfortunately, it is not at all straightforward or cheap to find the particular Ising model that fits a desired set of mean and correlation constraints. It is also difficult and expensive to sample binary vectors from an Ising model even when one is found (one has to resort to expensive methods like the "perfect sampling" Markov chain Monte Carlo simulation method [36]). Therefore, many other methods have been proposed for simulating such correlated binary vectors.

Examples would include [6] that proposed a method using look-up tables of size $O(d^3)$, [30] that introduced two methods – one based on setting up a linear programming problem and another based on Archimedean Copulas, [13] that introduced an "iterative proportional fitting algorithm", and [25] that represents a more recent copula approach to this problem.

3.2   Dichotomised Gaussian Simulation of Correlated Binary and Multary Vectors

The particular technique, the *dichotomised Gaussian* (DG) method, that we have elected to use has been described and utilized in several past papers, the first description possibly being in [11]. A more recent exposition of the method can be found in [31,32]. Those authors also argue that this model is "near maximum-entropy". This method can also easily be extended to the more general case of generating multary vectors with any given correlation structure and associated set of univariate marginal distributions.

The Basic Method. Suppose we are dealing with the general case of a d-dimensional multary search space $\Omega = \prod_{i=1}^{d} \mathbb{Z}_{a_i}$ where $\mathbb{Z}_{a_i} = \{0, \ldots, a_i - 1\}$, so that each $a_i \geq 2$ specifies the *arity* of the ith dependent variable (gene). The goal of the DG method is to allow the random generation of multary search space vectors $\omega \in \Omega$ so that these conform to a set of desired univariate marginal density functions $\left\{\hat{f}_i(c)\right\}_i$ and according to a target set of variable (gene) correlations r_{ij} given in a $d \times d$ gene correlation matrix $(R)_{i,j} = r_{ij}$.

Usually, R is a sample correlation matrix estimated from a sample population of selected search space points, and the $\hat{f}_i(c)$ are empirical univariate marginal densities estimated from normalized allele frequency counts in the population.

At the core of the DG method is a d-dimensional multivariate normal distribution $\mathcal{N}(0, \Sigma)$ where $(\Sigma)_{i,j} = \rho_{ij}$ is its $d \times d$ correlation matrix (not to be confused with R). The DG method also makes use of a set of threshold values (with $a_i - 1$ threshold values needed for each dimension i):

$$\mathcal{T} = \left\{t_i^b, i \in \{1, \ldots, d\}, b \in \{0, \ldots, (a_i - 2)\}\right\}$$

For each variable i, these $a_i - 1$ threshold values partition $\Re$ into a_i disjoint intervals:

$$K_i^0 = \left(-\infty, t_i^0\right], K_i^1 = \left(t_i^0, t_i^1\right], \ldots, K_i^k = \left(t_i^{k-1}, t_i^k\right], \ldots, K_i^{a_i-1} = \left(t_i^{a_i-2}, \infty\right)$$

To randomly generate a multary search space point $\omega \in \Omega$, we first generate a continuous d-dimensional random vector x from the multivariate normal distribution. We, then, use these thresholds to convert (or dichotomise) this vector into a multary search space point. At each position i, x_i must belong to one of the a_i disjoint thresholded intervals: $K_i^0, K_i^1, \ldots, K_i^{a_i-1}$, so if $x_i \in K_i^c$ then, at the ith position in the resulting multary vector ω, we set $\omega_i = c$.

Replicating the Marginal Univariate Densities. We can set these thresholds to exactly replicate the target univariate marginal densities $\left\{\hat{f}_i(c)\right\}_i$. Let $\hat{F}_i(c) = \sum_{d=0}^c \hat{f}_i(d)$ be the target univariate marginal *cumulative distribution function* (CDF) for variable i. If we then calculate the thresholds in $\mathcal{T}$ according to $t_i^b = \Phi^{-1}(\hat{F}_i(b))$ where $\Phi^{-1}(x)$ is the standard inverse normal CDF function, then it can be easily verified that the univariate marginal densities of the resulting randomly generated multary vectors ω will indeed equal $\left\{\hat{f}_i(c)\right\}_i$.

Replicating Gene Correlations. The next step in the DG method is to adjust each multivariate normal correlation value ρ_{ij} in Σ so that the resulting correlation $corr(\omega_i, \omega_j)$ between variables i and j in the simulated random multary vector ω equals the desired target gene correlation value r_{ij}.

We can use the efficient-to-evaluate standard bivariate normal CDF function $\Psi_2(x, y; \rho)$ to calculate bivariate marginal CDFs for the output vector ω as: $F_{ij}(b, c) = \text{Prob}\{\omega_i \leq b \cap \omega_j \leq c\} = \Psi_2\left(t_i^b, t_j^c; \rho_{ij}\right), i \neq j$. For convenience, if we also define $F_{ij}(b, c)$ to be 0 whenever $b < 0$ or $c < 0$, then it is easy to calculate the bivariate marginal densities $f_{ij}(b, c) = \text{Prob}\{\omega_i = b \cap \omega_j = c\}$ for ω as:

$$f_{ij}(b, c) = F_{ij}(b, c) - F_{ij}(b-1, c) - F_{ij}(b, c-1) + F_{ij}(b-1, c-1)$$

From these density values, the correlations $corr\,(\omega_i, \omega_j)$ between the variables of the generated search space points can be directly and easily calculated.

For each pair of variables, we need to solve for the unique ρ_{ij} that will produce a $\mathrm{corr}(\omega_i, \omega_j)$ value that matches the desired gene correlation r_{ij} in R. As pointed out in [31], these problems are monotonic and there is always a single unique solution for ρ_{ij}, guaranteed to lie within $[-1, 1]$. Straightforward and efficient one-dimensional bisection root-finding algorithms can be used to solve for each ρ_{ij}. In our implementation, we used Brent's root-finding bisection method, which on average converged within only six iterations. Alternative and more detailed descriptions of this approach can be found in [11,31].

Repairing the Correlation Matrix. The resulting Σ matrix may not always be positive semi-definite (in other words, may not be a valid correlation matrix). If it is not, however, then efficient algorithms exist to repair Σ by finding and replacing it with the nearest valid correlation matrix. A paper by Nicholas Higham [22] introduced the first algorithm for finding, for any arbitrary correlation matrix, its nearest valid correlation matrix. This method was based on Djikstra's "alternating projections method" and had linear convergence. However, later Newton-method based algorithms have been developed with fast quadratic convergence [37]. We used a publicly available[2] C-code version of this Newton-based algorithm in our implementation.

Generating Multary Search Space Points. To actually generate search space points ω, standard Gaussian simulation algorithms are used to sample continuous vectors from the multivariate normal distribution $\mathcal{N}(0, \Sigma)$ we constructed. The set of threshold values $\mathcal{T}$ is then used to dichotomise these random normal vectors into multary vectors, which will have the exact target univariate marginal densities and the desired (or at least very close to) gene correlation behaviour. This DG simulation process has an overall computational cost of $O(d^3)$. Calculating each individual ρ_{ij} and each individual threshold has a low fixed cost unrelated to the dimensionality d. The most expensive step is correlation matrix repair (due to the matrix operations involved) with cost $O(d^3)$. Pseudocode for this process is given in Algorithm 2.

3.3   Knowledge Incorporation

In our experiments, we used standard correlation matrix repair methods that found the correlation matrix that was nearest in terms of the Frobenius norm: $\|A\|_F = \sqrt{\sum_{i=1}^{m} \sum_{j=1}^{n} |a_{i,j}|^2}$. However, versions of these correlation repair algorithms are available that use various types of *weighted* Frobenius norms. For example, one such type of weighted Frobenius norm, dubbed the H-norm, is described in [22]: $\|A\|_H = \sqrt{\sum_{i=1}^{m} \sum_{j=1}^{n} w_{i,j} |a_{i,j}|^2}$ where $w_{i,j} \geq 0$. An efficient

---

[2] Downloadable from: http://www.math.nus.edu.sg/~matsundf/.

Algorithm 2. Pseudocode for the dichotomised Gaussian simulation of correlated binary and multary vectors

---

1: Estimate the empirical univariate marginal densities $\{\hat{f}_i(c)\}_i$ and the sample correlation matrix R from the selected population of search space points.
2: Calculate the set of threshold values $\mathcal{T}$ that will replicate the target univariate marginal densities.
3: Individually calculate, using a fast root-finding technique, the ρ_{ij} values in Σ that replicate the desired gene correlations.
4: If necessary, use a nearest correlation algorithm to repair the correlation matrix Σ.
5: Generate multary search space points by sampling random normal vectors from $\mathcal{N}(0, \Sigma)$, and dichotomising these into allele values using the thresholds in $\mathcal{T}$.

Newton-based nearest correlation matrix algorithm that uses this H-norm is presented in [38].

The use of such weights would allow us to naturally and easily incorporate into the DG model acquired/prior knowledge about the relative strengths or significances of individual bivariate interactions. We could assign larger weights to interactions we believe will have a greater impact on fitness. While not tested here, we plan to investigate versions of DICE that can incorporate prior knowledge of this type in the near future.

4   Experimental Setup

Our goal was to test and compare the performance this new dichotomised Gaussian EDA model with other existing discrete bivariate EDA models. To ensure an absolutely fair model comparison, we used the same basic EDA algorithm with identical settings with each EDA model.

We chose a test suite of seven challenging combinatorial optimization problem domains, deliberately selected so their dimensions could be easily varied.

4.1   EDA Algorithm Settings

All the EDAs used a population of 200 individuals. All algorithms were run for 100 generations. At each iteration, the probability model was used to generate 200 new individuals. The 100 fittest of these were then selected and used in updating the probability model. All the probabilistic EDA models were constructed, at each iteration t, using a set H_t^* of estimated univariate and/or bivariate marginal densities (estimated from current and previous selected populations). We used an exponentially-decaying weighted average to combine present and past density histograms. A model decay parameter $\tau \in [0, 1]$ was used to determine the factor at which the previous model was discounted at each iteration. Hence, the current model would be based on a weighted combination: $H_t^* = H_t + \tau H_{t-1} + \tau^2 H_{t-2} + \tau^3 H_{t-3} + \ldots$ of present and past univariate and/or bivariate marginal population histograms.

Extensive empirical testing determined that $\tau = 0.7$ was the best general setting for the EDAs we examined. An identical $\tau = 0.7$ setting was used for all runs. Batches of 100 runs were used to produce all the experimental results given below.

We compared our DG model against a simple *Univariate EDA* (UEDA) model and the three principal discrete bivariate EDA models available in the literature. These were the MST-based BMDA model (using the Pearson chi-squared statistic), the MST-based MIMIC model (scoring interactions using mutual information) and an inexpensive random tree (EDAM) model where a mixture of ten randomly chosen dependency tree structures was used (the same model used in [41]).

4.2   Problem Domain Set

Five well-known combinatorial optimization problem domains defined on bit-string search spaces were used; these are described in more detail in Table 1. Three NK-Landscape instances with $K = 2, 3$ and 4 resulted in a total test suite size of seven problem domains. We have also included results on the simple linear "Counting Ones" problem for comparison, but these are not included in the test suite averages. All of these problem domains generated new fitness functions for every run by randomly sampling a new set of weights. We deliberately chose such problem domains because they readily scale to higher dimensions, and we wanted to test the performance of these models on search spaces of varying dimensionalities.

Table 1. Problem domain set details

Problem domain	References	Fitness function formula/Details
Counting ones (OneMax)		$f(x) = \sum_{i=1}^{d} w_i(2x_i - 1),$ $w_i \sim \mathcal{N}(0, \frac{1}{d})$
QUBO (Quadratic Unconstrained Binary Optimization)	[5]	$f(x) = \sum_{i,j=1}^{d} w_{ij}(2x_i - 1)(2x_j - 1),$ $w_{ij} \sim \mathcal{N}(0, \frac{1}{d^2})$
CUBO (Cubic Unconstrained Binary Optimization)	[15]	$f(x) = \sum_{i,j,k=1}^{d} w_{ijk}(2x_i - 1)(2x_j - 1)(2x_k - 1),$ $w_{ij} \sim \mathcal{N}(0, \frac{1}{d^3})$
NK-Landscapes	[2]	"Random neighbourhood" model (without replacement); $K = 2, 3, 4$
K-Uniform MAX-SAT (with $20\,n$ random clauses)	[23]	$K = 3$ (variables per clause)
Weighted MAX-CUT	[21]	$f(x) = \sum_{i,j=1}^{d} w_{ij}(x_i \oplus x_j),$ $w_{ij} \sim \mathcal{U}(-\sqrt{\frac{3}{d^2}}, \sqrt{\frac{3}{d^2}})$

5 Results and Analysis

Figure 1 gives mean best run fitness performances for the EDA models averaged over the test suite for problem dimensions d = 25, 50, 75, 100, 150 and 200. Clearly, DICE, utilizing the DG model, has overall the best performances. Its mean test suite performance always is superior to its next nearest competitor. For $d = 25$, the narrow 2.4% performance gap to second-place MIMIC is significant using a 95% confidence interval in a two-tailed student-t test. The performance gap seems to gradually increase as the dimensionality increases. The performance gaps over its next competitor at higher dimensionalities are significant at a 99% level using the same significance test.

The accuracy gap between the DG model and the other models is only likely to become greater as dimensionality increases, as a greater and greater proportion of the bivariate interactions in the other models go unexploited. This may explain the seeming gradually increasing performance gap (the DG model is barely ahead of the nearest runner-up at $d = 25$ with a 2.4% gap, is 4.5% ahead at $d = 50$, is 7.0% ahead at $d = 75$, is 17.2% ahead at $d = 100$, and is 16.9% ahead at $d = 200$).

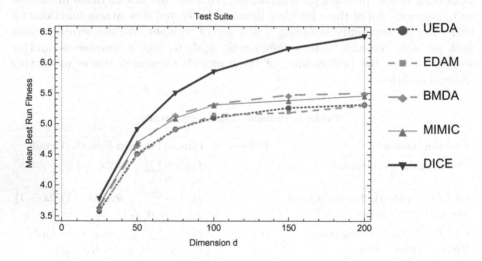

Fig. 1. Test suite mean best run fitnesses for the EDA models

Figures 2 and 3 provide individual plots of relative EDA model performances for all eight problem domains tested.

All EDA models seemed able to adequately cope with the simple One-Max "Counting Ones" problems. Similar performances were demonstrated by all algorithms.

Not a great deal separates the performances of the BMDA and MIMIC models (they essentially differ only in how they score bivariate interactions). Unsurprisingly, they are generally superior to the simpler univariate (UEDA) model.

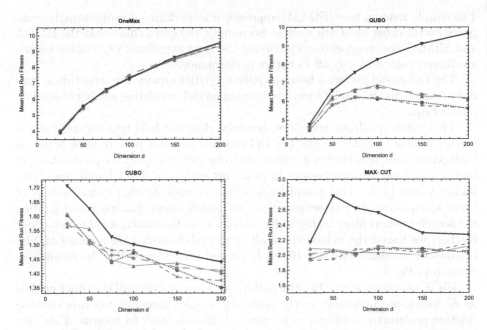

Fig. 2. Mean best run fitnesses for the EDA models on the OneMax, QUBO, CUBO and MAX-CUT problem domains

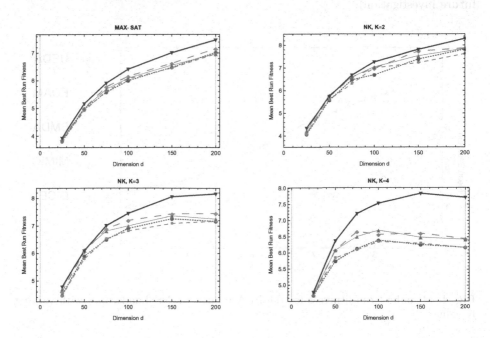

Fig. 3. Mean best run fitnesses for the EDA models on the MAX-SAT and NK-Landscape (with K = 2, 3 and 4) problem domains

The simple random tree (EDAM) approach also performs disappointingly compared to the other bivariate models. Seemingly, the extra effort that the BMDA and MIMIC models expend in identifying the most significant $O(d)$ of the bivariate interactions does pay off in better performance.

The DG model performs best on QUBO. QUBO's quadratic structure is similar in nature to DG model's own underlying model, consisting solely of bivariate interactions.

This purely quadratic structure, however, does not hold true for some of the other problem domains. While the DG model's superior performance is not as marked on these, nonetheless it still seems to be able to exploit the predominantly higher order interactions present in problems such as the NK-Landscapes with higher values of K. This promisingly seems to indicate that combinations of lower order bivariate interactions may be usefully approximating and guiding the search towards fitter higher order interactions. To investigate this behaviour further, we tested the behaviour of all of the EDA models on a range of NK-Landscape problems with $d = 100$ as K ranged from 5 up to 10. The results can be seen in Fig. 4.

DICE maintains a very healthy performance margin over all the other models as K increases. Intriguing, as the interaction order increases towards ten, the relative performance differences between all models start to narrow. This may be indicating that all of the models are becoming less capable of dealing with interactions involving increasingly large numbers of variables (a point worthy of future investigation).

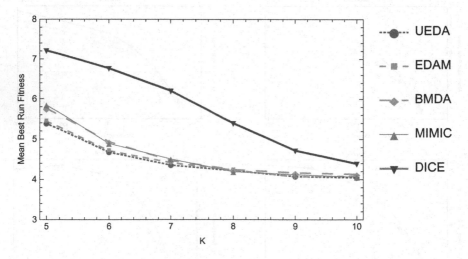

Fig. 4. Mean best run fitnesses for the EDA models on NK-Landscapes with varying K values

6 Conclusions

In this paper, we introduced a new (almost) fully bivariate model for discrete EDAs, based on dichotomised Gaussian models. At lower dimensions, DICE was competitive with otherwise identical EDAs that used other more established bivariate models (as found in MIMIC and BMDA). At intermediate dimensions, superior performance began to be exhibited by our model. With increasing dimensionality, this performance gap became even more pronounced. In this initial investigation, these models have exhibited much promise.

6.1 Future Work

A much more comprehensive investigation of this EDA modelling technique will be necessary on a much wider variety of problem domains.

It is very likely that memetic algorithm approaches could be profitably combined with DICE. Local search techniques are particularly useful for combinatorial optimization problems. The earlier COMIT EDA successfully combined a local hillclimber with its MST-based limited bivariate model.

We envisage that DG models could be usefully applied elsewhere in evolutionary computation. For example, it should be possible to construct crossover operators able to capture and respect arbitrary pairwise dependencies between variables (DG models could be used to generate crossover masks). This would provide increased opportunities to better tailor EA search operators to the characteristics of the problem domain at hand.

We are also investigating combining the DG model with CMA-ES, which is a popular and powerful EDA-like optimizer for continuous search spaces. Our DG model should be able to allow CMA-ES to be efficiently extended to discrete search spaces.

Acknowledgements. This work was supported, in part, by Science Foundation Ireland grant 10/CE/I1855 to Lero - the Irish Software Engineering Research Centre (www.lero.ie).

References

1. Aizerman, A., Braverman, E., Rozoner, L.: Theoretical foundations of the potential function method in pattern recognition learning. Autom. Remote Control **25**, 821–837 (1964)
2. Altenberg, L.: NK fitness landscapes. In: Back, T., Fogel, D., Michalewicz, Z. (eds.) Handbook of Evolutionary Computation, pp. B2.7:5–B2.7:10. Oxford University Press, New York (1997)
3. Baluja, S., Caruana, R.: Removing the genetics from the standard genetic algorithm. In: Machine Learning: Proceedings of the Twelfth International Conference, pp. 38–46 (1995)
4. Baluja, S., Davies, S.: Using optimal dependency-trees for combinational optimization. In: Proceedings of the Fourteenth International Conference on Machine Learning, pp. 30–38. Morgan Kaufmann Publishers (1997)

5. Boros, E., Hammer, P., Tavares, G.: Local search heuristics for quadratic unconstrained binary optimization (QUBO). J. Heuristics **13**(2), 99–132 (2007)
6. Caprara, A., Furini, F., Lodi, A., Mangia, M., Rovatti, R., Setti, G.: Generation
of antipodal random vectors with prescribed non-stationary 2-nd order statistics.
IEEE Trans. Sig. Process. **62**(6), 1603–1612 (2014)
7. Chang, Y.W., Hsieh, C.J., Chang, K.W., Ringgaard, M., Lin, C.J.: Training and
testing low-degree polynomial data mappings via linear SVM. J. Mach. Learn. Res.
11(Apr), 1471–1490 (2010)
8. Chow, C., Liu, C.: Approximating discrete probability distributions with dependence trees. IEEE Trans. Inform. Theory **14**(3), 462–467 (1968)
9. Cristianini, N., Shawe-Taylor, J.: An Introduction to Support Vector Machines and
Other Kernel-Based Learning Methods. Cambridge University Press, New York
(2000)
10. De Bonet, J., Isbell, C., Viola, P., et al.: MIMIC: finding optima by estimating
probability densities. In: Advances in Neural Information Processing Systems, pp.
424–430 (1997)
11. Emrich, L., Piedmonte, M.: A method for generating high-dimensional multivariate
binary variates. Am. Stat. **45**(4), 302–304 (1991)
12. Etxeberria, R., Larranaga, P.: Global optimization using Bayesian networks. In:
Second Symposium on Artificial Intelligence (CIMAF-99), Habana, Cuba, pp. 332–
339 (1999)
13. Gange, S.: Generating multivariate categorical variates using the iterative proportional fitting algorithm. Am. Stat. **49**(2), 134–138 (1995)
14. Genz, A., Bretz, F.: Computation of Multivariate Normal and t Probabilities, vol.
195. Springer Science & Business Media, New York (2009)
15. Glover, F., Hao, J.K., Kochenberger, G.: Polynomial unconstrained binary optimisation - part 2. Int. J. Metaheuristics **1**(4), 317–354 (2011)
16. Goldberg, Y., Elhadad, M.: SplitSVM: fast, space-efficient, non-heuristic, polynomial kernel computation for NLP applications. In: Proceedings of the 46th Annual
Meeting of the Association for Computational Linguistics on Human Language
Technologies: Short Papers, pp. 237–240. Association for Computational Linguistics (2008)
17. González-Fernández, Y., Soto, M.: A survey of estimation of distribution algorithms based on copulas. Technical report
18. Hansen, N., Kern, S.: Evaluating the CMA evolution strategy on multimodal test
functions. In: International Conference on Parallel Problem Solving from Nature,
pp. 282–291. Springer (2004)
19. Harik, G., Lobo, F., Goldberg, D.: The compact genetic algorithm. IEEE Trans.
Evol. Comput. **3**(4), 287–297 (1999)
20. Harik, G., Lobo, F., Sastry, K.: Linkage learning via probabilistic modeling in
the extended compact genetic algorithm(ECGA). In: Pelikan, M., Sastry, K.,
CantúPaz, E. (eds.) Scalable Optimization via Probabilistic Modeling, pp. 39–61.
Springer, New York (2006)
21. Heras, F., Larrosa, J., Oliveras, A.: MiniMaxSAT: an efficient weighted Max-SAT
solver. J. Artif. Intell. Res. (JAIR) **31**, 1–32 (2008)
22. Higham, N.: Computing the nearest correlation matrix: a problem from finance.
IMA J. Numer. Anal. **22**(3), 329–343 (2002)
23. Hoos, H., Stützle, T.: Stochastic Local Search: Foundations & Applications.
Elsevier, Amsterdam (2004)

24. Hyrš, M., Schwarz, J.: Multivariate Gaussian copula in estimation of distribution algorithm with model migration. In: 2014 IEEE Symposium on Foundations of Computational Intelligence (FOCI), pp. 114–119. IEEE (2014)
25. Jin, R., Wang, S., Yan, F., Zhu, J.: Generating spatial correlated binary data through a copulas method. Sci. Res. **3**(4), 206–212 (2015)
26. Lane, F., Azad, R., Ryan, C.: Principled evolutionary algorithm design and the kernel trick. In: Proceedings of the 2016 on Genetic and Evolutionary Computation Conference Companion, pp. 149–150. ACM (2016)
27. Lane, F., Azad, R., Ryan, C.: Principled evolutionary algorithm search operator design and the kernel trick. In: 2016 IEEE Symposium on Model Based Evolutionary Algorithms (IEEE MBEA 2016), part of the IEEE Symposium Series on Computational Intelligence 2016, pp. 1–9 (2016)
28. Larrañaga, P., Etxeberria, R., Lozano, J., Peña, J.: Combinatorial optimization by learning and simulation of Bayesian networks. In: Proceedings of the Sixteenth Conference on Uncertainty in Artificial Intelligence, pp. 343–352. Morgan Kaufmann Publishers Inc. (2000)
29. Larranaga, P., Lozano, J., Bengoetxea, E.: Estimation of distribution algorithms based on multivariate normal and Gaussian networks. Technical report, EHU-KZAA-IK-1 (2001)
30. Lee, A.: Generating random binary deviates having fixed marginal distributions and specified degrees of association. Am. Stat. **47**(3), 209–215 (1993)
31. Macke, J., Berens, P., Ecker, A., Tolias, A., Bethge, M.: Generating spike trains with specified correlation coefficients. Neural Comput. **21**(2), 397–423 (2009)
32. Macke, J., Murray, I., Latham, P.: How biased are maximum entropy models? In: Advances in Neural Information Processing Systems, pp. 2034–2042 (2011)
33. Mühlenbein, H.: The equation for response to selection and its use for prediction. Evol. Comput. **5**(3), 303–346 (1997)
34. Pelikan, M., Goldberg, D., Cantú-Paz, E.: BOA: the Bayesian optimization algorithm. In: Proceedings of the 1st Annual Conference on Genetic and Evolutionary Computation, vol. 1, pp. 525–532. Morgan Kaufmann Publishers (1999)
35. Pelikan, M., Mühlenbein, H.: The bivariate marginal distribution algorithm. In: Roy, R., Furuhashi, T., Chawdhry, P.K. (eds.) Advances in Soft Computing, pp. 521–535. Springer, New York (1999)
36. Propp, J., Wilson, D.: Exact sampling with coupled Markov chains and applications to statistical mechanics. Random Struct. Algorithms **9**(1–2), 223–252 (1996)
37. Qi, H., Sun, D.: A quadratically convergent Newton method for computing the nearest correlation matrix. SIAM J. Matrix Anal. Appl. **28**(2), 360–385 (2006)
38. Qi, H., Sun, D.: An augmented Lagrangian dual approach for the H-weighted nearest correlation matrix problem. IMA J. Numer. Anal. **31**(2), 491–511 (2011)
39. Rasmussen, C., Williams, C.: Gaussian Processes for Machine Learning. The MIT Press, Cambridge (2006)
40. Salinas-Gutiérrez, R., Hernández-Aguirre, A., Villa-Diharce, E.R.: Using copulas in estimation of distribution algorithms. In: Aguirre, A.H., Borja, R.M., Garciá, C.A.R. (eds.) MICAI 2009. LNCS (LNAI), vol. 5845, pp. 658–668. Springer, Heidelberg (2009). doi:10.1007/978-3-642-05258-3_58
41. Zhang, Q., Sun, J., Tsang, E., Ford, J.: Estimation of distribution algorithm based on mixture. Technical report

EvoNUM

Ranking Programming Languages for Evolutionary Algorithm Operations

Juan-Julián Merelo-Guervós[1]([☒]), Israel Blancas-Álvarez[6], Pedro A. Castillo[1],
Gustavo Romero[1], Pablo García-Sánchez[2], Victor M. Rivas[3],
Mario García-Valdez[4], Amaury Hernández-Águila[4], and Mario Román[5]

[1] CITIC and Computer Architecture and Technology Department,
University of Granada, Granada, Spain
{jmerelo,pacv,gustavo}@ugr.es

[2] Department of Computer Engineering, University of Cádiz, Cádiz, Spain
pablo.garciasanchez@uca.es

[3] Department of Computer Sciences, University of Jaén, Jaén, Spain
vrivas@ujaen.es

[4] Tijuana Institute of Technology, Tijuana, Mexico
{mario,amherag}@tectijuana.edu.mx

[5] University of Granada, Granada, Spain
mromang08@correo.ugr.es

[6] Real Time Innovations, Granada, Spain
iblancasa@gmail.com

Abstract. In this paper we measure the speed of several popular and recent programming languages performing the most usual operators in the canonical evolutionary algorithm, mutation and crossover, as well as an usual fitness function, OneMax. These three operations are representative of the kind of the ones performed in binary chromosomes. Our main objectives are, first, to create programs in programming languages that use the fastest available implementation. Second, to find out the differences in speeds for the different languages. Third, to find out whether the usual assumptions about the speed of languages really holds. And, finally, to find if the assumed order of speed in languages used in evolutionary algorithms holds true for all kinds of operations. In order to do that, we use available implementations or perform our own, concluding that the evolutionary algorithm scenario is more complex than usually assumed and finding out some surprising *winners* and *losers* among the languages tested.

Keywords: Benchmarking · Implementation of evolutionary algorithms · OneMax · Genetic operators · Programming languages · Performance measurements

1 Introduction

In the same spirit of the *No Free Lunch* theorem [23] we could consider there is a *no fast lunch* [10] hypothesis for the implementation of evolutionary optimization

© Springer International Publishing AG 2017
G. Squillero and K. Sim (Eds.): EvoApplications 2017, Part I, LNCS 10199, pp. 689–704, 2017.
DOI: 10.1007/978-3-319-55849-3_44

problems, in the sense that, while there are particular languages that might be the fastest for particular problem sizes and specially specific fitness functions there is no single language that is the fastest for all problem domains and design decisions.

That being the case, implementation decisions, and in many occasions reviewer reports, are based on common misconceptions such as thinking that a particular language is the fastest or that some other language is too slow for even being taken into consideration when implementing evolutionary algorithms. In many cases, that decision is based on features of the language the user knows, and the lack of information about new technologies and tools.

In fact, the current state of the art in application development eschews monolithic applications for loosely coupled set of processing components in the so-called *microservices architecture*, every one of them possibly written in a different language and running on the cloud [20,24,25]. In such an scenario, the possibility and even the likelihood of multiple parts of an evolutionary algorithm being written in different languages, every one of them suited to a particular component of the evolutionary algorithm, becomes higher [7]. Besides, as new languages become more familiar, it is interesting to have an estimation of their speed when running classical evolutionary algorithm operations. Furthermore, these asynchronous evolutionary algorithms with polyglot components might insert a component of asynchrony [12,19] that may have a positive impact on the overall performance of the algorithm.

After initial tests on a smaller number of languages [11] and several data structures, in this paper we test new languages, different data structures, new implementations, including some made using released evolutionary algorithm libraries, found and corrected some bugs and also updated language versions in those cases where new, and faster, ones have been released.

In order to make a fair comparison to the results we already had, we have re-used the same operations: crossover, mutation and fitness computation (One-Max). However, we have made an analysis that takes crossover and mutation in one hand and OneMax in another, since our preliminary results showed that there was sometimes a big difference between the speeds and their scale up found in one or the other.

We have used just these functions instead of implementing a whole evolutionary algorithm, first because it would have been impossible to achieve this breadth of languages; and second, because these operations, in fact, determine the total speed of an evolutionary algorithm program; indeed, it might be the case that [14] an Evolutionary Algorithm (EA) application will spend the most time running the fitness function and others, such as ranking the population; however, these are well covered by several general purpose benchmarks so they are not the focus of this paper.

A priori, results obtained here would generalize only to some implementations of genetic algorithms. However, in this paper we would like to present not only the result itself, which is interesting, but also a methodology to first assess new languages for implementing evolutionary algorithms for the value or insights they might give to the algorithm mechanism. Additionally, to make real-world measures and benchmark them to test their speed and performance relative to other common languages instead of choosing usual languages based only on past experience and common (maybe mis-) conceptions.

The rest of the paper is organized as follows: coming up next in Sect. 2, we will present the state of the art of the analysis of EA implementations. Next we will present in Sect. 3 the tests we have used in this paper and its rationale along with the languages we have chosen for carrying them out. Then, in Sect. 4 we will present the results obtained. Finally, we will explain the conclusions reached after these experiments and present future lines of work.

2 State of the Art

The point of benchmarking evolutionary algorithms is to discover which languages are more suitable for speedily running evolutionary experiments.

The first published benchmarks of evolutionary algorithms [8] focused on implementation details using C and C++, while other papers focused more on what kind of functions should be used to compare them [22].

Despite the growing importance given to best practices in the software creation process, there are not many publications on the subject, until recently when Alba et al. examined the performance of different data structures, all of them using the Java language, in [1]. [15] described the implementation of an evolutionary algorithm in Perl, also used in this paper, proving that, as a whole, Perl could run evolutionary algorithms almost as fast as Java, but if we took into consideration other factors like actual coding speed measured by single lines of code, Perl was better. [18] focused on the estimation of distribution algorithms, evaluating several metaheuristic packages having that particular option. However, it was not focused on speed, but on availability and languages used. Its survey did uncover the fact that most software packages used C or C++.

Most papers, if not all, including this one, focus on single-threaded procedural environments; for instance, a recent paper [17] centered on a single language, C++; despite this being a object-oriented language, this feature was not taken into account. In these cases *classical* languages, optimized for the execution of procedures and functions, not the dynamic creation of objects, have a certain advantage. However, innovation in software engineering has not only spawned new languages, but also new architectures like the Kappa architecture [4], microservices [16] or service-oriented frameworks [6,7] where we could envision that different parts of an evolutionary algorithm might be written in different languages, but also in new, domain specific, languages better suited for certain tasks. The *no fast lunch* principle enunciated above implies that different languages could be used for distributed systems, with the fastest or most appropriate language used for every part of it.

For instance, JavaScript is undoubtedly the best, if not the only, language, that can be run natively in browsers; a volunteer evolutionary computing system such as the one described by Desell [2,3] or Laredo [9] might leverage this fact to use mainly, or exclusively, this particular language. A *polyglot* analysis of languages for evolutionary algorithm such as the one done in this paper will allow us to find out not only which languages are the fastest in which environment, but also what is the actual difference so that we can trade the speed difference for the convenience of using a well-known tool ecosystem or a particular runtime environment.

All in all, existing literature focuses either on a single language and different data structures or different, and mainly popular, languages with a single data structure. In previously published research [11] we focused on fewer languages and mainly tried to measure their scaling behaviour across different lengths, and we found that Java, C# and C obtained the best results. However, we did not attempt to rank languages or measure relative speeds across all tests. This is what we do in this paper, extending the analysis of the previous paper with more languages and different implementations. Next we will explain how the experiment was set up and the functions used in it.

3 Experimental Setup

The main intention of this paper was to test new languages on these genetic operators, so we have had to program from scratch these functions, following in many cases instructions from experts so that we managed to extract the maximum speed out of the data and control structures for the particular language. As mentioned above, crossover, mutation are the most widely used operators for binary evolutionary algorithms; OneMax is also a widely used fitness function and one whose operations are representative or most binary fitness functions. In general, they exercise only a small part of the capabilities of the language, involving mainly integer and memory-access performance through loops. Their implementation of these operations is deceptively simple, specially for OneMax, a problem frequently used in programming job interviews but whose fastest implementation fully depends on the language.

Any of these operations use loops. Most languages include `for` loops; many can also perform *map* implicit loops where a function is applied to every component of a data structure, reducing sequential or random access to arrays. Other, more complex operations, such as *reduce*, which apply functions sequentially to all members of an array accumulating over an initial value, are sometimes available too. When available, we have used them. This implies that despite the simplicity of the benchmarking functions chosen, the results have wider applicability, except for floating point performance, which is not tested, mainly because it is a major component of many fitness functions, not so much of the evolutionary algorithm itself.

Data structures are the subject of these control structures; in this case we are dealing with a single one, the *chromosome*, which is widely accepted to be a list of zeros and ones. However, there are many possible ways of interpreting the meaning of "list" and of "zero" and "one".

Let us pay attention first to the structure itself, the *list*. In general, it will need to be a data structure that uses sequential access, a list or an array. However, for some fitness functions such as the one we are using here, a simple set will do. Mutation will be changing a single element in the set, crossover a group of elements. On the other hand, the "present"/"absent" concept can be represented by three type of atomic scalar data: a character (which is usually 1 or 0), an integer (1 or 0) or a Boolean value (true or false). Depending o the data structure chosen, we might have to choose a particular representation or not. The data structures we are actually using in this study can be divided into three different fields:

- *Strings*: representing a set bit by "1" and unset by "0", it is a data structure present in all languages and simple to use in most. In general, strings are used for its legibility and also the memory efficiency of storing values contiguosly. However, it need not be the most efficient one when computing fitness.
- *Vectors of Boolean values*, or Bit Vectors: not all languages have a specific primitive type for the Boolean false and true values; for those who have, sometimes they have specific implementations that make this data structure the most efficient. In some and when they Boolean values were not available, 1 or 0 were used. *Bitsets* are a special case, using bits packed into bytes for representing vector of bits, with 32 bits packed into a single 4 byte data structure and bigger number of bytes used as needed.
- *Lists* are accessed only sequentially, although running loops over them might be more efficient that using random-access methods such as the ones above. *Sequences* are functional data structures that differ from Lists in their finite size and the set of operations they are optimized for.

Besides, many languages, including functional ones, differentiate between Mutable and Constant or Immutable data structures, with different internal representations assigned to every one of them, and extensive optimizations used in Immutable or constant data structures. Immutable data structures are mainly used in functional languages, but some scripting languages like Ruby or Python use it for strings too. When available, we have also tested this type of data structures.

In this paper we have run the benhmarks in more than 20 different languages; additionally, another language, Rust, has been tested for one of them, and Clojure using persistent vectors was tested only for OneMax. This list includes 9 languages from the top 10 in the TIOBE index [21], with Visual Basic the only one missing, and 10 out of the top 20[1]. We have also added Perl6, which was in early releases in our previous papers and has advanced its speed greatly in the last releases. The list of languages and alternative implementations is shown in Table 1.

When available, available open source implementations of the operators and OneMax were used. In most cases, implementation took less than one hour and was inspired by the initial implementation made in Perl or in Lua; however, finetuning and improving from the last version published, as well as the testing

---

[1] Considering that Octave and Matlab actually use the same language. Besides, we have not measured proprietary implementations of languages such as that one.

Table 1. Languages, Versions, URLs, Data structures and Type of language used to carry out the benchmarks. No special flags were used for the interpreter or compiler.

Language	Version	URLs	Data structures	Type
C	4.8.2	http://git.io/v8T57	String	Compiled
C++	4.8.4	http://git.io/v8T57	Bit vector	Compiled
C#	mono 4.2	https://git.io/vzHDI	Bit vector	Compiled
Clojure	1.8.0	https://git.io/vzHDe	Bit vector	Compiled
Common lisp	0.13.7	https://git.io/vzHyR	Simple bit vector	Compiled
Dart	1.15.0	https://git.io/dEO	List	Interpreted
Go	go1.5.3	http://git.io/vBSYp	Bit vector	Compiled
Haskell	ghc 7.10.3	https://git.io/vzHMw	Mutable vector	Compiled
Java	1.8.0_66	http://git.io/v8TdR	Bitset	Compiled
JavaScript	node.js 5.0.0	http://git.io/vBSYd	String	Interpreted
JRuby	9.0.5.0 (2.2.3)	https://git.io/rEO	Bit vector	Interpreted
Julia	0.2.1	http://git.io/vBSOe	Bit vector	Interpreted
Kotlin	1.0.1	https://git.io/kEO	Bit vector	Compiled
Lua	5.3.3	http://git.io/vBSY7	String	Interpreted
Octave	3.8.1	http://git.io/v8T57	Bit vector	Interpreted
Pascal	Free Pascal 2.6.2-8	https://git.io/fpeo	Bit vector	Compiled
PHP	5.5.9	http://git.io/v8k9g	String	Interpreted
Perl	v5.24.0	http://git.io/bperl	String	Interpreted
Perl6	2016.09.1	http://git.io/bperl6	String, Bit vector	Interpreted
Python	2.7.3	http://git.io/vBSYb	String	Interpreted
Python 3	3.4.3	https://git.io/p3deap	Bit vector, List	Interpreted
Ruby	1.9.3p551	https://git.io/rEO	Bit vector	Interpreted
Rust	1.4.0	https://git.io/EOr	Bit vector	Compiled
Scala	2.11.7	http://git.io/vBSYH	String, Bit vector	Compiled

of several versions of the language to choose the fastest, took longer. Adequate data and control structures were used for running the application, which applies mutation to a single generated chromosome, or pair of them, a hundred thousand times. The length of the mutated string starts at 16 and is doubled until reaching 2^{15}, that is, 32768; in some cases we stopped at 2^{14} if it took more than one hour; we also extended it in some cases to 2^{16}.

In most cases, and especially in the ones where no implementation was readily available, we wrote small programs with very little overhead that called the functions directly. Using classes, function-call chains, and other artifacts, will add an overhead to the benchmark and will need to be different for each language. However, legibility or other constraints will make us use it anyway; this will have an influence in performance, but the differences will reflects what would be available for anyone implementing an evolutionary algorithm in a new language.

Every program uses native functions for measuring time, using system calls to check the time before and after operations were performed. These facilities used the maximum resolution available, which in some cases, namely Pascal, was somewhat inadequate. This was preferred to using external facilities since loading times, which are not important when running long experiments, will be different for compiled and interpreted languages; besides, external time will be more influenced by things like the hard drive state or other programs running.

In this paper, besides revising implementations of several functions with respect to [11], we have also added new languages and tested new versions of compilers and interpreters. The focus of this paper is also different: while in the previous papers our intention was to compute speeds, in this we aim to prove that there is no single implementation that beats all others in every aspect of an evolutonary algorithm.

4   Results and Analysis

All the results have been made available, with a free license, in the repository that holds this paper as well as some of the implementations, at https://git.io/bPPSN16. The Linux system we have used for testing runs the `3.13.0-34-generic #60-Ubuntu SMP` kernel on an `Intel(R) Core(TM)` `i7-4770 CPU @ 3.40GHz` CPU. Results for bitflip mutation, crossover and One-Max are shown in Figs. 1, 2 and 3. The graphs for crossover and mutation mainly show how time needed to perform varies more or less linearly with size; but in the case of some languages, the fact that they do not change that way make them show a stronger performance in the long run; for instance, Octave does not increase too much the time with size, making it faster at bigger sizes. The case of Java is really remarkable, in fact. We will examine aggregated results next.

To have a general idea of performance and be able to compare across benchmarks and sizes, we have used the language Julia, whose performance is more or less in the middle, as a baseline for comparison and expressed all times as the ratio between the time needed for a particular language and length and the time it takes the equivalent program in Julia. Ratios higher than 1 mean that the particular language+data structure is faster than Julia, <1 the opposite. The boxplot in Fig. 4 shows the average and standard deviation for all available lengths for the genetic operators; Fig. 5 shows the same for OneMax.

First result we wanted to find out, orders of magnitude in speed, can be checked by looking at the scale, which goes from faster and approximately 100 times as fast as Julia, to approximately 20 times as slow as Julia, that is, more than three orders of magnitude. In fact, the fastest is 10 times as fast as the 10th fastest for genetic operators, but almost a thousand times faster for One-Max. This also implies that fitness calculation is more speed-critical than genetic operators, but even so choosing a slow language might result in a program that is 100 or even one thousand times slower than the fastest. The second, is the comparison between languages, which, besides the usual suspects Java and C#, also show surprising entries: Haskell is the fastest running OneMax, and Go can

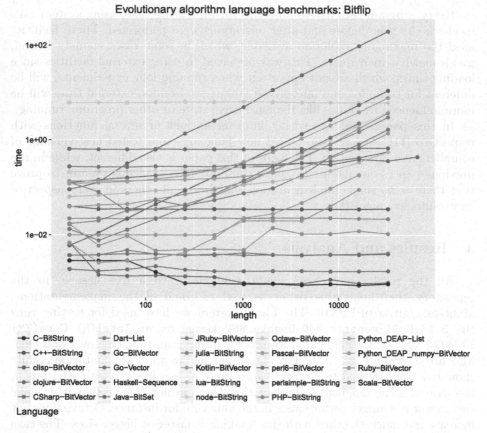

Fig. 1. Plot of the time needed to perform 100 K mutations in strings with lengths increasing by a factor of two from 16 to 2^{15}. Please note that x and y both have a logarithmic scale. Every language key includes the data structure used; it will be maintained in the rest of the paper.

be faster than C#; Kotlin and Go are also faster than C, and C++ is not as fast as would be expected.

Independently of the raw speed differences, let us have a look at all possible chromosome lengths and let us compute the average ranks, that is, the average position in which they fall for all possible tests and lengths. The averaged ranking for genetic operators is shown in Fig. 6 and for OneMax in Fig. 7 averages the position reached for all sizes and functions, and subtracts it from the total number of languages tested, so that bigger is better.

The first ranking for genetic operators shows C# as the first, on average, but also Go as the second and forth, depending on the data structure, with PHP as 4th and C as fifth. Due to its slow performance in the crossover operator, Java drops to 9th position, even if it performs very well in the mutation operator.

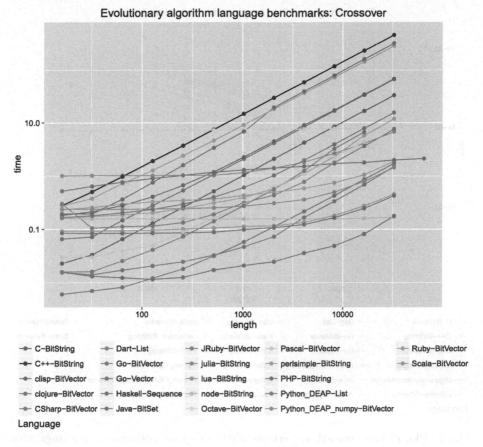

Fig. 2. Plot of the time needed to perform $100 \mathrm{K}$ crossovers in strings with lengths increasing by a factor of two from 16 to 2^{15}. Please note that x and y both have a logarithmic scale.

JRuby is the only interpreted language to show a strong performance, on average, in the top 10 area.

Except for C#, the top 5 for the OneMax operator is completely different, including Java as the first, Haskell and Clojure with two different representations. JRuby, Node and Octave are representatives of the interpreted languages crowd in the top 10.

In general, it is always compiled languages the ones that occupy the first positions. However, interpreted languages such as node.js, Perl, Lua and even PHP present a performance that, if not top, is at least relatively competitive with other compiled languages such as Pascal or C++. Thus, it is not always true that compiled languages are *always* faster than interpreted; but it can be said that the fastest languages are, consistently, compiled languages.

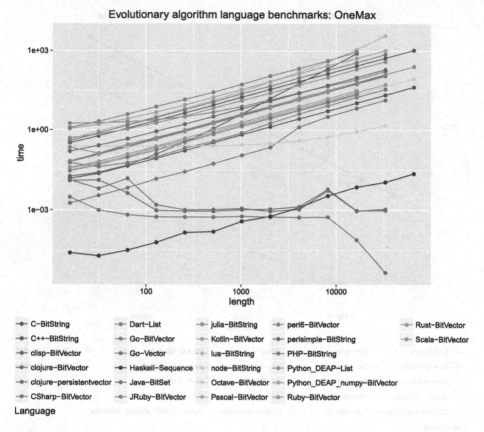

Fig. 3. Plot of time needed to perform 100 K OneMax evaluations in strings with lengths increasing by a factor of two from 16 to 2^{15}. Please note that x and y both have a logarithmic scale.

However, it is quite clear that the performance is not consistent across all operators for practically any language; Java is very fast evaluating OneMax, but slower than others using genetic operators; the case of Haskell is remarkable, because even being faster than Java on average evaluating OneMax, it is slower than even Perl6, the new entry in this paper, using genetic operators.

5   Conclusions

In this paper we have measured the performance of an extensive collection of languages in simple and common evolutionary algorithm operations: mutation, crossover and OneMax, with the objective of finding out which languages are faster at these operations and what are the actual differences across languages, operators and data structures, the main objective being giving EA practitioner elements of decision to choose which language or languages to use when implementing evolutionary algorithms.

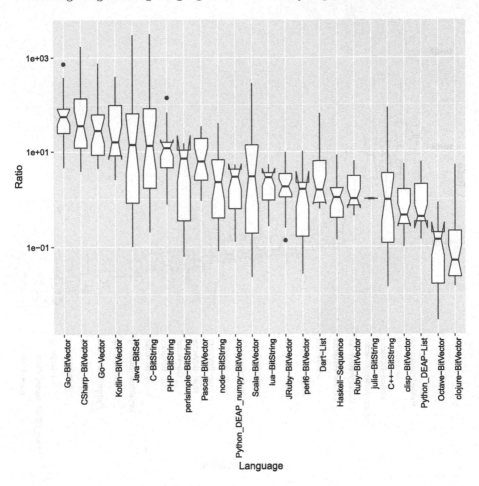

Fig. 4. Boxplot of scaled performance in mutation and crossover compared to the baseline language, which has been chosen to be Julia. Please note that y has a logarithmic scale. The strings indicate the language and the implementation; for instance, Python_DEAP_numpy is a python implementation using the operators in the DEAP framework [5] and numpy implementation for vectors.

In a development environment where different parts of the application might be performed using microservices [20], it is interesting to know which particular language is the best for specific operations. Pool based evolutionary algorithms [13] favor decomposition of concerns to different processing units following a microservices approach; in this case, a unit performing fitness evaluation might be different from other performing mutation or crossover. Modern cloud architectures also reduce ping and increase throughput so it is economical and sensible to perform this operation even if they are in different instances.

Bearing in mind this environment, we can conclude that functional languages such as Haskell or Clojure are the fastest evaluating fitness functions similar to

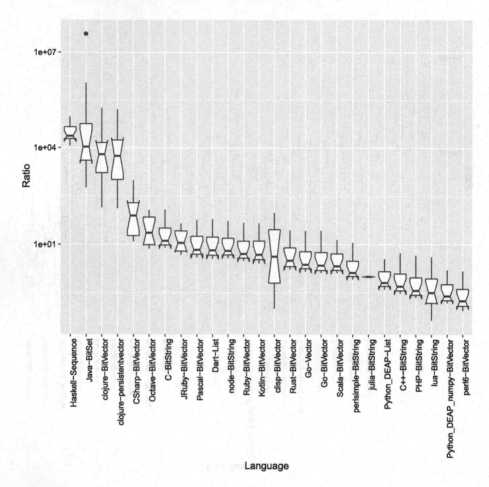

Fig. 5. Boxplot of scaled performance in the OneMax function compared to baseline Julia. Please note that y has a logarithmic scale.

OneMax; we could include here Royal Road, HIFF and other similar functions; Java and C# would be also strong contenders among the more popular languages, and JRuby would be the fastest among interpreted languages. On the other hand, Go is the best language processing genetic operators over binary strings, very close to the more popular languages Java and C#; as far as the interpreted languages is concerned, both PHP and Perl obtain the best results. Even if these results confirm that Java and C# are very fast at solving evolutionary algorithms, we have also proved that often overlooked languages such as Go and Kotlin should also be considered for implementing these monolithic applications.

That leads us to conclude that Java or C# would be the fastest choice in a canonical evolutionary algorithm, when solving problems similar to the OneMax.

Average rank

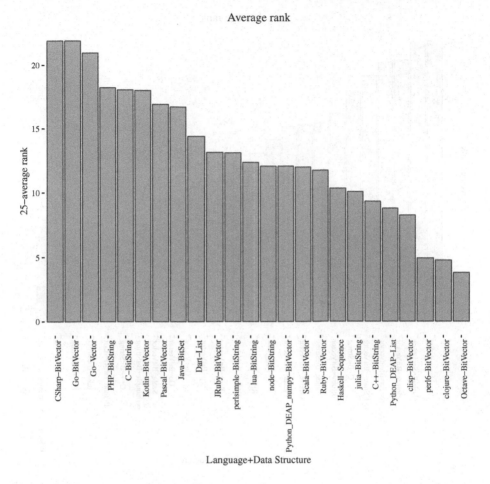

Fig. 6. Ranking averaged across all measures for genetic operators crossover and mutation, subtracted from the total number of measured languages, so bigger is better

However, evaluating binary fitness functions using a distributed microservices architecture would be better solved using Haskell or Clojure, while Go and even Perl might be better suited for performing genetic operators. In any case, this study shows that it is always a good practice to measure and compare the actual performance of the proposed implementation, and consider the possibility of using different data structures and even languages for our evolutionary algorithm application.

Future lines of work will include actual measurements in distributed applications to find the impact of the network on the final performance. These measurements will have to be taken in the whole system, so in advance a more extensive measurement of other operators such as tournament selection and other selection methods will have to be performed. *A priori*, these are essentially CPU integer

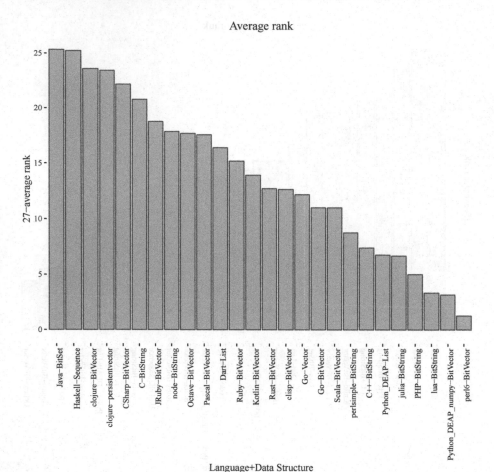

Fig. 7. Ranking averaged across all measures for OneMax, subtracted from the total number of measured languages, so bigger is better.

operations and their behavior might be, in principle, very similar to the one shown in these operations. Combining some compiled languages such as Go or C with others characterized by its speed in some string operations, like Perl or programming ease, like Python, might result in the best of both worlds: performance and rapid prototyping. Creating a whole multi-language framework along these lines is a challenge that might be interesting to carry out in the future.

Acknowledgements. This paper is part of the open science effort at the university of Granada. It has been written using knitr, and its source as well as the data used to create it can be downloaded from the GitHub repository https://github.com/JJ/2016-ea-languages-PPSN. It has been supported in part by GeNeura Team http://geneura.wordpress.com, projects TIN2014-56494-C4-3-P (Spanish Ministry of Economy and Competitiveness), Conacyt Project PROINNOVA-220590.

References

1. Alba, E., Ferretti, E., Molina, J.M.: The influence of data implementation in the performance of evolutionary algorithms. In: Moreno Díaz, R., Pichler, F., Quesada Arencibia, A. (eds.) EUROCAST 2007. LNCS, vol. 4739, pp. 764–771. Springer, Heidelberg (2007). doi:10.1007/978-3-540-75867-9_96
2. Desell, T., Anderson, D.P., Magdon-Ismail, M., Newberg, H., Szymanski, B.K., Varela, C.A.: An analysis of massively distributed evolutionary algorithms. In: IEEE Congress on Evolutionary Computation, pp. 1–8. IEEE (2010)
3. Desell, T., Magdon-Ismail, M., Szymanski, B., Varela, C.A., Newberg, H., Anderson, D.P.: Validating evolutionary algorithms on volunteer computing grids. In: Eliassen, F., Kapitza, R. (eds.) DAIS 2010. LNCS, vol. 6115, pp. 29–41. Springer, Heidelberg (2010). doi:10.1007/978-3-642-13645-0_3
4. Erb, B., Kargl, F.: A conceptual model for event-sourced graph computing. In: Proceedings of the 9th ACM International Conference on Distributed Event-Based Systems, DEBS 2015, pp. 352–355. ACM, New York, NY, USA (2015). http://doi.acm.org/10.1145/2675743.2776773
5. Fortin, F.A., Rainville, D., Gardner, M.A.G., Parizeau, M., Gagné, C., et al.: Deap: evolutionary algorithms made easy. J. Mach. Learn. Res. 13(1), 2171–2175 (2012)
6. García-Sánchez, P., González, J., Castillo, P., Merelo, J., Mora, A., Laredo, J., Arenas, M.: A distributed service oriented framework for metaheuristics using a public standard. In: González, J.R., Pelta, D.A., Cruz, C., Terrazas, G., Krasnogor, N. (eds.) Nature Inspired Cooperative Strategies for Optimization (NICSO 2010), vol. 284, pp. 211–222. Springer, Heidelberg (2010)
7. García-Sánchez, P., González, J., Castillo, P.A., García-Arenas, M., Merelo-Guervós, J.J.: Service oriented evolutionary algorithms. Soft Comput. 17(6), 1059–1075 (2013)
8. Jose Filho, L.R., Treleaven, P.C., Alippi, C.: Genetic-algorithm programming environments. Computer 27(6), 28–43 (1994)
9. Laredo, J.L.J., Bouvry, P., González, D.L., De Vega, F.F., Arenas, M.G., Merelo, J., Fernandes, C.M.: Designing robust volunteer-based evolutionary algorithms. Genet. Program. Evolvable Mach. 15(3), 221–244 (2014)
10. Merelo, J.J., García-Sánchez, P., García-Valdez, M., Blancas, I.: There is no fast lunch: an examination of the running speed of evolutionary algorithms in several languages, November 2015. ArXiv e-prints http://arxiv.org/abs/1511.01088
11. Merelo, J.J., et al.: Benchmarking languages for evolutionary algorithms. In: Squillero, G., Burelli, P. (eds.) EvoApplications 2016. LNCS, vol. 9598, pp. 27–41. Springer, Cham (2016). doi:10.1007/978-3-319-31153-1_3
12. Merelo, J.J., et al.: Testing the intermediate disturbance hypothesis: effect of asynchronous population incorporation on multi-deme evolutionary algorithms. In: Rudolph, G., Jansen, T., Beume, N., Lucas, S., Poloni, C. (eds.) PPSN 2008. LNCS, vol. 5199, pp. 266–275. Springer, Heidelberg (2008). doi:10.1007/978-3-540-87700-4_27
13. Merelo-Guervós, J.-J., Mora, A., Cruz, J.A., Esparcia, A.I.: Pool-based distributed evolutionary algorithms using an object database. In: Chio, C., et al. (eds.) EvoApplications 2012. LNCS, vol. 7248, pp. 446–455. Springer, Heidelberg (2012). doi:10.1007/978-3-642-29178-4_45
14. Merelo, J.J., Romero, G., Arenas, M.G., Castillo, P.A., Mora, A.M., Laredo, J.L.J.: Implementation matters: programming best practices for evolutionary algorithms. In: Cabestany, J., Rojas, I., Joya, G. (eds.) IWANN 2011. LNCS, vol. 6692, pp. 333–340. Springer, Heidelberg (2011). doi:10.1007/978-3-642-21498-1_42

15. Merelo-Guervós, J.J., Castillo, P.A., Alba, E.: `Algorithm::Evolutionary`, a flexible perl module for evolutionary computation. Soft Comput. **14**(10), 1091–1109 (2010). http://www.springerlink.com/content/8h025g83j0q68270/fulltext.pdf, http://sl.ugr.es/000K
16. Namiot, D., Sneps-Sneppe, M.: On micro-services architecture. Int. J. Open Inf. Technol. **2**(9), 24–27 (2014)
17. Nesmachnow, S., Luna, F., Alba, E.: An empirical time analysis of evolutionary algorithms as C programs. Softw. Pract. Experience **45**(1), 111–142 (2015)
18. Santana, R.: Estimation of distribution algorithms: from available implementations to potential developments. In: Proceedings of the 13th Annual Conference Companion on Genetic and Evolutionary Computation, pp. 679–686. ACM (2011)
19. Scott, E.O., De Jong, K.A.: Understanding simple asynchronous evolutionary algorithms. In: Proceedings of the 2015 ACM Conference on Foundations of Genetic Algorithms XIII, pp. 85–98. ACM (2015)
20. Swann, J., Hammond, K.: Towards 'metaheuristics in the large' (2015)
21. TIOBE team: Tiobe index for April 2016. Technical report, TIOBE, April 2016. http://www.tiobe.com/tiobe_index
22. Whitley, D., Rana, S., Dzubera, J., Mathias, K.E.: Evaluating evolutionary algorithms. Artif. Intell. **85**(1), 245–276 (1996). http://www.sciencedirect.com/science/article/pii/0004370295001247
23. Wolpert, D.H., Macready, W.G.: No free lunch theorems for optimization. IEEE Trans. Evol. Comput. **1**(1), 67–82 (1997). http://citeseer.nj.nec.com/wolpert96no.html
24. Wu, Q., Peng, C.: A least squares support vector machine optimized by cloud-based evolutionary algorithm for wind power generation prediction. Energies **9**(8), 585 (2016)
25. Zhang, G., He, R., Liu, Y., Li, D., Chen, G.: An evolutionary algorithm based on cloud model. Chin. J. Comput. **31**(7), 1082–1091 (2008)

Distance-Based Tournament Selection

Christian Oesch[✉]

Faculty of Business and Economics, University of Basel, Basel, Switzerland
christian.oesch@unibas.ch

Abstract. In this paper we analyze the performance of a novel genetic selection mechanism based on the classic tournament selection. This method tries to utilize the information present in the solution space of individuals, before mapping their solutions to a fitness measure. This allows to favour individuals dependent on what state the evolutionary search is in. If a population is caught up in several local optima, the correlation of the distance between the individuals and their performance tends to be lower than when the population converges to a single global optimum. We utilize this information by structuring the tournaments in a way favorable to each situation. The results of the experiments suggest that this new selection method is beneficial.

Keywords: Genetic algorithms · Tournament selection · Search space

1 Introduction

Multiple optima are still a challenge in many optimization problems. With standard approaches, one always balances exploitation of locality against exploration of the search space. In genetic algorithms [3] this is done by choosing the right evolutionary parameters and genetic operators. However, these values are fixed over the course of the optimization and do not take into account the current state of the population or where it is located in the search space. Genetic algorithms (GAs) base the guidance of their search on a single measure; the fitness. This single-value metric defines which individuals reproduce, and, over several generations, in which areas of the search space the population concentrates. In this study we want to open the discussion on using the genetic distribution of the population to guide the search process. To do this, we propose the use of genetic distances between individuals to modify the tournament composition in the selection stage of genetic algorithms. By measuring the correlation of the distances between individuals and their fitness, we believe that we can introduce mechanics which will enhance the algorithms performance.

This approach is related to niching methods [7,8] but does not rely on fixed distances and is adaptive to the state of the convergence process. It is an example of how to use additional information to guide the search process. In our method, depending on an individual's place in the population, only the chance of competing in a given tournament is modified. This results in a softer modification of the standard approach.

G. Squillero and K. Sim (Eds.): EvoApplications 2017, Part I, LNCS 10199, pp. 705–714, 2017.
DOI: 10.1007/978-3-319-55849-3_45

The rest of this article is structured as follows. In Sect. 2 the proposed method is presented. Section 3 describes the test cases and the evolutionary settings employed in this study. The results of the experiments are presented in Sects. 4 and 5 concludes this study and introduces further ideas and future areas of research.

2   Methodology

There are different ways to influence a GA's convergence behavior through additional information. In this study, we influence the convergence of the algorithm by modifying which opponents compete in a tournament. Note that this is an alternative approach to fitness sharing [12], fitness penalties [5] or other measures which directly change the selection probability of an individual. Instead, depending on the state of the genetic algorithm, we alter a tournament's opponents which can be genetically more or less diverse. In case of a very homogeneous tournament, meaning the individuals are similar, there is a high chance that the best individual of the local cluster will be selected. In more heterogeneous tournaments, as the individuals will not always have to compete against the best individual in the cluster, individuals in more distant regions of the search space have a higher chance of selection. Instead of modifying directly which individuals are selected, we basically give certain individuals a higher chance of participating in a tournament.

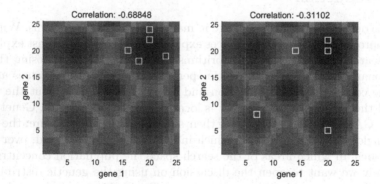

Fig. 1. The correlation of average distances to the other individuals and the individual's fitness. The dark blue spot around (20, 20) is the optimum. When the individuals gather in one optimum, the negative correlation of fitness to the average distance to other individuals tends to be stronger than in the case where some individuals are located in a local optima. (Color figure online)

Figure 1 shows an example for the two different cases of a negative correlation between the individual's average distance to each other and their fitness. In the left panel, the individuals gather in one optimum and the most central individual[1] of the population exhibits the highest fitness. On the right hand side, the correlation is weaker, as the best individual is no longer in the spatial center of the population. The optimal tournament will look different in both cases.

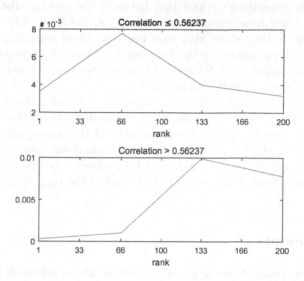

Fig. 2. Two probability transformations based on the rank distance to the initial tournament candidate. The x-axis shows the rank distance, the y-axis shows the probability of this rank's selection into the tournament.

In each tournament, the initial candidate is chosen at random. This is done uniformly and does not differ from standard tournament selection. However, once the initial candidate is chosen, the other constituents of the tournament are chosen based on their rank distance. To build the rank-distances between the individuals, we initially measure the Canberra-Distance [6] of their genomes. The Canberra-Distance is used such that the different dimensions have similar importance. It is defined by:

$$d(u, v) = \sum_{i=1}^{n} \frac{|u_i - v_i|}{|u_i| + |v_i|}, \tag{1}$$

where u and v are the vectors to compare, in this case the genomes. These distances are then turned into ranks r from 1 to N where N is the population size. Depending of the state of the algorithm a probability transformation is chosen to either favor individuals which are close to the initial candidate or solutions that are genetically further apart. This transformation is then applied to the rank distances to the other individuals and for each individual of the population a probability is assigned with which that individual is chosen for the current spot in the tournament. The probability of individual j to end up in a particular tournament p_j is then:

---

[1] The one with the lowest average distance to other individuals.

$$p_j = \begin{cases} g_1(r_j) & \text{if} \quad \rho \geq \alpha \\ g_2(r_j) & \text{if} \quad \rho < \alpha \end{cases} \quad (2)$$

where ρ is this generation's correlation between the average distance between individuals to their fitness score, and alpha is a threshold. The selection into the tournament is then done akin to a roulette wheel selection. This process is repeated for all opponents in the tournament. Once all opponents have been found, the tournament is performed and the tournament winner is determined and marked for reproduction and survival.

Figure 2 shows two probability transformations to select further individuals into the tournament. The x-axis shows the rank distance to the initial tournament candidate, and the y-axis the probability of the corresponding individual to be selected into the tournament. The transformations have been determined by Monte Carlo search over the Schwefel 1.2 problem ($f_2(x)$), shown in Sect. 3. This problem has been chosen as over the course of the runs, it has a wide range of values of ρ.

3   Experiments

To test the new concept, we apply it to most of the benchmark problems proposed in [14]. The functions are listed in Table 1. Functions f_1 to f_7 are unimodal, and the functions f_8 to f_{14} multimodal. The parameter n defines the dimensionality of the problem and S the range. $f_{\min}$ shows the minimum value of the optimization problem.

The functions are well-known benchmarks from the literature. $f_1(x)$ is a simple sphere model, $f_2(x)$, $f_3(x)$, $f_4(x)$ are Schwefel's problems 2.22, 1.2, and 2.21 [13]. $f_5(x)$ is the generalized Rosenbrock's function [11]. $f_6(x)$ is a step function and $f_7(x)$ is a quartic function with noise. A generalized version of Schwefel's problem 2.26 is given in $f_8(x)$. $f_9(x)$ is the generalized Rastrigin's function [10], and $f_{10}(x)$ Ackley's function [1]. The benchmark function $f_{11}(x)$ is the generalized Griewank function [4], and $f_{12}(x)$ Shekel's Foxholes function [9]. $f_{13}(x)$, f_{14}, and $f_{15}(x)$ are Kowalik's [14], Six-Hump Camel-Back [9], and Branin [2] functions.

All experiments are conducted with the same evolutionary parameters listed in Table 2. 300 runs are performed for both the standard tournament selection as well as for the novel distance-based tournament. The fitness is calculated by the mean-squared error (MSE). As noted in the previous section, problem $f_2(x)$ has been used to find a piecewise-linear probability transformation by Monte Carlo search. The parameters of the piecewise function are listed in Table 3. We apply two different probability transformations $g_1(r)$ and $g_2(r)$ depending on ρ. The ranks are split into three different segments, and the probabilities of selection into the tournament are interpolated based on the rank of the individuals.

Table 1. Benchmark functions

Test function	n	S	$f_{\min}$
$f_1(x) = \sum_{i=1}^{n} x_i^2$	30	$[-100, 100]^n$	0
$f_2(x) = \sum_{i=1}^{n} |x_i| + \prod_{n=1}^{n} |x_i|$	30	$[-10, 10]^n$	0
$f_3(x) = \sum_{i=1}^{n} (\sum_{j=1}^{i} x_j)^2$	30	$[-100, 100]^n$	0
$f_4(x) = \max_i \{|x_i|, 1 \le i \le n\}$	30	$[-100, 100]^n$	0
$f_5(x) = \sum_{i=1}^{n-1} \left[100(x_{i+1} - x_i^2)^2 + (x_i - 1)^2\right]$	30	$[-30, 30]^n$	0
$f_6(x) = \sum_{i=1}^{n} (|x_i + 0.5|)^2$	30	$[-100, 100]^n$	0
$f_7(x) = \sum_{i=1}^{n} i x_i^4 + \text{random}[0, 1)$	30	$[-1.28, 1.28]^n$	0
$f_8(x) = \sum_{i=1}^{n} -x_i \sin(\sqrt{|x_i|})$	30	$[-500, 500]^n$	-12569.5
$f_9(x) = \sum_{i=1}^{n} [x_i^2 - 10 \cos(2\pi x_i) + 10]$	30	$[-5.12, 5.12]^n$	0
$f_{10}(x) = -20 \exp(-0.2\sqrt{\frac{1}{n}\sum_{i=1}^{n} x_i^2})$ $- \exp(\frac{1}{n}\sum_{i=1}^{n} \cos(2\pi x_i)) + 20 + e$	30	$[-32, 32]^n$	0
$f_{11}(x) = \frac{1}{4000}\sum_{i=1}^{n} x_i^2 - \prod_{i=1}^{n} \cos(\frac{x_i}{\sqrt{i}}) + 1$	30	$[-600, 600]^n$	0
$f_{12}(x) = [\frac{1}{500} + \sum_{j=1}^{2} 5]\frac{1}{j+\sum_{i=1}^{2}(x_i-a_{ij})^6}$ $a_{ij} = \begin{bmatrix} -32 & -16 & 0 & 16 & 32 & -32 & 0 & 16 & 32 \\ -32 & -32 & -32 & -32 & -32 & -16 & 32 & 32 & 32 \end{bmatrix}$	2	$[-65.536, 65.536]^n$	1
$f_{13}(x) = \sum_{i=1}^{1} 1[a_i - \frac{x_1(b_i^2 + b_i x_2)}{b_i^2 + b_i x_3 + x_4}]$ $a_i = (0.1957, 0.1947, 0.1735, 0.1600, 0.0844,$ $0.0627, 0.456, 0.0342, 0.0323, 0.0235, 0.0246)$ $b_i^{-1} = (0.25, 0.5, 1, 2, 4, 6, 8, 10, 12, 14, 16)$	4	$[-5, 5]^n$	0.0003075
$f_{14}(x) = 4x_1^2 - 2.1x_1^4 + \frac{1}{3}x_1^6 + x_1 x_2 - 4x_2^2 + 4x_2^4$	2	$[-5, 5]^n$	-1.0316285
$f_{15}(x) = (x_2 - \frac{5.1}{4\pi^2}x_1^2 + \frac{5}{\pi}x_1 - 6)^2$ $+10(1 - \frac{1}{8}8\pi)\cos x_1 + 10$	2	$[-5, 10] \times [0, 15]$	0.398

4   Results

Table 4 shows the percentage of the mean-squared error in the distance-based tournament compared to the baseline runs for different quantiles and the mean. For example for problem $f_1(x)$ the minimum MSE at the end of the run was 64.4% of the baseline result. It is clear to see that our method dominates the standard implementation in most of the problems. Except for $f_{14}(x)$ and $f_{15}(x)$ the median of the MSE is smaller in the distance-based approach. Especially in the unimodal case, the new structure of the tournament performs well. Remember that in these cases, the correlation between the average distance to the other individuals and the fitness is most likely high. This means, the probability transformation $p_1(r)$ is applied predominantly. The method also outperforms the standard approach in the multimodal functions. However, the difference is not as large. Further performance improvements might be achieved by performing a more thorough search for the parameters of g_1 and g_2. The results are further presented in Fig. 3. The figure shows box plots of the results of all the benchmark problems. The reason for why the method does not work as well for functions

Table 2. Settings

Parameter	Value
Number of runs	300
Generations	400
Population size	200
Crossover probability	0.8
Mutation probability	0.065
Selection	Tournament
Tournament Size	8
Fitness	MSE

Table 3. Parameters of the probability transformation

	$p(r_{0.0})$	$p(r_{0.33})$	$p(r_{0.66})$	$p(r_{1.0})$
$g_1 : \rho > 0.562$	0.0035	0.0077	0.0040	0.0032
$g_2 : \rho \leq 0.562$	0.0003	0.0010	0.0099	0.0078

Table 4. Percentage of baseline MSE

	Min	$Q_{.25}$	$Q_{.5}$	$Q_{.75}$	Max	Mean
$f_1(x)$	64.4%	80.2%	79.9%	80.7%	75.3%	79.7%
$f_2(x)$	71.1%	91.4%	91.4%	92.2%	98.0%	91.9%
$f_3(x)$	68.6%	83.3%	81.4%	83.4%	66.9%	81.0%
$f_4(x)$	112.5%	92.3%	93.1%	93.9%	96.7%	93.6%
$f_5(x)$	75.0%	90.3%	89.9%	82.6%	107.6%	81.5%
$f_6(x)$	106.0%	83.4%	85.1%	87.5%	92.2%	84.5%
$f_7(x)$	99.5%	99.0%	98.8%	99.8%	100.0%	99.1%
$f_8(x)$	108.8%	83.9%	83.4%	82.6%	93.2%	84.1%
$f_9(x)$	89.8%	90.4%	91.5%	91.4%	105.7%	92.9%
$f_{10}(x)$	99.2%	92.5%	92.6%	92.7%	97.9%	92.7%
$f_{11}(x)$	98.8%	98.4%	98.5%	98.3%	97.6%	98.4%
$f_{12}(x)$	50.1%	97.2%	97.4%	101.2%	85.4%	98.3%
$f_{13}(x)$	128.2%	84.2%	84.9%	97.2%	104.5%	103.6%
$f_{14}(x)$	55.6%	125.7%	136.5%	99.5%	183.2%	111.9%
$f_{15}(x)$	1238.6%	112.8%	124.6%	127.6%	60.8%	124.2%

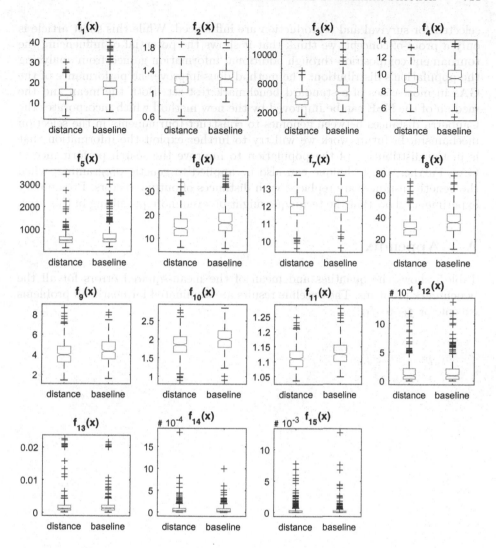

Fig. 3. The boxplots comparing distance-based tournament to the standard tournament selection.

$f_{13}(x)$ to $f_{15}(x)$ is not entirely clear. However, they all have a lower dimensionality in common. The loss of information from mapping low dimension genomes to the fitness might not be as large as in problems with higher dimensionality, dismantling the advantage of the distance-based method.

5   Conclusion

We have presented a new distance-based tournament for genetic algorithms. By influencing the chance of selection into the tournament, chances of being selected for survival and reproduction are influenced. While this short article is only a proof-of-concept, we think that it shows the potential of influencing the tournament composition through additional information gained from analyzing the population's distribution. The method does improve the performance of the GAs in most cases of a standard benchmark test set. Both the mean and the median of the MSE can be improved by the new method which incorporates the Canberra distances between genomes to construct tournaments in the selection mechanism. In future work we will try to further exploit the information that is in the distribution of the population to improve the search performance of GAs. Further, the technique can also be applied to genetic programing, when the genetic distances are replaced with distances of output vectors. Preliminary experiments show that the technique might be even more promising in this area.

A   Appendix

Table 5 shows the quantiles and mean of the mean-squared errors for all the benchmark problems. The baseline results are dominated for nearly all problems except for f_{13} to f_{15}.

Table 5. Mean-squared errors

Test function	Distance-based						Baseline					
	Min	Q.25	Q.5	Q.75	Max	Mean	Min	Q.25	Q.5	Q.75	Max	Mean
$f_1(x)$	3.67	11.24	13.65	16.64	29.90	14.38	5.69	14.01	17.09	20.61	39.71	18.04
$f_2(x)$	0.61	1.01	1.14	1.29	1.84	1.16	0.86	1.11	1.25	1.40	1.88	1.26
$f_3(x)$	1423.67	3028.80	3764.47	4791.36	7726.67	3910.02	2076.65	3635.05	4624.08	5747.95	11542.03	4826.56
$f_4(x)$	5.56	7.83	8.80	9.79	13.14	8.86	4.95	8.49	9.45	10.42	13.59	9.47
$f_5(x)$	167.17	395.45	503.46	658.47	3438.40	573.74	222.88	438.02	560.03	797.26	3195.39	703.98
$f_6(x)$	6.10	11.12	14.12	18.15	33.98	14.87	5.75	13.34	16.60	20.75	36.85	17.60
$f_7(x)$	9.56	11.55	12.05	12.53	13.76	12.00	9.61	11.67	12.20	12.56	13.76	12.11
$f_8(x)$	11.71	23.43	29.34	35.56	72.61	30.43	10.77	27.92	35.16	43.07	77.92	36.21
$f_9(x)$	1.45	3.23	3.96	4.80	8.64	4.11	1.62	3.57	4.33	5.25	8.18	4.42
$f_{10}(x)$	0.89	1.65	1.85	2.07	2.78	1.84	0.90	1.78	1.99	2.23	2.84	1.99
$f_{11}(x)$	1.04	1.08	1.11	1.14	1.25	1.11	1.05	1.10	1.13	1.16	1.28	1.13
$f_{12}(x)$	2.4E-07	3.0E-05	9.0E-05	2.1E-04	1.2E-03	1.6E-04	4.9E-07	3.0E-05	9.2E-05	2.1E-04	1.4E-03	1.7E-04
$f_{13}(x)$	1.4E-04	6.5E-04	1.2E-03	2.2E-03	2.3E-02	2.6E-03	1.1E-04	7.8E-04	1.4E-03	2.2E-03	2.2E-02	2.5E-03
$f_{14}(x)$	8.4E-08	1.1E-05	3.5E-05	8.7E-05	1.8E-03	7.5E-05	1.5E-07	8.6E-06	2.6E-05	8.7E-05	1.0E-03	6.7E-05
$f_{15}(x)$	4.0E-07	1.6E-05	5.8E-05	2.9E-04	7.7E-03	4.1E-04	3.2E-08	1.4E-05	4.6E-05	2.3E-04	1.3E-02	3.3E-04

References

1. Ackley, D.: A Connectionist Machine for Genetic Hillclimbing, vol. 28. Springer Science & Business Media (2012)
2. Dixon, L.C.W., Szegö, G.P.: The global optimization problem: an introduction. Towards Global Optim. **2**, 1–15 (1978)
3. Golberg, D.E.: Genetic Algorithms in Search, Optimization, and Machine Learning, p. 102. Addion wesley, Reading (1989)
4. Griewank, A.O.: Generalized descent for global optimization. J. Optim. Theory Appl. **34**(1), 11–39 (1981)
5. Homaifar, A., Qi, C.X., Lai, S.H.: Constrained optimization via genetic algorithms. Simulation **62**(4), 242–253 (1994)
6. Lance, G.N., Williams, W.T.: Computer programs for hierarchical polythetic classification (similarity analyses). Comput. J. **9**(1), 60–64 (1966)
7. Lee, C.-G., Cho, D.-H., Jung, H.-K.: Niching genetic algorithm with restricted competition selection for multimodal function optimization. IEEE Trans. Magn. **35**(3), 1722–1725 (1999)
8. Mahfoud, S.W.: Niching methods for genetic algorithms. Urbana **51**(95001), 62–94 (1995)
9. Molga, M., Smutnicki, C.: Test functions for optimization needs (2005)
10. Mühlenbein, H., Schomisch, M., Born, J.: The parallel genetic algorithm as function optimizer. Parallel Comput. **17**(6–7), 619–632 (1991)
11. Rosenbrock, H.H.: An automatic method for finding the greatest or least value of a function. Comput. J. **3**(3), 175–184 (1960)
12. Sareni, B., Krahenbuhl, L.: Fitness sharing and niching methods revisited. IEEE Trans. Evol. Comput. **2**(3), 97–106 (1998)
13. Schwefel, H.-P.P.: Evolution, Optimum Seeking: The Sixth Generation. Wiley, New York (1993)
14. Yao, X., Liu, Y., Lin, G.: Evolutionary programming made faster. IEEE Trans. Evol. Comput. **3**(2), 82–102 (1999)

Preferences-Based Choice Prediction
in Evolutionary Multi-objective Optimization

Manish Aggarwal[1], Justin Heinermann[2], Stefan Oehmcke[2],
and Oliver Kramer[2(✉)]

[1] Department of Information Systems,
Indian Institute of Management Ahmedabad, Ahmedabad, India
magwal8@gmail.com
[2] Computational Intelligence Group, Department of Computing Science,
University of Oldenburg, Oldenburg, Germany
{justin.heinermann,stefan.oehmcke,oliver.kramer}@uni-oldenburg.de

Abstract. Evolutionary multi-objective algorithms (EMOAs) of the type of NSGA-2 approximate the Pareto-front, after which a decision-maker (DM) is confounded with the primary task of selecting the best solution amongst all the equally good solutions on the Pareto-front. In this paper, we complement the popular NSGA-2 EMOA by posteriori identifying a DM's best solution among the candidate solutions on the Pareto-front, generated through NSGA-2. To this end, we employ a preference-based learning approach to learn an abstract ideal reference point of the DM on the multi-objective space, which reflects the compromises the DM makes against a set of conflicting objectives. The solution that is closest to this reference-point is then predicted as the DM's best solution. The pairwise comparisons of the candidate solutions provides the training information for our learning model. The experimental results on ZDT1 dataset shows that the proposed approach is not only intuitive, but also easy to apply, and robust to inconsistencies in the DM's preference statements.

Keywords: Multi-objective optimization · NSGA-2 · Preference-based learning · Solution selection

1 Introduction

In multi-objective optimization, the task is to approximate a Pareto-set of solutions given n conflictive objectives. The study of EMOAs has evoked a tremendous interest from researchers from different fields, with many EMOAs appearing in the recent times. Most evolutionary multi-objective approaches concentrate on computing a set of broadly distributed approximation of the Pareto-front for convenient a posteriori selection of alternative solutions. After the successful evolution of this set, a single solution needs to be chosen by a DM, which represents the best compromise by the DM among a set of conflicting objectives. Needless to say that each individual has his/her own way to make this

© Springer International Publishing AG 2017
G. Squillero and K. Sim (Eds.): EvoApplications 2017, Part I, LNCS 10199, pp. 715–724, 2017.
DOI: 10.1007/978-3-319-55849-3_46

compromise that is a reflection of the individual's priorities, values, attitudinal character (optimistic, pessimistic, tolerant, perfectionist), and the experience.

In the real applications, it is difficult for a DM to choose his/her *best solution*, directly from the Pareto-front yielded by an EMOA, because of the large number of candidate solutions comprising the Pareto-front, and large number of conflicting objectives. Instead, it is far more easier for the DM to apply his/her set of compromises on a subset of solutions, say a pair of solutions, at a time. Preference learning (PL) is an emerging subfield of machine learning, which deals with the learning of a predictive preference model of a DM from observed (or revealed) preference information. While evolutionary algorithms provide a multitude of equally good solutions in the form of Pareto-front, a machine learning algorithm is helpful to look deeper into the preference model of an individual decision-maker. Hence, both could be seen as complimentary with a potential to aid each other.

Combining PL with EMOA, our approach seeks to predict the best solution of a DM. That is, we intend to automate the entire process of making a decision, through generation of a vast number of solutions through EMOA, followed by the determination of the best solution, as it would have been done by the DM. The notable feature in the proposed approach is that it requires the DM's intervention only to train the model, and afterwards, the proposed approach is able to predict the DM's choices on its own. More specifically, we take as input the preference information of a DM, in the form of pairwise comparisons of the solutions on the Pareto-front, and uses the same to compute an ideal reference point (for the DM) on the objective space. It predicts the *best solution* on the basis of the closeness of the different solutions on the Pareto-front. This study is inspired from a recent study in the area of multi criteria decision making (MCDM) [1].

The proposed approach offers a convenient method for the DM to achieve a posteriori selection based on pairwise choices of alternative solutions. The paper is structured as follows. In Sect. 2 we shortly review related work in the field of EMOAs and integration of preference information. Section 3 introduces the preference learning approach that is basis of PL-NSGA-2, which is introduced in Sect. 4 and experimentally analyzed in Sect. 5. Results are summarized and discussed in Sect. 6.

2   Related Work

Many successful evolutionary multi-objective optimization algorithms have been introduced in the past. Most are first based on non-dominated sorting [2], which computes a domination rank for each solution. Among the solutions that are non-dominated or dominated by only one or a few other solutions in the population, a secondary criterion is applied to achieve a broad distribution among the Pareto-front.

The non-dominated sorting genetic algorithm (NSGA) in variant NSGA-2 [2] is maximizing the crowding distance, which for each solution represents the fitness difference of the two neighboring solutions w.r.t. each objective.

NSGA-2 is one of the most famous EMOAs with many applications and algorithmic extensions. In the experimental part of this work, we will also use NSGA-2 as optimization baseline. Further EMOAs have been introduced in the past like the strength Pareto evolutionary algorithm (SPEA) [3], which selects solutions w.r.t. the degree a solution is dominated and the density of the Pareto-front. Algorithms based on the hypervolume criterion maximize the dominated part of the whole population in the objective space [4].

Previous work on preference information integration of DMs can be divided into three categories. The first category concentrates on integrating preference information into the optimization process. For example, Friedrich *et al.* [5,6] assume that preference information is given as weights. The weight information is integrated into the measures that are basis of NSGA-2 and SPEA-based selection. In NSGA-2 weights are multiplied with the crowding distance. Unfortunately, the weight information is often not available or inconvenient to get from the DM. Ruiz *et al.* [7] approximate the region of interest on the Pareto- front with a reference point by using an achievement scalarizing function computed by DM preferences. also Filatovas *et al.* use scalarizing functions to narrow the search to parts of the Pareto-front.

The second category interactively integrates a DM's preference information into the optimization process by making use of the online decisions of the DM. For example, Branke *et al.* [8] let the DM take part interactively within the optimization process. At regular intervals, a DM is asked to rank the pairs of solutions, which updates an additive value function that speeds up the evolutionary optimization process. Also Jaszkiewicz [9] introduced an interactive approach that integrates pairwise comparisons during the evolutionary process into weight information that is basis for learning a preference function.

The third category helps the DM to select the solutions a posteriori from an evolved approximation of the Pareto-set. Chaudhari *et al.* [10] argue that the number of solutions that approximate the Pareto-front can be very large and propose clustering techniques to subsume groups of solutions on the front and offer cluster representatives to the DM. Zio and Bazzo [11] give an overview of approaches for a posteriori selection from the final front of solutions. The approach introduced in this work belongs to the third category.

3   Preference-Based Learning

In this section, we briefly give an overview of the proposed preference-based learning approach that is based on the computation of the ideal reference point $\mathbf{z}$, and is inspired from the study in [1]. Let $\mathcal{A}$ be a set of alternatives in a multi-criteria decision making (MCDM) scenario. We assume to have N pairwise comparison of the form

$$\mathbf{a}_i \succ \mathbf{a}_j \ , \tag{1}$$

where $\succ$ indicates that alternative $\mathbf{a}_i$ is preferred over $\mathbf{a}_j$, and $(\mathbf{a}_i, \mathbf{a}_j) \in \mathcal{A}$ forms a preference tuple obtained from a DM. The preference tuples of this kind are collected in a training set T.

Based on the preference tuples in T, an ideal reference point z and its distances to all the alternatives in $\mathcal{A}$ are computed. Figure 1 illustrates the ranking of the alternatives based on their closeness to the ideal reference point z. The alternatives are ranked in ascending order w.r.t. ascending distance to the reference point. That is, the closer an alternative is to the ideal reference point, the more preferred it is by the DM over other alternatives, and hence the better is its rank.

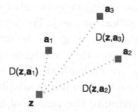

Fig. 1. Illustration of solution ranking with ideal reference point z. The alternative a_1 is closer to z than a_2 and a_3, ans a_2 is closer than a_3 resulting in $a_1 \succ a_2$, $a_1 \succ a_3$, and $a_2 \succ a_3$, i.e., ranking a_1, a_2, a_3.

We employ a variant of the popular Bradley-Terry model of discrete choice [12] that associates a utility function to each alternative, and finds out the probability of an alternative on the basis of the utility values. In the proposed approach, we use Euclidean distance $D(a, z)$ between the ideal reference point z and an alternative a as the utility function. Accordingly, the decision model is given by

$$P(a_i \succ a_j \mid z) = \frac{\exp(-D(a_i, z))}{\exp(-D(a_i, z)) + \exp(-D(a_j, z))}, \tag{2}$$

modeling all training set relations $a_i \succ a_j$ in T. This maximum likelihood model is optimized w.r.t. z yielding the reference point that our PL-NSGA-2 employs for the final ranking of solutions. In our optimization model, an alternative is a solution x_i in the final population with its evaluations on fitness functions $f = (f_1, \dots, f_n)$. Hence, z is an ideal point in the objective space.

Since, the proposed PL-based methodology makes use of pairwise comparison of alternatives, it is quite easy to apply in the real world problems. It is often easier for a DM to compare two competing alternatives, and identify the better of the two. The proposed algorithm provides an interesting method to decode a DM's rationale behind such a comparison in terms of a reference point that is used for predicting the DM's choices for any set of alternatives.

4   PL-Based Approach to Identify Best Solution

The proposed PL-based approach is based on the approximation of the Pareto-front with any of the EMOAs of the likes of NSGA-2, followed by the identification of the best solution among the candidate solutions on the Pareto-front.

For the evolved set of solutions, it offers a convenient way for the DM to finally choose a non-dominated solution. Algorithm 1 shows the pseudocode of our approach.

Algorithm 1. Proposed Approach to Identify Best Solution

1: $P \leftarrow$ optimization by EMOA
2: $T \leftarrow$ selection of N pairwise preference tuples by DM
3: $z \leftarrow$ ideal reference point with T
4: $x^* \in P \leftarrow$ w.r.t. distance to z

First, an EMOA like NSGA-2, SMS-EMOA, or SPEA computes an approximation of the Pareto-set, e.g., consisting of the last population P. From P, a pair of solutions are randomly chosen for the preference selection of a DM. This process is repeated N times. The result is a training set T of N pairwise preferences. The preference learning approach introduced in the previous section is applied to compute the ideal reference point $z \in \mathbb{R}^n$. A ranking of $P = \{x_i\}_{i=1}^n$ is computed based on the distance $D(z, f(x_i))$ in the objective space. In this study, we make use of NSGA-2 algorithm to generate the Pareto-front, and have applied our approach (henceforth referred to as PL-NSGA-2) to identify the best solution on the Pareto-front.

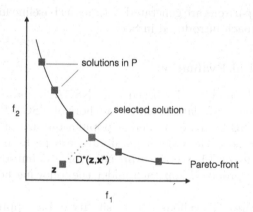

Fig. 2. Illustration of a posteriori selection of solutions from P based on closeness to reference point z, i.e., minimal distance $D^*(z, x^*)$.

PL-NSGA-2 banks upon the NSGA-2 efficiency in generating the Pareto-front and then identifies the best solution on the Pareto-front. The reference point directly helps to identify the preferred zone of a DM on the multi-objective space. A DM's reference point would shift on the objective space in accordance with the importance a DM places on an objective (Fig. 2).

5 Experimental Analysis

We dedicate this section for an empirical validation of our approach through a few experiments. For this sake, we first generate test data based on a typical evolutionary multi-objective optimization problem, namely ZDT1, followed by generating the Pareto-optimal front using NSGA-2 algorithm. We model a DM giving his pairwise preferences of the solutions with the help of a weight vector that defines a specific preference for objective functions. On the basis of such DM's pairwise preferences, we learn a ideal reference point of the DM in the objective space, and PL-NSGA-2 proposes that the *best solution* is closest to this reference point.

5.1 DM Modeling

We model a DM with dominance information and with weight $\mathbf{w}$ as follows. We consider minimization problems. A solution $\mathbf{x}_i$ is preferred to a solution $\mathbf{x}_j$, if $f_k(\mathbf{x}_i) < f_k(\mathbf{x}_j)$ for all $k = 1, \ldots, n$. For non-comparable, non-dominated solutions, the DM prefers the solution, for which it holds

$$\mathbf{w} \cdot \mathbf{f}(\mathbf{x}_i) < \mathbf{w} \cdot \mathbf{f}(\mathbf{x}_j) \tag{3}$$

Such pairwise comparisons are generated N times as baseline for the computation of $\mathbf{z}$ with the approach introduced in Sect. 3.

5.2 Experimental Evaluation

Our experimental analysis is based on NSGA-2, based on a MATLAB-implementation that is available from the authors of NSGA-2. We employ polynomial mutation, SBX crossover, and a population size of 200 parental and 200 offspring solutions. The experimental runs are performed on the popular benchmark problem ZDT1, see the Appendix for a definition. We analyze the performance of the proposed approach under the following heads:

Q0: Standard settings. To validate the feasibility of our approach, we first analyze, if our PL-NSGA-2 is able to identify solutions on the Pareto-front near the weights that reflect the DM model. For this sake we let NSGA-2 approximate the Pareto-set for 1000 generation with a population of size 200. Figure 3 shows some exemplary runs of PL-NSGA-2 on ZDT1 using different weights for the DM model. The figures show the final populations in the objective space, and the DM's preferred zone of solutions in corresponding to the associated weights $\mathbf{w}$ is shown through a solid red circle.

Q1: Effect of N on the ideal solution. We study the effect of N: number of preference tuples on the learning of DM's preferred zone. to this end, we run tests with different numbers of comparisons, i.e., $N = 100, 500, 4000$, and 6000

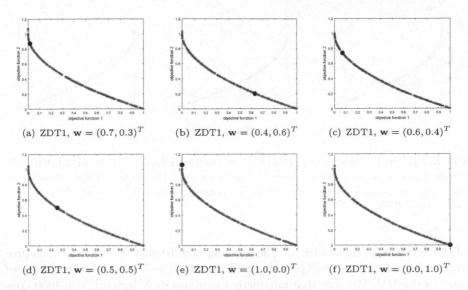

(a) ZDT1, $\mathbf{w} = (0.7, 0.3)^T$ (b) ZDT1, $\mathbf{w} = (0.4, 0.6)^T$ (c) ZDT1, $\mathbf{w} = (0.6, 0.4)^T$

(d) ZDT1, $\mathbf{w} = (0.5, 0.5)^T$ (e) ZDT1, $\mathbf{w} = (1.0, 0.0)^T$ (f) ZDT1, $\mathbf{w} = (0.0, 1.0)^T$

Fig. 3. Experimental analysis of PL-NSGA-2. The plots show the populations of solutions after 1000 generations of NSGA-2, and the preferred zone of the DM (by a solid red circle), on the basis of the vicinity to the DM's ideal reference point. on (a) ZDT1 and DM weights $\mathbf{w} = (0.7, 0.3)^T$, (b) ZDT1 and DM weights $\mathbf{w} = (0.4, 0.6)^T$, (c) ZDT1 and DM weights $\mathbf{w} = (0.6, 0.4)^T$, (d) ZDT1 and DM weights $\mathbf{w} = (0.5, 0.5)^T$, (e) ZDT1 and DM weights $\mathbf{w} = (1.0, 0.0)^T$, and (f) ZDT1 and DM weights $\mathbf{w} = (0.0, 1.0)^T$. (Color figure online)

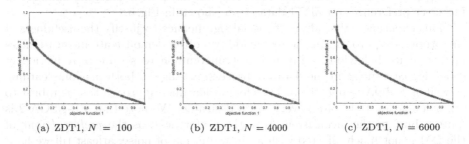

(a) ZDT1, $N = 100$ (b) ZDT1, $N = 4000$ (c) ZDT1, $N = 6000$

Fig. 4. Effect of the number of preference tuples on PL-NSGA-2. The plots show the preferred zone of solutions after 1000 generations of NSGA-2 on ZDT1 dataset, with (a) $N = 100$, (b) $N = 4000$, and (c) $N = 6000$.

with weight vector as $w = 0.6, 0.4$. Figure 4 shows some exemplary runs of PL-NSGA-2 on ZDT1 using different number of preference tuples in each run.

We observe that the preferred zone is sensitive to the number of tuples. This sensitivity decreases after $N = 4000$. In essence, it supports the intuitive fact that a minimum number of preference tuples are required to fully gather the preference model of the DM. In the current situation, we consider the population size as 200. Therefore, clearly, at $N = 100$, and $N = 500$, the preference information

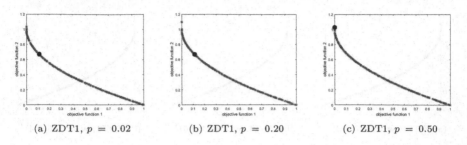

(a) ZDT1, $p = 0.02$ (b) ZDT1, $p = 0.20$ (c) ZDT1, $p = 0.50$

Fig. 5. Preferred solution of the DM obtained through PL-NSGA-2 on ZDT1, with different numbers of incorrect preferences. The plots show the preferred zone of solutions after 1000 generations of NSGA-2 on ZDT1 dataset, with (a) $p = 0.02$, (b) $p = 0.20$, and (c) $p = 0.50$.

of the DM is not fully captured. The learning stabilizes at $N = 4000$, which provides substantial number of pairwise preferences of the DM to infer the *preferred zone* of the DM. We note that any further increase in N beyond $N = 4000$ does not have a significant effect on the learnt *preferred zone* of the DM.

Q2: Robustness of the learning approach to inconsistencies in a DM's preferences. Lastly, we analyze the robustness of the approach w.r.t. to inconsistencies of pairwise DM decisions. For this sake, we add noise to the DM's preference decisions, by making inverse decisions with defined probabilities p, testing $p = 0.02, 0.20, 0.25, 0.5$. The plots obtained with different numbers of incorrect preferences on ZDT1 dataset are shown in Fig. 5.

This experimental study is of special significance to justify the usefulness of the proposed approach. In the real world, we often demonstrate inconsistencies in our choice behaviour. Also, it is not uncommon to see an introduction of some degree of noise in the data pre-processing stage in both machine learning as well as EMOA applications. Therefore, a learning approach that is robust to a particular level of noise is very much desirable. We note that PL-NSGA-2 is quite robust to the inconsistencies in the preferences, as the *preferred zone* of the DM is not much affected with an introduction of noise, atleast till we have $p = 0.20$, which makes the proposed approach potentially very much interesting.

Analysis of Results: It would be worthwhile to mention that the objective weights are only considered to simulate a DM's pairwise comparisons. In a real application, we do not require such weights, as a DM would apply his/her unique rationale (objective weight is only one component among many others of such rationale) to determine the better in such a pairwise comparison. Hence, though, in this study, apparently, we have reduced a multi-objective optimization problem to a single objective problem, in essence and in real applications, the problem is still a multi-objective optimization one. The proposed approach also helps to retain the diversity/shape of the Pareto-front for a deeper analysis of the same. We note from Fig. 3 that the reference point shifts in accordance with the objective weights. For instance, the reference points maximize the objectives on y and x axes with weights $(1.0, 0.0)$ and $(0.0, 1.0)$, respectively.

Once a DM's reference point is learned, PL-NSGA-2 can be straightaway applied to predict the DM's best solution for a new population of solutions (of the same domain and nature). It is interesting to note that PL-NSGA-2 can not only predict a DM's best solution, but it also help a DM to determine the best solution.

6   Conclusions

Introducing emerging algorithms from machine learning and MCDM to the field of EMOA, a predictive preference model is proposed to predict the best solution of a DM, among a multitude of equally good solutions for conflicting objectives. While a MCDM method helps to identify the best solution, the proposed PL-NSGA-2 approach is able to generate new solutions to approximate a broad coverage of the Pareto-set, and to predict the DM's best solution on this Pareto-front. The proposed approach is based on the pairwise preference-based learning of a DM's ideal reference point that leads to identifying the best solution on the basis of the closeness of the different solutions on the Pareto-front to this reference point.

The experimental analysis shows that the best solution is reflected through the pairwise preferences provided by a DM. Moreover, the proposed approach is intuitive, and easy to apply in practice. The experiments have further shown that PLEOMA requires roughly about 4000 pairwise comparisons for a population size of 200 and chromosome vector of length 5, and is remarkably robust against inconsistencies of the DM, as long as the inconsistency probability remains lesser than 20%.

The study has several real world applications. For instance, it can be used to analyze different decision behaviours of different individuals through reference points. The reference points learned through the proposed approach for different DMs reflect the DM's priorities and values. Such a study would be potentially useful in understanding consumer behaviour. Besides, it promises many interesting extensions. In the future, we plan to offer an alternative approach based on the determination of a weight factor based on pairwise rankings. We further plan to use the reference point as selection criterion during the run of the EMOA.

Acknowledgments. This work was carried out at Computational Intelligence Group, Department of Computing Science, University of Oldenburg, Germany with the support of German Academic Exchange Service (DAAD) to Manish Aggarwal as a visiting scientist and university academician.

A   Benchmark Function

Problem ZDT1 minimizes the two objective functions $f_1(\mathbf{x})$ and $f_2(\mathbf{x})$ with $f_1(\mathbf{x}) = x_1$ and $f_2(\mathbf{x}, \mathbf{z}) = g(\mathbf{z})h(f_1(\mathbf{x}), g(\mathbf{z}))$ with $g(\mathbf{z}) = 1 + \sum_{i=1}^{N} z_i / N$ and $h(f_1(\mathbf{x}), g(\mathbf{z})) = 1 - \sqrt{f_1(\mathbf{x})/g(\mathbf{z})}$.

References

1. Agarwal, M., Fallah Tehrani, A., Hullermeier, E.: Preference-based learning of ideal solutions in TOPSIS-like decision models. J. Multi-Criteria Decis. Anal. **22**(3–4), 175–183 (2015)
2. Deb, K., Agrawal, S., Pratap, A., Meyarivan, T.: A fast and elitist multiobjective genetic algorithm: NSGA-II. Trans. Evol. Comput. **6**(2), 182–197 (2002)
3. Zitzler, E., Thiele, L.: Multiobjective evolutionary algorithms: A comparative case study and the strength pareto approach. Trans. Evol. Comput. **3**(4), 257–271 (1999)
4. Beume, N., Naujoks, B., Emmerich, M.: SMS-EMOA: Multiobjective selection based on dominated hypervolume. Eur. J. Oper. Res. **181**(3), 1653–1669 (2007)
5. Friedrich, T., Kroeger, T., Neumann, F.: Weighted preferences in evolutionary multi-objective optimization. In: Wang, D., Reynolds, M. (eds.) AI 2011. LNCS (LNAI), vol. 7106, pp. 291–300. Springer, Heidelberg (2011). doi:10.1007/978-3-642-25832-9_30
6. Friedrich, T., Kroeger, T., Neumann, F.: Weighted preferences in evolutionary multi-objective optimization. Int. J. Mach. Learn. Cybern. **4**(2), 139–148 (2013)
7. Ruiz, A.B., Saborido, R., Luque, M.: A preference-based evolutionary algorithm for multiobjective optimization: the weighting achievement scalarizing function genetic algorithm. J. Glob. Optim. **62**(1), 101–129 (2015)
8. Branke, J., Greco, S., Slowinski, R., Zielniewicz, P.: Learning value functions in interactive evolutionary multiobjective optimization. Trans. Evol. Comput. **19**(1), 88–102 (2015)
9. Jaszkiewic, A.: Interactive multiobjective optimization with the pareto memetic algorithm. Found. Comput. Decis. Sci. **32**(1), 15–32 (2004)
10. Chaudhari, P., Dharaskar, R., Thakare, V.M.: Computing the most significant solution from pareto front obtained in multi-objective evolutionary. Int. J. Adv. Comput. Sci. Appl. (IJACSA) **1**(4), 1–6 (2010)
11. Zio, E., Bazzo, R.: A comparison of methods for selecting preferred solutions in multiobjective decision making. In: Kahraman, C. (ed.) Computational Intelligence Systems in Industrial Engineering. Atlantis Computational Intelligence Systems, vol. 6, pp. 23–43. Springer, Heidelberg (2012)
12. Bradley, R.A., Terry, M.E.: Rank analysis of incomplete block designs: I. the method of paired comparisons. Biometrika **39**(3/4), 324 (1952)

Numerical Optimization of ESA's Messenger Space Mission Benchmark

Martin Schlueter[1]([⊠]), Mohamed Wahib[2], and Masaharu Munetomo[1]

[1] Information Initiative Center, Hokkaido University, Sapporo 060-0811, Japan
schlueter@midaco-solver.com, munetomo@iic.hokudai.ac.jp
[2] RIKEN Advanced Institute for Computational Science, 7-1-26
Minatojima-minami-machi, Chuo-ku, Kobe, Hyogo 650-0047, Japan
mohamed.attia@riken.jp

Abstract. The design and optimization of interplanetary space mission trajectories is known to be a difficult challenge. The trajectory of the Messenger mission (launched by NASA in 2004) is one of the most complex ones ever created. The European Space Agency (ESA) makes available a numerical optimization benchmark which resembles an accurate model of Messengers full mission trajectory. This contribution presents an optimization approach which is capable to (robustly) solve ESA's Messenger full mission benchmark to its putative global solution within 24 h run time on a moderate sized computer cluster. The considered algorithm, named MXHPC, is a parallelization framework for the MIDACO optimization algorithm which is an evolutionary method particularly suited for space trajectory design. The presented results demonstrate the effectiveness of evolutionary computing for complex real-world problems which have been previously considered intractable.

Keywords: Interplanetary space trajectory · Optimization · GTOP · Messenger · CMAES, MIDACO · Parallelization

1 Introduction

Interplanetary trajectory optimization is a long standing challenge for space engineers and applied mathematicians alike. Since 2005 the Advanced Concept Team (ACT) of the European Space Agency (ESA) makes publicly available a comprehensive benchmark database of global trajectory optimization problems (GTOP) corresponding to real-world missions like Cassini, Rosetta and Messenger. The Messenger (full mission) benchmark in the GTOP database is notably the most difficult instance among those set, resembling a fully accurate model of the original trajectory of the Messenger mission launched by NASA in 2004.

The GTOP database expresses each benchmark as optimization problem (1) with box-constraints, whereas the objective function $f(x)$ is considered as nonlinear black-box function depending on a n-dimensional real valued vector of decision variables x. The GTOP database addresses researchers to test and compare their optimization algorithms on the benchmark problems.

© Springer International Publishing AG 2017
G. Squillero and K. Sim (Eds.): EvoApplications 2017, Part I, LNCS 10199, pp. 725–737, 2017.
DOI: 10.1007/978-3-319-55849-3_47

$$\text{Minimize} \quad f(x) \quad (x \in \mathbb{R}^n)$$

$$\text{subject to: } x_l \leq x \leq x_u \quad (x_l, x_u \in \mathbb{R}^n) \tag{1}$$

In [20] it was demonstrated that the MIDACO algorithm could solve many of the GTOP benchmarks to their putative best known solution within minutes to hours using its default parameters. However, in [20] it was also demonstrated, that the MIDACO algorithm failed to solve the hardest benchmark of this set, the Messenger (full mission) benchmark, to even a *near global* solution despite a massive run time of 24 h.

This contribution now addresses exclusively the Messenger (full mission) benchmark and demonstrates an optimization approach to robustly solve this benchmark within 24 h to its (putative) global optimal solution. The considered optimization approach is called MXHPC, which stands for *MIDACO Extension for High Performance Computing*. The MXHPC algorithm is a (massive) parallelization framework which executes and operates several instances of the MIDACO algorithm in parallel and has been especially developed for large-scale computer clusters.

This paper is structured as follows: The second section introduces the Messenger (full mission) benchmark and highlights its difficulty by presenting some preliminary numerical results obtained by CMAES [3] and MIDACO [18]. The third section describes the MXHPC algorithm in detail. The fourth section presents the numerical results obtained by MXHPC solving the Messenger (full mission) benchmark on a moderate computer cluster. Finally some conclusions are drawn.

2   The Messenger (Full Mission) Benchmark

The Messenger (full mission) benchmark models an multi-gravity assist interplanetary space mission from Earth to Mercury, including three resonant flyby's at Mercury. The sequence of fly-by planets for this mission is given by Earth-Venus-Venus-Mercury-Mercury-Mercury-Mercury, whereas the first item is the start planet and the last item is the final target planet. The objective of this benchmark is to minimize the total ΔV (change in velocity) accumulated during the full mission, which can be interpreted as reducing the fuel consumption. The benchmark invokes 26 continuous decision variables which are described as follows (for details on hyperbolic trajectories, see Kemble [14]) (Table 1):

The Messenger (full mission) benchmark does not contain constraints, except lower and upper bounds on the 26 decision variables. Table 2 displays the best known solution (corresponding to an objective function value of f(x) = 1.95863 km/s) together with the lower and upper bounds and their unit (if available). Note that the best known solution displayed in Table 2 corresponds closely to the data of the real Messenger trajectory and is believed to be globally optimal.

The Messenger (full mission) benchmark is part of the GTOP database which is a collection of (black-box) optimization problems resembling several real-world

Table 1. Description of optimization variables for Messenger benchmark

Variable	Description
1	Launch day measured from 1-Jan 2000 (MJD2000)
2	Initial excess hyperbolic speed (km/s)
3	Component of excess hyperbolic speed
4	Component of excess hyperbolic speed
5 ∼ 10	Time interval between events (e.g. departure, fly-by, capture)
11 ∼ 16	Fraction of the time interval after which DSM[a] occurs
17 ∼ 21	Radius of flyby (in planet radii)
22 ∼ 26	Angle measured in planet B plane of the planet approach vector

[a]DSM stands for *Deep Space Manoeuvre*

space mission trajectories. The instances of the GTOP database are known to be difficult to solve and have attracted a considerable amount of attention in the past. Many researchers have worked and published results on the GTOP database, for example [1,2,4–6,8,9,11–13,15,16,22,23]. A special feature of the GTOP database is that the actual global optimal solutions are in fact unknown and thus the ESA/ACT accepts and publishes any new solution that is at least 0.1% better (relative to the objective function value) than the current best known solution. Table 3 lists the individual GTOP benchmark instances (without the *Tandem* series) together with their number of solution submissions and the total time span between the first and last submission, measured in years.

From Table 3 it can be seen that it took the community in most cases several months to about a year to obtain the putative global optimal solution. From Table 3 it can also be seen that the Messenger (full mission) benchmark is an exception in this regard and stands out by the number of submitted solutions and the time span between its first and last submission. **Over 5 years** were required by the community to achieve the current best known solution to the Messenger (full mission) benchmark. This is a remarkable amount of time and reflects well the difficulty of this benchmark, about which the ESA states on their website [7]:

"it was hardly believable that a computer, given the fly-by sequence and an ample launch window, could design a good trajectory in complete autonomy without making use of additional problem knowledge".

ESA/ACT-GTOP website, 2016

2.1 Preliminary Numerical Results by CMAES and MIDACO

This sub-section further demonstrates the difficulty of the Messenger (full mission) benchmark by illustrating some preliminary numerical results achieved by the well-known CMAES [3] algorithm and the MIDACO [18] algorithm. Figure 1 presents a histogram of the solution objective function values obtained by 1000 independent test runs, performed once with CMAES and once with MIDACO.

Table 2. Best known solution for Messenger (full mission)

Variable	Lower bound	Solution value	Upper bound	Unit
1	1900	2037.8595972244	2300	MJD2000
2	2.5	4.0500001697	4.05	km/s
3	0	0.5567269199	1	n/a
4	0	0.6347532625	1	n/a
5	100	451.6575153013	500	days
6	100	224.6939374104	500	days
7	100	221.4390510408	500	days
8	100	266.0693628875	500	days
9	100	357.9584322778	500	days
10	100	534.1038782374	600	days
11	0.01	0.6378086222	0.99	days
12	0.01	0.7293472066	0.99	n/a
13	0.01	0.6981836705	0.99	n/a
14	0.01	0.7407197230	0.99	n/a
15	0.01	0.8289833176	0.99	n/a
16	0.01	0.9028496299	0.99	n/a
17	1.1	1.8337484775	6	n/a
18	1.1	1.1000000238	6	n/a
19	1.05	1.0499999523	6	n/a
20	1.05	1.0499999523	6	n/a
21	1.05	1.0499999523	6	n/a
22	$-\pi$	2.7481808788	π	n/a
23	$-\pi$	1.5952416573	π	n/a
24	$-\pi$	2.6241779073	π	n/a
25	$-\pi$	1.6276418577	π	n/a
26	$-\pi$	1.6058416537	π	n/a

The left side of Fig. 1 displays the histogram of 1000 solution objective function values obtained by CMAES. The X-axis represents the objective function value and the Y-axis represents the frequency of such values among all those solution. For the numerical tests, the original CMAES implementation from Hansen [10] was used, all parameters set to default. Table 4 lists detailed information on the obtained results by CMAES from all test runs.

In each performed test run the CMAES algorithm stopped by itself, if its internal standard deviation falls under a specific value (default 10^{-16} was used). On average the number of function evaluation performed by CMAES was 232780. Based on this number 1000 test runs were performed with MIDACO

Table 3. GTOP database benchmark problems

GTOP benchmark name	Number of submissions	Time between first and last submission
Cassini1	3	0.5 years
GTOC1	2	1.1 years
Messenger (reduced mission)	3	0.9 years
Messenger (full mission)	**10**	**5.7 years**
Cassini2	7	1.2 years
Rosetta	7	0.5 years
Sagas 2	1	*(only one submission)*

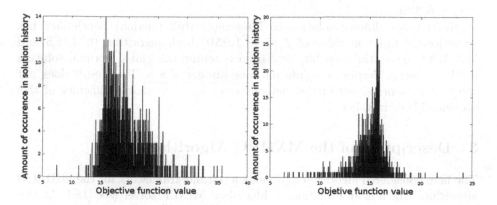

Fig. 1. Histogram of CMAES (left side) and MIDACO (right side) solutions

Table 4. CMAES results from 1000 test runs

Average solution $f(x)$	19.213 (ΔV)
Average function evaluation	232780
Average cpu-time	30.05 s
Overall best solution $f(x)$	7.379 (ΔV)
Overall execution time	8.3 h

(all parameters set to default), using a fixed maximal number of 232780 function evaluation in each such run. Table 5 lists detailed information on those test runs performed by MIDACO.

Comparing the results from the CMAES and MIDACO test runs, it can be seen that on average the CMAES algorithm stopped at a solution with an objective function value of 19.213, while the MIDACO algorithm stopped at a solution with an objective function value of 14.961. Both algorithms required a similar amount of time, which was about 30 second per run and totalled about

Table 5. MIDACO results from 1000 test runs

Average solution $f(x)$	14.961 (ΔV)
Average function evaluation	232780
Average cpu-time	29.01 s
Overall best solution $f(x)$	6.399 (ΔV)
Overall execution time	8.1 h

8 h for all 1000 test run executions. The overall best solution reported by CMAES corresponded to an objective function value of $f(x) = 7.379$. The overall best solution reported by MIDACO corresponded to an objective function value of $f(x) = 6.399$.

As the best known solution to Messenger (full mission) benchmark has an objective function value of $f(x) = 1.959$, both algorithm (CMAES and MIDACO) have still been far away from reaching the global optimal solution in above setup, despite a significant time budget of 8 h. This result does not come as a surprise, but further demonstrates the remarkable difficulty of this specific GTOP instance.

3   Description of the MXHPC Algorithm

The here considered algorithm represents a parallel framework for the MIDACO algorithm, which is an evolutionary black-box MINLP solver (see [18]). As this framework is particular suited for massive parallelization used in *High Performance Computing* (HPC) it is called MXHPC, which stands for *MIDACO Extension for HPC*. The basic purpose of the MXHPC algorithm is to execute several instances of MIDACO in parallel and manage the exchange of best known solution among those MIDACO instances.

Figure 2 illustrates how the MXHPC algorithm executes a number of S different instances of MIDACO in parallel. In regard to the well known Master/Slave concept in distributed computing, the individual MIDACO instances can be referred to as slaves, while the MXHPC algorithm can be referred to as master. In evolutionary algorithms such approach is also denoted as coarse-grained parallelization. Note in Fig. 2 that the best known solution is exchanged by MXHPC between individual MIDACO instances at a certain frequency (measured in function evaluation).

The MXHPC algorithm implies several individual parameters, this is the number of MIDACO instances, the exchange frequency of current best known solution and the survival rate of individual MIDACO instances at exchange times.

The considered exchange mechanism of best known solutions among individual MIDACO instances should be explained in more detail now, as this algorithmic step resembles the most sensitive part of the MXHPC algorithm. Let *survive* be the percentage (e.g. 25%) of surviving MIDACO instances at some

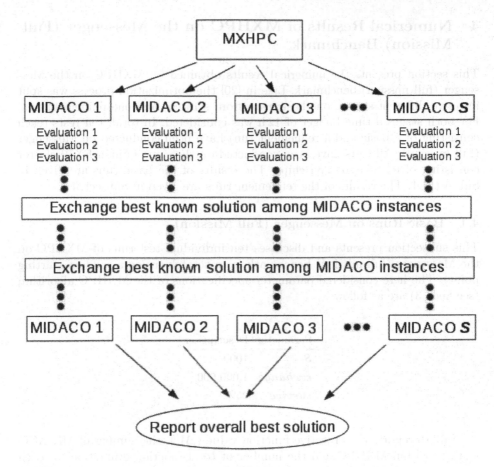

Fig. 2. Illustration of the MXHPC, executing S instances of MIDACO in parallel.

Parameter	Description
S	Number of MIDACO instances (also called *slaves*)
exchange	Solution exchange frequency among slaves
survive	Survival rate (in percentage) among slaves

exchange (e.g. 1,000,000 function evaluation) time of the MXHPC algorithm. Then, at an exchange time, MXHPC will first collect the current best solutions of each of the S individual MIDACO instances and identifies the *survive* (e.g. 25%) best among them. Those MIDACO instances, which hold one of those best solutions, will be unchanged (thus the instance "survives" the exchange procedure). All other MIDACO will be restarted using the overall best known solution as starting point.

Readers with a deeper interest in the algorithmic details of MIDACO are referred to Schlueter et al. [17].

4 Numerical Results of MXHPC on the Messenger (Full Mission) Benchmark

This section presents the numerical results obtained by MXHPC on the Messenger (full mission) benchmark. Like in [20] the optimization process was split into two different stages, one basic run (from scratch) and one refinement run. For both stages a time budget of 12 h was considered. In total, ten tests (each consisting of a basic and a refinement run) have been conducted on Messenger (full mission). All tests have been conducted on the same Fujitsu FX10 cluster consisting of 64 Sparc64 cpu chips. The results of the basic runs are given in Subsect. 4.1. The results of the refinement runs are given in Subsect. 4.2.

4.1 Basic Runs on Messenger (Full Mission)

This subsection presents and discusses ten individual test runs of MXHPC on the Messenger (full mission) benchmark from scratch (using a random starting point). The here considered parameter specifications of the MXHPC algorithm (see Sect. 3) are as follows:

Parameter	Description
S	1000
exchange	1,000,000
survive	25%

Table 6 reports the objective function value (ΔV), the number of MIDACO restarts within MXHPC and the number of total function evaluation for each of the ten individual basic runs of MXHPC on Messenger (full mission). Each test run setup differs only in the specific seed for the pseudo random number generator used within MXHPC. Furthermore, Table 6 displays the time, when MXHPC (b)reached the objective function value of 2.113, which corresponds to the overall best reported solution reported by a group (Stracquadanio et al. [22]) not associated with MIDACO. Note that given the difficulty of Messenger (full mission), an objective function value of 2.113 can already be considered as remarkable good, whereas such a solution is still around 8% above the overall best known one of 1.959.

From Table 6 it can be seen that in every test run a solution close to $f(x) = 2.0$ could be achieved, while the mark of $\Delta V = 2.113$ was (b)reached within one to six hours. It can be further seen that the number of total function evaluation necessary to achieve such objective function values ranges around 7×10^{10} (in words: seventy thousand million), which reflects well the complexity of this optimization problem. The number of MIDACO restarts within MXHPC ranged around fifty thousands. In addition to the results in Table 6, Fig. 3 illustrates the convergence curves of all ten runs in regard to the cpu time measured in seconds.

Table 6. 10 Test runs of MXHPC on MessFull

Seed	$f(x)$	Restarts	Total Eval	(B)reach $f(x) = 2.113$
1	2.0225	53,250	$70,000 \times 10^6$	9430 ($\sim$2.6 h)
2	2.0295	52,500	$69,000 \times 10^6$	7261 ($\sim$2.1 h)
3	2.0313	54,750	$72,000 \times 10^6$	13284 ($\sim$3.7 h)
4	2.0481	54,000	$71,000 \times 10^6$	12344 ($\sim$3.4 h)
5	2.0449	51,000	$67,000 \times 10^6$	5170 ($\sim$1.4 h)
6	2.0481	36,000	$47,000 \times 10^6$	14104 ($\sim$3.9 h)
7	2.0379	51,000	$67,000 \times 10^6$	3563 ($\sim$1.0 h)
8	2.0441	52,500	$69,000 \times 10^6$	7794 ($\sim$2.2 h)
9	2.0528	54,001	$71,000 \times 10^6$	23273 ($\sim$6.5 h)
10	2.0263	51,750	$68,000 \times 10^6$	6412 ($\sim$1.8 h)

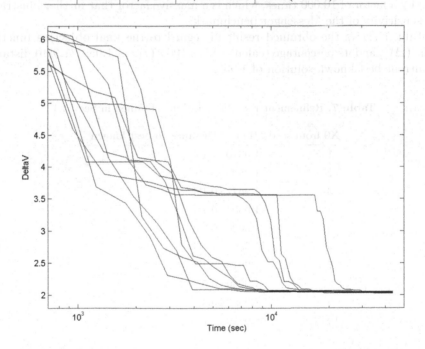

Fig. 3. Convergence curves of ten basic runs (semi-log scale)

In conclusion on Table 6 and Fig. 3 it can be stated that MXHPC is able to robustly solve Messenger (full mission) from scratch to an assumed near global solution, which is significantly better than the best result yet published by a different approach (see Stracquadanio et al. [22]).

4.2   Refinement Runs on Messenger (Full Mission)

This subsection presents the results of the refinement runs for each solution obtained by the previous basic run illustrated in Subsect. 4.1. Particular this means that each MXHPC solution from Table 6 (with an objective function value close above 2.0) was used as starting point for each individual refinement run presented in this subsection. The MXHPC algorithm setup is identical to the on used for the basic run, except one MIDACO parameter. This parameter is the *FOCUS* parameter (see [21]) which is used to concentrate the search process of each individual MIDACO instance within MXHPC around the submitted starting point (called $X0$). While in Subsect. 4.1 the default value of zero was assumed for FOCUS, here a value of 10,000[1] is used for all test runs. Note that a FOCUS value of 10,000 will imply a shrinking of the standard deviation in MIDACO's ACO multi-kernel gauss probability functions (see Schlueter et al. [17]) by a factor of 10,000 times, which is a massive factor that further illustrates the sensitivity of the Messenger benchmark.

Table 7 shows the obtained result in regard to the final objective function value (ΔV) and its percentage (calculated as $100 \times (f(x) - 1.959)/1.959$) distance to current best known solution of 1.959.

Table 7. Refinement runs for solutions obtained in Sect. 4.1

X0 from seed	$f(x)$	Distance to best known
1	1.9610	0.1%
2	1.9609	0.1%
3	1.9617	0.1%
4	1.9607	0.1%
5	1.9626	0.2%
6	1.9801	1.1%
7	1.9619	0.1%
8	1.9689	0.5%
9	1.9693	0.5%
10	1.9619	0.2%

From Table 7 it can be seen that in 5 out of 10 cases a final objective value close as 0.1% to the current best known one is obtained. In the worst case ($X0$ from seed 6), a solution with an objective close as 1.1% was obtained. In addition to the results in Table 7, Fig. 4 illustrates the convergence curves of all ten refinement runs. Note in Fig. 4 that the worst case run (corresponding to a final objective function value of about 1.98) appears as rather isolated result.

---

[1] Note that this is the same value for the FOCUS parameter as used for refinement runs in [20].

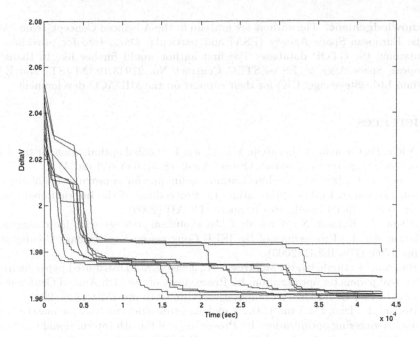

Fig. 4. Convergence curves of ten refinement runs (semi-log scale)

5   Conclusions

This contribution presented a rigorous study on the numerical optimization of ESA's Messenger (full mission) benchmark which is an exceptional difficult problem to solve. A novel algorithm, called MXHPC, was introduced. This algorithm acts as meta-algorithm on a computer cluster to operate in parallel several instances of the MIDACO algorithm. The MIDACO algorithm has previously shown to be efficient on interplanetary space mission design (see e.g. [19,20]). The numerical MXHPC results presented here demonstrate that it is possible to solve the Messenger (full mission) benchmark close to its putative global optimal solution within a single day. The results presented in Sect. 4 show that with a robustness of 5 out of 10 runs, a solution as close as 0.1% to the best known one was obtained within 24 h of run time on a 64 node Fujitsu FX10 cluster. In the worst case, a still remarkable good solution of just 1.1% above the best known one was obtained. These results further fortify the effectiveness of evolutionary computing for highly complex real-world applications that were previously considered intractable.

Future research might focus on both, improving the algorithmic performance of MXHPC and MIDACO as well as performing numerical test on larger computer clusters, having the ultimate goal to further reduce the overall required time to solve the Messenger (full mission) benchmark to few hours or even minutes.

Acknowledgement. The authors are grateful to the Advanced Concept Team (ACT) of the European Space Agency (ESA) and particular Dario Izzo for providing and maintaining the GTOP database. The first author would further like to thank the European Space Agency (ESA-ESTEC/Contract No. 21943/08/NL/ST) and EADS Astrium Ltd. (Stevenage, UK) for their support on the MIDACO development.

References

1. Addis, B., Cassioli, A., Locatelli, M., Schoen, F.: Global optimization for the design of space trajectories. Comput. Optim. Appl. **48**(3), 635–652 (2011)
2. Ampatzis, C., Izzo, D.: Machine learning techniques for approximation of objective functions in trajectory optimisation. In: Proceedings of the International Conference on Artificial Intelligence in Space (IJCAI) (2009)
3. Auger, A., Hansen, N.: A restart CMA evolution strategy with increasing population size. In: Proceedings of the IEEE Congress on Evolutionary Computation, pp. 1769–1776. IEEE (2005)
4. Biazzini, M., Banhelyi, B., Montresor, A., Jelasity, M.: Distributed hyper-heuristics for real parameter optimization. In: Proceedings of the 11th Annual Conference on Genetic and Evolutionary Computation (GECCO), pp. 1339–1346 (2009)
5. Biscani, F., Izzo, D., Yam, C.H.: A global optimisation toolbox for massively parallel engineering optimisation. In: Proceedings of the 4th International Conference on Astrodynamics Tools and Techniques (ICATT) (2010)
6. Danoy, G., Pinto, F.G., Dorronsoro, B., Bouvry, P.: New state-of-the-art results for Cassini2 global trajectory optimization problem. Acta Futura **5**, 65–72 (2012)
7. European Space Agency (ESA) and Advanced Concepts Team (ACT). GTOP database: Messenger (Full Mission) Instance (2016). Software http://www.esa.int/gsp/ACT/inf/projects/gtop/messenger_full.html
8. Gad, A.H.G.E.: Space trajectories optimization using variable-chromosome-length genetic algorithms. Ph.D.-Thesis, Michigan Technological University, USA (2011)
9. Gruber, A.: Multi Gravity Assist Optimierung mittels Evolutionsstrategien. BSc-Thesis, Vienna University of Technology, Austria (2009)
10. Hansen, N.: The CMA Evolution Strategy (2016). Sofware https://www.lri.fr/~hansen/cmaesintro.html
11. Henderson, T.A.: A Learning Approach To Sampling Optimization: Applications in Astrodynamics. Ph.D.-Thesis, Texas A & M University, USA (2013)
12. Islam, S.K.M., Roy, S.G.S., Suganthan, P.N.: An adaptive differential evolution algorithm with novel mutation and crossover strategies for global numerical optimization. IEEE Trans. Syst. Man Cybern. **42**(2), 482–500 (2012)
13. Izzo, D.: Global optimization and space pruning for spacecraft trajectory design. In: Conway, B. (ed.) Spacecraft Trajectory Optimization, pp. 178–199. Cambridge University Press, Cambridge (2010)
14. Kemble, S.: Interplanetary Mission Analysis and Design. Astronautical Engineering. Springer, Heidelberg (2006)
15. Lancinskas, A., Zilinskas, J., Ortigosa, P.M.: Investigation of parallel particle swarm optimization algorithm with reduction of the search area. In: Proceedings of the International Conference on Cluster Computing Workshops and Posters. IEEE (2010)
16. Musegaas, P.: Optimization of space trajectories including multiple gravity assists and deep space maneuvers. MSc Thesis, Delft University of Technology, Netherlands (2012)

17. Schlueter, M., Egea, J.A., Banga, J.R.: Extended ant colony optimization for non-convex mixed integer nonlinear programming. Comput. Oper Res. **36**(7), 2217–2229 (2009)
18. Schlueter, M., Gerdts, M., Rueckmann, J.J.: A numerical study of MIDACO on 100 MINLP benchmarks. Optimization **61**(7), 873–900 (2012)
19. Schlueter, M., Erb, S., Gerdts, M., Kemble, S., Rueckmann, J.J.: MIDACO on MINLP space applications. Adv. Space Res. **51**(7), 1116–1131 (2013)
20. Schlueter, M.: MIDACO software performance on interplanetary trajectory benchmarks. Adv. Space Res. **54**(4), 744–754 (2014)
21. Schlueter, M., Munetomo, M.: Introduction to MIDACO-SOLVER software. Technical report, HUSCAP, Hokkaido University, Japan (2013)
22. Stracquadanio, G., La Ferla, A., De Felice, M., Nicosia, G.: Design of robust space trajectories. In: Proceedings of the 31st International Conference on Artificial Intelligence (SGAI) (2011)
23. Vinko, T., Izzo, D.: Global Optimisation Heuristics and Test Problems for Preliminary Spacecraft Trajectory Design, European Space Agency. ACT Technical report, ACT-TNT-MAD-GOHTPPSTD (2008)

EvoPAR

A VNS with Parallel Evaluation of Solutions for the Inverse Lighting Problem

Ignacio Decia[⊠], Rodrigo Leira, Martín Pedemonte, Eduardo Fernández, and Pablo Ezzatti

Instituto de Computación, Universidad de la República, Montevideo, Uruguay
{idecia,rleira,mpedemon,eduardof,pezzatti}@fing.edu.uy

Abstract. Lighting design is a key issue in architectural design. The Inverse Lighting Problem (ILP) is an optimization problem that arises in lighting design and consist in finding the best configuration of lights that meets a set of goals that designers would like to achieve. In this paper, we present three different VNS that evaluate several solutions in parallel, improving the performance of a traditional VNS that has already been proposed for solving the ILP. These methods exploit the block matrix multiplication algorithms in order to increase the computational intensity of the algorithm and are specially well suited for parallel computation in GPUs architectures. The experimental analysis performed in two CPU/GPU hardware platforms for two scenarios with different complexity shows that the proposed methods provide fast results and are able to allow the interactive lighting design.

Keywords: Inverse Lighting Problems · Graphics processing unit · Variable neighborhood search · CUDA · GPGPU

1 Introduction

The Inverse Lighting Problem (ILP) is an optimization problem that arises in lighting design and consist in finding the best configuration of lights that meets a set of goals that designers would like to achieve. The ILP involves the calculation of the global illumination of the scene, and the search of an optimal solution from all the feasible solutions to the problem. Recently, a new method to address the ILP was presented in [1, 2]. This method uses the Low Rank Radiosity (LRR) [3] for calculating efficiently the global illumination associated to each candidate solution and a Variable Neighborhood Search (VNS) for solving the optimization problem. Despite the authors are able to solve ILPs in few minutes, the search process remains time consuming for complex scenes. Since parallel metaheuristics allow to reduce the search time [4], we study different parallelization strategies of the original VNS algorithm in order to speed up the process and improve the lighting design cycle.

In this work, we extend the classical VNS algorithm, which is a trajectory-based metaheuristic, with the evaluation of several solutions in parallel. Following this approach, the evaluation of the solutions can be transformed into a

© Springer International Publishing AG 2017
G. Squillero and K. Sim (Eds.): EvoApplications 2017, Part I, LNCS 10199, pp. 741–756, 2017.
DOI: 10.1007/978-3-319-55849-3_48

matrix-matrix multiplication. The block matrix multiplication algorithms, which are already part of numerical linear algebra libraries, increase the computational intensity and enhance the intrinsic parallelism of the algorithm. Our proposal consists in using these techniques for accelerating the VNS algorithm.

In the last decade, Graphic Processing Units (GPUs) have become an attractive platform for High Performance Computing due to their intrinsically parallel architecture and their relatively low economic cost [5]. As the block matrix multiplication algorithm over full matrices is specially suited for modern GPUs architecture, we also study implementations that compute the evaluation of the solutions using a GPU.

The VNS algorithms, with the evaluation of solutions in parallel, studied in this work, were able to obtain important reductions in the execution time of the original VNS algorithm for the two scenes considered in experimental evaluation. The implementation on GPU of the proposed methods were able to solve the ILP in about one minute, making possible the development of interactive design tools for the illumination of a scene.

2   Inverse Lighting Problems

Lighting design is an important issue in architectural design. Given an interior space to illuminate, the designer has to develop an illumination plan to meet some illumination goals. In this context, Light Intentions (LI) are the illumination goals that designers would like to achieve and comprise which surfaces should be illuminated with natural and artificial light, which ones should be in shadow and the maximum and minimum light intensities allowed on the surfaces. Besides the imposed LI, the restrictions can also include geometrical constraints. Traditional approaches for satisfying all LI usually require a complex process, often using the trial and error method, where the designer has to evaluate thousand of configurations until an acceptable solution is eventually found.

A particular lighting design problem is the Inverse Lighting Problem (ILP), which is further classified into problems of inverse emittance and inverse light positioning. In the former problems the unknowns are the emittances of a given subset of surfaces of the scene. In the latter problems the unknowns are the locations of the light sources in order to achieve a desired illumination. ILP solving techniques in general involve two computationally complex tasks, the simulation or calculation of the global illumination of the scene, and the search of an optimal solution from all the feasible solutions to the problem. Taken into consideration the high computational cost of both tasks, a key objective is the development of new algorithms to solve ILPs efficiently. One of such algorithms is the novel inverse lighting method presented in [1,2], which uses the LRR approximation to compute the global illumination and the VNS metaheuristic for efficient exploration of the search space. Next, we describe how the global illumination of the scene is calculated in this approach, and then in Sect. 3 we discuss how the VNS is used for solving the ILP.

In the radiosity methods, the global illumination calculation is simplified under the assumption of Lambertian diffuse reflection [6]. The scene is subdivided into n patches where the global illumination of the scene B is determined by the following equation:

$$B = (\mathbf{I} - \mathbf{RF})^{-1}E, \tag{1}$$

where B contains the radiosity value of each patch, $\mathbf{I}$ is the identity matrix, $\mathbf{R}$ is a diagonal matrix that stores the reflectivity of the patches, $\mathbf{F}$ is the form factor matrix (F_{ij} indicates the fraction of light reflected by patch i that arrives to patch j) and E is the emission vector with the emission value of each patch. All matrices have dimension $n \times n$.

In scenes where the geometry is static and the lighting is dynamic, the independent term E is the only term that varies, therefore the matrix $\mathbf{M} = (\mathbf{I} - \mathbf{RF})^{-1}$ is computed only once. Finding B using Eq. 1 involves a matrix-vector multiplication, requiring $O(n^2)$ operations. When $\mathbf{RF}$ has low numeric rank [3], $\mathbf{M}$ can be approximated by $\widetilde{\mathbf{M}} = (\mathbf{I} - \mathbf{Y}_k \mathbf{V}_k^T)$, where both $\mathbf{Y}_k$ and $\mathbf{V}_k$ are matrices $n \times k$, with $n \gg k$. The unknown $\widetilde{B}$ can now be computed following the next equation:

$$\widetilde{B} = (\mathbf{I} - \mathbf{Y}_k \mathbf{V}_k^T)E. \tag{2}$$

This low-rank approximation allows to finding the global illumination $\widetilde{B}$ performing only $O(nk)$ operations, providing a fast method for evaluating the ILP solutions. Under these circumstances, it is possible to formulate an optimization problem that is computationally affordable. In this work, we only consider inverse light positioning problems involving rectangular lights. This type of ILP can be formulated as the following optimization problem:

$$\max_{X} \quad f(\widetilde{B}, E, X)$$

$$\text{subject to:} \quad G(\widetilde{B}, E, X) \leq 0$$

$$E_i = \begin{cases} C_E & i \in \mathcal{E}(X) \\ 0 & \text{otherwise} \end{cases} \tag{3}$$

$$\widetilde{B} = \widetilde{\mathbf{M}}E,$$

where $X = (x_1, \ldots, x_d)$ are the decision variables of the problem that represent the coordinates that delimit the location of the light sources (for rectangular lights only the coordinates of the diagonally opposite corners are needed), G is the constraint function which enforces the LI and geometrical constraints imposed by the designer, C_E is the emission value of all emitter patches, and $\mathcal{E}$ are the set of patches that are within the areas of light, i.e., the patches that emit light. The goal of the optimization problem is to locate the lights in such a way that maximizes the objective function f subject to the constraints.

3   A VNS for the ILP

VNS is a metaheuristic widely used to solve a large variety of combinatorial optimization problems [4,7]. This method is based on the successive exploration of a set of neighborhoods $N_1(x), N_2(x), \ldots, N_{max}(x)$ to find the best solution. Each neighborhood $N_i(x)$ defines a set of candidate solutions around the point x. The algorithm starts from an initial solution x, and it computes a local search on the first neighborhood $N_1(x)$. If a better solution can not be found in the current neighborhood $N_l(x)$, the neighborhood structure is changed and the search continues in the next neighborhood $N_{l+1}(x)$; and so on. Otherwise, a better solution x' is found on the current neighborhood $N_l(x)$, the current solution x is replaced by x', and the local search is restarted in the first neighborhood $N_1(x')$. The algorithm usually ends when a maximum number of function evaluations is reached or when all the neighborhoods are explored and a better solution could not be found. Usually, the neighborhoods used in VNS are nested: $N_1(x) \subset N_2(x) \subset \ldots \subset N_{max}(x)$.

Algorithm 1 shows the VNS procedure used for solving the ILP previously presented in [1,2]. The decision variables of the problem are closely related to the neighbourhood structure. For this reason, we detail next how the decision variables are used to determine which patches are light emitters. In this work, we are only considering rectangular lights, the first pair of variables determines the first rectangle, where x_1 and x_2 are the opposite extremes of one of the diagonals of the rectangle. Then, the second pair of variables determines the second rectangle, and so on.

Each neighborhood N_k takes into account two parameters, the number of decision variables that can be modified at the same time (v) and a discretization (r) of the normalized range value of the variable that is being modified. For instance, when $v = 1$ and $r = 0.1$, a single decision variable x_i from x is randomly selected, and then a new value of x_i is chosen from the interval $x_i \pm 0.1(x_i^M - x_i^m)$, where x_i^M and x_i^m is the maximum and minimum possible values for x_i, respectively. In one step, a variable related to the position of the first light is modified; in the next step, a variable of the second light is modified; and so on. Following the parametric neighborhood definition, a grid of neighborhoods is defined, considering combinations of selected values of $v \in \{1, \ldots, nvar\}$ and $r \in \{0.1, 0.2, \ldots, 1\}$. Because all neighborhoods contain infinitely many elements, at each local search, the algorithm considers only a finite set of candidate solutions randomly selected from the current neighborhood $N_k(x)$. The number of candidates considered is proportional to the size of the current neighborhood.

4   Parallel Implementations of the VNS for the ILP

The evaluation of a candidate solution in the VNS algorithm for the ILP is computed using a matrix-vector product $\widetilde{B} = \widetilde{M}E$. This evaluation requires $O(nk)$ operations. Since in each local search t candidate solutions are evaluated, the complexity of exploring a single neighborhood is $O(tnk)$ operations.

Algorithm 1. VNS for the ILP based on [1, 2].

Input: A set of neighborhood structures N_k for $k = 1, \ldots, max$
Output: The best solution found
Pre-processing: Compute $\mathbf{Y}_k$, $\mathbf{V}_k^T$

```
 1  begin
 2  │   x ⟵ x₀                               /* Generate initial solution */
 3  │   while not stopping criteria do
 4  │   │   k ⟵ 1
 5  │   │   while k ≤ max do
 6  │   │   │   x^neigh ⟵ x
 7  │   │   │   for i ← 1 to p do            /* Local search with p tries */
 8  │   │   │   │   Generate feasible neighborhood solution x' :∈ Nₖ(x)
 9  │   │   │   │   Compute emission E of x'
10  │   │   │   │   Compute radiosity B̃ = (E − (Yₖ(VₖᵀE)))
11  │   │   │   │   Compute f(x') using B̃
12  │   │   │   │   if f(x') > f(x^neigh) then
13  │   │   │   │   │   x^neigh ⟵ x'
14  │   │   │   if f(x^neigh) > f(x) then
15  │   │   │   │   x ⟵ x^neigh
16  │   │   │   │   k ⟵ 1
17  │   │   │   else
18  │   │   │   │   k ⟵ k + 1
```

It is well known that even though computing m matrix-vector multiplications has the same order than computing a single matrix-matrix multiplication, the matrix-matrix product uses block matrix multiplication algorithms, which make a better use of cache memories, increasing the computational intensity (i.e., the number of *flops* per global memory access) [8]. This fact could be exploited in the VNS algorithm by simultaneously evaluating m candidate solutions. For this purpose, the m solutions can be combined in a matrix $\boldsymbol{E} = [E^1, E^2, \ldots, E^m]$, where E^i corresponds to the emission vector of the i solution. As a consequence, the m independent matrix-vector products is replaced by a matrix-matrix product $\boldsymbol{B} = \widetilde{\mathbf{M}} \boldsymbol{E}$, where $\boldsymbol{B} = [B^1, B^2, \ldots, B^m]$. Our proposal consists in exploring this idea through the use of techniques from numerical linear algebra area to reduce the runtime of the VNS algorithm. Since matrix-matrix multiplication is an operation highly suited for GPU platforms, we also take advantage of the massive parallelism available on modern GPUs with the aim of accelerating the computations involved in the global illumination calculation.

Based on the idea described below, we study three different approaches that are described next. For each of the approaches, two different implementations were developed, a CPU implementation with the aim of evaluating the benefits of the simultaneous evaluation of candidate solutions, and a CPU+GPU implementation that uses the GPU for accelerating the matrix-matrix multiplication.

In all the CPU+GPU implementations before generating the initial solution/s, $\mathbf{Y}_k$ and $\mathbf{V}_k^T$ are transferred from CPU to GPU. In all the implementations, $\mathbf{Y}_k$ and $\mathbf{V}_k^T$ are computed previously to the execution of the VNS.

All approaches can be divided in three main phases. In the *generation phase*, the neighbor solutions are generated from the current solution and neighborhood. Then, in the *evaluation phase* the candidate solutions are evaluated, and finally, in the *updating phase*, the best-so-far solution is updated if a better solution is found. *Generation* and *updating* phases are executed on the CPU, while in the case of the *evaluation* phase the execution platform depends on the implementation.

4.1   VNS with Parallel Local Search

In this approach the evaluation of the neighbor solutions is computed in parallel using the matrix-matrix multiplication. This approach will be referred as VNS$_{\text{PLS}}$. The main characteristics of this approach are:

1. *Generation phase*: A set of candidate solutions is built from the current neighborhood and the current solution. All the solutions from the set are feasible, i.e., if an unfeasible solution is constructed, it is discarded and a new solution is generated. Then, the emission matrix E is computed by calculating the emission vector for each solution.
2. *Evaluation phase*: The global illumination B is computed as the matrix-matrix product of $\widetilde{\mathbf{M}}$ and E (corresponding to several candidate solution of the same neighborhood) using a numerical linear algebra library, BLAS in the case of the CPU implementation and CUBLAS in the CPU+GPU counterpart. In the CPU+GPU implementation, the matrix E is transferred from CPU to GPU before the multiplication, and then B is transferred back to main memory. Finally, the function value $f(x)$ is computed for each B^i.
3. *Updating phase*: The algorithm iterates through the function values and it updates the current best-so-far solution if a better solution is found, i.e., a solution with a higher function value.

4.2   Parallel Independent Run of VNS

In this approach several independent VNS are run in parallel, i.e., the matrix-matrix multiplication is used for evaluating in parallel candidate solutions from different executions of VNS. This approach will be referred as VNS$_{\text{PIR}}$. The main characteristics of this approach are:

1. *Generation phase*: For each independent execution, a feasible candidate solution is selected from its current neighborhood. Then, the emission matrix E is computed by calculating the emission vector of each solution.
2. *Evaluation phase*: The evaluation phase of this approach is the same than in VNS$_{\text{PLS}}$ with the only difference that E is composed by several candidate solution, one from each independent execution.
3. *Updating phase*: For each independent run, the current best-so-far solution is updated if a better solution of the corresponding execution is found.

4.3   Parallel Independent Run of VNS with Parallel Local Search

This approach combines the two previous approaches, i.e., the matrix-matrix multiplication is used for evaluating in parallel candidate solutions from the neighborhood of the current solution of each of the different executions of VNS. This approach will be referred as VNS_{HYB}. Algorithm 2 presents the pseudocode of the CPU+GPU implementation of VNS_{HYB}. The main characteristics of this approach are:

1. *Generation phase*: For each independent run, a set of feasible candidate solutions is selected from its current neighborhood. Then, the emission matrix E is computed by calculating the emission vector for each candidate solution. This is shown in Algorithm 2 in lines 7 to 10.
2. *Evaluation phase*: The evaluation phase of this approach is the same than in VNS_{PLS} and in VNS_{PIR} with the only difference that E is composed by several candidate solution of each neighborhood from each independent run. This is shown in Algorithm 2 in lines 11 to 13. In the CPU implementation of VNS_{HYB} this phase is computed on the CPU.
3. *Updating phase*: For each independent run, the algorithm iterates through the function values of the neighborhood, and if a better solution is found, the current best-so-far solution of the execution is updated. This is shown in Algorithm 2 in lines 14 to 23.

5   Experimental Study

This section describes the experimental study used for evaluating the parallel implementations of VNS proposed in this work, including the test instances, the parameters setting, and the execution platforms. Then, the results regarding the numerical and computational efficiency of our proposals.

5.1   Test Instances

The optimization problem considered in this work consists in finding up to two lights which maximize the total light power reflected from the scene: $\sum_i A_i \widetilde{C}_i$, where A contains the area of each patch and $\widetilde{C} = \widetilde{B} - E$ is a vector with the reflected radiosity of each patch. The optimization problem also has the following restrictions: the two lights must be rectangular; the sum of their areas has to be less than 0.5 m^2; and they must be located on the ceiling of the scene.

For the experimental evaluation, we use two different scenarios, *Cornell Box* and *Sponza Atarium*, which are two widely used test scenes in the computer graphics research. Table 1 describes both scenarios, including the number of patches and the number of ceiling patches. The scenarios differ in the size, i.e., in the number of patches of the scene, and thus in the size of the matrices associated to the scenario, Sponza Atarium is significantly larger than Cornell Box. The percentage of the number of patches that are located in the ceiling is 2.3% for Sponza Atarium and 4.9% for Cornell Box.

Algorithm 2. CPU+GPU implementation of VNS$_{HYB}$.

Input: A set of neighborhood structures N_k for $k = 1, \ldots, max$
      m: the number of independent executions of VNS
Output: The best solution found
Pre-processing: Compute $\mathbf{Y}_k$, $\mathbf{V}_k^T$

1 **begin**
2   **Transfer $\mathbf{Y}_k$, $\mathbf{V}_k^T$ from CPU to GPU**
3   **for** $i \leftarrow 1$ to m **do**
4          $x^i \leftarrow x_0^i$ /* Generate initial solutions */
5          $k^i \leftarrow 1$ /* Initialize neighborhoods */
6   **while** *not stopping criteria* **do**
7   **for** $i \leftarrow 1$ to m **do**
8   **Generate p_i feasible neighborhood solutions** $\widehat{x}^i \in N_{k^i}(x^i)$
9          $\widehat{X} = [\widehat{x}_1^1, \ldots, \widehat{x}_{p_1}^1, \ldots, \widehat{x}_1^m, \ldots, \widehat{x}_{p_m}^m]$
10   **Compute emission E of $\widehat{X}$**
11   **Transfer E from CPU to GPU**
12   **Compute radiosity $\widetilde{B} = (E - (\mathbf{Y}_k(\mathbf{V}_k^T E)))$**
13   **Transfer $\widetilde{B}$ from GPU to CPU**
14   **for** $i \leftarrow 1$ to m **do**
15   **for** $j \leftarrow 1$ to p_i **do**
16   Compute $f(\widehat{x}_j^i)$ using $\widetilde{B}$
17   **Find the best neighbor solution** $\widehat{x}^i$ **of execution** i
18   **if** $f(\widehat{x}^i) > f(x^i)$ **then**
19                 $x^i \leftarrow \widehat{x}^i$
20                 $k^i \leftarrow 1$
21   **else**
22                 $k^i \leftarrow k^i + 1$
23   **if** $k^i > k_{max}$ **then** $k^i \leftarrow 1$

Table 1. Test scenarios used in the experimental evaluation.

Scenarios	Patches	Ceiling patches	Size of Y_k and V_k^T
Cornell Box	9216	448	9216×576
Sponza Atarium	79232	1802	79232×2668

5.2 Algorithms, Parameters Setting and Test Environment

In addition to the three VNS algorithms proposed in this paper, namely VNS$_{PLS}$, VNS$_{PIR}$, and VNS$_{HYB}$, we have also included an implementation of the original VNS proposed in [1,2] (referred as VNS$_{PW}$). Each of the VNS algorithms studied has been implemented both on CPU and CPU+GPU, except VNS$_{PW}$ that has only been implemented on CPU. The algorithms were implemented in Matlab R2011b (7.13.0.564) using MEX files for interacting with CUDA/CUBLAS.

The minimum number of feasible neighbor solutions built in VNS$_{PW}$ and VNS$_{PLS}$ is set to 500. The number of parallel independent runs of VNS used in VNS$_{PIR}$ is 500. The VNS$_{HYB}$ parameter values used are 50 for the minimum number of feasible neighbor solutions built and 10 for the number of parallel independent runs of VNS. The stopping criterion used for all the implementation of VNS used in this study is to reach a maximum number of function evaluations fixed a priori. The number of functions was set to 30000.

Two execution platforms are used for evaluating the algorithms. *Platform I* is a PC with a Quad Core Intel i7 2600 at 3.4 GHz with 8 GB RAM using Linux O.S. connected to a Nvidia Tesla C2070 GPU. *Platform II* is a PC with a Quad Core Intel i7 3770 at 3.4 GHz with 16 GB RAM using Linux O.S. connected to a Nvidia Geforce GTX 680. All the implementations use single-precision floating-point arithmetic. The transference times of data between CPU and GPU are included in the reported total run time of the CPU+GPU implementations.

5.3   Experimental Analysis

Since the VNS algorithm is a stochastic algorithm, we have followed the statistical procedure described next to provide the results with statistical significance. Thirty independent runs for each algorithm and each problem instance have been performed. The following statistical analysis has been performed to check if the distribution of the function values and the execution time of each algorithm is statistically different [9]. First, we perform a Kruskal-Wallis test for each instance independently. A post-hoc testing phase consisting in a pairwise comparison of all the cases compared using the Bonferroni-Dunn method on the Wilcoxon-Mann-Whitney test has also been performed. All the statistical tests are performed with a confidence level of 95%. The results are displayed in tabular form, where '◁' states that the algorithm of the row is statistically better than the column and '△' states that the opposite is true. When no statistically significant differences are found, the '−' symbol is used.

Numerical Efficiency. Let us begin with the analysis of the numerical efficiency of the VNS algorithms. Since the only operation that is computed on the GPU is the matrix-matrix multiplication, the CPU and CPU+GPU implementations of a certain variant have exactly the same numerical result. For this reason, we have only included in this analysis the CPU implementations of the algorithms. Table 2 presents the experimental results with respect to the quality of the solutions (median and interquartile range), while Table 3 presents in which instances the statistical confidence has been achieved.

The results obtained show that VNS$_{PLS}$ is slightly worse than the rest of the variants of VNS algorithm studied. In the Cornell scenario, there is no statistically difference between the results obtained by VNS$_{PW}$, VNS$_{PIR}$, and VNS$_{HYB}$. On the other hand, in the Sponza scene, VNS$_{PW}$ is slightly better than VNS$_{PIR}$ and VNS$_{HYB}$, which have similar results.

Table 2. Numerical efficiency of CPU versions of VNS algorithms (median (IQR)).

Scene	Plat.	VNS$_{PW}$	VNS$_{PLS}$	VNS$_{PIR}$	VNS$_{HYB}$
Cornell	I	19.334 (0.896e-2)	19.328 (0.113e-1)	19.334 (0.000e0)	19.334 (0.000e0)
	II	19.334 (0.896e-2)	19.328 (0.126e-1)	19.334 (0.675e-5)	19.334 (0.415e-2)
Sponza	I	4.737 (0.365e-2)	4.719 (0.972e-2)	4.729 (0.632e-2)	4.729 (0.816e-2)
	II	4.737 (0.365e-2)	4.719 (0.972e-2)	4.728 (0.396e-2)	4.730 (0.814e-2)

Table 3. Stat. significance for Cornell on I, Cornell on II, Sponza on I, Sponza on II.

	VNS$_{PLS}$				VNS$_{PIR}$				VNS$_{HYB}$			
VNS$_{PW}$	◁	◁	◁	◁	−	−	◁	◁	−	−	◁	◁
VNS$_{PLS}$ CPU					△	△	△	△	△	△	△	△
VNS$_{PIR}$ CPU									−	−	−	−

In summary, the extension of VNS with the parallel evaluation of solutions does not imply a strong reduction in the quality of the solutions obtained, specially in the VNS$_{PIR}$ and VNS$_{HYB}$ algorithms. A complete analysis on how the parameter configuration of the different algorithms (i.e., the minimum number of feasible neighbor solutions built and the number of parallel independent runs) is out of the scope of this work, since our main focus is the performance of the variants. However, the obtained results allow us to state there is no meaningful loss in the quality of the obtained solutions caused by the extension of VNS.

Computational Efficiency. Let us first analyze the performance of the evaluation phase of the different VNS algorithms. Table 4 shows the run time of the evaluation phase of VNS$_{PW}$ on CPU, and both implementations (CPU and CPU+GPU) of VNS$_{PLS}$, VNS$_{PIR}$, and VNS$_{HYB}$. The shortest execution time on each platform is indicated on bold. Table 5 presents in which cases the statistical confidence has been achieved.

The obtained results show that the run time of the evaluation phase of the VNS algorithm is drastically reduced when the matrix-matrix multiplication is used instead of the classical approach. This improvement is mainly explained by the better use of the cache memory achieved by the block matrix multiplication algorithm. The results also show that the implementations that use both CPU and GPU are the best performing algorithms, being able to execute in a shorter time than their corresponding counterparts that only execute on the CPU and than the original VNS. Regarding the different variants of VNS proposed, there is no algorithm that systematically has the shortest execution time with statistical confidence, which it makes impossible to conclude which strategy is better for all the scenes considered. Regarding the different scenarios, it is clear that the run time of the algorithms in the Sponza scene is considerably longer than in the Cornell scene, what is consistent with the difference on the size of the scenarios.

Table 4. Execution time in seconds of the evaluation phase (median $_{IQR}$).

Scene	Plat.	CPU implementation				CPU+GPU impl.		
		VNS_{PW}	VNS_{PLS}	VNS_{PIR}	VNS_{HYB}	VNS_{PLS}	VNS_{PIR}	VNS_{HYB}
Cornell	I	$71.02_{0.08}$	$4.75_{0.19}$	$4.33_{0.10}$	$\mathbf{3.96}_{0.10}$	$1.55_{0.05}$	$1.67_{0.02}$	$\mathbf{1.52}_{0.03}$
	II	$72.43_{1.05}$	$4.05_{0.27}$	$4.22_{0.61}$	$\mathbf{3.78}_{0.41}$	$1.93_{0.11}$	$1.96_{0.02}$	$2.54_{0.05}$
Sponza	I	$2752.46_{1.83}$	$\mathbf{152.48}_{4.40}$	$157.59_{1.64}$	$153.99_{2.24}$	$43.49_{1.78}$	$45.36_{0.22}$	$\mathbf{42.89}_{0.65}$
	II	$2789.07_{20.53}$	$\mathbf{136.42}_{5.03}$	$143.77_{4.66}$	$138.08_{5.65}$	$32.43_{0.92}$	$34.14_{0.41}$	$\mathbf{31.65}_{0.68}$

Table 5. Stat. significance for Cornell on I, Cornell on II, Sponza on I, Sponza on II.

	CPU implementation												CPU+GPU implementation											
	VNS_{PLS}				VNS_{PIR}				VNS_{HYB}				VNS_{PLS}				VNS_{PIR}				VNS_{HYB}			
VNS_{PW}	△	△	△	△	△	△	△	△	△	△	△	△	△	△	△	△	△	△	△	△	△	△	△	△
VNS_{PLS} CPU					△	—	◁	◁	△	—	—	—	△	△	△	△	△	△	△	△	△	△	△	△
VNS_{PIR} CPU									△	△	△	△	△	△	△	△	△	△	△	△	△	△	△	△
VNS_{HYB} CPU													△	△	△	△	△	△	△	△	△	△	△	△
VNS_{PLS} CPU+GPU																	◁	—	◁	◁	△	◁	—	△
VNS_{PIR} CPU+GPU																					△	◁	△	△

Table 6. Speedup in evaluation phase of VNS Algorithms vs. VNS_{PW}.

Scene	Platform	CPU impl.			CPU+GPU impl.		
		VNS_{PLS}	VNS_{PIR}	VNS_{HYB}	VNS_{PLS}	VNS_{PIR}	VNS_{HYB}
Cornell	I	14.95	16.40	**17.93**	45.82	42.53	**46.72**
	II	17.88	17.16	**19.16**	**37.53**	36.95	28.52
Sponza	I	**18.05**	17.47	17.87	63.29	60.68	**64.17**
	II	**20.44**	19.40	20.20	86.00	81.70	**88.12**

Table 6 shows the speedup of the evaluation phase of VNS algorithms proposed in this work vs. the original VNS (VNS_{PW}). The speedup values of the CPU implementations range from 14.95 × (VNS_{PLS} in Cornell scene run in Platform I) to 20.44 × (VNS_{PLS} in Sponza scene executed in Platform II), which represents an important reduction taking into account that these implementations use exactly the same hardware than VNS_{PW}. The speedup values of the implementations that use the GPU range from 28.52 × (VNS_{HYB} in Cornell scene run in Platform II) to 88.12 × (VNS_{HYB} in Sponza scene executed in Platform II), which represents an additional reduction in the run time of up to 4.36 × produced by computing the matrix-matrix multiplication on the GPU.

With regard to the scenarios, the speedup values are in general larger when solving the Sponza scene than for the Cornell scene. This is explained because larger scenarios produce larger tentative solutions, which allows the block matrix multiplication algorithms to better profit from parallel computation.

Let us now analyze the computational performance of the different VNS algorithms. Table 7 shows the total run time of the VNS Algorithms. The shortest execution time on each platform is indicated on bold. Table 8 presents in which cases the statistical confidence has been achieved.

Table 7. Execution time in seconds of the VNS algorithms (median $_{IQR}$).

Scene	Plat.	CPU implementation				CPU+GPU impl.		
		VNS_{PW}	VNS_{PLS}	VNS_{PIR}	VNS_{HYB}	VNS_{PLS}	VNS_{PIR}	VNS_{HYB}
Cornell	I	$82.50_{0.30}$	$\mathbf{10.61}_{0.36}$	$13.32_{0.25}$	$15.18_{2.35}$	$\mathbf{7.43}_{0.32}$	$10.65_{0.22}$	$12.78_{2.22}$
	II	$83.84_{1.62}$	$\mathbf{9.47}_{0.60}$	$12.76_{0.71}$	$14.95_{4.10}$	$\mathbf{7.34}_{0.36}$	$10.43_{0.34}$	$13.67_{4.08}$
Sponza	I	$2774.89_{2.48}$	$\mathbf{172.41}_{7.18}$	$179.02_{1.58}$	$178.63_{3.47}$	$\mathbf{63.26}_{2.83}$	$66.84_{0.35}$	$67.80_{3.13}$
	II	$2811.32_{21.14}$	$\mathbf{154.94}_{5.84}$	$164.08_{4.63}$	$161.13_{8.00}$	$\mathbf{51.19}_{2.34}$	$54.78_{0.41}$	$54.97_{4.60}$

Table 8. Stat. significance for Cornell on I, Cornell on II, Sponza on I, Sponza on II.

	CPU implementation												CPU+GPU implementation											
	VNS_{PLS}				VNS_{PIR}				VNS_{HYB}				VNS_{PLS}				VNS_{PIR}				VNS_{HYB}			
VNS_{PW}	△	△	△	△	△	△	△	△	△	△	△	△	△	△	△	△	△	△	△	△	△	△	△	△
VNS_{PLS} CPU					◁	◁	◁	◁	◁	◁	◁	◁	△	△	△	△	−	◁	△	△	◁	◁	△	△
VNS_{PIR} CPU									◁	◁	−	−	△	△	△	△	△	△	△	△	−	−	△	△
VNS_{HYB} CPU													△	△	△	△	△	△	△	△	△	−	△	△
VNS_{PLS} CPU+GPU																	◁	◁	◁	◁	◁	◁	◁	◁
VNS_{PIR} CPU+GPU																					◁	◁	−	−

The results obtained confirm that the run time of the VNS algorithms is highly reduced by changing the way in which the global illumination is calculated. With regard to the CPU+GPU implementations, they are also better performing algorithms than their CPU counterparts. However, the differences in the run time with the CPU implementations are relatively smaller than in the evaluation phase. When the total run time of the algorithms is considered, in most of the cases there is statistical confidence in the differences in the run time, showing that VNS_{PLS} implemented on CPU+GPU is systematically the best performing algorithm. Regarding the different scenarios, it also holds that the larger the scenario size, the larger the run time of the algorithm.

Table 9 shows the speedup of the VNS algorithms proposed in this work vs. VNS_{PW}. The speedup values of the CPU implementations range from 5.43 × (VNS_{HYB} in Cornell scene run in Platform I) to 18.14 × (VNS_{PLS} in Sponza scene executed in Platform II), while the speedup values of the implementations that use the GPU range from 6.13 × (VNS_{HYB} in Cornell scene run in Platform II) to 55.92 × (VNS_{PLS} in Sponza scene executed in Platform II). Even though run time reductions are important, they are inferior to the reductions obtained for the evaluation phase, specially in the Cornell scene. The speedup values obtained in the CPU+GPU variants (up to 3.03 ×) are superior to the CPU implementations but the improvements are only relevant in the Sponza scene.

Finally, since the run time reductions on the evaluation phase do not translate into similar reduction in the overall run time of the algorithms, we analyze how the total run time is divided into the run time of the evaluation, build, and update phases, and the rest of the algorithms. This is shown in Fig. 1. In each group of bars, the bars correspond to VNS_{PW}, VNS_{PLS}, VNS_{PIR}, and VNS_{HYB} on CPU, and VNS_{PLS}, VNS_{PIR}, and VNS_{HYB} on CPU+GPU, respectively.

Table 9. Speedup in total run time of VNS Algorithms vs. VNS$_{PW}$.

Scene	Platform	CPU impl.			CPU+GPU impl.		
		VNS$_{PLS}$	VNS$_{PIR}$	VNS$_{HYB}$	VNS$_{PLS}$	VNS$_{PIR}$	VNS$_{HYB}$
Cornell	I	**7.78**	6.19	5.43	**11.10**	7.75	6.46
	II	**8.85**	6.57	5.61	**11.42**	8.04	6.13
Sponza	I	**16.09**	15.50	15.53	**43.86**	41.52	40.93
	II	**18.14**	17.13	17.45	**54.92**	51.32	51.14

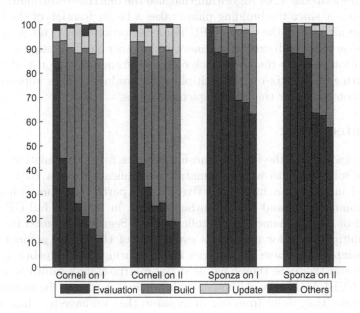

Fig. 1. Percentage of each phase over the total run time of the algorithms.

In VNS$_{PW}$, the execution time of the algorithm is dominated by the evaluation phase. The evaluation phase takes more than 85% and 99% of the total execution time for Cornell and Sponza scenes, respectively. This fact shows that the larger the scenario, the larger the weight of the evaluation phase in the overall run time. These results support the approach followed in this work that is based in reducing the run time involved in the evaluation phase.

In the Cornell scenario, the percentage of the total execution time that is dedicated to the evaluation phase in the implementations that use the matrix-matrix multiplication is less than half of the percentage that takes in the original algorithm. As a result, the building phase is no longer negligible and it represents more than 50% of the total execution time of the CPU implementations. For this reason, the high improvement in the performance of the evaluation phase produced by the use of the GPU does not translate into a high increase in the speedup of the complete algorithm.

On the other hand, in the Sponza scenario, even though the fraction of time of the total run time that is dedicated to the building phase is larger than in the original algorithm, it represents approximately 10% of the total execution time of the CPU implementations. This makes possible that the speedup values obtained by the CPU+GPU implementations for the complete algorithms are more similar to those attained in the evaluation phase.

From these results, it is clear that the CPU implementations of the VNS Algorithms that use the matrix-matrix multiplication for speeding up the evaluation phase outperform the VNS Algorithm that use the matrix-vector multiplication. In small scenes, since the building phase takes a larger fraction of the total run time of the algorithm, the CPU+GPU implementations could not lead to high reductions on the overall execution time. On the other hand, in large scenes when the evaluation phase is the bottleneck of the performance, the use of the GPU for computing the matrix-matrix multiplication produces a high improvement in the execution time over the CPU implementations.

6   Related Work

Up to our knowledge, the idea of transforming the fitness calculation of a population of solutions into a matrix-matrix multiplication on a GPU was first introduced in [10] for a multi-objective EA. In particular, the multiplication was programmed by hand by the authors. Later, in [11,12] a full GPU implementation of an EA (namely, a Systolic Genetic Search) also used the matrix-matrix multiplication for the fitness evaluation of the whole population. The authors pointed that there are libraries for computing linear algebra operations efficiently, and therefore they have used the matrix-matrix multiplication routine from CUBLAS library. Although both previous work use the matrix-matrix multiplication, they differ from our proposal in that we have to adapt the VNS algorithm, which is a single solution or trajectory based method, for working with several solutions to be able to use a similar approach. In this work, we have also shown that the performance of the algorithm can also benefit from using the matrix-matrix multiplication on the CPU.

Three different parallelization strategies for VNS have been proposed by García et al. [13]. In the Synchronous Parallel VNS (SPVNS), the local search is parallelized assigning the candidate solutions from the current neighborhood among the available processing units for their evaluation. In the Replicated Parallel VNS (RPVNS) strategy, multiple VNS are executed independently in parallel on the processors available. This allows to explore a wider region of the search space since each execution uses a different initial solution. Finally, in the Cooperative Neighborhood VNS, the current solution is sent to each available processor that computes an independent local search. Since the perturbation of the current solution computed by each processor can be different, each local search can potentially find different solutions. Our work is clearly aligned with the parallelization strategies defined by García et al., VNS_{PLS} and VNS_{PIR} implementations correspond to SPVNS and RPVNS strategies, respectively. VNS_{HYB} is an hybridization of the two aforementioned algorithms.

A population-based VNS was also proposed in [14]. In that approach, in each iteration, a population of solutions is used to simultaneously generate multiple candidate solutions from the current neighborhood to improve the search diversification. Although several speedup tricks to reduce computation time are presented, a parallel implementation of the VNS Algorithm is not discussed.

Finally, our proposal is also aligned with the guidelines for building efficient parallel metaheuristics on GPU presented by Luong [15]. In particular, for single solution metaheuristics like VNS, the author suggests to generate and evaluate the candidate solutions of the whole neighborhood on the GPU. The advantage of this approach is that a single solution has to be transferred from CPU to GPU, thus reducing drastically data transference. In this work, we only use the GPU for computing the whole neighborhood evaluation in parallel. The experimental results obtained regarding the grow in the fraction of the total execution time of the algorithms that is dedicated to the build phase makes clear that the generation of the neighborhood should also be ported to the GPU.

7   Conclusion and Future Work

In this work, we introduce a novel parallel VNS based in performing the evaluation of several candidate solutions simultaneously through a matrix-matrix multiplication for solving an ILP efficiently. Three different variants have been proposed and their CPU/GPU versions were evaluated on two scenarios with different complexity. The experimental results show that the proposed methods greatly outperform the original VNS algorithm that evaluates each solution independently, making clear the advantages of using block matrix multiplication algorithms. Additional improvements are obtained when the evaluation of solutions is performed on a GPU, especially in large scenes, in which the running time is dominated by the evaluation phase. The implementation on GPU of the proposed methods were able to solve the ILP in about one minute, making possible the interactive design of the illumination of a scene.

Some lines of future work have been identified. Since the generation of the candidate solutions of a neighborhood can be a bottleneck in the small scenes, one line of future work is to port the neighborhood generation to the GPU, reducing the data transfers. A second line of future work consists in taking advantage of the sparse structure of the emission matrix E (only patches that emit light are non-zero), which can lead to a better performance in computing the radiosity of the scene. Finally, the study of the shape of the search space could be benefical in order to select the best optimization strategy.

Acknowledgements. Authors acknowledge partial support from PEDECIBA – Uruguay and project ANII FSE_1_2014_1_102344.

References

1. Fernández, E., Besuievsky, G.: Inverse lighting design for interior buildings integrating natural and artificial sources. Comp. Graph. **36**(8), 1096–1108 (2012)
2. Fernández, E., Besuievsky, G.: Efficient inverse lighting: a statistical approach. Autom. Constr. **37**, 48–57 (2014)
3. Fernández, E.: Low-rank radiosity. In: Proceedings of the IV Iberoamerican Symposium in Computer Graphics, pp. 55–62 (2009)
4. Talbi, E.G.: Metaheuristics: From Design to Implementation. Wiley, Hoboken (2009)
5. Kirk, D.B., Wen-mei, W.H.: Programming Massively Parallel Processors: A Hands-on Approach. Newnes (2012)
6. Cohen, M., Wallace, J., Hanrahan, P.: Radiosity and Realistic Image Synthesis. Academic Press Professional Inc., San Diego (1993)
7. Mladenović, N., Hansen, P.: Variable neighborhood search. Comput. Oper. Res. **24**(11), 1097–1100 (1997)
8. Benner, P., Ezzatti, P., Quintana-Ortí, E., Remón, A.: On the impact of optimization on the time-power-energy balance of dense linear algebra factorizations. In: Aversa, R., Kołodziej, J., Zhang, J., Amato, F., Fortino, G. (eds.) ICA3PP 2013. LNCS, vol. 8286, pp. 3–10. Springer, Cham (2013). doi:10.1007/978-3-319-03889-6_1
9. Sheskin, D.J.: Handbook of Parametric and Nonparametric Statistical Procedures. Chapman and Hall/CRC, Boca Raton (2011)
10. Yoo, S., Harman, M., Ur, S.: Highly scalable multi objective test suite minimisation using graphics cards. In: Cohen, M.B., Ó Cinnéide, M. (eds.) SSBSE 2011. LNCS, vol. 6956, pp. 219–236. Springer, Heidelberg (2011). doi:10.1007/978-3-642-23716-4_20
11. Pedemonte, M., Luna, F., Alba, E.: Systolic genetic search for software engineering: the test suite minimization case. In: Esparcia-Alcázar, A.I., Mora, A.M. (eds.) EvoApplications 2014. LNCS, vol. 8602, pp. 678–689. Springer, Heidelberg (2014). doi:10.1007/978-3-662-45523-4_55
12. Pedemonte, M., Luna, F., Alba, E.: A systolic genetic search for reducing the execution cost of regression testing. Appl. Soft Comput. **49**, 1145–1161 (2016)
13. García López, F., Melián Batista, B., Moreno Pérez, J., Moreno Vega, J.: The parallel variable neighborhood search for the p-median problem. J. Heuristics **8**(3), 375–388 (2002)
14. Wang, X., Tang, L.: A population-based variable neighborhood search for the single machine total weighted tardiness problem. Comput. Oper. Res. **36**(6), 2105–2110 (2009)
15. Luong, T.V.: Parallel metaheuristics on GPU. Ph.D. thesis, INRIA Lille (2011)

Evolving Cut-Off Mechanisms and Other Work-Stealing Parameters for Parallel Programs

Alcides Fonseca$^{(\boxtimes)}$, Nuno Lourenço, and Bruno Cabral

CISUC, Department of Informatics Engineering, University of Coimbra,
Polo II - Pinhal de Marrocos, 3030 Coimbra, Portugal
{amaf,naml,bcabral}@dei.uc.pt

Abstract. Optimizing parallel programs is a complex task because the interference among many different parameters. Work-stealing runtimes, used to dynamically balance load among different processor cores, are no exception. This work explores the automatic configuration of the following runtime parameters: dynamic granularity control algorithms, granularity control cache, work-stealing algorithm, lazy binary splitting parameter, the maximum queue size and the unparking interval. The performance of the program is highly sensible to the granularity control algorithm, which can be a combination of other granularity algorithms. In this work, we address two search-based problems: finding a globally efficient work-stealing configuration, and finding the best configuration just for an individual program. For both problems, we propose the use of a Genetic Algorithm (GA). The genotype of the GA is able to represent combinations of up to three cut-off algorithms, as well as other work-stealing parameters.

The proposed GA has been evaluated in its ability to obtain a more efficient solution across a set of programs, in its ability to generalize the solution to a larger set of programs, and its ability to evolve single programs individually.

The GA was able to improve the performance of the set of programs in the training set, but the obtained configurations were not generalized to a larger benchmark set. However, it was able to successfully improve the performance of each program individually.

Keywords: Granularity · Cut-off mechanism · Parallel programming · Multicore · Genetic Algorithm

1 Introduction

Over the last decades, the number of cores per chip has been steadily increasing, while clock frequency has remained mostly the same. Thus, to take advantage of multi-core architectures, programmers have to create programs that are capable of executing in parallel.

Different parallel programming approaches rely on work-stealing runtimes to dynamically balance different tasks across the processor cores. These programming languages and extensions include Cilk [1], OpenMP [2], Java [3], X10 [4]

© Springer International Publishing AG 2017
G. Squillero and K. Sim (Eds.): EvoApplications 2017, Part I, LNCS 10199, pp. 757–772, 2017.
DOI: 10.1007/978-3-319-55849-3_49

and Æminium [5]. Regardless of whether parallelism comes from for-loops or recursive functions or whether it is regular or irregular, work-stealing runtimes are used to efficiently execute fine-grained tasks.

Programs written in these languages schedule tasks to the runtime. Tasks are independent blocks of code that can execute in parallel with each other. A parallel program is made of several tasks, that are scheduled across different native threads, each executing on each hardware thread. Work-stealing occurs when a thread does not find any tasks in its queue, and *steals* a task from the end of another queue instead. This mechanism allows threads that finish work early to help other threads, leading to an earlier completion time.

Work-stealing allows parallel programs to be agnostic to the hardware layout, delaying optimization and load balancing for run time. One optimization which has a large performance impact is the dynamic management of granularity. When scheduled, tasks are coarse-grained, but have the ability to recursively split in more tasks, which are executed asynchronously. How many times should a task split itself is decided at run time, according to a certain parameterized criterium. It is useful to schedule a few more tasks than can be executed at a given time, in order to use the work-stealing mechanism. However, too many tasks will lead to scheduling overheads. Choosing the wrong granularity control mechanism can slow down the program by orders of magnitude.

Related to the granularity control algorithm, there are two other parameters that have impact on the program. One value defines for how many calls will the decision whether to split a task or not be stored. The other value defines for how long will the decision be cached.

Unrelated to the granularity, there are four more parameters that can be used to impact performance. The first one, also with a large impact on performance, is the stealing algorithm. There are four alternative algorithms to select which task to steal from, with no algorithm performing better than the others in all programs. Another parameter is the maximum recursion level allowed in tasks, which reduces memory allocation overheads. The parking interval is another parameter that describes for how long will a workless thread wait to check for work again. The last parameter defines how many iterations of a loop will be execute in between task splits.

The granularity control algorithm and the other parameters define a configuration for the runtime that can be used to execute a given program. Since the goal is to reduce the execution time of programs, it is necessary to find an ideal configuration.

In this work two problems are tackled: finding a global configuration that can efficiently handle regular and irregular programs and finding the best configuration for each program. We defined a Genetic Algorithm (GA) to use for both problems. The genotype is represented of a combination of up to three parameterized cut-off conditions, a stealing algorithm and other values for runtime configuration. A random population is evolved using single-point recombination and mutation, and tournament and elitism are used for selecting individuals based on their performance.

Our contribution is a Genetic Algorithm for finding a configuration that minimizes execution time of a set of parallel programs.

We start by stating the problem and explaining how a parallel program can be optimized (Sect. 2). We then describe the evolutionary approach that we used, with the parameters of the GA detailed and explained (Sect. 3). We then evaluate the GA in different machines, using a large testing set composed by well-known benchmarks for evaluating the performance of parallel frameworks and platforms (Sect. 4). Finally, we draw the conclusions (Sect. 6).

2 Parallel Program Configuration

In this section we discuss two aspects of parallel programming that impact the performance of programs: work-stealing algorithms and granularity management.

2.1 Work-Stealing Algorithms

Most work-stealing algorithms are variations of the algorithm, introduced in Cilk [6]. In Cilk, function calls can be spawned instead of invoked. When a task is spawned, it is added to the queue of the current thread. With sync, a task awaits for the termination of its spawned tasks. In the meanwhile, tasks are executed in parallel by other threads. When a program starts executing, a number of threads is created matching the number of available cores in the machine. A thread tries to execute tasks in its own queue. If there is none, it tries to steal a task from other queues, following a stealing algorithm. If not, it parks for a given pre-configured interval. When tasks are generating too many-tasks, queues can be configured with a maximum size, after which new tasks are executed inline instead of being appended to the queue. In this work we use the implementation in Æminium Runtime [5], given its flexible configuration.

Figure 1 depicts a work-stealing mechanism in which the two first threads are executing tasks. Thread #3 has an empty queue, so it tries to steal from Thread #2, but it is also empty, so it steals a task from Thread #1. Thread #4 has no task, and cannot steal any from the other Threads, so it parks for a given interval.

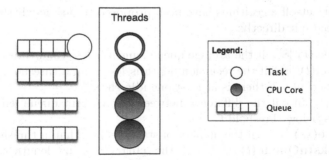

Fig. 1. Example of a work-stealing mechanism for a quad-core machine.

In the example, we used a stealing algorithm, **SequentialReverseScan**, that tried to steal tasks in reverse order, but there are other approaches. **Steal-FromMaxQueue** tries to steal from the largest queue, **MinLevel** tries to steal the task with the smallest depth in the calling graph, based on the assumption that it has more work, and **Revenge** tries to steal from tasks which stole from this task earlier, trying to maximize cache locality. The best stealing algorithm for a given program is not necessarily the same for another program.

Besides the stealing algorithm, there are other parameters that impact the performance of work-stealing schedulers. The **unparking interval** defines for how long will a thread that has not found any task to execute wait until it looks for more tasks again. Another parameter is the **maximum queue size**. Whenever a queue reaches its maximum size, tasks are executed instead of being scheduled to a queue. This limit prevents queues from growing indefinitely, allocating more and more memory.

These parameters are dependent on each other, preventing each of them to be optimized individually.

2.2 Cut-Off Algorithm

When recursively dividing tasks in half, the execution time of each task reduces to half, plus the overhead of partitioning, scheduling and merging. Dividing tasks until they cannot be split typically leads to overheads larger than the resulting tasks. Thus, there is a trade-off in splitting tasks, between maximizing parallelism and load balancing and not splitting to prevent unprofitable scheduling overheads. For instance, a program for computing the Fibonacci sequence with the finest granularity possible will have slow downs because the smaller tasks possible are several times smaller than the scheduling overhead. Defining a maximum queue size prevents tasks from being appended to the queue, but not from being created. Task creation includes memory allocation, which is unnecessary overhead in this case.

Cut-off algorithms leverage this trade-off by deciding whether to spawn tasks or to inline calculations, preventing the creation of new tasks. This technique is called Lazy Task Creation [7] and allows for a dynamically increase of task granularity. The main difficulty in applying this technique is in selecting the criterium used to stop task splitting.

Different cut-off algorithms have been proposed to decide whether to split a task, or execute it directly:

- **MaxTasks**(t) [8] - if the average queue length is less than threshold t
- **MaxLevel**(l) [8] - if the recursion depth is less than a threshold l
- **LoadBased** [9] - if there is at least one idle thread
- **Surplus**(t) [3] - if the difference between the current queue length and the average is below threshold t
- **StackSize**(ss) [10] - if the number of stacks is less than a threshold ss
- **MaxTasksInQueue**(t) [10] - if the current queue length is less than threshold t

Additionally, combinations of two cut-off algorithms have also been presented:

- **ATC(*t*, *l*)** [9] - a combination of MaxTasks(*t*) and MaxLevel(*l*)
- **MaxTasksWithStackSize(*t*, *ss*)** [10] - a combination of TasksTasks(*t*) with StackSize(*ss*)

2.3   Summary

The work-stealing configuration for a given program can be defined by the following parameters:

- Cut-off algorithm and its parameters, or a combination of several cut-offs
- Cut-off algorithm cache duration, either by number of calls or duration
- The *PPS* threshold for Lazy Binary Splitting
- The stealing algorithm
- The maximum queue size
- The unparking interval

In order to optimize a parallel program, it is important to find the best values for these parameters.

3   An Evolutionary Algorithm for Parallel Program Optimization

Given the infeasibility of testing all work-stealing and granularity configurations, and the interdependencies among configuration parameters, we propose an evolutionary algorithm as an heuristic to find a configuration that is acceptable.

3.1   Genotype

Representing a work-stealing configuration is not trivial, specially if custom hybrid granularity control algorithms should be considered. Work-stealing and PPS parameters could be represented as integers, but the cut-off algorithm requires a more complex representation.

On an early version, we considered using a Genetic Programming (GP) approach, using a typed AST that could be compiled to a runtime Java expression was considered. However, in preliminary results we noticed that most of the iterations introduced bloat instead of improving the quality of solutions. Since evaluating cut-off algorithms is very time consuming, a more strict GA can be used to replace GP.

Existing cut-off algorithms can be expressed using an expression similar to: $Var_1 < Threshold_1 \dagger_1 Var_2 < Threshold_2 \dagger_2 Var_3 < Threshold_3$. While this expression is able to represent combinations of up to 3 conditions, only combinations of two have been presented before. While a cut-off algorithm could have more than 3 conditions, using all conditions in one call would increase the overhead. † represents either the **and** or the **or** binary operators, following the Java semantics. *Threshold* can represent any number from 0 to 100, which is a sensible maximum for any of the possible variables. *Var* could take any of the following values available in the runtime listed in Table 1. The *true* option was introduced to allow cut-offs with less than three conditions, resulting in a condition where −1000 is always less than any number between 0 and 100.

The final genotype is described in Table 2.

Table 1. Possible cut-off variables

Variable	Description
queueSize	Length of the current queue
level	Depth of the parallel recursion
stacksize	Number of allocated stacks
activeThreads	Number of threads executing tasks
idleThreads	Number of threads not executing tasks
surplus	Length difference between local and average queues
totalTasks	Number of active and pending tasks
emptyQueues	Number of empty queues
memory	Percentage of used memory in the machine
cpuLoad	Percentage of CPU load in the machine
true	−1000, so the condition is always true

3.2   Operators and General Configurations

Recombination is performed by a single point crossover between two parents. A random point of the genotype is selected, and the child inherits the genes before that point from parent 1, and the remaining from parent 2. The mutation operator is different per gene. The mutation of non-integer genes randomly selects an option from the alternative list. In the case of integers, it has a 75% chance of adding or subtracting a number within 5% of the maximum value, and 25% chance of replacement by a random integer within the range of that gene. This mutation simulates a partial local-searching around that threshold.

The population size of the GA was set to 25, which is small. The reason for this, is that evaluating each configuration is very time-consuming, thus a larger population would penalize execution time. The algorithm executes 100 iterations, which is enough for fitness to stabilize. Even with smaller numbers, the overall evaluation consists of more than two months of execution time.

The recombination rate is 90% in order to test several combinations of cut-offs and other configurations. The mutation rate is 50%, higher than the traditional for the same reason. Mutating granularity thresholds is desirable as they have a large impact in program performance.

Table 2. Genotype

Gene	Description
var_1	One of 11 options in Table 1
$threshold_1$	Integer between 0 and 100
$\dagger_1$	**and** or **or** binary operators
var_2	One of 11 options in Table 1
$threshold_2$	Integer between 0 and 100
$\dagger_2$	**and** or **or** binary operators
var_3	One of 11 options in Table 1
$threshold_3$	Integer between 0 and 100
$granularityCacheCalls$	Integer between 0 and 1000
$granularityCacheTime$	Integer between 0 and 1000
PPS	Integer between 0 and 100
$Stealing$	One of: StealFromMaxQueue, MinLevel,
	Revenge and SequentialReverseScan
$maxQueueSize$	Integer between 0 and 1000
$unparkingInterval$	Integer between 0 and 1000

In order to keep the best approach until the final generation, elitism was defined with value 2, and to always introduce new genetic material and avoid local minima, a new random individual is introduced at each generation.

3.3 Fitness Evaluation

In order to evaluate the generalization capability of the GA, we defined a training and a testing dataset. The training and testing datasets consists of the programs described in Table 3, belonging to the Æminium Benchmark suite [10]. In the training set, programs have smaller inputs in order to reduce the evaluation time. The testing set will be used to evaluate the generalization capability of our algorithm.

Fitness evaluation includes compiling the cut-off expression to Java source code, and writing the other parameters to a configuration file. Then, each of the programs is executed once and recorded. Parallel programs can have a high standard deviation in regards to execution time. However, if two cut-off approaches are similar, either one or both can be kept, as the elitism value is 2. Additionally, there is a timeout of 10 s per evaluation because the training benchmarks were designed to last 1 s with a reasonably good cut-off and default parameters. Programs that exceeded 500 s were terminated, and the timeout value was used.

For each individual, the fitness is the sum of the execution times of all programs in the benchmark set. This set could be made of just one program, or many.

Table 3. Description of the programs used in the benchmark

Program	Training input size	Testing input size	Type	Balance
BFS		d = 26, w = 2	Recursive	Regular
BlackScholes	1000^2	10000^2	For-loop	Regular
Convex-Hull		10000^2	Recursive	Regular
Do-All	1 million	100 million	For-loop	Regular
FFT	131072	8388608	Recursive	Regular
Fibonacci	n = 41	n = 51	Recursive	Skewed
Genetic Knapsack		g = 100, p = 100	For-loop	Regular
Health	l = 4	l = 7	For-loop	Regular
Heat	1000×1000, it = 1024	4096×4096, it = 1024	For-loop	Regular
Integrate	error = 10^{-11}	error = 10^{-14}	Recursive	Skewed
KDTree		10 million	Recursive	Regular
LUD		4096×4096	Recursive	Regular
Matrix Multiplication	p = 10000, q = r = 1024	p = 10000, q = r = 1000	For-loop	Regular
MergeSort		100 million	Recursive	Regular
MolDyn		it = 1 size = 40	For-loop	Recursive
MonteCarlo		10000×60000	Recursive	Regular
N-Body	n = 50, it = 3	n = 50000, it = 3	For-loop	Skewed
N-U Knapsack		items = 30, corr = 3	Recursive	Skewed
NeuralNet		it = 500000	Recursive	Regular
N-Queens	n = 13	n = 8..15	For-Loop	Irregular
Pi	100.000	100 million	For-loop	Regular
Quicksort		10 million	Recursive	Regular
RayTracer		2000	Loop	Regular

3.4   Selection Operator

For selecting an individual for recombination, or for the next generation, a tournament operator [11] is used. Initially, a roulette wheel [12] was being used, but at generation 50 all the population had the same genotype. A tournament among 4 individuals revealed to be a solution with higher diversity and achieved better results. However, the implemented tournament did not consider their fitness. Instead, each tournament compared the performance of different individuals in a single random benchmark. The reason for this custom tournament is to try to cross algorithms that solve different types of programs together.

4   Evaluation

In this section, the GA proposed is evaluated considering its ability to evolve a configuration for a set of programs, its ability to generalize the evolved configuration to a larger set of programs, and its ability to evolve individual programs.

4.1   Experimental Settings

These experiments were conducted on 3 different machines, each with different characteristics, featured in Table 4. *server32* and *server24* had Ubuntu 14.04 installed. The experiments executed on top of the Æminium Runtime [5], executing on the Java HotSpot 64-Bit Server VM 1.8.

Table 4. Details of the hardware used in the experiments.

Name	Processor	CPU cores	Threads	RAM
server32	Intel(R) Xeon(R) CPU E5-2650 @ 2.00 GHz	16 cores	32 threads	32 GB
server24	Intel(R) Xeon(R) CPU X5660 @ 2.80 GHz	12 cores	24 threads	24 GB

The time measure was for the parallel algorithm alone and runtime overheads, excluding the data setup required. Because of being time-consuming experiences, only one execution of each configuration-program pair was executed. In some cases, several seeds were used in the GA, and the results mention that.

4.2   Evolving a Configuration for a Set of Heterogenous Programs

One of the problems is the identification of a global configuration that would perform well across all programs. This configuration would not necessarily be the best configuration for each program, but would serve as a default configuration for parallel platforms, such as Cilk, OpenMP or Æminium.

Figure 2 show the fitness of the best individual of each generation. Five different seeds are used to show the effects of randomness in the algorithm. Only five seeds were used for time constraints, as it would have required one and half year of computation to evaluate 30 seeds. In all five seeds, the performance of whole benchmark is improving. The elitism used guarantees that fitness values only decrease, which was not true otherwise.

While the overall fitness decreased, the execution time of individual programs could have increased, as long as other programs would reduce the execution time even more.

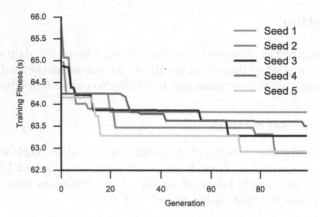

Fig. 2. Fitness of the best individual of each generation of the training dataset on *server32*.

4.3   The Generalization Ability of the Evolved Configurations

Given that the performance impact of granularity and stealing algorithms depends on the specific program, it is not clear whether an evolved configuration from a specific set of programs can be successfully applied to other programs.

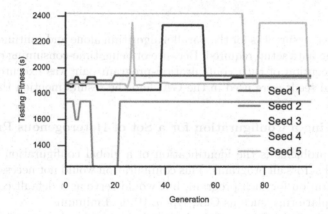

Fig. 3. Fitness in the testing dataset of the best individual of each generation of the training dataset on *server32*.

Figure 3 shows the performance of the best configuration of each generation on the training dataset, but evaluated on the testing dataset. Since the testing dataset includes unseen programs, these results show the poor generalization capability of the GA. The testing-based fitness does not always decrease over time, and remains relatively stable for most seeds. In the case of Seed 2, a better configuration was found in early generations, but a better one was found in the training dataset, which was not reflected on the testing programs. These results confirm the heavy dependency of cut-off algorithms on the parallel program [10].

4.4   Evolving Configurations for an Individual Program

While its generalization capability might be poor, the GA can improve the performance of a set of programs. In this evaluation we consider sets of just one program. In the case of long-running programs, it is important to optimize the most frequently used functions. The GA can be used to improve functions that are frequently called.

Figure 4 shows the performance of the best individuals of each generation, using the GA with a single program for fitness evaluation. The performance of all programs was improved, with different gains. Each program has its own overheads, which results in different percentages of time saved. Most of the programs were able to reduce most of the time within 40 generations, while a minority took longer to optimize.

5   Related Work

The impact of cut-off algorithms has been a recurrent concern over the years. When proposing MaxTasks and MaxLevel, Duran et al. [8] have found that, in OpenMP, these algorithms performed differently on different programs, with no algorithm being considered better than the other. The study also concluded that choosing the wrong cut-off could have a negative impact in performance, making the program run longer than when no cut-off was being used. The authors also suggest that depth first schedulers should be the default, since they are specially well suited to handle cut-off techniques, avoiding high levels of recursion whenever there is a significant allocation of memory. Duran et al. were not able to conclude which cut-off algorithm is the best for each class of application.

Olivier et al. [13] studied unbalanced workloads, concluding that different parameters of MaxTasks and MaxLevel yield different results. Unfortunately, they also observed that there was no unique cut-off parameter capable of achieving the best results for all scheduling policies. It is important to notice that the evaluation used machines with just 2 cores, which is not representative of the machines available today.

Duran also studied the behavior of ATC in [9], confirming that the best cut-off algorithm is program dependent. The adaptive approach was introduced in an attempt to limit the problems with both MaxTasks and MaxLevel algorithms. MaxLevel did not create tasks in depth, not making use of the potential parallelism in the program. MaxTasks, on the other hand, would create too many tasks, introducing an undesirable overhead. The main objective of combining the two was not to improve performance, but rather to minimize the penalty of both approaches.

Fonseca et al. [10] evaluated all the mentioned cut-off algorithms in a larger benchmark suite. The benchmark suite consisted of heterogenous programs diverse in their nature. It included programs with loop- and recursive-based parallelism, irregular and regular parallelism, memory-intensive and CPU-intensive programs. Since cut-off algorithms are sensible to all these parameters, there

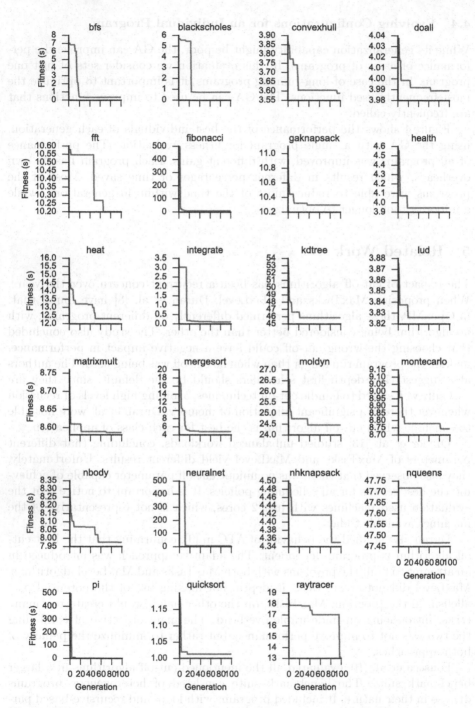

Fig. 4. Fitness of the best individual over different instances of GA, one for each individual program, on *server24*

is no single algorithm that outperforms all the others. Thus, the best cut-off algorithm is program-dependent.

Tchiboukdjian et al. [14] evaluated a window-based granularity for scheduling loops on a work-stealing runtime. The window-method was evaluated on the extraction of an isosurface in an unstructured mesh using the marching tetrahedra algorithm. Testing powers of two for the grain size, between 2^2 and 2^{14} found a quadratic-like curve, with a minimum in 2^9. Different applications would have a different minimum.

In X10, the work-stealing mechanism [15] allows stealing batches of tasks, instead of single tasks. The goal of this approach was to support irregular graph analysis, through the stealing of coarser tasks. However, there is a need to configure the batch size, which also results in a need for automatic configuration.

Wang et al. [16] propose an adaptive approach for work-stealing, which considers tasks that have the potential for generating more tasks as *special tasks*. While this approach improves the performance of the Cilk runtime, it also relies on a manual definition of a cut-off value to switch from regular tasks to a sequential mode, when the task granularity is fine.

Chen et al. [17] have shown how task granularity impacts the performance on memory-bound programs, and suggests an empirical profiling-based approach for automatically obtaining the right granularity. This approach finds a static granularity threshold, while our proposed approach uses a dynamic granularity algorithm, which can adapt to the program during execution. Furthermore, the granularity-finding algorithm does not consider other factors, which would be improved by the usage of a genetic-algorithm to reduce the computing-time of testing all combinations of parameters.

Genetic algorithms have been used for optimizing parallel programs. The most common case is finding the best program schedule, mapping tasks to processors, which is a NP-complete problem. Ahmad et al. [18] propose the first genetic algorithm to optimize the schedule of programs, by using the task priority as a chromosome. Kwok et al. [19] propose another genetic algorithm that uses a task-processor encoding for schedules. This algorithm was able to find the optimal schedule in half of the cases. The paper also identified finding the ideal genetic algorithm parameters (population size, mutation rate, crossover rate) as an open problem, which also applies to this work. Wang et al. [20] proposed a similar approach for the same problem, but considering a cluster of machines. This approach outperformed a human and two non-evolutionary heuristic approaches. Correa et al. [21] combines a genetic approach with a list-heuristic to improve solution quality over the two pure approaches, although having an higher execution time. Omara et al. [22] improve the schedule genetic algorithm with a second fitness function which evaluates load-balancing, reducing the search time of the genetic program.

Mezmaz et al. [23] extend the genetic algorithm for a bi-criteria multi-objective problem. Instead of just minimizing the execution time, this algorithm also minimizes energy consumption. Sheik et al. [24] propose a multi-objective genetic algorithm that minimizes execution time, energy consumption and temperature. It maps each processor to a task and a clock frequency as encoding.

Evolutionary algorithms can also be used to optimize parallel programs through the rewriting of code. Langdon et al. [25] have used genetic programming to evolve a CUDA program to reduce the execution time successfully. This is a variation of the GenProg [26] automatic program repair technique, applied to a parallel program.

Ryan et al. [27, 28] have proposed a genetic programming algorithm to rewrite a sequential program into a parallel program with the same semantics. This is done using through program transformations on a grammar representation of the program.

6 Conclusions

We have proposed a GA for the optimization of parallel programs based on the following configurations: combination of cut-off criteria, cut-off decision caching, Lazy Binary Splitting intermediate iterations, workstealing algorithm, maximum recursion level and unparking interval.

The GA has been applied to a small training benchmark composed of 11 programs with small input sizes. The GA was able to successfully find a configuration that optimized the whole benchmark. The performance of some of the programs was degraded over the generations in order to greatly improve others. When the best individuals of each generation were tested against the whole 23 program benchmark, the overall performance did not improve.

Additionally, the GA has also been applied to individual programs successfully, with all programs improving their performance, with different gains. Most of the programs were able to achieve the best configuration within 40 generations.

Finally, it has been shown that despite the lack of generation of the GA for finding a universal configuration, when evaluating with this specific training and testing sets using global execution time as a metric, most of the programs were improved. Furthermore, individually applying the GA with a small number of generations (50) does improve the performance of programs and can be used for finding the best configuration for a long-running program. The proposed approach can use other metrics instead of just using the execution time, such as energy consumption.

Acknowledgments. The first author was supported by the Portuguese National Foundation for Science and Technology (FCT) through a Doctoral Grant (SFRH/BD/84448/2012).

References

1. Blumofe, R.D., Joerg, C.F., Kuszmaul, B.C., Leiserson, C.E., Randall, K.H., Zhou, Y.: Cilk: an efficient multithreaded runtime system. J. Parallel Distrib. Comput. **37**(1), 55–69 (1996)
2. Dagum, L., Menon, R.: Openmp: an industry standard api for shared-memory programming. IEEE Comput. Sci. Eng. **5**(1), 46–55 (1998)

3. Lea, D.: A java fork/join framework. In: Proceedings of the ACM 2000 Conference on Java Grande, pp. 36–43. ACM (2000)

4. Charles, P., Grothoff, C., Saraswat, V., Donawa, C., Kielstra, A., Ebcioglu, K., Von Praun, C., Sarkar, V.: X10: an object-oriented approach to non-uniform cluster computing. In: ACM Sigplan Notices, vol. 40, pp. 519–538. ACM (2005)

5. Stork, S., Naden, K., Sunshine, J., Mohr, M., Fonseca, A., Marques, P., Aldrich, J.: Æminium: a permission-based concurrent-by-default programming language approach. ACM Trans. Program. Lang. Syst. (TOPLAS) 36(1), 2 (2014)

6. Frigo, M., Leiserson, C.E., Randall, K.H.: The implementation of the cilk-5 multithreaded language. In: ACM Sigplan Notices, vol. 33, pp. 212–223. ACM (1998)

7. Mohr, E., Kranz, D.A., Halstead, R.H.: Lazy task creation: a technique for increasing the granularity of parallel programs. IEEE Trans. Parallel Distrib. Syst. 2(3), 264–280 (1991)

8. Duran, A., Corbalán, J., Ayguadé, E.: Evaluation of OpenMP task scheduling strategies. In: Eigenmann, R., Supinski, B.R. (eds.) IWOMP 2008. LNCS, vol. 5004, pp. 100–110. Springer, Heidelberg (2008). doi:10.1007/978-3-540-79561-2_9

9. Duran, A., Corbalán, J., Ayguadé, E.: An adaptive cut-off for task parallelism. In: Proceedings of the 2008 ACM/IEEE Conference on Supercomputing, p. 36. IEEE Press (2008)

10. Fonseca, A., Cabral, B.: Evaluation of runtime cut-off approaches for parallel programs. In: VECPAR 2016 Proceedings (2016)

11. Miller, B.L., Goldberg, D.E.: Genetic algorithms, tournament selection, and the effects of noise. Complex Syst. 9(3), 193–212 (1995)

12. DeJong, K.: An analysis of the behavior of a class of genetic adaptive systems. Ph.D. Thesis, University of Michigan (1975)

13. Olivier, S.L., Prins, J.F.: Evaluating OpenMP 3.0 run time systems on unbalanced task graphs. In: Müller, M.S., Supinski, B.R., Chapman, B.M. (eds.) IWOMP 2009. LNCS, vol. 5568, pp. 63–78. Springer, Heidelberg (2009). doi:10.1007/978-3-642-02303-3_6

14. Tchiboukdjian, M., Danjean, V., Gautier, T., Mentec, F., Raffin, B.: A work stealing scheduler for parallel loops on shared cache multicores. In: Guarracino, M.R., et al. (eds.) Euro-Par 2010. LNCS, vol. 6586, pp. 99–107. Springer, Heidelberg (2011). doi:10.1007/978-3-642-21878-1_13

15. Cong, G., Kodali, S., Krishnamoorthy, S., Lea, D., Saraswat, V., Wen, T.: Solving large, irregular graph problems using adaptive work-stealing. In: 2008 37th International Conference on Parallel Processing, pp. 536–545. IEEE (2008)

16. Wang, L., Cui, H., Duan, Y., Lu, F., Feng, X., Yew, P.C.: An adaptive task creation strategy for work-stealing scheduling. In: Proceedings of the 8th Annual IEEE/ACM International Symposium on Code Generation and Optimization, pp. 266–277. ACM (2010)

17. Chen, S., Gibbons, P.B., Kozuch, M., Liaskovitis, V., Ailamaki, A., Blelloch, G.E., Falsafi, B., Fix, L., Hardavellas, N., Mowry, T.C., et al.: Scheduling threads for constructive cache sharing on cmps. In: Proceedings of the Nineteenth Annual ACM Symposium on Parallel Algorithms and Architectures, pp. 105–115. ACM (2007)

18. Ahmad, I., Dhodhi, M.K.: Multiprocessor scheduling in a genetic paradigm. Parallel Comput. 22(3), 395–406 (1996)

19. Kwok, Y.K., Ahmad, I.: Efficient scheduling of arbitrary task graphs to multiprocessors using a parallel genetic algorithm. J. Parallel Distrib. Comput. 47(1), 58–77 (1997)

20. Wang, L., Siegel, H.J., Roychowdhury, V.P., Maciejewski, A.A.: Task matching and scheduling in heterogeneous computing environments using a genetic-algorithm-based approach. J. Parallel Distrib. Comput. **47**(1), 8–22 (1997)
21. Corrêa, R.C., Ferreira, A., Rebreyend, P.: Scheduling multiprocessor tasks with genetic algorithms. IEEE Trans. Parallel Distrib. Syst. **10**(8), 825–837 (1999)
22. Omara, F.A., Arafa, M.M.: Genetic algorithms for task scheduling problem. J. Parallel Distrib. Comput. **70**(1), 13–22 (2010)
23. Mezmaz, M., Melab, N., Kessaci, Y., Lee, Y.C., Talbi, E.G., Zomaya, A.Y., Tuyttens, D.: A parallel bi-objective hybrid metaheuristic for energy-aware scheduling for cloud computing systems. J. Parallel Distrib. Comput. **71**(11), 1497–1508 (2011)
24. Sheikh, H.F., Ahmad, I., Fan, D.: An evolutionary technique for performance-energy-temperature optimized scheduling of parallel tasks on multi-core processors. IEEE Trans. Parallel Distrib. Syst. **27**(3), 668–681 (2016)
25. Langdon, W.B., Harman, M.: Genetically improved CUDA C++ software. In: Nicolau, M., Krawiec, K., Heywood, M.I., Castelli, M., García-Sánchez, P., Merelo, J.J., Rivas Santos, V.M., Sim, K. (eds.) EuroGP 2014. LNCS, vol. 8599, pp. 87–99. Springer, Heidelberg (2014). doi:10.1007/978-3-662-44303-3_8
26. Le Goues, C., Nguyen, T., Forrest, S., Weimer, W.: Genprog: a generic method for automatic software repair. IEEE Trans. Software Eng. **38**(1), 54–72 (2012)
27. Ryan, C., Ivan, L., Koza, J.R., Banzhaf, W.: Automatic parallelization of loops in sequential programs using genetic programming. In: Genetic Programming 1998: Proceedings of the Third, pp. 344–349. Morgan Kaufmann (1998)
28. Ryan, C., Ivan, L.: Automatic parallelization of arbitrary programs. In: Poli, R., Nordin, P., Langdon, W.B., Fogarty, T.C. (eds.) EuroGP 1999. LNCS, vol. 1598, pp. 244–254. Springer, Heidelberg (1999). doi:10.1007/3-540-48885-5_21

Issues on GPU Parallel Implementation of Evolutionary High-Dimensional Multi-objective Feature Selection

Juan José Escobar, Julio Ortega[✉], Jesús González, Miguel Damas, and Beatriz Prieto

Department of Computer Architecture and Technology, CITIC, University of Granada, Granada, Spain
{jjescobar,jortega,jesusgonzalez,mdamas,beap}@ugr.es

Abstract. The interest on applications that analyse large volumes of high dimensional data has grown recently. Many of these applications related to the so-called *Big Data* show different implicit parallelism that can benefit from the efficient use, in terms of performance and power consumption, of Graphics Processing Unit (GPU) accelerators. Although the GPU microarchitectures make possible the acceleration of applications by exploiting parallelism at different levels, the characteristics of their memory hierarchy and the location of GPUs as coprocessors require a careful organization of the memory access patterns and data transferences to get efficient speedups. This paper aims to take advantage of heterogeneous parallel codes on GPUs to accelerate evolutionary approaches in Electroencephalogram (EEG) classification and feature selection in the context of Brain Computer Interface (BCI) tasks. The results show the benefits of taking into account not only the data parallelism achievable by GPUs, but also the memory access patterns, in order to increase the speedups achieved by superscalar cores.

Keywords: EEG classification · Feature selection · GPU · Heterogeneous parallel architectures · Multi-objective optimization · OpenCL

1 Introduction

Multi-objective optimization provides a suitable approach to cope with data mining applications such as classification, clustering, and feature selection where several objectives such as accuracy, simplicity and comprehensibility of models, among others, should be jointly taken into account. Nevertheless, the computational cost required by multi-objective optimization algorithms could prevent its use on many present applications, especially those related with the Big Data realm that comprise high dimensional patterns, unless efficient parallel codes would make possible an efficient exploitation of present high-performance computer architectures. In the present paper, we consider some of the issues related with the development of GPU parallel codes for evolutionary multi-objective

© Springer International Publishing AG 2017
G. Squillero and K. Sim (Eds.): EvoApplications 2017, Part I, LNCS 10199, pp. 773–788, 2017.
DOI: 10.1007/978-3-319-55849-3_50

feature selection in the classification of high-dimensional patterns. Our codes have been evaluated on EEG classification, which is a good example of such applications that process high-dimensional patterns and requires feature selection techniques to remove noisy or irrelevant features or to improve the learning accuracy and result comprehensibility, mainly whenever the number of features in the input patterns is higher than the number of available patterns.

Thus, our approach to EEG classification for BCI tasks [1] includes an evolutionary multi-objective optimization algorithm and a clustering algorithm applied to a set of high-dimensional patterns that usually requires high-volume storage and different kinds of inherent parallelism. As GPUs implement characteristics which are common in the current processors architecture approaches to take advantage of technology improvements [2], their use has been previously proposed to accelerate parallel metaheuristics and evolutionary computation [3]. With respect to the GPU implementations of evolutionary multi-objective procedures, we have the papers of Sharma et al. [4] and Wong et al. [5]. There are also many papers that have approached the parallelization of the K-means algorithm on GPUs [6–8]. However, the parallelization on GPUs of a whole data mining application with the characteristics of our target application is less frequent in the literature. With respect to our previous papers [9,10], here we show not only the relevance of taking into account the memory access patterns in the algorithms but also a more detailed analysis of the resources use that makes possible to take advantage of the data parallelism available in the codes.

After this introduction, Sect. 2 describes the evolutionary multi-objective optimization approach to feature selection, whose implementation has been parallelized. Section 3 summarizes the GPU characteristics which are relevant to this work and Sect. 4 analyses the main issues to develop efficient parallel codes in heterogeneous platforms, and the details of our proposed OpenCL [11] codes. Then, Sect. 5 describes the experimental results and compares the behaviour of different considered alternatives and finally Sect. 6 summarizes the conclusions.

2   Evolutionary Multi-objective Unsupervised Feature Selection

This paper tackles feature selection in unsupervised classification of patterns characterized by a high number of features. Moreover, we are interested in applications where the number of patterns to be classified is usually far lower than the number of features, and thus it is required to cope with a curse of dimensionality problem [12]. The most relevant features should be selected to achieve an adequate performance of the classifier, to decrease the computational complexity of the classification, and to remove irrelevant/redundant features. Nevertheless, optimal feature selection is an NP-hard problem that requires efficient metaheuristics, especially in high-dimensional classification problems. Here, we apply multi-objective optimization to feature selection and propose the use of heterogeneous parallel architectures to accelerate it.

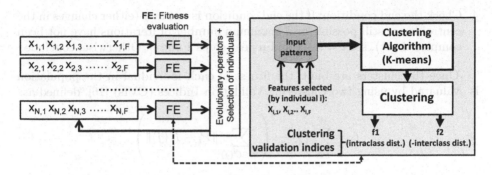

Fig. 1. Wrapper procedure for unsupervised feature selection by means of evolutionary multi-objective optimization (and K-means as clustering algorithm)

Multi-objective optimization can be applied to data mining applications as it is shown in [13,14]. The benefits from a multi-objective approach to feature selection in both supervised and unsupervised classification have been reported elsewhere [15]. However, as the number of features involved in the applications here considered is large, a multi-objective optimization approach would imply high computational costs, and the execution time is an important issue to consider.

Figure 1 shows our approach to a wrapper procedure for feature selection in unsupervised classification of EEG patterns. A multi-objective evolutionary procedure evolves a population of individuals that codify different feature selections. Given a feature selection (an individual in the population of the evolutionary algorithm), the P patterns included in the database, DS, will be used to define the set training patterns by choosing the components corresponding to the number of features, F, selected. This way, the K-means algorithm has been applied to the P patterns $P_i = (p_i^1, ..., p_i^F)(i = 1, ..., P)$ to determine the centroids $K^t(j)(j = 1, .., W)$ of the W possible clusters (W is known in our classification problem, and it is equal to the number of classes).

K-means algorithm is a well-known clustering algorithm. Its steps are described below:

1. Initialize centroids: Set $t = 0$ and generate W initial centroids $K^t(j)(j = 1, .., W)$ (as many centroids as clusters or classes), by randomly selecting them among the P patterns in the database.
2. Clustering: Assign each pattern to the cluster corresponding to its nearest centroid. Thus, the sets $C^t(j)(j = 1, .., W)$ are built as follows:

$$C^t(j) = \left\{ P_i \in DS : \|P_i - K^t(j)\| < \|P_i - K^t(l)\| \right\} (l = 1, .., W) \quad (1)$$

3. Update centroids: Calculate the new cluster centroids, $K^{t+1}(j)(j = 1, .., W)$ according to (2):

$$K^{t+1}(j) = \frac{1}{|C^t(j)|} \sum_{P_i \in C^t(j)} P_i \quad (2)$$

4. Check the end condition: If the end condition is not met (either changes in the centroids are still possible or a maximum number of iterations have not been completed yet), set $t = t + 1$ and repeat steps 2 and 3. Otherwise, conclude.

Once the clusters are built, the fitness of each individual in the population is evaluated by using two Clustering Validation Indices (CVIs) [16], defined as:

$$f_1 = \sum_{j=1}^{W} \frac{1}{|C(j)|} \left(\sum_{P_i \in C(j)} \|P_i - K(j)\| \right) \tag{3}$$

$$f_2 = - \sum_{j=1}^{W-1} \left(\sum_{i>j} \|K(i) - K(j)\| \right) \tag{4}$$

where (3) and (4) correspond to the intraclass and minus the interclass distances, respectively. In these equations, $|C(j)|$ is the number of patterns in cluster $C(j)(j = 1, .., W)$ whose centroid is $K(j)$, and $\|P_i - K(j)\|$ is the Euclidean distance between the pattern P_i and the centroid $K(j)$.

3   The GPU Microarchitecture and the OpenCL Framework

In this section, the GPU characteristics relevant to our work are described. We will also relate this description with the terms used by OpenCL [11] to provide a more consistent introduction as the codes proposed in this paper have been implemented in such programming language.

The basic computing elements or cores of the GPU are the so-called *Stream Processors* (SPs). They do not contain instruction units and only are able to execute scalar operations. Several SPs along with one or more instruction units and a register file comprise a multiprocessor, also called *Streaming Multiprocessor* (SMX). A GPU can include multiple SMXs, which allows the simultaneous execution of the same program on different data, i.e. the Single Program Multiple Data (SPMD) model. The threads are organized within thread blocks in such a way that all the threads in a block are assigned to a single SMX. Moreover, the blocks are also partitioned into *warps* containing threads with consecutive and increasing identity number that start together at the same program address. While the threads in a block are able to cooperate and share the instruction unit, the register file and some low latency memory, threads in different blocks can only communicate with each other through the off-chip memory. Models relevant to performance optimization of applications on GPUs have been proposed in [17–19]. Precisely, the availability of accurate performance models constitutes an important topic to distribute the application workload in order to achieve optimal performance.

The OpenCL framework allows platform-independent parallel programming through programs executed in a host that launch functions, called *kernels*, to

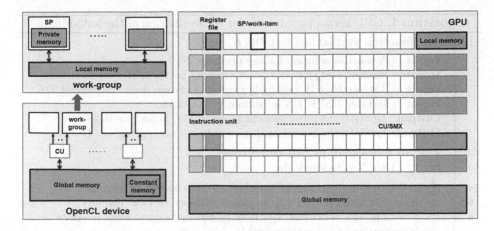

Fig. 2. Elements of the OpenCL device (left block) and schematic diagram of a GPU architecture (right block)

other OpenCL devices, such as Central Processing Units (CPUs) or GPUs. A device in OpenCL is an array of functionally independent *Computing Units* (CUs) divided into *work-items*, which are the minimum units of concurrent execution. Several work-items can execute the same instruction over different data items according to a Single Instruction Multiple Data (SIMD) model, and they can be also organized as a *work-group*, in such a way that several work-groups can be executed according to a SPMD model, which are distributed through the available CUs. The GPU scheme previously shown can be translated to the OpenCL terms. This way, the SMXs are computing units, the SP cores are work-items and the thread blocks are work-groups. The abstract memory model of OpenCL defines memory spaces that also resemble the usual memory hierarchies. Thus, the *global memory* (off-chip memory) is visible to all computing units in the device, as the *constant memory*, included in the global memory to store variables whose values do not change. All work-items in a given work-group share the corresponding *local memory*, while the *private memory* is only accessed by a work-item. Figure 2 relates the main GPU and OpenCL framework terms and elements.

4   The Proposed OpenCL GPU Kernel

In this section, we provide our parallel approach to take advantage of GPUs architectures performing the role of a coprocessor connected, through a bus (usually PCI Express), to a host including multiple superscalar cores that share the main memory.

From Fig. 1 and Sect. 2, it is clear that our application involves both evolutionary multi-objective and clustering algorithms. In [20] we have proposed several approaches to parallelize the application through different parallel

---

Algorithm 1. GPU kernel pseudocode for the evaluation of the individuals

1 **Kernel function** evaluation($S(i), DS, K, DS^t$)

| **Input**   : A possible solution for the problem, $S(i)$
| **Input**   : Dataset $DS(j); \forall j = 1, ..., P$ training patterns of F components
| **Input**   : The set K of W centroids randomly chosen from the dataset DS
| **Input**   : Dataset DS^t is DS in column-major order
| **Output**: $f_1(S(i))$, the intraclass distances in $S(i)$ according to (3)
| **Output**: $f_2(S(i))$, the interclass distances in $S(i)$ according to (4)

2 | $<<$ *All work-groups, All work-items* $>>$
3 | **for** $i \leftarrow 1$ **to** N individuals **do**
4 | | $<<$ *work-groupID, All work-items in work-groupID* $>>$
5 | | $K_l \leftarrow$ Copy the centroids from global memory to local memory
6 | | $I \leftarrow$ Copy the individual $S(i)$ from global memory to local memory
7 | | Initialization of the mapping table, $MT \leftarrow 0$
8 | | **repeat**
9 | | | $<<$ *work-groupID, work-itemID* $>>$
10 | | | $MT \leftarrow$ Each pattern is assigned to the nearest cluster using DS^t
11 | | | $D \leftarrow$ Nearest Euclidean distance is stored for each pattern
12 | | | Check if the pattern has been assigned to another centroid
13 | | | $<<$ *work-groupID, All work-items in work-groupID* $>>$
14 | | | $K_l \leftarrow$ Update the centroids using the dataset DS
15 | | **until** *stop criterion is not reached*;
16 | | $<<$ *work-groupID, Work-item number 0* $>>$
17 | | $f_1(S(i)) \leftarrow$ intraclass(K_l, DS)
18 | | $f_2(S(i)) \leftarrow$ interclass(K_l, DS)
19 | **end**
20 | **return** $(f_1(S(i)), f_2(S(i)))$
21 **End**

---

evolutionary multi-optimization options, but we did not parallelize the fitness computation for the individuals in the population. This issue is considered here by taking advantage of the GPU resources to run data parallel codes. Thus, a core in the CPU (i.e. the host) launches a kernel in the GPU to evaluate the fitness (the two cost functions) of the individuals in the population. The GPU kernel implements two levels of parallelism: parallel evaluation of the population (implemented as a master-worker parallel evolutionary algorithm) and the data parallel evaluation of the cost functions for each individual. In [21] it is shown another OpenCL implementation of a genetic algorithm for feature selection in a biometric recognition application. Although the paper does not implement a multi-objective algorithm and its fitness function differs from the couple of functions here considered, its approach follows a quite similar strategy. Moreover, this paper describes some optimizations we have applied to our first approach described in [9].

Table 1. Memory (in bytes) used by (Ref) code [9] and our proposed code (Opt). N, W, F and P are the number of individuals, centroids, features and patterns respectively

Mem. type		Global		Constant		Local		
Description		Population	Databases	Centroids		Indiv.	Tables	Distances
Array		S_{pop}	S_{DB}	S_W	S_{K_l}	S_{ind}	S_{MT}	S_D
Size	Ref	$N \times F$	$4 \times P \times F$	$4 \times W \times F$	$4 \times W \times F$	F	$3 \times W \times P$	$4 \times W \times P$
	Opt		$8 \times P \times F$	$4 \times W$			P	$4 \times P$
Total	Ref	$N \times F + 4 \times P \times F$		$4 \times W \times F$		$4 \times W \times F + 7 \times W \times P + F$		
size	Opt	$N \times F + 8 \times P \times F$		$4 \times W$		$4 \times W \times F + 5 \times P + F$		

Algorithm 1 shows the pseudocode for the implemented kernel to evaluate the fitness of the individuals (the K-means algorithm and the computation of the intraclass and interclass distances defining the two cost functions of the multi-objective optimization procedure). As it has been described above, individuals are evaluated in parallel by different work-groups in the OpenCL GPU kernel, thus implementing the first level of parallelism of the algorithm (line 3 in Algorithm 1). Besides, the GPU kernel also implements a second level of parallelism as each work-group is composed by warps of, for example, 32 work-items each in the case of the GPU used for the experimental part of this work. This second level of parallelism corresponds to the parallel implementation of the K-means algorithm (lines 5–15), whose main steps were described in Sect. 2, and the computation of the cost functions f_1 and f_2 (lines 17 and 18 in Algorithm 1) according to (3) and (4). Table 1 provides the amount of memory required by our GPU kernel in comparison with the approach used as reference and described in [9], which does not take into account the memory access patterns of the algorithm to improve its performance. In what follows, we describe the main details of the new proposed GPU kernel and, in Sect. 5, we argument that these optimizations have allowed efficient data parallel performances.

1. Initialize centroids: The GPU kernel receives the input parameters provided by the host code: the individuals of the population, the dataset (only once at the beginning of the algorithm), and the initial centroids for the K-means algorithms (at the beginning of each generation of the evolutionary multi-objective algorithm). An individual, $S(i)$, is a one-dimensional array of contiguous 0's and 1's (according to the selection or not of the corresponding feature) stored in global memory. It will be copied into local memory (line 6 in Algorithm 1) as this on-chip memory is faster than global memory. The global memory used is $S_{Pop} = N \times F$ bytes, where N is the number of individuals and F is the whole number of features (among which the selection is to be done). The datasets DS and DS^t include the P training patterns, each characterized by F features. Both sets are stored in global memory due to their large sizes, in a one-dimensional array of $P \times F$ elements normalized by the host program. In DS the patterns are organized in row-major order while column-major order is used in DS^t (DS^t is the transpose of DS). Each dataset needs $S_{DB} = 4 \times P \times F$ bytes of global memory. The initial

values of the W centroids are randomly selected among the patterns of the dataset, and their corresponding indices are copied from the host memory to the GPU constant memory. Thus, the amount of required constant memory is $S_W = 4 \times W$, while in the reference code [9] $S_W = 4 \times W \times F$ bytes are necessary. As the positions of the centroids are modified along the iterations of the K-means algorithm (otherwise K-means would end), each centroid is obtained from its index in constant memory and stored into local memory whenever a new individual is going to be evaluated (line 5). The operations of lines 5 and 6 are executed in parallel by all work-items of the corresponding work-group. The centroids need $S_{K_l} = 4 \times W \times F$ bytes of local memory.

2. Clustering: To implement this step of the K-means algorithm, each work-item obtains the nearest centroid for a specific pattern by using the Euclidean distances between patterns and centroids. As it has been indicated, the array DS^t is stored in the GPU global memory to accelerate this task. The P first memory addresses of DS^t store the values of the first feature for all patterns, the following P memory addresses store the values of the second feature, and so on. Therefore, as each work-item handles a different pattern in a given time, consecutive work-items will request consecutive memory addresses, thus allowing full coalescence of the accesses to global memory. Coalescence is a technique in which consecutive threads of a warp request data stored in global memory, in consecutive logical addresses. It aims to minimize the number of transaction segments requested from global memory by taking advantage of the memory bus width to get multiple data in a single transaction. We have been able to use coalescence as consecutive work-items in the same work-group request data stored in consecutive logical addresses of the global memory. When the WI work-items in the work-group process the first WI data, the next WI data are repeatedly requested and processed, until the whole dataset has been processed. Moreover, when the nearest centroid to a given pattern and the corresponding distance are obtained, they can be written, respectively in the structures MT and D with the minimum number of memory bank conflicts. The mapping table MT contains the centroid assigned to each pattern along the K-means iterations, thus requiring $S_{MT} = P$ bytes of local memory, being P the number of patterns in the dataset DS, as each pattern only stores the index of its corresponding centroid, K_i. The initialization of MT is carried out by all work-items (line 7). Moreover, through the mapping table MT, it is easier to check the K-means convergence by taking into account whether a pattern has been assigned to another centroid (line 12), instead of doing that at the end of the iteration (if there are not changes in the centroid assignments). As MT, the array D is stored in local memory including the Euclidean distances between each pattern and its closest centroid, occupying a total of $S_D = 4 \times P$ bytes. In the reference algorithm [9] a table of $W \times P$ bytes was used to store the nearest centroid to a given pattern in iteration i and two more tables with the same sizes were also required to store the nearest centroids for the patterns in iteration $i - 1$, and to interchange the tables for iterations i and $i-1$. In addition, the reference algorithm requires $4 \times W \times P$ bytes to store the distances between each pattern and the different centroids.

3. Update centroids: The most complex step of K-means in terms of data parallelization is to update the centroids (line 14). We assign each work-item to add the same feature of all patterns belonging to the corresponding centroid. Some approaches [22,23] propose to perform this step sequentially in the host, although the cost per iteration associated to transfer the centroids to the host, process them, and return them could be too high, especially in applications with high-dimensional patterns. The structure of the dataset DS^t is not adequate as consecutive work-items compute consecutive features. Now, DS is used because its first F memory addresses contain all the features of the first pattern, the following F addresses contain the features of the second pattern, and so on. Thus, the coalescence of global memory accesses can be achieved and the memory bank conflicts are minimized when a centroid is updated in local memory. Figure 3 shows the relation between DS and DS^t and the work-item accesses to these structures according to the steps 2 and 3 of the K-means algorithm.
4. Check the end condition: Once the end condition of the K-means is met, the GPU kernel returns the fitness values of the individuals (lines 17 and 18) according to (3) and (4) of Sect. 2. The data parallelism available in these equations can be easily exploited by taking advantage of all work-items available at each SMX.

5   Experimental Results

In this section, we analyse the performance of our OpenCL (version 1.2) codes running on Linux CentOS 6.7 operating system, in a node with 32 GB of DDR3 memory and two Intel Xeon E5-2620 processors at 2.1 GHz including six cores per socket with Hyper-Threading, thus comprising 24 threads. The node also has a Tesla K20c with 5 GB of global memory, 208 GB/s as maximum memory bandwidth and 2496 CUDA cores at 705.5 MHz, distributed into 13 SMXs, thus including 192 cores per SMX. In our experiments, we have used two benchmarks extracted from the datasets recorded in the BCI Laboratory at the University of Essex and described in [24].

The data benchmark b480a includes 178 patterns (EEGs) with 480 features corresponding to the subject coded as 110 in the dataset. We have also considered another larger data file for the same subject, the b3600a, including 178 patterns (EEGs) with 3600 features.

The multi-objective optimization has been implemented by using the well-known algorithm NSGA-II [25] including two-point crossover with a probability of 0.9, a mutation by inversion of the selected bit with probability of 0.1, and selection by binary tournament. The hypervolumes [26] are obtained with $(1, 1)$ as reference point, and the minimum values for the cost functions f_1 and f_2 are respectively 0 and -1, i.e. $(0, -1)$. We have made 10 repetitions of each experiment, to accomplish the corresponding statistical analysis of the results. Thus, after analysing the obtained hypervolume results by applying the Kolmogorov-Smirnov and the Kruskal-Wallis tests, it has been observed that there are not

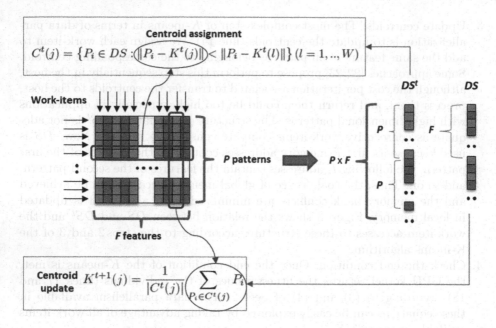

Fig. 3. Work-items accesses to DS and DS^t in the different steps of the GPU kernel

Table 2. Mean execution times and standard deviation (* means statistically significant difference) between CPU (12 cores) and GPU (12 SMXs) with the dataset b3600a. it $\equiv$ iteration; ind $\equiv$ individual

$\times 10^4$ ms	CPU 1 core	GPU 12 SMXs	CPU 12 cores
20 it. 120 ind.	6.78 ± 0.13	$*\mathbf{0.71 \pm 0.02}$	0.76 ± 0.02
20 it. 240 ind.	13.11 ± 0.26	$*\mathbf{1.38 \pm 0.01}$	1.44 ± 0.04
50 it. 120 ind.	17.57 ± 0.04	$*\mathbf{1.83 \pm 0.04}$	1.94 ± 0.04
50 it. 240 ind.	33.26 ± 0.06	$\mathbf{3.64 \pm 0.07}$	3.78 ± 0.22

statistically significant differences with respect to the results obtained by the sequential procedure with the same number of individuals in the population and generations. This is expected, as our OpenCL codes implement a master-worker parallel approach that keep the behaviour of the base sequential algorithm.

Table 2 compares the mean execution times of the GPU kernel executed with 12 SMXs and 1024 work-items and the corresponding CPU kernel executed in 12 cores. The CPU kernel only implements the master-worker parallel evolutionary multi-objective algorithm but does not take advantage of the data parallelism that is also exploited by the GPU kernel. The table shows that the GPU provides better execution times despite it runs at 705.5 MHz while the CPU cores run at 2.1 GHz as GPU takes advantage of the data parallelism available in the fitness evaluation of the individuals in the population. The statistical analysis shows significant differences in all but one of the considered alternatives. On the other hand, Fig. 4 shows the corresponding speedups for the times in Table 2.

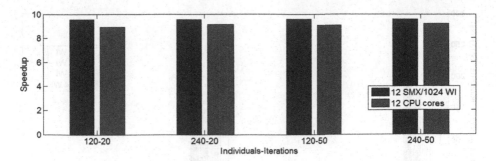

Fig. 4. Speedups between CPU (12 cores) and GPU (12 SMXs/1024 work-items) with the dataset b3600a

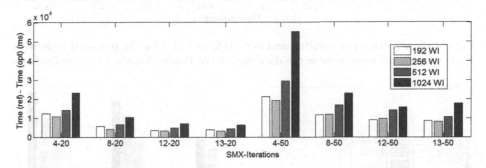

Fig. 5. Time reduction achieved by the optimized code in the data file b480a with a population size of 240 individuals

In what follows, we analyse the behaviour of the GPU kernel here proposed in Sect. 4 with respect to the previously mentioned reference parallel code evaluated in [9]. From Table 1, the optimized code implies an increase in the required global and constant memory equal to $4 \times (F \times (P - W) + W)$ bytes, as in our application P is greater than W, and a decrease in the required local memory equal to $P \times (7 \times W - 5)$ bytes. Nevertheless, the optimized GPU kernel here proposed requires less running time than the reference code in all the experiments accomplished under the same conditions of SMXs and work-items. As an example of the obtained results, Fig. 5 shows the reduction in the running time achieved by our proposed optimized version for different number of SMXs and work-items for the dataset b480a. As it can be seen, from 256 work-items, the amount of time-cutting provided by the optimized GPU-kernel grows as more work-items are used due to the effect of the applied coalescence technique.

Figure 6 shows the time-cutting provided by the optimized version shown in Fig. 5 divided by the number of SMXs and iterations. As it can be seen, the results per iteration and SMX multiprocessor are approximately the same for similar number of work-items.

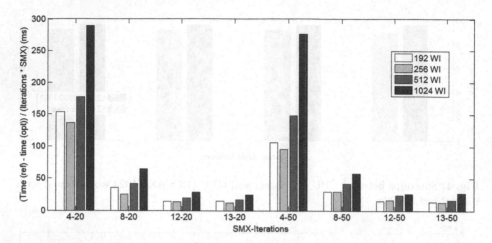

Fig. 6. Time-cutting per iteration and per SMX provided by the proposed code with respect to the reference code in the data file b480a. Population size of 240 individuals

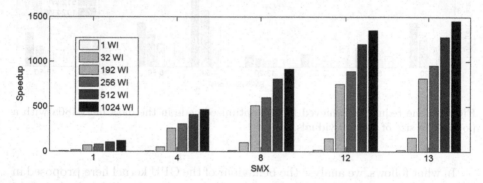

Fig. 7. Speedups in the data file b480a. Population size of 240 individuals

Figure 7 provides the speedups obtained by the optimized code here proposed for different SMXs multiprocessors and work-items with respect to the running time of a work-item in only one SMX multiprocessor. It can be seen that the speedups grow with the number of SMXs and work-items. To get some insight into the effect of the number of these SMXs and work-items, Figs. 8 and 9 provide several efficiency measures obtained when the speedups are respectively divided by the number of SMXs or the number of work-items. As it can be seen from Fig. 8, the speedups per SMXs are quite similar given a number of work-items (there is only a slight decrease as the number of work-items grows). Figure 9 shows that the speedups per work-item grow as more SMXs are used although, for a given number of SMXs, they decrease as more work-items are considered.

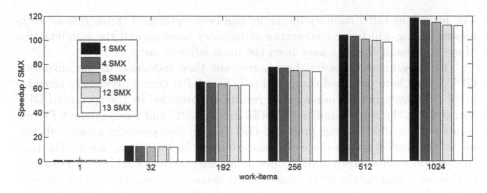

Fig. 8. Speedup per number of SMXs in the data file b480a. Population size of 240 individuals

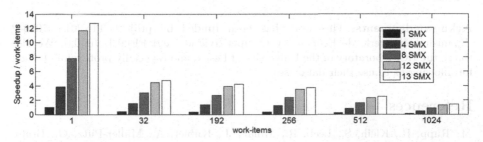

Fig. 9. Speedup per number of work-items in the data file b480a. Population size of 240 individuals

6   Conclusions

Many works in the literature have shown important speedups achieved by different parallel evolutionary algorithms implemented on GPUs. Nevertheless, fewer details have been reported about the benefits of such many-core architectures in data mining applications with high dimensional patterns and/or high volume data. This paper proposes parallel OpenCL codes for heterogeneous platforms including GPU architectures of a multi-objective approach to high-dimensional feature selection for EEG classification on BCI tasks. More specifically, the application to be parallelized is based on a multi-objective optimization evolutionary algorithm with two cost functions. Thus, the fitness evaluation for a given individual implies the computation of two validation indices for the clustering obtained through a K-means algorithm applied to the patterns in the dataset.

Our OpenCL GPU kernel extracts two kinds of parallelism. The first one corresponds to a master-worker parallel multi-objective evolutionary algorithm that distributes the evaluation of the individuals among the available threads or SMXs. The second approach entails the parallelization of the evaluation function. This way, the individuals are distributed among the SMXs of the GPU and the K-means algorithm is parallelized among different work-items in the SMXs.

The use of the GPU memory hierarchy has been optimized through some techniques among which the coalescence of memory accesses and the minimization of memory bank conflicts have been the most efficient ones.

The experimental results show a relevant time reduction in the optimized GPU kernel here proposed compared to a first GPU kernel previously provided in [9]. Moreover, better running time results are provided by the optimized GPU kernel when the same number of SMXs in the GPU and cores in the CPU are compared. In addition, our proposed GPU kernel also provides a more efficient use of the work-items as more of them are used. Nevertheless, despite the relatively good results shown in this paper, more alternatives should be also explored to take advantage of the heterogeneous parallelism. Among them, the implementation of evolutionary subpopulations through island approaches could offer new insights about the possibilities of the GPUs in the type of applications here considered.

Acknowledgements. This work has been funded by project TIN2015-67020-P (Spanish "Ministerio de Economá y Competitividad" and FEDER funds). We also thank the BCI laboratory of the University of Essex, and especially prof. John Q. Gan, for allowing us to use their databases.

References

1. Rupp, R., Kleih, S., Leeb, R., Millan, J., Kübler, A., Müller-Putz, G.: Brain-computer interfaces and assistive technology. In: Grübler, G., Hildt, E. (eds.) Brain-Computer-Interfaces in their Ethical, Social and Cultural Contexts. The International Library of Ethics, Law and Technology, pp. 7–38. Springer, Heidelberg (2014)
2. Collet, P.: Why GPGPUs for evolutionary computation? In: Tsutsui, S., Collet, P. (eds.) Massively Parallel Evolutionary Computation on GPGPUs. Natural Computing Series, pp. 3–14. Springer, Heidelberg (2013)
3. Alba, E., Luque, G., Nesmachnow, S.: Parallel metaheuristics: recent advances and new trends. Int. Trans. Oper. Res. **20**(1), 1–48 (2013)
4. Sharma, D., Collet, P.: Implementation techniques for massively parallel multi-objective optimization. In: Tsutsui, S., Collet, P. (eds.) Massively Parallel Evolutionary Computation on GPGPUs. Natural Computing Series, pp. 267–286. Springer, Heidelberg (2013)
5. Wong, M., Cui, G.: Data mining using parallel multi-objective evolutionary algorithms on graphics processing units. In: Tsutsui, S., Collet, P. (eds.) Massively Parallel Evolutionary Computation on GPGPUs. Natural Computing Series, pp. 287–307. Springer, Heidelberg (2013)
6. Baramkar, P., Kulkarni, D.: Review for k-means on graphics processing units (GPU). Int. J. Eng. Res. Technol. **3**(6), 1911–1914 (2014)
7. Wu, R., Zhang, B., Hsu, M.: Clustering billions of data points using gpus. In: Hast, A., Buchty, R., Tao, J., Weidendorfer, J. (eds.) Proceedings of the Combined Workshops on UnConventional High Performance Computing workshop plus Memory Access Workshop, pp. 1–6. UCHPC-MAW 2009. ACM, Ischia, May 2009
8. Zechner, M., Granitzer, M.: Accelerating k-means on the graphics processor via CUDA. In: Proceedings of the First International Conference on Intensive Applications and Services, INTENSIVE 2009, pp. 7–15. IEEE, Valencia, April 2009

9. Escobar, J.J., Ortega, J., González, J., Damas, M.: Assessing parallel heterogeneous computer architectures for multiobjective feature selection on EEG classification. In: Ortuño, F., Rojas, I. (eds.) IWBBIO 2016. LNCS, vol. 9656, pp. 277–289. Springer, Heidelberg (2016). doi:10.1007/978-3-319-31744-1_25

10. Escobar, J.J., Ortega, J., González, J., Damas, M.: Improving memory accesses for heterogeneous parallel multi-objective feature selection on eeg classification. In: Proceedings of the 4th International Workshop on Parallelism in Bioinformatics, PBIO 2016. Springer, Grenoble, France (2016)

11. Khronos Group: Khronos opencl registry. https://www.khronos.org/registry/cl/. Accessed: 30 November 2015

12. Bellman, R.: Adaptive Control Processes: A Guided Tour. Princeton University Press, Princeton (1961)

13. Mukhopadhyay, A., Maulik, U., Bandyopadhyay, S., Coello Coello, C.: A survey of multiobjective evolutionary algorithms for data mining: Part I. IEEE Trans. Evol. Comput. **18**(1), 4–19 (2014)

14. Mukhopadhyay, A., Maulik, U., Bandyopadhyay, S., Coello Coello, C.: A survey of multiobjective evolutionary algorithms for data mining: Part II. IEEE Trans. Evol. Comput. **18**(1), 20–35 (2014)

15. Handl, J., Knowles, J.: Feature subset selection in unsupervised learning via multiobjective optimization. Int. J. Comput. Intell. Res. **2**(3), 217–238 (2006)

16. Arbelaitz, O., Gurrutxaga, I., Muguerza, J., Pérez, J., Perona, I.: An extensive comparative study of cluster validity indices. Pattern Recogn. **46**(1), 243–256 (2013)

17. Lopez-Novoa, U., Mendiburu, A., Miguel-Alonso, J.: A survey of performance modeling and simulation techniques for accelerator-based computing. IEEE Trans. Parallel Distrib. Syst. **26**(1), 272–281 (2015)

18. Hong, S., Kim, H.: An analytical model for a GPU architecture with memory-level and thread-level parallelism awareness. In: Proceedings of the 36th Annual International Symposium on Computer Architecture, pp. 152–163. ISCA 2009. ACM, New York, June 2009

19. Dao, T., Kim, J., Seo, S., Egger, B., Lee, J.: A performance model for gpus with caches. IEEE Trans. Parallel Distrib. Syst. **26**(7), 1800–1813 (2015)

20. Kimovski, D., Ortega, J., Ortiz, A., Baños, R.: Leveraging cooperation for parallel multi-objective feature selection in high-dimensional eeg data. Concurrency Comput. Pract. Experience **27**(18), 5476–5499 (2015)

21. Fazendeiro, P., Padole, C., Sequeira, P., Prata, P.: OpenCL implementations of a genetic algorithm for feature selection in periocular biometric recognition. In: Panigrahi, B.K., Das, S., Suganthan, P.N., Nanda, P.K. (eds.) SEMCCO 2012. LNCS, vol. 7677, pp. 729–737. Springer, Heidelberg (2012). doi:10.1007/978-3-642-35380-2_85

22. Dhanasekaran, B., Rubin, N.: A new method for GPU based irregular reductions and its application to k-means clustering. In: Proceedings of the Fourth Workshop on General Purpose Processing on Graphics Processing Units, pp. 729–737. GPGPU-4, ACM, Newport Beach, March 2011

23. Gunarathne, T., Salpitikorala, B., Chauhan, A., Fox, G.: Optimizing OpenCL kernels for iterative statistical algorithms on GPUs. In: Proceedings of the Second International Workshop on GPUs and Scientific Applications, GPUScA 2011, pp. 33–44. Galveston Island, October 2011

24. Asensio-Cubero, J., Gan, J., Palaniappan, R.: Multiresolution analysis over simple graphs for brain computer interfaces. J. Neural Eng. **10**(4) (2013)

25. Deb, K., Agrawal, S., Pratap, A., Meyarivan, T.: A fast elitist non-dominated sorting genetic algorithm for multi-objective optimization: NSGA-II. In: Schoenauer, M., Deb, K., Rudolph, G., Yao, X., Lutton, E., Merelo, J.J., Schwefel, H.-P. (eds.) PPSN 2000. LNCS, vol. 1917, pp. 849–858. Springer, Heidelberg (2000). doi:10.1007/3-540-45356-3_83
26. Fonseca, C., López-Ibáñez, M., Paquete, L., Guerreiro, A.: Computation of the hypervolume indicator. http://lopez-ibanez.eu/hypervolume. Accessed: 30 November 2015

Embedded Grammars for Grammatical Evolution on GPGPU

J. Ignacio Hidalgo[1]([✉]), Carlos Cervigón[1], J. Manuel Velasco[1],
J. Manuel Colmenar[2], Carlos García-Sánchez[3], and Guillermo Botella[3]

[1] Adaptive and Bioinspired Systems Research Group,
Universidad Complutense de Madrid, 28040 Madrid, Spain
`hidalgo@dacya.ucm.es`
[2] Rey Juan Carlos University, Tulipán s/n, 28933 Mstoles, Madrid, Spain
[3] ArTeCS Group, Universidad Complutense de Madrid, 28040 Madrid, Spain

Abstract. This paper presents an implementation of Grammatical Evolution on a GPU architecture. Our proposal, *Embedded Grammars*, implements the grammar directly in the code. Although more rigid, it allows to compute the decodification in parallel with the evaluation of the individuals. We tested three different grammars with a set of eight symbolic regression problems. The symbolic regression problems consists on obtaining a mathematical expression in the form $y = f(x)$, in our case, from a set of 288 pairs x, y. The analysis of the results shows that *Embedded Grammars* are better not only in terms of execution time, but also in quality when compared with an implementation on a CPU. Speed-up results are also better than those presented in the literature.

Keywords: Grammatical evolution · Model identification · Symbolic regression · Graphic processing unit

1 Introduction

Currently one of the aspects that appear repeatedly, regardless of the application area, is the processing of data and information, including identifying patterns and modeling using mathematical expressions. Evolutionary algorithms (EAs) are search and optimization tools based on the natural selection and evolution process that have proven their usefulness in many fields of application in science and engineering [1]. In particular, Genetic Programming (GP) in its original form [2] and its variants, such as Grammatical Evolution (GE) [3], have proven to be a very efficient tool in obtaining mathematical expressions that fit a data set, by solving problems known as symbolic regression (SR). GE have the peculiarity of using a grammar to decode the solutions to the problem, allowing to narrow the search spaces by incorporating knowledge to the optimization process. For this reason, they are especially useful in model identification and modeling problems.

As it is well known, EAs work with a set of solutions in an iterative process by applying a set of operators that simulate the processes that nature uses to

© Springer International Publishing AG 2017
G. Squillero and K. Sim (Eds.): EvoApplications 2017, Part I, LNCS 10199, pp. 789–805, 2017.
DOI: 10.1007/978-3-319-55849-3_51

evolve. One of the issues that can arise when real problems are tackled by EAs is the increase in execution time, since the evaluation of a large number of individuals has to be done. In addition, in GE, this time can be even greater, since an additional process of translation through the grammar is needed to obtain the meaning and fitness of the solutions. Fortunately, one of the features of EAs is that they are embarrassingly parallel. In the last years different options have appeared to accelerate the execution of these algorithms [4]. Among them, there are some methods that make use of General Purpose Graphic Processing Units (GPGPU or simply GPU) [5]. The use of GPGPUs in this field is due to its ability to work with multiple data in a single instruction, a type of computation widely used in the treatment of high parallelism at data level.

However, the necessity of using a grammar makes the efficient parallelization of GE a difficult task. The only work in the literature, [6], only presented results with one instance and identified several problems in the parallelization process. The objective of our work is to investigate the effectiveness of new implementations of GE on GPGPUs. The type of problems to be worked on are symbolic regression, which consists of finding an equation $y = f(x)$ given the regression of x on y in a discrete number of points. This work proposes an implementation of GE on GPU in which a specific implementation is performed for each one of the use grammars, taking advantage of the large number of multiprocessors of this type of hardware. Although this solution is more rigid and reduces the versatility, it allows us to optimize the implementation for a specific problem in terms of computing time.

In order to verify the effectiveness of this proposal, a set of tests has been carried out on SR problems commonly used in the literature. Measurements have been made on the quality of the solutions obtained and on the execution times. The results show that the execution time on GPU is reduced by 966.94% on average with respect to the CPU implementation, with an average of 0.18 seconds less per generation (Pearson correlation $= 0.6$). The quality of the obtained solutions is increased by 11.87 % on average.

The rest of the paper is organized as follows: Sect. 2, briefly introduces Grammatical Evolution and Sect. 3 explain the main features of Graphic Processing Units. In Sect. 4 we explain our approach which is tested in Sect. 5. We conclude the paper with Sect. 6.

2   Grammatical Evolution

GE [3,7] is a relatively new way of treating GP, one of the paradigms of EAs. Its main difference with traditional GP is how to decode the solutions. In traditional GPs, the chromosome encodes a solution in the form of a tree, while in GE a new level of abstraction is added, making each chromosome to code the productions that will be applied through a grammar. In other words, the decoding process is determined by the grammar, usually represented in BNF (Backus Naur Format) form [7–9].

BNF is a way for expressing context-free grammars. The BNF is a specification of a language composed by a set of derivation rules, in the form:

```
<symbol> ::= <expression>
```

Figure 1 represents an example of a grammar in BNF used for SR problems similar to the grammars (not in BNF) that we will apply in this work. Figures 2 and 3 represent the other two grammars that we embedded in the code for running our experiments and will be cited later in the text. We can describe the BNF format in the following way:

- A grammar is represented by the 4-Tuple {N, T, P, S}, being N the non-terminal set, T is the terminal set, P the production rules for the assignment of elements on N and T, and S is a start symbol which should appear in N.
- The production rules are sequences of terminals and non-terminals.
- The options within a production rule are separated by a "|" symbol.
- The decoding process starts with the Start symbol, S.
- The decoding process, when finished, give us the phenotype, which is the closed form of the expression in SR.

As we can see in Fig. 1, $S = program$, which indicates that we are looking for a program in the form of an expression for this problem. After that, we will apply the rule in the grammar for $program$. The genotype is used to map the expression by applying the module operator to the genes in the following way:

$$Choice_i = (CIV) \; MOD \; (\# \; of \; choices_i)$$

where $Choice_i$ is the choice selected for non-terminal i, CIV is the value of the gene we are decoding, MOD is the module function, and $(\# \; of \; choices_i)$ is the number of possible choices at rule for the non-terminal i. This mapping function was proposed in [10] and takes the integer value of the chromosome, computes the module function in relation to the number of the choices of a rule, and selects the choice according to that result. Given that the module function will return values from 0 to $(\# \; of \; choices_i) - 1$, the first choice will correspond to the first value, 0, the second to 1, and so on. Combining those rules and the genes in the chromosome we will reach to a mathematical expression in this grammar. Obviously, the higher the number of rules in the BNF, the higher the complexity of the process and probably, of the final expression. We will use the EA to evolve chromosomes, $i.e.$, genotypes. We refer the interested reader to [11] for a detailed example of the decoding process in GE and to [3] for a complete reference to GEs.

3 Graphic Processing Units - GPUs

GPUs are processors with a high computation power at affordable costs. Actually, desktop GPUs initially designed for 3D rendering processing are also used for scientific proposes. The scientists have also used this type of devices to accelerate their own applications, coined the term GPGPU (General-Purpose Computing on Graphics Processing Units). Due to this scientific interest, there exist

```
<program> ::= <expr>
<expr>::= <expr> <op> <expr>|<unop> <expr>|<const>| <var>
<op>    ::= + | - | * | /
<unop>      ::=  sin | cos | -
<const>     ::=  1 | 0.1 | 10.0
<var>       ::=  x
```

Fig. 1. Grammar 1 in BNF format designed for symbolic regression.

```
<program> ::= <expr>
<expr>       ::= <expr> <op> <expr> | <unop> <expr> |   <var>
<op>         ::= + | - | *
<unop>       ::=  sin | cos | exp | log
<var>        ::=  x
```

Fig. 2. Grammar 2 in BNF format designed for symbolic regression.

```
<program> ::= <expr>
<expr>       ::= <expr> <op> <expr> | <unop> <expr> | <const>|
                 <var>
<op>         ::= + | - | * | /
<unop>       ::=  sin | cos | -
<const>      ::= 1.0
<var>        ::=  x
```

Fig. 3. Grammar 3 in BNF format designed for symbolic regression.

GPUs that do not have graphical output, since their main objective is to perform calculations with high parallelism at data level. This apparently contradiction name-utility allows to take advantage of the high number of processors available in the most efficient way. GPUs are optimized for a very specific set of arithmetic operations, for which they offer a better performance than general-purpose CPUs. They were designed for the execution of graphical applications and in the past were utilized exclusively for the rapid rendering of graphical primitives with simulations of interactive 3D spaces, removing workload to the CPU. They are devoted to the calculation with floating-point values, since 3D space representation uses mathematical environments in $\mathbb{R}^3$.

The architecture of GPGPU has a complex hardware implementation with many differences from conventional general purpose processors. The GPU processor is generally assembled on an internal board with a connection to the main memory through a PCI-Express bus connector. While a few high performance cores are usually present in a CPU, the GPU paradigm is quite different and involves the inclusion of a large number arithmetic-logic units that can be seen as a vector processing unit. From the architectural point of view, a single GPU is organized in blocks of ALUs, denoted multiprocessors. Usually each multiprocessor has an important number of ALUs, a fast shared memory and its own instructions scheduler. The schedule picks a single *warp* per cycle which means that 32 *threads* replicates instruction execution on the correspondent ALU. This process can be considered as SIMD (Single Instruction Multiple Data) parallelism. Moreover, to hide high latencies on DRAM-memory, each multiprocessor runs many *threads* on fly that are processed in batches (threads are grouped into *warps*) from time to time as in fine multi-threading processor. From the memory hierarchy point of view, a GPU incorporates a read-write high latency DRAM-memory, a shared memory accessible at a single multi-processor level, a private memory accessible by a single core and an only read memory (constant memory).

CUDA (Compute Unified Device Architecture), is an NVIDIA parallel computing architecture that leverages the great power of the GPU to provide an outstanding increase in system performance [12]. CUDA includes the architecture specifications and an associated programming model. CUDA offers a simplified control of multiple threads, being able to deal with hundreds or even thousands of threads. CUDA can be consider an extension of standard C language. It follows the host-device model. The host (CPU) is in charged GPU-memory transfers and GPU execution by means of kernel invocation. Kernel defines the workload distribution on GPU-multiprocessor. In CUDA jargon, the parallelism is defined with kernel execution: the number of *CUDA-blocks* and number of *CUDA-threads*. Each *CUDA-block* is mapped into a multiprocessor and the *CUDA-threads* are grouped into *warps*. Shared memory is commonly used to share information between all *CUDA-threads* in a single *CUDA-blocks*. In this paper, we use a modern Maxwell Architecture GPU whose main features are summarized in Table 1.

4   Embedded Grammars

As we already mentioned, in GE, chromosomes are translated into solutions using grammars. When implementing this translation process on a GPU, it is necessary to take into account the particularity of CUDA and to study the parallelization of both the translation and the evaluation processes. In the implementation made in this work, the grammar is not read from an external file, which is the most used form, but is included in the code itself. To make this possible, we use a recursive implementation in C and CUDA. Although an implementation in BNF could be more readable, our contribution takes advantage of the parallelization process, both in decoding and evaluating solutions.

Hence, we opted for what we call an *Embedded Grammar*. This type of implementation has two major drawbacks: readability and modularity. Obviously, a grammar in BNF notation is much more accessible for reading than a recursive program that uses numerous global constants and memory pointers. On the other hand if we need to change the grammar we have to modify the code and recompile the project. A proposed solution for a future update is the inclusion of several files with pre-compiled grammars that offer the possibility to select the

Table 1. GTX 960 Engine Specs

Feature	Value
CUDA cores	1024
Base clock (MHz)	1127
Boost clock (MHz)	1178
Texture fill rate (GigaTexels/sec)	72
GbpsMemory clock	7.0
Standard memory config	2 GB
Memory interface	GDDR5
Memory interface width	128-bit
Memory bandwidth (GB/sec)	112
OpenGL	4.4
CUDA	Yes
Bus support	PCI express 3.0
Maximum digital resolution	5120 × 3200
Maximum VGA resolution	2048 × 1536
Maximum GPU tempurature (in C)	98 C
Graphics card power (W)	120 W

grammar depending on the problem that is facing the algorithm. This problem could also be solved by providing the grammar as a separate program that interacts with the rest of the application, so that if we need to modify the grammar, we only will need to recompile that file. However, our approach has a main characteristic that justifies its use: the code can be executed in parallel on a GPU. Figure 4 shows a portion of the code where the grammar is embedded.

In this paper we are dealing with symbolic regression problems. We deal with a set of regression points to evaluate the quality of the solutions in the population. The codification of the grammar allows us to perform the decoding and evaluation of the individuals in a concurrent way, key steps in the programming of evolutionary grammars. At each step of the recursion process, a part of both problems are thrown out and at the end of the execution of the kernel we obtain the fitness value for all individuals. Making the same number of recursive calls with different data means that the process runs in parallel as many threads as regression data the problem instance has. This allows a greater occupancy of the multiprocessors of the GPU. Thus, when a high number of regression points have to be evaluated for a single chromosome or solution, CUDA runs as many threads as regression points are in the data set, and all translations and transcripts are carried out simultaneously.

The implementation of the GPU algorithm has followed a similar scheme to the one proposed by the article *Acceleration of Grammatical Evolution Using Graphics Processing Units* [6], proposed by Pospichal et al., that includes a small

```
__device__ float expresion(int * population, int * i, float * variables, int
    currCrom, int sizeCromosome){

    if (*i >= sizeCromosome) return FLT_MAX;
    int gene= population[currCrom + (*i)] % NUMEXP; *i += 1;

    switch (gene){

    case 0: // Binary operator <OP>
            gene = population[currCrom + (*i)] % NUMOPS;
            *i += 1;
            float a = expresion(population, i, variables, currCrom,
                    sizeCromosome);
            float b = expresion(population, i, variables, currCrom,
                    sizeCromosome);

            if (a >= FLT_MAX || b >= FLT_MAX) return FLT_MAX;

            switch (gen){
            case 0:
                    return  a * b;
            case 1:
                    return a + b;
            case 2:
                    return a - b;
            case 3:
                    if (b == 0) return FLT_MAX;
                    return a / b;
            }

    case 1: //VALOR
            gene= population[currCrom + (*i)] % NUMCONST;
            *i += 1;

            switch (gen){
                    case 0:
                            return 0.1;
                    case 1:
                            return 1.0;
                    case 2:
                            return 10.0;
            }

    case  2: //VARIABLE
            gene= population[currCrom + (*i)] % NUMVAR;
            *i += 1;

            switch (gen){
            case 0:
                    return variables[0];
            case 1:
                    return variables[1];
            case 2:
                    return variables[2];
            }

    case 3: //Unary Operator
            gene= population[currCrom + (*i)] %NUMUNOPS;
            *i += 1;

            float c = expresion(population, i, variables, currCrom,
                    sizeCromosome);
            if (c >= FLT_MAX) return FLT_MAX;

            switch (gen){
                    case 0: //SIN(EXP)
                            return sinf(c);
                    case 1: //COS(EXP)
                            return cosf(c);
                    case 2:
                            return -c;
            }
    }

%/*
%       This method will receive a population of chromosomes, a set of
%       variables and an empty but allocated array. The utility of
%       this function is to decode the phenotype of the chromosomes, storing
%       the result on a variable. The variables used into the decodification
%       step are received via "variables" and the  decoded population will be
%       "population".
%*/
```

Fig. 4. An extract of the code with the grammar embedded on it.

stage for control of the CPU between some of its steps. Pospichal proposes the transfer of the entire population to main memory after each generation. In our case, it has been decided to make a much smaller transfer, containing only the best individual. The goal is to minimize the use of the PCI-Express bus, which would produce a bottleneck in the GPU-CPU data transfer. Pospichal proposes to perform only the evaluation in the GPU. However, given that our transfer through the bus is minimal we can move the execution to the GPU in order to boost the execution time. Therefore, our proposal performs an implementation of almost the whole program in the GPU. Another difference with [6] is that while in its implementation they executed as many blocks as chromosomes exist in the population, here we can perform the process of each individual in a different thread. This approach saves the context changes of blocks, which would have a computational cost, for the benefit of a context switch by threads, which are automatically switched. Nevertheless, the main difference is the use of an embedded grammar in the code, given that [6] uses the classic BNF grammar approximation.

5   Experimental Results

The experimental results are presented in Tables 4 and 5 and collect the information corresponding to the execution of three different implementations of evolutionary grammars on GPU and CPU. The three grammars are represented in Figs. 1, 2 and 3. These grammars have been used to solve 8 different univariate symbolic regression problems, whose target expressions are shown in Table 3. We have done 10 runs of each one of the instances of the problems considering all the configurations. The parameters of the algorithms are show in Table 2. Tables 4 and 5 summarize the relevant information for the analysis in 8 columns: *Gram*, specifies grammar; *Best*, best solution found; *Avg*, average value; *Worst*, worst value; *AvgTime*, average execution time; *#Gen*, number of generations in which optimal fitness is obtained; *#Opt*, number of times the overall optimum is found; and *Desv*: standard deviation of the solutions.

We use Mean Squared Error as a fitness function, computing the values of y given by the decoded solutions with the 288 points of x in the input data. Tables 4 and 5 indicate through the column *AvgTime*, that the GPU implementation is better for the 8 problems. In terms of the quality numbers we can see that GPU implementations are better for problems 1, 3 and 8, while CPU algorithms seems to be better for problems 2 and 4. Both GPU and CPU perform equal for the easiest problems 5, 6 and 7. In addition, Table 6 shows the ranks of the Friedman test for all the algorithm configurations under study. The computed Friedman p-value is 0.775, so we can not affirm that one grammar or one hardware system (CPU or GPU) is better than another. However, as the final row suggests, all the methods performs similar. This results was expected since the grammars are specially indicated for these problems and the evolutionary process is not changed with the *GPU-Embedded Grammars*.

We can extract more information from Figs. 5, 6 and 7. Figure 5 shows the number of optimal values obtained with each of the grammars (G1, G2 and G3),

Table 2. Parameters of the evolutionary algorithms.

Parameter	Value
Population size	512
Chromosome length	256 genes
Codon values	0–255
Data points	288
Generations	see table
Crossover probability	65%
Mutation probability	5%
Regeneration frequency	100 generations
Regeneration percentage	10%

Table 3. Benchmark problems and number of generations used for the test.

Problem	Expression	#Generations
1	$cos(2x)$	1000
2	$cos(x) + x + 1$ dx	15000
3	$sin(x + 2)$	1000
4	$x^2 + x - 3$	1000
5	$x^3 + (2x)^2 - x - 2$	7000
6	$(x^4 + x^3 + (2x)^2 + x$	7000
7	$x^2 + x$	1000
8	$x + 7$	1000

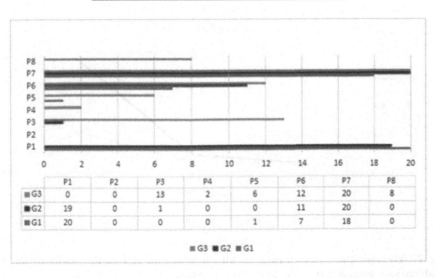

	P1	P2	P3	P4	P5	P6	P7	P8
G3	0	0	13	2	6	12	20	8
G2	19	0	1	0	0	11	20	0
G1	20	0	0	0	1	7	18	0

Fig. 5. Number of optimal values obtained with each of the grammars (G1, G2 and G3), for each of the problems (P1 to P8)

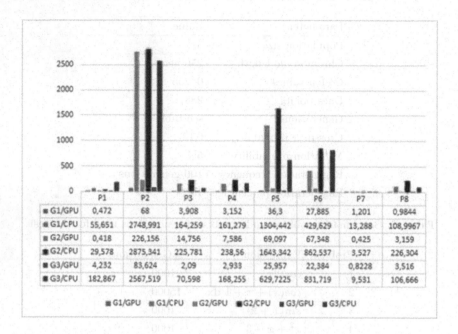

Fig. 6. Averaged execution times (in seconds) for different number of generations.

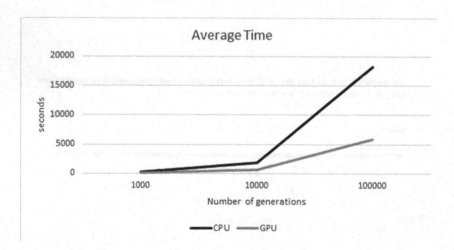

Fig. 7. Averaged time over 10 runs for all the problems (P1 to P8) and with all the combinations grammar (G1, G2 and G3) / hardware GPU or CPU).

Table 4. Experimental results for benchmarks 1 to 4.

Problem 1							
Gram	Best	Avg	Worst	AvgTime	#Gen	#Opt	Desv
GPU1	0	0	0	0.472	120.7	10	0
GPU2	0	0	0	0.418	40.4	10	0
GPU3	0.0005	0.093	0.27	4.232	1000	0	0.0842
CPU1	0	7.3E-06	0.000073	55.651	319.3	9	0.000023
CPU2	0	0.047	0.47	29.578	149.1	9	0.1486
CPU3	0.01	0.171	0.34	182.867	1000	0	0.129

Problem 2							
Gram	Best	Avg	Worst	AvgTime	#Gen	#Opt	Desv
GPU1	82.03	378.97	1524.54	68	15000	0	513.5471
GPU2	211.02	2557.6	4791.16	226.156	15000	0	1687.1364
GPU3	91.76	146.663	355.66	83.624	15000	0	76.3056
CPU1	76.33	126.105	271.19	2748.991	15000	0	55.3189
CPU2	91.77	3105.356	4416.64	2875.341	15000	0	1365.2586
CPU3	83.23	147.299	446.91	2567.519	15000	0	115.0694

Problem 3							
Gram	Best	Avg	Worst	AvgTime	#Gen	#Opt	Desv
GPU1	0.0007	0.03	0.2	3.908	1000	0	0.062
GPU2	0.05	0.198	0.26	14.756	1000	0	0.0808
GPU3	0	0.036	0.09	2.09	616.7	6	0.0464
CPU1	0.005	0.0654	0.2	164.259	1000	0	0.0554
CPU2	0	0.18	0.26	225.781	998.5	1	0.0983
CPU3	0	0.027	0.09	70.598	446	7	0.0434

Problem 4							
Gram	Best	Avg	Worst	AvgTime	#Gen	#Opt	Desv
GPU1	0.06	16.327	140.5	3.152	1000	0	43.6661
GPU2	0.82	3.583	12.64	7.586	1000	0	3.2813
GPU3	1.24	16.378	140.54	2.933	1000	0	43.6305
CPU1	0.64	161.279	3	161.279	1000	0	0.8854
CPU2	0.28	2.584	3	238.56	1000	0	0.9001
CPU3	0	1.46	3.15	168.255	922.9	2	1.2473

Table 5. Experimental results for benchmarks 5 to 8.

Problem 5							
Gram	Best	Avg	Worst	AvgTime	#Gen	#Opt	Desv
GPU1	0	36.3	890.19	36.3	6896	1	275.4861
GPU2	1.88	24.375	145.49	69.097	7000	0	44.3206
GPU3	0	237.8	237.8	25.957	6556.3	2	86.8194
CPU1	0	72.88	369	1304.442	6443.2	2	128.8588
CPU2	0.44	34.624	145.5	1643.342	7000	0	53.39
CPU3	0	289.79	1541.53	629.7225	4991.3	4	612.414
Problem 6							
Gram	Best	Avg	Worst	AvgTime	#Gen	#Opt	Desv
GPU1	0	31.195	275.04	27.885	5840.5	3	85.8272
GPU2	0	9.26	52.67	67.348	6390.6	4	16.55
GPU3	0	7.638	57.94	22.384	4886.2	5	18.1994
CPU1	0	0.137	1.37	429.629	2350.4	9	0.4332
CPU2	0	0.896	8.94	862.537	3670.7	7	2.8263
CPU3	0	6.708	54.25	831.719	4163.6	7	17.1834
Problem 7							
Gram	Best	Avg	Worst	AvgTime	#Gen	#Opt	Desv
GPU1	0	5.57	55.7	1.201	338	8	17.61
GPU2	0	0	0	0.425	35.7	10	0
GPU3	0	0	0	0.8228	280.9	10	0
CPU1	0	0	0	13.288	105.8	10	0
CPU2	0	0	0	3.527	18.6	10	0
CPU3	0	0	0	9.531	63.3	10	0
Problem 8							
Gram	Best	Avg	Worst	AvgTime	#Gen	#Opt	Desv
GPU1	0.004	6.263	2.65	0.9844	1000	0	0.894
GPU2	0.03	3.159	6.18	3.159	1000	0	2.01
GPU3	0.02	2.518	5.32	3.516	1000	0	2.3086
CPU1	0	0.8744	3	108.9967	911.9	1	1.1703
CPU2	0.69	2.51	4.73	226.304	1000	0	1.2907
CPU3	0	0.5	5	106.666	738.9	8	1.5763

Table 6. Friedman test for comparing the 6 implementations: 3 grammars on GPU and CPU.

Problem	GPU/G1	$R_{GPU/G1}$	CPU/G1	$R_{CPU/G1}$	GPU/G2	$R_{GPU/G2}$	CPU/G2	$R_{CPU/G2}$	GPU/G3	$R_{GPU/G3}$	CPU/G3	$R_{CPU/G3}$
1	0	1.5	7E-06	3	0.	1.5	0.05	4	0.1	5	0.2	6
2	378.9	4	126.1	1	2557.6	5	3105.3	6	146.6	2	147.299	3
3	0.03	2	0.06	4	0.2	6	0.2	5	0.04	3	0.027	1
4	16.3	4	161.2	6	3.5	3	2.5	2	16.3	5	1.46	1
5	36.3	3	72.9	4	24.3	1	34.6	2	237.8	5	289.79	6
6	31.195	6	0.137	1	9.26	5	0.896	2	7.638	4	6.708	3
7	5.57	6	0	3	0	3	0	3	0	3	0	3
8	6.3	6	0.9	2	3.2	5	2.5	3	2.5	4	0.5	1
Avg	59.3	4.063	45.2		324.8	3.658	393.3	3.375	51.4	3.875	55.8	
Rank	4	6	1	2	5	4	6	3	2	5	3	2

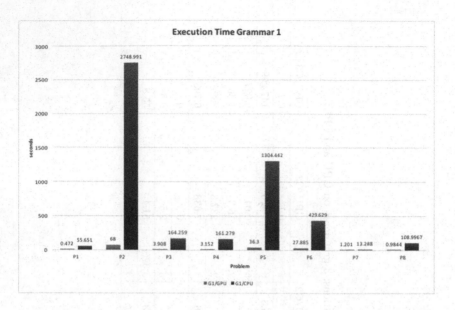

Fig. 8. GPU and CPU executions time, Grammar 1, problems P1 to P8.

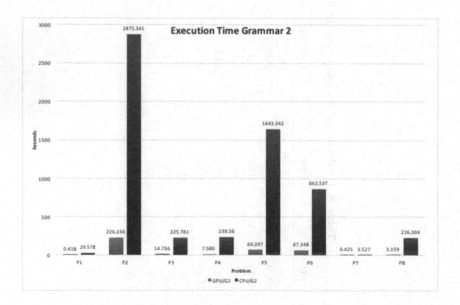

Fig. 9. GPU and CPU executions time, Grammar 2, problems P1 to P8.

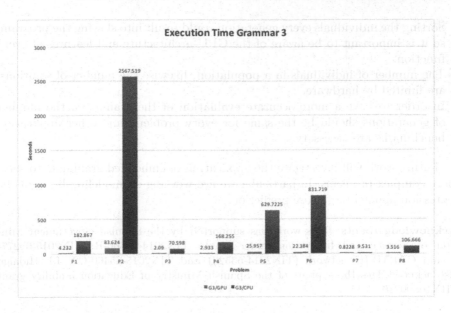

Fig. 10. GPU and CPU executions time, Grammar 3, problems P1 to P8.

for each of the problems (P1 to P8). The plot confirms what was stated in the previous paragraph. On Fig. 7 we can see averaged execution times (in seconds) for different number of generations. The GPU is more useful as the number of generations increases. Figure 6 shows the averaged time over 10 runs for all the problems (P1 to P8), with all the combinations of grammars (G1, G2 and G3) and hardware (GPU or CPU). Finally, Figs. 8, 9 and 10 compare GPU and CPU executions times for Grammar 1, 2 and 3 respectively

6 Conclusions

In this work a new proposal has been made in order to implement grammatical evolution on GPUs. The aim of this approach was to decrease the execution time on an effective way. We named the proposal as *Embedded Grammars*, since we implemented the grammar directly into the code. Although more rigid, it allows to compute the decodification in parallel with the evaluation of the individuals. A total of three different grammars over eight symbolic regression problems were tested. We showed that *GPU-Embedded Grammars* are better than CPU in terms of execution time and quality. More precisely, we can state that:

- It is possible and useful to design and develop a GE taking advantage of the massive multiparallelism of the SIMD scheme and the programming features provided by the CUDA architecture.
- With the implementation presented in this paper, a greater number of generations can be run within the same wall-clock time, increasing the differences on performance between GPU and CPU.

- Sorting the individuals every generation could result into slowing the program, so it is important to be aware of the GPU-architecture and features of every function.
- The number of individuals in a population, likewise the number of solutions, are limited by hardware.
- In order to have a more accurate evaluation of the grammars, the number of generations should be the same for every problem, and other application benchmarks are necessary.

Future work will investigate the application of embedded grammars to solve more complex problems. In particular we are working on modeling by symbolic regression applied to glucose prediction.

Acknowledgements. This work was supported by the Spanish Government Minister of Science and Innovation under grants TIN2014-54806-R, TIN2015-65277-R and CAPAP-H5 network (TIN2014-53522) and TIN2015-65460-C2. J.I. Hidalgo also acknowledges the support of the Spanish Ministry of Education mobility grant PRX16/00216.

References

1. Hidalgo, J.I., Fernndez, R., Colmenar, J.M., Cioffi, F., Risco-Martn, J.L., Gonzlez-Doncel, G.: Using evolutionary algorithms to determine the residual stress profile across welds of age-hardenable aluminum alloys. Appl. Soft Comput. **40**, 429–438 (2016)
2. Koza, J.R.: Genetic Programming. The MIT Press, Cambridge (1992)
3. O'Neill, M., Ryan, C.: Grammatical Evolution: Evolutionary Automatic Programming in an Arbitrary Language. Kluwer Academic Publishers, Dordrecht (2003)
4. Alba, E., Tomassini, M.: Parallelism and evolutionary algorithms. IEEE Trans. Evol. Computat. **6**(5), 443–462 (2002)
5. Tsutsui, S., Collet, P.: Massively Parallel Evolutionary Computation on GPGPUs. Springer, Heidelberg (2013)
6. Pospichal, P., Murphy, E., O'Neill, M., Schwarz, J., Jaros, J.: Acceleration of grammatical evolution using graphics processing units: computational intelligence on consumer games and graphics hardware. In: Proceedings of the 13th Annual Conference Companion on Genetic and Evolutionary Computation, GECCO 2011, pp. 431–438. ACM, NY (2011)
7. O'Neill, M., Ryan, C.: Grammatical evolution. IEEE Trans. Evol. Computat. **5**(4), 349–358 (2001)
8. Ryan, C., O'Neill, M., Collins, J.J.: Grammatical evolution: solving trigonometric identities. In: Proceedings of Mendel 1998: 4th International Conference on Genetic Algorithms, Optimization Problems, Fuzzy Logic, Neural Networks and Rough Sets, pp. 111–119 (1998)
9. Ryan, C., Nicolau, M., O'Neill, M.: Genetic algorithms using grammatical evolution. In: Foster, J.A., Lutton, E., Miller, J., Tettamanzi, C. (eds.) EuroGP 2002. LNCS, pp. 278–287. Springer, Heidelberg (2002). doi:10.1007/3-540-45984-7_27

10. Ryan, C., Collins, J.J., Neill, M.O.: Grammatical evolution: evolving programs for an arbitrary language. In: Banzhaf, W., Poli, R., Schoenauer, M., Fogarty, T.C. (eds.) EuroGP 1998. LNCS, vol. 1391, pp. 83–96. Springer, Heidelberg (1998). doi:10.1007/BFb0055930
11. Hidalgo, J.I., Maqueda, E., Risco-Martín, J.L., Cuesta-Infante, A., Colmenar, J.M., Nobel, J.: glucmodel: a monitoring and modeling system for chronic diseases applied to diabetes. J. Biomed. Inform. **48**, 183–192 (2014)
12. CUDA Nvidia. Programming guide (2008)

A Performance Assessment of Evolutionary Algorithms in Volunteer Computing Environments: The Importance of Entropy

Juan J. Merelo[1,2]([✉]), Paloma de las Cuevas[1,2], Pablo García-Sánchez[3], and Mario García-Valdez[4]

[1] Department of Computer Architecture and Technology,
University of Granada, Granada, Spain
{jmerelo,palomacd}@ugr.es
[2] CITIC, University of Granada, Granada, Spain
[3] Department of Computer Engineering, University of Cádiz, Cádiz, Spain
pablo.garciasanchez@uca.es
[4] Department of Graduate Studies,
Instituto Tecnológico de Tijuana, Tijuana, Mexico
{amherag,mario}@tectijuana.edu.mx

Abstract. In a volunteer distributed computing system, users run a program on their own machine to contribute to a common effort. If the program is embedded in a web page, collaboration is straightforward, but also ephemeral. In this paper, we analyze a volunteer evolutionary computing system called NodIO, by running several experiments, some of them massive. Our objective is to discover rules that encourage volunteer participation and also the interplay of these contributions with the dynamics of the algorithm itself, making it more or less efficient. We will show different measures of participation and contribution to the algorithm, as well as how different volunteer usage patterns and tweaks in the algorithm, such as restarting clients when a solution has been found, contribute to improvements and leveraging of these contributions. We will also try to find out what is the key factor in the early termination of the experiments, measuring entropy in the contributions and other large scale indicators.

1 Introduction

The World Wide Web provides not only a platform for content distribution, but also, thanks to the maturity and reliability of the HTTP protocol, an increasingly reliable and high-performance operating system for running distributed applications. Besides the protocol itself, there are two factors that contribute to this fact: the JavaScript virtual machine every browser runs [21] and the simplified standard interface for interacting with servers exemplified by the REST application interface convention [16]. Thus creating a distributed computing experiment is just a matter of making a JavaScript application interchange information with a server, by using REST. From the point of view of the programmer, this involves

© Springer International Publishing AG 2017
G. Squillero and K. Sim (Eds.): EvoApplications 2017, Part I, LNCS 10199, pp. 806–821, 2017.
DOI: 10.1007/978-3-319-55849-3_52

relatively common skills and no special libraries, since the interface is built in the browser, and a simple application that responds to those requests on the server side; both involve just a few dozens lines of code additionally to whatever business logic the application has. But, more importantly and from the point of view of the user, that application can be run by simply visiting a web page.

Using this approach for creating distributed experiments is called *volunteer*, *cycle-scavenging*, or *opportunistic* computing [25] and it dates back, in different shapes and underlying mechanisms, to the origin of the web [2]. Our interest here, however, is to use it as a resource for evolutionary computation, as our group has done for a long time [22].

In this line of research that uses volunteer computing for evolutionary algorithms, there are several pending issues. The first and maybe most important is approaching volunteer computing as a socio-technical system [27] which integrates user decisions and behavioral patterns in the system model; this includes trying to optimize the number of users in a particular experiment. The second line of research, although related to the first, is more focused on the evolutionary algorithm itself and how different design decisions will affect its performance. We have approached the first issue in our previous work [22], but in this paper our focus will be in the second aspect: we will try to design a decentralized system that, at the same time, is able to use all available resources for finding the solution of an evolutionary algorithm. This design will be done incrementally by changing client and the server and measuring its impact on the overall performance: time and evaluations needed to find the solution. Eventually, we want to find a system that, whatever the number of users available to perform the experiment, is able to maximize their contribution to the evolutionary algorithm, at the same time that the evolutionary algorithm itself makes the most of those contributions and is able to find the solution to the problem in a minimum time, with the least number of contributions.

The rest of the paper is organized as follows: Next we will briefly present the state of the art in opportunistic distributed evolutionary computation (EC). Section 3 will describe the framework and problem used in the experiments, which are publicly available under a free license. We will present the results of the different steps in the incremental design in Sect. 4, to finally wrap up with the conclusions.

2   State of the Art

Volunteer computing involves users deciding to run a program that acts as a client or as a peer in an experiment and, as such, has been deployed in many different ways from the beginning of the Internet, starting with the SETI@home framework for processing extraterrestrial signals [2], or a high-throughput queuing system such as HTCondor [8]. However, the dual facts of the introduction of JavaScript as a universal language for the browser and the browser itself as both an ubiquitous web and Internet client has made this combination the most popular for volunteer computing frameworks such as the one we are using here, and whose first version was described in [18]. Systems based on the JavaScript/browser combination emphasize the ephemerality, ease of use, and universality, while systems such as HTCondor or BOINC might be more adequate for work that require higher availability of volunteer resources, achieving this with downloadable clients which in some cases, like HTCondor, need administration access to the resources.

Several authors have already described systems using JavaScript either for unwitting [4,6,10] or volunteer [12,17] distributed evolutionary computation and it has been used ever since by several authors, including more recent efforts [7,9,15,20,24]. In fact, this last paper [20] performs an analysis of what it calls *Gray computing* doing an analysis of feasibility, cost-effectiveness, change in the user experience and architectural optimization needed, concluding that the computing power available can be vast and it that it can be cost-effective to use it.

Using a peer to peer approach, the SPACE framework [14] distributes fitness evaluations across a heterogeneous pool of cloud compute nodes and volunteer peer computers running a browser. In SPACE peers establish a bi-directional communication with the server using the `Socket.io` JavaScript library. As an experiment they provide an `ASM.js` compiled version of the RoboGen software platform, showing that JavaScript can be used in a broad spectrum of applications.

Recent works have been using crowdsourcing in order to train robots for human interaction, a representative work of this trend is that of Anetsberger and Bongard [3] in which they propose training simulated robots for the grounding of language symbols. They do this by using human observers that issue arbitrary commands to these robots via the web, providing positive or negative reinforcement in response to the robots resulting actions. For interaction, they use the Twitch video streaming platform where users can issue commands through the platform's integrated chat service. Subjects were incentivized to interact with the system by GUI features that provided participants with a sense of involvement with the simulation. This kind of systems could add additional dynamics, because users can collaborate or even compete with each other when issuing their commands.

Most of these papers focused on testing the system by itself as proofs of concepts, more than on its performance or their actual influence on the result of an evolutionary algorithm. In fact, some of them do not even work in as a distributed computing system [24], describing the expressive capabilities of JavaScript for evolutionary computation.

The proofs of concept described above do not go further than trying to find out how many users join the effort and how many the system is able to support. In fact, systems described in [17] had serious scaling issues; some of them also tried to find out how much time was needed to find the solution or, alternatively, how many users would be needed to be competitive with single-user single-computer implementations of the same algorithm. However, the latest systems try to emphasize the seamless integration of peer and volunteer computing systems [14].

This latest system offloads evaluation to browsers so the actual algorithm runs in some other place; in general, most researchers do not try to assess the performance of the algorithm itself in the precise conditions they find in a volunteer computing system, although papers such as the one by Laredo et al. [13], using models, try to find out the resulting performance when the users are changing continuously according to a Weibull distribution. In the case of Klein and Spector [10], the algorithm is actually run on the server, using the browser mainly for fitness evaluation, and thus no actual contribution to the evaluation of the evolutionary algorithm itself is made.

There is another factor that should be taken into account: since the user has control of the browser, there is a limited amount of interaction with it, namely, the fact that by reloading the webpage they can apply a kind of hypermutation, killing the current population and generating new individuals some of which will make their way to the common pool via migration. In that sense, volunteer computing is also a way of *human computation* [23], a concept that has also been applied to evolutionary algorithms [11], in this case extensively and with all operators. It is quite difficult to find out how many times this happens and what is their effect on the overall algorithm, but this only reaffirms the fact that there is a long list of issues with volunteer evolutionary computation, and that the volunteer him or herself is at the center of many of them.

In this paper we will make contributions towards the design of efficient volunteer evolutionary algorithms by studying the effect of several design decisions on performance. In the next Section we will present the general framework and the initial setup.

3   Description of the Framework

In this section we present NodIO, a distributed volunteer-based evolutionary computation system implemented in JavaScript. All parts of the framework are free and available with a free license from https://github.com/JJ/splash-volunteer.

The architecture of the NodIO system is divided in two tiers:

1. A REST (representational state transfer) server that responds to HTTP requests made by the browsers. These HTTP requests use JSON for information encoding, in this case chromosomes and related information sent by the clients, and responses returned by the server. The server has the capability to run a single experiment, storing the incoming chromosomes in a key-value cache that uses as key the chromosome string itself and is reset when the solution is found. This cache has a finite size that erases the oldest chromosomes once it has been filled to its maximum capacity.
2. A client that includes the evolutionary algorithm as JavaScript code embedded in a web page that displays the fitness and other graphs, some additional links, and information on the experiment. This code runs an evolutionary algorithm *island* that starts with a random population, then after every

100 generations, it sends the best individual back to the server (via a PUT request), and then requests a random individual back from the server (via a GET request). We have kept the number of generations between migrations fixed since it is a way of finding out how much real work every client is doing. In the version of the server used in this paper, we implemented a policy by which the combination IP-fitness chromosome could only be inserted once into the cache. That means that if a particular IP sends a fitness value of 99 into the server, it will be accepted only once. The main intention of this policy was to avoid *overlapping* of contributions, with clients still running an *old* run of the experiment contributing after a new one had started. This however did not completely avoid these contributions: if the clients of the *old* run increased their new fitness, it would still be allowed.

Algorithm 1. Algorithm for each of the clients in a web browser.

Input: *ea, period, population_size*
Output: *best*
    Initialization :
1: create a random population of *ea.population.size = population_size*
2: generation_count = 0
    EA LOOP:
3: **while** (*ea.population.best ≠ best_fitness*) **do**
4:    *ea.generation()*
5:    *generation_count + +*
6:    **if** ((*generation_count* mod *period*) == 0) **then**
7:       **GET** *random*
8:       ea.population.add(random)
9:       **PUT** ea.population.best
10:      **GET** statistics
11:      update GUI with statistics
12:    **end if**
13: **end while**
14: **return** *ea.population.best*

Figure 1 describes the general system architecture; the algorithm is described in Algorithm 1. Different JavaScript libraries, such as JQuery or `Chart.js` have been used to build the user interface elements of the framework, which should be running in http://nodio-jmerelo.rhcloud.com, a free resource hosted in the OpenShift Platform as a Service[1].

NodIO needs a fitness function to work with, in this case the classical Trap function [1] has been used. The evolutionary algorithm that uses Trap as fitness function is completely run in the browser, but the server also includes, as a configuration option, a subroutine that checks if the solution has been found. In all cases we are using 50 Traps, a problem that is difficult enough to need the

---

[1] It is not guaranteed to be running, or running the same version, when you read this, however; you can always get the sources from GitHub and set it up yourself.

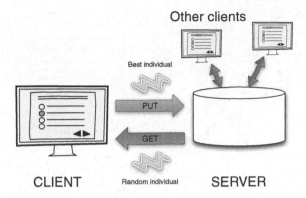

Fig. 1. Description of the NodIO system. Clients execute a JavaScript EA in the browser, which, every 100 generations, sends the best individual and receives a random one back from the server.

intervention of several users for an extended amount of minutes. For every new individual the clients send to the cache, several pieces of metadata are stored: a time stamp, the client IP, the chromosome and fitness value, the cache size in that particular moment, and also if that individual actually updated the cache or not.

All experiments are announced in the same way: we use social networks, mainly Twitter, to announce the start of a new experiment. LinkedIn, Facebook, and also private groups in Telegram and WhatsApp have been used for announcements too. We also encourage friends and followers to put their own posts for announcing it, instead of just sharing, in the way allowed by the platform, our original ones. For instance, when using Twitter, to include the URL of the experiment inside a tweet of their own, instead of just sharing it via a retweet (RT). During the running of the experiments, users are engaged, questions answered, and all kind of explanations given if requested. In general, announcements have been made in Spanish, but in some cases English was used too. This makes for a certainly unreliable experimentation framework, but it is a realistic one. The steps in the design of the evolutionary algorithm will be explained next.

4 Experiments and Results

Since the point of using a volunteer computing system is to cut costs, all experiments were set up using the OpenShift PaaS, which provides a free tier, making the whole experiment cost equal to nil. In fact, the NodIO system can be deployed to any Platform or Infrastructure as a Service system as long as it can run `node.js` and can store logs on the same place or in some other Log as a Service. Local storage can be used, but it is not a requisite and, in fact, Heroku does not allow persistent storage of files in its service. All these logs are available upon request. Processed files are available in the same repository that hosts this paper, as well as the scripts needed to process them.

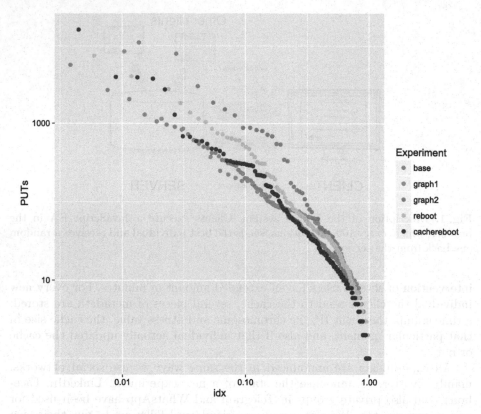

Fig. 2. Log-log plot of ranked and normalized number of contributions (PUTs) per IP.

Every run had slightly different conditions, although in some cases it was just a server reboot and a new round of announcements. Each run batch included at least 30 completions, that is, evolution until the solution was found. The number of runs was controlled by polling an URL that indicated the number of runs made in the present batch so far. Every volunteer contributed a certain number of individuals (represented by the PUT HTTP request in Fig. 1) to the server. The ranked number of contributions per unique IP is shown in Fig. 2 in a log-log scale. Besides following the usual Zipf's law found in our previous work and thus having a very similar appearance for all 5 sets, it is interesting to see how some sets have a number of contributions per IP that are slightly superior to the rest, especially so in graph2. The last two sets, reboot and cachereboot, also show a regime in the middle of the graph which shows that some users are contributing more than in other similar sets. In general, these differences in behavior are due more to the specific users that show up in these experiments than to general laws, but it should also be noted that those behaviors can be encouraged by design.

A summary of the experiments and their results is shown in Table 1. This table shows the median time needed to find the solution as well as the median

Table 1. Summary of results for the 5 sets of experiments.

Experiment	Median time (ms)	Median IPs		Median PUTs			#Runs	Unique IPs	Puts/IP
		Total	Used	Total	Used	Ratio			
base	120056.0	10	4	256.0	21.0	0.1290323	81	262	21.33333
graph1	152619.5	9	4	212.5	26.5	0.1282238	36	96	24.30000
graph2	1173561.5	6	4	761.5	22.0	0.0520509	36	73	129.04545
reboot	796214.0	9	6	646.0	67.0	0.0955121	45	168	75.88889
cachereboot	392917.0	12	12	576.0	79.0	0.1575092	55	225	43.28571

number of IPs and PUTs. In this case we distinguish between the total number of clients participating in every particular run, and the *actual* number whose contributions were accepted into the cache, which was set up to accept those only if *new* chromosomes were sent to the server in order to avoid overlaps between one run and the next. That is why, in both cases, the "Contributing" column includes a value that is less than the total number. The next column includes the total number of runs in that particular batch, finished roughly after a minimum number of 30 was reached.

The baseline, called *base* in the Table, uses the mechanism of dropping contributions from clients if they are repeated to avoid overlap. Clients still get a random chromosome from the server, so they can in fact proceed with the algorithm and even finish it. However, this was not known to the volunteer, so the fact that they were not contributing to the pool was conveyed by inserting a graph in the client that represented the size of the cache, labeled "How am I contributing". The user could then realize there was no contribution and do something about it. These sets of runs are labeled graph1 and 2. However, a stuck client could still add to the pool if it found a new optimum, so we added a mechanism for rebooting the client, that is, reloading the page, if the cache size was found to be less than 1, which indicated a run recently started. This batch of runs is labelled reboot. This size of the cache was not really noticed by some slow clients or too fast runs, so that in the last case, labeled cachecrash, clients rebooted if the cache collapsed by more than a certain length, indicating a cache that had been voided and was filling again. Our objective was twofold: to encourage engagement by the users and also to increase the involvement of every client in the common experiment, eliminating at the same time overlaps between runs.

The first thing we will have to check is whether we have effectively eliminated those overlaps. In order to do that, we will have to establish a threshold under which we can reasonably expect that the solution cannot be found. In every evolutionary algorithm it might happen, by chance, that the solution is found in just a few evaluations, but that is usually not the case. By looking at the logs in the last case we have established the minimum at 16 PUTs; in less than 1600 generations no solution to that difficult problem will be found. Let us

Table 2. Experiments with *overlapped* runs filtered out: summary of results.

Experiment	Median time (ms)	Median IPs		Median PUTs		#Runs	Puts/IP
		Total	Used	Total	Used		
base	293685	13.0	8.0	483.0	57.0	47	35.50000
graph1	768053	12.0	5.0	601.0	79.0	21	45.84615
graph2	1477969	6.0	4.0	901.0	52.0	25	149.42857
reboot	799471	9.5	6.5	656.5	67.0	44	76.48016
cachereboot	463347	12.0	12.0	638.5	80.5	52	44.25911

filter then the runs, eliminating those that used less than 1600 generations to find the solution which can reasonably be said that they did so because some browser "carried over" a chromosome from the previous run. The results are shown in Table 2. The first change is in the column #Runs, which shows that most of the runs in the initial configurations found the solution thanks to these carried over clients. However, in the last two rows, the ones that rebooted clients when they detected changes in cache, the difference is minimal. This means that one objective has been reached: if clients reboot when they detect changes in the cache that imply a new run, overlaps are almost eliminated. Going back to Table 1, we can see than the ratio of effective contributions, those that feed the cache, increases from around 13% in the first case to almost 16% in the last, reaching lows of less than 6% in some cases (graph2). This indicates that rebooting the clients has the positive effect of increasing the contribution of clients to the common pool. However, we should remark that the clients will still stop contributing if they get stuck in a particular solution, so the ratio keeps being low resulting in a slow change in the cache and a lower diversity of clients that tap that cache. At any rate, an increased number of effective PUTs will have a positive impact on the algorithm.

Table 3. Minute-wise correlation for number of participating volunteers.

Experiment	correlation
base	0.8408602
graph1	0.7346538
reboot	0.7280738
cachereboot	0.4657099

We can check this impact by looking at the column that refers to median time in Table 2 and its relation to the median number of PUTs, which reflects the number of evaluations performed by the clients. The last two rows have a low number of evaluations, around 650, which is higher than the first two, probably due to the lower volunteer supply, but better than the middle one; besides, the amount is remarkably similar. But in the last case, it takes much less time to find the solution *using the same number of evaluations*; the same situation applies if we compare `graph1` to `cachereboot`. All variables are difficult to control in this environment, but it might be due to the fact that parallelism has increased, there are more volunteers contributing at the same time. In fact, as it can be seen in the last column, the median number of contributions per user is the lowest for `cachereboot`, which needs less contributions by users to find the same solution. Besides, the last row shows that *all* users actively contribute to the cache, while in the `reboot` strategy 30% of users do not. This might be due to the fact that `reboot` only does so when cache size is less than one, indicating that this strategy is only partly successful in avoiding overlaps.

In fact, Table 3, which shows the correlation between the number of IPs from one minute to the next, presents a similar behavior for all experiments but the last one. A high correlation indicating that the number of volunteers changes slowly from one minute to the next; however, the `cachereboot` experiment correlation indicates a bigger dynamism, with volunteers joining and leaving the experiment all the time, maybe because experiments take less time and need less resources.

5   Finding the Keys to a Good Performance

In order to have enough data to perform more analysis on it, a new experiment was performed along several days with, eventually, several hundreds of persons participating on it. It was announced by several popular Twitter figures and found its way into Reddit. The number of PUTs per minute are shown in Fig. 3. Usually, sudden peaks in them are due to new announcements in social networks, usually. This is one of the problems with this kind of volunteer computing systems: they feed on the continuous influx of new users; however, this can be automatized and also encouraged, resulting, as shown, in that once enough users have participated it is sometimes easier to find new ones.

The dot color in Fig. 3 corresponds to the *ratio* or, as indicated above, the actual number of contributing PUTs, those that have not been discarded due to repeated sending by clients or (briefly) belonging to the previous instance of the experiment. It reveals that, in some cases where the amount of PUTs really increases, they are actually not contributing so much, while light dots, corresponding to a ratio close to 1, usually stay in the lowest part of the graphic.

This is interesting in the sense that it indicates that there might be something more to performance than just the number of volunteers contributing. Therefore, in this experiment we include an additional measure: user-contribution entropy, which is measured by computing the compression entropy of every user contribution for the whole experiment. This is computed converting the sequence of the number of PUTs into a string and then compressing it using `Zlib`, a standard compression library. Since the compression rate is related to the randomness of the sequence, a higher compression rate will correspond to an experiment with a low entropy, while a lower compression rate will indicate that there has been

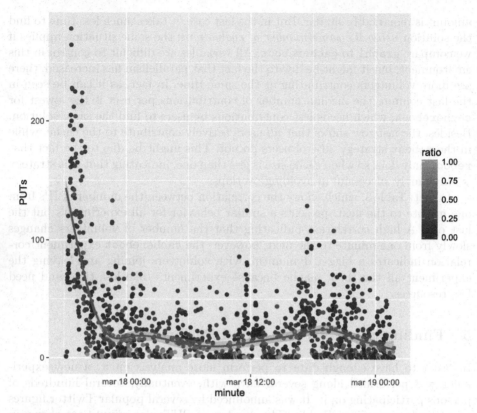

Fig. 3. Plotting the contributions per minute in a new and massive experiment, as well as the real number as color. Lighter color indicates that all PUTs contributed new individuals to the experiment, darker color few to none. (Color figure online)

a certain amount of unexpected changes during the experiment. Although less popular than Jenssen-Shannon entropy, this way of measuring it is widely used [19] in case where we want to compute the entropy of sequences of events, such as arrhythmias [5]. Unlike Jenssen-Shannon entropy, the range of the compression entropy will vary between 0 (lower, or worse compression rate) and 1 (no compression).

The graph that plots the time to solution of every instance of the experiment vs. entropy is shown in Fig. 4. There is a clear trend towards experiments with lower entropy taking more time and experiments with higher entropy taking more time, which indeed can be statistically fit to a linear model. This dependence on entropy is much clearer than the assumed dependence on the number of users, which is represented in the graph by dot color, and even the number of PUTs or contributions, which is represented by dot size. You can see a clearly blue and big dot, meaning more than 40 different IPs participating and around 1500 PUTs in the high end of the graph, showing that it took the longest to find the solution. On the other hand, clearly red and small dots are on the lowest end of

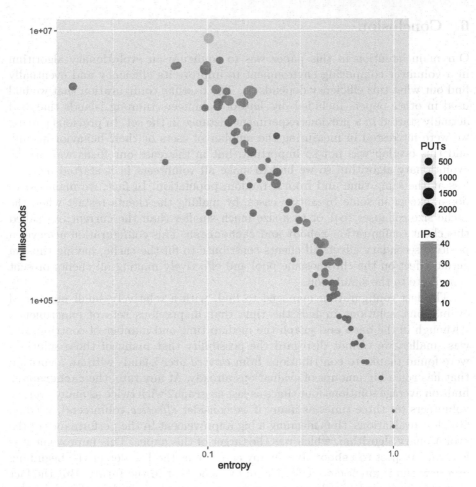

Fig. 4. Entropy of the user contribution vs. time to solution in the volunteer computing experiment. The fit to a linear model is significant.

the graph, indicating that it took a short time to find the solution as long as the entropy is high.

This is a very significant result which has many implications on volunteer computing experiment design, and is clearly something that has to do more with the fact that we are dealing with an evolutionary algorithm where creating and maintaining diversity is an important part of its exploration component, than with the fact that it is a volunteer computing experiment. This is why we claim that volunteer computing setups are, in some cases, a better option than synchronous and distributed implementations with a similar computing capability, because if diversity is kept high, the performance achieved can be much better than in similar synchronous and parallel experiments.

6   Conclusion

Our main intention in this paper was to configure an evolutionary algorithm in a volunteer computing environment to improve its efficiency and eventually find out what this efficiency depends on. The baseline configuration that we had used in other papers included *overlaps* or volunteers running islands that had actually started in a previous experiment instance in the set. In previous papers, we were interested in measuring the number of users or their behavior in bulk and this overlap was not so important, but in this case our focus was on the evolutionary algorithm so we had to make all volunteers in it started more or less at the same time and from a random population. In fact, we managed to do so, except in some byzantine cases, by making the clients restart when the cache size collapses to 1 or to a size much smaller than the current; we called this client configuration `reboot` and `cachecrash`. This configuration achieves a positive secondary effect: all clients contribute to fill the cache, having thus an actual effect on the chromosome pool and effectively making all clients present contribute to the simulation.

The last configuration managed to find, with a relatively small number of evaluations, solutions in half the time that in previous sets of experiments. Although in the `base` and `graph` the median time and number of contributions was smaller, we cannot disregard the possibility that many of those solutions were found thanks to contributions from *carried over* islands with an algorithm that has run a big amount of evaluations already. At any rate, the `cachereboot` finds on average solutions four times as fast as `graph2` with twice as many average volunteers (or three times as many if we consider *effective* volunteers), needing 50% less evaluations, thus meaning a big improvement in the performance of the evolutionary algorithm, which was the target of this paper. This improvement is less with respect to `reboot`, but in any case the method to detect the beginning of a new run is much more effective and will be kept in the future. But the fact that this happened was due to the *entropy* as proved in the last section of this paper.

We have also proved in this paper, through an experiment with a massive number of users, that in fact the single factor predicting the time needed to reach the solution is the compression entropy, meaning that it is not so much the raw number of users, but the fact that they contribute fit individuals to the pool in such a way that it increases its diversity early in the experiment; that is, it is much better a few users with different types of computers and browsers contributing at the same time that more users with exactly the same computer and browser contributing more or less synchronously. This also implies that it is obviously better to manage as many users as possible to contribute at the same time and at the beginning of the experiment, which might not really be possible; however, the reboot strategy used in the latest versions really contributed to this early boost in diversity. It is interesting also to note that this boost in performance due to client contribution diversity is due to the fact that we are running an evolutionary algorithm, where diversity is an essential component.

These last result has also got implications for architecture design. For instance, it might be interesting to combine clients in the browser with other kind of clients that contribute mainly to diversity. In fact, early experiments with other type and more difficult problem point in this direction. Besides, user-interaction strategies attracting users to experiment instances at the very beginning, like announcing it in social media, might help too to achieve higher performance.

This is one of the changes we intend to explore in the future, which holds many challenges, such as gathering more users and improving the efficiency of the algorithm run in an asynchronous way by the users. In the first case, it will be interesting to make it more *social* by comparing local performance to other's contributions, and showing it in a graph or being able to tweet advances or the fact that the solution has been found. Anything that keeps the users running the system and attracts new users will contribute to the speed of finding the solution. And the algorithm will have to be improved, mainly by making the population more diverse. Right now there is a rigid policy of contribution to the pool: send the best individual, but this could be relaxed. Some other policies could also be tested, as well as running heterogeneous algorithms in the same way that was done in [26]. Diversity, as in any other evolutionary algorithm, seems to be the key, but there are many ways of approaching it.

All these avenues of experimentation will be done openly following the Open Science policy of our group, which, in fact, contributes to establish trust and security between us and volunteers and is an essential feature of the system. That is why this paper, as well as the data and processing scripts, are published with a free license in GitHub at https://git.io/gecco-es-15.

Acknowledgments. This work has been supported in part by TIN2014-56494-C4-3-P (Spanish Ministry of Economy and Competitivity). We are also grateful to @otisdriftwood for his help gathering users for the new experiments.

References

1. Ackley, D.H.: A Connectionist Machine for Genetic Hillclimbing. Kluwer Academic Publishers, Norwell (1987)
2. Anderson, D.P., Cobb, J., Korpela, E., Lebofsky, M., Werthimer, D.: SETI@home: an experiment in public-resource computing. Commun. ACM **45**(11), 56–61 (2002)
3. Anetsberger, J., Bongard, J.: Robots can ground crowd-proposed symbols by forming theories of group mind. In: Proceedings Alife XV (2016)
4. Apolónia, N., Ferreira, P., Veiga, L.: Enhancing online communities with cycle-sharing for social networks. In: Abraham, A., Hassanien, A.-E. (eds.) Computational Social Networks, pp. 161–195. Springer, Heidelberg (2012)
5. Baumert, M., Baier, V., Haueisen, J., Wessel, N., Meyerfeldt, U., Schirdewan, A., Voss, A., et al.: Forecasting of life threatening arrhythmias using the compression entropy of heart rate. Methods Inf. Med. (Methodik der Information in der Medizin) **43**(2), 202 (2004)
6. Boldrin, F., Taddia, C., Mazzini, G.: Distributed computing through web browser. In: 2007 IEEE 66th Vehicular Technology Conference, VTC-2007 Fall, pp. 2020–2024. IEEE (2007)

7. Duda, J., Dłubacz, W.: Distributed evolutionary computing system based on web browsers with JavaScript. In: Manninen, P., Öster, P. (eds.) PARA 2012. LNCS, vol. 7782, pp. 183–191. Springer, Heidelberg (2013). doi:10.1007/978-3-642-36803-5_13

8. Fajardo, E.M., Dost, J.M., Holzman, B., Tannenbaum, T., Letts, J., Tiradani, A., Bockelman, B., Frey, J., Mason, D.: How much higher can htcondor fly? J. Phys. Conf. Ser. **664**(6), 062014 (2015). http://stacks.iop.org/1742-6596/664/i=6/a=062014

9. Gonzalez, D.L., de Vega, F.F., Trujillo, L., Olague, G., de la O, F.C., Cardenas, M., Araujo, L., Castillo, P.A., Sharman, K.: Increasing GP computing power via volunteer computing. CoRR abs/0801.1210 (2008)

10. Klein, J., Spector, L.: Unwitting distributed genetic programming via asynchronous JavaScript and XML. In: Proceedings of the 9th Annual Conference on Genetic and Evolutionary Computation, GECCO 2007, pp. 1628–1635. ACM, New York (2007)

11. Kosorukoff, A.: Human based genetic algorithm. In: 2001 IEEE International Conference on Systems, Man, and Cybernetics, vol. 5, pp. 3464–3469 (2001)

12. Langdon, W.B.: Pfeiffer - a distributed open-ended evolutionary system. In: Edmonds, B., Gilbert, N., Gustafson, S., Hales, D., Krasnogor, N. (eds.) AISB 2005: Proceedings of the Joint Symposium on Socially Inspired Computing (METAS 2005), 12–15 April 2005, pp. 7–13. University of Hertfordshire, Hatfield, UK (2005). http://www.cs.ucl.ac.uk/staff/W.Langdon/ftp/papers/wbl_metas2005.pdf. sSAISB 2005 Convention

13. Laredo, J.L.J., Castillo, P.A., Mora, A.M., Merelo, J.J., Fernandes, C.: Resilience to churn of a peer-to-peer evolutionary algorithm. Int. J. High Perform. Syst. Architect. **1**(4), 260–268 (2008)

14. Leclerc, G., Auerbach, J.E., Iacca, G., Floreano, D.: The seamless peer and cloud evolution framework. In: Proceedings of the 2016 on Genetic and Evolutionary Computation Conference, pp. 821–828. ACM (2016)

15. Martınez, G.J., Val, L.: Capataz: A framework for distributing algorithms via the World Wide Web. CLEI Electron. J. **18**(2), 1 (2015)

16. Masse, M.: REST API Design Rulebook. O'Reilly Media, Inc., Sebastopol (2011)

17. Merelo, J.J., García, A.M., Laredo, J.L.J., Lupión, J., Tricas, F.: Browser-based distributed evolutionary computation: performance and scaling behavior. In: Proceedings of the 2007 GECCO Conference Companion on Genetic and Evolutionary Computation, GECCO 2007, pp. 2851–2858. ACM, New York (2007)

18. Merelo-Guervós, J.J., García-Sánchez, P.: Designing and modeling a browser-based distributed evolutionary computation system. In: Laredo, J.L.J., Silva, S., Esparcia-Alcázar, A.I. (eds.) Genetic and Evolutionary Computation Conference, GECCO 2015, Madrid, Spain, July 11–15, 2015, Companion Material Proceedings, pp. 1117–1124. ACM (2015). http://doi.acm.org/10.1145/2739482.2768465

19. Ornstein, D.S., Weiss, B.: Entropy and data compression schemes. IEEE Trans. Inf. Theory **39**(1), 78–83 (1993)

20. Pan, Y., White, J., Sun, Y., Gray, J.: Gray computing: an analysis of computing with background javascript tasks. In: Proceedings of the 37th International Conference on Software Engineering, vol. 1, pp. 167–177. IEEE Press (2015)

21. Paulson, L.D.: Building rich web applications with ajax. Computer **38**(10), 14–17 (2005)

22. Peñalver, J.G., Merelo, J.J.: Optimizing web page layout using an annealed genetic algorithm as client-side script. In: Eiben, A.E., Bäck, T., Schoenauer, M., Schwefel, H.-P. (eds.) PPSN 1998. LNCS, vol. 1498, pp. 1018–1027. Springer, Heidelberg (1998). doi:10.1007/BFb0056943

23. Quinn, A.J., Bederson, B.B.: Human computation: a survey and taxonomy of a growing field. In: Proceedings of the SIGCHI Conference on Human Factors in Computing Systems, pp. 1403–1412. ACM (2011)

24. Rivas, V.M., Guervós, J.J.M., López, G.R., Arenas-García, M., Mora, A.M.: An object-oriented library in javascript to build modular and flexible cross-platform evolutionary algorithms. In: Esparcia-Alcázar, A.I., Mora, A.M. (eds.) EvoApplications 2014. LNCS, vol. 8602, pp. 853–862. Springer, Heidelberg (2014). doi:10.1007/978-3-662-45523-4_69

25. Sarmenta, L.F.: Volunteer computing. Ph.D. thesis, Massachusetts Institute of Technology (2001)

26. Valdez, M.G., Trujillo, L., Merelo-Guervós, J.J., de Vega, F.F., Olague, G.: The evospace model for pool-based evolutionary algorithms. J. Grid Comput. **13**(3), 329–349 (2015). http://dx.doi.org/10.1007/s10723-014-9319-2

27. Vespignani, A., et al.: Predicting the behavior of techno-social systems. Science **325**(5939), 425 (2009)

EvoROBOT

EvoROBOT

Overcoming Initial Convergence in Multi-objective Evolution of Robot Control and Morphology Using a Two-Phase Approach

Tønnes F. Nygaard[(✉)], Eivind Samuelsen, and Kyrre Glette

Department of Informatics, University of Oslo, Oslo, Norway
{tonnesfn,eivinsam,kyrrehg}@ifi.uio.no

Abstract. Co-evolution of robot morphologies and control systems is a new and interesting approach for robotic design. However, the increased size and ruggedness of the search space becomes a challenge, often leading to early convergence with sub-optimal morphology-controller combinations. Further, mutations in the robot morphologies tend to cause large perturbations in the search, effectively changing the environment, from the controller's perspective. In this paper, we present a two-stage approach to tackle the early convergence in morphology-controller co-evolution. In the first phase, we allow free evolution of morphologies and controllers simultaneously, while in the second phase we re-evolve the controllers while locking the morphology. The feasibility of the approach is demonstrated in physics simulations, and later verified on three different real-world instances of the robot morphologies. The results demonstrate that by introducing the two-phase approach, the search produces solutions which outperform the single co-evolutionary run by over 10%.

1   Introduction

Evolutionary robotics (ER) is an approach for automatic design and adaptation of robot bodies and control systems, through the use of evolutionary algorithms (EAs). This has the potential for improving future robot design processes, as well as improving the resilience and adaptability of robots [1,2].

While most work in evolutionary robotics concerns the optimization of robotic control systems, there has also been an effort, mainly through the use of software simulations, into simultaneously optimizing robotic bodies and control systems [3]. While examples of such systems are still limited, it is believed that optimizing both aspects simultaneously could lead to interesting and robust behaviors, even when limited control and actuation is available. Most examples of the potential of co-evolution of morphologies and controllers are found within the field of virtual creatures, where a physical counterpart of the simulated system may not be available [4,5]. However, there have also been some examples of evolution in simulation leading to instantiation of working physical robots [3,6,7], and recently even simulationless evolution of robotic morphologies [8].

© Springer International Publishing AG 2017
G. Squillero and K. Sim (Eds.): EvoApplications 2017, Part I, LNCS 10199, pp. 825–836, 2017.
DOI: 10.1007/978-3-319-55849-3_53

Optimizing robot morphologies together with control systems is a difficult task, and we have only so far seen relatively simple results, even though significant amounts of computational resources have been allocated [3]. One of the reasons for this difficulty is the increased dimensionality of the search space that comes with the freedom to design the body, in addition to the control system. In effect this requires a much larger amount of exploration to find the desired quality of solutions. However, another aspect of the difficulty is that the co-evolution of morphology and control also leads to a much more difficult search – the search landscape is much more rugged, and small changes in the morphology can easily offset the performance of a previously found good body-controller combination. An interesting view on this, based on the theory of embodied cognition, can be found in [9]. Here, a morphological change is seen as scrambling of the interface between the controller and its physical interface to the environment.

With similar observations in our own work on co-evolving morphologies and control systems [10], in this paper we demonstrate a simple approach to reduce this effect. We demonstrate that it is possible to improve the solution quality after convergence of a morphology-controller evolutionary run by freezing the morphology, and allowing a second phase of continued evolution on the control system alone. This approach leads to significant improvements in the final solutions with a modest number of further evaluations, and indicates that phases of optimizing only the control system can be beneficial. Our method can easily be combined with other approaches, like novelty search [11] or various methods of encouraging behavioral diversity [12]. We demonstrate the approach for a realistic robot design, and validate the method by producing and evaluating two of the evolved robot designs in the real world. The performances of the evolved designs are compared to a hand-designed robot within the same framework.

2   Background

The perhaps most well-known example of co-evolution of morphology and control is Sims' work on virtual creatures [4]. Here, virtual creatures were evolved in a rigid body physics simulation, displaying diverse and natural behaviors. While these virtual creatures were not targeted for instantiation in the physical world, the setting of virtual creatures has been popular for exploring various aspects of co-evolving morphologies and control. Examples include: evolution of soft bodied creatures [13], evolution of artificial muscle-based creatures [5], diversity-enhanced morphology evolution [14], and investigations of the relationships between environment and body complexity [15].

While results from simulations can give a number of insights, being able to automatically design physical robot morphologies is inarguably even more interesting, and could eventually lead to useful techniques in robot engineering. However, going from the already difficult task of designing virtual creatures to designing physically instantiable robots is challenging. The encoding of the solutions need to take into account physically realizable body parts and actuators, and a sufficiently accurate simulation of these. Further, actually producing the robots can be a relatively cumbersome and time-consuming task, and usually only a handful of the results from simulation can therefore be evaluated as real-world robots.

Finally, the combined morphology-controller robots are prone to reality gap issues, potentially even more so than when control systems only are evolved. In particular, it seems to often be the case that some morphology-controller combinations work relatively as expected from simulation, while other combinations suffer from a large reality gap [3,6,7].

Experiments on evolving morphologies and controllers employ a variety of different building blocks, from convenient physics simulation primitives in the case of virtual creatures [4,13], to building blocks which are convenient to prototype and integrate with actuators in the case of physical instantiation [3,6,7,16]. In these cases, focus has been more on the evolutionary design process, and the resulting physical robots are mostly meant to validate the approach.

However, there have also been some attempts at evolutionary morphology design with an engineering perspective in mind, range from rather free-form structures, which are given large design freedom, to structures inspired by more "realistic" robot shapes, which are intended to solve a task or carry a payload. These include the design of a variety of shapes for robotic manipulators [17], or parametric legged robots [18]. It should be noted that while these works worked on realistic robot shapes, they have so far only been validated in simulation. There are also some good examples of parametric design optimizations for bio-inspired robot morphologies, such as the optimization of the caudal fin dimensions for a robotic fish [19], or the optimization of leg parameters for an octopus-inspired robot [20].

It has been pointed out that co-evolution of morphologies and controllers is difficult [9]. Methods which have been explored to tackle this challenge includes generative encodings [6,10,13], morphological diversity-enhanced algorithms [10, 14,20], and more complex environments [15].

3   Implementation

3.1   The Robot

Six legged robots with three degrees of freedom for each leg were used for all experiments. The legs are arranged in a spider configuration, and vacant slots for tools or two more legs were added to the front of the robot for versatility and future experiments.

A parametric blueprint was defined from which each robot was defined. The choice of parameters was limited by the computational complexity of the increasing solution space, while the ambition of a more general robot system provides a contrast with the demand for more dimensions. The final compromise assumes symmetry along the movement direction of the robot to allow a sufficiently complex robot with fewer parameters. The lengths of the two outer leg segments can be set, with minimum lengths, given by the size of the servos used, and the maximum given by the manufacturing equipment available. Six legs with two

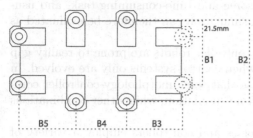

Fig. 1. Drawing of the base, showing all parameters.

Table 1. The parameters used in morphology.

Parameter	#	Lower	Upper
Tibia length	3	80 mm	254 mm
Femur length	3	80 mm	254 mm
B1	1	52.65 m	94 mm
B2	1	83 mm	284 mm
B3	1	61.5 mm	254 mm
B4	1	52.65 mm	254 mm
B5	1	61.5 m	254 mm

configurable segment lengths each yields 12 parameters, but assuming symmetry reduces this to 6. The placement of each servo on the base plate was also made parameterizable, as seen in Fig. 1. A total of 11 parameters defines the complete morphology of the robot, with details given in Table 1.

The physical instantiation of each robot is built using plastic parts printed in ABS by a Fortus 250mc 3d printer. The parts were designed for high strength and low weight, and FEM simulation was used extensively in the design process. Rapid prototyping principles were used to reduce risk of design errors and encourage good project progression, and the first manually designed robot can be seen in Fig. 2. We chose Dynamixel AX-18A smart servos as actuators for their ease of use and relatively high power, and implemented the whole control scheme on a windows based computer.

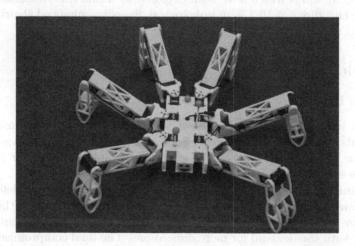

Fig. 2. Image of the printed and assembled hand designed robot. The face was added for recruitment events, to make the robot seem less frightening to children.

3.2   Control System

We implemented a simple control system that serves as an extension of a popular wave controller [21]. The traditional controller contains a collection of amplitude and a phase parameters that together with the source wave signal generates commands for all actuators. We also needed an offset value for each servo, but through initial tests found the resulting controller to be hard to limit and evolve. We therefore introduced two new equations that uses v as minimum angle and w as maximum angle, as seen in Eq. 1. An offset ϕ is added to provide the full controller equation, given in Eq. 2. The time t is given in seconds. Symmetry was also used in the control system, and each pair of servos was thus defined by its minimum movement, maximum movement, and phase offset. This results in a total of 36 parameters to define the movement of the robot, as seen in Table 2.

$$\alpha = \frac{(v - w)}{2}$$
$$\beta = \frac{(v + w)}{2} \tag{1}$$

$$\chi(t, v, w, \phi) = \frac{(v - w)}{2} \times tanh(4 \times sin(2 \times \pi \times (t + \phi))) + \frac{(v + w)}{2} \tag{2}$$

Table 2. Table showing search space for morphology at the top and control at the bottom. Coxa movement$_1$ is moving along the side of the robot, while Coxa movement$_2$ is moving behind the robot.

Coxa movement$_1$	4	−0.81	1.64
Coxa movement$_2$	2	−1.64	1.64
Femur movement	6	−2.49	2.49
Tibia movement	6	−2.49	2.49
Phases	18	−π	π

3.3   Evaluation

The main goal of each individual is a fast walking gait, but the weight of individuals was also used in the evolutionary algorithm to ensure a higher degree of variation in the resulting population, and to aid in the evolutionary search by providing two partially conflicting objectives [22].

A custom in-house developed simulation framework was used to rapidly test a range of different individuals. The framework acts as an interface to Nvidia PhysX library, and generates a simplified robot morphology based on the morphological parameters. It uses the same controller code as used in hardware tests. The evolutionary framework ParadisEO [ref] is used for running the evolutionary algorithm.

Real world evaluations were done in the University of Oslo's motion capture lab. It features an OptiTrack motion capture system to efficiently estimate the position and pose of the robot, using infrared cameras and the light from reflective spheres mounted on the robot. Each gait is evaluated for four seconds. A wiring harness was built to ensure that the robot did not trip in its own power and command wires, and turning gaits were evolved and used to ensure the robot stays within the area covered by the cameras at all times. We achieved a fully autonomous testing system that needs no human intervention during testing or evolutionary experiments, which allowed for prolonged tests in hardware.

3.4 Evolutionary Setup

We chose NSGA-II [23] as the evolutionary algorithm for our experiments. 32 bit floating point numbers were used to represent all parameters in the genome.

We used non-uniform mutation using the normal distribution with standard deviations 0.025 and 0.01 for control and morphology mutation respectively. Random reset mutation was used with a per-gene probability of 0.02. Tests with several different crossover operators did not yield significant advantages, so these were not used.

4   Experiments and Results

4.1   Experiments

The main co-evolutionary runs in simulation were done using 1024 generations of 256 individuals. A total of 20 runs were done, to reduce statistical anomalies. Two morphologies were then selected from the results, and were, together with the hand designed robot, selected for further evolution. Control systems for these three robots were then evolved with three new groups of runs, using the same evolutionary parameters as before. Morphology was locked, and the controllers were all reset to random values at the start of the new runs. A smaller number of evolutionary runs were then conducted on each morphology to generate turning gaits needed for continuous automated tests in hardware without human intervention.

The best performing individual from each of the three control-exclusive evolutionary runs were 3d printed and built according to their evolved morphology. The performance was then verified in hardware by running the gait on the physical platform in the motion capture lab, and movement was recorded and compared to performance in simulation. Each individual gait speed was recorded over 4 s, and two sets of 128 evaluations were done for each individual. The two sets were done at different times with other tests in between, to reduce the effect of noise in the test setup.

4.2   Results

Figure 3 shows a typical development of fitness over the run time for an EA. We can see from the relatively low increase during the last generations that the algorithm is close to convergence. We also see a fairly large difference between the global best distance and the average best distance of the 20 evolutionary runs.

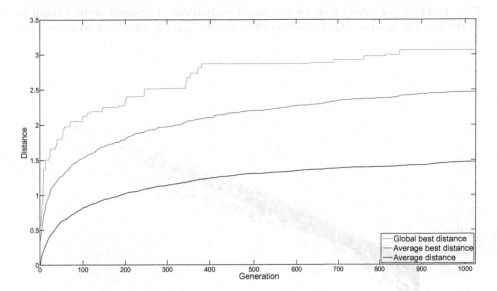

Fig. 3. The distance travelled for morphology runs. Highest fitness across all runs is shown in green, while the blue line shows the average of the maximum fitness for all runs. Average distance of all last generation individuals is seen in red. (Color figure online)

Two robots were selected from the runs, one smaller and one larger than the hand designed robot. The smaller evolved robot had a 6% lower body weight (not including servos), while the larger robot had a 2% higher weight. The robots can be seen in Fig. 4

Table 3 shows the improvement of the additional control-exclusive phase, compared to the single co-evolutionary run. We see that the two robots with evolved morphologies gets a considerable improvement at 15.5% and 11.7%. The manually designed robot only achieves a 3.2% increase over the best performing individual from the co-evolutionary run.

Figure 5 shows the results of the co-evolutionary runs, with the Pareto front marked in red. The results from the evolution of control is seen in green, which outperforms the co-evolutionary runs significantly. As in Table 3, we also here see that the manually designed robot, in the middle green line, does not show the same improvement over the Pareto front as the other two (Fig. 6).

Fig. 4. The three robots used for real world evaluations. The small evolved robot is to the left, the hand designed robot is in the middle, and the large evolved robot is to the right.

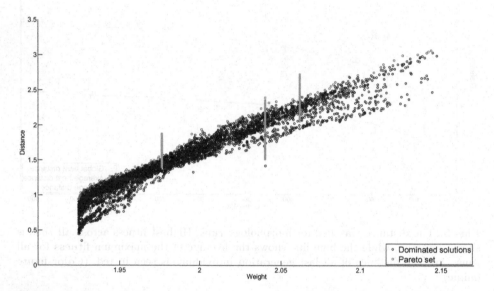

Fig. 5. The Pareto front of the final morphology runs, compared to the three groups of evolutionary runs for the robot control systems. (Color figure online)

Table 3. The performance of the 1st phase (co-evolutionary run), 2nd phase (control-exclusive evolutionary run) and the percentage increase when compared to the Pareto front. A 1st phase result is missing from the manually designed robot since this morphology is not picked from the Pareto front of the co-evolutionary run. The improvement is compared to the highest performing robot of comparable weight.

Robot	1st phase result	2nd phase result	Improvement
Manually designed	-	0.299 m/s	3.2%*
Small evolved robot	0.203 m/s	0.234 m/s	15.5%
Large evolved robot	0.304 m/s	0.339 m/s	11.7%

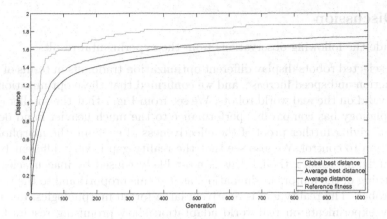

Fig. 6. The evolution of control for the small evolved robot. The original top fitness is marked in purple, and is surpassed already at generation 126. (Color figure online)

The performance of the robots tested in the real world can be seen in Fig. 7. We see that the evolved gait for the manually designed robot does not outperform the manually designed gait, though the variance in measured speed is greater. We see that the speed of the smaller evolved robot is slightly lower than the manually designed robot, and that the large evolved robot outperforms both. This is consistent with the simulation results. The original fitness values in the simulation is seen in green, and shows a fairly large reality gap between simulation and real world.

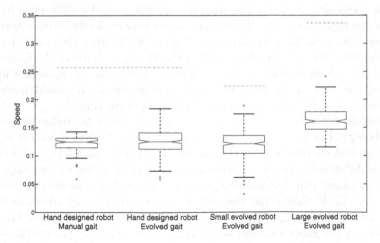

Fig. 7. Box plot of the speeds from the motion capture of evolved gaits on all robots. The green dashed line indicates the speed of the robot in simulation. (Color figure online)

5   Discussion

We made the following observations from the experimental results:

- The selected robots display different optimization trade-offs in terms of weight reduction and speed increase, and we confirmed that these optimizations were still valid on the real world robots. We see from Fig. 7 that the smaller evolved morphology has comparable performance to the much heavier hand designed robot, giving further proof of the effectiveness of evolving the morphology in addition to control. We also see that the reality gap is very different between the different robots, though this is most likely caused by inaccuracies in the modeling of the motors in simulation, as it seems proportional to the weight of the robot. The reality gap is relatively large for all morphologies, but preliminary experiments on real-world adaptation show promising results towards reducing the performance loss.
- We see from Table 3 and Fig. 5 that the hand designed robot performs worse than the two evolved robots when compared to the Pareto front of the co-evolutionary run. This is due to the evolutionary algorithm finding better morphologies than the hand designed version, and the comparison of the hand designed robot with an evolved controller to an arbitrary co-evolved robot with similar weight only yields a slight improvement.
- We see from Fig. 3 that the evolutionary algorithm has most likely converged on local optima after 1024 generations, and we do not expect considerable jumps in fitness if we were to run this algorithm for another 1024 generations. The two stage evolution we propose adds a second run of controller only optimization, and there are mainly two features of this second run that could explain the increase in the quality of the solutions found: A reduced search space due to the frozen morphology genes, and a difference in fitness landscape ruggedness. Smaller search spaces may typically require fewer evaluations before convergence, but do not necessarily affect the ability to escape local optima. We therefore believe that the changed shape of the fitness landscape may be an important factor here, in line with the thoughts in [9] of locking the controller's interface to the environment. It would however be necessary to do further experiments to fully confirm this.
- The second evolutionary run works in a smaller search space due to the locked morphology, but another aspect of this approach is that it also starts with new, random control systems. We originally did not expect this step to make a large difference, since we are using random reset mutation throughout the co-evolutionary run, but early experiments showed significant improvements. This most likely shows that the ability to surpass the original convergence is both due to the changes in landscape, and partial reset of genes. The action of resetting the genomes could be viewed as spreading out the initial solutions over the entirety of the now morphologically frozen search landscape, and may thus lead to better exploration towards optimal solutions, as compared to a less diversified population of already converged control genes.
- While it may not be required to do a full evolutionary run in the second phase, the experiments demonstrate that there is room for adaptation and

performance increase after the morphology has been frozen, which warrants further explorations into different types of controller optimizations combined with the co-evolutionary search for morphology and control.

6 Conclusion and Future Work

In this paper, we investigated using a two-phase evolution method to exceed the initial convergence found in the single co-evolutionary case. We saw that locking morphology and doing a re-evolution of control on two different morphologies showed continued improvement of between 10% and 15%, which was unlikely to be found by extending the original co-evolutionary run. Tests in hardware showed that the gaits and morphologies found worked also in the real world.

It would be interesting to further investigate the inner workings of why we are able to exceed the initial fitness found, and if this could be implemented as an operator within a single evolutionary run. Perhaps using either some sort of random mutation operator to emulate the reset of controllers between runs, or an operator that locks the morphology for some number of generations, might show some improvement over traditional co-evolutionary techniques. Expanding on this two-phase evolutionary method by using many alternating phases might show an even higher ability to escape local minima than we found here, and might allow continued evolution on not only the controller, but the morphology as well. It would also be natural to consider lifetime learning schemes, i.e. allowing the controller to adapt to the morphology before the fitness value is recorded. We already have some promising results from using such schemes for fixed morphologies [24]. In any case, these approaches could also be combined with other methods for preventing premature convergence, such as diversity-enhancing search methods [14].

References

1. Bongard, J.C.: Evolutionary robotics. Commun. ACM **56**(8), 74–83 (2013)
2. Doncieux, S., Bredeche, N., Mouret, J.B., Eiben, A.E.G.G.: Evolutionary robotics: what, why, and where to. Front. Robot. AI **2**, 4 (2015)
3. Lipson, H., Pollack, J.B.: Automatic design and manufacture of robotic lifeforms. Nature **406**(6799), 974–978 (2000)
4. Sims, K.: Evolving virtual creatures. In: Proceedings of the 21st Annual Conference on Computer Graphics and Interactive Techniques, pp. 15–22. ACM (1994)
5. Lessin, D., Risi, S.: Soft-body muscles for evolved virtual creatures: the next step on a bio-mimetic path to meaningful morphological complexity. In: European Conference on Artificial Life, pp. 761–762 (2015)
6. Hornby, G.S., Lipson, H., Pollack, J.B.: Generative representations for the automated design of modular physical robots. IEEE Trans. Robot. Autom. **19**(4), 703–719 (2003)
7. Samuelsen, E., Glette, K.: Real-world reproduction of evolved robot morphologies: automated categorization and evaluation. In: Mora, A.M., Squillero, G. (eds.) EvoApplications 2015. LNCS, vol. 9028, pp. 771–782. Springer, Heidelberg (2015). doi:10.1007/978-3-319-16549-3_62

8. Brodbeck, L., Hauser, S., Iida, F.: Morphological evolution of physical robots through model-free phenotype development. PLoS ONE **10**(6), 1–17 (2015)
9. Cheney, N., Bongard, J., Sunspiral, V., Lipson, H.: On the difficulty of co-optimizing morphology and control in evolved virtual creatures. In: Proceedings of the Artificial Life Conference 2016 (ALIFE XV), pp. 226–234. MIT Press (2016)
10. Samuelsen, E., Glette, K.: Some distance measures for morphological diversification in generative evolutionary robotics. In: GECCO 2014 - Proceedings of the 2014 Genetic and Evolutionary Computation Conference, pp. 721–728 (2014)
11. Lehman, J., Stanley, K.O.: Abandoning objectives: evolution through the search for novelty alone. Evol. Comput. **19**(2), 189–223 (2011)
12. Mouret, J.B., Doncieux, S.: Encouraging behavioral diversity in evolutionary robotics: an empirical study. Evol. Comput. **20**(1), 91–133 (2012)
13. Cheney, N., MacCurdy, R., Clune, J., Lipson, H.: Unshackling evolution: evolving soft robots with multiple materials and a powerful generative encoding. In: Proceedings of the 15th Annual Conference on Genetic and Evolutionary Computation, pp. 167–174. ACM (2013)
14. Lehman, J., Stanley, K.O.: Evolving a diversity of virtual creatures through novelty search and local competition. In: Proceedings of the 13th Annual Conference on Genetic and Evolutionary Computation, pp. 211–218. ACM (2011)
15. Auerbach, J.E., Bongard, J.C.: Environmental influence on the evolution of morphological complexity in machines. PLoS Comput. Biol. **10**(1), e1003399 (2014)
16. Lund, H.H.: Co-evolving control and morphology with LEGO robots. In: Hara, F., Pfeifer, R. (eds.) Morpho-functional Machines: The New Species, pp. 59–79. Springer, Heidelberg (2003)
17. Leger, C.: Automated synthesis and optimization of robot configurations: an evolutionary approach. Ph.D. thesis, Carnegie Mellon University (1999)
18. Passault, G., Rouxel, Q., Fabre, R., N'Guyen, S., Ly, O.: Optimizing morphology and locomotion on a corpus of parametric legged robots. In: Lepora, N., Mura, A., Mangan, M., Verschure, P., Desmulliez, M., Prescott, T.J.J. (eds.) Living Machines 2016. LNCS (LNAI), vol. 9793, pp. 227–238. Springer, Heidelberg (2016). doi:10.1007/978-3-319-42417-0_21
19. Clark, A.J., Moore, J.M., Wang, J., Tan, X., McKinley, P.K.: Evolutionary design and experimental validation of a flexible caudal fin for robotic fish. Artif. Life **13**, 325–332 (2012)
20. Corucci, F., Calisti, M., Laschi, C.: Novelty-based evolutionary design of morphing underwater robots. In: Proceedings of Genetic and Evolutionary Computation Conference, pp. 145–152 (2015)
21. Koos, S., Cully, A., Mouret, J.B.: Fast damage recovery in robotics with the T-resilience algorithm. Int. J. Robot. Res. **32**(14), 1700–1723 (2013)
22. Deb, K., Srinivasan, A.: Innovization: discovery of innovative design principles through multiobjective evolutionary optimization. In: Knowles, J., Corne, D., Deb, K., Chair, D. (eds.) Multiobjective Problem Solving from Nature. Natural Computing Series, pp. 243–262. Springer, Heidelberg (2008)
23. Deb, K., Pratap, A., Agarwal, S., Meyarivan, T.: A fast and elitist multiobjective genetic algorithm: NSGA-II. Trans. Evol. Comput. **6**(2), 182–197 (2002)
24. Ruud, E.L., Samuelsen, E., Glette, K.: Memetic robot control evolution and adaption to reality. In: Proceedings of ICES: 2016 IEEE International Conference on Evolvable Systems (2016)

Evolutionary Adaptation to Social Information Use Without Learning

James M. Borg$^{(\boxtimes)}$ and Alastair Channon

School of Computing and Mathematics, Keele University, Keele, UK
{j.borg,a.d.channon}@keele.ac.uk

Abstract. Social information can provide information about the presence, state and intentions of other agents; therefore it follows that the use of social information may be of some adaptive benefit. As with all information, social information must be interpretable and relatively accurate given the situation in which it is derived. In both nature and robotics, agents learn which social information is relevant and under which circumstances it may be relied upon to provide useful information about the current environmental state. However, it is not clear to what extent social information alone is beneficial when decoupled from a within-lifetime learning process, leaving evolution to determine whether social information provides any long term adaptive benefits. In this work we assess this question of the adaptive value of social information when it is not accompanied by a within-lifetime learning process. The aim here is to begin to understand when social information, here expressed as a form of public information, is adaptive; the rationale being that any social information that is adaptive without learning will be a good base to allow the learning processes associated with social information to evolve and develop later. Here we show, using grounded neuroevolutionary artificial life simulations incorporating simulated agents, that social information can in certain circumstances provide an adaptive advantage to agents, and that social information that more accurately indicates success confers more reliable information to agents leading to improved success over less reliable sources of social information.

Keywords: Social information · Public information · Evolutionary adaptation · Neuroevolution · Artificial life

1 Social Information, Learning and Evolution

Social information can broadly be thought of as information derived from the behaviours, actions, cues or signals of other agents [1]. As social information necessarily involves the direct or indirect broadcasting of information in to the public domain, it is sometimes known as (or conflated with) public information [2]. Here we assess whether the use of social information in populations of simulated neuroevolutionary agents is adaptive when decoupled from within-lifetime learning processes. Within-lifetime learning processes confer significant adaptive

© Springer International Publishing AG 2017
G. Squillero and K. Sim (Eds.): EvoApplications 2017, Part I, LNCS 10199, pp. 837–852, 2017.
DOI: 10.1007/978-3-319-55849-3_54

advantages to agents employing them, be it through the development of a set of robust and flexible behaviours, the rapid adaptation to new environments or circumstances, the quick incorporation of new information, or the guiding of the evolutionary process itself [3]. The adaptive advantages of learning are particularly potent when social information is incorporated alongside innovation and individual learning [4], resulting in social learning and potentially even cultural evolution [5]. However, as beneficial as within-lifetime social learning processes are, it is unclear to what extent social or public information has an adaptive benefit when decoupled from these learning processes and evolution is left to determine the value of social information. Is the incorporation of social information alone enough to gain an adaptive advantage over non-social agents? Or are learning processes necessary to allow social information to confer any benefits? These are the questions that we address in this paper.

Social learning is seen widely in nature [6] in a range of species as diverse as humans and nine-spined stickleback fish [7]. The mechanisms and processes that underpin social learning are themselves broad, ranging from teaching, imitation and emulation to stimulus enhancement and exposure [8], with any of these mechanisms potentially leading to the formation of traditions and cultures [5,9]. However, within each social learning category there is some dependence on who information is obtained from, be it a teacher or which agent is unintentionally (or intentionally) exposing an individual to new information. As social learning is necessarily conformist, a poor social information model may result in the discovery and propagation of sub-optimal behaviours [10]. Despite the potential pitfalls of over-conformist social learning, including sub-optimal behaviour development [10] and even population collapse [11,12], social learning, and therefore social information transfer, can be of great benefit to agents, thus explaining why even simple forms of social information transfer are seen so widely in nature [8,13,14] and have been shown to produce complex behaviours that are easily attributed to more complex social learning mechanisms like imitation [15]. At the heart of the problem being addressed here are three core arguments. (1) Information is a fitness enhancing resource [16], even when information suppression is seen to be adaptive [17] or when information is encoded or interpreted incorrectly [16] - any new information about the world enables populations of agents to better adapt to the world they are in, even if this means disregarding or suppressing information. (2) Incremental evolution is not a process of unguided random variations, but a process that itself can adapt in a way that is analogous to the kind of learning seen in cognitive organism [18], leading to complex and robust adaptive traits in nature, autonomous robots [19] and simulated agents [20] in the same way that learning can lead to complex and adaptive behaviours (though on a different time scale). (3) Inadvertently expressed public information and simple mechanisms of social information transfer can lead to behaviours that are sufficiently complex to enable cultural evolutionary processes [5,21]. These three core arguments give us good reason to believe that social information without within-lifetime learning processes should still be adaptive, and therefore lead to evolution adopting the use of social information to the benefit of social agents over non-social agents. Though we must still be mindful that social information may be at odds with personal beliefs [21] or lead to population-level conformism to sub-optimal behaviours [10], thus leading to a trade-off between the accommodation of social information and the evolution of robust evolved behaviours.

This leads us to the hypothesis that agents making use of social information should outperform non-social agents: any additional information, that is not just noise, that provides more information about the environment should lead agents to an improved "performance" in the environment over agents without access to such information. However, social information may only be useful when it accurately indicates success or indirectly leads to success, and therefore may provide little or no concrete benefit in complicated or less predictable environments - in these more challenging environments learning may be necessary to allow temporarily useful social information to be quickly adopted and then rejected when it is no longer relevant. This hypothesis will be tested by modelling populations of agents who have no social information available to them and populations of agents with various forms of social information available to them. Each social information strategy will be tested against the non-social strategy, starting initially with the most basic strategy available: presence, with the null hypothesis in each case being that the social population does not show an improved ability to solve the task at hand compared to non-social agents. The social information strategies used here are: presence, action, health and age. Presence social information simply enables agents to detect the presence of other agents (non-social agents are essentially blind to other agents); action enables agents to see what other agents are currently doing; health enables agents to see the current energy or battery state of others; and age information enables agents to see how long others have lived for.

2   EnVar and Environmental Set-Up

The task world used here is known as EnVar. EnVar is a bounded (non-toroidal) 2D environment containing a variety of consumable resources known as plants. Plants are recognised by agents simply as an RGB value. Plants are divided into a number of species, each with a base RGB value and a radius in RGB space. Plants are generated within these RGB regions and identified as belonging to the nearest species according to euclidean distance in RGB space. Each plant species is assigned an energy value, which is transferred to agents if the plant of that species is consumed; energy values may be positive or negative. Notionally the EnVar world is broken up in to cells, though here each cell represents a pixel and therefore the world can be considered to be continuous. Plants in the world take up a number of cells, forming a block, with each block only being able to be eaten a certain number of times before being exhausted (here set to be 200 eating events). Once a plant block has been exhausted it is no longer consumable and therefore removed from the world to be replaced by a new block from a random plant species somewhere else in the world - this maintains a constant number of food blocks in the world at any time. Agents are permitted to share space with a plant resource but cannot overlap with each other, thus removing the possibility of agents piling up on top of one another on valuable food resources. In this work EnVar is set up to create a 700 × 700 pixel sized cell world, containing five hundred 10 × 10 pixel blocks of plants. In order to test our hypothesis we test populations of social and no social agents in a set of increasingly difficult environments. Environmental difficulty is dictated by the ratio of positive food resources to negative food resources. The simplest world used here has an equal (1:1) ratio of positive food species to negative food species. Tests get progressively harder by increasing the number of negative food species, whilst maintaining only one positive food species, resulting in the most difficult world used here having a 1:9 ratio of positive food species to negative food species. As each plant species has a equal chance of appearing in the world, and covers approximately the same portion of RGB space, agents in the most difficult environment are nine times more likely to experience a negative plant resources than a positive plant resource. In the results section below environment 1 relates to a 1:1 ratio environment, with environment 9 relating to a 1:9 ratio environment. For all tests here negative food species come with an energy value $E_{neg} = -10.0$, with positive food species contributing an energy value of $E_{pos} = 1.0$ when consumed. This provides a strong evolutionary pressure to avoid eating negative food species.

3   Neuroevolutionary Model

Agents in the EnVar simulation world are grounded 2D simulated agents, controlled by a hybrid neural network architecture known as the *Shunting Model*[1]. The shunting model uses two interacting neural networks to determine agent behaviours, here represented as a discrete set of agent actions. The two interacting networks are known as the *Decision Network* and the *Shunting Network*. The decision network is simply a feed-forward neural network comprising of an input layer, one hidden layer and an output layer. Outputs from the decision network are used to produce a locally-connected, topologically-organised network of neurons known as the shunting network, which simply places and organises agent preferences for environmental features and states in such a way to allow the agent to hill climb in a shunting space (known as the activity landscape) that directly maps on to their immediate neighbourhood. The shunting network weights are fixed for all agents, whereas the decision network is genetically encoded and is subject to change via evolution (See footnote 1).

3.1   The Shunting Network

The shunting network is a locally-connected, topologically-organised network of neurons that was originally used for collision free motion planning in robots [22] and has been subsequently applied in a number of 2D and 3D artificial life models

---

[1] For a detailed overview of the Shunting Model architecture please see [22–24].

[4,10,23,24]. Here the shunting network's topology is simply superimposed on to the environment, with each cell in the network topology directly relating to a pixel within an agent's visual field. Using the shunting equation (see Eq. 1) values for each cell (which can be interpreted as representing an environmental feature or state, and are initially set by the Iota output I obtained from the decision network) are propagated across the neurons/cells of the network, producing an activity landscape with peaks and valleys representing desirable and undesirable features in the environment. The result is a landscape which allows the agent to follow a route determined by the higher Iota values while avoiding undesirable valleys. A mock-up example of an activity landscape with a snapshot of the visual field it represents can been seen in Fig. 1.

$$\frac{dx_i}{dt} = -Ax_i + \sum_{j \in N_i} w_{ij} [x_j]^+ + I_i \tag{1}$$

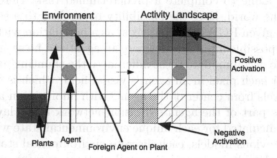

Fig. 1. Mock-up transition from agent visual field to shunting network activity landscape: The left-hand grid shows the agent's visual field with two plant objects and one other agent occupying the same space as a plant. The right-hand grid shows an example activity landscape for the visual field. The agent determines that an agent on a plant is an interesting feature and therefore assigns it a strong positive Iota value (I), whereas the purple plant is seen negatively and is therefore assigned a strong negative Iota value. These Iota values propagate over the activity landscape using Eqs. 1 and 2. The central agent then chooses to move within its immediate Moore neighbourhood to the cell with highest activity value.

In Eq. 1 each node in the shunting network corresponds to one pixel within an agent's visual field; x_i is the activation of neuron i; A is the passive decay rate; N_i in the receptive field of i; w_{ij} is the connection strength from neuron j to i, specified to be set by a monotonically decreasing function of the Euclidean distance between cells i and j; the function $[x]^+$ is $max(0, x)$; and I_i is the external input to neuron i (known as the Iota value). The shunting network is advantageous as it exhibits computational efficiency by not explicitly searching over all possible paths. In line with the work of Stanton and Channon [24], we use a simplified, stable solution for Eq. 1 as seen in Eq. 2. Here constant $x_i^{new} = x_i$ for all i. The maximum Iota value is $maxI = 15$, with the resulting value for

x_i^{new} also being capped at a minimum Iota value $minI = -15$. This stops Iota values growing out of control, whilst providing a large enough maximum value (and a small enough minimum value) to ensure activity propagation across the network. In order to allow propagation to occur within a time-step, the shunting equation must be run a number of times, we take this number of iterations to be equal to the diameter of the visual field.

$$x_i^{new} = min\left(\frac{1}{8}\sum_{j\epsilon N_i}[x_j]^+ + I_i, maxI\right) \qquad (2)$$

The shunting model implemented here differs in a number of significant ways from previous Artificial Life implementations [4,10,23,24]. In these previous implementations agents see their entire environment, have a set number of discrete environmental features and states to set Iota values for, and are in the environment alone to complete a predetermined task. Here agents have a limited view of the world, have the possibility of needing to a set an Iota value for a plant of any given RGB value, and exist as a population within the environment (leading to possible input states where an agent can be seen on a particular plant). In order to accommodate these differences the shunting model here is run independently for each pixel in an agent's visual field, which is set here to have a radius of 30 pixels from center of the agent, with information about that pixel being included as part of the agent's decision network input layer. In this way an Iota value is calculated for each unique environmental state within an agent's visual field (in previous models, each discrete environmental state was included as an output, with only an agent's internal state or current cell's state being accommodated in the input layer of the decision network). This change does not change the resulting behaviour of the shunting model or activity landscape, just the way in which information is passed to the shunting network from the decision network. In order to minimise the amount of processing time required to populate and create the activity landscape, Iota values are only collected for unique states experienced by an agent - for a state to be unique it must be a newly experienced set of decision network inputs (discussed below). To further optimise processing time, an agent will only produce an activity landscape if its outputs determine that it should move in the current time step; agents that are not moving do not need an activity landscape.

3.2   The Decision Network, Neuroevolution and Reproduction

Evolution in the model is applied only to the decision network. The decision network here is a feed-forward neural network comprised of seven standard input nodes, and an additional social input node in social information tests, eight hidden units, and two output nodes, resulting in 112–128 weights. Each network layer is fully connected, with floating point weights in the range $[-1:1]$ being directly encoded from an agent's genotype. A standard sigmoid activation function is used at each hidden and output node, though outputs processed for deriving agent actions are then scaled to be within the range [0:1] and the Iota output is scaled to be within the range [minI:maxI]. As the agent is expected to produce an Iota value to feed in to the shunting network for each unique environmental feature or state within its visual field, inputs into the decision network must accommodate both the internal state of the agent, the state of their current environment, and the state of the environmental feature they are assessing; this leads to there being two sets of input nodes. The first set of input nodes are simply plant RGB inputs - if the agent is viewing empty space these inputs are set to −1, else they are set to be the normalised RGB of the plant being viewed. Following these inputs are a series of generic inputs, which are dependent on the agent's internal state and the current environmental state. These inputs are the agent's current battery level in the normalised range [0:1], a moving average of the agent's battery level over the previous 100 time steps, the agent's current external environmental state and a moving average environmental state, which are both set to be +1 and do not change in the tests presented here (the model is set-up to accommodate external environmental change which is not used here). In social information tests agents have an additional input based on the agent they of viewing.

The genotype, which is essentially an array of weights, is subjected to both mutation and crossover should a reproduction event take place. The crossover mechanism used here is single point crossover, with per locus mutation occurring with probability $p_{mut} = 1/L$, where L is the length of the genotype. Mutation is achieved by way of Gaussian random noise, with a value taken from a normal distribution with $\mu = 0, \sigma = 0.01$ being either subtracted or added to the floating point value at the loci to be mutated. All weight values are bounded in the range [−1:1]. Reproduction events take place only in response to a death event. Agents can die if they run out of energy, or if they are in the lowest 10% of agents ranked by energy at the end of an epoch. The first method for removing agents from the population ensures that agents cannot remain in the population with no energy, the second method ensures space is made for new agents to be created even if the population as a whole is successful at maintaining above zero energy levels, thus maintaining a selection pressure for task improvement. Both methods of death are not directly related to task ability as it is possible for a good agent to be unlucky and never, or rarely, experience a positive food resource whereas less able agents may have the fortune to be born near an abundance of food resources or be born relatively close to the end of an epoch. This method of reproduction maintains a constant population size of 200 agents. The new agent, or child, created to replace the removed agent is the progeny of two agents, one of whom is selected in a tournament, the other of which is selected randomly from the remaining population. The tournament selection mechanism applied here takes two agent from the population, compares their current energy levels, and selects the agent with the higher energy level as a parent. Like in nature this isn't a perfect measure of fitness as it is possible the agent is young and therefore has not yet had time to loose significant amounts of energy, or the agent could have simply been lucky or unlucky with available food sources. However, in general agents with more effective behaviours will on average find themselves with a better energy levels than agents with less effective behaviours, thus driving evolution toward behaviours that are more suited to the task or environment at hand. The second parent is selected randomly to ensure the population doesn't become dominated by the progeny of a small sub-set of the population, thus maintaining a level of exploration in the genotypic search space. New agents are placed in the world within the visual field of one of their parents.

3.3   Agent Actions and Action Energy Costs

The agents in the model have a set of simple, discrete, actions available to them, through the output layer of their decision networks: wait, eat or move. The decision network has two outputs, an Iota output to be fed into the shunting network and an eat/wait output. The agent first considers its current input state at its current position - if the agent produces an Iota value above the threshold $\theta_a = 0.5$ it indicates the agent if happy with it's current state and position and therefore does not move (an activity landscape is therefore not calculated as it not needed). The agent's eat/wait output is then considered; if the output produces a value above the threshold $\theta_b = 0.5$ the agent attempts to eat whatever may be at its current position; agents are welcome to try and eat at locations where no plant is present, but no benefit for this action is conferred, and the eat action is considered to be an unsuccessful eating attempt rather than a wait action. If an agent decided to eat at a location containing a plant, the plant's energy is transferred to the agent, this does not necessarily lead to the exhaustion of the plant resource, as plants are considered as a mass. The Iota output is in the range $[-1:1]$, which is then scaled to be within the range $[minI:maxI]$ for use in the shunting network, whereas the eat/wait output is limited to the range $[0:1]$. If the eat/wait output gives an output below the expected threshold the agent simply waits at its current location. Waiting and eating both reduce an agents energy by 0.1 energy units (though eating may result in a net energy gain), with moving using up 0.2 energy units per time step. Agents will only move if their Iota output for their current location is below threshold θ_a, in this case an activity landscape is created based on the Iota outputs for all visible environmental features. Agents are born with, and are able to achieve, a maximum energy level of 100 units. As epochs here constitute 1000 time steps, an agent would be able to survive for a maximum of one epoch, or one thousand time steps by remaining inactive. In order to avoid moving agents moving around in circles, or moving backwards and forwards, in neutral space (where there is no activity gradient from the activity landscape) consecutive neutral move actions maintain the same direction of travel with probability $p_{dir} = 0.9$.

Measurements are taken to determine whether an eat event was successful or unsuccessful. Any eat action that does not result in a non-negative energy providing food source being consumed is considered to be unsuccessful, so only eating non-energy reducing plants is a successful eating action. In order to measure a population of agents' success in a given environment, the difference between successful and unsuccessful eating actions is measured. This difference measure is useful as it is possible for agents to spend an equal amount of time eating successfully and unsuccessfully, which would demonstrate a strong performance on measure of successful eating, but a weak performance on a measure of unsuccessful eating - the difference instead demonstrates a neutral performance, so a population that spends very little time eating, but all of that time eating successfully (so a picky eating strategy) would be a better performing population than a locust like population that eats everything in sight.

3.4   Social Information Strategies

Populations of agents using social information differs only very slightly from non-social populations; social information populations have an additional input unit for social information, thus non-social agents are rendered blind to other agents in the world. The social information strategies explored here, including the no social strategy are discussed below:

NO SOCIAL: No input node is available to the agent to enable social information to be used by the agent's decision network. Agents proceed with no information about other agents.

PRESENCE: The social information input node receives an input of +1 if another agent if present within the visual field. No other information about the agent being viewed is used. This strategy is not dissimilar to the Inadvertent Information strategy used by agents in the work by Mitri et al. [17], though the agents explored in the work presented here do not have a choice about whether they express social information or not (this is the case for all social information strategies presented here).

ACTION: An input representing the current action state of the agent being viewed. The wait action is input as a value of 0, eat is input as 0.5 and move is represented as 1.

HEALTH: The current energy levels of the agent being viewed are normalised to be within the range [0:1] and input to the viewing agent's decision network.

AGE: The age (in time steps) of agent being viewed is normalised using a hyperbolic tangent function of the logarithm of the age, which is then normalised to be within the range [0:1]. See formula (3) where a represents agent age in time steps.

$$input_a = (\tanh(\log(a)) + 1)/2 \tag{3}$$

4   Results and Discussion

Forty populations of each social information strategy (including no social) were tested on each environment $(1 \rightarrow 9)$. Each population was permitted to evolve in the environment for 100 epochs of 1000 time steps. Reproduction and death events occurred both within and at epoch, meaning all populations were a mix of young and older agents at all stages of evaluation, with agents having no maximum age limit. Population data was accumulated for each epoch, and collected at the end of each epoch. As we are primarily interested here in the final test performance achieved by a population, not the pathway toward this achievement, average metrics were taken for each population, for each environment, for the last 25 epochs of a test, by which point performance had stabilised across measures. The results presented here are the median values of the 40 populations' average last 25 epochs of data - as this data was rarely normally distributed the medians were considered to be of more use than means. In order to derive the statistical significance between population data for each social information strategy a Mann-Whitney U test was used, with p values being derived from the resulting Z-scores. Figure 2 presents Z-score values on an inverted secondary y-axis, with p-value being represented by highlighting over Z-score data points. In order to test our hypothesis, that populations of agents making use of social information should outperform non-social agents, we measure the difference between how often agents successfully and unsuccessfully apply their eat actions, thus allowing us to measure the effectiveness of the eating behaviour within populations. Only comparisons for each social information strategy against the no social strategy are undertaken to see if any statistically significant differences arise. We go on to further analyse a wider array of metrics, including successful and unsuccessful eating actions in isolation, agent turnover, and average agent age.

4.1   Eat Action Performance

In Fig. 2 we can see the difference between successful and unsuccessful eating actions for each social information strategy compared to results for non-social populations. Looking first at populations with no social information (black line on all graphs in Fig. 2) we see that the median difference crosses zero, and therefore indicates the eat action is being applied unsuccessfully more often than successfully, at environment 3 (a 1:3 positive to negative food ratio). All social information strategies manage to maintain the eat action in favour of successful eating until a more difficult environment - this is most notable for both the Health and Age social information strategies where eat actions do not begin to favour unsuccessful eating until environment 5, with the Health strategy recrossing zero briefly, and the Age strategy maintaining an almost neutral profile for all environments after environment 5. This suggests there is a benefit to social information in that social information may allow populations to maintain successful behaviours in more challenging and difficult environments. However, if we look more closely at the resulting Z-scores and p-values we see that both the Presence and Action strategies rarely demonstrate a significantly better difference in eat actions over populations of no social agents, and even when significant differences are seen they are with relatively weak and therefore lead us to the conclusion that we cannot say with any certainty that either the Presence or Action social information strategy provides a significant improvement over having no social information at all. Despite the poor performance seen for all strategies in later environments, all strategies were capable of enabling at least one population to achieve a positive eat profile in all environments. It is also worth noting the inconsistent results observed with regard to the No Social strategy in environments 7 and 8. Despite the median result fluctuating in a way that suggest environment 8 was less challenging than environment 7, there was no statistically significant difference between the distribution of results for these environments.

Despite Presence and Action social information being of dubious value, it does seem that both Health and Age social information provide a more convincing benefit. We can see in Fig. 2(c) that populations using social information about the health of other agents demonstrate a significantly better difference in eating actions until environment 7, this performance difference is most noticeable in less difficult environments (environments and 1 and 2) where we see a p value < 0.01. Populations using social information about age (as seen in Fig. 2(d)) also demonstrate a significantly better difference in eating action in less difficult environments, though the statistical significance over environments is less consistent. However, the two most significant Z-scores seen relate to no social information vs. age social information on environments 1 and 2, which suggest that social information about age is particularly useful in these less difficult, but still challenging environments. From this data we can begin to see the potential advantages of certain types of social information.

4.2   Social Information Performance in Less Difficult Environments

In Fig. 2 we see that environment 1, where there is a 1:1 ratio of positive to negative plant resources, gives rise to a significant difference in eating performance when social information populations are compared to populations with no access to social information, with this result being extended to environment 2 (a 1:2 ratio) for both Health and Age social information populations. This suggests a particular benefit to using social information in less difficult environments. It is worth noting here that whilst environment 1 and 2 are less difficult than later environments used here, they are still themselves reasonably challenging given that we could have tested in environments with positive plant resources in abundance. Having a 1:1 or 1:2 ratio of positive to negative plant resources provides a reasonable challenge, so much so that in environment 3 we see that non-social populations, relying on evolution alone and having no access to social information, now begin to struggle at the task. Figure 3 shows a wider range of performance metrics for environment 1, including the breakdown of successful and unsuccessful eating actions in isolation. Here we see that the success of social information populations is as a result of both higher eat success rates and lower eat failure rates, though it is interesting to note that Age, Presence and Action social information populations are capable of demonstrating very low levels of eat success, even when compared to No Social populations, when the

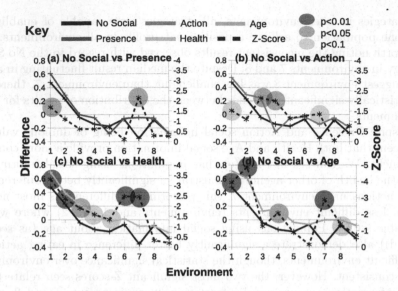

Fig. 2. Difference between successful and unsuccessful eat actions: Graphs showing the difference in % of actions that qualified as successful eating actions and % of actions that qualified as unsuccessful eating actions in each environment, for each social information strategy compared against no social information. All graphs show the Z-score from an Mann-Whitney U test on the secondary y axis, with highlighting included to indicate statistical significance. Each data point represents the median of the average results for forty populations.

full data range is considered. The main driving force behind the success of social populations, especially Health and Age, seems to be consistently low eat fail rates across populations - the upper quartile ranges for both of these strategies not exceeding 0.02 (2% of actions). This suggests that social information is often being used to help agents avoid or not consume negative plant resources. Age and Health information may be particularly useful for this purpose as it would allow agents to avoid or ignore young or unhealthy agents whilst developing a preference for healthy and older agents. Whilst Presence or Action information may also be useful for the purposes of discrimination (move towards areas of high agent presence, or follow moving agents for example), they are both potentially riskier sources of information compared to Health or Age which both provide information about agent success. Figure 4, which shows performance metrics for environment 2, also shows that for Age social information this ability to maintain consistently low rates of unsuccessful eating alongside a strong eating success performance is maintained in slightly harder environments. We can also see that for unsuccessful eating actions, the upper quartile range for social information strategies is comparable to the median for no social populations.

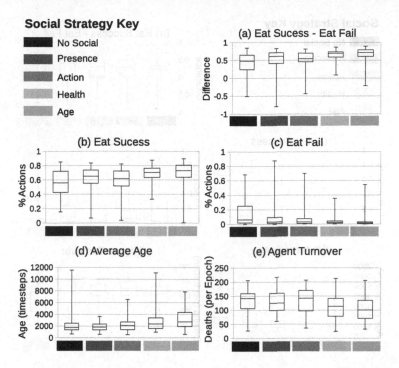

Fig. 3. Environment 1 box plots: Box plots for the eat action and other population metrics, including a breakdown of successful and unsuccessful eating actions, average agent age, and agent turnover, in environment 1.

Alongside information about eating, both Figs. 3 and 4 also give information on average agent age and agent turnover. For both environments 1 and 2 we see both Age and Health social information enabling populations to accomplish a high average agent age with an accompanying reduction in agent turnover (fewer agents dying within an epoch due to running out of energy), though the median agent turnover for Health social information is comparable to the no social tests. Both Presence and Action populations fail to distinguish themselves from No Social populations, suggesting the improvements in eating performance seen most notably in environment 1 do not necessarily translate directly to improved survival, this suggests there must be other underlying behaviours that are causing these populations to use more energy thus resulting in lower average ages and a higher agent turnover when compared to the Age and Health social information populations. We suspect the indeterminate quality of both Presence and Action information causes agents using this information to be less discerning about which agents and plant resources they move towards, resulting in less informed movement and therefore less efficient energy expenditure - though further analysis will have to be done to confirm these suspicions.

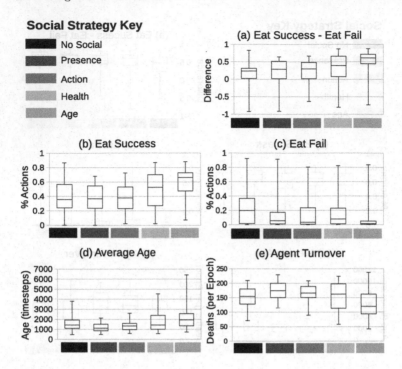

Fig. 4. Environment 2 box plots: Box plots for the eat action and other population metrics, including a breakdown of successful and unsuccessful eating actions, average agent age, and agent turnover, in environment 2.

5   Conclusions and Further Work

The work presented here, alongside results from of Mitri et al. [17], contribute to the discussion on the adaptive value of social information for evolved simulated agents by demonstrating that social information can provide an adaptive benefit to a neuroevolutionary process when decoupled from a within-lifetime learning process. However, we do see that social information is only of an consistent adaptive benefit in less difficult environments, and when the social information itself is informative. This work also demonstrates the potential adaptive benefits of simple social and public information strategies such as social influence, social facilitation, stimulus enhancement, and local enhancement [8,13,14,25], adding further weight to the work by Noble and Todd [15] in which it was argued that simple social learning mechanisms are capable of producing complex adaptive behaviours that may easily be confused for the resulting behaviours of more complex social learning mechanisms. The social information strategies implemented here could be argued to be mechanisms of stimulus and local enhancement as the social information inadvertently expressed here by agents could be used by others as an attractor to unfamiliar plant resources or a promoter of eating (or other) behaviours. However, we also see evidence of social information potentially being used to ignore locations or being used to suppress eating (or other) behaviours, which may indicate some level of information suppression [17]. Moving forward we intend to undertake a greater analysis of the behaviours being expressed by agents in this work. It would be of interest to see how often non eating actions are utilised by agents and whether the amount of movement undertaken by agents is promoted by having social information, with further investigations being necessary to ascertain whether this movement results in greater or lesser agent grouping, as evidence from other fields suggests that social information should result in larger groups, thus promoting more informed individual decision making based on the larger quantities of social information made available as a result of having a larger social group [1].

References

1. King, A.J., Cowlishaw, G.: When to use social information: the advantage of large group size in individual decision making. Biol. Lett. **3**(2), 137–139 (2007)
2. Bonnie, K.E., Earley, R.L.: Expanding the scope for social information use. Anim. Behav. **74**(2), 171–181 (2007)
3. Nolfi, S., Floreano, D.: Learning and evolution. Auton. Rob. **7**(1), 89–113 (1999)
4. Borg, J.M., Channon, A., Day, C.: Discovering and maintaining behaviours inaccessible to incremental genetic evolution through transcription errors and cultural transmission. In: ECAL 2011: Proceedings of the Eleventh European Conference on the Synthesis and Simulation of Living Systems, pp. 101–108. MIT Press (2011)
5. Whiten, A., Van Schaik, C.P.: The evolution of animal cultures and social intelligence. Philos. Trans. Roy. Soc. B: Biol. Sci. **362**(1480), 603–620 (2007)
6. Reader, S.M., Biro, D.: Experimental identification of social learning in wild animals. Learn. Behav. **38**(3), 265–283 (2010)
7. Kendal, J.R., Rendell, L., Pike, T.W., Laland, K.N.: Nine-spined sticklebacks deploy a hill-climbing social learning strategy. Behav. Ecol. **20**(2), 238–244 (2009)
8. Galef, B.G.: Social learning and traditions in animals: evidence, definitions, and relationship to human culture. Wiley Interdisc. Rev.: Cogn. Sci. **3**(6), 581–592 (2012)
9. Zwirner, E., Thornton, A.: Cognitive requirements of cumulative culture: teaching is useful but not essential. Sci. Rep. **5** (2015). Article no. 16781
10. Jolley, B.P., Borg, J.M., Channon, A.: Analysis of social learning strategies when discovering and maintaining behaviours inaccessible to incremental genetic evolution. In: Tuci, E., Giagkos, A., Wilson, M., Hallam, J. (eds.) SAB 2016. LNCS (LNAI), vol. 9825, pp. 293–304. Springer, Heidelberg (2016). doi:10.1007/978-3-319-43488-9_26
11. Whitehead, H., Richerson, P.J.: The evolution of conformist social learning can cause population collapse in realistically variable environments. Evol. Hum. Behav. **30**(4), 261–273 (2009)
12. Borg, J.M., Channon, A.: Testing the variability selection hypothesis - the adoption of social learning in increasingly variable environments. In: ALIFE 13: The Thirteenth Conference on the Synthesis and Simulation of Living Systems, pp. 317–324. MIT Press (2012)
13. Rendell, L., Fogarty, L., Hoppitt, W.J., Morgan, T.J., Webster, M.M., Laland, K.N.: Cognitive culture: theoretical and empirical insights into social learning strategies. Trends Cogn. Sci. **15**(2), 68–76 (2011)

14. van der Post, D.J., Franz, M., Laland, K.N.: Skill learning and the evolution of social learning mechanisms. BMC Evol. Biol. **16**(1), 166 (2016)
15. Noble, J., Todd, P.M.: Imitation or something simpler? Modeling simple mechanisms for social information processing. In: Nehaniv, C.L., Dautenhahn, K. (eds.) Imitation in Animals and Artifacts, pp. 423–439. MIT Press, Cambridge (2002)
16. McNamara, J.M., Dall, S.R.: Information is a fitness enhancing resource. Oikos **119**(2), 231–236 (2010)
17. Mitri, S., Floreano, D., Keller, L.: The evolution of information suppression in communicating robots with conflicting interests. Proc. Nat. Acad. Sci. **106**(37), 15786–15790 (2009)
18. Watson, R.A., Szathmáry, E.: How can evolution learn? Trends Ecol. Evol. **31**(2), 147–157 (2016)
19. Floreano, D., Keller, L.: Evolution of adaptive behaviour in robots by means of darwinian selection. PLoS Biol. **8**(1), e1000292 (2010)
20. Channon, A.D., Damper, R.: The evolutionary emergence of socially intelligent agents. In: Edmonds, B., Dautenhahn, K. (eds.) Socially Situated Intelligence: A Workshop Held at SAB 1998, University of Zurich Technical Report, pp. 41–49 (1998)
21. Danchin, É., Giraldeau, L.A., Valone, T.J., Wagner, R.H.: Public information: from nosy neighbors to cultural evolution. Science **305**(5683), 487–491 (2004)
22. Yang, S.X., Meng, M.: An efficient neural network approach to dynamic robot motion planning. Neural Netw. **13**(2), 143–148 (2000)
23. Robinson, E., Ellis, T., Channon, A.: Neuroevolution of agents capable of reactive and deliberative behaviours in novel and dynamic environments. In: Almeida e Costa, F., Rocha, L.M., Costa, E., Harvey, I., Coutinho, A. (eds.) ECAL 2007. LNCS (LNAI), vol. 4648, pp. 345–354. Springer, Heidelberg (2007). doi:10.1007/978-3-540-74913-4_35
24. Stanton, A., Channon, A.: Incremental neuroevolution of reactive and deliberative 3D agents. In: ECAL 2015: Proceedings of the Thirteenth European Conference on the Synthesis and Simulation of Living Systems, pp. 341–348. MIT Press (2015)
25. Acerbi, A., Marocco, D., Nolfi, S.: Social facilitation on the development of foraging behaviors in a population of autonomous robots. In: Almeida e Costa, F., Rocha, L.M., Costa, E., Harvey, I., Coutinho, A. (eds.) ECAL 2007. LNCS (LNAI), vol. 4648, pp. 625–634. Springer, Heidelberg (2007). doi:10.1007/978-3-540-74913-4_63

Interactive Evolution of Complex Behaviours Through Skill Encapsulation

Pablo González de Prado Salas$^{(\boxtimes)}$ and Sebastian Risi

IT University of Copenhagen, Copenhagen, Denmark
{pago,sebr}@itu.dk

Abstract. Human-based computation (HBC) is an emerging research area in which humans and machines collaborate to solve tasks that neither one can solve in isolation. In evolutionary computation, HBC is often realized through interactive evolutionary computation (IEC), in which a user guides evolution by iteratively selecting the parents for the next generation. IEC has shown promise in a variety of different domains, but evolving more complex or hierarchically composed behaviours remains challenging with the traditional IEC approach. To overcome this challenge, this paper combines the recently introduced ESP (*encapsulation, syllabus and pandemonium*) algorithm with IEC to allow users to intuitively break complex challenges into smaller pieces and preserve, reuse and combine interactively evolved sub-skills. The combination of ESP principles with IEC provides a new way in which human insights can be leveraged in evolutionary computation and, as the results in this paper show, IEC-ESP is able to solve complex control problems that are challenging for a traditional fitness-based approach.

Keywords: Evolutionary computation · Interactive evolutionary computation · Modular networks · Neuroevolution

1 Introduction

A promising approach to solve complex control problems is *neuroevolution* [1,2], an iterative process that takes natural evolution as inspiration to train artificial neural networks (ANNs). Each generation produces new networks through mutations, and selection guides this process to create ANNs that produce specific behaviours. While neuroevolution has shown promise in a variety of tasks [1,3], a major problem with the traditionally employed objective functions in evolutionary computation is that they can be vulnerable to deception wherein evolution converges to a suboptimal solution [4,5]. Fitness evaluations can also be problematic for abstract tasks, for which designing an efficient evaluation function may be almost as challenging as solving the problem itself.

One way to deal with deception in evolution is to involve humans in the loop to evaluate candidate solutions, a method known as *interactive evolutionary computation* (IEC; [6]). Especially when combined with more open-ended

© Springer International Publishing AG 2017
G. Squillero and K. Sim (Eds.): EvoApplications 2017, Part I, LNCS 10199, pp. 853–869, 2017.
DOI: 10.1007/978-3-319-55849-3_55

search methods such as novelty search [4,7], it is possible to create synergistic effects between humans and automated processes to solve more complex tasks [8,9]. However, most IEC systems suffer from two drawbacks. First, a significant problem is human fatigue [6], which means that users can only evaluate a limited set of candidates at a time. Second, in most existing IEC systems it is difficult to incrementally elaborate on previously evolved behaviours or to create hierarchically composed behaviours [6,8,9].

This paper introduces a method that aims to scale IEC approaches to more complex domains and behaviours. Our approach builds on the ESP (*encapsulation, syllabus and pandemonium*) method that allows a complex task to be broken down into intermediate learning tasks, together with mechanisms for preservation, reuse, and combination of previously learned skills [10,11]. While the original ESP method relied on multiple pre-defined fitness functions, the new method *IEC-ESP* allows users to break down a task into smaller sub-tasks based on their human-level domain knowledge; modules for the sub-skills can then be evolved separately and protected from further evolution through encapsulation. Regulatory modules orchestrate when the different modules should be activated. Once the basic behaviours are evolved interactively, regulatory modules can be evolved interactively as well. These skills can in turn be encapsulated and used as a unit for further evolution.

While other research areas have been able to exploit a large range of human intuition in the context of human-based computation [12] (a prominent example being the Foldit game, in which users need to determine the three-dimensional structure of proteins [13]), current IEC systems limit the user to solely "nudging" evolution by deciding between a discrete choice of candidates. The new approach presented in this paper goes a step further and also allows users to use their intuition in breaking down complex behaviors into microtasks (often employed in human computation), which could extend the reach of IEC to more complex problems in the future.

2   Background

This section reviews IEC and the module-based ESP method for evolving hierarchically composed neural networks. These are the key ingredients and motivation behind the IEC-ESP method presented in this paper. Evolution of individual modules is based on NEAT [14], which is reviewed next.

2.1   NEAT

Neuroevolution of Augmented Topologies (NEAT) has proven successful in a variety of domains and was originally proposed by Stanley and Miikkulainen [14] as a way to evolve ANNs capable of solving complex control tasks. NEAT is based on three main concepts: (1) NEAT gives a principled way to crossover different topologies; (2) It keeps track of and preserves innovation; (3) It is based on the principle of minimal structure, which ensures that all complexity in a topology is justified. For a more complete review of NEAT see Stanley and Miikkulainen [14].

2.2   ESP Method

ESP is a neuroevolution method to create complex and hierarchically composed behaviours introduced by Lessin et al. [10,11]. ESP stands for *encapsulation, syllabus and pandemonium*, which are the key ingredients for this method. A *syllabus* in ESP allows complex behaviour to be broken down into more approachable tasks by a human designer. *Encapsulation* allows sub-skills to be preserved throughout further evolution by freezing parts of the ANN. Finally, conflicts between competing modules can be resolved by placing them in a *pandemonium* relationship, in which only the module with highest stimulation will be active, while the rest of the modules will be suppressed.

Task-decomposition strategies similar to ESP have been employed in multiple related field. Brooks's subsumption architecture is a prominent example in artificial intelligence and robotics [15]. In reinforcement learning and evolutionary computation, work such as layered learning and hierarchical task decomposition [16–18] explore similar concepts.

However, a drawback of the original ESP method (and many related approaches) is that the experimenter has to design and fine-tune individual fitness functions for each of the different modules, which can become laborious for complex behaviours. Therefore, the idea in this paper is to evolve those modules through interactive evolution, which is explained next.

2.3   Interactive Evolutionary Computation (IEC)

Typically, IEC frameworks offer the user a set of candidates to evaluate. Users select individuals based on their preference, which are then combined and mutated to produce the next generation of candidates [6]. One advantage of this form of human-based evaluation is its flexibility and expressiveness compared to the explicitly defined mathematical fitness functions traditionally employed in evolutionary computation. For this reason, IEC is used in domains were goals are hard to define mathematically, or were goals might be subjective, such as in creating two-dimensional images [19], three-dimensional forms [20], or musical compositions [21]. Perhaps the most common problem with IEC is user-fatigue; according to Takagi even 10 to 20 iterations may be enough to produce user-fatigue [6], although this depends on the specific details of the task at hand.

A way to alleviate the problem of user fatigue is to combine the intuition of humans with the speed of machines to limit the number of candidates the user has to evaluate [22,23]. IEC has recently also been combined with novelty search [4], which allows users to focus on evaluating a limited set of *novel* behaviours [8]. A similar set-up was further explored by Löwe and Risi [9] to facilitate the evolution of more adaptive agent behaviours. However, while most related works aim to reduce the number of user evaluations needed, how to create more complex and *hierarchically* composed behaviours has so far received limited attention, which the approach presented in this paper tries to address.

3   Approach: IEC-ESP

The main idea in the presented approach is to allow users to (1) break down complex tasks into smaller sub-tasks, (2) interactively evolve behaviours for these sub-tasks, and (3) interactively evolve regulatory modules that learn when to use each sub-tasks. In this context, the proposed approach allows humans to apply their intuition at two different levels of abstraction. First, as in traditional IEC, humans have the ability to identify promising stepping-stones through the interactive selection process. Second, humans often have a good intuition in how to divide a task into smaller, easier solvable sub-tasks.

3.1   IEC-ESP Algorithm

This section explains the approach in more detail based on a step-by-step example of how IEC-ESP can evolve an agent that can drive through a car track and stop when encountering red traffic lights (Fig. 1).

First, the user decides how to break down the task into smaller components that can be solved using IEC. When a new module is created, the user can also optionally select the input and outputs to which it will be connected. By default, the module will connect to all inputs and outputs, but in some domains it might be useful to limit the available inputs and thereby the evolutionary search space. Determining which inputs and outputs are relevant for a module may be intuitive for a human user, but not directly obvious for automatic approaches.

Individual modules are evolved by NEAT using IEC (Fig. 1.1). During the interactive step users can mark individuals they find interesting or individuals that should be removed. When the selection is complete, users can call for a new generation of individuals, in which candidates that were selected get a higher fitness (10.0 for the experiments in this paper) and therefore have a higher chance to reproduce than unselected candidates (who receive a fitness of 1.0). Basic behaviours can easily be evolved in this way, such as *Drive* (Fig. 1.1) and *Stop* (Fig. 1.2). These basic behaviours can then be orchestrated by regulation modules, which are evolved to decide when their child modules are active (Fig. 1.3). Regulation modules encapsulate everything within them and can be treated as basic modules themselves, allowing for increasingly complex behavioural hierarchies. Alternatively, users can decide on a fixed strategy when modules should be activated, such as "this module will be active/inactive when this [selected] input is active/inactive".

As an advanced feature, users can also directly regulate the contribution of each module to the final result. One module-specific value adjusts all the weights connecting the local outputs of the module to the final global outputs. For most tasks this is not necessary, but it enables fine-grain control over how modules should be combined. For example, by using a negative contribution, it is possible to "subtract" the behaviour of a module (see Sect. 5.1).

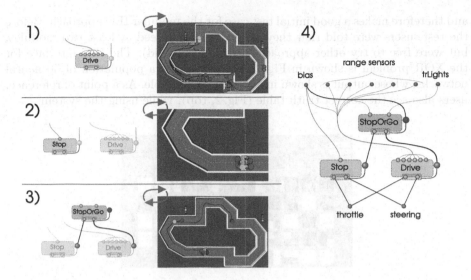

Fig. 1. Incremental Evolution with IEC-ESP. The evolution of the first module that drives regardless of traffic lights is shown in (1). The user can select interesting drivers (yellow) and mark others for deletion (red). The user continues evolving a "stop" module (2), and then a regulation module (3), which decides when *Drive* and *Stop* are active. This module is evolved in the same IEC fashion. A schematic representation of the final neural network is shown in (4). (Color figure online)

4   Experiments

We compare the IEC-ESP approach to a regular fitness-based approach and regular IEC without the ability to encapsulate behaviours on three different domains. The first and most simple domain is the well-known XOR logic gate. The second domain is composed of four driving tasks with variable difficulty and the last domain is a garbage collection scenario, which involves sequential and conditional tasks. Based on feedback during the XOR tests, the program was redesigned to make the UI more intuitive.

In addition to an expert user (one of the authors), five users participated in the XOR experiment, and seven in the garbage collection task. To get to know the program, users were shown how to evolve a solution in the car racing domain before they tried the garbage collection task. While the user tests are at this point anecdotal regarding the number of participants and the fact that they did not always have precisely the same conditions, they did demonstrate the potential of the IEC-ESP approach.

4.1   XOR

The goal in the XOR domain is to reproduce the characteristic XOR truth table. Because the tasks is non-linear separable it requires at least one hidden neuron and therefore makes a good initial test case for the modular IEC approach. Before the test, users were told that they would probably need at least two modules, but were free to try other approaches (which they did). The IEC interface for the XOR problem is shown in Fig. 2. Users evaluate a population of 50 neural networks, whose output is shown in form of a truth table. As a point of reference, users also see the correct truth table (Fig. 2, top), while using the system.

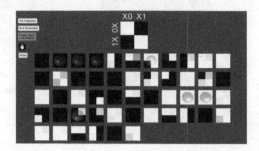

Fig. 2. XOR IEC-ESP Interface. Users are presented with a total of 50 individuals they can choose from (bottom). The truth table for a correct XOR gate is shown on top as reference (1.0 = black, 0.0 = white)

For the fitness-based approach, evaluation is based on: $F = (1 - |t - x|)$ if $|t - x| > 0.5$, and $F = 1.0$ otherwise, where t is the expected output and x is the network's output. The final fitness is the sum over all four input-output pairs.

4.2 Car Navigation

The car domain includes four tracks with increasing levels of difficulty, which should test IEC-ESP ability to create complex and hierarchically composed behaviours. In the first track (Fig. 3a) the only goal is to drive around the track. This racing track is included in the original SharpNEAT port to the Unity platform by Daniel Jallov[1], upon which the system presented here builds. The second track includes traffic lights (Fig. 3b). The two traffic lights are always set to opposite states to reduce the chance of cars encountering two green lights. The third track adds left-right junctions (Fig. 3c), in which junction sensors inform cars of the path they should take (some of these change randomly while the cars are driving through the track). The final track includes both traffic lights and different types of junctions such as T-junctions and dead-ends (Fig. 3d).

Cars are equipped with five short-range proximity sensors that respond to obstacles in different directions (forward, left, right and forward-left and forward-right at 45° angles). Another sensor responds to near-by traffic lights, and is set to 0.5 for orange lights, 1.0 for red lights, and 0.0 otherwise. An additional sensor indicates which direction the car should take at junctions (set to 0.33 for left turns, 0.66 to continue straight and 1.0 for turning right).

---

[1] https://github.com/lordjesus/UnityNEAT.

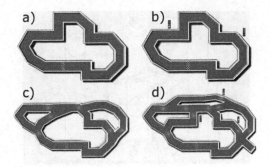

Fig. 3. Car Navigation Tasks. In the simplest track (a) the only goal is to drive around the track as fast as possible. Tracks (b) and (d) include traffic lights. In (c) and (d) green arrows indicate the direction the cars are supposed to follow at junctions. (Color figure online)

For the fitness-based approach $F = [d \cdot c_d - w \cdot c_w - l \cdot c_l] \frac{1}{T}$, where d is the number of road segments advanced, w is the number of collisions with walls and l depends on the behaviour with respect to traffic lights. If the car moves during a green light (or no traffic light is visible) l is decreased one unit, or increased if the vehicle is not moving. The opposite is true for red lights (± 600). The c constants that were found to work best through prior experimentation are ($c_d = 20, c_w = 0.5, c_l = 0.025$). T is the length of the simulation, which was set to a value that would allow good controllers to complete slightly over one lap.

4.3   Garbage Collection

In this task, robots need to transport garbage from two different loading bays to an unload area (Fig. 4). A clock alternates between *red* and *blue* periods, indicating the correct loading bay at that specific time. During IEC the users can change the clock manually, while it changes with a period of 80 time units (experiment length is 150 time units) in the automated setup. After picking up cargo, the robot needs to proceed to the unloading area.

Robots have three range sensors, one pointing straight ahead and two pointing at $\pm 45°$. These sensors only respond to walls and the borders of coloured areas, and return a value between [0.0, 1.0] according to the distance to the obstacle. Their range is limited to about a quarter of the arena length. Three additional long-range sensors provide information about the loading bays and the unloading area. Each sensor responds to one of the three areas and returns a value that is higher the closer the robot is to the corresponding area. Robots also have a sensor that detects cargo (1.0 for cargo, 0.0 otherwise) and another one for the clock state (1.0 for red period, 0.0 for blue). Robots do not interact (or sense) each other during interactive evolution.

Fitness for the automated approach is set to $F = \bar{s} \cdot c_s - [w \cdot c_w + fit] \frac{1}{T}$, where $\bar{s}$ is the average speed of the robot, and w are the collisions with walls, which is also increased when walls are within the proximity-sensor range, using

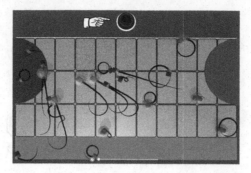

Fig. 4. Garbage Collection Domain. The goal in the garbage collection-domain is to pick up garbage from either the red or blue area (depending on the current clock setting shown at the top), and drop it off at the unloading area at the bottom. The IEC framework allows users to give behaviours either a high (robots shown in yellow) or low fitness (red). For clarity, only 20 individuals are shown in this figure, while 50 are used during the experiments. Black lines show the recent robot paths. (Color figure online)

$1 - \frac{dist}{range}$. The variable fit accumulates values depending on the displayed robot behaviours: $+40$ for picking up cargo, -80 for entering the wrong bay, -20 for entering a bay with cargo, $+50$ for delivering cargo and -10 for entering the delivery area without cargo. Finally, T is the simulation length, and the constants are $(c_s = 0.3, c_w = 0.03)$.

4.4 Parameters

IEC-ESP experiments use a population of 50 individuals classified into 10 species using the k-means algorithm. For the fitness-based simulations we also tested larger population sizes of 150 individuals with 30 species. In the initial population connections from local input to local output neurons are formed with a chance of 99%. 20% of the genomes in each species are copied without changes to the next generation. Parents for the next generation are taken from the fittest 20% individuals in the specie with a chance that is proportional to their fitness value. 20% of the offspring will be produced by asexual reproduction (mutations on a single parent genome). Of the remaining sexual reproduction, 0,1% will be intra-species (parents from different species). In sexual reproduction, common traits are copied from one parent at random. Other traits are always copied from the fittest parent, and all non-common genes from the least fit parent will be copied with 10% chance.

Offspring (except elites) is mutated with a 3% chance of node and 5% chance of connection addition. Connections are removed with 0,4% chance. With 80% probability connection weights are changed. In this case, 99.1% of the time 90% of the connection weights suffer small variations ($\sigma = 0,02$) while 0.9% of the time 10% of the connections will be reset to a random value within the allowed range from −5 to +5. Recurrent connections are allowed. The network is activated five times at each step.

5   Results

The results reported in this section include many trials by the authors, some small-scale user tests and fitness-based simulations. The reported number of generations for the IEC approaches are measured in how many times the user selected the desired candidates and called for a new iteration (offspring creation). A video of the IEC-ESP system in action can be found at: https://goo.gl/VyGE9p.

5.1   XOR Results

In a set of ten independent evolutionary runs, fitness-based search was able to solve the task in an average of 31 generations (sd = 18). To solve the task through IEC-ESP, the five testers needed 24, 18, 9, 4 and 16 generations respectively, taking between 30 min and one hour (including introduction and set-up). Users reported that becoming familiar with the program was more problematic than solving the challenge itself. After this experiment, the user interface was redesigned thoroughly with the goal to make it more intuitive. At least two users (as well as the expert user) tried to find a solution using traditional IEC; all failed, even after evolving networks for more than 40 generations.

Some different solutions discovered by the users are shown in Fig. 5. Users first interactively evolved two modules with complementary patterns, and then fixed the relative contribution of each one to achieve the desired result.

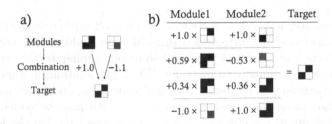

Fig. 5. XOR IEC-ESP Solutions. Schematic decomposition of a XOR gate is shown in (a). Modules are combined with different user-defined weights. Different solutions for the XOR problem are shown in (b). The last solution is from the expert user.

5.2   Garbage Collection Results

While the fitness-based approach can solve XOR consistently, it does not reliably find a solution for the garbage collection task. A variety of different fitness functions were tried, all with limited success.

With the best combination (see Sect. 4.3), fitness-based evolution solved the task in 2 out of 15 runs. In another three runs (Fig. 6b) one of the two clock periods resulted in a faulty behaviour (typically this involves a wide loop that passes through both loading areas in each cycle, which results in a penalty per loop). In 10 out of 13 runs only partial solutions were discovered, such as the one in Fig. 6a. These partial solutions work well for one of the clock periods and remain idle for the other. Simulations with a larger population (150 vs. 50) perform better, but the trend is the same (Fig. 7).

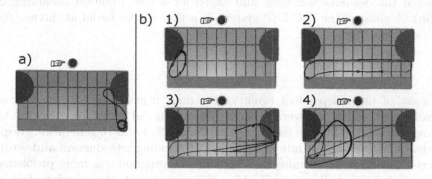

Fig. 6. Typical Partial Solutions for Fitness-based Search. The partial solution in (a) fails when the clock has changed to blue, resulting in a tight-loops idle state. A better approximated solution is shown in (b). The blue loop (1) is almost perfect, while the red unloads too far (2). The red-to-blue transition (3, 4) is problematic for units that were on the way to load. These will go once into the red bay during the blue clock (penalty) and twice into the unloading area without cargo (double penalty). (Color figure online)

The expert user was able to solve the garbage collection task in all 20 trials it was tried. Traditional IEC attempts (using only one module) were not successful and, in the best case, resulted in partial solutions similar to the one shown in Fig. 6b. The most common strategy for IEC-ESP solutions (either expert or inexperienced users) was to create three main modules, one to navigate to each of the relevant areas (blue, red and pink). A fourth may be added, since the module navigating to the unloading area usually goes to either the left or right corner of the wide unloading area, which will be inefficient from either the blue or the red bays. This way of approaching the solution results in behaviours that look different from those evolved using a fitness function. A solution found by the expert user is shown in Fig. 8.

The results of the seven non-experienced users were less consistent and they struggled more with the program, which is likely due to the fact that they had to learn how to use the interface on top of solving the task; however, a few solutions (3) were in fact found. For these solutions, each module required in the range of 2 to 50 generations to evolve. Figure 9 shows such a solution by an inexperienced user that, surprisingly, does not rely on range-finder sensors,

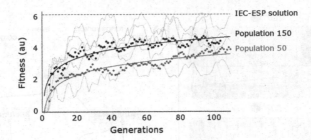

Fig. 7. Average Best Fitness over Generations in the Garbage Collection Task. Light lines are individual simulations (smoothed using 2-generation averages). Full points and continuous lines are average values and logarithmic fit, for experiments with population sizes of 150 and 50. For reference, the average testing performance (sd = 0.4) of the IEC-ESP solution (Fig. 9) on 14 trials is also shown (dashed line). Different trials result in slightly different results because of the noisy Unity-based simulation environment.

resulting in smaller modules. This result demonstrates that even inexperienced users during their first attempts may offer valuable insight for experts, but also shows that getting accustomed to the user interface is key. The main result is that both pure IEC and fitness-based approaches fail when the task requires to elaborate on partial solutions, while IEC-ESP allows especially expert users to interactively and incrementally evolve increasingly complex behaviours.

5.3 Car Navigation Results

The simplest car navigation track (Fig. 3a) is not very challenging for any of the compared approaches. In fact, it is not uncommon to find approximate solutions even from the initial IEC candidates. In the ten independent runs, fitness-based search found a solution in 9.2 generations on average (sd = 9.7; Fig. 10a).

The track with traffic lights (Fig. 3b) proved significantly harder for the fitness-based approach (no perfect solution was found in 30 evolutionary runs, Fig. 10b). Tracks with junctions proved even more challenging in our fitness-based attempts, so we chose to focus on the easier task with only traffic lights.

The expert user was able to find a IEC-ESP solution for the traffic light track (Fig. 3b) in all 20 attempted trials. Figure 1 shows an IEC-ESP solution, which is composed of one module that drives with no regard to the traffic lights (Fig. 1.1) and one that allows cars to stop. Notice this is a trivial behaviour, because it needs not decide *when* to stop, but just *how* to stop. For stopping (basically doing nothing) only bias is used as input. The last element is a regulation module that decides whether to drive or stop depending on the value of incoming traffic lights.

A possible strategy to solve the more complex track with junctions (Fig. 3c) is to first evolve two simple driving modules that tend to follow right and left walls. A regulation module is evolved next, which allows the car to switch between the two modules when entering junctions.

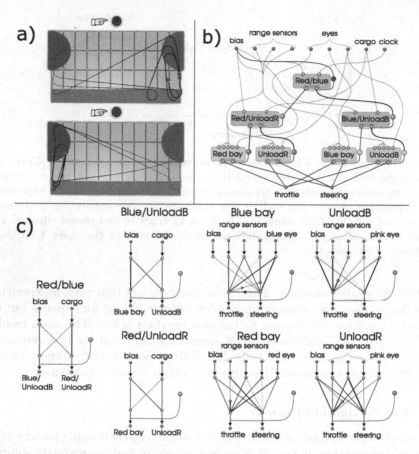

Fig. 8. Expert User Solution for the Garbage collection Task. (a) Behaviour for both periods with trails after clock transitions. (b) Network diagram. Regulatory neurons are at the right side of each module, and share colour when they are in a "pandemonium" (only one in a group may be active at any time). (c) Network connections within modules. Red/UnloadR connections are shown twice as intense for clarity. (Color figure online)

Figure 11 shows two schematic solutions for the track with traffic lights and junctions by an expert user (Fig. 3d). One of the solutions includes a regulation module that decides among *Left*, *Straight* and *Right* (where normal driving is *Left* or *Right* which drives closer to left or right walls respectively). The straight-driving module is necessary for certain T-junctions in this track. This module scheme seems like a good idea, but in practice regulatory modules with more than two children can be challenging to evolve. Although it looks more convoluted, it is actually easier to develop a solution that uses a two-step regulation process. In the second example in Fig. 11, the first module decides between *Left* and other driving modules. If Left is not chosen, then a second regulatory module chooses between *Straight* and *Right*. This approach is easy to scale.

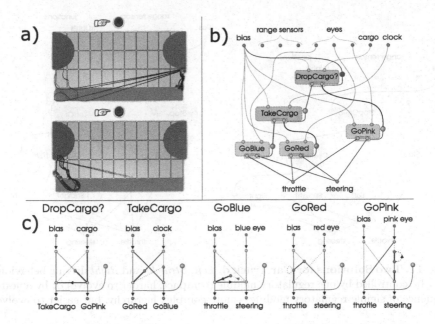

Fig. 9. Non-expert User Solution for the Garbage Collection Task. (a) Correct behaviour for red and blue clock periods. Trails show the transition from the other period. (b) Schematic network view. Regulatory neurons are represented at the right side of each module. Regulatory neurons of the same colour share a "pandemonium", allowing only one in the group to be active at the same time. (c) Network connections within modules. Note this solution does not use range sensors at all. (Color figure online)

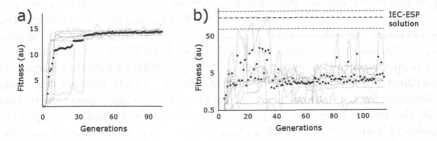

Fig. 10. Average Performance. Fitness over generations for the tracks without (a) and with traffic lights (b). Black dots show averaged fitness over ten independent evolutionary runs. Dashed lines in (b) show the average test performance of a IEC-ESP solution evaluated on 40 trials together with ± sd.

6 Discussion

This paper presents an approach that combines IEC with the ESP method [10,11], which allows evolved skills to be protected and reused as part of a

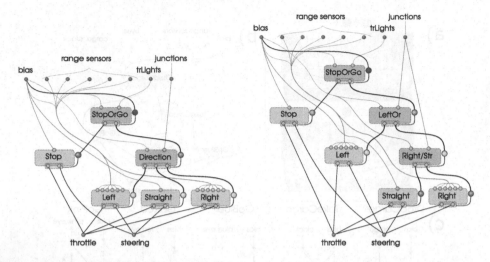

Fig. 11. Two Solutions for Car Track d. *Left, Straight* and *Right* driving behaviours may be controlled by one regulatory module (compact, harder to evolve) or by a nested sequence of simple regulatory modules (more complex hierarchy, but easier to evolve).

larger network. The results suggest that the approach facilitates the evolution of hierarchically composed behaviours, which is difficult with the traditional form of IEC. The presented method takes a step towards exploiting a larger part of our human intuition in the IEC process, by allowing users to break down the given task into intermediate and therefore easier to solve sub-tasks. Deciding on the inherent problem structure of a task requires high-level abstract reasoning, a problem where humans currently still surpass machines. In the future it will be interesting to use the computational speed of the machine to a fuller extend. For example, a novelty-assisted IEC approach [8] could continuously generate novel behaviours to accelerate the IEC aspect of our IEC-ESP approach.

Comparing the different approaches, it is interesting to note that humans and algorithms have a very different concept of difficulty. The traffic light task is more challenging for the automated approach than the garbage collection problem, while the reverse is true for humans. This difference does hint at the potential benefits of learning how to combine human and computer intelligence efficiently. In particular, we believe the failure in the driving task is more related to the unpredictable environment and noisy evaluations rather than the complexity of the behaviours involved. This is problematic for the fitness-based approach, but not for IEC-ESP. While a different fitness function, incremental evolution or a more deterministic environment could alleviate these problems, it shows the versatility of the presented approach that succeeds without any such restrictions.

Although the results are promising, some IEC-ESP solutions for the most complex track have small shortcomings. While the best solutions can perform several laps without any mistakes, sometimes transitions between different modules can be problematic and result in unexpected behaviours (e.g. loops or driving in the wrong direction). Mitigating problems that can result from the combination of apparently successful modules is an important future research direction.

An interesting insight from this work is the importance of training the users to use the particular interface and getting to know the program and domain. As the results show, while an expert user with intimate knowledge of the system and underlying algorithms can consistently solve the tasks, the same is not true for the non-expert users. In the future it will be important to alleviate this problem by making the user interface more intuitive but also providing a step-by-step and easy to understand tutorial.

One exciting promise of the approach is that the modular-network structure makes it possible for multiple users to collaborate on their design. In case of a monolithic neural networks, reusing parts of a network for a new problems would be significantly more challenging. For example, an interactively evolved module that processes information from ten light-sensitive neurons could be used in any project that implements such sensors, without the rest of the network interfering.

The experiments reported here are preliminary and unfortunately do not allow for a proper statistical analysis. Therefore, important future work is to apply IEC-ESP to relevant problems and to conduct rigorous and extensive user-experience experiments.

7   Conclusions

This paper introduced a combination of IEC and the module-based ESP method for preserving, combining and reusing previously learned skills. The new IEC-ESP method was evaluated on a variety of different tasks that proved challenging to evolve with a traditional fitness-based approach. IEC-ESP requires the experimenter to decompose the overall task into smaller sub-tasks, which fits naturally with our human abilities of high-level abstraction. Importantly, the defined sub-tasks can then be evolved efficiently through interactive evolution. The main conclusion is that the approach now allows more complex domains to be solved than have heretofore been possible with IEC, and adds more evidence to the synergistic effects in combining human and machine capabilities.

Acknowledgements. We thank Fundación Ramón Areces for funding as part of their postdoc fellowship program.

References

1. Floreano, D., Dürr, P., Mattiussi, C.: Neuroevolution: from architectures to learning. Evol. Intel. **1**(1), 47–62 (2008)
2. Yao, X.: Evolving artificial neural networks. Proc. IEEE **87**(9), 1423–1447 (1999)
3. Risi, S., Togelius, J.: Neuroevolution in games: state of the art and open challenges. IEEE Trans. Comput. Intell. AI Games **PP**(99), 1–1 (2015)
4. Lehman, J., Stanley, K.O.: Exploiting open-endedness to solve problems through the search for novelty. In: Proceedings of the Eleventh International Conference on Artificial Life. Alife XI, MIT Press (2008)

5. Goldberg, D.E.: Simple genetic algorithms and the minimal, deceptive problem. Genet. Algorithms Simul. Annealing **74**, 88 (1987)
6. Takagi, H.: Interactive evolutionary computation: fusion of the capacities of EC optimization and human evaluation. Proc. IEEE **89**, 1275–1296 (2001)
7. Lehman, J., Stanley, K.O.: Abandoning objectives: evolution through the search for novelty alone. Evol. Comput. **19**(2), 189–223 (2011)
8. Woolley, B.G., Stanley, K.O.: A novel human-computer collaboration: combining novelty search with interactive evolution. In: Proceedings of the 2014 Annual Conference on Genetic and Evolutionary Computation, GECCO 2014, pp. 233–240. ACM, New York (2014)
9. Löwe, M., Risi, S.: Accelerating the evolution of cognitive behaviors through human-computer collaboration. In: Proceedings of the Genetic and Evolutionary Computation Conference 2016, GECCO 2016, pp. 133–140. ACM, New York (2016)
10. Lessin, D., Fussell, D., Miikkulainen, R.: Open-ended behavioral complexity for evolved virtual creatures. In: Proceedings of the 15th Annual Conference on Genetic and Evolutionary Computation, GECCO 2013, pp. 335–342. ACM, New York (2013)
11. Lessin, D., Fussell, D., Miikkulainen, R., Risi, S.: Increasing behavioral complexity for evolved virtual creatures with the ESP method. arXiv preprint arXiv:1510.07957 (2015)
12. Michelucci, P., Dickinson, J.L.: The power of crowds. Science **351**(6268), 32–33 (2016)
13. Khatib, F., Dimaio, F., Cooper, S., Kazmierczyk, M., Gilski, M., Krzywda, S., Zabranska, H., Pichova, I., Thompson, J., Popović, Z., Jaskolski, M., Baker, D.: Crystal structure of a monomeric retroviral protease solved by protein folding game players. Nat. Struct. Mol. Biol. **18**(10), 1175–1177 (2010)
14. Stanley, K.O., Miikkulainen, R.: Evolving neural networks through augmenting topologies. Evol. Comput. **10**(2), 99–127 (2002)
15. Brooks, R.: A robust layered control system for a mobile robot. IEEE J. Robot. Autom. **2**(1), 14–23 (1986)
16. Doucette, J.A., Lichodzijewski, P., Heywood, M.I.: Hierarchical task decomposition through symbiosis in reinforcement learning. In: Proceedings of the 14th Annual Conference on Genetic and Evolutionary Computation, pp. 97–104. ACM (2012)
17. Whiteson, S., Kohl, N., Miikkulainen, R., Stone, P.: Evolving keepaway soccer players through task decomposition. In: Cantú-Paz, E., et al. (eds.) GECCO 2003. LNCS, vol. 2723, pp. 356–368. Springer, Heidelberg (2003). doi:10.1007/3-540-45105-6_41
18. Lee, W.P., Hallam, J., Lund, H.H.: Applying genetic programming to evolve behavior primitives and arbitrators for mobile robots. In: IEEE International Conference on Evolutionary Computation, pp. 501–506, April 1997
19. Secretan, J., Beato, N., D'Ambrosio, D.B., Rodriguez, A., Campbell, A., Folsom-Kovarik, J.T., Stanley, K.O.: Picbreeder: a case study in collaborative evolutionary exploration of design space. Evol. Comput. **19**(3), 373–403 (2011)
20. Clune, J., Lipson, H.: Evolving 3D objects with a generative encoding inspired by developmental biology. SIGEVOlution **5**(4), 2–12 (2011)
21. Hoover, A.K., Szerlip, P.A., Norton, M.E., Brindle, T.A., Merritt, Z., Stanley, K.O.: Generating a complete multipart musical composition from a single monophonic melody with functional scaffolding. In: Proceedings of the Third International Conference on Computational Creativity, Dublin, Ireland, pp. 111–118, May 2012

22. Bernatskiy, A., Hornby, G., Bongard, J.: Improving robot behavior optimization by combining user preferences. In: Proceedings of the Fourteenth International Conference on the Synthesis and Simulation of Living Systems, ALIFE 2014 (2014)
23. Wagy, M.D., Bongard, J.C.: Combining computational and social effort for collaborative problem solving. PLoS ONE **10**(11), e0142524 (2015)

Evolution and Morphogenesis of Simulated Modular Robots: A Comparison Between a Direct and Generative Encoding

Frank Veenstra[(⊠)], Andres Faina, Sebastian Risi, and Kasper Stoy

IT University of Copenhagen, Copenhagen, Denmark
{frve,anfv,sebr,ksty}@itu.dk

Abstract. Modular robots offer an important benefit in evolutionary robotics, which is to quickly evaluate evolved morphologies and control systems in reality. However, artificial evolution of simulated modular robotics is a difficult and time consuming task requiring significant computational power. While artificial evolution in virtual creatures has made use of powerful generative encodings, here we investigate how a generative encoding and direct encoding compare for the evolution of locomotion in modular robots when the number of robotic modules changes. Simulating less modules would decrease the size of the genome of a direct encoding while the size of the genome of the implemented generative encoding stays the same. We found that the generative encoding is significantly more efficient in creating robot phenotypes in the initial stages of evolution when simulating a maximum of 5, 10, and 20 modules. This not only confirms that generative encodings lead to decent performance more quickly, but also that when simulating just a few modules a generative encoding is more powerful than a direct encoding for creating robotic structures. Over longer evolutionary time, the difference between the encodings no longer becomes statistically significant. This leads us to speculate that a combined approach – starting with a generative encoding and later implementing a direct encoding – can lead to more efficient evolved designs.

Keywords: Modular robots · Evolutionary algorithms · Direct and generative encodings

1 Introduction

Evolutionary Robotics has covered a vast amount of research on the automated design of Robotic entities via artificial evolution [1–3]. To rapidly explore different robotic morphologies and control systems that can be physically assembled in the real world, robotic modules are useful as evolutionary building blocks. A robotic module being an independent unit that encapsulates part of its functionality [4]. This encapsulation is important for the (re)configuration of modular robot compositions. In contrast to static robotic entities, modular robots can

© Springer International Publishing AG 2017
G. Squillero and K. Sim (Eds.): EvoApplications 2017, Part I, LNCS 10199, pp. 870–885, 2017.
DOI: 10.1007/978-3-319-55849-3_56

be reconfigured enabling researchers to quickly explore different morphologies. However, it is difficult to design a representation of the genotype to phenotype mapping of a modular robot and we can either evolve all parameters of every simulated module or reuse parts of the genome to construct and control a modular robot. The latter approach – a generative encoding – would require a smaller genome and could in turn evolve decent morphologies and control more quickly. In contrast, evolving all parameters of every robotic module enables us to fine tune behavioral parameters but also increases the search space.

In nature, most multicellular organisms develop from a *zygote* [5]. The zygote and its genome comprises the developmental representation of the organism [6]. The resulting developmental process allows for the reuse of genes which can give rise to recursive structures in the phenotype. Computational models representing an artificial organism's phenotype either use a direct or generative encoding (also indirect encoding). A direct encoding constitutes a one-to-one mapping of genotypic components into the phenotype meaning that the genes encode for every simulated module. In contrast, generative encodings – similar to the development of an organism from a zygote – reuse elements of the genome for constructing the phenotype. Generative encodings have a smaller genotypic state space due to this reuse of genes.

Since the morphological search space in modular robots is limited to the amount of connection sites available on each module, encodings that directly map the assembling process of modular building blocks have been implemented for the generation of robot morphologies [7–9]. Usually, these direct encodings implement an additional symmetry operator that increases the effectiveness of artificial evolution. Simple generative encodings [2,10–16] have been shown to quickly lead to useful robot morphologies. It is, however, unclear whether designing platforms that evolve modular robot morphologies should rather use a direct or generative representation and if the generative encoding is still useful when just a few modules are being used. A generative encoding should no longer have an advantage if the genetic state space in both encodings is of similar size since the amount of mutable parameters are equal.

In this paper we investigate whether a generative encoding or a direct encoding is more useful for evolving modular robots for locomotion. Both encodings make use of evolutionary algorithms to optimize the simulated robots. The direct encoding utilizes the 'Evolutionary designer of heterogeneous modular robots' (Edhmor; see Sect. 2.2) [8] system. The generative encoding is based on a parallel rewriting system called a Lindenmayer System (L-System) [17]. As mentioned earlier, the size of the search space of the direct encoding grows exponentially considering the amount of mutatable parameters (in our case the amount of modules) while the search space of the generative encoding stays roughly the same size. The ability of the direct encoding to mutate parameters of individual modules enables more local improvements. In contrast, since small mutations in the generative encoding can lead to drastic phenotypic changes, the generative encoding might be more prone to stagnate in local optima. Though the scope of this paper does not encompass transferability, the implemented encodings serve as a stepping stone towards evolving feasible modular robotic entities in reality.

2   Methodology

Many modular robotic systems make use of central pattern generators for controlling the modules [15,18,19]. These central pattern generators are derived from their natural equivalents seen in biology [20,21]. The implementation of modifiable central pattern generators seems a logical step towards evolving modular robots, however, we think that this convolutes the search space of the evolutionary system unnecessarily for the aim of this paper. To still achieve a patterned output in our modular system, sinusoidal functions control each module individually in a decentralized manner. By fixing the morphological parameters of the simulated modules and limiting the control parameters of the modules to sinusoidal functions, we are able to analyze how the different encodings can be implemented for evolving robotic structures. For evolving simulated robot morphologies, two evolutionary platforms were used to evaluate the direct and the generative encoding. Both platforms employ the robotics simulator 'Virtual Robot Experimentation Platform' (V-REP; version 3.32) [22]. The next sections will discuss the common elements as well as the differences for each platform.

2.1   Common Elements for both Platforms

Both encodings simulate the exact same modules modeled in V-REP. A cube module and a servo module were designed for the platforms. The modules are based on earlier designs of physical modules (Fig. 1a; developed at the IT University of Copenhagen). In turn, the simulated modules (Fig. 1b) are modeled according to the physical properties of these modular units. The real modules can be attached to one another via magnets and the breaking force and torque parameters resulting from these connections is modeled in the simulated modules.

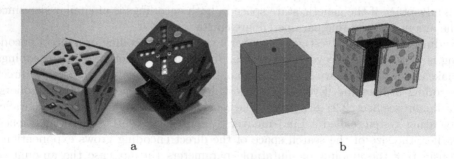

a   b

Fig. 1. Illustration of the modules created in the real world (a) and in the simulator (b).

The modules contain male and female connection sites that enable the modules to connect together. The connections are modeled with a force sensor in V-REP. If the force on a connection site exceeds 1.7 N m of torque or 80.0 N of force, the force sensor between the modules breaks leading to the fragmentation of the morphology. 10 consecutive threshold violations for the force sensor had to be registered before a connection could break.

The cube module (dimensions x, y, z is 55 mm, 55 mm, 55 mm; weight is 100 g) is used as an initial building block for the modular robot to which other modules are attached. This cube has five female conection sites (top, right, left, front, back). The servo module (dimensions x, y, z is 55 mm, 55 mm, 80 mm; weight is 160 g) has three female connection sites (top, right, left) and one male attachment site (bottom). The bottom male connection site of the servo module is thus able to connect to any of the female connection sites of other cube or servo modules.

The joint of the servo module implements a PI controller (P is 0.1 and I is 0.01) and could exert a maximum torque of 1.5 N m. A sinusoidal wave function controls the position of the joint in the servo module. The maximum amplitude of the sinusoidal wave function ranged from $-90°$ and $+90°$ from its original position. The offset, phase and amplitude of the sinusoidal function are mutable parameters. When a new module is added to the simulation, only the male connection site of the new module can be connected to any female connection site of the robot. The new module has four different orientations in which it can attach to a new connection site (note that the amount of orientations is a bit different in the direct encoding: Sect. 2.2). The servo modules implemented the default simulation material while the cube module used the "rest_stack_grasp_material" as material types simulated by V-REP.

The goal of the simulated robots was to move as far away from its initial position in a horizontal direction as possible within 20 s of simulation time. This distance is measured by the horizontal distance that the initial cube module has traveled. Before starting a simulation in V-REP, modules are joined together to form a robot morphology. The entire robot is then shifted upwards so that its lowest point is 0.1 mm above the simulated ground. To take into account the movement due to the robot simply falling over, the distance traveled in the first 2.5 s of the simulation is discarded. An additional cost function was added to compensate for modules that were disconnected due to the breaking of a connection site. The fitness value of each individual is directly correlated to the horizontal distance traveled multiplied by the amount of connections broken between the modules to the power 0.8 and can be derived from Eq. 1.

$$F = \sqrt{(p_e x - p_1 x)^2 + (p_e y - p_1 y)^2} * \eta^{0.8} \tag{1}$$

Where F represents the fitness value obtained by calculating the eventual position (p_e) minus the position after 2.5 s (p_1) traveled in both x and y directions. η represents the amount of broken module connections of the morphology after 20 s of simulation time.

A simulation environment consisted of a default floor and was simulated using the bullet dynamics engine (version 2.78). The dynamics settings were set to accurate (default) with a time-step of 50 ms. Six experiments were done comparing the different encodings. Three of the experiments ran twelve evolutionary runs whereby a maximum of 5, 10 or 20 servo modules and one cube module were allowed. These three experiments were done to see how the direct encoding performed. The other three experiments analyzed the efficiency of the generative encoding and was also composed of twelve evolutionary runs simulating a maximum of 5, 10 or 20 modules. The runs are limited to a fixed amount of evaluations. In the simulations that could simulate a maximum of five modules, 12,500 evaluations were done. The other runs were limited to 25,000 evaluations; more evaluations were performed in these runs since the search space is larger when increasing the amount of simulated modules. 25,000 evaluations were chosen as a trade-of between performance and computational requirements. Since a high end physics simulator is used, the computational requirements are considerable. The next sections will cover the direct and indirect encodings in more detail.

2.2 Direct Encoding

The 'Evolutionary designer of heterogeneous modular robots' (Edhmor) [8,23] system is used as the direct encoding strategy to assemble and evaluate robot morphologies. The Edhmor system is organized as a tree representation, where nodes represent control parameters of a module and its type and edges represent how a module is attached to a parent module. The direct encoding is used together with a constructive algorithm. This algorithm starts building a random population of robots with just a few modules. Afterwards, different mutation phases are applied cyclically. The mutation phases of the algorithm are:

- *Add Module:* Add a module into a morphology.
- *Mutate morphology:* Change the orientations or the place where some modules are connected.
- *Mutate control:* Change the control parameters of some modules.
- *Prune robot:* Test all the morphologies generated by removing a module and its children.

In every phase, a mutation operator is applied several times to produce different random mutations of the same individual which are tested in the simulator. For example, when adding a new module to a robot, five different robots are generated and each of them have a new module placed in different positions and orientations. These phases revert to the previous robot if the mutation does not increase the fitness of the robot, except in the add module phase. This phase forces morphological evolution to take place which has been shown to be advantageous when evolving virtual creatures [24].

The evolutionary algorithm of Edhmor is furthermore generational, the 10% worst performing robots are removed from the population every cycle. Half of them are replaced by random robots with a low number of modules, the other half is generated by applying symmetry operators to the best robots. The symbolic representation and its phenotype are depicted in Fig. 2. A more detailed overview of the system can be found in [8].

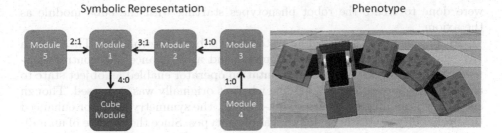

Fig. 2. Representation of the direct encoding. (left) Symbolic representation of the direct encoding: each rectangle represents a module and each arrow represents a connection between modules. There are two numbers for each connection, which indicate the face of the parent where the child node is attached and the orientation of the child node. (right) The symbolic representation of the direct encoding that encodes for a phenotype.

2.3 Generative Encoding

The implemented generative encoding is based on a context sensitive Lindenmayer-System (L-System) [17,25] – a parallel rewriting system. In our case, the variables used in the L-System represent the modules employed to construct a robot (Fig. 3), similar to [26]. In the simulation environment, each variable represents a specific module *state* which encompasses all the parameters of the morphology, control and attachment rules inherent to a module state. The genome of the generative encoding is thus composed of a fixed amount of module states predefined before an individual is generated and evaluated in the simulation environment. The relevant genetic parameters of the module state are used to create a new module. These genetic parameters include the attachment rules for modules. The attachment rules of the cube module included the information of which module is connected to what connection site and in which orientation. The same attachment rules are possible in the servo modules but the servo modules only contain three attachment sites. The implemented attachment rules are in essence similar to the rewriting rules of a normal context sensitive L-System [36]. It is context sensitive since a module cannot be placed at an attachment site if another module is already occupying it. Furthermore, modules cannot be created if this causes a collision with other created modules.

The generative encoding was limited to using five different module states. The first state (the axiom) represents the cube module and the four other states represent the servo module. The four states that represent a servo module encode for the same module but can differ in their mutable parameters responsible for the sinusoidal function that controls the servo module. The internal sinusoidal function that controlled the PI controller of the modules could be mutated in the genome of the module states. This means that the robot can actually not have more than four distinct sinusoidal controllers. For illustrating the different object states, they are colored in the phenotype. The modules could either be red, yellow, blue or pink depending on their state. Four iterations of the L-System were done to create the robot phenotypes starting with the cube module as the axiom.

All parameters of the module states were subject to evolution. There was a 15% chance of a morphological parameter and a 5% chance of a control parameter to be mutated. A symmetry mutation operator enabled an object state to arise at the opposite site of a module where it originally was expressed. Though symmetry is an inherent trait to an L-System, the symmetry operator enhanced the probability of creating symmetrical phenotypes. Since the genome of an individual is represented by different module states, a crossover operator enabled different states to be exchanged between individuals. The crossover function had a 20% chance that a module state of an individual came from a different individual than its original parent.

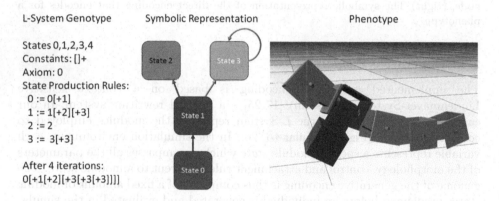

Fig. 3. Representation of the generative encoding. (left) The L-System parameters form the genotype of the morphology whereby the variables of L-Systems are replaced by module states. The '+' constant represents the placing of the next module at the specific attachment sites of a module. The symbolic representation of the genotype (middle) serves as a visualization on how the genotype constructs the phenotype (right).

3   Results

The results of the different evolutionary runs were divided in a performance analysis and a phenotype analysis. The performance analysis was done to get a clear insight in the efficiency of the encodings. Knowing a bit of what type of phenotypes resulted from the evolutionary runs gives us more insight in what prominent evolved characteristics were and how we can ultimately improve the simulator for the design of actual modular robots.

3.1   Performance Analysis

As can be seen in Fig. 5, the average fitness values – as well as the averages of the maximum fitness values – of the evolutionary runs is quite different per encoding. The generative encoding seems to be able to quickly find decent behaviors that are rewarded with a high fitness value. A Mann-Whitney U test has been performed at specified intervals to check whether the encodings performed significantly different. The performance difference was measured using the average fitness values of the maximum fitness of each individual evolutionary run at a specified time. The test resulted in a significant difference between evolved populations after 6,250 evaluations (p-value: 0.000612) and 12,500 evaluations (p-value: 0.003674) when simulating a maximum of 5 modules. There was also a significant difference between the two encodings at 6,250 evaluations (p-value: 0.00328), not at 12,500 evaluation (p-value: 0.0124106) but again at 25,000 evaluations (p-value: 0.001617) when evolving a maximum of 10 modules. The runs of the simulation evolving a maximum of 20 modules was also statistically different at evaluation 6,250 (0.00332) but not at evaluation 12,500 (p-value: 0.177805) and also not at evaluation 25,000 (p-value: 0.209462). The maximum and average fitness values of the individual runs can be seen in Fig. 4.

3.2   Phenotypes

Different distinct phenotypic behaviors emerged after a certain amount of evolutionary time. The direct encoding evolved various kinds of strategies though the generative encoding had evolved more simple, distinct types of locomotion due to the similarity in behavior seen in several modules. Caterpillar like behavior could be seen evolved conglomerates that were composed of a single chain of modules Fig. 7b. A single chain of modules could also result in a different type of rolling locomotion Fig. 6a, b. For some evolved robots there was no apparent logic to how they moved. Two robots tossed their weight around which resulted in complex rolling (Figs. 6c, 7c and d) and one robot performed a crawling (Fig. 7e) behavior. The types of behavior should become more evident when consulting the supplied video [27].

The constructive strategy of the direct encoding has a tendency to add modules to the robot. This results in the best individual of all the different evolutionary runs to be composed of 5 modules when simulating a maximum of 5 modules. In the case that the maximum number of modules is 10, 8 out of 12 runs have reached the maximum number of modules and the average is 9 modules. When 20 modules are allowed, the average is 12.33 with a standard deviation of 2.87. In this experiment, the amount of modules are limited by the fact that the excess of torque breaks the connections between the modules, which are heavily penalized by the fitness function.

All the robots with a maximum of five modules developed similar morphologies, linear structures, with a rolling behavior. One of them is shown in Fig. 6a. With a limit of 10 modules, branches in the structure of the robots appear. Despite the fact that the rolling behavior is still predominant, a crawling behavior can be found in some individuals (Fig. 6b). When increasing the maximum number of modules to 20, some unspecified conglomerates of modules are found but most of the behaviors roll or crawl as in Fig. 6c.

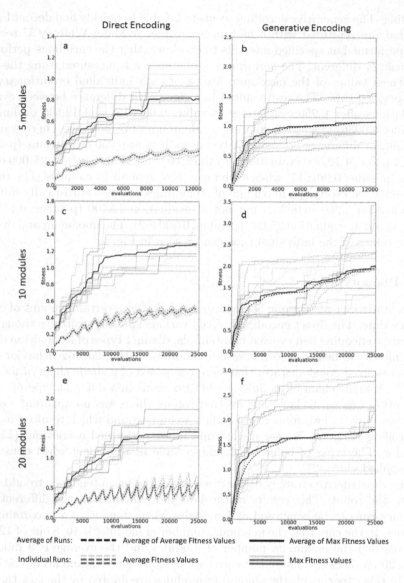

Fig. 4. The graphs represent the individual runs done for each experiment. The six graphs are represent the direct encoding simulating a maximum of 5 servo modules (a); generative encoding simulating a maximum of 5 modules (b); direct encoding simulating a maximum of 10 servo modules (c); generative encoding simulating a maximum of 10 modules (d); direct encoding simulating a maximum of 20 servo modules (e), generative encoding simulating a maximum of 20 modules (f). The bold black line represents the average maximum fitness values for all runs while the black dotted line represents the average of the average fitness values of all runs. The colored lines represent individual runs, where the solid line represents the maximum fitness value of the population and the dotted line the average fitness of the population. (Color figure online)

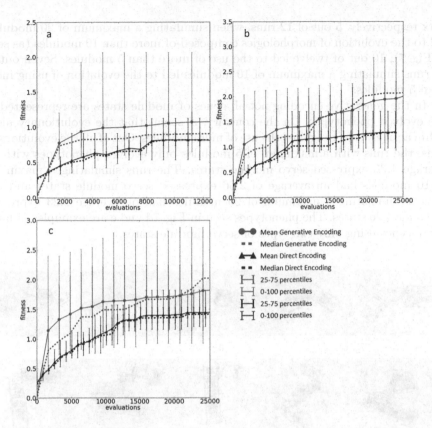

Fig. 5. The graphs display the average maximum fitness values of the different evolutionary runs when simulating a maximum of 5 modules (a), 10 modules (b) and 20 modules (c). The solid blue line marked with circles represents the average maximum fitness value of all the runs of the generative encoding. The red solid line marked with triangles represents the average maximum fitness values of the direct encoding. The dotted lines represent the median of the two types of encodings. The thick error bars depict the 25–75 percentiles and the thin error bars depict the 0–100 percentiles. (Color figure online)

In the generative encoding there was a recurrence of simple friction based phenotype (Fig. 7a) when simulating a maximum of 5 modules. This friction based phenotype seemed to exploit friction parameters of the simulator. Exactly half of the evolutionary runs that allowed for a maximum of 5 servo modules stagnated in a local optima with this kind of phenotype. Moreover, the fitness values of these individuals were quite low while other simple more effective morphologies, such as the phenotype shown in Fig. 7b, were possible to evolve. Considering the amount of modules of the resulting phenotypes, the amount of modules present in all robots was considerably smaller in the generative encoding compared to the direct encoding. The average amount of modules in the best evolved individuals of all runs was 3.5, 6.83 and 8.615 for the runs allowing 5, 10 and 20 modules max respectively. 5 out of 12 runs, when simulating a maximum of 20 modules, led to the evolution of morphologies composed of more than 10 modules (as seen in Fig. 7); 10 out of twelve led to the use of more than 5 modules. Seven out of 12 runs simulating a maximum of 10 modules led to the evolution of using more than 5 modules.

In the generative encoding not all genes of module states are represented in the evolved phenotypes. On the contrary, it seems that the evolutionary algorithm actively selects against the use of more modules. Out of all the evolutionary runs, the runs with a maximum of 5 modules only evolved phenotypes with on average 1.33 expressed servo module states. The runs simulating a maximum of 10 modules had an average of 2.66 expressed servo module states and the runs of simulating a maximum of 20 modules had on average 2.23 expressed servo module states. The phenotypes seen in Fig. 7d and e are examples of large phenotypes using only two types of servo module states.

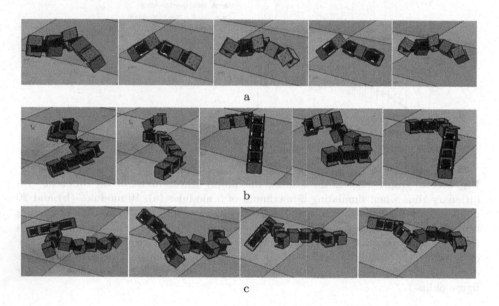

a

b

c

Fig. 6. Phenotypes obtained through the direct encoding. Resulting phenotypes simulated with a maximum of 5 modules (a), 10 modules (b) and 20 modules (c). For a more detailed visualization of the phenotypes, see [27]

4   Discussion

As can be derived from the graphs (Figs. 4 and 5) there is a difference in performance between the generative and direct encoding. The most striking difference in performance can be seen in the initial phase of the generative encoding where it outperforms the direct encoding. Over time, the direct encoding was able to catch up with the generative encoding and the performance differences were no

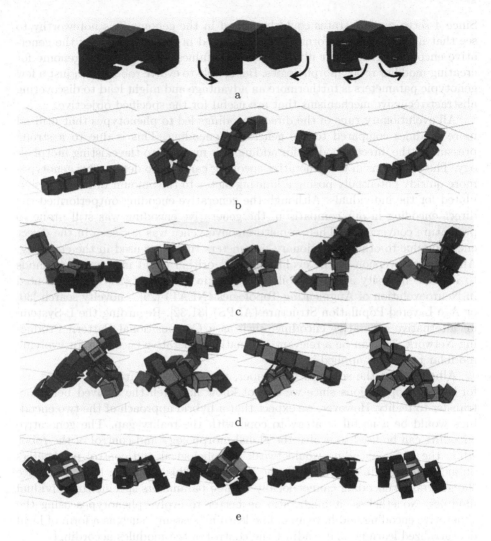

Fig. 7. Various phenotypes acquired through the generative encoding. Resulting phenotypes simulated with a maximum of five modules (a), ten modules (b) and 20 modules (c; d). For a more detailed visualization of the phenotypes, see [27]

longer statistically significant. The generative encoding still had an advantage in the long run when only a maximum of 5 modules could be simulated. This result was counter intuitive since we expected the generative encoding to perform better in the long run when more modules could be simulated.

A smaller portion of the genome of the generative encoding can lead to modular robots containing more modules than the direct encoding. The amount of servo module states used in the generative encoding was 2.23 on average in the final evaluations of the evolutionary runs of the generative encoding.

Since 4 servo module states could be stored in the genome it is noteworthy to see that not all genetic information is expressed in the phenotype of the generative encoding. This result illustrates the usefulness of reusing the genome for creating modular robot morphologies. Being able to evolve robots with just a few genotypic parameters is furthermore an advantage and might lead to discovering abstract recursive mechanisms that are useful for the specified objective.

All evolutionary runs of the direct encodings led to phenotypes that utilized more modules compared to the generative encoding. This is due to a strong pressure in the direct encoding for adding new modules to the existing morphology. The mutations in the generative encoding can lead to destructive genotypes more quickly potentially posing a limiting factor to the amount of modules simulated for the individuals. Although the generative encoding outperformed the direct encoding in our comparison, the generative encoding was still prone to premature convergence. This premature convergence was not seen in the direct encoding due to other evolutionary parameters that were used in the encoding. An improved version of the evolutionary algorithm could implement methods to increase diversity and evolvability as done in speciation [28] – implemented in Neuroevolution of Augmenting Topologies (NEAT) [29] – novelty search [30] or Age Layered Population Structure (ALPS) [31,32]. Regarding the L-System, an alternative generative encoding, such as a Compositional Pattern Producing Network [33], can be a relevant alternative generative encoding for evolving modular robots (as applied in [16]).

Albeit out of the scope of this paper, the presented data is of limited use for robotic applications since we do not know how well the evolved behaviors transfer to reality. However, we expect that a hybrid approach of the two encodings would be a useful strategy to cope with the reality gap. The generative encoding can be used to evolve the global morphology and control of the robot while the direct encoding would tweak morphological and control parameters online or in a feedback loop with the simulator. This would be beneficial since the generative encoding cannot locally change parameters specific to individual modules. Nonetheless, it might also be better to evolve phenotypes using the generative encoding and have an online learning system – such as a form of local decentralized learning [34] – adjust the control of the modules accordingly.

The presented semi-homogeneous modular robot system presents a promising step in the direction of evolving feasible modular robots. Increasing the heterogeneity in the system would give us additional insight in how we should model or modules in the future to produce even better robots. One could think of applying additional structural modules that have a variable stiffness. Since many organisms exploit various biomechanical attributes – be it elasticity, friction, strength – adding this type of module can enable evolution to come up with morphological solutions [35] and reduces the need for every part of the robot morphology to be actuated. Additionally, sensory modules can be implemented to extent the functionality of the system giving the robot inputs to its control system. The products of evolution of these potentially evolved hetegeneous modular robots can become experimental platforms that can be consulted before designing and building a non-modular equivalent.

5   Conclusion

Much work in evolutionary robotics is devoted to brain-body optimization strategies though few studies take into account the transferability of the evolved morphologies and control systems. We try to decrease this gap and enable researchers to have a fast way of evolving and evaluating robots in simulation and reality. Our robotic platform that simulates conglomerates of modules showed that a generative encoding, despite, having less optimization freedom, is more effective for evolving locomotion in simulated robots. The reuse of genes in the generative encoding seems to work well for the evolution of robot morphologies and control. This is a great advantage when constructing a robot out of many modules since many of them can be assigned with the same control parameters. We conceive that the generative encoding is able to evolve more abstract and simple robots and suspect that a hybrid system would be ideal for experimenting with the reality gap of the evolved robots. This hybrid system can initially use a generative encoding in simulation followed up by a direct encoding that locally optimizes parameters in a real robot.

Acknowledgement. This project was in part funded by Project 'flora robotica' which has received funding from the European Unions Horizon 2020 research and innovation program under the FET grant agreement, no. 640959. Computation/simulation for the work described in this paper was supported by the DeIC National HPC Centre, SDU. Special thanks to Rodrigo Moreno Garca (Universidad Nacional de Colombia) and Ceyue Liu (China University of Mining & Technology) that helped shape the design and implementation of the robotic Modules.

References

1. Lipson, H., Pollack, J.B.: Automatic design and manufacture of robotic lifeforms. Nature **406**(6799), 974–978 (2000)
2. Hornby, G.S., Lipson, H., Pollack, J.B.: Generative representations for the automated design of modular physical robots. IEEE Trans. Robot. Autom. **19**(4), 703–719 (2003)
3. Eiben, A.E., Bredeche, N., Hoogendoorn, M., Stradner, J., Timmis, J., Tyrrell, A.M., Winfield, A.F.T.: The triangle of life: evolving robots in real-time and real-space. In: Advances in Artificial Life, ECAL 2013, pp. 1056–1063 (2013)
4. Stoy, K.: The deformatron robot: a biologically inspired homogeneous modular robot. In: Proceedings - IEEE International Conference on Robotics and Automation, pp. 2527–2531, May 2006
5. Reece, J.B., Urry, L.A., Cain, M.L., Wasserman, S.A., Minorsky, P.V., Jackson, R.B.: Campbell Biology. Pearson, Boston (2010)
6. Floreano, D., Mattiussi, C.: Bio-Inspired Artificial Intelligence. MIT Press, Cambridge (2008)
7. Marbach, D., Ijspeert, A.J.: Online optimization of modular robot locomotion. In: IEEE International Conference Mechatronics and Automation, vol. 1, pp. 248–253, July 2005
8. Faíña, A., Bellas, F., López-Peña, F., Duro, R.J.: EDHMoR: evolutionary designer of heterogeneous modular robots. Eng. Appl. Artif. Intell. **26**(10), 2408–2423 (2013)

9. Guettas, C., Cherif, F., Breton, T., Duthen, Y.: Cooperative co-evolution of configuration and control for modular robots. In: 2014 International Conference on Multimedia Computing and Systems, ICMCS 2014, pp. 26–31, October 2015

10. Sims, K.: Evolving virtual creatures. In: Proceedings of the 21st Annual Conference on Computer Graphics and Interactive Techniques, pp. 15–22, July 1994

11. Sims, K.: Evolving 3D morphology and behavior by competition. Artif. Life 1(4), 353–372 (1994)

12. Hornby, G., Pollack, J.: The advantages of generative grammatical encodings for physical design. In: Proceedings of the 2001 Congress on Evolutionary Computation (IEEE Cat. No. 01TH8546), vol. 1, pp. 600–607 (2001)

13. Auerbach, J.E., Bongard, J.C.: Evolving complete robots with CPPN-NEAT: the utility of recurrent connections. In: Proceedings of the 13th Annual Genetic and Evolutionary Computation Conference, GECCO 2011, pp. 1475–1482 (2011)

14. Cheney, N., MacCurdy, R., Clune, J., Lipson, H.: Unshackling evolution: evolving soft robots with multiple materials and a powerful generative encoding. In: Proceeding of the Fifteenth Annual Conference on Genetic and Evolutionary Computation, GECCO 2013, p. 167 (2013)

15. Bonardi, S., Vespignani, M., Moeckel, R., Kieboom, J.V.D., Pouya, S., Sproewitz, A., Ijspeert, A.J.: Automatic generation of reduced CPG control networks for locomotion of arbitrary modular robot structures. In: Proceedings of Robotics: Science and Systems (2014)

16. Auerbach, J.E., Heitz, G., Kornatowski, P.M., Floreano, D.: Rapid evolution of robot gaits. In: GECCO 2015, pp. 743–744 (2015)

17. Lindenmayer, A.: Mathematical models for cellular interactions in development I. Filaments with one-sided inputs. J. Theor. Biol. 18(3), 280–299 (1968)

18. Kamimura, A., Kurokawa, H., Yoshida, E., Murata, S., Tomita, K., Kokaji, S.: Automatic locomotion design and experiments for a modular robotic system. IEEE/ASME Trans. Mechatron. 10(3), 314–325 (2005)

19. Sproewitz, A., Moeckel, R., Maye, J., Ijspeert, A.J.: Learning to move in modular robots using central pattern generators and online optimization. Int. J. Robot. Res. 27(3–4), 423–443 (2008)

20. Still, S., Hepp, K., Douglas, R.J.: Neuromorphic walking gait control. IEEE Trans. Neural Netw. 17(2), 496–508 (2006)

21. Ijspeert, A.J.: Central pattern generators for locomotion control in animals and robots: a review. Neural Netw. 21(4), 642–653 (2008)

22. Rohmer, E., Singh, S.P.N., Freese, M.: V-REP: a versatile and scalable robot simulation framework. In: IEEE International Conference on Intelligent Robots and Systems, pp. 1321–1326 (2013)

23. Faiña, A., Orjales, F., Bellas, F., Duro, R.: First steps towards a heterogeneous modular robotic architecture for for intelligent industrial operation. In: IEEE/RSJ International Conference on Intelligent Robots and Systems, IROS 2011 (2011)

24. Cheney, N., Bongard, J., Sunspiral, V., Lipson, H.: On the difficulty of co-optimizing morphology and control in evolved virtual creatures. In: Proceedings of the Artificial Life Conference 2016, ALIFE XV, pp. 226–234 (2016)

25. Lindenmayer, A., Jürgensen, H.: Grammars of development: discrete-state models for growth, differentiation, and gene expression in modular organisms. In: Rozenberg, G., Salomaa, A. (eds.) Lindenmayer Systems: Impacts on Theoretical Computer Science, Computer Graphics, and Developmental Biology, pp. 3–21. Springer, Heidelberg (1992)

26. Veenstra, F., Faina, A., Stoy, K., Risi, S.: Generating artificial plant morphologies for function and aesthetics through evolving L-Systems. In: Proceedings of the Artificial Life Conference 2016, pp. 692–699. MIT Press (2016)

27. Veenstra, F., Faina, A., Risi, S., Stoy, K.: Video: evolving modular robots using direct and generative encodings (2017). https://www.youtube.com/watch?v=HCDftic1AdA

28. Cook, O.F.: Factors of species-formation. Science **23**(587), 506–507 (1906)

29. Stanley, K.O., Miikkulainen, R.: Efficient evolution of neural network topologies. In: Proceedings of the 2002 Congress on Evolutionary Computation, CEC 2002, pp. 1757–1762 (2002)

30. Lehman, J., Stanley, K.O.: Exploiting open-endedness to solve problems through the search for novelty. In: Artificial Life XI, pp. 329–336 (2008)

31. Hornby, G.S.: ALPS: the age-layered population structure for reducing the problem of premature convergence. In: Proceedings of the 8th Annual Conference on Genetic and Evolutionary Computation, pp. 815–822 (2006)

32. Hornby, G.S.: The age-layered population structure (ALPS) evolutionary algorithm. In: Proceedings of the 9th Annual Conference on Genetic and Evolutionary Computation (2009)

33. Stanley, K.O.: Compositional pattern producing networks: a novel abstraction of development. Genet. Program. Evolvable Mach. **8**(2), 131–162 (2007)

34. Christensen, D.J., Schultz, U.P., Stoy, K.: A distributed and morphology-independent strategy for adaptive locomotion in self-reconfigurable modular robots. Robot. Auton. Syst. **61**(9), 1021–1035 (2013)

35. Pfeifer, R., Iida, F.: Morphological computation: connecting body, brain and environment. Japan. Sci. Mon. **58**(2), 48–54 (2005)

36. Prusinkiewicz, P., Lindenmayer, A.: The algorithmic beauty of plants. Plant Sci. **122**(1), 109–110 (1997). doi:10.1016/S0168-9452(96)04526-8

Continual and One-Shot Learning Through Neural Networks with Dynamic External Memory

Benno Lüders, Mikkel Schläger, Aleksandra Korach, and Sebastian Risi$^{(\boxtimes)}$

IT University of Copenhagen, Copenhagen, Denmark
{blde,mihs,akor,sebr}@itu.dk

Abstract. Training neural networks to quickly learn new skills without forgetting previously learned skills is an important open challenge in machine learning. A common problem for adaptive networks that can learn during their lifetime is that the weights encoding a particular task are often overridden when a new task is learned. This paper takes a step in overcoming this limitation by building on the recently proposed *Evolving Neural Turing Machine* (ENTM) approach. In the ENTM, neural networks are augmented with an external memory component that they can write to and read from, which allows them to store associations quickly and over long periods of time. The results in this paper demonstrate that the ENTM is able to perform *one-shot learning* in reinforcement learning tasks without catastrophic forgetting of previously stored associations. Additionally, we introduce a new ENTM *default jump* mechanism that makes it easier to find unused memory location and therefor facilitates the evolution of continual learning networks. Our results suggest that augmenting evolving networks with an external memory component is not only a viable mechanism for adaptive behaviors in neuroevolution but also allows these networks to perform continual and one-shot learning at the same time.

Keywords: Neural Turing Machine · Continual learning · Adaptive neural networks · Plasticity · Memory · Neuroevolution

1 Introduction

An important open challenge in AI is the creation of agents that can continuously adapt to novel situations and learn new skills within their lifetime without catastrophic forgetting of previous learned ones [1]. While much progress has been made recently in diverse areas of AI, addressing the challenge of continual learning – a hallmark ability of humans – has only received little attention. Some notable approach exist, such as the recently introduced *progressive neural network* approach [2], which takes a step towards continual learning but requires the manual identification of tasks. Earlier approaches include the *cascade-correlation algorithm* [3] that can incrementally learn new feature detectors while avoiding

© Springer International Publishing AG 2017
G. Squillero and K. Sim (Eds.): EvoApplications 2017, Part I, LNCS 10199, pp. 886–901, 2017.
DOI: 10.1007/978-3-319-55849-3_57

forgetting. Another recently introduced method called *elastic weight consolidation* [4], allows neural networks to learn multiple tasks sequentially by slowing down learning on weights that are important for previously learned tasks.

The approach presented in this paper is based on neuroevolution (NE), i.e. the artificial evolution of artificial neural networks (ANNs), which has shown promise in creating adaptive agent behaviors for a wide variety of tasks [5–7]. In order to enable these evolving ANNs to learn during their lifetime, efforts have been made to allow them to adapt online and learn from past experience [8–17]. Adaptive neural networks can either change through local Hebbian learning rules [18], in which connection weights are modified based on neural activation [8,9,14], or recurrent neural networks (RNNs) that store activation patterns through recurrent connections [10]. However, a common problem for these techniques is their inability to sustain long-term memory. The network weights that encode a particular task are often overridden when a new task is learned, resulting in catastrophic forgetting [19]. Recently, Ellefsen et al. [11] showed that by encouraging the evolution of modular neural networks together with neuromodulated plasticity [14], catastrophic forgetting in networks can be minimized, allowing them to learn new skills while retaining the ones already learned. Here we present a complementary approach that does not require mechanisms to encourage neural modularity, because memory and control are separated by design.

More specifically, we build on a recent method by Graves et al. [20] that tries to overcome the limitation of neural networks to store data over long timescales by augmenting them with an external read-write memory component. The differentiable architecture of their *Neural Turing Machine* (NTM) can be trained through gradient descent and is able to learn simple algorithms such as copying, sorting and recall from example data. Instead of the original NTM, which requires differentiability throughout, here we employ the evolvable version of the NTM (ENTM) that can be trained through neuroevolution and allows the approach to be directly applied to reinforcement learning domains [21]. Additionally, by evolving the topology and weights of the neural networks starting from a minimal structure, the optimal network structure is found automatically.

This paper also introduces a new ENTM mechanism, called *default jump*, with the goal to make unused memory locations easier accessible to the ENTM. The motivation for such an approach is that especially tasks requiring continual learning should benefit from a mechanism that prevents overriding previously learned knowledge. We test the ENTM approach on two different tasks. The first one is a Morris water maze navigation tasks, which does not require continual learning but adds further evidence to the adaptive capabilities of the ENTM. The main task is the season task [11], which tests an agent's ability to withstand catastrophic forgetting. In this task the agent has to learn to eat nutritious food items while avoiding poisonous food. Different food items are presented during different seasons, requiring the agent to remember what it learned during previous seasons in order to perform well. The results show that the ENTM is in fact able to learn new associations without catastrophic forgetting by using its external memory component. Additionally, in contrast to the approach by Ellefsen et al., in which associations are learned over multiple network presentations [11], our method can learn new associations in one-shot.

While the previously established methodologies for evolving adaptive networks were either plastic synapses or recurrent connections, this paper adds further evidence that the emerging class of memory augmented neural networks in machine learning [20,22,23], also benefit networks trained through evolution. Evolving adaptive networks has been a long-standing problem in NE that has only seen limited progress; networks with an external read-write memory could now make other adaptive tasks solvable that have heretofore been inaccessible for NE.

2   Background

In this section we review work that the approach in this paper builds upon, such as neuroevolution techniques and Neural Turing Machines.

2.1   Neuroevolution

The weights and topologies of the Artificial Neural Networks (ANNs) in this paper are trained by the Neuroevolution of Augmenting Topologies (NEAT) approach [24]. The main challenge with evolving neural networks is that some of the primary principles of Evolutionary Algorithms (EAs), mainly crossover, are difficult to apply to networks with arbitrary topologies. NEAT solves this problem by using historical markers for all genes in the chromosome; every time a new mutation is performed it receives a historical marking, which is a unique identifying number. This way networks with arbitrary topologies can be combined in a meaningful way.

Additionally, NEAT begins with simple networks (i.e. networks with no hidden nodes and inputs directly connected to the network's outputs), and augments them during the evolutionary process through mutations (adding nodes and connections) and crossover. NEAT uses speciation, which is designed to protect innovation. When a new gene is added through mutation, the resulting phenotype will typically decrease in fitness initially, causing the individual to be eliminated from the population. Speciation avoids this by assigning newly formed topologies to separate species based on genetic diversity, which will not have to compete with older, currently fitter species. This way, potentially innovative networks will get a chance to evolve, preserving diversity. Inside each species, the individuals compete with other species members instead of the entire population, using a technique called *fitness sharing*. This is analogous to *niching* in natural evolution, where species avoid competing with others, by discovering unexplored ways to exploit the environment.

2.2 Neural Turing Machines (NTMs)

A Turing Machine (TM) is an abstract machine that reads and writes information from/to a tape, according to rules emitted by a controller. A Neural Turing Machine (NTM) is a TM where the controller is an ANN [20]. The controller determines what is written to and read from the tape. At each time step, the ANN emits a number of different signals, including a data vector and various control inputs. These signals allow the NTM to focus its read and write heads on different parts of the external memory. The write heads modify the tapes content and the information from the read heads is used as input to the ANN during the next time step. At the same time, the ANN receive input from its environment and can interact with it through its outputs.

The original NTM introduced by Graves et al. [20] is trained end-to-end through gradient descent, and therefore has to be differentiable throughout. This is achieved by blurry read and write operations that interact with every location on the tape at once, requiring a fixed tape length. Each read and write operation has weightings associated with every location on the tape. The read and write heads act individually, so weightings have to be calculated for each head. The tape can be addressed with two mechanisms: content-based and location-based. In content-based addressing, the location is found by comparing the tape's content and the read/write vector, where greater similarity results in higher weighting. Location based addressing employs a shift mechanism, that can shift all weightings to one side, while rotating border values to the opposite end of the tape. This mechanism is implemented through an interpolation gate output assigned to each head, which controls interpolation between the current weighting and the weighting of the previous time step. After the interpolation, the shift is performed by using special shift outputs from the head. In the final NTM step, the resulting weights can be sharpened to favor locations with greater weights.

2.3 Evolvable Neural Turing Machines (ENTMs)

Based on the principles behind NTMs, the recently introduced Evolvable Neural Turing Machine (ENTM) uses NEAT to learn the topology and weights of the ANN controller [21]. That way the topology of the network does not have to be defined a priori (as is the case in the original NTM setup) and the network can grow in response to the complexity of the task. As demonstrated by Greve et al. [21], the ENTM often finds compact network topologies to solve a particular task, thereby avoiding searching through unnecessarily high-dimensional spaces. Because the network does not have to be differentiable, it can use hard attention and shift mechanisms, allowing it to generalize perfectly to longer sequences in a copy task. Additionally, a dynamic, theoretically unlimited tape size is now possible.

Figure 1 shows the ENTM setup in more detail. The ENTM has a single combined read/write head. The network emits a write vector w of size M, a write interpolation control input i, a content jump control input j, and three shift control inputs s_l, s_0, and s_r (left shift, no shift, right shift). The size of the

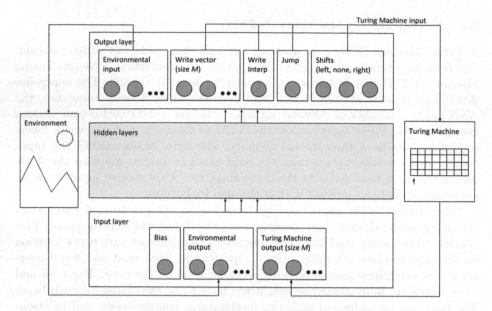

Fig. 1. Evolvable Neural Turing Machine. This figure shows the activation flow between the ANN, the memory bank and the external environment. Extra ANN outputs determine the vector to be written to memory and the movement of the read and write heads. The ANN receives the content of the current memory location as input at the beginning of the next time-step. In addition to the NTM specific inputs and outputs, the ANN has domain dependent actuators and sensors. The structure of the hidden layers is automatically determined by the NEAT algorithm.

write vector M determines the size of each memory location on the tape. The write interpolation component allows blending between the write vector and the current tape values at the write position, where $M_h(t)$ is the content of the tape at the current head location h, at time step t, i_t is the write interpolation, and w_t is the write vector, all at time step t:

$$M_h(t) = M_h(t-1) \cdot (1 - i_t) + w_t \cdot i_t. \qquad (1)$$

The content jump determines if the head should be moved to the location in memory that most closely resembles the write vector. A content jump is performed if the value of the control input exceeds 0.5. The similarity between write vector w and memory vector m is determined by:

$$s(w, m) = \frac{\sum_{i=1}^{M} |w_i - m_i|}{M}. \qquad (2)$$

At each time step t, the following actions are performed in order:

1. Record the write vector w_t to the current head position h, interpolated with the existing content according to the write interpolation i_t.

2. If the content jump control input j_t is greater than 0.5, move the head to location on the tape most similar to the write vector w_t.
3. Shift the head one position left or right on the tape, or stay at the current location, according to the shift control inputs s_l, s_0, and s_r.
4. Read and return the tape values at the new head position.

3   Evolvable Neural Turing Machines for Continual Learning

In the original ENTM setup [21], the tape has an initial size of one and its size is increased if the head shifts to a previously unvisited location at either end. This is the only mechanism to increase the tape size in the original setup. Thus to create a new memory, the ENTM write head has to first jump to one end of the tape, and then perform a shift into the correct direction to reach a new, untouched memory location. This procedure also requires marking the end of the tape, to identify it as the target for a subsequent content jump.

In this paper we introduce a new *default jump* mechanism that should facilitate creating new memories without catastrophic overriding learned associates. The default jump utilizes a single pre-initialised memory location (in this paper the vector is initialized to values of 0.5), which is always accessible at one end of the tape. It can provide an efficient, consistent opportunity for the write head to find an unused memory location during a content jump, in which a new memory must be recorded. Once the default memory location is written to, a new default memory is created at the end of the tape. Additionally, we introduce a minimum similarity threshold for the content jumps; if a content jump is performed, and no location on the tape meets the minimum similarity threshold, the head will instead jump to the default location.

4   Water Maze Task

To further test the basic learning capabilities of the ENTM, we initially performed experiments on a task that does not necessarily require continual learning. An experiment was set up for a discrete grid-world version of the water maze domain. This domain, which is also known as the Morris water navigation task, is usually used to study spatial learning and memory in rodents [25], and therefore a good test domain for our ENTM. In these experiments, a rodent is typically placed at the center of a circular pool of water, and the objective is to find an invisible platform to escape from the pool, which is sometimes relocated.

In our setup, the platform (or goal) can appear in any of the four corners of the grid (Fig. 2). During the course of the experiment, the platform is relocated, and the agent has to explore the environment to relocate it. A step limit was imposed to prevent the agent from searching for the goal indefinitely. However, it is sufficiently large to allow ample time for the agent to discover the platform.

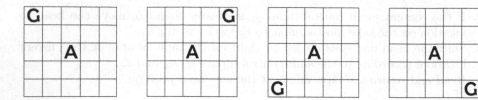

Fig. 2. Water Maze. The agent starts at position A and has to reach the four possible goal (G) positions on a 5×5 grid.

4.1   Neural Network Inputs/Outputs

The network has four outputs to determine the direction of movement (left, right, up, down). The network receives as input the agent's x and y positions, wall sensors for all of the four sides, as well as sensors that indicate when the goal is found. The memory bank vector size is set to two and the default jump mechanisms was not employed for this task.

4.2   Evaluation

Every individual is evaluated on ten rounds in the water maze environment. At the beginning of each round, the agent is put in the center, and the goal in one of the corners. The corner chosen during the first round remains the same for six rounds. In the seventh round, the goal is relocated to one of the other corners. This process – one iteration – is repeated 12 times to ensure that every specimen is tested on all possible permutations of goal positions. Tests were performed on two grid sizes, 5×5 and 9×9.

Agents are scored as follows: If the goal was not previously discovered, reaching the water maze platform yields a maximum number of points for this round, normalized to 1.0, regardless of the path taken. If the limit of steps is reached before finding the goal, a score of 0.1 is awarded. In a situation where the goal was discovered in previous rounds, the agent is scored by proximity. The closer the agent is to the goal at the end of the round, the higher the awarded reward. However, diverging from the shortest path to the goal and taking additional steps results in a punishment. In more detail, moving towards the goal adds a number of points equal to the difference between the maximum possible Manhattan distance from the goal and the agent's current distance. Moving away subtracts the difference between the maximum distance and the agent's previous distance and a further punishment of 0.4 times previous distance. Moreover, an additional -1 is taken from the score at the end of the round for every extra step over the possible minimum required number of steps. The score cannot drop below 0 and is normalized between 0.0 and 1.0. The fitness function for a single round can be expressed as the following sum:

$$F = \sum_{i=1}^{m}[(1 - g^s)(g_i^f + 0.1 \cdot (1 - g_i^f)) + g^s \cdot (c_i \cdot (d^{max} - d_i^{cur})$$
$$- (1 - c_i)(d^{max} - d_i^{prev} + 0.4 \cdot d_i^{prev}))] - s_{exc} \cdot (s_{made} - s_{min}), \quad (3)$$

where m describes the maximum number of steps, $g^s \in \{0, 1\}$ states if the goal was seen in previous rounds, $g_i^f \in \{0, 1\}$ states whether the goal was found as a result of taking step i, $c_s \in \{0, 1\}$ states if the agent moved closer to the goal in step i, d^{max} is the maximum possible Manhattan distance between the agent and the goal, d_i^{cur} is the agent's current distance from the goal, d_i^{prev} is the agent's previous distance from the goal, $s_{exc} \in \{0, 1\}$ states if the agent took more steps than required, s_{made} is the number of steps made, and s_{min} is the minimum number of steps needed to reach the goal. Given a large number of moves available to the agent to ease the discovery process, it is possible to end such a round with a rating equal to 0.

4.3 NEAT Parameters

For the water maze the population is 300. Connection weight mutation rate is set to 60%, connection addition probability to 2%, and connection removal probability to 5%. Nodes are added with a probability of 2%. The maximum number of generations is set to 10,000. The ENTM ANJI 2.0 NEAT implementation[1] was used for the water maze task.

5 Season Task

The main test for the agents in this paper is the *season task* [11], which tests an agent's ability to withstand catastrophic forgetting (Fig. 3). During its lifetime, the agent is presented with a number of different food items. Some are *nutritious*, some are *poisonous*. Rewards are given for eating nutritious and avoiding poisonous food items, while punishment is given for eating poisonous and avoiding nutritious food. The goal of the agent is to learn and remember which food items can be eaten. The task is split into *days*, *seasons* and *years*. Each day, every food item will be presented in a random order. After a certain number of days, the season will change from summer to winter. During winter, a different set of food items will be presented. Again, some are poisonous and some are not, and the agent has to learn the new associations. After the winter season, the season will change back to summer. The agent now has to remember what it learned during the previous summer season to achieve the highest possible score. Both seasons constitute a *year*. To successfully solve the season task, the agents needs to learn to store information about the food items it encounters in its external memory. A hand-designed system might consider one memory location per food item, which the agent reads from to determine the correct action. If the agent encounters food it has not seen before, it should use the reinforcement learning signals to create a new memory at a new location.

Following Ellefsen et al. [11], each lifetime has three years, and each year has two seasons. Each season has four food items (presented in a random order), of which two are poisonous. In Ellefsen's experiments, there is a fixed number of five days per season. In this paper we use a random number of days between one and five to prevent overfitting to a certain sequence length.

---

[1] https://goo.gl/P4unLh.

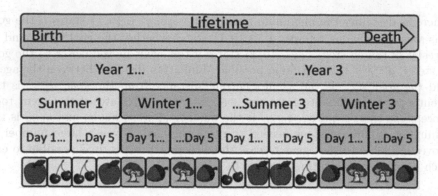

Fig. 3. Season Task. Example of a season task environment for one individual's lifetime. The lifetime lasts three years. Each year has two seasons: winter and summer. Each season consists of five days. Each day, the season's food items are presented to the individual in a random order. Figure from Ellefsen et al. [11].

5.1   Neural Network Inputs/Outputs

The ANNs environmental inputs consist of inputs 1–4 to encode which summer item is presented, and inputs 5–8 to encode the winter items. Additionally, one reward input is activated when the agent makes the correct decision, and one punishment input is activated when the wrong decision is made. The ENTM read/write vector size M is set to 10. The ANN has one output o connected to the environment, which determines whether a food item should be eaten ($o > 0.7$) or not ($o < 0.3$). If $0.3 < o \leq 0.7$, neither reward nor punishment inputs are activated.

For each time step, i.e. one activation of the ANN, only a single location can be read from the tape. Therefore, the memory associated with a food item has to be stored in a single location. When recalling from memory, the head has to perform a content jump to the relevant location; shifting alone would not be sufficient to reliably reach the correct location of memorized food items, given the random ordering in which they are presented. Because the ENTM needs time to perform a content jump after it receives the relevant input vector, at least two time steps are required per food item to successfully retrieve stored information. If the ENTM records feedback from the environment, another step is required, totaling three time steps. We introduce redundancy in the form of additional time steps per food item to facilitate the evolution of this relatively complex algorithm. Through prior experimentation we found that four time steps per food item work well in practice. The input nodes encoding the current food item are activated during all four steps. The reward calculation is based on the response of the network in the third step and given to the network in form of reward or punishment in step four.

5.2   Evaluation

Each individual is evaluated on 50 randomly generated sequences. To avoid noisy evaluations, the same 50 random sequences are used throughout the evolutionary process. However, we also perform a generalization test on the last generation networks on unseen and longer sequences (40 seasons with 4–10 days in testing, compared to six seasons with 2–5 days during evolutionary training).

The agents are scored based on how often they choose the correct action for eating or ignoring a food item. The first encounter with each food item (the first day of each season in the first year) is not included in the score because the agent has no way of knowing the initial random associations. Each scored day, an agent will receive a point for making the correct decision. The resulting total fitness is scaled into the range $[0.0, 1.0]$, with $F = \frac{c}{T}$, where c is the number of correct decisions made during the lifetime, and T is the total number of scored time steps. Thus, an agent with a fitness of 1.0 will have eaten all nutritious food items, and no poisonous food items past the exploration days, solving the task perfectly.

5.3   NEAT Parameters

We use a population size of 250. The selection proportion is 20%, and the elitism proportion is 2%. Connection weight range is $[-10, 10]$. The initial interconnection proportion is set to 30%. The experiments run for a maximum of $10,000$ generations. Through prior experimentation, the optimal mutation parameters were found to be 98.8% connection weight mutation probability (default SharpNEAT setting), 9% connection addition probability, 5% connection removal probability. The node addition probability is set to 0.5%. The code for the ENTM SharpNEAT implementation can be found here: https://github.com/BLueders/ENTM_CSharpPort.

Complexity Regulation Strategy. The NEAT implementation SharpNEAT uses a complexity regulation strategy for the evolutionary process, which has proven to be quite impactful on our results. A threshold defines how complex the networks in the population can be (here defined as the number of genes in the genome and set to 350 in our experiments), before the algorithm switches to a simplifying phase, where it gradually reduces complexity. During the simplification phase, sexual offspring is deactivated, to reduce genome augmentation through crossover. This emphasizes pruning of redundant complexity in the population. The algorithm will switch back to a complexification phase when the simplification stalls, i.e. when the simplified offspring in the population do not score high enough to be selected.

6   Results

This section first presents the results on the water maze task, which tests the basic learning capabilities of the ENTM, and then results on the season task, which evaluates its continual and one-shot learning abilities.

6.1   Water Maze Results

For the 5 × 5 grid, a perfect solution was found in seven out of ten evolutionary runs, while the remaining three runs still reached a high fitness of over 0.9. As for the 9 × 9 grid size, solutions were found in five out of ten instances. Fitness scores of the remaining five tests varied from 0.95 to 0.98. Among the seven successful 5 × 5 runs, it took 3,834 generations on average to find a solution (sd = 2,585). Four solutions were found in under 5,000 generations, with two of them discovered relatively fast, within 270 and 570 generations respectively.

In the 9 × 9 domain, the average number of generations to find a solution was 3,607 (sd = 1,691). Again, four solutions were discovered in under 5,000 generations, but none in less than a 1,000.

The controller came up with an efficient strategy for solving the problem. The agent would start the exploration from the lower-right corner, and then continue moving counterclockwise, following the edge. The complete order would be lower-right, upper-right, upper-left, and lower-left. If a goal was found, then in subsequent rounds the controller would go straight for the relevant corner. In the relocation round, the agent would first look for the goal in the previously discovered position, and upon finding out it is not there, it would continue along the edge. Figure 4 presents paths taken by the exemplary 5 × 5 controller at different stages of the run with the reward positioned first in the lower-left, then in the upper-left corner. These results add to the growing body of evidence [21], that ENTMs offer an efficient alternative adaptation mechanism for evolving neural networks.

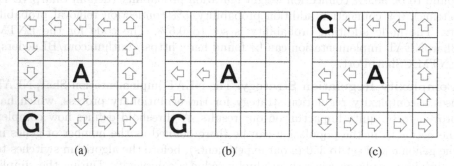

Fig. 4. Maze Solution Behavior. (a) The agent's path during exploration on a 5 × 5 grid. (b) The agent's path after the goal was found. (c) The agent's path after goal relocation.

6.2   Season Task Results

A total of 30 independent evolutionary runs were performed. The average final fitness of the ENTMs with default jump was 0.827 ($sd = 0.081$), while the average fitness without it was 0.794 ($sd = 0.066$). While this difference is not significant (according to the Mann-Whitney U test), the methods perform significantly different during testing on 50 random sequences ($p < 0.05$), confirming

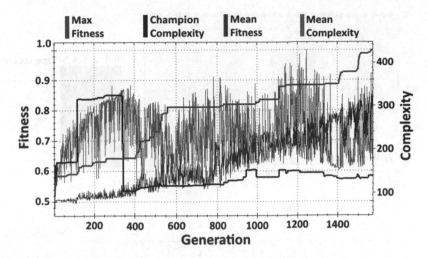

Fig. 5. Season Task Performance. Fitness and network complexity of an example solution during evolution in the season task. Notice the low champion complexity relative to the population mean.

the benefits of the new jump mechanism. In this case ENTMs with default jump scores 0.783 on average ($sd = 0.103$), while the method without default jump has a score of 0.706 ($sd = 0.085$).

Most high-performing networks connect the punishment input to the write interpolation output. This behavior only produces memories if an incorrect decision is made. If the default behavior is correct, the agent does not have to create a memory to alter its behavior. In some cases, agents do not ever write to the tape. They express a congenital or instinctive behavior and alter it only if necessary. If the environment overlaps with the instincts, nothing has to be learned; if the world differs, those differences are explored by making the wrong decisions. This triggers a punishment, which causes the creation of a new memory, which in turn alters the agent's behavior.

The best evolved network has a total of 138 connections and six hidden nodes. Figure 5 shows its fitness and complexity during evolution. The periodic increases and decreases in mean fitness mirror the complexification and simplification phases. The champion complexity drops below the average complexity around generation 350 and stays below average for the rest of the run. The initial drop is closely followed by the steepest improvement phase in fitness of the run.

The champion network is able to learn new associations in *one-shot*, without catastrophic forgetting of earlier learned associations (Fig. 6a). The network records the information about the food items in four memory locations, two for each season (Fig. 6c). The agent initially *ignores* all food items. Since it is punished for ignoring nutritious items, the agent then memorizes the food items it gets wrong and has to eat in the future. Each nutritious item is saved into its own memory location, summing up to the four locations used. Memorisation is accomplished by connecting the punishment input to the write interpolation output.

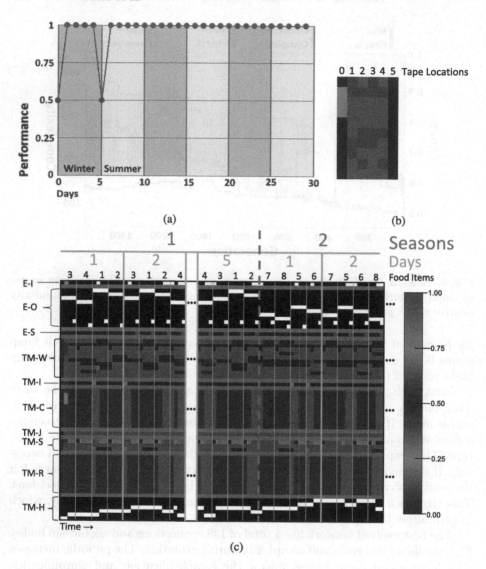

Fig. 6. Evolved Solution Example. (a) The best evolved network quickly learns the correct food associations and reaches a perfect score of 1.0, displaying one-shot learning abilities. Additionally, the associations learned in earlier seasons are still remembered in later ones. The memory content at the end of the lifetime is shown in (b). Note the initial redundant recording at location 0, and the Default Jump location at location 5. Locations 1–4 contain the associations to the nutritious food items. Memory usage during learning is shown in (c). Days 3 and 4 of season 1, and everything past day 2 in season 2 are not shown but solved perfectly. Legend: **E-I:** ANN output that determines if the food item should be eaten. **E-O:** ANN inputs from the environment; summer item (1–4), winter item (5–8), reward (9), punishment (10). **E-S:** Score indicator. **TM-W:** Write vector. **TM-I:** Write interpolation. **TM-C:** Content of the tape at the current head position after write. **TM-J:** Content jump input. **TM-S:** The three shift values, in descending order: left, none, right. **TM-R:** Read vector. **TM-H:** Current head position (after control operations).

The agent makes extensive use of the default jump location and can almost generalize perfectly to never before seen sequences, reaching a testing score of 0.988. Whenever a food item is encountered which does not have a recorded memory association, the network jumps to the default jump location, reads the pre-initialized vector, which results in the agent deciding to not eat the food item. If this triggers a punishment, because the food item was nutritious, a new memory is recorded. Whenever that item is then encountered later on during its lifetime, the correct memory will be recalled. It is worth noting that the default location is overwritten when a new food item is saved, which will result in a new default location being created at the end of the tape. During day one, when food item 3 is presented (first food item), tape position 2 (from the bottom) is the default location (see Fig. 6a). Later, when food item 4 is presented, it is overwritten, because the agent received a punishment for not eating it. Tape position 3 is now the new default location, and is overwritten later with information about food item 2, at the end of day one. At the beginning of season two, the agent successfully writes to the default Jump location again, storing the information about food item 8 in memory location 4. Food item 5 is stored in location 5. This concludes all food items that have to be stored. Food items 1, 3, 6 and 7 are poisonous, so whenever these are encountered, the agent jumps to the current default location and decides not to eat them. The final learned food associations as they are stored in memory are shown in Fig. 6b.

7   Discussion

While plastic neural networks with local learning rules can learn the correct associations in the season task gradually over multiple days [11], the ENTM-based agents can learn much faster. The evolved ENTM solutions allow successful one-shot-learning during the first day and can perfectly distinguish each food item afterwards. Memories are generated instantly, and do not need multiple iterations to form.

During evolution, some runs overfit to the most frequent associations of food items, i.e. which food items are poisonous and which are nutritious. To prevent noisy evaluations, all agents in each of the 30 evolutionary runs are always evaluated on the same 50 randomly created sequences. We distinguish two different variations of overfitting. In the first, agents overfit towards certain associations during evolution, causing them to fail during testing. In the other case, agents can solve most sequences, but fail when food items appear in a very specific order over multiple days. In the future it will be important to device strategies that produce general solutions more consistently and compare ENTM networks to solutions based on Hebbian learning in terms of robustness.

In some cases, the dynamic nature of ENTM's memory will cause the agents to continually expand their memory throughout their lifetime. This potentially unnecessary expansion can slow down the simulation significantly. In the future a cost could be introduced for expanding the memory, encouraging a more efficient memory usage.

8   Conclusion

Moving beyond the original demonstration of the ENTM [21] in the T-Maze domain, which did not require the agent to learn new associations during its lifetime, this paper shows how the ENTM is able to overcome catastrophic forgetting in a reinforcement learning task. The new capability to continually learn was demonstrated in a task requiring the agent to learn new associations while preserving previously acquired ones. Additionally, we introduced the ENTM default jump mechanism that makes it easier for the ENTM to find unused memory locations and therefore facilitates the evolution of learning agents. Importantly and in contrast to previous Hebbian-based approaches, the ENTM is able to perform continual and one-shot learning at the same time. The hope is that memory-augmented networks such as the ENTM will reinvigorate research on evolving adaptive neural networks and can serve as a novel and complementary model for lifetime learning in NE.

Acknowledgment. Computation/simulation for the work described in this paper was supported by the DeIC National HPC Centre, SDU.

References

1. Kumaran, D., Hassabis, D., McClelland, J.L.: What learning systems do intelligent agents need? Complementary learning systems theory updated. Trends Cogn. Sci. **20**(7), 512–534 (2016)
2. Rusu, A.A., Rabinowitz, N.C., Desjardins, G., Soyer, H., Kirkpatrick, J., Kavukcuoglu, K., Pascanu, R., Hadsell, R.: Progressive neural networks. Preprint arXiv:1606.04671 (2016)
3. Fahlman, S.E., Lebiere, C.: The cascade-correlation learning architecture. In: Proceedings of the Advances in Neural Information Processing Systems 2 (1989)
4. Kirkpatrick, J., Pascanu, R., Rabinowitz, N., Veness, J., Desjardins, G., Rusu, A.A., Milan, K., Quan, J., Ramalho, T., Grabska-Barwinska, A., et al.: Overcoming catastrophic forgetting in neural networks. arXiv preprint arXiv:1612.00796 (2016)
5. Floreano, D., Dürr, P., Mattiussi, C.: Neuroevolution: from architectures to learning. Evol. Intell. **1**(1), 47–62 (2008)
6. Yao, X.: Evolving artificial neural networks. Proc. IEEE **87**(9), 1423–1447 (1999)
7. Risi, S., Togelius, J.: Neuroevolution in games: state of the art and open challenges. IEEE Trans. Comput. Intell. AI Games **PP**(99), 1–1 (2015)
8. Stanley, K.O., Bryant, B.D., Miikkulainen, R.: Evolving adaptive neural networks with and without adaptive synapses. In: The 2003 Congress on Evolutionary Computation, CEC 2003, vol. 4, pp. 2557–2564. IEEE (2003)
9. Floreano, D., Urzelai, J.: Evolutionary robots with on-line self-organization and behavioral fitness. Neural Netw. **13**(4), 431–443 (2000)
10. Blynel, J., Floreano, D.: Exploring the T-Maze: evolving learning-like robot behaviors using CTRNNs. In: Cagnoni, S., Johnson, C.G., Cardalda, J.J.R., Marchiori, E., Corne, D.W., Meyer, J.-A., Gottlieb, J., Middendorf, M., Guillot, A., Raidl, G.R., Hart, E. (eds.) EvoWorkshops 2003. LNCS, vol. 2611, pp. 593–604. Springer, Heidelberg (2003). doi:10.1007/3-540-36605-9_54

11. Ellefsen, K.O., Mouret, J.B., Clune, J.: Neural modularity helps organisms evolve to learn new skills without forgetting old skills. PLoS Comput. Biol. **11**(4), e1004128 (2015)

12. Risi, S., Stanley, K.O.: Indirectly encoding neural plasticity as a pattern of local rules. In: Doncieux, S., Girard, B., Guillot, A., Hallam, J., Meyer, J.-A., Mouret, J.-B. (eds.) SAB 2010. LNCS (LNAI), vol. 6226, pp. 533–543. Springer, Heidelberg (2010). doi:10.1007/978-3-642-15193-4_50

13. Silva, F., Urbano, P., Correia, L., Christensen, A.L.: odNEAT: an algorithm for decentralised online evolution of robotic controllers. Evol. Comput. **23**(3), 421–449 (2015)

14. Soltoggio, A., Bullinaria, J.A., Mattiussi, C.: Drr, P., Floreano, D.: Evolutionary advantages of neuromodulated plasticity in dynamic, reward-based scenarios. In: Bullock, S., Noble, J., Watson, R., Bedau, M.A., (eds.): Proceedings of the 11th International Conference on Artificial Life (Alife XI), pp. 569–576. MIT Press, Cambridge (2008)

15. Risi, S., Stanley, K.O.: A unified approach to evolving plasticity and neural geometry. In: The 2012 International Joint Conference on Neural Networks (IJCNN), pp. 1–8. IEEE (2012)

16. Norouzzadeh, M.S., Clune, J.: Neuromodulation improves the evolution of forward models. In: Proceedings of the Genetic and Evolutionary Computation Conference 2016, GECCO 2016, pp. 157–164. ACM, New York (2016)

17. Löwe, M., Risi, S.: Accelerating the evolution of cognitive behaviors through human-computer collaboration. In: Proceedings of the Genetic and Evolutionary Computation Conference 2016, GECCO 2016, pp. 133–140. ACM, New York (2016)

18. Hebb, D.O.: The Organization of Behavior. Wiley & Sons, New York (1949)

19. McCloskey, M., Cohen, N.: Catastrophic interference in connectionist networks: the sequential learning problem. In: Bower, G.H. (ed.) The Psychology of Learning and Motivation, vol. 24, pp. 109–164 (1989)

20. Graves, A., Wayne, G., Danihelka, I.: Neural turing machines. arXiv:1410.5401 (2014)

21. Greve, R.B., Jacobsen, E.J., Risi, S.: Evolving neural turing machines for reward-based learning. In: Proceedings of the Genetic and Evolutionary Computation Conference 2016, GECCO 2016, pp. 117–124. ACM, New York (2016)

22. Weston, J., Chopra, S., Bordes, A.: Memory networks. Preprint arXiv:1410.3916 (2014)

23. Graves, A., Wayne, G., Reynolds, M., Harley, T., Danihelka, I., Grabska-Barwińska, A., Colmenarejo, S.G., Grefenstette, E., Ramalho, T., Agapiou, J., et al.: Hybrid computing using a neural network with dynamic external memory. Nature **538**(7626), 471–476 (2016)

24. Stanley, K.O., Miikkulainen, R.: Evolving neural networks through augmenting topologies. Evol. Comput. **10**(2), 99–127 (2002)

25. Foster, D., Morris, R., Dayan, P., et al.: A model of hippocampally dependent navigation, using the temporal difference learning rule. Hippocampus **10**(1), 1–16 (2000)

Erratum to: Large Scale Problems in Practice: The Effect of Dimensionality on the Interaction Among Variables

Fabio Caraffini, Ferrante Neri, and Giovanni Iacca

Erratum to:
Chapter "Large Scale Problems in Practice:
The Effect of Dimensionality on the Interaction Among
Variables" in: G. Squillero and K. Sim et al. (Eds.):
Applications of Evolutionary Computation, **Part I, LNCS 10199,**
https://doi.org/10.1007/978-3-319-55849-3_41

The original version of the paper starting on p. 636 was revised. An acknowledgement has been added. The original chapter was corrected.

The updated online version of this chapter can be found at
https://doi.org/10.1007/978-3-319-55849-3_41

© Springer International Publishing AG 2018
G. Squillero and K. Sim (Eds.): EvoApplications 2017, Part I, LNCS 10199, p. E1, 2017.
https://doi.org/10.1007/978-3-319-55849-3_58

Author Index